76% of introduction to psychology instructors state that student reading of text chapters is very or extremely important for success in their courses.

> *Psychology: The Science of Mind and Behavior* supports student reading and comprehension of material through its print pedagogy: chapter focal questions/chapter outlines, *Test Yourself* questions, and chapter summary and key terms; adaptive questioning diagnostic that helps students create individualized study plans; exercises that support concept comprehension; and optional e-book format, which may appeal to students on the go or those who prefer reading in small chunks.

If you would like to participate in any of the McGraw-Hill research initiatives, please contact us at **www.mhhe.com/faculty-research.**

Psychology

The Science of Mind and Behavior

fifth edition

Psychology

The Science of Mind and Behavior

Michael W. Passer
University of Washington

Ronald E. Smith
University of Washington

McGraw Hill

Connect
Learn
Succeed™

The McGraw·Hill Companies

Connect
Learn
Succeed™

Published by McGraw-Hill, an imprint of The McGraw-Hill Companies, Inc., 1221 Avenue of the Americas, New York, NY 10020. Copyright © 2011, 2009, 2007, 2004, 2001. All rights reserved. No part of this publication may be reproduced or distributed in any form or by any means, or stored in a database or retrieval system, without the prior written consent of The McGraw-Hill Companies, Inc., including, but not limited to, in any network or other electronic storage or transmission, or broadcast for distance learning.

This book is printed on acid-free paper.

3 4 5 6 7 8 9 0 DOW/DOW 9 8 7 6 5 4 3 2

ISBN: 978-0-07-353212-7
MHID: 0-07-353212-6

Vice President Editorial: *Michael Ryan*
Editorial Director: *Beth Mejia*
Publisher: *Mike Sugarman*
Executive Editor: *Krista Bettino*
Executive Marketing Manager: *Julia Flohr Larkin*
Marketing Manager: *Yasuko Okada*
Director of Development: *Dawn Groundwater*
Development Editors: *Cara Labell and John Sisson*
Editorial Coordinator: *Julie Kuljurgis*
Permissions Editor: *Marty Moga*
Production Editor: *Catherine Morris*
Manuscript Editor: *Andrea McCarrick*
Design Manager: *Allister Fein*
Text Designer: *Amanda Kavanagh*
Cover Designer: *Allister Fein*
Illustrators: *John and Judy Waller*
Lead Photo Research Coordinator: *Alexandra Ambrose*
Photo Researcher: *David Tietz*
Buyer II: *Tandra Jorgensen*
Composition: *10/12 pt Palatino by MPS Limited, A Macmillan Company*
Printing: *45# New Era Thin Plus, R. R. Donnelley & Sons*

Cover: *mandj98/iStockphoto; Talshiar/Istockphoto*

Credits: The credits section for this book begins on page C-1 and is considered an extension of the copyright page.

Library of Congress Cataloging-in-Publication Data

Passer, Michael W.
　Psychology : the science of mind and behavior / Michael W. Passer, Ronald E. Smith.—5th ed.
　　p. cm.
　Includes bibliographical references and index.
　ISBN-13: 978-0-07-353212-7 (alk. paper)
　ISBN-10: 0-07-353212-6 (alk. paper)
　1. Psychology—Textbooks. I. Smith, Ronald E. II. Title.
　BF121.P348 2011
　150—dc22

2010020291

The Internet addresses listed in the text were accurate at the time of publication. The inclusion of a Web site does not indicate an endorsement by the authors or McGraw-Hill, and McGraw-Hill does not guarantee the accuracy of the information presented at these sites.

www.mhhe.com

To Bev and Kay, for their endless love and support.

About the Authors

MICHAEL W. PASSER

Michael Passer coordinates the introductory psychology program at the University of Washington, which enrolls about 2,500 students per year, and also is the faculty coordinator of training for new teaching assistants (TAs). He received his bachelor's degree from the University of Rochester and his PhD in Psychology from the University of California, Los Angeles, with a specialization in social psychology. Dr. Passer has been a faculty member at the University of Washington since 1977. A former Danforth Foundation Fellow and University of Washington Distinguished Teaching Award finalist, Dr. Passer has had a career-long love of teaching. Each academic year he teaches introductory psychology twice and a required pre-major course in research methods. Dr. Passer developed and teaches a graduate course on the Teaching of Psychology, which prepares students for careers in the college classroom, and also has taught courses in social psychology and attribution theory. He has published more than 20 scientific articles and chapters, primarily in the areas of attribution, stress, and anxiety, and has taught the introductory psychology course for over 20 years.

RONALD E. SMITH

Ronald E. Smith is Professor of Psychology and Director of Clinical Psychology Training at the University of Washington, where he also has served as Area Head of the Social Psychology and Personality area. He received his bachelor's degree from Marquette University and his PhD from Southern Illinois University, where he had dual specializations in clinical and physiological psychology. His major research interests are in anxiety, stress and coping, and in performance enhancement research and intervention. Dr. Smith is a Fellow of the American Psychological Association. He received a Distinguished Alumnus Award from the UCLA Neuropsychiatric Institute for his contributions to the field of mental health. He has published more than 200 scientific articles and book chapters in his areas of interest and has authored or coauthored 29 books on introductory psychology, human performance enhancement, and personality, including *Introduction to Personality: Toward an Integration*, with Walter Mischel and Yuichi Shoda (Wiley, 2004). An award-winning teacher, he has more than 15 years of experience in teaching the introductory psychology course.

Contents in Brief

Contents

CHAPTER 3

Genes, Environment, and Behavior 65

CHAPTER 4

The Brain and Behavior 95

CHAPTER 5

Sensation and Perception 129

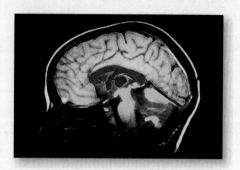

CHAPTER 8

Memory 252

CHAPTER 11

Motivation and Emotion 367

CHAPTER 12

Development over the Life Span 414

CHAPTER 13

Personality 458

CHAPTER 14

Health and Well-Being 504

CHAPTER 15

Psychological Disorders 546

Preface

Mind and behavior. A more fascinating area of study is hard to imagine, yet as students we didn't recognize this when we entered college. In fact, the study of psychology wasn't on either of our radar screens. Michael planned to major in physics, Ron in journalism. Then something unexpected occurred. Each of us took an introductory psychology course, and suddenly our life paths changed. Because of instructors who brought psychology to life, we were hooked, and that initial enthusiasm has never left us.

Now, through *Psychology: The Science of Mind and Behavior*, we have the pleasure and privilege of sharing our enthusiasm with you and a new generation of students. Our goal is to spark a passion for psychology in today's students. We believe that the study of psychology has something to offer everyone, whether it is the development of a new lens for viewing everyday life, an appreciation for the myriad ways psychological research has changed and illuminated human understanding, or an enthusiastic engagement with new concepts and theories. We want students to experience, as we did, the intellectual excitement and relevance of studying the mind and behavior.

FOLLOWING WHERE THE SCIENCE LEADS . . . TO CRITICAL EXAMINATION

As psychologists and instructors of introductory psychology, a challenge we face is engaging students in the critical examination of the course topics. However, in order to support critical examination, we must first help students understand the content. We must decide how to address psychology's enormous breadth and diverse approaches within an academic time frame that always seems too short. Moreover, as we move from topic to topic—from chapter to chapter—we don't want to leave students feeling that psychology is merely a massive collection of disjointed facts. And, to enthusiastic students who may be expecting simple answers to important personal and intellectual questions—or who may already believe they know the answers thanks to what they've learned from the Web or other media—we must convey the message that because behavior is complex, answers to such questions often are not black and white.

To meet these challenges, we start with the science. By following where the science leads, students learn course material and are ushered through the process of critical examination. At the center of this approach is the recognition that psychologists study behavior from multiple vantage points that emphasize biological, psychological, and environmental determinants. This approach shows students that despite the myriad topics psychologists study and the diverse approaches they use, there is an underlying commonality to how any topic can be examined. To further show students "where the science leads," and how to follow the trail, *Psychology: The Science of Mind and Behavior* marries the best of print and digital formats to help students develop some basic tools of critical examination, including:

- **An understanding of how research leads to discovery.** To help students understand the research process, each chapter's *Research Close-up* presents a specific research study in the format of a simplified journal article. These high-interest studies and their accompanying "Research Design" graphics help students understand how correlational and experimental research are carried out. The "Discussion" section provides a brief critical analysis of the study and its methodology. The *Research Close-ups* support the critical examination of information by showing the nuts and bolts of psychological research and the knowledge research brings to the analysis. *Research Close-up* topics include "Sex Differences in the Ideal Mate: Evolution or Social Roles?" (Chapter 3), "Memory Illusions: Remembering Things That Never Occurred" (Chapter 8), and "Drug versus Psychological Treatments for Depression" (Chapter 16).

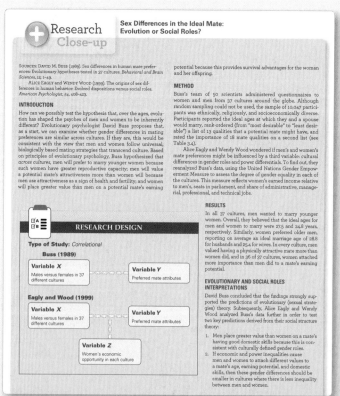

- **Knowledge that an accurate understanding of behavior is based on science.** Because introductory psychology students often take widely accepted "facts" at face value, the new *Myth or Reality?* presents a compelling question that students may think they know the answer to based on common or popular knowledge. *Myth or Reality?* demonstrates that one cannot know the answer to a question without examining the relevant research. Additionally, *Myth or Reality?* encourages critical thinking by modeling how students might approach questions or issues they address in their everyday lives. *Myth or Reality?* topics range from "Subliminal Stimuli Can Program Our Minds" (Chapter 5) to "The Aging Brain Is Like a Muscle: Use It or Lose It" (Chapter 12) to "Criminal Profiling Is a Useful Investigative Tool" (Chapter 13).

introductions and fuller descriptions of each area of analysis. Behaviors explored include "Sleep and Dreaming" (Chapter 6), "Intellectual Functioning" (Chapter 10), and "Stress and Resilience" (Chapter 14).

- **An understanding of how information can be applied.** In addition to the many applications discussed throughout the textbook's narrative, *Applying Psychological Science* demonstrates how knowledge derived from basic research can be applied at both personal and societal levels. To illustrate this science-into-application theme, several of these features focus on skills that can enhance learning and performance. These topics include research-derived principles for studying effectively (Chapter 1), behavioral self-modification (Chapter 7), and memory enhancement (Chapter 8). Additionally, online video clips show what concepts may look like in the real world.

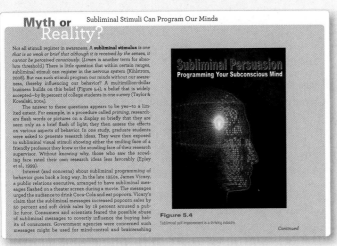

Myth or Reality? Subliminal Stimuli Can Program Our Minds

Not all stimuli register in awareness. A **subliminal stimulus** *is one that is so weak or brief that although it is received by the senses, it cannot be perceived consciously.* (Limen is another term for absolute threshold.) There is little question that within certain ranges, subliminal stimuli can register in the nervous system (Kihlstrom, 2008). But can such stimuli program our minds without our awareness, thereby influencing our behavior? A multimillion-dollar business builds on this belief (Figure 5.4), a belief that is widely accepted—by 85 percent of college students in one survey (Taylor & Kowalski, 2004).

The answer to these questions appears to be yes—to a limited extent. For example, in a procedure called *priming,* researchers flash words or pictures on a display so briefly that they are seen only as a brief flash of light; they then assess the effects on various aspects of behavior. In one study, graduate students were asked to generate research ideas. They were then exposed to subliminal visual stimuli showing either the smiling face of a friendly professor they knew or the scowling face of their research supervisor. Without knowing why, those who saw the scowling face rated their own research ideas less favorably (Epley et al., 1999).

Interest (and concerns) about subliminal programming of behavior goes back a long way. In the late 1950s, James Vicary, a public relations executive, arranged to have subliminal messages flashed on a theater screen during a movie. The messages urged the audience to drink Coca-Cola and eat popcorn. Vicary's claim that the subliminal messages increased popcorn sales by 50 percent and soft drink sales by 18 percent aroused a public furor. Consumers and scientists feared the possible abuse of subliminal messages to covertly influence the buying habits of consumers. Government agencies were concerned such messages might be used for mind-control and brainwashing.

Continued

Figure 5.4
Subliminal self-improvement is a thriving industry.

Applying Psychological Science How to Enhance Your Academic Performance

College life presents many challenges, and working smart can be as important as working hard. The following strategies can help you increase your learning and academic performance (Figure 1.26).

EFFECTIVE TIME MANAGEMENT
If you efficiently allocate study time, you will have a clear conscience when it's time for recreational activities and relaxation. First, *develop a written schedule;* this forces you to decide how to allocate time and increases your commitment to the plan. Write down your class schedule and other responsibilities. Then block in periods for study, avoiding times you are likely to be tired.

Distribute study times throughout the week. Schedule some study times immediately before enjoyable activities, which you can use as rewards for studying.

Second, *prioritize your tasks.* Don't procrastinate by working on simple tasks while putting off the toughest tasks. This can result in never getting to the major tasks (e.g., writing term papers, studying for exams) until too little time remains. Each day, ask "What is the most important thing to get done?" Do that first, then move to the next most important task, and so on.

Third, *break large tasks into smaller parts.* Important tasks often are too big to complete all at once. Break them down into a set of specific and realistic goals (e.g., number of pages to be read).

- **The ability to consider multiple factors to understand behavior.** *Levels of Analysis* emphasizes how psychologists examine the interplay of biological, psychological, and environmental factors in their quest to understand behavior. New in this edition are contextual

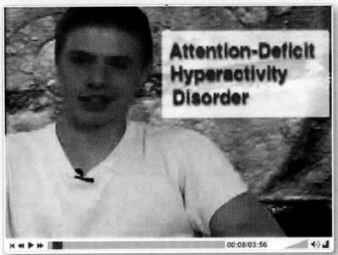

Attention-Deficit Hyperactivity Disorder

00:08:03:56

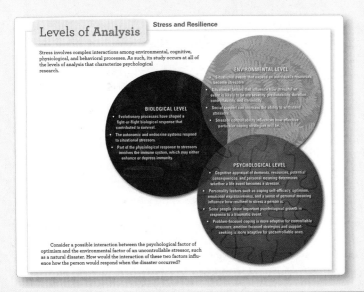

Levels of Analysis Stress and Resilience

Stress involves complex interactions among environmental, cognitive, physiological, and behavioral processes. As such, its study occurs at all of the levels of analysis that characterize psychological research.

ENVIRONMENTAL LEVEL
- Situational events that exceed an individual's resources become stressors.
- Situational factors that influence how stressful an event is likely to be are severity, predictability, duration controllability, and chronicity.
- Social support can increase the ability to withstand stressors.
- Stressor controllability influences how effective particular coping strategies will be.

BIOLOGICAL LEVEL
- Evolutionary processes have shaped a fight-or-flight biological response that contributed to survival.
- The autonomic and endocrine systems respond to situational stressors.
- Part of the physiological response to stressors involves the immune system, which may either enhance or depress immunity.

PSYCHOLOGICAL LEVEL
- Cognitive appraisal of demands, resources, potential consequences, and personal meaning determines whether a life event becomes a stressor.
- Personality factors such as coping self-efficacy, optimism, emotional expressiveness, and a sense of personal meaning influence how resilient to stress a person is.
- Some people show important psychological growth in response to a traumatic event.
- Problem-focused coping is more adaptive for controllable stressors; emotion-focused strategies and support-seeking is more adaptive for uncontrollable ones.

Consider a possible interaction between the psychological factor of optimism and the environmental factor of an uncontrollable stressor, such as a natural disaster. How would the interaction of these two factors influence how the person would respond when the disaster occurred?

To practice the use of these tools, students can apply their developing critical-examination skills to *Thinking Critically* activities. These activities question a belief or information presented in the text, or pose a situation that requires analysis, and then ask students to construct an answer using their critical-examination tools. Students can then compare their answer to one provided at the end of the chapter. Topics include "Would Perfect Memory Be a Gift or a Curse?" (Chapter 8), "Hypnosis and Amazing Feats" (Chapter 6), and "Do I Have That Disorder?" (Chapter 15).

CONNECTING WITH TODAY'S STUDENTS: ADAPTIVE DIAGNOSTIC TOOL AND PEDAGOGY THAT SUPPORT LEARNING

We recognize that today's students are as different from the learners of the last generation as today's discipline of psychology is different from the field 30 years ago. Students now learn in multiple modalities. Rather than sitting down and reading traditional printed chapters in linear fashion from beginning to end, they tend to prefer materials that are more visual and more interactive, and they often read and study in short bursts. For many students, a traditionally formatted printed textbook is no longer enough when they have instant, 24/7 access to news and information from around the globe. *Psychology: The Science of Mind and Behavior* responds to contemporary students' needs through an adaptive diagnostic tool and several pedagogical elements.

Adaptive Diagnostic Tool

Connect Psychology's groundbreaking adaptive diagnostic tool helps students "know what they know" while helping them learn what they don't know through engaging interactivities, exercises, video clips, and readings. Instructors using Connect Psychology report that their students' performance is improving by a letter grade or more.

Through this unique tool, *Psychology: The Science of Mind and Behavior* gives instructors the ability to identify struggling students quickly and easily, *before* the first exam. Connect Psychology's adaptive diagnostic tool develops an individualized learning plan for every student. Confidence levels tailor the next question to each individual, helping students to identify what they don't know. If your student is doing well, the adaptive diagnostic tool challenges the student with more applied and conceptual questions. If your student is struggling, the system identifies problem areas and directs the student to the exact page he or she needs to read. In doing so, it works like a GPS, helping students master key concepts

efficiently and effectively. Regardless of individual study habits, preparation, and approaches to the course, Connect Psychology's adaptive diagnostic tool provides them with a customized road map to success.

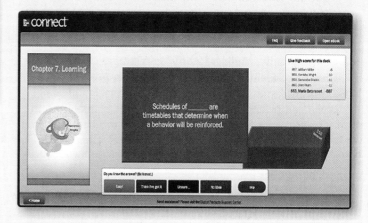

Pedagogical Elements

Psychology: The Science of Mind and Behavior supports student learning of concepts throughout each chapter.

- Chapter outlines and accompanying focal questions begin each chapter. These elements preview the content to come and focus students' attention on key issues that will be discussed in the chapter.

- *Test Yourself* quizzes allows students to confirm that they understand key concepts of the chapter before moving forward.

- Online exercises and pre- and post-tests give students the opportunity to apply what they have learned.

- The chapter-ending *Chapter Summary* and *Key Terms and Concepts* sections point students to key ideas.

- Detailed study questions, available online for instructors who wish to provide or assign study questions to their students, can be customized to best fit teaching goals and student needs.

INTEGRATED LEARNING SYSTEM

The resources listed here may accompany *Psychology: The Science of Mind and Behavior*, 5th edition. Please contact your McGraw-Hill representative for details concerning policies, prices, and availability.

Adaptive Diagnostic Tool

What if . . .

- you could re-create the one-on-one experience of working through difficult concepts in office hours with every one of your students without having to invest any office-hour time to do so?
- you could see at a glance how well each of your students (or sections) was performing in each segment of your course?
- you had all of the assignments and resources for your course pre-organized by learning objective and with point-and-click flexibility?

Over the course of developing *Psychology: The Science of Mind and Behavior,* we asked these questions and many more. We did not stop at simply asking questions. We visited with faculty across the country and also observed what you do to prepare and deliver your courses. We observed students as they worked through assignments and studied for exams. The result of these thousands of hours of research and development is a adaptive diagnostic tool that bolsters student performance at the same time it makes instructors' lives easier and more efficient.

This diagnostic tool is an unparalleled, intelligent learning system based on cognitive mapping that *diagnoses* your students' knowledge of a particular subject and then creates an individualized learning path geared toward student success in your course. It offers individualized assessment by delivering appropriate learning material in the form of questions at the right time, helping students attain mastery of the content. Whether the system is assigned by you or used independently by students as a study tool, the results can be recorded in an easy-to-use grade report that allows you to measure student progress at all times and coach your students to success. As an added benefit, all content covered in this adaptive diagnostic tool is tied to learning objectives for your course so that you can use the results as evidence of subject mastery. This tool also provides a personal study plan that allows the student to estimate the time it will take and number of questions required to learn the subject matter. Your students will learn faster, study more efficiently, and

retain more knowledge when using the adaptive diagnostic tool in concert with *Psychology: The Science of Mind and Behavior.* To experience this environment for yourself, please visit www.mcgraw-hillconnect.com.

Online Learning Center for Instructors

The password-protected instructor side of the Online Learning Center (www.mhhe.com/passer5e) contains the Instructor's Manual, Test Bank files, PowerPoint slides, Classroom Performance System (CPS, or "clicker") Questions, Image Gallery, and other valuable material to help you design and enhance your course. See more information about specific assets below. Ask your local McGraw-Hill representative for password information.

Instructor's Manual, by Laura Gruntmeir, Redlands Community College. This comprehensive guide provides all the tools and resources instructors need to present and enhance their introductory psychology course. The Instructor's Manual contains detailed lecture launchers, learning objectives, interesting lecture and media presentation ideas, student assignments, and handouts. The many tips and activities in this manual can be used with any class, regardless of size or teaching approach.

Test Banks.
   Test Bank 1, by Kim Maclin, University of Northern Iowa, and Dwight Peterson, University of Nevada, Reno, includes factual, conceptual, and applied questions. This comprehensive resource offers more than 3,500 items in all, including multiple-choice, true-false, and fill-in-the-blank questions.
   Test Bank 2, by Veronica Rowland, comprises more than 2,500 factual, conceptual, and applied questions and multiple-choice items.
   Test Bank 3, by Martha Hubertz, Florida Atlantic University, offers 40 questions per chapter (680 in total), the majority of which are applied questions.

PowerPoint Presentations, by Jenel Cavazos, University of Oklahoma. These presentations cover the key points of the chapter and include figures and charts from the text where relevant. They can be used as is or modified to meet your needs.

Classroom Performance System (CPS), updated by Patricia Lanzon, Henry Ford Community College. The Classroom Performance System (CPS) from eInstruction allows instructors to gauge immediately what students are learning during lectures. CPS includes both comprehension questions to check understanding and polling or opinion questions. In addition, CPS facilitates taking attendance, giving and grading pop quizzes, and giving multiple versions of formal, printed class tests using CPS for immediate grading.

Image Gallery. More than 100 figures from the text can be downloaded from the Image Gallery on the Instructor's Online Learning Center.

Online Learning Center for Students

This companion website at http://www.mhhe.com/passer5e offers a variety of student resources including multiple choice and true/false quizzes to reinforce key principles and cover all the major concepts discussed throughout the text. Entirely different from the test items in the Test Bank, these quiz questions, written by Patricia Lanzon, Henry Ford Community College, assess students and also help them learn. Key terms from the text are presented as flashcards, as well as in a glossary of terms.

Annual Editions: Psychology 10/11

Edited by William Buskist, Auburn University. This annually updated reader provides convenient, inexpensive access to current articles selected from the best of the public press. Organizational features include an annotated listing of selected Web sites, an annotated table of contents, a topic guide, a general introduction, brief overviews for each section, a topical index, and an instructor's resource guide with testing materials.

Classic Edition Sources: Psychology, 4th edition

Edited by Terry Pettijohn, Ohio State University–Marion. This reader provides more than 40 selections of enduring intellectual value—classic articles, book excerpts, and research studies—that have shaped the study of psychology and our contemporary understanding of it.

Taking Sides: Clashing Views on Controversial Psychological Issues, 16th edition

Edited by Brent Slife, Brigham Young University. This reader presents current controversial issues in a debate-style format designed to stimulate student interest and develop critical-thinking skills. Each issue is thoughtfully framed with an issue summary, an issue introduction, and a postscript. An instructor's manual with testing material is available for each volume.

ACKNOWLEDGMENTS

A project having the scope of an introductory psychology text is truly a team enterprise, and we have been the fortunate recipients of a great team effort. We want to thank and acknowledge the contributions of the many people who made this book possible, beginning with Krista Bettino and Mike Sugarman, McGraw-Hill Higher Education's executive editor and publisher for Psychology, respectively. We are indebted to Krista and Mike for their strong faith in this project and their unwavering support. We have been blessed with superlative developmental editors. Senior Development Editor Cara Labell with Development Editor John Sisson helped to conceive the direction for the revision and provided guidance in implementing our shared vision throughout the process. Similarly, our copy editor, Andrea McCarrick, was splendid, and her input went well beyond the normal call of duty.

On the production end, thanks go to Catherine Morris, our project manager, for coordinating the endless production details; to Allister Fein, our design manager, for creating the fabulous cover and attractive layout of the book; and to Robin Mouat, our art editor. David Tietz, our photo researcher, worked diligently to acquire many of the excellent and unique photos in this edition. We also thank Julia Flohr and Yasuko Okada, our marketing managers, who have worked tirelessly to create an imaginative marketing program.

Outstanding supplements are a critical element in the success of any textbook program, but our supplement authors have gone beyond excellence in implementing the total integration of the supplements. We are in great debt to Laura Gruntmeir for developing an absolutely first-class Instructor's Manual that not only includes a wealth of useful material for novice and experienced instructors alike, but also coordinates outstanding audio/visual and electronic resources. Jenel Taylor (University of Oklahoma) developed a highly innovative set of media-rich PowerPoint slides that instructors can use to spark their lectures. Content for the CPS ("clicker") system and the student quizzes were prepared by Patricia Lanzon (Henry Ford Community College).

Finally, Kim Maclin (University of Northern Iowa), Dwight Peterson (University of Nevada, Reno), Veronica Rowland, and Martha Hubertz (Florida Atlantic University) did an excellent job revising the three test banks that are second to none in quality and breadth.

We would like to thank Amanda Patrick for assisting us with the formatting of references, and we also owe special thanks to the distinguished corps of colleagues who provided review feedback—on both the textbook and its supplements—as we prepared *Psychology: The Science of Mind and Behavior*, 5th edition. Many of the improvements in the book are the outgrowth of their comments about what they want in an introductory psychology textbook for their courses. In this regard, we sincerely appreciate the time and effort contributed by the following instructors:

Manuscript Reviewers

Evelyn Armbrust, *California State University–Sacramento*

Ted Barker, *Northwest Florida State College*

Ralph Braithwaite, *St. Joseph College*

Clifford Brown, *Wittenberg University*

Daniel Chen, *University of Puget Sound*

Deborah Y. Chun, *Western Washington University*

Andrea Clements, *East Tennessee State University–Johnson City*

Mark Covey, *Concordia College*

Jared P. Dempsey, *Oklahoma State University–Stillwater*

Matthew Fanetti, *Missouri State University*

Johnathan Forbey, *Ball State University*

Charla R. Hall, *Southeastern Oklahoma University*

Elizabeth Yost Hammer, *Xavier University of Louisiana*

Gregory E. Harris, *Polk Community College*

Jennifer Hicks, *Southeastern Oklahoma University*

Michelle Hodges, *Lamar State College–Orange*

Bobby Hutchinson, *Modesto Junior College*

Christopher Jones, *University of Puget Sound*

Kathy Judge, *Cleveland State University*

Elizabeth Katz, *Towson University*

Kevin King, *University of Washington*

Chad Lakey, *East Tennessee State University–Johnson City*

Gerald Latcher, *Long Island University–C. W. Post*

Jacob Leonisio, *University of Washington*

Stephanie Little, *Wittenberg University*

Mike Mangan, *University of New Hampshire*

Amy Martin, *Rockford College*

Christopher Mayhorn, *North Carolina State University*

Wanda McCarthy, *University of Cincinnati–Clermont*

Daniel McConnell, *University of Central Florida*

Deborah Meadows, *Columbia Basin College*

David Perkins, *University of Louisiana–Lafayette*

Jeffrey Ratliff-Crain, *University of Minnesota–Morris*

Marilyn Rodriguez, *University of Miami*

Sharleen Sakai, *Michigan State University–East Lansing*

Jacob Schoenholtz, *Camden County College*

Jay Schumacher, *Texas A&M University*

Beth Seebach, *Saint Mary's University*

Michael Serra, *Texas Tech University*

Maria Shpurik, *Florida International University–Miami*

Pat Somers, *College of DuPage*

Jeremy Tyler, *Towson University*

Ben Wallace, *Cleveland State University*

Eric Weiser, *Curry College*

C. Mark Wessinger, *University of Nevada–Reno*

Jonathan Westfall, *University of Toledo*

Stuart White, *University of New Orleans*

Josephine Wilson, *Wittenberg University*

Reviewers of Past Editions

Bill Adler, *Collin County Community College–Plano*

Mark D. Alicke, *Ohio University*

Ronald Baenninger, *Temple University*

Susan Baillet, *University of Portland*

Jeffrey Baker, *Rochester Institute of Technology*

David R. Barkmeier, *Northeastern University*

Robert S. Baron, *University of Iowa–Iowa City*

Tammy D. Barry, *University of Southern Mississippi*

David Baskind, *Delta College*

Ute J. Bayen, *University of North Carolina–Chapel Hill*

Daniel Bellack, *Trident Technical College*

Pam Birrell, *University of Oregon*

Adriel Boals, *Duke University*

Edward Brady, *Southwestern Illinois College*

Angela Bragg, *Mt. Hood Community College*

Mark Brechtel, *University of Florida*

Deborah S. Briihl, *Valdosta State University*

Cody Brooks, *Denison University*

Josh Burk, *College of William and Mary*

David Burrows, *Beloit College*

Adam Butler, *University of Northern Iowa*

James F. Calhoun, *University of Georgia*

Marc Carter, *Hofstra University*

Walter Cegelka, *St. Thomas University*

P. Niels Christensen, *San Diego State University*

Michael Clump, *Marymount University*

Perry L. Collins, *Wayland Baptist University*

Laura Da Costa, *University of Illinois–Springfield*

Dan Daughtry, *Texas A&M University*

Betty Davenport, *Campbell University*

M. Catherine DeSoto, *University of Northern Iowa*

Rochelle Diogenes, *Montclair, NJ*

Joan Doolittle, *Anne Arundel Community College*

Tracy Dunne, *Boston University*

Amanda Emo, *University of Cincinnati*

William Fabricius, *Arizona State University*

Marte Fallshore, *Central Washington University*

Phil Finney, *Southeast Missouri State University*

Barry Fritz, *Quinnipiac University*

Dean E. Frost, *Portland State University*

Perry Fuchs, *University of Texas–Arlington*

Ray Fuller, *Trinity College of Dublin*

Janet Gebelt, *University of Portland*

Glenn Geher, *State University of New York–Albany*

Andrew Getzfeld, *New Jersey City University*

Adam Goodie, *University of Georgia*

Shepard B. Gorman, *Nassau Community College*

Gary J. Greguras, *Louisiana State University*

Carlos Grijalva, *University of California–Los Angeles*

Tresmaine Grimes, *Iona College*

Laura Gruntmeir, *Redlands Community College*

Michael Hackett, *Westchester Community College*

Michelle Haney, *Berry College*

Jason W. Hart, *Indiana University of Pennsylvania*

Bert Hayslip Jr., *University of North Texas*

Brett Heintz, *Delgado Community College*

Dwight Hennessy, *Buffalo State College*

Michael Hillard, *Central New Mexico Community College*

Jennifer Hodges, *Louisiana Tech University*

Debra L. Hollister, *Valdosta Community College*

Steven W. Horowitz, *Central Connecticut State University*

Charles Huffman, *James Madison University*

Timothy B. Jay, *Massachusetts College of Liberal Arts*

Robert A. Johnston, *College of William and Mary*

Deana Julka, *University of Portland*

Robert Kaleta, *University of Wisconsin–Milwaukee*

Rick Kasschau, *University of Houston*

Rosalie Kern, *Michigan Technological University*

Gary King, *Rose State College*

Pat King, *Del Mar College*

Karen Kopera-Frye, *Buchtel College of Arts and Sciences*

F. Scott Kraly, *Colgate University*

Mark Krause, *University of Portland*

Cynthia D. Kreutzer, *Georgia Perimeter College–Lawrenceville*

Holly Krueger, *University of Oregon*

Gert Kruger, *University of Johannesburg*

Kevin Larkin, *West Virginia University*

Kristin Lazarova, *Northeast State Technical Community College*

Dianne Leader, *Georgia Institute of Technology*

Christopher W. LeGrow, *Marshall University*

Ting Lei, *Borough of Manhattan Community College*

Estevan R. Limon, *City University of New York, Hunter College*

Alan J. Lipman, *Georgetown University*

Paul Lipton, *Boston University*

Mary Livingston, *Louisiana Tech University*

Mark Ludorf, *Stephen F. Austin State University*

Derek Mace, *Penn State University–Erie*

Kim MacLin, *University of Northern Iowa*

Stephen Madigan, *University of Southern California*

Laura Madson, *New Mexico State University*

Brian Malley, *University of Michigan*

Kathleen Malley-Morrison, *Boston University*

Gregory Manley, *University of Texas–San Antonio*

Michael Jason McCoy, *Cape Fear Community College*

Anne McCrea, *Sinclair Community College*

David McDonald, *University of Missouri–Columbia*

Cheryl McNeil, *West Virginia University*

Mary Meiners, *San Diego Miramar College*

David B. Mitchell, *Loyola University–Chicago*

Kevin Moore, *DePauw University*

Joseph Morrissey, *State University of New York–Binghamton*

Nancy Olson, *Mt. Hood Community College*

Phil Pegg, *Western Kentucky University*

Edison Perdomo, *Central State University*

Brady Phelps, *South Dakota State University*

Richard Pisacreta, *Ferris State University*

Deborah Podwika, *Kankakee Community College*

Donald J. Polzella, *University of Dayton*

Gary Poole, *Simon Fraser University*

Daren S. Protolipac, *St. Cloud State University*

J. T. Ptacek, *Bucknell University*

Jacqueline T. Ralston, *Columbia College*

Janice L. Rank, *Portland Community College*

Lauretta Reeves, *University of Texas–Austin*

Scott Ronis, *University of Missouri*

Melani Russell, *Louisiana Tech University*

Richard Sandargas, *University of Tennessee*

Catherine Sanderson, *Amherst College*

Stephen Saunders, *Marquette University*

Nancy Schaab, *Delta College*

Christopher Scribner, *Lindenwood University*

William G. Shadel, *University of Pittsburgh*

Rebecca Shiner, *Colgate University*

Jennifer Siciliani, *University of Missouri–St. Louis*

Alice H. Skeens, *University of Toledo*

John Skowronski, *Northern Illinois University*

Steven M. Smith, *Texas A&M University*

Sheldon Solomon, *Skidmore College*

Mary Hellen Spear, *Prince George's Community College*

Claire St. Peter-Pipkin, *West Virginia University*

Jennifer Stevens, *College of William and Mary*

Carla Strassle, *York College*

Content Revisions

Following are the chapter-by-chapter changes that were made in this edition of *Psychology: The Science of Mind and Behavior.*

Chapter 1: The Science of Psychology

- The chapter now begins with a "word task" that was widely circulated via the Web; it is used later in the chapter to illustrate the importance of critical thinking and the pervasiveness of misconceptions about behavior. The former "Ray and Kira" opening vignette has been shortened and moved to the section on "Perspectives on Behavior," where it then continues to be used to illustrate each of psychology's major historical perspectives.

- The chapter's first main section, "The Nature of Psychology," now includes descriptions of eight major psychological subfields to give students a better and more immediate understanding of psychology's breadth.

- A new section on "Psychology's Scientific Approach" then describes psychology's empirical approach, identifies pitfalls in everyday thinking that can lead to misconceptions about behavior, and discusses how a scientific approach seeks to minimize these pitfalls.

- Building on this discussion of "psychology as a science," a new section on "Thinking Critically about Behavior" uses the chapter-opening jumbled word exercise to emphasize the importance of critically evaluating conclusions and thinking about alternative explanations for behavior. Potential costs of "uncritical thinking" and pseudoscience are discussed.

- A new *Myth or Reality?* critically examines the popular belief that when it comes to changing answers on multiple-choice and true-false tests, students typically should stick with their first instinct. Research by Kruger et al. (2005) is featured.

- A separate section on "Basic and Applied Research" now follows the discussion of "Goals of Psychology." In both sections, Kruger et al.'s (2005) research provides the focal example and replaces the previous examples of the Robber's Cave study and cooperative learning/jigsaw groups. (Cooperative learning is discussed in the section on prejudice reduction in Chapter 17.)

- Coverage of psychology's historical perspectives has been shortened slightly (by about 5 percent), but the topic is still a prominent component of the chapter. In discussing the sociocultural perspective, the social psychological approach is now explicitly described in a separate section and precedes the discussion of cultural psychology.

- In the section on psychology as "A Global Science and Profession," the table that describes psychological subfields has been shortened. Subfields now described in the narrative at the beginning of the chapter have been deleted to avoid redundancy, and two new subfields (health psychology and forensic psychology) have been added.

- The section "Psychology and Your Life" has been changed to "Psychology, Society, and Your Life" and adds two new examples to the already existing discussion of "Psychology and Public Policy": how psychological research has improved airline safety, and President Obama's formation of a "behavioral dream team" to provide consultation during the 2008 presidential election campaign.

Chapter 2: Studying Behavior Scientifically

- The opening vignette includes a new (2009) example of bystander nonintervention.

- The discussion of "Defining and Measuring Variables" now describes how researchers can use multiple measures within a single study to operationally define a variable.

- The new example used to illustrate unobtrusive measurement states more explicitly why a measure is or is not unobtrusive.

- The *Myth or Reality?* reports findings from the most recent (2005) Gallup poll on Americans' paranormal beliefs and provides examples of paranormal media content. Possible reasons for widespread belief in the paranormal are cited, along with the disagreement about the standard of proof. The description of the Ganzfeld procedure is improved. Additional meta-analytic results and research findings are noted.

Chapter 3: Genes, Environment, and Behavior

- New content has been added on epigenetics, the ways in which internal and external environmental factors can influence genotypic expression and be carried across generations (Masterpasqua, 2009).

- New content on evolution includes the recent discovery of *Ardipithecus ramidus,* the earliest bipedal hominid on whom we have extensive fossil evidence.

- Updated information on evolution, culture, and sex roles includes evidence that financially independent women, like men, choose younger, attractive romantic partners rather than older, affluent ones (Bower, 2009).

- The treatment of genetic and environmental influences on intelligence and personality development has been updated.

- A new *Applying Psychological Science* discusses "Gene Manipulations and Therapies."
- A new *Myth or Reality?* analyzes the proposition that "Human Behavior Reflects Nature's Plan."

Chapter 4: The Brain and Behavior

- The *Applying Psychological Science* presents updated information on the psychopharmacology of psychoactive drugs and how they affect neurotransmitter systems and brain functioning.
- A new *Research Close-up* focuses on Sperry's pioneering split-brain research and its implications for understanding the brain.
- New information on sex differences in the cerebral lateralization of language has been added.

Chapter 5: Sensation and Perception

- A new *Myth or Reality?* considers the question of whether (and to what extent) subliminal stimuli can program our behavior, affect, and thinking.
- Much of the basic information on pain previously presented in Chapter 14 has been updated and moved into this chapter. The applied information on pain-control methods remains in Chapter 14, "Health and Well-Being."
- The *Applying Psychological Science* on sensory prosthetics contains a description of the recently developed SmartHand, which provides amputees with both sensory input and precise motor control.
- New evidence (Lin et al., 2009) that humans have a special visual system that processes threatening information, as suggested in the George W. Bush shoe-ducking incident in Iraq, is discussed.
- The *Thinking Critically* guides students through a fascinating visual illusion and then asks them to analyze their experience.

Chapter 6: States of Consciousness

- The discussion of the emotional unconscious no longer includes the case of the amnesiac patient reported by Claparède (1911).
- In describing how dreams play a key role in the social fabric of some traditional cultures, the reference to the Timiar (Senoi) of Malaysia has been replaced by a more recent study of the indigenous inhabitants of Dominica in the Caribbean Islands (George-Joseph & Smith, 2008). Cross-cultural findings on dream content have been added, along with an accompanying table.
- The discussion of dream theories now includes findings (and a figure) from a recent cross-cultural study examining how college students in America, South Korea, and India view the validity of various dream theories (Morewedge & Norton, 2009).

- The coverage of drug-induced states now includes the most recent available national prevalence data (Johnston et al., 2008) on American college students' use of specific drugs.
- Hypnosis is now defined as a procedure rather than as a state, in accordance with APA's (2005) recommended definition.
- A new *Myth or Reality?* examines whether hypnosis enhances eyewitness memory. This replaces the former *Beneath the Surface* discussion of "When Dreams Come True."
- The discussion of the "hypnotized brain" has been streamlined and now mentions findings concerning the brain's response to pain-reducing hypnotic suggestions.

Chapter 7: Learning: The Role of Experience

- The chapter now opens with two, rather than three, brief vignettes (concerning a classically conditioned fear of cars and the operant conditioning of prosocial and gambling behaviors). The vignette about the teenage boys who wrestle has been dropped.
- The discussion of classically conditioned allergic reactions now notes that such reactions not only can be acquired but also reduced in strength via pairing procedures (Goebel et al., 2008). To reduce length, the 1956 "case of the asthma patient and the goldfish" has been dropped.
- The *Myth or Reality?* on "Spanking Is a Necessary Evil" substantially updates the previous *Beneath the Surface* discussion of "Spare the Rod, Spoil the Child." It includes more current information on the prevalence of spanking and new citations on spanking outcomes, and it specifically notes the argument that other forms of discipline also can have negative developmental outcomes.
- Shaping is illustrated in detail with a new and more current example involving the production of speech in a boy with selective mutism (Facon et al., 2008). The figure presenting data from this study now directly illustrates the shaping process, whereas the figure based on the previous study did not. Moreover, the figure now is placed to accompany the narrative description, whereas in prior editions it was located in a later section on applied behavior analysis.
- The discussion of the role of awareness in operant conditioning has been streamlined by dropping coverage of Spielberger and DeNike's (1966) study on verbal conditioning.

Chapter 8: Memory

- The separate *Levels of Analysis* features for "Remembering" and for "Forgetting" have been combined into one *Levels of Analysis* titled "Memory."
- The *Myth or Reality?* explores the relation between memory confidence and memory accuracy, focusing

primarily on the topic of flashbulb memory. Recent findings on flashbulb memories of 9/11, based on a nationally representative sample of Americans, are discussed (Conway et al., 2009).

- The discussion of implicit memory no longer includes the case of the amnesiac patient reported by Claparède (1911).

- The discussion of memory construction includes recent findings on memory distortion in college alumni's recollections of their college grades (Bahrick et al., 2008). The *Research Close-up*, which examines false memories on the Deese-Roediger-McDermott critical lure task by people with memories of alien abduction, now describes a successful conceptual replication involving people who claim memories of past lives (Meyersburg et al., 2009).

- Updates have been added to the coverage of children's recall of traumatic events in relation to the recovered-memory controversy (Goodman et al., 2010).

- The discussion of "Culture and Memory Construction" mentions two studies that replicate earlier findings on cross-cultural differences in the age of earliest autobiographical memories (Fiske & Pillemer, 2006; Wang, 2006).

Chapter 9: Language and Thinking

- A new chapter-opening vignette ties the themes of language and decision making into the "Miracle on the Hudson" (the successful 2009 ditching of U.S. Airways Flight 1549 in the Hudson River).

- The concept of double entendre is added to the discussion of the surface and deep structure of language.

- In the section on "Acquiring a First Language," the description of Chomsky's position has been simplified. The key terms *language acquisition device* and *language acquisition support system* (Bruner, 1983) have been deleted.

- The discussion of bilingualism now mentions not only potential benefits of learning a second language (L2) on cognitive skills, but also potential negative effects on vocabulary size (Bialystok & Feng, 2009).

- New findings are reported about the bilingual brain and the relation between the age of L2 learning and fluency. A recent study and new figure are highlighted, addressing the question of whether late L2 learners can achieve full nativelike L2 proficiency (Abrahamsson & Hyltenstam, 2009).

- An entirely new section on learning to read discusses the concept of phonological awareness and describes findings on how we recognize words (Pammer, 2009).

- The new *Myth or Reality?* examines the belief that dyslexia is a "reading backwards" disorder and discusses other misconceptions about dyslexia.

- A new example involving medical diagnosis is used to illustrate the difference between inductive and deductive reasoning.

- The discussion of the representativeness heuristic, the availability heuristic, and confirmation bias includes new secondary or primary examples to help students better grasp these concepts.

- The discussion of "The Nature of Expertise" now uses the Miracle on the Hudson vignette to illustrate the role that schemas play in expertise and also mentions how experts' schemas can sometimes interfere with optimal problem solving.

- A figure that illustrates the major components of wisdom (Baltes & Smith, 2008) has been added to the section on "What Is Wisdom?"

Chapter 10: Intelligence

- A section on multiple intelligences includes new content on the nature and measurement of personal intelligence (Mayer, 2008).

- The *Myth or Reality?* considers the relations that have now been found between brain size and intelligence, plus new findings regarding neural efficiency and IQ.

- New information is presented on how Blacks and Whites differ in their conceptions of intelligence and its genetic, environmental, and personal-choice causes (Jayaratne et al., 2009).

- New evidence is reviewed on how sex hormones activated by stereotype-threat and stereotype-lift conditions can affect cognitive performance of men and women.

Chapter 11: Motivation and Emotion

- The chapter opens with the inspiring story of The Three Doctors, African American youth from the inner city who made a pact to become doctors and succeeded in doing so.

- A new section on "Self-Determination Theory" reviews the causes and consequences of intrinsic and extrinsic motivation, including 2009 studies by Deci, Ryan, and others.

- The *Applying Psychological Science* reviews the evidence for the efficacy of systematic goal-setting procedures and shows students how to apply these principles in their own lives.

- The *Myth or Reality?* is titled, "The Lie Detector Can Tell if You're Guilty or Innocent."

- The *Research Close-up* presents the classic studies of Lazarus and Schachter exploring causal relations between cognition and emotional arousal.

Chapter 12: Development over the Life Span

- *Fetal alcohol spectrum disorders* has been added as a key term and is defined. *Fetal alcohol syndrome* is retained as a key term and is identified as a disorder within the spectrum.

- In discussing childhood, a new section on "Social Skill Development" (Berry & O'Connor, 2010) now follows the discussion of "Early Emotions and Emotion Regulation" and relates emotional and social-skill development to socialization.

- In Figure 12.23 on parenting styles, the label "Neglectful" replaces "Neglecting" in order to match the key term used in the narrative and reflect the term in more common use today.

- The *Myth or Reality?* is titled "The Aging Brain Is Like a Muscle: Use It or Lose it." It includes recent scientific references and adds examples of how the "mental exercise hypothesis" has generated popular products that claim to build mental power.

- Following the *Research Close-up* on "What Does It Take to Become an Adult?" a new section titled "Emerging Adulthood Beliefs across Cultures" discusses cross-cultural similarities and differences in beliefs about the criteria deemed necessary for attaining adulthood.

Chapter 13: Personality

- As before, the chapter opens with a historical description of mass killer Charles Whitman. Following treatment of the biological, psychodynamic, phenomenological-humanistic, trait, and social cognitive perspectives, the *Applying Psychological Science* uses concepts and propositions from each of these perspectives to piece together a coherent personality description of Whitman and the likely causal factors in his murderous acts.

- This chapter's *Myth or Reality?* challenges the proposition that trained psychological profilers are helpful in solving crimes and analyzes the reasons they have such credibility in the mass media and law enforcement domains. Part of this discussion introduces clinical versus actuarial prediction and the operation of cognitive heuristics previously covered in Chapter 9.

Chapter 14: Health and Well-Being

- Thoroughly reorganized and revised, this chapter has a positive psychology orientation in focusing on physical and psychological wellness and the factors that influence it.

- The *Myth or Reality?* tackles the misconception shared by many college students that binge drinking is harmless fun.

- A new section on resilience follows the material on stress and its effects on physical and psychological well-being. The *Research Close-up* presents a recent study of coping strategies that influenced the relation between life stress and illness in young athletes.

- A new section has been included on posttraumatic growth (PTG).

- A new updated section on happiness has been moved from Chapter 11, "Motivation and Emotion." The *Applying Psychological Science* presents research-derived guidelines for increasing one's subjective well-being.

Chapter 15: Psychological Disorders

- This chapter has been extensively restructured and updated, including not only a treatment of the major psychological disorders of adults and children, but also an analysis of scientific and social issues in psychiatric diagnosis.

- Our levels-of-analysis approach considers the causal factors of each class of disorders from a biological, psychological, and environmental vantage point.

- The *Myth or Reality?* explores the proposition that people with psychological disorders are especially dangerous.

- The *Research Close-up* presents a recent study by Adrian Raine's group on differences in prefrontal brain characteristics between successful (not apprehended) and unsuccessful (imprisoned) psychopaths.

- A restructured section on psychiatric diagnosis considers the differences between categorical and dimensional approaches to description and diagnosis, considers the changes coming in DSM-V, and shows how the newly proposed (February 2010) DSM-V revision makes use of dimensional rating scales to diagnose personality disorders.

Chapter 16: Treatment of Psychological Disorders

- This chapter, like all others, is completely updated, including nearly 40 new citations from 2008 to 2010.

- A new section on "third-wave" cognitive-behavioral therapies describes mindfulness approaches, Dialectical Behavior Therapy, and Acceptance and Commitment Therapy, reviewing the evidence for their efficacy.

- Costantino et al.'s (2009) research on how cultural congruence (between treatment and cultural beliefs) influences treatment outcomes for minorities is reviewed.

- The *Myth or Reality?* considers the efficacy and safety of antidepressant medications for depression, including the 2010 Fournier et al. study that showed that only the most depressed patients exhibited drug effects that exceeded those of patients who had taken placebos.

- An expanded section on treatment research methods applies scientific principles to this high-interest topic.

Chapter 17: Social Thinking and Behavior

- In the section on "Norms, Conformity, and Obedience," the brief discussion of social norms governing personal space has been deleted.

- In the *Research Close-up* on Milgram's obedience research, the content of the "Research Design" box has been simplified by focusing solely on his overall program as "experimental" and deleting mention of the "descriptive" nature of each individual study.

- In the section on "Detecting and Resisting Compliance Techniques," the norm of reciprocity is still covered, but the accompanying example and photo pertaining to the Hare Krishna Society's use of this norm in the 1970s has been deleted.

- In the section on "Behavior in Groups," the description of Ringelmann's rope-pulling experiment has been dropped from the social loafing section. New findings related to social loafing and groupthink are noted (e.g., Pearsall et al., 2010; Troyer & Youngreen, 2009).

- A recent study on speed dating (Luo & Zhang, 2009) is now discussed in the section on "Spellbound by Beauty"; Walster et al.'s (1966) classic study is described more briefly.

- The section on "Media Violence and Aggression" and the *Myth or Reality?* on video game violence contain many new references (e.g., Anderson et al., 2010). New meta-analytic and longitudinal findings on video game violence are described. While retaining the conclusion that exposure to violent media and video games increases the risk of aggression, dissenting viewpoints are noted (e.g., Ferguson, 2009).

chapter one

The Science of Psychology

Myth or Reality?™

When Taking Tests, Stick with Your First Instinct (page 8)

Psychology is a science that directly applies to your life. Read how researchers have critically examined this popular test-taking advice, and use what you learn the next time you take an exam.

Let's begin our exploration of psychology with a quick exercise. Please read the paragraph below, unscrambling the words as you proceed.

Aoccdrnig to a rscheearch at Cmabrigde Uinervtisy, it deosn't mttaer waht oredr the ltteers in a wrod are, the olny iprmoatnt tihng is taht the frist and lsat ltteres are at the rghit pclae. The rset can be a toatl mses and you can sitll raed it wouthit a porbelm. Tihs is bcuseae we do not raed ervey lteter by istlef but the wrod as a wlohe.

Type "jumbled words," "jumbled paragraph," or "scrambled letters" into a Web browser, dig around, and you'll find multiple sites and blogs about this paragraph. Back in 2003 it was all the rage, and it has been in the news since then (*Daily Telegraph*, 2009, April 1). The paragraph spread across the Internet (with the misspelling, "rscheearch") and reached countless e-mail inboxes as people—amazed by how easily they could read it—passed it along. When we showed the paragraph to our students, most breezed through it, though some struggled (if you had trouble, that's OK; see the unscrambled version on page 30). Show the paragraph to people you know, and see how they do.

Do you accept the claim that if the first and last letters of a word remain intact, "The rset can be a toatl mses and you can sitll raed it wouthit a porbelm"? From the paragraph's immense popularity, we speculate that many people did. After all, the evidence is concrete; it's right before our eyes. Well, whether you do or don't accept it, here's a challenge: can you think of reasons why this particular jumbled paragraph is easy to read? Even better, can you create a short jumbled paragraph—keeping the first and last letters of words intact—that people would find hard to read? We'll return to this challenge on page 6.

So what does a jumbled paragraph have to do with psychology? If you personally view *psychology* as synonymous with *therapy*, *shrinks*, or *couches*, then your answer might be "not much." But as we'll see, psychologists study a tremendous diversity of topics, and language—including how we recognize words—is one of them (Mousikou et al., 2010).

The paragraph raises other key psychological issues, such as how we acquire knowledge and form beliefs about our world, that we'll discuss shortly. Among the countless beliefs we hold and claims we hear about human nature and behavior, how do we separate fact from fiction, myth from reality? The science of psychology leads us to engage these questions.

THE NATURE OF PSYCHOLOGY

Psychology *is the scientific study of behavior and the mind.* The term *behavior* refers to actions and responses that we can directly observe, whereas the term *mind* refers to internal states and processes—such as thoughts and feelings—that cannot be seen directly and that must be inferred from observable, measurable responses. For example, we cannot directly see a person's feeling of love or admiration for someone else, but we can infer how the person feels based on observable verbal statements ("I love you," "I really admire you").

To many people, when you say the word *psychologist*, the first image that comes to mind is that of a therapist. This reaction is understandable, as a large number of psychologists work in a subfield called **clinical psychology:** *the study and treatment of mental disorders.* Many clinical psychologists diagnose and treat people with psychological problems in clinics, hospitals, and private practice. Some also are scientists who conduct research on the causes of mental disorders and the effectiveness of various treatments. Yet many psychologists have no connection with therapy and instead conduct research in other subfields (Figure 1.1). For example, **cognitive psychology** *specializes in the study of mental processes, especially from a model that views the mind as an information processor.* Cognitive psychologists examine topics such as consciousness, attention, memory, decision making, and problem solving. An area within cognitive psychology, called *psycholinguistics,* focuses on the psychology of language. The jumbled-word exercise relates directly to psycholinguistics.

To illustrate psychology's diversity, here are a few other subfields:

- **Biopsychology** *focuses on the biological underpinnings of behavior.* Biopsychologists examine how brain processes, genes, and hormones influence our actions, thoughts, and feelings. Some biopsychologists seek to explain how evolution has shaped our psychological capabilities (e.g., our capacity for advanced thinking and language) and behavioral tendencies (e.g., acting aggressively or altruistically).

- **Developmental psychology** *examines human physical, psychological, and social development across the life span.* For example, some developmental psychologists explore the infant's emotional world, while others study how different parenting styles psychologically affect children or how our mental abilities change during adolescence and adulthood.

- **Experimental psychology** *focuses on basic processes such as learning, sensory systems (e.g., vision, hearing), perception, and motivational states (e.g., sexual motivation, hunger, thirst).* Most research in this subfield involves laboratory experiments, often with nonhuman animals. Although this subfield is called "experimental" psychology, be aware that researchers in many psychological subfields conduct experiments.

- **Industrial-organizational (I/O) psychology** *examines people's behavior in the workplace.* I/O psychologists study leadership, teamwork, and factors that influence employees' job satisfaction, work motivation, and performance. They develop tests to help employers identify the best job applicants and design systems that companies use to evaluate employee performance.

Figure 1.1

Psychologists study diverse topics. Subfields that may not immediately occur to you include aviation and space psychology, educational psychology, and psychology and the law.

- **Personality psychology** *focuses on the study of human personality*. Personality psychologists seek to identify core personality traits and the way different traits relate to one another and influence behavior. They also develop tests to measure personality.

- **Social psychology** *examines people's thoughts, feelings, and behavior pertaining to the social world:* the world of other people. Social psychologists study how people influence one another, behave in groups, and form impressions and attitudes. They study social relationships involving attraction and love, prejudice and discrimination, helping, and aggression.

Note that topics studied in different subfields often overlap. Consider decision making, which is examined in all of the areas mentioned above. For example, a cognitive psychologist might study how wording the same information in different ways affects people's decisions, a social psychologist might study decision making in groups, and a developmental psychologist could examine how children's decision-making strategies change with age (Joslyn et al., 2009; Toma & Butera, 2009). Moreover, many psychologists have interests that bridge different subfields. Thus a clinical

psychologist might be interested in the biological bases of how adolescents with anxiety disorders make decisions. She could have adolescents who do and who don't have an anxiety disorder perform decision-making tasks, and use brain-imaging techniques to compare the neural activity of the two groups (Krain et al., 2008).

We'll encounter other branches of psychology throughout the chapter, but we hope you already get the picture. Psychologists do study the causes of mental disorders, provide therapy, and evaluate therapy effectiveness, but their interests and research span the entire realm of behavior. Indeed, the scope of modern psychology stretches from the borders of medicine and the biological sciences to those of the social sciences (Figure 1.2).

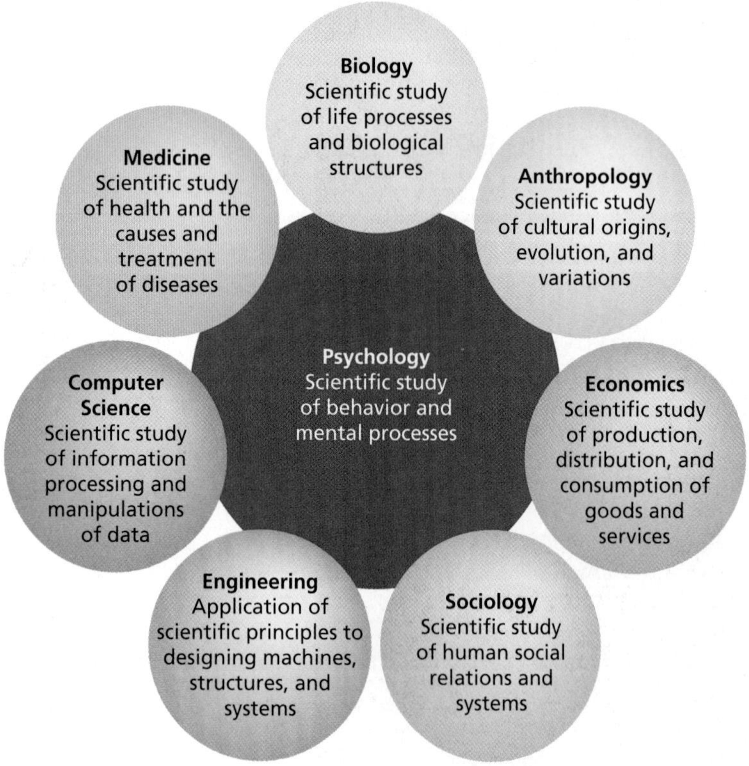

Psychology's Scientific Approach

Across psychology's diverse subfields, researchers share a common underlying scientific approach to studying behavior. *Science* is a process that involves systematically gathering and evaluating empirical evidence to answer questions and test beliefs about the natural world. *Empirical evidence* is evidence gained through experience and observation; it includes evidence obtained from manipulating or "tinkering around" with things and then observing what happens (this is the essence of experimentation). For example, if we want to know how people's intellectual abilities change as they age, we don't rely on intuition, pure reasoning, or folk wisdom to obtain an answer. Rather, we collect empirical data by exposing people to intellectual tasks and observing how they perform. Moreover, in science these observations need to be *systematic* (i.e., performed according to a system of rules or conditions) so that they will be as objective and precise as possible (Shaughnessy et al., 2010).

Understanding Behavior: Some Pitfalls of Everyday Approaches

Science is only one of many ways that we learn about human behavior. Family and friends, great works of literature, secular and religious teachings, the Internet and popular media—all provide us with messages about human nature. Mix in our own intuitions, the knowledge that each of us acquires from years of personal experience interacting with people, and so-called conventional or folk wisdom, and we have potent ingredients for generating our personal beliefs about what makes people tick.

Figure 1.2

Psychology as a scientific hub.
Psychology links with and overlaps many sciences.

Problem is, in everyday life there are many ways in which these sources can end up promoting misconceptions. Other people—via conversations, books, the Internet, and popular media—may provide us with information and insights that they believe to be accurate but which really are not. Even personal experiences can lead us to form inaccurate beliefs. Although our experiences and everyday observations provide us with empirical information, unlike scientific observations, everyday observations are usually casual rather than systematic. Our own experiences also may be atypical and not representative of what most people experience.

As we'll explore in later chapters, misconceptions also can result from our own faulty thinking. For example:

- We often take *mental shortcuts* when forming judgments, shortcuts that sometimes serve us poorly (White, 2009). Judging someone's personality based solely on stereotypes about his or her physical appearance would be an example of a mental shortcut.

- Because many factors in real life may operate simultaneously to influence behavior, we may *fail to consider alternative explanations* for a behavior and assume that one factor has caused it when in fact some less obvious factor was the major cause (Lassiter et al., 2007).

- Once our beliefs are established, we often fail to test them further. In this vein, we tend to display a *confirmation bias* by selectively paying attention to information that is consistent with our beliefs and downplaying or ignoring information that is inconsistent with them (Hart et al., 2009).

Using Science to Minimize Everyday Pitfalls

Yes, scientists are human too and may fall victim to all these pitfalls and to others that we'll discuss in the next chapter. But by adopting a scientific approach, psychologists can take concrete steps to avoid or at least minimize biases and problems that can lead to inaccurate conclusions. For example, rather than relying on imprecise casual observations, psychologists use various instruments (e.g., video recorders, questionnaires, brain-imaging devices) to objectively and precisely record people's responses. When directly watching people, several researchers can independently observe the same behaviors and compare their findings to ensure that their observations were reliable. To further reduce subjectivity psychologists typically use statistics to analyze their data.

To minimize erroneous conclusions about what has caused what, psychologists often are able to examine behavior under highly controlled experimental conditions in which they intentionally manipulate one factor, try to keep other factors constant, and see how the manipulated factor influences behavior.

Science also is a public affair, as occurs when psychologists publish their findings. This enables scientists to scrutinize and challenge each other's findings if they wish. Collectively, this reduces the risk of confirmation bias. As new studies are conducted, the original findings are put to the test and may be contradicted, forcing scientists to modify their beliefs and to conduct further research to sort out the reason for the contradictory results.

To be sure, science has limitations and its own pitfalls. It is ideally suited to examining testable questions about the natural world. Psychologists can study questions such as "Do happy people differ from unhappy people in their degree of religiousness or spirituality?" and "What do people believe gives their life meaning?" But science cannot answer questions such as "Does God exist?" and "What is the meaning of life?" The former is a question of faith that is beyond scientific measurement; the latter is a question answered by personal values. As for pitfalls, poorly designed or poorly executed studies can produce misleading data that lead to invalid conclusions.

Even when studies are designed well and conducted properly, "false starts" can occur in which other researchers later are unable to duplicate the original researchers' findings. Additionally, over time, new research often modifies or completely overturns existing scientific beliefs. But it's important to realize that these aren't weaknesses of the scientific approach. Rather, they reveal one of its great strengths: *in principle, science ultimately is a self-correcting process.* At any point in history, scientific knowledge represents a best estimate of how the world operates. As better or more complete information is gathered, that best estimate may continue to be supported, or it may need to be changed. Understandably, to many people such change can be frustrating or confusing, as illustrated by the public uproar in 2009 when an expert medical panel issued new breast-cancer screening guidelines (Kolata, 2009). The panel stated that most women should start having regular mammogram tests at age 50, not at age 40 as recommended by prior, long-standing guidelines. To scientists, however, such change represents an evolution of knowledge called "scientific progress."

Thinking Critically about Behavior

Because behavior is so complex, its scientific study poses special challenges. As you become familiar with the kinds of evidence necessary to validate scientific conclusions, you will become a better-informed consumer of the many claims made in the name of psychology. For one thing, this course will teach you that many widely held beliefs about behavior are inaccurate. Can you distinguish the valid claims from the invalid ones in Table 1.1?

Perhaps more important than the concepts you learn in this course will be the habits of thought that you acquire—habits that involve *critical thinking*. Critical thinking involves taking an active role in understanding the world around you, rather than merely receiving information. It's important to reflect on what that information means, how it fits in with your experiences, and what implications it has for your life and society. Critical thinking also means evaluating the validity of something presented to you as fact (Levy, 2010). For example, when someone makes a claim or asserts a new "fact," ask yourself the following questions, just as a scientist would:

- What, exactly, is the claim or assertion?
- Who is making the claim? Is the source credible and trustworthy?
- What's the evidence, and how good is it?
- Are other explanations possible? If so, can I evaluate them?
- What is the most appropriate conclusion?

Table 1.1 | Widely Held Beliefs about Behavior: Fact or Fiction?

Directions: Decide whether each statement is true or false.

1. Most people with exceptionally high IQs are well adjusted in other areas of their life.
2. In romantic relationships, opposites usually attract.
3. Overall, married adults are less happy than adults who aren't married.
4. Graphology (handwriting analysis) is a valid method for measuring people's personality.
5. A person who is innocent of a crime has nothing to fear from a lie detector test.
6. People who commit suicide usually have signaled to others their intention to do so.
7. When you negatively reinforce someone's behavior, the person becomes more likely to behave that way.
8. On some types of mental tasks, people perform as well or better when they are 70 years old than when they are 20 years old.
9. Usually it is safe to awaken someone who is sleepwalking.
10. A schizophrenic is a person who has two or more distinct personalities, hence the term *split personality*.

ANSWERS: Items 1, 6, 8, and 9 are supported by psychological research. Item 7 is true by definition. The remaining items are false. (If you correctly answered nine or ten of these items, you've done significantly better than random guessing.)

The Jumbled-Word Challenge

Let's think critically about the jumbled-word paragraph presented earlier. First, *what's the claim?* There are three, actually: (1) that people can read jumbled words without a problem as long as the first and last letters stay in the same place, (2) that this occurs because we read "words as a whole" rather than read each letter by itself, and (3) that this finding is based on research at Cambridge University.

Second, *who is making the claim?* Unfortunately, the jumbled-paragraph's author is anonymous, which is *caution flag #1*. We can't evaluate the author's credibility and trustworthiness.

Third, *what's the evidence, and how good is it?* The evidence begins with a claim implying that research was conducted at Cambridge. No reference information (researchers' names, publication location or date) is given: this is *caution flag #2*. Indeed, it seems that there was no such research done at Cambridge, although unpublished research at another university may have been the source (Davis, 2003; Rawlinson, 1999).

There's also the dramatic evidence of your own experience: reading the jumbled paragraph easily. But this is only one short paragraph. Also, overall, the transposition (i.e., switched ordering) of letters is minimal. This is *caution flag #3* and leads to the next question.

Fourth, *are other explanations possible* for why the paragraph is easy to read? We'll discuss reading more fully in Chapter 9. For now, consider this:

- Sixty-five percent of the words either aren't jumbled (because they have only one to three letters), or—with four-letter words—there is only one possible transposition (switching the second and third letters), which makes unscrambling them easy.
- For the words with five or six letters, in all but one case, the transposition is minor because only a single letter is out of sequence (e.g., for "mttaer," only the "a" is out of order).
- Thus, in total, 83 percent of the words are either unjumbled or have only minor transpositions. This preserves much of the way the words sound when we read them. Further, these words provide contextual information that makes it easier to anticipate the meaning of some of the few longer scrambled words.

In everyday life, you're unlikely to conduct a scientific study to test these alternative explanations, but you can gather additional evidence by constructing sentences with longer words and more complex transpositions and having some people try to read them. Try reading this paragraph (page 30 reveals the unjumbled version), and see if it changes your belief about the ease of reading jumbled words.

A plciaiiotn dieend the mtnaalueghsr of a clgaloeue, but was coincetvd and dlepoeevd sreeve macedil cdointonis in posirn, wrhee he deid. Arnodiistitman of agctannloauit dgurs ptttnaioeed the eefctfs of atehonr durg, and rprsoiearty frliaue rleeutsd.

Lastly, *what is the most appropriate conclusion to draw?* The claim that it's relatively easy to read words as long as the first and last letters are intact appears to be too broad, too absolute. Stated as such, it's clearly wrong. Stated in qualified terms of "under some conditions," the claim has support, although one study found that even minor transpositions of interior letters slowed reading speed by 11 percent (Rayner et al., 2006). In some languages, however, such interior transpositions may make words very difficult, if not impossible, to read (Davis, 2003).

Of Astrology and Asstrology: Potential Costs of Uncritical Thinking

Suppose someone swallows the bait of the original jumbled-word paragraph and now erroneously believes that it's always easy to read words with transposed letters. Unless it's a smart-aleck student or worker who plans to turn in jumbled school papers or work reports (citing "scientific justification" for doing so), what's the harm in holding this little false belief? Perhaps the immediate personal consequences are minimal, but misconceptions can add up and contribute to an increasingly misguided view of how the world operates.

Unfortunately, people uncritically accept many misconceptions that do have concrete harmful consequences. For example, in the hope of making their babies smarter, consumers shelled out about 200 million dollars annually to purchase Baby Einstein videos that the Walt Disney Company advertised as educational, despite a lack of scientific support for such educational claims (Zimmerman et al., 2007). Under government and consumer-group pressure, Disney eventually dropped the "educational" claim and later agreed to partially refund consumers (Lewin, 2009).

Despite a lack of scientific evidence, people spend untold amounts of their hard-earned money to have their personalities analyzed and their futures forecasted by astrologers,

Figure 1.3

The popularity of pseudoscience.

Source: ScienceCartoonsPlus.com. Reprinted with permission.

graphologists (handwriting analyzers), tea-leaf readers, and other so-called fortune tellers—including "rumpologists" (sometimes referred to as "asstrologers"), who "read" people's buttocks to obtain their presumed psychic insights (Wyman & Vyse, 2008). Money aside, it's impossible to estimate how many people have made major life decisions based on fortune tellers' bogus advice. It's also hard to know how many people have not only wasted money on bogus therapies for ailments, diseases, and mental disorders but also experienced needless continued distress or further bodily harm by failing to employ scientifically validated treatments. Unfortunately, *pseudoscience—* fields such as astrology, graphology, rumpology, and so on that are dressed up to look like science but which lack credible scientific evidence— appears to attract many believers (Figure 1.3).

Each chapter of this textbook contains a special section called "Myth or Reality?" in which we'll examine a popular psychological claim in depth. We've already discussed the jumbled-words claim, but now let's examine a claim that may be familiar to you and perhaps is already influencing your behavior—with potential costs. See the next page.

Goals of Psychology

As a science, psychology has four central goals: *description, explanation, control,* and *application.* Description is the most basic goal; psychologists seek to describe how people behave, think, and feel. Second, psychologists strive to explain—to understand—why people act as they do. Explanations typically take the form of hypotheses and theories that specify the causes of behavior. Third,

Myth or Reality?

When Taking Tests, Stick with Your First Instinct

Double-check your answers, but only change an answer if you misread the question or found something in the test that indicates your first answer was incorrect. Otherwise, stick with your first guess because research shows it's usually the right answer. (Hutton, 2009; education.com, 2009)

Does this advice sound familiar? Many test-taking tips Web sites offer similar advice: if you're unsure about your initial answer, "stick with your first instinct." In other words, if you change answers, you're more likely to switch a right answer to a wrong one than a wrong answer to a right one. Most students and many instructors agree with this claim: they believe that changing answers will more likely lower than raise exam scores (Kruger et al., 2005).

What Happens When Students Switch Answers?

In 1929, C. O. Mathews analyzed almost 40,000 answers that college students marked on multiple-choice and true-false tests. Of the answers students had changed, switching from wrong to right was far more common (59 percent of switches) than switching from right to wrong (27 percent of switches). The remaining switches were from one wrong answer to another wrong answer. Decades later, psychologists reviewed 33 studies on this topic and concluded that in every study "(a) the majority of answer changes are from incorrect to correct and (b) most students who change their answers improve their test scores" (Benjamin et al., 1984).

More recently, psychologists Justin Kruger, Derrick Wirtz, and Dale Miller (2005) obtained similar findings in a study of 1,561 college students. By a 2:1 ratio, more changed answers went from wrong to right than from right to wrong, and by nearly a 3:1 ratio more students who changed answers ended up with higher rather than lower exam scores (Figure 1.4). Yet most students still believed that as a general test-taking strategy, changing answers was harmful. Kruger et al. called this "the first instinct fallacy."

The First Instinct Fallacy

Before concluding that the first instinct strategy is indeed a fallacy, let's think critically. Benjamin et al. (1984) note two cautions. First, in some instances students may have changed answers (and gone from wrong to right) because they simply misread the question or mismarked their answer. Researchers typically can't tell why students changed exam answers, so this means that analyzing students' changed answers on exams isn't a pure test of the "stick with your first hunch" strategy. Second, scrutinizing exam forms for changed answers doesn't tell us about the answers that students thought about changing but didn't change. Perhaps by following the first instinct strategy, students got most of those items right. Last, we'll add that if the first instinct strategy is a myth, it would help to have a convincing psychological explanation for why so many people believe it to be reality.

Fortunately, Kruger, Wirtz, and Miller's research (2005) addressed these issues. In three studies, they tested and found support for an explanation of why people perceive the first instinct fallacy to be true. Imagine that on an exam item you thought about switching answers, decided not to, and would have gotten it right if you had switched. On another item, you had the right answer but switched to a wrong answer. As the researchers predicted, given these two outcomes,

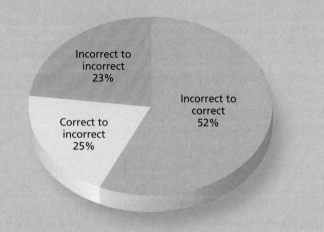

Figure 1.4

Changing answers on multiple-choice tests.
Researchers analyzed the eraser marks on 6,412 exams taken by introductory psychology students. Contrary to popular wisdom, changing one's answer was twice as likely to result in gaining points than in losing points. Source: Based on Kruger et al., 2005.

many more students said that switching from right to wrong would be the more frustrating outcome. "Geez I had it right. If only I hadn't switched!" This frustration then leads to a memory bias in which we are more likely to remember instances of right-to-wrong switches than instances when we should have switched but didn't. In turn, the memory bias leads students to believe that sticking with one's first instinct generally is the best strategy. This four-stage model appears below:

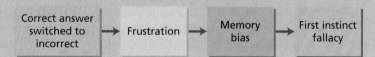

Moreover, in one of their studies, Kruger et al. (2005) were able to identify instances in which students were unsure of their multiple-choice answers but stuck with their initial choices rather than switching to a second choice they thought might be correct. Indeed, students stuck with their first instinct most of the time, and it cost them: their "first instinct answers" were almost twice as likely to be wrong as they were to be right.

Conclusions

Based on available evidence, "stick with your first instinct" appears to be more myth than reality. If upon reflection you have doubts about an initial exam answer and think that another answer is more likely to be correct, don't be afraid to change it. This doesn't guarantee that on any single exam, or even over the long haul, you'll be better off switching answers. Guarantees like that don't exist. Odds are that being willing to switch answers will benefit you in the long run, but some students do obtain lower scores by switching. What you can do is gather your own evidence from several exams. Act like a scientist. For exam items you were unsure about, note whether you "stayed" or "switched." How often did each strategy help or hurt your score? Keep a tally of the outcomes, and then you'll have some personal evidence to guide your future test-taking strategy.

psychologists exert control by designing experiments or other types of research to test whether their proposed explanations are accurate. Finally, many psychologists apply psychological knowledge in ways that enhance human welfare.

Consider Kruger et al.'s (2005) research on the first instinct fallacy. They first determined that although students are more likely to change multiple-choice answers from wrong to right than from right to wrong, they still erroneously believe that the best exam strategy is to "go with your first instinct" (description). Next, they proposed a model to explain why many students hold this belief (explanation). To test each part of their model, Kruger et al. conducted additional studies in which they carefully controlled the situations and questions to which participants were exposed (control). Their findings supported the model. The knowledge gained has already led other psychologists and educators to offer correct advice to students about answer-switching strategies (Social Psychology Network, 2010). Now you can apply this knowledge to your own test-taking behavior as well.

Basic and Applied Research

Science involves **basic research,** *which reflects the quest for knowledge for its own sake,* and **applied research,** *which is designed to solve specific, practical problems.* For psychologists, most basic research examines how and why people behave, think, and feel the way they do. Kruger et al.'s (2005) research on the first instinct fallacy represents basic research. Their main intent was to test a hypothetical model and thereby increase our understanding of why the first instinct fallacy exists. Although the knowledge gained from their study has obvious applied relevance, the purpose of their study was not to apply that knowledge or directly modify students' beliefs or behavior. Basic research may be carried out in laboratories or real-world settings, with human participants or other species. Psychologists who study other species usually attempt to discover principles that ultimately will shed light on human behavior, but some study animal behavior for its own sake.

In applied research, psychologists often use basic scientific knowledge to design interventions. For example, we could use the basic knowledge obtained from Kruger et al.'s (2005) research to design and test the effectiveness of an intervention program aimed at altering college students' misconceptions about changing exam answers. Similarly, researchers have used basic research findings—such as principles concerning

how people learn by observing the behavior of others—to design and implement HIV/AIDS-prevention programs in North America, Africa, and Asia (Lerdboon et al., 2008).

Psychology's Broad Scope: A Simple Framework

Because we are biological creatures living in a complex social world, psychologists study an amazing array of factors to understand why people behave, think, and feel as they do. At times, this diversity of factors may seem a bit overwhelming, but we would like to provide you with a framework that will greatly simplify matters. We call it *levels of analysis:* behavior and its causes can be examined at the *biological level* (e.g., brain processes, genetic influences), the *psychological level* (e.g., our thoughts, feelings, and motives), and the *environmental level* (e.g., past and current physical and social environments to which we are exposed).

Here is a brief example of how the framework can be applied. Consider a behavior that you engage in every day: eating (Figure 1.5). At the biological level, various chemicals, neural circuits, and structures in your brain respond to bodily signals and help regulate whether you feel hungry or full. At the psychological level, your moods, food preferences, and motives affect eating. Do you ever eat when you're not hungry, perhaps because you feel stressed or bored? The environmental level of analysis calls attention to specific stimuli (such as the appearance or aroma of different foods) that may trigger eating and to cultural customs that influence our food preferences. Does the aroma of freshly baked treats ever make your stomach growl? How about the sight of duck feet or a mound of fish gills on a plate? To most Westerners, duck feet and fish gills may not be appetizing, but during a stay in China we discovered that our hosts considered them delicious.

Mind-Body and Nature-Nurture Interactions

Form a mental picture of a favorite food, and you may trigger a hunger pang. Focus on positive thoughts when facing a challenging situation, and you may keep your bodily arousal in check; dwell instead on negative thoughts, and you can rapidly stimulate the release of stress hormones (Borod, 2000). These examples illustrate what traditionally have been called *mind-body interactions*—the relations between mental processes in the brain and the functioning of other bodily systems. Mind-body interactions focus our attention on the fascinating interplay between the psychological

The Biological Level

The Psychological Level

The Environmental Level

Figure 1.5

(*left*) **Biological level.** This rat weighs about triple the weight of a normal rat. As we (or rats) eat, hunger decreases as certain brain regions regulate the sensation of becoming full. Those regions in this rat's brain have been damaged, causing it to overeat and become obese. (*center*) **Psychological level.** At times we may eat out of habit, stress, or boredom. With candy bar in hand and other candies lined up, this student is ready for some autopilot munching. (*right*) **Environmental level.** Does a plateful of insect-topped crackers sound appetizing to you? Cultural norms influence food preferences.

Figure 1.6

Youth and beauty? Or maturity and wisdom?

What we perceive depends on our perspective. If you examine this drawing, you will see either a young woman or an old one. Now try changing your perspective. The ear and necklace of the young woman are the left eye and mouth of the old woman.

and biological levels of analysis. This topic has a long history within psychology, and as you will see throughout the textbook, it remains one of psychology's most exciting frontiers.

The levels-of-analysis framework also addresses an issue that has been debated since antiquity: is our behavior primarily shaped by nature (our biological endowment) or by nurture (our environment and learning history)? The pendulum has swung toward one end or the other at different times in history, but today, growing interest in cultural influences and advances in genetics and brain research keep the nature-nurture pendulum in a more balanced position.

Perhaps most important, modern research increasingly reveals that nature and nurture interact (Moffitt et al., 2006). Just as our biological capacities affect how we behave and experience the world, our experiences influence our biological capacities. For humans and rats alike, continually depriving a newborn of physical contact, or providing a newborn with an enriched environment in which to grow, can influence its brain functioning and biological development (Rosenzweig, 1984). Thus, while it may be tempting to take sides, "nature *or*

nurture?" usually is the wrong question. As the levels-of-analysis framework implies, nature, nurture, and psychological factors must all be taken into account to gain the fullest understanding of behavior. Later in the chapter, we'll provide a more detailed example of how looking at behavior from multiple levels enhances our understanding.

PERSPECTIVES ON BEHAVIOR

Psychologists' focus on the biological, psychological, and environmental factors that influence behavior is not new; it has been an integral part of psychology's history. But just how did psychology's scope become so broad? In part, it happened because psychology has roots in such varied disciplines as philosophy, medicine, and the biological and physical sciences. As a result, different ways of viewing people, called *perspectives*, became part of psychology's intellectual traditions (Figure 1.6).

In science, new perspectives are engines of progress. Advances occur as existing beliefs are challenged, a debate ensues, and scientists seek

test yourself   **The Nature of Psychology**

The titles of five research articles from psychological journals are listed below. Based on the title, identify whether each study is most likely to represent *basic* or *applied* research.

1. Two forms of spatial imagery: Neuroimaging evidence
2. The prevention of depressive symptoms in low-income minority children: Two-year follow-up
3. Increasing seat belt use on a college campus: An evaluation of two prompting procedures
4. Facial structure is a reliable cue of aggressive behavior
5. Recognizing speech under a processing load: Dissociating energetic from informational factors

ANSWERS: 1-basic, 2-applied, 3-applied, 4-basic, 5-basic

new evidence to resolve the debate. Sometimes, the best-supported elements of contrasting perspectives are merged into a new framework, which in turn will be challenged by still newer viewpoints.

If you have ever met someone who views the world differently from the way you do, you know that perspectives matter. Similarly, perspectives serve as lenses through which psychologists examine and interpret behavior. To illustrate this point, consider the case of Ray, a shy student when he first entered college. Ray knew he was shy, especially around women, yet he wasn't sure why. He had been nervous on the few dates he had gone on in high school. During his first college semester, Ray met some women he liked but was afraid to ask them out. He didn't make male friends either. By winter, he was depressed and his schoolwork suffered. After a good spring-break visit with his family, Ray turned things around. He studied hard, did well in class, and made friends with some guys in the dorm. His mood improved, and soon thereafter he met Kira. Kira was attracted to Ray but sensed his shyness, so she asked Ray out. They've been dating for a year, and Ray is happy. He and Kira have even discussed marriage.

Soon we'll briefly look at Ray's case through the lens of six psychological perspectives. But first, to better understand how these perspectives evolved, let's examine psychology's roots and two of its earliest schools of thought.

Psychology's Intellectual Roots

Humans have long sought to understand themselves, and for ages the *mind-body problem* has occupied the center of this quest. Is the mind—the inner agent of consciousness and thought—a spiritual entity separate from the body, or is it a part of the body's activities?

Many early philosophers held a position of *mind-body dualism,* the belief that the mind is a spiritual entity not subject to physical laws that govern the body. But if the mind is not composed of physical matter, how could it become aware of bodily sensations, and how could its thoughts exert control over bodily functions? French philosopher and scientist René Descartes (1596–1650) proposed that the mind and body interact through the brain's tiny pineal gland. Although Descartes placed the mind within the brain, he maintained that the mind was a spiritual, non-material entity. Dualism implies that no amount of research on the physical body (including the brain) could ever hope to unravel the mysteries of the nonphysical mind.

Another view, *monism* (from the Greek word *monos,* meaning "one"), holds that mind and body are one and that the mind is not a separate spiritual entity. To monists, mental events correspond to physical events in the brain, a position advocated by English philosopher Thomas Hobbes (1588–1679). Monism helped set the stage for psychology because it implied that the mind could be studied by measuring physical processes within the brain. The stage was further set by John Locke (1632–1704) and other philosophers from the school of **British empiricism,** *which held that all ideas and knowledge are gained empirically—that is, through the senses.* According to empiricists, observation is a more valid approach to knowledge than is pure reason, because reason is fraught with the potential for error. This idea bolstered the development of modern science, whose methods are rooted in empirical observation.

Discoveries in physiology (an area of biology that examines bodily functioning) and medicine also paved the way for psychology's emergence. By 1870, European researchers were electrically stimulating the brains of laboratory animals and

Figure 1.7

At the University of Leipzig in 1879, Wilhelm Wundt (*far right*) established the first laboratory of experimental psychology to study the structure of the mind.

Figure 1.8

William James, a leader of functionalism, helped establish psychology in North America. His multivolume book, *Principles of Psychology* (1890/1950), greatly expanded the scope of psychology.

Figure 1.9

Mary Whiton Calkins founded a psychology laboratory at Wellesley College, where she taught for over 30 years. She studied memory and dreams and, in 1905, became the first female president of the American Psychological Association.

mapping the surface areas that controlled various body movements. Additionally, medical reports were linking damage in different areas of patients' brains with various behavioral and mental impairments. This mounting evidence of the relation between brain and behavior supported the view that empirical methods of the natural sciences could be used to study mental processes. Indeed, in the mid-1800s German scientists had already established a new field called *psychophysics*, the study of how psychologically experienced sensations depend on the characteristics of physical stimuli (e.g., how the perceived loudness of a sound changes as its physical intensity increases).

Around this time, Charles Darwin's (1809–1882) theory of evolution was generating societal shock waves. Opponents attacked his theory because it seemed to contradict philosophical and religious beliefs about the exalted nature of human beings. Evolution implied that the mind was not a spiritual entity but rather the product of biological continuity between humans and other species. Darwin's theory also implied that scientists might gain insight about human behavior by studying other species. By the late 1800s, a convergence of intellectual forces provided the impetus for psychology's birth.

Early Schools: Structuralism and Functionalism

The infant science of psychology emerged in 1879, when Wilhelm Wundt (1832–1920) established the first experimental psychology laboratory at the University of Leipzig in Germany (Figure 1.7). One of his graduate students, Englishman Edward Titchener (1867–1927), later established a psychology laboratory in the United States at Cornell University. Wundt and Titchener believed that the mind could be studied by breaking it down into its basic components, as a chemist might break down a complex chemical compound. Their approach came to be known as **structuralism,** *the analysis of the mind in terms of its basic elements.*

In their experiments, structuralists used the method of *introspection* ("looking within") to study sensations, which they considered the basic elements of consciousness. They exposed participants to all sorts of sensory stimuli—lights, sounds, tastes—and trained them to describe their inner experiences. Although this method of studying the mind was criticized as being too subjective and died out after a few decades, the structuralists left an important mark by establishing a scientific tradition for studying cognitive processes.

In the United States, structuralism eventually gave way to **functionalism,** *which held that psychology should study the functions of consciousness rather than its elements.* Here's a rough analogy to explain the difference between structuralism and functionalism: Consider your hands. A structuralist would try to explain their movement by studying how muscles, tendons, and bones operate. In contrast, a functionalist would ask, "Why do we have hands? How do they help us adapt to our environment?" The functionalists asked similar questions about mental processes and behavior. They were influenced by Darwin's evolutionary theory, which stressed the importance of adaptation in helping organisms survive and reproduce in their environment.

William James (1842–1910), a leader in the functionalist movement, taught courses in physiology, psychology, and philosophy at Harvard University (Figure 1.8). James helped widen the scope of psychology to include the study of various biological and mental processes and overt behavior. Like Wundt, James trained psychologists who went on to distinguished careers. Among them was Mary Whiton Calkins (1863–1930), who became the first female president of the American Psychological Association in 1905 (Figure 1.9). Although functionalism no longer exists as a school of thought within psychology, its tradition endures in two modern-day fields: *cognitive psychology*, which studies mental processes, and *evolutionary psychology*, which emphasizes the adaptiveness of behavior.

The Psychodynamic Perspective: The Forces Within

Have you ever been mystified by why you behaved or felt a certain way? Recall the case of Ray, the student described earlier in the chapter who could not understand why he was so shy. The **psychodynamic perspective** *searches for the causes of behavior within the inner workings of our personality (our unique pattern of traits, emotions, and motives), emphasizing the role of unconscious processes.* Sigmund Freud (1856–1939) developed the first and most influential psychodynamic theory (Figure 1.10).

Psychoanalysis: Freud's Great Challenge

In late 19th-century Vienna, Freud was a young physician intrigued by the brain's mysteries. Some of his patients experienced symptoms such as blindness, pain, paralysis, and phobias (intense unrealistic fears) that were not caused by any apparent bodily malfunction or disease. Thus Freud reasoned that the causes must be psychological. Moreover, if patients were not producing their symptoms consciously, Freud reasoned that the causes must be hidden from awareness—they must be unconscious. Freud eventually treated his patients by using a technique called *free association,* in which the patient expressed any thoughts that came to mind. To Freud's surprise, patients eventually described painful and long-"forgotten" childhood experiences, often sexual in nature. After patients remembered and mentally "relived" these traumatic experiences, their symptoms often improved.

Freud became convinced that an unconscious part of the mind profoundly influences behavior, and he developed a theory and a form of psychotherapy called **psychoanalysis**—*the analysis of internal and primarily unconscious psychological forces.* He also proposed that humans have powerful inborn sexual and aggressive drives and that because these desires are punished in childhood, we learn to fear them and become anxious when we are aware of their presence. This leads us to develop *defense mechanisms,* which are psychological techniques that help us cope with anxiety and the pain of traumatic experiences. *Repression,* a primary defense mechanism, protects us by keeping unacceptable impulses, feelings, and memories in the unconscious depths of the mind. All behavior, whether normal or "abnormal," reflects a largely unconscious and inevitable conflict between the defenses and internal impulses. This ongoing psychological struggle between conflicting forces is dynamic in nature, hence the term *psychodynamic.* To explain Ray's extreme shyness around women, Freud might have explored whether Ray is unconsciously afraid of his sexual impulses and therefore avoids putting himself into dating situations where he would have to confront those hidden impulses.

Freud's theory stirred great controversy. Even some of his followers disagreed with aspects of the theory, especially its heavy emphasis on childhood sexuality. Other psychologists viewed the theory as difficult to test. Nevertheless, Freud's ideas stimulated research on topics such as dreams, memory, aggression, and mental disorders. One review of over 3,000 scientific studies examining Freud's ideas found support for some aspects of his theory, whereas other aspects were unsupported or contradicted (Fisher & Greenberg, 1996). But even where Freud's theory wasn't supported, it ultimately led to important discoveries. Additionally, Freud's work forever broadened the face of psychology to include the study and treatment of psychological disorders.

Modern Psychodynamic Theory

Modern psychodynamic theories continue to explore how unconscious and conscious aspects of personality influence behavior. However, they downplay the role of hidden sexual and aggressive motives and focus more on how early relationships with family members and other caregivers shape the views that people form of themselves and others (Kernberg, 2000; Levine, 2010). In turn, these views can unconsciously influence a person's relationships with other people throughout life.

To explain Ray's shyness, a modern psychodynamic psychologist might examine Ray's conceptions of himself and his parents. Ray's shyness may stem from a fear of rejection of which he is unaware. This fear may be based on conceptions that he developed of his parents as being rejecting and disapproving, views that now unconsciously shape his expectations of how relationships with women and men will be.

The psychodynamic perspective dominated thinking about personality, mental disorders, and psychotherapy for the first half of the 20th century, and it continues to influence psychology and the practice of psychotherapy (Ryle, 2010). Although most contemporary psychological scientists reject Freud's particular version of the unconscious mind, modern psychological research has identified brain mechanisms that produce unconscious emotional reactions and has shown that many aspects of information processing occur outside of awareness (Bargh & Morsella, 2010; Debiec & LeDoux, 2009).

The Behavioral Perspective: The Power of the Environment

The **behavioral perspective** *focuses on the role of the external environment in governing our actions.* From this perspective, our behavior is jointly determined by habits learned from previous life experiences and by stimuli in our immediate environment.

Origins of the Behavioral Perspective

The behavioral perspective has roots in the philosophical school of British empiricism. According to the early empiricist John Locke, at birth the human mind is a *tabula rasa*—a "blank tablet" or "slate"—upon which experiences are written. In this view, human nature is shaped purely by the environment.

In the early 1900s, experiments by Russian physiologist Ivan Pavlov (1849–1936) revealed how learning occurs when events are associated

Figure 1.10

Sigmund Freud founded psychoanalysis. For more than 50 years, he probed the hidden recesses of the mind.

Figure 1.11

John B. Watson founded the school of behaviorism. He published *Psychology as a Behaviorist Views It* in 1913.

with one another. Pavlov found that dogs automatically learned to salivate to the sound of a new stimulus, such as a tone, if that stimulus was repeatedly paired with food. Meanwhile, American psychologist Edward Thorndike (1874–1949) examined how organisms learn through the consequences of their actions. According to Thorndike's (1911) *law of effect*, responses followed by satisfying consequences become more likely to recur, and those followed by unsatisfying consequences become less likely to recur. Thus learning is the key to understanding how experience molds behavior.

Behaviorism

Behaviorism, *a school of thought that emphasizes environmental control of behavior through learning,* began to emerge in 1913. John B. Watson (1878–1958), who led the new movement, strongly opposed the "mentalism" of the structuralists, functionalists, and psychoanalysts (Figure 1.11). He argued that the proper subject matter of psychology was observable behavior, not unobservable inner consciousness. Humans, he said, are products of their learning experiences, and he issued the following challenge:

> Give me a dozen healthy infants, well-formed, and my own specialized world to bring them up in and I'll guarantee you to take any one of them at random and train him to become any type of specialist I might select—doctor, lawyer, artist, merchant-chief and, yes, even beggar-man and thief, regardless of his talents, penchants, tendencies, abilities, vocations, and race of his ancestors. (1925, p. 82)

Behaviorists sought to discover laws that govern learning, and they believed that the same basic principles of learning applied to all organisms. B. F. Skinner (1904–1990) was a leading 20th-century behaviorist (Figure 1.12). Although Skinner didn't deny that people have thoughts and feelings, he maintained that "no account of what is happening inside the human body, no matter how complete, will explain the origins of human behavior" (1989a, p. 18). Skinner believed that the real causes of behavior reside in the outer world: "A person does not act upon the world, the world acts upon him" (1971, p. 211). His research, based largely on studying rats and pigeons under controlled laboratory conditions, examined how behavior is influenced by the rewarding and punishing consequences that it produces.

In the case of Ray, our shy college student, a behaviorist might focus on Ray's past dating experiences. In high school, the first time Ray invited

Figure 1.12

B. F. Skinner, a leading behaviorist, argued that mentalistic concepts were not necessary to explain behavior and that learning principles could be used to enhance human welfare.

a girl to a dance he was turned down. Later, he had a crush on a girl and they went out once, after which she turned him down. Though nervous, he asked out a few girls after that but was turned down each time. Such punishing consequences decreased the likelihood that Ray would ask someone out in the future. Fortunately, Kira asked Ray out, and the positive consequences they experienced on their first date reinforced their behavior, increasing the odds that they would go out again.

Skinner believed that through "social engineering," society could harness the power of the environment to change behavior in beneficial ways. His approach, known as *radical behaviorism,* was considered extreme by many psychologists, but he was esteemed for his scientific contributions and for focusing attention on how environmental forces could be used to enhance human welfare. In the 1960s, behaviorism inspired powerful techniques known collectively as *behavior modification.* These techniques, aimed at decreasing problem behaviors and increasing positive behaviors by manipulating environmental factors, are still used widely today (Eldevik et al., 2010).

Behaviorism's insistence that psychology should focus only on observable stimuli and responses resonated with many who wanted psychology to model itself on the natural sciences. Behaviorism dominated North American research on learning into the 1960s, challenged psychodynamic views about the causes of psychological disorders, and led to effective treatments for some disorders. But radical behaviorism's influence waned after the 1970s as interest in studying mental processes expanded (Robins et al., 1999). Still, behaviorists continue to make important contributions, and their discovery of basic laws of learning was one of the greatest contributions made by 20th-century American psychology.

Cognitive Behaviorism

In the 1960s and 1970s, a growing number of psychologists showed that cognitive processes such as attention and memory could be rigorously studied by using sophisticated experiments. This led some behaviorists to challenge radical behaviorism's view that mental life was off-limits as a topic for scientific study. They developed a modified view called **cognitive behaviorism,** *which proposes that learning experiences and the environment influence our expectations and other thoughts and, in turn, that our thoughts influence how we behave* (Bandura, 1969, 2008). Cognitive behaviorism remains an influential viewpoint to this day (Figure 1.13).

A cognitive behaviorist might say that Ray's past dating rejections were punishing and led him to expect that further attempts at romance would be doomed. In turn, these expectations of social rejection inhibited him from asking women out and even from making male friends.

Figure 1.13

Albert Bandura has played a key role in developing cognitive behaviorism, which merges the behavioral and cognitive perspectives.

? thinking **critically**

ARE THE STUDENTS LAZY?

Imagine that you are a high school teacher. Whenever you try to engage your students in a class discussion, they gaze into space and hardly say anything. You start to think that they're just a bunch of lazy kids. From a radical behavioral perspective, is your conclusion reasonable? How might you improve the situation? Think about it, then see page 29.

The Humanistic Perspective: Self-Actualization and Positive Psychology

In the mid-20th century, as the psychodynamic and behavioral perspectives vied for dominance within psychology, a new viewpoint called *humanism* arose to challenge them both. The **humanistic perspective (humanism)** *emphasized free will, personal growth, and the attempt to find meaning in one's existence.*

Humanists rejected psychodynamic concepts of humans as being controlled by unconscious forces and rejected behaviorism's view of humans as mere reactors to the environment. Instead, humanistic theorists such as Abraham Maslow (1908–1970) proposed that each of us has an inborn force toward *self-actualization,* the reaching of one's individual potential (Figure 1.14). When people develop in a supportive environment, their positive inner nature emerges. In contrast, misery and pathology occur when environments frustrate people's innate tendency toward self-actualization. Humanists emphasized the importance of personal choice, responsibility, personality growth, and positive feelings of self-worth. To humanists, the meaning of our existence resides squarely in our own hands.

Thinking about Ray's shyness and loneliness, a humanist might say that no matter how often Ray was rejected in the past, he must take personal responsibility for turning things around. A humanist also might wonder whether, in his freshman year, Ray's happiness and sense of self-worth were resting too heavily on his hope for a good romantic relationship. By focusing on building a few friendships, Ray wisely found another way to satisfy what Maslow (1954) called "belongingness," our basic human need for social acceptance and companionship.

Few early humanists were scientists, and, historically, humanism has had a more limited impact on mainstream psychological science than have other perspectives. Still, it has inspired important areas of research. Humanist Carl Rogers (1902–1987) identified key aspects of psychotherapy that led to constructive changes in clients. Humanistic concepts have also stimulated research on self-esteem and self-concept (Verplanken & Holland, 2002).

Figure 1.14

The humanistic perspective emphasizes the human ability to surmount obstacles in the drive toward self-actualization.

Humanism's focus on self-actualization and growth is seen in today's growing **positive psychology movement,** *which emphasizes the study of human strengths, fulfillment, and optimal living* (Park et al., 2010). Rather than focusing on "what's wrong with our world" (e.g., mental disorders, conflict, prejudice), positive psychology examines how we can nurture what is best within ourselves and society to create a happy and fulfilling life.

The Cognitive Perspective: The Thinking Human

The **cognitive perspective** *examines the nature of the mind and how mental processes influence behavior.* In this view, humans are information processors whose actions are governed by thought.

Origins of the Cognitive Perspective

Two of psychology's earliest schools of thought, structuralism and functionalism, reflected the cognitive perspective. Recall that structuralists attempted to identify the basic elements of consciousness, while functionalists explored the purposes of consciousness. Other pioneering cognitive psychologists, such as Hermann Ebbinghaus (1850–1909), studied memory.

By the 1920s, German scientists had formed a school of thought known as *Gestalt psychology,* which examined how the mind organizes elements of experience into a unified or "whole" perception (*Gestalt* roughly translates as "whole" or "organization"). They argued that perceptions are organized so that "the whole is greater than the sum of its parts." Consider the painting in Figure 1.15. Many people initially perceive it as a whole—as a portrait of a strange-looking person—rather than as a mosaic of individual sea creatures. Gestalt psychology stimulated interest in topics such as perception and problem solving, but like structuralism and functionalism, it eventually disappeared as a scientific school. As behaviorism's antimentalistic stance strengthened in North America during the 1920s and 1930s, the study of the mind was relegated to the back burner.

Renewed Interest in the Mind

In the 1950s, interest in studying cognitive processes regained ground. In part, this interest stemmed from psychologists' involvement during World War II in designing information displays, such as gauges in airplane cockpits, that enabled military personnel (e.g., pilots) to recognize and interpret that information quickly and accurately. Computer technology, in its infancy at that time, provided new information-processing concepts and terminology that psychologists adapted to the study of memory and attention (Broadbent, 1958). A new metaphor developed—the mind as a system that processes, stores, and retrieves information—and it remains influential today.

On another front in the 1950s, behaviorists and linguists debated how children acquire language. The behaviorists, led by Skinner, claimed that language is acquired through basic principles of learning. The linguists, led by Noam Chomsky (b. 1928), argued that humans are biologically "preprogrammed" to acquire language and that children come to understand language as a set of "mental rules." This heated debate convinced many psychologists that language was too complex to be explained by behavioral principles and instead needed to be examined from a cognitive perspective.

Interest in cognition grew in other areas. For example, a theory by Swiss psychologist Jean Piaget (1896–1980), which explained how children's thinking becomes more sophisticated with age, gained widespread recognition in North America. Overall, psychologists' interest in mental processes swelled in the 1960s and 1970s—a period that sometimes is referred to as the "cognitive revolution."

The Modern Cognitive Perspective

Cognitive psychology, which focuses on the study of mental processes, embodies the cognitive perspective. Cognitive psychologists study the processes by which people reason, make decisions, solve problems, form perceptions, and produce and understand language. Many, such as Elizabeth Loftus, study memory and factors that distort it (Figure 1.16). Cognitive psychologists explore the nature of attention and consciousness and have increasingly studied how unconscious processes influence behavior.

Cognitive neuroscience, *which uses sophisticated electrical recording and brain-imaging techniques to examine brain activity while people engage in cognitive tasks,* is a rapidly growing area that represents the intersection of cognitive psychology and the biological perspective within psychology. Cognitive neuroscientists seek to determine how the brain goes about its business of learning language, acquiring knowledge, forming memories, and performing other cognitive activities (Nyhus & Curran, 2010).

From a cognitive perspective, we can examine Ray's shyness in terms of how he processes information. The few times he went on dates, Ray's nervousness may have caused him to focus

Figure 1.15

This painting illustrates the Gestalt principle that the whole is greater than the sum of its parts. The individual elements are sea creatures, but the whole is perceived as a portrait of a face. *The Water,* by Arcimboldo, from Kunsthistorisches Museum, Vienna.

Figure 1.16

Cognitive psychologist Elizabeth Loftus studies the nature of memory and how memories become distorted.

on the slightest things that weren't going well, while failing to notice other cues that suggested his date was having a good time. Ray also may be remembering those events as much more unpleasant than they actually were, and his interpretation of past dating failures may be based on faulty reasoning. Ray believes he was rejected because of his personal qualities ("I'm not interesting enough") and therefore expects that future dates will also be unsuccessful. If Ray correctly attributed the rejections to some situational factor ("Clarissa was already interested in someone else"), then he would not necessarily expect other women to reject him in the future.

The Sociocultural Perspective: The Embedded Human

Humans are social creatures. Embedded within a culture, each of us encounters ever changing social settings that shape our actions and values, our sense of identity, our very conception of reality. The **sociocultural perspective** *examines how the social environment and cultural learning influence our behavior, thoughts, and feelings.*

The Social Psychological Component

For over a century, *social psychologists* have studied how the presence of other people influences our behavior, thoughts, and feelings (Rubin & Badea, 2010; Triplett, 1898). The word *presence* connotes actual physical presence (e.g., you're in a group), implied presence (e.g., you're dressing for a party, aware that at the party people will evaluate how

you look), and imagined presence (e.g., driving a car, you slow down because you incorrectly think the car behind you is an unmarked police car). The social psychological approach overlaps with many other perspectives. For example, like behaviorism, social psychology pays special attention to how the environment influences our behavior, but its emphasis is narrowed to the social environment. Consistent with a cognitive perspective, much social psychological research examines social cognition: how people form impressions of one another, how attitudes form and can be changed, how our expectations affect our behavior, and so forth. Intersecting the biological perspective (which we discuss next), social psychologists have increasingly examined the biological bases of social thinking and behavior. For example, it appears that social pain—as can occur when people reject or ostracize us—shares many of the same brain circuits that underlie physical pain (Lieberman & Eisenberger, 2009).

The Cultural Component

Culture refers to the enduring values, beliefs, behaviors, and traditions that are shared by a large group of people and passed from one generation to the next. All cultural groups develop their own social **norms,** *which are rules (often unwritten) that specify what behavior is acceptable and expected for members of that group.* Norms exist for all types of social behaviors, such as how to dress, respond to people of higher status, or act as a woman or man (Figure 1.17). For culture to endure, each new generation must internalize, or adopt, the norms and values of the group as their own. *Socialization* is the process by which culture is transmitted to new members and internalized by them.

Throughout much of the 20th century, psychological research largely ignored non-Western groups. Even within Western societies, for decades participants in psychological research typically were White and came from middle- or upper-class backgrounds. There were important exceptions, however, such as Kenneth Clark (1914–2005), Mamie Clark (1917–1983), and others, who examined how discrimination and prejudice influenced the personality development of African American children (Clark & Clark, 1947; Figure 1.18).

Over time, psychologists increasingly began to study diverse ethnic and cultural groups. Today the growing field of **cultural psychology** (sometimes called **cross-cultural psychology**) *explores how culture is transmitted to its members and examines psychological similarities and differences among people from diverse cultures* (Norenzayan et al., 2010).

Figure 1.17

Social norms differ across cultures and over time within cultures. The idea of women engaging in aggressive sports or military combat is unthinkable in many cultures. A few generations ago, it was also unthinkable in the United States.

Figure 1.18

Psychologists Kenneth B. Clark and Mamie P. Clark studied the development of racial identity among African American children. Kenneth Clark also wrote books on the psychological impact of prejudice and discrimination.

One important difference among cultures is the extent to which they emphasize individualism versus collectivism (Triandis & Suh, 2002). Most industrialized cultures of northern Europe and North America promote *individualism*, an emphasis on personal goals and self-identity based primarily on one's own attributes and achievements. In contrast, many Asian, African, and South American cultures nurture *collectivism*, in which individual goals are subordinated to those of the group and personal identity is defined largely by the ties that bind one to the extended family and other social groups. This difference is created by social learning experiences that begin in childhood and continue in the form of social customs.

Thinking about Ray's lonely first year in college, the sociocultural perspective again leads us to Ray's expectations of social rejection and beliefs about why it occurred before. We also can ask how his cultural upbringing and other social factors contributed to his shy behavior. Throughout his teen years, cultural norms for male assertiveness may have put pressure on Ray. His shyness may have evoked teasing and other negative reactions from his high school peers, increasing his feelings of inadequacy by the time he reached college. As for Ray and Kira's dating relationship, we might examine how norms regarding courtship and marriage differ across cultures.

In each chapter of this book, a "Research Close-up" provides you with a highly condensed, in-depth look at an important study, paralleling the format of research articles published in psychological journals. We give you background information about the study, describe its method and key results, and discuss (evaluate) key aspects of the study. On the next page, our first "Research Close-up" examines cross-cultural attitudes about love and marriage.

The Biological Perspective: The Brain, Genes, and Evolution

The **biological perspective** *examines how brain processes and other bodily functions regulate behavior.* Biological psychology has always been a prominent part of the field, but its influence has increased dramatically over recent decades.

Behavioral Neuroscience

Ray and Kira are in love. They study and eat together. They hold hands and kiss. Yet a year earlier, Ray was depressed. What brain regions, neural circuits, and bodily chemicals enable us to feel love, pleasure, and depression; to read, study, and feel hunger? These questions pertain to **behavioral neuroscience** (also called *physiological psychology*), *which examines brain processes and other physiological functions that underlie our behavior, sensory experiences, emotions, and thoughts* (Rolls, 2010).

An early pioneer of biological psychology, American Karl Lashley (1890–1958), trained rats

Research Close-up

Would You Marry Someone You Didn't Love?

SOURCE: ROBERT LEVINE, SUGURU SATO, TSUKASA HASHIMOTO, and JYOTI VERMA (1995). Love and marriage in eleven cultures. *Journal of Cross-Cultural Psychology, 26,* 554–571.

INTRODUCTION

Would you marry someone you did not love? According to one theory, people in individualistic cultures are more likely to view romantic love as a requirement for marriage, because love is a matter of personal choice (Goode, 1959). In collectivistic cultures, concern for the extended family plays a larger role in marriage decisions.

Psychologist Robert Levine and his colleagues (1995) examined college students' views about love and marriage. Whereas previous research focused on American students, these authors studied students from 11 countries. They also examined whether students from collectivistic and economically poorer countries would be less likely to view love as a prerequisite to marriage.

METHOD

The researchers administered language-appropriate versions of the same questionnaire to 1,163 female and male college students from 11 countries. The key question was, "If someone had all the other qualities you desired, would you marry this person if you were not in love with him/her?" The students responded "No," "Yes," or "Not Sure." The researchers determined each country's economic status and collectivistic versus individualistic orientation from data gathered by previous cross-cultural investigators.

RESULTS

Within each country, the views of female and male students did not differ significantly. In contrast, beliefs across countries varied strongly (Table 1.2). In India, Thailand, and Pakistan, most students said they would marry or at least consider marrying someone they did not love. In the Philippines and Japan, a sizable minority—just over a third—felt the same way. In contrast, students from the other countries overwhelmingly rejected the notion of marrying somebody they did not love. Overall, students from collectivistic and economically poorer countries were less likely to view love as a prerequisite to marriage.

Table 1.2 | Love and Marriage in Eleven Cultures

If someone had all the other qualities you desired, would you marry this person if you were not in love with him/her?

Country	Percentage		
	No	**Yes**	**Not Sure**
India	24	49	27
Thailand	34	19	47
Pakistan	39	50	11
Philippines	64	11	25
Japan	64	2	34
Hong Kong	78	6	16
Australia	80	5	15
Mexico	83	10	7
England	84	7	9
Brazil	86	4	10
United States	86	4	10

SOURCE: Levine et al., 1995.

DISCUSSION

Among most of our own students, the notion that you marry someone you love is a truism. They are surprised—as perhaps you are—that many students in other countries would consider marrying someone they did not love. This study reminds us that as members of a particular culture, it is easy to mistakenly assume that "our way" is the "normal way."

As in all research, we must think critically and interpret the results carefully. For example, among those students who said they would marry someone without being in love, would it be accurate to conclude that they view love as irrelevant to marriage? Not necessarily, because other research has found that "mutual attraction/love" is viewed across most cultures as a desirable quality in a mate (Buss, 1989). Thus the results of this study suggest only that in some cultures love is not viewed as an *essential prerequisite* to enter into marriage.

to run mazes and then measured how surgically produced lesions (damage) to various brain areas affected the rats' learning and memory. His research inspired other psychologists to map brain regions involved in specific psychological functions (Figure 1.19). Another pioneer, Canadian Donald O. Hebb (1904–1985), proposed that changes in the connections between nerve cells in the brain provide the biological basis for learning, memory, and perception. His influential theory inspired research that eventually led to the discovery of **neurotransmitters,** *which are chemicals released by nerve cells that allow them to communicate with one another.*

Figure 1.19

Karl Lashley was a pioneer of physiological psychology (behavioral neuroscience). He examined how damage to various brain regions affected rats' ability to learn and remember.

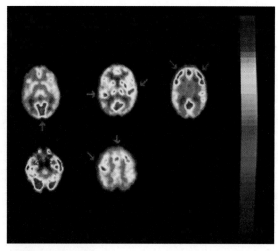

Figure 1.20

Behavioral neuroscientists use positron-emission tomography (PET) scans to measure brain activity as people perform various tasks. Viewed from above, each image pictures a horizontal slice of the brain with the front of the brain at the top. Yellow and red indicate regions of greatest activity: (*top left*) visual task, (*top center*) auditory task, (*top right*) cognitive task, (*bottom left*) memory task, and (*bottom right*) motor task.

Today, modern brain-imaging techniques allow psychologists to watch activity in specific brain areas as people experience emotions, perceive stimuli, and perform tasks (Figure 1.20). These advances have led to new areas of study that link various psychological perspectives. For example, *cognitive neuroscience*—the study of brain processes that underlie thinking and information processing—represents an intersection of cognitive psychology and behavioral neuroscience.

Behavior Genetics

Psychologists have had a long-standing interest in **behavior genetics,** *the study of how behavioral tendencies are influenced by genetic factors* (Plomin & Haworth, 2009). Animals can be selectively bred not only for physical traits but also for behavioral traits such as aggression. This is done over generations by mating highly aggressive males and females. In Thailand, where gambling on fish fights is a national pastime, selective breeding has produced the highly aggressive Siamese fighting fish. The male of this species will instantly attack his own image in a mirror.

Identical human twins, who result from the splitting of a fertilized egg and therefore have the same genetic makeup, are more similar to one another on many behavioral traits than are fraternal twins, who result from two different fertilized eggs and therefore are no more similar genetically than are nontwin siblings. This greater behavioral similarity is found even when identical twins

Figure 1.21

Charles Darwin, a British naturalist, formulated a theory of evolution that revolutionized scientific thinking.

have been reared in different homes and dissimilar environments (Lykken, 2006).

Thinking about Ray, perhaps he inherited a tendency to be shy. Some infants display an extremely shy, inhibited emotional style that seems to be biologically based and persists into adulthood (Kagan, 1989; Newman et al., 1997). Dating rejections may have reinforced Ray's natural reluctance to ask women out.

Evolutionary Psychology

In his theory of evolution, Darwin (1859) noted that within a species some members possess specific traits to a greater extent than do other members (Figure 1.21). Through a process he called **natural selection,** *if an inherited trait gives certain members an advantage over others* (such as increasing their ability to attract mates or escape from danger), *these members will be more likely to survive and pass these characteristics on to their offspring.* In this way, species evolve as the presence of adaptive traits increases within the population over generations. Traits that put certain members at a disadvantage tend to become less common within a species over time, because members having those traits will be less likely to survive and reproduce. As environments change, the adaptiveness of a trait may increase or decrease. Thus, through natural selection, a species' biology evolves in response to environmental conditions (Figure 1.22).

Evolutionary psychology *seeks to explain how evolution shaped modern human behavior* (Simpson & Beckes, 2010). Evolutionary psychologists stress that human mental abilities and behavioral tendencies evolved along with a changing body (Tooby & Cosmides, 2005). According to one theory, as our humanlike ancestors developed new physical abilities (such as the ability to walk upright, thus freeing the use of the arms and hands), they began to use tools and weapons and live in social groups (Pilbeam, 1984). Certain psychological abilities—thought, language, the capacity to learn and solve problems—became more important to survival as our ancestors had to adapt to new ways of living.

Within any generation, genetically based variations in brain structure and functioning occur among individuals. Ancestors whose brain characteristics better supported adaptive mental abilities were more likely to survive and reproduce. Thus, through natural selection, adaptations to new environmental demands contributed to the development of the brain, just as brain growth contributed to the further development of human behavior.

Evolutionary psychologists also attempt to explain human social behavior. Recall that Ray and Kira are contemplating marriage. Why is it that across the world, on average, men desire a younger mate and women tend to seek an older mate? As we'll discuss more fully in Chapter 3, whereas sociocultural psychologists argue that socialization and economic gender inequality cause most sex differences in mate preferences, some evolutionary psychologists propose that through natural selection, men and women have become biologically predisposed to seek somewhat different qualities in a mate (Buss, 1989, 2007).

test yourself   Perspectives on Behavior

Match each numbered psychological perspective to the most appropriate primary emphasis on the right.

Perspective	Primary Emphasis (i.e., major causes of behavior)
1. behavioral	a. brain processes; genes; evolution
2. biological	b. social norms; socialization; presence of other people
3. cognitive	c. unconscious motives, conflicts, and defenses
4. humanistic	d. thinking and information processing; memory
5. psychodynamic	e. learning, rewarding/punishing consequences of behavior
6. sociocultural	f. choice and free will; search for personal meaning

ANSWERS: 1-e, 2-a, 3-d, 4-f, 5-c, 6-b

Figure 1.22

Natural-selection pressures result in physical changes. The peppered moth's natural color is that of the lighter insect. However, over many generations, peppered moths that live in polluted urban areas have become darker, not from the pollution but because moths that inherited slightly darker coloration blended better into their grimy environment. Thus, they were more likely to survive predators and pass their "darker" genes on to their offspring. However, a trip into the countryside to visit their light-colored relatives could easily prove fatal for these darker urban insects.

USING LEVELS OF ANALYSIS TO INTEGRATE THE PERSPECTIVES

As summarized in Table 1.3, psychology's six major perspectives (presented in the order we discussed them) provide differing conceptions of human nature. Fortunately, we can distill their essence into the simple three-part framework that we introduced earlier. Behavior can be examined at biological, psychological, and environmental levels. At the *biological level of analysis*, we can study behavior and its causes in terms of brain functioning, hormones, and genetic factors shaped over the course of evolution. At the *psychological level of analysis*, we might look to the cognitive perspective and analyze how thought, memory, and planning influence behavior. Borrowing from the psychodynamic and humanistic perspectives, we can examine how motives and personality traits influence behavior. Finally, at the *environmental*

Table **1.3** | **Comparison of Six Major Perspectives on Human Behavior**

	Psychodynamic	Behavioral	Humanistic	Cognitive	Sociocultural	Biological
Conception of human nature	The human as controlled by inner forces and conflicts	The human as reactor to the environment	The human as free agent, seeking self-actualization	The human as thinker	The human as social being embedded in a culture	The human animal
Major causal factors in behavior	Unconscious motives, conflicts, and defenses; early childhood experiences and unresolved conflicts	Past learning experiences and the stimuli and behavioral consequences that exist in the current environment	Free will, choice, and innate drive toward self-actualization; search for personal meaning of existence	Thoughts, anticipations, planning, perceptions, attention, and memory processes	Social forces, including norms, social interactions, and group processes in one's culture and social environment	Genetic and evolutionary factors; brain and biochemical processes
Predominant focus and methods of discovery	Intensive observations of personality processes in clinical settings; some laboratory research	Study of learning processes in laboratory and real-world settings, with an emphasis on precise observation of stimuli and responses	Study of meaning, values, and purpose in life; study of self-concept and its role in thought, emotion, and behavior	Study of cognitive processes, usually under highly controlled laboratory conditions	Study of behavior and mental processes of people in different cultures; experiments examining people's responses to social stimuli	Study of brain-behavior relations; role of hormones and biochemical factors in behavior; behavior genetics research

level of analysis, the behavioral and sociocultural perspectives lead us to examine how stimuli in the physical and social environment shape our behavior, thoughts, and feelings.

Realize that a full understanding of behavior often moves us back and forth between these three levels. Consider Ray and Kira. When we describe the culture in which they were raised, such as its religious values and social customs, we are operating at the environmental level of analysis. However, if Ray and Kira adopt those cultural values and make them part of their identities, this represents the psychological level of analysis. Similarly, we might describe a family environment as abusive, but an abused child's tendency to worry and feel anxious—and the chemical changes in the brain that underlie this anxiety—move us to the psychological and biological levels of analysis.

An Example: Understanding Depression

To appreciate how the levels-of-analysis framework can help us understand behavior, let's briefly examine a common but complex psychological problem: depression. Most people experience sadness, grief, or the blues at some time in their lives. These feelings often are normal responses to significant negative events or losses that we experience. However, when these emotions are intense, persist over a long period, and are accompanied by thoughts of hopelessness and an inability to experience pleasure, we have crossed the boundary between a normal reaction and clinical depression.

Looking first at the biological level, genetic factors appear to predispose some people toward developing depression (Edvardsen et al., 2009). In one study, relatives of people who had developed major depression before age 20 were 8 times more likely to become depressed at some point than were relatives of nondepressed people (Weissman et al., 1984). Biochemical factors also play a role. For many depressed people, certain neurotransmitter systems that send signals between the brain's nerve cells do not operate normally, and the most effective antidepressant drugs restore neurotransmitter activity to more normal levels.

Moving to a psychological level, cognitive viewpoints emphasize that depression is associated with a pessimistic thinking style (Strunk & Adler, 2009). Depressed people can find the black cloud surrounding every silver lining. They tend to blame themselves for negative things that occur in their lives, take little credit for the good things, view the future as bleak, and may have perfectionistic expectations that make them overly sensitive to how other people evaluate

them (Bieling et al., 2004). Psychodynamic theorists believe that severe loss, rejection, or trauma in childhood helps create a personality style that causes people to overreact to setbacks, setting the stage for future depression (Bowlby, 2000).

At the environmental level, behaviorists propose that depression often begins as a reaction to an environment that provides fewer rewards for the person. As depression intensifies, some people stop doing things that ordinarily give them pleasure. They also may complain a lot and seek excessive social support, eventually causing other people to avoid them. The net result is a vicious cycle: an environment with even fewer rewards, reduced support from other people, and worsening depression (Hopko & Mullane, 2008; Lewinsohn et al., 1985). Sociocultural factors also affect depression. Although depression is found across cultures and ethnic groups, its symptoms, causes, and prevalence may reflect cultural differences (Jackson & Williams, 2006). For example, in North America, feelings of sadness typically are a major component of depression. In some regions of China, however, many depressed people report feelings of boredom or internal pressure but not sadness (Kleinman, 2004).

We'll discuss depression more fully in Chapter 15. For now, let's summarize the causal factors in depression that we've discussed by grouping them into the three levels of analysis, as shown in the figure on the next page.

Summary of Major Themes

Our excursion through psychology's major perspectives and levels of analysis reveals several principles that you will encounter repeatedly as we explore the realm of behavior:

- As a science, psychology relies on *systematic empiricism* to study behavior.

- Although committed to studying behavior objectively, psychologists recognize that our personal experience of the world is *subjective.*

- Behavior is determined by *multiple causal factors,* including our biological endowment ("nature"), the environment and our past learning experiences ("nurture"), and psychological factors that include our thoughts and motives.

- Behavior is a means of *adapting* to environmental demands; capacities have evolved over each species' history because they facilitated adaptation and survival.

- Behavior and mental processes are affected by the *social and cultural environments* in which we develop and live.

Levels of Analysis

Causal Factors in Depression

It's important to realize that some of the factors we describe can act as a cause but also can be an effect. For example, depression (cause) may lead to a decrease in social support (effect), and in turn decreased social support (cause) can deepen the person's depression (effect). Also recognize that the causes of depression may vary from case to case and that multiple causes can combine or interact with one another. **Interaction** *means that the way in which one factor influences behavior depends on the presence of another factor.* For example, someone who experiences a minor setback may become depressed if she or he has a strong biological predisposition for depression or a highly pessimistic thinking style. The same setback might barely faze a person who has a weak biological predisposition for depression or an optimistic thinking style. Thus, just as boiling water softens celery and hardens an egg, the same environmental factor can affect two people differently, depending on their biological and psychological makeup.

You've now seen how a levels-of-analysis approach can be applied to examining depression. Earlier in the chapter, we briefly described how it could be applied to the everyday behavior of eating. Focus on another aspect of human behavior that interests you the most, and think about how it might be examined at the biological, psychological, and environmental levels.

ENVIRONMENTAL LEVEL

- Prior losses and rejections, especially early in life, may lead people to overreact to current losses or rejections.
- A significant decrease in pleasurable experiences may help trigger depression.
- Social support may decrease if people avoid the depressed person.
- Cultural norms may influence how people react to negative events and express unhappiness.

BIOLOGICAL LEVEL

- People's genetic inheritance influences their susceptibility toward developing depression.
- Abnormal activity of neurotransmitters in the brain can cause depression.
- Antidepressant drugs restore more normal levels of neurotransmitter activity and relieve symptoms of depression for many people.

PSYCHOLOGICAL LEVEL

- A pessimistic thinking style and negative interpretations of events may trigger or intensify depression.
- Perfectionistic expectations can make people overly sensitive to how other people evaluate them.
- Heightened sensitivity to loss or rejection may lead people to overreact to setbacks.

test yourself

Levels of Analysis

Each of the following psychologists is studying factors related to depression from which level of analysis: *biological, psychological,* or *environmental*?

1. Dr. Rios studies whether the odds of developing depression depends on being an only child or having siblings.
2. Dr. Todd hypothesizes that, as compared to nondepressed people, when depressed people fail at a task they will be more likely to attribute their failure to a lack of ability.
3. Dr. Ito compares the brain activity of depressed and nondepressed people while they perform the same task. She finds that certain brain areas in depressed people are underactive.

ANSWERS: 1-environmental, 2-psychological, 3-biological

Figure 1.23

Shelley Taylor studies people's biological responses to stress and illness. She is a leading researcher in health psychology and social psychology.

PSYCHOLOGY TODAY

As a science and profession, psychology today is more diversified and robust than ever before. Because of psychology's enormous breadth, no psychologist can be an expert on all aspects of behavior. You have already encountered some of psychology's major subfields throughout the chapter, and Table 1.4 introduces six more. Remember, however, that psychological research often cuts across subfields. For example, psychologist Shelley Taylor (Figure 1.23) explores how people's biological responses to stress and illness vary depending on their beliefs, values, and social relationships. Her work draws on several traditional subfields of psychology—including social psychology, personality psychology, and biopsychology—as well as a newer subfield, called *health psychology,* that she helped pioneer (and that you will learn about in Chapter 14).

A Global Science and Profession

Modern psychology is diversified in terms of geography, ethnicity, and gender. A century ago, psychological research was conducted almost entirely in Europe, North America, and Russia by White males. Today these regions remain scientific powerhouses, but you will find women and men from diverse backgrounds conducting psychological research and providing psychological services around the globe. Founded in 1951 to support psychology worldwide, the International Union of Psychological Science consists of major psychological organizations from 71 countries (IUPsyS, 2009). Moreover, across the world,

college students are eagerly studying psychology. In the United States, psychology ranks among the top five fields in the number of undergraduate degrees and doctoral degrees awarded annually (National Center for Education Statistics, 2008).

The American Psychological Association (APA), founded in 1892, is the largest individual psychological association in the world. Its 150,000 members and 56 divisions represent not only the subfields we've already discussed and those shown in Table 1.4 but also areas that focus on psychology's relation to the arts, religion, the military, the environment, sports, social policy issues, public service, and the media (APA, 2010a). The American Psychological Society (APS), a newer organization consisting primarily of researchers, has grown to 20,000 members in just two decades (APS, 2010). Both APA and APS have international members in dozens of countries.

A career in most psychological subfields requires a doctoral degree based on four to six years of training beyond the bachelor's degree. Graduate training includes broad exposure to knowledge in psychology, concentrated study in one or more subfields, and extensive training in research methods. In some areas (such as clinical, counseling, school, and industrial-organizational psychology), additional supervised practical experience in a hospital, clinic, school, or workplace setting is generally required. Please note, however, that psychologists who perform mental health services are not the same as psychiatrists. *Psychiatrists* are medical doctors who, after completing their general training in medicine, receive additional training in diagnosing and treating mental disorders.

Besides its fascinating subject matter, psychology attracts many people with its rich variety of career options. Figure 1.24 shows the major settings in which psychologists work. Many psychologists teach, engage in research, or apply psychological principles and techniques to help solve personal or social problems. For more information on careers in psychology, visit the Online Learning Center (OLC) that accompanies this book.

Psychology, Society, and Your Life

Most Americans have a positive view of psychology and are at least somewhat aware that beyond providing therapy, psychologists contribute to solving other societal problems (Mills, 2009). Still, many people don't realize the range and depth of psychology's applied contributions or how they affect our lives. Many people also fail to recognize that such contributions are rooted in scientific research. Let's consider some examples.

Table **1.4** | **Some Additional Subfields within Psychology**

Specialty	Major Focus
Animal behavior (comparative psychology)	Study of nonhuman species in natural or laboratory environments; includes genetics, brain processes, social behavior, evolutionary processes
Counseling psychology	Consultation with clients on issues of personal adjustment; vocational and career planning; interest and aptitude testing
Educational psychology	Study of psychological aspects of the educational process; curriculum and instructional research; teacher training
Forensic psychology	Application and study of psychological principles pertaining to the criminal justice system, including law enforcement and the courts
Health psychology	Study of psychological and behavioral aspects of physical health and illness, and mental health and well-being; development of programs that promote healthy behavior
Quantitative psychology	Study of measurement and data-analysis issues; development of mathematical models of behavior

Fly the Friendly Skies . . . Safely

The next time you board an airplane or know someone who does, you might reflect for a moment on the work of several types of research psychologists who have made air travel safer, but who you've probably never heard about: *aviation psychologists* and *human factors psychologists* (*human factors* is the study of human-machine interfaces). They've helped develop and assess training programs to improve the teamwork of cockpit crews, and as you'll read in Chapter 5, years ago they identified a nighttime visual illusion that led pilots to misjudge their plane's altitude while landing and resulted in several fatal crashes. For decades, these psychologists also have helped design instrument displays so that pilots can quickly and accurately process the information provided by the many dials, gauges, and digital readouts crammed into the cockpits of commercial and military planes (Casner, 2009). Because these contributions partly rest on the shoulders of experimental, cognitive, and social psychologists who for decades have studied the basic nature of human vision, information processing, and social interaction, we all might tip our proverbial hats to them as well (Monk et al., 2008). We're guessing that most people would appreciate psychological science's contribution to air safety, if only they knew about it.

President Obama's "Behavioral Dream Team"

If you live in the United States, and perhaps even if not, the outcome of U.S. presidential elections can affect your life through the president's domestic and international policies (Figure 1.25). In 2008, Barack Obama's presidential-election campaign team secretly assembled a group, called the Consortium of Behavioral Scientists, to provide advice on issues such as fund-raising and increasing voter turnout. This "behavioral dream team," as *Time* magazine reporter Michael Grunwald (2009) called it, included social psychologist Robert Cialdini, an expert who has conducted basic and applied research on persuasion. The team also included Nobel Prize–winning cognitive psychologist Daniel Kahneman, an expert in the thought processes and biases that affect people's decision making.

When dream team members provided Obama's campaign with recommendations, they included reference citations to the scientific research on which that advice was based. Mike Moffo, a field director in the campaign, noted that "it was amazing to have these bullet points telling us what to do and the science behind it. . . . These guys really know what makes people tick" (Grunwald, 2009, p. 29).

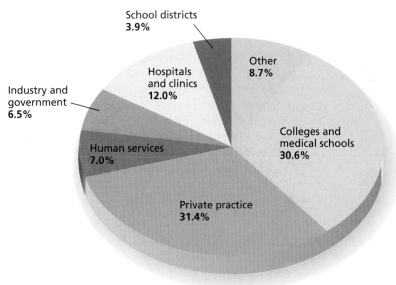

Figure 1.24

Work settings of psychologists.

Source: 2009 APA Directory. Compiled by Center for Workforce Studies.

President Obama's reliance on behavioral science didn't end with his election. In trying to get people to "go green," for example, the Obama administration (like other administrations before it) is dealing with the fundamental issue of changing people's habits. As you'll see in upcoming chapters, psychological science has a lot to say about behavior change.

Figure 1.25

President Barack Obama speaking to an audience in Virginia.

Psychology and Public Policy

Modern society faces a host of complex social problems, many of which may affect you directly or indirectly. Psychology, as a science and profession, is poised to help solve them. Through basic research, psychologists provide fundamental knowledge about behavior. In applied research, they use this knowledge to design, implement, and assess intervention programs. Together, basic research and applied research are pillars for *evidence-based public policies* that affect the lives of millions of people.

Increasingly, psychologists are being called on to tackle social issues and shape public policy. Consider these examples:

- *Education:* From grade school through college, how can we best teach students? In 2002, psychologist Grover Whitehurst became the first director of the U.S. Institute of Education Sciences, a new research unit within the U.S. Department of Education. The institute's mission "is to provide rigorous and relevant evidence on which to ground education practice and policy" (Institute of Education Sciences, 2010).

- *Violence prevention:* Based on decades of aggression research, the APA and other organizations are conducting a program to provide children with nonviolent role models and to improve the violence-prevention skills of teachers, parents, and other caregivers (APA, 2009b). Training sessions are held nationally and in local communities.

- *Mental health:* When research indicated that college students needed greater access to on-campus mental health care, the APA crafted the Campus Care and Counseling Act to help meet this need. Some provisions of this act were incorporated into legislation that was passed by the U.S. Congress in 2004.

Psychologists also influence national policy by helping politicians craft legislation dealing with a host of other social issues, from preventing AIDS and obesity to enhancing child care and homeland security. Moreover, their influence is not limited to the United States. School bullying, for example, is a serious problem in several countries. Norwegian psychologist Dan Olweus, a leading researcher on bullying, developed a prevention program that the Norwegian government makes available to all of its public schools (Olweus, 2004). Some American schools also have adopted it.

Applying Psychology to Your Life

We're biased, of course, but to us, psychology is the most fascinating subject around, and we hope that some of this enthusiasm rubs off on you. Beyond the immensely important goals of satisfying people's intellectual curiosity about human behavior and helping to solve societal problems, psychological research yields many principles that you can actively apply to enhance your own life. You've already seen that the truism to "trust your first instinct" on multiple-choice and true-false exams is actually more myth than reality, and may be harming your exam performance if you follow it blindly. Other research by behavioral, cognitive, and educational psychologists on learning and memory provides additional guidelines that can improve your academic performance. To conclude this chapter, our first "Applying Psychological Science" feature describes some of these guidelines.

Applying Psychological Science

How to Enhance Your Academic Performance

College life presents many challenges, and working smart can be as important as working hard. The following strategies can help you increase your learning and academic performance (Figure 1.26).

EFFECTIVE TIME MANAGEMENT

If you efficiently allocate study time, you will have a clear conscience when it's time for recreational activities and relaxation. First, *develop a written schedule*; this forces you to decide how to allocate time and increases your commitment to the plan. Write down your class schedule and other responsibilities. Then block in periods for study, avoiding times you are likely to be tired.

Distribute study times throughout the week. Schedule some study times immediately before enjoyable activities, which you can use as rewards for studying.

Second, *prioritize your tasks*. Don't procrastinate by working on simple tasks while putting off the toughest tasks. This can result in never getting to the major tasks (e.g., writing term papers, studying for exams) until too little time remains. Each day, ask "What is the most important thing to get done?" Do that first, then move to the next most important task, and so on.

Third, *break large tasks into smaller parts*. Important tasks often are too big to complete all at once. Break them down into a set of specific and realistic goals (e.g., number of pages to be read).

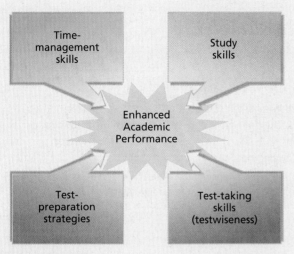

Figure 1.26

Improving academic performance.
Academic performance-enhancement methods include strategies for managing time, studying more effectively, preparing for tests, and taking tests.

Successfully completing each goal is rewarding, strengthens your study skills, and increases your feelings of mastery.

STUDYING MORE EFFECTIVELY

After planning your study time, use that time effectively. *Choose a study place where there are no distractions and where you do nothing but study,* say, a quiet library rather than a busy cafeteria. In time, you will learn to associate that location with studying, and studying there will become even easier (Watson & Tharp, 1997). To enhance your memory of the material, distribute your studying over multiple sessions (Rohrer & Taylor, 2006).

How you study is vital to your academic success. Don't read material passively and hope that it will just soak in. Instead, *use an active approach to learning.* For example, when reading a textbook chapter, first look over the chapter outline, which will give you a good idea of the information you are going to be processing. As you read the material, think about how it applies to your life or how it relates to other information that you already know (Higbee, 2001).

PREPARING FOR TESTS AND ASSESSING YOUR UNDERSTANDING

Contrary to what many students believe, introductory psychology is not an easy course. It covers a lot of diverse material, and many new concepts must be mastered. Many students entering college don't realize that the academic demands far exceed those of high school. Moreover, many students don't realize how hard high achievers actually work. In one study, researchers found that failing students spent only one third as many hours studying as did A-students (who studied about two hours for every hour spent in class). Yet the failing students *thought* they were studying as much as anyone else, and many wondered why they were not doing well (Watson & Tharp, 1997).

As we noted earlier, a written study schedule helps spread your test preparation over time and helps avoid last-minute cramming. Cramming is less effective because it is fatiguing, taxes your memory, and may increase test anxiety, which interferes with learning and test performance (Chapell et al., 2005).

In preparing for tests, repeatedly assess your knowledge. Unfortunately, some studies reveal that students are not highly accurate in judging how well they comprehend textbook material (Dunlosky & Lipko, 2007). This can lead to overconfidence. Therefore, take concrete steps to monitor your understanding. For example, in each textbook chapter you'll find several Test Yourself inserts. When you take these self-tests, don't rely on a vague impression such as "I got most of them right." Rather, score your performance (i.e., percent correct) for each chapter. Likewise, use the list of key terms at the end of each chapter to help assess your understanding of important concepts. Write an explanation of each term and check your accuracy by re-reading the relevant textbook material. To determine how well you truly know and remember the material, be sure to assess your understanding after a time delay, such as after completing all the readings (Thiede & Anderson, 2003). Also realize that the Test Yourself items and key terms only focus on a portion of the content in each chapter. Thus, your studying should extend beyond these items.

TEST-TAKING STRATEGIES

Some students are more effective test takers than others. They know how to approach different types of tests (e.g., multiple choice or essay) to maximize their performance. Such skills are called *testwiseness* (Fagley, 1987). Here are some strategies that testwise students use:

- Use time wisely. Check your progress occasionally during the test. Answer the questions you know first (and, on essay exams, the ones worth the most points). Do not get bogged down on a question you find difficult. Mark it, and come back to it later.
- On essay exams, outline the points you want to make before you begin writing, then cover the key points in enough detail to communicate what you know.
- On multiple-choice tests, read each question and try to answer it before reading the answer options. If you find your answer among the alternatives, that alternative is probably the correct one. Still, read all the other alternatives to make sure that you choose the best one.
- As the "Myth or Reality?" feature discussed, don't be reluctant to change an answer if you believe that the alternative is better.
- Some multiple-choice questions have "all of the above" as an alternative. If one of the answer choices is clearly incorrect, eliminate the "all of the above" option; if you are sure that at least two of the answer choices are correct but are not sure about the third, choose "all of the above."

Time management, study skills, test-preparation strategies, and testwiseness are not acquired overnight; they require effort and practice. Look ahead to the "Applying Psychological Science" and "Research Close-up" features in the following chapters; they discuss additional principles that can help you enhance your academic performance:

Chapter 7: modifying your study behavior (page 236)

Chapter 8: improving memory (page 288)

Chapter 9: solving problems creatively (page 320)

Chapter 9: recognizing whether you understand the textbook material you've read (page 324)

Chapter 11: setting goals (page 394)

test yourself   Psychology Today

True or False?

1. A career in most subfields of psychology requires a doctoral degree.
2. Psychiatry is a subfield of medicine—not a subfield of psychology—that specializes in studying and treating mental disorders.
3. As scientists, psychologists strictly avoid providing input about matters of public policy.
4. On multiple-choice tests, if you start to think that another answer to a question might be better than your original answer, don't switch. Usually, you're better off sticking with your first instinct.

ANSWERS: 1-true, 2-true, 3-false, 4-false

Chapter Summary

THE NATURE OF PSYCHOLOGY

- Psychology is the scientific study of behavior and the mind. Psychologists systematically gather and evaluate empirical evidence to answer questions about how people behave, think, and feel.
- Psychology's systematic approach yields more accurate knowledge about behavior than do everyday casual observations and conventional folk wisdom, which have generated many misconceptions and myths about human nature.
- Description, explanation, control, and application are the main goals of psychological science. Basic research reflects the quest for knowledge for its own sake. Applied research focuses on solving practical problems.
- Because psychologists study biological, psychological, and environmental factors that affect a wide array of behaviors, psychological science intersects with many other disciplines.

PERSPECTIVES ON BEHAVIOR

- Several major perspectives have shaped psychology's scientific growth. In the late 1800s, Wundt and James helped found psychology. Structuralism, which examined the basic components of consciousness, and functionalism, which focused on the purposes of consciousness, were psychology's earliest schools of thought.
- The psychodynamic perspective proposes that unconscious motives, conflicts, and defense mechanisms influence our behavior. Freud emphasized how unconscious sexual and aggressive impulses and childhood experiences shape personality. Modern psychodynamic theories focus

on how early family relationships and our sense of self unconsciously influence our behavior.
- The behavioral perspective emphasizes how the external environment and learning shape behavior. Watson and Skinner believed that psychology should study only observable stimuli and responses, not unobservable mental processes. Cognitive behaviorists believe that learning experiences influence our thoughts, which in turn influence our behaviors.
- The humanistic perspective emphasizes personal freedom and choice, psychological growth, and self-actualization. Humanism has contributed to research on the self, the process of psychotherapy, and today's positive psychology movement.
- The cognitive perspective, embodied by the subfield of cognitive psychology, views humans as information processors who think, judge, and solve problems. Cognitive neuroscience examines brain processes that occur as people perform mental tasks.
- The sociocultural perspective examines how the social environment and cultural learning influence our behavior and thoughts. Cultural psychologists study how culture is transmitted to its members and examine similarities and differences among people from various cultures.
- The biological perspective examines how bodily functions regulate behavior and psychological characteristics. Behavioral neuroscientists study brain activity and hormonal influences, behavior geneticists examine the role of heredity, and evolutionary psychologists seek to explain how evolution has biologically predisposed modern humans toward certain ways of behaving.

USING LEVELS OF ANALYSIS TO INTEGRATE THE PERSPECTIVES

- Factors that influence behavior can be organized into three levels of analysis. The biological level examines brain processes, hormonal and genetic influences, and evolutionary adaptations. The psychological level focuses on mental processes and psychological motives. The environmental level examines physical and social stimuli, including cultural factors, that shape our behavior and thoughts.

- Biological, psychological, and environmental factors contribute to depression and also interact with one another. Interaction means that the way in which one factor (e.g., a personal setback) influences behavior depends on the presence of another factor (e.g., a weak or strong biological vulnerability to develop depression).

PSYCHOLOGY TODAY

- Modern psychologists work in many settings. They teach, conduct research, perform therapy and counseling, apply psychological principles to enhance human welfare, and help shape public policy.

- To enhance your learning and chances of performing well on tests, you can apply scientific psychological principles regarding time management, strategies for studying more effectively, test-preparation strategies, and techniques for taking tests.

KEY TERMS AND CONCEPTS

Each term has been boldfaced and defined in the chapter on the page indicated in parentheses.

applied research (p. 9)
basic research (p. 9)
behavioral neuroscience (p. 18)
behavioral perspective (p. 13)
behavior genetics (p. 20)
behaviorism (p. 14)
biological perspective (p. 18)
biopsychology (p. 3)
British empiricism (p. 11)
clinical psychology (p. 2)
cognitive behaviorism (p. 15)
cognitive neuroscience (p. 16)

cognitive perspective (p. 16)
cognitive psychology (p. 3)
cultural (cross-cultural) psychology (p. 17)
developmental psychology (p. 3)
evolutionary psychology (p. 20)
experimental psychology (p. 3)
functionalism (p. 12)
humanistic perspective (humanism) (p. 15)
industrial-organizational (I/O) psychology (p. 3)

interaction (p. 23)
natural selection (p. 20)
neurotransmitters (p. 19)
norms (p. 17)
personality psychology (p. 4)
positive psychology movement (p. 16)
psychoanalysis (p. 13)
psychodynamic perspective (p. 12)
psychology (p. 2)
social psychology (p. 4)
sociocultural perspective (p. 17)
structuralism (p. 12)

? thinking **critically**

ARE THE STUDENTS LAZY? (Page 15)

It may be tempting to blame the students' unresponsiveness on laziness, but a radical behaviorist would not focus on internal mental states to explain their inaction. First, to say that students are unresponsive *because* they're lazy doesn't explain anything. Consider this reasoning: How do we know that the students are lazy? Answer: because they are unresponsive. Therefore, if we say that students are lazy because they're unresponsive and then turn around and conclude that students are unresponsive because they are lazy, all we are really saying is that "students are unresponsive because they are unresponsive." This is not an explanation at all but rather an example of circular reasoning.

From a behavioral perspective, people's actions are shaped by the environment and learning experiences. Put yourself in the hypothetical role of the high school teacher: You may not realize it, but when students sit quietly, you

smile and seem more relaxed. When students participate in class discussions, you are quick to criticize their ideas. In these ways you may have taught your students to behave passively.

To change their behavior, you can modify their educational environment so that they will learn new responses. Reward behaviors that you want to see (raising hands, correctly answering questions, and so on). For example, praise students not only for giving correct answers but also for participating. If an answer is incorrect, point this out in a nonpunitive way while still reinforcing the student's participation.

Modifying the environment to change behavior is often not as easy as it sounds, but this example illustrates one way a behaviorist might try to rearrange the environmental consequences rather than jump to the conclusion that the situation is hopeless.

Jumbled-Word Paragraphs: Unscrambled Versions

Jumbled Paragraph 1 (page 2): According to a researcher at Cambridge University, it doesn't matter what order the letters in a word are, the only important thing is that the first and last letters are at the right place. The rest can be a total mess and you can still read it without a problem. This is because we do not read every letter by itself but the word as a whole. (*NOTE:* in the jumbled version, the author of the original paragraph misspelled *researcher* by adding an extra "ch" and omitting an "er".)

Jumbled Paragraph 2 (page 7): A politician denied the manslaughter of a colleague, but was convicted and developed severe medical conditions in prison, where he died. Administration of anticoagulant drugs potentiated the effects of another drug, and respiratory failure resulted.

chapter two

Studying Behavior Scientifically

Myth or Reality?

ESP Exists (page 55)

Many people believe in the paranormal, including ESP (extra-sensory perception). Is belief in ESP merely wishful thinking, or have scientists consistently found evidence that ESP exists?

Winter was around the corner, and Teryl's Sunday-morning drive to Oregon City was about to take an unexpected twist. The pickup truck in front of her hit a slick spot, veered off the road, and went over the edge. Teryl, who has paralyzed legs and only partial use of her arms, stopped her minivan, lowered herself into her wheelchair, and headed to the crash site. She then got out of her wheelchair, slid down the wet embankment, crawled to reach the bleeding, dazed driver, and administered first aid until the paramedics arrived. Said Teryl, "I think anybody would have done that. You see a car go down a ditch, and I can't imagine not stopping to help" (*Seattle Times,* 1997, December 11). Yet unfortunately, as we shall see over and over again, the unimaginable does indeed occur.

On a Saturday night in October 2009, several teenagers and young adults beat and gang-raped a student for two hours after she left her high school homecoming dance near San Francisco. More than a dozen people witnessed the on-campus attack. Some recorded it on their cell phones, but none helped the victim or called the police. Finally, someone dialed 911, telling the dispatcher: "People . . . have seen her, but nobody wants to call the cops" (Lopez, 2009, November 6). Two years earlier, in Detroit, a 91-year-old man was hospitalized after being severely beaten by a carjacker. Bystanders witnessed the beating but failed to intervene. A store surveillance camera captured the incident on video. The victim's son remarked in disbelief after viewing the video, "I'll never get over those other guys standing around. I never thought I'd see anything like that" (Schmitt, 2007, May 15).

These and other similar incidents spark the memory of the infamous case of Kitty Genovese, who in March 1964 was attacked by a knife-wielding assailant as she returned from work to her New York City apartment. The attack occurred around 3 A.M. and lasted about 30 minutes, during which time many neighbors heard Genovese's screams and pleas for help. Some went to their windows to find out what was happening. Yet nobody assisted her, and by the time the police arrived, she had died. The incident drew international attention from a shocked public, and commentators expressed outrage over "bystander apathy" and people's refusal to "get involved."

"Bystander apathy" is an easy and popular explanation for people's failure to help, but a scientist would ask "What's the evidence?" A curious scientist also would consider whether plausible alternative explanations exist and think of ways to test them. We'll soon see how two psychologists did just that.

Figure 2.1

What determines whether a bystander will help a victim?

Science frequently has all the mystery of a detective story. Consider the psychological puzzle of bystander intervention. If you were in trouble and needed help from bystanders, would you receive it? Ordinary citizens like Teryl often act decisively to help someone in need (Figure 2.1). But, as other tragedies illustrate, people do not always come to the aid of others. Why do bystanders sometimes risk injury and death to assist a stranger yet at other times fail to intervene—even when helping or calling the police entails little personal risk? We will return to this puzzle shortly.

In this chapter we explore principles and methods that form the foundation of psychological science. These principles also promote a way of thinking—critical thinking—that can serve you well in many aspects of your life.

SCIENTIFIC PRINCIPLES IN PSYCHOLOGY

At its core, science is an approach to asking and answering questions about the universe around us. Certainly, there are other ways we learn about our world and ourselves: through reason, intuition, and common sense; religion and spirituality; the arts; and the teachings of family, friends, and others. What distinguishes science from these approaches is a process guided by certain principles.

Scientific Attitudes

Curiosity, skepticism, and open-mindedness are driving forces behind scientific inquiry. Like a child who constantly asks "Why?", the good scientist is intensely curious. And like a master detective, the good scientist is an incurable skeptic. Each claim is met with the reply "Show me your evidence." Scientists also must remain open-minded to conclusions supported by facts, even if those conclusions refute their own beliefs.

Following the Kitty Genovese murder, two psychology professors in New York City, John Darley and Bibb Latané, met for dinner. They were so curious about how dozens of people could witness a violent crime and not even call the police that they decided to investigate further. Darley and Latané also were skeptical of the media's "bystander apathy" explanation; they believed it unlikely that all of the bystanders could have been apathetic. They noted that the bystanders could see that other neighbors had turned on their lights and were looking out their windows. Each bystander might have been concerned about Kitty Genovese's plight but assumed that someone else surely would help or call the police.

Darley and Latané reasoned that the presence of multiple bystanders produced a *diffusion of responsibility*, a psychological state in which each person feels decreased personal responsibility for intervening. Then they performed several experiments to test their explanation.

Gathering Evidence: Steps in the Scientific Process

Science involves a continuous interplay between observing and explaining events. Figure 2.2 shows the following five steps that reflect how scientific inquiry often proceeds.

Step 1: Identify a Question of Interest   Curiosity sparks the first step: identifying a question of interest. From personal experiences, news events, scientific articles and books, and other sources, scientists observe something that piques their interest, and they ask a question about it. Darley and Latané observed that nobody helped Kitty Genovese and then asked "Why?"

Step 2: Gather Information and Form a Hypothesis   Next, scientists examine whether any studies, theories, and other information already exist that might help answer their question. Then they form a hypothesis. Noting that each bystander probably knew that other bystanders were witnessing Kitty Genovese's plight, Darley and Latané proposed that a diffusion of responsibility reduced the likelihood that any one bystander would intervene. This tentative explanation is then translated into a **hypothesis,** *a specific prediction about some phenomenon* that often takes the form of an "If-Then" statement: "in an emergency, IF multiple bystanders are present, THEN the likelihood that any one bystander will intervene is reduced."

Step 3: Test the Hypothesis by Conducting Research   The third step is to test the hypothesis by conducting research. Darley and Latané (1968) staged an "emergency" in their laboratory and recorded people's responses. Male undergraduate participants were told that they would be discussing "college experiences." To ensure privacy, they would be in separate rooms, they would communicate through an intercom system, and the experimenter would not listen to their conversation. The students understood that they would take turns speaking for several rounds. In each round, a student would have 2 minutes to speak, during which time the others would be unable to interrupt or be heard, because their microphones would be turned off.

As the discussion began over the intercom, a speaker described his difficulties adjusting to college life and disclosed that he suffered from seizures. During the next round, this same speaker began to gasp, saying: "'. . . Could somebody-er-er—help . . . [choking sounds] . . . I'm gonna die-er-er—help . . . seizure' [chokes, then silence]" (Darley & Latané, 1968, p. 379).

Unbeknownst to the students, they were actually listening to a recording. This ensured that all of them were exposed to the identical "emergency." To test how the number of bystanders influences helping, Darley and Latané assigned students to one of three conditions on a random basis. Each student was alone but was led to believe that, on the intercom system, (1) he was alone with the victim, (2) another listener was present, or (3) four other listeners were present. The students believed that the seizure was real and serious. But did they help?

Step 4: Analyze Data, Draw Tentative Conclusions, and Report Findings   At the fourth step, researchers analyze the information (called *data*) they collect, draw tentative conclusions, and report their findings to the scientific community.

USING THE SCIENTIFIC METHOD

Examining bystander intervention: Why do people sometimes fail to help a victim in need during an emergency, even when there is little or no personal risk? What factors increase or decrease the likelihood that a bystander will intervene?

STEP **1** **IDENTIFY** ·

Identify Question of Interest
Kitty Genovese is murdered. The attack lasts over 30 minutes. Neighbors fail even to call the police until it is too late. The public is shocked. *Why did no one help?*

STEP **2** **HYPOTHESIZE**

Gather Information and Form Hypothesis
A diffusion of responsibility may have occurred. Hypothesis: IF multiple bystanders are present, THEN each bystander's likelihood of intervening will decrease.

STEP **3** **TEST**

Test Hypothesis by Conducting Research
Conduct an experiment by creating an emergency in a controlled setting. Manipulate (control) the number of other bystanders that each participant believes to be present, and then measure whether and how quickly each participant helps the victim.

STEP **4** **ANALYZE**

Analyze Data, Draw Tentative Conclusions, and Report Findings
The data reveal that helping decreases as the perceived number of bystanders increases. The hypothesis is supported. (If the data are found not to support the hypothesis, revise hypothesis or procedures and retest.)

STEP **5** **BUILD**

Build a Body of Knowledge; Ask Further Questions; Conduct More Research; Develop and Test Theories
Additional experiments support the hypothesis. A theory of social impact is developed based on these findings. The theory is then tested directly by deriving new hypotheses and conducting new research.

Figure 2.2

Using the scientific method.

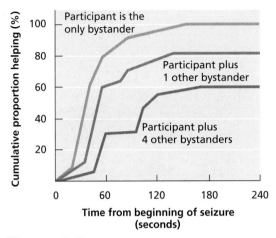

Figure 2.3

Helping in an emergency.
Participants who believed that they were the only bystander who could hear a seizure victim's plea for help were more likely to take action than were participants who believed that either one or four additional bystanders were listening. Source: Data from Darley & Latané, 1968.

As Figure 2.3 shows, Darley and Latané found that all participants who thought they were alone with the victim helped within 3 minutes of the seizure. As the number of presumed bystanders increased, the proportion of actual participants who helped decreased, and those who helped took longer to respond. These findings support the diffusion-of-responsibility explanation and illustrate how research can contradict commonsense adages such as "There's safety in numbers."

Darley and Latané then submitted a report describing their research to a scientific journal. Expert reviewers favorably judged the quality and importance of the research, so the journal published the article. Publishing research is essential to scientific progress. It allows fellow scientists to learn about new ideas and findings, to evaluate the research, and to challenge or expand on it.

Step 5: Build a Body of Knowledge At the fifth step, scientists build a body of knowledge about the topic in question. They ask further questions (e.g., "What other factors affect bystander intervention?"), formulate new hypotheses, and test those hypotheses by conducting more research. As evidence mounts, scientists may attempt to build theories. A **theory** *is a set of formal statements that explains how and why certain events are related to one another.* Theories are broader than hypotheses. For example, dozens of experiments revealed that diffusion of responsibility occurred across many situations. Latané then combined the principle of

diffusion of responsibility with other principles of group behavior to develop a broader *theory of social impact,* which has been used to explain a variety of social behaviors (Latané & Bourgeois, 2001). Scientists use theories to formulate new hypotheses, which are then tested by conducting more research. In this manner, the scientific process becomes self-correcting. If research consistently supports the hypotheses derived from a theory, confidence in the theory increases. If predictions made by the theory are not supported, then it will need to be modified or, ultimately, discarded.

Two Approaches to Understanding Behavior

Humans have a strong desire to understand why things happen. Why do scientists favor the preceding step-by-step approach to understanding behavior over the approach typically involved in everyday common sense: hindsight?

Hindsight (After-the-Fact Understanding)

Many people erroneously believe that psychology is nothing more than common sense. "I knew that all along!" is a common response to some psychological research. For example, decades ago a *New York Times* book reviewer criticized a report titled *The American Soldier* (Stouffer et al., 1949a, 1949b), which summarized the results of a study of the attitudes and behavior of U.S. soldiers during World War II. The reviewer blasted the government for spending a lot of money to "tell us nothing we don't already know."

Consider the following statements. How would you account for each of them?

1. Compared to White soldiers, Black soldiers were less motivated to become officers.

2. During basic training, soldiers from rural areas had higher morale and adapted better than soldiers from large cities.

3. Soldiers in Europe were more motivated to return home while the fighting was going on than they were after the war ended.

You should have no difficulty explaining these results. Typical reasoning might go something like this: (1) Due to widespread prejudice, Black soldiers knew that they had little chance of becoming officers. Why should they torment themselves wanting something that was unattainable? (2) It's obvious that the rigors of basic training would seem easier to people from farm settings, who were used to hard work and rising at the crack of dawn. (3) Any sane person would have wanted to go home while bullets were flying and people were dying.

Did your explanations resemble these? If so, they are perfectly reasonable. There is one catch, however. The results of the actual study were the *opposite* of the preceding statements. In fact, Black soldiers were more motivated than White soldiers to become officers, city boys had higher morale than farm boys during basic training, and soldiers were more eager to return home after the war ended than during the fighting. When told these actual results, our students quickly find explanations for them. In short, it is easy to arrive at reasonable after-the-fact explanations for almost any result.

In everyday life, *hindsight* (after-the-fact explanation) is probably our most common method of trying to understand behavior. The Danish philosopher Søren Kierkegaard noted, "Life is lived forwards, but understood backwards." The major limitation of relying solely on hindsight is that past events usually can be explained in many ways, and there is no sure way to know which—if any—of the explanations is correct. Despite this drawback, after-the-fact understanding can provide insights and is often the foundation on which further scientific inquiry is built. For example, Darley and Latané's diffusion-of-responsibility explanation was initially based on after-the-fact reasoning about the Kitty Genovese murder.

Understanding through Prediction, Control, and Theory Building

Whenever possible, scientists prefer to test their understanding of "what causes what" more directly. If we truly understand the causes of a given behavior, then we should be able to predict the conditions under which that behavior will occur in the future. Furthermore, if we can control those conditions (e.g., in the laboratory), then we should be able to produce that behavior.

Darley and Latané's research illustrates this approach. They predicted that due to a diffusion of responsibility, the presence of multiple bystanders during an emergency would reduce individual helping. Next, they carefully staged an emergency and controlled participants' beliefs about the number of bystanders present. Their prediction was supported. Understanding through prediction and control is a scientific alternative to after-the-fact understanding.

"IT MAY VERY WELL BRING ABOUT IMMORTALITY, BUT IT WILL TAKE FOREVER TO TEST IT."

Figure 2.4

The importance of testability.
Is the scientist's claim of discovering an "eternal life potion" a testable hypothesis? Yes, because it is possible to show the hypothesis to be false. If people drink it but still die at some point in time, then we have refuted the hypothesis. Therefore it is testable. It is, however, impossible to absolutely prove true. If a person drinks the potion, then no matter how long she or he lives—even a million years—she or he might die the next day. Thus, we cannot prove that the potion can make you live forever. Source: ScienceCartoonsPlus.com. Reprinted with permission.

Theory building is the strongest test of scientific understanding, because good theories generate an integrated network of predictions. A good theory has several important characteristics.

- It incorporates existing knowledge within a broad framework; that is, it organizes information in a meaningful way.

- It is testable. It generates new hypotheses whose accuracy can be evaluated by gathering new evidence (Figure 2.4).

- The predictions made by the theory are supported by the findings of new research.

- It conforms to the *law of parsimony:* If two theories can explain and predict the same phenomenon equally well, the simpler theory is the preferred one.

Even when a theory is supported by many successful predictions, it is never regarded as an absolute truth. It is always possible that future observations will contradict it or that a newer, more accurate theory will displace it. The displacement of old beliefs and theories by newer ones is the essence of scientific progress.

Finally, although scientists use prediction as a test of "understanding," this does not mean that prediction requires understanding. Even a child can predict that thunder will follow lightning without knowing why it does so. But prediction based on understanding (i.e., theory building) has advantages: it satisfies our curiosity and generates principles that can be applied to new situations.

Defining and Measuring Variables

Psychologists study variables and the relations among them. A **variable,** quite simply, *is any characteristic or factor that can vary.* People's height, hair color, income, age, sex, and grade point average are variables: they vary from one person to another, and many also vary within a given person over time.

Many variables that psychologists study represent abstract concepts that cannot be observed directly. For example, "self-esteem," "stress," and "intelligence" are concepts that refer to people's internal qualities. We might say that Tyra has high self-esteem, Shaun is intelligent, and Claire feels stressed, but how do we know this? We can't directly look inside their heads and see "self-esteem," "intelligence," or "stress," yet such concepts must be capable of being measured if we are to study them scientifically.

Because any variable may mean different things to different people, scientists must define their terms clearly. And when conducting research, scientists must also define variables operationally. An **operational definition** *defines a variable in terms of the specific procedures used to produce or measure it.* Operational definitions translate abstract concepts into something observable and measurable.

To illustrate, suppose we want to study the relation between stress and academic performance among college students. How shall we operationally define our variables? "Academic performance" could mean a single test score, a course grade, or one's overall grade point average. So, for our study, let's operationally define it as students' final exam scores in an introductory chemistry course. We also have many options for operationally defining exam stress. See the "Levels of Analysis" on page 38 to consider how exam stress can be defined from biological, psychological, and environmental perspectives.

Measurement is challenging, because psychologists study incredibly varied and complex processes. Some processes are directly observable, but others are not. Fortunately, psychologists have numerous measurement techniques at their disposal (Figure 2.5).

(a)

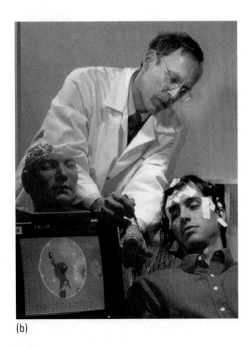
(b)

(c)

Figure 2.5

(a) Self-report, (b) physiological, and (c) behavioral measures are important scientific tools for psychologists.

Levels of Analysis

Measuring Exam Stress

In measuring exam stress, we do not have to limit ourselves to one operational definition of stress or of academic performance. Incorporating multiple levels of analysis, we might measure students' pre-exam stress hormones and self-reported worry, their nervous habits during the exam, and the exam's difficulty. We can then examine how these different stress measures relate to immediate exam performance and students' overall grade point averages.

ENVIRONMENTAL LEVEL

We can measure aspects of the academic environment that create greater or lesser demands on students, such as

- The difficulty of the exam and of the overall course grading scale
- Time pressures and room noise during the exam
- The level of achievement expectations set by the students' parents

BIOLOGICAL LEVEL

Before, during, and after the final exam, we can physiologically measure students'

- Stress hormone levels
- Heart rate and respiration rate
- Muscle tension and sweating

PSYCHOLOGICAL LEVEL

- Two weeks before the final exam, we can administer a personality test to students that measures their self-reported, general level of anxiety over taking exams.
- Just before the final exam, we can ask students to report their level of worry, tension, and anxiety.
- During the exam, we can directly observe "nervous behaviors" such as fingernail biting, foot wiggling, and hair pulling.

This strategy of measuring a conceptual variable (i.e., a "construct") in multiple ways can yield a much more complete picture than does using a single type of measure. If you were designing a research study, what measures would you choose to operationally define exam stress?

Self-Reports and Reports by Others

Self-report measures ask people to report on their own knowledge, attitudes, feelings, experiences, or behavior. This information is often gathered through interviews or questionnaires. The accuracy of self-reports hinges on people's ability and willingness to respond honestly. Especially when questions focus on sensitive topics, such as sexual habits or drug use, self-reports may be distorted by **social desirability bias,** *the tendency to respond in a socially acceptable manner rather than according to how one truly feels or behaves.* Researchers try to minimize this bias by establishing rapport with participants and allowing them to respond confidentially or anonymously. Questionnaires can also be designed to reduce social desirability bias.

We also can get information about someone's behavior by obtaining *reports made by other people,* such as parents, spouses, and teachers who know the person. For example, job supervisors might be asked to rate workers' competence. As with self-reports, researchers try to maximize participants' honesty in reporting about other people.

Measures of Overt Behavior

Another measurement approach is to *record overt (i.e., directly observable) behavior.* In an experiment on learning, we might measure how many errors a person makes while performing a task. In an experiment on drug effects, we might measure people's *reaction time*—how rapidly they respond to a stimulus (such as the onset of a light)—after ingesting various amounts of alcohol. In Darley and Latané's (1968) bystander emergency experiment, they recorded whether and how quickly college students helped a seizure victim.

Psychologists also develop *coding systems* to record different categories of behavior. While a parent and child jointly perform a task, we might code the parent's behavior into categories such as "praises child," "assists child," and "criticizes child." Observers must be trained to use the coding system properly so that their measurements will be *reliable* (i.e., consistent). If two observers watching the same behaviors repeatedly disagree in their coding, then the data are unreliable and of little use.

Humans and other animals may behave differently when they know they are being observed. To counter this problem, researchers may disguise their presence or use **unobtrusive measures,** *which record behavior in a way that keeps participants unaware that certain responses are being measured.* For example, if we ask people to report their mood on a questionnaire, then they are aware that we're measuring their mood. In contrast, we could have people perform tasks—such as rating pleasant and emotionally neutral pictures and reading various types of words—that actually assess people's moods but do so in a way that is not obvious to the participants; the measures are unobtrusive (Kiecolt-Glaser et al., 2008).

Psychologists also gather information about behavior by using **archival measures,** *which are records or documents that already exist.* For example, to evaluate the effectiveness of a program to reduce schoolchildren's disruptive classroom behaviors, researchers examined school records (e.g., student suspensions, trips to the principal's office) gathered before and after the program was implemented (Pelham et al., 2005).

Psychological Tests

Psychologists develop and use specialized tests to measure many types of variables. For example, *personality tests,* which assess personality traits, often contain questions that ask how a person typically feels or behaves (e.g., "True or False: I prefer to be alone rather than in social gatherings."). In essence, such tests are specialized self-reports. Other personality tests present ambiguous stimuli (e.g., pictures that could have different meanings), and personality traits are judged based on how a person interprets these stimuli.

Other psychological tests consist of performance tasks. For example, *intelligence tests* may ask people to assemble objects or solve arithmetic problems. *Neuropsychological tests* help diagnose normal and abnormal brain functioning by measuring how well people perform mental and physical tasks, such as recalling lists of words or manipulating objects (Abramowitz & Caron, 2010).

Physiological Measures

Psychologists also record physiological responses to assess what people are experiencing. Measures of heart rate, blood pressure, respiration rate, hormonal secretions, and brain functioning have long been the mainstay of biopsychology, but these measures have become increasingly important in many other areas of psychology.

Physiological responses can have their own interpretive problems, the main one being that we don't always understand what they mean. For example, if a person shows increased heart rate and brain activity in a particular situation, what emotion or thought is being expressed? Nevertheless, our knowledge about links between patterns of physiological activity and specific psychological processes is rapidly expanding (Rolls, 2010).

In sum, psychologists can measure behavior in many ways, each with advantages and disadvantages. To gain greater confidence in their findings, researchers may use several types of measures within a single study.

ETHICAL PRINCIPLES IN RESEARCH

When designing their research, psychologists must weigh the knowledge and possible applications to be gained against potential risks to research participants. To safeguard the rights of participants, researchers must adhere to ethical standards set by government regulations and national psychological organizations. Animal subjects must also be treated in accord with established ethical guidelines. At academic and research institutions, special committees review the ethical issues involved in research proposals. If a proposed study is considered ethically questionable, it must be modified or the research cannot be conducted.

The *Ethics Code* of the American Psychological Association (APA) builds on work by international and national commissions charged with developing ethical guidelines for biomedical and behavioral research. The APA code sets forth five broad ethical principles that represent ideals toward which all psychologists should strive. These principles include:

- *Beneficence:* seeking to benefit other people
- *Responsibility:* performing professional duties with utmost care
- *Integrity:* being honest and accurate
- *Justice:* enhancing all people's access to the benefits of psychological knowledge
- *Respect:* respecting people's dignity and rights to confidentiality and self-determination (APA, 2002)

Ethical Standards in Human Research

The APA's *Ethics Code* also provides specific guidelines for conducting research (Figure 2.6).

According to the ethical standard of **informed consent,** *before people agree to participate in research, they should be informed about:*

- *the study's purpose and procedures;*
- *the study's potential benefits;*
- *potential risks to participants;*
- *the right to decline participation and withdraw at any time without penalty;*
- *whether responses will be confidential and, if not, how privacy will be safeguarded.*

The principle of informed consent emphasizes the importance of *risk/benefit analysis:* a proposed study's potential risks must be identified and weighed against its potential benefits. When children, seriously disturbed mental patients, or other people who cannot give true informed consent are involved, consent must be obtained from their parents or guardians. To safeguard participants' right to privacy, researchers typically gather and report data in ways that keep participants' identity anonymous or confidential.

Deception, which occurs when participants are misled about the nature of a study, is controversial. Consider the Darley and Latané (1968) bystander experiment. Participants were not told that the study was going to examine how they would respond to an emergency, nor were they informed that the procedure (someone presumably having a seizure) might cause them stress.

Deception violates the principle of informed consent, but its proponents argue that when studying certain types of behaviors, deception is the only way to obtain natural, spontaneous responses from participants. Darley and Latané's participants, for example, had to believe that the emergency was significant and real.

Figure 2.6

Ethical standards are designed to protect the welfare of humans and nonhumans in psychological research.

Guidelines permit deception only when no other feasible alternative is available and the study has benefits that clearly outweigh the ethical costs of deceiving participants. When deception is used, the true purpose of the study should be explained to participants after it is over. The overwhelming majority of psychological studies do not involve deception.

Ethical Standards in Animal Research

According to the APA's Committee on Animal Research and Ethics (CARE, 2005), animals are subjects in 7 to 8 percent of psychological studies. This includes research done in the wild and in controlled settings. Rodents and birds comprise 90 percent of the animals studied; nonhuman primates comprise 5 percent.

Some psychologists study animals to discover principles that shed light on human behavior, and some do so to learn about other species. The vast majority of psychologists and college psychology majors believe that animal research is necessary for scientific progress in psychology (Plous, 1996a, 1996b). As in medical research, however, some studies expose animals to conditions considered too hazardous for humans.

APA and federal government guidelines require that animals be treated humanely and that the potential importance of the research clearly justifies the risks to which they are exposed. This determination, however, is not always easy to make. For example, should researchers be allowed to inject a drug into an animal in order to learn whether that drug might permanently impair memory? Before animal research can be conducted, it must be reviewed and approved by panels that often include nonscientists.

Animal research is debated both outside and within the psychological community (Herzog, 2005). Psychologists agree that it is morally wrong to subject animals to needless suffering. Many scientists, however, do not agree with the former head of the American Anti-Vivisection Society who maintained that animals should never be used in research "which is not for the benefit of the animals involved" (Goodman, 1982, p. 61). Proponents point to numerous important medical and psychological advances made possible by animal research. They ask, "Does the prospect of finding a cure for cancer or of identifying harmful drug effects or the causes of psychological disorders justify exposing some animals to harm?"

Proponents also note that animal research has benefited animals. For example, using knowledge discovered in studies with dogs, researchers have changed the behavior of coyotes, bears, and other wild animals that were endangering humans or livestock, thereby sparing those wild animals from being shot and killed (Gustavson & Gustavson, 1985).

Although animal research has declined slightly in recent decades, the ethical questions remain as vexing as ever. What is most encouraging is that the welfare of animals in research is receiving the careful attention it deserves.

METHODS OF RESEARCH

Like detectives searching for clues to solve a case, psychologists conduct research to gather evidence about behavior and its causes. The research method chosen depends on the problem being studied, the investigator's objectives, and ethical principles.

Descriptive Research: Recording Events

The most basic goal of science is to describe phenomena. In psychology, **descriptive research** *seeks to identify how humans and other animals behave, particularly in natural settings.* Such research provides valuable information about the diversity of behavior and may yield clues about potential cause-effect relations that are later tested experimentally. Case studies, naturalistic observation, and surveys are research methods commonly used to describe behavior.

Case Studies: The Hmong Sudden Death Syndrome

A **case study** *is an in-depth analysis of an individual, group, or event.* By studying a single case in detail, researchers typically hope to discover principles that hold true for people or situations in general. Data may be gathered through observation, interviews, psychological tests, physiological recordings, or task performance.

Case studies have several advantages. First, when a rare phenomenon occurs, this method enables scientists to study it closely. Second, a case study may challenge the validity of a theory or widely held scientific belief. Third, a case study can be a vibrant source of new ideas that may subsequently be examined using other research methods. Consider the following example.

Vang is a former Hmong (Laotian) soldier who resettled in Chicago in 1980 after escaping the ravages of war in Laos. Vang had traumatic memories of wartime destruction and severe guilt about leaving his brothers and sisters behind when he fled with his wife and child (Figure 2.7). The culture shock created by moving from rural Laos to urban Chicago increased Vang's stress. According to a mental health team, Vang experienced problems almost immediately:

> [He] could not sleep the first night in the apartment, nor the second, nor the third. . . . Vang came to see his resettlement worker . . . Moua Lee. Vang told Moua that the first night he woke suddenly,

Figure 2.7

Many Hmong refugees who escaped the ravages of war in their homeland experienced great stress and guilt when they resettled in North America. This stress, combined with cultural beliefs about angry spirits, may have contributed to the Hmong sudden death syndrome, which eventually claimed more than 40 lives.

short of breath, from a dream in which a cat was sitting on his chest. The second night . . . a figure, like a large black dog, came to his bed and sat on his chest . . . and he grew quickly and dangerously short of breath. The third night, a tall, white-skinned female spirit . . . lay on top of him. Her weight made it . . . difficult for him to breathe . . . After 15 minutes, the spirit left him and he awoke, screaming. (Tobin & Friedman, 1983, p. 440)

Vang's report attracted scientific interest because about 25 Laotian refugees in the United States already had died of what was termed the "Hmong sudden death syndrome." The cases were similar to Vang's: a healthy person died in his or her sleep after exhibiting labored breathing, screaming, and frantic movements. The U.S. Centers for Disease Control concluded that the deaths were triggered by the combined stress of resettlement, guilt over abandoning family in Laos, and the Hmong's cultural beliefs about angry spirits.

Researchers concluded that Vang might have been a survivor of the sudden death syndrome. The role of cultural beliefs is suggested by what happened next. Vang went for treatment to a Hmong woman regarded as a shaman (a person, acting as both doctor and priest, who is believed to work with spirits and the supernatural). She told him his problems were caused by unhappy spirits and performed ceremonies to release the spirits. Vang's nightmares and breathing problems during sleep ceased.

Vang's case study suggests that cultural beliefs and stress may profoundly influence physical well-being. This work was followed by other studies of Hmong immigrants and stimulated interest in the relation between cultural beliefs and health (Maher & Ho, 2009).

The major limitation of a case study is that it is a poor method for determining cause-effect relations. In most case studies, explanations of behavior occur after the fact and there is little opportunity to rule out alternative explanations. The fact that Vang's symptoms ended after seeing a shaman might not have had anything to do with his cultural beliefs; it could have been pure coincidence, or other changes in Vang's life could have been responsible.

A second potential drawback concerns the *generalizability* of the findings: will the principles uncovered in a case study hold true for other people or in other situations? The question of generalizability pertains to all research methods, but drawing broad conclusions from a case study can be particularly risky. The key issue is the degree to which the case under study is representative of other people or situations.

A third drawback is the possible lack of objectivity in the way data are gathered and interpreted. Such bias can occur in any type of research, but case studies can be particularly worrisome because they are often based largely on the researcher's subjective impressions. A skeptical attitude requires that claims based on case studies be followed up by more controlled methods before they are accepted. In everyday life, we should adopt a similarly skeptical view. When you encounter claims based on case examples or anecdotes, remember that the case may be atypical or the person making the claim may be biased. Try to seek out other evidence to evaluate the claim.

Naturalistic Observation: Bullies in the Schoolyard

In **naturalistic observation,** *the researcher observes behavior as it occurs in a natural setting, and attempts to avoid influencing that behavior* (Figure 2.8). For example, by observing African chimpanzees in the wild, British researcher Jane Goodall (1986) and other scientists found that chimpanzees display behaviors, such as making and using tools, that were formerly believed to lie only within the human domain (Lonsdorf, 2006).

Naturalistic observation is also used to study human behavior. Consider bullying, a topic that has received increasing attention from psychologists (Poteat & Rivers, 2010). Were you ever bullied at school? If so, did any schoolmates step in to help? In a three-year study, psychologists recorded children's playground interactions during recess and lunch periods at two elementary schools in Toronto (Hawkins et al., 2001). Their main goal was to describe peer interventions during episodes of schoolyard bullying. How often do schoolmates intervene? What strategies do they use? Are peer interventions effective?

Figure 2.8
Psychologists conduct naturalistic observations in many settings, including the schoolyard.

To answer these questions, the researchers developed coding systems so that the children's behavior could be classified into meaningful categories. To illustrate, here are 3 of 10 categories representing different intervention strategies:

- Verbal assertion: verbally requesting that the bullying stop, without verbally attacking the bully or victim (e.g., "Stop it," "Knock it off.")
- Physical assertion: physically stepping in to separate the bully and victim but not physically attacking either one
- Physical aggression: hitting, pushing, shoving, or otherwise physically engaging the bully or victim

Overall, of the 306 bullying episodes observed, schoolmates were present 88 percent of the time but intervened in only 19 percent of the episodes. In order, the three most common types of intervention were verbal assertion alone, physical aggression alone, and verbal assertion combined with physical assertion.

Like case studies, naturalistic observation does not permit clear causal conclusions. In the real world, many variables simultaneously influence behavior, and they cannot be disentangled with this research technique. There also is the possibility of bias in how researchers interpret what they observe. Finally, even the mere presence of an observer may disrupt a person's or animal's behavior. Thus, researchers may disguise their presence so that participants are not aware of being observed. Fortunately, when disguise is not feasible, people and other animals typically adapt to and ignore the presence of an observer as time passes. This process is called *habituation,* and researchers

may delay their data collection until participants have habituated to the observers' presence.

Survey Research: Adolescents' Exposure to Abuse and Violence

In **survey research,** *information about a topic is obtained by administering questionnaires or interviews to many people.* Political polls are a well-known example, but surveys also ask about participants' behaviors, experiences, and attitudes on wide-ranging issues. For example, in a carefully conducted national survey of 12- to 17-year-old Americans, 40 percent of these adolescents reported that they had witnessed violence either at home or in their community, and 8 percent and 23 percent, respectively, indicated that they had personally been the victims of sexual and physical assault (Hanson et al., 2006). This survey studied 3,097 adolescents, who were interviewed at length by telephone. How is it possible to make an accurate estimate of the responses of an entire population of 25 million American adolescents based on these data (U.S. Census Bureau, 2005a)?

In survey research, a **population** *consists of all the individuals who we are interested in drawing a conclusion about,* such as "American adolescents." Because it is often impractical to study the entire population, we would administer the survey to a **sample,** *which is a subset of individuals drawn from the larger population.*

To draw valid conclusions about a population from a survey, the sample must be representative: a **representative sample** *is one that reflects the important characteristics of the population* (Figure 2.9). A sample composed of 80 percent males would not be representative of the student body at a college where only

Figure 2.9

Surveys and sampling.
A representative sample possesses the important characteristics of the population in the same proportions. Data from a representative sample are more likely to generalize to the larger population than are data from an unrepresentative sample.

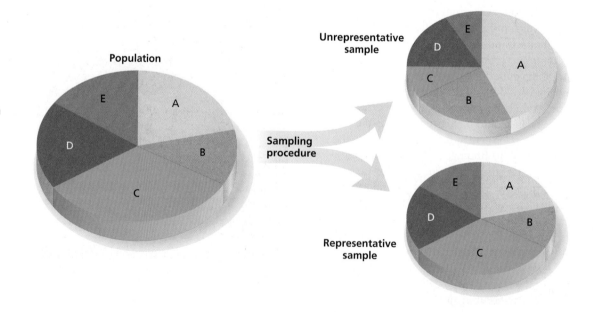

50 percent of the students are men. To obtain a representative sample, survey researchers typically use a procedure called **random sampling,** *in which every member of the population has an equal probability of being chosen to participate in the survey.* A common variation of this procedure, called *stratified random sampling,* is to divide the population into subgroups based on characteristics such as gender or ethnic identity. Suppose the population is 55 percent female. In this case, 55 percent of the spaces in the sample would be allocated to women and 45 percent to men. Random sampling is then used to select the individual women and men who will be in the survey.

When a representative sample is surveyed, we can be confident (though never completely certain) that the findings closely portray the population as a whole. This is the strongest advantage of survey research. Modern political opinion polls typically use such excellent sampling procedures that, just prior to elections, they can reasonably predict who will win a national election from a sample of about 1,000 people.

In contrast, unrepresentative samples can produce distorted results. It is better to have a smaller representative sample than a larger, unrepresentative one. In one famous example, a mail survey of almost 2 million voters in 1936 by *Literary Digest* magazine predicted that Republican presidential candidate Alf Landon would easily defeat Democratic candidate Franklin Roosevelt. When the election took place, Roosevelt won in a landslide!

How could a prediction based on 2 million people be so massively wrong? The answer is that the survey's sample was unrepresentative of the population that actually voted. The researchers obtained names and addresses from telephone directories, automobile registration lists, and magazine subscription lists. In 1936, most poorer Americans did not have telephones, cars, or magazine subscriptions. Thus the sample underrepresented poorer socioeconomic groups and overrepresented wealthier people: bad sample, bad prediction. In sum, always consider the nature of the sample when interpreting survey results.

In scientific research, surveys are an efficient method for collecting a large amount of information about people's opinions, experiences, and lifestyles, and they can reveal changes in people's beliefs and habits over many years. But there also are several major drawbacks to surveys. First, survey data cannot be used to draw conclusions about cause and effect. Second, surveys rely on participants' self-reports, which can be distorted by social desirability bias, by interviewer bias, by people's inaccurate perceptions of their own behavior, and by misinterpreting survey questions. Third, unrepresentative samples can lead to faulty generalizations about how an entire population would respond. And finally, even when surveys use proper random sampling procedures, once in a while—simply by chance—a sample that is randomly chosen will turn out not to be representative of the larger population. Overall, in properly conducted professional and scientific surveys, this happens less than 5 percent of the time, but it does happen.

? thinking **critically**

SHOULD YOU TRUST INTERNET AND POP MEDIA SURVEYS?

Tom fills out a political-attitude survey posted on the Internet. Claire mails in a dating-satisfaction survey that came in a fashion magazine to which she subscribes. Sam responds to a local TV news phone-in survey on a tax issue ("Call our number, press '1' to agree, '2' to disagree"). For each survey, can the results be trusted to reflect the general public's attitudes? Think about it, then see page 63.

Correlational Research: Measuring Associations between Events

What factors distinguish happily married couples from those headed for divorce? Do firstborn children differ in personality from later-born children? Is monetary wealth related to happiness? These and countless other psychological questions ask about associations between naturally occurring events or variables. To examine such relationships, scientists typically conduct **correlational research,** which in its simplest form has three components:

1. The researcher *measures one variable* (X), such as people's birth order.

2. The researcher *measures a second variable* (Y), such as a personality trait.

3. The researcher *statistically determines whether X and Y are related.*

Remember that correlational research involves measuring variables, not manipulating them.

Naturalistic observation and surveys are often used not only to describe events but also to study associations between variables. For example, in the naturalistic observation study of schoolyard bullying, the researchers examined associations between the children's sex and peer intervention (Hawkins et al., 2001). They found that girls were more likely to intervene when the bully and victim were female and that boys were more likely to intervene when the bully and victim were male.

Other types of studies also fall under the correlational umbrella, as our "Research Close-up" illustrates.

Research Close-up   **Very Happy People**

SOURCE: ED DIENER and MARTIN E. P. SELIGMAN (2002). Very happy people. *Psychological Science, 13*, 81–84.

INTRODUCTION

What characteristics distinguish very happy people from other people? Thousands of studies have examined depressed, anxious, or otherwise unhappy people. Yet according to psychologists Ed Diener and Martin Seligman, this study is the first to explore factors correlated with high happiness. In the spirit of critical thinking, let's test your common sense. Which of the following statements do you expect to be true?

In college, compared to students who experience average happiness, the happiest students

- worry less about things in general.
- have more satisfying close friendships, family relationships, and romantic relationships.
- generally are more outgoing.
- have more money.
- have higher grades.
- are more physically attractive.

METHOD

At a midwestern American university, 222 students completed questionnaires and psychological tests measuring their general levels of positive and negative emotions, personality traits, social relationships, satisfaction with life, and other characteristics. People who knew the students rated how often the students experienced positive and negative emotions. For 51 days, students also recorded their daily emotions in a diary.

Based on these measures, the researchers identified the 10 percent of students who consistently were the happiest, the 10 percent who consistently were the unhappiest, and a group (27 percent) that displayed average happiness. The "Research Design" figure summarizes key aspects of the method.

RESULTS

Compared to the other participants, very happy students reported spending the greatest amount of time socializing with people and having the most satisfying social relationships with close friends, family, and romantic partners. Ratings from other people also indicated that very happy students had the most satisfying social relationships. Conversely, the unhappiest students reported the least satisfying social relationships and spent the most time alone.

Very happy students also were more outgoing and agreeable and worried less about things in general. However, compared to average-happiness peers, the happiest students did not differ in how much money they said they had. College transcripts revealed that, overall, they did not have a higher grade point average, nor did independent observers rate them as being more physically attractive.

DISCUSSION

Although strong social relationships were related to greater happiness, they did not guarantee happiness; some unhappy students also had satisfying social relationships. Diener and Seligman found a similar pattern for the other variables in their study and concluded that "there appears to be no single key to high happiness that automatically produces this state" (p. 83). Instead, high levels of happiness seem to involve a combination of social and psychological factors.

Were all of your predictions accurate? As you might imagine, had the results shown that the happiest students had more money and higher grades and were more physically attractive, many people would likely say "Big deal, that's just common sense." But the findings did not support these conclusions, illustrating why scientists gather data—rather than rely solely on intuition—to answer the questions they pose.

This study also illustrates basic characteristics of correlational research. The researchers measured several variables—happiness, social relationships, and so on—and then examined whether these variables were statistically related to one another. In contrast to experiments, correlational studies only *measure* variables that occur naturally. Diener and Seligman did not *manipulate* any variables; they didn't try to influence people's happiness or relationships. As we will now discuss, the correlational approach has advantages and limitations.

RESEARCH DESIGN

Question: What characteristics distinguish very happy people from other people?

Type of Study: *Correlational*

Variable X	**Variable Y**
Personal Characteristic (e.g., satisfaction with social relationships; physical attractiveness)	Degree of Happiness (very happy, average happiness, least happy)

Correlation Does Not Establish Causation

As just described, Diener and Seligman (2002) found that very happy people had stronger, more satisfying social relationships than unhappy people (Figure 2.10a). It is tempting to conclude from these findings that stronger social relationships cause people to be happier, but correlational research does not allow us to draw such a conclusion. First, the direction of causality could be the opposite. Perhaps being happy causes people to have stronger social relationships. For example, maybe happiness makes a person more receptive to going out and forming close relationships. In correlational research, you must consider the possibility that variable X (social relationships) has caused variable Y (happiness), that Y has caused X, or that both variables have influenced each other. This interpretive problem is called the *bidirectionality (i.e., two-way causality) problem* (Figure 2.10b).

Second, the association between social relationships and happiness may be artificial, or what scientists call *spurious* (not genuine). Although social relationships and happiness are statistically related, it may be that neither variable has any causal effect on the other. A third variable, Z, may really be the cause of why some people have better social relationships and also why those people are happier. For example, Z might be a certain personality style. Recall that very happy people in Diener and Seligman's study were, in general, more outgoing and agreeable and tended to worry less. Perhaps this personality style makes it easier for people to establish good social relationships. At the same time, this style may help people soak up more joy from life and therefore feel happier. Thus, on the surface it looks as if social relationships and happiness are causally linked, but in reality this may only be due to Z (in this case, personality style).

This interpretive problem is called the *third-variable problem:* Z is responsible for what looks like a relation between X and Y (Figure 2.10c). As Z varies, it causes X to change. As Z varies, it also causes Y to change. The net result is that X and Y change in unison, but this is caused by Z—not by any direct effect of X or Y on each other. In sum, we cannot draw causal conclusions from correlational data, and this is the major disadvantage of correlational research.

The Correlation Coefficient

A **correlation coefficient** *is a statistic that indicates the direction and strength of the relation between two variables.* Variables can be correlated either positively or negatively. A **positive correlation** *means that higher*

? thinking **critically**

DOES EATING ICE CREAM CAUSE PEOPLE TO DROWN?

Nationally, ice cream consumption and drownings are positively correlated. Over the course of the year, on days when more ice cream is consumed, there tend to be more drownings. Are these two variables causally related? What causal possibilities should you consider? Think about it, then see page 64.

scores on one variable are associated with higher scores on a second variable. Thus social relationships and happiness are positively correlated such that more satisfying relationships are associated with higher levels of happiness. Similarly, people's height and weight are positively correlated (i.e., in general, taller people tend to weigh more).

A **negative correlation** *occurs when higher scores on one variable are associated with lower scores on a second variable.* Job satisfaction and job turnover are negatively correlated, which means that workers who are more satisfied with their jobs tend to have lower rates of turnover (e.g., quitting, being fired). Likewise, students' test anxiety and exam performance are negatively correlated

(a) Social relationships and happiness are correlated

(b) Bidirectionality problem

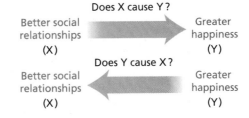

(c) Third-variable problem

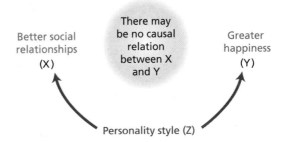

Figure 2.10

Correlation does not establish causation.

(a) Students who have better social relationships are happier. But why does this association occur? (b) Good social relationships could cause people to become happier, or, conversely, being a happier person could make it easier to form good social relationships. This is the bidirectionality problem. (c) There may be no causal link between social relationships and happiness. Other variables, such as personality traits (e.g., having a more outgoing, agreeable disposition) may be part of the true common origin of better social relationships and of happiness. This is the third-variable problem.

Figure 2.11

Scatterplots depicting correlations.

A scatterplot depicts the correlation between variables. The horizontal axis represents variable X, the vertical axis variable Y. Each data point represents a specific pair of X and Y scores, such as the number of hours a week a student studies (X) and that student's grade point average (Y). The three scatterplots show (a) a strong positive correlation, (b) a zero correlation (0.00), and (c) a strong negative correlation for hypothetical sets of data.

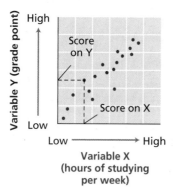

(a) A positive correlation

Variable Y (grade point)

High / Low

Score on Y

Score on X

Low → High

**Variable X
(hours of studying
per week)**

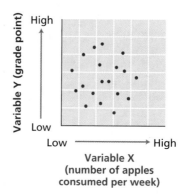

(b) Zero correlation

Variable Y (grade point)

High / Low

Low → High

**Variable X
(number of apples
consumed per week)**

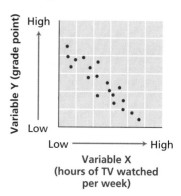

(c) A negative correlation

Variable Y (grade point)

High / Low

Low → High

**Variable X
(hours of TV watched
per week)**

(students with higher levels of test anxiety tend to perform more poorly on exams).

Correlation coefficients range from values of +1.00 to −1.00. The plus or minus sign tells you the direction of a correlation (i.e., whether the variables are positively or negatively correlated). The absolute value of the statistic tells you the strength of the correlation. The closer the correlation is to +1.00 (a perfect positive correlation) or −1.00 (a perfect negative correlation), the more strongly the two variables are related. Therefore, a correlation of −.59 indicates a stronger association between X and Y than does a correlation of +.37. A zero correlation (0.00) means that X and Y are not related statistically: as scores on X increase or decrease, scores on Y do not change in any orderly fashion. Figure 2.11 illustrates three **scatterplots,** *graphs that show the correlation between two variables.* (For more detailed information about the correlation coefficient, see the Appendix that follows Chapter 17.)

Correlation as a Basis for Prediction

Why conduct correlational research if it does not permit clear cause-effect conclusions? One benefit is that correlational research can help establish whether relations found in the laboratory generalize to the outside world. For example, suppose that laboratory experiments show that talking on a telephone while operating a driving simulator causes people to get into more simulated crashes. Correlational studies, while not demonstrating cause-effect, can at least establish whether there is a real-world association between driver cell-phone usage and automobile accident rates. (By the way, there is.) A second benefit is that correlational research can discover associations that are subsequently studied under controlled laboratory conditions. Third, for practical or ethical reasons, some questions cannot be studied with experiments but can be examined correlationally. We

cannot experimentally manipulate how religious someone is, but we can measure people's religiousness and determine if it is associated with other variables, such as personality traits.

Another benefit is that correlational data allow us to make predictions. If two variables are correlated, either positively or negatively, knowing the score of one variable helps us estimate the score on the other variable. For example, students who apply to college in North America typically take a national test that assesses academic aptitude and skills, such as the SAT. Scores on such tests help admissions officers estimate how well a student is likely to do in college, as the scatterplot in Figure 2.12 shows.

You can see that higher SAT scores are associated with higher first-year grade point averages (GPAs). The scatterplot also shows that this positive correlation is not perfect. Some students who do well on the SAT end up having an average

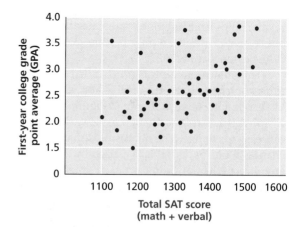

Figure 2.12

Correlation of SAT scores with first-year college GPAs.

This scatterplot represents data for a hypothetical sample of 50 students. The horizontal axis represents variable X, SAT scores. The vertical axis represents variable Y, these same students' overall grade point averages (GPAs) for their first year in college. Variables X and Y are moderately correlated.

or poor GPA; conversely, others have low SAT scores but excel in college. Still, even a moderate SAT-GPA correlation is useful to admissions officers, especially when SAT scores are used with other variables—such as high school GPAs—that also help estimate college performance. Remember, we are not saying that higher SAT scores *cause* better first-year performance, only that they help predict it. Similarly, business, government, and military organizations spend millions of dollars developing screening tests that correlate with work performance and therefore help predict how well applicants will do on the job.

Experiments: Examining Cause and Effect

Do you ever drive while talking on a cell phone? Fueling the fire of a sometimes passionate public and political debate, several correlational studies have found that hand-held and hands-free cell phone use while driving is associated with a substantially increased risk of having a vehicular collision (McEvoy et al., 2005). But as you just learned, correlation does not establish causation. How then can we obtain a clearer causal picture?

In contrast to descriptive and correlational methods, experiments are a powerful tool for examining cause-and-effect relations. An **experiment** has three essential characteristics:

1. The researcher *manipulates (i.e., controls) one or more variables.* In the simplest possible experiment, the researcher manipulates one variable by creating two different conditions to which participants are exposed. For example, we could create a variable called "cell-phone use" by randomly assigning half of our participants to drive without talking on a cell phone and assigning the other participants to drive while conversing on a hands-free cell phone. These would represent the two groups (conditions) of the experiment (i.e., drive condition, drive + phone condition).

2. The researcher *measures whether this manipulation influences other variables* (i.e., variables that represent the participants' responses). For simplicity, let's focus on just one measure of driving performance, called "braking reaction time": how quickly a driver depresses the car's brake pedal when another vehicle in front of the car slows down.

3. The researcher *attempts to control extraneous factors that might influence the outcome of the experiment.* For example, while each participant is driving, there will be no passengers

Figure 2.13

A simulator used in several experiments that examine how talking on a cell phone while driving affects drivers' performance. The simulator can be programmed to display various driving conditions, such as city (shown here) and highway traffic.

and no CD or radio playing. It also would be ideal to expose the drive and drive + phone participants to the same travel routes and also the same traffic and weather (temperature, visibility) conditions. By doing so, any differences we find in braking performance between the two groups could not possibly be due to these extraneous environmental factors. To achieve this type of rigorous environmental control, and also for ethical reasons of safety, let's do what most researchers have done: employ a highly advanced, realistic driving simulator in a laboratory environment, rather than have people drive in actual traffic (see Figure 2.13).

The logic behind this approach is straightforward:

- Start out with equivalent groups of participants.
- Treat them equally in all respects except for the variable that is of particular interest (in this case, cell-phone use).
- Isolate this variable and manipulate it (create drive and drive + phone conditions).
- Measure how the groups respond (braking reaction time).

If the groups respond differently, then the most plausible explanation is that these differences were caused by the manipulated variable (Figure 2.14).

Independent and Dependent Variables

The term **independent variable** *refers to the factor that is manipulated or controlled by the experimenter.*

Figure 2.14

The logic of designing an experiment.

The experimenter manipulates whether people talk on a cell phone while driving, measures their driving performance, and attempts to treat them equally in every other way. This creates an experimental group and a control group.

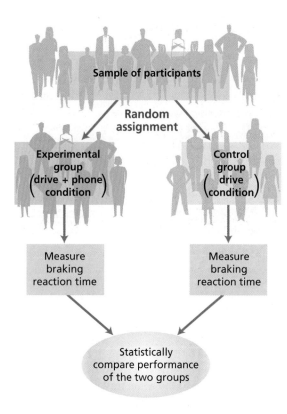

In our example, cell-phone use is the independent variable. The **dependent variable** *is the factor that is measured by the experimenter and that may be influenced by the independent variable.* In this experiment, braking reaction time is the dependent variable. An easy way to keep this distinction clear is to remember that the dependent variable *depends on* the independent variable. Presumably, braking reaction time will depend on whether the driver is talking on a cell phone. The independent variable is the cause, and the dependent variable is the effect.

Our experiment thus far has only one dependent variable, but we could have many. In addition to braking reaction time, we could measure driving speed, how frequently drivers fail to detect lights or road signs, and so on. This way, we could gain more knowledge about how cell-phone use affects driving performance.

Experimental and Control Groups

The terms *experimental group* and *control group* are often used when discussing experiments. An **experimental group** *is the group that receives a treatment or an active level of the independent variable.* A **control group** *is not exposed to the treatment or receives a zero-level of the independent variable.* The purpose of the control group is to provide a standard of behavior to which the experimental group can be compared. In our experiment, participants

in the drive + phone group represent the experimental group (or experimental condition), and participants in the drive condition represent the control group (or control condition).

Experiments with one independent variable often include more than two experimental groups. In our driving-performance study, we could add a third condition in which other participants talk on a hand-held cell phone (rather than a hands-free phone) while driving, and even add other conditions in which participants don't converse on a phone but instead listen to the radio or talk with a passenger. The drive-only participants would still represent the control group, and we could now compare how various types of potential distractions affect driver performance.

Two Basic Ways to Design an Experiment

One common way to design an experiment is to have different participants in each condition. To draw meaningful conclusions, the various groups of participants must be equivalent at the start of the study. For example, suppose that in our experiment the drive + phone group displayed poorer driving performance than the drive group. If the participants in the drive + phone group, on average, happened to have less driving experience or poorer vision than the drive participants, then these factors—not talking on a cell phone—might have been why they performed more poorly.

To address this issue, researchers typically use **random assignment,** *a procedure in which each participant has an equal likelihood of being assigned to any one group within an experiment.* Thus, a participant would have a 50 percent chance of being in the drive + phone group and a 50 percent chance of being in the drive group; that determination would be made randomly. This procedure does not eliminate the fact that participants differ from one another in driving experience, visual acuity, or other personal factors. Instead, random assignment is used to *balance these differences* across the various conditions of the experiment. It increases our confidence that, at the start of an experiment, participants in the various conditions are equivalent overall.

A second way to design experiments is to expose each participant to all the conditions of an independent variable. For example, we could measure how skillfully the same people drive when talking on a cell phone versus when not talking on a phone. By doing so, factors such as the participants' driving experience and visual acuity are held constant across the different conditions of the experiment, and therefore we can rule them out as alternative explanations for any results we obtain.

This approach, however, can create problems if not used properly. Suppose that every participant drove the simulation the first time without conversing on the phone and then drove it the second time while having phone conversations. If participants drove more poorly while talking on the phone, what would be the cause? Distraction created by the phone conversation? Perhaps. But perhaps the participants became bored, fatigued, or overconfident by the time they drove the route for the second time. To avoid this problem, researchers use **counterbalancing,** *a procedure in which the order of conditions is varied so that no condition has an overall advantage relative to the others.* Half the participants would drive the simulation first while having phone conversations and then drive it again without phone conversations. For the remaining participants, this order would be reversed.

Manipulating Two Independent Variables: Effects of Cell-Phone Use and Traffic Density on Driving Performance

To better capture the complexity of real life, researchers often study several causal factors within a single experiment by manipulating two or more independent variables simultaneously. Suppose we want to know how cell-phone use *and* traffic density influence drivers' performance. We could design separate experiments—one to examine cell-phone use and the other traffic density—but it typically is better to manipulate both independent variables within the same experiment. This approach allows us to examine not only (a) how cell-phone use and traffic density each independently influence drivers' performance, but also (b) whether cell-phone use has different effects depending on whether traffic is heavier or lighter. In scientific terms, we are asking whether there is an interaction between cell-phone use and traffic density. The concept of *interaction* means that the way in which one independent variable (X_1; e.g., cell-phone use) influences the dependent variable (Y; e.g., driving performance) differs depending on the various conditions of another independent variable (X_2; e.g., traffic density).

As before, our first independent variable would be cell-phone use (drive only versus drive + phone). But now we would add a second independent variable, traffic density, by creating two or more conditions that differ in the amount of traffic that the driver encounters. For example, let's create "low density" and "high density"

conditions by programming our driving simulator to display only one other car on the travel route or many other cars on the route.

We now have two independent variables, each of which has two conditions: cell-phone use (drive, drive + phone) and traffic density (low, high). As Figure 2.15a shows, combining these two independent variables within the same experiment creates four unique conditions: (1) driving in low-density traffic; (2) driving in high-density traffic; (3) driving while talking on the phone in low-density traffic; and (4) driving while talking on the phone in high-density traffic.

David Strayer and his colleagues (2003) conducted such an experiment. College undergraduates drove a simulated 40-mile route that had multiple lanes in each direction. Every student had cell-phone conversations in some sections of the route and no phone conversations in the remaining sections. All phone conversations took place with a research assistant.

Each student's task was to follow a "pace car" traveling in the right lane. The low and high traffic-density conditions were created by randomly assigning each student to drive the entire route either with no other cars on the highway (other than the pace car) or with a steady flow of cars appearing in the left lane (high-density condition).

For every student, the pace car braked and slowed down 32 times over the course of the route. If the student failed to brake in response, he or she would eventually collide with the pace car. The researchers measured several aspects of driving performance, including students' braking reaction time and whether they had any collisions.

Figure 2.15b shows the results for one of the dependent variables, braking reaction time. When traffic density was high, on average it took participants 179 milliseconds longer to depress their brake pedal when talking on the hands-free phone than when not talking on the phone. When traffic density was low, braking reaction times were only 29 milliseconds slower when talking on the phone. Strayer and his colleagues (2003) concluded that, overall, talking on a cell phone while driving caused drivers' responses to be more sluggish, especially when traffic density was high. In fact, three accidents occurred in the high-density, drive + phone condition, all involving participants' cars rear-ending the pace car. No accidents occurred in the other conditions.

Table 2.1 summarizes key features of the research methods we have discussed, as well as some limitations of experiments, which we will discuss next.

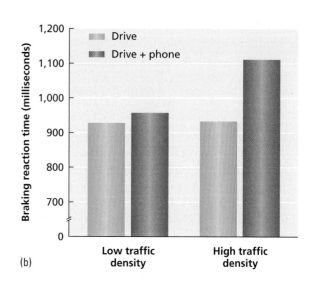

Cell-Phone Use
(independent variable #1)

Traffic Density (independent variable #2)	Drive	Drive + phone
Low traffic density	Drive in low traffic density	Drive + phone in low traffic density
High traffic density	Drive in high traffic density	Drive + phone in high traffic density

(a)

(b)

Figure 2.15

Cell-phone use, traffic density, and driving performance.

(a) Simultaneously manipulating two independent variables—cell-phone use and traffic density—creates four conditions in this design. (b) Average braking reaction time in response to multiple decelerations by a simulated pace car.
SOURCE: Data from Strayer et al., 2003.

Table 2.1 | An Overview of Research Methods

Method	Primary Features	Main Advantages	Main Disadvantages
Case study	An individual, group, or event is examined in detail, often using several techniques (e.g., observations, interviews, psychological tests).	Provides rich descriptive information, often suggesting hypotheses for further study. Can study rare phenomena in depth.	Poor method for establishing cause-effect. The case may not be representative. Often relies on the researcher's subjective interpretations.
Naturalistic observation	Behavior is observed in the setting in which it naturally occurs.	Can provide detailed information about the nature, frequency, and context of naturally occurring behaviors.	Poor method for establishing cause-effect relations. Observer's presence, if known, may influence participants' behavior.
Survey	Questions or tests are administered to a sample drawn from a larger population.	A properly selected, representative sample typically yields accurate information about the broader population.	Unrepresentative samples may yield misleading results. Interviewer bias and social desirability bias can distort the findings.
Correlational study	Variables are measured, and the strength of their association is determined. (Naturalistic observation and surveys are often used to examine associations between variables.)	Correlation allows prediction. May help establish how well findings from experiments generalize to more natural settings. Can examine issues that cannot be studied ethically or practically in experiments.	Correlation does not imply causation, due to the bidirectionality problem and the third-variable problem (which can create a confounding of variables).
Experiment	Independent variables are manipulated, and their effects on dependent variables are measured.	Optimal method for examining cause-effect relations. Ability to control extraneous factors helps rule out alternative explanations.	Confounding of variables, placebo effects, and experimenter expectancies can threaten the validity of causal conclusions.

THREATS TO THE VALIDITY OF RESEARCH

Although the experimental approach is a powerful tool for examining causality, researchers must avoid errors that can lead to faulty conclusions. **Internal validity** *represents the degree to which an experiment supports clear causal conclusions.* If an experiment is designed and conducted properly, we can be confident that it was the independent variable that caused the differences in the dependent variable. In this case, the experiment has high internal validity. However, if an experiment contains important flaws, it will have low internal validity because we can no longer be sure what caused the differences in the dependent variable.

Confounding of Variables

Consider a fictitious experiment in which Dr. Starr examines how listening to different types of music influences people's feelings of relaxation. The independent variable is the type of music: new age, country, or rock. Sixty college students are randomly assigned to listen to one of the three types of music for 20 minutes. Afterward, they rate how relaxed they feel on a questionnaire.

Dr. Starr believes that the experiment will be more realistic if the new age music is played at a low volume, the country music at a moderate volume, and the rock music at a loud volume. The results show that students who listened to the new age music felt most relaxed, while those who listened to the rock music felt least relaxed. Dr. Starr concludes that of the three types of music, new age music is the most relaxing.

What is wrong with Dr. Starr's conclusion that the type of music caused the differences in how relaxed students felt? Stated differently, can you identify another major factor that could have produced these results? Perhaps students who listened to new age music felt most relaxed because their music was played at the lowest, most soothing volume. Had they listened to it at a high volume, maybe they would have felt no more relaxed than the students who listened to the rock music. We now have two variables that, like the strands of a rope, are intertwined: the independent variable (the type of music) that Dr. Starr really was interested in and a second variable (the volume level) that Dr. Starr was not interested in but foolishly did not keep constant.

Confounding of variables *means that two variables are intertwined in such a way that we cannot determine which one has influenced a dependent variable.* In this experiment, the music's volume level is called a *confound* or a *confounding variable,* and it presents an alternative explanation for what caused Dr. Starr's results.

	Group 1	Group 2	Group 3
Independent variable (type of music)	New age	Country	Rock
Confounding variable (volume level)	Low	Moderate	High

The key point to remember is that this confounding of variables prevents Dr. Starr from drawing clear causal conclusions, thereby ruining the internal validity of the experiment. Dr. Starr can eliminate this problem by keeping the volume level constant across the three music conditions.

Confounding, by the way, is a key reason why causal conclusions cannot be drawn from correlational research. Recall the third-variable problem (see page 47). If variables X (e.g., level of happiness) and Y (e.g., quality of social relationships) are correlated, a third variable, Z (e.g., personality style), may be mixed up with X and Y, so we cannot tell what has caused what. Thus Z is just another type of confounding variable.

Placebo Effects

In medical research, the term **placebo** *refers to a substance that has no pharmacological effect.* In experiments testing the effectiveness of new drugs for treating diseases, one group of patients—the *treatment group*—receives the actual drug (e.g., through pills or injections). A second group, the *placebo control group,* receives a placebo (e.g., pills composed of inactive ingredients or injections of saline). Typically, participants are told that they will be given either a drug or a placebo, but they are not told which one. In another control group, patients receive neither the drug nor a placebo.

The rationale for using placebos is that patients' symptoms may improve solely because they expect that a drug will help them. If 40 percent of the drug patients, 38 percent of the placebo control patients, and only 5 percent of the other control patients improve, then we have evidence of a **placebo effect:** *people receiving a treatment show a change in behavior because of their expectations, not because the treatment itself had any specific benefit* (Figure 2.16).

Placebo effects decrease internal validity by providing an alternative explanation for why responses change after exposure to a treatment. This problem applies to evaluating all types of treatments, not just those that test the effectiveness of drugs. For example, suppose that depressed patients improve (i.e., become less depressed) while receiving psychotherapy. Is this due to the specific procedures and content of the psychotherapy itself, or might it merely be a placebo effect resulting from their positive expectations that the therapy would help them? Experiments that include the proper control groups can examine this question, as we will discuss in Chapter 16.

Figure 2.16

Throughout history, placebo effects have fostered the commercial success of many products that had no proven physiological benefit. Herbal medicines are one of today's "health crazes." Do they really work? If so, is it because of placebo effects or the herbs' chemical properties? The best way to answer this question is through experiments that include placebo control groups.

Experimenter Expectancy Effects

Researchers typically have a strong commitment to the hypothesis they are testing. In psychology, the term **experimenter expectancy effects** *refers to the subtle and unintentional ways a researcher influences participants to respond in a manner that is consistent with the researcher's hypothesis.* Scientists can take several steps to avoid experimenter expectancy effects. For example, researchers who interact with participants in a study or who record participants' responses are often kept blind to (i.e., not told about) the hypothesis or the specific condition to which a participant has been assigned. This makes it less likely that these researchers will develop expectations about how participants "should" behave.

The **double-blind procedure,** *in which both the participant and experimenter are kept blind as to which experimental condition the participant is in,* simultaneously minimizes participant placebo effects and experimenter expectancy effects. In research testing drug effects, each participant receives either a real drug or a placebo but does not know which. People who interact with the participants (e.g., those who dispense the drugs or measure participants' symptoms) also are kept unaware of which participants receive the drug or placebo. This procedure minimizes the likelihood that the researchers will behave differently toward the two groups of participants, and it reduces the chance that participants' own expectations will influence the outcome of the experiment (Figure 2.17).

"IT WAS MORE OF A 'TRIPLE-BLIND' TEST. THE PATIENTS DIDN'T KNOW WHICH ONES WERE GETTING THE REAL DRUG, THE DOCTORS DIDN'T KNOW, AND I'M AFRAID, <u>NOBODY</u> KNEW"

Figure 2.17

The double-blind procedure is useful, but scientists try to avoid the infamous "triple-blind procedure." Source: ScienceCartoonsPlus.com. Reprinted with permission.

Replicating and Generalizing the Findings

Returning to our hypothetical experiment on cell-phone use, let's suppose that participants' driving performance was impaired while they talked on a cell phone. If our experiment was conducted properly, it will have high internal validity and thus we can be confident that talking on the phone, and not some other factor, caused the driving impairment. There remain, however, other questions that we must ask. Would the results be similar with other types of participants or when driving under different road or traffic conditions?

These questions focus on **external validity,** *which is the degree to which the results of a study can be generalized to other populations, settings, and conditions.* Typically, judgments about external validity are most concerned about the *generalizability of underlying principles.* If talking on a cell phone impairs braking reaction time by 140 milliseconds in our experiment but only by 120 milliseconds in a subsequent experiment with younger drivers, then the 20-millisecond difference is not the key issue. Rather, it's that the principle—"talking on a cell phone impairs driving"—has successfully generalized to younger drivers.

To determine external validity, either we or other scientists need to replicate our experiment. **Replication** *is the process of repeating a study to determine whether the original findings can be duplicated.* If our findings are successfully replicated, especially when studying other types of participants and driving conditions, we become more confident in concluding that cell-phone use impairs driving performance. Indeed, in simulation experiments, talking on a cell phone while driving has been found to interfere with driving performance in rural and urban environments of varying complexity, among younger and older drivers, and when using hand-held and hands-free phones (Strayer & Drews, 2004; Törnros & Bolling, 2006). Increasingly, psychologists are paying more attention to *cross-cultural replication*—examining whether findings generalize across different cultures.

When research findings fail to replicate, it may lead to better research and new discoveries as scientists search for clues to explain why the results turned out differently in one study versus another. For example, although many experiments suggest that cell-phone use interferes with optimal driving performance, not all experiments do. Further research will be needed to sort out the factors, such as different driving conditions, that might account for such results.

Studies that consistently fail to replicate the results of earlier research may suggest that the original research was flawed or that the finding was a fluke. Even so, the scientific process has done its job and prevented us from getting caught in a blind alley. To see why replication is such an important component of the scientific process, let's look at the following "Myth or Reality?"

Myth or Reality?   ESP Exists

Do you believe in ESP (extrasensory perception), such as telepathy (directly transmitting thoughts between minds), clairvoyance (remotely sensing a current object or event), or precognition (foretelling the future)? How about other paranormal phenomena? Across the globe, many people believe. A nationally representative Gallup poll found that 73 percent of American adults believed in at least one of the phenomena in Table 2.2; 32 percent believed in four or more items (Moore, 2005). Many Canadian and British adults also hold paranormal beliefs (Lyons, 2005). Compared to nonbelievers, believers tend to be more open to new experiences and are more fantasy prone (Smith et al., 2009).

Should such beliefs surprise us? For decades, a steady diet of movies, TV shows, and novels has fed our imagination with characters who possess psychic abilities such as telepathy (e.g.,

Professor Xavier, *X-Men*; Matt Parkman, *Heroes*; Edward Cullen, *Twilight/New Moon*) and psychokinesis, the direct mental influence of physical objects and systems (e.g., Yoda, *Star Wars*; Jean Grey, *X-Men*; Sylar, *Heroes*). Both correlational research and experiments suggest an association between exposure to paranormal media content and belief in paranormal phenomena (Sparks & Miller, 2001).

Paranormal beliefs also have other sources. For one thing, many people claim to have had a paranormal experience (Kunzendorf et al., 2007). For another, popular books and Web sites written by parapsychologists (i.e., scientists from various fields who study paranormal phenomena) proclaim strong scientific support for several paranormal phenomena, including ESP (Parapsychology Association, 2008; Radin, 2006).

Continued

Table 2.2 | **Belief in the Paranormal among American Adults**

Phenomenon	Believe (%)	Not Sure (%)	Don't Believe (%)
ESP	41	25	32
Haunted houses	37	16	46
Ghosts/spirits	32	19	48
Telepathy	31	27	42
Clairvoyance	26	24	50
Astrology	25	19	55
Extraterrestrial visits to Earth	24	24	51
Mental communication with a dead person	21	23	55
Witches	21	12	66
Reincarnation	20	20	59
Channeling/allowing a spirit to assume temporary control of one's body	9	20	70

Does research convincingly demonstrate that ESP exists? That's the claim, but the reality is that while many parapsychologists say "absolutely," many scientists and other skeptics say "absolutely not" (Alcock, 2010). Believers and skeptics disagree about the rigor of some parapsychological research and about how high the standards of scientific evidence should be set: should we apply the same standards used to assess other phenomena, or should extraordinary claims of psychic phenomena require "extraordinary proof" (Gracely, 1998)? Either way, the ability of independent investigators to replicate initial research findings is a central scientific standard.

When tested under controlled conditions in well-designed experiments and replications, claim after claim of psychic ability has evaporated. The Committee for Skeptical Inquiry, founded in 1976, consists of psychologists, other scientists, philosophers, and magicians expert in the art of fakery. To conclude that a phenomenon is psychic, the committee requires that presently known natural physical or psychological explanations be ruled out. To date, it has not judged any psychic claims to be valid.

What about demonstrations by self-proclaimed psychics, such as using mental powers to bend spoons? In 1964, James Randi, a magician and expert in the art of psychic fraud, began offering $1,000 to anyone who could demonstrate paranormal ability under his scrutiny. Today the offer is $1 million, and still no one has collected. Predictions made by leading psychics in national newspapers also yield dismal results (Emery Jr., 2001).

In 1994, however, an article in a major psychological journal provided evidence of telepathy based on an overall statistical analysis—called *meta-analysis*—of 11 studies using the *ganzfeld procedure* (Bem & Honorton, 1994). In this approach, a participant (the "receiver") listens to white noise played through earphones and sees red light through translucent goggles. Parapsychologists believe this makes the receiver more sensitive to telepathy signals. In a separate, acoustically shielded room, a "sender" concentrates on a visual target (e.g., a photograph) selected randomly by computer from among many stimuli. Meanwhile, the receiver's thoughts are verbally recorded. Then the receiver is shown four stimuli (e.g., photographs), not told which is the target, and rates how well each one matched her or his thoughts. In these studies, the target stimulus received the highest rating of the four stimuli on 32 percent of the trials, a statistically significant increase above the chance level of 25 percent.

Does the ganzfeld procedure—which over time added many rigorous controls—provide solid evidence of ESP? Psychologists Julie Milton and Richard Wiseman (1999) analyzed 30 ganzfeld studies conducted by seven independent laboratories and concluded that the studies did not provide replicable laboratory evidence of ESP. When authors of a larger meta-analysis subsequently concluded support for ESP (Storm & Ertel, 2001), Milton and Wiseman (2001) argued that this broader analysis was flawed because it included many early ganzfeld experiments that lacked rigorous controls. As newer studies are published—including attempts to use brain-recording techniques to find evidence of telepathy—scientists continue to debate the status of ESP (Alcock, 2010; Watt & Irwin, 2010).

Critical thinking requires us to have a reasoned skepticism that demands solid scientific evidence, but not a blind skepticism that rejects the unknown as impossible. In our opinion, at present there is no generally accepted, conclusive scientific evidence to support the existence of ESP. Research continues, and while the burden of proof lies with those who believe in the paranormal, evaluations of their claims should be based on scientific evidence rather than on preconceived positive or negative expectations.

ANALYZING AND INTERPRETING DATA

Around election time, do you feel like you're swimming in a sea of statistics from endless voter polls and political advertisements? As a student, you live in a world of grade point averages. And on the Internet you'll find loads of statistics about athletes, teams, the economy, and stock prices.

Statistics are woven into the fabric of modern life, and they are integral to psychological research. We'll explain why statistics are important by focusing on a few basic concepts. The Appendix that follows Chapter 17 provides more information about these and other concepts.

Being a Smart Consumer of Statistics

Suppose that a neighborhood group wants your support for a new crime-watch program. To convince you, the group quotes statistics from a nearby town, showing that this program will reduce your chance of being robbed by a whopping 50 percent. Sounds impressive, but would you be impressed if you learned that in 2009 this town had two robberies and that after adopting the crime-watch program in 2010 they had only one? Because the number of robberies was so low to begin with, this percentage change doesn't mean much. In everyday life, it helps to ask about the number of cases or observations that stand behind percentages.

Now consider a fictitious consumer study that asked 1,000 people to taste three cola drinks from competing companies and choose the one they liked best. The two *bar graphs* in Figure 2.18 show the same results but make a different visual impression. It's always wise to look at the fine print, including the scale of measurement, that accompanies graphs and charts.

Lastly, imagine that you apply for a consulting job at Honest Al's Consulting Firm. You ask Al how much money his consultants make. Al replies, "Our consultants' average salary is $75,000." "Wow," you think to yourself. Now look at the list of 10 salaries in Table 2.3. Is the job still as attractive to you? This is another example of why it is important to think critically about statistics. Honest Al was indeed being honest, but as you will now see, by asking questions about a few other statistics, you come away with a more accurate understanding of the situation.

Using Statistics to Describe Data

In contrast to the information in Table 2.3, psychological research often involves a large number of measurements. Typically it is difficult to make much sense out of the *data* (i.e., the information collected) by examining the individual scores of each participant. **Descriptive statistics** *allow us to summarize and describe the characteristics of a set (or distribution) of data.* You are already familiar with one descriptive statistic—the correlation coefficient, which we discussed on pages 47–48. Now we'll introduce two other types of descriptive statistics.

Measures of Central Tendency

Given a set of data, *measures of central tendency* address the question "What's the typical score?" One measure, the **mode,** *is the most frequently occurring score in a distribution.* At Honest Al's the modal salary is $263,000. While the mode is easy to identify, it may not be the most representative score. Clearly, $263,000 is not the typical salary of the 10 consultants.

Figure 2.18

Manipulating visual impressions of data.

Suppose that 30 percent of 1,000 taste testers preferred Cola A, 20 percent preferred Cola B, and 17 percent preferred Cola C. (Note that 33 percent had no preference and thus their results are not graphed.) Look at the Y-axis (the vertical axis) of each graph. The left-hand graph (a), where the Y-axis scale goes from zero to 100 percent, makes this difference seem small. The right hand graph (b), with a Y-axis scale of zero to 30 percent, makes this difference seem large. As marketing director for Cola A, which graph would you put in your advertisements?

Percentage of people in taste test who prefer each cola

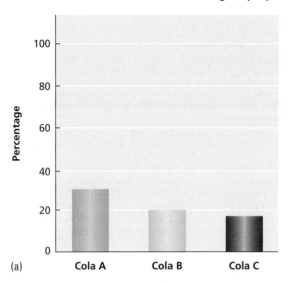

(a)

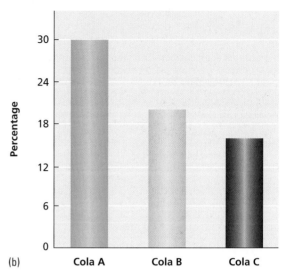

(b)

Table 2.3 | Salaries of 10 Consultants at Honest Al's Consulting Firm

Consultant	Annual Salary	
1. Al's brother	$263,000	Mode, most frequent score
2. Al's sister	263,000	
3. Johnson	30,500	
4. Rodriguez	29,500	
5. Jones	29,000	Median, middle score $28,500
6. Chen	28,000	
7. Brown	27,500	
8. Carter	27,000	
9. Mullins	26,500	
10. Watson	26,000	
Mean (average salary)	$= \dfrac{\$750,000}{10 \text{ scores}} = \$75,000$	

A second measure of central tendency is the **median,** *the point that divides a distribution of scores in half when those scores are arranged in order from lowest to highest.* Half of the scores lie above the median, half below it. In Table 2.3, because there is an even number of scores, the median is $28,500—the point halfway between employee 5 ($29,000) and employee 6 ($28,000).

Finally, the **mean** *is the arithmetic average of a set of scores.* To determine the mean, you simply add up all the scores in a distribution and divide by the number of scores. The $75,000 average that Honest Al quoted was the mean salary.

Be aware that the mean has a disadvantage: It is affected by extreme scores. The $263,000 salaries of Al's brother and sister inflate the mean, making it less representative of the typical salary.

The median, in contrast, is not affected by extreme scores. Changing the top salary to $1 million does not change the median but further inflates the mean. Still, the mean has a key advantage over the median and mode: it captures information from every score. In Table 2.3, if Johnson and Rodriguez each received a $50,000 salary increase, the median and mode would not change. However, the mean would increase and reflect the fact that Honest Al was now paying some of his employees better salaries.

Because the mean takes all the information in a set of scores into account, it is the most commonly used measure of central tendency in research, and perhaps in everyday life as well. But keep in mind that extreme scores will distort the mean. When you go for that job interview, also ask about the median and modal salaries.

Measures of Variability

To describe a set of data, we want to know not only the typical score but also whether the scores cluster together or vary widely. *Measures of variability* capture the degree of variation, or spread, in a distribution of scores. Look at Table 2.4, which lists Honest Al's salaries alongside those of 10 consultants from Claire's Consulting Firm. The mean salary is the same at both firms, but notice how Claire's salaries are closer to one another—less variable—than are Al's. The simplest but least informative measure of variability is the **range,** *which is the difference between the highest and lowest scores in a distribution.* At Honest Al's, the salary range is $237,000; at Claire's the range is only $11,000.

A more important statistic, the **standard deviation,** *takes into account how much each score in*

Table 2.4 | **Annual Salaries of Ten Consultants at Two Consulting Firms**

Honest Al's Firm		Claire's Firm
$263,000		$81,000
263,000		78,000
30,500		76,000
29,500		76,000
29,000		76,000
28,000		75,000
27,500		73,000
27,000		73,000
26,500		72,000
26,000		70,000
$75,000	Mean	$75,000
$237,000	Range	$11,000
$94,009	Standard deviation	$3,000

a distribution differs from the mean. At Honest Al's, the standard deviation is $94,009; at Claire's, it's only $3,000. We need not be concerned here with how the standard deviation is calculated. Rather, the key point is that it uses information from every score, whereas the range takes into account only the highest and lowest scores.

Using Statistics to Make Inferences

Descriptive statistics allow researchers to efficiently summarize data, but researchers typically want to go beyond mere description and draw *inferences* (conclusions) from their data. To illustrate, suppose we conduct an experiment to examine how noise affects adults' ability to learn new factual information. Each of 80 participants is placed alone in the same room. Half of the participants are randomly assigned to perform a reading-comprehension task while recorded traffic noise is played in the background. For the remaining participants, the room is kept quiet. We find that, on average, adults in the noisy room perform more poorly than adults in the quiet room.

At this point we would like to make a general inference: "noise impairs people's ability to learn new factual material." However, we must first wrestle with a key issue: even if our experiment had all the proper controls and there were no confounding variables, perhaps the noise really had no effect on performance, and our findings were merely a chance outcome. Perhaps, for example, just by random chance we happened to end up with 40 adults in the noisy room who would have performed this poorly anyway, even if they had been in a quiet room.

Inferential statistics *tell us how confident we can be in making inferences about a population based on findings obtained from a sample.* In our case, they help determine the probability that we would obtain similar results if our experiment were repeated over and over with other samples from the same population. Inferential statistics tell researchers whether their findings are statistically significant. **Statistical significance** *means that it is very unlikely that a particular finding occurred by chance alone.* Psychologists typically consider results to be statistically significant only if the results could have occurred by chance alone fewer than 5 times in 100.

Keep in mind that statistical significance does not mean that a finding is scientifically or socially important. If thousands of adults took our reading comprehension test in either a noisy or quiet room, and if the variability (the standard deviation) within each condition was small, then even a tiny difference between the average test performance of these groups might be statistically significant but trivial for practical purposes. Yet a psychological technique that helps athletes run or swim faster by one hundredth of a second might make the difference between winning the gold medal or no medal at the Olympics. Statistical significance only means it is unlikely that the results of study are due to chance. The scientific or social significance of the findings must be judged within a broader context.

Meta-analysis: Combining the Results of Many Studies

As research on a topic accumulates, scientists must reach overall conclusions about how variables are related. Often experts on a topic will review the number and quality of studies that support, or fail to support, a particular relation and then draw conclusions that they believe are best supported by the facts.

Increasingly, these expert reviews are being supplemented by **meta-analysis,** *a statistical procedure for combining the results of different studies that examine the same topic.* In a typical study, the responses of each participant are analyzed. In a meta-analysis, each study is treated as a "single participant," and its overall results are analyzed with those of other studies. A meta-analysis tells researchers about the direction and statistical strength of the relation between two variables.

For example, would you expect gender differences in how often people recall nighttime dreams? One meta-analysis combined the results of 175 studies and found that overall, among adolescents and adults, women recalled dreams somewhat more often than did men (Schredl & Reinhard, 2008).

Researchers who use meta-analysis must decide which studies to include and describe their common limitations. Many researchers consider meta-analysis to be the most objective way to integrate the findings of multiple studies and reach overall conclusions about behavior.

test yourself   Analyzing Data

True or false?

1. Ten students were asked "How many dates did you go on last month?" Their answers were: 0, 0, 0, 1, 2, 2, 3, 4, 4, 8. The median for this set of data equals 2.

2. The mode in the preceding set of data equals 0.

3. The mode, median, and mean are measures of variability.

4. Statistics that summarize the characteristics of a set of scores are called "descriptive statistics."

5. If the finding of a study is found to be "statistically significant," it is very unlikely that this finding is due simply to chance.

ANSWERS: 1-true, 2-true, 3-false, 4-true, 5-true

CRITICAL THINKING IN SCIENCE AND EVERYDAY LIFE

In today's world, we are exposed to a great deal of information about human behavior—some of which is accurate and much of which is not. Especially in the popular media, we encounter oversimplifications, overgeneralizations, and *pseudoscientific misinformation*—bunk and psychobabble that is made to sound scientific. To be an informed consumer, you must be able to critically evaluate research and identify factors that limit the validity of conclusions. Critical-thinking skills can also help you avoid being misled by claims made in everyday life, such as those in advertisements. Thus, enhancing your critical-thinking skills is an important benefit that you can derive from your psychology course.

Throughout this chapter, you have seen how critical thinking, a healthy dose of skepticism, and the scientific method help scientists solve puzzles of mind and behavior. As critical thinkers, we should recognize that our beliefs and emotions can act as psychological blinders that allow us to accept inadequate evidence uncritically, especially when this evidence supports our current views. This does not mean that we should be so skeptical of everything that we end up believing nothing at all. Rather, we need to balance openmindedness with a healthy skepticism and evaluate evidence for what it is worth (Figure 2.19).

Figure 2.19

Modern society bombards us with scientific and pseudoscientific claims. A good dose of critical thinking often can help us tell good science from junk science, and some publications do promote healthy skepticism and critical thinking, such as *Skeptical Inquirer* magazine.

To exercise your critical-thinking skills, read the following descriptions of a research study, an advertisement, and a newspaper article. Have some fun and see if you agree with the claims made.

Write down your answers, and compare them with the answers provided at the end of the box. You can facilitate critical thinking by asking yourself the following questions:

1. What claim is being made?
2. Who is making the claim? Is the source trustworthy and credible?
3. What evidence is presented? How good is it?
4. Are there other plausible explanations for the conclusions being drawn? What additional evidence would help to reach a clearer conclusion?
5. What is the most reasonable conclusion to draw?

SOME INTERESTING CLAIMS

Example 1: A Lot of Bull

Deep inside the brains of humans and other mammals is a structure called the *caudate nucleus*. Years ago, a prominent researcher hypothesized that this part of the brain is responsible for turning off aggressive behavior. The scientist was so confident in his hypothesis that he bet his life on it. A microelectrode was implanted inside the caudate nucleus of a large, aggressive bull. The researcher stood before the bull and, like a Spanish matador, waved a cape to incite the bull to charge. As the bull thundered toward him, the researcher pressed a button on a radio transmitter that he held in his other hand. This sent a signal that caused the microelectrode to stimulate the bull's caudate nucleus. Suddenly, the bull broke off its charge and stopped. Each time this sequence was repeated, the bull stopped its charge. The researcher concluded that the caudate nucleus was the "aggression-off" center of the brain.

Stimulating the caudate nucleus caused the bull to stop charging, but does this demonstrate that the caudate nucleus is an aggression-off center? Why or why not? (*Hint:* What other bodily functions might the caudate nucleus help regulate that would cause the bull to stop charging?)

Example 2: Vacations and Burglaries

A newspaper advertisement appeared in several American cities. The headline "While You're on Vacation, Burglars Go to Work" was followed by this statement: "According to FBI statistics, over 26 percent of home burglaries take place between Memorial Day and Labor Day" (U.S. holidays in late May and early September). The ad then offered a summer sale price for a home security system. In sum, the ad implied that burglaries are particularly likely to occur while people are away on summer vacation. How do you feel about this claim and its supporting evidence?

Example 3: Will Staying up Late Cause You to Forget What You Have Studied?

The headline of a newspaper article read, "Best Way to Retain Complex Information? Sleep on It, Researcher Says." The article began, "Students who study hard Monday through Friday and then party all night on weekends may lose much of what they learned during the week, according to a sleep researcher." The researcher was then quoted as saying, "It appears skewing the sleep cycle by just two hours can have this effect. Watching a long, late movie the night following a class and then sleeping in the next morning will make it so you're not learning what you thought. You'll not lose it all—just about 30 percent."

Next, the experiment was described. College students learned a complex logic game and then were assigned to one of four sleep conditions. Students in the control condition were allowed to have a normal night's sleep. Those in Condition 2 were not allowed to have any sleep, whereas students in Conditions 3 and 4 were awakened only when they went into a particular stage of sleep. (We'll learn about sleep stages in Chapter 6.) A week later, everyone was tested again. Participants in Conditions 3 and 4 performed 30 percent worse than the other two groups.

Reexamine the experimental conditions, then identify what's wrong with the claims in the first paragraph.

CRITICAL ANALYSES OF THE CLAIMS

Analysis 1: A Lot of Bull

Perhaps the caudate nucleus plays a role in vision, memory, or movement, and stimulating it momentarily caused the bull either to become blind, to forget what it was doing, or to alter its movement. Perhaps the bull simply became dizzy or experienced pain. These are all possible explanations for why the bull stopped charging. In fact, the caudate nucleus helps regulate movement; it is not an aggression-off center in the brain.

Analysis 2: Vacations and Burglaries

First, how much is "over 26 percent"? We don't know for sure but can assume that it is less than 27 percent, because it would be to the advertiser's advantage to state the highest number possible. The key problem is that the time period between Memorial Day and Labor Day typically represents between 26 and 29 percent of the days of the year. Therefore, about 26 percent of burglaries occur during about 26 percent of the year. Wow! Technically the ad is correct: burglars do go to work in the summer while you're on vacation. But the ad also may have misled people. Burglars seem to be just as busy at other times of the year.

Analysis 3: Will Staying up Late Cause You to Forget What You Have Studied?

It could be true that going to bed and waking up later than usual might cause you to forget more of what you have studied. However, the article does not provide evidence for this claim. Look at the four conditions carefully. To test this claim, an experiment would need to include a condition in which participants went to bed later than usual, slept through the night, and then awakened later than usual. But in this experiment, the control group slept normally, and the three experimental conditions examined only the effects of getting no sleep or losing certain types of sleep.

When you read newspaper or magazine articles, look beyond the headlines and think about whether the claims are truly supported by the evidence. Were you able to pick out some flaws in these claims before you read the analyses? Critical thinking requires practice, and you will get better at it if you keep asking yourself the five critical-thinking questions listed earlier.

Chapter Summary

SCIENTIFIC PRINCIPLES IN PSYCHOLOGY

- The scientific process proceeds through several steps: (1) identifying a question of interest; (2) formulating a tentative explanation and a testable hypothesis; (3) conducting research to test the hypothesis; (4) analyzing the data, drawing a tentative conclusion, and reporting one's findings to the scientific community; and (5) building a body of knowledge by asking further questions, conducting more research, and developing and testing theories.

- In everyday life, we typically use hindsight to explain behavior. Hindsight is flawed because there may be many possible explanations and no way to assess which is correct. Psychologists prefer to test their understanding through prediction, control, and theory building.

- A good theory organizes known facts, gives rise to additional hypotheses that are testable, is supported by the findings of new research, and is parsimonious.

- An operational definition defines a concept or variable in terms of the specific procedures used to produce or measure it.

- To measure behavior, psychologists obtain people's self-reports and reports from others who know the participants, directly observe behavior, use unobtrusive measures, analyze archival data, administer psychological tests, and measure physiological responses.

ETHICAL PRINCIPLES IN RESEARCH

- Psychological researchers follow extensive ethical guidelines. In human research, key standards include obtaining informed consent, ensuring the participants' right to privacy, minimizing potential risks to participants, and minimizing the use of deception.

- Animals must be treated humanely. As in human research, the risks to which they are exposed must be justified by the potential importance of the research.

- Before human or animal research can be conducted, it must be approved by ethics review boards.

METHODS OF RESEARCH

- Descriptive research describes how organisms behave. Case studies involve the detailed study of a person, group, or event. They often suggest ideas for further research but are a poor method for establishing cause-effect relations.

- Naturalistic observation can yield rich descriptions of behavior in real-life settings and permits examination of relations between variables. Researchers try to avoid influencing the participants they observe.

- Surveys involve administering questionnaires or interviews to many people. Many surveys study a sample that is randomly drawn from the larger population. Representative samples allow researchers to estimate the responses of the entire population. Unrepresentative samples can lead to inaccurate estimates.

- Correlational research measures the relation between naturally occurring variables. A positive correlation means that higher scores on one variable are associated with higher scores on a second variable. A negative correlation occurs when higher scores on one variable are associated with lower scores on a second variable. Causal conclusions cannot be drawn from correlational data. Variable X may cause Y, Y may cause X, or some third variable (Z) may be the true cause of X and Y.

- A well-designed experiment is the best way to examine cause-effect relations. Experiments have three essential characteristics: (1) one or more variables—called *independent variables*—are manipulated, (2) their effects on other variables—called *dependent variables*—are measured, and (3) extraneous factors are controlled so that cause-effect conclusions can be drawn. The independent variable is viewed as the cause; the dependent variable, as the effect.

- In some experiments, different participants are randomly assigned to each condition. In other experiments, the same participants are exposed to all the conditions, but the order in which the conditions are presented is counterbalanced. Researchers can study several causal factors within one experiment by simultaneously manipulating two or more independent variables.

THREATS TO THE VALIDITY OF RESEARCH

- An experiment has high internal validity when it is designed well and permits clear causal conclusions. Confounding occurs when the independent variable becomes mixed up with an uncontrolled variable. This ruins internal validity because we can no longer tell which variable caused the changes in the dependent variable.

- Placebo effects (in which the mere expectation of receiving a treatment produces a change in behavior) and experimenter expectancy effects (which are subtle ways a researcher influences participants to behave consistently with the hypothesis being tested) threaten a study's internal validity.

- The double-blind procedure prevents placebo effects and experimenter expectancy effects from biasing research results.

- External validity is the degree to which the findings of a study generalize to other populations, settings, and conditions. Researchers establish a study's external validity by replicating it under different circumstances.

ANALYZING AND INTERPRETING DATA

- Descriptive statistics summarize the characteristics of a set of data. Measures of central tendency identify the typical score. The mode is the most frequent score. When all the scores are arranged from lowest to highest, the median is the middle score. The mean is the arithmetic average of the scores.
- Measures of variability assess whether scores are clustered together or spread out. The range is the difference between the highest and lowest scores. The standard deviation takes into account how much each score differs from the mean.
- Inferential statistics allow researchers to determine whether their findings are statistically significant, which means that it is very unlikely that a particular finding occurred by chance alone.
- Meta-analysis statistically combines the results of many studies that examine the same variables.

CRITICAL THINKING IN SCIENCE AND EVERYDAY LIFE

- Critical thinking is an important life skill. It can prevent us from developing false beliefs and from being duped by unsubstantiated claims.
- When you encounter a claim, consider the source of the claim, the quality of the evidence, whether other plausible explanations exist for the conclusions being drawn, and whether more evidence is needed to reach a clearer conclusion.

KEY TERMS AND CONCEPTS

Each term has been boldfaced and defined in the chapter on the page indicated in parentheses.

archival measures (p. 39)
case study (p. 42)
confounding of variables (p. 53)
control group (p. 50)
correlational research (p. 45)
correlation coefficient (p. 47)
counterbalancing (p. 51)
dependent variable (p. 50)
descriptive research (p. 42)
descriptive statistics (p. 57)
double-blind procedure (p. 54)
experiment (p. 49)
experimental group (p. 50)
experimenter expectancy effects (p. 54)
external validity (p. 55)

hypothesis (p. 33)
independent variable (p. 49)
inferential statistics (p. 59)
informed consent (p. 40)
internal validity (p. 53)
mean (p. 58)
median (p. 58)
meta-analysis (p. 59)
mode (p. 57)
naturalistic observation (p. 43)
negative correlation (p. 47)
operational definition (p. 37)
placebo (p. 54)
placebo effect (p. 54)
population (p. 44)

positive correlation (p. 47)
random assignment (p. 50)
random sampling (p. 45)
range (p. 58)
replication (p. 55)
representative sample (p. 44)
sample (p. 44)
scatterplot (p. 48)
social desirability bias (p. 38)
standard deviation (p. 58)
statistical significance (p. 59)
survey research (p. 44)
theory (p. 35)
unobtrusive measures (p. 39)
variable (p. 37)

 thinking **critically**

SHOULD YOU TRUST INTERNET AND POP MEDIA SURVEYS? (Page 45)

Recall the *Literary Digest* survey we just discussed. Even with 2 million people responding, the survey was inaccurate because the sample did not represent the overall population.

Typical Internet, magazine, and phone-in surveys share two major problems. First, people who choose to respond are entirely *self-selected* (rather than selected by the researcher), and the resulting samples likely do not even represent the entire population of people who use the Internet, subscribe to that magazine, or watch that TV show, respectively. Perhaps those who respond are more motivated, have a more helpful personality, or differ in some other important way from those who don't respond.

Second, it is unlikely that samples of Internet users, magazine subscribers, and TV news viewers represent the population at large (e.g., American adults). For example, at the time one massive Internet study was conducted, about 25 percent of Americans were Black or Latino. Yet just under 5 percent of the people who participated in the study were Black or Latino (Gosling et al., 2004). Do you think that the readers of *Cosmopolitan, Playboy, Guns & Ammo,* or any magazine typify the general population? In sum, because Internet and pop media surveys do not use random sampling, they are likely to generate samples that are not representative of the broader population.

Continued

Surely, many news organizations sponsor high-quality surveys conducted by professional pollsters. The key is that these surveys, such as political polls, use appropriate random-sampling procedures to obtain representative samples.

Finally, be aware that some psychologists—especially those who study people's personality and social behaviors—are increasingly using the Internet to collect research data. As users surf the Web, they may find a site that invites them to participate in an experiment or take a psychological test. These studies are not surveys that critically depend on having representative samples of the broader population. Rather, they typically examine relations among variables and underlying psychological principles. Some researchers question the validity of such Internet-based studies, but proponents have shown that most of these concerns are unfounded. More research is needed, but thus far it seems that Internet-based studies of this type yield findings that are consistent with those obtained from more traditional types of methods (Best et al., 2001; Gosling et al., 2004).

DOES EATING ICE CREAM CAUSE PEOPLE TO DROWN? (Page 47)

Just because two variables are correlated, we cannot conclude that they are causally related. First, consider the bidirectionality problem. We don't see any likely way that drownings could cause the rest of the public to eat more ice cream, so let's rule that out. Can we conclude, then, that more ice cream consumption causes more drownings? We suppose that, in a few cases, gorging on ice cream shortly before swimming might enhance the risk of drowning. But nationally, how often is this likely to happen?

Now consider the third-variable problem. What other factors might cause people to eat more ice cream and also lead to an increase in drownings? The most obvious third variable is "daily temperature" (or "month of the year"). Summer months bring hotter days, and people eat more ice cream in hot weather. Likewise, on hotter days drownings increase simply because so many more people go swimming. In short, the most reasonable conclusion is that the ice cream–drowning correlation is due to a third variable.

chapter three

Genes, Environment, and Behavior

Myth or Reality?

Human Behavior Reflects Nature's Plan (page 92)

As evidence mounts for the prominent role of genetic factors, evolutionary accounts of human behavior have gained new impetus. To what extent are human characteristics a programmed expression of "nature's plan"?

65

Figure 3.1

Jim Springer and Jim Lewis are identical twins who were separated when 4 weeks old and raised in different families. When reunited in adulthood, they showed striking similarities in personality, interests, and behavior. They both favored poodles as pets, and both had built benches around trees in their yards.

Warm sunlight filtered through his windows as Jim Springer opened his back door and stepped outside. It was indeed a fine September Saturday, a good day to spend some time on his favorite hobby, woodworking. He was about finished with his pet project, an unusual bench that encircled a large tree in his yard. He reached into his pocket and removed a pack of Salem cigarettes. "I really should give these things up," he thought, but as he looked at his bench with pride, he decided to enjoy a smoke to toast his success. He had purchased a can of redwood stain and had been blessed with a nice warm day to apply it to his bench. It was going to look great.

Fifty miles away, Jim Lewis had gotten up early to put on a pot of coffee. His wife, Betty, came into the kitchen and commented on the aroma. "Let's go outside. It's a great morning." Jim poured two mugs of the steaming coffee and they walked outside, where the sun splashed through the canopy of leaves provided by a large oak tree. As the couple sat down on the white bench that encircled the tree, Jim lit up a Salem to enjoy with his coffee.

Jim Lewis and Jim Springer first met in 1979 after 39 years of being separated. They had grown into adulthood oblivious to the existence of one another until Jim Lewis felt a need to learn more about his family of origin. After years of searching through court records, Jim Lewis finally found his twin brother, Jim Springer. When they met, Lewis said it was "like looking into a mirror," but the similarities went far beyond their nearly identical appearance. When they shared their stories, they found that both had childhood dogs named Toy. Both had been nail biters and fretful sleepers, suffered from migraine headaches, and had high blood pressure. Both Jims had married women named Linda, had been divorced, and married second wives named Betty. Lewis named his first son James Allen; Springer named his James Alan. For years, they both had taken holidays at the same Florida beach. Both of the Jims worked as sheriff's deputies. They both drank Miller Lite, smoked Salem cigarettes, loved stock car racing, hated baseball, left regular love notes to their wives, made doll furniture in their basements, and had constructed benches around the trees in their backyards (Figure 3.1).

Jim Springer and Jim Lewis became the first participants in a landmark University of Minnesota study of twins who had been separated early in life and reared apart. The Minnesota researchers found that the twins' habits, facial expressions, brain waves, heartbeats, and handwriting were nearly identical. When given a series of psychological tests, they were strikingly similar in intelligence and personality traits (Tellegen et al., 1988).

For psychologists, the connections between the twins' biological and behavioral similarities raise fascinating questions about factors that underlie human development. In this chapter, we investigate the relationships between genes, environment, intelligence, and evolution.

How can we explain the behavioral similarities in Jim Springer and Jim Lewis? In fact, they had been brought up quite differently; the Minnesota researchers found that the adoptive families of the Jim twins differed in important ways. What the Jims did have in common, however, were their identical genes. Although it is always possible that the behavioral commonalities of the Jim twins were coincidental, the Minnesota researchers found that other identical-twin pairs separated early in life also showed striking similarities. For example, when a pair of twin housewives from England met one another in Minneapolis for their week-long battery of psychological and medical tests, they found to their amazement that each was wearing seven rings, two bracelets on one wrist, and a watch and bracelet on the other. Another pair of men, one raised in Germany and the other in the Caribbean, shared a host of unusual behaviors, such as reading magazines from back to front, flushing toilets before using them, and dipping buttered toast in their coffee. Whether raised together or apart, the identical twins were far more similar in personality and intelligence test scores than were siblings (including nonidentical twins) raised in the same families (Tellegen et al., 1988).

It has been said that each of us is (1) what all humans are, (2) what some other humans are, and (3) what no other human in the history of the world has been, is, or will be (Kluckhohn & Murray, 1953). In this chapter we examine important biological and environmental factors that produce the behavioral commonalities and differences among humans. First, we will examine the role of the genes passed on to you at conception by your parents. Next, we will explore how learning helps you adapt to your environment and how it is related to culture and evolution. As we will see, genetic and environmental factors interact to influence many of your psychological characteristics, including intelligence and personality. Finally, we will explore the role of evolutionary forces that, millions of years before your birth, helped forge some of what you are today. Here again, we will see that biological and environmental factors interacted in complex ways, setting into place the pieces of the puzzle that is the human being and helping to account for both our similarities and our differences.

GENETIC INFLUENCES ON BEHAVIOR

From antiquity, humans have wondered how physical characteristics are transmitted from parents to their offspring. The answer was provided in the 1860s by Gregor Mendel, an Austrian monk trained in both physics and plant physiology. Mendel, renowned as a plant breeder, was fascinated with the variations he saw in plants of the same species. For example, the garden pea can have either white or purple flowers, yellow or green seeds, wrinkled or smooth skins, and different pod shapes (Figure 3.2). Best of all from his research perspective, pea plants (which normally fertilize themselves) could be artificially cross-fertilized to combine the features of plants that differed in physical characteristics. In a series of elegantly controlled experiments, Mendel did exactly that, carefully recording the features of the resulting offspring. His beautifully conducted experiments showed that heredity must involve the passing on of specific "organic factors," not a simple blending of the parents' characteristics. For example, if he fertilized a plant with purple flowers with pollen from a white-flowered plant, he did not get offspring with light purple flowers, but various percentages of purple- and white-flowered plants. Moreover, these specific factors might produce visible characteristics in the offspring, or they might simply be carried for possible transmission to another generation. In any case, Mendel showed that in the humble pea plant, as in humans, the offspring of one set of parents

Figure 3.2

The elegant experiments performed by Gregor Mendel revolutionized scientific thinking and spurred the development of the science of genetics. His research was done on the inheritance of physical characteristics in garden peas, which can have either purple or white flowers, as well as variations in other characteristics.

do not all inherit the same traits, as is evident in the differences we see among brothers and sisters.

Early in the 20th century, geneticists made the important distinction between **genotype,** *the specific genetic makeup of the individual,* and **phenotype,** *the individual's observable characteristics.* A person's genotype is like a computer software code. At a biological level, genes direct the process of development by programming the formation of protein molecules, which can vary in infinite ways. Some of the genes' directives are used on one occasion, some on another. Some are never used at all, either because they are contradicted by other genetic directives or because the environment never calls them forth. For example, geneticists discovered that chickens have retained the genetic code for teeth (Kollar & Fisher, 1980). Yet because the code is prevented from being phenotypically expressed (converted into a particular protein), there's not a chicken anywhere that can sink its teeth into a mailman. Genotype is present from conception, but phenotype can be affected both by other genes and by the environment. Thus, genotype is like the software commands in your word processing program that allow you to type an e-mail; phenotype is like the content of the e-mail that appears on your computer screen.

Chromosomes and Genes

What exactly are Mendel's "organic factors," and how are they transmitted from parents to offspring? The egg cell from the mother and sperm cell from the father carry within their nuclei the material of heredity in the form of rodlike units called *chromosomes.* A **chromosome** *is a double-stranded and tightly coiled molecule of deoxyribonucleic acid (DNA).* Indeed, the DNA is so tightly coiled that if the DNA in a single human cell (visible only under a microscope) were stretched out, it would be 6 feet long (Masterpasqua, 2009). All of the information of heredity is encoded in the combinations of four chemical bases—adenine, thymine, guanine, and cytosine—that occur throughout the chromosome. Within each DNA molecule, the sequence of the four letters of the DNA alphabet—A, T, G, and C—creates the specific commands for every feature and function of your body. Human DNA has about 3 billion chemical base pairs, arranged as A-T or G-C units (Human Genome Project, 2007). The ordering of 99.9 percent of these bases is the same in all people.

The DNA portion of the chromosome carries the **genes,** *the biological units of heredity* (Figure 3.3). The average gene has about 3,000 ATGC base pairs, but sizes vary greatly; the largest gene has 2.4 million bases. Each gene carries the ATGC codes for manufacturing specific proteins, as well as when and where in the body they will be made. These proteins can take many forms and functions, and they underlie every bodily structure and chemical process. It is estimated that about half of all genes target brain structure and functions (Kolb & Whishaw, 2003). Every moment of every day, the strands of DNA silently transmit their detailed instructions for cellular functioning.

With one exception, every cell with a nucleus in the human body has 46 chromosomes. The exception is the *sex cell* (the egg or sperm), which has only 23. At conception, the 23 chromosomes from the egg combine with the 23 corresponding chromosomes from the sperm to form a new cell, the *zygote,* containing 46 chromosomes. Within each chromosome, the corresponding genes received from each parent occur in matched pairs. Every cell nucleus in your body contains the genetic code for your entire body, as if each house in your community contained the architect's plans for every building and road in the entire city.

Dominant, Recessive, and Polygenic Effects

Alternative forms of a gene that produce different characteristics are called **alleles.** Thus, there is an allele

Figure 3.3

The ladder of life.
Chromosomes consist of two long, twisted strands of DNA, the chemical that carries genetic information. With the exception of egg and sperm cells, every cell in the body carries within its nucleus 23 pairs of chromosomes, each containing numerous genes that regulate every aspect of cellular functioning.

Each chromosome contains numerous **genes,** segments of DNA that contain instructions to make proteins— the building blocks of life.

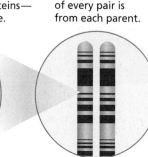

One **chromosome** of every pair is from each parent.

Each nucleus contains 46 **chromosomes,** arranged in 23 pairs.

Each human cell (except red blood cells) contains a **nucleus.**

The human body contains 100 trillion **cells.**

that produces blue eyes and a different one that produces brown eyes. The reason genotype and phenotype are not identical is that some genes are dominant and some are recessive. If a gene in the pair received from both the mother and father is **dominant,** *the particular characteristic that it controls will be displayed.* If, however, a gene received from one parent is **recessive,** *the characteristic will not show up unless the partner gene inherited from the other parent is also recessive.* In humans, for example, brown eyes are dominant over blue eyes. A child will have blue eyes only if both parents have contributed recessive genes for blue eyes. If Nathan inherits a dominant gene for brown eyes from one parent and a recessive gene for blue eyes from the other, he will have brown eyes, and the blue-eyed trait will remain hidden in his genotype. Eventually, this brown-eyed child may pass the recessive gene for blue eyes to his own offspring.

In a great many instances, *a number of gene pairs combine their influences to create a single phenotypic trait. This is known as* **polygenic transmission,** and it complicates the straightforward picture that would occur if all characteristics were determined by one pair of genes. It also magnifies the number of possible variations in a trait that can occur. Despite the fact that about 99.9 percent of human genes are identical among people, it is estimated that the union of sperm and egg can result in about 70 trillion potential genotypes, accounting for the great diversity of characteristics that occurs even among siblings.

The Human Genome

At present, our knowledge of phenotypes greatly exceeds our understanding of the underlying genotype, but that may soon change. In 1990, geneticists began the Human Genome Project, a coordinated effort to map the DNA, including all the genes, of the human organism. The genetic structure in every one of the 23 chromosome pairs has now been mapped by methods that allow the investigators to literally disassemble the genes on each chromosome and study their specific sequence of bases (A, T, G, and C; see Figure 3.3).

The first results of the genome project provided a surprise: the human genome consists of approximately 25,000 genes rather than the 100,000 previously estimated (Human Genome Project, 2007). That result told geneticists that gene interactions are even more complex than formerly believed and that it's highly unlikely that a single gene could account for a complex condition such as anorexia or schizophrenia. Even given this reduced number of genes, the 3.1 billion ATGC combinations in the entire human genome, if printed consecutively, would add about 150,000 pages to this book.

The "book of life" revealed by the Human Genome Project has given us greater knowledge of which specific genes or gene combinations are involved in normal and abnormal characteristics (McGuffin et al., 2005). The location and structure of more than 80 genes that contribute to hereditary diseases have already been identified through gene mapping (Human Genome Project, 2007). On another front, behavioral scientists are exploring the gene combinations that underlie behavior and, in some cases, are modifying those genes.

A Genetic Map of the Brain

In September 2006, the Allen Institute for Brain Science in Seattle announced the culmination of a $40 million project to map the genetic workings of the mouse brain. The mouse's brain is 99 percent identical to the human brain and is therefore frequently used by neuroscientists to study human brain function. Using a robotic system to analyze 16,000 paper-thin brain slices per week, the Institute's scientists took only three years to determine where in the brain 21,000 genes are turned on, or expressed, and to develop a genetic atlas of the brain that is now available to all scientists online. (You can view the atlas at www.brain-map.org.) Almost every cell in the mouse body contains the full genotype. What a particular cell will become and how it will function is determined by which genes are switched on, so that a liver cell will look and function differently than will a skin cell or a brain cell. The Allen Institute researchers discovered that about 80 percent of all mouse genes are switched on somewhere in the brain and that there are probably more cell types within the brain than in all the other organs of the body combined (National Institutes of Health, 2010). Using human cadaver brains and bits of living tissue removed by brain surgeons during tumor removal or aneurism repair, the researchers next plan to develop a genetic map of the human cerebral cortex, the seat of our higher mental functions. Knowing where and how genes are switched on in the brain will provide new insights on both normal brain functions and diseases of the brain and may herald the development of revolutionary new treatment and prevention techniques.

Genetics research has allowed us not only to describe the structure and functions of genes as never before, but it has also had other scientific and applied benefits. These include genetic testing of individuals and the ability to alter the genes themselves.

Applying Psychological Science

Until recently, biological psychologists had to be content with studying genetic phenomena that occurred in nature. Aside from selectively breeding plants and animals for certain characteristics or studying the effects of genetic mutations, scientists had no ability to influence genes directly. Today, however, technological advances enable them not only to map the human genome and measure the genotypes of individuals but also to duplicate and modify the structures of genes themselves (Peacock, 2010).

Some gene-manipulation research involves transplanting genes from one species into another. Such studies have shown how closely we humans are related to other living creatures. For example, both humans and insects have eyes, although the eyes differ markedly in their structural characteristics (see Figure 3.4). Some years ago, geneticists identified a human gene called *Pax6* that is responsible for eye development. If this gene is not switched on at a critical time in development, people do not develop eyes. Researchers wondered what would happen if they transplanted human Pax6 genes at various locations along the body of a fruit fly and let them express themselves in that biological environment. Amazingly, numerous small eyes appeared on the fruit fly's body that looked just like the multifaceted eye of the insect itself, demonstrating how the biological environment in which a gene resides can determine its phenotypic expression (Hartwell et al., 2010). This is an example of **epigenetics,** *changes in gene expression that are independent of the DNA itself and are caused instead by environmental factors.* Epigenetic researchers have discovered that the environment, both physical and social, can cause changes in molecular structures that regulate gene expression so that an unchanging genotype can have differing phenotypic effects (Masterpasqua, 2009).

In another gene-manipulation approach, researchers use certain enzymes (proteins that create chemical reactions) to cut the long threadlike molecules of genetic DNA into pieces, combine it with DNA from another organism, and insert it into a host organism,

such as a bacterium. Inside the host, the new DNA combination continues to divide and produce many copies of itself. Researchers can also insert new genetic material into viruses that can infiltrate the brain and modify the genetic structure in brain tissue.

Recent gene-modification research by psychologists has focused on processes such as learning, memory, emotion, and motivation. One procedure done with animals (typically mice) is to alter a specific gene in a way that prevents it from carrying out its normal function. This is called a **knockout procedure** *because that particular function of the gene is knocked out, or eliminated.* The effects on behavior are then observed. For example, psychologists can insert genetic material that will prevent neurons from responding to a particular brain chemical or neurotransmitter. They can then measure whether the animal's ability to learn or remember is subsequently affected. This can help psychologists determine the importance of particular transmitter substances in relation to the behaviors of interest (Jang et al., 2003; Thomas & Palmiter, 1997). Researchers can also use a **knock-in procedure** *to insert a new gene into an animal during the embryonic stage and study its impact on behavior after the animal is born.*

GENETIC COUNSELING AND THERAPY

As we learn more about the human genome and about the genetic combinations that contribute to both physical and psychological disorders, the assessment and modification of genes heralds new advances in the form of genetic screening and therapy. Gene testing has already improved lives. Currently, more than 1,000 DNA-based genetic tests for specific diseases, including susceptibility to Alzheimer's disease, have now been developed (National Institutes of Health, 2010). Some tests are used to assist in diagnosis and direct a physician toward appropriate treatments. Other tests allow couples to avoid conceiving children with devastating diseases or identify people at high risk for conditions like cancers and heart disease that can be countered by lifestyle interventions focused on smoking, diet, or exercise.

However, this capability also brings with it some serious practical, ethical, and life-altering issues that may confront you in your lifetime. For example, the tests are not infallible (and many tell you only whether you are susceptible to developing a particular disorder), and a misinterpretation of results could cause great psychological suffering. Medical ethics experts also fear what would happen if insurance companies and employers were able to require genetic testing and base employment and insurability decisions on test results. Finally, embryonic screening will give parents increased knowledge of what their offspring might be like. Are parents entitled to make abortion decisions based not only on information that identifies a devastating disease in the fetus but also on results that tell them whether a normal child is likely to be emotionally reactive, possibly obese, or not possessed of the blue eyes desired by the parents (Valverde, 2010)? Issues like these are in the forefront of current moral and ethical debates about gene testing.

Right now, gene testing is far ahead of gene therapy. As of 2010, the U.S. Food and Drug Administration had not approved

Figure 3.4

The eyes of insects and humans differ considerably in their structural characteristics. However, when the human Pax6 gene that initiates eye development in people is implanted in the fruit fly *Drosophila*'s side, it produces a multifaceted eye that looks like the eye of the insect itself, showing how the biological environment in which a gene operates can influence its expression. This demonstration also shows the relatedness of species as dissimilar as insects and humans.

any gene therapy product for general use. Current gene therapy is experimental and has not proven very successful in clinical trials (National Institutes of Health, 2010). However, scientific work continues on the development of effective therapies. Gene-modification techniques may one day enable us to alter genes that contribute to psychological disorders, such as depression and schizophrenia (McGuffin et al., 2005). Many continue to echo the words of behavior geneticists Robert Plomin and John Crabbe: "We predict that DNA will revolutionize psychological research and treatment early in the twenty-first century" (2000, p. 825).

Behavior Genetics

The activities of genes lie behind every structure and process in the body, and behavior reflects a continuous interplay between a biological being and the environment in which it operates. Researchers in the field of **behavior genetics** *study how heredity and environmental factors influence psychological characteristics*. More specifically, they try to determine the relative influence of genetic and environmental factors in accounting for individual differences in behavior. For example, a behavior geneticist might ask, "How important are genetic factors in aggression, intelligence, personality characteristics, and various types of psychological disorders?"

The key to answering such questions lies in the fact that the degree of relatedness to one another tells us how genetically similar people are. Recall that children get half of their genetic material from each parent. Thus the probability of sharing any particular gene with one of your parents is 50 percent, or .50. If you have brothers and sisters, you also have a .50 probability of sharing the same gene with each of them, since they get their genetic material from the same parents. Of course, as we have seen, if you are an identical twin, you have a 1.00 probability of sharing any particular gene with your twin. And what about a grandparent? Here, the probability of a shared gene is .25 because, for example, your maternal grandmother passed half of her genes on to your mother, who passed half of hers on to you. Thus the likelihood that you inherited a specific gene from your grandmother is .50 × .50, or .25. The probability of sharing a gene is also .25 for half siblings, who share half of their genes with the common biological parent but none with the other parent.

Theoretically, an adopted child differs genetically from his or her adoptive parents, and the same is true for unrelated people. These facts about genetic similarity give us a basis for studying the role of genetic factors in physical and behavioral characteristics.

Family, Adoption, and Twin Studies

Many studies have shown that the more similar people are genetically, the more similar they are likely to be psychologically, although this level of similarity differs depending on the characteristic in question. In **family studies,** *researchers study relatives to determine if genetic similarity is related to similarity on a particular trait*. If people who are more closely related to one another (i.e., share more genes) are more similar on the trait in question, this points to a possible genetic contribution.

Another research method used to estimate the influence of genetic factors is the **adoption study,** *in which people who were adopted early in life are compared on some characteristic with both their biological parents, with whom they share genetic endowment, and with their adoptive parents, with whom they share no genes*. If adopted people are more similar to a biological parent (with whom they share 50 percent of their genes) than to an adoptive parent (with whom they share a common environment but no genes), a genetic influence on that trait is indicated. If they're more similar to their adoptive parents, environmental factors are judged to be more important for that particular characteristic.

Twin studies, *which compare trait similarities in identical and fraternal twins*, are one of the more powerful techniques used in behavior genetics. Because *monozygotic*, or identical, twins develop from the same fertilized egg, they are genetically identical (Figure 3.5). Approximately 1 in 250 births produces identical twins. *Dizygotic*, or fraternal, twins develop from two fertilized eggs, so they share 50 percent of their genetic endowment, like any other set of brothers and sisters. Approximately 1 in 150 births produces fraternal twins.

Twins, like other siblings, are usually raised in the same familial environment. Thus, we can compare **concordance** rates, *or trait similarity*, in samples of identical and fraternal twins. We assume that if the identical twins are far more similar to one another than are the fraternal twins in a specific characteristic, a genetic factor is likely to be involved. Of course, the fly in this ointment is the possibility that because identical twins are more similar to one another in appearance than fraternal twins are, they are treated more alike and therefore share a more similar environment. This could partially account for greater behavioral similarity in identical twins.

Figure 3.5

Identical (monozygotic) twins come from a single egg and sperm as a result of a division of the zygote. They have all of their genes in common. Fraternal (dizygotic) twins result from two eggs fertilized by two sperm. They share only half of their genes as a result.

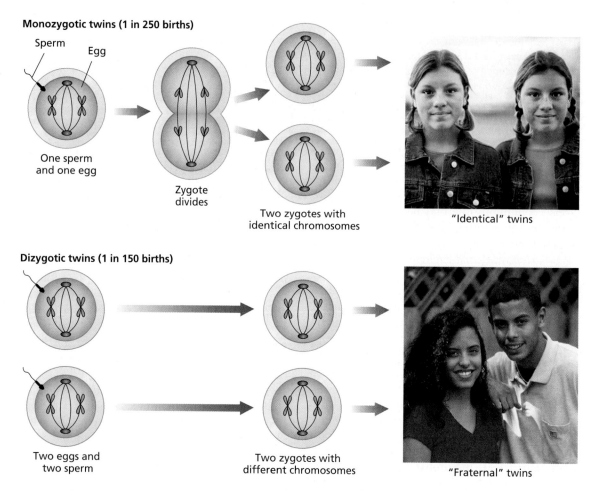

Monozygotic twins (1 in 250 births)

Sperm

Egg

One sperm and one egg

Zygote divides

Two zygotes with identical chromosomes

"Identical" twins

Dizygotic twins (1 in 150 births)

Two eggs and two sperm

Two zygotes with different chromosomes

"Fraternal" twins

To rule out this environmental explanation, behavior geneticists have adopted an even more elegant research method. Sometimes, as in the University of Minnesota study in which the Jim twins participated, researchers are able to find and compare sets of identical and fraternal twins who were separated very early in life and raised in *different* environments (Bouchard et al., 1990). By eliminating environmental similarity, this research design permits a better basis for evaluating the respective contributions of genes and environment.

As we shall see, many (but not all) psychological characteristics, including intelligence, personality traits, and certain psychological disorders, have a notable genetic contribution (Bouchard, 2004). Adopted children are typically found to be more similar to their biological parents than to their adoptive parents on these measures, and identical twins tend to be more similar to one another than are fraternal twins, even if they were separated early in life and reared in different environments (Bazzett, 2008; Loehlin, 1992; Plomin & Spinath, 2004). On the other hand, identical twins reared together still tend to be somewhat more similar on some characteristics than those reared apart, indicating that the environment also makes a difference.

Heritability: Estimating Genetic Influence

Using adoption and twin studies, researchers can apply a number of statistical techniques to estimate the extent to which differences among people are due to genetic differences. A **heritability coefficient** *estimates the extent to which the differences, or variation, in a specific phenotypic characteristic within a group of people can be attributed to their differing genes.* For example, heritability for height is very high, around 80 percent. It's important that you understand what this .80 heritability estimate really means. This result does *not* mean that 80 percent of a particular person's height is due to genetic factors and the other 20 percent to the environment. Heritability applies only to differences *within particular groups* (and estimates can and do vary, depending on the group).

Table 3.1 shows the wide range of heritability that has been found for height and for various other physical and psychological characteristics.

Table **3.1** | Heritability Estimates for Various Human Characteristics

Trait	Heritability Estimate
Height	.80
Weight	.60
Smoking	.52
Likelihood of being divorced	.50
Antisocial behavior	.41
School achievement	.40
Activity level	.40
Major depression	.37
Anxiety disorder	.35
Problem drinking	.26
Preferred characteristics in a mate	.10
Religious attitudes	.00

Sources: Bouchard et al., 1990; Dunn & Plomin, 1990; Malouf et al., 2008.

Subtracting each heritability coefficient from 100 provides an estimate of the proportion of group variability that is attributable to the environment in which people develop. For height, environment accounts for only about 100 minus 80, or 20 percent, of the variation within groups, but for religious attitudes, environment accounts for virtually all differences among people.

Even while they try to estimate the contributions of genetic factors, behavior geneticists realize that genes and environment are not really separate determinants of behavior. Instead, they operate as a single, integrated system. Gene expression is influenced on a daily basis by the environment. For example, two children of equal intellectual potential may have differences in IQs as great as 15 to 20 points if one is raised in an impoverished environment and the other in an enriched one (Plomin & Spinath, 2004). And high or low environmental stress can be responsible for turning on or off genes that regulate the production of stress hormones (Taylor, 2006a). We will have occasion to view gene-environment interactions in virtually every chapter of this book. For now, however, let us consider the role of the environment in adaptation.

test yourself   **Genetic Influences on Behavior**

True or False?

1. Your genotype is your specific genetic makeup, whereas your resulting observable characteristics are your phenotype.
2. Every cell in your body, including the egg and sperm cells, has 46 chromosomes.
3. In polygenic transmission, a number of genes combine their influences to create a particular trait.
4. Epigenetic research shows that environmental influences can alter an individual's genotype.
5. Adopted children tend to be more similar to their adoptive parents than to their biological parents if they were adopted early in life.

ANSWERS: 1-true, 2-false, 3-true, 4-false, 5-false

ADAPTING TO THE ENVIRONMENT: THE ROLE OF LEARNING

We encounter changing environments, each with its unique challenges, from the moment we are conceived. Some challenges, such as acquiring food and shelter, affect survival. Others, such as deciding where to go on a date, do not. But no matter what the challenge, we come into this world with biologically based abilities to respond adaptively. These mechanisms allow us to perceive our world, to think and problem solve, to remember past events, and to profit from our experiences. If evolution can be seen as *species adaptation* to changing environments, then we can view learning as a process of *personal adaptation* to the circumstances of our lives. Learning allows us to use our biological gifts to profit from experience and adapt to our environment.

How Do We Learn? The Search for Mechanisms

For a long time, the study of learning proceeded along two largely separate paths, guided by two different perspectives on behavior: *behaviorism* and *ethology* (Bolles & Beecher, 1988). Within psychology, behaviorism dominated learning research from the early 1900s through the 1960s. Behaviorists assumed that there are laws of learning that apply to virtually all organisms. For example, each species they studied—whether birds, reptiles, rats, monkeys, or humans—responded in predictable ways to patterns of reward or punishment.

Behaviorists treated the organism as a *tabula rasa*, or "blank tablet," on which learning experiences were inscribed. Most of their research was conducted with nonhuman species in controlled laboratory settings. Although they acknowledged biological differences among species, to behaviorists, the environment was preeminent.

Why Do We Learn? The Search for Functions

While behaviorism flourished in early- to mid-20th-century America, a specialty area called *ethology* arose in Europe within the discipline of biology (Lorenz, 1937; Tinbergen, 1951). Ethologists focused on animal behavior in the natural environment and noted striking differences among species in how they behaved in order to survive. Ethologists viewed the organism as anything but a blank tablet, arguing that because of evolution, every species comes into the world biologically prepared to act in certain ways. Ethologists focused on the *functions* of behavior, particularly its **adaptive significance**—*how behavior influences an organism's chances of survival and reproduction in its natural environment.*

Consider how newly hatched herring gulls beg for food by pecking at a red mark on their parents' bills. Parents respond by regurgitating food, which the chicks ingest. Seeing the red mark and long shape of a parent's bill automatically triggers the chicks' pecking. This behavior is so strongly prewired that chicks will peck just as much at long inanimate models or objects with red dots or stripes (Figure 3.6). Ethologists call this instinctive behavior a **fixed action pattern,** *an unlearned response automatically triggered by a particular stimulus.*

As ethology research proceeded, several things became clear. First, some fixed action patterns are modified by experience. Unlike herring gull hatchlings, older chicks have learned what an adult gull looks like and will not peck at an inanimate object unless it resembles the head of an adult gull (Hailman, 1967). Second, in many cases what appears to be instinctive behavior actually involves learning. For example, the indigo

bunting is a songbird that migrates between North and Central America. As if by pure instinct, it knows which direction to fly by using the North Star to navigate. (The North Star is the only stationary star in the Northern Hemisphere that maintains a fixed compass position.) In fall, the buntings migrate south by flying away from the North Star; they return in the spring by flying toward it.

To study whether any learning is involved in the buntings' navigational behavior, Steven Emlen (1975) raised birds in a planetarium with either a true sky or a false sky in which a star other than the North Star was the only stationary one. In the fall, the buntings became restless in their cages as migration time approached. When the birds raised in the planetarium with the true sky were released, they flew away in the direction opposite the North Star. In contrast, those exposed to the false sky ignored the North Star and instead flew away in the direction opposite the "false" stationary star. Emlen concluded that although the indigo bunting is genetically prewired to navigate by a fixed star, it has to learn through experience which specific star in the nighttime sky is stationary.

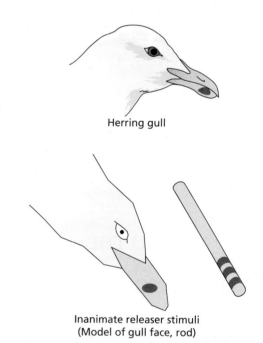

Herring gull

Inanimate releaser stimuli
(Model of gull face, rod)

Figure 3.6

A herring gull hatchling will peck most frequently at objects that are long and have red markings, even if they are inanimate models and do not look like adult gulls. This innate fixed action pattern is present from birth and does not require learning. The stimuli that trigger a fixed action pattern, such as the red markings on the inanimate objects and on the beak of the real herring gull shown here, are called releaser stimuli. Source: Adapted from Hailman, 1969.

Learning and Evolution

The separate paths of behaviorism and ethology have increasingly converged (Papini, 2002), reminding us that the environment shapes behavior in two fundamental ways: through *species adaptation* and through *personal adaptation*. Our personal adaptation to life's circumstances occurs through the laws of learning that the behaviorists and other psychologists have examined, and it results from our interactions with immediate and past environments.

When you drive or go out on a date, your behavior is influenced by the immediate environment (e.g., traffic, your date's smiles) and by capabilities you acquired through past experiences (e.g., driving skills, social skills). Because culture plays an ongoing role in shaping our present and past experiences, it strongly affects what we learn. Cultural socialization influences our beliefs and perceptions, our social behavior and sense of identity, the skills that we acquire, and countless other characteristics (Figure 3.7).

The environment also influences species adaptation. Over the course of evolution, environmental conditions faced by each species help shape its biology. This does not occur directly. Learning, for example, does not modify an organism's genes, and therefore learned behaviors do not pass genetically from one generation to the next. But through natural selection, genetically based characteristics that enhance a species' ability to adapt to the environment—and thus to survive and reproduce—are more likely to be passed on to the next generation. Eventually, as physical features (e.g., the red mark on the adult gull's beak) and behavioral tendencies (e.g., the chick's pecking the mark) influenced by those genes become more common, they become a part of a species' very nature.

Theorists propose that as the human brain evolved, it acquired adaptive capacities that enhanced our ability to learn and solve problems (Chiappe & MacDonald, 2005; Cosmides & Tooby, 2002). In essence, we have become prewired to learn. Of course, so have other species. Because all species face some common adaptive challenges, we might expect some similarity in their libraries of learning mechanisms. Every environment is full of events, and each organism must learn

- which events are, or are not, important to its survival and well-being;
- which stimuli signal that an important event is about to occur; and
- whether its responses will produce positive or negative consequences.

These adaptive capacities are present to varying degrees in all organisms. Even the single-celled paramecium can learn to jerk backward in its avoidance pattern in response to a vibration that has been paired with electric shock (Hennessey et al., 1979). As we move up the phylogenetic scale from simpler to more complex animals, learning abilities become more sophisticated, reaching their highest level in humans. Learning is the mechanism through which the environment exerts its most profound effects on behavior, and we will explore learning processes in depth in Chapter 7. For now, let's look at a few key concepts.

Shared and Unshared Environments

Environment is a very broad term, referring to everything from the prenatal world of the womb and the simplest physical environment to the complex social systems in which we interact with

Figure 3.7

People in different cultures learn specific behaviors in order to adapt to their environment. Even the same general skill will take on different forms, depending on unique environmental features and demands.

multiple people, places, and things. Some of these environments, such as our family household or school classroom, are shared with other people, such as our siblings and classmates. This is called a **shared environment** *because the people who reside in them experience many of their features in common.* Siblings living in the same home are exposed to a common physical environment, the availability or unavailability of books, a TV, or a computer. They share the quality of food in the home, exposure to the attitudes and values transmitted by parents, and many other experiences. However, each of us also has *experiences that are unique to us,* or an **unshared environment.** Even children living in the same home have their own unique experiences, including distinct relationships with their parents and siblings.

Twin studies (especially those that include twins raised together and apart) are particularly useful for estimating the extent to which genotype, shared environment, and unshared environment contribute to group variance on a particular characteristic (see Figure 3.8). As we shall see, such studies have provided new insights on the factors that influence a wide range of human characteristics.

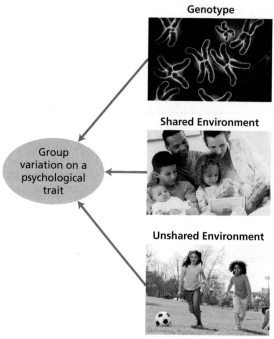

Figure 3.8

Behavior genetics research methods permit the estimation of three sources of variation in a group's scores on any characteristic. It is therefore possible to estimate from results of twin and adoption studies the contributions of genetic factors and of shared and unshared environmental factors.

test yourself   **Adapting to the Environment**

True or False?

1. The extent to which a behavior influences an organism's chances of survival and reproduction in its natural environment is known as its adaptive significance.

2. Learning cannot alter an organism's genome, but it could, through natural selection, influence a species' genome over time.

3. Hilary and her sister have different friends, teachers, and activities. Behavior geneticists refer to these differences as their shared environment.

ANSWERS: 1-true, 2-true, 3-false

BEHAVIOR GENETICS, INTELLIGENCE, AND PERSONALITY

Of the many psychological characteristics that we possess, few if any are more central to our personal identity and our successful adaptation than intelligence and personality. Although we consider these topics in much greater detail in Chapters 10 and 13, respectively, intelligence and personality are particularly relevant to our

current discussion because the genetic and environmental factors that influence them have been the subject of considerable research.

Genes, Environment, and Intelligence

To what extent are differences in intelligence (as defined by an IQ score derived from a general intelligence test) due to genetic factors? This seemingly simple question has long been a source of controversy and, at times, bitter debate. The answer has important social as well as scientific consequences.

Heritability of Intelligence

Let's examine the genetic argument. Suppose that intelligence were totally heritable, that is, suppose that 100 percent of the intellectual variation in the population were determined by genes. (No psychologist today would maintain that this is so, but examining the extreme view can be instructive.) In that case, any two individuals with the same genotype would have identical intelligence test scores, so the correlation in IQ between identical (monozygotic) twins would be 1.00. Nonidentical brothers and sisters (including fraternal twins, who result from two fertilized eggs) share only half of their genes. Therefore, the correlation between the test scores of fraternal twins and other siblings should be substantially lower. Extending the argument, the correlation between a parent's test scores and his or her children's scores should be about the same as that between siblings, because a child inherits only half of his or her genes from each parent.

What do the actual data look like? Table 3.2 summarizes the results from many studies. As you can see, the correlations between the test scores of identical twins are substantially higher than any other correlations in the table (but they are not 1.00). Identical twins separated early in life and reared apart are of special interest because they have identical genes but experienced different environments. Note that the correlation for identical twins raised apart is nearly as high as that for identical twins reared together. It is also higher than that for fraternal twins raised together. This pattern of findings is a powerful argument for the importance of genetic factors (Bouchard et al., 1990; Plomin et al., 2007).

Adoption studies are also instructive. As Table 3.2 shows, IQs of adopted children correlate as highly with their biological parents' IQs as they do with the IQs of the adoptive parents who reared them. Overall, the pattern is quite clear: the more genes people have in common, the more similar their IQs tend to be. This is very strong evidence that genes play a significant role in intelligence, accounting for 50 to 70 percent of group variation in IQ (Petrill, 2003; Plomin & Spinath, 2004). However, analysis of the human genome shows that there clearly is not a single "intelligence" gene (Plomin & Craig, 2002). The diverse abilities measured by intelligence tests are undoubtedly influenced by large numbers of interacting genes, and different combinations seem to underlie specific abilities (Luciano et al., 2001; Plomin & Spinath, 2004).

Environmental Determinants

Because genotype accounts for only 50 to 70 percent of the IQ variation among people in the United States, genetics research provides a strong argument for the contribution of environmental factors to intelligence (Plomin & Spinath, 2004). A good place to look for such factors is in the home and school environments.

Shared Family Environment   How important to intelligence level is the shared environment of the home in which people are raised? If home environment is an important determinant of intelligence, then children who grow up together should be more similar than children who are reared apart. As Table 3.2 shows, siblings who are raised together are indeed more similar to one another than those reared apart, whether they are identical twins or biological siblings. Note also that there is a correlation of .32 between unrelated adopted children reared in the same home. Overall, it appears that between a quarter and a third of the population's individual differences in intelligence can be attributed to shared environmental factors.

The home environment clearly matters, but there may be an important additional factor. Recent research suggests that differences within home environments are much more important at lower socioeconomic levels than they are in upper-class families. This may be because lower socioeconomic families differ more among themselves in the intellectual richness of the home environment than do upper-class families (Turkheimer et al., 2003). Indeed, a lower-income family that has books in the house, can't afford video games, and encourages academic effort may be a very good environment for a child with good intellectual potential.

Table **3.2** | **Correlations in Intelligence among People Who Differ in Genetic Similarity and Who Live Together or Apart**

Relationship	Percentage of Shared Genes	Correlation of IQ Scores
Identical twins reared together	100	.86
Identical twins reared apart	100	.75
Nonidentical twins reared together	50	.57
Siblings reared together	50	.45
Siblings reared apart	50	.21
Biological parent–offspring reared by parent	50	.36
Biological parent–offspring not reared by parent	50	.20
Cousins	12.5	.15
Adopted child–adoptive parent	0	.19
Adopted children reared together	0	.32

SOURCES: Based on Bouchard & McGue, 1981; Bouchard et al., 1990; Scarr, 1992.

Environmental Enrichment and Deprivation Another line of evidence for environmental effects comes from studies of children who are removed from deprived environments and placed in middle- or upper-class adoptive homes. Typically, such children show a gradual increase in IQ on the order of 10 to 12 points (Scarr & Weinberg, 1977; Schiff & Lewontin, 1986). Conversely, when deprived children remain in their impoverished environments, either they show no improvement in IQ or they actually deteriorate intellectually over time (Serpell, 2000). Scores on general intelligence tests correlate around .40 with the socioeconomic status of the family in which a child is reared (Lubinski, 2004).

Educational Experiences As we might expect, educational experiences, perhaps best viewed as a nonshared variable, can also have a significant impact on intelligence. Many studies have shown that school attendance can raise IQ and that lack of attendance can lower it. A small decrease in IQ occurs over summer vacations, especially among low-income children. IQ scores also drop when children are unable to start school on time due to teacher shortages or strikes, natural disasters, or other reasons (Ceci & Williams, 1997). It appears that exposure to an environment in which children have the opportunity to practice mental skills is important in solidifying those skills.

Where intelligence is concerned, we've seen that genetic factors, shared environment, and unique experiences all contribute to individual differences in intelligence. Does the same apply to personality differences?

Personality Development

The comedian Rodney Dangerfield recounted the day his son came home from kindergarten looking very troubled. When asked why he seemed so depressed, the little boy replied that they had learned a new saying in school that day: "Like father, like son."

If this old saying has validity, what causes similarities in personality between fathers and sons (and mothers and daughters)? Is it genes, environment, or both?

Heritability of Personality

Behavior genetics studies on personality have examined genetic and environmental influences on relatively broad personality traits. One prominent personality trait theory is called the Five Factor Model (see Chapter 13). Five-factor theorists like Robert McCrae and Paul Costa (2003)

Table **3.3**	Heritability of the Big Five Personality Factors Based on Twin Studies

Trait	Heritability Coefficient
Extraversion	.54
Neuroticism	.48
Conscientiousness	.49
Agreeableness	.42
Openness to Experience	.57

SOURCE: Bouchard, 2004.

believe that individual differences in personality can be accounted for by variation along five broad personality dimensions, or traits, known as the Big Five: (1) *Extraversion-Introversion* (sociable, outgoing, adventuresome, spontaneous versus quiet, aloof, inhibited, solitary), (2) *Agreeableness* (cooperative, helpful, good natured versus antagonistic, uncooperative, suspicious); (3) *Conscientiousness* (responsible, goal-directed, dependable versus undependable, careless, irresponsible); (4) *Neuroticism* (worrying, anxious, emotionally unstable versus well-adjusted, secure, calm); and (5) *Openness to Experience* (imaginative, artistically sensitive, refined versus unreflective, crude and boorish, lacking in intellectual curiosity).

What results are obtained if we compare the Big Five traits in identical and fraternal twins who were raised together and those who were raised apart? Table 3.3 shows heritability estimates of the Big Five personality factors described above. These results are consistent with studies of other personality variables as well, indicating that between 40 and 50 percent of the personality variations among people are attributable to genotype differences (Bouchard, 2004). Although personality characteristics do not show as high a level of heritability as the .70 figure found for intelligence, it is clear that genetic factors account for a significant amount of personality difference.

Environment and Personality Development

If genetic differences account for only about 40 to 50 percent of variations in personality, then surely environment is even more important than it is in the case of intelligence. Researchers expected that the shared environment might be even more important for personality than it is for intelligence. Over the years, virtually every theory of personality has embraced the assumption that experiences within the family, such as the amount of love expressed by parents and other child-rearing practices, are critical determinants of personality development.

Imagine, therefore, the shock waves generated by the finding from the Minnesota Twins Study and other research that shared features of the family environment account for little or no variance in major personality traits (Bouchard, 2004; Plomin, 1997). The key finding was that twins raised together and apart, whether identical or fraternal, did not differ in their degree of personality similarity (although identical twins were always more similar to one another than were fraternal twins). In fact, researchers have found that pairs of children who are raised within the same family are as different from one another as are pairs of children who are randomly selected from the population (Plomin & Caspi, 1999).

Adoption studies support a similar conclusion. In adoption studies, the average correlation for personality variables between adopted siblings who are genetically dissimilar but do share much of their environment, including the parents who raise them, the schools they attend, the religious training they receive, and so on, is close to .00 (Plomin et al., 2007). Except at child-rearing extremes, where children are abused or seriously neglected, parents probably get more credit when children turn out well personality-wise—and more blame when they don't—than they deserve (Scarr, 1992).

However, the surprising findings concerning shared environments do not mean that experience is not important. Rather than the general family environment, it seems to be the individual's unique or unshared environment, such as his or her unique school experiences (e.g., being in Mr. Jones's classroom in fifth grade, where conscientiousness and openness to experience were stressed) and interactions with specific peers (such as Jeremy, who fostered extraverted relationships with others) that account for considerable personality variance. Even within the same family, we should realize, siblings have different experiences while growing up, and each child's relationship with his or her parents and siblings may vary in important ways. It is these unique experiences that help shape personality development. Whereas behavior geneticists have found important shared-environment effects in intelligence, attitudes, religious beliefs, occupational preferences, notions of masculinity and femininity, political attitudes, and health behaviors such as smoking and drinking (Larsen & Buss, 2007), these shared-environment effects do not extend to general personality traits such as the Big Five. At this point, we don't know whether there are some crucial unshared-environment variables that researchers have missed because of their preoccupation with shared-environment factors, or whether there are countless small variables that make the difference. This question will be an important frontier in future personality research.

test yourself
Behavior Genetics, Intelligence, and Personality

True or False?

1. IQ correlations for identical twins reared apart are higher than those for fraternal twins reared in the same home.
2. Genetic factors account for about 30 percent of the IQ variation between people living in the U.S.
3. Genetic factors so strongly influence intelligence that environmental enrichment or deprivation has virtually no effect on IQ.
4. Although genetic factors are important, heritability is generally lower for personality traits than for intelligence.
5. Shared family environment seems to have little impact on the development of personality traits.

ANSWERS: 1-true, 2-false, 3-false, 4-true, 5-true

GENE-ENVIRONMENT INTERACTIONS

Genes and environment both influence intelligence, personality, and other human characteristics. But, as we've stressed throughout this chapter, they rarely operate independently. Even the prenatal environment can influence how genes express themselves, as when the mother's drug use or malnutrition retards gene-directed brain development. In the critical periods following birth, enriched environments, including the simple touching or massaging of newborns, can influence the unfolding development of premature infants (Field, 2001) and the future "personality" of young monkeys (Harlow, 1958). Although they can't modify the genotype itself, by influencing how the genotype creates proteins, environmental conditions can influence how genetically based characteristics express themselves phenotypically throughout the course of development (Plomin et al., 2007). Epigenetic effects on psychological functions can also be carried across future generations (Masterpasqua, 2009).

Just as environmental effects influence phenotypic characteristics, genes can influence how the individual will experience the environment and respond to it (Hernandez & Blazer, 2007; Plomin & Spinath, 2004). Let us examine some of these two-way relations between genes and experience.

How the Environment Can Influence Gene Expression

First, genes produce a range of potential outcomes. The concept of *reaction range* provides one useful framework for understanding gene-environmental interactions. The **reaction range** *for a genetically influenced trait is the range of possibilities—the upper and lower limits—that the genetic code allows.* For example, to say that intelligence is genetically influenced does not mean that intelligence is fixed at birth. Instead, it means that an individual inherits a *range* for potential intelligence that has upper and lower limits. Environmental effects will then determine where the person falls within these genetically determined boundaries.

At present, genetic reaction ranges cannot be measured directly, and we do not know if their sizes differ from one person to another. The concept has been applied most often in the study of intelligence. Studies of IQ gains associated with environmental enrichment and adoption programs suggest that the ranges could be as large as 15 to 20 points on the IQ scale (Dunn & Plomin, 1990). If this is indeed the case, then the influence of environmental factors on intelligence may be highly significant. A shift this large can move an individual from a below-average to an average intellectual level, or from an average IQ that would not predict college success to an above-average one that would predict success.

Some practical implications of the reaction range concept are illustrated in Figure 3.9. First, consider persons B and H. They have identical reaction ranges, but person B develops in a very deprived environment and H in an enriched environment with many cultural and educational advantages. Person H is able to realize her innate potential and has an IQ that is 20 points higher than person B's. Now compare person C and person I. Person C

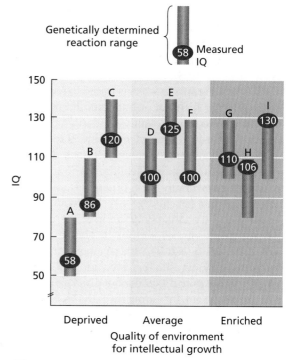

Figure 3.9

Reaction range is an example of how environmental factors can influence the phenotypic expression of genetic factors. Genetic endowment is believed to create a range of possibilities within which environment exerts its effects. Enriched environments are expected to allow a person's intelligence to develop to the upper region of his or her reaction range, whereas deprived environments may limit intelligence to the lower portion of the range. Where intelligence is concerned, the reaction range may cover as much as 15 to 20 points on the IQ scale.

actually has greater intellectual potential than person I but ends up with a lower IQ as a result of living in an environment that does not allow that potential to develop. Finally, note person G, who was born with high genetic endowment and reared in an enriched environment. His slightly-above-average IQ of 110 is lower than we would expect, suggesting that he did not take advantage of either his biological capacity or his environmental advantages. This serves to remind us that intellectual growth depends not only on genetic endowment and environmental advantage but also on interests, motivation, and other personal characteristics that affect how much we apply ourselves or take advantage of our gifts and opportunities.

As noted earlier, heritability estimates are not universal by any means. They can vary, depending on the sample being studied, and they may be influenced by environmental factors. This fact was brought home forcefully in research by Eric Turkheimer and colleagues (2003) mentioned earlier. They found in a study of 7-year-old identical and fraternal twins that the proportions of IQ variation attributable to genes and environment varied by social class. In impoverished families, fully 60 percent of the IQ variance was accounted for by the shared (family) environment, and the contribution of genes was negligible. In affluent families, the result was almost the reverse, with shared environment accounting for little variance and genes playing an important role. Clearly, genes and social-class environment seem to be interacting in their contribution to IQ.

It seems quite likely that there are genetically based reaction ranges for personality factors as well. This would mean that, personality-wise, there are biological limits to how malleable, or changeable, a person is in response to environmental factors. However, this hardly means that biology is destiny. Depending on the size of reaction ranges for particular personality characteristics—and even, perhaps, for different people—individuals could be quite susceptible to the impact of unshared-environmental experiences.

How Genes Can Influence the Environment

Reaction range is a special example of how environment can affect the expression of genetically influenced traits. But there are other ways in which genetic and environmental factors can interact with one another. Figure 3.10 shows three ways in which genotype can influence the environment, which, in turn, can influence the development of personal characteristics (Scarr & McCartney, 1983).

First, genetically based characteristics may influence aspects of the environment to which the child is exposed. For example, we know that intelligence has strong heritability. Thus, a child born to highly intelligent parents is also likely to have good intellectual potential. If, because of their own interests in intellectual pursuits, these parents provide an intellectually stimulating environment with lots of books, educational toys, computers, and so on, this environment may help foster the development of mental skills that fall at the top of the child's reaction range. The resulting bright child is thus a product of both the genes shared with the parents and of his or her ability to profit from the environment they provide.

A second genetic influence on the environment is called the **evocative influence,** *meaning that a child's genetically influenced behaviors may evoke certain responses from others.* For example, some children are very cuddly, sociable, and outgoing almost from birth; whereas others are more aloof, shy, and don't like to be touched or approached. These characteristics are in part genetically based (Kagan, 1999; Plomin et al., 2007).

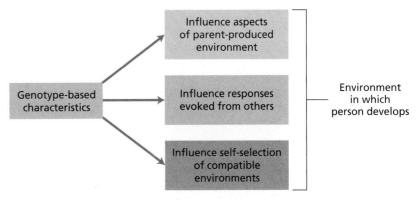

Figure 3.10

Three ways in which a person's genotype can influence the nature of the environment in which the person develops. Source: Based on Scarr & McCartney, 1983.

Think of how you yourself would be most likely to respond to these two types of babies. The outgoing children are likely to be cuddled by their parents and evoke lots of friendly responses from others as they mature, creating an environment that supports and strengthens their sociable and extraverted tendencies. In contrast, shy, aloof children typically evoke less-positive reactions from others, and this self-created environment may strengthen their genotypically influenced tendency to withdraw from social contact.

In both of these examples, genotype helped create an environment that reinforces already-existing biologically based tendencies. However, a behavior pattern can also evoke an environment that counteracts the genetically favored trait and discourages its expression. We know, for example, that activity level has moderate heritability of around .40 (Table 3.1). Thus, parents of highly active, "off the wall" children may try to get them to sit still and calm down, or those of inactive children may press them into lots of physical activities designed to increase physical well-being, in both instances opposing the natural tendencies of the children. Thus the environment may either support or discourage the expression of a person's genotype.

Finally, people are not simply passive responders to whatever environment happens to come their way. We actively seek out certain environments and avoid others. Genetically based traits may therefore affect the environments that we select, and these environments are likely to be compatible with our traits. Thus a large, aggressive child may be attracted to competitive sports with lots of physical contact, and a highly intelligent child will seek out intellectually stimulating environments; whereas a shy, introverted child may shun social events and prefer solitary activities or a small number of friends. These varied self-selected environments may have very different effects on subsequent development. We therefore see that how people develop is influenced by both biology and experience and that these factors combine in ways that are just beginning to be understood.

EVOLUTION, CULTURE, AND BEHAVIOR

In the misty forests and verdant grasslands of past eons, our early human ancestors faced many environmental challenges as they struggled to survive. If even one of your ancestors had not behaved effectively enough to survive and reproduce, you would not be here to contemplate your existence. In this sense, each of us is an evolutionary success story. As descendants of those successful forebears, we carry within us genes that contributed to their adaptive and reproductive success.

The vast majority (99.9 percent) of genes we share with all other humans creates the "human nature" that makes us like all other people. We enter the world with innate **biologically based mechanisms** *that enable us to take in, process, and respond to information, predisposing us to behave, to feel, and even to think in certain ways* (Stearns & Hoekstra, 2005). In humans, these inborn capacities allow us to learn, to remember, to speak a language, to perceive certain aspects of our environment at birth, to respond with universal emotions, and to bond with other humans. Most scientists view these biological characteristics as products of an evolutionary process. Evolutionary theorists also believe that important aspects of social behavior, such as aggression, altruism, sex roles, protecting kin, and mate selection are influenced by biological mechanisms that have evolved during the development of our species (Figure 3.11). Says evolutionary psychologist David Buss: "Humans are living fossils—collections of mechanisms produced by prior selection pressures" (1995, p. 27).

Evolution of Adaptive Mechanisms

Evolution *is a change over time in the frequency with which particular genes—and the characteristics they produce—occur within an interbreeding population.* As particular genes become more or less frequent in a population, so do the characteristics they influence. Some genetic variations arise in a population through **mutations,** *random events and accidents in*

NOW SHOWING
PLANET OF THE HUMANS

THERE ARE SIMILARITIES—THE WAY THEY USE THEIR HANDS, THEIR PRIMITIVE PROBLEM-SOLVING SKILLS. REALLY GIVES YOU THE WILLIES, DOESN'T IT?

Figure 3.11

These days, evolutionary principles are widely discussed. Cartoon by Don Wright. Reprinted by permission of Tribune Media Services.

gene reproduction during the division of cells. If mutations occur in the cells that become sperm and egg cells, the altered genes will be passed on to offspring. Mutations help create variation within a population's physical characteristics. It is this variation that makes evolution possible.

Natural Selection

Long before Charles Darwin published his theory of evolution in 1859, people knew that animals and plants could be changed over time by selectively breeding members of a species that shared desired traits (see Figure 3.12). A visit to a dog show illustrates the remarkably varied products of selective breeding of pedigree animals.

Just as plant and animal breeders "select" for certain characteristics, so too does nature. According to Darwin's principle of **natural selection,** *characteristics that increase the likelihood of survival and reproduction within a particular environment will be more likely to be preserved in the population and therefore will become more common in the species over time.* As environmental changes produce new and different demands, various new characteristics

Figure 3.12

Human-initiated selective breeding over a number of generations produced this tiny horse. A similar process could occur through natural selection if for some reason a particular environment favored the survival and reproductive ability of smaller members of the equine population.

may contribute to survival and the ability to pass on one's genes (Barrow, 2003). In this way, natural selection acts as a set of filters, allowing certain characteristics of survivors to become more common. Conversely, characteristics of nonsurvivors become less common and, perhaps, even extinct over time. The filters also allow neutral variations that neither facilitate nor impede fitness to be preserved in a population. These neutral variations, sometimes called *evolutionary noise,* could conceivably become important in meeting some future environmental demand. For example, people differ in their ability to tolerate radiation (Vral et al., 2002). In today's world, these variations are of limited importance, but they clearly could affect survivability if future nuclear war were to increase levels of radioactivity around the world. As those who could tolerate higher levels of radiation survived and those who could not perished, the genetic basis for high-radiation tolerance would become increasingly more common in the human species. Thus, for natural selection to work, there must be individual variation in a species characteristic that influences survival or the ability to reproduce.

Evolutionary Adaptations   The products of natural selection are called **adaptations,** *physical or behavioral changes that allow organisms to meet recurring environmental challenges to their survival, thereby increasing their reproductive ability.* In the final analysis, the name of the natural selection game is to pass on one's genes, either personally or through kin who share at least some of them (Dawkins, 2006). Evolutionary theorists believe this is why animals and humans may risk or even sacrifice their lives in order to protect their kin and the genes they carry.

In the animal kingdom, we find fascinating examples of adaptation to specific environmental conditions. For example, the tendency for one species of cannibalistic spider to eat its own kind decreases markedly if other food supplies are available. Genetically identical butterflies placed in different environments can take on completely different physical appearances depending on local climatic conditions during the larval stage of development. And in several species of tropical fish, imbalances in the ratio of males to females can actually result in males changing into females or females into males (Schaller, 2006). If environmental factors can trigger such profound changes in insects and fish, should we be surprised if a species as remarkably flexible as humans would also adapt to environmental changes and evolve over time?

Applying concepts of natural selection and adaptation to human evolution begins with the notion that an organism's biology determines its behavioral capabilities, and that its behavior (including its mental abilities) determines whether or not it will survive. One theory is that when dwindling vegetation in some parts of the world forced apelike animals down from the trees and required that they hunt for food on open, grassy plains, chances for survival were greater for those capable of *bipedal locomotion,* the ability to walk on two legs (Figure 3.13). By freeing the hands, bipedalism fostered the development and use of tools and weapons that could kill at a distance (Lewin, 1998). Hunting in groups and avoiding dangerous predators encouraged social organization, which required the development of specialized social roles (such as "hunter and protector" in the male and "nurturer of children" in the female) that still exist in most cultures. These environmental challenges also favored the development of language, which enhanced social communication and the transmission of knowledge.

In this manner, successful human behavior evolved along with a changing body (Geary, 2005; Tooby & Cosmides, 1992).

Brain Evolution   Tool use, bipedal locomotion, and social organization put new selection pressures on many parts of the body. These included the teeth, the hands, and the pelvis, all of which changed over time in response to the new dietary and behavioral demands. But the greatest pressure was placed on the brain structures involved in the abilities most critical to the emerging way of life: attention, memory, language, and thought. These mental abilities became important to survival in an environment that required quick learning and problem solving. In the evolutionary progression from *Australopithecus* (an early human ancestor who lived about 4 million years ago) through *Homo erectus* (1.6 million to 100,000 years ago) to the human subspecies Neandertal of 75,000 years ago, the brain tripled in size, and the most dramatic growth occurred in the parts of the brain that are the seat of the higher mental processes (Figure 3.14). Thus, evolved changes in behavior seem to have contributed to the development of the brain, just as the growth of the brain contributed to evolving human behavior (Striedter, 2005).

Surprisingly, perhaps, today's human brain does not differ much from the Stone Age brain of our ancient ancestors. In fact, Neandertal had a slightly larger brain than we have. Yet the fact that we perform mental activities that could not have been imagined in those ancient times tells us that human capabilities are not solely determined by the brain; cultural evolution is also important in the development of adaptations. From an evolutionary perspective, culture provides important environmental inputs to evolutionary mechanisms.

Evoked Culture   According to the evolutionary concept of **evoked culture,** *cultures may themselves be the product of biological mechanisms that evolved to meet specific adaptation challenges faced by specific groups of people in specific places at specific times.* Through this process, a culture could develop in a setting in which survival depended on the male's success in game hunting, differing in important ways from a culture that developed in a farming community in which survival depended on women sharing the breadwinner role (Gangestad et al., 2006). In the shared-breadwinner culture, we might expect less sharply defined sex roles. Once established by successful adaptation, a culture is transmitted to future members through social

Figure 3.13

This female *Ardipithecus ramidus,* which lived about 4.4 million years ago in what is now Ethiopia, is the earliest bipedal hominid on whom we have extensive fossil evidence. Anthropologists believe that Ardi's feet illustrate a transitional evolutionary phase, as their handlike structure facilitated the apelike behavior of climbing through trees.

Australopithecus
(4 million years ago)

The brain capacity ranges from 450 to 650 cubic centimeters (cc).

Homo erectus
(1.6 million to 100,000 years ago)

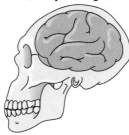

Further development of the skull and jaw is evident, and brain capacity is 900 cc.

Neandertal
(75,000 years ago)

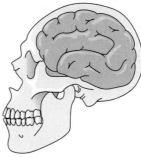

The human skull has now taken shape: the skull case has elongated to hold a complex brain of 1,450 cc.

Homo sapiens

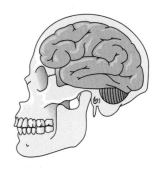

The deeply convoluted brain reflects growth in areas concerned with higher mental processes.

Figure 3.14

The human brain evolved over a period of several million years. The greatest growth occurred in those areas concerned with the higher mental processes, particularly memory, thought, and language.

learning, as has occurred for all of us in our own process of development. This serves to remind us of another truism: the creation of new environments through our own behavior is another important part of the evolutionary equation (Boyd & Richerson, 2005). Through our own behaviors, humans can create environments that influence subsequent natural selection of biological traits suited to the new environments (Bandura, 1997).

? thinking **critically**

NATURAL SELECTION AND GENETIC DISEASES

If Darwin was right about natural selection, then why do we have so many harmful genetic disorders? Consider, for example, cystic fibrosis, a hereditary disorder of European origin that clogs one's lungs with mucus and prevents digestion, typically causing death before age 30. Another example is sickle-cell anemia, which causes early deaths in many people of African descent. Can you reconcile the existence of such disorders with "survival of the fittest"? Think about it, then see page 94.

Evolution and Human Nature

To evolutionary psychologists, what we call human nature is the expression of inborn biological tendencies that have evolved through natural selection. There exists a vast catalogue of human characteristics and capabilities that unfold in a normally developing human being. Consider, for example, this brief preview of commonalities in human behavior that will be discussed in greater detail in later chapters.

- Infants are born with an innate ability to acquire any language spoken in the world (see Chapter 9). The specific languages learned depend on which ones they are exposed to. Deaf children have a similar innate ability to acquire any sign language, and their language acquisition pattern parallels the learning of spoken language. Language is central to human thought and communication.

- Newborns are prewired to perceive specific stimuli (see Chapter 5). For example, they are more responsive to pictures of human faces than to pictures of the same facial features arranged in a random pattern (Fantz, 1961). They are also able to discriminate the odor of their mother's milk from that of other women (McFarlane, 1975). Both adaptations improve human bonding with caregivers.

- At one week of age, human infants show primitive mathematical skills, successfully discriminating between two and three objects. These abilities improve with age in the absence of any training. The brain seems designed to make "greater than" and "less than" judgments, which are clearly important in decision making (Geary, 2005).

- According to Robert Hogan (1983), establishing cooperative relationships with a group was critical to the human species' survival and reproductive success. Thus humans seem to have a need to belong and strongly fear being ostracized from the group (see Chapter 11). Social anxiety (fear of social disapproval may be an adaptive mechanism to protect against doing things that will prompt group rejection (Baumeister & Tice, 1990).

- As a species, humans tend to be altruistic and helpful to one another, especially to children and relatives (see Chapter 17). Research shows that altruism varies according to degree of relatedness. Evolutionary theorists suggest that helping family members and relatives increases the likelihood that those people will be able to pass on the genes they share with you. People are also more likely to help younger people than older ones (Burnstein et al., 1994), perhaps because, from a species perspective, younger people have more reproductive value than do older people.

- As we will see in Chapter 11, there is much evidence for a set of basic emotions that are universally recognized (Ekman, 1973). Smiling, for example, is a universal expression of happiness and goodwill that typically evokes positive reactions from others (Figure 3.15). Emotions are important means of social communication that trigger mental, emotional, and behavioral mechanisms in others (Ketellar, 1995).

- In virtually all cultures, males are more violent and more likely to kill others (particularly other males) than are females. The differences are striking, with male-male killings outnumbering female-female killings, on average, by about 30 to 1 (Daly & Wilson, 1988). Evolutionary researchers suggest that male-male violence is rooted in hunting, establishing dominance hierarchies, and competing successfully for the most fertile mates, all of which enhanced personal and reproductive survival as our species evolved.

Having sampled from the wide range of behavioral phenomena that have been subjected to an evolutionary analysis, let us focus in greater detail on two areas of current theorizing that relate to both commonalities and differences among people—sex and self. Before doing so, however, we should emphasize a most important principle: *behavior does not occur in a biological vacuum; it always involves a biological organism acting within (and often in response to) an environment.* That environment may be inside the body in the form of interactions with other genes, influencing how genes and the protein molecules through which they operate express themselves. It may be inside the mother's womb, or it may be "out there," in the form of a physical environment or a culture. Although everyone agrees that biological and environmental factors interact with one another, most of the debates in evolutionary psychology concern two issues: (1) how general or specific are the biological mechanisms that have evolved? and (2) how much are these mechanisms influenced in their expression by the environment?

Sexuality and Mate Preferences

The name of the evolutionary game is to continue the species, and the only way this can occur is through reproduction. In order to pass on one's genes and maintain the species, people must mate. We should not be surprised, therefore, that evolutionary theorists and researchers have devoted great attention to sexuality, differences between men and women, and mate-seeking. This topic also has generated considerable debate about the relative contributions of evolutionary and sociocultural factors to this domain of behavior.

One of the most important and intimate ways that humans relate to one another is by seeking a mate. Marriage seems to be universal across the globe (Buss & Schmitt, 1993). In seeking mates,

Figure 3.15

The human smile seems to be a universal expression of positive emotion and is universally perceived in that way. Evolutionary psychologists believe that expressions of basic emotions are hardwired biological mechanisms that have adaptive value as methods of communication.

however, women and men display different mating strategies and preferences. Compared with women, men typically show more interest in short-term mating, prefer a greater number of short-term sexual partners, and have more permissive sexual attitudes and more sexual partners over their lifetimes (Schmitt et al., 2001). In one study of 266 college undergraduates, two thirds of the women said that they desired only one sexual partner over the next 30 years, but only about half of the men shared that goal (Pedersen et al., 2002). These attitudinal differences also extend to behavior. In research done at three different colleges, Russell Clark and Elaine Hatfield (1989; Clark, 1990) sent male and female research assistants of average physical attractiveness out across campus. Upon seeing an attractive person of the opposite sex, the assistant approached the person, said he or she found the person attractive, and asked, "Would you go to bed with me tonight?"

Women approached in this manner almost always reacted very negatively to the overture and frequently dismissed the assistants with such endearing terms as "creep" and "pervert." Not a single woman agreed to have sex. In contrast, three in every four men enthusiastically agreed, often asking why it was necessary to wait until that night. Other findings show that compared to women, men think about sex about three times more often, desire more frequent sex, and initiate more sexual encounters (Baumeister et al., 2001; Laumann et al., 1994). They also are much more likely to interpret a woman's friendliness as a sexual come-on, apparently projecting their own sexual desires onto the woman (Johnson et al., 1992).

Despite these differences, most men and women make a commitment at some point in their lives to a long-term mate. What qualities do women and men seek in such a mate? Once again, we see sex differences. Men typically prefer women somewhat younger than themselves, whereas women prefer somewhat older men. This tendency is exaggerated in the "trophy wives" sometimes exhibited by wealthy and famous older men. In terms of personal qualities, Table 3.4 shows the overall results of a worldwide study of mate preferences in 37 cultures (Buss et al., 1990). Men and women again show considerable overall agreement, but some differences emerge. Men place greater value on a potential mate's physical attractiveness and domestic skills, whereas women place greater value on a potential mate's earning potential, status, and ambitiousness. The question is "Why?"

Table **3.4** | **Characteristics of a Mate**

Women and men rated each characteristic on a 4-point scale. From top to bottom, the following numbers represent the order (rank) of most highly rated to least highly rated items for Buss's worldwide sample. How would you rate their importance?

Characteristic Desired in a Mate	Rated by	
	Women	Men
Mutual attraction/love	1	1
Dependable character	2	2
Emotional stability/maturity	3	3
Pleasing disposition	4	4
Education/intelligence	5	6
Sociability	6	7
Good health	7	5
Desire for home/children	8	8
Ambitious	9	11
Refinement	10	9
Similar education	11	14
Good financial prospect	12	13
Good looks	13	10
Social status	14	15
Good cook/housekeeper	15	12
Similar religion	16	17
Similar politics	17	18
Chastity	18	16

Source: Based on Buss et al., 1990.

According to an evolutionary viewpoint called **sexual strategies theory** (and a related model called **parental investment theory**), *mating strategies and preferences reflect inherited tendencies, shaped over the ages in response to different types of adaptive problems that men and women faced* (Buss & Schmitt, 1993; Trivers, 1972). In evolutionary terms, our most successful ancestors were those who survived and passed down the greatest numbers of their genes to future generations. Men who had sex with more partners increased the likelihood of fathering more children, so they were interested in mating widely. Men also may have taken a woman's youth and attractive, healthy appearance as signs that she was fertile and had many years left to bear his children (Buss, 1989).

In contrast, ancestral women had little to gain and much to lose by mating with numerous men. They were interested in mating wisely, not widely. In humans and other mammals, females typically make a greater investment than males: they carry the fetus, incur health risks and possible birth-related death, and nourish the newborn. Engaging in short-term sexual relationships with multiple males can in the end create uncertainty about which one is the father, thereby decreasing a male's willingness to commit resources to helping a mother raise the child. For these reasons, women maximized their reproductive success—and the survival chances for themselves and their offspring—by being selective and choosing mates who were willing and able to commit time, energy, and other resources (e.g., food, shelter, protection) to the family. Women increased their likelihood of passing their genes into the future by mating wisely, and men by mating widely. Through natural selection, according to evolutionary psychologists, the differing qualities that maximized men's and women's reproductive success eventually became part of their biological nature (Buss, 2007).

Steven Gangestad, Martie Haselton, and David Buss (2006) found that some of these mate-preference patterns are more pronounced in parts of the world with historically high levels of pathogens (disease-causing germs) that endangered survival than in areas that had historically low levels of pathogens. Where diseases like malaria, plague, and yellow fever are more prevalent, male factors such as physical attractiveness and robustness, intelligence, and social dominance—all presumably signs of biological fitness—seem especially important to women even today. Gangestad et al. suggest that in such environments, women seem willing to sacrifice some degree of male investment in their offspring in favor of a mate who has a higher probability of giving them healthy children. To men, a woman's attractiveness and healthiness (and that of her family) also are more important in high-pathogen environments, presumably because these historically were signs of a woman who would be more likely to give birth to healthy children and live long enough to rear them.

Not all scientists have bought into this evolutionary explanation for human mating patterns and other social behaviors. Again, the disagreement revolves around the relative potency of interacting biological and environmental factors. In the case of mate selection, proponents of **social structure theory** *maintain that men and women display different mating preferences not because nature impels them to do so, but because society guides them into different social roles* (Eagly & Wood, 1999, 2006). Adaptive behavior patterns may have been passed from parents to children not through genes but through learning. Social structure theorists point out that despite the shift over the past several decades toward greater gender equality, today's women still have generally less power, lower wages, and less access to resources than men do. In a two-income marriage, the woman is more likely to be the partner who switches to part-time work or becomes a full-time homemaker after childbirth. Thus society's division of labor still tends to socialize men into the breadwinner role and women into the homemaker role. An older male–younger female age gap is favorable because older men are likely to be further along in earning power and younger women are more economically dependent, and this state of affairs conforms to cultural expectations of marital roles (Figure 3.16).

We now have two competing explanations for sex differences in mating behavior: the evolution-based sexual strategies approach and the social structure view. Our "Research Close-up" looks at one attempt to compare predictions derived from the two theories.

Figure 3.16

Marriages in which the woman is much younger than the man are far more common than are marriages in which the woman is far older. CNN broadcaster Larry King poses with his seventh wife, Shawn Southwick, who is 26 years younger. Is the tendency for women to marry men older than themselves a remnant of evolutionary influences or a product of sociocultural forces?

Research Close-up

Sex Differences in the Ideal Mate: Evolution or Social Roles?

SOURCES: DAVID M. BUSS (1989). Sex differences in human mate preferences: Evolutionary hypotheses tested in 37 cultures. *Behavioral and Brain Sciences, 12,* 1–49.

ALICE EAGLY and WENDY WOOD (1999). The origins of sex differences in human behavior: Evolved dispositions versus social roles. *American Psychologist, 54,* 408–423.

INTRODUCTION

How can we possibly test the hypothesis that, over the ages, evolution has shaped the psyches of men and women to be inherently different? Evolutionary psychologist David Buss proposes that, as a start, we can examine whether gender differences in mating preferences are similar across cultures. If they are, this would be consistent with the view that men and women follow universal, biologically based mating strategies that transcend culture. Based on principles of evolutionary psychology, Buss hypothesized that *across cultures,* men will prefer to marry younger women because such women have greater reproductive capacity; men will value a potential mate's attractiveness more than women will because men use attractiveness as a sign of health and fertility; and women will place greater value than men on a potential mate's earning potential because this provides survival advantages for the woman and her offspring.

METHOD

Buss's team of 50 scientists administered questionnaires to women and men from 37 cultures around the globe. Although random sampling could not be used, the sample of 10,047 participants was ethnically, religiously, and socioeconomically diverse. Participants reported the ideal ages at which they and a spouse would marry, rank-ordered (from "most desirable" to "least desirable") a list of 13 qualities that a potential mate might have, and rated the importance of 18 mate qualities on a second list (see Table 3.4).

Alice Eagly and Wendy Wood wondered if men's and women's mate preferences might be influenced by a third variable: cultural differences in gender roles and power differentials. To find out, they reanalyzed Buss's data, using the United Nations Gender Empowerment Measure to assess the degree of gender equality in each of the cultures. This measure reflects women's earned income relative to men's, seats in parliament, and share of administrative, managerial, professional, and technical jobs.

RESULTS

In all 37 cultures, men wanted to marry younger women. Overall, they believed that the ideal ages for men and women to marry were 27.5 and 24.8 years, respectively. Similarly, women preferred older men, reporting on average an ideal marriage age of 28.8 for husbands and 25.4 for wives. In every culture, men valued having a physically attractive mate more than women did, and in 36 of 37 cultures, women attached more importance than men did to a mate's earning potential.

EVOLUTIONARY AND SOCIAL ROLES INTERPRETATIONS

David Buss concluded that the findings strongly supported the predictions of evolutionary (sexual strategies) theory. Subsequently, Alice Eagly and Wendy Wood analyzed Buss's data further in order to test two key predictions derived from their social structure theory:

1. Men place greater value than women on a mate's having good domestic skills because this is consistent with culturally defined gender roles.
2. If economic and power inequalities cause men and women to attach different values to a mate's age, earning potential, and domestic skills, then these gender differences should be smaller in cultures where there is less inequality between men and women.

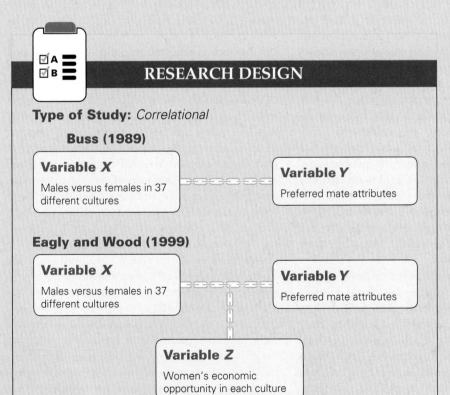

RESEARCH DESIGN

Type of Study: *Correlational*

Buss (1989)

Variable X
Males versus females in 37 different cultures

Variable Y
Preferred mate attributes

Eagly and Wood (1999)

Variable X
Males versus females in 37 different cultures

Variable Y
Preferred mate attributes

Variable Z
Women's economic opportunity in each culture

Continued

As reported by Buss, the potential-mate characteristic "good cook/housekeeper" produced large overall gender differences, with men valuing it more highly. Could this overall trend, however, depend on differences in cultural roles or power differentials? As predicted by the social structure model, Eagly and Wood found that in cultures with greater gender equality, men showed less of a preference for younger women, women displayed less of a preference for older men, and the gender gap decreased in mate preferences for a "good cook/housekeeper" and "good financial prospect." On the other hand, cultural gender equality did not influence the finding that men value physical attractiveness more than women do; that gender difference was *not* smaller in cultures with greater gender equality.

DISCUSSION

Both Buss (Gangestad et al., 2006) and Eagly and Wood (2006) share an interactionist perspective on mate selection that simultaneously takes nature and nurture into account. They differ, however, on how specific and strongly programmed the biological dispositions are thought to be. When Buss found remarkably consistent sex differences in worldwide mate preferences, he interpreted this cross-cultural consistency as evidence that men and women follow universal, biologically based mating strategies. Yet Eagly and Wood (1999, 2006) insist that consistency in behavior across cultures does not, by itself, demonstrate *why* those patterns occur. They view the mate-selection preferences not as biologically preprogrammed, but rather as reflecting evolved but highly flexible dispositions that depend heavily on social input for their expression. In support of this position, they found that a commonly found social condition across cultures, gender inequality, accounts for some—but not all—of the sex differences in mating preferences. Later studies have found that financially independent women, like many men, prefer attractive "hotties" to men with big bank accounts (Bower, 2009).

In science, such controversy stimulates opposing camps to find more sophisticated ways to test their hypotheses. Ultimately, everyone's goal is to arrive at the most plausible explanation for behavior. This is why scientists make their data available to one another, regardless of the possibility that their peers may use the data to bolster an opposing point of view.

Although men and women differ in some of their mating preferences and strategies, the similar overall order of mate preferences shown in Table 3.4 indicates that we are talking once again about shades of the same color, not different colors. In fact, Buss and his coworkers (1990) found that "there may be more similarity between men and women from the same culture than between men and men or women and women from different cultures" (p. 17). Universal proclamations are now being replaced by "it depends" statements.

Evolution and Human Individuality

Evolutionary theory emphasizes what humans (and animals) have in common because of natural-selection pressures. However, a basic fact of human nature is that we also differ from one another psychologically. Can evolutionary theory also account for human individuality?

Earlier in this chapter, we described the Five Factor Model of personality, the leading current trait theory. Because these five trait dimensions—extraversion, agreeableness, conscientiousness, neuroticism, and openness to experience—have been found in people's descriptions of themselves and others in virtually all cultures, some theorists regard them as universal among humans. And because evolutionary theory addresses human universals, the Big Five traits have been the major focus of evolutionary personality theory.

Why should these traits be found so consistently in the languages and behaviors of cultures around the world? According to David Buss (1999), they exist in humans because they have helped us achieve two overriding goals: physical survival and reproductive success. Traits such as extraversion and emotional stability would have been helpful in attaining positions of dominance and mate selection. Conscientiousness and agreeableness are important in group survival, as well as in reproduction and the care of children. Finally, because openness to experience may be the basis for problem solving and creative activities that could affect the ultimate survival of the species, there has always been a need for intelligent and creative people. Evolutionary theorists therefore regard the behaviors underlying the Big Five as sculpted by natural selection until they ultimately became part of human nature.

So much for commonalities in the personality traits that people exhibit. But what about the individual differences in these traits that we witness every day and that define individual personalities? If natural selection is a winnowing process that favors certain personal characteristics over others, would we not expect people to become more alike over time and personality differences to be minimal? Here we turn to another important evolutionary concept called **strategic pluralism,** *the idea that multiple—even contradictory—behavioral strategies* (e.g., introversion and extraversion) *might be adaptive in certain environments and would therefore be maintained through natural selection.*

Daniel Nettle (2006) theorizes that we see variation in the Big Five traits because all of them have adaptive trade-offs (a balance of potential benefits and costs) in the outcomes they may produce. For example, the trait of agreeableness brings with it the benefits of harmonious social relationships and the support of others, but also the risks of being exploited or victimized by others. Another potential cost of agreeableness arises from not sufficiently pursuing one's own personal interests; a little selfishness can be adaptive. Even neuroticism, which is generally viewed as a negative trait, has both costs and benefits that could relate to survival. On the cost side, neuroticism involves anxiety, depression, and stress-related illness that could shorten the life span and drive potential mates away. But the fitness trade-off of neuroticism is a vigilance to potential dangers that could be life-saving, as well as fear of failing and a degree of competitiveness that could have adaptive achievement outcomes. Nettle believes that these trade-offs favor evolutionary variation in the Big Five traits and that the specific environment in which our ancestors evolved made it more or less adaptive to be an extravert or an introvert, agreeable or selfish, fearful or fearless, conscientious or immoral, and so on. This would help account for genes favoring individual differences on personality dimensions and for the great diversity we see in personality trait patterns.

Evolutionary theorists also account for individual differences in personality traits by focusing on gene-environment interactions. Evolution may provide humans with species-typical behavior patterns, but environmental inputs influence how they are manifested. For example, dominance may be the behavior pattern encouraged by innate mechanisms in males, but an individual male who has many early experiences of being subdued or dominated may develop a submissive personality. For evolutionists who assume that the innate female behavior pattern is submissiveness, an individual female who has the resources of high intelligence and physical strength may be

Levels of Analysis

Gene-Environment Research

Although the focus of this chapter has been on genetics and behavior, all three scientific levels of analysis—biological, psychological, and environmental—are involved in the context of discovery.

ENVIRONMENTAL LEVEL

- Evolutionary researchers focus on the environmental factors that fostered behavioral adaptations through natural-selection pressures.

- Epigenetic research reveals how internal and external environmental factors influence how genes express themselves phenotypically.

- Twin studies (especially of twins raised apart) provide insights into the relative roles of genetic factors as well as shared and unshared environmental factors.

- Research on the manner in which genetic factors influence the learning environments that people select or create through their own behavior sheds new light on gene-environment interactions.

- Cross-cultural research shows how cultural learning can affect the expression of gene-influenced behaviors.

BIOLOGICAL LEVEL

- Human genome research is unlocking the secrets of our genetic structure and has already dispelled long-held beliefs, such as that concerning the number of genes in the genome.

- Studies on how genes are switched on and off provide insights into how genetic processes determine the development of biological structures such as the brain. Such knowledge may be the basis for revolutionary new medical treatments.

- Investigations of polygenetic effects may help unravel the complex ways in which genes interact with one another to influence behavior.

PSYCHOLOGICAL LEVEL

- The psychological products of gene-environment interactions cannot be studied without an understanding of the behaviors and psychological processes of interest. This requires psychological research and the development of methods for measuring the psychological characteristics of interest.

- Adoption and twin studies allow researchers to estimate the relative contributions of genes and environment on specific psychological variables. These contributions have been shown to differ widely, depending on the behavior of interest.

- Other research focuses on the specific ways in which environmental and genetic factors exert their individual and combined effects on behavior.

Suppose the entire world was consumed by a deadly plague that killed most humans. How would the human genotype be expected to change as a result of this event? By what process would this occur?

quite willing and able to behave in a competitive and dominant fashion.

As we have seen throughout this chapter, genetic factors underlie evolutionary changes, and they strongly influence many aspects of our human behavior. Genes do not act in isolation, however, but in concert with environmental factors, some of which are created by nature and some of which are of human origin. Together, these forces have forged the human psychological capabilities and processes that are the focus of psychological science. The "Levels of Analysis" feature on page 91 summarizes the causes of behavior at the biological, psychological, and environmental levels.

Myth or Reality?

Human Behavior Reflects Nature's Plan

Evolutionary theory is an important and influential force in modern psychology. However, it is not without its controversial issues, which are both scientific and philosophical in nature. There also exist some widespread misconceptions about evolutionary theory.

"It Exists, Therefore It Evolved"

First, some scientific issues. One has to do with the standards of evidence for or against evolutionary psychology. Adaptations are forged over a long period of time—perhaps thousands of generations—and we cannot go back to prehistoric times and determine with certainty what the environmental demands were. For this reason, evolutionary theorists are often forced to infer the forces to which our ancestors adapted, leading to after-the-fact speculation that is difficult to prove or disprove. A challenge for evolutionary theorists is to avoid the logical fallacy of circular reasoning:

"Why does behavioral tendency X exist?"
"Because of environmental demand Y."
"How do we know that environmental demand Y existed?"
"Because otherwise behavior X would not have developed."

Evolutionary theorists also remind us that it is fallacious to attribute every human characteristic to natural selection (Clark & Grunstein, 2005; Lloyd & Feldman, 2002). In the distant past, as in the present, people created environments that shaped behavior, and those behaviors were often passed down through cultural learning instead of through natural selection. Likewise, a capability that evolved in the past for one reason may now be adaptive for something else. For example, the ability to discern shapes was undoubtedly advantageous for prehistoric hunters trying to spot game in the underbrush. Today, however, few humans in our culture need to hunt in order to survive, but those shape-discriminating capabilities are critical in perceiving letters and learning to read.

Evolutionary theorists have sometimes been accused of giving insufficient weight to cultural learning factors, and many debates about evolutionary explanations center around this issue (Regal, 2005). Witness, for example, the dizzying changes that have occurred in U.S. culture in the past 50 years as humans have altered their own environment. Modern evolutionary theorists acknowledge the role of both *remote causes* (including past evolutionary pressures that may have prompted natural selection) and *proximate* (more recent) *causes*, such as cultural learning and the immediate environment, that influence current behavior. Human culture evolves as both a cause and an effect of brain and behavioral evolution (Boyd & Richerson, 2005). In other words, genes and environment affect one another over time.

"My Genes Are My Destiny"

In thinking about behavior from an evolutionary point of view, it is important to avoid two other fallacies. One is **genetic determinism,** *the idea that genes have invariant and unavoidable effects that can't be altered.* It makes no sense to conclude that because something in nature (such as males' greater tendency to be violent) is influenced by our genes, it is either unavoidable, natural, or morally right. Although evolutionary theorists themselves argue against this view, it has been used to defend the status quo and also to conclude that if "survival of the fittest" (a term actually coined by Herbert Spencer, not by Darwin) is the rule of nature, then those at the top of the social ladder are somehow the most fit of all and therefore "the best people." This notion of genetic superiority has had destructive consequences, not the least of which was the *eugenics* movement of the early twentieth century to prevent the "less biologically fit" (particularly immigrants) from breeding, and Nazi Germany's program of selective breeding designed to produce a "master race." As for the notion that genetically based behaviors are unalterable and therefore must be accepted, we should remember that all behaviors are a function of both the person's biology and the environment. In many cases, what we consider to be self-control or morality requires that we override "natural" biologically based inclinations. Our ability to regulate our own behavior and to exercise moral control is often just as important to our survival (i.e., as adaptive) as are our biological tendencies. Likewise, we can choose to alter the environment in order to override undesired behavioral tendencies, and many of the laws and sanctions that societies enact serve exactly that purpose.

"It's All Part of Mother Nature's Plan"

A final fallacy is the view that evolution is purposive, or "has a plan." There is, in fact, no plan in evolutionary theory; there is only adaptation to environmental demands and the natural selection process that results. The "nature's plan" concept has sometimes been used to support the morality of certain acts, even destructive ones. The usual strategy is for proponents of some idea to find an example of what they believe to be a comparable behavior occurring in the natural world and to use that example to support their own behavior or cause as "in accord with nature." To use this argument to define what is ethically or morally correct is not appropriate. Although there are regularities in natural events that define certain "laws of nature," judgments of morality are most appropriately based on cultural standards and philosophical considerations and not on biological imperatives.

test yourself — Evolution, Culture, and Behavior

Fill in the blank.

1. _____ refers to changes over time in the frequency with which certain genes and their associated characteristics occur within an interbreeding population.
2. In natural selection the physical or behavioral changes that increase the likelihood of survival and reproductive success are _____.
3. _____ theory provides an interpretation of male-female differences that focuses on the role of cultural learning.
4. The notion that multiple and even contradictory behaviors may be adaptive in specific environments, contributing to individuality in personality traits, is called _____.

ANSWERS: 1-Evolution, 2-adaptations, 3-Social structure, 4-strategic pluralism

Chapter Summary

GENETIC INFLUENCES ON BEHAVIOR

- Hereditary potential is carried in the genes, whose commands trigger the production of proteins that control body structures and processes.
- Genotype (genetic structure) and phenotype (outward appearance) are not identical, in part because some genes are dominant, while others are recessive. Many characteristics are polygenic in origin; that is, they are influenced by the interactions of multiple genes.
- Genetic manipulation allows scientists to duplicate and alter genetic material or, potentially, to repair dysfunctional genes. These procedures promise groundbreaking advances in understanding genetic mechanisms and in treating physical and psychological disorders. Moreover, our ability to analyze people's genotypes allows for genetic screening and raises a host of practical issues.
- Although the genotype itself is unchangeable, epigenetic environmental factors can influence how the genotype is translated into the resulting phenotype.
- Behavior geneticists study how genetic and environmental factors contribute to the development of psychological traits and behaviors. Adoption and twin studies are the major research methods used to disentangle hereditary and environmental factors. Especially useful is the study of identical and fraternal twins who were separated early in life and raised in different environments. Identical twins are more similar on a host of psychological characteristics, even when reared apart. Many psychological characteristics have significant heritability.

ADAPTING TO THE ENVIRONMENT: THE ROLE OF LEARNING

- The environment exerts its effects largely through learning processes made possible by innate biological mechanisms. Humans and other animals can learn which stimuli are important and which responses are likely to result in goal attainment, thereby allowing them to regulate their behavior and adapt to the environment.
- Because learning always occurs within environments, it is important to distinguish between different kinds of environments. Behavior geneticists make an important distinction between shared (by more than one person) and unshared (more or less unique) environmental influences.

BEHAVIOR GENETICS, INTELLIGENCE, AND PERSONALITY

- Intelligence has a strong genetic basis, with heritability coefficients in the .50 to .70 range. Shared family environment is also important (particularly at lower socioeconomic levels), as are educational experiences.
- Personality also has a genetic contribution, though not as strong as that for intelligence. Shared family environment seems to have little impact on the development of personality traits. Unshared individual experiences are far more important environmental determinants.

GENE-ENVIRONMENT INTERACTIONS

- Genetic and environmental factors rarely operate alone. They interact with one another in important ways. Genetic factors may influence how different people experience the same environment, and the environment can influence how genes express themselves.
- Genetic reaction range sets upper and lower limits for the impact of environmental factors. Where intelligence is concerned, environmental factors may create differences as large as 20 IQ points.
- Genetic factors can influence the environment in three important ways. First, genes shared by parents and children may be expressed in how the parents behave and in the environment they create. Second, genes may produce characteristics (for example, extraversion or hostility) that influence how others respond to the person. Finally, people may

self-select or create environments that are consistent with their genetic characteristics, as when an intelligent person seeks out intellectually stimulating situations.

EVOLUTION, CULTURE, AND BEHAVIOR

- Evolutionary psychology focuses on biologically based mechanisms sculpted by evolutionary forces as solutions to the problems of adaptation faced by species. Some of these genetically based mechanisms are general (e.g., the ability to learn from the consequences of our behavior), whereas others are thought to be domain-specific, devoted to solving specific problems (e.g., mate selection).

- Evolution is a change over time in the frequency with which particular genes—and the characteristics they produce—occur within an interbreeding population. Evolution represents an interaction between biological and environmental factors.

- The cornerstone of Darwin's theory of evolution is the principle of natural selection. According to this principle, biologically based characteristics that contribute to survival and reproductive success increase in the population over time, because those who lack the characteristics are less likely to pass on their genes. The concept of evoked culture implies that cultures also develop in response to adaptive demands specific to various human populations.

- Among the aspects of human behavior that have received evolutionary explanations are human mate selection and personality traits. In research on mate selection, evolutionary explanations have been tested against hypotheses derived from social structure theory, which emphasizes the role of cultural factors.

- Myths about evolution abound. Critical thinking helps counter circular reasoning about evolutionary causes and effects and challenges genetic determinism and social Darwinism. We should also recognize that harmful genetically based behavior tendencies can be overridden by human decision and self-control.

KEY TERMS AND CONCEPTS

Each term has been boldfaced and defined in the chapter on the page indicated in parentheses.

adaptations (p. 83)
adaptive significance (p. 74)
adoption study (p. 71)
alleles (p. 68)
behavior genetics (p. 71)
biologically based mechanisms (p. 82)
chromosome (p. 68)
concordance (p. 71)
dominant gene (p. 69)
epigenetics (p. 70)
evocative influence (p. 81)
evoked culture (p. 84)

evolution (p. 82)
family study (p. 71)
fixed action pattern (p. 74)
genes (p. 68)
genetic determinism (p. 92)
genotype (p. 68)
heritability coefficient (p. 72)
knock-in procedure (p. 70)
knockout procedure (p. 70)
mutations (p. 82)
natural selection (p. 83)
phenotype (p. 68)

polygenic transmission (p. 69)
reaction range (p. 80)
recessive gene (p. 69)
sexual strategies (parental investment) theory (p. 87)
shared environment (p. 76)
social structure theory (p. 88)
strategic pluralism (p. 90)
twin study (p. 71)
unshared environment (p. 76)

 thinking critically

NATURAL SELECTION AND GENETIC DISEASES (Page 85)

Genetics research shows that in most cases, there's not a one-to-one relation between a particular gene and a particular trait. Most traits involve the influence of many genes, and a given gene can contribute to many traits. Traits, therefore, come in packages, with some of the traits in the package being adaptive and others maladaptive. In fact, cystic fibrosis (CF) is one such example. CF is the most commonly inherited disorder among people of European descent. Why would such a damaging genetic trait survive in the gene pool?

Geneticists have found that people with CF also have a trait that slows the release of salts into the intestine (Allen, 2010). Some scientists believe that this related trait might have helped save carriers from severe dehydration and death from the diarrheal diseases that killed 7 out of every 10 newborns in medieval Europe. Perhaps CF was preserved in the population because another part of the trait package made carriers more likely to survive and pass on their genes.

Let's consider sickle-cell anemia. Many people of African descent suffer from this genetically caused blood disorder that lowers one's life expectancy. Why would a disorder that decreases survival be preserved in a population? The answer may be that despite its negatives, the sickle-cell gene has an important redeeming quality: it makes people more resistant to malaria, the most lethal disease in the African environment. Because it enhanced survival from malaria, the sickle-cell trait became more common among Africans and can therefore be seen as a product of natural selection.

These examples show us that we should be careful not to oversimplify the concept of adaptation and assume that any trait that survives, whether physical or psychological, is of immediate benefit to the species.

chapter four

The Brain and Behavior

CHAPTER OUTLINE

Myth or Reality?

We Use Only Ten Percent of Our Brain Power (page 123)

The brain is one of the most complex structures in the universe, and its activity underlies our every thought, emotion, and behavior. How often have you heard that we use only a small portion of its neural capacity? Is this true?

The year was 1848. As the Vermont winter approached, a railroad construction crew hurried to complete its work on a new track. The men could not know that they were about to witness one of the most celebrated incidents in the annals of neuroscience.

As a blasting crew prepared its charges, the dynamite accidentally exploded. A 13-pound spike more than 3 feet long was propelled through the head of Phineas Gage, a 25-year-old foreman. The spike entered through the left cheek, passed through the brain, and emerged through the top of the skull (Figure 4.1). Dr. J. M. Harlow, who treated Gage, described the incident:

> The patient was thrown upon his back by the explosion, and gave a few convulsive motions of the extremities, but spoke in a few minutes. He . . . seemed perfectly conscious, but was becoming exhausted from the hemorrhage, . . . the blood pouring from the top of his head. . . . He bore his sufferings with firmness, and directed my attention to the hole in his cheek, saying, "the iron entered there and passed through my head." (1868, pp. 330–332)

Miraculously, Gage survived. Or did he?

> His physical health is good, and I am inclined to say that he has recovered. Has no pain in his head, but says it has a queer feeling that he is not able to describe. Applied for his situation as foreman, but is undecided whether to work or travel. His contractors, who regarded him as the most efficient and capable foreman in their employ previous to his injury, considered the change in his mind so marked that they could not give him his place again. The equilibrium or balance, so to speak, between his intellectual faculties and animal propensities, seems to have been destroyed. He is fitful, irreverent, indulging at times in the grossest profanity (which was not previously his custom), manifesting but little deference for his fellows, impatient of restraint or advice when it conflicts with his desires . . . devising many plans of future operations, which are no sooner arranged than they are abandoned in turn for others. . . . His mind is radically changed, so decidedly that his friends and acquaintances say that he is "no longer Gage." (pp. 339–340)

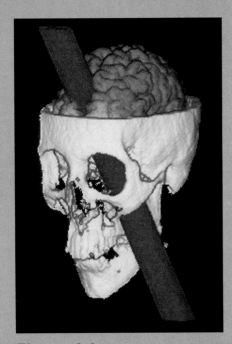

Figure 4.1

The brain damage suffered by Phineas Gage seemed to change him into a new person. The red image shows the path of the spike that shot through Gage's brain.

Mind and body, body and mind. The tragic story of Phineas Gage illustrates the intimate connection between brain, mind, and behavior. Physical damage to Gage's brain changed his thinking and behavior so radically that he became, psychologically, a different person, "no longer Gage." Is our personal identity so thoroughly locked inside our skull? Is who we are and what we do reducible to the electrochemical activities of the nervous system? Most neuroscientists would not hesitate to answer yes. After you read this chapter, you will probably agree.

The evolutionary history of our species, the genes you inherited from your parents, and your life experiences have shaped who you are. From a psychological perspective, your most important physical organ is your brain, a grapefruit-sized mass of tissue that feels like jelly and has the gnarled appearance of a grayish walnut. One of the true marvels of nature, the brain has been termed "our three-pound universe," for every experience is represented within our skull (Hooper & Teresi, 1986). To understand how the brain controls our experience and behavior, we must first understand how its individual cells function and how they communicate with one another.

NEURONS

Specialized cells called **neurons** *are the basic building blocks of the nervous system.* The estimated 100 billion nerve cells in your brain and spinal cord are linked together in circuits, not unlike the electrical circuits in a computer. Each neuron has three main parts: a cell body, dendrites, and an axon (Figure 4.2). The cell body, or *soma,* contains the biochemical structures needed to keep the neuron alive, and its nucleus carries the genetic information that determines how the cell develops and functions. Emerging from the cell body are branchlike fibers called **dendrites** (from the Greek word meaning "tree"), *specialized receiving units like antennae that collect messages from neighboring neurons and send them on to the cell body.* There, the incoming information is combined and processed. The many branches of the dendrites can receive input from 1,000 or more neighboring neurons. The surface of the cell body also has receptor areas that can be directly stimulated by other neurons. All parts of a neuron are covered by a protective membrane that controls the exchange of chemical substances between the inside and outside of the cell. These exchanges play a critical role in the electrical activities of nerve cells.

Extending from one side of the cell body is a single **axon,** *which conducts electrical impulses away from the cell body to other neurons, muscles, or glands.* The axon branches out at its end to form a number of *axon terminals*—as many as several hundred in some cases. Each axon terminal may connect with dendrites from numerous neurons, making it possible for a single neuron to pass messages to as many as 50,000 other neurons (Simon, 2007). Given the structure of the dendrites and axons, it is easy to see how there can be trillions of interconnections in the brain, making it capable of performing the complex activities that are of interest to psychologists.

Neurons can vary greatly in size and shape. Researchers using electron microscopes have viewed more than 200 different types of nerve cells. A neuron with its cell body in your spinal cord may have an axon that extends several feet to one of your fingertips, whereas a neuron in your brain may be no more than a thousandth of an inch long. Regardless of their shape or size, neurons have been exquisitely sculpted by nature to perform their function of receiving, processing, and sending messages.

Neurons are supported in their functions by *glial cells* (from the Greek word meaning "glue"). Glial cells do not send or receive nerve impulses, but they surround neurons and hold them in place. The glial cells also manufacture nutrient chemicals that neurons need, and they absorb toxins and waste materials that would damage or kill neurons. During prenatal brain development, as new neurons are being formed through cell division, glial cells send out long fibers that guide newly divided neurons to their targeted places in the brain (Fenichel, 2006). Within the brain, glial cells outnumber neurons about 10 to 1.

The Electrical Activity of Neurons

Neurons do two important things. Like tiny batteries, they generate electricity that creates nerve

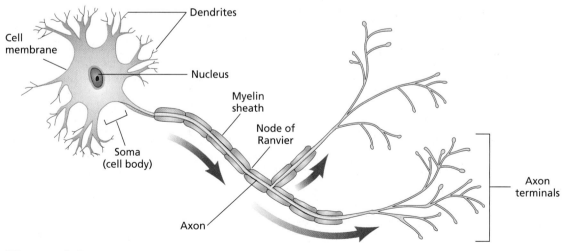

Figure 4.2

Structural elements of a typical neuron.
Stimulation received by the dendrites or soma (cell body) may trigger a nerve impulse, which travels down the axon to stimulate other neurons, muscles, or glands. Some axons have a fatty myelin sheath interrupted at intervals by the nodes of Ranvier. The myelin sheath helps increase the speed of nerve conduction.

impulses. They also release chemicals that allow them to communicate with other neurons and with muscles and glands.

Let's first consider how nerve impulses occur. Nerve activation involves three basic steps:

1. At rest, the neuron has an electrical *resting potential* due to the distribution of positively and negatively charged chemical ions inside and outside the neuron.

2. When stimulated, a flow of ions in and out through the cell membrane reverses the electrical charge of the resting potential, producing an *action potential,* or nerve impulse.

3. The original ionic balance is restored, and the neuron is again at rest.

Let's now flesh out the details of this remarkable process. Like other cells, neurons are surrounded by body fluids and separated from this liquid environment by a protective membrane. This cell membrane is a bit like a selective sieve, allowing certain substances in the body fluid to pass through *ion channels* into the cell while refusing or limiting passage to other substances.

The chemical environment inside the neuron differs from its external environment in significant ways, and the process whereby a nerve impulse is created involves the exchange of electrically charged atoms called *ions.* In the salty fluid outside the neuron are positively charged sodium ions (Na^+) and negatively charged chloride ions (Cl^-). Inside the neuron are large negatively charged protein molecules (*anions,* or A^-) and positively charged potassium ions (K^+). The high concentration of sodium ions in the fluid outside the cell, together with the negatively charged protein ions inside, results in an uneven distribution of positive and negative ions that makes the interior of the cell negative compared to the outside (Figure 4.3a). *This internal difference of around 70 millivolts (mV) is called the neuron's* **resting potential.** At rest, the neuron is said to be in a state of *polarization.*

Nerve Impulses: The Action Potential

In research that won them the 1963 Nobel Prize, neuroscientists Alan Hodgkin and Andrew Huxley found that if they stimulated the neuron's axon with a mild electrical stimulus, the interior voltage differential shifted instantaneously from −70 millivolts to +40 millivolts. *This electrical shift, which lasts about a millisecond (1/1,000 of a second), is called the* **action potential,** *or nerve impulse.*

What happens in the neuron to cause the action potential? Hodgkin and Huxley found that the key mechanism is the action of sodium and potassium ion channels in the cell membrane.

Figure 4.3 shows what happens. In a resting state, the neuron's sodium and potassium channels are closed, and the concentration of Na^+ ions is 10 times higher outside the neuron than inside it (see Figure 4.3a). But when a neuron is stimulated sufficiently, nearby sodium channels open up. Attracted by the negative protein ions inside, positively charged sodium ions flood into the axon, creating a state of *depolarization* (see Figure 4.3b). In an instant, the interior now becomes positive (by about 40 millivolts) in relation to the outside, creating the action potential. In a reflex action to restore the resting potential, the cell closes its sodium channels, and positively charged potassium ions flow out through their channels, restoring the negative resting potential (see Figure 4.3c). Eventually, the excess sodium ions flow out of the neuron, and the escaped potassium ions are recovered. The resulting voltage changes are shown in Figure 4.3d.

Once an action potential occurs at any point on the membrane, its effects spread to adjacent sodium channels, and the action potential flows down the length of the axon to the axon terminals. Immediately after an impulse passes a point along the axon, however, there is a recovery period as the K^+ ions flow out of the interior. During this **absolute refractory period,** *the membrane is not excitable and cannot discharge another impulse.* This places an upper limit on the rate at which nerve impulses can occur. In humans, the limit seems to be about 300 impulses per second (Kolb & Whishaw, 2005).

It's All or Nothing   One other feature of the action potential is noteworthy. In accordance with the so-called **all-or-none law,** *action potentials occur at a uniform and maximum intensity, or they do not occur at all.* Like firing a gun, which requires that a certain amount of pressure be placed on the trigger, the negative potential inside the axon has to be changed from −70 millivolts to about −50 millivolts (the *action potential threshold*) by the influx of sodium ions into the axon before the action potential will be triggered. *Changes in the negative resting potential that do not reach the −50 millivolt action potential threshold are called* **graded potentials.** Under certain circumstances, graded potentials created by several neurons can add up to trigger an action potential in an adjacent neuron.

For a neuron to function properly, sodium and potassium ions must enter and leave the membrane at just the right rate. Drugs that alter this transit system can decrease or prevent neural functioning. For example, local anesthetics such as Novocain and Xylocaine attach themselves to the sodium channels, stopping the flow of sodium ions into the

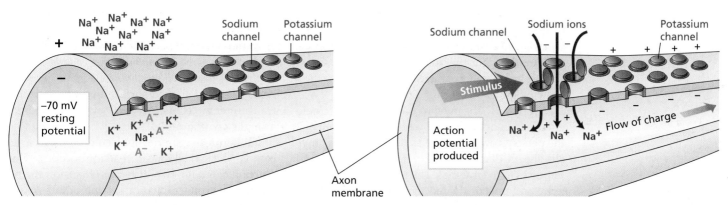

(a) The 10:1 concentration of sodium (Na⁺) ions outside the neuron and the negative protein (A⁻) ions inside contribute to a resting potential of –70 mV.

(b) If the neuron is sufficiently stimulated, sodium channels open and sodium ions flood into the axon. Note that the potassium channels are still closed.

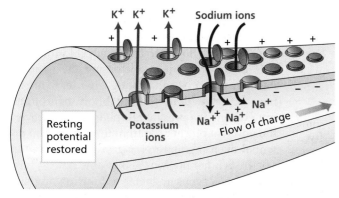

(c) Sodium channels that were open in (b) have now closed and potassium channels behind them are open, allowing potassium ions to exit and restoring the resting potential at that point. Sodium channels are opening at the next point as the action potential moves down the axon.

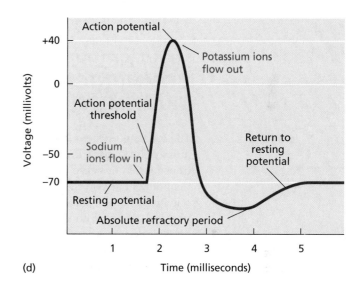

(d)

Figure 4.3

From resting potential to action potential.
When a neuron is not being stimulated, a difference in electrical charge of about −70 millivolts (mV) exists between the interior and the surface of the neuron. (a) This resting potential is caused by the uneven distribution of positively and negatively charged ions, with a greater concentration of positively charged sodium ions kept outside the cell by closed sodium channels and the presence of negatively charged protein (A⁻) ions inside the cell. In addition, the action of sodium-potassium pumps helps maintain the negative interior by pumping out three sodium (Na⁺) ions for every two positively charged potassium (K⁺) ions drawn into the cell. (b) Sufficient stimulation of the neuron causes an action potential. Sodium channels open for an instant and Na⁺ ions flood into the axon, reversing the electrical potential from −70 mV to +40 mV. (c) Within a millisecond, the sodium channels close and many K⁺ ions flow out of the cell through open potassium channels, helping to restore the interior negative potential. As adjacent sodium channels are opened and the sequence in (b) and (c) is repeated, the action potential moves down the length of the axon. (d) Shown here are the changes in electrical potential that would be recorded from a particular point on the axon. After a brief refractory period during which the neuron cannot be stimulated, another action potential can follow.

neurons. This stops pain impulses from being sent by the neurons (Ray & Ksir, 2004).

The Myelin Sheath Many axons that transmit information throughout the brain and spinal cord are covered by a tubelike **myelin sheath,** *a whitish, fatty insulation layer derived from glial cells during development.* Unmyelinated axons are gray in color, hence the term *gray matter.* Myelinated fibers are sometimes called *white matter.*

Because the myelin sheath is interrupted at regular intervals by the *nodes of Ranvier,* where the

myelin is either extremely thin or absent, myelinated axons look a bit like sausages placed end to end (see Figure 4.2). In axons lacking the myelin sheath, the action potential travels down the axon length in a point-to-point fashion like a burning fuse. But in myelinated axons, the nodes of Ranvier are close enough to one another so that depolarization at one node can activate the next node, allowing electrical conduction to jump from node to node at higher speeds.

The myelin sheath is most commonly found in the nervous systems of higher animals. In many neurons, the myelin sheath is not completely formed until some time after birth. The resulting efficiency of neural transmission is partly responsible for the gains that infants exhibit in muscular coordination and cognitive functioning as they grow older (Cabeza et al., 2005).

Damage to the myelin coating can have tragic effects. In people afflicted with multiple sclerosis, the person's own immune system attacks the myelin sheath, disrupting the delicate timing of nerve impulses to the muscles. The result is increasingly jerky and uncoordinated movements and, in the final stages, paralysis (Toy, 2007).

We've now seen how nerve impulses are created. However, the activity of a single neuron means little unless it can communicate its message to other neurons. This is where the chemical activities of neurons come into play.

HOW NEURONS COMMUNICATE: SYNAPTIC TRANSMISSION

The nervous system operates as a giant communications network, and its action requires the transmission of nerve impulses from one neuron to another. Early in the history of brain research, scientists thought that the tip of the axon made physical contact with the dendrites or cell bodies of other neurons, passing electricity directly from one neuron to the next. With the advent of the electron microscope, however, researchers discovered a **synaptic space,** *a tiny gap between the axon terminal and the next neuron.* This discovery raised new and perplexing questions: If neurons do not physically touch the other neurons to which they send signals, how does communication occur? If the action potential does not cross the synapse, what does? What carries the message?

Neurotransmitters

In addition to generating electricity, neurons produce **neurotransmitters,** *chemical substances that carry messages across the synaptic space to other neurons, muscles, or glands.* This process of chemical communication involves five steps: synthesis, storage, release, binding, and deactivation. In the *synthesis* stage, the transmitter molecules are formed inside the neuron. The molecules are then *stored* in **synaptic vesicles,** *chambers within the axon terminals.* When an action potential comes down the axon, these vesicles move to the surface of the axon terminal and the molecules are *released* into the fluid-filled space between the axon of the

presynaptic (sending) neuron and the membrane of the *postsynaptic* (receiving) neuron. The molecules cross the synaptic space and *bind* themselves to **receptor sites,** *large protein molecules embedded in the receiving neuron's cell membrane.* Each receptor site has a specially shaped surface that fits a specific transmitter molecule, just as a lock accommodates a single key (Figure 4.4).

When a transmitter molecule binds to a receptor site, a chemical reaction occurs. This reaction can have two different effects on the receiving neuron—excitation or inhibition. When an *excitatory* transmitter is at work, the chemical reaction causes the postsynaptic neuron's sodium channels to open. As sodium ions flood into the cell and depolarize it, they create either a graded potential or an action potential as just described. An *inhibitory* neurotransmitter will do the opposite. It may cause positive potassium ions to flow out of the neuron or negative chloride ions from the exterior to flow into it through chloride channels in the membrane, increasing the neuron's negative potential and making it harder to fire the neuron. The action of an inhibitory neurotransmitter from one presynaptic neuron may prevent the postsynaptic neuron from firing an action potential even if it is receiving excitatory stimulation from other neurons at the same time.

If the nervous system is to function properly, it must maintain a fine-tuned balance between excitation and inhibition. Even such a simple act as bending your arm requires excitation of your biceps muscles and simultaneous inhibition of your triceps so those muscles can relax.

Once a neurotransmitter molecule binds to its receptor, it continues to excite or inhibit the neuron until it is *deactivated,* or shut off. This occurs in two major ways (Simon, 2007). Some transmitter molecules are deactivated by other chemicals located in the synaptic space that break them down into their chemical components. In other instances, the deactivation mechanism is **reuptake,** *in which the transmitter molecules are taken back into the presynaptic axon terminals.* Some antidepressant medications inhibit reuptake of the excitatory transmitter serotonin, allowing serotonin to continue to excite neurons and thereby reduce depression.

Specialized Neurotransmitter Systems

Through the use of chemical transmitters, nature has found an ingenious way of dividing up the brain into systems that are uniquely sensitive to certain messages. There is only one kind of electricity, but there are many shapes that can be assumed by transmitter molecules. Because the

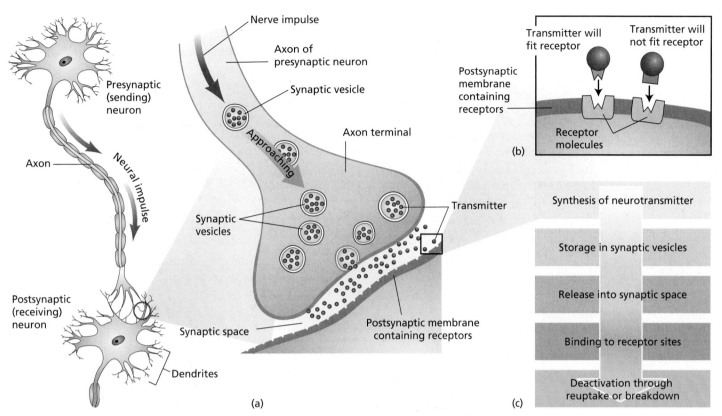

Figure 4.4

A synapse between two neurons.

The action potential travels to the axon terminals, where it stimulates the release of transmitter molecules from the synaptic vesicles. These molecules travel across the synapse and bind to specially keyed receptor sites on the cell body or dendrite of the postsynaptic neuron (a). The lock-and-key nature of neurotransmitters and receptor sites is shown in (b). Only transmitters that fit the receptor will influence membrane potentials. The sequence of neurotransmitter activity, from synthesis to deactivation, is shown in (c). If the neurotransmitter has an excitatory effect on the neuron, the chemical reaction that occurs creates a graded or an action potential. If the transmitter substance is inhibitory, it increases the negative potential inside the neuron and makes it more difficult to fire it.

various systems in the brain recognize only certain chemical messengers, they are immune to cross talk from other systems.

There are many different neurotransmitter substances, some of which can coexist within the same neuron. A given neuron may use one transmitter at one synapse and a different one at another synapse. Moreover, different transmitters can be found within the same axon terminal or in the same synapse, adding another layer of complexity (Kolb & Whishaw, 2005). Each substance has a specific excitatory or inhibitory effect on certain neurons. Some neurotransmitters (for example, norepinephrine) can have either excitatory or inhibitory effects, depending on which receptor sites they bind to.

Table 4.1 lists several of the more important neurotransmitters that have been linked to psychological phenomena. We'll encounter all of these substances in this and future chapters. For the moment, we'll focus on **acetylcholine (ACh),** *a neurotransmitter involved in muscle activity and memory,* to illustrate the diversity of neurotransmitter mechanisms.

Underproduction of ACh is an important factor in Alzheimer's disease, a degenerative brain disorder that afflicts 5 to 10 percent of people over 65 years of age (Morris & Becker, 2005). Reductions in ACh weaken or deactivate neural circuitry that stores memories, creating profound memory impairments. ACh is also an excitatory transmitter at the synapses where neurons activate muscle cells, helping to account for the tremors and severe motor impairments found in the later stages of Alzheimer's disease.

Drugs that block the action of ACh can prevent muscle activation and cause paralysis. One example occurs in botulism, a serious type of food poisoning that can result from improperly canned food. The toxin formed by the *botulinum* bacteria blocks the release of ACh from the axon terminal, resulting in a potentially fatal paralysis of the muscles, including those of the respiratory system. A mild form of the toxin, known as Botox, is used cosmetically to remove skin wrinkles by paralyzing the muscles whose contraction causes wrinkles.

Table **4.1** | **Some Neurotransmitters and Their Effects**

Neurotransmitter	Major Function	Disorders Associated with Malfunctioning	Additional Discussion
Acetylcholine (ACh)	Excitatory at synapses involved in muscular movement and memory	Memory loss in Alzheimer's disease (undersupply); paralysis (absence); violent muscle contractions and convulsions (oversupply)	Chapter 8
Norepinephrine	Excitatory and inhibitory functions at various sites; involved in neural circuits controlling learning, memory, wakefulness, and eating	Depression (undersupply); stress and panic disorders (overactivity)	Chapters 6, 14
Serotonin	Inhibitory or excitatory; involved in mood, sleep, eating, and arousal, and may be an important transmitter underlying pleasure and pain	Depression; sleeping and eating disorders (undersupply); obsessive-compulsive disorder (overactivity)	Chapters 6, 13, 15, 16
Dopamine	Excitatory; involved in voluntary movement, emotional arousal, learning, memory, and experiencing pleasure or pain	Parkinson's disease and depression (undersupply); schizophrenia (overactivity)	Chapters 6, 15, 16
GABA (gamma-aminobutyric acid)	Inhibitory transmitter in motor system	Destruction of GABA-producing neurons in Huntington's disease produces tremors and loss of motor control, as well as personality changes	Chapter 6
Endorphin	Inhibits transmission of pain impulses (a neuromodulator)	Insensitivity to pain (oversupply); pain hypersensitivity, immune problems (undersupply)	Chapters 5, 6, 14

The opposite effect on ACh occurs with the bite of the black widow spider. The spider's venom triggers a torrent of ACh, resulting in violent muscle contractions, convulsions, and possible death. Some chemical agents, such as the deadly sarin gas released into the Tokyo subway system by terrorists in 1995, also raise havoc by allowing ACh to run wild in the nervous system. Sarin and similar nerve gas agents prevent the activity of an enzyme that normally degrades ACh at the synapse. The result is uncontrolled seizures and convulsions that can kill.

Most neurotransmitters have their excitatory or inhibitory effects only on specific neurons that have receptors for them. Others, called **neuromodulators**, *have a more widespread and generalized influence on synaptic transmission.* These substances circulate through the brain and either increase or decrease (i.e., modulate) the sensitivity of thousands, perhaps millions, of neurons to their specific transmitters. The best known neuromodulators are the *endorphins,* which travel through the brain's circulatory system and inhibit pain transmission while enhancing neural activity that produces pleasurable feelings. We'll examine the endorphins in greater detail in Chapter 5. Other neuromodulators play important roles in functions such as eating, sleeping, and coping with stress.

Knowledge about neurotransmitter systems has many important applications. For one thing, it helps us understand the mechanisms that underlie the effects of **psychoactive drugs,** *chemicals that produce alterations in consciousness, emotion, and behavior.* The following "Applying Psychological Science" feature focuses on mechanisms of drug effects within the brain.

Applying Psychological Science

Understanding How Drugs Affect Your Brain

Drugs affect consciousness and behavior by influencing the activity of neurons (Ettinger, 2009). A survey of 55,000 students at 132 colleges in the United States revealed that in the prior year, 47 percent had used tobacco; 84 percent, alcohol; 33.6 percent, marijuana; and 5 to 10 percent, cocaine, amphetamines, hallucinogenic drugs such as LSD, and designer drugs such as Ecstasy (Core Institute, 2002).

Most psychoactive drugs produce their effects by either increasing or decreasing the synthesis, storage, release, binding, or deactivation of neurotransmitters. An **agonist** *is a drug that increases the activity of a neurotransmitter.* Agonists may (1) enhance a neuron's ability to synthesize, store, or release neurotransmitters; (2) mimic the action of a neurotransmitter by binding with and stimulating postsynaptic receptor sites; (3) bind with and stimulate postsynaptic receptor sites; or (4) make it more difficult for neurotransmitters to be deactivated, such as by inhibiting reuptake.

An **antagonist** *is a drug that inhibits or decreases the action of a neurotransmitter*. An antagonist may (1) reduce a neuron's ability to synthesize, store, or release neurotransmitters or (2) prevent a neurotransmitter from binding with the postsynaptic neuron by fitting into and blocking the receptor sites on the postsynaptic neuron.

With the distinction between agonist and antagonist functions in mind, let us consider how some commonly used drugs work within the brain. Alcohol is a depressant drug having both agonist and antagonist effects. As an agonist, it stimulates the activity of the inhibitory transmitter GABA, thereby depressing neural activity. As an antagonist, it decreases the activity of glutamate, an excitatory transmitter (Levinthal, 2007). The double-barreled effect is a neural slowdown that inhibits normal brain functions, including clear thinking, emotional control, and motor coordination. Sedative drugs, including barbiturates and tranquilizers, also increase GABA activity, and taking them with alcohol can be deadly when their depressant effects on neural activity are combined with those of alcohol (Schatsberg et al., 2010).

Caffeine is a stimulant drug that increases the activity of neurons and other cells. It is an antagonist for the transmitter adenosine, which inhibits the release of excitatory transmitters. By reducing adenosine activity, caffeine helps produce higher rates of cellular activity and more available energy. Although caffeine is a stimulant, it is important to note that contrary to popular belief, caffeine does *not* counteract the effects of alcohol and sober people up. What your drunken friend needs is a ride home with a driver who is sober—not a cup of coffee.

Nicotine is an agonist for the excitatory transmitter acetylcholine. Its chemical structure is similar enough to that of ACh to allow it to fit into ACh binding sites and create action potentials. At other receptor sites, nicotine stimulates dopamine activity, which seems to be an important chemical mediator of energy and pleasure. This may help account for nicotine's powerful addictive properties. Researchers are working to develop medications that could wean people off cigarettes and other tobacco products by blocking or occupying the specific receptor sites that trigger dopamine release (Self & Staley, 2009).

Amphetamines are stimulant drugs that boost arousal and mood by increasing the activity of the excitatory neurotransmitters dopamine and norepinephrine. They do so by causing presynaptic neurons to release greater amounts of these neurotransmitters and by inhibiting reuptake, allowing dopamine and norepinephrine to keep stimulating postsynaptic neurons (Ksir et al., 2008). Cocaine produces excitation, a sense of increased muscular strength, and euphoria. Like amphetamines,

cocaine increases the activity of norepinephrine and dopamine, but it does so in only one major way: it blocks their reuptake. Thus, amphetamines and cocaine have different mechanisms of action on the dopamine and norepinephrine transmitter systems, but both drugs produce highly stimulating effects on mood, thinking, and behavior.

We should comment on two other drugs that, unfortunately, are also found on college campuses. Rohypnol (flunitrazepam, known as "roofies" or "rope") and GHB (gamma hydroxybutyrate, known as "easy lay") are so-called date-rape drugs. Partygoers sometimes add these drugs to punch and other drinks in hopes of lowering drinkers' inhibitions and facilitating nonconsensual sexual conquest. The drugs are powerful sedatives that suppress general neural activity by enhancing the action of the inhibitory transmitter GABA (Levinthal, 2007). Rohypnol is about 10 times more potent than Valium. At high doses or when mixed with alcohol or other drugs, these substances may lead to respiratory depression, loss of consciousness, coma, and even death. Rohypnol also attacks neurotransmission in areas of the brain involved in memory, producing an amnesia effect that may prevent users from remembering the circumstances under which they ingested the drug or what happened to them afterward. GHB, which makes its victim appear drunk and helpless, is now a restricted drug, and slipping it into someone's drink is a criminal act. The bottom line is that these drugs are neither good to give nor good to receive (Figure 4.5). Increasingly, women are being advised against accepting opened drinks from fellow revelers or leaving their own drinks unattended at parties.

Figure 4.5

As these college students consume alcohol, they are increasing the activity of the inhibitory transmitter GABA and decreasing the activity of an excitatory transmitter, thus depressing brain functions that influence judgment. The possibility of a drink having been spiked with a "date rape" drug could place these women at great risk.

test yourself

Neurons and How They Communicate

Match each numbered neurotransmitter to its effect on the right.

1. acetylcholine
2. serotonin
3. norepinephrine
4. endorphins
5. GABA

a. a neuromodulator that inhibits pain impulses

b. excitatory; voluntary movement, learning, memory, emotional arousal; oversupply associated with stress, panic disorders

c. excitatory at synapses involved in muscular movement and memory; undersupply in Alzheimer's disease

d. inhibitory transmitter in motor system; undersupply produces tremors, loss of motor control

e. inhibitory or excitatory; involved in mood, sleep, eating, emotional arousal, and pleasure/pain; undersupply in depression

ANSWERS: 1-c, 2-e, 3-b, 4-a, 5-d

THE NERVOUS SYSTEM

The nervous system is the body's control center. Three major types of neurons carry out the system's input, output, and integration functions. **Sensory neurons** *carry input messages from the sense organs to the spinal cord and brain.* **Motor neurons** *transmit output impulses from the brain and spinal cord to the body's muscles and organs.* Finally, there are neurons that link the input and output functions. These **interneurons,** which far outnumber sensory and motor neurons, *perform connective or associative functions within the nervous system.* For example, interneurons would allow us to recognize a friend by linking the sensory input from the visual system with the memory of that person's characteristics stored elsewhere in the brain. The activity of interneurons makes possible the complexity of our higher mental functions, emotions, and behavioral capabilities.

The nervous system can be broken down into several interrelated subsystems (Figure 4.6). The two major divisions are the peripheral and central nervous systems.

The Peripheral Nervous System

The **peripheral nervous system** *contains all the neural structures that lie outside of the brain and spinal cord.* Its specialized neurons help carry out (1) the input functions that enable us to sense what is going on inside and outside our bodies and (2) the output functions that enable us to respond with our muscles and glands. The peripheral nervous system has two major divisions, the somatic nervous system and the autonomic nervous system.

The Somatic Nervous System

The **somatic nervous system** *consists of sensory neurons that are specialized to transmit messages from the eyes, ears, and other sensory receptors, and motor neurons that send messages from the brain and spinal cord to the muscles that control voluntary movements.* The axons of sensory neurons group together like many strands of a rope to form *sensory nerves,* and motor-neuron axons combine to form *motor nerves.* As you read this page, sensory neurons in your eyes are sending impulses into a complex network of specialized visual tracts that course through your brain. (Inside the brain and spinal cord, nerves are called *tracts.*) At the same time, motor neurons are stimulating the eye movements that allow you to scan the lines of type and turn the pages. The somatic system thus allows you to sense and respond to your environment.

The Autonomic Nervous System

The body's internal environment is regulated largely through the activities of the **autonomic nervous system,** *which senses the body's internal functions and controls the glands and the smooth (involuntary) muscles that form the heart, the blood vessels, and the lining of the stomach and intestines.* The autonomic system is largely concerned with involuntary functions, such as respiration, circulation, and digestion; it is also involved in many aspects of motivation, emotional behavior, and stress responses. It consists of two subdivisions, the *sympathetic nervous system* and the *parasympathetic nervous system* (Figure 4.7). Typically, these two divisions affect the same organ or gland in opposing ways.

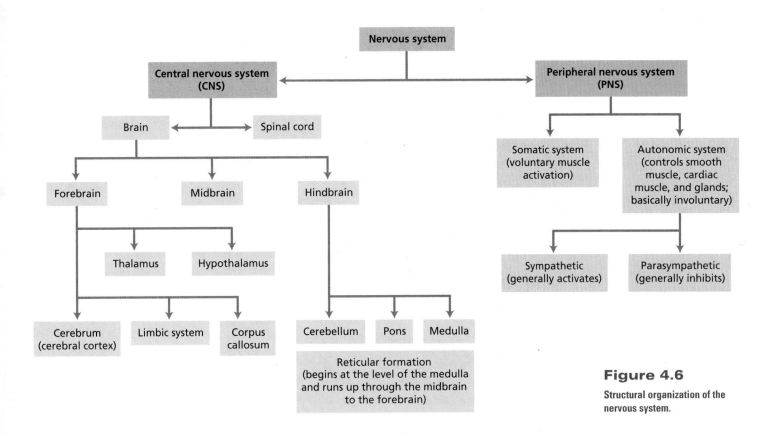

Figure 4.6

Structural organization of the nervous system.

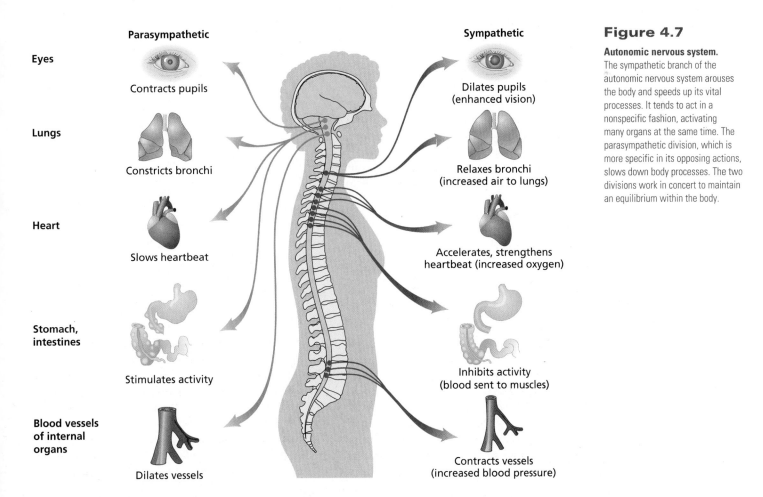

Figure 4.7

Autonomic nervous system.
The sympathetic branch of the autonomic nervous system arouses the body and speeds up its vital processes. It tends to act in a nonspecific fashion, activating many organs at the same time. The parasympathetic division, which is more specific in its opposing actions, slows down body processes. The two divisions work in concert to maintain an equilibrium within the body.

The **sympathetic nervous system** *has an activation or arousal function, and it tends to act as a total unit.* For example, when you encounter a stressful situation, your sympathetic nervous system helps you confront the stressor in several ways. It speeds up your heart rate so that it can pump more blood to your muscles, dilates your pupils so that more light can enter your eyes and improve your vision, slows down your digestive system so that blood can be transferred to the muscles, increases your rate of respiration so that your body can get more oxygen, and, in general, mobilizes your body. This is sometimes called the *fight-or-flight response.*

Compared with the sympathetic branch, which tends to act as a unit, the **parasympathetic nervous system** *is far more specific in its opposing actions, affecting one or a few organs at a time. In general, it slows down body processes and maintains a state of tranquility.* Thus, your sympathetic system speeds up your heart rate; your parasympathetic system slows it down. By working together to maintain equilibrium in your internal organs, the two divisions can maintain **homeostasis,** *a delicately balanced or constant internal state.* In addition, sympathetic and parasympathetic activities sometimes coordinate to enable us to perform certain behaviors. For example, sexual function in the male involves penile erection (through

parasympathetic dilation of blood vessels) followed by ejaculation (a primarily sympathetic function; Masters et al., 1988).

The Central Nervous System

More than any other system in our body, the central nervous system distinguishes us from other creatures. This **central nervous system** *contains the brain and the spinal cord, which connects most parts of the peripheral nervous system with the brain.*

The Spinal Cord

Most nerves enter and leave the central nervous system by way of the spinal cord, a structure that is 16 to 18 inches long and about 1 inch in diameter in a human adult. The vertebrae (bones of the spine) protect the spinal cord's neurons. When the spinal cord is viewed in cross section (Figure 4.8), its central portion resembles an H or a butterfly. The H-shaped portion consists largely of gray-colored neuron cell bodies and their interconnections. Surrounding the gray matter are white-colored myelinated axons that connect various levels of the spinal cord with each other and with the higher centers of the brain. Entering the back side of the spinal cord along its length are sensory nerves. Motor nerves exit the spinal cord's front side.

Some simple stimulus-response sequences, known as *spinal reflexes,* can be triggered at the level of the spinal cord without any involvement of the brain. For example, if you touch something hot, sensory receptors in your skin trigger nerve impulses in sensory nerves that flash into your spinal cord and synapse inside with interneurons. The interneurons then excite motor neurons that send impulses to your hand, so that it pulls away (see Figure 4.8). Other interneurons simultaneously carry the "Hot!" message up the spinal cord to your brain. But it is a good thing that you don't have to wait for the brain to tell you what to do in such emergencies. Getting messages to and from the brain takes slightly longer, so the spinal cord reflex system significantly reduces reaction time and, in this case, potential tissue damage.

The Brain

The three pounds of protein, fat, and fluid that you carry around inside your skull is the real you. It is also the most complex structure in the known universe. Neuroscientists estimate that this three-pound powerhouse contains about 3 million miles of neural connections (Conlan, 1999). If lined up to form a neural trail, it would take you 5.7 years to drive an auto at 60 mph, 24 hours a day, from one end to the other.

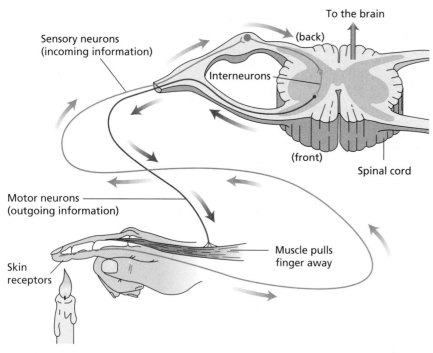

Figure 4.8

A cross section of the spinal cord.
Sensory and motor nerves enter and exit the spinal cord on both sides of the spinal column. Interneurons within the H-shaped spinal gray matter can serve a connective function, as shown here, but in many cases, sensory neurons can also synapse directly with motor neurons. At this level of the nervous system, reflex activity is possible without involving the brain.

As befits this biological marvel, your brain is the most active energy consumer of all your body organs. Although your brain accounts for only about 2 percent of your total body weight, it consumes about 25 percent of your body's oxygen and 70 percent of its glucose. Moreover, the brain never rests; its rate of energy metabolism is relatively constant day and night. In fact, when you dream, the brain's metabolic rate actually increases slightly (Simon, 2007).

How can this rather nondescript blob of grayish tissue discover the principle of relativity, build the Hubble Space Telescope, and produce great works of art, music, and literature? Answering such questions requires the ability to study the brain and how it functions. To do so, neuroscientists use a diverse set of tools and procedures.

Unlocking the Secrets of the Brain

Because of scientific and technical advances, more has been learned about the brain in the past four decades than was known throughout all the preceding ages. Neuroscientists use four different methods to study the brain's structures and activities.

Neuropsychological Tests Psychologists have developed a variety of *neuropsychological tests* to measure verbal and nonverbal behaviors of people who may have suffered brain damage through accident or disease (Strauss et al., 2006). They are also important research tools. For example, Figure 4.9 shows a portion of a Trail Making Test, used to test memory and planning. Scores on the test give an indication of a person's type and severity of brain damage. Neuropsychological tests of this kind have provided much information about brain-behavior relations. They also are used to assess learning disabilities and developmental disorders.

Destruction and Stimulation Techniques Experimental studies are another useful method of learning about the brain (Tatlisumak & Fisher, 2006). Researchers can produce brain damage (lesions) in which specific nervous tissue is destroyed with electricity, with cold or heat, or with chemicals. They also can surgically remove some portion of the brain and study the consequences. Most experiments of this kind are performed on animals, but humans also can be studied when accident or disease produces a specific lesion or when abnormal brain tissue must be surgically removed.

An alternative to destroying neurons is chemically or electrically stimulating them, which typically produces effects opposite to destruction. In chemical stimulation, a tiny tube, or *cannula*, is

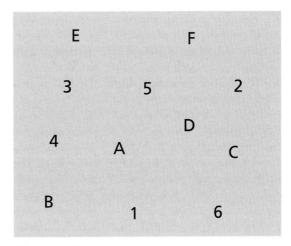

Figure 4.9

The Trail Making Test.
The Trail Making Test is used by psychologists to assess brain functioning. It consists of a randomly scattered set of numbers and letters. On this timed test, the patient must connect the numbers and letters consecutively with a continuous line, or "trail" (i.e., A to 1 to B to 2 to C to 3 and so on). People with certain kinds of brain damage have trouble alternating between the numbers and letters because they cannot retain a plan in memory long enough.

inserted into a precise area of the brain so that chemicals, including neurotransmitters, can be delivered directly and their effects on behavior studied. A specific region of the brain can also be stimulated by a mild electric current. Electrodes can be permanently implanted so that the region of interest can be stimulated repeatedly. Some electrodes are so tiny that they can stimulate individual neurons.

In one electrical-stimulation study, placement of electrodes on a specific region of the brain's outer surface above the right ear produced a surprising effect. The woman experienced herself as floating in the air above her body (Blanke et al., 2002). Neuroscientists wonder if the researchers may have accidentally discovered a neural basis for "near death" and other so-called paranormal out-of-body experiences that have been reported by many people.

Electrical Recording Because electrodes can record brain activity as well as stimulate it, scientists can eavesdrop on the electrical "conversations" occurring within the brain. Neurons' electrical activity can be measured by inserting small electrodes in particular areas of the brain, and some recording electrodes are so tiny that they can be inserted into individual neurons.

In addition to measuring individual "voices," scientists can tune in to "crowd noise." The **electroencephalograph (EEG)** *measures the activity of large groups of neurons through a series of large electrodes placed on the scalp* (Figure 4.10a, b). Although the EEG is a rather nonspecific measure that taps the electrical activity of thousands of neurons in many parts of the brain, specific EEG patterns correspond to certain states of consciousness, such as wakefulness and sleep. Clinicians also use the EEG to detect abnormal electrical patterns that signal the presence of brain pathology.

Brain Imaging   The newest tools of discovery are imaging techniques that permit neuroscientists to peer into the living brain (Figure 4.10c–g). The most important of these are *CT scans, PET scans, MRIs,* and *fMRIs.* CT scans and MRIs are used to visualize brain structure, whereas PET scans and fMRIs allow scientists to view brain activity (Bremner, 2005).

Developed in the 1970s, **computerized axial tomography (CT, or CAT) scans** *use X-ray technology to study brain structures.* A highly focused beam of X-rays takes pictures of narrow slices of the brain. A computer analyzes the X-rayed slices and creates pictures of the brain's interior from many different angles (Figure 4.10d). Pinpointing where deterioration or injuries have occurred helps clarify relations between brain damage and psychological functioning. CT scans are 100 times more sensitive than standard X-ray procedures, and the technological advance was so dramatic that its developers, Allan Cormack and Godfrey Hounsfield, were awarded the 1979 Nobel Prize for Medicine.

Magnetic resonance imaging (MRI) *creates images based on how atoms in living tissue respond to a magnetic pulse delivered by the device.* When the magnetic field is shut off, the magnetic energy absorbed by the atoms in the tissue emits a small electrical voltage that is relayed to a computer for analysis. MRI provides color images of the tissue and can make out details one tenth the size of those detected by CT scans (Figure 4.10e).

Whereas CT scans and MRIs provide pictures of brain structures, **positron-emission tomography (PET) scans** *measure brain activity, including metabolism, blood flow, and neurotransmitter activity.* Glucose, a natural sugar, is the major nutrient of neurons, so when neurons are active, they consume more glucose. To prepare a patient for a PET scan, a radioactive (but harmless) form of glucose is injected into the bloodstream and travels to the brain, where it circulates in the blood supply. The PET scan measures the energy emitted by the radioactive substance, and the data, fed into a computer, produce a color picture of the brain on a display screen (Figure 4.10g). If the patient is performing a reasoning task, for example, a researcher can tell by the colored glucose-concentration pattern which parts of the brain are most heavily activated.

The conventional MRI yields pictures taken several minutes apart. An important advance in MRI technology is **functional MRI (fMRI),** *which can produce pictures of blood flow in the brain taken within seconds of one another.* Active brain tissue uses more oxygen; thus, scanning the oxygen concentration of blood in the brain provides a vivid picture of brain activity without the need to inject a radioactive substance into the brain (Huettel et al., 2005). Researchers can now, quite literally, watch real-time presentations as different regions of the brain light up when participants perform various tasks (Figure 4.10f).

Advances in brain research represent an important frontier of psychology. Driven by its intense desire to "know thyself," the brain is beginning to yield its many secrets. Yet many important questions remain. This should not surprise us, for as one observer noted, "If the brain were so simple that we could understand it, we would be so simple that we couldn't" (Pugh, 1977).

test yourself   The Nervous System

True or False?

1. The nervous system carries out its functions with three types of neurons: sensory, motor, and interneurons.
2. The parasympathetic nervous system slows down the activities of internal organs and glands, and it acts as a unit, affecting many organs at once.
3. When a physician taps a patient's kneecap with a hammer, she is testing a spinal reflex.
4. The EEG is used to measure the electrical activity of a few neurons.
5. Researchers use fMRI to measure the activity of a brain region as it occurs in real time.

ANSWERS: 1-true, 2-false, 3-true, 4-false, 5-true

(a)

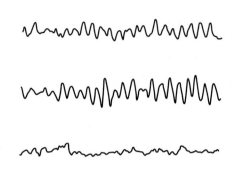

(b)

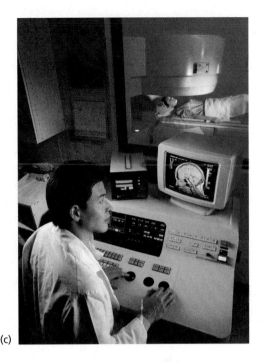

(c)

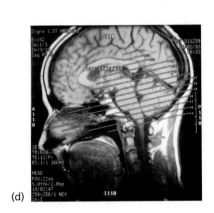

(d)

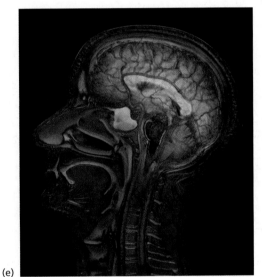

(e)

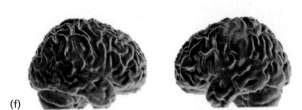

(f)

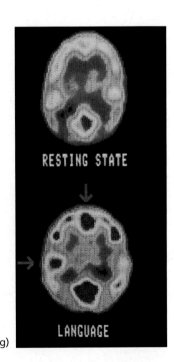

(g)

Figure 4.10

Measuring brain activity.

The electroencephalograph (EEG), shown in (a), permits the electrical recording of the activity of large groups of neurons in the brain through a series of electrodes attached to the scalp. An EEG readout is shown in (b). Various brain scanning machines, such as the one shown in (c), produce a number of different images. (d) The CT scan uses narrow beams of X-rays to construct a composite picture of brain structures. (e) MRI scanners produce vivid pictures of brain structures. (f) Functional MRI (fMRI) procedures take images in rapid succession, showing neural activity as it occurs. (g) PET scans assess brain activity by recording the amount of radioactive substance that collects in various brain regions.

THE HIERARCHICAL BRAIN: STRUCTURES AND BEHAVIORAL FUNCTIONS

In an evolutionary sense, your brain is far older than you are, for it represents perhaps 500 million years of evolutionary development and fine-tuning. The human brain is like a living archaeological site, with the more recently developed structures built atop structures from the distant evolutionary past (Striedter, 2005). The structures at the brain's core, which we share with all other vertebrates, govern the basic physiological functions that keep us alive, such as breathing and heart rate. Built upon these basic structures are newer systems that involve progressively more complex functions—sensing,

emoting, wanting, thinking, reasoning (Brogdal, 2010). Evolutionary theorists believe that as genetic variation sculpted these newer structures over time, natural selection favored their retention, because animals who had them were more likely to survive in changing environments. The crowning feature of brain development is the *cerebral cortex*, the biological seat of Einstein's scientific genius, Mozart's creativity, Osama bin Laden's brutality, and Mother Teresa's compassion; it is what makes you a unique human being.

The major structures of the human brain, together with their psychological functions, are shown in Figure 4.11. The brain has traditionally been viewed as having three major subdivisions: the hindbrain; the midbrain, which lies above the hindbrain; and the forebrain.

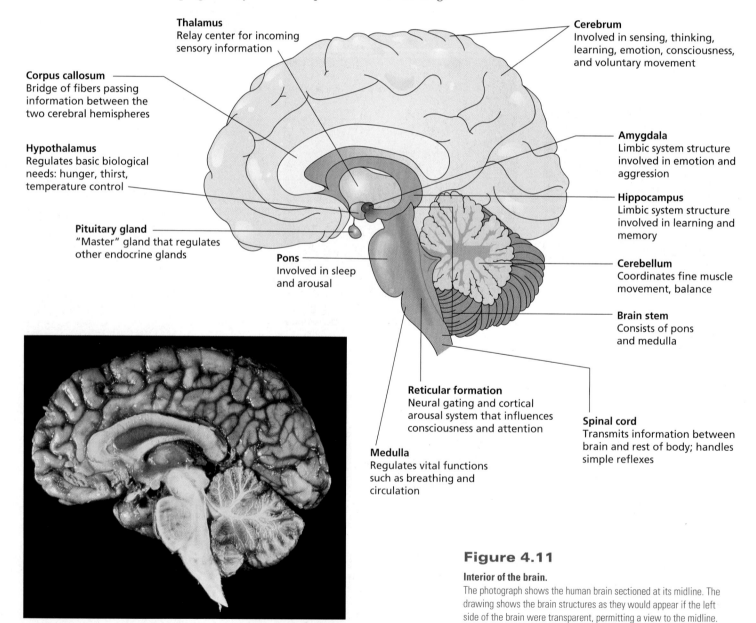

Thalamus
Relay center for incoming sensory information

Corpus callosum
Bridge of fibers passing information between the two cerebral hemispheres

Hypothalamus
Regulates basic biological needs: hunger, thirst, temperature control

Pituitary gland
"Master" gland that regulates other endocrine glands

Pons
Involved in sleep and arousal

Medulla
Regulates vital functions such as breathing and circulation

Reticular formation
Neural gating and cortical arousal system that influences consciousness and attention

Cerebrum
Involved in sensing, thinking, learning, emotion, consciousness, and voluntary movement

Amygdala
Limbic system structure involved in emotion and aggression

Hippocampus
Limbic system structure involved in learning and memory

Cerebellum
Coordinates fine muscle movement, balance

Brain stem
Consists of pons and medulla

Spinal cord
Transmits information between brain and rest of body; handles simple reflexes

Figure 4.11

Interior of the brain.
The photograph shows the human brain sectioned at its midline. The drawing shows the brain structures as they would appear if the left side of the brain were transparent, permitting a view to the midline.

The Hindbrain

The **hindbrain** *is the lowest and most primitive level of the brain.* As the spinal cord enters the brain, it enlarges to form the structures that compose the stalk-like brain stem. Attached to the brain stem is the other major portion of the hindbrain, the *cerebellum.*

The Brain Stem: Life-Support Systems

The structures of the **brain stem** *support vital life functions.* Included are the *medulla* and the *pons.* The 1.5-inch-long medulla is the first structure above the spinal cord. Well developed at birth, the **medulla** *plays an important role in vital body functions such as heart rate and respiration.* Because of your medulla, these functions occur automatically. Damage to the medulla usually results in death or, at best, the need to be maintained on life-support systems. Suppression of medulla activity can occur at high levels of alcohol intoxication, resulting in death by heart or respiratory failure (Blessing, 1997).

The medulla is also a two-way thoroughfare for all the sensory and motor nerve tracts coming up from the spinal cord and descending from the brain. Most of these tracts cross over within the medulla, so the left side of the brain receives sensory input from and exerts motor control over the right side of the body, and the right side of the brain serves the left side of the body. Why this crossover occurs is one of the unsolved mysteries of brain function.

The **pons** (meaning "bridge" in Latin) *lies just above the medulla and carries nerve impulses between higher and lower levels of the nervous system.* The pons also has clusters of neurons that help regulate sleep. Like the medulla, the pons helps control vital functions, especially respiration, and damage to it can produce death.

The Cerebellum: Motor-Coordination Center

Attached to the rear of the brain stem, the cerebellum ("little brain" in Latin) does indeed look like a miniature brain. Its wrinkled *cortex,* or covering, consists mainly of gray cell bodies (gray matter). The **cerebellum** *is concerned primarily with muscular movement coordination, but it also plays a role in learning and memory.*

Specific motor movements are initiated in higher brain centers, but their timing and coordination depend on the cerebellum (De Zeeuw & Cicirata, 2005). The cerebellum regulates complex, rapidly changing movements that require precise timing, such as those of a ballet dancer or a competitive diver. Within the animal kingdom, cats have an especially well-developed cerebellum,

Figure 4.12

The cerebellum's movement-control functions are easily disrupted by alcohol, providing the neural basis for the sobriety tests administered by police.

helping to account for their ability to move gracefully (Altman & Bayer, 1996).

The motor-control functions of the cerebellum are easily disrupted by alcohol, producing the coordination difficulties that police look for in roadside sobriety tests. Intoxicated people may be unable to walk a straight line or touch their noses with their index fingers (Figure 4.12). Physical damage to the cerebellum results in severe motor disturbances characterized by jerky, uncoordinated movements, as well as an inability to perform habitual movements such as walking.

The Midbrain

Lying just above the hindbrain, the **midbrain** *contains clusters of sensory and motor neurons.* The sensory portion of the midbrain contains important relay centers for the visual and auditory systems. Here, nerve impulses from the eyes and ears are organized and sent to forebrain structures involved in visual and auditory perception. The midbrain also contains motor neurons that control eye movements.

The Reticular Formation: The Brain's Gatekeeper

Buried within the midbrain is a finger-shaped structure that extends from the hindbrain up into the lower portions of the forebrain. This structure receives its name from its resemblance under a microscope to a *reticulum,* or net. The **reticular formation** *acts as a kind of sentry, both alerting higher centers of the brain that messages are coming and then either blocking those messages or allowing them to go forward.* The reticular formation has an *ascending* part, which sends input to higher regions of the brain to alert it, and a *descending* portion, through which higher brain centers can either admit or block out sensory input.

The reticular formation plays a central role in consciousness, sleep, and attention. Without reticular stimulation of higher brain regions, sensory messages do not register in conscious awareness even though the nerve impulses may reach the appropriate higher areas of the brain. It is as if the brain is not awake enough to notice them. In fact, some general anesthetics work by deactivating neurons of the ascending reticular formation so that sensory impulses that ordinarily would be experienced as pain never register in the sensory areas of the brain (Simon, 2007).

The reticular formation also affects sleep and wakefulness. In a classic series of experiments in the late 1940s, researchers discovered that electrical stimulation of different portions of the reticular formation can produce instant sleep in a wakeful cat and sudden wakefulness in a sleeping animal (Marshall & Magoun, 1997). Severe damage to the reticular formation can produce a permanent coma (Pendlebury, 2007).

Attention is an active process during which only important or meaningful sensory inputs get through to our consciousness. Other inputs have to be toned down or completely blocked out or we'd be overwhelmed by stimulation. The descending reticular formation plays an important part in this process, serving as a kind of gate through which some inputs are admitted while others are blocked out by signals coming down from higher brain centers (Van Zomeren & Brouwer, 1994).

The Forebrain

The **forebrain** *is the brain's most advanced portion from an evolutionary standpoint.* Its major structure, the **cerebrum,** *consists of two large hemispheres, a left side and a right side,* that wrap around the brain stem as the two halves of a cut grapefruit might wrap around a large spoon. The outer portion of the forebrain has a thin covering, or cortex. Within are a number of important structures buried in the central regions of the hemispheres.

The Thalamus: The Brain's Sensory Switchboard

The *thalamus* is located above the midbrain. It resembles two small footballs, one within each cerebral hemisphere. The **thalamus** *has sometimes been likened to a switchboard that organizes inputs from sensory organs and routes them to the appropriate areas of the brain.* The visual, auditory, and body

senses (balance and equilibrium) all have major relay stations in the thalamus (Jones, 2006).

Because the thalamus plays such a key role in routing sensory information to higher brain regions, individuals with disrupted functioning in the thalamus often experience a highly confusing world. In research at the National Institute of Mental Health (NIMH) carried out by Nancy Andreason and her coworkers (1994), MRIs from 39 schizophrenic men were compared with those of 47 normal male volunteers. The brain images showed specific abnormalities in the thalamus of the schizophrenic brains, suggesting that the thalamus may have been sending garbled sensory information to the higher regions of the brain and creating the confusing sensory experiences and hallucinations reported by many patients.

The Hypothalamus: Motivation and Emotion

The *hypothalamus* (literally, "under the thalamus") consists of tiny groups of neuron cell bodies that lie at the base of the brain, above the roof of the mouth. The **hypothalamus** *plays a major role in many aspects of motivation and emotion, including sexual behavior, temperature regulation, sleeping, eating, drinking, and aggression.* Damage to the hypothalamus can disrupt all of these behaviors (Toy, 2007). For example, destruction of one area of a male's hypothalamus results in a complete loss of sex drive; damage to another portion produces an overwhelming urge to eat that results in extreme obesity (Morrison, 2006).

The hypothalamus has important connections with the *endocrine system,* the body's collection of hormone-producing glands (discussed later in this chapter). Through its connection with the nearby *pituitary gland* (the master gland that exerts control over the other glands of the endocrine system), the hypothalamus directly controls many hormonal secretions that regulate sexual development and sexual behavior, metabolism, and reactions to stress.

The hypothalamus is also involved in our experiences of pleasure and displeasure. The discovery of this fact occurred quite by accident. In 1953, psychologist James Olds was conducting an experiment to study the effects of electrical stimulation in a rat's midbrain reticular formation. One of the electrodes missed the target and was mistakenly implanted in the hypothalamus. Olds noticed that whenever this rat was stimulated, it repeated whatever it had just done, as if it had been rewarded for that behavior. Olds then implanted electrodes in the hypothalamus of other animals and exposed them to a variety of learning situations. He found that they also learned and performed behaviors

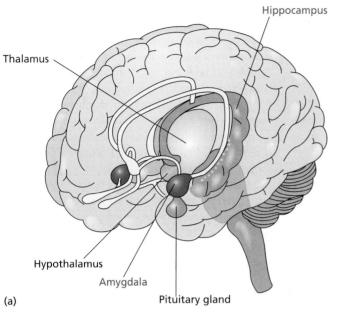

Thalamus

Hippocampus

Hypothalamus

Amygdala

Pituitary gland

(a)

(b)

Figure 4.13

Limbic system structures.

(a) The amygdala and hippocampus are major structures of the limbic system (indicated by red type). The hippocampus is important in the establishment of memories. (b) Electrical stimulation of the amygdala, which organizes emotional responses, can evoke an immediate aggressive response.

in order to receive what was clearly an electrical reward. In fact, some of the rats pressed a pedal up to 5,000 times in an hour until they dropped from exhaustion. Stimulation of other nearby areas produced just the opposite effect—a tendency to stop performing any behavior that was followed by stimulation, as if the animal had been punished. Olds and other researchers who replicated his work concluded that they had discovered what they called "reward and punishment areas" in the brain, some of which were in the hypothalamus. Later research revealed that the "reward" areas are rich in neurons that release dopamine, which seems to be an important chemical mediator of pleasure (Kolb & Whishaw, 2005).

Humans who have had electrodes implanted in their brains to search for abnormal brain tissue have reported experiencing pleasure when these reward regions were electrically stimulated. One patient reportedly proposed marriage to the experimenter while being so stimulated (Heath, 1972). Thus, a misplaced electrode in James Olds's laboratory led to a discovery that neural events occurring in the hypothalamus and adjacent areas have important roles in motivation.

The Limbic System: Memory, Emotion, and Goal-Directed Behavior

As we continue our journey up through the brain, we come to the *limbic system*, a set of structures lying deep within the cerebral hemispheres

(Figure 4.13). The **limbic system** *helps coordinate behaviors needed to satisfy motivational and emotional urges that arise in the hypothalamus. It also is involved in memory.*

Two key structures in the limbic system are the *hippocampus* and the *amygdala*. The **hippocampus** *is involved in forming and retrieving memories.* Damage there can result in severe memory impairment for recent events (Isaacson, 2002). The **amygdala** (from the Greek word for "almond") *organizes motivational and emotional response patterns, particularly those linked to aggression and fear* (LeDoux, 1998). Electrically stimulating certain areas of the amygdala causes animals to snarl and assume aggressive postures (see Figure 4.13b), whereas stimulation of other areas results in a fearful inability to respond aggressively, even in self-defense. For example, a normally aggressive and hungry cat will cower in fear from a tiny mouse placed in its cage. The amygdala can also produce emotional responses without the higher centers of the brain "knowing" that we are emotionally aroused, providing a possible explanation for unconscious emotional responses (LeDoux, 1998).

The amygdala is a key part of a larger control system for anger and fear that also involves other brain regions (Siegel, 2005). It has important interconnections with the hippocampus, and amygdala stimulation is important in the hippocampus's creation of emotional memories. Without amygdala activity, emotional memories are not well established. One patient whose amygdala was removed could not recall emotional scenes from movies seen a day earlier, although he was able to remember the nonemotional scenes.

Finally, like the hypothalamus, the limbic system contains reward and punishment areas that have important motivational functions. Certain drugs, such as cocaine and marijuana, seem to induce pleasure by stimulating limbic reward areas that use dopamine as their neurotransmitter (LeMoal, 1999).

The Cerebral Cortex: Crown of the Brain

The **cerebral cortex,** *a 1/4-inch-thick sheet of gray (unmyelinated) cells that form the outermost layer of the human brain,* is the crowning achievement of brain evolution. Fish and amphibians have no cerebral cortex, and the progression from more primitive to more advanced mammals is marked by a dramatic increase in the proportion of cortical tissue. In humans, the cortex constitutes fully 80 percent of brain tissue (Simon, 2007).

The cerebral cortex is not essential for physical survival in the way that the brain stem structures are, but it is essential for human functioning. How much so is evident in this description of patients who, as a result of an accident during prenatal development, were born without a cerebral cortex:

> Some of these individuals may survive for years, in one case of mine for twenty years. From these cases, it appears that the human [lacking a cortex] sleeps and wakes; . . . reacts to hunger, loud sounds, and crude visual stimuli by movement of eyes, eyelids, and facial muscles; . . . may see and hear, . . . may be able to taste and smell, to reject the unpalatable and accept such food as it likes. . . . [They can] utter crude sounds, can cry and smile, showing displeasure when hungry and pleasure, in a babyish way, when being sung to; [they] may be able to perform spontaneously crude [limb] movements. (Cairns, 1952, p. 109)

Because the cortex is wrinkled and convoluted, like a wadded-up piece of paper, a great amount of cortical tissue is compressed into a relatively small space inside the skull. If we could remove the cortex and smooth it out, the tissue would cover an area roughly the size of a pillowcase. Perhaps 75 percent of the cortex's total surface area lies within its *fissures,* or canyonlike folds. Three of these fissures are important landmarks. One large fissure runs lengthwise across the top of the brain, dividing it into a right and a left hemisphere. Within each hemisphere, a *central fissure* divides the cerebrum into front and

rear halves, and a third fissure runs from front to rear along the side of the brain. On the basis of these landmarks, neurologists have divided each hemisphere into four lobes: *frontal, parietal, occipital,* and *temporal.* A fist made with your right hand (with the side of your thumb facing you) can serve as a rough orientation to these lobes. The bend in your fingers represents the frontal lobe, your knuckles the parietal lobe, your wrist area the occipital lobe, and your thumb the temporal lobe of the left hemisphere.

As shown in Figure 4.14, each of the cerebral lobes is associated with particular sensory and motor functions, as well as with speech understanding and speech production (Biller et al., 2006). The large areas in Figure 4.14 that are not associated with sensory or motor functions (about three fourths of the cortex) make up the *association cortex,* involved in mental processes such as thought, memory, and perception. (We will discuss the association cortex in more detail shortly.)

The Motor Cortex   The **motor cortex** *controls the 600 or more muscles involved in voluntary body movements.* If all of these muscles were activated at once, they would generate enough power to lift 11 tons (Daniels et al., 2007).

The motor cortex lies at the rear of the frontal lobes adjacent to the central fissure. Because the nerve tracts from the motor cortex cross over at the level of the medulla, each hemisphere governs movement on the opposite side of the body. Thus, severe damage to the right motor cortex would produce paralysis in the left side of the body. The left side of Figure 4.15 shows the relative organization of function within the motor cortex. As you can see, specific body areas are represented in upside-down fashion within the motor cortex, and the amount of cortex devoted to each area depends on the complexity of the movements that are carried out by the body part. For example, the amount of cortical tissue devoted to your fingers is far greater than that devoted to your torso, even though your torso is much larger. If we electrically stimulate a particular point on the motor cortex, movements occur in the muscles governed by that part of the cortex.

The Sensory Cortex   Specific areas of the cortex receive input from our sensory receptors. With the exception of taste and smell, at least one specific area in the cortex has been identified for each of the senses.

The **somatic sensory cortex** *receives sensory input that gives rise to our sensations of heat, touch, and cold and to our senses of balance and body movement (kinesthesis).* It lies at the front portion of the

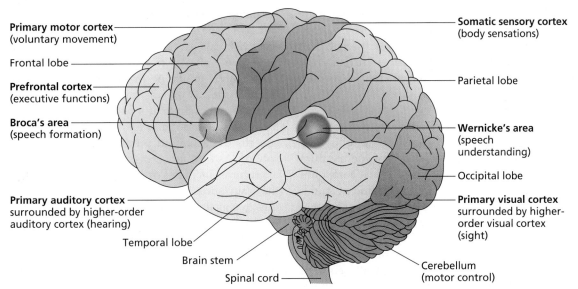

Primary motor cortex
(voluntary movement)

Frontal lobe

Prefrontal cortex
(executive functions)

Broca's area
(speech formation)

Primary auditory cortex
surrounded by higher-order
auditory cortex (hearing)

Temporal lobe

Brain stem

Spinal cord

Somatic sensory cortex
(body sensations)

Parietal lobe

Wernicke's area
(speech
understanding)

Occipital lobe

Primary visual cortex
surrounded by higher-
order visual cortex
(sight)

Cerebellum
(motor control)

Figure 4.14

Lobes of the brain.
Division of the brain into frontal
(blue), parietal (green), occipital
(purple), and temporal (yellow) lobes.
This figure shows localization of
sensory, motor, and some important
language functions in the cortex. The
remainder is primarily association
cortex, consisting of interneurons
of complex psychological functions,
such as perception and reasoning.

Figure 4.15

Cortical organization.
Both the somatic sensory and the
motor cortex are highly specialized
so that every site is associated with
a particular part of the body. The
amount of cortex devoted to each
body part is proportional to the
sensitivity of that area's motor or
sensory functions. Both the sensory
and motor cortex are arranged in an
upside-down fashion and serve the
opposite side of the body. SOURCE:
Adapted from Penfield/Rasmussen. *The
Cerebral Cortex of Man.* © 1950 Gale, a
part of Cengage Learning, Inc. Reproduced
by permission. www.cengage.com/
permissions.

parietal lobe just behind the motor cortex, separated from it by the central fissure. As in the case of the motor system, each side of the body sends sensory input to the opposite hemisphere. Like the motor area next to it, the somatic sensory area is basically organized in an upside-down fashion, with the feet being represented near the top of the brain. Likewise, the amount of cortex devoted to each body area is directly proportional to that region's sensory sensitivity. The organization of the sensory cortex is shown on the right side of Figure 4.15, as is the proportion of cortex devoted

to each body area. As far as your sensory cortex is concerned, you are mainly fingers, lips, and tongue. Notice also that the organization of the sensory cortex is such that the body structures it serves lie side by side with those in the motor cortex, an arrangement that enhances sensory-motor interactions in the same body area.

The senses of hearing and sight are well represented in the cortex. As shown in Figure 4.14, the auditory area lies on the surface of the temporal lobe at the side of each hemisphere. Each ear sends messages to the auditory areas of both

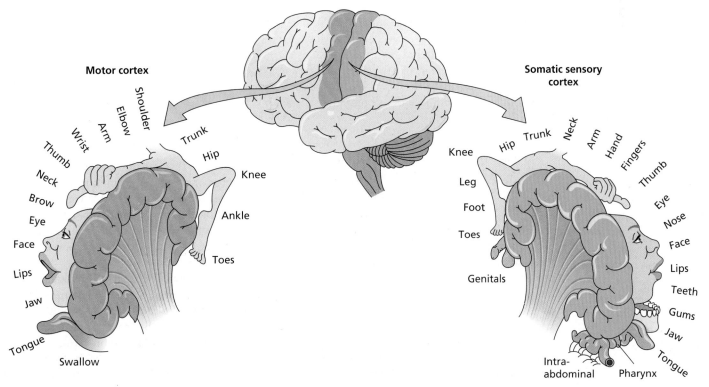

Motor cortex

Shoulder
Elbow
Arm
Wrist
Thumb
Neck
Brow
Eye
Face
Lips
Jaw
Tongue
Swallow
Trunk
Hip
Knee
Ankle
Toes

Somatic sensory
cortex

Neck
Arm
Hand
Fingers
Thumb
Eye
Nose
Face
Lips
Teeth
Gums
Jaw
Tongue
Pharynx
Intra-
abdominal
Genitals
Toes
Foot
Leg
Knee
Hip
Trunk

hemispheres, so the loss of one temporal lobe has little effect on hearing. The primary sensory area for vision lies at the rear of the occipital lobe. Here, messages from the eyes are analyzed, integrated, and translated into sight. As in the auditory system, each eye sends input to both hemispheres.

Within each sensory area, neurons respond to particular aspects of the sensory stimulus; they are tuned in to specific aspects of the environment. Thus, certain cells in the visual cortex fire only when we look at a particular kind of stimulus, such as a vertical line or a corner (Hubel & Wiesel, 1979). In the auditory cortex, some neurons fire only in response to high tones, whereas others respond only to tones having other specific frequencies. Many of these neuronal responses are present at birth, suggesting that we are prewired to perceive many aspects of our sensory environment (Noback et al., 2005). Nonetheless, the sensory cortex, like other parts of the brain, is also sensitive to experience. For example, when people learn to read Braille, the area in the sensory cortex that receives input from the fingertips increases in size, making the person more sensitive to the tiny sets of raised dots (Pool, 1994).

Speech Comprehension and Production   Two specific areas that govern the understanding and production of speech are also located in different lobes of the left hemisphere (see Figure 4.14). **Wernicke's area,** *in the temporal lobe, is primarily involved in speech comprehension.* Damage to this cortical region leaves patients unable to understand written or spoken speech. Scott Moss, a psychologist who suffered temporary aphasia from a left-hemisphere stroke (blockage or bursting of blood vessels in the brain that results in death of neurons from lack of oxygen), described his experience:

> I recollect trying to read the headlines of the Chicago Tribune but they didn't make any sense to me at all. I didn't have any difficulty focusing; it was simply that the words, individually or in combination, didn't have meaning. (Moss, 1972, p. 4)

Broca's area, *in the frontal lobe, is mainly involved in the production of speech through its connections with the motor cortex region that controls the muscles used in speech.* Damage to this area leaves patients with the ability to comprehend speech but not to express themselves in words or sentences. These two speech areas normally work in concert when you are conversing with another person. They allow you to comprehend what the other person is saying and to express your own thoughts.

Association Cortex   The **association cortex** *is involved in many important mental functions, including perception, language, and thought.* These areas are sometimes referred to as "silent areas" because electrically stimulating them does not give rise to either sensory experiences or motor responses. Damage to specific parts of the association cortex causes disruption or loss of functions such as speech, understanding, thinking, and problem solving. As we might expect, the amount of association cortex increases dramatically as we move up the brain ladder from lower animals to human beings. It constitutes about 75 percent of the human cerebral cortex and accounts for people's superior cognitive abilities. One scientist has described our mass of association cortex as "evolution's missing link" (Skoyles, 1997). He suggests that its flexibility and learning capacity have allowed us to acquire new mental skills specific to our human way of life, such as reading and mathematics, far more quickly than could have occurred through natural selection alone.

The importance of the association cortex is demonstrated in people who suffer from *agnosia,* the inability to identify familiar objects. One such case is described by the neurologist Oliver Sacks (1985, p. 123):

> Dr. P. [one of Sacks's patients] was a talented and accomplished musician whose behavior was quite normal except for one glaring exception: Although his vision was perfect, he often had difficulty recognizing familiar people and objects. Thus, he would chat with pieces of furniture and wonder why they did not reply, or pat the tops of fire hydrants, thinking they were children. One day, while visiting Sacks's office for an examination, Dr. P. looked for his hat as he was ready to depart. He suddenly reached out and grabbed his wife's head, trying to lift it. He had mistaken his wife for his hat! His wife smiled tolerantly; she had become accustomed to such actions on his part.

Dr. P. had suffered brain damage that left him unable to connect the information sent to the visual cortex with information stored in other cortical areas that concerned the nature of objects. The associative neurons responsible for linking the two types of information no longer served him.

The Frontal Lobes: The Human Difference   Some neuroscientists suggest that the entire period of human evolutionary existence could well be termed the "age of the frontal lobe" (Krasnegor et al., 1997). This brain region hardly exists in mammals such as mice and rats. The frontal lobes compose about 3.5 percent of the cerebral cortex in the cat, 7 percent in the dog, and 17 percent in the chimpanzee. In a human, the frontal lobes constitute 29 percent of the cortex. The frontal lobes—the site of such human qualities as self-awareness, planning, initiative, and responsibility—are in some respects the most mysterious and least understood part of the brain.

Much of what we know about the frontal lobes comes from detailed studies of patients who have experienced brain damage. Frontal-lobe damage results not so much in a loss of intellectual abilities as in an inability to plan and carry out a sequence of actions, even when patients can verbalize what they should do. This can result in an inability to correct actions that are clearly erroneous and self-defeating (Shallice & Burgess, 1991).

The frontal cortex is also involved in emotional experience. In people with normal brains, PET scans show increased activity in the frontal cortex when people are experiencing feelings of happiness, sadness, or disgust (Lane et al., 1997). In contrast, patients with frontal-lobe damage often exhibit attitudes of apathy and lack of concern. They simply don't seem to care about anything. Consider the following episode reported by a neurologist who was testing a patient with frontal-lobe damage:

> Testing left-right discrimination was oddly difficult, because she said left or right indifferently. When I drew her attention to this, she said, "Left/right. Right/left. Why the fuss? What's the difference?"
>
> "Is there a difference?" I asked.
>
> "Of course," she said with a chemist's precision. . . . "But they mean nothing to me. They're no different *for me*. Hands . . . Doctors . . . Sisters," she added, seeing my puzzlement. "Don't you understand? They mean nothing—nothing to me. *Nothing means anything*, at least to me."
>
> Mrs. B, though acute and intelligent, was somehow not present—"desouled"—as a person. (Sacks, 1985, p. 174)

A region of the frontal lobe has received increasing attention in recent years. The **prefrontal cortex,** *located just behind the forehead, is the seat of the so-called executive functions.* Executive functions are mental abilities—such as goal setting, judgment, strategic planning, and impulse control—that allow people to direct their behavior in an adaptive fashion. Deficits in executive functions seem to underlie a number of problem behaviors. People with prefrontal-cortex disorders seem oblivious to the future consequences of their actions and seem to be governed only by immediate consequences (Zald & Rauch, 2006). As you may have guessed by now, Phineas Gage, the railroad foreman described in our chapter-opening case, suffered massive prefrontal damage when the spike tore through his brain (see Figure 4.1). Thereafter he exhibited classic symptoms of disturbed executive functions, becoming behaviorally impulsive and losing his capacity for future planning.

A more ominous manifestation of prefrontal dysfunction—the capacity to kill—was discovered by researchers using PET-scan technology. Jacqueline Stoddard and colleagues (1997) studied 41 people who had committed impulsive homicides, or manslaughter. Compared to nonviolent controls, the violent people showed low prefrontal activation while working on a task that requires frontal-lobe planning and behavioral inhibition. Later studies of impulsively violent individuals suggested disordered prefrontal control of limbic system areas that organize aggressive behavior (Steuber et al., 2006).

test yourself   The Hierarchical Brain

Match each numbered brain structure with its function on the right.

1. thalamus
2. cerebral cortex
3. reticular formation
4. hypothalamus
5. hippocampus
6. cerebellum
7. prefrontal cortex

a. regulates basic biological needs and emotional reactions
b. alerts and arouses the brain and selectively inhibits stimulus input
c. routes sensory information to the brain
d. coordinates muscle movement and balance
e. site of higher mental functions; has sensory, motor, and association areas
f. involved in goal setting, self-control, and other executive functions.
g. limbic structure involved in memory and learning

ANSWERS: 1-c, 2-e, 3-b, 4-a, 5-g, 6-d, 7-f

HEMISPHERIC LATERALIZATION: THE LEFT AND RIGHT BRAINS

The left and right cerebral hemispheres are connected by a broad white band of myelinated nerve fibers. The **corpus callosum** *is a neural bridge consisting of white myelinated fibers that acts as a major communication link between the two hemispheres and allows them to function as a single unit* (see Figure 4.11). Despite the fact that they normally act in concert, however, there are important differences between the psychological functions of the two cerebral hemispheres (Hugdahl & Davidson, 2005). **Lateralization** *refers to the relatively greater localization of a function in one hemisphere or the other.*

Medical studies of patients who suffered various types of brain damage provided the first clues that certain complex psychological functions were lateralized on one side of the brain or the other. The deficits observed in people with damage to either the left or right hemisphere suggested that, for most people, verbal abilities and speech are localized in the left hemisphere, as are mathematical and logical abilities (Springer, 1997). When Broca's or Wernicke's speech areas in the left hemisphere are damaged, the result is **aphasia,** *the partial or total loss of the ability to communicate.* Depending on the location of the damage, the problem may lie in recognizing the meanings of words, in communicating verbally with others, or in both functions.

When the right hemisphere is damaged, the clinical picture is quite different. Language functions are not ordinarily affected, but the person has great difficulty perceiving spatial relations. A patient may have a hard time recognizing faces and may even forget a well-traveled route or, as in the case of Dr. P., mistake his wife for a hat (Sacks, 1985). It appears that mental imagery, musical and artistic abilities, and the ability to perceive and understand spatial relations are primarily right-hemisphere functions (Biller et al., 2006).

The two hemispheres differ not only in the cognitive functions that reside in them but also in their links with positive and negative emotions. EEG studies have shown that the right hemisphere is relatively more active when negative emotions such as sadness and anger are being experienced. Positive emotions such as joy and happiness are accompanied by relatively greater left-hemisphere activation (Marshall & Fox, 2000).

Despite the lateralization of specific functions in the two cerebral hemispheres, the brain normally functions as a unified whole because the two hemispheres communicate with one another through the corpus callosum. To illustrate, extend your two hands straight out in front of you, separated by about one foot. Now focus on the point between them. You'll find that you can still see both hands in your peripheral vision and that you have a unified view of the scene. It therefore might surprise you to know that your left hand is being "seen" only by your right hemisphere and your right hand only by your left hemisphere. To see how this occurs, examine Figure 4.16, which shows that some of the fibers of the optic nerve from each eye cross over at the *optic chiasma* and travel to the opposite brain hemisphere. Fibers that transmit messages from the right side of the visual field project to the left hemisphere; fibers from the visual field's left side project to the right hemisphere. Because the two hemispheres are in constant communication

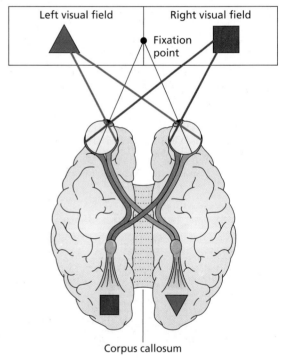

Figure 4.16

The split brain.
The visual system's anatomy made studies of split-brain subjects possible. Images entering the eye are reversed by the lens, so that light waves from the right visual field fall on the left side of the retina and light waves from the left visual field fall on the right side of the retina. Optic nerve fibers from the inner portion of the retina (toward the nose) cross over at the optic chiasma, whereas the fibers from the outer portion of the retina do not. As a result, the right side of the visual field projects to the visual cortex of the left hemisphere, whereas the left visual field projects to the right hemisphere. When the corpus callosum is cut, the two hemispheres no longer communicate with each other. By presenting stimuli to either side of the visual fixation point, researchers can control which hemisphere receives the information.

with one another, most of the knowledge of lateralized functions in humans was based on studies of people with brain damage that affected one of the hemispheres.

Suppose it was somehow possible to study each of the two hemispheres in isolation. A series of Nobel Prize–winning studies by psychobiologist Roger Sperry (1982) and his associates did exactly this.

Are There Sex Differences in Lateralization of Language?

Although the "men are from Mars, women are from Venus" notion is in large part a popular psychology myth, the two sexes do differ in some significant ways, including how their brains operate. Language-related differences have been one focus of research. One robust finding is that men

Research Close-up

Splitting the Brain: One Body, Two Minds?

SOURCE: ROGER W. SPERRY (1982). Some effects of disconnecting the cerebral hemispheres. *Science, 217,* 1223–1226, 1250.

INTRODUCTION

Like many scientific advances, Sperry's startling discoveries resulted from human misfortune. Some patients suffer from a form of epilepsy in which a seizure that begins as an uncontrolled electrical discharge of neurons on one side of the brain spreads to the other hemisphere. Years ago, neurosurgeons found that by cutting the nerve fibers of the corpus callosum, the band of myelinated fibers that connects the two hemispheres, they could prevent the seizure from spreading from one hemisphere to the other. Moreover, the operation did not seem to disrupt other major psychological functions. Sperry realized that the disconnected hemispheres in these patients provided an unusual opportunity to test the functions of the two hemispheres.

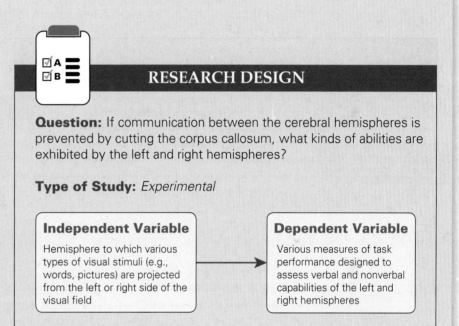

RESEARCH DESIGN

Question: If communication between the cerebral hemispheres is prevented by cutting the corpus callosum, what kinds of abilities are exhibited by the left and right hemispheres?

Type of Study: *Experimental*

Independent Variable

Hemisphere to which various types of visual stimuli (e.g., words, pictures) are projected from the left or right side of the visual field

Dependent Variable

Various measures of task performance designed to assess verbal and nonverbal capabilities of the left and right hemispheres

METHOD

Sperry and his colleagues developed some simple but ingenious ways to test the functions of the two hemispheres after the corpus callosum was cut and the patients had recovered from their surgery. They selected right-handed men and women so that they could be quite certain that verbal abilities were localized in the left hemisphere.

The experimental apparatus is shown in Figure 4.17. The patients were seated in front of a screen. In the center of the screen was a fixation point. They were instructed to focus on the fixation point in the center of the screen. Words or pictures were briefly flashed by a slide projector to either the right or left side of the visual field, sending the image through the visual system to either the left or right hemisphere. The patients were asked to respond verbally or with movements of either hand. The patients' hands were concealed beneath the apparatus so that they could not be seen by the patients.

RESULTS

Sperry found that the split-brain operation had in some ways created two minds in one body. When words were flashed to the right side of the visual field, resulting in their being sent to the language-rich left hemisphere, subjects could verbally describe what they had seen. They could also write what they had seen with their right hand (which is controlled by the left hemisphere). However, if words were flashed to the left side of the visual field and sent on to the right hemisphere, the subjects could neither describe them verbally nor write what they had seen with their left hand. This pattern of findings indicated that the right hemisphere does not have well-developed language abilities.

The inability to identify objects verbally did not mean, however, that the right hemisphere was incapable of recognizing them. If a picture of an object (e.g., a spoon) was flashed to the right hemisphere and the left hand (controlled by the right hemisphere) was allowed to feel many different objects behind the screen, the person's hand would immediately select the spoon and hold it up. As long as the person continued to hold the spoon in the left hand, sending sensory input about the object to the "nonverbal" right hemisphere, the subject was unable to name it. However, if the spoon was transferred to the right hand, the person could immediately name it. In other words, until the object was transferred to the

Continued

Picture of hairbrush
flashed on screen

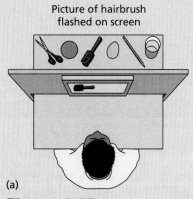

(a)

"What did you see?"

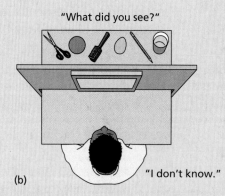

(b)   "I don't know."

"With your left hand, select the object you
saw from those behind the screen."

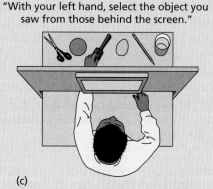

(c)

Figure 4.17

A split-brain patient.

A split-brain patient focuses on the fixation point in the center of the screen. (a) A picture of a hairbrush is briefly projected to the left side of the visual field, thus sending the information to the right hemisphere. (b) The patient is asked to report verbally what she saw. She cannot name the object. In (c), she is asked to select the object she saw, and quickly finds it with her left hand. What would happen if the object were to be transferred to her right hand or if the word were to be projected to the right side of the visual field? In either case, the information would be sent to the language-rich left hemisphere, and she would be able to name the object.

right hand, the left hemisphere had no knowledge of what the right hemisphere was experiencing.

Other studies have shown the right hemisphere's definite superiority over the left in another important ability, the recognition of patterns. In one demonstration, three split-brain patients were presented with photographs of similar-looking faces projected in either the left or right visual field. On each trial, the patients were asked to select the photo they had just seen from a set of 10 cards. On this task, the spatially oriented right hemisphere was far more accurate than the linguistic left hemisphere in correctly identifying the photos (Figure 4.18). Apparently, the faces were too similar to one another to be differentiated very easily by left-hemisphere

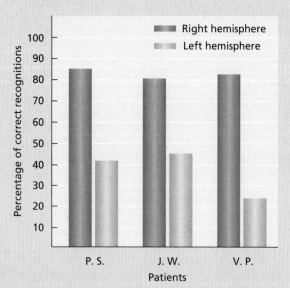

Figure 4.18

Facial-recognition accuracy by the left and right hemispheres of three split-brain patients.

Patients show greater accuracy when information is flashed to the right hemisphere, which has stronger pattern recognition abilities. Source: Data from Gazzaniga & Smylie, 1983.

verbal descriptions, but the spatial abilities of the right hemisphere could differentiate among them (Gazzaniga & Smylie, 1983).

DISCUSSION

Some psychologists have suggested that what we call the conscious self resides in the left hemisphere, because consciousness is based on our ability to verbalize about the past and present. Is the right hemisphere, then, an unconscious (nonverbal) mind? Yes, these psychologists answer, except when it communicates with the left hemisphere across the corpus callosum (Ornstein, 1997). But when the major interhemispheric communication highway is closed, each hemisphere, in a sense, can have a "mind of its own," and the two minds do not always agree on things. One split-brain patient learned to use Scrabble letters to communicate from his right hemisphere using his left hand. To test the dual-mind hypothesis, researchers asked the two hemispheres the same questions and found that the answers often disagreed. For example, when asked what occupation he would prefer, the left hemisphere responded verbally, "a draftsman." But the right hemisphere used the Scrabble pieces to spell out "race car driver" (LeDoux et al., 1977).

Keep in mind that in daily life, these psychological disconnects do not occur, because split-brain patients learn to compensate for their disconnected hemispheres. For example, they can scan the visual environment so that visual input from both the left and right visual fields gets into both hemispheres. The dual-mind phenomena shown in the laboratory appeared because the patients were tested under experimental conditions that were specifically designed to isolate the functions of the two hemispheres.

Nonetheless, the results of split-brain research were so dramatic that they led some people (and even some scientists) to promote a conception of brain functions as being highly localized and restricted to one hemisphere or the other. Even today, we hear about "right-brain" education programs and the untapped potentials that they can release. Certainly, there is some degree of localization of brain functions, but a far more important principle is that in the normal brain, most functions involve many areas of the brain working together. The brain is an exquisitely integrated system, not a collection of localized functions.

are about 23 percent more likely than women to be left-handed, which would affect lateralization of language (Papadatou-Pastou et al., 2008). Based on clinical and neuroscience research, some researchers also believe that right-handed men and women may differ in the extent to which language is localized in the left hemisphere. Clinicians have observed that men who suffer left-hemisphere strokes are far more likely than women to show severe aphasic symptoms, or loss in language capacity. In women with left-hemisphere damage, language functions are more likely to be spared, suggesting that more of their language function is shared with the right hemisphere (McGlone, 1977).

These clinical observations have been followed up using modern fMRI scanning techniques. In a study that launched this line of investigation (Shaywitz et al., 1995), right-handed men and women viewed pairs of randomly arranged vowels and consonants and were asked to decide whether or not the two "nonsense" words rhymed with each other. This task was chosen because it required the subjects to "sound out" the words in their minds to form a representation of the word sounds, a function that is critical in understanding language. The fMRIs showed that the rhyming task increased cortical activity in a region of the left hemisphere that is known to be involved in language. For males, this neural activity was restricted to the left hemisphere, but for females, the activity was represented in the corresponding areas of both hemispheres (Figure 4.19). Later imaging studies report similar findings, although the differences are often subtle. This finding, together with the clinical observations of stroke victims, suggests that there may be sex differences in lateralization of certain aspects of language (Ciarello et al., 2009; Clements et al., 2006; Lindell & Lamb, 2008). On the whole, however, whether based on anatomical or brain-imaging studies, the brains of men and women are far more similar than they are different (Wallentin, 2009). Nonetheless, the subtle differences that do occur continue to intrigue neuroscientists.

? thinking critically

DO THE SEXES DIFFER?

Does the evidence for greater activation of the right hemisphere in the nonsense-word study by Shaywitz et al. (1995) prove that women require the use of both hemispheres for some language functions? What kinds of evidence would provide further information on this question? Think about it, then see page 128.

PLASTICITY IN THE BRAIN: THE ROLE OF EXPERIENCE AND THE RECOVERY OF FUNCTION

Learn to walk, acquire speech, begin to read, fall in love, and your brain changes in ways that make you a different person from who you were before. Learning and practicing a mental or physical skill may change the size or number of brain areas involved and alter the neural pathways used in the skill (Adams & Cox, 2002; Posner & Rothbart, 2007a). This process of brain alteration begins in the womb and continues throughout life. It is governed in important ways by genetic factors but is also strongly influenced by the environment.

Neural plasticity *refers to the ability of neurons to change in structure and function* (Huttenlocher, 2002). Two aspects of neural plasticity—the effects of early experience on brain development and recovery from brain damage—are at the forefront of current research.

How Experience Influences Brain Development

Brain development is programmed by complex commands from our genes, but how these genetic commands express themselves can be powerfully affected by the environment in which we develop, including the environment we are exposed to in the womb (Fenichel, 2006). Consider the following research findings:

- For the fetus in the womb, exposure to high levels of alcohol ingested by the pregnant mother can disrupt brain development and produce the lifelong mental and behavioral damage seen in fetal alcohol syndrome. Drinking during the first weeks of pregnancy—sometimes before a woman is even aware that she's pregnant—is particularly risky in this regard (Streissguth et al., 1985).

- Compared with the brains of normally reared rats, the brains of rat pups raised in a stimulating environment with lots of toys and playmates weighed more and had larger neurons, more dendritic branches, and greater concentrations of acetylcholine, a neurotransmitter involved in motor control and in memory (Rosenzweig, 1984).

- Prematurely born human infants who were caressed and massaged on a regular basis

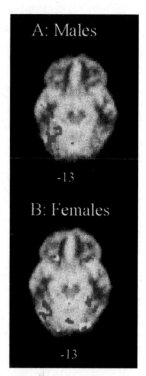

Figure 4.19

Brain activation, as recorded by fMRI, is shown in the red areas. For males, the left hemisphere is more active than the right hemisphere during this language task. Females' activation patterns are distributed in corresponding areas of both the left and right hemispheres, indicating less lateralization of language functions than in the males' brains. The yellow activation patterns occurred in response to a control (nonlanguage) task. SOURCE: Rossell et. al., 2002.

showed faster neurological development than did those given normal care and human contact (Field et al., 1986).

- MRI recordings revealed that experienced violinists and other string-instrument players who do elaborate movements on the strings with their left hands had a larger right-hemisphere somatosensory area devoted to these fingers than did nonmusicians. The corresponding left-hemisphere (right-hand) cortical areas of the musicians and nonmusicians did not differ. The earlier in life the musicians had started playing their instruments, the greater the cortical differences (Elbert et al., 1995).

- Chronic alcoholism inhibits the production of new neural connections in the hippocampus, thereby impairing learning, memory, and other cognitive functions. After weeks of abstinence, the process of forming new synapses begins to return to normal (Nixon & Crews, 2004).

- Some theorists believe that life stress has a similar negative effect on neuron formation in the brain, thereby causing or maintaining clinical depression. Antidepressant medications increase serotonin action in the brain, and serotonin increases neuron production in the brain (Jacobs, 2004).

- Cultural factors may affect brain development as well. For example, the Chinese language uses complex pictorial images (rather than words) to represent objects or concepts. Because pictorial stimuli are processed in the right hemisphere, we might expect less left-hemisphere lateralization of language among speakers of Chinese than among people who speak English or other alphabet-based languages. There is evidence to support this hypothesis in the areas of reading and writing (Tzeng et al., 1979).

- Cultural factors also influence people's brain-activation patterns as well. Americans, from an individualistic culture, and Chinese, from a collectivistic culture that emphasizes interconnectedness with others (see page 18), made trait ratings of themselves, their mothers, and an unacquainted famous person while fMRI readings of blood oxygen recorded brain activation. Both Americans and Chinese showed greater activation in an area of the prefrontal cortex involved in judging the self-relevance of stimuli when they rated themselves than when they rated the famous person. However, as shown in

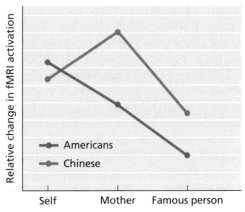

Figure 4.20

Culture influences brain function.
This graph shows the pattern of fMRI recordings of prefrontal-cortex activation in Americans and Chinese as they made trait ratings of themselves, their mothers, and an unrelated famous person.
Source: Based on Zhu et al., 2007.

Figure 4.20, the Chinese showed even higher activation when rating their mothers, reflecting the interconnectedness of their self-identity with their family. Americans showed no such pattern (Zhu et al., 2007).

These and other findings show that in a very real sense, each person's brain goes through its own personal evolutionary process. In numerous ways, the brain changes and adapts as it is sculpted by life experiences (Posner & Rothbart, 2007b).

Studies using the electron microscope help explain why such plasticity is possible early in life. A 1- to 2-year-old child has about 50 percent more brain synapses than mature adults do (Lomber & Eggermont, 2006). This greater availability of synapses may help explain why children can recover from brain damage more quickly and completely than adults. Sadly, the days of synaptic riches don't last forever. Unused or weaker synapses deteriorate with age, so that the brain loses some of its plasticity (Hobert, 2009). Moreover, cell death is programmed into every neuron by its genes, and what some neuroscientists refer to as the neuron's "suicide apparatus" is activated by a lack of stimulation from other neurons and by many other factors that are not yet known. As a result, adults actually have fewer synapses than do children, despite their more advanced cognitive and motor capabilities. However, the remaining neurons form new connections in response to experiences and the formation of new memories.

Healing the Nervous System

The brain's ability to adapt in the event of damage is one of its remarkable characteristics. When nerve tissue is destroyed or neurons die as part of the aging process, surviving neurons can restore functioning by modifying themselves either structurally or biochemically (Lomber & Eggermont, 2006). They can alter their structure by sprouting enlarged networks of dendrites or by extending axons from surviving neurons to form new synapses (Shepherd, 1997). Surviving neurons may also make up for the loss by increasing the volume of neurotransmitters they release (Dwyer, 2007). Moreover, research findings have disproved the long-standing assumption of brain scientists that dead neurons cannot be replaced in the mature brain (Kempermann, 2005). *The production of new neurons in the nervous system is called* **neurogenesis.** Neurogenesis occurs in both the immature and the adult brain. In the adult brain, the birth of new cells has been established only in the hippocampus and olfactory bulb (a relay center for the sense of smell) so far, but it may occur in other areas as well. The study of neurogenesis is an exciting research frontier. Biochemical strategies to enhance hippocampal neurogenesis in the brains of Alzheimer's patients may help counteract the loss of neurons that occurs in that disease (Schaeffer et al., 2009).

One revolutionary neurogenesis technique involves the transplantation into the brain of **neural stem cells,** *immature "uncommitted" cells that can mature into any type of neuron or glial cell needed by the brain.* These cells, found in both the developing and adult nervous systems, can be put into a liquid medium and injected directly into the brain. Once in the brain, they can travel to any of its regions, especially developing or degenerating areas. There they can detect defective or genetically impaired cells and somehow convert themselves into healthy forms of the defective cells. Stem cells have been successfully transplanted into the spinal cords of injured animals, where they have taken hold and organized themselves into neural networks (Jung et al., 2009). This success may herald an eventual ability to do what has never before been possible: repair the severed spinal cord.

Myth or Reality?

We Use Only Ten Percent of Our Brain Power

How often have you heard that we use only 10 percent of our brain capacity? Is there any truth to this notion?

Let's apply what we've learned in this chapter to critically evaluate that statement. One principle of critical thinking is to test an idea by trying to find evidence against it. The reason is that we can find something to support almost any statement, even if it's false. In contrast, one disconfirming piece of evidence tells us the statement is not true as is.

First, let's consider what we know about brain activity from PET and fMRI imaging studies. Do they show that only 10 percent of the brain is active at any time? Certainly not. Instead, the brain exhibits widespread activity even during sleep. Although certain functions may use only a small part of the brain at one time, any sufficiently complex set of activities or thought patterns involves many parts of the brain. For any given activity, such as eating, watching television, walking, or reading this book, you may use a few specific parts of your brain. Over the course of a whole day, however, just about all of the brain is used at one time or another. Thus brain activity data fly in the face of the 10-percent truism.

Next, we might consider what we know about brain damage. Does the 10-percent principle mean that we would be just fine if 90 percent of our brain were removed? Hardly. It is well known that damage to a relatively small area of the brain, such as that caused by a stroke, can produce devastating disabilities. Yet the damage caused by such a condition is far less than what would occur if 90 percent of the brain were removed. As a prominent neurologist told us, "If a surgeon tells you he or she is going to remove the 90 percent of the brain you don't need, run like hell."

We might also apply what we've learned about neural development, particularly the "use it or lose it" principle. The process of brain development involves pruning synapses that are not used, thereby fine-tuning brain functioning. Many studies have shown that if the input to a particular neural system is eliminated, then neurons in this system will not function properly. If we were really using only 10 percent of the brain, we could expect the other 90 percent to atrophy over time.

Where did the 10-percent idea come from in the first place? Perhaps it was inspired in part by the work of psychologist Karl Lashley in the 1920s and 1930s. Lashley removed large areas of the cerebral cortex in rats and found that these animals could still relearn specific tasks. This did not mean, however, that other functions were not severely affected. But psychics and other "human potential" marketeers found the idea intriguing and have kept it alive over the decades. After all, if we use only 10 percent of our brain, imagine the untapped psychic abilities that lie dormant, just waiting to be released using their products. Psychics often attribute their special, if fraudulent, gifts to the release of brain potential that other people have not accessed.

This does not mean that we don't have untapped potential; it's just that, if realized, it would be represented in the form of new synapses within brain tissue that you're already using. A final reason why the myth persists is that it's been repeated so often over the years in the mass media, it has become a part of popular culture, an unquestioned factoid that's taken on a life of its own. However, there's no question that the 10-percent principle is a myth without scientific foundation.

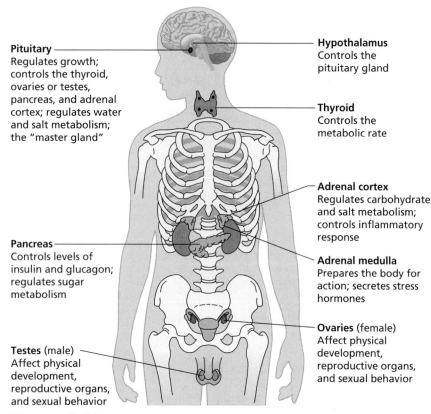

Pituitary
Regulates growth; controls the thyroid, ovaries or testes, pancreas, and adrenal cortex; regulates water and salt metabolism; the "master gland"

Pancreas
Controls levels of insulin and glucagon; regulates sugar metabolism

Testes (male)
Affect physical development, reproductive organs, and sexual behavior

Hypothalamus
Controls the pituitary gland

Thyroid
Controls the metabolic rate

Adrenal cortex
Regulates carbohydrate and salt metabolism; controls inflammatory response

Adrenal medulla
Prepares the body for action; secretes stress hormones

Ovaries (female)
Affect physical development, reproductive organs, and sexual behavior

Figure 4.21

The endocrine system.
The glands that compose the endocrine system and the effects of their hormones on bodily functions.

The fact that transplanted stem cells can apparently go anywhere in the brain and become any kind of cell suggests the possibility of revolutionary treatments for diseases involving neural degeneration and dysfunction. These include Alzheimer's disease, multiple sclerosis, strokes, mental disorders, and genetically based birth defects, all of which have serious psychological consequences (Wernig & Brustle, 2002). Stem cells may also hold the key to countering the effects of aging on brain functioning. In one study, human stem cells transplanted into the brains of aged rats migrated to the hippocampus and cortex. Four weeks later, these rats showed improved performance in a water-maze task, suggesting improved learning and memory ability (Qu et al., 2001). Much more research is needed, but, at long last, we may be on the threshold of being able to heal the damaged brain and restore lost psychological functions (Brazel & Rao, 2004). A key to doing so will be to discover why it is that stem cells, which have the potential to produce new neurons and are found throughout the adult brain, are not utilized more widely by the brain to repair itself. It may be that altering stem cells through drug-based or genetic interventions will increase their ability to repair the damaged brain (Kempermann, 2005).

INTERACTIONS WITH THE ENDOCRINE SYSTEM

The nervous system interacts with another communication system within the body: the endocrine system (Gundelfinger et al., 2006). This communication has major influences on behavior and on psychological and physical well-being.

The **endocrine system** *consists of numerous hormone-secreting glands distributed throughout the body* (Figure 4.21). Like the nervous system, the endocrine system's function is to convey information from one area of the body to another. Rather than using nerve impulses, however, the endocrine system conveys information in the form of **hormones,** *chemical messengers that are secreted from its glands into the bloodstream.* Just as neurons have receptors for certain neurotransmitters, cells in the body (including neurons) have receptor molecules that respond to specific hormones from the endocrine glands (Porterfield & White, 2007). Many of the hormones secreted by these glands affect psychological development and functioning.

Endocrine messages trigger responses in the brain, and mental processes within the brain can affect endocrine functioning. For example, negative thoughts about a stressful situation can quickly trigger the secretion of stress hormones within the body (Borod, 2000).

The nervous system transmits information rapidly, with the speed of nerve impulses. In contrast, the endocrine system is much slower because the delivery of its messages depends on the rate of blood flow. Nonetheless, hormones travel throughout the body in the bloodstream and can reach billions of individual cells. Thus, when the brain has important information to transmit, it has the choice of sending it quickly and directly in the form of nerve impulses to a relatively small number of neurons or indirectly by means of hormones to a large number of cells. Often both communication networks are used, resulting in both immediate and prolonged stimulation.

Hormones begin to influence our development, capacities, and behavior long before we're born. In the third to fourth month of pregnancy, genetically programmed releases of sex hormones in the fetus determine sex-organ development, as well as differences in the structure and function of several parts of the nervous system. Females have a greater density of neurons in language-relevant areas of the temporal lobe, which may contribute to the small overall superiority they manifest in verbal skills (Collins & Kimura, 1997). Other hormonally produced brain differences, as yet undiscovered,

Levels of Analysis

Brain, Behavior, and Environment

The focus of this chapter has been on the physiology of the nervous system. This is the province of neuroscience. Yet neuroscientists realize that their work at the biological level of analysis is only part of the fascinating and abiding mystery of how brain creates mind, indeed of how brain *is* mind. Consider some of the findings we have reviewed in this chapter:

ENVIRONMENTAL LEVEL

- Early environment, whether enriched or deprived, influences brain development and behavior capabilities.
- Environmental rewards and punishments influence what we learn and the neural representations of that learning
- The stimuli present at any particular moment trigger both biological (e.g., brain-activation, hormonal, and neurotransmitter) and behavioral processes.
- The culture in which we grow up plays an important role in psychological development and, as recent research shows, in how the brain operates.

BIOLOGICAL LEVEL

- Every thought, feeling, or behavior involves the action of the nervous system. In a real sense, our brain *is* the locus of who and what we are as a person.
- The biological level of analysis provides us with tools, such as brain scans, to study and directly measure the activity of the nervous system.
- Clinical studies of brain-damaged individuals by neurologists have provided much evidence concerning normal brain functions.

PSYCHOLOGICAL LEVEL

- The psychological perspective provides discoveries on the nature and causes of both normal and abnormal cognition, emotion, and behavior. These provide the basic phenomena that the biological perspective studies.
- The psychological perspective provides the measures of psychological functions that allow us to relate them to biological factors, such as genetic or brain-activation variables.
- Plasticity research (page 121) shows us that psychological factors influence the brain just as the brain influences behavior. New thought and behavior patterns create the changes in the brain that underlie what we call learning, motivation, emotion, and personality development. Even playing a stringed instrument influences thought and behavior patterns.

In summary, biological, psychological, and environmental factors are all involved in most behaviors, typically interacting with one another, and all of them can serve as either cause or effect.

Try making a list of modern environmental factors—only ones that have existed since you were born—that may influence brain and psychological development.

---

may help account for the fact that language functions are less localized in the left hemisphere in females (Rossell et al., 2002). These sex differences will be discussed in greater detail in Chapter 9.

Of special interest to psychologists are the **adrenal glands,** *twin structures perched atop the kidneys that serve, quite literally, as hormone factories, producing and secreting about 50 different hormones* that regulate many metabolic processes within the brain and other parts of the body. The adrenals produce the neurotransmitter dopamine, as well as several stress hormones. In an emergency, the adrenal glands are activated by the sympathetic branch of the autonomic nervous system. Stress hormones are then secreted into the bloodstream, mobilizing the body's emergency-response system. Because hormones remain in the bloodstream for some time, the action of these adrenal hormones is especially important under conditions of prolonged stress. If not for the long-term influence of hormones, the autonomic nervous system would have to produce a constant barrage of nerve impulses to the organs involved in responding to stress (Fink, 2010).

test yourself

Neural Plasticity and the Endocrine System

True or false?

1. Plasticity is the ability of the nervous system to form new neurons.
2. Rats raised in a stimulating early environment showed faster brain growth. However, early stimulation has no similar effects on humans.
3. Brain research supports the widely proclaimed belief that most people use only about 10 percent of their brain capacity.
4. The adrenal gland is strongly involved in the release of stress hormones.
5. The endocrine system conveys information in the form of hormones from one area of the body to another.

ANSWERS: 1-false, 2-false, 3-false, 4-true, 5-true

Chapter Summary

NEURONS

- Each neuron has dendrites, which receive nerve impulses from other neurons; a cell body, which controls the vital processes of the cell; and an axon, which conducts nerve impulses to adjacent neurons, muscles, and glands.
- Neural transmission is an electrochemical process. The nerve impulse, or action potential, is a brief reversal in the electrical potential of the cell membrane from negative to positive as sodium ions from the surrounding fluid flow into the cell through sodium ion channels. The action potential obeys the all-or-none law, firing completely or not at all. The myelin sheath increases the speed of neural transmission.

HOW NEURONS COMMUNICATE: SYNAPTIC TRANSMISSION

- Passage of the impulse across the synapse is mediated by chemical transmitter substances. Neurons are selective in the neurotransmitters that can stimulate them. Some neurotransmitters excite neurons, whereas others inhibit firing of the postsynaptic neuron. The nervous system requires a delicate balance of excitation and inhibition of neurons.
- Psychoactive drugs such as caffeine, alcohol, nicotine, and amphetamines produce their effects by either increasing or decreasing the action of neurotransmitters. Agonists can mimic or increase the action of neurotransmitters, whereas antagonists inhibit or decrease the action of neurotransmitters.

THE NERVOUS SYSTEM

- The nervous system contains sensory neurons, motor neurons, and interneurons. Its two major divisions are the central nervous system, consisting of the brain and spinal cord, and the peripheral nervous system. The peripheral system is divided into the somatic system (which is responsible for sensory and motor functions) and the autonomic nervous system (which directs the activity of the body's internal organs and glands).
- The autonomic nervous system consists of sympathetic and parasympathetic divisions. The sympathetic system has an arousal function and tends to act as a unit. The parasympathetic system slows down body processes and is more specific in its actions. Together, the two divisions maintain a state of homeostasis, or internal balance.
- The spinal cord contains sensory neurons and motor neurons. Interneurons inside the spinal cord serve a connective function between the two. Simple stimulus-response sequences can occur as spinal reflexes.
- Neuropsychological tests, destruction and stimulation techniques, electrical recording, and brain imaging have facilitated discoveries about brain-behavior relations. Recently developed methods for producing computer-generated pictures of structures and processes within the living brain include the CT scan, PET scan, MRI, and fMRI.

THE HIERARCHICAL BRAIN: STRUCTURES AND BEHAVIORAL FUNCTIONS

- The brain is divided structurally into the hindbrain, the midbrain, and the forebrain. This organization reflects the evolution of increasingly complex brain structures related to behavioral capabilities.
- Major structures within the hindbrain include the medulla, which monitors and controls vital body functions; the pons,

which contains important groups of sensory and motor neurons; and the cerebellum, which is concerned with motor coordination.

- The reticular formation, located in the midbrain, plays a vital role in consciousness, attention, and sleep. Activity of the ascending reticular formation excites higher areas of the brain and prepares them to respond to stimulation. The descending reticular formation acts as a gate, determining which stimuli enter into consciousness.

- The forebrain consists of two cerebral hemispheres and a number of subcortical structures. The cerebral hemispheres are connected by the corpus callosum.

- The thalamus acts as a switchboard through which impulses originating in sense organs are routed to the appropriate sensory-projection areas. The hypothalamus plays a major role in many aspects of motivational and emotional behavior. The limbic system seems to be involved in organizing the behaviors involved in motivation and emotion.

- The cerebral cortex is divided into frontal, parietal, occipital, and temporal lobes. Some areas of the cerebral cortex receive sensory input, some control motor functions, and others (the association cortex) are involved in higher mental processes in humans. The frontal lobes are particularly important in such executive functions as planning, voluntary behavior, and self-awareness.

HEMISPHERIC LATERALIZATION: THE LEFT AND RIGHT BRAINS

- Although the two cerebral hemispheres ordinarily work in coordination with one another, they appear to have different functions and abilities. Studies of split-brain patients, whose corpus callosa have been cut, indicate that the left hemisphere commands language and mathematical abilities, whereas the right hemisphere has well-developed spatial abilities but a generally limited ability to communicate through speech.

- Positive emotions are linked to relatively greater left-hemisphere activation, and negative emotions are linked to relatively greater right-hemisphere involvement.

- Despite hemispheric localization, however, most behaviors involve interactions between both hemispheres; the brain normally operates as a highly integrated system.

PLASTICITY IN THE BRAIN: THE ROLE OF EXPERIENCE AND THE RECOVERY OF FUNCTION

- Neural plasticity refers to the ability of neurons to change in structure and function. Environmental factors, particularly early in life, have notable effects on brain development. There are often periods during which environmental factors have their greatest (or only) effects on plasticity.

- A person's ability to recover from brain damage depends on several factors. Other things being equal, recovery is greatest early in life and declines with age.

- When neurons die, surviving neurons can alter their structure and functions to recover the ability to send and receive nerve impulses. Neurons can also increase the amount of neurotransmitters they release. Recent findings suggest that the brains of mature primates and humans are capable of producing new neurons (neurogenesis).

- Current advances in the treatment of neurological disorders include experiments on neurogenesis and the injection of neural stem cells into the brain, where they find and replace diseased or dead neurons.

INTERACTIONS WITH THE ENDOCRINE SYSTEM

- The nervous and endocrine systems have extensive neural and chemical means of communication, and each is capable of affecting and being affected by the other.

- The endocrine system secretes hormones into the bloodstream. These chemical messengers affect many bodily processes, including those associated with the central and autonomic nervous systems. Because of the adrenal glands' relation to functions of the nervous system, they are of particular interest to psychologists. Hormonal effects in the womb may produce brain differences in males and females that influence sex differences in certain psychological functions.

KEY TERMS AND CONCEPTS

Each term has been boldfaced and defined in the chapter on the page indicated in parentheses.

absolute refractory period (p. 98)
acetylcholine (ACh) (p. 101)
action potential (p. 98)
adrenal glands (p. 125)
agonist (p. 102)
all-or-none law (p. 98)
amygdala (p. 113)
antagonist (p. 103)
aphasia (p. 118)

association cortex (p. 116)
autonomic nervous system (p. 104)
axon (p. 97)
brain stem (p. 111)
Broca's area (p. 116)
central nervous system (p. 106)
cerebellum (p. 111)
cerebral cortex (p. 114)
cerebrum (p. 112)

computerized axial tomography
 (CT or CAT) scan (p. 108)
corpus callosum (p. 118)
dendrites (p. 97)
electroencephalograph (EEG) (p. 107)
endocrine system (p. 124)
forebrain (p. 112)
functional MRI (fMRI) (p. 108)
graded potentials (p. 98)

hindbrain (p. 111)
hippocampus (p. 113)
homeostasis (p. 106)
hormones (p. 124)
hypothalamus (p. 112)
interneurons (p. 104)
lateralization (p. 118)
limbic system (p. 113)
magnetic resonance imaging (MRI) (p. 108)
medulla (p. 111)
midbrain (p. 111)
motor cortex (p. 114)
motor neurons (p. 104)

myelin sheath (p. 99)
neural plasticity (p. 121)
neural stem cells (p. 123)
neurogenesis (p. 123)
neuromodulators (p. 102)
neurons (p. 97)
neurotransmitters (p. 100)
parasympathetic nervous system (p. 106)
peripheral nervous system (p. 104)
pons (p. 111)
positron-emission tomography (PET)
  scan (p. 108)
prefrontal cortex (p. 117)

psychoactive drugs (p. 102)
receptor sites (p. 100)
resting potential (p. 98)
reticular formation (p. 111)
reuptake (p. 100)
sensory neurons (p. 104)
somatic nervous system (p. 104)
somatic sensory cortex (p. 114)
sympathetic nervous system (p. 106)
synaptic space (p. 100)
synaptic vesicles (p. 100)
thalamus (p. 112)
Wernicke's area (p. 116)

 # thinking **critically**

DO THE SEXES DIFFER? (Page 121)

First, you may have recognized that although the right hemisphere of women was more active during the language task, what we have so far is a correlation between task performance and biological activity. Does this activity play a causal role in task performance? Is it essential for task performance? We simply don't know at this point. Another question we might ask is whether women are more likely than men to suffer language deficits if they suffer right-hemisphere damage. If so, this would indicate that right-hemisphere activation is more important in women. In fact, we know that women are *not* more likely than men to become aphasic if they suffer right-hemisphere damage (Brogdal, 2010). Perhaps women use both hemispheres for the performance of certain language tasks but can fall back on one if damage occurs to the other. Clearly, we have more to learn about possible sex differences in lateralization, but we are learning which questions to ask.

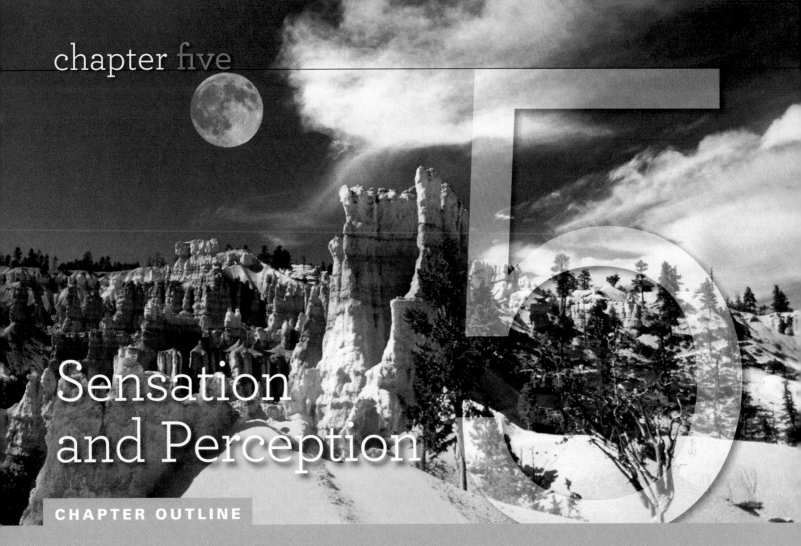

chapter five

Sensation and Perception

Myth or Reality?

Subliminal Stimuli Can Program Our Minds (page 133)

Need to improve your study habits? Quit smoking? Enhance your sex life? Many people try subliminal programming as a means to self-improvement. Subliminal stimuli can be embedded in advertisements and political ads. How much can stimuli that don't register in awareness influence our thoughts, attitudes, and behaviors?

129

I walked up to an ice cream vendor and asked what flavors she sold. But she answered in such a tone that a whole pile of coals, of black cinders, came bursting out of her mouth and I couldn't bring myself to buy any ice cream after she answered that way.

Nature gives us a marvelous set of sensory connections with our world. If our sense organs are not defective, we experience light waves as colors and levels of brightness, air vibrations as sounds, pressure as touch sensations, chemical substances as colors or tastes, and so on. However, such is not the case for people with a rare condition called **synesthesia,** *which means, quite literally, "mixing of the senses"* (Cytowic, 2002; Harrison & Baron-Cohen, 1997). Individuals with synesthesia may experience sounds as colors or tastes as touch sensations of different shapes. One man reported that when he listens to an orchestra, he doesn't just hear music; he also sees it. The sounds of a violin trigger a shiny rich burgundy color, like a red wine, whereas a cello's music produces a flowing golden yellow hue, like honey (CNN, 2009, February 9).

Russian psychologist A. R. Luria (1968) studied a highly successful writer and musician whose life was a perpetual stream of mixed-up sensations. On one occasion, Luria asked him to report on his experiences while listening to electronically generated musical tones. In response to a medium-pitched tone, the man experienced a brown strip with red edges, together with a sweet and sour flavor. A very high-pitched tone evoked the following sensation: "It looks something like a fire-works tinged with a pink-red hue. The strip of color feels rough and unpleasant, and it has an ugly taste— rather like that of a briny pickle. . . . You could hurt your hand on this." Mixed sensations like these frequently occurred in the man's daily life, and they were sometimes disconcerting, as in his description of his encounter with the ice cream vendor.

How is it possible for sensory experience to become so jumbled, for sensory input to somehow get routed to the wrong parts of the brain? The answer to this question is not fully understood, but its answer will require knowledge of the sensory systems—what stimulates them, how they operate, and how sensory input is sent to the brain and transformed into the perceptual experiences we take so much for granted. By the time you finish this chapter, you'll be able to answer many of these questions.

People who experience synesthesia provide glimpses into different aspects of how we sense and understand our world. These processes, previewed in Figure 5.1, begin when specific types of stimuli activate specialized sensory receptors. Whether the stimulus is light, sound waves, a chemical molecule, or pressure, your sensory receptors must translate the information into the only language your nervous system understands: the language of nerve impulses. This process is called *transduction*. Once this translation occurs, specialized neurons called *feature detectors* break down and analyze the specific features of the stimulus. At the next stage, these numerous stimulus features are reconstructed into a neural representation that is then compared with previously stored information, such as our knowledge of how particular objects look, smell, or feel. This matching of a new stimulus with our internal storehouse of knowledge allows us to recognize the stimulus and give it meaning. We then consciously experience a perception.

How does this process help us understand the mysterious mixing of the senses in synesthesia? We know that specific parts of the brain are specialized for different sensory functions. In people with synesthesia, there is some sort of cross-wiring, so that activity in one part of the brain evokes responses in another part of the brain dedicated to another sensory modality

(Ward, 2008). Functional MRI studies have shown that for people with synesthesia with word-color linkages, hearing certain words is associated with neural activity in parts of the visual cortex. This does not occur in people without synesthesia, even if they are asked to imagine colors in association with certain words (Nunn et al., 2002).

Several explanations have been offered for the sensory mixing (Cytowic & Eagleman, 2009; Hubbard & Ramachandran, 2005). One theory is that the pruning of neural connections that occurs in infancy has not occurred in people with synesthesia, so that brain regions retain connections that are absent in most people. In support of this theory, diffusion tensor imaging, which lights up white matter pathways in the brain, has revealed increased connectivity in patients with synesthesia (Rouw & Scholte, 2007). Another theory is that with synesthesia, there is a deficit in neural inhibitory processes in the brain that ordinarily keep input from one sensory modality from "overflowing" into other sensory areas and stimulating them.

Whatever the processes involved, both normal perceptual processes and synesthesia relate to one of the big mysteries in cognitive neuroscience called the "binding problem." How do we bind all of our perceptions into one complete whole while keeping its sensory elements separate? When you hold a rose in your hand, see its colored petals, feel their velvety quality, and smell its aroma, these disparate sensory experiences are somehow fused into your total experience of the rose. People with synesthesia may create additional perceptions of that rose that are inconsistent with its physical properties.

In some ways, sensation and perception blend together so completely that they are difficult to separate, for the stimulation we receive through our sense organs is instantaneously organized and transformed into the experiences that we refer to as perceptions. Nevertheless, psychologists do distinguish between them. **Sensation** *is the stimulus-detection process by which our sense organs respond to and translate environmental stimuli into nerve impulses that are sent to the brain.* **Perception**—*making "sense" of what our senses tell us—is the active process of organizing this stimulus input and giving it meaning* (Mather, 2006; May, 2007).

Because perception is an active and creative process, the same sensory input may be perceived in different ways at different times. For example, read the two sets of symbols in Figure 5.2. The middle symbols in both sets are exactly the same, and they sent identical input to your brain, but you probably perceived them differently. Your interpretation, or perception, of the characters was influenced by their context—that is, by the characters that preceded and followed them and by your learned expectation of what normally follows the letter A and the number 12. This is a simple illustration of how perception takes us a step beyond sensation.

SENSORY PROCESSES

The particular stimuli to which different animals are sensitive vary considerably. The sensory equipment of any species is an adaptation to the environment in which it lives. Many species have senses that humans lack altogether. Carrier pigeons, for example, use the earth's magnetic field to find their destination on cloudy nights when they can't navigate by the stars. Sharks sense electric currents leaking through the skins of fish hiding in undersea crevices, and rattlesnakes find their prey by detecting infrared radiation given off by small rodents. Whatever the source of stimulation, its energy must be converted into nerve impulses, the only language the nervous system understands (Liedtke, 2006). **Transduction** *is the process whereby the characteristics of a stimulus are converted into nerve impulses.* We now consider the range of stimuli to which humans and other mammals are attuned and the manner in which the various sense organs carry out the transduction process.

As a starting point, we might ask how many senses there are in humans. Certainly there appear to be more than the five classical senses: vision, audition (hearing), gustation (taste), olfaction (smell), and touch. For example, there are senses that provide information about balance and body position. Also, the sense of touch can be subdivided into separate senses of pressure,

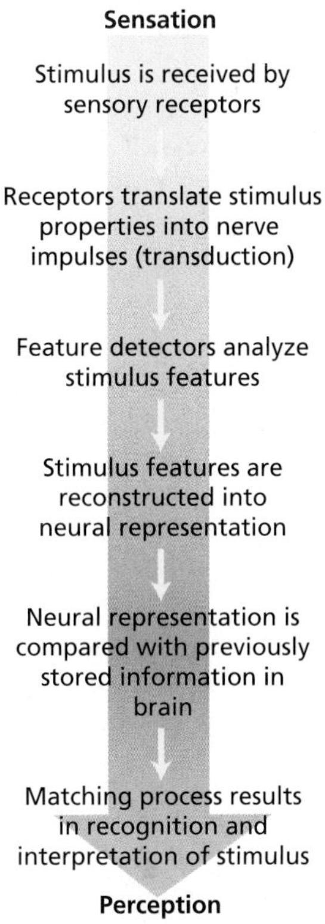

Sensation

Stimulus is received by sensory receptors

↓

Receptors translate stimulus properties into nerve impulses (transduction)

↓

Feature detectors analyze stimulus features

↓

Stimulus features are reconstructed into neural representation

↓

Neural representation is compared with previously stored information in brain

↓

Matching process results in recognition and interpretation of stimulus

Perception

Figure 5.1

Sensation becomes perception. Sensory and perceptual processes proceed from the reception and translation of physical stimuli into nerve impulses. Then occurs the active process by which the brain receives the nerve impulses, organizes and confers meaning on them, and constructs a perceptual experience.

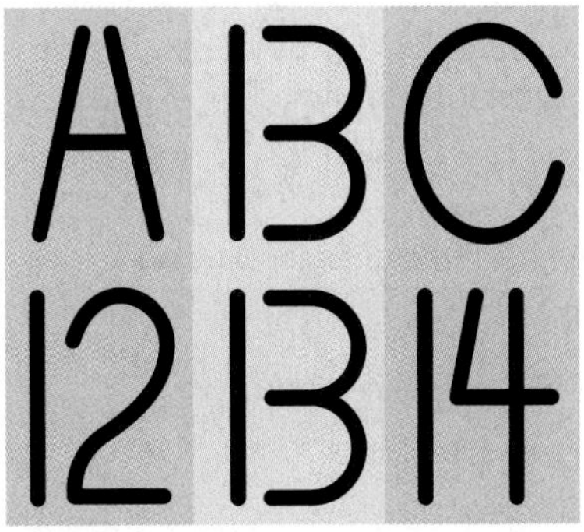

Figure 5.2

Context and perception.
Quickly read these two lines of symbols out loud. Did your perception of the middle symbol in each line depend on the symbols that surrounded it?

pain, and temperature. Receptors deep within the brain monitor the chemical composition of our blood. The immune system also has sensory functions that allow it to detect foreign invaders and to receive stimulation from the brain.

Like those of other organisms, human sensory systems are designed to extract from the environment the information that we need to function and survive. Although our survival does not depend on having eyes like eagles or owls, noses like bloodhounds, or ears as sensitive as those of the worm-hunting robin, we do have specialized sensors that can detect many different kinds of stimuli with considerable sensitivity. The scientific area of **psychophysics,** *which studies relations between the physical characteristics of stimuli and sensory capabilities,* is concerned with two kinds of sensitivity. The first concerns the absolute limits of sensitivity. For example, what is the dimmest light, the faintest sound, or the weakest salt solution that humans can detect? The second kind of sensitivity has to do with differences between stimuli. What is the smallest difference between two tones that we can detect?

Stimulus Detection: The Absolute Threshold

How intense must a stimulus be before we can detect its presence? Researchers answer this question by systematically presenting stimuli of varying intensities to people and asking whether they can detect them. Researchers designate the **absolute threshold** *as the lowest intensity at which a stimulus can be detected 50 percent of the time.* Thus the lower the absolute threshold, the greater the sensitivity. From studies of absolute thresholds, we can estimate the general limits of human sensitivity for the five major senses. Some examples are presented in Table 5.1. As you can see, many of our absolute thresholds are surprisingly low. Yet some other species have sensitivities that far surpass those of humans. For example, a female

silkworm moth who is ready to mate needs to release only a billionth of an ounce of an attractant chemical molecule per second to attract every male silkworm moth within a mile's radius.

At one time, scientists thought that although some people have greater sensory acuity than others, each person has a more or less fixed level of sensitivity for each sense. But psychologists who study stimulus detection found that an individual's apparent sensitivity can fluctuate quite a bit. The concept of a fixed absolute threshold is inaccurate because there is no single point on the intensity scale that separates nondetection from detection of a stimulus. There is instead a range of uncertainty, and people set their own **decision criterion,** *a standard of how certain they must be that a stimulus is present before they will say they detect it.* The decision criterion can also change from time to time, depending on such factors as fatigue, expectation (e.g., having watched a horror movie), and the potential significance of the stimulus. **Signal-detection theory** *is concerned with the factors that influence sensory judgments.*

In a typical signal-detection experiment, participants are told that after a warning light appears, a barely perceptible tone may or may not be presented. Their task is to tell the experimenter whether or not they hear the tone. Under these conditions, there are four possible outcomes, as shown in Figure 5.3. When the tone is in fact presented, the participant may say "yes" (a hit) or "no" (a miss). When no tone is presented, the participant may also say "yes" (a false alarm) or "no" (a correct rejection).

At low stimulus intensities, both the participant's and the situation's characteristics influence the decision criterion (Colonius & Dzhafarov, 2006; Methot & Huitema, 1998). Bold participants who frequently say "yes" have more hits, but they also

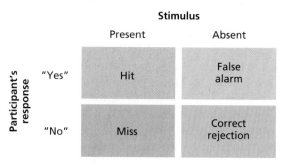

Figure 5.3

Signal-detection research.

This matrix shows the four possible outcomes in a signal-detection experiment in which participants decide whether a stimulus has been presented or not presented. The percentages of responses that fall within each category can be affected by both characteristics of the participants and the nature of the situation.

Table **5.1** | **Some Approximate Absolute Thresholds for Humans**

Sensory Modality	Absolute Threshold
Vision	Candle flame seen at 30 miles on a clear, dark night
Hearing	Tick of a watch under quiet conditions at 20 feet
Taste	1 teaspoon of sugar in 2 gallons of water
Smell	1 drop of perfume diffused into the entire volume of a large apartment
Touch	Wing of a fly or bee falling on a person's cheek from a distance of 1 centimeter

SOURCE: Based on Galanter, 1962.

have more false alarms than do conservative participants. Researchers can influence participants to become bolder or more conservative by manipulating the rewards and costs for giving correct or incorrect responses. Increasing the rewards for hits or the costs for misses results in lower detection thresholds (more "yes" responses at low intensities). Thus a Navy radar operator may be more likely to notice a faint blip on her screen during a wartime mission—when a miss could have disastrous consequences—than during a peacetime voyage. Conversely, like physicians who will not perform a risky medical procedure without strong evidence to support their diagnosis, participants become more conservative in their "yes" responses as costs for false alarms are increased, resulting in higher detection thresholds (Irwin & McCarthy, 1998). Signal-detection research shows us that perception is, in part, a decision.

What happens when stimuli register in the nervous system but cannot be consciously perceived? Can they nonetheless affect our behavior? Is this myth or reality?

The Difference Threshold

Distinguishing between stimuli can sometimes be as important as detecting stimuli in the first place. When we try to match the colors of paints or clothing, small stimulus differences can be very important. Likewise, a slight variation in taste might signal that food is tainted or spoiled. Professional wine tasters and piano tuners make their living by being able to make subtle discriminations.

The **difference threshold** *is defined as the smallest difference between two stimuli that people can perceive 50 percent of the time.* The difference threshold is sometimes called the *just noticeable difference (jnd).* German physiologist Ernst Weber discovered in the 1830s that there is some degree of lawfulness in the range of sensitivities within our sensory systems. **Weber's law** *states that the difference threshold,*

Myth or Reality?

Subliminal Stimuli Can Program Our Minds

Not all stimuli register in awareness. A **subliminal stimulus** *is one that is so weak or brief that although it is received by the senses, it cannot be perceived consciously.* (*Limen* is another term for absolute threshold.) There is little question that within certain ranges, subliminal stimuli can register in the nervous system (Kihlstrom, 2008). But can such stimuli program our minds without our awareness, thereby influencing our behavior? A multimillion-dollar business builds on this belief (Figure 5.4), a belief that is widely accepted—by 85 percent of college students in one survey (Taylor & Kowalski, 2004).

The answer to these questions appears to be yes—to a limited extent. For example, in a procedure called *priming*, researchers flash words or pictures on a display so briefly that they are seen only as a brief flash of light; they then assess the effects on various aspects of behavior. In one study, graduate students were asked to generate research ideas. They were then exposed to subliminal visual stimuli showing either the smiling face of a friendly professor they knew or the scowling face of their research supervisor. Without knowing why, those who saw the scowling face rated their own research ideas less favorably (Epley et al., 1999).

Interest (and concerns) about subliminal programming of behavior goes back a long way. In the late 1950s, James Vicary, a public relations executive, arranged to have subliminal messages flashed on a theater screen during a movie. The messages urged the audience to drink Coca-Cola and eat popcorn. Vicary's claim that the subliminal messages increased popcorn sales by 50 percent and soft drink sales by 18 percent aroused a public furor. Consumers and scientists feared the possible abuse of subliminal messages to covertly influence the buying habits of consumers. Government agencies were concerned such messages might be used for mind-control and brainwashing

Figure 5.4

Subliminal self-improvement is a thriving industry.

Continued

purposes. The National Association of Broadcasters reacted by outlawing subliminal messages on American television. Canada soon followed suit.

The outcries were, in large part, false alarms. Several attempts to reproduce Vicary's results under controlled conditions failed, and many other studies conducted in laboratory settings, on TV and radio, and in movie theaters indicated that there is little reason to be concerned about significant or widespread control of consumer behavior through subliminal stimulation (Dixon, 1981; Durkin, 1998). Years later, Vicary admitted that his study was a hoax, designed to revive his foundering advertising agency. However, his false report did stimulate a great deal of useful research on the power of subliminal stimuli to influence behavior. Where consumer behavior is concerned, the conclusion is that persuasive stimuli above the perceptual threshold are far more influential than are subliminal attempts to sneak into our subconscious mind. Nonetheless, subliminal messages may have at least short-term behavioral effects if they are relevant to a person's momentary goal state. Thirsty participants exposed to subliminal Lipton Ice messages showed an increased desire for that drink relative to thirsty controls who saw other words, but the message had no effect on non-thirsty participants (Karremans et al., 2006).

Although subliminal stimuli cannot control consumer behavior, research suggests that such stimuli do affect more subtle phenomena, such as perceptions and attitudes (Greenwald & Banaji, 1995; Kihlstrom, 2008). In one study, college students who were exposed to subliminal presentations of aggressively toned words like *hit* and *attack* later judged ambiguous behaviors of others as more aggressive. They also were more likely to behave aggressively than were participants who had been exposed to subliminal nonaggressive words (Todorov & Bargh, 2002). There is little doubt that subliminal stimuli can also have subtle effects on attitudes, judgments, and behavior. Perhaps this explains the motivation behind a Republican attack ad shown on television during the 2000 presidential campaign. In the ad, criticizing the health care reform plan proposed by Al Gore and running mate Joseph Lieberman, a very brief subliminal flash of the word *RATS* was closely associated in time with images of Gore and Lieberman (Figure 5.5). When the image was discovered through a frame-by-frame analysis of the ad, Democrats cried foul and accused the Republicans of waging subliminal warfare against their candidates. The ad's producer denied any wrongdoing, claiming that the word's appearance was simply a production error in which a fragment of the word *BUREAUCRATS*, which also appeared in the ad (but in much smaller letters), had mysteriously found its way into the finished product. Technical experts declared that explanation most unlikely (Della Sala, 2007).

Would you like to improve your self-concept, program yourself for success, enhance your sex life, or quit smoking? Many people believe that subliminal methods can also be a means to

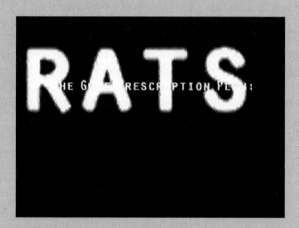

Figure 5.5

This subliminal frame was embedded in a 2000 political ad attacking the Gore-Lieberman proposal to reform health care.

self-improvement by programming the unconscious mind to guide one's adaptive behavior. To test the efficacy of subliminal self-improvement, Anthony Greenwald and coworkers (1991) purchased two commercially marketed subliminal tapes, one for memory improvement, the other to increase self-esteem. They then recruited participants who said they wanted to improve in one of those areas and gave them memory and self-esteem tests. Each person seeking memory improvement was then given a subliminal tape labeled "memory improvement" and told to use it once a day for a month. Similarly, the self-esteem seekers were each given a tape labeled "self-esteem improvement." Unbeknownst to the participants, however, half of each group actually received the other tape.

A month later, the researchers brought the people back and retested them on the memory and self-esteem measures. Theoretically, if change were being produced by the subliminal messages, people should improve only in the area addressed by the tape they actually heard. But that's not what the researchers found. Participants improved in both areas, but self-esteem improvement was actually greater for those who listened to the memory-improvement tape, and those who listened to the self-esteem tape improved more in memory than they did in self-esteem. Thus the power of an expectancy, or a placebo effect, explains the results better than does the power of subliminal programming of the unconscious mind. Although subliminal products may appeal to some people as a relatively effortless way to change, they remain unproven scientifically, especially in comparison with other behavior-change methods (Lilienfeld et al., 2010). Personally, we have much greater faith in the effectiveness of the techniques presented in this book's "Applying Psychological Science" features, because they're backed by scientific evidence.

Table **5.2** | **Weber Fractions for Various Sensory Modalities**

Sensory Modality	Weber Fraction
Audition (tonal pitch)	1/333
Vision (brightness, white light)	1/60
Kinesthesis (lifted weights)	1/50
Pain (heat produced)	1/30
Audition (loudness)	1/20
Touch (pressure applied to skin)	1/7
Smell (India rubber)	1/4
Taste (salt concentration)	1/3

SOURCE: Based on Teghtsoonian, 1971.

or jnd, is directly proportional to the magnitude of the stimulus with which the comparison is being made and can be expressed as a *Weber fraction.* For example, the jnd value for weights is a Weber fraction of approximately 1/50 (Teghtsoonian, 1971). This means that if you lift a weight of 50 grams, a comparison weight must be at least 51 grams in order for you to be able to judge it as heavier. If the weight were 500 grams, a second weight would have to be at least 510 grams (i.e., 1/50 = 10 g/500 g) for you to discriminate between them.

Although Weber's law breaks down at extremely high and low intensities of stimulation, it holds up reasonably well within the most frequently encountered range, thereby providing a useful barometer of our abilities to discern differences in the various sensory modalities. Table 5.2 lists Weber fractions for the various senses. The smaller the fraction, the greater the sensitivity to differences. As highly visual creatures, humans show greater sensitivity in their visual sense than they do in, for example, their sense of smell. Undoubtedly many creatures who depend on their sense of smell to track their prey would show quite a different order of sensitivity. Weber fractions also show that humans are highly sensitive to differences in the pitch of sounds but far less sensitive to loudness differences.

Sensory Adaptation

From a survival perspective, it's important to know when some new development requires your attention. If you were relaxing outdoors, you would want to be aware of the whine of an approaching mosquito. Because changes in our environment are usually noteworthy, sensory systems are finely attuned to changes in stimulation (Rensink, 2002). Sensory neurons are engineered to respond to a constant stimulus by decreasing

their activity, and *the diminishing sensitivity to an unchanging stimulus is called* **sensory adaptation.**

Adaptation (sometimes called *habituation*) is a part of everyday experience. After a while, monotonous background sounds are largely unheard. The feel of your wristwatch against your skin recedes from awareness. When you dive into a swimming pool, the water may feel cold at first because your body's sensors respond to the change in temperature. Over time, however, you become used to the water temperature.

Adaptation occurs in all sensory modalities, including vision. Indeed, were it not for tiny involuntary eye movements that keep images moving about the retina, stationary objects would simply fade from sight if we stared at them. In an ingenious demonstration of this type of adaptation, R. M. Pritchard (1961) attached a tiny projector to a contact lens worn by each participant (Figure 5.6a). This procedure guaranteed that visual images presented through the projector would maintain a constant position on the retina, even when the eye moved. When a stabilized image was projected through the lens onto the retina, participants reported that the image appeared in its entirety for a time and then began to vanish and reappear as parts of the original stimulus (Figure 5.6b).

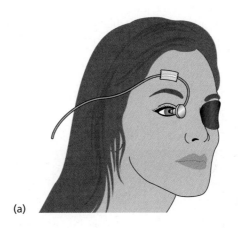

(a)

(b)

Figure 5.6

Demonstrating visual adaptation.
(a) To create a stabilized retinal image, a person wears a contact lens to which a tiny projector has been attached. Despite tiny eye movements, images are cast on the same region of the retina. (b) Under these conditions, the stabilized image is clear at first and then begins to fade and reappear in meaningful segments as the receptors fatigue and recover.
SOURCE: Adapted from Pritchard, 1961.

Although sensory adaptation may reduce our overall sensitivity, it is adaptive, for it frees our senses from the constant and the mundane, allowing them to pick up informative changes in the environment that could be important to our well-being or survival.

VISION

The normal stimulus for vision is electromagnetic energy, or light waves, which are measured in nanometers (nm), or one billionth of a meter. In addition to that tiny portion of light waves that humans can perceive, the electromagnetic spectrum encompasses X-rays, television and radio signals, and infrared and ultraviolet rays (Figure 5.7). Bees are able to see ultraviolet light, and rattlesnakes, as mentioned earlier, can detect infrared energy. Our visual system is sensitive only to wavelengths extending from about 700 nanometers (red) down to about 400 nanometers (blue-violet). (You can remember the order of the spectrum, from higher wavelengths to lower ones, with the name ROY G. BIV—red, orange, yellow, green, blue, indigo, and violet.)

The Human Eye

Light waves enter the eye through the *cornea*, a transparent protective structure at the front of the eye (Figure 5.8). Behind the cornea is the *pupil*, an

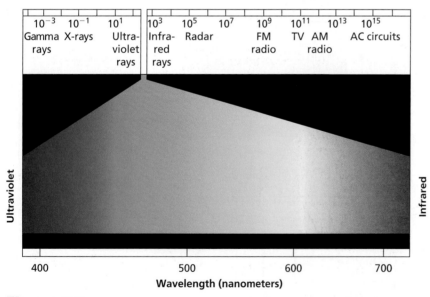

Figure 5.7

Light energy.
Of the full spectrum of electromagnetic radiation, only the narrow band between 400 and 700 nanometers (nm) is visible to the human eye. One nanometer equals one 1,000,000,000th of a meter.

adjustable opening that can dilate or constrict to control the amount of light that enters the eye. The pupil's size is controlled by muscles in the colored *iris* that surrounds the pupil. Low levels of illumination cause the pupil to dilate, letting more light into the eye to improve optical clarity; bright light makes the pupil constrict.

Behind the pupil is the **lens,** *an elastic structure that becomes thinner to focus on distant objects and thicker to focus on nearby objects.* Just as the lens of a camera focuses an image on a photosensitive material (film), so the lens of the eye focuses the visual image on the **retina,** *a multilayered light-sensitive tissue at the rear of the fluid-filled eyeball.* As seen in Figure 5.8a, the lens reverses the image from right to left and top to bottom when it is projected upon the retina, but the brain reverses the visual input into the image that we perceive.

The ability to see clearly depends on the lens's ability to focus the image directly onto the retina (Pedrotti & Pedrotti, 1997). If you have good vision for nearby objects but have difficulty seeing faraway objects, you probably suffer from *myopia* (nearsightedness). In nearsighted people, the lens focuses the visual image in front of the retina (or too near the lens), resulting in a blurred image for faraway objects. This condition generally occurs because the eyeball is longer (front to back) than normal. In contrast, some people have excellent distance vision but have difficulty seeing close-up objects clearly. *Hyperopia* (farsightedness) occurs when the lens does not thicken enough and the image is therefore focused on a point behind the retina (or too far from the lens). Eyeglasses and contact lenses are designed to correct for the natural lens's inability to focus the visual image directly onto the retina.

Photoreceptors: The Rods and Cones

The retina, with its specialized sensory neurons, is actually an extension of the brain (Bullier, 2002). It contains two types of light-sensitive receptor cells, called *rods* and *cones* because of their shapes (see Figure 5.8b). There are about 120 million rods and 6 million cones in the human eye.

The **rods,** *which function best in dim light, are primarily black-and-white brightness receptors.* They are about 500 times more sensitive to light than are the cones, but they do not give rise to color sensations. The retinas of some nocturnal creatures, such as owls, contain only rods, giving them exceptional vision in very dim light but no color vision (Dossenbach & Dossenbach, 1998). The **cones,** *which are color receptors, function best in bright illumination.* Some creatures that are active

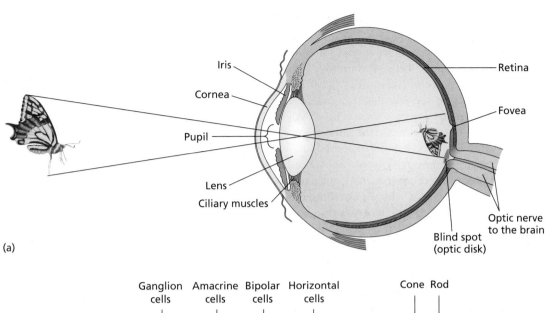

(a)

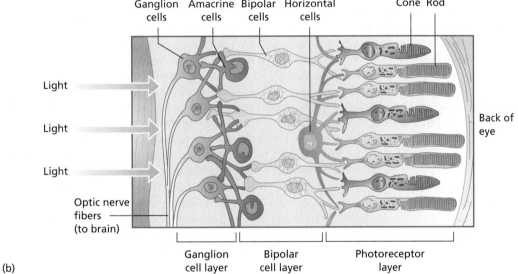

(b)

Figure 5.8

The human eye.

(a) This cross section shows the major parts of the human eye. The iris regulates the size of the pupil. The ciliary muscles regulate the shape of the lens. The image entering the eye is reversed by the lens and cast on the retina, which contains the rod and cone photoreceptor cells. The optic disk, where the optic nerve exits the eye, has no receptors and produces a blind spot, as demonstrated in Figure 5.9. (b) Photoreceptors in the retina, the rods and cones, synapse with bipolar cells, which in turn synapse with ganglion cells whose axons form the optic nerve. The horizontal and amacrine cells allow sideways integration of retinal activity across areas of the retina.

only during the day, such as pigeons and chipmunks, have only cones in their retinas, so they see the world in living color but have very poor night vision (Dossenbach & Dossenbach, 1998). Animals that are active both day and night, as humans are, have a mixture of rods and cones. In humans, rods are found throughout the retina except in the **fovea,** *a small area in the center of the retina that contains no rods but many densely packed cones.* Cones decrease in concentration the farther away they are from the center of the retina, and the periphery of the retina contains mainly rods.

Rods and cones send their messages to the brain via two additional layers of cells. The rods and cones have synaptic connections with *bipolar cells,* which in turn synapse with a layer of about 1 million *ganglion cells, whose axons are collected into a bundle to form the* **optic nerve.** Thus input from more than 126 million rods and cones is eventually funneled into only 1 million traffic lanes leading out of the retina toward higher visual centers. Figure 5.8b shows how the rods and cones are connected to the bipolar and ganglion cells. One interesting aspect of these connections is the fact that the rods and cones not only form the rear layer of the retina, but their light-sensitive ends actually point away from the direction of the entering light so that they receive only a fraction of the light energy that enters the eye.

The manner in which the rods and cones are connected to the bipolar cells accounts for both the greater importance of rods in dim light and our greater ability to see fine detail in bright illumination, when the cones are most active. Typically, many rods are connected to the same bipolar cell. They can therefore combine, or funnel, their individual electrical messages to the bipolar cell, where the additive effect of the many signals may be enough to fire it. That is why we can more easily detect a faint stimulus, such as a dim star, if we look slightly to one side so that its image falls not on the fovea but on the peripheral portion of the retina, where the rods are packed most densely.

Like the rods, the cones that lie in the periphery of the retina share bipolar cells. In the fovea, however, the densely packed cones each have their own "private line" to a single bipolar cell. As a result, our **visual acuity,** *or ability to see fine detail,* is greatest when the visual image projects directly onto the fovea. Such focusing results in the firing of a large number of cones and their private-line bipolar cells. Some birds of prey, such as eagles and hawks, are blessed with two foveas in each eye, contributing to a visual acuity that allows them to see small prey on the ground as they soar hundreds of feet above the earth (Tucker, 2000).

The optic nerve formed by the axons of the ganglion cells exits through the back of the eye not far from the fovea, producing a blind spot where there are no photoreceptors. You can demonstrate the existence of your blind spot by following the directions in Figure 5.9. Ordinarily, we are unaware of the blind spot because our perceptual system fills in the missing part of the visual field (Rolls & Deco, 2002).

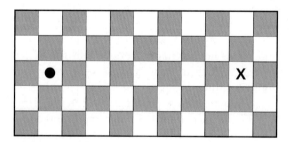

Figure 5.9

Find your blind spot.

Close your left eye and, from a distance of about 12 inches, focus steadily on the dot with your right eye as you slowly move the book toward your face. At some point the image of the X will cross your optic disk (blind spot) and disappear. It will reappear after it crosses the blind spot. Note how the checkerboard remains wholly visible even though part of it falls on the blind spot. Your perceptual system fills in the missing information.

Visual Transduction: From Light Waves to Nerve Impulses

Rods and cones translate light waves into nerve impulses through the action of protein molecules called **photopigments** (Stryer, 1987; Wolken, 1995). The absorption of light by the photopigments produces a chemical reaction that changes the rate of neurotransmitter release at the receptor's synapse with the bipolar cells. The greater the change in transmitter release, the stronger the signal passed on to the bipolar cell and, in turn, to the ganglion cells whose axons form the optic nerve. If a stimulus triggers nerve responses at each of the three levels (rod or cone, bipolar cell, and ganglion cell), the message is instantaneously on its way to the visual relay station in the thalamus and then on to the visual cortex of the brain.

Brightness Vision and Dark Adaptation

As noted earlier, rods are far more sensitive than cones under conditions of low illumination. Nonetheless, the sensitivity of both the rods and the cones to light intensity depends in part on the wavelength of the light. Research has shown that rods have a much greater sensitivity than cones throughout the color spectrum except at the red end, where rods are relatively insensitive. Cones are most sensitive to low illumination in the greenish-yellow range of the spectrum (Valberg, 2006). These findings have prompted many cities to change the color of their fire engines from the traditional red (to which rods are insensitive) to a greenish yellow in order to increase the vehicles' visibility to both rods and cones in dim lighting.

Although the rods are by nature sensitive to low illumination, they are not always ready to fulfill their function. Perhaps you have had the embarrassing experience of entering a movie theater on a sunny day, groping around in the darkness, and finally sitting down in someone's lap. Although one can meet interesting people this way, most of us prefer to stand in the rear of the theater until our eyes adapt to the dimly lit interior.

Dark adaptation *is the progressive improvement in brightness sensitivity that occurs over time under conditions of low illumination.* After absorbing light, a photoreceptor is depleted of its pigment molecules for a period of time. If the eye has been exposed to conditions of high illumination, such as bright sunlight, a substantial amount of photopigment will be depleted. During dark adaptation, the photopigment molecules are regenerated and the receptor's sensitivity increases greatly.

Vision researchers have plotted the course of dark adaptation as people move from conditions

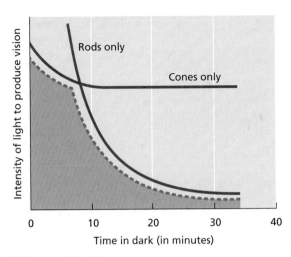

Figure 5.10

Adapting to the dark.
The course of dark adaptation is graphed over time. The curve has two parts, one for the cones and one for the rods. The cones adapt completely in about 10 minutes, whereas the rods continue to increase their sensitivity for another 20 minutes.

of bright light into darkness (Carpenter & Robson, 1999). By focusing light flashes of varying wavelengths and brightness on the fovea (which contains only cones) or on the periphery of the retina (where rods reside), they discovered the two-part curve shown in Figure 5.10. The first part of the curve is due to dark adaptation of the cones. As you can see, the cones gradually become sensitive to fainter lights as time passes, but after about 5 to 10 minutes in the dark, their sensitivity has reached its maximum. The rods, whose photopigments regenerate more slowly, do not reach their maximum sensitivity for about half an hour. It is estimated that after complete adaptation, rods are able to detect light intensities 1/10,000 as great as those that could be detected before dark adaptation began (May, 2007).

Color Vision

We are blessed with a world rich in color. The majesty of a glowing sunset, the rich blues and greens of a tropical bay, the brilliant colors of fall foliage are all visual delights. Human vision is finely attuned to color; our difference thresholds for light wavelengths are so small that we are able to distinguish an estimated 7.5 million hue variations (Medieros, 2006). Historically, two different theories of color vision have tried to explain how this occurs.

The Trichromatic Theory

Around 1800 it was discovered that any color in the visible spectrum can be produced by some combination of the wavelengths that correspond

to the colors blue, green, and red. This fact was the basis for an important trichromatic (three-color) theory of color vision advanced by Thomas Young, an English physicist, and Hermann von Helmholtz, a German physiologist. According to the **Young-Helmholtz trichromatic theory,** *there are three types of color receptors in the retina.* Although all cones can be stimulated by most wavelengths to varying degrees, individual cones are most sensitive to wavelengths that correspond to either blue, green, or red (Figure 5.11). Presumably, each of these receptor classes sends messages to the brain, based on the extent to which they are activated by the light energy's wavelength. The visual system then combines the signals to re-create the original hue. If all three cones are equally activated, a pure white color is perceived.

Although the Young-Helmholtz theory was consistent with the laws of color mixture, there are several facts that did not fit the theory. Take our perception of yellow, for example. According to the theory, yellow is produced by the activity of red and green receptors. Yet certain people with red-green color blindness, who are unable to perceive either color, are somehow able to experience yellow. A second phenomenon that posed

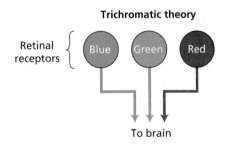

Figure 5.11

Two classic theories of color vision.
The Young-Helmholtz trichromatic theory proposed three different receptors, one for blue, one for green, and one for red. The ratio of activity in the three types of cones yields our experience of a particular hue, or color. Hering's opponent-process theory also assumed that there are three different receptors: one for blue-yellow, one for red-green, and one for black-white. Each of the receptors can function in two possible ways, depending on the wavelength of the stimulus. Again, the pattern of activity in the receptors yields our perception of the hue.

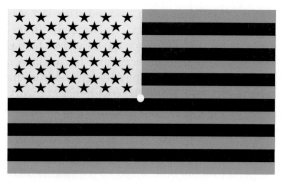 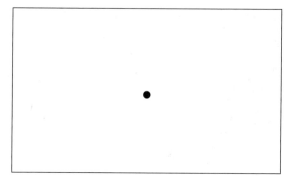

Figure 5.12

Opponent processes at work.

Negative color afterimages demonstrate opponent processes occurring in the visual system. Stare steadily at the white dot in the center of the flag for about a minute, then shift your gaze to the dot in the blank space. The opponent colors should appear.

problems for the trichromatic theory was the color afterimage, in which an image in a different color appears after a color stimulus has been viewed steadily and then withdrawn. To experience an afterimage, follow the instructions for Figure 5.12. Trichromatic theory cannot account for what you'll see.

Opponent-Process Theory

A second influential color theory, formulated by Ewald Hering in 1870, also assumed that there are three types of cones. **Hering's opponent-process theory** *proposed that each of the three cone types responds to two different wavelengths.* One type responds to blue or yellow, another to red or green, and a third to black or white. For example, a red-green cone responds with one chemical reaction to a green stimulus and with its other chemical reaction (opponent process) to a red stimulus (see Figure 5.11). You have experienced one of the phenomena that support the existence of opponent processes if you did the exercise in Figure 5.12. The afterimage that you saw in the blank space contains the colors specified by opponent-process theory: The green portion of the flag appeared as red; the black, as white; and the yellow, as blue. According to opponent-process theory, as you stared at the green, black, and yellow colors, the neural processes that register those colors became fatigued. Then when you cast your gaze on the white surface, which reflects all wavelengths, a rebound opponent reaction occurred as each receptor responded with its opposing red, white, or blue reactions.

Dual Processes in Color Transduction

Which theory—the trichromatic theory or the opponent-process theory—is correct? Two centuries of research have yielded verifying evidence for each theory. Today's **dual-process theory** *combines the trichromatic and opponent-process theories to account for the color transduction process* (Valberg, 2006).

The trichromatic theorists Young and Helmholtz were right about the cones. The cones do indeed contain one of three different protein photopigments that are most sensitive to wavelengths roughly corresponding to the colors blue, green, and red (Valberg, 2006). Different ratios of activity in the blue-, green-, and red-sensitive cones can produce a pattern of neural activity that corresponds to any hue in the spectrum (Backhaus et al., 1998). This process is similar to that which occurs on your TV screen, where color pictures (including white hues) are produced by activating combinations of tiny blue, green, and red dots.

Hering's opponent-process theory was also partly correct, but opponent processes do not occur at the level of the cones, as he maintained. When researchers began to use microelectrodes to record from single cells in the visual system, they discovered that ganglion cells in the retina, as well as neurons in visual relay stations and the visual cortex, respond in an opponent-process fashion by altering their rate of firing (Knoblauch, 2002). For example, if a red light is shone on the retina, an opponent-process ganglion cell may respond with a high rate of firing, but a green light will cause the same cell to fire at a very low rate. Other neurons respond in a similar opponent fashion to blue and yellow stimuli.

The red-green opponent processes are triggered directly by input from the red- or green-sensitive cones in the retina (Figure 5.13). The blue-yellow opponent process is a bit more complex. Activity of blue-sensitive cones directly stimulates the blue process further along in the visual system. And yellow? The yellow opponent process is triggered not by a yellow-sensitive cone, as Hering proposed, but rather by simultaneous input from the red- and green-sensitive cones (Valberg, 2006).

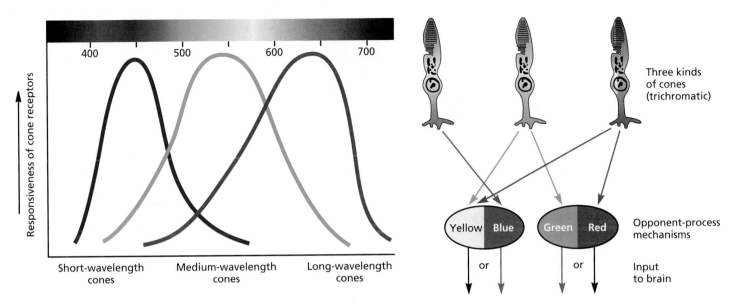

Figure 5.13

Dual color vision processes.
Color vision involves both trichromatic and opponent processes that occur at different places in the visual system. Consistent with trichromatic theory, three types of cones are maximally sensitive to short (blue), medium (green), and long (red) wavelengths, respectively. However, opponent processes occur further along in the visual system, as opponent cells in the retina, visual relay stations, and the visual cortex respond differentially to blue versus yellow, red versus green, and black versus white stimuli. Shown here are the inputs from the cones that produce the blue-yellow and red-green opponent processes.

Color-Deficient Vision

People with normal color vision are referred to as *trichromats*. They are sensitive to all three systems: blue-yellow, red-green, and black-white. However, about 7 percent of the male population and 1 percent of the female population have a deficiency in the blue-yellow system, the red-green system, or both. This deficiency is caused by an absence of hue-sensitive photopigment in certain cone types. A *dichromat* is a person who is color-blind in only one of the systems (blue-yellow or red-green). A *monochromat* is sensitive only to the black-white system and is totally color-blind. Most color-deficient people are dichromats and have their deficiency in the red-green system. Color-blindness tests typically employ sets of colored dots such as those in Figure 5.14. Depending on the type of deficit, a color-blind person cannot discern the numbers embedded in one of the two circles.

Analysis and Reconstruction of Visual Scenes

Once the transformation of light energy to nerve impulses occurs, the process of combining the messages received from the photoreceptors into the perception of a visual scene begins. As you read this page, nerve impulses from countless neurons are being analyzed and the visual image that you perceive is being reconstructed. Moreover,

you know what these black squiggles on the page mean. How does this occur?

From the retina, the optic nerve sends impulses to a visual relay station in the thalamus, the brain's sensory switchboard. From there, the input is routed to various parts of the cortex, particularly the primary visual cortex in the occipital lobe at the rear of the brain. Microelectrode studies have shown that there is a point-to-point correspondence between tiny regions of the retina

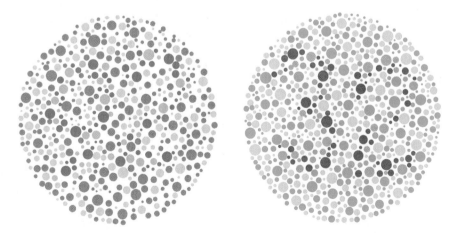

Figure 5.14

Test your color vision.
These dotted figures are used to test for color-deficient vision. The left one tests for blue-yellow color blindness, the right one for red-green color blindness. Because the dots in the picture are of equal brightness, color is the only available cue for perceiving the numbers in the circles. Can you see them?

and groups of neurons in the visual cortex. As you might expect, the fovea, where the one-to-one synapses of cones with bipolar cells produce high visual acuity, is represented by a disproportionately large area of the visual cortex. Somewhat more surprising is the fact that there is more than one cortical map of the retina; there are at least 10 duplicate mappings. Perhaps this is nature's insurance policy against damage to any one of them, or perhaps the duplicate maps are somehow involved in the integration of visual input (Bullier, 2002).

Groups of neurons within the primary visual cortex are organized to receive and integrate sensory nerve impulses originating in specific regions of the retina. Some of these cells, known as **feature detectors,** *fire selectively in response to visual stimuli that have specific characteristics* (May, 2007). Discovery of these feature detectors won David Hubel and Torsten Wiesel of Harvard University the 1981 Nobel Prize. Using tiny electrodes to record the activity of individual cells of the visual cortex of animals, Hubel and Wiesel found that certain neurons fired most frequently when lines of certain orientations were presented. One neuron might fire most frequently when a horizontal line was presented; another neuron, in response to a line of a slightly different orientation; and so on "around the clock." For example, the letter A could be constructed from the response of feature detectors that responded to three different line orientations: /, \, and –. Within the cortex, this information is integrated and analyzed by successively more complex feature-detector systems to produce our perception of objects (Palmer, 2002).

Other classes of feature detectors respond to color, to depth, or to movement (Livingstone & Hubel, 1994; Zanker, 2010). These feature-detector "modules" subdivide a visual scene into its component dimensions and process them

simultaneously. Thus as a red, white, and green beach ball sails toward you, separate but overlapping modules within the brain are simultaneously analyzing its colors, shape, distance, and movement by engaging in parallel processing of the information and constructing a unified image of its properties (Hubel & Wiesel, 2005). The final stages in the process of constructing a visual representation occur when the information analyzed and recombined by the primary visual cortex is routed to other cortical regions known as the *visual association cortex,* where features of the visual scene are combined and interpreted in light of our memories and knowledge (Grossberg et al., 2005). If all goes correctly, a process that began with nerve impulses from the rods and cones now ends with our recognizing the beach ball for what it is and catching it. Quite another conscious experience and response would probably occur if we interpreted the oncoming object as a water balloon.

Recently, scientists have discovered that neurons in the brain respond selectively not only to basic stimulus characteristics like corners and colors, but also to complex stimuli that have acquired special meaning through experience. For example, brain scientists at the University of California–Los Angeles who were recording from single neurons in the amygdala of a brain-damaged patient found a neuron that responded electrically to only 3 of 50 visual scenes. All of the 3 scenes involved former president Bill Clinton, but they differed considerably. One was a portrait, another a group picture that included Clinton, and the third was a cartoonist's representation of the president. Pictures of other celebrities, animals, landscapes, and geometric forms evoked no response (Figure 5.15). This neuron was likely part of a neural circuit that was created within the brain to register this particular celebrity (Koch, 2004).

Figure 5.15

A Bill Clinton feature detector?
Single-neuron electrical recording in a patient's amygdala (which receives extensive visual input) revealed a neuron that responded to depictions of Bill Clinton but not to 47 other pictures showing other presidents, celebrities (e.g., Michael Jordan, *far right*), objects, landscapes, and geometric shapes. This neuron was apparently part of a neuronal network that had learned to recognize and represent the former president.
Source: Koch, 2004.

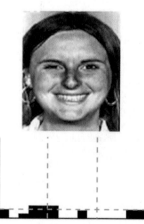 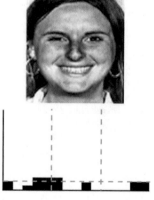  

Neuron's Electrical Response

Sensory Processes and Vision

Match each numbered term to the correct definition on the right.

1. cones	a. opponent processes
2. feature detectors	b. acronym for the color spectrum
3. optic nerve	c. sensory relay station in brain
4. ROY G BIV	d. retinal color receptors
5. Hering's theory	e. respond to specific stimulus characteristics
6. thalamus	f. information conduit from the visual receptors to the brain
7. jnd	g. key concept of Weber's law

ANSWERS: 1-d, 2-e, 3-f, 4-b, 5-a, 6-c, 7-g

AUDITION

The stimuli for our sense of hearing are sound waves, a form of mechanical energy. What we call *sound* is actually pressure waves in air, water, or some other conducting medium. When a stereo's volume is high enough, you can actually see cloth speaker covers moving in and out. The resulting vibrations cause successive waves of compression and expansion among the air molecules surrounding the source of the sound. These sound waves have two characteristics: frequency and amplitude (Figure 5.16).

Frequency *is the number of sound waves, or cycles, per second.* The **hertz (Hz)** *is the technical measure of cycles per second; 1 hertz equals 1 cycle per second.* The sound waves' frequency is related to the pitch that we perceive; the higher the frequency (hertz), the higher the perceived pitch. Humans are capable of detecting sound frequencies from 20 to 20,000 hertz (about 12,000 hertz in older people). Most common sounds are in the lower frequencies. Among musical instruments, the piano can play the widest range of frequencies, from 27.5 hertz at the low end of the keyboard to 4,186 hertz at the high end. An operatic soprano's voice, in comparison, has a range of only about 250 to 1,100 hertz (Aiello, 1994).

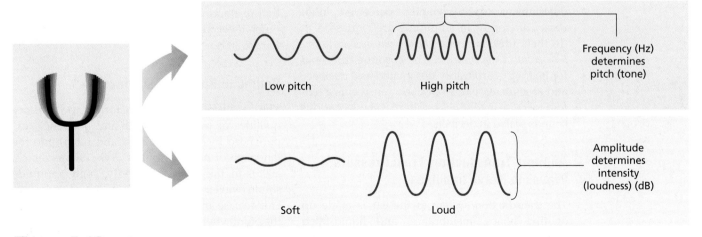

Figure 5.16

Auditory stimuli.
Sound waves are a form of mechanical energy. As the tuning fork vibrates, it produces successive waves of compression and expansion of air molecules. The number of maximum compressions per second (cycles per second) is its frequency, measured in hertz (Hz). The height of the wave above zero air pressure represents the sound's amplitude. Frequency determines pitch; amplitude determines loudness, measured in decibels (dB).

Table **5.3** | Decibel Scaling of Common Sounds

Level in Decibels (dB)	Common Sounds	Threshold Levels
140	50-horsepower siren at a distance of 100 feet, jet fighter taking off 80 feet away	Potential damage to auditory system
130	Boiler shop	
120	Air hammer at position of operator, portable music player at maximum volume, jet aircraft at 500 feet overhead	Human pain threshold
110	Trumpet automobile horn at 3 feet	
100	Crosscut saw at position of operator	
90	Inside subway car	Hearing damage with prolonged exposure
80	Train whistle at 500 feet	
70	Inside automobile in city	
60	Downtown city street (Chicago), average traffic	
50	Restaurant, business office	
40	Classroom, church	
30	Hospital room, quiet bedroom	
20	Recording studio	Threshold of hearing (young men)
10		
0		Minimum threshold of hearing

NOTE: The decibel scale relates a physical quantity—sound intensity—to the human perception of that quantity—sound loudness. It is a logarithmic scale—that is, each increment of 10 dB represents a tenfold increase in loudness. The table indicates the decibel ranges of some common sounds as well as thresholds for hearing, hearing damage, and pain. Prolonged exposure at 150 dB causes death in laboratory rats.

Amplitude *refers to the vertical size of the sound waves—that is, the amount of compression and expansion of the molecules in the conducting medium.* The sound wave's amplitude is the primary determinant of the sound's perceived loudness. Differences in amplitude are expressed as **decibels (dB),** *a measure of the physical pressures that occur at the eardrum.* The absolute threshold for hearing is arbitrarily designated as 0 decibels, and each increase of 10 decibels represents a tenfold increase in loudness. Table 5.3 shows various sounds scaled in decibels.

Auditory Transduction: From Pressure Waves to Nerve Impulses

The transduction system of the ear is made up of tiny bones, membranes, and liquid-filled tubes designed to translate pressure waves into nerve impulses (Figure 5.17). At a speed of about 750 mph, sound waves travel into an auditory canal leading to the *eardrum,* a membrane that vibrates in response to the sound waves. Beyond the eardrum is the *middle ear,* a cavity housing three tiny bones (the smallest in the body, each the size of a grain of rice). The vibrating activity of these bones—the *hammer (malleus), anvil (incus),* and *stirrup (stapes)*—amplifies the sound waves more than 30 times. The first bone, the hammer, is attached firmly to the eardrum, and the stirrup is attached to another membrane, the *oval window,* which forms the boundary between the middle ear and the inner ear.

The inner ear contains the **cochlea,** *a coiled, snail-shaped tube about 3.5 centimeters (1.4 inches) in length that is filled with fluid and contains the* **basilar membrane,** *a sheet of tissue that runs its length.* Resting on the basilar membrane is the **organ of Corti,** *which contains about 16,000 tiny hair cells that are the actual sound receptors.* The tips of the hair cells are attached to another membrane, the *tectorial membrane,* that overhangs the basilar membrane along the entire length of the cochlea. The hair cells synapse with the neurons of the auditory nerve, which in turn send impulses via an auditory relay station in the thalamus to the temporal lobe's auditory cortex (Ando, 2009).

When sound waves strike the eardrum, pressure created at the oval window by the hammer, anvil, and stirrup of the middle ear sets the fluid inside the cochlea into motion. The fluid waves that result vibrate the basilar membrane and the tectorial membrane, causing a bending of the hair cells in the organ of Corti (see Figure 5.17b). This bending of the hair cells triggers the release of neurotransmitters into the synaptic space between the hair cells and the neurons of the auditory nerve, resulting in nerve impulses that are sent to the brain. Within the auditory cortex are feature-detector neurons that respond to specific kinds of auditory input, much as occurs in the visual system (Musiek & Baran, 2006).

Coding of Pitch and Loudness

The auditory system transforms the sensory qualities of wave amplitude and frequency (experienced by us as loudness and pitch) into the language of nerve impulses (Syka & Merzenich, 2005). In the case of intensity, high-amplitude sound waves cause the hair cells to bend more and release more neurotransmitter substance at the point where they synapse with auditory nerve cells, resulting in a higher rate of firing within the auditory nerve. Also, certain receptor neurons have higher thresholds than others, so that they will fire only when the hair cells bend considerably in response to an intense sound. Thus what

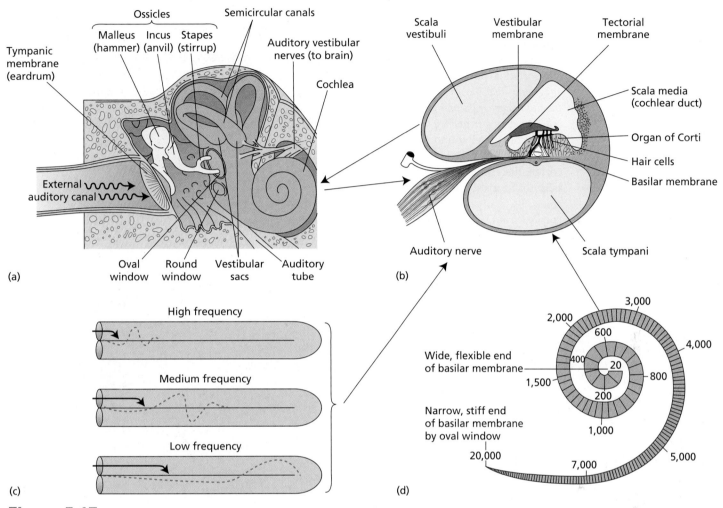

Figure 5.17

The ear.

(a) A cross section of the ear shows the structures that transmit sound waves from the auditory canal to the cochlea. (b) In the cochlea, sound waves are translated into fluid waves that stimulate hair cells in the organ of Corti. The resulting nerve impulses reach the brain via the auditory nerve. The semicircular canals and vestibular sacs of the inner ear contain sense organs for equilibrium. (c) Fluid waves are created by different sound frequencies. (d) Varying frequencies maximally stimulate different areas of the basilar membrane. High-frequency waves peak quickly and stimulate the membrane close to the oval window.

we experience as loudness is coded in terms of both the rate of firing in the axons of the auditory nerve and the specific hair cells that are sending messages (Carney, 2002).

The coding of wave frequency that produces our perception of pitch also involves two different processes, one for frequencies below about 1,000 hertz (two octaves below the top of the piano keyboard) and another for higher frequencies. Historically, as in the case of color vision, two competing theories were advanced to account for pitch perception. According to the **frequency theory of pitch perception,** *nerve impulses sent to the brain match the frequency of the sound wave.* Thus a 30-hertz (30 cycles per second) sound wave from a piano should send 30 volleys of nerve impulses per second to the brain.

Unfortunately, frequency theory encounters a major problem. Because neurons are limited in their rates of firing, individual impulses or volleys of impulses fired by groups of neurons cannot produce high enough frequencies of firing to match sound-wave frequencies above 1,000 hertz. How then do we perceive higher frequencies, such as a 4,000-hertz note from the same piano? Experiments conducted by Georg von Bekesy (1957) uncovered a second mechanism for coding pitch that earned him the 1961 Nobel Prize. Bekesy cut tiny holes in the cochleas of guinea pigs and human cadavers and observed through a microscope what happened inside the fluid-filled cochlea when he stimulated the eardrum with tones of varying frequencies. He found that high-frequency sounds produced an abrupt fluid wave (Figure 5.17c) that peaked close to the oval window, whereas lower-frequency vibrations produced a slower fluid wave that peaked farther down the cochlear canal. Bekesy's observations supported a **place theory of pitch perception,** *suggesting that the specific point in the cochlea where the fluid wave peaks and most strongly bends the hair cells serves as a frequency coding cue* (Figure 5.17d). Researchers later found that, similar to the manner in which the retina is mapped onto the visual cortex, the auditory cortex has a tonal-frequency map that corresponds to specific areas of the cochlea. By analyzing the specific location of the cochlea from which auditory nerve impulses are being received, the brain can code pitches like our 4,000-hertz piano note (Musiek & Baran, 2006).

Thus, like trichromatic and opponent-process theories of color vision, which were once thought to contradict one another, frequency and place theories of pitch perception both proved applicable in their own ways. At low frequencies, frequency theory holds true; at higher frequencies, place theory provides the mechanism for coding the frequency of a sound wave.

Sound Localization

Have you ever wondered why you have two ears, one located on each side of your head? As is usually the case in nature's designs, there is a good reason. Our very survival can depend on our ability to locate objects that emit sounds. The nervous system uses information concerning the time and intensity differences of sounds arriving at the two ears to locate the source of sounds in space (Luck & Vecera, 2002).

Sounds arrive first and loudest at the ear closest to the sound. When the source of the sound is directly in front of us, the sound wave reaches both ears at the same time and at the same intensity, so the source is perceived as being straight ahead. Our binaural (two-eared) ability to localize sounds is amazingly sensitive. For example, a sound 3 degrees to the right arrives at the right ear only 300 millionths of a second before it arrives at the left ear, and yet we can tell which direction the sound is coming from (Yin & Kuwada, 1984).

Other animals have even more exotic sound-localization systems. For example, the barn owl comes equipped with ears that are exquisitely tailored for pinpoint localization of its prey during night hunting. Its right ear is directed slightly upward, its left ear slightly downward. This allows it to localize sounds precisely in both the vertical and horizontal planes and thereby to zero in on its prey with deadly accuracy.

? thinking critically

NAVIGATING IN FOG: PROFESSOR MAYER'S TOPOPHONE

The device shown in Figure 5.18 is called a *topophone.* It was used in the late 1880s to help sailors locate sounds while navigating in thick fog. Based on what you've learned about the principles of sound localization, can you identify two features of this instrument that would assist sailors in detecting and locating sounds? Think about it, then see page 172.

PROFESSOR MAYER'S TOPOPHONE.

Figure 5.18

An early "hearing aid."
The topophone, used in the late 1800s by sailors to increase their ability to locate sounds while navigating in thick fog, assisted in two ways. Can you identify the relevant principles?

Hearing Loss

In the United States alone, more than 20 million people suffer from impaired hearing. Of these, 90 percent were born with normal hearing (Sataloff & Thayer, 2006). They suffer from two major types of hearing loss. **Conduction deafness** *involves problems with the mechanical system that transmits sound waves to the cochlea.* For example, a punctured eardrum or a loss of function in the tiny bones of the middle ear can reduce the ear's capacity to transmit vibrations. Use of a hearing aid, which amplifies the sounds entering the ear, may correct many cases of conduction deafness.

An entirely different matter is **nerve deafness,** *caused by damaged receptors within the inner ear or damage to the auditory nerve itself.* Nerve deafness cannot be helped by a hearing aid because the problem does not lie in the transmission of sound waves to the cochlea. Although aging and disease can produce nerve deafness, exposure to loud sounds is one of its leading causes. Repeated exposure to loud sounds of a particular frequency (as might be produced by a machine in a factory) can eventually cause the loss of hair cells at a particular point on the basilar membrane, thereby causing hearing loss for that frequency.

Extremely loud music can also take a serious toll on hearing (Naff, 2010). Even brief exposure to sounds exceeding 140 decibels can cause irreversible damage to the receptors in the inner ear, as can more continuous sounds at lower decibel levels. In 1986, a rock concert by The Who reached 120 decibels at a distance of 164 feet from the speakers. Although this earned The Who a place in the Guinness Book of Records for the all-time loudest concert, it inflicted severe and permanent hearing damage to many in the audience. The Who's lead guitarist, Pete Townshend, eventually suffered severe hearing loss from prolonged noise exposure. An iPod or similar portable music player can generate this decibel level through its earphones (Ballard, 2010).

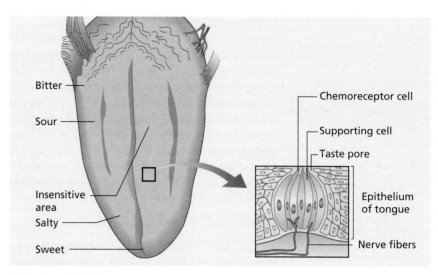

Figure 5.19

Taste organs.

The receptors for taste are specialized cells located in the tongue's taste buds. The tongue's 9,000 taste buds are found on the tip, back, and sides of the tongue. As this figure shows, certain areas of the tongue are especially sensitive to chemical stimuli that produce particular taste sensations. However, these different sensitivities are a matter of degree, as all kinds of taste buds are found in most areas of the tongue. The center of the tongue is relatively insensitive to chemical stimuli for taste.

TASTE AND SMELL: THE CHEMICAL SENSES

Gustation, *the sense of taste,* and **olfaction,** *the sense of smell,* are chemical senses; their receptors are sensitive to chemical molecules rather than to some form of energy. These senses are so intertwined that some scientists consider them a "common chemical sense" (Halpern, 2002). Enjoying a good meal usually depends on the simultaneous activity of taste and odor receptors, as becomes apparent when we have a stuffy nose and our food tastes bland. People who lose their sense of smell typically believe they have lost their sense of taste as well (Beauchamp & Bartoshuk, 1997).

Gustation: The Sense of Taste

People who consider themselves gourmets are frequently surprised to learn that their sense of taste responds to only four qualities: sweet, sour, salty, and bitter. Every other taste experience combines these qualities and those of other senses, such as smell, temperature, and touch. For example, part of the taste of popcorn includes its complex texture, its crunchiness, and its odor. In addition to its chemical receptors, the tongue is richly endowed with tactile (touch) and temperature receptors.

Taste buds *are chemical receptors concentrated along the tip, edges, and back surface of the tongue* (Figure 5.19). Each taste bud is most responsive to one or two of the basic taste qualities but responds weakly to the others as well. An additional taste sensation, called *umami,* increases the intensity of other taste qualities. This sensory response is activated by certain proteins, as well as by monosodium glutamate, a substance used by some restaurants for flavor enhancement.

Humans have about 9,000 taste buds, each one consisting of several receptor cells arranged like the segments of an orange. A small number of receptors are also found in the roof and back of the mouth, so that even people without a tongue can taste substances. Hairlike structures project from the top of each cell into the taste pore, an opening to the outside surface of the tongue. When a substance is taken into the mouth, it interacts with saliva to form a chemical solution that flows into the taste pore and stimulates the receptor cells. A taste results from complex patterns of neural activity produced by the four types of taste receptors (Halpern, 2002).

The sense of taste not only provides us with pleasure but also has adaptive significance in discriminating between nutrients and toxins (Scott, 1992). Our response to some taste qualities is innate. For example, newborn infants respond positively to sugar water placed on the tongue and negatively to bitter substances such as quinine

(Davidson & Fox, 1988). Many poisonous substances in nature have bitter tastes, so this emotional response seems to be hardwired into our physiology. In nature, sweet substances are more likely to occur in high-calorie (sugar-rich) foods. Unfortunately, many humans now live in an environment that is different from the food-scarce environment in which preferences for sweet substances evolved (Scott & Giza, 1993). As a result, people in affluent countries overconsume sweet foods that are good for us only in small quantities.

Olfaction: The Sense of Smell

Humans are visually oriented creatures, but the sense of smell (olfaction) is of great importance for many species. Bloodhounds, for example, have poor eyesight but a highly developed olfactory sense that is about 2 million times more sensitive than ours (Thomas, 1974). A bloodhound can detect a person's scent in a footprint that is four days old, something no human could do.

The receptors for smell are long cells that project through the lining of the upper part of the nasal cavity and into the mucous membrane. Humans have about 40 million olfactory receptors, dogs about 1 billion. Unfortunately, our ability to discriminate among different odors is not well understood. The most popular current theory is that olfactory receptors recognize diverse odors individually rather than by mixing the activity of a smaller number of basic receptors, as occurs in taste (Wilson et al., 2004). Olfactory receptors have structures that resemble neurotransmitter binding sites on neurons. Any of the thousands of potential odor molecules can lock into sites that are tailored to fit them (Buck & Axel, 1991). The receptors that fire send their input to the **olfactory bulb,** *a forebrain structure immediately above the nasal cavity.* Each odorous chemical excites only a limited portion of the olfactory bulb, and odors are apparently coded in terms of the specific area of the olfactory bulb that is excited (Dalton, 2002).

The social and sexual behavior of animals is more strongly regulated by olfaction than is human behavior (Alcock, 2005). For example, many species use urine to mark their territories; we humans find other ways, such as erecting fences or spreading our belongings over the table we are using in the library. Nonetheless, like animals, we have special receptors in the nose that send impulses to a separate olfactory area in the brain that connects with brain structures involved in social and reproductive behavior. Some researchers believe that **pheromones,** *chemical signals found in natural body scents,* may affect human behavior in subtle ways (Beauchamp & Bartoshuk, 1997).

One interesting phenomenon known as **menstrual synchrony** *is the tendency of women who live together or are close friends to become more similar in their menstrual cycles.* Psychologist Martha McClintock (1971) tested 135 college women and found that during the course of an academic year, roommates moved from a mean of 8.5 days apart in their periods to 4.9 days apart. Another study of 51 women who worked together showed that close friends had menstrual onsets averaging 3.5 to 4.3 days apart, whereas those who were not close friends had onsets that averaged 8 to 9 days apart (Weller et al., 1999). Are pheromones responsible for synchrony? In one experiment, 10 women with regular cycles were dabbed under the nose every few days with underarm secretions collected from another woman. After 3 months, the recipients' cycles began to coincide with the sweat donor's cycles. A control group of women who were dabbed with an alcohol solution rather than sweat showed no menstrual synchrony with a partner (Preti et al., 1986). In other studies, however, menstrual synchrony was not found for cohabitating lesbian couples or for Bedouin women who spent most of their time together, indicating that prolonged and very intensive contact may not be conducive to menstrual synchrony (Weller et al., 1999; Weller & Weller, 1997).

Do odors make us sexually attractive? The marketers of various "pheromone" perfumes tell us they do. And if you have ever owned a dog or cat that went into heat, you can attest to the effects of such odors in animals. However, researchers have yet to find any solid evidence to back the claims of commercial products promising instant sexual attraction. For humans, it appears that a pleasant personality and good grooming are a better bet than artificially applied pheromones when it comes to finding a mate.

THE SKIN AND BODY SENSES

The skin and body senses include the senses of touch, kinesthesis (muscle movement), and equilibrium. The last two are called *body senses* because they inform us of the body's position and movement. They tell us, for example, if we are running or standing still, lying down or sitting up.

The Tactile Senses

Touch is important to us in many ways. Sensitivity to extreme temperatures and to pain enables us to escape external danger and alerts us to disorders within our body. Tactile sensations are also a source of many of life's pleasures, including sexual orgasm. As discussed in Chapter 3, massage enhances newborn babies' development (Cigales et al., 1997; Field, 2000). Conversely, it has been shown that a lack of tactile contact with a caretaking adult retards physical, social, and emotional development (Harlow, 1958).

Humans are sensitive to at least four tactile sensations: pressure (touch), pain, warmth, and cold. These sensations are conveyed by receptors in the skin and in our internal organs. Mixtures of these four sensations form the basis for all other common skin sensations, such as itch.

Considering the importance of our skin senses, surprisingly little is known about how they work. The skin, a multilayered elastic structure that covers 2 square yards and weighs between 6 and 10 pounds, is the largest organ in our body. As shown in Figure 5.20, it contains a variety of receptor structures, but their role in specific sensations is less clear than for the other senses. Many sensations probably depend on specific patterns of activity in the various receptors (Schiff & Foulke, 2010). We do know that the primary receptors for pain and temperature are the *free nerve endings*, simple nerve cells beneath the skin's surface that resemble bare tree branches (Gracely et al., 2002). *Basket cell fibers* situated at the base of hair follicles are receptors for touch and light pressure (Heller & Schiff, 1991).

The brain can locate sensations because skin receptors send their messages to the point in the somatosensory cortex that corresponds to the area of the body where the receptor is located. As we saw in Chapter 4, the amount of cortex devoted to each area of the body is related to that part's sensitivity. Our fingers, lips, and tongue are well represented, accounting for their extreme sensitivity to stimulation (Figure 5.21; see also Figure 4.15).

Sometimes the brain "locates" sensations that cannot possibly be present. This occurs in the puzzling phantom-limb phenomenon, in which amputees experience vivid sensations coming from the missing limb (Warga, 1987). Apparently an irritation of the nerves that used to originate in the limb fools the brain into interpreting the resulting nerve impulses as real sensations. Joel Katz and Ronald Melzack (1990) studied 68 amputees who insisted that they experienced pain from the amputated limb that was as vivid and real as any pain they had ever felt. This pain was not merely a recollection of what pain used to feel like in the limb; it was actually experienced in the present. The phantom-limb phenomenon can be

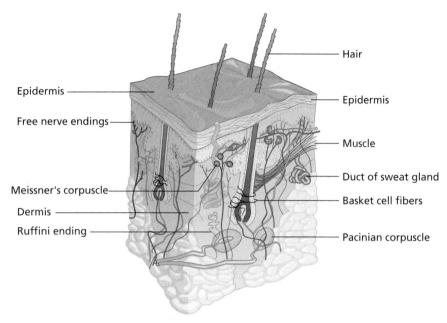

Figure 5.20

Skin receptors.

A variety of sensory receptors in the human skin and internal tissues allow us to sense touch and temperature. Basket cell fibers around hair follicles detect bending of the hair in light touch, and Meissner's corpuscles provide the same information in hairless areas. Pacinian corpuscles and Ruffini endings provide deeper touch sensations, and the free nerve endings respond to temperature and painful stimuli. Source: Adapted from Smith, 1998.

quite maddening. Imagine having an intense itch that you never can scratch or an ache that you cannot rub. When amputees are fitted with prosthetic limbs and begin using them, phantom pain tends to disappear (Gracely et al., 2002).

Figure 5.21

World-renowned percussionist Evelyn Glennie became deaf many years ago. She now uses her tactile sense to detect distinct vibrations that correspond with individual tones. Though deaf, she is capable of perfect tonal discrimination.

Pain

Pain receptors are found in all body tissues with the exception of the brain, bones, hair, nails, and nonliving parts of the teeth. Free nerve endings in the skin and internal organs respond to intense mechanical, thermal, or chemical stimulation and then send nerve impulses into the spinal cord, where sensory tracts carry pain information to the brain. Once in the brain, the sensory information about pain intensity and location is relayed by the thalamus to the somatosensory and frontal areas of the cerebral cortex (Fields, 2005). Reflecting the adaptive value of pain, brain recordings reveal that cerebral processing of pain occurs faster than for other kinds of tactile stimuli, permitting a more rapid response (Ploner et al., 2006). Other tracts from the thalamus direct nerve impulses to the limbic system, which is involved in motivation and emotion. These tracts seem to control the emotional component of pain (Zanker, 2010). Thus pain has both a sensory and an emotional component. *Suffering* occurs when both painful sensations and a negative emotional response are present (Fordyce, 1988; Turk, 2001).

Spinal and Brain Mechanisms

Gate control theory, developed by Canadian psychologist Ronald Melzack and physiologist Patrick Wall (1982), was a major advance in the study of pain. **Gate control theory** *proposes that the experience of pain results from the opening and closing of gating mechanisms in the nervous system* (Turk & Melzack, 2001). Events in the spinal cord can open a system of spinal cord "gates" and allow the nerve impulses to travel toward the brain. However, other sensory input can partially or completely close the gates and blunt our experiencing of pain. For example, rubbing a bruise or scratching an itch can produce relief. Gate control theorists also suggest that acupuncture achieves its pain-relieving effects because the acupuncture needles stimulate mostly tactile receptors that close the pain gates.

From a psychological perspective, perhaps the most intriguing feature of gate control theory is that nerve impulses in fibers descending from the brain can also influence the spinal gates, thereby increasing or decreasing the flow of pain stimulation to the brain. This *central control mechanism* allows thoughts, emotions, and beliefs to influence the experience of pain and helps explain why pain is a psychological phenomenon as well as a physical one.

Gate control and other theorists have traditionally viewed pain as solely reflecting the action of neurons. However, the immune system also plays a role in pain. Recent research has shown that *glial cells*, which structurally support and service neurons within the spinal cord, are involved in the creation and maintenance of pathological pain (Watkins & Maier, 2003). These glial cells become activated by immune challenges (viral or bacterial infection) and by substances released by neurons within the pain pathway. They then amplify pain by releasing *cytokines* (messenger molecules) that promote inflammation. This may help account for that "ache all over" sensation that many of us experience when we are ill.

The Endorphins

In 1680, an English physician wrote, "Among the remedies which it has pleased Almighty God to give man to relieve his suffering, none is so universal and so efficacious as opium" (quoted in Snyder, 1977). Opiates (such as opium, morphine, and heroin) have been used for centuries to relieve pain, and they strongly affect the brain's pain and pleasure systems. In the 1970s, scientists discovered that opiates produce their effects by locking into specific receptor sites in brain regions associated with pain perception.

But why would the brain have built-in receptors for opiates unless there were some natural chemical in the brain for the receptor to receive? Later research disclosed what had to be true: the nervous system has its own built-in analgesics (painkillers) with opiatelike properties. These natural opiates were named **endorphins** (meaning *endogenous, or internally produced, morphines*). Endorphins exert some of their painkilling effects by inhibiting the release of neurotransmitters involved in the synaptic transmission of pain impulses from the spinal cord to the brain (Fields, 2005). Endorphins are of great interest to psychologists because they may help explain how psychological factors "in the head" can have such strong effects on pain and suffering.

In 2001, John-Kar Zubieta and coworkers published a landmark study that showed the endorphins in action within the brain. They injected a radioactive form of an endorphin into volunteer participants, then stimulated them with painful injections of saltwater into the jaw muscles. Brain scans allowed the researchers to see which areas of the brain lit up from endorphin activity and to relate this activity to pain reports given by the participants every 15 seconds. The scans revealed a surge of endorphin activity within several brain regions, including the thalamus (the sensory switchboard), the amygdala (an emotion center), and a sensory area of the cortex. As the endorphin surge continued over 20 minutes of

Figure 5.22

Acupuncture is a proven pain-reduction procedure. Gate control theory attributes its effects to the stimulation of sensory fibers that close sensory gates in the pain system. In addition, there is evidence that acupuncture stimulates endorphin release.

pain stimulation, participants reported decreased sensory and emotional ratings of pain.

Acupuncture (Figure 5.22) is an effective pain-reduction technique that ultimately may be understood in terms of endorphin mechanisms. Injections of naloxone, a drug that counteracts the effects of endorphins, greatly decrease the pain-reducing effects of acupuncture (Oleson, 2002). This suggests that acupuncture normally releases endorphins to blunt pain sensations.

The Body Senses

We would be totally unable to coordinate our body movements were it not for the sense of **kinesthesis,** *which provides us with feedback about our muscles' and joints' positions and movements.* Kinesthetic receptors are nerve endings in the muscles, tendons, and joints. The information this sense gives us is the basis for making coordinated movements. Cooperating with kinesthesis is the **vestibular sense,** *the sense of body orientation, or equilibrium.*

The vestibular receptors are located in the vestibular apparatus of the inner ear (see Figure 5.17). One part of the equilibrium system consists of three semicircular canals, which contain the receptors for head movement. Each canal lies in a different plane: left-right, backward-forward, or up-down. These canals are filled with fluid and lined with hairlike cells that function as receptors. When the head moves, the fluid in the appropriate canal shifts, stimulating the hair cells and sending messages to the brain. The semicircular canals respond only to acceleration and deceleration; when a constant speed is reached (no matter how high), the fluid and the hair cells return to their normal resting state. That's why airplane takeoffs and landings give a sense of movement whereas cruising along at 500 miles per hour does not. Located at the base of the semicircular canals, the vestibular sacs also contain hair cells that respond to the position of the body and tell us whether we are upright or tilted at an angle. These structures form the second part of the body-sense system (Dolins & Mitchell, 2010).

You have now learned a considerable amount about the principles underlying stimulus detection and transduction. As the following "Applying Psychological Science" section shows, these principles have not only informational value for understanding how our sensory systems operate, but also applied value in helping people with sensory impairments.

Applying Psychological Science

Sensory Prosthetics: Restoring Lost Functions

Millions of people suffer from blindness and deafness, living in sightless or soundless worlds. War, accidents, or illness result in amputations that cost others important aspects of their sense of touch. Psychological research on the workings of the sensory systems is now being combined with technical advances in bioengineering, resulting in **sensory prosthetic devices** *that provide sensory input that can, to some extent, substitute for what cannot be supplied by a person's sensory receptors* (Patil & Turner, 2008). In considering these devices, we should remind ourselves that we don't see with the eyes, hear with the ears, or feel with touch receptors. We see, hear, and feel with our brain. The nerve impulses sent from the retina, the organ of Corti, or the skin are no different from those sent from anywhere else in the body.

SEEING WITH THE EARS

One device, known as a Sonicguide, provides new "eyes" through the ears, capitalizing on principles of auditory localization. The Sonicguide (Figure 5.23) works on the same principle as *echolocation,* the sensory tool used by bats to navigate in total darkness. A pair of eyeglasses contains a transmitter that emits high-frequency sound waves beyond the range of human hearing. These waves bounce back from objects in the environment and are transformed by the Sonicguide

Continued

Figure 5.23

The Sonicguide allows a blind person to perceive the size, distance, movement, shape, and texture of objects through sound waves that represent the visual features of objects.

into sounds that can be heard through earphones. Different sound qualities match specific features of external objects, and the wearer must learn to interpret the sonic messages. For example, the sound's pitch tells the person how far away an object is; a low pitch signals a nearby object and becomes higher as the distance to the object increases. The loudness of the sound tells how large the object is, and the clarity of the sound (ranging from a staticlike sound to a clear tone) signals the texture of the object, from very rough to very smooth. Finally, the sound-localization principle described earlier tells the person where the object is located in the environment by means of differences in the time at which sounds arrive at the two ears.

In the first laboratory tests of the Sonicguide, psychologists Stuart Aitken and T. G. R. Bower (1982) used the apparatus with six blind babies who ranged in age from 5 to 16 months. Within hours or days, all of the babies using the Sonicguide could reach for objects, walk or crawl through doorways, and follow the movements of their own hands and arms. Moreover, abilities such as reaching for

objects, recognizing favorite toys, and reaching out to be picked up when mother (but not someone else) approached seemed to occur on the same developmental timetable as in sighted children. Aitken and Bower concluded that blind infants can extract the same information from sonic cues as sighted babies do from visual cues.

Older children and adults can learn to use the device too, but not as easily as babies can. Children trained with the device can easily find objects, such as water fountains and specific toys. They can thread their way through crowded school corridors and can even play hide-and-seek. The Sonicguide is now being used by visually impaired children in schools and other natural settings, as well as by adults (Hill et al., 1995).

THE SEEING TONGUE

At the University of Wisconsin, Paul Bach-y-Rita (2004) developed a tactile tongue-based, electrical input sensor as a substitute for visual input. The tongue seems an unlikely substitute for the eye, hidden as it is in the dark recess of the mouth. Yet in many ways it may be the second-best organ for providing detailed input, for it is densely packed with tactile receptors, thus allowing the transmission of high-resolution data. Moreover, its moist surface is a good conducting medium for electricity, meaning that minimum voltage is required to stimulate the receptors.

The current stimulator, shown in Figure 5.24a, receives digital data from a camera and provides patterns of stimulation to the tongue through a 144-electrode array. The array can transmit shapes that correspond to the main features of the visual stimulus. Initial trials with blindfolded sighted people and blind people show that with about 9 hours of training, users can "read" the letters of a Snellen eye chart with an acuity of 20/430, a modest but noteworthy beginning (Simpaio et al., 2001).

With continued development, a miniature camera attached to eyeglasses will transmit wireless data to a more densely packed electrode array attached to a dental retainer. In addition to helping people who are blind, the device could have both military and civilian applications. For example, it could help soldiers locate objects in pitch-black environments, such as caves, where night-vision devices are useless. It could also aid firefighters as they search smoke-filled buildings for people to rescue.

Figure 5.24

Two approaches to providing artificial vision for the blind. (a) Bach-y-Rita's device converts digitized stimuli from a camera to a matrix of electrodes, which stimulate tactile receptors in the tongue to communicate spatial information to the brain. (b) Tiny electrodes implanted into individual neurons in the visual cortex produce patterns of phosphenes that correspond to the visual scene observed through the video camera and encoder. Note how the cortical image is reversed as in normal visual input.

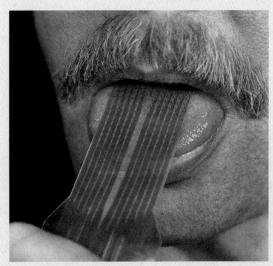

(a)

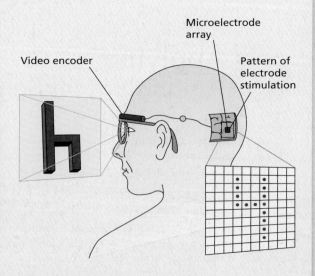

(b)

CORTICAL IMPLANTS

When cells in the visual cortex are stimulated electrically, discrete flashes of light called *phosphenes* are experienced by both sighted and blind people. Because sensory neurons in the visual cortex are arranged in a manner that corresponds to the organization of the retina, a specific pattern of stimulation applied to individual neurons in the cortex can form a phosphene pattern that conforms to the shapes of letters or objects (Weiland & Humayun, 2008). The acuity of the pattern depends on the area of the visual cortex that is stimulated (the portion receiving input from the densely packed fovea produces greatest acuity) and on the number of stimulating electrodes in the array.

Building on this approach, researchers have developed the device shown in Figure 5.24b. It consists of a silicon strip containing thousands of tiny stimulating electrodes that penetrate directly into individual neurons in the visual cortex, where they can stimulate phosphene patterns. Eventually, a tiny television camera mounted in specially designed eyeglasses will provide visual information to a microcomputer that will analyze the scene and then send the appropriate patterns of electrical stimulation through the implanted electrodes to produce corresponding phosphene patterns in the visual cortex. The researchers have shown that sighted participants who wear darkened goggles that produce phosphenelike patterns of light flashes like those provided by cortical stimulation can quickly learn to navigate through complex environments and are able to read text at about two thirds their normal rate (Liu et al., 2008; Normann et al., 1996, 1999). Blind people with the stimulating electrodes implanted in the visual cortex have also been able to learn a kind of cortical Braille for reading purposes. Although still experimental, a commercially available intracortical prosthetic device should appear in the near future.

COCHLEAR IMPLANTS

People with hearing impairments have also been assisted by the development of prosthetic devices. The cochlear implant is for people suffering from nerve deafness, who cannot be helped by mere sound amplification provided by normal hearing aids. A set of 22 electrodes is implanted in coillike fashion around the cochlea in order to directly stimulate the auditory nerve. A microphone sends sound waves to a processor implanted in the bone behind the ear, and the processor breaks the sound down into its principal frequencies and sends electrical signals to cochlear areas associated with particular frequencies (Fayad et al., 2008). Electrical recording of cortical responses to sounds in people who had been deaf for more than two decades showed that in the months following installation of a cochlear implant, sounds increasingly "registered" in the auditory cortex (Pantev et al., 2006). With a cochlear implant, deaf people like radio personality Rush Limbaugh can hear everyday sounds such as sirens, and many can understand speech (Meyer et al., 1998; Parkinson et al., 1998). Although the substitution of 22 electrodes for the more than 16,000 hair cells that populate the intact cochlea cannot produce normal auditory experience, cochlear implants have helped many people partially restore their sense of hearing.

THE BIONIC HAND THAT RESTORES TACTILE SENSATIONS

In 2009, researchers in Sweden and Italy announced the development of the SmartHand, a prosthetic device that restores the sense of touch in people who have lost their hands (*ScienceDaily*, 2009, November 11). The SmartHand contains 40 sensors that are connected to the sensory nerves in the arm of an amputee (Figure 5.25). Four motors, also linked to the brain through their attachment to motor nerves in the arm, allow patients to move the fingers in very precise ways. This is the first prosthetic hand that allows the level of control of movement that comes only through tactile feedback. With it, an amputee can actually experience the feeling of stroking a loved one's cheek and can handle delicate objects with just the right amount of pressure. Among the first to receive the device when it is available commercially will be returning soldiers from Iraq and Afghanistan who have lost their hands in battle.

Sensory prosthetics illustrate the ways in which knowledge about sensory phenomena such as phosphenes, the organization of the visual cortex, sound localization, and the place theory of pitch perception can provide the information needed to take advantage of new technological advances. Yet even with all our ingenuity, prosthetic devices are not substitutes for our normal sensory systems, a fact that should increase our appreciation for what nature has given us.

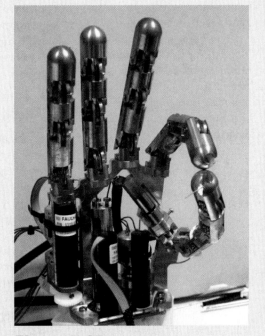 

Figure 5.25

Shown here without its skinlike covering, the SmartHand's leads connect to both sensory and motor nerves in the arm. The resulting motor control, combined with sensory feedback from the bionic hand's movements, allows an amputee to perform this precision act without dropping or crushing the soft plastic bottle.

Audition, Chemical, Skin, and Body Senses

True or false?

1. The frequency theory of pitch perception is limited to frequencies up to about 4,000 hertz.
2. High-frequency sound stimulates the portion of the cochlea close to the oval window.
3. The absolute threshold of hearing for young men is at about 20 decibels.
4. Taste buds are found only on the edges of the tongue.
5. Free nerve endings are pain receptors.
6. Cochlear implants are used for conduction deafness.

ANSWERS: 1-false, 2-true, 3-true, 4-false, 5-true, 6-false

PERCEPTION: THE CREATION OF EXPERIENCE

Sensory systems provide the raw materials from which experiences are formed. Our sense organs do not select what we will be aware of or how we will experience it; they merely transmit as much information as they can through our nervous system. Yet our experiences are not simply a one-to-one reflection of what is external to our senses. Different people may experience the same sensory information in radically different ways, because perception is an active, creative process in which raw sensory data are organized and given meaning.

To create our perceptions, the brain carries out two different kinds of processing functions (Figure 5.26). In **bottom-up processing,** *the system takes in individual elements of the stimulus and then combines them into a unified perception.* Your visual system operates in a bottom-up fashion as you read. Its feature detectors analyze the elements

in each letter of every word and then recombine them into your visual perception of the letters and words. In **top-down processing,** *sensory information is interpreted in light of existing knowledge, concepts, ideas, and expectations.* Top-down processing is occurring as you interpret the words and sentences constructed by the bottom-up process. Here you make use of higher-order knowledge, including what you have learned about the meaning of words and sentence construction. Indeed, a given sentence may convey a different personal meaning to you than to another person if you relate its content to some unique personal experiences. Top-down processing accounts for many psychological influences on perception, such as the roles played by our motives, expectations, previous experiences, and cultural learning.

Perception Is Selective: The Role of Attention

As you read these words, 100 million sensory messages may be clamoring for your attention. Only a few of these messages register in awareness; the rest you perceive either dimly or not at all. But you can shift your attention to one of those unregistered stimuli at any time. (For example, how does the big toe of your right foot feel right now?) Attention, then, involves two processes of selection: (1) focusing on certain stimuli and (2) filtering out other incoming information (Luck & Vecera, 2002).

These processes have been studied experimentally through a technique called *shadowing*. Participants wear earphones and listen simultaneously to two messages, one sent through each earphone. They are asked to repeat (or shadow) one of the messages word for word as they listen. Most participants can do this quite successfully, but only at the cost of not remembering what the other message was about. Shadowing experiments demonstrate

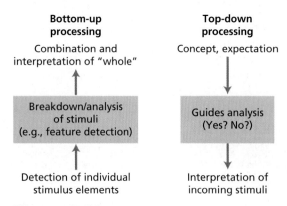

Figure 5.26

Perceptual processing.
Bottom-up perceptual processing builds from an analysis of individual stimulus features to a unified perception. Top-down processing begins with a perceptual whole, such as an expectation or an image of an object, then determines the degree of fit with the stimulus features.

that we cannot attend completely to more than one thing at a time. But we can shift our attention rapidly back and forth between the two messages, drawing on our general knowledge to fill in the gaps (Bonnel & Hafter, 1998; Sperling, 1984).

Inattentional Blindness

Electrical recording and brain-imaging studies have shown that unattended stimuli register in the nervous system but do not enter into immediate experience (Itti & Rees, 2005). In the visual realm, scientists have coined the term **inattentional blindness** *to refer to the failure of unattended stimuli to register in consciousness* (Mack, 2003). We can look right at something without "seeing" it if we are attending to something else. In one study, several experienced pilots training on flight simulators were so intent on watching the landing instruments, such as the air-speed indicator on the plane's windshield, that they directed their plane onto a runway containing another aircraft (Haines, 1991). In another instance, research participants who were counting the number of passes made during a videotaped basketball game did not notice a woman wearing a gorilla suit who walked across the court, even though she remained in clear sight for more than 5 seconds (Simons & Chabris, 1999). Inattentional blindness is surely relevant to findings that cell phone conversations significantly reduce driving performance in experimental studies (e.g., Golden et al., 2003). It's a bad idea to drive and yack at the same time. It's also a bad idea to drink and drive, as alcohol ingestion increases inattentional blindness (Clifasefi et al., 2006).

Environmental and Personal Factors in Attention

Attention is strongly affected by both the nature of the stimulus and by personal factors. Stimulus characteristics that attract our attention include intensity, novelty, movement, contrast, and repetition. Sexually oriented stimuli are especially attention-grabbing (Krishna, 2009). Advertisers use these properties in their commercials and packaging. Internal factors, such as our motives and interests, act as powerful filters and influence which stimuli in our environment we will notice. For example, when we are hungry, we are especially sensitive to food-related cues. A botanist walking through a park is particularly attentive to the plants; a landscape architect attends primarily to the layout of the park.

People are especially attentive to stimuli that have relevance to their well-being, a tendency that clearly has biological survival value (Oehman et al., 2001). This tendency is shown in experiments in which researchers measure how quickly people focus on and react to threatening versus nonthreatening stimuli. Thus people are quicker to identify an angry-looking face in a crowd than a smiling face (Hansen & Hansen, 1988). If a fearful face or figure is projected on one side of the visual field and a neutral face or figure on the other, measurements of eye movements show faster movements toward the fearful stimulus, showing the capacity of threat-relevant stimuli to capture visual attention (Bannerman et al., 2009).

In the sport of baseball, batters are sometimes forced to avoid pitched balls that might hit them. In an analog of this process, Jeffrey Lin and coworkers (2009) seated participants in front of a video display, then measured their reaction times in response to spherical images that sped from the background. The observers had significantly faster reaction times when the speeding object was coming toward their heads than when its trajectory would barely miss their heads. The investigators suggested that humans have developed a special visual system that unconsciously triggers protective responses to stimuli that are interpreted as threatening. As a real-life illustration of this principle, they point to the 2008 incident shown in Figure 5.27, when an Iraqi

Figure 5.27

President Bush reflexively ducks as an Iraqi reporter hurls a shoe toward the podium, but Iraqi Prime Minister al-Maliki does not.

Figure 5.28

Advertisers use attention-attracting stimuli in their advertisements. Personal characteristics of potential customers are also important. What kinds of individuals would be most attentive to this ad?

reporter hurled his shoes at president George Bush during a joint news conference with Iraqi Prime Minister Nouri al-Maliki. Commenting on this scene, Lin stated, "If you look at the shoe-throwing video, you will see that the prime minister doesn't flinch at all. His brain has already categorized the shoe as non-threatening which does not require evasive action. But Bush has categorized the shoe as threatening and triggers an evasive dodge, all within a fraction of a second" (Schwarz, 2009).

Advertisers are adept at using attention-getting stimuli to attract potential customers to their products (Figure 5.28). Sometimes, however, the process backfires, as in the following case.

> A famous model glides down a staircase, removing articles of clothing as she goes. Once inside the car being promoted in this British advertisement, she removes her panties and flings them out the window. The only problem with this wildly popular ad? An informal survey by a Welsh psychologist revealed that the visual image was so compelling that virtually no one remembered the brand of car being advertised. (Clay, 2002, p. 38)

Perceptions Have Organization and Structure

Have you ever stopped to wonder why we perceive the visual world as being composed of distinct objects? After all, the information sent by the retina reflects nothing but an array of varying intensities and frequencies of light energy. The light rays reflected from different parts of a single object have no more natural "belongingness" to one another than those coming from two different objects. Yet we perceive scenes as involving separate objects, such as trees, buildings, and people. These perceptions must be a product of an organization imposed by our nervous system (Jenkin & Harris, 2005; Matthen, 2007). This top-down process of perceptual organization occurs so automatically that we take it for granted. But Dr. Richard, a prominent psychologist who suffered brain damage in an accident, no longer does.

> There was nothing wrong with his eyes, yet the input he received from them was not put together correctly. Dr. Richard reported that if he saw a person, he sometimes would perceive the separate parts of the person as not belonging together in a single body. But if all the parts moved in the same direction, Dr. Richard then saw them as one complete person. At other times, he would perceive people in crowds wearing the same color clothes as "going together" rather than as separate people. He also had difficulty putting sights and sounds together. Sometimes, the movement of the lips did not correspond to the sounds he heard, as if he were watching a badly dubbed foreign movie. Dr. Richard's experience of his environment was thus disjointed and fragmented. (Sacks, 1985, p. 76)

Another, more extreme example of perceptual organization gone awry is synesthesia, which we described at the beginning of this chapter. What, then, are the processes whereby sensory nonsense becomes perceptual sense?

Gestalt Principles of Perceptual Organization

Early in the 20th century, psychologists from the German school of Gestalt psychology set out to discover how we organize the separate parts of our perceptual field into a unified and meaningful whole. *Gestalt* is the German term for "pattern," "whole," or "form." Gestalt theorists were early champions of top-down processing, arguing that the wholes we perceive are often more than (and frequently different from) the sum of their parts. Thus your perception of the photo in Figure 5.29 is likely to be more than "people on a football field."

The Gestalt theorists emphasized the importance of **figure-ground relations,** *our tendency to organize stimuli into a central or foreground figure*

Figure 5.29

As Gestalt psychologists emphasized, what we perceive (in this case, the name spelled out by the band) is more than simply the sum of its individual parts.

and a background. In vision, the central figure is usually in front of or on top of what we perceive as background. It has a distinct shape and is more striking in our perceptions and memory than the background. We perceive borders or contours wherever there is a distinct change in the color or brightness of a visual scene, but we interpret these contours as part of the figure rather than background. Likewise, we tend to hear instrumental music as a melody (figure) surrounded by other chords or harmonies (ground).

Separating figure from ground can be challenging (Figure 5.30), yet our perceptual systems are usually equal to the task. Sometimes, however, what's figure and what's ground is not completely obvious, and the same stimulus can give rise to two different perceptions. Consider Figure 5.31, for example. If you examine it for a while, two alternating but equally plausible perceptions will emerge, one based on the inner portion and the other formed by the two outer portions. When the alternative perception occurs, what was previously the figure becomes the background.

In addition to figure-ground relations, the Gestalt psychologists were interested in how separate stimuli come to be perceived as parts of larger wholes. They suggested that people group and interpret stimuli in accordance with four **Gestalt laws of perceptual organization:** *similarity, proximity, closure, and continuity.* These organizing principles are illustrated in Figure 5.32.

What is your perception of Figure 5.32a? Do you perceive 16 unrelated dots or two triangles formed by different-sized dots? If you see triangles, your perception obeys the Gestalt *law of similarity,* which says that when parts of a configuration are perceived as similar, they will be perceived as belonging together. The *law of proximity* says that elements that are near each other are likely to be perceived as part of the same configuration. Thus most people perceive Figure 5.32b as three sets of two lines rather than six separate lines. Illustrated in Figure 5.32c is the *law of closure,* which states that people tend to close the open edges of a figure or fill in gaps in an incomplete figure, so that their identification of the form (in this case, a circle) is more complete than what is actually there. Finally, the *law of continuity* holds that people link individual elements together so they form a continuous line or pattern that makes sense. Thus Figure 5.32d is far more likely to be seen as combining components a-b and c-d rather than a-d and c-b, which have poor continuity. Or consider Fraser's spiral,

Figure 5.30

Figure-ground relations are important in perception. These amazing body paintings were created by Liu Bolin of Beijing. In a series known as "camouflage," the artist paints people from head to toe so they will blend in with the background.

Figure 5.31

One stimulus, two perceptions. This reversible figure illustrates alternating figure-ground relations. It can be seen as a vase or as two people facing one another. Whichever percept exists at the moment is seen as figure against background.

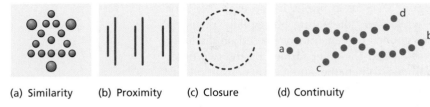

(a) Similarity   (b) Proximity   (c) Closure   (d) Continuity

Figure 5.32

Gestalt perceptual laws.
Among the Gestalt principles of perceptual organization are the laws of (a) similarity, (b) proximity, (c) closure, and (d) continuity. Each principle causes us to organize stimuli into wholes that are greater than the sums of their parts.

shown in Figure 5.33, which is not really a spiral at all! (To demonstrate, trace one of the circles with a pencil.) We perceive the concentric circles as a spiral because, to our nervous system, a spiral gives better continuity between individual elements than does a set of circles. The spiral is created by us, not by the stimulus.

Perception Involves Hypothesis Testing

Recognizing a stimulus implies that we have a **perceptual schema**—*a mental representation or image containing the critical and distinctive features of a person, object, event, or other perceptual phenomenon.* Schemas provide mental templates that allow us to classify and identify sensory input in a top-down fashion.

Imagine, for example, that a person approaches you and calls out your name. Who is this person? If the stimuli match your internal schemas of your best friend's appearance and voice closely enough, you identify the person as your

Figure 5.33

A spiral that isn't.
Fraser's spiral illustrates the Gestalt law of continuity. If you follow any part of the "spiral" with a pencil, you will find that it is not a spiral at all but a series of concentric circles. The "spiral" is created by your nervous system because that perception is more consistent with continuity of the individual elements.

friend (McAdams & Drake, 2002). Many political cartoonists have an uncanny ability to capture the most noteworthy facial features of famous people so that we can easily recognize the person represented by even the simplest line sketch.

Perception is, in this sense, an attempt to make sense of stimulus input, to search for the best interpretation of sensory information we can arrive at based on our knowledge and experience. Likening perception to the scientific process described in Chapter 2, Richard L. Gregory (1966, 2005) suggested that each of our perceptions is essentially a hypothesis about the nature of the object or, more generally, the meaning of the sensory information. The perceptual system actively searches its gigantic library of internal schemas for the interpretation that best fits the sensory data. In some instances, sensory information fits two different internal representations, and there is not enough information to permanently rule out one of them in favor of the other. For example, examine the Necker cube, shown in Figure 5.34. If you stare at the cube for a while, you will find that it changes before your very eyes as your nervous system tries out a new perceptual hypothesis.

Perception Is Influenced by Expectations: Perceptual Sets

During a Mideast crisis in 1988, the warship USS *Vincennes* was engaged in a pitched battle with several Iranian gunboats. Suddenly, the *Vincennes's* advanced radar system detected an aircraft taking off from a military-civilian airfield in Iran and heading straight toward the American vessel. Radar operators identified the plane as an Iranian F-14 fighter, known to carry lethal missiles

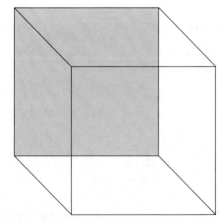

Figure 5.34

Reversible perceptions.
The same stimulus can give rise to different perceptions. Stare at this Necker cube for a while; the front of the cube will suddenly become the back, and it will appear as if you're viewing the cube from a different angle.

used earlier in a damaging attack on another U.S. warship. Repeated requests to the plane to identify itself yielded no response. The plane was now only 10 miles from the ship and, according to the crewmen watching the radar, descending toward the *Vincennes* on an attack course. When a final warning evoked no response, the *Vincennes*'s captain gave the command to fire on the plane. Two surface-to-air missiles streaked into the sky. Moments later, all that remained of the plane was a shower of flaming debris.

The jubilation and relief of the *Vincennes*'s crew was short-lived. Soon the awful truth was known. The plane they had shot down was not an attacking F-14 warplane but a commercial airliner carrying 290 passengers, all of whom died when the aircraft was destroyed. Moreover, videotape recordings of the electronic information used by the crew to identify the plane and its flight pattern showed conclusively that the aircraft was not an F-14 and that it had actually been climbing to its cruising altitude rather than descending toward the ship.

How could such a tragic error have been made by a well-trained and experienced crew with access to the world's most sophisticated radar equipment? At a congressional hearing on the incident, several prominent perception researchers reconstructed the psychological environment that could have caused the radar operators' eyes to lie.

Clearly, the situation was stressful and dangerous. The *Vincennes* was already under attack by Iranian gunboats, and other attacks could be expected. It was easy for the radar operators, observing a plane taking off from a military field and heading toward the ship, to interpret this as a prelude to an air attack. The *Vincennes*'s crew was determined to avoid the fate of the other American warship, producing a high level of vigilance for any stimuli that suggested an impending attack. Fear and expectation thus created a psychological context within which the sensory input from the computer system was interpreted in a top-down fashion. The perception that the aircraft was a warplane and that it was descending toward the ship fit the crew's expectations and fears, and it became the reality that they experienced. They had a **perceptual set**—*a readiness to perceive stimuli in a particular way.* Sometimes, believing is seeing.

Stimuli Are Recognizable under Changing Conditions: Perceptual Constancies

When a closed door suddenly swings open, it casts a different image on our retina, but we still perceive it as a door. Our perceptual hypothesis remains the same. Were it not for **perceptual constancies,** *which allow us to recognize familiar stimuli under varying conditions,* we would have to literally rediscover what something is each time it appeared under different conditions. Thus you can recognize a tune even if it is played in a different octave, as long as the relations among its notes are maintained. You can detect the flavor of a particular spice even when it occurs in foods having very different tastes.

In vision, several constancies are important. *Shape constancy* allows us to recognize people and other objects from many different angles, as in the case of the swinging door. Perhaps you have had the experience of sitting up front and off to one side of the screen in a crowded movie theater. At first the picture probably looked distorted, but after a while your visual system corrected for the distortion and objects on the screen looked normal again.

Because of *brightness constancy,* the relative brightness of objects remains the same under different conditions of illumination, such as full sunlight and shade. Brightness constancy occurs because the ratio of light intensity between an object and its surroundings is usually constant. The actual brightness of the light that illuminates an object does not matter, as long as the same light intensity illuminates both the object and its surroundings.

When we take off in an airplane, we know that the cars on the highway below are not shrinking and becoming the size of ants. *Size constancy* is the perception that the size of objects remains relatively constant even though images on our retina change in size with variations in distance. Thus a man who is judged to be 6 feet tall when standing 5 feet away is not perceived to be 3 feet tall at a distance of 10 feet, even though the size of his image on the retina is reduced to half its original size (Figure 5.35).

(?) thinking **critically**

WHY DOES THAT RISING MOON LOOK SO BIG?

Just before bedding down for the night on a backpacking trip, a friend of ours poked his head outside of his tent and gasped to his wife, "Look at the moon! Just look at that moon!" Indeed, a gorgeous full moon had just come over the horizon, and it was so enormous that it dwarfed the mammoth peaks surrounding them. The couple gazed at it in wonder for a few minutes and then retired into their tent. Later that night, they looked outside again only to see a rather small, ordinary full moon approaching the zenith.

You too may have exclaimed over the size of a rising moon, only to notice later that the moon, well above the horizon, seemed to have shrunk. What can explain this phenomenon? Think about it, then see page 172.

Figure 5.36

The demands faced by a batter in judging the speed, distance, and movements of a pitched baseball within thousandths of a second underscore the capabilities of the visual perceptual system.

Figure 5.35

Who's bigger?

Size constancy based on distance cues causes us to perceive the person in the background as being of normal size. When the same stimulus is seen in the absence of the distance cues, size constancy breaks down. The two men no longer look similar in size, nor do the photographic images of the man in the blue shirt.

PERCEPTION OF DEPTH, DISTANCE, AND MOVEMENT

The ability to adapt to a spatial world requires that we make fine distinctions involving distances and the movement of objects within the environment. Humans are capable of great precision in making such judgments. Consider, for example, the perceptual task faced by a baseball batter (Figure 5.36). A fastball thrown by the pitcher at 90 miles per hour from 60 feet will reach the batter who is trying to hit it in about 42/100 of a second. A curveball thrown at 80 miles per hour will reach the hitting zone in 47/100 of a second, a difference of only 5/100 of a second but a world of difference for timing and hitting the pitch. Within the first 6 to 8 feet of a ball's flight from the pitcher's hand (an interval of about 25/1,000 of a second), the batter must correctly judge the speed, spin, and location of the pitch. If any of the judgments are wrong, the hitter will probably be unable to hit a fair ball, for the ball will be in the bat's contact zone for only 2/1,000 of a second (Adair, 1990). The perceptual demands of such a task are imposing indeed—as are the salaries earned by those who can perform this task consistently. How does the visual perception system make such judgments?

Depth and Distance Perception

One of the more intriguing aspects of visual perception is our ability to perceive depth. The retina receives information in only two dimensions (length and width), but the brain translates these cues into three-dimensional perceptions. It does this by using both **monocular depth cues,** *which require only one eye,* and **binocular depth cues,** *which require both eyes.*

Monocular Depth Cues

Judging the relative distances of objects is one important key to perceiving depth. When artists paint on a flat canvas, they depend on a variety of monocular cues to create perceptions of depth in their pictures. One such cue is *patterns of light and shadow.* The 20th-century artist M. C. Escher skillfully used light and shadow to create the three-dimensional effect shown in Figure 5.37. The depth effect is as powerful when you close one eye as it is when you use both.

Another cue, *linear perspective,* refers to the perception that parallel lines converge, or angle toward one another, as they recede into the distance. Thus, if you look down railroad tracks, they appear to angle toward one another with increased distance, and we use this as a depth cue. The same occurs with the edges of a highway or the sides of an elevator shaft. *Interposition,* in which objects closer to us may cut off part of our view of more distant objects, provides another cue for distance and depth.

An object's *height in the horizontal plane* provides another source of information. For example, a ship 5 miles offshore appears in a higher plane

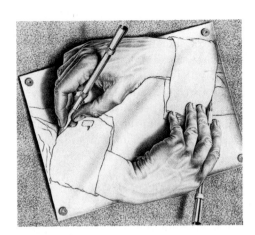

Figure 5.37

Patterns of light and shadow can serve as monocular depth cues, as shown in *Drawing Hands,* by M. C. Escher.

Figure 5.38

In this mural, painted on the Mississippi River flood wall at Cape Girardeau, Missouri, the artist has skillfully used seven monocular depth cues to create a striking 3-dimensional depth effect. (1) Linear perspective is produced by the converging lines of the plank. (2) The people and objects in the background are smaller than those in the foreground (relative size). (3) The background is in a higher horizontal plane than the foreground. (4, 5) The objects in the background are less detailed than the "closer" ones (texture and clarity). (6) The people and objects in the foreground cut off parts of those "behind" them in the background (interposition). (7) Light and shadow are also used to create a depth effect.

and closer to the horizon than does one that is only 1 mile from shore. *Texture* is a fifth cue, because the texture or grain of an object appears finer as distance increases. Likewise, *clarity* can be an important cue for judging distance; we can see nearby hills more clearly than ones that are far away, especially on hazy days.

Relative size is yet another basis for distance judgments. If we see two objects that we know to be of similar size, then the one that looks smaller will be judged to be farther away. For example, this cue may figure prominently in the moon illusion.

None of these monocular cues involve movement of the object(s), but a final monocular cue, *motion parallax,* tells us that if we are moving, nearby objects appear to move faster in the opposite direction than do faraway ones. Like the other monocular cues, motion provides us with information that we can use to make judgments about distance and therefore about depth.

Figure 5.38 illustrates all of the monocular cues just described, with the exception of motion parallax.

Binocular Depth Cues

The most dramatic perceptions of depth arise with binocular depth cues, which require the use of both eyes. For an interesting binocular effect, hold your two index fingers about 6 inches in front of your eyes with their tips about 1 inch apart. Focus on your fingers first, then focus beyond them across the room. Doing so will produce the image of a third finger between the other two. This third finger will disappear if you close either eye.

Most of us are familiar with the delightful depth experiences provided by View-Master slides and 3-D movies watched through special glasses. These devices make use of the principle of **binocular disparity,** *in which each eye sees a slightly different image.* Within the brain, the visual input from the two eyes is analyzed by feature detectors that are attuned to depth (Howard, 2002; Livingstone & Hubel, 1994). Some of the feature detectors respond only to stimuli that are either in front of or behind the point on which we are fixing our gaze. The responses of these depth-sensitive neurons are integrated to produce our perception of depth (Goldstein, 2002).

A second binocular distance cue, **convergence,** *is produced by feedback from the muscles that turn your eyes inward to view a close object.* You can experience this cue by holding a finger about 1 foot in front of your face and then moving it slowly toward you. Messages sent to your brain by the eye muscles provide it with a depth cue.

Perception of Movement

The perception of movement is a complex process, sometimes requiring the brain to integrate information from several different senses. To demonstrate, hold a pen in front of your face. Now, while holding your head still, move the pen back and forth. You will perceive the pen as moving. Now hold the pen still and move your head back and forth at the same rate of speed. In both cases, the image of the pen moved across your retina in about the same way. But when you moved your head, your brain took into account input from your kinesthetic and vestibular systems and concluded that you were moving but the pen was not.

The primary cue for perceiving motion is the movement of the stimulus across the retina (Sekuler et al., 2002). Under optimal conditions, a retinal image need move only about one fifth the diameter of a single cone for us to detect movement (Nakayama & Tyler, 1981). The relative movement of an object against a structured background is also a movement cue (Gibson, 1979). For example, if you fixate on a bird in flight, the relative motion of the bird against its background is a strong cue for perceived speed of movement.

The illusion of smooth motion can be produced if we arrange for the sequential appearance of two or more stimuli. Gestalt psychologist Max Wertheimer (1912) demonstrated this in his studies of **stroboscopic movement,** *illusory movement produced when a light is briefly flashed in darkness and then, a few milliseconds later, another light is flashed nearby.* If the timing is just right, the first light seems to move from one place to the other in a manner indistinguishable from real movement.

Stroboscopic movement (termed the "phi phenomenon" by Wertheimer) has been used commercially in numerous ways. For example, think of the strings of successively illuminated lights on theater marquees that seem to move endlessly around the border or that spell out messages in a moving script. Stroboscopic movement is also the principle behind motion pictures, which consist of a series of still photographs, or frames, that are projected on a screen in rapid succession with dark intervals in between (Figure 5.39). The rate at which the frames are projected is critical to our perception of smooth movement. Early movies, such as the silent films of the 1920s, projected the stills at only 16 frames per second, and the movements appeared fast and jerky. Today the usual speed is 24 frames per second, which more perfectly produces an illusion of smooth movement. Television presents at 30 images per second.

ILLUSIONS: FALSE PERCEPTUAL HYPOTHESES

Our analysis of perceptual schemas, hypotheses, sets, and constancies allows us to understand some interesting perceptual experiences known as **illusions,** *compelling but incorrect perceptions.* Such perceptions can be understood as erroneous perceptual hypotheses about the nature of a stimulus. Illusions are not only intriguing and sometimes delightful visual experiences, but they also provide important information about how our perceptual processes work under normal conditions (Gregory, 2005).

Ironically, most visual illusions can be attributed to perceptual constancies that ordinarily help us perceive more accurately (Frisby, 1980). For example, size constancy results in part from our ability to use distance cues to judge the size of objects. But as we saw in the discussion of the moon illusion, distance cues can sometimes fool us. In the Ponzo illusion, shown in Figure 5.40, the depth cues of linear perspective (the tracks converging) and height of the horizontal plane provide distance cues that make the upper bar appear farther away than the lower bar. Because it seems

Figure 5.39

Stroboscopic movement is produced in moving pictures as a series of still photographs projected at a rate of 24 per second.

Figure 5.40

The Ponzo illusion.

Which of the white lines is longer? Measure them and see. The distance cues provided by the converging railroad tracks affect size perception and disrupt size constancy.

(a)

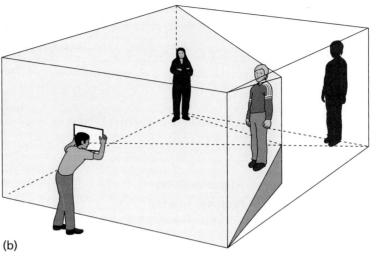

(b)

Figure 5.41

A size illusion.

(a) The Ames Room produces a striking size illusion because it is designed to appear rectangular. (b) The room, however, is actually trapezoidal, and the figure on the left is actually much farther away from the viewer than the one on the right and thus appears smaller. We perceive the boy as if he were the purple figure, making him appear very large.

thinking **critically**

EXPLAIN THIS STRIKING ILLUSION

We'd like you to experience a truly interesting illusion. To do so, all you need is a piece of fairly heavy paper and a little patience. Fold the piece of paper lengthwise down the middle, and set it on a table with one of the ends facing you like an open tent, as shown in Figure 5.43. Close one eye and, from slightly above the object, stare at a point midway along the top fold of the paper. After a while the paper will suddenly "stand up" and look like a corner viewed from the inside. When this happens, gently move your head back and forth while continuing to view with one eye. The movement will produce a striking perception. Can you explain what you now see? For a discussion of this illusion, see page 172.

Figure 5.43

Try this visual experience.

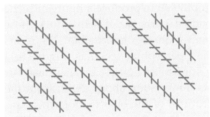

The long lines are actually parallel, but the small lines make them appear crooked.

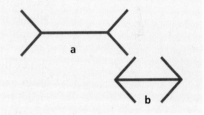

The Müller-Lyer illusion. Which line, a or b, is longer? Compare them with a ruler.

Figure 5.42

Context-produced geometric illusions.

farther away, the perceptual system concludes that the bar in the background must be larger than the bar in the foreground, despite the fact that the two bars cast retinal images of the same size.

Distance cues can be manipulated to create other size illusions. To illustrate this, Adelbert Ames constructed a special room. Viewed through a peephole with one eye, the room's scene presents a startling size reversal (Figure 5.41a). Our perceptual system assumes that the room has a normal rectangular shape because, in fact, most rooms do. Monocular depth cues do not allow us to see that, in reality, the left corner of the room is twice as far away as the right corner (Figure 5.41b). As a result, size constancy breaks down, and we base our judgment of size on the sizes of the retinal images cast by the two people.

The study of perceptual constancies shows that our perceptual hypotheses are strongly influenced by the context, or surroundings, in which a stimulus occurs. Figure 5.42 shows two

 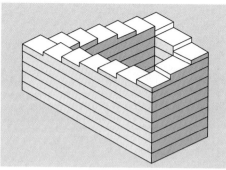 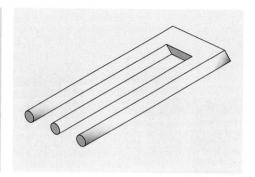

Figure 5.44

Things that couldn't be.

Monocular depth cues are cleverly manipulated to produce an impossible triangle, a never-ending staircase, and the "devil's tuning fork."

examples of how context can produce illusory perceptions.

Some of the most intriguing perceptual distortions are produced when monocular depth cues are manipulated to produce a figure or scene whose individual parts make sense but whose overall organization is "impossible" in terms of our existing perceptual schemas. Figure 5.44 shows three impossible figures. In each case, our brain extracts information about depth from the individual features of the objects, but when this information is put together and matched with our existing schemas, the percept that results simply doesn't make sense. The "devil's tuning fork," for

example, could not exist in our universe. It is a two-dimensional image containing paradoxical depth cues. Our brain, however, automatically interprets it as a three-dimensional object and matches it with its internal schema of a fork—a bad fit indeed. The never-ending staircase provides another compelling example of an impossible scene that seems perfectly reasonable when we focus only on its individual elements.

Illusions are not only personally and scientifically interesting, but they can have important real-life implications. Our "Research Close-up" describes one scientist's search for an illusion having life-and-death implications.

Research Close-up   Stalking a Deadly Illusion

SOURCE: CONRAD L. KRAFT (1978). A psychophysical contribution to air safety: Simulator studies of illusions in night visual approaches. In H. L. Pick, Jr., H. W. Leibowitz, J. E. Singer, A. Steinschneider, and H. W. Stevenson (Eds.), *Psychology: From research to practice.* New York: Plenum.

INTRODUCTION

When the Boeing Company introduced the 727 jet airliner in the mid-1960s, it was the latest word in aviation technology. The plane performed well in test flights, but four fatal crashes soon after it was placed in service raised fears that there might be a serious flaw in its design.

The first accident occurred as a 727 made its approach to Chicago over Lake Michigan on a clear night. The plane plunged into the lake 19 miles offshore. About a month later, another 727 glided in over the Ohio River to land in Cincinnati. Unaccountably, it struck the ground

about 12 feet below the runway elevation and burst into flames. The third accident occurred as an aircraft approached Salt Lake City over dark land. The lights of the city twinkled in the distance, but the plane made too rapid a descent and crashed short of the runway. Months later, a Japanese airliner approached Tokyo at night. The flight ended tragically as the plane, its landing gear not yet lowered, struck the waters of Tokyo Bay 6 miles from the runway.

Analysis of these four accidents, as well as others, suggested a common pattern. All occurred at night under clear weather conditions, so the pilots were operating under visual flight rules rather than performing instrument landings. In each instance, the plane was approaching city lights over dark areas of water or land. In all cases, the lights in the background terrain sloped upward to varying degrees. Finally, all of the planes crashed short of the runway. These observations led a Boeing industrial psychologist, Conrad L. Kraft,

Figure 5.45

Conrad Kraft, a Boeing psychologist, created an apparatus to study how visual cues can affect the simulated landings of airline pilots. Pilots approached Nightertown in a simulated cockpit. The computer-controlled city could be tilted to reproduce the illusion thought to be responsible for fatal air crashes.

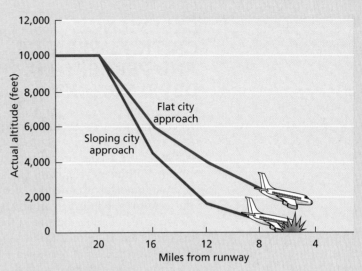

Figure 5.46

Misperceptions of experienced pilots.

The illusion created by upward-sloping city lights caused even highly experienced pilots to overestimate their altitude, and 11 of the 12 flight instructors crashed short of the runway. When the lights were flat, all the pilots made perfect approaches. Source: Based on Kraft, 1978.

to suspect that the cause of the crashes might be pilot error based on some sort of visual illusion.

METHOD

To test this possibility, Boeing engineers constructed an apparatus to simulate night landings (Figure 5.45). It consisted of a cockpit and a miniature lighted city named Nightertown. The city moved toward the cockpit on computer-controlled rollers, and it could be tilted to simulate various terrain slopes. The pilot could control simulated air speed and rate of climb and descent, and the Nightertown scene was controlled by the pilot's responses just as a true visual scene would be.

The participants were 12 experienced Boeing flight instructors who made virtual-reality landings at Nightertown under systematically varied conditions created by the computerized simulator. All of their landings were visual landings so as to be able to test whether a visual illusion was occurring. Every aspect of their approach and the manner in which they controlled the aircraft were measured precisely.

RESULTS

The flight instructors' landings were nearly flawless until Kraft duplicated the conditions of the fatal crashes by having the pilots approach an upward-sloping distant city over a dark area. When this occurred, the pilots were unable to detect the upward slope, assumed that the background city was flat, and consistently overestimated their approach altitude. On a normal landing, the preferred altitude at 4.5 miles from the runway is about 1,240 feet. As Figure 5.46 shows, the pilots approached at about this altitude when the simulated city was in a flat position. But when it was sloped upward, 11 of the 12 experienced pilot instructors crashed about 4.5 miles short of the runway.

CRITICAL DISCUSSION

This study, considered a classic by many psychologists, shows the value of studying behavior under highly controlled conditions and with precise

measurements. By simulating the conditions under which the fatal crashes had occurred, Kraft identified the visual illusion that was the source of pilot error. He showed that the perceptual hypotheses of the flight instructors, like those of the pilots involved in the real crashes, were tragically incorrect. It would have been ironic if one of the finest jetliners ever built had been removed from service because of presumed mechanical defects while other aircraft remained aloft and at risk for tragedy.

Kraft's research not only saved the 727 from months—or perhaps years—of needless mechanical analysis but, more important, it also identified a potentially deadly illusion and the precise conditions under which it occurred. On the basis of Kraft's findings, Boeing recommended that pilots attend carefully to their instruments when landing at night, even under perfect weather conditions. Today, commercial airline pilots are required to make instrument landings not only at night but also during the day.

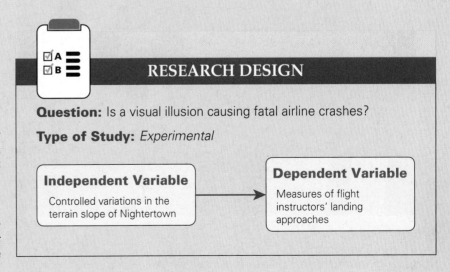

RESEARCH DESIGN

Question: Is a visual illusion causing fatal airline crashes?

Type of Study: *Experimental*

Independent Variable	**Dependent Variable**
Controlled variations in the terrain slope of Nightertown	Measures of flight instructors' landing approaches

EXPERIENCE, CRITICAL PERIODS, AND PERCEPTUAL DEVELOPMENT

Development of sensory and perceptual systems results from the interplay of biological and experiential factors. Genes program biological development, but this development is also influenced by environmental experiences. For example, if you were to be blinded in an accident and later learned to read Braille, the area of the somatosensory cortex that is devoted to the fingertips would enlarge over time as it borrowed other neurons to increase its sensitivity (Pool, 1994). By the time they are old enough to crawl, children placed on a "visual cliff" formed by a glass-covered table that suddenly drops off beneath the glass will not ordinarily venture over the edge (Figure 5.47). This aversion may result from the interaction of innate depth-perception abilities and previous experience (Gibson & Walk, 1960).

What might a lifetime of experience in a limited environment do to perceptual abilities that seem innate? Sometimes, conditions under which people live create natural experiments that help provide answers. For example, the

BaMbuti pygmies, who live in the rain forests of Central Africa, spend their lives in a closed-in green world of densely packed trees without open spaces. The anthropologist C. M. Turnbull (1961) once brought a man named Kenge out of the forest to the edge of a vast plain. A herd of buffalo grazed in the distance. To Turnbull's surprise, Kenge remarked that he had never seen insects of that kind. When told that they were buffalo, not insects, Kenge was deeply offended and felt that Turnbull was insulting his intelligence. To prove his point, Turnbull drove Kenge in his jeep toward the animals. Kenge stared in amazement as the "insects" grew into buffalo before his eyes. To explain his perceptual experience to himself, he concluded that witchcraft was being used to fool him. Kenge's misperception occurred as a failure in size constancy. Having lived in an environment without open spaces, he had no experience in judging the size of objects at great distances.

As noted earlier, when light passes through the lens of the eye, the image projected on the retina is reversed, so that right is left and up is down. In 1896, perception researcher George Stratton created a special set of glasses that undid this reversal, thereby becoming the first human ever to have a right-side-up image on his retina while standing upright. Reversing how nature and a lifetime of experience had fashioned his perceptual system disoriented Stratton at first. The ground and his feet were now up, and he had to put on his hat from the bottom up. He had to reach to his left to touch something he saw on his right. Stratton suffered from nausea and couldn't eat or get around for several days. Gradually, however, he adapted to his inverted world, and by the end of 8 days he was able to successfully reach for objects and walk around. Years later, people who wore inverting lenses for longer periods of time did the same. Some were able to ski down mountain slopes or ride motorcycles while wearing the lenses, even though their visual world remained upside down and never became normal for them. When they removed the inverting lenses, they had some initial problems but soon readapted to the normal visual world (Dolezal, 1982).

Cross-Cultural Research on Perception

As far as we know, humans come into the world with the same perceptual abilities regardless of where they are born. From that point on, however, the culture they grow up in helps determine the kinds of perceptual learning experiences they

Figure 5.47

Eleanor Gibson and Richard Walk constructed this "visual cliff" with a glass-covered drop-off to determine whether crawling infants and newborn animals can perceive depth. Even when coaxed by their mothers, young children refuse to venture onto the glass over the cliff. Newborn animals also avoid the cliff.

(a)

(b)

Figure 5.48

Does culture influence perception?

(a) What is the object above the woman's head? East Africans had a far different answer than did North Americans and Europeans. (b) Cultural differences also occurred when people were asked which animal the archer was about to shoot. Sources: (a) Adapted from Gregory & Gombrich, 1973; (b) Adapted from Hudson, 1960.

have. Cross-cultural research can help identify which aspects of perception occur in all people, regardless of their culture, as well as perceptual differences that result from cultural experiences (Posner & Rothbart, 2007b). Although there are far more perceptual similarities than differences among the peoples of the world, the differences that do exist show us that perception can indeed be influenced by experience.

Consider the perception of a picture that depends on both the nature of the picture and characteristics of the perceiver. In Figure 5.48a, what is the object above the woman's head? In one study, most North Americans and Europeans instantly identified it as a window. They also tended to see the family sitting inside a dwelling. But when the same picture was shown to East Africans, nearly all perceived the object as a basket or box that the woman was balancing on her head. To them, the family was sitting outside under a tree (Gregory & Gombrich, 1973). These interpretations were more consistent with their own cultural experiences.

In our earlier discussion of monocular depth cues, we used paintings such as the flood wall mural in Figure 5.38 to illustrate monocular depth perception. In Western culture, we have constant exposure to two-dimensional pictures that our perceptual system effortlessly turns into three-dimensional perceptions. Do people who grow up in cultures that do not expose them to pictures have the same perceptions? When presented with the picture in Figure 5.48b and asked which animal the hunter was about to

shoot, tribal African people answered that he was about to kill the "baby elephant." They did not use the monocular cues that cause Westerners to perceive the man as hunting the antelope and to view the elephant as an adult animal in the distance (Hudson, 1960).

Illusions occur when one of our common perceptual hypotheses is in error. Earlier we showed you the Müller-Lyer illusion (see Figure 5.42), in which a line appears longer when the V-shaped lines at its ends radiate outward rather than inward. Westerners are very susceptible to this illusion. They have learned that in their "carpentered" environment, which has many corners and square shapes, inward-facing lines occur when corners are closer and outward-facing lines occur when they are farther away. But when people from other cultures who live in more rounded environments are shown the Müller-Lyer stimuli, they are more likely to correctly perceive the lines as equal in length (Segall et al., 1966). They do not fall prey to a perceptual hypothesis that normally is correct in an environment like ours that is filled with sharp corners but wrong when applied to the lines in the Müller-Lyer illusion (Deregowski, 1989).

Cultural learning affects perceptions in other modalities as well. Our perceptions of tastes, odors, and textures are strongly influenced by our cultural experiences. A taste that might produce nausea in one culture may be considered delicious in another. The taste and gritty texture experienced when chewing a large raw insect or the rubbery texture of a fish eye may appeal far less to you than it would to a person from a culture in which that food is a staple.

Critical Periods: The Role of Early Experience

The examples in the preceding section suggest that experience is essential for the development of perceptual abilities. For some aspects of perception, there are also **critical periods** *during which certain kinds of experiences must occur if perceptual abilities and the brain mechanisms that underlie them are to develop normally.* If a critical period passes without the experience occurring, it is too late to undo the deficit that results.

Earlier we saw that the visual cortex has feature detectors composed of neurons that respond only to lines at particular angles. What would happen if newborn animals grew up in a world in which they saw some angles but not others? In a classic experiment, British researchers Colin Blakemore and Grahame Cooper (1970) created such a world for newborn kittens. The animals were raised in the dark except for a 5-hour period each day during which they were placed in round chambers that had either vertical or horizontal stripes on the walls. Figure 5.49a shows one of the kittens in a vertically striped chamber. A special collar prevented the kittens from seeing their own bodies while they were in the chamber, guaranteeing that they saw nothing but stripes.

When the kittens were 5 months old, Blakemore and Cooper presented them with bars of light at differing angles and used microelectrodes to test the electrical responses of individual feature-detector cells in their visual cortex. The results for the kittens raised in the vertically striped environment are shown in Figure 5.49b. As you can see, the kittens had no cells that fired in response to horizontal stimuli, resulting in visual impairments. They also acted as if they could not see a pencil when it was held in a horizontal position and moved up and down in front of them. However, as soon as the pencil was rotated to a vertical position, the animals began to follow it with their eyes as it was moved back and forth.

As you might expect, the animals raised in the horizontally striped environment showed the opposite effect. They had no feature detectors for vertical stimuli and did not seem to see them. Thus the cortical neurons of both groups of kittens developed in accordance with the stimulus features of their environments.

Other visual abilities also require early exposure to the relevant stimuli. Yoichi Sugita (2004) raised infant monkeys in rooms illuminated with only monochromatic light. As adults, these monkeys were clearly deficient in color perception. They had particular difficulty with color constancy, being unable to recognize the same colors under changing brightness conditions.

Some perceptual abilities are influenced more than others by restricted stimulation. In other research, monkeys, chimpanzees, and kittens were raised in an environment devoid of shapes. The animals distinguished differences in size, brightness, and color almost as well as normally reared animals do, but for the rest of their lives they performed poorly on more complex tasks, such as distinguishing different types of objects and geometric shapes (Riesen, 1965).

Restored Sensory Capacity

Scientists have studied the experiences of visually impaired people who acquired the ability to see later in life. For example, people born with cataracts grow up in a visual world without form. The clouded lenses of their eyes permit them to perceive light but not patterns or shapes. One such person was Virgil, who had been almost totally blind since childhood. He read Braille, enjoyed listening to sports on the radio and conversing with other people, and had adjusted quite well to his disability. At the urging of his fiancee, Virgil agreed to undergo surgery to remove his thick cataracts. The day after the surgery, his bandages were removed. Neurologist Oliver Sacks (1999) recounts what happened next.

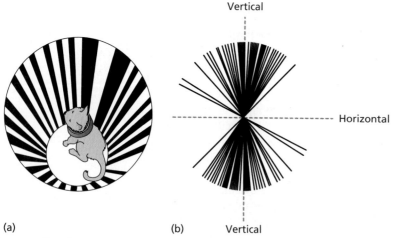

(a)   (b)

Figure 5.49

Effects of visual deprivation.

(a) Kittens raised in a vertically striped chamber, such as the one shown here, lacked cortical cells that fired in response to horizontal stimuli. (b) The kittens' perceptual "holes" are easily seen in this diagram, which shows the orientation angles that triggered nerve impulses from feature detectors. Source: Adapted from Blakemore & Cooper, 1970.

There was light, there was color, all mixed up, meaningless, a blur. Then out of the blur came a voice that said, "Well?" Then, and only then . . . did he finally realize that this chaos of light and shadow was a face—and, indeed, the face of his surgeon. . . . His retina and optic nerve were active, transmitting impulses, but his brain could make no sense of them. (p. 132)

Virgil was never able to adjust to his new visual world. He had to touch objects in order to identify them. He had to be led through his own house and would quickly become disoriented if he deviated from his path. Eventually, Virgil lost his sight once again. This time, however, he regarded his blindness as a gift, a release from a sighted world that was bewildering to him.

Virgil's experiences are characteristic of people who have their vision restored later in life. A German physician, Marius von Senden (1960), compiled data on patients born with cataracts who were tested soon after their cataracts were

Levels of Analysis

Sensation and Perception

The processes involved in sensation and perception illustrate the interaction of biological, psychological, and environmental factors.

ENVIRONMENTAL LEVEL

- Environmental stimulation is needed during early critical periods for development of the sensory systems.
- Environmental stimuli activate sensory receptors that are tailored to receive and transduce them.
- Past learning experiences allow us to impart meaning to environmental events.
- Cultural experiences influence in important ways how we perceive and respond to particular environmental events.

BIOLOGICAL LEVEL

- Evolutionary processes have resulted in sensory systems that make contact with the environment possible. These structures receive stimuli and transduce them into nerve impulses.
- Sensory way stations route nerve impulses from receptors to specific areas within the brain.
- Within the brain, sensory input is analyzed by feature detectors and interpreted in terms of top-down and bottom-up processes.

PSYCHOLOGICAL LEVEL

- Stimuli are given psychological meaning. We are especially attentive to stimuli that are relevant to our well-being.
- Gestalt principles of perceptual organization operate as top-down cognitive processes.
- Cognitive schemas and hypotheses are the basis for interpreting physical stimuli.
- Perceptual sets prepare us to perceive in certain ways.
- Psychological characteristics influence selective attention and perceptions.

Imagine you are designing a research study on perception. Which perceptual process will you study and which psychological and environmental factors will you include as independent variables? Try to describe the possible interactions between the factors you've selected.

surgically removed in adulthood. These people were immediately able to perceive figure-ground relations, to scan objects visually, and to follow moving targets with their eyes, indicating that such abilities are innate. However, they could not visually identify objects, such as eating utensils, that they were familiar with through touch; nor were they able to distinguish simple geometric figures without counting the corners or tracing the figures with their fingers.

After several weeks of training, the patients were able to identify simple objects by sight, but their perceptual constancies were very poor. Often they were unable to recognize the same shape in another color, even though they could discriminate between colors. Years later, some patients could identify only a few of the faces of people they knew well. Many also had great difficulty judging distances. Apparently, no amount of subsequent experience could make up for their lack of visual experience during the critical period of childhood.

More recently, a woman in India was studied 20 years after she had cataracts removed at age 12 (Ostrovsky et al., 2007). Although the patient's visual acuity was below par, she did surprisingly well on complex visual tasks. This suggests that the human brain retains an impressive capacity for visual learning, even for children who are blind until early adolescence.

All of these lines of evidence—cross-cultural perceptual differences, animal studies involving visual deprivation, and observations of congenitally impaired people whose vision has been restored—suggest that biological and experiential factors interact in complex ways. Some of our perceptual abilities are at least partially present at birth, but experience plays an important role in their normal development. How innate and experiential factors interact promises to be a continued focus of perception research. Thus perception is very much a biopsychological process whose mysteries are best explored by examining them from biological, psychological, and environmental levels of analysis.

test yourself

Perception, Illusions, and Perceptual Development

True or false?

1. People show faster reaction times to threat-related stimuli.
2. Fraser's spiral illustrates the Gestalt law of continuity.
3. Visual illusions can be attributed to perceptual constancies.
4. Movies utilize the principle of stroboscopic movement.
5. Motion parallax is a binocular depth cue.
6. The Ames Room is designed to distort size constancy.
7. Animals will venture onto the "visual cliff," but human babies won't.

ANSWERS: 1–true, 2–true, 3–true, 4–true, 5–false, 6–true, 7–false

Chapter Summary

SENSORY PROCESSES

- Sensation is the process by which our sense organs receive and transmit information, whereas perception involves the brain's processing and interpretation of the information.
- The absolute threshold is the lowest intensity at which a stimulus is detected 50 percent of the time. Signal-detection theory is concerned with factors that influence decisions about whether or not a stimulus is present.

- The difference threshold, or just noticeable difference (jnd), is the amount by which two stimuli must differ for them to be perceived as different 50 percent of the time. Weber's law states that the jnd is proportional to the intensity of the original stimulus and is constant within a given sense modality.
- Sensory systems are particularly responsive to changes in stimulation, and adaptation occurs in response to unchanging stimuli.

VISION

- Light-sensitive visual receptor cells are located in the retina. The rods are brightness receptors, and the less numerous cones are color receptors. Light energy striking the retina is converted into nerve impulses by chemical reactions in the photopigments of the rods and cones. Dark adaptation involves the gradual regeneration of photopigments that have been depleted by brighter illumination.
- Color vision is a two-stage process having both trichromatic and opponent-process components.
- Visual stimuli are analyzed by feature detectors in the primary visual cortex, and the stimulus elements are reconstructed and interpreted in light of input from the visual association cortex.

AUDITION

- Sound waves, the stimuli for audition, have two characteristics: frequency, measured in terms of cycles per second, or hertz (Hz); and amplitude, measured in terms of decibels (dB). Frequency is related to pitch, amplitude to loudness.
- Loudness is coded in terms of the number and types of auditory nerve fibers that fire. Pitch is coded in two ways, explained by frequency and place theories.
- Hearing loss may result from conduction deafness, produced by problems involving the structures of the ear that transmit vibrations to the cochlea, or from nerve deafness, in which the receptors in the cochlea or the auditory nerve are damaged.

TASTE AND SMELL: THE CHEMICAL SENSES

- The receptors for taste and smell respond to chemical molecules. Taste buds are responsive to four basic qualities: sweet, sour, salty, and bitter. The receptors for smell (olfaction) are long cells in the upper nasal cavity.

THE SKIN AND BODY SENSES

- The skin and body senses include touch, kinesthesis, and equilibrium. Receptors in the skin and body tissues are sensitive to pressure, pain, warmth, and cold. Kinesthesis functions by means of nerve endings in the muscles, tendons, and joints. The sense organs for equilibrium are in the vestibular apparatus of the inner ear.
- Pain receptors are free nerve endings. Gate control theory takes account of downward influences from the brain. Endorphins decrease pain.
- Principles derived from the study of sensory processes have been applied in developing sensory prosthetics for people who are blind, hearing impaired, or have lost their hands.

PERCEPTION: THE CREATION OF EXPERIENCE

- Perception involves both bottom-up processing, in which individual stimulus fragments are combined into a perception, and top-down processing, in which existing knowledge and perceptual schemas are applied to interpret stimuli.

- We cannot attend completely to more than one thing at a time, but we are capable of rapid attentional shifts. Inattentional blindness refers to a failure to perceive certain stimuli when attending to other stimulus elements. The perceptual system appears to be especially vigilant to stimuli that denote threat or danger.
- Gestalt psychologists identified a number of principles of perceptual organization, including figure-ground relations and the laws of similarity, proximity, closure, and continuity. Gregory suggested that perception is essentially a hypothesis about what a stimulus is, based on previous experience and the nature of the stimulus.
- Perceptual sets involve a readiness to perceive stimuli in certain ways, based on our expectations, assumptions, motivations, and current emotional state.
- Perceptual constancies allow us to recognize familiar stimuli under changing conditions. In the visual realm, there are three constancies: shape, brightness, and size.

PERCEPTION OF DEPTH, DISTANCE, AND MOVEMENT

- Monocular cues to judge distance and depth include patterns of light and shadow, linear perspective, interposition, height in the horizontal plane, texture, clarity, relative size, and motion parallax.
- Binocular disparity occurs as slightly different images are viewed by each eye and acted on by feature detectors for depth. Convergence of the eyes provides a second binocular cue.
- The basis for perception of movement is absolute movement of a stimulus across the retina or relative movement of an object in relation to its background. Stroboscopic movement is illusory.

ILLUSIONS: FALSE PERCEPTUAL HYPOTHESES

- Illusions are erroneous perceptions, or incorrect perceptual hypotheses. Perceptual constancies help produce many illusions.

EXPERIENCE, CRITICAL PERIODS, AND PERCEPTUAL DEVELOPMENT

- Perceptual development involves both physical maturation and learning. Some perceptual abilities are innate or develop shortly after birth, whereas others require particular experiences early in life in order to develop.
- Cultural factors can influence certain aspects of perception, including picture perception and susceptibility to illusions. However, many aspects of perception seem constant across cultures.
- Visual-deprivation studies, manipulation of visual input, and studies of restored vision have shown that the normal biological development of the perceptual system depends on certain sensory experiences at early periods of development.

KEY TERMS AND CONCEPTS

Each term has been boldfaced and defined in the chapter on the page indicated in parentheses.

absolute threshold (p. 132)
amplitude (p. 144)
basilar membrane (p. 144)
binocular depth cues (p. 160)
binocular disparity (p. 161)
bottom-up processing (p. 154)
cochlea (p. 144)
conduction deafness (p. 146)
cones (p. 136)
convergence (p. 161)
critical periods (p. 168)
dark adaptation (p. 138)
decibel (dB) (p. 144)
decision criterion (p. 132)
difference threshold (p. 133)
dual-process theory (p. 140)
endorphins (p. 150)
feature detectors (p. 142)
figure-ground relations (p. 156)
fovea (p. 137)
frequency (p. 143)

frequency theory of pitch perception (p. 145)
gate control theory (p. 150)
Gestalt laws of perceptual organization (p. 157)
gustation (p. 147)
Hering's opponent-process theory (p. 140)
hertz (Hz) (p. 143)
illusions (p. 162)
inattentional blindness (p. 155)
kinesthesis (p. 151)
lens (p. 136)
menstrual synchrony (p. 148)
monocular depth cues (p. 160)
nerve deafness (p. 146)
olfaction (p. 147)
olfactory bulb (p. 148)
optic nerve (p. 137)
organ of Corti (p. 144)
perception (p. 131)
perceptual constancies (p. 159)
perceptual schema (p. 158)

perceptual set (p. 159)
pheromones (p. 148)
photopigments (p. 138)
place theory of pitch perception (p. 146)
psychophysics (p. 132)
retina (p. 136)
rods (p. 136)
sensation (p. 131)
sensory adaptation (p. 135)
sensory prosthetic devices (p. 151)
signal-detection theory (p. 132)
stroboscopic movement (p. 162)
subliminal stimulus (p. 133)
synesthesia (p. 130)
taste buds (p. 147)
top-down processing (p. 154)
transduction (p. 131)
vestibular sense (p. 151)
visual acuity (p. 138)
Weber's law (p. 133)
Young-Helmholtz trichromatic theory (p. 139)

thinking critically

NAVIGATING IN FOG: PROFESSOR MAYER'S TOPOPHONE (Page 146)

The device shown in Figure 5.18 made use of two principles of sound localization. First, because the two ear receptors were much larger than human ears, they could capture more sound waves and funnel them to the sailor's ears. Second, the wide spacing between the two receptors increased the time difference between the sound's arrival at the two human ears, thus increasing directional sensitivity.

WHY DOES THAT RISING MOON LOOK SO BIG? (Page 159)

To begin with, let's emphasize the obvious: the moon is not actually larger when it's on the horizon. Photographs show that the size of the image cast on the retina is exactly the same in both cases. So what psychologists call the moon illusion must be created by our perceptual system. Though not completely understood, the illusion seems to be a false perception caused by cues that ordinarily contribute to maintaining size constancy. The chief suspect is apparent distance, which figures importantly in our size judgments. One theory holds that the moon looks bigger as it's rising over the horizon because we use objects in our field of vision, such as trees, buildings, and landscape features, to estimate its distance. Experiments have shown that objects look farther away when viewed through filled spaces than they do when viewed through empty spaces (such as the sky overhead). Filled space can make objects look as much as 2.5 to 4 times farther away. According to the theory, the perceptual system basically says, "If the size of the retinal image is the same but it's farther away, then it must be bigger."

This explanation can't be the whole story, however, because some people perceive the moon on the horizon as being closer, rather than farther away. If something the same size seems closer, it will look larger even though it isn't. It may be that there are individual differences in the size-judgment processes that cause the illusion, so that no single explanation applies to everybody.

EXPLAIN THIS STRIKING ILLUSION (Page 163)

To analyze your experience, it is important to understand that both the "tent" and the "corner" cast identical images on your retina. After perceiving the tent for a while, your brain shifted to the second perceptual hypothesis, as it did in response to the Necker cube shown in Figure 5.34. When the object looked like a tent, all the depth information was consistent with that perception. But when you began to see it as a corner and then moved your head slowly back and forth, the object seemed to twist and turn as if it were made of rubber. This occurred because, when you moved, the image of the near point of the fold moved across your retina faster than the image of the far point. This is the normal pattern of stimulation for points at different depths and is known as motion parallax. Thus, when you were seeing a tent, the monocular cue of motion parallax was consistent with the shape of the object. But when the object was later seen as standing upright, all the points along the fold appeared to be the same distance away, yet they were moving at different rates of speed! The only way your brain could maintain its "corner" perception in the face of the motion parallax cues was to see the object as twisting and turning. Again, as in other illusions, forcing all of the sensory data to fit the perceptual hypothesis produced an unusual experience.

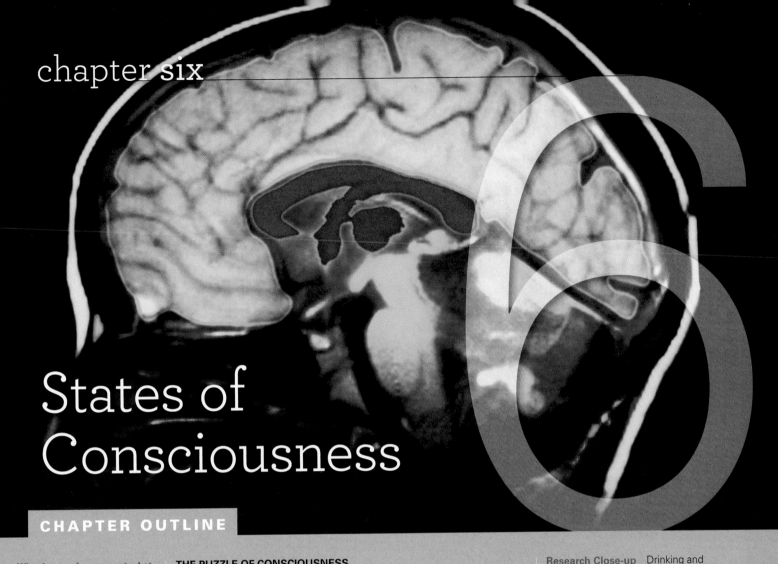

chapter six

States of Consciousness

Myth or Reality?

Hypnosis Uncovers Eyewitnesses' Hidden Memories (page 207)

A person witnesses a crime but can't remember much about it. Under hypnosis the person recalls more details, which helps the police solve the crime. That's the popular conception of forensic hypnosis, but does it really improve eyewitness memory?

Figure 6.1

Perception without conscious awareness.
A rectangular slot was rotated to different angles on a series of trials. When asked simply to hold and tilt a rectangular card to match the slot's angle, D. F. performed poorly. She could not consciously recognize the orientation of the slot. Despite this, when asked to rapidly insert the card into the slot, as illustrated here, she performed well. Source: Goodale, 1995.

Three unrelated people, whom we'll call Sondra, Jason, and Ellen, had an unusual problem: eating while asleep. Each night they would sleepwalk to the kitchen. Sondra would

> consume cat food or salt sandwiches, buttered cigarettes and . . . large quantities of peanut butter, butter, salt and sugar. . . . Once she awakened while struggling to open a bottle of ammonia cleaning fluid, which she was prepared to drink. (Schenck et al., 1991, p. 430)

While sleepwalking, Jason and Ellen also ate odd foods (such as raw bacon), and sometimes Jason spoke coherently with his wife. Upon awakening, they couldn't remember their experiences.

After evaluation by sleep specialists, Sondra received medication and Jason was referred to his primary physician. Neither drugs nor psychotherapy helped Ellen, so a new plan was tried: locking the kitchen door at bedtime, hiding the key, and placing crackers and a pitcher of water by the bed. Usually, when Ellen awoke in the morning, the crackers and water would be gone, and she had no memory of having consumed them (Whyte & Kavey, 1990).

In contrast to Sondra, Jason, and Ellen's sleepeating, D. F.'s unusual problem takes center stage when she's awake. One day, D. F. lost consciousness and suffered brain damage from carbon-monoxide exposure. As psychologist Melvin Goodale (2000) describes, when D. F. regained consciousness,

> she was unable to recognize the faces of her relatives and friends or identify the visual form of common objects. In fact, she could not even tell the difference between . . . a square and a triangle. At the same time, she had no difficulty recognizing people from their voices or identifying objects placed in her hands; her perceptual problems appeared to be exclusively visual. (p. 367)

D. F.'s condition is called **visual agnosia,** *an inability to visually recognize objects.* It's not blindness: D. F. can see. Rather, brain damage has "left her unable to perceive the size, shape, and orientation of objects" (Goodale, 2000).

But how, then, is D. F. able to walk across a room while easily avoiding obstacles? And if she can't consciously perceive the difference in shape and size between, say, a spoon and a glass, how does she know to open her hand to the proper width to grasp objects? On a laboratory task, how is D. F. able to rapidly insert an object into a tilted rectangular slot when, just moments before, she could not consciously recognize the slot's orientation (Figure 6.1)?

Sleepeating and visual agnosia are intriguing conditions, and they offer potential insights into the nature of consciousness. Psychologists would explore whether these disorders are as far removed from our everyday states of consciousness as we might think. They would be especially interested in how Sondra, Jason, Ellen, and D. F. could perform tasks that seem to require attention and monitoring—making sandwiches or conversing while asleep, grasping objects—yet do so without conscious awareness.

How can someone be asleep yet find the kitchen and prepare food? Well, consider this: Why don't you fall out of bed at night? You are not consciously aware of your many postural shifts when you are sound asleep, yet a part of you somehow knows where the edge of the bed is. And what of D. F.'s ability, while awake, to avoid obstacles and grasp objects without conscious awareness of their shape or size? Again, consider this: Have you ever spaced out while driving because you were deeply engrossed in thought? Suddenly you snap out of it, with no memory of the miles you've just driven. While you were consciously focused inward, some part of you—without conscious awareness—kept track of the road and controlled your hand movements at the wheel.

(a)

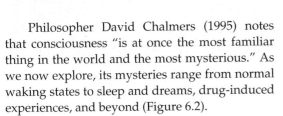

(b)

Figure 6.2

(a) During a Sufi religious ceremony in Istanbul, Turkey, whirling dervishes perform a spinning dance—a prayer in motion—that induces an altered state of consciousness. (b) Buddhists believe that meditation produces inner peace, facilitates insight and enlightenment, and opens a path to different dimensions of consciousness.

Philosopher David Chalmers (1995) notes that consciousness "is at once the most familiar thing in the world and the most mysterious." As we now explore, its mysteries range from normal waking states to sleep and dreams, drug-induced experiences, and beyond (Figure 6.2).

THE PUZZLE OF CONSCIOUSNESS

When psychology was founded in the late 1800s, its "great project" was to unravel some of the puzzles of consciousness (Natsoulas, 1999). This interest waned during behaviorism's mid-20th century dominance, but resurgence of the cognitive and biological perspectives has led us to rethink long-standing conceptions about the mind.

Characteristics of Consciousness

In psychology, **consciousness** *is often defined as our moment-to-moment awareness of ourselves and our environment.* Among its characteristics, consciousness is:

- *subjective and private:* Other people cannot directly know what reality is for you, nor can you enter directly into their experience.
- *dynamic (ever changing):* We drift in and out of various states throughout each day. Moreover, although the stimuli of which we are aware constantly change, we typically experience consciousness as a continuously flowing stream of mental activity, rather than as disjointed perceptions and thoughts (James, 1890/1950).

- *self-reflective and central to our sense of self:* The mind is aware of its own consciousness. Thus no matter what your awareness is focused on—a lovely sunset or an itch on your back—you can reflect on the fact that you are the one who is conscious of it.

Finally, consciousness is *intimately linked to selective attention,* discussed in Chapter 5. William James noted that "the mind is at every stage a theatre of simultaneous possibilities. Consciousness consists in . . . the selection of some, and the suppression of the rest by the . . . agency of Attention" (1879, p. 13). **Selective attention** *is the process that focuses awareness on some stimuli to the exclusion of others.* If the mind is a theater of mental activity, then consciousness reflects whatever is illuminated at the moment—the bright spot on the stage—and selective attention is the spotlight or mechanism behind it (Baars, 1997).

Measuring States of Consciousness

Scientists who study consciousness must operationally define private inner states in terms of measurable responses. *Self-report measures* directly ask people to describe their inner experiences, but self-reports are not always verifiable or possible to obtain. While asleep, most of us (thankfully) do not speak; nor can we fill out self-report questionnaires.

Behavioral measures record, among other things, performance on special tasks. By examining D. F.'s performance on the card-slot task under different conditions (see Figure 6.1), researchers concluded that despite being unable to consciously perceive the slot's orientation, her brain nonetheless

Figure 6.3

Gordon Gallup (1970) exposed 4 chimps to a mirror. By day 3, they used it to inspect hard-to-see parts of their own bodies. To further test whether the chimps knew the mirror image was their own reflection, Gallup anesthetized them and put a red mark on each of their foreheads. Later, with no mirror, the chimps rarely touched the red mark. But upon seeing it when a mirror was introduced, they touched the red spot almost 30 times in 30 minutes, suggesting that the chimps had some self-awareness. A similar test in which a red mark was placed on the tip of infants' noses revealed that infants begin to recognize themselves in a mirror around 18 months of age.

processed this information. Behavioral measures are objective, but they require us to infer the person's state of mind. Figure 6.3 illustrates another clever behavioral measure.

Physiological measures establish the correspondence between bodily processes and mental states. Through electrodes attached to the scalp, the electroencephalograph (EEG) measures brain-wave patterns that reflect the ongoing electrical activity of large groups of neurons. Different patterns correspond to different states of consciousness, such as whether you are alert, relaxed, or asleep. Brain imaging allows scientists to more precisely examine brain activity that underlies various mental states. Physiological measures cannot tell us what a person is experiencing subjectively, but they have been invaluable for probing the inner workings of the mind.

Levels of Consciousness

Much of what occurs within your brain is beyond conscious access. You don't consciously perceive the brain processes that lull you to sleep. You're aware of your thoughts but not of how your brain creates them. What else lies outside of conscious awareness?

The Freudian Viewpoint

Sigmund Freud (1900/1953) proposed that the mind consists of three levels of awareness. The *conscious* mind contains thoughts and perceptions of which we are currently aware. *Preconscious* mental events are outside current awareness but can easily be recalled. For instance, you may not have thought about a friend for years, but when someone mentions your friend's name, you become aware of pleasant memories. *Unconscious* events cannot be brought into conscious awareness under ordinary circumstances. Freud proposed that some unconscious content—such as unacceptable sexual and aggressive urges, traumatic memories, and threatening emotional conflicts—is *repressed*; that is, it is kept out of conscious awareness because it would arouse anxiety, guilt, or other negative emotions.

Behaviorists roundly criticized Freud's ideas. After all, they sought to explain behavior without invoking conscious mental processes, much less unconscious ones. Cognitive psychologists and many contemporary psychodynamic psychologists also take issue with specific aspects of Freud's theory. However, as we will see, research supports Freud's general premise that unconscious processes can affect behavior.

The Cognitive Viewpoint

Cognitive psychologists reject the notion of an unconscious mind driven by instinctive urges and repressed conflicts. Rather, they view conscious and unconscious mental life as complementary forms of information processing that work in harmony (Hassin et al., 2005). For example, many activities, such as planning a vacation or studying, require controlled (conscious) processing, *the conscious use of attention and effort.* Other activities involve automatic (unconscious) processing *and can be performed without conscious awareness or effort.* Automatic processing occurs most often when we carry out routine actions or very well-learned tasks.

In everyday life, learning to write, drive, and type on a computer keyboard all involve controlled processing; at first you have to pay a lot of conscious attention to what you are doing. With practice, performance becomes more automatic and certain brain areas involved in conscious thought become less active (Saling & Phillips, 2007). Through years of practice, athletes and musicians program themselves to execute highly complex skills with a minimum of conscious thought.

Automatic processing, however, has a key disadvantage because it can reduce our chances of finding new ways to approach problems (Langer, 1989). Controlled processing is more flexible and open to change. Still, many well-learned behaviors seem to be performed faster and better when our mind is on autopilot, with controlled processing taking a backseat. The baseball player Yogi Berra captured this idea in his classic statement, "You can't think and hit at the same time." At tasks ranging from putting a golf ball to playing video games, too much self-focused thinking can hurt performance and cause people to choke under pressure (Beilock & Carr, 2001).

Automatic processing also facilitates divided attention, *the capacity to attend to and perform more than one activity at the same time.* We can talk while we walk, type as we read, and so on. Yet divided attention has limits and is more difficult when two tasks require similar mental resources. For example, we cannot fully attend to separate messages delivered simultaneously through two earphones.

Unconscious Perception and Influence

The concept of unconscious information processing is widely accepted today, but this was not always the case. It has taken painstaking research to reveal that stimuli can be perceived without conscious awareness and influence how we behave or feel. Consider these examples.

Visual Agnosia

Studies of people with brain damage provide scientists with insights into how the mind works. Recall that D. F., the woman with visual agnosia, could not consciously perceive the shape, size, or orientation of objects yet had little difficulty performing a card-insertion task and avoiding obstacles when she walked across a room. To perform these tasks easily, her brain must have processed accurate information about the properties of the various objects. If she professed no conscious awareness of these properties, then this information processing must have occurred unconsciously (Goodale, 2000).

There are many types of visual agnosia. For example, people with *prosopagnosia* can visually recognize objects but not faces. When some of these patients look in the mirror, they do not consciously recognize their own faces. Yet in laboratory tests these patients display different patterns of brain activity, arousal, and eye movements when they look at familiar rather than unfamiliar faces (Young, 2003). In other words, their brains are recognizing a difference between familiar and unfamiliar stimuli, but this recognition doesn't reach conscious awareness.

Blindsight

People with agnosia are not blind, but those with a rare condition called blindsight *are blind in part of their visual field yet in special tests respond to stimuli in that field despite reporting that they can't see those stimuli* (Kentridge et al., 2004). For example, due to left-hemisphere damage, a blindsight patient may be blind in the right half of the visual field. A stimulus (e.g., a photograph, a vertical line) is flashed on a screen so that it appears within the patient's blind visual field. On trial after trial, the patient reports seeing nothing. But when asked to point to where the stimulus was, she or he guesses at rates much higher than chance, suggesting that the stimulus was perceived unconsciously. On some tasks, guessing accuracy may reach 80 to 100 percent (Radoeva et al., 2008).

Priming

Here's a simple task. Starting with the two letters *ho_____* (this is called a *word stem*), what is the first word that comes to your mind? Was it *hot, how, home, house, hope, hole,* or *honest*? Clearly, you had these and many other words to choose from.

Now imagine that just before completing this word stem you had looked at a screen on which the word *hose* (or perhaps a picture of a hose) was presented *subliminally* (it was displayed so rapidly or weakly that it was below your threshold for conscious perception).

Suppose we conduct an experiment with many participants and many word stems (e.g., *ho_____, gr_____, ma_____,* etc.). We find that compared to people who are not exposed to subliminal words such as *hose, gripe,* and *manage,* people who are subliminally exposed are more likely to complete the word stems with those particular words. This provides evidence of a process called **priming**: *Exposure to a stimulus influences (i.e., primes) how you subsequently respond to that same or another stimulus.* Thus even if people do not consciously see *hose*, the subliminal word or image primes their response to *ho____*.

Subliminal stimuli can prime more than our responses to word stems. For example, when people are shown photographs of a person, the degree to which they evaluate that person positively is influenced by whether they have first been subliminally exposed to pleasant or unpleasant images, such as photos of other faces that are happy or fearful (Sweeny et al., 2009). Likewise, being subliminally exposed to words with an aggressive theme causes people to judge another person's ambiguous behavior as being more aggressive (Todorov & Bargh, 2002).

The Emotional Unconscious

Modern psychodynamic psychologists emphasize that beyond the types of unconscious processing we've just discussed, emotional and motivational processes also operate unconsciously and influence behavior (Westen, 1998). Numerous experiments support the view that unconscious processes can have an emotional and motivational flavor (LaBar & LeDoux, 2006). For example, have you ever been in a bad or a good mood and wondered why you were feeling that way? Perhaps it is because you were influenced by events in your environment of which you were not consciously aware.

In one study, Tanya Chartrand and her colleagues (2002) subliminally presented college students with nouns that were either strongly negative (e.g., *cancer, cockroach*), mildly negative (e.g., *Monday, worm*), mildly positive (e.g., *parade, clown*), or strongly positive (e.g., *friends, music*). Later, students rated their moods on psychological tests. Although not consciously aware of seeing the nouns, students shown the strongly negative words reported the saddest mood, whereas those who had seen the strongly positive words reported the happiest mood.

Why Do We Have Consciousness?

Why have we evolved into conscious beings? Surely the subjective richness of your life might evaporate if you lost the ability to consciously reflect on your feelings, thoughts, and memories. But how does consciousness help us adapt to, and survive in, our environment?

In his book *The Quest for Consciousness*, Christof Koch (2004) notes that, "consciousness goes hand-in-hand with the ability to plan, to reflect upon many possible courses of action, and to choose one" (p. 205). Koch suggests that consciousness serves a summarizing function. At any instant, your brain processes many external stimuli (e.g., sights, sounds, etc.) and internal stimuli (e.g., bodily sensations). Conscious awareness provides a summary—a single mental representation—of what is going on in your world at each moment, and it makes this summary available to brain regions involved in planning and decision making. Other scientists agree that consciousness aids the distribution of information to many brain areas (Shanahan & Baars, 2005).

On another front, consciousness helps us override potentially dangerous behaviors governed by impulses or automatic processing. Without the capacity to reflect, you might lash out after every provocation. Without the safety net of consciousness, Sondra almost drank ammonia during a sleepwalking episode.

Consciousness also allows us to deal flexibly with novel situations and helps us plan responses to them (Koch, 2004; Langer, 1989). Self-awareness—coupled with communication—also enables us to express our needs to other people and coordinate actions with them.

The Neural Basis of Consciousness

Within our brains, where does consciousness arise? And if no individual brain cell is conscious (as far as we know), then how does brain activity produce consciousness?

Windows to the Brain

Some researchers have examined the brain functioning of patients who have visual agnosia, blindsight, or other disorders that impair conscious perception. Let's return to the case of D. F. Brain imaging revealed that D. F.'s primary visual cortex was largely undamaged from carbon-monoxide exposure. Why, then, could she not consciously recognize objects and faces?

The answer builds on prior research in which psychologists discovered multiple brain pathways for processing visual information (Ungerleider & Mishkin, 1982). One pathway, extending from the primary visual cortex to the parietal lobe, carries information to support the unconscious guidance of movements (Gabbard & Ammar, 2008). A second pathway, extending from the primary visual cortex to the temporal lobe, carries information to support

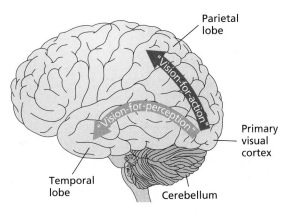

Figure 6.4

Action and perception.

The neural pathway shown in red is sometimes called the *vision-for-action pathway* because it carries information used in the visual control of movement, such as reaching for and grasping something or inserting a card into a slot. The pathway shown in green is sometimes called the *vision-for-perception pathway* because it carries information that helps us recognize objects (Koch, 2004; Milner & Dijkerman, 2001). Both pathways ultimately make connections to the prefrontal cortex.

the conscious recognition of objects (Figure 6.4). Consistent with this view, imaging of D. F.'s brain indicated that parts of this second visual pathway were badly damaged (Goodale, 2000).

Scientists study the neural basis of consciousness in other creative ways. Some explore conscious perceptions created when specific brain areas are electrically stimulated, while others examine how consciousness is lost and regained when patients are put under and recover from anesthesia (Lee et al., 2009). Still others have used a procedure called *masking* (Figure 6.5) to control whether people perceive a stimulus consciously or unconsciously. In experiments, participants undergo brain imaging while exposed to masked and unmasked stimuli. This enables scientists to assess how brain activity differs depending on whether the same stimuli (e.g., photos of angry faces) are consciously or unconsciously perceived.

Building on this technique, neuroscientists have found that emotionally threatening stimuli are processed consciously and unconsciously through different neural pathways. The pathway that produces conscious recognition involves the prefrontal cortex and several other brain regions that are bypassed in the pathway for unconscious processing (Morris & Dolan, 2001).

Consciousness as a Global Workspace

Many neuroscientists believe that there is no single place in the brain that gives rise to consciousness. Instead, they view the mind as a collection of largely separate but interacting information-processing

modules that perform tasks related to sensation, perception, memory, movement, planning, problem solving, emotion, and so on. The modules process information in parallel—that is, simultaneously and largely independently. However, there also is cross talk between them, as when the output from one module is carried by neural circuits to provide input for another module. For example, a formula recalled from memory can become input for problem-solving modules that allow you to compute answers during a math exam.

According to one view, consciousness is a *global workspace* that represents the unified activity of multiple modules in different areas of the brain (Baars, 2007). In essence, of the many brain modules and connecting circuits that are active at any instant, a particular subset becomes joined in unified activity that is strong enough to become a conscious perception or thought (Koch, 2004). The specific modules and circuits that make up this dominant subset can vary as our brain responds to changing stimuli—sights, sounds, smells, and so on—that compete for conscious attention.

Subjectively, of course, we experience consciousness as unitary, rather than as a collection of modules and circuits. This is somewhat akin to listening to a choir sing. We are aware of the integrated, harmonious sound of the choir rather than the voice of each individual member. As we now see, many factors influence these modules and, in so doing, alter our consciousness.

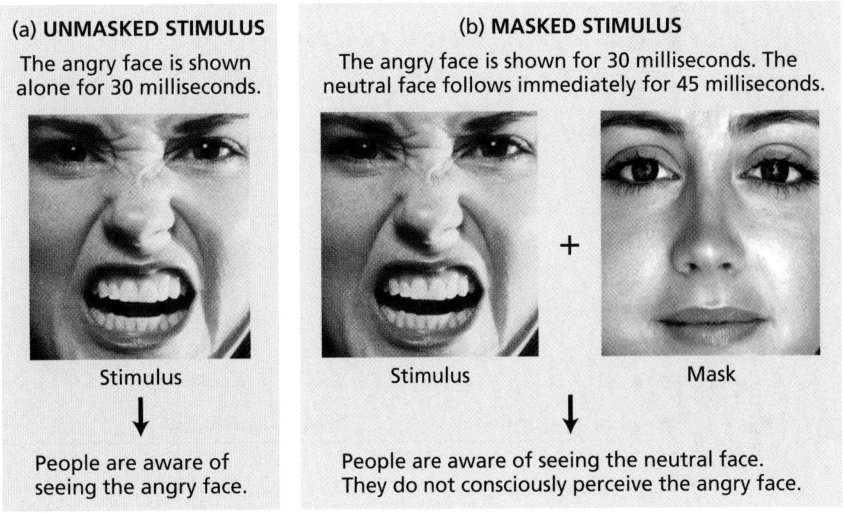

(a) UNMASKED STIMULUS
The angry face is shown alone for 30 milliseconds.

Stimulus

↓

People are aware of seeing the angry face.

(b) MASKED STIMULUS
The angry face is shown for 30 milliseconds. The neutral face follows immediately for 45 milliseconds.

Stimulus   +   Mask

↓

People are aware of seeing the neutral face. They do not consciously perceive the angry face.

Figure 6.5

An example of masking.

(a) If a picture of an angry face is flashed on a screen for 30 milliseconds, people report seeing it. In this case, the picture is not masked. (b) If the angry face is immediately followed by a photo of a neutral face shown for a longer time (e.g., 45 milliseconds), people report seeing the neutral face but not the angry face. In this approach—called *backward masking*—the presentation of the second photo masks the conscious perception of the first photo. Masking works with many types of stimuli, not just photos of faces. Source: Adapted from Morris & Dolan, 2001.

test yourself   **The Puzzle of Consciousness**

test yourself   **The Puzzle of Consciousness**

True or false?

1. Self-report measures are the only valid way to measure states of consciousness.
2. According to Freud, the preconscious mind consists of mental events that cannot be brought into conscious awareness.
3. Controlled processing requires the conscious use of attention and effort.
4. Visual agnosia, blindsight, and priming all support the concept of unconscious processing.
5. The brain has a single "consciousness center" located in the right prefrontal cortex.

ANSWERS: 1-false, 2-false, 3-true, 4-true, 5-false

CIRCADIAN RHYTHMS: OUR DAILY BIOLOGICAL CLOCKS

Like other animals, humans have adapted to a world with a 24-hour day-night cycle. Every 24 hours our body temperature, certain hormonal secretions, and other bodily functions undergo a rhythmic change that affects our alertness and readies our passage back and forth between waking consciousness and sleep (Figure 6.6). These *daily biological cycles are called* **circadian rhythms.**

Keeping Time: Brain and Environment

Most circadian rhythms are regulated by the brain's **suprachiasmatic nuclei (SCN),** located in the hypothalamus. SCN neurons have a genetically programmed cycle of activity and inactivity, functioning like a biological clock. They link to the tiny pineal gland, which secretes **melatonin,** *a hormone that has a relaxing effect on the body.* SCN neurons become active during the daytime and reduce the pineal gland's secretion of melatonin, raising body temperature and heightening alertness. At night, SCN neurons are inactive, allowing melatonin levels to increase and promoting relaxation and sleepiness (Zee & Lu, 2008).

Our circadian clock is biological, but environmental cues such as the day-night cycle help keep SCN neurons on a 24-hour schedule. Your eyes have neural connections to the SCN, and after a night's sleep, the light of day increases SCN activity and helps reset your 24-hour biological clock. What would happen, then, if you lived in a laboratory or underground cave without clocks and could not tell whether it was day or night outside? In experiments in which people did just that, most participants drifted into a natural wake-sleep cycle, called a *free-running circadian rhythm*, that is longer than 24 hours (Hillman et al., 1994).

For decades, research suggested that our free-running rhythm was about 25 hours long. In these studies, however, the bright room lights that participants kept on artificially lengthened their circadian rhythms. Under more controlled conditions, the free-running rhythm averages around 24.2 hours (Lavie, 2000). Yet even this small deviation from the 24-hour day is significant. If you were to follow your free-running rhythm, two months from now you would be going to bed at noon and awakening at midnight.

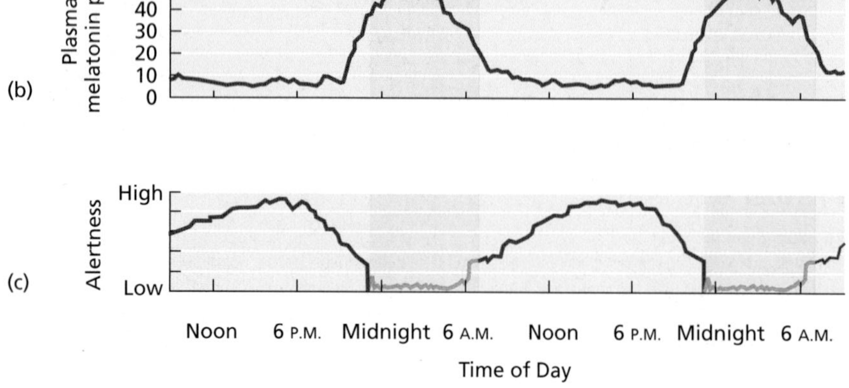

Early Birds and Night Owls

Circadian rhythms also influence our tendency to be a morning person or a night person (Emens et al., 2009). Compared to night people ("night owls"), morning people ("early birds") go to bed

Figure 6.6

Circadian rhythms.
(a) Changes in our core body temperature, (b) levels of melatonin in our blood, and (c) degrees of alertness are a few of the bodily functions that follow a cyclical 24-hour pattern called a *circadian rhythm.* Humans also have longer and shorter biological cycles, such as the 28-day female menstrual cycle and a roughly 90-minute brain activity cycle during sleep. SOURCE: Adapted from Monk et al., 1996.

Table 6.1 | **Morningness among College Students from Six Countries**

Country	Morningness Score
Colombia	42.4
India	39.4
Spain	33.9
England	31.6
United States	31.4
Netherlands	30.1

NOTE: Scores can range from 13 ("extreme evening type") to 55 ("extreme morning type").
SOURCE: Smith et al., 2002.

and rise earlier, and their body temperature, blood pressure, and alertness peak earlier in the day.

Cultures may differ in their overall tendency toward "morningness." Carlla Smith and her co-workers (2002) used questionnaires to measure the degree of morningness among college students from six countries. They predicted and found that students from Colombia, India, and Spain—regions with warmer annual climates—exhibited greater morningness than students from England, the United States, and the Netherlands (Table 6.1).

thinking **critically**

EARLY BIRDS, CLIMATE, AND CULTURE

Is this study of morningness correlational or experimental? What factors other than climate might explain why people from warmer regions display greater morningness? Think about it, then see page 212.

Environmental Disruptions of Circadian Rhythms

Environmental changes can disrupt our circadian rhythms. Jet lag is a sudden circadian disruption caused by flying across several time zones in one day. Flying east, you lose hours from your day; flying west extends your day to more than 24 hours. Jet lag, which often causes insomnia and decreased alertness, is a significant concern for businesspeople, athletes, airline crews, and others who frequently travel across many time zones (Reilly, 2009). The body naturally adjusts about one hour or less per day to time-zone changes. Typically, people adjust faster when flying west, presumably because lengthening the travel day is more compatible with our natural free-running circadian cycle (Revell & Eastman, 2005).

Night-shift work is the most problematic circadian disruption for society. Imagine beginning an 8-hour work shift at 11 P.M. or midnight, a time when your biological clock is promoting sleepiness. After work you head home in morning daylight, making it harder to alter your biological clock (Sasseville et al., 2009). Daytime becomes bedtime, and you may sleep less than you did before. Over time you may become fatigued, stressed, and more accident-prone (Folkard, 2008). On days off, reverting to a typical day-night schedule to spend time with family and friends will disrupt any hard-earned circadian adjustments you have made. If you work for a company that requires employees to rotate shifts every few days or weeks, then after adapting to night work, you'll have to switch to a day or evening shift and readjust your biological clock again.

These circadian disruptions, combined with fatigue from poor daytime sleep, can be a recipe for disaster. Job performance errors, fatal traffic accidents, and engineering and industrial disasters peak between midnight and 6 A.M. (Akerstedt et al., 2001). In some cases, night operators at nuclear power plants have been found asleep at the controls. On-the-job sleepiness is also a major concern among long-distance truck drivers, airline crews, doctors and nurses, and others who work at night.

Seasonal affective disorder (SAD) *is a cyclic tendency to become psychologically depressed during certain seasons of the year.* In most cases, SAD begins in fall or winter, when there is less daylight, and then lifts in spring (Rosenthal & Rosenthal, 2006). The circadian rhythms of SAD sufferers may be particularly sensitive to light, so as sunrises occur later in winter, the daily onset time of their circadian clocks may be pushed back to an unusual degree. On late-fall and winter mornings, when many people must arise for work and school in darkness, SAD sufferers remain in sleepiness mode long after the morning alarm clock sounds (Figure 6.7).

Figure 6.7

The latitude puzzle.
In North America, the rates of winter SAD and milder depression ("winter blues") increase at more northerly latitudes, where the hours of daylight diminish more severely in late fall and winter. Yet European studies report lower winter SAD rates and a weaker SAD–latitude relation. In fact, most studies in Sweden, Norway, Finland, and Iceland report winter SAD rates similar to those in the southern United States. The reason for this discrepancy is not clear. SOURCES: Data adapted from Mersch et al., 1999. Map graphic from *The New York Times*, 29 December 1993, p. B7; copyright © 1993 The New York Times.

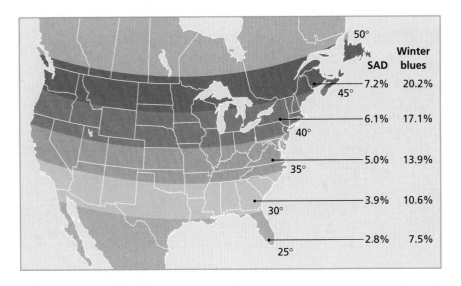

	SAD	Winter blues
50°		
45°	7.2%	20.2%
40°	6.1%	17.1%
35°	5.0%	13.9%
30°	3.9%	10.6%
25°	2.8%	7.5%

Applying Psychological Science

Outsmarting Jet Lag, Night-Work Disruptions, and Winter Depression

Circadian research provides important insights on the nature of consciousness. It also offers several treatments for circadian disruptions affecting millions of people.

CONTROLLING EXPOSURE TO LIGHT

Reducing Jet Lag

Flying east across time zones, your body's internal clock falls behind the time at your destination. Exposure to outdoor light in the morning—and avoiding light late in the day—moves the circadian clock forward and helps it catch up to local time. (Think of morning light as jump-starting your circadian clock at a time when you would be asleep back home.) Flying west, your body clock moves ahead of local time. So to reduce jet lag, you want to delay your circadian cycle by avoiding bright light in the morning and exposing yourself to light in the afternoon or early evening. These are general rules, but the specific timing of light exposure depends on the number of time zones crossed (Waterhouse & Reilly, 2009). For jet travelers, spending time outside (even on cloudy days) is the easiest way to get the needed exposure to light.

Adjusting to Night Work

When night employees go home after work, their circadian adjustment can be increased by (1) keeping the bedroom dark and quiet to foster daytime sleep and (2) maintaining a schedule of daytime sleep even during days off (Boulos, 1998). Day sleepers are advised to install light-blocking window shades, unplug the phone, and use earplugs.

Treating SAD

Many experts believe that phototherapy, which involves properly timed exposure to specially prescribed bright artificial lights, is an effective treatment for SAD (Strong et al., 2009). Several hours of daily phototherapy, especially in the early morning, can shift circadian rhythms by as much as 2 to 3 hours per day (Neumeister, 2004). The fact that phototherapy effectively treats SAD is the strongest evidence that SAD is triggered by winter's lack of sunlight rather than by its colder temperatures (Figure 6.8).

MELATONIN TREATMENT: USES AND CAUTIONS

The hormone melatonin is a key player in the brain's circadian clock. Melatonin also exists in pill or capsule form; it is a prescription drug in some countries and is unavailable to the public in others. In the United States, it is a nonprescription dietary supplement. Depending on when it is taken, oral melatonin can shift some circadian cycles forward or backward by as much as 30 to 60 minutes per day of use. Melatonin treatment has been used with some success to decrease jet lag, help employees adapt to night-shift work, and alleviate SAD (Arendt, 2009; Lewy et al., 2006).

Figure 6.8

For many people, the depression from SAD can be reduced by daily exposure to bright fluorescent lights.

But there is reason for caution. Doses of 0.1 to 0.5 milligram are often sufficient to produce circadian shifts, but tablet doses are often 3 to 5 milligrams, producing blood melatonin levels that are more than 10 times the normal concentration (Sack et al., 1997). Melatonin use is supervised during research, but individuals who self-administer it may do more harm than good. Taking melatonin at the wrong time can backfire and make circadian adjustments more difficult. Daytime use may decrease alertness (Graw et al., 2001).

REGULATING ACTIVITY SCHEDULES

Properly timed physical exercise may help shift the circadian clock (Mistlberger et al., 2000). For example, compared to merely staying up later than normal, exercising when you normally go to bed may push back your circadian clock, as you would want to do when flying west (Baehr, 2001). To reduce jet lag, you can also begin synchronizing your biological clock to the new time zone in advance. To do so, adjust your sleep and eating schedules by 1 to 2 hours per day, starting several days before you leave (Eastman et al., 2005). Schedule management also applies to night-shift work. For workers on 8-hour rotating shifts, circadian disruptions can be reduced by a forward-rotating shift schedule—moving from day to evening to night shifts—rather than a schedule that rotates backward from day to night to evening shifts (Driscoll et al., 2007). Forward schedules take advantage of free-running circadian rhythms. When work shifts change, it is easier to extend the waking day than to compress it.

SLEEP AND DREAMING

Sweet, mysterious sleep. We spend much of our lives in this altered state, relinquishing conscious control of our thoughts, dreaming and remembering little of it upon awakening. Yet sleep, like other behaviors, can be studied at biological, psychological, and environmental levels.

Stages of Sleep

Circadian rhythms promote a readiness for sleep by decreasing alertness, but they do not regulate sleep directly. Instead, roughly every 90 minutes while asleep, we cycle through different stages in which brain activity and other physiological responses change in a generally predictable way (Dement, 2005; Kleitman, 1963).

Sleep research is often carried out in specially equipped laboratories where sleepers' physiological responses are recorded (Figure 6.9). EEG recordings of your brain's electrical activity would show a pattern of **beta waves** *when you are awake and alert.* Beta waves have a high frequency (of about 15 to 30 cycles per second, or cps) but a low amplitude, or height (Figure 6.10). As you close your eyes, *feeling relaxed and drowsy, your brain waves slow down and* **alpha waves** occur at about 8 to 12 cps.

Stage 1 through Stage 4

As sleep begins, your brain-wave pattern becomes more irregular, and slower *theta waves* (3.5 to 7.5 cps) increase. You are now in *stage 1*, a form of light sleep from which you can easily be awakened. You'll probably spend just a few minutes in stage 1, during which time some people experience dreams, vivid images, and sudden body jerks. As sleep becomes deeper, *sleep spindles*—periodic

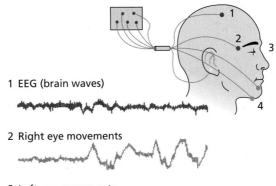

1 EEG (brain waves)

2 Right eye movements

3 Left eye movements

4 Muscle tension

Figure 6.9

The sleep laboratory.
In a modern sleep laboratory, people sleep while their physiological responses are monitored. Electrodes attached to the scalp record the person's EEG brain-wave patterns. Electrodes attached beside the eyes record eye movements during sleep. Electrodes attached to the jaw record muscle tension. A neutral electrode is attached to the ear.

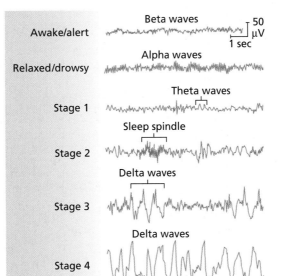

Figure 6.10

Stages of sleep.
Changing patterns of brain-wave activity help define the various stages of sleep. Note that brain waves become slower as sleep deepens from stage 1 through stage 4. SOURCE: Based on Hauri, 1982.

1- to 2-second bursts of rapid brain-wave activity (12 to 15 cps)—begin to appear. Sleep spindles indicate that you are now in *stage 2* (see Figure 6.10). Your muscles are more relaxed, breathing and heart rate are slower, dreams may occur, and you are harder to awaken.

Sleep deepens as you move into *stage 3*, marked by the regular appearance of *very slow (0.5 to 2 cps) and large* **delta waves.** As time passes, they occur more often, and when delta waves dominate the EEG pattern, you have reached *stage 4*. *Together, stage 3 and stage 4 are often referred to as* **slow-wave sleep.** Your body is relaxed, activity in various parts of your brain has decreased, you are hard to awaken, and you may have dreams. After 20 to 30 minutes of stage-4 sleep, your EEG pattern changes as you go back through stages 3 and 2, spending a little time in each. Overall, within 60 to 90 minutes of going to sleep, you have completed a cycle of stages: 1-2-3-4-3-2. At this point, a remarkably different sleep stage ensues.

REM Sleep

In 1953, Eugene Aserinsky and Nathaniel Kleitman of the University of Chicago struck scientific gold when they identified a unique sleep stage called **REM sleep,** *characterized by rapid eye movements (REM), high arousal, and frequent dreaming.* They found that every half minute or so during REM sleep, bursts of muscular activity caused sleepers' eyeballs to vigorously move back and forth beneath their closed eyelids. Moreover, sleepers awakened from REM periods almost always reported a dream—including people who swore they "never had dreams." At last, scientists could examine dreaming more closely. Wait for REM, awaken the sleeper, and catch a dream.

During REM sleep, physiological arousal may increase to daytime levels. The heart rate quickens, breathing becomes more rapid and irregular, and brain-wave activity resembles that of active wakefulness. Regardless of dream content (most dreams are not sexual), men have penile erections and women experience vaginal lubrication. The brain also sends signals making it more difficult for voluntary muscles to contract. As a result, muscles in the arms, legs, and torso lose tone and become relaxed. These muscles may twitch, but in effect you are paralyzed, unable to move. This state is called *REM sleep paralysis* and, because of it, REM sleep is sometimes called *paradoxical sleep:* your body is highly aroused, yet it looks like you are sleeping peacefully because there is so little movement.

Although each cycle through the sleep stages takes an average of 90 minutes, Figure 6.11 shows that as the hours pass, stage 4 and then stage 3 drop out and REM periods become longer.

Getting a Night's Sleep: From Brain to Culture

The brain steers our passage through sleep, but it has no single "sleep center." Certain areas at the base of the forebrain (called the *basal forebrain*) and within the brain stem regulate our falling asleep. Other brain stem areas—including where

Figure 6.11

Cycling through a night's sleep. This graph shows a record of a night's sleep. The REM stages are shown in blue. People typically average four to five REM periods during the night, and these tend to become longer as the night wears on. On this night, the REM 5 period has been cut short because the person awakened.

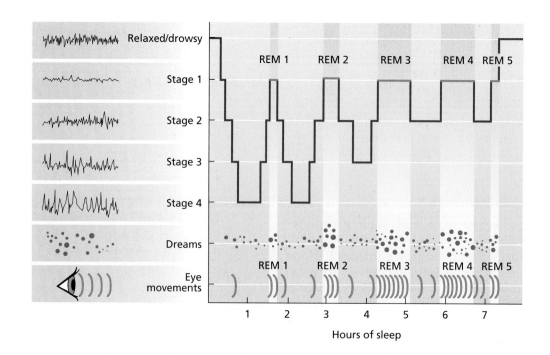

The Brain During REM Sleep

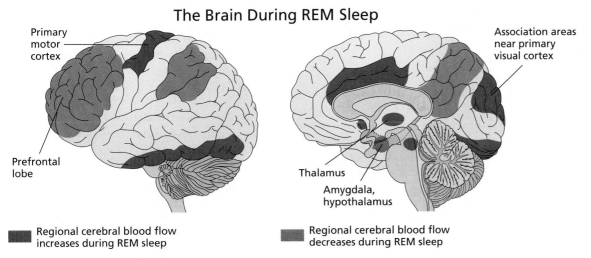

Primary motor cortex

Prefrontal lobe

Association areas near primary visual cortex

Thalamus

Amygdala, hypothalamus

■ Regional cerebral blood flow increases during REM sleep

■ Regional cerebral blood flow decreases during REM sleep

Figure 6.12

Brain activity during REM sleep.

During REM sleep, as compared to wakefulness, several brain regions display markedly decreased (blue) and increased (rust) activity. Note the decreased activation in certain prefrontal lobe regions and increased activity in parts of the amygdala and hypothalamus, thalamus, primary motor cortex, and association areas near the primary visual cortex in the occipital lobe. Source: Schwartz & Maquet, 2002.

the reticular formation passes through the pons (called the *pontine reticular formation*)—play a key role in regulating REM sleep (Izac & Eeg, 2006). This region contains neurons that periodically activate other brain systems, each of which controls a different aspect of REM sleep, such as eye movement and muscular paralysis.

Brain images taken during REM sleep reveal intense activity in limbic system structures, such as the amygdala, that regulate emotions. This pattern may reflect the emotional nature of many REM-sleep dreams (Figure 6.12). The primary motor cortex is active, but its signals for movement are blocked and don't reach our limbs. Association areas near the primary visual cortex are active, which may reflect the processing of visual dream images. In contrast, decreased activity occurs in regions of the prefrontal cortex involved in high-level mental functions, such as planning and logical analysis. This may indicate that our sleeping mind does not monitor and organize its mental activity as carefully as when awake, enabling dreams to be illogical and bizarre (Hobson et al., 2000).

Environmental factors, such as changes in season, also affect sleep. In fall and winter, most people sleep about 15 to 60 minutes longer per night. Shift work, stress at work and school, and nighttime noise can decrease sleep quality (Saremi et al., 2008).

Several aspects of sleep, such as its timing and length, vary across cultures. One study of 818 Japanese and Slovak adolescents found that, on average, the Japanese teenagers went to sleep later at night and slept for a shorter time than their Slovak peers (Iwawaki & Sarmany-Schuller, 2001). Many people, particularly those living in cultures in tropical climates, enjoy the traditional ritual of a 1- to 2-hour midday nap and reduce the length of nighttime sleep (Kribbs, 1993).

Cultural norms also influence several behaviors related to sleep. Do you sleep on a cushioned bed? In some cultures, people sleep on floors or suspended in hammocks (Figure 6.13). *Co-sleeping*, in which children sleep with their parents in the same bed or room, is not common in the United States, as children's sleeping alone is

Figure 6.13

In warmer regions of the Americas, the use of hammocks for sleeping has been common among various indigenous peoples for centuries. This photo shows a Mayan family in the Yucatán, Mexico.

seen as a way to foster independence. But in many cultures, co-sleeping is common (Li et al., 2009).

How Much Do We Sleep?

The question seems simple, as does the answer for many of us: not enough! In reality, the issue is complex. First, Figure 6.14 reveals that there are differences in how much people sleep at various ages. Newborns average 16 hours of sleep a day, almost half of it in REM. As we age, three important changes occur:

- We sleep less; 19- to 30-year-olds average around 7 to 8 hours of sleep a night, and elderly adults average just under 6 hours.
- REM sleep decreases dramatically during infancy and early childhood but remains relatively stable thereafter.
- Time spent in stages 3 and 4 declines. By old age we get relatively little slow-wave sleep.

Second, individual differences in the amount of sleep occur at every age. For example, sleep surveys indicate that one-third of preschoolers sleep between 10 and 10.9 hours a night (National Sleep Foundation, 2004). About 2 percent sleep 14 hours or more a night and 3 percent less than 8 hours.

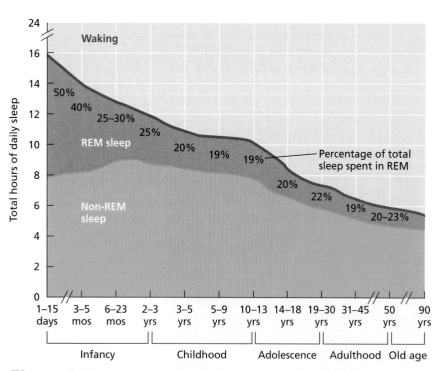

Figure 6.14

Aging and sleep.

Daily total sleep time and the percentage of sleep time in REM and non-REM sleep change with age.

SOURCE: Adapted from Roffwarg, H. P., Muzio, J. N., & Dement, W. C. (1966). Ontogenic development of human dream-sleep cycle. *Science, 152,* 604, figure 1. Copyright © American Association for the Advancement of Science. Reprinted with permission.

Do We Need Eight Hours of Nightly Sleep?

Sleep surveys describe how much sleep people believe they get, not how much they need. Still, it appears that the adage, "everyone needs 8 hours of sleep a night," isn't true (Monk et al., 2001). Indeed, studies reveal that a few people function well on little sleep. Researchers in London examined a healthy, energetic 70-year-old woman who claimed to sleep less than 1 hour a night (Meddis et al., 1973). Over five consecutive nights at the sleep lab, she averaged 67 minutes of sleep a night and showed no ill effects. Such extreme short-sleepers, however, are rare.

What accounts for differences in how much we sleep? Part of the answer appears to reside in our genes. Surveys of thousands of twins in Finland and Australia reveal that identical twins have more similar sleep lengths, bedtimes, and sleep patterns than do fraternal twins (Heath et al., 1990). Using selective breeding, researchers have developed some genetic strains of mice that are long- versus short-sleepers, other strains that spend more or less time in REM, and still others that spend more or less time in slow-wave sleep (Ouyang et al., 2004).

Studies indicate that sleep length and sleep patterns are also related to nongenetic factors. Differences in marital status, employment, work hours, and lifestyle pressures are some of the many factors contributing to the variability in people's sleep (Vincent et al., 2009).

Sleep Deprivation

Sleep deprivation is a way of life for many college students and other adults (National Sleep Foundation, 2009). June Pilcher and Allen Huffcutt (1996) meta-analyzed 19 studies in which participants underwent either "short-term total sleep deprivation" (up to 45 hours without sleep), "long-term total sleep deprivation" (more than 45 hours without sleep), or "partial deprivation" (being allowed to sleep no more than 5 hours a night for one or more consecutive nights). The researchers measured participants' mood (e.g., irritability) and responses on mental tasks (e.g., logical reasoning, word memory) and physical tasks (e.g., manual dexterity, treadmill walking).

What would you predict? Would all types of deprivation affect behavior, and which behaviors would be affected the most? In fact, all three types of sleep deprivation impaired functioning. The typical sleep-deprived person functioned only as well as someone in the bottom 9 percent of nondeprived participants. Overall, mood suffered most, followed by cognitive and then physical performance, although sleep loss significantly impaired *all three* behaviors.

What about students who pull all-nighters and claim they still perform as well as ever? June Pilcher and Amy Walters (1997) found that college students deprived of one night's sleep performed more poorly on a critical-thinking task than students allowed to sleep—yet incorrectly perceived that they had performed better. In short, the students underestimated the negative effects of sleep loss on performance.

Most total-sleep-deprivation studies with humans last less than 5 days, but 17-year-old Randy Gardner set a world record (since broken) of staying awake for 11 days for his 1964 high school science-fair project in San Diego. Grateful sleep researchers received permission to study him (Gulevich et al., 1966). Contrary to a popular myth that Randy suffered few negative effects, at times during the first few days he became irritable, forgetful, and nauseated. By the fifth he had periods of disorientation and mild hallucinations. Over the last 4 days he developed finger tremors and slurred speech. Still, in his final day without sleep he beat sleep researcher William Dement 100 consecutive times at a pinball-type game. When Randy finally went to bed, he slept almost 15 hours the first night and returned to his normal amount of sleep within a week. In general, it takes several nights to recover from extended sleep deprivation, and we do not make up all the sleep time that we have lost.

Why Do We Sleep?

Given that we spend almost a third of our lives sleeping, it must serve an important purpose. But what might that purpose be?

Sleep and Bodily Restoration

According to the **restoration model,** *sleep recharges our run-down bodies and allows us to recover from physical and mental fatigue* (Hess, 1965; Walker, 2008). Sleep-deprivation research supports this view, indicating that we need sleep to function at our best.

If the restoration model is correct, activities that increase daily wear on the body should increase sleep. Evidence is mildly supportive. A study of 18- to 26-year-old ultramarathon runners found that they slept much longer and spent a greater percentage of time in slow-wave sleep on the two nights following their 57-mile run (Shapiro et al., 1981). For the rest of us mere mortals, a meta-analysis of 38 studies found that we tend to sleep longer by about 10 minutes on days we have exercised (Youngstedt et al., 1997).

What is it that gets restored in our bodies while we sleep? We don't know precisely, but many researchers believe that a cellular waste product called *adenosine* plays a role (Alam et al., 2009). Like a car's exhaust emissions, adenosine is produced as cells consume fuel. As adenosine accumulates, it inhibits brain circuits responsible for keeping us awake, thereby signaling the body to slow down because too much cellular fuel has been burned. During sleep, our adenosine levels decrease.

Sleep as an Evolved Adaptation

Evolutionary/circadian sleep models *emphasize that sleep's main purpose is to increase a species' chances of survival in relation to its environmental demands* (Webb, 1974). Our prehistoric ancestors had little to gain—and much to lose—by being active at night. Hunting, food gathering, and traveling were accomplished more easily and safely during daylight. Leaving the protection of one's shelter at night would have served little purpose other than to become dinner for nighttime predators.

Over the course of evolution, each species developed a circadian sleep-wake pattern that was adaptive in terms of its status as predator or prey, its food requirements, and its methods of defense from attack. For small prey animals such as mice and squirrels, which reside in burrows or trees safely away from predators, spending a lot of time asleep is adaptive. For large prey animals such as horses, deer, and zebras, which sleep in relatively exposed environments and whose safety from predators depends on running away, spending a lot of time asleep would be hazardous (Figure 6.15). Sleep may also have evolved as a mechanism for conserving energy. Our body's overall metabolic rate during sleep is about 10 to 20 percent slower than during waking rest (Wouters-Adriaens & Westerterp, 2006). The restoration and evolutionary theories highlight complementary functions of sleep, and both contribute to a two-factor model of why we sleep (Webb, 1994).

Sleep and Memory Consolidation

Do specific sleep stages have special functions? To answer this question, imagine volunteering for a sleep-deprivation study in which we will awaken you only when you enter REM sleep; you will be undisturbed through the other sleep stages. How will your body respond? First, on successive nights, we will have to awaken you more often,

Figure 6.15

Daily hours of sleep.
The average daily hours of sleep vary across species.

experiments, including brain-imaging studies, the issue remains controversial (Saxvig et al., 2008). For example, the consolidation hypothesis is contradicted by the fact that although many antidepressant drugs greatly suppress or nearly eliminate REM sleep, patients taking these drugs do not show impaired abilities to remember new information, experiences, or skills.

Some researchers argue that the function of REM sleep—particularly the high brain activation of REM sleep—is to keep the brain healthy by offsetting the periods of low brain arousal during restful slow-wave sleep (Vertes & Eastman, 2003). At present, the unique functions of REM and other sleep stages are still being debated (Schabus, 2009).

Sleep Disorders

As the sleepeating cases of Sondra, Jason, and Ellen illustrate, the processes that regulate sleep are complex and can go wrong in many ways. In a national survey, 64 percent of the American adults sampled felt that they had some type of sleep problem (National Sleep Foundation, 2009).

Insomnia

True or False: someone who falls asleep easily can still have insomnia. The statement is true because **insomnia** *refers to chronic difficulty in falling asleep, staying asleep, or experiencing restful sleep.* If you occasionally have trouble getting a good night's sleep, don't worry. Almost everyone does. People with true insomnia have frequent and persistent sleep troubles.

Insomnia is the most common sleep disorder, experienced by 10 to 40 percent of the population of various countries (Bartlett et al., 2008). Some people are genetically predisposed toward insomnia. Moreover, medical conditions, mental disorders such as anxiety and depression, and many drugs can disrupt sleep, as can general worrying, stress at home and work, poor lifestyle habits, and circadian disruptions such as jet lag and night-shift work.

Psychologists have pioneered many nondrug treatments to reduce insomnia and improve sleep quality. One treatment, called *stimulus control,* involves conditioning your body to associate stimuli in your sleep environment (such as your bed) with sleep, rather than with waking activities and sleeplessness (Bootzin, 2002). For example, if you are having sleep difficulties, do not study, watch TV, or snack in your bedroom. Use your bed only for sleeping. If you cannot fall asleep

because your brain will fight back to get REM sleep. Second, when the study ends, for the first few nights you probably will experience a *REM-rebound effect,* a tendency to increase the amount of REM sleep after being deprived of it.

This suggests that the body needs REM sleep, and similar effects are found for slow-wave sleep. But for what purpose? Many researchers believe that these sleep stages help us remember important information by enhancing **memory consolidation,** *a gradual process by which the brain transfers information into long-term memory* (Verleger et al., 2008; Winson, 1990). Despite many supportive within 10 minutes, get up and leave the bedroom. Do something relaxing until you feel sleepy, then return to bed. Table 6.2 contains more guidelines from sleep experts for reducing insomnia and achieving better sleep.

Narcolepsy

About 1 out of every 2,000 people suffers not from an inability to sleep but from an inability to stay awake (Ohayon, 2008). **Narcolepsy** *involves extreme daytime sleepiness and sudden, uncontrollable sleep attacks that may last from less than a minute to an hour.* No matter how much they rest at night, individuals with narcolepsy may experience sleep attacks at any time. When a sleep attack occurs, they may go right into a REM stage.

People with narcolepsy also may experience attacks of *cataplexy*, a sudden loss of muscle tone often triggered by excitement and other strong emotions. In severe cases, the knees buckle and the person collapses, conscious but unable to move for a few seconds to a few minutes. Cataplexy is an abnormal version of the normal muscular paralysis that takes place during nighttime REM sleep, and some experts view narcolepsy as a disorder in which REM sleep intrudes into waking consciousness.

Narcolepsy can be devastating. People with narcolepsy are more prone to accidents, feel that their quality of life is impaired, and may be misdiagnosed by doctors as having a mental disorder rather than a sleep disorder (Rovere et al., 2008).

Some people may be genetically predisposed toward developing narcolepsy. It can be selectively bred in dogs (Figure 6.16). In humans, if one identical twin has narcolepsy, the other has a 30-percent chance of developing it (Mignot, 1998). At present there is no cure for narcolepsy, but stimulant drugs and daytime naps often reduce daytime sleepiness, and antidepressant drugs (which suppress REM sleep) can decrease attacks of cataplexy.

REM-Sleep Behavior Disorder

Kaku Kimura and his colleagues in Japan (1997) reported the case of a 72-year-old woman who, during a night in a sleep laboratory, repeatedly sang and waved her hands during REM sleep. One episode lasted 3 minutes. She was experiencing **REM-sleep behavior disorder (RBD),** *in which the loss of muscle tone that causes normal REM-sleep paralysis is absent.* If awakened, RBD patients often report dream content that matches their behavior, as if they were acting out their dreams: "A 67-year-old man . . . was awakened one night by his wife's yelling as he was choking her. He was

Table 6.2 | How to Improve the Quality of Your Sleep

Sleep experts recommend a variety of procedures to reduce insomnia and improve the general quality of sleep.

- Maintain a regular sleep-wake pattern to establish a stable circadian rhythm.
- Get the amount of sleep you need during the week, and avoid sleeping in on weekends, as doing so will disrupt your sleep rhythm. Even if you sleep poorly or not at all one night, try to maintain your regular schedule the next.
- If you have trouble falling asleep at night, avoid napping if possible. Evening naps should be especially avoided because they will make you less sleepy when you go to bed.
- Avoid stimulants. This includes not just tobacco products and coffee but also caffeinated soft drinks and chocolate (sorry), which contain caffeine. It can take the body 4 to 5 hours to reduce the amount of caffeine in the bloodstream by 50 percent.
- Avoid alcohol and sleeping pills. As a depressant, alcohol may make it easier to go to sleep, but it disrupts the sleep cycle and interferes with REM sleep. Sleeping pills also impair REM sleep, and their constant use can lead to dependence and insomnia.
- Try to go to bed in a relaxed state. Muscle-relaxation techniques and meditation can reduce tension, remove worrisome thoughts, and help induce sleep.
- Avoid physical exercise before bedtime because it is too stimulating. If you are unable to fall asleep, do not use exercise to try to wear yourself out.
- If you are having sleep difficulties, avoid performing nonsleep activities in your bedroom.

Sources: Bootzin, 2002; King et al., 2001.

dreaming of breaking the neck of a deer he had just knocked down" (Schenck et al., 1989, p. 1169).

RBD sleepers may kick violently, throw punches, or get out of bed and move about wildly, leaving the bedroom in shambles. Many RBD patients have injured themselves or their sleeping partners. Research suggests that brain abnormalities may interfere with signals from the brain stem that normally inhibit movement during REM sleep, but in many cases the causes of RBD are unknown (Iranzo & Aparicio, 2009).

Figure 6.16

This dog lapses suddenly from alert wakefulness into a limp sleep while being held by sleep researcher William Dement. Using selective breeding, researchers at Stanford's Sleep Disorders Center have established a colony of narcoleptic canines.

Sleepwalking

Sleepwalking usually occurs during a stage-3 or stage-4 period of slow-wave sleep (Zadra et al., 2008). Sleepwalkers often stare blankly and are unresponsive to other people. Many seem vaguely conscious of the environment as they navigate around furniture, yet they can injure themselves accidentally, such as by falling down stairs. The pattern, however, is variable. Recall that Jason, while eating during his sleepwalking episodes, could have intelligible conversations with his wife. People who sleepwalk often return to bed and awaken in the morning with no memory of the event.

About 10 to 30 percent of children sleepwalk at least once, but less than 5 percent of adults do. If you did not sleepwalk as a child, the odds are less than 1 percent that you will do so as an adult (Hublin et al., 1997).

A tendency to sleepwalk may be inherited, and daytime stress, alcohol, and certain illnesses and medications can increase sleepwalking (Pressman, 2007). Treatments may include psychotherapy and awakening children before the time they typically sleepwalk (Frank et al., 1997). For children, the most common approach is simply to wait for the child to outgrow it while creating a safe sleep environment to prevent injury.

Nightmares and Night Terrors

Nightmares are bad dreams, and virtually everyone has them. Like all dreams, they occur more often during REM sleep. Arousal during nightmares typically is similar to levels experienced during pleasant dreams.

Night terrors *are frightening dreams that arouse the sleeper to a near-panic state.* In contrast to nightmares, night terrors are most common during slow-wave sleep (stages 3 and 4), are more intense, and involve greatly elevated physiological arousal; the heart rate may double or triple. In some cases the terrified sleeper may suddenly sit up, scream, or flee the room—as if trying to escape from something. Come morning the sleeper usually has no memory of the episode (Szelenberger et al., 2005).

Up to 6 percent of children, but only 1 to 2 percent of adults, experience night terrors (Ohayon et al., 1999). In most childhood cases, treatment is simply to wait for the night terrors to diminish with age.

Sleep Apnea

People with **sleep apnea** *repeatedly stop and restart breathing during sleep.* Stoppages usually last 20 to 40 seconds but can continue for 1 to 2 minutes. In severe cases they occur 400 to 500 times a night. Sleep apnea is most commonly caused by an obstruction in the upper airways, such as sagging tissue as muscles lose tone during sleep. The chest and abdomen keep moving, but no air gets through to the lungs. Finally, reflexes kick in and the person gasps or produces a loud, startling snore, followed by a several-second awakening. The person typically falls asleep again without remembering having been awake.

About 3 percent of people have obstructive sleep apnea, which is most common among overweight, middle-aged males (Krishnan & Collop, 2006). Surgery may be performed to remove the obstruction, and sleep apnea sometimes is treated by having the sleeper wear a mask that continuously pumps air to keep the air passages open (Villar et al., 2009).

The Nature of Dreams

Dreaming is highly valued in many traditional cultures. In the Caribbean island nation of Dominica, for example, indigenous inhabitants believe that dreams can reveal the future and guide current actions, and they interpret dreams using symbols passed down orally across generations (George-Joseph & Smith, 2008). Even in industrialized societies that generally attach less importance to dreams, many people believe that dreams can be meaningful (Morewedge & Norton, 2009).

When Do We Dream?

Mental activity occurs throughout the sleep cycle. When Jason Rowley and his colleagues (1998) awakened college students merely 45 seconds after sleep onset, about 25 percent of the students reported that they had been experiencing visual hallucinations (visual images that seemed real). As this *hypnagogic state*—the transitional state from wakefulness through early stage-2 sleep—continued, mental activity became less "thought-like" and more "dreamlike."

Throughout the night we dream most often during REM sleep, when activity in many brain areas is highest. Awaken a REM sleeper and you have about an 80- to 85-percent chance of catching a dream. In contrast, people awakened from non-REM (NREM) sleep report dreams about 15 to 50 percent of the time. Also, our REM dreams are more likely to be vivid, bizarre, and storylike than NREM dreams.

Despite these REM-NREM differences, don't believe the fallacy (often reinforced by the popular media) that dreaming happens only during REM sleep. Figure 6.17 shows an analysis of 1,576 reports collected from 16 college students awakened from various sleep stages (Fosse et al., 2001). Even during NREM sleep, hallucinatory images were more common than non-dreamlike thoughts. By some estimates, about 25 percent of the vivid dreams we have each night actually occur during NREM periods (Solms, 2002).

What Do We Dream About?

Much of our knowledge about dream content derives from 45 years of research using a coding system developed by Calvin Hall and Robert Van de Castle (1966). Analyzing 1,000 dream reports (mostly from college students), they found that although some dreams certainly are bizarre, overall dreams are not nearly as strange as they are stereotyped to be. Most take place in familiar settings and often involve people we know.

Given the stereotype of "blissful dreaming," it may surprise you that across many cultures, most dreams contain negative content (Domhoff & Schneider, 2008). Hall and Van de Castle (1966) found that 80 percent of dream reports involved negative emotions, almost half contained aggressive acts, and a third involved some type of misfortune. Also, women dreamt almost equally about male and female characters, whereas about two thirds of men's dream characters were male. Although the reason for this gender difference is not clear, a similar pattern has been found across several cultures and age groups.

Our life experience and current concerns can shape dream content (Bulkeley & Kahan, 2008). Pregnant women, for example, have dreams with many pregnancy themes, and in the weeks following the September 11, 2001, terrorist attacks, a study of 1,000 residents of Manhattan found that 1 in 10 experienced distressing dreams about the attacks (Galea et al., 2002).

Cross-culturally, dream content displays commonalities and differences. For example, negatively themed dreams are prevalent, and in dreams that involve aggressive content the dreamer more often is the victim than the perpetrator (Domhoff & Schneider, 2008). Yet, although dreams that involve physical and nonphysical aggression (e.g., verbal threats) are found across cultures, Table 6.3 shows that the percentage of physically aggressive dream content (out of all aggressive dream content) varies widely across societies. In part, this reflects differences in how often people from various cultural groups have dreams that involve

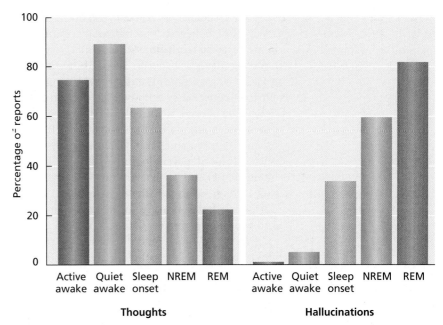

Figure 6.17

Mental activity during sleep.

This graph shows the percentage of verbal reports that reflected thoughts and visual hallucinations recorded during active and quiet wakefulness and when awakened during sleep onset, REM sleep, and NREM sleep.
Source: Adapted from Fosse et al., 2001.

fights or attacks between humans and animals (Domhoff & Schneider, 2008).

Why Do We Dream?

Questions about the purpose and meaning of dreams have intrigued humankind for ages. Let's examine a few viewpoints.

Table 6.3	In Dreams, the Percentage of Aggressive Acts That Involve Physical (versus Nonphysical) Aggression	
Society	**Men's Dreams**	**Women's Dreams**
Yir Yiront (Australia)	92	n/a*
Baiga (India)	86	n/a*
Navaho (North America)	77	n/a*
Skolt (Finland)	70	68
Ifaluk (Micronesia)	60	40
Tinguian (Philippines)	55	46
Alor (Indonesia)	53	61
United States	50	34
Hopi (North America)	40	39
French Canadians	n/a*	31
The Netherlands	32	14
Switzerland	29	23

*These data are based on earlier studies by various researchers of dream content in preindustrial and industrial societies, and "n/a" means that data were not available.
Source: Domhoff & Schneider 2008, Table 1, p. 1260.

Freud's Psychoanalytic Theory Sigmund Freud (1900/1953) believed that the main purpose of dreaming is **wish fulfillment,** *the gratification of our unconscious desires and needs.* These desires include sexual and aggressive urges that are too unacceptable to be consciously acknowledged and fulfilled in real life. Freud distinguished between (1) a dream's *manifest content,* the surface story that the dreamer reports, and (2) its *latent content,* which is its disguised psychological meaning. Thus a dream about being with a stranger on a train that goes through a tunnel (manifest content) might represent a hidden desire for sexual intercourse with a forbidden partner (latent content).

Dream work was Freud's term for the process by which a dream's latent content is transformed into the manifest content. It occurs through symbols (e.g., train = penis; tunnel = vagina) and by creating individual dream characters who combine features of several people in real life. This way unconscious needs can be fulfilled, and because they are disguised within the dream, the sleeper does not become anxious and can sleep peacefully.

Although dreams often reflect ongoing emotional concerns, many researchers reject the specific postulates of Freud's theory. They find little evidence that dreams have disguised meaning or that their general purpose is to satisfy forbidden, unconscious needs and conflicts (Domhoff, 1999). Critics of dream analysis say that it is highly subjective; the same dream can be interpreted differently to fit the particular analyst's point of view.

Cognitive Theories According to **problem-solving dream models,** *because dreams are not constrained by reality they can help us find creative solutions to our problems and ongoing concerns* (Cartwright, 1977). Self-help books and numerous Web sites promote this idea, and history offers some intriguing examples of inventors, scientists, and authors who allegedly came upon creative ideas or solutions to problems in a dream (Figure 6.18). But critics argue that because so many of our dreams don't focus on personal problems, it's difficult to see how problem solving can be the broad underlying reason for *why* we dream. They also note that just because a problem shows up in a dream does not mean that the dream involved an attempt to solve it. We may think about our dreams after awakening and obtain new insights; in this sense dreams may help us work through ongoing concerns. However, this is not the same as solving problems *while* dreaming (Squier & Domhoff, 1998).

Cognitive-process dream theories *focus on the process of how we dream and propose that dreaming and waking thought are produced by the same mental systems in the brain* (Foulkes, 1982). There is more similarity between dreaming and waking mental processes than is commonly believed (Domhoff, 2005). For example, one reason many dreams appear bizarre is because their content shifts rapidly. "I was dreaming about an exam and suddenly, the next thing I knew, I was in Hawaii on the beach." (Don't we wish!) Yet if you reflect on the contents of your waking thoughts—your stream of consciousness—you will realize they also shift suddenly. About half of REM dream reports involve rapid content shifts, but when people are awake and placed in the same environmental conditions as sleepers (a dark, quiet room), about 90 percent of their reports involve rapid content shifts (Antrobus, 1991). Thus, rapid shifting of attention is a process common to dreaming and waking mental activity.

Hand-held needle

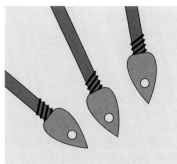

Spears in Howe's dream

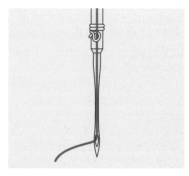

Sewing machine needle

Figure 6.18

Dreams and problem solving.

In 1846, American inventor Elias Howe patented a sewing machine that could sew 250 stitches per minute. He had struggled unsuccessfully for years to figure out how to get a machine to stitch using a needle with the threading hole in the back (blunt) end—as in a traditional hand-held needle. Allegedly, one night he had a dream that he was being pursued by spear-throwing tribesmen. In the dream he saw that each spearhead had a hole in it. When Howe awoke, he recognized that, for a sewing machine to work, the threading hole needed to be at the front (sharp) end of the needle, as it had been on the spears.

Activation-Synthesis Theory Is it possible that dreams serve no special purpose? In 1977, J. Allan Hobson and Robert McCarley proposed a physiological theory of dreaming.

According to the **activation-synthesis theory,** *dreams do not serve any particular function—they are merely a by-product of REM neural activity.* When we are awake, neural circuits in our brain are activated by sensory input—sights, sounds, tastes, and so on. The cerebral cortex interprets these patterns of neural activation, producing meaningful perceptions. During REM sleep the brain stem bombards our higher brain centers with random neural activity (the activation component). Because we are asleep, this neural activity does not match any external sensory events, but our cerebral cortex continues to perform its job of interpretation. It does this by creating a dream—a perception—that provides the best fit to the particular pattern of neural activity that exists at any moment (the synthesis component). This helps to explain the bizarreness of many dreams, as the brain is trying to make sense out of random neural activity. Our memories, experiences, desires, and needs can influence the stories that our brain develops, and therefore dream content may reflect themes pertaining to our lives. In this sense, dreams can have meaning, but they serve no special function (McCarley, 1998).

Critics claim that activation-synthesis theory overestimates the bizarreness of dreams and pays too little attention to NREM dreaming (Solms, 2002). Nevertheless, this theory revolutionized dream research by calling attention to a physiological basis for dreaming (Domhoff, 2005; Hobson et al., 2000).

So Why *Do* We Dream? In the court of popular opinion, Freudian dream theory may reign supreme. As Figure 6.19 shows, in a recent study (Morewedge & Norton, 2009), American, South Korean, and Indian college students were far more likely to endorse a key Freudian principle—that dreams allow unconscious content to rise to the surface—than theories that explain dreams as solutions to problems, as by-products of random neural activation, or as a means of helping the brain discard unwanted information (a "learning theory" of dreams).

Popular opinion, however, doesn't determine why dreaming actually occurs. But among scientists there is still no agreement as to why we dream, and the explosion of brain research on sleep hasn't dampened the debate (Hobson, 2007; Solms, 2007). Still, neuroscience research indicates that dreaming involves an integration of perceptual, emotional, motivational, and cognitive processes performed by various brain modules. *Neurocognitive theories,* such as activation-synthesis, bridge the cognitive and biological perspectives by attempting to explain how subjective aspects of dreaming correspond to physiological changes that occur during sleep (Hobson et al., 2000). These models acknowledge that motivational factors—our needs and desires—can influence how the brain attaches meaning and emotion to the neural activity that underlies our dreams (Hobson, 2007).

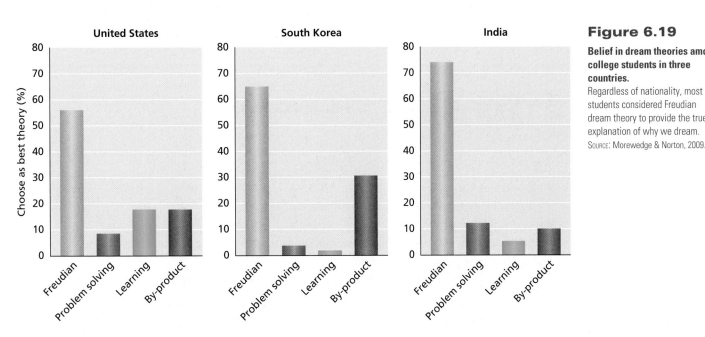

Figure 6.19

Belief in dream theories among college students in three countries.

Regardless of nationality, most students considered Freudian dream theory to provide the truest explanation of why we dream.
SOURCE: Morewedge & Norton, 2009.

Levels of Analysis   Sleep and Dreaming

We've seen that science has unraveled some, though certainly not all, of the mysteries surrounding sleep and dreaming. Let's review how the study of sleep and dreaming spans the biological, psychological, and environmental levels of analysis.

ENVIRONMENTAL LEVEL

- The day-night cycle and time cues help regulate our circadian rhythms and sleep readiness.
- Night-shift work and jet travel across time zones can disrupt circadian rhythms and impair sleep.
- A noisy sleep environment can impair sleep quality.
- Experiences from waking life can show up in our dream content.
- Cultural norms influence sleep-related behaviors (e.g., co-sleeping) and the meaning attached to dreams.

BIOLOGICAL LEVEL

- Circadian rhythms affect our readiness for sleep.
- Different species have evolved different sleep-wake cycles.
- Certain brain circuits actively promote falling asleep, while others regulate various sleep stages.
- Sleep stages are marked by distinct patterns of physiological activity.
- Heredity partly accounts for differences among people in sleep length and the likelihood of developing sleep disorders.

PSYCHOLOGICAL LEVEL

- Worries and stress may hinder falling asleep or contribute to other sleep problems.
- Learned sleep habits can facilitate or impair a sound night's sleep.
- Mental activity occurs throughout sleep, ranging from fragmented thoughts and images to storylike dreams.
- Ongoing psychological problems or concerns may show up in our dream content.
- Dreaming has been theorized to serve various psychological functions, including memory consolidation, unconscious wish fulfillment, and problem solving.

How do environmental and psychological factors affect your own sleep and dreaming? Do personal experiences or events show up in your dreams? Do environmental or psychological factors ever impair your ability to fall or stay asleep?

test yourself   Sleep and Dreaming

True or false?

1. Delta waves occur primarily in stage-2 sleep.
2. During REM sleep, voluntary muscles become paralyzed.
3. As we age, average nightly REM sleep time increases.
4. The evolutionary/circadian model proposes that sleep's purpose is to help us recover from fatigue.
5. Dreaming occurs only during REM sleep.
6. Activation-synthesis theory proposes that dreams have no special function.

ANSWERS: 1-false, 2-true, 3-false, 4-false, 5-false, 6-true

DRUG-INDUCED STATES

Three thousand years ago, the Aztecs considered hallucinogenic mushrooms to be a sacred substance for communicating with the spirit world. Today drugs are a cornerstone of medical practice and, as Figure 6.20 shows, a pervasive part of social life. They alter consciousness by modifying brain chemistry, but drug effects are also influenced by psychological, environmental, and cultural factors (Kassel et al., 2010).

Drugs and the Brain

Drugs enter the bloodstream and are carried throughout the brain by small blood vessels called capillaries. Capillaries contain a **blood-brain barrier,** *a special lining of tightly packed cells that lets vital nutrients pass through so neurons can function.* The blood-brain barrier screens out many foreign substances, but some, including various drugs, can pass through. Once inside, they alter consciousness by facilitating or inhibiting synaptic transmission (Julien, 2008).

How Drugs Facilitate Synaptic Transmission

Synaptic transmission involves several basic steps. First, neurotransmitters are synthesized inside presynaptic (sending) neurons and stored in vesicles. Next, they are released into the synaptic space, where they bind with and stimulate receptor sites on postsynaptic (receiving) neurons.

Finally, neurotransmitter molecules are deactivated by enzymes or by reuptake.

An **agonist** *is a drug that increases the activity of a neurotransmitter.* Figure 6.21 shows that agonists may

- enhance a neuron's ability to synthesize, store, or release neurotransmitters;
- bind with and stimulate postsynaptic receptor sites (or make it easier for neurotransmitters to stimulate these sites);
- make deactivation more difficult, such as by inhibiting reuptake.

Consider two examples. First, *opiates* (such as morphine and codeine) are effective pain relievers. The brain contains its own chemicals, endorphins, which promote pain relief. Opiates have a molecular structure similar to that of endorphins. They bind to and activate receptor sites that receive endorphins. To draw an analogy, think of opening a lock with a key. Normally an endorphin molecule acts as the key, but due to its similar shape, an opiate molecule can fit into the lock and open it.

Second, *amphetamines* boost arousal and mood by causing neurons to release greater amounts of dopamine and norepinephrine and by inhibiting reuptake. During reuptake, neurotransmitters in the synapse are absorbed back into presynaptic neurons through special channels. As shown in Figure 6.21c, amphetamine molecules block this process. Therefore, dopamine and norepinephrine remain in the synaptic space longer and keep stimulating postsynaptic neurons.

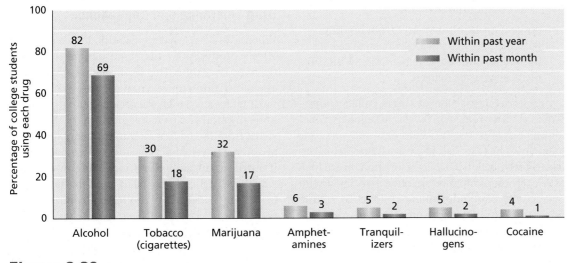

Figure 6.20

Drug use among college students.

This graph illustrates nonmedical drug use among American college students who are 1 to 4 years beyond high school. These data are based on a nationally representative survey. Source: Johnston et al., 2009.

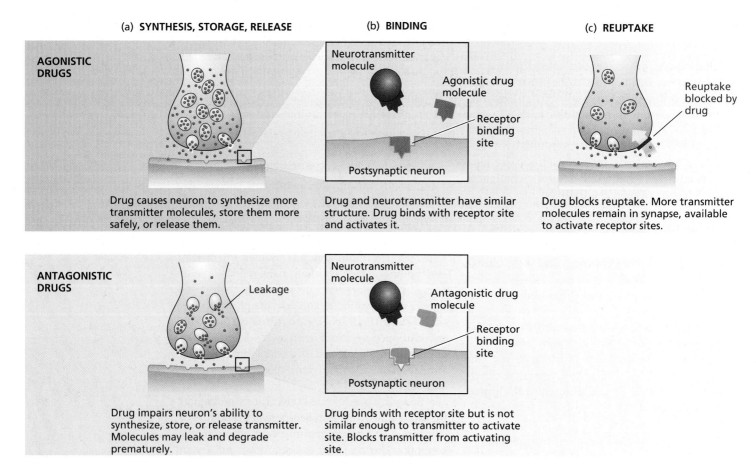

(a) SYNTHESIS, STORAGE, RELEASE

(b) BINDING

(c) REUPTAKE

AGONISTIC DRUGS

Drug causes neuron to synthesize more transmitter molecules, store them more safely, or release them.

Neurotransmitter molecule

Agonistic drug molecule

Receptor binding site

Postsynaptic neuron

Drug and neurotransmitter have similar structure. Drug binds with receptor site and activates it.

Reuptake blocked by drug

Drug blocks reuptake. More transmitter molecules remain in synapse, available to activate receptor sites.

ANTAGONISTIC DRUGS

Leakage

Drug impairs neuron's ability to synthesize, store, or release transmitter. Molecules may leak and degrade prematurely.

Neurotransmitter molecule

Antagonistic drug molecule

Receptor binding site

Postsynaptic neuron

Drug binds with receptor site but is not similar enough to transmitter to activate site. Blocks transmitter from activating site.

Figure 6.21

How drugs affect neurotransmitters.
(*top*) Agonistic drugs increase the activity of a neurotransmitter. (*bottom*) Antagonistic drugs decrease the activity of a neurotransmitter.

How Drugs Inhibit Synaptic Transmission

An **antagonist** *is a drug that inhibits or decreases the action of a neurotransmitter.* As Figure 6.21 shows, an antagonist may

- reduce a neuron's ability to synthesize, store, or release neurotransmitters; or
- prevent a neurotransmitter from binding with the postsynaptic neuron, such as by fitting into and blocking the receptor sites on the postsynaptic neuron.

Consider the action of drugs called *antipsychotics* used to treat *schizophrenia,* a severe psychological disorder whose symptoms may include hallucinations (e.g., hearing voices) and delusions (clearly false beliefs, such as believing you are Joan of Arc). These symptoms are often associated with overactivity of the dopamine system. To restore dopamine activity to more normal levels, pharmaceutical companies have developed drugs with a molecular structure similar to dopamine, but not too similar. Returning to the lock-and-key analogy, imagine finding a key that fits into a lock but won't turn. The key's shape is close enough to the real key to get in but not to open the lock. Similarly,

antipsychotic drugs fit into dopamine receptor sites but not well enough to stimulate them. While they occupy the sites, dopamine released by presynaptic neurons is blocked and cannot get in, and the schizophrenic symptoms usually decrease.

Drug Tolerance and Dependence

When a drug is used repeatedly, the intensity of effects produced by the same dosage level may decrease over time. This *decreasing responsivity to a drug is called* **tolerance.** As it develops, the person must take increasingly larger doses to achieve the same physical and psychological effects. Tolerance stems from the body's attempt to maintain a state of optimal physiological balance, called *homeostasis.* If a drug changes bodily functioning in a certain way, say by increasing heart rate, the brain tries to restore balance by producing **compensatory responses,** *which are reactions opposite to that of the drug* (e.g., reactions that decrease heart rate).

What happens when drug tolerance develops and the person suddenly stops using the drug? The body's compensatory responses may continue and, no longer balanced out by the drug's effects, the person can experience strong reactions

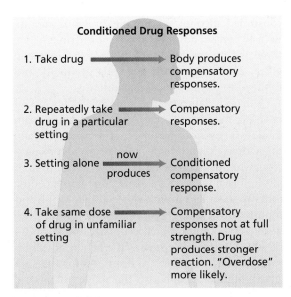

Figure 6.22

Conditioned drug responses and overdose.
Environmental stimuli that are repeatedly paired with the use of a drug can eventually trigger compensatory responses on their own. If the same drug dose is now taken in a new setting, compensatory responses will not be at full strength, thereby increasing the risk of an "overdose" reaction.

opposite to those produced by the drug. This *occurrence of compensatory responses after discontinued drug use is known as* **withdrawal.** For example, in the absence of alcohol's sedating and relaxing effects, a chronic drinker may experience anxiety and hypertension.

Learning, Drug Tolerance, and Overdose

Tolerance for various drugs depends partly on the familiarity of the drug setting. Figure 6.22 illustrates how environmental stimuli associated with repeated drug use begin to elicit compensatory responses through a learning process called *classical conditioning.* As drug use continues, the physical setting triggers progressively stronger compensatory responses, increasing the user's tolerance. This helps explain why drug addicts often experience cravings when they enter a setting associated with drug use. The environmental stimuli trigger compensatory responses that, without drugs to mask their effect, cause the user to feel withdrawal symptoms (Bradizza & Stasiewkz, 2009).

There is a hidden danger in this process, particularly for experienced drug users. Compensatory responses serve a protective function by physiologically countering part of the drug's effects. If a user takes his or her usual high dose in a familiar environment, the body's compensatory responses are at full strength—a combination of compensatory reactions to the drug itself and

also to the familiar, conditioned environmental stimuli. But in an *unfamiliar* environment, the conditioned compensatory responses are weaker, and the drug has a stronger physiological net effect than usual (Siegel et al., 2000).

Shepard Siegel (1984) interviewed people addicted to heroin who had experienced near-fatal overdoses. He found that in most cases they had not taken a dose larger than their customary one. Rather, they had injected a normal dose in an unfamiliar environment. Siegel concluded that the addicts were not protected by their usual compensatory responses, resulting in an "overdose" reaction.

Drug Addiction and Dependence

Drug addiction, which is formally called **substance dependence,** *is a maladaptive pattern of substance use that causes a person significant distress or substantially impairs that person's life.* Substance dependence is diagnosed as occurring with *physiological dependence* if drug tolerance or withdrawal symptoms have developed. The term *psychological dependence* is often used to describe situations in which people strongly crave a drug because of its pleasurable effects, even if they are not physiologically dependent. However, this is not a diagnostic term, and some drug experts feel it is misleading. Drug cravings do have a physical basis; they are rooted in patterns of brain activity (Sun & Rebec, 2005).

Misconceptions about Substance Dependence Many people mistakenly believe that if a drug doesn't produce tolerance or withdrawal, one can't become dependent on it. In reality, neither tolerance nor withdrawal is needed for a diagnosis of substance dependence.

The popular media image of a shaking alcoholic desperately searching for a drink reinforces another misconception, namely that the motivation to avoid or end withdrawal symptoms is the primary cause of addiction. Such physiological dependence contributes powerfully to drug dependence, but consider these points:

- People can become dependent on drugs, such as cocaine, that produce only mild withdrawal (Kampmann et al., 2002). The drug's pleasurable effects—often produced by boosting dopamine activity—play a key role in causing dependence.

- Many drug users who quit and make it through withdrawal eventually start using again, even though they are no longer physiologically dependent.

Table **6.4** | **Behavioral Effects of Alcohol**

BAL	Hours to Leave Body	Behavioral Effects
.03	1	Decreased alertness, impaired reaction time in some people
.05	2	Decreased alertness, impaired judgment and reaction time, good feeling, release of inhibitions
.10	4	Severely impaired reaction time, motor function, and judgment; lack of caution
.15	10	Gross intoxication, worsening impairments
.25	?	Extreme sensory and motor impairment, staggering
.30	?	Stuporous but conscious, cannot comprehend immediate environment
.40	?	Lethal in over 50 percent of cases

- Many factors influence drug dependence, including genetic predispositions, religious beliefs, family and peer influences, and cultural norms (Ehlers et al., 2010).

Depressants

Depressants *decrease nervous system activity.* In moderate doses, they reduce tension and anxiety and produce euphoria. In extremely high doses, depressants can slow down vital life processes to the point of death.

Alcohol

Alcohol is the most widely used recreational drug in many cultures. A national survey of American college students found that 69 percent had consumed alcohol within the previous month, with 40 percent binging (five or more drinks at one time) within the previous two weeks (Johnston et al., 2009). Tolerance develops gradually and can lead to physiological dependence.

Alcohol dampens the nervous system by increasing the activity of GABA, the brain's main inhibitory neurotransmitter, and by decreasing the activity of glutamate, a major excitatory neurotransmitter (Kumar et al., 2009). Why, then, if alcohol is a depressant drug, do many people initially seem less inhibited when they drink and report getting a high from alcohol? In part, the weakening of inhibitions occurs because alcohol's neural slowdown depresses the action of inhibitory control centers in the brain. As for the subjective high, alcohol boosts the activity of several neurotransmitters, such as dopamine, that produce feelings of pleasure and euphoria (Tupala & Tiihonen, 2004). At higher doses, however, the brain's control centers become increasingly disrupted, thinking and physical coordination become disorganized, and fatigue may occur as blood alcohol level (BAL) rises (Table 6.4).

The *blood-alcohol level (BAL)* is a measure of alcohol concentration in the body. Elevated BALs impair reaction time, coordination, and decision making and also increase risky behaviors (Figure 6.23). Thirty-nine percent of American and Canadian traffic accident deaths involve alcohol (National Highway Traffic Safety Administration, 2006).

Why do intoxicated people often act in risky ways that they wouldn't when sober? It is not simply a matter of lowered inhibitions. Alcohol

Figure 6.23

Drinking, driving, and accident risk.
At .08 to 0.10 BAL, the legal definition of intoxication in most American states and Canadian provinces, the risk of having an auto accident is about 6 times greater than at 0.00, and the risk climbs to 25 times higher at a BAL of 0.15. SOURCE: Based on National Safety Council, 1992.

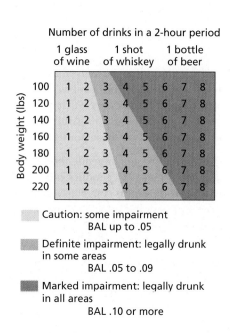

Number of drinks in a 2-hour period

Caution: some impairment
BAL up to .05

Definite impairment: legally drunk in some areas
BAL .05 to .09

Marked impairment: legally drunk in all areas
BAL .10 or more

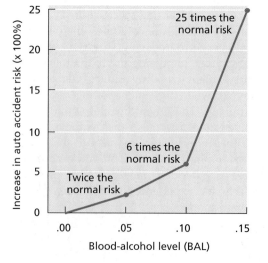

also produces **alcohol myopia,** *shortsighted thinking caused by the inability to pay attention to as much information as when sober* (Davis et al., 2007; Steele & Josephs, 1990). People who drink start to focus only on aspects of the situation (cues) that stand out. In the absence of strong cautionary cues (such as warnings) to inhibit risky behavior, they don't think about long-term consequences of their actions as carefully as when they are sober. Our "Research Close-up" illustrates this effect.

Research
Close-up

Drinking and Driving: Decision Making in Altered States

SOURCE: TARA K. MACDONALD, MARK P. ZANNA, and GEOFFREY T. FONG (1995). Decision making in altered states: Effects of alcohol on attitudes toward drinking and driving. *Journal of Personality and Social Psychology, 68,* 973–985.

INTRODUCTION

Most people have negative attitudes about drunk driving and say they would not do it. They realize that the cons (e.g., risk of accident, injury, death, and police arrest) far outweigh the pros (e.g., not having to ask someone for a lift). Why, then, do so many people decide to drive after becoming intoxicated?

Based on alcohol-myopia principles, Tara Mac-Donald and her colleagues reasoned that when intoxicated people decide whether to drive, they may focus on the pros or the cons but do not have the attentional capacity to focus on both. If a circumstance that favors driving (a *facilitating cue*) is called to the intoxicated person's attention (e.g., "It's only a short distance"), she or he will latch onto it and fail to consider the cons. But in general situations that do not contain facilitating cues, intoxicated people's feelings about driving should remain as negative as when they were sober.

The authors made two predictions. First, intoxicated and sober people will have equally negative *general attitudes* and intentions toward drinking and driving. Second, intoxicated people will have less negative attitudes and greater intentions toward drinking and driving than sober people in situations that contain a facilitating cue.

intentions (e.g., "I will drink and drive the next time that I am out at a party or bar with friends"). Other items contained a facilitating cue, a special circumstance that suggested a possible reason for drinking and driving ("If I had only a short distance to drive home . . . / If my friends tried to persuade me to drink and drive . . . I would drive while intoxicated"). Participants rated each item on a 9-point scale (1 = "strongly disagree"; 9 = "strongly agree").

RESEARCH DESIGN

Question: If sober people hold negative attitudes toward drinking and driving, then why after becoming intoxicated do they decide to drive? Does focusing on "special circumstances" play a role?

Type of Study: *Experimental*

Independent Variables	Dependent Variables
• Alcoholic state (intoxicated versus sober) • Drinking-driving situation (special circumstance versus general situation)	• Attitude toward "drinking and driving" • Intention to drive while intoxicated

METHOD

Laboratory Experiment

Fifty-seven male introductory psychology students, all regular drinkers who owned cars, participated. They were randomly assigned to either the sober condition, in which they received no alcohol, or the alcohol condition, in which they received 3 alcoholic drinks within 1 hour (the average BAL was .074 percent, just below the .08 percent legal driving limit in Ontario, Canada).

Participants then completed a drinking-and-driving questionnaire. Some items asked about general attitudes and

Party/Bar Diary Study

Fifty-one male and female college students recorded a telephone diary while at a party or bar where they were going to drink alcohol. Some were randomly assigned to record the diary when they first arrived; others, just before they left. Based on participants' descriptions of how much alcohol they had consumed, the researchers estimated their BAL and identified two groups: "sober participants" (average BAL .01) and "intoxicated participants" (average BAL .11).

Continued

RESULTS

The findings from both studies supported the predictions. Sober participants and intoxicated participants both expressed negative general attitudes about drinking and driving and indicated they would not drive when intoxicated. But when the questions presented a special circumstance, intoxicated participants expressed more favorable attitudes and a greater intention to drive than did sober participants.

DISCUSSION

This study nicely illustrates how a person's physiological state (sober versus intoxicated) and an environmental factor (general situation versus special circumstance) interact to influence psychological functioning (attitudes and decision making). However, let's think critically about the results. Was it really narrowed attention—leading to a failure to consider negative consequences—that caused the results? The authors anticipated two alternative explanations. First, perhaps people who drink do not realize how intoxicated they are. Second, perhaps intoxicated people overestimate their driving ability, a belief called *drunken invincibility*. The authors tested and ruled out these explanations. Intoxicated participants believed they were *more* intoxicated than they actually were and also estimated that they would drive *more poorly* than the average person.

Is it possible that the findings were caused by participants' expectations about alcohol rather than its chemical effects? The authors conducted a placebo control experiment in which some participants were convincingly misled to believe they were intoxicated. Results showed that the alcohol-myopia effect occurred only for participants who truly had consumed alcohol. It was not caused by participants' expectations.

What practical value do these findings have? The researchers suggest that a sign saying "Drinking and Driving Kills," or a large photograph of a police officer administering a breathalyzer test, be made highly visible near the exit of a bar. Alcohol myopia should cause intoxicated people to narrow their focus of attention to these *inhibiting cues*, causing them to rethink any decision to drink and drive. In subsequent research, MacDonald and coworkers (2003) found that making strong inhibiting cues salient did indeed lead intoxicated people to behave more cautiously.

Barbiturates and Tranquilizers

Physicians prescribe barbiturates (sleeping pills) and tranquilizers (antianxiety drugs, such as Valium) as sedatives and relaxants. Like alcohol, they depress the nervous system by increasing the activity of the inhibitory neurotransmitter GABA (Grasshoff et al., 2008).

Barbiturates and tranquilizers are widely overused, and tolerance and physiological dependence can occur. As tolerance builds, addicted people may take up to 50 sleeping pills a day. At high doses, barbiturates trigger initial excitation, followed by slurred speech, loss of coordination, depression, and memory impairment. Overdoses may cause unconsciousness, coma, and even death. Users often don't recognize that they have become dependent until they try to stop and experience serious withdrawal symptoms, such as anxiety, insomnia, and possibly seizures.

Stimulants

Stimulants *increase neural firing and arouse the nervous system.* They increase blood pressure, respiration, heart rate, and overall alertness. While they can elevate mood to the point of euphoria, they also can heighten irritability.

Amphetamines

Amphetamines are powerful stimulants prescribed to reduce appetite and fatigue, decrease the need for sleep, and reduce depression. Unfortunately, they are widely overused to boost energy and mood (Ghodse, 2007).

Amphetamines increase dopamine and norepinephrine activity. Tolerance develops, and users may crave their pleasurable effects. Eventually, many heavy users start injecting large quantities, producing a sudden surge of energy and rush of intense pleasure. With frequent injections, they may remain awake for a week, their bodily systems racing at breakneck speed. Injecting amphetamines greatly increases blood pressure and can lead to heart failure and cerebral hemorrhage (stroke); repeated high doses may cause brain damage (Ksir et al., 2008).

There is an inevitable crash when heavy users stop taking the drug. They may sleep for 1 to 2 days, waking up depressed, exhausted, and irritable. This crash occurs because the neurons' norepinephrine and dopamine supplies have become depleted.

Cocaine

Cocaine is a powder derived from the coca plant, which grows mainly in western South America. Usually inhaled or injected, it produces excitation, a sense of increased muscular strength, and euphoria. Cocaine increases the activity of norepinephrine and dopamine by blocking their reuptake.

(a)

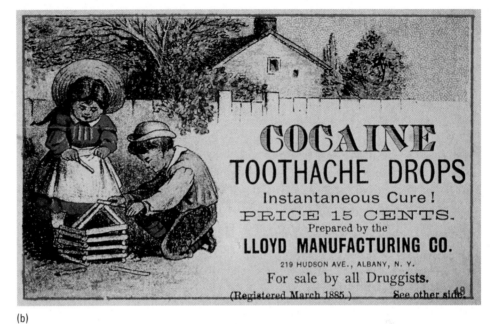

(b)

Figure 6.24

(a) Until 1903, there was a clear reason why Coca-Cola "relieved fatigue": it contained cocaine, which was then replaced by caffeine.
(b) Before it was made illegal, cocaine was found in a variety of medicinal products.

Cocaine was once widely used as a local anesthetic in eye, nose, and throat surgery. Novocain, a synthetic form of cocaine, is still used in dentistry as an anesthetic. Due to its stimulating effects, cocaine found its way into health potions sold to the public, before it was made illegal. In 1885 John Pemberton developed Coca-Cola by mixing cocaine with the kola nut and syrup (Figure 6.24).

In large doses, cocaine can produce vomiting, convulsions, and paranoid delusions (Smith et al., 2009). A depressive crash may occur after a cocaine high. Tolerance develops to many of cocaine's effects, and chronic use has been associated with an increased risk of cognitive impairments and brain damage (Franklin et al., 2002). Crack is a chemically converted form of cocaine that can be smoked, and its effects are faster and more dangerous. Overdoses can cause sudden death from cardiorespiratory arrest.

Ecstasy (MDMA)

Ecstasy, also known as MDMA (methylenedioxymethamphetamine), is artificially synthesized and has a chemical structure that partly resembles both methamphetamine (a stimulant) and mescaline (a hallucinogen). Ecstasy produces feelings of pleasure, elation, empathy, and warmth. In the brain, it primarily increases serotonin functioning, which boosts one's mood but may cause agitation. After the drug wears off, users often feel sluggish and depressed—a rebound effect partly due to serotonin depletion (Travers & Lyvers, 2005). They may have to take increasingly stronger doses to overcome tolerance to Ecstasy.

In experiments with laboratory rats, Ecstasy has produced long-lasting damage to the axons of neurons that release serotonin (Mechan et al., 2002). Human studies suggest a similar possibility (Figure 6.25), but it is not clear whether such damage is permanent (de Win et al., 2008). In the long run, Ecstasy may produce consequences that are anything but pleasurable. Continued use has been associated with impaired memory and sleep difficulties (Indlekofer et al., 2009).

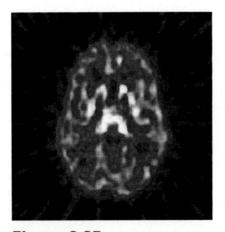

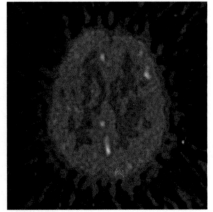

Figure 6.25

Frequent Ecstasy use and the brain.

(*left*) This PET-scan image shows the brain of a person who never used Ecstasy. (*right*) This image shows the brain of a person who used Ecstasy 70 times or more over a period of at least 1.5 years but who stopped using the drug for several weeks before these images were taken. Areas of lighter color indicate a higher density of special proteins (called *transporters*) necessary for normal serotonin reuptake. The darker image of the brain on the right suggests that there is damage to the serotonin reuptake system. SOURCE: McCann et al., 1998.

Opiates

Opium is a product of the opium poppy. *Opium and drugs derived from it, such as morphine, codeine, and heroin, are called* **opiates.** Opiates have two major effects: they provide pain relief and cause mood changes, which may include euphoria. Opiates stimulate receptors normally activated by endorphins, thereby producing pain relief. Opiates also increase dopamine activity, which may be one reason they induce euphoria (Flores et al., 2006).

In medical use, opiates are the most effective agents known for relieving intense pain. Heroin was developed in 1889 by the Bayer company (which today produces aspirin). Initially thought to be a nonaddictive painkiller, heroin is, like other opiates, highly addictive. In the 1920s, it was made illegal in the United States.

Heroin users feel an intense rush within several minutes of an injection, but they often pay a high price for this transient pleasure. High doses may lead to coma, and overdoses can cause death (Morgan et al., 2008).

Hallucinogens

Hallucinogens *are powerful mind-altering drugs that produce hallucinations.* Some derive from natural sources and have been considered sacred in many tribal cultures because of their ability to produce contact with spiritual forces (Figure 6.26). Other hallucinogens, such as LSD (lysergic acid diethylamide, or "acid") and phencyclidine ("angel dust") are synthetic.

Hallucinogens distort sensory experience and can blur the boundaries between reality and fantasy. Users may speak of having mystical experiences and feeling exhilarated. They may also experience violent outbursts, paranoia, and panic and have flashbacks after the "trip" has ended. The mental effects of hallucinogens are unpredictable, which constitutes their greatest danger (Johnson et al., 2008).

LSD is a powerful hallucinogen that causes a flooding of excitation in the nervous system. Tolerance develops rapidly but decreases quickly. It increases the activity of serotonin and dopamine at certain receptor sites, but scientists still do not know precisely how LSD produces its effects (Passie et al., 2008).

Marijuana

Marijuana, a product of the hemp plant (*Cannabis sativa*), is the most widely used and controversial illegal drug in the United States (Figure 6.27). **THC (tetrahydrocannabinol)** *is marijuana's major active ingredient,* and it binds to receptors on neurons throughout the brain. But why does the brain have receptor sites for a foreign substance such as marijuana? The answer is that the brain produces its own THC-like substances called *cannabinoids.* With chronic use, THC may increase GABA activity, which slows down neural activity and produces relaxing effects (Ksir et al., 2008). THC also increases dopamine activity, which may account for some of its pleasurable subjective effects (Maldonado & Rodriguez de Fonseca, 2002).

Misconceptions about Marijuana

One misconception about marijuana is that chronic use causes people to become unmotivated and apathetic, a condition called *amotivational syndrome.* Another misconception is that marijuana causes people to start using more dangerous

Figure 6.26

In some cultures, hallucinogenic drugs are thought to have spiritual powers. Under the influence of peyote, this Indian shaman prepares to conduct a religious ceremony.

Figure 6.27

Marijuana is illegal in the United States at the federal level, but some jurisdictions have legalized marijuana use for certain medical purposes. Although the U.S. Supreme Court ruled against the medical legalization of marijuana in 2005, the issue remains hotly debated.

drugs. Neither statement is supported by the scientific evidence (Ksir et al., 2008; Rao, 2001). A third misconception is that using marijuana has no significant dangers. In fact, marijuana smoke contains more cancer-causing substances than does tobacco smoke. At high doses, users may experience negative changes in mood, sensory distortions, and feelings of panic and anxiety. While users are high, marijuana can impair their reaction time, thinking, memory, learning, and driving skills (Hall & Degenhardt, 2009).

Another misconception is that users can't become dependent on marijuana. Actually, repeated marijuana use produces tolerance, and at typical doses, some chronic users may experience withdrawal symptoms, such as restlessness. People who use chronically high doses and suddenly stop may experience vomiting, disrupted sleep, and irritability. About 5 to 10 percent of people who use marijuana develop dependence (Anthony, 2006).

From Genes to Culture: Determinants of Drug Effects

Table 6.5 lists some typical drug effects but, as we now discuss and as the Levels of Analysis graphic on the next page summarizes, a user's reaction depends on more than the drug's chemical structure.

Biological Factors

Animal research indicates that genetic factors influence sensitivity and tolerance to drugs'

effects (Radcliffe et al., 2009). The most extensive research has focused on alcohol. Rats and mice can be genetically bred to inherit a strong preference for drinking alcohol instead of water. Even in their first exposure to alcohol, these rats show greater tolerance than normal rats.

Among humans, identical twins have a higher concordance rate for alcoholism than do fraternal twins (Lyons et al., 2006). Moreover, people who grow up with alcoholic versus nonalcoholic parents respond differently to drinking alcohol under laboratory conditions. Adults who had alcoholic parents typically display faster hormonal and psychological reactions as blood-alcohol levels rise, but these responses drop off more quickly as blood-alcohol levels decrease (Newlin & Thomson, 1997). Compared with other people, they must drink more alcohol over the course of a few hours to maintain their feeling of intoxication. Overall, many scientists see evidence for a genetic role in determining human responsiveness to alcohol (Kuo et al., 2009).

Psychological Factors

People's beliefs and expectancies can influence drug reactions and drug use (George et al., 2000; Metrik et al., 2009). Experiments show that people may behave as if drunk if they simply think they have consumed alcohol but actually have not. If a person's fellow drinkers are gregarious, he or she

Table **6.5** | **Effects of Some Major Drugs**

Class	Typical Effects	Risks of High Doses and/or Chronic Use
Depressants		
Alcohol	Relaxation, lowered inhibition, impaired physical and psychological functioning	Disorientation, unconsciousness, possible death at extreme doses
Barbiturates, tranquilizers	Reduced tension, impaired reflexes and motor functioning, drowsiness	Shallow breathing, clammy skin, weak and rapid pulse, coma, possible death
Stimulants		
Amphetamines, cocaine, Ecstasy	Increased alertness, pulse, and blood pressure; elevated mood; suppressed appetite; agitation; sleeplessness	Hallucinations, paranoid delusions, convulsions, long-term cognitive impairments, brain damage, possible death
Opiates		
Opium, morphine, codeine, heroin	Euphoria, pain relief, drowsiness, impaired motor and psychological functioning	Shallow breathing, convulsions, coma, possible death
Hallucinogens		
LSD, mescaline, phencyclidine	Hallucinations and visions, distorted time perception, loss of contact with reality, nausea	Psychotic reactions (delusions, paranoia), panic, possible death
Marijuana	Mild euphoria, relaxation, enhanced sensory experiences, increased appetite, impaired memory and reaction time	Fatigue, anxiety, disorientation, sensory distortions, possible psychotic reactions, exposure to carcinogens

may feel it's expected to respond the same way. Personality factors also influence drug reactions and usage. People who have difficulty adjusting to life's demands or whose contact with reality is marginal may be particularly vulnerable to negative drug reactions and addiction (Ray & Ksir, 2004).

Environmental Factors

The setting in which a drug is taken can influence a user's reactions. As noted earlier, merely being in a familiar drug-use setting can trigger compensatory physiological responses and cravings. The behavior of other people who are sharing the drug experience provides cues for how to respond, and a hostile environment may increase the chances of a bad trip with drugs such as LSD (Palfai & Jankiewicz, 1991).

Cultural learning also affects how people respond to a drug (Bloomfield et al., 2002). In many Western cultures, increased aggressiveness and sexual promiscuity are commonly associated with drunken excess. In contrast, members of the Camba culture of Bolivia customarily drink large quantities of a 178-proof beverage, remaining cordial and nonaggressive between episodes of passing out. In the 1700s, Tahitians introduced to alcohol by European sailors reacted at first with pleasant relaxation when intoxicated, but after witnessing the violent aggressiveness exhibited

Levels of Analysis — Drug-Induced States

Drug-induced states involve an interplay of biological, psychological, and environmental factors. Let's summarize some of these factors.

ENVIRONMENTAL LEVEL

- Cultural norms and experiences can shape users' drug attitudes and expectations.
- Repeated drug use in a particular setting can produce conditioned compensatory stimuli.
- The social context and behavior of other drug users who are present can affect how a person responds to a drug.

BIOLOGICAL LEVEL

- Drugs increase or decrease the activity of particular neurotransmitter systems.
- The body produces compensatory responses to counteract a drug's effect, possibly leading to tolerance.
- Withdrawal symptoms occur when drug use stops, but the body's compensatory responses continue.
- Genetic factors influence biological reactivity to specific drugs.

PSYCHOLOGICAL LEVEL

- Drugs can alter numerous aspects of psychological functioning, including mood, memory, attention, decision making, social inhibitions, and pain awareness.
- Users' attitudes and expectations about drugs can influence their psychological reactions to a drug.
- A user's level of personal adjustment can influence the likelihood of a negative drug reaction.

Suppose a person consumes enough alcoholic drinks within 30 minutes to reach a blood-alcohol level of .08. In one case, suppose all the drinks are the same: all beers or all the same kind of wine. In another case, suppose each drink is different: beer, red wine, and tequila. Would you expect the person to feel equally intoxicated in both cases?

by drunken sailors, they too began behaving aggressively (MacAndrew & Edgerton, 1969).

Cultural factors also affect drug consumption. Traditionally, members of the Navajo tribe do not consider drinking any amount of alcohol to be normal, whereas drinking wine or beer is central to social life in some European countries (Tanaka-Matsumi & Draguns, 1997). In some cultures, hallucinogenic drugs are feared and outlawed, whereas in others they are used in medicinal or religious contexts to seek advice from spirits (Dalgarno, 2009).

test yourself   Drug-Induced States

True or false?

1. Agonists are drugs that increase neurotransmitter activity.
2. Compensatory bodily responses to a drug produce tolerance.
3. Drug dependence can occur only with withdrawal symptoms.
4. Alcohol myopia is the principle that intoxication causes attention to narrow.
5. Amphetamines increase dopamine and norepinephrine activity.
6. Cocaine is classified as an opiate drug.

ANSWERS: 1-true, 2-true, 3-false, 4-true, 5-true, 6-false

HYPNOSIS

In 18th-century Vienna, physician Anton Mesmer gained fame for using magnetized objects to cure patients. He claimed that illness was caused by blockages of an invisible bodily fluid and that his technique of "animal magnetism" (later named *mesmerism* in his honor) would restore the fluid's normal flow. A scientific commission discredited mesmerism, but its use continued. Decades later, Scottish surgeon James Braid investigated the fact that mesmerized patients often went into a trance in which they seemed oblivious to their surroundings. Braid concluded that mesmerism was a state of "nervous sleep" produced by concentrated attention, and he renamed it *hypnosis*, after Hypnos, the Greek god of sleep.

The Scientific Study of Hypnosis

Hypnosis *is a procedure in which "one person (the subject) is guided by another (the hypnotist) to respond to suggestions for changes in subjective experience, alterations in perception, sensation, emotion, thought or behavior"* (APA, 2005, para. 1). Hypnosis draws great interest because some mental health practitioners use it as an aid in conducting therapy. Basic scientists explore whether hypnosis produces a unique state of consciousness and put its claims to rigorous test.

Hypnotic induction is a process that creates a context for hypnosis. A hypnotist may ask the subject to sit down and gaze at an object on the wall, and then, in a quiet voice, suggest that the subject's eyes are becoming heavy. The goal is to relax the subject and increase her or his concentration.

Contrary to popular belief, people cannot be hypnotized against their will. Even when people want to be hypnotized, they differ in how susceptible (i.e., responsive) they are to hypnotic suggestions. **Hypnotic susceptibility scales** *contain a standard series of pass-fail suggestions that are read to a subject after a hypnotic induction* (Table 6.6). The subject's score is based on the number of passes. Across many cultures, about 5 percent of subjects respond to few or none of the suggestions, 10 percent pass all or nearly all of the items, and the rest fall in between (Sanchez-Armass & Barabasz, 2005).

Hypnotic Behaviors and Experiences

Does hypnosis alter people's psychological functioning and behavior? Let's examine some claims.

Involuntary Control and Behaving against One's Will

Hypnotized people *subjectively experience* their actions to be involuntary (Kirsch, 2001). For example, look at the second item in Table 6.6. To hypnotized subjects, it really feels like their hands are being pushed apart by a mysterious force,

Table **6.6** | **Sample Test Items from the Stanford Hypnotic Susceptibility Scale, Form C**

Item	Suggested Behavior	Criterion for Passing
Lowering Arm	Right arm is held out; subject is told arm will become heavy and drop	Arm is lowered by 6 inches in 10 seconds
Moving Hands Apart	With hands extended and close together, subject is asked to imagine a force pushing them apart	Hands are 6 or more inches apart in 10 seconds
Mosquito Hallucination	It is suggested that a mosquito is buzzing nearby and lands on subject	Any grimace or acknowledgment of mosquito
Posthypnotic Amnesia	Subject is awakened and asked to recall suggestions after being told under hypnosis that he or she will not remember the suggestions	Three or fewer items recalled before subject is told, "Now you can remember everything."

Source: Based on Wertzenhoffer & Hilgard, 1962.

Figure 6.28

The human-plank demonstration, a favorite of stage hypnotists, seems to demonstrate the power of hypnosis. Are you convinced?

rather than by their conscious control. If this is so, then can a hypnotist make people perform acts that are harmful to themselves or others? In a classic experiment, Martin Orne and Frederick Evans (1965) found that hypnotized subjects could be induced to dip their hands briefly in a foaming solution they were told was acid and then to throw the "acid" in another person's face. This might appear to be a striking example of the power of hypnosis to get people to act against their will. However, Orne and Evans tested a control group of subjects who were asked to simply pretend that they were hypnotized. These subjects were just as likely as hypnotized subjects to put their hands in the "acid" and throw it at someone.

Hypnosis does not involve a unique power to get people to behave against their will (Wagstaff, 2008). A legitimate authority figure can induce people to commit out-of-character and dangerous acts whether they are hypnotized or not.

Amazing Feats

Have you seen or heard about stage hypnotists who get an audience member to perform an amazing physical feat, such as the "human plank" (Figure 6.28)? A subject, usually male, is hypnotized and lies outstretched between two chairs. He is told that his body is rigid and then, amazingly, another person successfully stands on the subject's legs and chest.

Similarly, hypnosis can have striking physiological effects. Consider another classic experiment involving 13 people who were strongly allergic to the toxic leaves of a certain tree (Ikemi & Nakagawa, 1962). Five of them were hypnotized, blindfolded, and told that a leaf from a harmless tree to which they were not allergic was touching

one of their arms. In fact, the leaf really was toxic, but 4 out of the 5 hypnotized people had no allergic reaction. Next, the other arm of each hypnotized person was rubbed with a leaf from a harmless tree, but he or she was falsely told that the leaf was toxic. All 5 people responded to the harmless leaf with allergic reactions.

Should we attribute the human-plank feat and the unusual responses of the allergic people to unique powers of hypnosis? Here is where a healthy dose of critical thinking is important.

(?) thinking **critically**

HYPNOSIS AND AMAZING FEATS

In the case of the human plank and in the allergy experiment, what additional evidence do you need to determine whether these amazing feats and responses really are caused by hypnosis? How could you gather this evidence? Think about it, then see page 212.

Pain Tolerance

Scottish surgeon James Esdaile performed more than 300 major operations in the mid-1800s using hypnosis as the sole anesthetic (Figure 6.29). Experiments confirm that hypnosis often increases pain tolerance and that this is not due merely to a placebo effect (Milling, 2008). For patients who experience chronic pain, hypnosis can produce relief that lasts for months or even years

We do not know exactly how hypnosis produces its painkilling effects, although the positive expectancies it creates for pain reduction play some role (Milling, 2008). It also may influence the release of endorphins, distract patients from their pain, or somehow help them separate the pain from conscious experience (Barber, 1998).

Hypnotic Amnesia

You may have seen TV shows or movies in which hypnotized people are given a suggestion that they will not remember something (such as a familiar person's name), either during the session itself (*hypnotic amnesia*) or after coming out of hypnosis (*posthypnotic amnesia*). A reversal cue also is given, such as a phrase ("You will now remember everything") that ends the amnesia once the person hears it. Is this Hollywood fiction?

Research indicates that about 25 percent of hypnotized college students can be led to experience amnesia (Kirsch, 2001). Although researchers agree that hypnotic and posthypnotic amnesias occur, they debate the causes. Some believe it results from voluntary attempts to avoid thinking about certain information, and others believe it is caused by an altered state of consciousness that weakens normal memory systems (Kihlstrom, 2007; Spanos, 1996).

In contrast to hypnotic amnesia, can hypnosis enhance memory? Let's examine whether this is myth or reality.

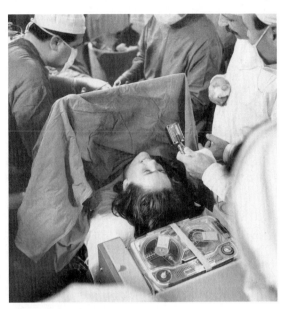

Figure 6.29

This patient is having her appendix removed with hypnosis as the sole anesthetic. Her verbal reports that she feels no pain are being recorded.

(Patterson, 2004). Brain-imaging research reveals that hypnosis modifies neural activity in brain areas that process painful stimuli, but nonhypnotic techniques, such as mental imagery and performing distracting cognitive tasks, also alter neural functioning and reduce pain (Petrovic & Ingvar, 2002).

Myth or Reality?

Hypnosis Uncovers Eyewitnesses' Hidden Memories

In a 2007 episode of the popular TV show *Mythbusters*, one of the show's hosts, Adam Savage, noted: "There is one [hypnosis myth] I've always wanted to try. Well, it's that you can remember more material under hypnosis than under normal circumstances. Like the police could put you under hypnosis and you'd remember all sorts of things about a crime you witnessed that you had no conscious memory of witnessing." As the show's narrator added, "it's one of the most pervasive myths associated with hypnosis. But can going under really unleash a vast resource of hidden memories?" (2007, April 11, episode 76).

Many people believe hypnosis can do just that. Psychologist Joseph Green and his colleagues, for example, found that college students in Australia, Germany, Iran, and the United States endorsed the view that hypnosis "can make subjects remember things that they could not normally remember" (2006, p. 271). In the popular media, from science-fiction TV shows like *Star Trek: The Next*

Generation, to modern crime dramas like *The Mentalist*, hypnosis has been portrayed as a technique for uncovering hidden memories. And some real-life cases seem to back it up.

In a bizarre mass kidnapping, later dramatized in a book and television movie, a school bus from Chowchilla, California, carrying 26 children and its driver disappeared from a country road in 1976. The victims, buried underground in an abandoned moving van by three kidnappers, escaped 16 hours later. Afterward, a police expert hypnotized the bus driver and asked him to recall the ordeal. The driver formed a vivid image of the kidnappers' white van and could "read" all but one digit on the van's license plate. This information allowed the authorities to track down the kidnappers.

On *Mythbusters*, three employees witnessed a staged altercation between two men and later recalled more details of the event while hypnotized than when not hypnotized. The show's conclusion about hypnosis as a forensic memory aid: "confirmed." But unfortunately,

Continued

their hypnosis test was flawed. Aside from testing only three people, the participants were told ahead of time about the memory hypothesis being tested. Memory while under hypnosis was always tested second, after the three had first tried to recall the events while not hypnotized. Perhaps their better memory resulted merely from a second attempt at recalling the events, not from hypnosis. Further, the first memory test was solely by written questionnaire. For the second test, the hypnotist verbally presented the questions. In short, the hypnosis test was entertaining, but not solid science.

Despite some success stories like the Chowchilla case, there are also real-life failures of forensic hypnosis. The most rigorous testing, performed in controlled experiments, has revealed overall that hypnosis does not reliably improve memory (Lynn et al., 2009; Whitehouse et al., 2009). In some experiments, participants watched videotapes of simulated bank robberies or other crimes. Next, while hypnotized or not, they were questioned by researchers, or even by actual police investigators or criminal lawyers. Hypnotized people displayed better recall than unhypnotized people in some studies but no better recall in others. In still other experiments, hypnotized participants performed more poorly than unhypnotized controls. They recalled more information, but much of that extra recall was inaccurate and, to make matters worse, the fact that they recalled these memories under hypnosis may have convinced people that their memories must have been accurate (Burgess & Kirsch, 1999; Wagstaff et al., 2008).

A related concern is that some memories recalled under hypnosis may be *pseudomemories*, false memories *created* during hypnosis

by statements or leading suggestions made by the forensic examiner (Lynn et al., 2009). In some experiments, hypnotized and nonhypnotized subjects were intentionally exposed to false information about an event (e.g., about a bank robbery). Later, after the hypnotized subjects had been brought out of hypnosis, all participants were questioned. Highly suggestible people who had been hypnotized were more likely to report the false information as being a true memory (Sheehan et al., 1992; Wagstaff, 2009).

So, is the claim that forensic hypnosis uncovers hidden memories a myth or reality? Unlike *Mythbusters*, we view the claim as mostly "busted," due to the unreliable effects of hypnosis on eyewitness memory. Efforts by psychologists and others are under way, however, to examine whether hypnotic induction instructions can be modified, or specific elements of the hypnosis procedure (e.g., just closing one's eyes) can be used, to improve the overall accuracy of memories recalled in forensic interviews (Wagstaff et al., 2008; Whitehouse et al., 2009)

Many North American courts have banned or limited testimony obtained under hypnosis (Patry et al., 2009; Wagstaff, 2009). A chief concern is that the increased suggestibility of hypnotized eyewitnesses makes them particularly susceptible to memory distortion caused by leading questions, and they may honestly come to believe facts that never occurred (Scoboria et al., 2002). Similarly, if a therapist uses hypnosis to help patients recall long-forgotten memories of sexual abuse, what shall we conclude? Are the horrible memories real, or are they pseudomemories created during therapy? We explore this issue in Chapter 8.

Theories of Hypnosis

Hypnos may have been the Greek god of sleep, but studies of brain physiology reveal that hypnosis definitely *is not* sleep. What is hypnosis, and how does it produce its effects?

Dissociation Theories

Several researchers propose **dissociation theories** *that view hypnosis as an altered state involving a division (dissociation) of consciousness* (Kihlstrom, 2007). Ernest Hilgard (1994) proposed that hypnosis creates a division of awareness in which the person simultaneously experiences two streams of consciousness that are cut off from one another. One stream responds to the hypnotist's suggestions, while the second stream—the part of consciousness that monitors behavior—remains in the background but is aware of everything that goes on. Hilgard refers to this second part of consciousness as the *hidden observer*.

Suppose a hypnotized subject is given a suggestion that she will not feel pain. Her arm is lowered into a tub of ice-cold water for 45 seconds, and every few seconds she reports the amount

of pain. In contrast to nonhypnotized subjects, who find this experience moderately painful, she probably will report feeling little pain. But suppose the procedure is done differently. Before lowering the subject's arm, the hypnotist says, "Perhaps there is another part of you that is more aware than your hypnotized part. If so, would that part of you report the amount of pain." In this case, the subject's other stream of consciousness, the hidden observer, will report a higher level of pain (Figure 6.30).

For Hilgard, this dissociation explained why behaviors that occur under hypnosis seem involuntary or automatic. Given the suggestion that "your arm will start to feel lighter and will begin to rise," the subject intentionally raises his or her arm, but only the hidden observer is aware of this. The main stream of consciousness that responds to the command is blocked from this awareness and perceives that the arm is rising all by itself.

Social-Cognitive Theories

To other theorists, hypnosis does not represent a special state of dissociated consciousness

(Dienes et al., 2009). Instead, **social-cognitive theories** *propose that hypnotic experiences result from expectations of people who are motivated to take on the role of being hypnotized* (Kirsch, 2001; Spanos, 1996). Most people believe that hypnosis involves a trancelike state and responsiveness to suggestions. People motivated to conform to this role develop a readiness to respond to the hypnotist's suggestions and to perceive hypnotic experiences as real and involuntary.

In a classic study, Martin Orne (1959) illustrated the importance of expectations about hypnosis. During a classroom demonstration, college students were told that hypnotized people frequently exhibit spontaneous stiffening of the muscles in the dominant hand. (Actually, this rarely occurs.) An accomplice of the lecturer pretended to be hypnotized and, sure enough, he "spontaneously" exhibited hand stiffness. When students who had seen the demonstration were later hypnotized, 55 percent of them exhibited stiffening of the hand without any suggestion from the hypnotist. Control-group participants saw a demonstration that did not mention or display hand stiffening. Not one of these students exhibited hand stiffening when they were hypnotized.

Does social-cognitive theory imply that hypnotized people are faking or playacting? Not at all. Role theorists emphasize that when people immerse themselves in the hypnotic role, their responses are completely real and may indeed represent altered experiences (Kirsch, 2001). Our expectations strongly influence how the brain organizes sensory information. Often we literally see what we expect to see. According to social-cognitive theory, many effects of hypnosis represent an extension of this principle. The hypnotized subject whose arm automatically rises in response to a suggestion genuinely perceives the behavior to be involuntary because this is what the subject expects and because attention is focused externally on the hypnotist and the hypnotic suggestion.

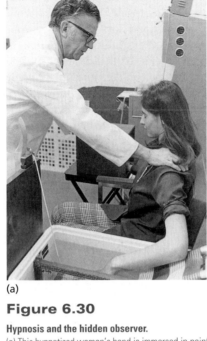
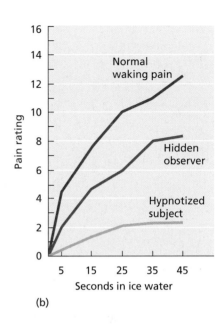

(a)   (b)

Figure 6.30

Hypnosis and the hidden observer.

(a) This hypnotized woman's hand is immersed in painfully cold ice water. Placing his hand on her shoulder, Ernest Hilgard contacts her dissociated hidden observer. (b) This graph shows pain-intensity ratings given by a woman when she is not hypnotized, when she is under hypnosis, and by her hidden observer in the same hypnotic state. The hidden observer reports more pain than the hypnotized woman but less than the subject when she is not hypnotized. Source: Based on Hilgard, 1977, 1994.

The Hypnotized Brain

Can peering inside the brain reveal the nature of hypnosis? To find out, look at the colored and gray-scale drawings in Figure 6.31. Now:

1. Look at the colored drawing again, form a mental image of it, and try to drain the color out of it. In other words, try to visualize it as if it were a gray-scale figure.

2. Next, look at the gray-scale drawing, form a mental picture of it, and try to add color to it.

Stephen Kosslyn and coworkers (2000) identified 8 people who scored high in hypnotic susceptibility and who reported they could drain away

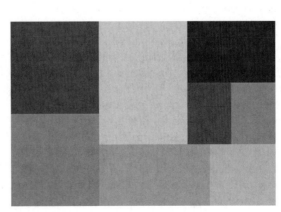

Figure 6.31

Color perception and the hypnotized brain.

These color and gray-scale drawings are similar to the ones used by Kosslyn and his colleagues (2000).

or add color to their mental images of such drawings. Subjects then performed these tasks while inside a PET scanner. On some trials they were hypnotized, and on other trials they were not.

The PET scans revealed that whether subjects were hypnotized or not, an area in the right hemisphere that processes color information was more active when subjects visualized the gray drawing as having color (Task 2) than when they visualized the color drawing as gray (Task 1). In the left hemisphere, however, visualizing the gray drawing as having color increased brain activation in one particular region only when the subjects were hypnotized. As the researchers noted, "The right hemisphere appeared to respond to imagery per se, whereas the left required the additional boost provided by hypnosis" (Kosslyn et al., 2000, p. 1283).

Other brain-imaging studies reveal that giving hypnotized subjects pain-reducing suggestions not only decreases their subjective reports of pain but also decreases activity in several brain regions that process pain signals (Milling, 2008). These results and other physiological findings suggest an important conclusion: hypnotized people are not faking it but rather are experiencing altered brain activity that matches their verbal reports (Dienes et al., 2009). But does this brain activity reflect a state of dissociation?

Social cognitive theorists argue that these findings don't resolve the issue (Kirsch, 2001). They note that hypnotic experiences are subjectively real, and if hypnosis alters brain activity, this does not contradict the position that people's expectations are what lead them to become hypnotized in the first place. In sum, cognitive neuroscience provides insights into the hypnotized brain, but it will take more research to resolve the debate about hypnosis (Dienes et al., 2009).

test yourself   Hypnosis

True or false?

1. Hypnosis is a state of sleep.
2. Forensic hypnosis reliably improves eyewitness memory.
3. According to social-cognitive theory, hypnotic experiences result from people's expectations and highly motivated role-playing.
4. According to dissociation theory, hypnosis creates two independent streams of consciousness.

ANSWERS: 1-false, 2-false, 3-true, 4-true

Chapter Summary

THE PUZZLE OF CONSCIOUSNESS

- *Consciousness* refers to our moment-to-moment awareness of ourselves and the environment. It is subjective, dynamic, self-reflective, central to our sense of identity, and linked to selective attention. Scientists use self-report, behavioral, and physiological measures to measure states of consciousness.
- Freud viewed the unconscious mind as a reservoir of unacceptable desires and repressed experiences. Cognitive psychologists view it as an information-processing system and distinguish between controlled and automatic processing. Research on visual agnosia, blindsight, and priming reveals that information processed unconsciously can influence people's behavior and emotions.

- Consciousness has adaptive value. It facilitates planning and decision making, helps us cope with novel situations, and lets us override impulsive and automated behaviors. The brain contains at least several separate neural circuits for conscious versus unconscious information processing.
- Global-workspace models propose that the mind consists of separate but interacting information-processing modules. Consciousness arises from the unified activity of multiple modules located in different brain areas.

CIRCADIAN RHYTHMS: OUR DAILY BIOLOGICAL CLOCKS

- Circadian rhythms are 24-hour biological cycles that help regulate bodily processes and influence our alertness.

The suprachiasmatic nuclei (SCN) are the brain's master circadian clock. Free-running circadian rhythms are about 24.2 hours. The day-night cycle and other environmental factors reset our daily clocks to a 24-hour schedule.

- Circadian rhythms influence our tendency to be a morning or night person. Cultural factors may also play a role.
- In general, our alertness is lowest in the early morning hours. Job performance errors, major industrial accidents, and fatal auto accidents peak during these hours.
- Jet lag, night-shift work, and seasonal affective disorder (SAD) involve circadian disruptions. Treatments include controlling one's exposure to light, taking oral melatonin, and regulating one's daily activity schedule.

SLEEP AND DREAMING

- Sleep has five main stages. Stages 1 and 2 are lighter sleep; stages 3 and 4 are deeper, slow-wave sleep. High physiological arousal and rapid eye movement characterize stage-5 REM sleep. Several brain regions regulate sleep, and genetic, psychological, and environmental factors affect sleep duration and quality.
- Sleep deprivation negatively affects mood and performance.
- The restoration model proposes that we sleep to recover from physical and mental fatigue. Evolutionary/circadian models state that each species developed a sleep-wake cycle that maximized its chance of survival.
- Insomnia, narcolepsy, REM-sleep behavior disorder, sleepwalking, night terrors, and sleep apnea can have serious consequences. Sleepwalking typically occurs during slow-wave sleep, whereas nightmares most often occur during REM sleep. Night terrors create a near-panic state of arousal and typically occur in slow-wave sleep.
- Dreams occur throughout sleep but are most common during REM periods. Our cultural background, current concerns, and recent events influence what we dream about.
- Freud proposed that dreams fulfill unconscious wishes. Cognitive-process dream theories view dreams and waking thoughts as products of the same mental systems. Activation-synthesis theory views dreaming as the brain's attempt to fit a story to random neural activity.

DRUG-INDUCED STATES

- Drugs alter consciousness by modifying neurotransmitter activity. Agonists increase a neurotransmitter system's activity; antagonists decrease it.

- Tolerance develops when the body produces compensatory responses to counteract a drug's effects. When drug use is stopped, compensatory responses continue and produce withdrawal symptoms. Substance dependence is a maladaptive pattern of drug use.
- Depressants, such as alcohol, barbiturates, and tranquilizers, decrease neural activity. Stimulants, such as amphetamines, cocaine, and Ecstasy, increase arousal and boost mood. Repeated use may produce serious negative psychological effects and bodily damage.
- Opiates increase endorphin activity, producing pain relief and mood changes. Opiates are highly addictive. Hallucinogens powerfully distort sensory experience and can blur the line between reality and fantasy.
- Marijuana produces relaxation at low doses but can cause anxiety and sensory distortions at higher doses. It can impair thinking and reflexes.
- A drug's effect depends on its chemical actions, the physical and social setting, cultural norms and learning, and the user's genetic predispositions, expectations, and personality.

HYPNOSIS

- Hypnosis involves an increased receptiveness to suggestions. Hypnotized people experience their actions as involuntary, but hypnosis has no unique power to make people behave against their will or perform amazing feats. Hypnosis increases pain tolerance, as do other psychological techniques.
- Some people can be led to experience hypnotic amnesia and posthypnotic amnesia. The use of hypnosis to improve memory is controversial. Hypnosis increases the risk that people will develop distorted memories about events in response to leading questions.
- Dissociation theories view hypnosis as an altered state of divided consciousness. Social-cognitive theories state that hypnotic experiences occur because people have strong expectations about hypnosis and are highly motivated to enter a hypnotized role.
- Brain imaging reveals that hypnotized people display changes in neural activity consistent with their subjectively reported experiences. This supports the view that hypnosis involves an altered state but doesn't establish whether it is a dissociated state.

KEY TERMS AND CONCEPTS

Each term has been boldfaced and defined in the chapter on the page indicated in parentheses.

activation-synthesis theory (p. 193)
agonist (p. 195)
alcohol myopia (p. 199)

alpha waves (p. 183)
antagonist (p. 196)
automatic (unconscious) processing (p. 177)

beta waves (p. 183)
blindsight (p. 177)
blood-brain barrier (p. 195)

thinking critically

EARLY BIRDS, CLIMATE, AND CULTURE (Page 181)

As a critical thinker, keep in mind that correlation does not establish causation. This is a correlational study. The major variables (climate, students' morningness) were not manipulated; they were only measured. The association between climate and morningness might be causal, but we must consider other possible explanations.

First, why might climate affect morningness? The researchers hypothesized that to avoid performing daily activities during the hottest part of the day, people who live in warmer climates adapt to a pattern of rising early in the morning, a finding consistent with a prior study that revealed strong tendencies toward morningness among Brazilians (Benedito-Silva et al., 1989).

Second, as the authors note, these results could be due to factors other than climate. The Netherlands, England, and the United States share a northern-European heritage, and perhaps some aspect of this common background predisposes people toward less morningness. Yet, say the authors, India's cultural traditions are distinct from those of Spain and Colombia, so it's difficult to apply the "common cultural heritage" argument to explain the greater morningness found among students from these countries. If not cultural heritage, perhaps the greater industrialization and summertime use of air-conditioned home and work environments in the Netherlands, England, and the United States reduce the necessity for residents to adapt circadian cycles to local climate conditions. Aware of their study's limitations, the authors suggest that climate may be just one of several factors that contribute to cross-cultural differences in morningness.

HYPNOSIS AND AMAZING FEATS (Page 206)

For any causal claim, as critical thinkers it's important to think about the concept of control groups. You should keep this question in mind: What would have happened anyway, even without this special treatment or intervention? Applied to hypnosis, the key question is whether people can exhibit these same amazing feats when they are not hypnotized. When a stage hypnotist gets someone to perform the human plank, the audience attributes this feat to the hypnotic trance. What the audience doesn't know is that an average man suspended in this manner can support 300 pounds on his chest with little discomfort and no need of a hypnotic trance. Indeed, Figure 6.28 shows The Amazing Kreskin, a professional performer and self-proclaimed "mentalist," standing on someone who is not hypnotized.

As for the allergy experiment, we must ask whether allergic people might show the same reactions if they were not hypnotized. Indeed, the experiment included 8 nonhypnotized control participants (Ikemi & Nakagawa, 1962). When blindfolded and exposed to a toxic leaf but misled to believe that it was harmless, they did not show an allergic response. Conversely, when their arm was rubbed with a harmless leaf but they were falsely told it was toxic, they had an allergic reaction. In short, the nonhypnotized people responded the same way as the hypnotized subjects.

Other research shows that under hypnosis, vision can improve and stomach acidity can increase. However, well-controlled studies show that nonhypnotized subjects can exhibit these same responses (Spanos & Chaves, 1988). As with placebo effects and other mind-body interactions, people's beliefs and expectations can produce real physiological effects.

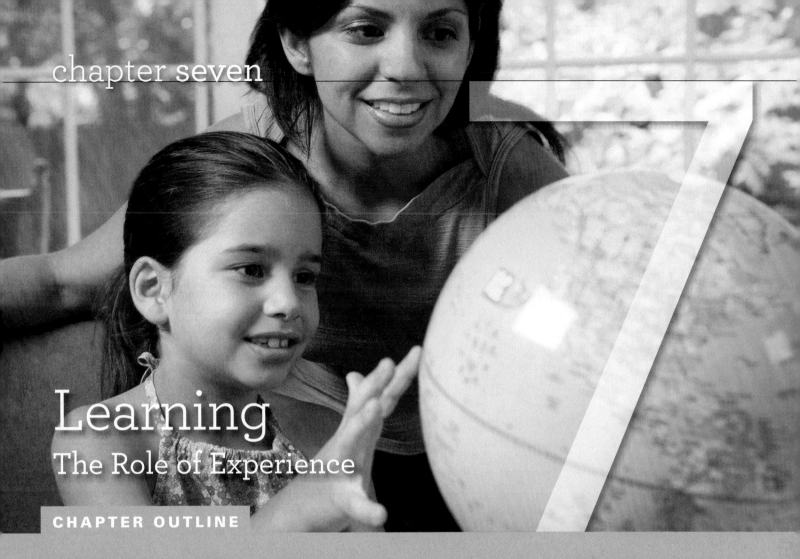

chapter **seven**

Learning
The Role of Experience

CHAPTER OUTLINE

Myth or Reality?

Spanking Is a Necessary Evil (page 227)

The well-known adage "spare the rod, spoil the child" has been used to justify spanking and other physical punishment as discipline for misbehaving children. Is physical punishment a necessary evil, or does scientific research suggest otherwise?

Thanks to six sessions of psychotherapy, Carol's life is normal again. She is now free from the intense fear of something most of us take for granted: riding in a car. Carol was severely injured in a car crash and hospitalized for months. A year later, she described to a therapist how the fear began when her husband came to take her home from the hospital.

> As we walked toward the new car he had bought, I began to feel uneasy. I felt nervous all the way home. It started to get worse after that. I found myself avoiding riding in the car, and couldn't drive it at all. I stopped visiting friends and tried to get them to come to our house. . . . After a while, even the sight of a car started to make me nervous. . . . You know, this is the first time I've left the house in about four months.

To help Carol, the therapist used a highly successful procedure based, in part, on century-old principles of learning discovered in laboratory investigations of salivating dogs.

A thousand miles away, on a sidewalk outside a Las Vegas casino, a woman volunteers her time soliciting donations for a local charity. Though hot and tired, she remains upbeat and thanks each person who drops money in her collection can. Inside, exhausted and down to his last dollar, a man has been playing the slot machines for 36 hours. A casino guard mutters to a cocktail waitress, "I'll never understand what keeps these guys going."

Humans are not biologically programmed to fear cars, solicit monetary donations, or play slot machines. Although our genetic endowment creates the potential for such actions to occur, these diverse behaviors are all learned. A psychologist would want to discover the principles that govern learning and seek ways to apply these principles to enhance people's well-being.

Reflect for a moment on how much of your behavior is learned: telling time, getting dressed, driving, reading, using money, and so on. Beyond such skills, learning affects our emotional reactions, perceptions, and physiological responses. Through experience, we learn to think, act, and feel in ways that contribute richly to our individual identity.

Learning is a process by which experience produces a relatively enduring change in an organism's behavior or capabilities. The term capabilities highlights a distinction made by many theorists: "knowing how" versus "doing." For example, experience may provide us with immediate knowledge (e.g., we receive instructions on how to perform a skill), but in science we must measure learning by actual changes in responses (e.g., later in the day we perform the skill).

In this chapter we explore four basic learning processes. The first, habituation, involves a change in behavior that results merely from repeated exposure to a stimulus. Next, we examine two types of conditioning, which involves learning associations between events. Classical conditioning occurs when two stimuli become associated with one another (say, being inside a car and being severely burned) such that one stimulus (being in a car) now triggers a response (intense fear) that previously was triggered by the other stimulus (being burned). In operant conditioning, organisms learn to associate their responses with specific consequences (e.g., asking for a charitable donation leads to a monetary gift). Lastly, we consider observational learning, in which observers imitate the behavior of a model (e.g., children imitate a behavior they see on TV).

Many learning principles that we will discuss reflect key discoveries made by behaviorists. Within psychology, behaviorism dominated research on learning during the early to middle twentieth century. Behaviorists assumed that there are laws of learning that apply to virtually all organisms. They explained learning solely in terms of directly observable events and avoided speculating about an organism's unobservable mental state. Yet, although this chapter focuses on how environmental experiences modify behavior, you will see that biological and cognitive factors play important roles in learning (Shanks, 2010). You also will find many examples of how psychologists have creatively applied learning principles to enhance human welfare.

ADAPTING TO THE ENVIRONMENT

The concept of learning, like that of evolution, calls attention to the importance of adapting to the environment. But whereas evolution focuses on species' adaptations passed down biologically across generations, learning represents a process of *personal adaptation*. That is, learning focuses on how an organism's behavior changes in response to environmental stimuli encountered during its lifetime. In humans, much of what we learn varies across cultures—different skills, customs, languages, and so forth. Likewise, the contents of learning vary across species. We have yet to encounter a deer that has learned to order take-out food. Still, all animal species face some common adaptive challenges, such as finding food. Because environments contain many events, each organism must learn (a) which events are, or are not, important to its survival and well-being, (b) which stimuli signal that an important event is about to occur, and (c) whether its responses will produce positive or negative consequences. The learning processes examined in this chapter enable humans and other species to respond to one or more of these adaptive challenges. Consider, for example, *habituation*.

Imagine that you are a participant in an experiment. You're sitting alone in a quiet laboratory when suddenly (as part of the experiment) a loud sound startles you. Your body jerks slightly, you become aroused, and you look toward the source of the sound. Over time, as you hear it again and again, your startle response diminishes until eventually you ignore the sound.

Habituation *is a decrease in the strength of response to a repeated stimulus.* It may be the simplest form of learning and occurs across species ranging from humans to dragonflies to sea snails (Glanzman, 2009). Touch the skin of a sea snail in a certain location, and it will reflexively contract its gill. With repeated touches, this response habituates, and the gill no longer retracts. Habituation serves a key adaptive function. If an organism responded to every stimulus in its environment, it would rapidly become overwhelmed and exhausted. By learning not to respond to uneventful familiar stimuli, organisms conserve energy and can attend to other stimuli that are important.

Habituation plays a key role in enabling scientists to study behavior. Whether observing animals in the wild or schoolchildren, a researcher's mere presence may initially disrupt participants' natural responses. Thus, before collecting data, observers often allow people and animals to habituate to their presence.

CLASSICAL CONDITIONING: ASSOCIATING ONE STIMULUS WITH ANOTHER

Life is full of interesting associations. Do you ever hear songs on the radio or find yourself in places that instantly make you feel good because they're connected to special times you've had? When you smell the aroma of popcorn or freshly baked cookies, does your mouth water or your stomach growl? These examples illustrate a learning process called **classical conditioning,** *in which an organism learns to associate two stimuli* (e.g., a song and a pleasant event), *such that one stimulus* (the song) *comes to elicit a response* (feeling happy) *that originally was elicited only by the other stimulus* (the pleasant event).

Like habituation, classical conditioning is a basic form of learning that even occurs in insects (Watanabe et al., 2008). Its discovery dates back to the late 1800s and an odd twist of fate.

Pavlov's Pioneering Research

In the 1860s, Ivan Pavlov was studying theology in a Russian seminary when his plans to join the priesthood unexpectedly changed. A new government policy allowed the translation of Western scientific publications into Russian. Pavlov read Darwin's theory of evolution and other works, which sparked a strong interest in the sciences (Windholz, 1997). Pavlov became a renowned physiologist, conducting research on digestion in dogs that won him the Nobel Prize in 1904.

To study digestion, Pavlov presented food to dogs and measured their salivary response (Figure 7.1). As often occurs in science, Pavlov made an accidental but important discovery. He noticed that with repeated testing, the dogs began to salivate before the food was presented, such as when they heard the footsteps of the approaching experimenter.

Further study by Pavlov's (1923/1928) research team confirmed this observation. Dogs have a natural reflex to salivate to food but not to tones. Yet when a tone or other stimulus that ordinarily did not cause salivation was presented just before food powder was squirted into a dog's mouth, soon the sound of the tone alone made the dog salivate. This process of learning

(a)

(b)

Figure 7.1

Pavlov's method of measuring salivation in dogs.

(a) Ivan Pavlov (*with the white beard*) is shown here with colleagues and one of his canine subjects. (b) In his early research, Pavlov measured salivation using a simple device similar to the one shown here. In later research, a collection tube was inserted directly into the salivary gland.

by association came to be called *classical*, or *Pavlovian, conditioning.* Many psychologists regard Pavlov's discovery as one of the most important in psychology's history (Wills, 2005). But why all the fuss about dogs salivating to tones?

This question raises a major point about basic scientific research: typically, it is the *underlying principle*—not the specific findings—that is paramount. Classical conditioning performs a key adaptive function: it alerts organisms to stimuli that signal the impending arrival of an important event. As Pavlov noted, if salivation could be conditioned, so might bodily processes that affect diseases and mental disorders.

Basic Principles

What factors influence the acquisition and persistence of conditioned responses? Let's examine some basic principles of conditioning.

Acquisition

Acquisition refers to the period during which a response is being learned. Suppose we wish to condition a dog to salivate to a tone. Sounding the tone initially may cause the dog to perk up its ears but not to salivate. At this time, the tone is a *neutral stimulus* because it does not elicit salivation (Figure 7.2). If, however, we place food in the dog's mouth, the dog will salivate. This salivation response to food is *reflexive*—it's what dogs do by nature. Because no learning is required for food to produce salivation, the food is an **unconditioned stimulus (UCS),** *a stimulus that elicits a reflexive or innate response (the UCR) without prior learning.* Salivation is an **unconditioned response (UCR),** *a reflexive or innate response that is elicited by a stimulus (the UCS) without prior learning.*

Next the tone and the food are paired—each pairing is called a *learning trial*—and the dog salivates. After several learning trials, if the tone is presented by itself, the dog salivates even though there is no food. The tone has now become a **conditioned stimulus (CS),** *a stimulus that, through*

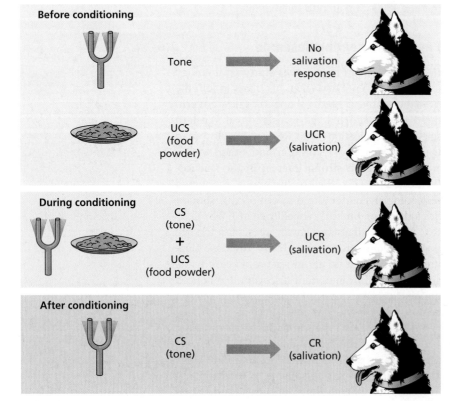

Figure 7.2

The classical conditioning process.

In classical conditioning, after a neutral stimulus such as a tone is repeatedly associated with food (unconditioned stimulus), the tone becomes a conditioned stimulus capable of eliciting a salivation response (conditioned response).

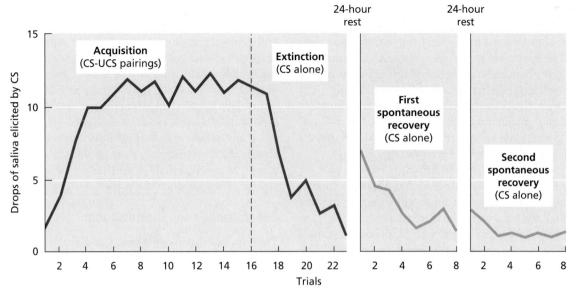

Figure 7.3

Acquisition, extinction, and spontaneous recovery.
The strength of the CR (salivation) increases during the acquisition phase as the CS (tone) and the UCS (food) are paired on each trial. During the extinction phase, only the CS is presented, and the strength of the CR decreases and finally disappears. After a rest period following extinction, presentation of the CS elicits a weaker CR (spontaneous recovery) that extinguishes more quickly than before.

association with a UCS, comes to elicit a conditioned response similar to the original UCR. Because the dog is now salivating to the tone, salivation has become a **conditioned response (CR),** *a response elicited by a conditioned stimulus.* Notice that when the dog salivates to food, this natural (unconditioned) reflex is called a UCR. But when it salivates to a tone, this learned (conditioned) response is called a CR.

During acquisition, a CS typically must be paired multiple times with a UCS to establish a strong CR (Figure 7.3). Pavlov also found that a tone became a CS more rapidly when it was followed by greater amounts of food. Indeed, when the UCS is intense and aversive—such as an electric shock or a traumatic event—conditioning may require only one CS-UCS pairing (Richard et al., 2000). Carol's car phobia illustrates this *one-trial (single-trial) learning.* As she explains to the therapist, her automobile accident was very traumatic:

> My car went out of control. It crashed into a light pole, rolled over, and began to burn. I . . . couldn't get out . . . I'm sorry, doctor, but even thinking about it is horrible. I had a broken pelvis and third-degree burns over half my body.

In Carol's example, a stimulus (riding in or seeing a car) became a CS after only one pairing with an intense UCS (an extremely painful crash). Fear was the UCR, and it became a CR triggered by the sight of cars (Figure 7.4).

The sequence and time interval of the CS-UCS pairing also affect conditioning. Learning usually occurs most quickly with a *forward short-delay pairing:* the CS (tone) appears first and is still present when the UCS (food) appears. In *forward trace*

Figure 7.4

Classical conditioning and Carol's car phobia.
It is likely that Carol's phobia of cars was acquired through classical conditioning.

pairing, the tone sounds and then stops, and afterward the food is presented. In forward pairing, it is often optimal for the CS to appear no more than 2 or 3 seconds before the UCS (Klein & Mowrer, 1989). Forward pairing has adaptive value because the CS signals the impending arrival of the UCS. Typically, presenting the CS and UCS at the same time (*simultaneous pairing*) produces less rapid conditioning, and learning is slowest when the CS is presented after the UCS (*backward pairing*).

Once a CR is established, it may persist for a long time. After her horrible accident, Carol's fear of cars persisted for months despite the fact that she was in no further crashes. Similarly, in posttraumatic stress disorder, exposure to stimuli (CS) associated with the traumatic event (UCS) can trigger stress responses long after the trauma occurred (Taylor, 2010).

To summarize, classical conditioning usually is strongest when (1) there are repeated CS-UCS pairings, (2) the UCS is more intense, (3) the sequence involves forward pairing, and (4) the time interval between the CS and UCS is short.

Extinction and Spontaneous Recovery

If classical conditioning is to help organisms adapt to their environment, there must be a way to eliminate the CR when it is no longer appropriate. Indeed, there is. **Extinction** *is a process in which the CS is presented repeatedly in the absence of the UCS, causing the CR to weaken and eventually disappear.* Each occurrence of the CS without the UCS is called an *extinction trial.* When Pavlov repeatedly presented the tone without the food, the dogs eventually stopped salivating to the tone (see Figure 7.3). Occasional re-pairings of the CS (e.g., tone) and the UCS (e.g., food) usually are required to maintain a CR.

Perhaps it seems inconsistent to you that Pavlov's dogs would eventually stop salivating to the tone if food no longer was presented with it, whereas Carol's phobia of cars persisted for months even though she was not in any additional crashes. How can we explain this?

thinking critically

WHY DID CAROL'S CAR PHOBIA PERSIST?
Reread the definition of extinction carefully. In Carol's case, identify the CS, UCS, and CR. Can you explain why her fear of cars did not extinguish on its own? Think about it, then see page 251.

Even when a CR extinguishes, not all traces of it are necessarily erased. Suppose we condition a dog to salivate to a tone. Then we repeatedly present the tone without food, and the dog eventually stops salivating to the tone. Later, if we present the tone alone, the dog may salivate once again. This is called **spontaneous recovery,** *the reappearance of a previously extinguished CR after a rest period and without new learning trials.* As Figure 7.3 shows, the spontaneously recovered CR usually is weaker than the initial CR and extinguishes more rapidly in the absence of the UCS.

Generalization and Discrimination

Thus far we have explained Carol's car phobia as a case of one-trial conditioning in which being in a car was paired with a traumatic experience. But why would Carol fear other cars when it was her old car—now long gone—that was in the accident?

Pavlov found that once a CR is acquired, the organism often responds not only to the original CS but also to stimuli that are similar to it. The greater the stimulus similarity, the greater the chance that a CR will occur. A dog that salivates to a medium-pitched tone is more likely to salivate to a new tone slightly different in pitch than to a very low- or high-pitched tone. Learning theorists call this **stimulus generalization:** *stimuli similar to the initial CS elicit a CR* (Figure 7.5).

Stimulus generalization serves critical adaptive functions. An animal that ignores the sound of rustling bushes and then is attacked by a hidden predator will (assuming it survives) become alarmed by the sound of rustling bushes in the future. If stimulus generalization did not occur, then

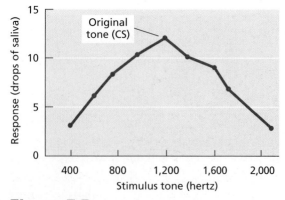

Figure 7.5

Stimulus generalization.
An animal will salivate most strongly to the CS that was originally paired with the UCS. Progressively weaker conditioned responses occur as stimuli become less similar to the CS, as seen here with tones of lower or higher frequencies (pitch).

the next time the animal heard rustling it would become alarmed only if the sound was identical to the rustling that preceded the earlier attack. This would be of little value to the animal's survival. Through stimulus generalization, however, the animal develops an alarm response to a range of rustling sounds. Some will be false alarms, but safe is better than sorry.

Unfortunately, maladaptive responses can occur when generalization spreads too far. The car involved in Carol's crash was gone, but after leaving the hospital her fear immediately generalized to the new car her husband had bought. Over time, stimulus generalization continued, although the fear was weaker:

> *Carol:* After a while, even the sight of a car started to make me nervous.
>
> *Therapist:* As nervous as riding in one?
>
> *Carol:* No, but still nervous. It's so stupid. I'd even turn off the TV during scenes involving car crashes.

To prevent stimulus generalization from running wild, organisms must be able to discriminate between irrelevant stimuli and those that may signal danger. An animal that became alarmed at every sound would exhaust itself from stress. In classical conditioning, **discrimination** *is demonstrated when a CR* (such as an alarm reaction) *occurs to one stimulus* (a sound) *but not to others.* Carol's fear of cars did not occur when she saw bicycles or trains.

When my mother was a girl, a large dog bit her several times. From then on, she feared dogs. Years later, when my brother wanted a dog, my mother would have none of it. But he pleaded endlessly. How could our family satisfy my brother's wish yet not trigger my mother's fear? The solution: get a dog as dissimilar as possible to the large dog that bit her, in hopes that her fear would display stimulus discrimination. We adopted a tiny Chihuahua puppy, and the plan half-succeeded. My mother was not afraid and adored the dog. Alas, my brother's fondness for big dogs failed to generalize to Chihuahuas, and he repeatedly called it a "yippity oversized rat."

Higher-Order Conditioning

Imagine that we expose a dog to repeated tone-food pairings and the tone becomes a CS that elicits a strong salivation response. Next, suppose that we present a neutral stimulus, such as a black square, and the dog does not salivate. Now, we present the black square just prior to the tone, but do not present any food. After repeated

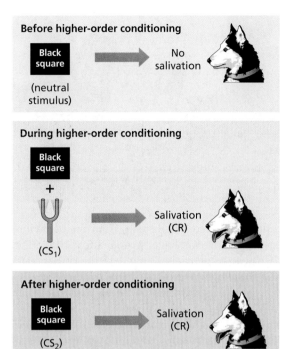

Figure 7.6

Higher-order conditioning. Once a tone has become a conditioned stimulus that triggers salivation, we can now use it to condition a salivation response to a new neutral stimulus: a black square. The tone is the CS_1. The black square becomes the CS_2.

square-tone pairings, the square will become a CS and elicit salivation by itself (Figure 7.6). This process is called **higher-order conditioning:** *a neutral stimulus becomes a CS after being paired with an already established CS.* Typically, a higher-order CS produces a CR that is weaker and extinguishes more rapidly than the original CR: the dog will salivate less to the black square than to the tone, and its response to the square will extinguish sooner.

Higher-order conditioning greatly expands the influence of conditioned stimuli (Hussaini et al., 2007). It can affect what we come to value, fear, like, or dislike. For example, political candidates try to get voters to like them by associating themselves with patriotic symbols, cuddly babies, famous people, and other conditioned stimuli that already trigger positive emotional reactions.

Applications of Classical Conditioning

Pavlov's belief that salivation was merely the tip of the classical conditioning iceberg has proven correct. Conditioning principles help us understand many human behaviors and problems.

Acquiring and Overcoming Fear

Building on Pavlov's discoveries, pioneering behaviorist John B. Watson challenged Freud's view of the causes of mental disorders, such as phobias. To explain Carol's car phobia, no assumptions about hidden unconscious conflicts or repressed

Figure 7.7

John Watson and Rosalie Rayner examine how Little Albert reacts to a furry mask.

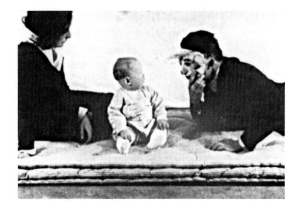

| Table 7.1 | Using Exposure Training to Reduce Fear |

This table lists 10 of 17 steps Mary Cover Jones used to eliminate Peter's fear of rabbits in a classic study.

Step	Peter's Progress
1.	Rabbit anywhere in room triggers fear.
2.	Rabbit 12 feet away tolerated.
4.	Rabbit 3 feet away tolerated.
5.	Rabbit close in cage tolerated.
6.	Rabbit free in room tolerated.
8.	Rabbit touched when free in room.
10.	Rabbit allowed on tray of high chair.
12.	Holds rabbit on lap.
16.	Fondles rabbit affectionately.
17.	Lets rabbit nibble his fingers.

Source: Adapted from Jones, 1924.

traumas are needed. Instead, from the behaviorist viewpoint, cars have become a fear-triggering CS due to a one-trial pairing with the UCS (crash) and subsequent stimulus generalization.

Does this explanation seem reasonable? It may, but almost any explanation can seem plausible in hindsight. Therefore, John B. Watson and Rosalie Rayner (1920) set out to obtain stronger evidence that fear could be conditioned. They studied an 11-month-old infant named Albert. One day, as Little Albert played in a hospital room, Watson and Rayner showed him a white rat. Albert displayed no sign of fear. Later, knowing that Albert was afraid of loud noises, they hit a steel bar with a hammer, making a loud noise as they showed Albert the rat. The noise scared Albert and made him cry. After several rat-noise pairings, the sight of the white rat alone made Albert cry.

To examine stimulus discrimination and generalization, Watson and Rayner exposed Albert to other test stimuli several days later. Albert displayed no fear when shown colored blocks, but furry white or gray objects, such as a rabbit and a bearded Santa Claus mask, made him cry (Figure 7.7). By the time Albert's mother took him from the hospital, he had not been exposed to any treatment designed to extinguish his fear. Unfortunately, we do not know what became of Albert after that.

Two other sources of evidence suggest that at least some fears are conditioned. First, laboratory experiments show that humans and other mammals become afraid of neutral stimuli that are paired with electric shock (Merz et al., 2010). Second, behavioral treatments partly based on classical conditioning principles are among the most effective psychotherapies for phobias (Eelen & Vervliet, 2006). The assumption is that if phobias are learned, they can be unlearned.

In 1924, psychologist Mary Cover Jones successfully treated a boy named Peter who had a strong fear of rabbits. Jones gradually extinguished Peter's fear using the procedure shown in Table 7.1. Her approach foreshadowed current behavior

therapies, called **exposure therapies,** *in which a patient is exposed to a stimulus (CS) that arouses an anxiety response (such as fear) without the presence of the UCS, allowing extinction to occur.* In reality, the origin of a patient's phobia is often unknown, and psychologists debate whether all phobias are learned (Coelho & Purkis, 2009). But, even so, in most cases, exposure treatments are effective.

Mental imagery, real-life situations, or both can be used to present the phobic stimulus. In one approach, *systematic desensitization,* the patient learns muscle relaxation techniques and is gradually exposed to the fear-provoking stimulus (Wolpe, 1958). Another approach, sometimes called *flooding,* immediately exposes the person to the phobic stimulus (Kneebone & Al-Daftary, 2006). In Carol's case, her therapist extinguished the car phobia in six sessions of flooding. He asked her to imagine vivid scenes in which she drove in freeway traffic and traveled on narrow mountain roads. As Carol's initially strong anxiety decreased, she was able to sit in her car and eventually drive it. Exposure therapies are highly effective and represent one of behaviorism's important applied legacies (Hamm, 2009).

thinking critically

WAS THE "LITTLE ALBERT" STUDY ETHICAL?

Review boards that oversee research ethics did not exist in the 1920s. Would you have approved Watson and Rayner's request to conduct the Little Albert study? Why or why not? Think about it, then see page 251.

Attraction and Aversion

Classical conditioning influences what attracts and pleasurably arouses us. Consider sexual arousal. The comment "It really turns me on when you wear that" reflects how a garment or scent of a partner's cologne can become a CS for arousal. People, fish, birds, and rats become more sexually aroused to originally neutral stimuli after those stimuli have been paired with a naturally arousing UCS (Domjan, 2000b).

Classical conditioning also can decrease our arousal and attraction to stimuli. This principle is used in **aversion therapy,** *which attempts to condition an aversion (a repulsion) to a stimulus that triggers unwanted behavior by pairing it with a noxious UCS.* To treat pedophiles (child molesters), a therapist may pair pictures of children with strong electric shock, and to reduce an alcoholic's attraction to alcohol, the patient may be given a drug that induces severe nausea when alcohol is consumed. Aversion therapies yield mixed results, often producing short-term changes that extinguish over time (Garbutt, 2009).

Conditioned attraction and aversion also influence our attitudes. By repeatedly pairing a CS with pleasant or unpleasant stimuli, we may develop a favorable or unfavorable attitude toward that CS. Advertising executives carefully link products to attractive and famous people, humor, and pleasurable interactions with family, friends, and the opposite sex (Figure 7.8). Marketing experiments show that the products become conditioned stimuli that elicit favorable consumer attitudes (Priluck & Till, 2004).

Sickness and Health

Through classical conditioning, our bodies can learn to respond in ways that either promote or harm our health. Let's look at three examples.

Allergic Reactions   Classical conditioning often can account for the appearance of physical symptoms that do not seem to have a medical cause. For example, by consistently pairing a neutral stimulus (e.g., a distinct odor) with a substance that naturally triggers an allergic reaction, the neutral stimulus can become a CS that elicits a similar allergic response (Irie et al., 2001). Conversely, by pairing a neutral stimulus (e.g., a novel-tasting drink) with an antiallergy substance (e.g., antihistamine), that stimulus can become a CS that reduces an allergic reaction such as a runny nose or skin rash (Goebel et al., 2008).

Anticipatory Nausea and Vomiting   Chemotherapy and radiation therapy save countless lives in the fight against cancer but often cause nausea and vomiting. Many cancer patients eventually develop **anticipatory nausea and vomiting (ANV):** *they become nauseated and may vomit anywhere from minutes to hours* before *a treatment session.*

ANV is a classically conditioned response (Parker et al., 2006). Initially neutral stimuli, such as hypodermic needles, the hospital room, or even the sight of a hospital, become associated with the treatment (the UCS) and act as conditioned stimuli that trigger nausea and vomiting (the UCR). Fortunately, as with conditioned fear, psychological treatments can help patients unlearn the ANV response (Edser, 2002). The patient may first be taught how to relax physically, and then the conditioned stimuli that trigger ANV are paired with relaxation and pleasant mental imagery.

The Immune System   As psychologist Robert Ader (2003; Ader & Cohen, 1975) discovered decades ago, even the immune system can be classically conditioned, affecting susceptibility to disease and fatal illness. As Figure 7.9 shows,

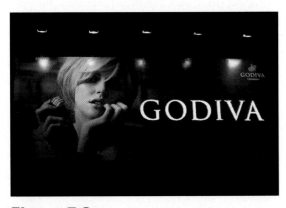

Figure 7.8

Advertisers attempt to classically condition favorable consumer attitudes to products by associating the products with other positive stimuli, such as physically attractive models.

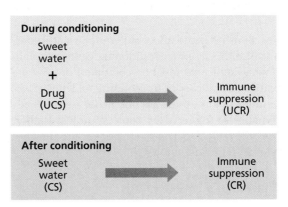

Figure 7.9

The immune system can be classically conditioned.

After being paired with an immune-suppressant drug, sweet water becomes a CS that triggers a reduced immune response.

when rats drink sweetened water (a neutral stimulus) that is paired with injections of a drug (the UCS) that suppresses immune activity (the UCR), the sweetened water becomes a CS that suppresses immune activity.

Conversely, conditioning can also increase immune functioning (DeMoranville et al., 2000). German researchers gave sweet sherbet to an experimental group of volunteers, along with an injection of epinephrine (i.e., adrenaline), which increases the activity of immune-system cells that attack tumors. Compared with control groups, people receiving the sherbet-epinephrine pairings subsequently reacted to the sherbet alone with a stronger immune response (Buske-Kirschbaum et al., 1992, 1994).

Classical conditioning also helps fight disease (Ader, 2003). One experiment involved mice suffering from a normally fatal illness that caused their immune systems to attack their own bodies (Ader & Cohen, 1982). By classically conditioning a sweet taste (CS) to trigger immune suppression (CR), the researchers reduced the mice's mortality rate. Later, a similar conditioning procedure was used along with drug therapy to successfully treat an 11-year-old girl who had a life-threatening disease in which her immune system was overactive (Olness & Ader, 1992).

test yourself   **Classical Conditioning**

A dog salivates to food but not to a bright light. After the light is paired with food for 15 trials, the dog salivates when the light is presented alone. After many "light only" trials, the dog stops salivating to the light. The next day, when the light is turned on (without food) the dog salivates.

Match the numbered term to the correct item on the right.

1. conditioned stimulus
2. unconditioned stimulus
3. spontaneous recovery
4. unconditioned response
5. extinction
6. conditioned response

a. salivation, to the food
b. salivation, to the light
c. the food
d. the light
e. salivation to the light stops
f. salivation to the light resumes

ANSWERS: 1-d, 2-c, 3-f, 4-a, 5-e, 6-b

OPERANT CONDITIONING: LEARNING THROUGH CONSEQUENCES

For all its power to affect our emotions, attitudes, and health, classical conditioning cannot explain how a dog learns to sit on command or how we learn to drive cars or use computers. Unlike salivating to a tone, these are not *elicited responses* automatically triggered by some stimulus. Rather, they are *emitted (voluntary) responses,* and they are learned in a different way.

Thorndike's Law of Effect

While Pavlov was studying classical conditioning, American psychology student Edward L. Thorndike (1898) was exploring how animals learn to solve problems. He built a special cage, called a *puzzle box,* that could be opened from the inside by pulling a string or stepping on a lever (Figure 7.10). Thorndike placed a hungry animal, such as a cat, inside the box. Food was put outside, and to get it the animal had to learn how to open the box. The cat scratched and pushed the bars, paced, and tried to dig through the floor. By chance, it eventually stepped on the lever, opening the door. Performance slowly improved with repeated trials, and over time the cat learned to press the lever soon after the door was shut.

Because performance improved slowly, Thorndike concluded that the animals did not attain *insight* into the solution. Rather, with trial and error, they gradually eliminated responses that failed to open the door and became more likely to perform the actions that worked. Thorndike (1911) called this process *instrumental learning* because an organism's behavior is instrumental in bringing about certain outcomes. He also proposed the

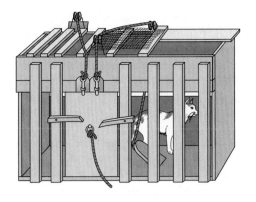

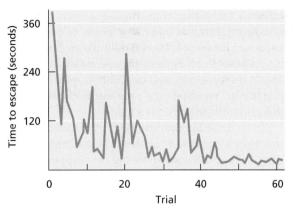

Figure 7.10

Thorndike's puzzle box.
Through trial and error, a cat eventually learns to open Thorndike's puzzle box in order to obtain food.
SOURCE: Based on Thorndike, 1898, 1911.

law of effect, *which states that in a given situation, a response followed by a satisfying consequence will become more likely to occur and a response followed by an annoying consequence will become less likely to occur.*

Skinner's Analysis of Operant Conditioning

Harvard psychologist B. F. Skinner, who built on and expanded Thorndike's work, was America's leading proponent of behaviorism throughout much of the 20th century. Skinner coined the term *operant behavior,* meaning that an organism *operates* on its environment in some way.

Operant conditioning *is a type of learning in which behavior is influenced by the consequences that follow it* (Skinner, 1938, 1953). Skinner designed

what has come to be known as a **Skinner box,** *a special chamber used to study operant conditioning experimentally.* A lever on one wall is positioned above a small cup. When the lever is depressed, a food pellet automatically drops into the cup. As shown in Figure 7.11, a hungry rat is put into the chamber and, as it moves about, it accidentally presses the lever. A food pellet clinks into the cup, and the rat eats it. We record the rat's behavior on a cumulative recorder, which shows that the rat presses the bar more frequently over time.

Skinner identified several types of consequences. For now, we will focus on two: *reinforcement* and *punishment.* With **reinforcement,** *a response is strengthened by an outcome that follows it.* Typically, the term *strengthened* is operationally defined as an increase in the frequency of a

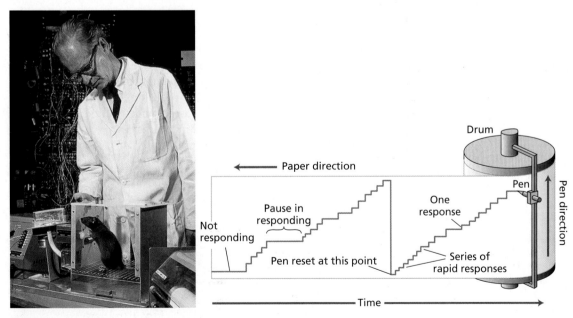

Figure 7.11

Measuring and reinforcing an operant response.
With B. F. Skinner watching, a rat raises up and presses a lever in an operant experimental chamber (Skinner box). This turns on a light inside the chamber. (Notice the silver lever just below the rat's front paws and the orange light to the left of its paws.) A food reinforcer is automatically delivered by the apparatus to the left of the box, and the rat's performance is displayed on a cumulative recorder. Today, a computer would record the responses.

response. The outcome (a stimulus or event) that increases the frequency of a response is called a *reinforcer*. Food pellets are reinforcers because they increase the rat's frequency of lever pressing. Once a response becomes established, reinforcers maintain it: the rat keeps pressing the lever because it continues to receive food.

In contrast to reinforcement, **punishment** *occurs when a response is weakened by outcomes that follow it.* Take our lever-pressing rat. Suppose we change things so that pressing the lever delivers a brief electric shock rather than food. If lever pressing decreases (which it will), then the electric shock represents a *punisher,* a consequence that weakens the behavior. Notice that reinforcers and punishers are defined in terms of their observable effects on behavior. If the food doesn't increase lever pressing, then it is not a reinforcer for this rat at this time.

Following Darwin's notion of natural selection, which applies to species adaptation, Skinner viewed operant conditioning as a type of natural selection that facilitates an organism's personal adaptation to the environment. Through operant conditioning, organisms generally learn to increase behaviors that are followed by favorable consequences and reduce behaviors that are followed by unfavorable consequences, a pattern consistent with Thorndike's law of effect.

Skinner's analysis of operant behavior involves three kinds of events that form a three-part contingency: (1) *antecedents*, which are stimuli that are present before a behavior occurs, (2) *behaviors* that the organism emits, and (3) *consequences* that follow the behaviors. Thus,

> IF antecedent stimuli are present (IF I say, "Sit!")
>
> AND behavior is emitted (AND my dog Jessie sits),
>
> THEN consequences will occur (THEN Jessie will receive a treat).

The relation between the behavior and the consequence is called a *contingency*. After I say, "Sit!" the consequence of receiving food is contingent on Jessie's response of sitting.

Distinguishing Operant from Classical Conditioning

Despite accurately learning all of the terms involved in classical and operant conditioning, some students still have difficulty distinguishing between these two types of learning. As we explore operant conditioning more closely, keep in mind these differences between classical and operant conditioning:

- Classical conditioning focuses on *elicited* behaviors: the conditioned response (e.g., salivation) is triggered involuntarily, almost like a reflex, by the conditioned stimulus (e.g., a tone). Operant conditioning focuses on *emitted* behaviors: in a given situation, the organism generates responses (e.g., pressing a lever) that are under its physical control.

- In classical conditioning, learning occurs through CS-UCS pairings. In other words, one stimulus (e.g., a tone) becomes associated with another stimulus (e.g., food). In operant conditioning, behavior changes when responses made by the organism (e.g., pressing a lever) become associated with certain consequences (e.g., receiving food).

- In classical conditioning, the CS (e.g., tone) occurs before the CR (e.g., salivation) and triggers it. In operant conditioning, the reinforcing or punishing consequences occur *after* a response is made. Table 7.2 summarizes these differences.

Also realize that although classical and operant conditioning are different processes, many learning

Table **7.2** | **Some Differences between Classical and Operant Conditioning**

Question	Classical Conditioning	Operant Conditioning
What type of behavior is involved?	Elicited: CR is a reflexlike response (e.g., salivation, fear) triggered by CS (e.g., tone, sight of cars)	Emitted: response (e.g., lever pressing, sitting down) operates on the environment and is under the organism's control
How does learning occur?	Through CS-UCS pairings, one stimulus (CS; tone) is associated with another stimulus (UCS; food)	Organism's responses are associated with reinforcing, punishing, or neutral consequences
What is the sequence of events?	The CS occurs *before* the CR and triggers it (e.g., tone triggers salivation; sight of car triggers fear)	Consequences *follow* an organism's response (e.g., food is delivered after a lever is pressed); antecedent stimuli may set the occasion for emitting certain responses

situations involve both. Have you ever had a teacher who squeaked chalk when writing on a blackboard? One of your authors had a high school teacher who was a pro at this. Soon the mere sight of him raising the chalk to the board became a CS that automatically triggered a CR of shivers up the spine. It also was a signal for the students to put their fingers in their ears (an operant response), which was reinforced by the consequence of reducing the squeaking sound. Thus one stimulus (raising the chalk) can have classical as well as operant functions.

Antecedent Conditions: Identifying When to Respond

In operant conditioning, the antecedent may be a general situation or a specific stimulus. Let's return to our lever-pressing rat. At present, simply being in the Skinner box is the antecedent condition. In this situation, the rat will press the lever. Suppose we place a light on the wall above the lever. When the light is on, pressing the lever dispenses food, but when the light is off, no food is given. The rat

will soon learn to press the lever only when the light is on. The light becomes a **discriminative stimulus,** *a signal that a particular response will now produce certain consequences.* Discriminative stimuli set the occasion for operant responses. The sight of the teacher raising chalk to the blackboard was—in operant conditioning terms—a discriminative stimulus signaling it was time for the students to put their fingers in their ears.

Discriminative stimuli guide much of your everyday behavior. Food on your plate, classroom bells, the words people speak to you, and the sight of a friend's face are all discriminative stimuli that set the occasion for you to make certain responses.

Consequences: Determining How to Respond

Behavior is governed by its consequences. Two major types of reinforcement strengthen responses, and two major types of punishment weaken them. Operant behavior also is weakened by extinction. Figure 7.12 shows these processes.

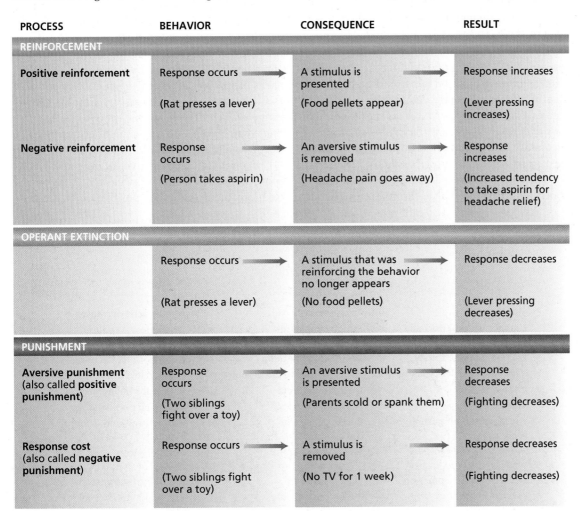

PROCESS	BEHAVIOR	CONSEQUENCE	RESULT
REINFORCEMENT			
Positive reinforcement	Response occurs → (Rat presses a lever)	A stimulus is presented → (Food pellets appear)	Response increases (Lever pressing increases)
Negative reinforcement	Response occurs (Person takes aspirin)	An aversive stimulus is removed → (Headache pain goes away)	Response increases (Increased tendency to take aspirin for headache relief)
OPERANT EXTINCTION			
	Response occurs → (Rat presses a lever)	A stimulus that was reinforcing the behavior no longer appears → (No food pellets)	Response decreases (Lever pressing decreases)
PUNISHMENT			
Aversive punishment (also called **positive punishment**)	Response occurs → (Two siblings fight over a toy)	An aversive stimulus is presented → (Parents scold or spank them)	Response decreases (Fighting decreases)
Response cost (also called **negative punishment**)	Response occurs → (Two siblings fight over a toy)	A stimulus is removed → (No TV for 1 week)	Response decreases (Fighting decreases)

Figure 7.12

Five major operant processes: positive reinforcement, negative reinforcement, operant extinction, aversive punishment, and response cost.

Positive Reinforcement

Positive reinforcement *occurs when a response is strengthened by the subsequent presentation of a stimulus.* A rat receives food pellets when it presses a lever and eventually begins to press the lever more often. A new employee, praised by her boss for completing a small project quickly, begins to complete more of her projects on time. The stimulus that follows and strengthens the response is called a *positive reinforcer.* Food, drink, comforting physical contact, attention, praise, and money are common positive reinforcers. In our chapter-opening vignette, the volunteer's behavior of soliciting money for charity is positively reinforced by each donation, by the praise of fellow workers at the charity, and by her feeling of pride in helping people.

The term *reward* is often misused as a synonym for the term *positive reinforcer.* Behaviorists prefer *positive reinforcer* because it focuses on how consequences affect behavior. In many instances, rewards do not function as positive reinforcers. Parents may give a child a reward (such as a new toy) for cleaning her room, but if the child does not clean her room in the future, then the toy was not a positive reinforcer for that behavior.

Primary and Secondary Reinforcers Psychologists distinguish between two broad types of positive reinforcers: **Primary reinforcers** *are stimuli, such as food and water, that an organism naturally finds reinforcing because they satisfy biological needs.* **Secondary (conditioned) reinforcers** *are stimuli that acquire reinforcing properties through their association with primary reinforcers.* Money is a conditioned reinforcer. Similarly, chimpanzees learn to value, work for, and even hoard tokens (a secondary reinforcer) that they can place into a vending machine to obtain raisins.

Secondary reinforcers illustrate how behavior often depends on both classical and operant conditioning. Consider dog training. Correct responses, such as sitting on command, initially are operantly reinforced with food. But just before delivering food, the trainer enthusiastically says, "Good Dog!" At first the phrase "Good Dog!" is just meaningless sounds to the dog. But by repeatedly pairing "Good Dog!" with food each time the dog sits, "Good Dog!" becomes a classically conditioned stimulus that elicits excitement (salivation, tail wagging). Now the trainer can use the phrase "Good Dog!" as a secondary reinforcer, instead of always having to carry and provide food.

Negative Reinforcement

B. F. Skinner noted that when a response pays off, it is more likely to occur in the future. In everyday life, our behaviors pay off not only when they lead to the presentation of praise, money, and so on, but also when they enable us to get rid of or avoid something we find aversive. For example, taking aspirin pays off because it relieves a headache. This process is called **negative reinforcement:** *a response is strengthened by the subsequent removal (or avoidance) of an aversive stimulus* (see Figure 7.12). The aversive stimulus that is removed (e.g., the headache) is called a *negative reinforcer.* Figure 7.13 presents other examples of negative reinforcement.

Do not confuse negative reinforcement with punishment. Punishment weakens a response. Reinforcement—whether positive or negative—

Figure 7.13

Negative reinforcement in everyday life.
Here are some common examples of negative reinforcement. In each case, the consequence strengthens the behavior. There are countless other examples. Can you think of a few?

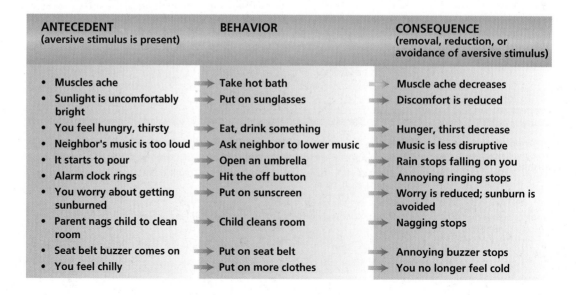

ANTECEDENT (aversive stimulus is present)	BEHAVIOR	CONSEQUENCE (removal, reduction, or avoidance of aversive stimulus)
• Muscles ache	Take hot bath	Muscle ache decreases
• Sunlight is uncomfortably bright	Put on sunglasses	Discomfort is reduced
• You feel hungry, thirsty	Eat, drink something	Hunger, thirst decrease
• Neighbor's music is too loud	Ask neighbor to lower music	Music is less disruptive
• It starts to pour	Open an umbrella	Rain stops falling on you
• Alarm clock rings	Hit the off button	Annoying ringing stops
• You worry about getting sunburned	Put on sunscreen	Worry is reduced; sunburn is avoided
• Parent nags child to clean room	Child cleans room	Nagging stops
• Seat belt buzzer comes on	Put on seat belt	Annoying buzzer stops
• You feel chilly	Put on more clothes	You no longer feel cold

strengthens a response (or maintains it once it has reached full strength). When it comes to the terms *positive reinforcement* and *negative reinforcement*, the adjectives *positive* and *negative* do not mean "good" and "bad." Rather, they refer to procedures: *positive* refers to presenting a stimulus; *negative* refers to removing a stimulus.

Negative reinforcement plays a key role in helping us learn to escape from and avoid aversive situations. While showering, have you ever heard someone flush a toilet, only to have your shower water turn scalding hot? Your response of backing away is negatively reinforced—strengthened—by the escape from (i.e., removal of) the scalding water. Soon the mere sound of the flush becomes a signal—a discriminative stimulus—for you to back away. You successfully avoid the scalding water, which negatively reinforces your response of backing away as soon as you hear the flush.

Operant Extinction

Operant extinction *is the weakening and eventual disappearance of a response because it is no longer reinforced.* When previously reinforced behaviors no longer pay off, we are likely to abandon and replace them with more successful ones. If pressing a lever no longer results in food pellets, the rat will eventually stop making this response.

The degree to which nonreinforced responses persist is called *resistance to extinction*. Nonreinforced responses may stop quickly (low resistance), or they may keep occurring hundreds or thousands of times (high resistance). People who solicit charitable donations, like the woman in Las Vegas, do not stop just because 100 passersby in a row fail to give money. As we explain later, resistance to extinction is strongly influenced by the pattern of reinforcement that has previously maintained the behavior.

Operant extinction often provides a good alternative to punishment as a method for reducing undesirable behaviors. Consider the case of "Pascal the Rascal" (author's files):

> Mrs. Adams sought help at a child guidance clinic because her 4-year-old son, Pascal, delighted in misbehaving. She had tried to reason with him. Then she resorted to yelling. When that failed, Mrs. Adams began spanking Pascal. Even that did not work.

The intended punishments failed because they actually reinforced Pascal with what he wanted most: attention. The psychologist told Mrs. Adams that as difficult as it might be at times, she needed to ignore Pascal when he misbehaved, thereby depriving him of attention. Mrs. Adams was also told to reinforce Pascal's desirable behaviors by paying attention to him when he acted accordingly. Soon thereafter, Pascal was no longer a rascal.

Aversive Punishment

Like reinforcement, punishment comes in two forms. One involves actively *applying* aversive stimuli, such as painful slaps, electric shock, and verbal reprimands. This is called **aversive punishment** (also called **positive punishment,** or **punishment by application**): *a response is weakened by the subsequent presentation of a stimulus.* Spanking and scolding a child for misbehaving are obvious examples, but so is a child's touching a hot stovetop burner. The pain delivered by the burner makes it less likely that the child will touch it in the future. Likewise, a high school student wears a new blouse, her friends' facial expressions say "ugh," and she tosses the blouse into the back of her closet.

Aversive punishment can produce rapid results, an important consideration when it is necessary to stop a particularly dangerous behavior, such as an animal or person attacking someone. Although aversive punishment often works, the use of spanking and other forms of physical punishment for disciplinary purposes is controversial. Let's explore this issue.

Myth or Reality?   Spanking Is a Necessary Evil

Growing up, were you spanked or slapped for misbehaving? If you were an American child, your answer likely is yes. In a national survey of American parents, 94 percent reported spanking their children by age 4 (Straus & Stewart, 1999). Similarly, 91 percent of American undergraduates surveyed at one university said they were physically punished growing up (Chang et al., 2006). Most American parents today still spank or slap (Feigelman et al., 2009).

Should they? Sweden banned all child corporal (i.e., physical) punishment in 1979, and 23 other countries have followed suit (Straus, 2008). Moreover, 100 countries ban corporal punishment in schools. In the United States, 49 of 50 states allow parents to use physical punishment, and 21 permit it in public schools (Gershoff, 2008b). The spanking debate is a hot topic that keeps surfacing in U.S. media outlets such as *Fox News.com* (2010), *MSNBC.com*

Continued

(Snyderman, 2009), *Newsweek* (Kalb, 2008), NBC's *The Today Show* (2009), and CBS's *The Early Show* (2009). As one reporter notes, "It's a topic that riles up emotions and opinions. . . . Online message boards are flooded" (Kalb, 2008, para. 1).

Traditional wisdom claims, "Spare the rod, spoil the child." What's the evidence? In a landmark report, psychologist Elizabeth Gershoff (2002) meta-analyzed 88 studies on parental use of corporal punishment, involving about 36,000 participants. Most studies were correlational. Five examined whether corporal punishment, overall, temporarily suppressed children's misbehavior; only three found that it did. In contrast, corporal punishment was consistently associated with negative outcomes including:

- decreased quality of the parent-child relationship;
- poorer internalization of moral standards;
- greater aggressive, delinquent, and antisocial behavior in childhood and, later, in adulthood;
- poorer mental health during childhood and adulthood;
- increased risk of childhood physical abuse and of later becoming a physically abusive adult.

Subsequent studies have found similar and other associations with negative child development outcomes (Berlin et al., 2009; Zolotor et al., 2008).

Are their alternative explanations? As a critical thinker, recall that correlation does not establish causation. Consider the punishment—aggression association. It's possible that corporal punishment causes children to behave more aggressively. Many psychologists express this concern because physical punishment may send a message to the child that aggression is appropriate and effective (Gershoff, 2008b). But we also must consider the bidirectionality problem. Perhaps children who aggress and misbehave more cause their parents to be more physically punitive. Further, we must consider the third-variable problem. Maybe something else—an inherited or environmental factor—causes children to behave more aggressively and also causes parents to punish more physically, making it seem as though aggression and corporal punishment are causally related when in fact they are not (Larzelere & Kuhn, 2005). Some correlational studies use procedures to partly reduce these interpretive problems, although many do not.

What additional evidence would be helpful? After Sweden banned child corporal punishment, did children become poorly socialized? It appears that the first Swedish generation raised after the ban committed an unusually high frequency of criminal assaults against minors (Larzelere, 2008). But, more broadly, teenage rates of theft, rape, narcotics trafficking, drug use, and suicide all declined (Durrant, 2000). Economic and other national factors likely influenced these results, so we can't conclude that banning corporal punishment caused these changes. Yet as Joan Durrant (2000) notes, whatever the cause, "Swedish youth have not become more unruly, undersocialized, or self-destructive following the . . . ban. In fact, most measures demonstrated a substantial improvement in youth well-being" (p. 451).

Consider one final point: spanking isn't the only disciplinary method linked to negative child development outcomes. When other techniques are compared directly to "customary" (nonsevere) spanking, similar child development outcomes are often found (Larzelere & Kuhn, 2005). Still, if spanking and the most effective nonphysical punishment methods often produce similar results for some outcomes, then why spank?

Is spanking a necessary evil? To some American and Canadian child-rearing researchers, "evil," yes; "necessary," no (Durrant et al., 2009; Straus, 2008). They favor a ban on child corporal punishment, arguing that such punishment has mixed short-term and little long-term effectiveness in improving children's behavior, yet increases the risk for negative child development outcomes (Gershoff, 2008b). Not so fast, say other psychologists. While not advocating the broad use of corporal punishment, they feel the evidence doesn't support an outright ban and instead demonstrates that there are some circumstances in which customary disciplinary spanking is effective and appropriate: for example, as a backup when time-outs or other nonphysical disciplinary techniques fail with children who have behavior problems (Larzelere & Baumrind, 2010).

But even if so, at least in most situations, the current evidence suggests it's a myth that child discipline needs to be physical. As for legal bans, such decisions involve more than scientific evidence. They invoke beliefs and values about child rearing, family privacy, parental freedoms, and children's rights (Holden, 2010). After examining the preceding evidence, what are your views?

Response Cost

Loss of privileges, groundings, and monetary fines represent another approach to modifying behavior. They take away something that an individual finds satisfying. In **response cost** (also called **negative punishment,** or **punishment by removal**), *a response is weakened by the subsequent removal of a stimulus* (i.e., "that'll cost you"). A child who misbehaves may be punished with a time-out, in which he or she has to sit quietly (possibly in isolation) for a period of time; this temporarily removes opportunities to play, watch TV, or participate in other enjoyable activities. Response cost, of course, is not limited to disciplining children or teenagers, as any automobile driver who has paid a fine for speeding knows (that'll *really* cost you). And even adults can receive a time-out (Figure 7.14).

Many psychologists who counsel parents on modifying children's behavior favor response cost over physical punishment (Gershoff, 2008a). Still, all types of disciplinary punishment have limitations. They may suppress behavior but do not cause an organism to forget how to make the response. Because they tell us what not to do but don't necessarily help us learn what to do, it is important to use positive reinforcement to strengthen desirable alternative responses directly. Finally, punishment may arouse negative emotions, such as fear and anger (Jay et al., 2006). This can produce dislike and avoidance of the person delivering the punishment.

Skinner (1953) believed that punishing behavior was not an effective way to produce long-term change. Yet research indicates that under some conditions, punishment can promote enduring changes in behavior (Domjan, 2000a). As psychologist George Holden (2002) notes, "To be effective, it must occur after every transgression, be immediate, be intense at least for the first transgression, and not be signaled by a discriminative stimulus," (p. 591) such as a threat or warning. Unfortunately, as Holden also notes, "These conditions represent a tall order for parents; in fact, it is likely parents are destined to fail on all four counts." For example, parents cannot always be present when children transgress.

Reinforcing desired responses and operantly extinguishing misbehavior often provide good alternatives to punishment (recall the case of Pascal the Rascal). But these approaches also have limits. Reinforced behaviors may extinguish or fail to generalize (as when children act politely only when parents are present), and attempts to operantly extinguish misbehavior may fail.

Immediate, Delayed, and Reciprocal Consequences

In general, a consequence that occurs immediately after a behavior has a stronger effect than one that is delayed. Training animals typically requires immediate reinforcement so that they associate the correct response, rather than a subsequent behavior, with the reinforcer.

Because humans can imagine future consequences, our behavior is less rigidly controlled by the timing of consequences. Still, the power of immediate reinforcement helps explain why many people continue to engage in behaviors with maladaptive long-term consequences. Chronic drug users usually find it difficult to stop because the immediate reinforcing consequences of the drug override the delayed benefits of not using the drug (e.g., being healthier). With many drugs, use is positively reinforced by feelings of pleasure

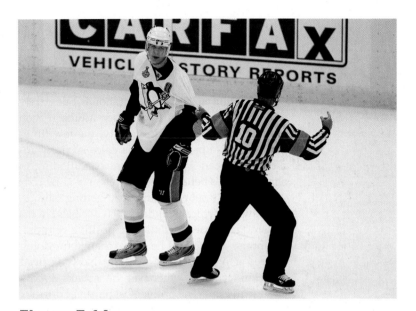

Figure 7.14

In ice hockey, misbehavior can earn a time-out in the penalty box.

that result from enhanced dopamine activity (Julien, 2005). Powerful negative reinforcers also play a role. Chronic cigarette smokers experience increased tension as the nicotine level in their blood drops after their last cigarette. When they smoke again, tension decreases. Thus smoking is negatively reinforced by the removal of unpleasant tension (Battista et al., 2008).

Finally, realize that in everyday life, learning frequently is a reciprocal process—a two-way street involving a sequence of responses between organisms. Whether it's friends hanging out or a tiger chasing a gazelle, each response by one organism may reinforce, punish, help extinguish, or classically condition the other organism's behavior.

? thinking critically

CAN YOU EXPLAIN THE "SUPERMARKET TANTRUM"?

At the market, a child asks his dad to buy candy. He refuses. The child screams and won't stop. Soon the father can't stand it, buys the candy, and the child's tantrum ends. A week later this scene repeats, but the father gives in as soon as the tantrum starts. The next time the child asks for candy, the father just says, "okay." Use concepts of reinforcement and punishment to explain this sequence of events. Then, see page 251.

Shaping and Chaining: Taking One Step at a Time

Sami is a shy 12-year-old boy diagnosed with developmental delays. For years, he has displayed *selective mutism:* he speaks at home but rarely with children, teachers, or other adults (Facon et al., 2008). In a day-care facility, the few times he moves his lips to speak, his voice is barely audible. How can we use operant conditioning to change Sami's behavior?

First, let's set a specific goal: getting Sami to speak with "typical" loudness (70 decibels) in his classroom. Second, let's select positive reinforcers: praise and tokens he can exchange for doing desired activities (e.g., bike riding). Now, we need to reinforce Sami whenever he speaks loudly enough in class. The problem is, he never does so.

Fortunately, Skinner discovered a powerful process for overcoming such problems: **shaping,** *which involves reinforcing "successive approximations" toward a final response.* One-on-one with Sami, we reinforce him for speaking single words at a low decibel level (44 dB). This is the first approximation toward our final goal (Figure 7.15). Next, we reinforce him only if he speaks a little more loudly (say, 47 dB). This is the second approximation. We continue this process in small decibel increments until he is speaking words at 70 dB or louder. Next, we move on to sentences, then to sentences in the presence of multiple people, and eventually to speaking in his classroom. Based on a similar shaping procedure, Sami learned to speak and become more socially interactive at day care (Facon et al., 2008).

Even when behaviors can be learned through trial and error—such as a rat learning to press a lever for food—shaping can speed up the process. By reinforcing successive approximations—such as standing near the lever, raising a front paw, touching the lever, and finally depressing the lever—acquisition time is reduced.

Another procedure, **chaining,** *is used to develop a sequence (chain) of responses by reinforcing each response with the opportunity to perform the next response.* Suppose a rat has learned to press a lever when a light is on to receive food. Next we place a bell nearby. By accident, the rat bumps into and rings the bell, which turns on the light. Seeing the light, the rat runs to and presses the lever. Over time, the rat will learn to ring the bell because this response is reinforced by the light turning on, which provides the opportunity to press the lever for food. As in this example, chaining often begins with the final response in the sequence and works backward toward the first response (Williams & Burkholder, 2008). Figure 7.16 shows another example.

The behaviors that we display in everyday life often develop through shaping and chaining. Recall the father who initially refused his child's

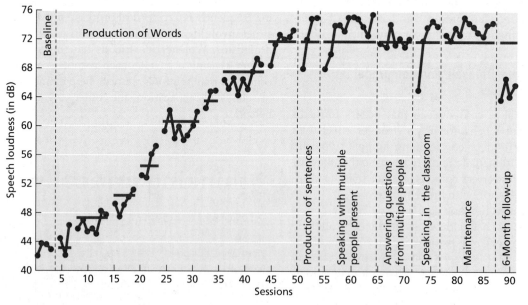

Figure 7.15

Using shaping to treat selective mutism.

Before treatment (baseline), researchers ask Sami questions and record how loudly (in decibels) he replies. Next, Sami is reinforced each time at least a one-word response meets or exceeds progressively higher decibel criteria (the horizontal lines). Shaping then proceeds to more challenging contexts and reaches the target situation of Sami speaking in the classroom. During the maintenance phase, reinforcement is gradually reduced so that Sami's behavior won't extinguish when the treatment ends. At a 6-month follow-up, Sami still can easily be heard. Source: From Facon et al., 2008.

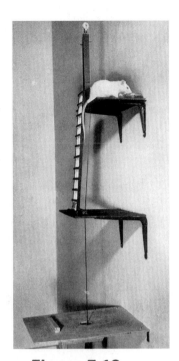

Figure 7.16

Chaining a sequence of responses.

Through chaining, this rat has learned to climb a ladder to reach a string, pull on the string to raise the ladder, and then climb the ladder again to reach food at the top. Often, this training begins with the last step in the chain. Then, working backward, each prior step in the chain is reinforced by the opportunity to perform the next step.

request for candy, then gave in after a lengthy tantrum, then gave in as soon as a tantrum started, and finally just said okay to the request. In essence, his response of agreeing immediately was shaped. Instructors who teach musical, athletic, and academic skills often shape their students' performance by starting with a simple response and reinforcing progressively closer approximations to the complex response that is ultimately desired.

Generalization and Discrimination

As in classical conditioning, operant responses may generalize to similar antecedent situations. A dog taught by its owner to "Sit!" will likely start sitting when other people give the command. A young child who touches a hot stovetop burner learns to avoid touching not only that burner but other hot burners as well. Thus, in **operant generalization,** *an operant response occurs to a new antecedent stimulus or situation that is similar to the original one.*

Through experience, we also learn to discriminate between antecedent conditions. Children learn to raid the cookie jar only when the parents are not in the kitchen. We learn to board buses and trains marked by specific symbols (79: Express) and avoid otherwise identical vehicles with different symbols (78: Local). **Operant discrimination** *means that an operant response will occur to one antecedent stimulus but not to another.* These antecedent stimuli—parents' presence or absence, bus markings—are discriminative stimuli. *A behavior that is influenced by discriminative stimuli is said to be under* **stimulus control.** The sight of a police car exerts stimulus control over most people's driving behavior.

The concept of operant discrimination gives science a powerful tool for examining the perceptual and cognitive abilities of human infants and nonhuman species. We can't ask infants and animals to tell us if they can distinguish between different colors, sounds, faces, and so on. But by using a procedure called *operant discrimination training*, we can teach an organism, for example, that pressing a lever when a red light is on produces a food reinforcer. Now all we have to do is change the color of the light and not reinforce any response when that light is on. If the organism learns to respond to one color and not the other, we infer that it can discriminate between them.

Schedules of Reinforcement

In daily life, reinforcement comes in different patterns and frequencies. These patterns, called *schedules of reinforcement*, have strong and predictable effects on learning, extinction, and performance (Ferster & Skinner, 1957; Haluk & Wickman, 2010). The most basic distinction is between continuous and partial reinforcement. With **continuous reinforcement,** *every response of a particular type is reinforced.* Every press of the lever results in food pellets. Every $1.25 deposit in the soda machine results in a can of cool, bubbly drink. With **partial (intermittent) reinforcement,** *only a* *portion of the responses of a particular type are reinforced.* (Hereafter, when discussing reinforcement schedules, we will simply use the term *response* to refer to the particular behavior of interest.)

Partial reinforcement schedules can be categorized along two important dimensions. The first is ratio versus interval schedules. On *ratio schedules,* a certain percentage of responses are reinforced. For example, we might decide to reinforce only 50 percent of the rat's lever presses with food. The key factor is that ratio schedules are based on the number of responses: more responses, more reinforcement. On *interval schedules,* a certain amount of time must elapse between reinforcements, regardless of how many responses might occur during that interval. We might reinforce lever pressing only once per minute, whether the rat presses the lever 5, 10, or 60 times. The key factor is that interval schedules are based on the passage of time.

The second dimension is fixed versus variable schedules. On a *fixed schedule,* reinforcement always occurs after a fixed number of responses or after a fixed time interval. On a *variable schedule,* the required number of responses or the time interval between them varies at random around an average. Combining these two dimensions creates four types of reinforcement schedules (Figure 7.17).

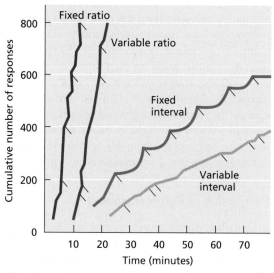

Figure 7.17

Partial reinforcement schedules affect performance.
Each type of positive reinforcement schedule produces a typical cumulative response curve. The hash marks indicate the delivery of a reinforcer. Ratio schedules produce a high rate of responding, as shown in the steep slopes of the curves. Variable schedules typically produce a steadier rate of responding than fixed schedules. Notice the prominent scalloped pattern in the fixed-interval schedule; responding decreases immediately after reinforcement and then increases as the time for the next reinforcement approaches.

Fixed-Ratio Schedule

On a **fixed-ratio (FR) schedule,** *reinforcement is given after a fixed number of responses.* For example, FR-3 means that reinforcement occurs after every third response, regardless of how long it takes for those responses to occur.

If we told you that you would receive $1 every 3 times you pressed a lever, would you work hard? Skinner found that fixed-ratio schedules produce high rates of responding. That is one reason why some businesses prefer paying employees' wages based on a set number of items produced. If the ratio is gradually increased over time, many responses can be obtained with relatively few reinforcements. Pigeons in a Skinner box have been known to wear down their beaks pecking a disc on an FR-20,000 schedule (one reinforcer per 20,000 responses).

FR schedules have a second characteristic effect. As shown in Figure 7.17, the organism may pause briefly after each reinforcement, perhaps because the next response (or responses) is never reinforced.

Variable-Ratio Schedule

On a **variable-ratio (VR) schedule,** *reinforcement is given after a variable number of responses, all centered around an average.* A VR-3 schedule means that, *on average,* 3 responses are required for reinforcement. For example, for the first 12 responses, reinforcement might occur after responses 2, 3, 6, and 11.

VR schedules, like FR schedules, produce a high rate of responding. But because reinforcement is less predictable (the next response *might* be reinforced), there often is less pausing after reinforcement and a steadier rate of responding, as shown in Figure 7.17. VR schedules also are highly resistant to extinction because the organism learns that long periods of no payoff will eventually be followed by reinforcement.

Gambling activities are maintained by VR schedules. For example, the gambler in our opening vignette plays a slot machine programmed to pay off an average of every 20 pulls (VR-20). After 8 pulls, he receives a 10-coin jackpot. After 2 more attempts, he hits a 15-coin jackpot. But then, after 30 more attempts, nothing. He's frustrated but still hooked by the VR schedule. That next attempt just might be the one that pays off, so he plays again . . . and again.

Fixed-Interval Schedule

On a **fixed-interval (FI) schedule,** *the first response that occurs after a fixed time interval is reinforced.*

Suppose a rat is pressing a lever on an FI-3 (3-minute) schedule. After a lever press is reinforced, for the next 3 minutes it makes no difference how many more times the rat responds. There will be no further reinforcement. Once these 3 minutes elapse, the next lever press is reinforced. The FI schedule's characteristic response pattern is shown in Figure 7.17. Notice the pronounced scalloping after each reinforcement. Responding slows after reinforcement and becomes more frequent as the time for the next reinforcement draws near.

In college, many instructors give exams at equal (or nearly equal) intervals, perhaps one exam every 3 or 4 weeks. Does your study behavior resemble the scalloped pattern shown in Figure 7.17, reflecting little studying immediately following each exam and cramming just before the next one? This uneven performance rate is typical of FI schedules.

For students who are motivated solely by the prospect of getting good grades, and not by the goal of acquiring knowledge in a particular course or by other goals, exams that occur at regular intervals (e.g., every two weeks) reinforce study behavior on a fixed-interval schedule. In other words, studying for an exam often calls for responding to questions about the course material (e.g., on practice tests, study guide tests, self-made flash cards, or other verbal rehearsal). However, correct responses are reinforced with actual grade points only after a fixed time interval has passed, and the students are taking a new, official course exam.

Variable-Interval Schedule

On a **variable-interval (VI) schedule,** *reinforcement is given for the first response that occurs after a variable time interval, centered around an average.* A VI-3 schedule means that, *on average,* there is a 3-minute interval between opportunities to obtain reinforcement. Sometimes, responses a few seconds apart may be reinforced; at other times, the interval may be many minutes. As Figure 7.17 shows, because the availability of reinforcement is less predictable than on an FI schedule, the VI schedule produces a steadier response rate.

Pop quizzes represent a VI schedule. A course might average a quiz every week, but the unpredictable timing will likely produce a steadier approach to studying than regularly scheduled quizzes. Random drug testing and roadside speed traps also reflect VI schedules. They reinforce desired behaviors (staying drug-free, driving within the speed limit) by appearing at unpredictable intervals. Of course, they also punish undesired behaviors with suspensions and fines!

Reinforcement Schedules, Learning, and Extinction

Continuous reinforcement has a key advantage over partial reinforcement: it produces more rapid learning because the association between a behavior and its consequences is easier to perceive. However, it also has a disadvantage: continuously reinforced responses usually extinguish more rapidly, because the sudden shift to no reinforcement is easier to perceive (Valles et al., 2006).

Partial reinforcement produces behavior that is learned more slowly but is more resistant to extinction. Especially when reinforcement has been unpredictable in the past, it takes longer to learn that it is gone forever. People do not continue to drop coins into a soda machine that doesn't deliver, because vending machines are supposed to operate on a continuous schedule. But it would take many pulls on a slot machine to recognize that it had stopped paying off completely. To sum up, the best way to promote fast learning and high resistance to extinction is to begin reinforcing a desired behavior on a continuous schedule until the behavior is well established and then shift to a partial (preferably variable) schedule that is gradually made more demanding.

Escape and Avoidance Conditioning

Behavior often involves escaping from or avoiding aversive situations. Escape occurs when we take medications to relieve pain or put on more clothes when we are cold. Avoidance occurs when we put on sunscreen to prevent sunburn or obey traffic laws to avoid tickets. You can probably think of many more examples.

In **escape conditioning,** *the organism learns a response to terminate an aversive stimulus.* Escape behaviors are acquired and maintained through negative reinforcement. If you're cold, putting on a sweater is negatively reinforced by the desirable consequence that you no longer shiver. Taking a pain reliever is negatively reinforced by the reduction of pain. In **avoidance conditioning,** *the organism learns a response to avoid an aversive stimulus.* We learn to dress warmly to avoid feeling cold in the first place.

Escape and avoidance conditioning can be demonstrated experimentally (Van der Borght et al., 2005). For example, researchers may place an animal in a *shuttlebox,* a rectangular chamber

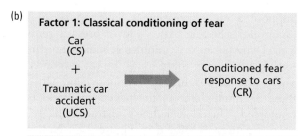

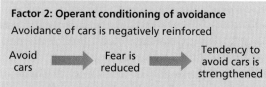

Figure 7.18

(a) Researchers use the shuttlebox to study escape and avoidance learning. (b) The two-factor theory of avoidance learning would account for Carol's car phobia in terms of two sets of learning processes: classical conditioning of a fear response and the negative reinforcement of avoidance of cars through fear reduction.

divided into two compartments and connected by a doorway (Figure 7.18a). The floor is a grid through which electric shock can be delivered to either compartment. When the animal receives a shock in its compartment, it attempts to escape. Eventually, it runs through the door and into the other compartment. When shock is delivered to that compartment, the animal can escape by running back to the original side. Running through the door removes the shock, which negatively reinforces this escape behavior. Over a few trials, the animal learns to escape as soon as the shock is administered.

To study avoidance conditioning experimentally, researchers introduce a discriminative stimulus—a warning signal such as a light—that precedes the shock by a few seconds. After a few trials, the animal learns that the light signals impending shock. It runs to the other compartment as soon as it sees the light and thereby avoids being shocked.

Once this avoidance response is learned, it often is hard to extinguish, even when the animal no longer experiences any shock after the light is turned on. We saw the same situation with Carol's car phobia: she continued to avoid cars even though the intense pain from her accident was no longer experienced. What makes avoidance so resistant to extinction?

According to one model, the **two-factor theory of avoidance learning,** *both classical and operant conditioning are involved in avoidance learning* (Mowrer, 1947; Rescorla & Solomon, 1967). For our rat, the warning light is initially a neutral stimulus paired with a shock (UCS). Through classical conditioning, the light becomes a CS that elicits fear. Now operant conditioning takes over. Fleeing from the light is negatively reinforced by the termination of fear. This strengthens and maintains the avoidance response. Now if we permanently turn off the shock, the avoidance response prevents extinction from taking place. Seeing the light

come on, the animal will not hang around long enough to learn that the shock no longer occurs.

In similar fashion, Carol's fear of cars was classically conditioned. The mere sight of a car (like the light for the rat) elicits fear and she flees, thereby avoiding riding in or driving the car. This avoidance is negatively reinforced by fear reduction, so it remains strong (Figure 7.18b). Extinction is difficult because Carol doesn't give herself the opportunity to be in the car without experiencing physical pain and trauma. This is why exposure therapies for phobias are so effective. By preventing avoidance responses, they provide the key ingredient for extinction: exposure to the CS (car) in the absence of the UCS (pain, trauma).

The two-factor theory helps us understand how many avoidance behaviors develop (Eelen & Vervliet, 2006). However, it has trouble explaining some aspects of avoidance, such as why people develop phobic avoidance to some stimuli (e.g., snakes) more easily than to others (e.g., flowers). As we shall explore later, other factors also regulate our avoidance responses.

Applications of Operant Conditioning

In his best-selling books *Walden Two* (1948) and *Beyond Freedom and Dignity* (1971), Skinner set forth his utopian vision of how a "technology of behavior" based on positive reinforcement could end war, improve education, and solve other social problems. To his critics, Skinner's ideas conjured up images of people being manipulated like rats. But Skinner's point was that social influence is a natural part of human existence. Parents and children influence each other, as do employees and employers, teachers and students, friends, and romantic partners. To behaviorists, individual and societal problems are created by the *haphazard* use of reinforcement and overreliance on punishment (Catania, 2001).

Specialized Animal Training

Through shaping and chaining, animals can learn to perform some truly remarkable behaviors. Some are trained to be TV, movie, or circus performers, whereas others learn to assist people with disabilities (Figure 7.19). Police dogs assist officers on routine patrol, and other dogs learn to use their sense of smell to help locate hidden bombs, illegal drugs, and missing persons (Gazit & Terkel, 2003). The U.S. Navy has trained sea lions to retrieve sunken test weapons and dolphins to patrol waters around nuclear submarine bases (Morrison, 1988). Operantly trained dolphins also patrolled the waters around some U.S. ships during the Vietnam and Persian Gulf Wars.

Education and the Workplace

Walk into a computer store, and you likely will find shelves of educational software teaching everything from math to foreign languages. Computerized instruction rests on two principles championed by Skinner: *immediate performance feedback* and *self-paced learning*.

Skinner was deeply concerned about the inefficiency of traditional instructional methods (1968, 1989b). Long before the advent of personal computers, he developed mechanical teaching machines. Each machine presented material, quizzed the student, and provided immediate feedback. Students who did not learn the material the first time could repeat steps; those who did could advance to the next set of information. Today, personal computers have made Skinner's vision an educational reality. Computer-assisted instruction also is found in business, industry, and the military (Tung et al., 2009).

Skinner's work increased society's attention to the issue of motivation. A key behaviorist assumption is that poor performance should not be attributed to laziness or a bad attitude. Instead, we should view the environment as not providing the proper consequences to reinforce desired behaviors. Many corporations invest in training programs to enhance managers' effectiveness in reinforcing desired worker behaviors. Incentive systems—from stock options to bonuses for meeting performance goals—are now common in business and professional sports.

Token economies, *in which desirable behaviors are reinforced with tokens* (e.g., points, gold stars) *that are later turned in for other reinforcers* (e.g., prizes, recreation time), have been used to enhance academic and job performance (Athens et al., 2007). In one study, a token economy reduced work injuries among open-pit mine workers (Fox et al., 1987). Miners received stamp awards for making safety suggestions and avoiding injuries, and lost stamps for unsafe behaviors. Stamps were later traded in for tangible reinforcers. The program cost money, but far less than the cost of worker absenteeism due to accidents.

Modifying Problem Behaviors

Operant conditioning research gave rise to a field called **applied behavior analysis,** *which combines a behavioral approach with the scientific method to solve individual and societal problems* (Kazdin, 1975; Matson, 2009). Essentially, applied behavior analysts design and implement a program to change behavior, and they measure its effectiveness objectively by gathering data before and after the program is in place (see Figure 7.15, page 230).

Figure 7.19

(*left*) A trainer uses a laser to point out an object for the monkey to pick up. (*right*) Because of injuries suffered in an accident, this woman cannot move her arms or legs. The monkey has been operantly trained to assist her with basic chores, such as eating.

The procedures (e.g., reinforcement, shaping) that are used to change behavior are collectively known as *behavior modification*.

Applied behavior analysis has reduced an incredible range of behavior problems, from chronic hair pulling to drivers' failure to use seat belts (Byrd et al., 2002). It has improved students' social skills, increased employee productivity, reduced workplace injuries, and increased energy conservation (Wilder et al., 2009).

Operant conditioning demonstrates the environment's power in shaping behavior. But this doesn't mean we are at its mercy. Our "Applying Psychological Science" feature describes how you can use learning principles to gain greater control over your own behavior.

Applying Psychological Science

Using Operant Principles to Modify Your Behavior

People often blame the inability to overcome bad habits or maladaptive behaviors on vague concepts such as poor willpower and lack of self-control. Behaviorists prefer the more optimistic assumption that we can acquire *self-regulation*, which means using learning principles to change our behavior (Kanfer & Goldstein, 1991). This approach has helped people overcome addictions, lose excess weight, reduce their risk of heart disease, and improve their lives in many other ways. Let's examine how a college student could use self-regulation principles to increase the amount and effectiveness of studying.

STEP 1: SPECIFY THE PROBLEM

The first step in a self-regulation program is to pinpoint the behaviors you want to change (Watson & Tharp, 1997). This may be more challenging than it sounds, because we often use vague words to describe our problems. Here's how one of our students described her study problem: "I'm just not motivated to study hard." With a little help, she redefined her problem in more specific behavioral terms: "Between 7 and 10 P.M. I don't spend enough time at my desk reading and outlining my textbook."

Whenever possible, design your program to positively reinforce desirable behaviors (i.e., studying) rather than punish undesirable ones (i.e., not studying). Therefore we define this student's *target behavior* (the specific goal) as follows: "Four nights a week, between 7 and 10 P.M., spend $2\frac{1}{2}$ hours studying."

STEP 2: COLLECT BASELINE DATA

The next step is to collect *baseline (preintervention) data* on your behavior. Baseline data provide information about how frequently the target behavior currently occurs. Without it, you have no way of measuring how much you change after starting your program. The most effective approach is to plot data on a graph. Figure 7.20 shows data collected by one of our students.

STEP 3: IDENTIFY ANTECEDENTS AND CONSEQUENCES

While you collect baseline data, try to identify *antecedent* factors that disrupt study behavior, such as friends calling or stopping by (Watson & Tharp, 1997). Also focus on the *consequences* of your behavior. Does studying produce outcomes that are satisfying?

STEP 4: DEVELOP A PLAN TO MODIFY THE ANTECEDENTS AND CONSEQUENCES

Once you have identified key antecedents and consequences, you are in position to modify either or both.

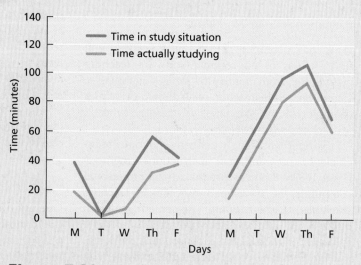

Figure 7.20

Using self-reinforcement to increase study time.
This student graphed the amount of time he spent in the study environment and the time he actually spent studying. Study time increased when he began to self-reinforce study behavior in the second week.

Altering the Antecedents

You can modify the environment so that different stimuli control your behavior. To increase studying, select a specific place where you do nothing but study. If your attention wanders, get up and leave the study area. Your objective is to condition yourself to study in response to the stimuli present in the study area. B. F. Skinner used this technique throughout his own career: he did all of his writing at a particular desk and did nothing else there.

Altering the Consequences

Consequences determine whether a behavior will be repeated. Fortunately, we have the power to arrange many of our own consequences. Self-administered *positive reinforcement* should be the cornerstone of most programs. Find an effective reinforcer that you can control, and make it available only if you engage in the desired behavior. Almost any activity or object you enjoy can serve as a reinforcer, but it must be potent enough to maintain the desired behavior. Awarding yourself a penny for each hour of study time is unlikely to modify your behavior, whereas a 30-minute credit toward a recreational activity might be very effective. After selecting a reinforcer, decide how to use it. Draw up and sign a contract with yourself. The contract should precisely state

- how often or how long you must perform the target behavior (or refrain from performing it if the goal is to reduce an undesirable behavior), and
- the kind and amount of reinforcement you will receive for specific achievements.

Use Reinforcers Effectively

Immediately reinforce the target behavior whenever possible. If your reinforcer cannot be available immediately, use tokens that can later be converted into a reinforcer. One student who wanted to increase her study time awarded herself 1 point per 15 minutes of study time. Points were redeemed for rewards that varied in their reinforcement value. For example, 1 point was worth 15 minutes of TV viewing, but 15 points earned the right to "do anything I want to, all day." Behavior analysts have used token economies successfully with workers, children, patients in mental hospitals, prison inmates, and other groups (Tarbox et al., 2006). If it works for them, it can work for you.

Use Shaping

If you collect good baseline data, you will know the level at which you currently perform your target behavior. Begin at this level or slightly beyond it and move *slowly* toward your final goal, reinforcing yourself at each step. For example, begin by reinforcing yourself for each 10-minute increase in study time. If you have trouble, reduce the size of your steps. Attaining each small goal along the way can be reinforcing and provides motivation to continue (Locke & Latham, 2002). The objective is to bring about gradual change while enjoying plenty of reinforcers, as well as the satisfaction that comes from increasing self-mastery. *The way you arrange reinforcement contingencies is the most critical determinant of whether you will achieve your goal.*

STEP 5: IMPLEMENT THE PROGRAM AND KEEP MEASURING BEHAVIOR

Most people experience occasional setbacks or plateaus when progress seems to stop. If this happens repeatedly, it is not a sign of weak willpower but rather a need to modify the program. Yes, self-regulation programs can fail, but failure calls for resourcefulness rather than despair. If need be, change the terms of your contract, but always operate under a specific contract. Keep recording and graphing the target behavior. This is the only way to identify your progress accurately.

This five-step process is one of several behavioral approaches to gaining greater control of our lives. Psychologists continue to design and test methods to increase self-regulation, adding new meaning to the phrase "Power to the people."

---

test yourself — Operant Conditioning

Match each numbered term to the correct situation on the right.

1. positive reinforcement
2. response cost
3. discriminative stimulus
4. aversive punishment
5. negative reinforcement
6. operant extinction

a. A boss yells at a worker for showing up late; the tardiness stops.
b. A student tries a new coffee shop, the coffee is great, and she returns next week.
c. A teen who stays out past curfew loses driving privileges for a week.
d. When a police officer is present, people don't jaywalk.
e. Symptoms are relieved by a new medication, so a person keeps taking it.
f. A medication stops working, so a person stops taking it.

ANSWERS: 1-b, 2-c, 3-d, 4-a, 5-e, 6-f

CROSSROADS OF CONDITIONING

Behaviorists built much of the foundation on which our knowledge of learning principles rests, and behaviorism remains influential today (Marr, 2007). Over the years, however, psychologists who viewed behavior from biological and cognitive perspectives enriched our understanding of learning by challenging some of behaviorism's key assumptions.

Biological Constraints: Evolution and Preparedness

Behaviorists never suggested that a rat could learn to fly, but for decades they assumed that they could condition virtually any behavior an organism was physically capable of performing. Yet evidence mounted that "conditioned" animals did not always respond as they were supposed to. The behaviorist assumption was wrong because it ignored a key principle discussed at the outset of this chapter: Behavior is influenced by an organism's evolutionary history, and this places biological constraints on learning.

Martin Seligman's (1970) concept of *preparedness* captures this idea. **Preparedness** *means that through evolution, animals are biologically predisposed (prewired) to learn some associations more easily than others.* In general, behaviors related to a species' survival are learned more easily than behaviors contrary to an organism's natural tendencies. Let's consider some examples.

Constraints on Classical Conditioning: Learned Taste Aversions

Imagine eating or drinking something, then becoming sick to your stomach and throwing up. Perhaps it is a case of the flu, or it could be food poisoning. When a food is associated with nausea or vomiting, that particular food can become a CS that triggers a **conditioned taste aversion,** *a conditioned response in which the taste (and sometimes the sight and smell) of a particular food becomes disgusting and repulsive* (Garcia et al., 1985). The very thought of it may even make us feel queasy, and we learn to avoid it. During pregnancy many women experience nausea and vomiting, and they may develop aversions to foods associated with these symptoms (Bayley et al., 2002). Cancer patients may develop aversions to foods they eat before chemotherapy or radiation therapy sessions, even when they know that the food did not cause their posttreatment stomach upset. Like other conditioned responses, the aversion develops involuntarily.

Psychologist John Garcia pioneered numerous taste-aversion experiments that challenged two basic assumptions of classical conditioning. First, behaviorists had assumed that the CS-UCS time interval had to be relatively short: usually a few seconds. Garcia showed that animals learned taste aversions even though the food (CS) was consumed up to several hours—or even a day—before they became ill (in this case, the UCS).

Second, in a classic experiment, Garcia illustrated how biological preparedness influences learned aversions (Garcia & Koelling, 1966). Whenever rats licked a drinking tube, they were simultaneously exposed to three neutral stimuli: sweet-tasting water, a bright light, and a buzzer (Figure 7.21). The rats were then divided into two conditions. In one condition, the rats were exposed to X-rays upon drinking the water, which later made them ill (UCS). Would the rats develop an aversion to all three neutral stimuli? No, they avoided the sweet water but not the light or buzzer. Why did only the sweet taste become a

Stage 1: All Rats
When rats touch the drinking tube, sweet water is delivered and a light and buzzer turn on.

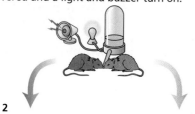

Stage 2

Illness condition	Fear condition

Group 1 rats get nauseating X-rays when they drink.

Group 2 rats get electric shocks when they drink.

Stage 3

Group 1 rats avoid the sweet water and prefer the plain water with the light and buzzer.

Group 2 rats still drink the sweet water, but avoid the plain water with the light and buzzer.

Figure 7.21

Biological preparedness in classical conditioning. This figure illustrates the design and main results of Garcia and Koelling's (1966) aversion experiment.

CS? Because rats are biologically primed to form taste-illness associations, which means that in nature they most easily identify poisonous or bad food by its taste (or smell). In nature, sounds and lights don't make rats sick.

When rats in the second condition licked the tube, the light, buzzer, and sweet taste were all paired with an electric shock. Would these rats learn to fear all three neutral stimuli? No, they avoided the light and buzzer but kept drinking the sweet water. This also makes adaptive sense. In nature, sights and sounds—but not how food and drink taste—signal fear-provoking situations (e.g., a cat about to pounce).

The same principle applies to humans. When a food makes us violently sick, we may develop an aversion to it but not to the friends we ate with. Further, seeing the food again may repulse us but not make us afraid.

Psychologists have applied knowledge about conditioned aversions to save animals' lives. To prevent coyotes from killing ranchers' sheep, scientists (Gustavson et al., 1974) laced pieces of meat with lithium chloride, a nausea-inducing drug. They wrapped the meat in sheep hide and left it out for coyotes to eat. The coyotes ate it, became ill, and developed an aversion to the meat, thereby becoming less likely to kill sheep. This saved the lives of sheep—and also of the coyotes, who otherwise would have been shot by the ranchers. Figure 7.22 illustrates nature's own wildlife management based on learned taste aversions.

Applying taste-aversion principles to children with cancer, psychologists gave young patients an unusual-tasting candy before their chemotherapy sessions (Broberg & Bernstein, 1987). As hypothesized, the candy acted as a scapegoat and protected the children from developing aversions to their normal foods. Thus the candy—rather than their normal food—became the aversive CS.

Are We Biologically Prepared to Fear Certain Things?

Seligman (1971) and others (Öhman, 2008) propose that like other animals, humans are biologically prepared to acquire certain fears more readily than others. In one case, a 4-year-old girl saw a snake in a park but wasn't frightened by it (Marks, 1977). She returned to the family car and accidentally smashed her hand in the car door. She subsequently developed a phobia not of car doors or cars, but of snakes!

In the laboratory, Swedish psychologists showed people pictures of various stimuli, flashing each picture on a screen and pairing it with electric shock (the UCS). Next, they measured people's physiological responses when those stimuli were presented alone (Öhman & Soares, 1998). When the pictures showed snakes, spiders, or angry faces, people quickly acquired conditioned fear responses to these stimuli, even when the pictures were flashed too briefly to be consciously perceived. But participants who received shocks while looking at slides of flowers, houses, or happy faces displayed much weaker fear conditioning.

Humans develop phobias to many stimuli, but most often we fear things that seem to have greater evolutionary significance: snakes, spiders, and potentially dangerous animals and places (Hofmann et al., 2004). Is this the result of evolution-based biological preparedness, or might it be due to learning experiences that teach

Figure 7.22

A conditioned aversion in nature.

This blue jay has never eaten a monarch butterfly but doesn't pass up an easy meal. Soon, toxins in the butterfly cause food poisoning. The jay feels discomfort, vomits, and develops a conditioned aversion triggered by the sight of the monarch's brightly patterned wings. From now on, it will leave monarchs alone. Source: Photos courtesy of Lincoln P. Brower.

us to expect that some stimuli can be dangerous? Multiple factors may affect fear conditioning, but one thing is clear: fear can be conditioned much more easily to some stimuli than to others.

Constraints on Operant Conditioning: Animals That "Won't Shape Up"

Two of B. F. Skinner's students, Keller and Marian Breland (1961, 1966), became famous animal trainers. They successfully used shaping and chaining to train thousands of animals for circuses, TV shows, and movies, but sometimes the animals simply refused to behave according to the laws of operant conditioning.

On one occasion, the Brelands tried to train a chicken to play baseball. A small ball would roll toward home plate, and the chicken would pull a chain to swing a small metal bat. If the ball was hit, a bell would ring and the chicken was supposed to run to first base to get a food reinforcer. The Brelands easily trained the chicken to pull the chain that swung the bat and to run to first base when it heard the bell. But when the ball was introduced into the game, utter chaos ensued. If the chicken hit the ball, instead of running to first base it chased the ball all over the field, pecking at it furiously and flapping its wings. Try as they might, the Brelands could not extinguish these behaviors. End of training and end of the chicken's baseball career. This and other similar cases suggest that in operant conditioning (as in classical conditioning), organisms are biologically prepared to learn some types of associations more readily than others.

The Brelands also found that once a particular stimulus came to represent food, animals began to act as if it were food. The chicken pecked at the ball as if it were something to eat. In another case, raccoons had learned to deposit tokens into a box to receive a food reinforcer. But soon, instead of depositing the tokens, the raccoons kept rubbing them as if they were washing real food. This washing behavior was so deeply rooted that it simply overrode the conditioning procedure. The Brelands called this **instinctive drift,** *the tendency for a conditioned response to drift back toward instinctive behavior.*

Research provides other evidence of instinctive drift. For example, wild rats trained to press a lever for food will often drift back to instinctive behaviors and instead scratch and bite the lever (Powell & Curley, 1976).

Instinctive drift also has practical importance. People who adopt wild animals as pets or who train them for circuses face some personal risk no matter how hard they try to domesticate these animals. An acquaintance of ours once rescued a baby raccoon and raised it lovingly for nearly a year, at which time the raccoon unexpectedly reverted to its more instinctive, aggressive behavior. Our friend, now known as "Three Fingers," returned his pet to the wild.

Cognition and Conditioning

Early behaviorists believed that learning involves the relatively automatic formation of bonds between stimuli and responses. This viewpoint came to be known as *S-R (stimulus-response) psychology.* Behaviorists opposed explanations of learning that went beyond observable stimuli and responses. They did not deny that people had thoughts and feelings but argued that behavior could be explained without referring to such mentalistic concepts (Skinner, 1953, 1990).

Even in psychology's early years, some learning theorists challenged the S-R model, arguing that in between stimulus and response there is something else: the organism's (*O*) cognitive representation of the world (Figure 7.23). This came to be known as the *S-O-R,* or *cognitive, model of learning.* Today the cognitive perspective represents an important force in learning theory.

Early Challenges to Behaviorism: Insight and Cognitive Maps

In the 1920s, German psychologist Wolfgang Köhler (1925) challenged Thorndike's behaviorist assumption that animals learn to perform tasks only by trial and error. Köhler exposed

THE FAR SIDE® BY GARY LARSON

"Stimulus, response! Stimulus, response! Don't you ever *think?*"

Figure 7.23

Some psychologists who challenged behaviorism's S-R model argued that to best explain human and animal behavior (though, obviously, not the activity of amoebae), the organism's cognitive representations must be taken into account.

chimpanzees to novel learning tasks and concluded that they were able to learn by **insight,** *the sudden perception of a useful relationship that helps to solve a problem.* Figure 7.24 shows how one of his apes solved the problem of how to retrieve bananas that were dangling beyond reach. Köhler emphasized that the apes often spent time staring at the bananas and available tools, as if they were contemplating the problem, after which the solution suddenly appeared.

Behaviorists argued that insight actually represents the combining of previously learned responses (Epstein et al., 1984). Imagine a pigeon placed inside a chamber where a miniature model of a banana dangles from the ceiling, out of reach. A small box sits in the corner of the chamber. Similar to Köhler's apes, the pigeon looks around, goes to the box, moves it under the banana by pushing it with its beak, then stands on the box and pecks the banana. Without knowing the pigeon's behavioral history (just as we don't know the entire behavioral history of Köhler's apes), we might conclude that this is a novel behavior reflecting remarkable insight. But instead, the pigeon has simply combined several independent behaviors (e.g., pushing a box, stepping onto a

Figure 7.24

Sultan seems to study the hanging bananas that are out of reach. After looking around, Sultan suddenly grabs some crates, stacks them, and obtains his tasty reward.

box) that researchers had operantly conditioned using reinforcement. Although the debate about insight continues to this day, Köhler's work nevertheless helped place the cognitive learning viewpoint on the map.

Another cognitive pioneer, American learning theorist Edward Tolman, studied spatial learning in rats. Look at the maze in Figure 7.25a. A rat runs to an open circular table, continues across, and follows the only path available to a goal box containing food. After 12 trials, the rat easily negotiates the maze. Next, the maze is changed. The rat runs its usual route and reaches a dead end (Figure 7.25b). What will the rat do?

Tolman found that rats returned to the table, briefly explored most of the 18 new paths for just a few inches, and then chose one. By far, the largest number—36 percent—chose the fourth path to the right of their original route, which took them closest to where the goal box had been. In short, the rats behaved as you would, given your advantage of seeing the maps.

Tolman (1948) argued that reinforcement theory could not explain this behavior but that he could: the rats had developed a **cognitive map,** *a mental representation of the spatial layout.* The concept of cognitive maps supported Tolman's belief that learning does not merely "stamp in" stimulus-response connections. Rather, learning provides knowledge, and based on their knowledge, organisms develop an expectancy, a cognitive representation, of "what leads to what."

Behaviorists disagreed with Tolman's interpretations and, as with insight, the debate over cognitive maps continues (Jeffery, 2008; Jensen, 2006). Still, Tolman's concept of expectancy remains a cornerstone of cognitive approaches to classical and operant conditioning.

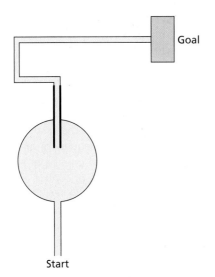

(a)   Start

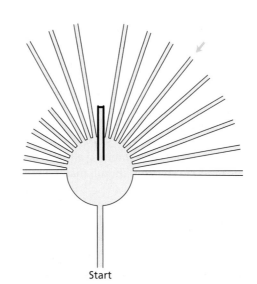

(b)   Start

Figure 7.25

Cognitive maps in rats.
(a) Rats first learned to run the simple maze. (b) When the maze was switched, many rats chose the fourth path to the right of the original route. Tolman proposed that the rats had developed a cognitive map of the maze. Source: Adapted from Tolman, 1948.

Cognition in Classical Conditioning

Early American behaviorists believed that classical conditioning created a direct reflexlike connection between the CS (e.g., tone) and CR (e.g., salivation). Interestingly, Pavlov held a different view, proposing that a neural bond is formed between the CS and the UCS. Thus, for Pavlov's dogs, the tone triggered an association with food, which then triggered salivation (Shanks, 2010).

Cognitive learning theorists also believe that classical conditioning forms a CS-UCS link. In cognitive terminology, the link is an expectancy that the CS will be followed by the UCS. This *expectancy model* states that the most important factor in classical conditioning is not how often the CS and the UCS are paired, but how well the CS predicts (i.e., signals) the appearance of the UCS (Lovibond, 2006; Rescorla & Wagner, 1972).

Robert Rescorla (1968) tested this principle in a fear-conditioning experiment. Rats in one condition received electric shocks (UCS), and each shock was preceded by a tone. As usual, the tone soon became a CS that elicited a fear response when presented alone. In a second condition, rats received the same number of tone-shock pairings as the first group, but they also received as many shocks that were not preceded by the tone. Would the tone become a CS for fear? According to traditional learning theory, the answer should be yes, because the number of tone-shock pairings was the same as in the first group. But the expectancy model predicts no, because the tone does not reliably predict when the shock will occur. The results supported Rescorla's hypothesis: the tone did not elicit a fear response for the second group.

CS-UCS inconsistency also explains why we don't become conditioned to all the neutral stimuli that are present just before a UCS appears. For example, when Pavlov's dogs were presented with tone-food pairings, there was light in the room. Why didn't the dogs learn to salivate whenever they saw light? The key is that when the room was lit, the dogs often were *not* receiving food. When a neutral stimulus does not consistently predict the arrival of the UCS, it is less likely to become a CS. This is highly adaptive; if it were not the case, you and I (along with Pavlov's dogs) would be twitching, salivating, and exhibiting all sorts of reflexive responses to so many stimuli that it would be difficult to function.

Other evidence supports the expectancy model. For example, recall that forward pairing (e.g., a tone followed by food) typically produces the strongest learning, whereas backward pairing (e.g., food followed by a tone) produces the weakest learning. This makes sense based on the expectancy model. In forward pairing, the tone predicts the imminent arrival of the food; it is a signal that something meaningful is about to happen. In backward pairing, the tone has no predictive value because the food has already arrived. In sum, the expectancy model has been highly influential and provides good evidence that cognition plays a role in classical conditioning (Lovibond, 2006).

Cognition in Operant Conditioning

S-O-R theorists believe that cognitive processes also play a key role in operant conditioning. Let's examine three issues.

The Role of Awareness   To demonstrate operant conditioning, an introductory psychology instructor sent a student, Kyle, out of the room and told another student how to shape the response of flicking a light switch on and off, using small chocolate candies as the reinforcer. When Kyle returned, he was given a piece of chocolate first for looking at the wall that held the light switch, then for approaching the wall, and so on. After 25 minutes of shaping, Kyle was flicking the switch.

Another student then asked if she could serve as experimenter. A new participant, Jeff, left the room while the class decided that he should be shaped to erase the blackboard. When Jeff returned, the new experimenter said, "Jeff, if you'll erase the blackboard, I'll give you this bag of candy." This time, it took all of 5 seconds to produce the desired behavior.

Cognitive theorists emphasize that organisms develop an *awareness,* or *expectancy,* of the relations between their responses and probable consequences. From this viewpoint, Kyle and Jeff developed an expectation that flicking the light switch and erasing the blackboard would produce a delicious consequence.

The concept of awareness implies that the best predictor of behavior is the perceived contingency, not the actual one (Figure 7.26). Often the two are identical, but sometimes people perceive contingencies that do not actually exist. One example is *superstitious behavior.* In cognitive terms, the organism misperceives that a specific behavior produces favorable consequences or helps avoid bad ones. Humans often engage in superstitious behaviors to gain a sense of control over environmental events (Foster et al., 2006). One traveler we know eats ice cream prior to taking any trip on a train because this supposedly will guarantee a safe journey. This superstitious behavior, of course, has been reinforced each time by a safe arrival.

Latent Learning Tolman's research, illustrated in Figure 7.25, suggested that the rats developed cognitive maps when they were reinforced with food for running a maze. Tolman also believed that cognitive maps could be learned without reinforcement, posing an even greater challenge to the behaviorist viewpoint. In one experiment, three groups of rats learned the correct path through a complex maze (Tolman & Honzik, 1930). Rats in the first group found food each time they reached the goal box. Rats in the second group found the goal box empty each time they reached it. Rats in the third group found no food at the end of the maze for the first 10 days but did find food in the goal box starting on the eleventh day.

Figure 7.27 shows the results, and the key finding is this: on Day 11, the rats in the third group discovered food in the goal box for the first time. The next day, they were performing just as well as the first group, which had been reinforced all along. What could explain this sudden performance improvement? According to Tolman, during Days 1 to 10, rats in the third group were learning the spatial layout of the maze as they wandered about. They were not being reinforced by food, but they gained knowledge about the maze's spatial layout. This learning remained *latent* (hidden) until the rats discovered a good reason on Day 11 to get to the goal box quickly; it was then immediately displayed in performance the next day. Behaviorists disagreed with Tolman's interpretation and proposed alternative stimulus-response explanations (Jensen, 2006). But to cognitive (S-O-R) theorists, Tolman's experiments support the concept of **latent learning,** *which refers to learning that occurs but is not demonstrated until later, when there is an incentive to perform* (Blodgett, 1929). We may learn how to do something at one time but not display that knowledge until we perform a task at a future time.

Self-Evaluations as Reinforcers and Punishers Students called him "Holy Hubert," and he visited our college campus for over 10 years. His fire-and-brimstone warnings to repent often evoked amusement, insults, and ridicule. One could hardly imagine less positive consequences for an evangelist. One day, we asked Hubert why he continued to preach when students reacted so negatively. He answered, "I don't care what they say. When I know I'm doing the Lord's work, I feel so good."

Hubert's persistence illustrates that external reinforcement and punishment are not the only consequences controlling behavior. We often feel pride for doing something even if others do not know or approve of our deeds. We may also disapprove of ourselves for failing to live up to our own

"Boy, do we have this guy conditioned. Every time I press the bar down he drops a pellet in."

Figure 7.26

Perception versus reality.

Source: Cartoon by H. Mazzeo & P. Gardner, from *Columbia Jester*, Nov. 1950, vol. 50, no. 4, p. 9. Courtesy of the University Archives, Columbia University in the City of New York.

standards. These *cognitive self-evaluations* represent important internal reinforcers and punishers (Scott & Cervone, 2002). Think back to the woman in Las Vegas who solicits charitable donations. Her strong belief that she is doing something valuable may be all the positive reinforcement she needs.

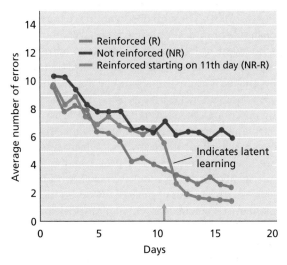

Figure 7.27

Tolman's demonstration of latent learning.

Rats had one trial in the maze per day. Group R was reinforced with food every time they reached the end of the maze. Group NR never received reinforcement. The critical group, NR-R, received food reinforcement on Day 11. Their immediate performance improvement suggested that they had learned the maze prior to the introduction of reinforcement. Source: Tolman & Honzik, 1930.

OBSERVATIONAL LEARNING: WHEN OTHERS SHOW THE WAY

How did you learn to write, dance, and drive a car, or even to spread peanut butter and jelly across a piece of bread rather than piling it up in the center? Reinforcement certainly was involved, but so was **observational learning,** *the learning that occurs by observing the behavior of a model.* Teachers, parents, and coaches often help us learn by intentionally modeling skills, but observational learning extends beyond such contexts. We also learn fears, prejudices, likes and dislikes, and social behaviors by watching others (Olsson & Phelps, 2004). Through observation we may learn desirable or undesirable behaviors. When parents who swear in front of their children complain to one another, "Where did our kids learn that damn language?" the answer should be apparent.

Observational learning can be highly adaptive. By observing others, an organism can learn which events are important, which stimuli signal that such events are about to occur, and which responses are likely to produce positive or negative consequences. For example, monkeys may learn adaptive fears—such as a fear of snakes—by observing other monkeys react with fear (Öhman & Mineka, 2001).

Humans' capacity to learn by observation, which is also called *modeling,* far outstrips that of other creatures. It helps us bypass the potentially time-consuming and dangerous process of trial and error. For example, we wouldn't want each new generation of brain surgeons or airline pilots to learn their crafts only through trial and error!

Bandura's Social-Cognitive Theory

As you've seen, research on biological preparedness and cognitive factors in conditioning challenged

behaviorism's S-R view of learning. Psychologist Albert Bandura's pioneering research and theorizing on observational learning also helped carry the S-O-R challenge to behaviorism's gate. Bandura's **social-cognitive theory,** also known by its former name **social-learning theory,** *emphasizes that people learn by observing the behavior of models and acquiring the belief that they can produce behaviors to influence events in their lives* (Bandura, 1969, 2006b).

The Modeling Process and Self-Efficacy

Bandura views modeling as a four-step process that includes several cognitive factors:

- *Attention:* First, we must pay attention to the model's behavior.

- *Retention:* Second, we must retain that information in memory so that it can be recalled when needed.

- *Reproduction:* Third, we must be physically capable of reproducing the model's behavior or something similar to it.

- *Motivation:* Fourth, we must be motivated to display the behavior.

According to Bandura, **self-efficacy,** *which represents people's belief that they have the capability to perform behaviors that will produce a desired outcome,* is a key motivational factor in observational learning. Recall that at the beginning of the chapter we defined learning as a change in an organism's behavior or capabilities based on experience. According to Bandura, the knowledge or capability to perform a behavior may be acquired at one time but not displayed until a later time when the motivational conditions are favorable.

Tolman's research on latent learning in rats demonstrated this point, and a classic experiment by Bandura (1965) on modeling demonstrated the learning-versus-performance distinction in

Figure 7.28

In Bandura's (1965) experiment, most children who watched an aggressive model attack a Bobo doll later imitated that behavior. These photos show only one of several specific actions that the children spontaneously imitated.

humans. In this experiment, children watched a film in which a model acted aggressively toward a "Bobo doll" (an inflatable plastic clown), punching, kicking, and hitting it with a mallet. One group saw the model rewarded with praise and candy, a second group saw the model reprimanded for aggression, and a third group saw no consequences for the model. After the film, each child was placed in a room with various toys, including a Bobo doll (Figure 7.28).

Children who saw the model punished performed fewer aggressive actions toward the Bobo doll than did children in the other two groups. Does this mean that this group failed to learn how to respond aggressively? To find out, the experimenter later offered the children attractive prizes if they could do what the model had done. All of the children quickly reproduced the model's aggressive responses. Note that just as Tolman showed that rats apparently learned the layout of a maze while they were not receiving reinforcement, Bandura demonstrated that regardless of whether the model was reinforced or punished, children had indeed learned the model's behavior.

Imitation of Aggression and Prosocial Behavior

Bandura's work helped stir a societal controversy that was brewing in the 1960s and continues to this day: What effect does viewing aggressive models on TV or in movies have on our attitudes and behavior? We will discuss this issue more fully in Chapter 17. In brief, research suggests that viewing media violence

- decreases viewers' concerns about the suffering of victims;
- habituates us to the sight of violence; and
- provides aggressive models that increase some viewers' tendency to act aggressively (Eron, 2000; Huesmann et al., 2003).

If watching media violence can enhance our tendency to act aggressively, might watching prosocial models who do good deeds increase our tendency to help others? Psychologist Joyce Sprafkin and her colleagues (1975) conducted a classic experiment on this issue. They found that by exposing children to a TV show in which an action hero helps save a young puppy, the children became more likely to help what they believed were real puppies in danger, even though helping meant giving up the opportunity to win prizes at a game. Many studies indicate that exposure to prosocial models enhances people's helping behavior (Hearold, 1986).

Applications of Observational Learning

In everyday life, we learn many skills from observing models. Elementary school teachers model how to write, pronounce, and use words. In college, foreign-language instructors do the same. Parents, teachers, business managers, and athletic coaches model how to solve problems and perform tasks. If you play sports or video games, you may have picked up strategies or moves by watching other players.

Psychologists have also used observational learning to enhance prosocial behavior. For example, researchers showed high school students an audiovisual program that featured models (other students) who donated blood; donations to a blood bank subsequently increased by 17 percent (Sarason et al., 1991).

More ambitiously, observational learning has been used to address global social problems. Miguel Sabido, a vice president in charge of research at Mexico's largest media company, used Bandura's theory to help develop the first project of its kind in 1975 (Smith, 2002). When a national literacy program in Mexico failed to draw a good turnout, Sabido created a TV soap opera to give the literacy program a boost. The popular soap opera aired for a year and featured a literate female character who, as part of the national program, organized a self-study group for teenagers and adults who struggled with illiteracy.

Sabido hoped that the soap opera characters' learning to read would provide viewers with positive role models, increase viewers' self-efficacy that they could learn to read, and motivate viewers to enroll in the literacy program. His hope bore fruit. After one episode in which viewers were directly asked to enroll, "about 25,000 people descended on the distribution center in Mexico City to get their reading materials" (Bandura, 2002b, p. 224). New annual enrollments in the literacy program jumped from 100,000 in the previous year to over 900,000 in the year the soap opera aired and decreased to about 400,000 the year after the soap opera ended.

Mass media programs incorporating social-cognitive learning principles have since tackled social problems in South America, Africa, India, and Asia (Bandura, 2006a). Our "Research Close-up" describes an experiment that implemented and evaluated one of these programs.

Research Close-up

Using Social-Cognitive Theory to Prevent AIDS: A National Experiment

SOURCE: PETER W. VAUGHAN, EVERETT M. ROGERS, ARVIND SINGHAL, and RAMADHAN M. SWALEHE (2000). Entertainment-education and HIV/AIDS prevention: A field experiment in Tanzania. *Journal of Health Communication*, 5, 81–100.

INTRODUCTION

In the 1990s, the African nation of Tanzania faced a growing AIDS crisis that was fueled by risky sexual practices and widespread misinformation about HIV transmission (Bandura, 2002b). HIV/AIDS was widely spread through heterosexual contact between truck drivers and prostitutes who frequented the areas where truckers made stops.

To combat this crisis, the Tanzanian government and Radio Tanzania produced 208 episodes of a radio soap opera over several years. The content took advantage of principles from social-cognitive theory. In this 5-year study, Peter Vaughan and his colleagues (2000) measured the effects of the radio program on listeners' attitudes and sexual practices.

METHOD

The soap opera featured three types of role models. Positive role models were knowledgeable about HIV/AIDs, minimized risky sex, and ultimately attained rewarding social outcomes. Transitional role models began by acting irresponsibly but eventually adopted safer sexual practices. Negative role models engaged in risky sex that led to adverse outcomes, including death from contracting HIV/AIDS.

The program's content was designed to (1) make listeners realize that they were at risk for contracting HIV/AIDS, (2) increase listeners' self-efficacy by showing them how to control the risk, and (3) get listeners to reduce their number of sexual partners and use condoms when having sex.

This prime-time soap opera was broadcast twice weekly to six geographic regions (e.g., the experimental regions) of Tanzania for 5 years. A seventh geographic region served as a control region for the first 3 years and received the radio program for only the final 2 years. Each year interviewers gathered information about participants' attitudes, sexual behaviors, and personal characteristics. One or more family members from roughly 2,750 randomly chosen households participated.

RESULTS

In the six experimental regions, the typical listener heard 108 of the 204 episodes, and about 80 percent said that the program helped them learn about preventing HIV/AIDS. Compared to people not exposed to the program, those who tuned in became more likely to believe that they were at risk for contracting HIV/AIDS but could control this risk through safer sexual practices. Listeners spoke more often with their partners about HIV/AIDS, reduced their number of sexual partners, and increased their use of condoms. These findings were replicated in the seventh geographic region after it was switched from being a control group to an experimental group.

DISCUSSION

This study illustrates how a scientific theory can guide the development of a treatment program that addresses a major societal problem. By cleverly turning the comparison region into an experimental region after 3 years, the researchers were able to test whether their initial findings would replicate.

Conducting large-scale research in the real world presents difficult challenges that can threaten a study's internal validity. Within each experimental

RESEARCH DESIGN

Question: Can a radio soap opera series, designed using social-cognitive learning principles, change people's attitudes and behavior regarding risky sex?

Type of Study: *Field experiment (an experiment conducted in a natural setting)*

Independent Variable

Immediate (all 5 years) versus delayed (final 2 years only) exposure to a radio soap opera series

Dependent Variables

- Attitudes about risky sex and HIV/AIDS
- Self-efficacy for reducing risk of AIDS
- Sexual practices

region, the researchers could not control who tuned in to the radio programs. Indeed, listeners and nonlisteners differed in several ways (e.g., listeners were somewhat better educated and wealthier). To minimize the chance that such factors would distort the results, the researchers statistically adjusted for these factors when they analyzed the data.

The study also relied heavily on participants' self-reports. But by gathering some objective data (such as increases in the number of condoms distributed in these regions), these researchers were able to corroborate some of the self-report measures.

THE ADAPTIVE BRAIN

We began this chapter by noting that learning represents your personal adaptation to the circumstances you encounter throughout your life. To close the chapter, we'd like to emphasize that your ability to learn and adapt depends not only on networks of brain structures and circuits but also on the brain's own ability to adapt—to modify its structure and functioning—in response to experience.

No single part of the brain controls learning. For example, the hypothalamus and neural pathways involving dopamine play a key role in regulating our ability to experience reward (Olds, 1958; Rolls, 2000). Humans report pleasure when specific areas of the hypothalamus are electrically stimulated, and both humans and rats will learn to repeatedly press a button or lever to receive these electrical reinforcers. The cerebellum plays an important role in acquiring some classically conditioned movements, such as conditioned eyeblink responses, whereas the amygdala is centrally involved in acquiring conditioned fears (LaBar & LeDoux, 2006). We'll take a closer look at brain processes that underlie learning when we discuss memory in the next chapter.

Biology affects learning, but learning also influences brain functioning (Fanselow & Poulos, 2005). As we noted in the last chapter, as you make the transition on a new task from inexperienced novice to experienced master, your brain is able to rely less on conscious processing and instead process more information nonconsciously. Highly trained athletes and musicians can execute incredibly complex skills with a minimum of conscious thought. No doubt you can think of skills that seem almost automatic to you now (perhaps driving a car or typing on a keyboard) but which required considerable effort when you first learned them. As we gain experience at novel tasks, the brain's frontal lobes—the seat of executive functions such as decision making and planning—tend to exercise less control and become less active (Eliassen et al., 2003). Indeed, notice in Figure 7.29 how a video-game player's brain activity generally decreased after practicing the game.

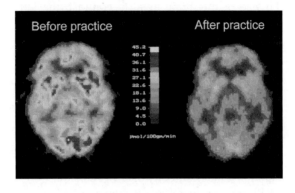

Before practice   After practice

pmol/100gm/min

Figure 7.29

While learning a computer game, the brain of a novice player is highly active and uses a lot of energy, as indicated by the large yellow and red areas in the left PET scan. As the right scan shows, energy consumption decreases with experience.

Learning also etches its imprints on the brain's physical structure. During countless hours of practice and performance, a violinist makes continuous, precise movements with the fingers of his or her left hand while the right hand moves the bow (Figure 7.30). This constant fingering of the strings

Figure 7.30

The precise, constant left-hand movements involved in fingering the strings provides a great deal of sensory stimulation to this violinist's right-hemisphere somatosensory cortex.

provides a great deal of sensory stimulation to the somatosensory cortex of the right hemisphere. By using brain imaging, researchers found that the area in this brain region that is devoted to representing the fingers was larger among string-instrument musicians (who averaged almost 12 years of experience) than among nonmusicians. Moreover, the earlier in life that the musicians had started to play their instruments, the greater the size of this brain area. In contrast, the left-hemisphere somatosensory area representing the right-hand fingers of the musicians and nonmusicians did not differ (Elbert et al., 1995).

Because these findings are correlational, they can't clearly establish cause and effect. Perhaps it wasn't playing music that caused the brain differences. Maybe it was the other way around: pre-existing brain differences helped these individuals become musicians. Yet controlled experiments with animals do indeed show that learning leaves its mark not only on the somatosensory cortex but on other parts of the brain as well. For example, when monkeys and rats learn skilled movements that require them to use their fingers and paws, respectively, the representations of these body parts in the motor cortex change (Kleim et al., 2002).

Levels of Analysis   Learning

Although this chapter has highlighted the centrality of environmental experiences on learning, as we now recap, learning also involves key factors at the biological and psychological levels of analysis.

ENVIRONMENTAL LEVEL

- Cultural norms and socialization affect the content of what we learn.
- The pairing of neutral stimuli with unconditioned stimuli can produce classically conditioned responses.
- The consequences of an operant behavior, the pattern of those consequences, and the presence of antecedent stimuli affect where and how often the behavior will recur.
- The behavior of other people—live or in the media—may be imitated or provide knowledge.

BIOLOGICAL LEVEL

- Heredity determines each species' potential to learn via habituation, classical and operant conditioning, and modeling.
- Evolution has biologically predisposed each species to learn some associations more readily than others.
- Multiple brain regions and neurotransmitters underlie our capacity to learn, such as dopamine pathways that help regulate our ability to experience reward.
- Learning produces changes in brain activity and neural circuitry.

PSYCHOLOGICAL LEVEL

- Awareness plays a role in learning. Organisms develop expectancies of CS-UCS associations and response-consequence contingencies.
- As illustrated by superstitious behavior, perceived associations can influence behavior even when they are inaccurate.
- Learning can provide knowledge, which may be demonstrated overtly in behavior at a later time.
- Self-evaluations, which may generate feelings of pride and shame, can serve as internal reinforcers and punishers.

Reflecting on your emotional reactions, other bodily responses to specific stimuli, and your likes and dislikes, can you identify any that may have resulted from classical conditioning experiences? Can you think of examples of behaviors (including skills and the attitudes that you express) that you have acquired due to operant conditioning or observational learning?

Learning's effects on the brain occur throughout the life cycle. Compared to newborn rats that grow up in standard cages, litter mates that grow up in enriched environments—with toys and greater opportunities to learn—develop heavier brains whose neurons have more dendrites and synapses and greater concentrations of various neurotransmitters (Rosenzweig, 1984). In turn, this increased brain development enables animals to perform better on subsequent learning tasks (Meaney et al., 1991). And in humans, exposure to stimulating environments and new learning opportunities during late adulthood seems to slow declines in brain functioning, as measured by better performance on intellectual and perceptual tasks (Newson & Kemps, 2006; Schaie, 2005). In a sense, then, every day you are alive, your brain adapts and continues its own personal evolution; its neural networks and patterns of activity are affected not only by your genetic endowment but also by your learning experiences.

In closing, the Levels of Analysis feature on the preceding page summarizes some of the environmental, psychological, and biological factors that play key roles in learning.

Chapter Summary

ADAPTING TO THE ENVIRONMENT

- Learning is a process by which experience produces a relatively enduring change in an organism's behavior or capabilities. Learning is measured by changes in an organism's responses and is a form of personal adaptation to the environment. Habituation is a decrease in the strength of a response to a repeated stimulus. It allows organisms to attend to other stimuli that are more important.

CLASSICAL CONDITIONING: ASSOCIATING ONE STIMULUS WITH ANOTHER

- Classical conditioning involves pairing a neutral stimulus with an unconditioned stimulus (UCS) that elicits an unconditioned response (UCR). Through pairing, the neutral stimulus becomes a conditioned stimulus (CS) that evokes a conditioned response (CR) similar to the original UCR.
- Acquisition involves CS-UCS pairings. Extinction represents the disappearance of the CR when the CS is presented repeatedly without the UCS. After extinction, spontaneous recovery of the CR may occur when the CS is presented after a rest period.
- Stimulus generalization occurs when a CR is elicited by a stimulus similar to the original CS. Discrimination occurs when a CR occurs to one stimulus but not another. In higher-order conditioning, once a stimulus (e.g., a tone) becomes a CS, it can be used in place of the original UCS (food) to condition other neutral stimuli.
- Bodily and psychological responses can be classically conditioned, including fears, sexual attraction, positive and negative attitudes, nausea, and immune system responses. Techniques based on classical conditioning are highly successful in treating phobias.

OPERANT CONDITIONING: LEARNING THROUGH CONSEQUENCES

- Thorndike's law of effect states that responses followed by satisfying consequences are strengthened, whereas those followed by annoying consequences are weakened. Skinner analyzed operant conditioning in terms of antecedents, behaviors, and consequences. Discriminative stimuli are antecedents that signal the likely consequences of particular behaviors in a given situation.

- Reinforcement occurs when a response is strengthened by its consequences. With positive reinforcement, a response is strengthened by the subsequent presentation of a stimulus. With negative reinforcement, a response is strengthened by the removal of an aversive stimulus. In operant extinction, a response weakens and eventually disappears because it no longer is reinforced.

- Punishment occurs when a response is weakened by its consequences. With aversive punishment, the consequence involves the presentation of an aversive stimulus. With response cost, the consequence involves withdrawing a rewarding stimulus. The use of corporal punishment with children is controversial.

- Shaping involves reinforcing successive approximations that increasingly resemble the final desired behavior. Chaining develops a sequence of responses by reinforcing each response with the opportunity to perform the next response.

- Operant generalization occurs when behavior changes in one situation due to reinforcement or punishment, and the new response carries over to similar situations. Operant discrimination occurs when an operant response occurs to one discriminative stimulus but not to another.

- On a continuous reinforcement schedule, every target response is reinforced. Partial reinforcement may occur on a ratio schedule or interval schedule. In general, ratio schedules produce higher rates of performance than interval schedules. On a fixed-ratio schedule, reinforcement occurs after a fixed number of responses. On a fixed-interval schedule, it occurs after a fixed time interval. On variable schedules, the required number of responses or time interval varies around some average.

- Escape conditioning and avoidance conditioning result from negative reinforcement. According to the two-factor theory of avoidance learning, fear is acquired through classical conditioning. This fear motivates escape and avoidance, which are negatively reinforced by fear reduction. Operant conditioning principles have been applied in many settings to enhance performance and reduce behavior problems.

CROSSROADS OF CONDITIONING

- An organism's evolutionary history places biological constraints on learning. Organisms show faster classical conditioning when a CS has evolutionary significance. It also is difficult to operantly condition animals to perform behaviors contrary to their evolved natural tendencies. Instinctive drift occurs when an operantly conditioned response reverts to a more natural response.

- Köhler's studies of animal insight and Tolman's research on cognitive maps suggested that cognition plays a role in learning. Cognitive interpretations of classical conditioning propose that organisms learn an expectancy that the CS will be followed by the UCS. Cognitive learning theorists view operant conditioning as the development of an expectancy that certain behaviors will produce certain consequences under certain conditions. Research on latent learning indicates that learning can occur without reinforcement.

OBSERVATIONAL LEARNING: WHEN OTHERS SHOW THE WAY

- Observational learning occurs by watching the behavior of a model. Bandura's social-cognitive theory proposes that modeling involves attention, retention, reproduction, and motivation. Observing successful models can increase people's self-efficacy and motivate them to perform the modeled behavior.

- Children can learn aggressive and prosocial behaviors by watching models, and modeling is an instructional technique in everyday skill-learning situations. Psychologists have applied modeling concepts to increase adults' prosocial behavior. Social-cognitive theory has stimulated intervention programs to address social problems, such as illiteracy and HIV/AIDS.

THE ADAPTIVE BRAIN

- The brain's ability to adapt and modify itself in response to experience underlies our ability to learn. No single brain structure regulates all learning. The hypothalamus and dopamine pathways play a role in enabling us to experience reward. The cerebellum and amygdala are involved in acquiring different types of classically conditioned responses. Research demonstrates that learning alters the brain.

KEY TERMS AND CONCEPTS

Each term has been boldfaced and defined in the chapter on the page indicated in parentheses.

anticipatory nausea and vomiting (ANV) (p. 221)
applied behavior analysis (p. 235)
aversion therapy (p. 221)

aversive punishment (positive punishment, punishment by application) (p. 227)
avoidance conditioning (p. 233)
chaining (p. 230)

classical conditioning (p. 215)
cognitive map (p. 241)
conditioned response (CR) (p. 217)
conditioned stimulus (CS) (p. 216)

? thinking critically

WHY DID CAROL'S CAR PHOBIA PERSIST?
(Page 218)

We can't know for sure why Carol's fear reaction failed to extinguish, but a strong possibility is that she was not exposed to sufficient extinction trials. The key to extinction is the presentation of the CS (car) without the UCS (events of the crash). If Carol avoided cars after her accident, then there was little opportunity for the CS to occur without the UCS. This is the unfortunate irony of phobias: people avoid the stimulus they fear, thereby depriving themselves of extinction trials. Thus the key ingredient to extinction is not the mere passage of time but repeated presentation of the CS without the UCS.

WAS THE "LITTLE ALBERT" STUDY ETHICAL?
(Page 220)

Imagine that we are reviewing this research proposal in 1918.

(1) If you initially thought that you would not approve this study, consider the following:

- Suppose the experimenters obtain Albert's parents' informed consent.

- Although Albert will experience short-term stress, consider the enormous potential benefits of this study. It may revolutionize thinking about phobias and lead to effective treatments that benefit countless people with phobias.

- Suppose the experimenters promise to use learning principles to extinguish Albert's phobia immediately after the study.

Would you now approve the study?

(2) If your initial (or new) judgment is to approve this study, consider the following:

- Based on learning theory, isn't there a long-term risk that the phobia will generalize to other stimuli?

- If a phobia is successfully conditioned, is it guaranteed that Albert will receive treatment to eliminate it? Has the treatment been tested with humans? What is the failure rate? If there already is good evidence that it's effective, why conduct this study?

Applying today's ethical standards, we believe this research proposal would have been rejected. There was insufficient evidence at the time to support the effectiveness of phobia extinction treatment with humans. An ethical alternative approach would have been to study whether learning-based treatments could effectively treat patients who already had phobias.

CAN YOU EXPLAIN THE "SUPERMARKET TANTRUM"? (Page 229)

The father's initial refusal to buy candy is followed by an aversive stimulus (the tantrum). This punishes the father's response, and after two tantrums he no longer refuses the request. When the father eventually gives in, this removes the aversive stimulus (the tantrum), which negatively reinforces (strengthens) the response of giving in. Thus the father's response of refusing to buy candy is weakened by punishment, and the response of giving in is strengthened by negative reinforcement. Just as important, the child has learned that throwing a tantrum pays off. The tantrum was positively reinforced by the consequence of getting candy.

chapter eight

Memory

CHAPTER OUTLINE

Myth or Reality?

If You Can Confidently Recall Something, That Memory Is Accurate (page 269)

Do you have memories of events in your life that you can recall so clearly, so confidently, that it seems as if those memories were etched in your mind with a permanent marker? We simply can't forget the details of such vivid memories. Or can we?

(a)

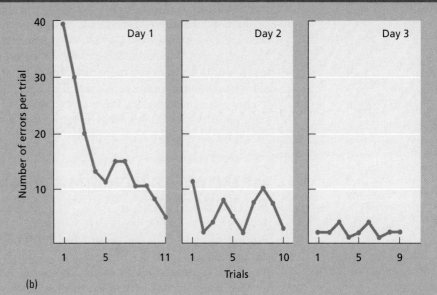

(b)

Figure 8.1

Learning without consciously remembering.
(a) On this complex task, a participant traces a pattern while looking at its mirror image, which also shows the writing hand moving in the direction opposite to its actual movement. (b) H. M.'s performance on this task rapidly improved over time—he made fewer and fewer errors—indicating that he had retained a memory of how to perform the task. Yet each time he performed it, he stated that he had never seen the task before and had to have the instructions explained again. SOURCE: Adapted from Milner, 1965.

At age 5, Rajan Mahadevan sauntered outside his home in India one day while his parents entertained about 40 to 50 guests at a party. Rajan studied the guests' parked cars, returned to the party, and then recited all the license plate numbers from memory, matching each to the proper guest in the order they had parked. While in college, Rajan set a world record by flawlessly recalling the first 31,811 digits of pi. He averaged 3.5 digits per second! Yet in most other ways, Rajan's memory is ordinary. As he notes, "Unless I put my glasses, wallet and keys together near the door before I leave to start my day, I will surely forget them" (Harris, 2002).

Whereas Rajan achieved fame for his extraordinary remembering, H. M. became one of the most famous cases in neuropsychology because of his extraordinary forgetting (MacKay et al., 2009). At age 27, H. M. had most of his hippocampus and surrounding brain tissue surgically removed to reduce his severe epileptic seizures. The operation succeeded but unexpectedly left H. M. with severe *amnesia* (memory loss).

For the most part, H. M.'s memories from his childhood, teens, and early 20s were still intact. What he lost was the ability to form new memories that he could consciously recall. Typically, once an experience or fact left his immediate train of thought, he could not remember it. Spend the day with H. M., depart and return minutes later, and he would not recall having met you. He read magazines over and over as if he had never seen them before. H. M. couldn't remember being told that a favorite uncle had died. Thus every time H. M. asked how his uncle was, he experienced shock and grief as if hearing of his uncle's death for the first time.

H. M.'s surgery took place in 1953, and researchers studied him for more than 50 years (Steinvorth et al., 2005). No matter how many years passed up until his death in 2008, his memory of new events contained little after 1953.

A psychologist would ask what these two extraordinary cases tell us about the complexity of human memory. How does Rajan perform such amazing feats of numerical memory? Does he have truly rare memory ability? If so, why can't he remember where he places his keys? Why is it, as Figure 8.1 shows, that with practice H. M. can remember the skilled movements needed to perform a new task, yet swear each time he encounters the task that he has never seen it before (Milner, 1965)?

In this chapter we explore the fascinating nature of memory. **Memory** *refers to the processes that allow us to record, store, and later retrieve experiences and information.* Memory adds richness and context to our lives, but even more fundamentally, it allows us to learn from experience and thus adapt to changing environments. From an evolutionary standpoint, without the capacity to remember we would not have survived as a species.

MEMORY AS INFORMATION PROCESSING

Psychological research on memory has a rich tradition, dating back to late-19th-century Europe. By the 1960s, computer advances and the cognitive revolution in psychology had led to a new metaphor that continues to guide memory research: the mind as a processing system that encodes, stores, and retrieves information. **Encoding** *refers to getting information into the system by translating it into a neural code that your brain processes.* This is a little like what happens when you type on a computer keyboard, as your keystrokes are translated into an electrical code that the computer can understand and process. **Storage** *involves retaining information over time.* Once in the system, information must be filed away and saved, as happens when a computer stores information temporarily in RAM (random access memory) and more permanently on a hard drive. Finally, **retrieval** *refers to processes that access stored information.* On a computer, retrieval occurs when you give a software command (e.g., "open file") that transfers information from the hard drive back to RAM and the screen, where you can scroll through it. Keep in mind, however, that this analogy between human and computer is crude. For one thing, people routinely forget and distort information and sometimes "remember"

events that never occurred (Laney & Loftus, 2010). Human memory is dynamic, and its complexity cannot be fully captured by any existing information-processing model.

Encoding, storage, and retrieval represent what our memory system does with information. Before exploring these processes more fully, let's examine some basic components of memory.

A Three-Stage Model

The model in Figure 8.2, developed by Richard Atkinson and Richard Shiffrin (1968) and subsequently modified, depicts memory as having three major components: sensory memory, working (short-term) memory, and long-term memory. Other models have been proposed, but this three-stage framework has been the most influential.

Sensory Memory

Sensory memory *briefly holds incoming sensory information.* It comprises different subsystems, called *sensory registers,* which are the initial information processors. Our visual sensory register is called the *iconic store,* and in 1960 George Sperling conducted a classic experiment to assess how long it holds information. On one task, Sperling arranged 12 letters in three rows and four columns, like those in Figure 8.3. He flashed the array on a screen for $\frac{1}{20}$ of a second, after which participants immediately recalled as many letters as they could. Typically, they were able to recall only 3 to 5 letters.

Why was recall so poor? Did participants have too little time to scan all the letters, or had they seen the whole array, only to have their iconic memory fade before they could report all the letters? To find out, Sperling added another experimental condition. This time, just as the letters were flashed off, participants heard either a

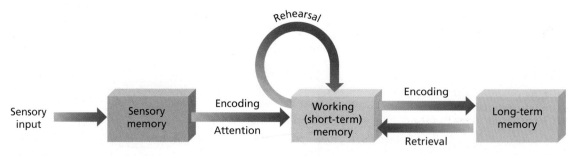

Figure 8.2

The three-stage model of memory.

In this model, memory has three major components: (1) sensory memory, which briefly holds incoming sensory information; (2) working (short-term) memory, which processes certain information received from sensory memory and information retrieved from long-term memory; and (3) long-term memory, which stores information for longer periods of time. SOURCE: Adapted from Atkinson & Shiffrin, 1968.

Fixation

Display (1/20 sec.) plus tone

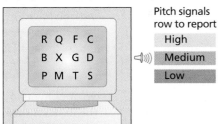

Pitch signals
row to report

| High |
| Medium |
| Low |

Report

Figure 8.3

Sperling's classic study of iconic memory.
After a participant fixates on a screen, a matrix of letters is flashed for $\frac{1}{20}$ of a second. In one condition, participants do not hear any tone and must immediately report as many letters as they can. In another condition, a high-, medium-, or low-pitched tone signals the participant to report either the top, middle, or bottom row. If the tone occurs just as the letters are flashed off, participants typically can report 3 or all 4 letters, no matter which row is signaled.

high-, medium-, or low-pitched tone, which signaled the participants to report either the top, middle, or bottom row of letters.

In this case, participants often could report all 4 letters in whichever row was signaled. Their not knowing which row would be signaled ahead of time implies that their iconic memory had stored an image of the whole array, and they now had time to "read" their iconic image of any one line before it rapidly disappeared. If this logic is correct, then participants should have done poorly if the signaling tone was delayed. Indeed, with just a 1-second delay, performance was no better than without the tone. As Figure 8.4 illustrates, it is difficult, perhaps impossible, to retain complete information in purely visual form for more than a fraction of a second. In contrast, our auditory sensory register, called the *echoic store,* can hold information about the precise details of a sound for several seconds (Winkler et al., 2002).

Working/Short-Term Memory

Most information in sensory memory rapidly fades away. But according to the original three-stage model, through selective attention some information enters **short-term memory,** *a memory store that temporarily holds a limited amount of information.*

Memory Codes   Once information leaves sensory memory, it must be represented by some type of code if it is to be retained in short-term memory. For example, the words that someone just spoke to you ("I like your new haircut") must somehow become represented in your mind. **Memory codes** *are mental representations of some type of information or stimulus,* and they can take various forms. We may try to form mental images (*visual codes*), code something by sound (*phonological codes*), or focus

on the meaning of a stimulus (*semantic codes*). For physical actions, such as learning sports or playing musical instruments, we code patterns of movement (*motor codes*).

The form of a memory code often does not correspond to the form of the original stimulus. As you read these words (visual stimuli), you are probably not storing images of the way the letters look. Rather, you are likely forming phonological codes (as you say the words silently) and semantic codes (as you think about their meaning) (Lee, 2009). Thus when people are presented with lists of words or letters and asked to recall them immediately, they often make phonetic errors. They

Figure 8.4

The arc of light that you see traced by a twirling sparkler or the lingering flash that you see after observing a lightning bolt results from the brief duration of information in iconic memory. Because your iconic memory stores complete information for only a fraction of a second, the image quickly vanishes.

Table **8.1** | Digit-Span Test

Directions: Starting with the top sequence, read these numbers at a steady rate of one per second. Immediately after saying the last number in each series, signal the person to recall the numbers in order. Most people can recall a maximum sequence of 5 to 9 digits.

8 3 5 2

4 3 9 3 1

7 1 4 9 3 7

5 4 6 9 2 3 6

1 5 2 4 8 5 8 4

9 3 2 6 5 8 2 1 4

6 8 1 3 1 9 4 7 3 5

4 2 4 6 9 5 2 1 7 4 3

3 7 9 8 4 6 1 7 2 4 9 5

might mistakenly recall a *V* as a *B* because of the similarity in how the letters sound.

Capacity and Duration Short-term memory can hold only a limited amount of information at a time. Depending on the stimulus, such as a series of unrelated numbers or letters, most people can hold no more than five to nine meaningful items in short-term memory, leading George Miller (1956) to set the capacity limit at "the magical number seven, plus or minus two." To demonstrate this, try administering the digit-span test in Table 8.1 to some people you know.

If short-term memory capacity is so limited, how can we remember and understand sentences as we read? For a partial answer, read the letters below (one per second); then cover them up and write down as many letters as you can remember, in the order presented.

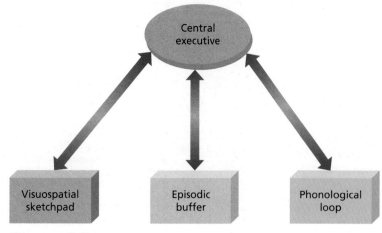

Figure 8.5

Components of working memory.

According to Baddeley's most recent model, working memory has four components. Source: Adapted from Repovs & Baddeley, 2006.

BIRCDERYKAEUQSASAWTI

Did you have any trouble? Now, with the order of the letters reversed (and a few spaces added), try to remember all 20 letters.

IT WAS A SQUEAKY RED CRIB

No doubt you found the second task much easier. The limit on short-term storage capacity concerns the number of meaningful *units* that can be recalled, and the 20 letters have been combined into 6 meaningful units (words). *Combining individual items into larger units of meaning is called* **chunking,** which aids recall.

Short-term memory is limited in duration as well as capacity. Have you ever been introduced to someone and then, moments later, realized that you've forgotten her or his name? Without rehearsal, information in short-term memory generally has a shelf life of up to 20 seconds (Peterson & Peterson, 1959). However, by rehearsing information—such as when you look up a telephone number and keep saying it to yourself while waiting to use a phone—you can extend its duration in short-term memory.

Putting Short-Term Memory to Work The original three-stage model viewed short-term memory as a temporary holding station along the route from sensory to long-term memory. Information that remained in short-term memory long enough presumably was transferred into more permanent storage. Cognitive scientists now reject this view as too passive. Instead, they view short-term memory as **working memory,** *a limited-capacity system that temporarily stores and processes information* (Baddeley, 2007). In other words, working memory is a mental workspace that stores information, actively manipulates it, supports other cognitive functions such as problem solving and planning, and interacts with long-term memory (Baddeley, 2010).

Components of Working Memory According to one influential model, working memory has several components, as shown in Figure 8.5 (Baddeley, 2007; Baddeley & Hitch, 1974). One component, the *phonological loop*, briefly stores mental representations of sounds. The phonological loop is active when you listen to a spoken word or when you sound out a word to yourself as you read. Silently repeating the name of the person to whom you're being introduced will briefly refresh the acoustic codes stored in the phonological loop.

A second component, the *visuospatial sketchpad*, briefly stores visual and spatial information, as occurs when you form a mental image of someone's face or of the spatial layout of your bedroom. Note that the phonological loop and visuospatial sketchpad can be active simultaneously. For example, you can silently repeat the word *sunset* while at the same time holding a mental image of a sunset or, for that matter, of an elephant.

A third component, called the *episodic buffer*, provides a temporary storage space where information from long-term memory and from the phonological and/or visuospatial subsystems can be integrated, manipulated, and made available for conscious awareness. For example, after reading or hearing me say "How much is 87 plus 36?" your phonological loop initially maintains the acoustic codes for the sounds of 87 and 36 in working memory. Your visuospatial sketchpad also might maintain a mental image of the numbers. But to do this task, the rules for performing addition must be retrieved from your long-term memory and temporarily stored in the episodic buffer, where they are integrated with (i.e., applied to) information from the phonological and visuospatial subsystems. This creates the ingredients for the conscious perceptions that you experience as you perform the mental addition (e.g., "7 + 6 = 13, carry the 1 . . . ").

The episodic buffer also comes into play when you chunk information. British psychologist Alan Baddeley (2002) notes that despite the phonological loop's very limited acoustic storage capacity, people can routinely listen to and then repeat novel sentences that are 15 or 16 words long. It is within the episodic buffer, he proposes, that groups of words are chunked into meaningful phrases and stored (and phrases can be further chunked into sentences), enabling us to recall relatively long sections of prose.

The fourth component of working memory, called the *central executive,* directs the overall action. When solving arithmetic problems, for example, the central executive doesn't store the numbers or rules of addition. Instead, it plans and controls the sequence of actions that need to be performed, divides and allocates attention to the other subsystems, and integrates information within the episodic buffer. It also may monitor the progress as interim steps are completed (DeStefano & LeFevre, 2004).

Long-Term Memory

Long-term memory *is our vast library of more durable stored memories.* As far as we know, long-term storage capacity essentially is unlimited, and once formed, a long-term memory can endure for up to a lifetime.

Are short-term and long-term memory really distinct? Case studies of amnesia victims like H. M. suggest so. If you told H. M. your name or some fact, he could remember it briefly but could not form a long-term memory of it. Experiments in which people with normal memory learn lists of words also support this distinction. Suppose that we present you with a series of 15 unrelated words, one word at a time. Immediately after seeing or hearing the last word, you are to recall as many words as you can, in any order you wish. As Figure 8.6 illustrates, most experiments find that words at the end and beginning of a list are the easiest to recall. This U-shaped pattern is called the **serial position effect,** *meaning that the ability to recall an item is influenced by the item's position in a series.* The serial position effect has two components: a *primacy effect*, reflecting the superior recall of the earliest items, and a *recency effect*, representing the superior recall of the most recent items.

What causes the primacy effect? According to the three-stage model, as the first few words enter short-term memory, we can quickly rehearse them and transfer them into long-term memory. However, as the list gets longer, short-term memory rapidly fills up and there are too many words to keep

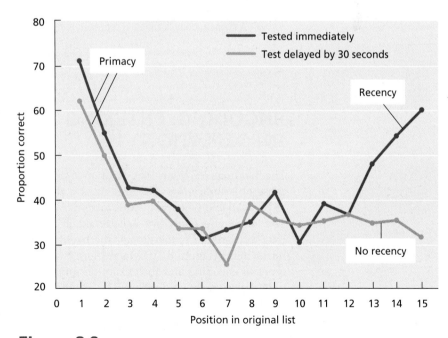

Figure 8.6

The serial position effect.
Immediate recall of a word list produces a serial position curve, where primacy and recency effects are both evident. However, even a delay of 15 to 30 seconds in recall (during which rehearsal is prevented) eliminates the recency effect, indicating that the later items in the word list have disappeared from short-term memory.
Source: Adapted from Glanzer & Cunitz, 1966.

repeating before the next word arrives. Therefore, beyond the first few words, it is harder to rehearse the items and they are less likely to get transferred into long-term memory. If this hypothesis is correct, then the primacy effect should decrease if we are prevented from rehearsing the early words, say, by being presented with the list at a faster rate. Indeed, this is what happens (Glanzer, 1972).

As for the recency effect, the last few words still linger in short-term memory and have the benefit of not being bumped out by new information. Thus if we try to recall the list immediately, all we have to do is recite the last words from short-term memory before they decay (i.e., fade away). In sum, according to the three-stage model, the primacy effect is due to the transfer of early words into long-term memory, whereas the recency effect is due to the continued presence of information in short-term memory.

If this explanation is correct, then it must be possible to wipe out the recency effect—but not the primacy effect—by eliminating the last words from short-term memory. This happens when the recall test is delayed, even for as little as 15 to 30 seconds, *and* we are prevented from rehearsing the last words. To prevent rehearsal, we might be asked to briefly count a series of numbers immediately after the last word is presented (Glanzer & Cunitz, 1966; Postman & Phillips, 1965). Now by the time we try to recall the last words, they will have faded from short-term memory or been bumped out by the numbers task (6 . . . 7 . . . 8 . . . 9 . . .). Figure 8.6 shows that under delayed conditions, the recency effect disappears while the primacy effect remains.

Having examined some basic components of memory, let us now explore more fully how information is encoded, stored, and retrieved.

test yourself — Memory as Information Processing

True or false?

1. Iconic sensory memory typically stores complete information about a stimulus for up to 30 seconds.
2. According to Baddeley, working memory has separate visuospatial and phonological components.
3. When people immediately recall a list of words they've heard, both primacy and recency effects typically occur.
4. A memory code is a mental representation of information or some stimulus.

ANSWERS: 1-false, 2-true, 3-true, 4-true

ENCODING: ENTERING INFORMATION

The holdings of your long-term memory, like those of a library, must be organized if they are to be available when you want to retrieve them. The more effectively we encode material into long-term memory, the greater the likelihood of retrieving it (Figure 8.7). Let's explore two basic types of encoding and then examine some ways to optimize encoding quality.

Effortful and Automatic Processing

Think of the parade of information that you have to remember every day: names, meeting times, and mountains of schoolwork. Remembering it all involves *effortful processing*, encoding that is initiated intentionally and requires conscious attention (Adam et al., 2005). When you rehearse information, make lists, and take notes, you are engaging in effortful processing.

In contrast, have you ever been unable to answer an exam question and thought, "I should know this! I can even picture the diagram on the upper corner of the page!"? In this case, you have apparently transferred information about the diagram's location on the page (which you were not trying to learn) into your long-term memory through *automatic processing*, encoding that occurs without intention and requires minimal attention. Information about the frequency, spatial location, and sequence of events is often encoded automatically (Gallivan et al., 2009).

Levels of Processing: When Deeper Is Better

Imagine that you are participating in a laboratory experiment and are about to be shown a list of

"The matters about which I'm being questioned, Your Honor, are all things I should have included in my long-term memory but which I mistakenly inserted in my short-term memory."

Figure 8.7

Ineffective encoding can have practical as well as theoretical significance. Source: Copyright © Ed Fisher/The New Yorker Collection/cartoonbank.com.

words, one at a time. Each word will be followed by a question, and all you have to do is answer yes or no. Here are three examples:

1. POTATO "Is the word in capital letters?"

2. HORSE "Does the word rhyme with *course*?"

3. TABLE "Does the word fit in the sentence 'The man peeled the ____'?"

Each question requires effort but differs from the others in an important way. Question 1 requires superficial *structural encoding,* as you only have to notice how the word looks. Question 2 requires a little more effort. You must engage in *phonological* (also called *phonemic*) *encoding* by sounding out the word to yourself and then judging whether it matches the sound of another word. Question 3 requires *semantic encoding* because you must pay attention to what the word means.

Like the three examples above, the words you are about to be presented with in this experiment will be followed by a question that requires either structural, phonological, or semantic encoding. Unexpectedly, you will then be given a memory test in which you will be shown a list of words and asked to identify which words were presented earlier. Which group of words will you recognize most easily? Those processed structurally, phonologically, or semantically?

According to the concept of **levels of processing,** *the more deeply we process information, the better we will remember it* (Craik & Lockhart, 1972, 2008). Thus you should best remember those words that you processed semantically, as shown in Figure 8.8. Merely perceiving the structural properties of the words (e.g., uppercase versus lowercase) involves shallow processing, and phonemically encoding words is intermediate. Semantic encoding, however, involves the deepest processing because it requires us to focus on the meaning of information.

Although many experiments have replicated this finding, at times depth of processing can be difficult to measure. If some students prepare for an exam by creating hierarchical outlines while others create detailed flashcards, which method involves deeper processing? Still, the levels-of-processing model has stimulated much research (Froger et al., 2008). There are situations in which few would argue with at least a broad distinction between shallow and deep processing. Here is one of them.

Exposure and Rehearsal

Years ago one of our students sought advice after failing an exam. He said that he had been to all the lectures and read each chapter three times. Yet not a word in his textbook had been underlined or highlighted. When asked whether he took notes as

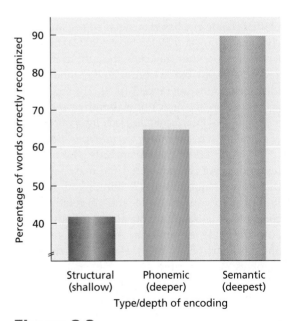

Figure 8.8

Depth of processing and memory.

Participants were shown words and asked questions that required (1) superficial structural processing, (2) somewhat deeper phonemic processing, or (3) even deeper semantic processing of each word. Depth of processing increased later recognition of the words in a larger list. Source: Based on Craik & Tulving, 1975.

he read the text or paused to reflect on the information, he said no. Instead, he read and reread each chapter quickly, much like a novel, and assumed that the information would somehow sink in.

Unfortunately, mere exposure to a stimulus without focusing on it represents shallow processing. To demonstrate, try drawing from memory a picture of a coin (e.g., a U.S. penny), accurately locating all the markings. Few people can do this. Even thousands of shallow exposures to a stimulus do not guarantee long-term retention.

Rehearsal goes beyond mere exposure. When we rehearse information, we are thinking about it. But not all rehearsals are created equal. Have you ever seen a live performance of a play and been amazed at the actors' flawless recall of volumes of material in front of live audiences? You may picture the actors reading the script and saying the words over and over, day after day, until they've memorized their lines. This approach, called **maintenance rehearsal,** *involves simple, rote repetition,* and some students rely on it to learn their course material.

Maintenance rehearsal keeps information active in working memory, as when someone tells you a phone number and you repeat it to yourself as you place the call. However, rote memorization usually is not an optimal method to transfer information into long-term memory.

What, then, is a better method? Professional actors begin not by memorizing but by studying the script in great depth, trying to get into the mindset of their characters. Based on detailed research, psychologists Tony and Helga Noice (2002a) note that actors, "before they gave any thought to memorization, stressed the notion of understanding the ideas behind the utterances" (p. 9). The techniques actors use are examples of **elaborative rehearsal,** *which involves focusing on the meaning of information or expanding (i.e., elaborating) on it in some way.*

If your study habits include (1) organizing and trying to understand the material rather than just memorizing it, (2) thinking about how it applies to your own life, and (3) relating it to concepts or examples you already know, then you are using elaboration. According to Craik and Lockhart (1972, 2008), elaborative rehearsal involves deeper processing than maintenance rehearsal, and experiments show that it is more effective in transferring information into long-term memory (Benjamin & Bjork, 2000).

Organization and Imagery

J. C. is an awe-inspiring restaurant waiter. Perhaps you would like a filet mignon, medium-rare, a baked potato, and Thousand Island dressing on your salad? Whatever you order, it represents only 1 of more than 500 options (7 entrees × 5 serving temperatures × 3 side dishes × 5 salad dressings) available at the restaurant where J. C. works. Yet you and 20 of your friends can place your selections with J. C., and he will remember them perfectly without writing them down.

Psychologists K. Anders Ericsson and Peter Polson (1988) studied J. C. and found that he invented an organizational scheme to aid his memory. He divided customers' orders into four categories (entree, temperature, side dish, dressing) and used a different system to encode the orders in each category. For example, he encoded dressings by their initial letter, so orders of Thousand Island, oil and vinegar, blue cheese, and oil and vinegar would become *TOBO*. Organizational schemes are an excellent way to enhance memory.

Hierarchies and Chunking

Organizing material in a *hierarchy* takes advantage of the principle that memory is enhanced by associations between concepts (Herrmann et al., 2002). A logical hierarchy enhances our understanding of how individual items are related; as we proceed from top to bottom, each category serves as a cue that triggers our memory for the items below it. Because hierarchies have a visual organization, imagery can be used as a supplemental memory code. The hierarchy in Figure 8.9, for example, may help you remember some concepts about encoding.

As noted earlier, chunking refers to combining individual items into larger units of meaning. To refresh your memory, read the letters below (one per second), then try to recall as many as you can in the same sequence.

I R S Y M C A I B M C I A F B I

If you recalled 5 to 9 letters in order, you did well. Now let's reorganize these 16 letters into 5 larger, more meaningful chunks: IRS, YMCA, IBM, CIA, and FBI. These chunks are easier to rehearse, keep active in working memory, and transfer into long-term memory. When learning a new telephone number (e.g., 123-456-7890), you probably encode it in chunks.

Visual Imagery

What did your sixth-grade classmates look like? To answer this question, you might construct mental images in your working memory, based on information that you draw out of long-term memory.

Allan Paivio (1969, 2006) proposes that information is stored in long-term memory in two forms: verbal codes and visual codes. According

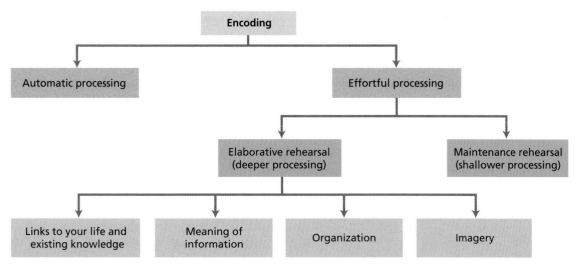

Figure 8.9

Meaningful hierarchical organization enhances memory.
Placing information into a meaningful hierarchy enhances encoding and memory. This hierarchy could be developed further by adding a fifth level of boxes under "Organization" labeled *Hierarchies, Chunking, Acronyms*, and *Rhymes*. A box labeled *Method of loci* could be added under "Imagery," although it also organizes information.

to his **dual coding theory,** *encoding information using both verbal and visual codes enhances memory because the odds improve that at least one of the codes will be available later to support recall.* Dual coding, however, is harder to use with some types of stimuli than others. Try to construct a mental image of (1) a fire truck and (2) jealousy. You probably found the second task more difficult because jealousy represents an abstract concept rather than a concrete object (Fliessbach et al., 2006).

Memory experts recommend using imagery to dual-code information. The ancient Greeks developed the **method of loci** (*loci* is Latin for "places"), *a memory aid that associates information with mental images of physical locations.* To use this technique, imagine a place that has distinct locations, such as your campus. Next, link each location with an item you are trying to remember. For example, to remember the components of working memory, imagine walking to the administration building (central executive), an art studio (visuospatial sketchpad), a music room (phonological loop), and the campus newspaper room (episodic buffer). It takes practice to use this technique effectively, but many studies support its effectiveness (Massen et al., 2009).

Other Mnemonic Devices

The term *mnemonics* (*nee-MON-iks*) refers to the art of improving memory, and a **mnemonic device** *is a memory aid.* Mnemonic devices reorganize information into more meaningful units and provide extra cues to help retrieve information from

long-term memory. Hierarchies, chunking, visual imagery, and the method of loci are mnemonic devices. So are *acronyms*, which combine one or more letters (usually the first letter) from each piece of information you want to remember. For example, many students learn the acronym ROY G. BIV to help remember the hues in the visible spectrum (the colors of the rainbow: red, orange, yellow, green, blue, indigo, violet).

Even putting information in a rhyme may enhance memory (Whalen, 2003). Some students use rhyming when they study, and advertisers often include rhyming jingles in their messages. In one experiment, adults exposed to rhymes in advertisements remembered more product information than did adults exposed to the same advertisements without the rhymes (Smith & Phillips, 2001).

How Prior Knowledge Shapes Encoding

Can you recall the paragraph you just read word for word? Typically, when we read, listen to someone speak, or experience some event, we do not precisely encode every word, sentence, or moment. Rather, we usually encode the *gist*—the general theme (e.g., "rhymes can enhance memory")—of that information or event.

Schemas: Our Mental Organizers

The themes that we extract from events and encode into memory are often organized around *schemas*. A **schema** *is a mental framework—an organized pattern of thought—about some aspect of the world*

(Bartlett, 1932; Silva et al., 2006). For example, the concepts "dog," "shopping," and "love" serve as schemas that help you organize your world. To see more clearly what a schema is and how it can influence encoding, read the following paragraph.

> The procedure is actually quite simple. First you arrange things into different groups. Of course, one pile may be sufficient depending on how much there is to do. If you have to go somewhere else due to lack of facilities, that is the next step; otherwise you are pretty well set . . . it is better to do too few things at once than too many. In the short run this might not seem important, but complications can easily arise. A mistake can be expensive as well. . . . After the procedure is completed, one arranges the materials into different groups again. Then they can be put into their appropriate places. Eventually they will be used once more, and the whole cycle will have to be repeated. (Bransford & Johnson, 1972, p. 722)

Asked to recall the details of the preceding paragraph, you would probably have trouble. However, suppose we tell you that the paragraph is about a common activity: washing clothes. Now if you read the paragraph again, you will find that the abstract and seemingly unrelated details suddenly make sense. Your schema for "washing clothes" helps you organize and encode these details as a meaningful pattern and thus remember more of them.

Schemas, Encoding, and Expertise

When most people look at a musical score, they see sheets of uninterpretable information. In contrast, musicians see organized patterns that they can easily encode. In music, as in other fields, acquiring *expertise* is a process of developing schemas that help encode information into meaningful patterns (Boschker et al., 2002).

William Chase and Herbert Simon (1973) demonstrated this point in a classic study. Three chess players—an expert ("master"), an intermediate player, and a beginner—were allowed 5 seconds to look at a chessboard containing about 25 pieces. Then they looked away and, on an empty board, attempted to reconstruct the placement of the pieces from memory. This was repeated over several trials, each with a different arrangement of pieces. On some trials, the chess pieces were arranged in *meaningful positions* that actually might occur in game situations. With only a 5-second glance, the expert typically recalled 16 pieces, the intermediate player 8, and the novice only 4. But when the pieces were in *random positions,* each player did poorly, accurately recalling only 2 or 3 pieces.

What explains these results? We have to reject the idea that the expert had better overall memory than the other players, because he performed no better than they did with the random arrangements. But the concepts of schemas and chunking do explain the findings (Gobet & Simon, 2000). When the chess pieces were arranged in meaningful positions, the expert could apply well-developed schemas to recognize patterns and group pieces together. For example, he would treat as a unit all pieces that were positioned to attack the king. The intermediate and novice players, who did not have well-developed chess schemas, could not construct the chunks and had to try to memorize the position of each piece.

However, when the pieces were not in positions that would occur in a real game, they were no more meaningful to the expert than to the other players. When that happened, the expert lost the advantage of schemas and had to approach the task on a piece-by-piece basis just as the other players did. Similarly, football coaches show much better recall than novices do after looking at diagrams of football plays (patterns of Xs and Os), but only when the plays are logical (Figure 8.10).

Encoding and Exceptional Memory

A **mnemonist** (or **memorist**) *is a person who displays extraordinary memory skills.* It's tempting to assume that mnemonists like waiter J. C. or pi-master Rajan Mahadevan have an innate, photographic memory. But K. Anders Ericsson and his colleagues (2004; Hu et al., 2009) argue that exceptional memory is a highly learned skill that involves extensive practice and efficient encoding, storage, and retrieval.

Mnemonists take advantage of basic memory principles. Many create visual images or stories to help them encode information. They often chunk information into larger units, combine smaller chunks into larger ones, and elaborate on the material by associating chunks with other meaningful information. Thus, 194473862001 might become "1944 = World War II; 73 and 86 = two old people; 2001 = famous movie." Combining techniques like these with 190 hours of practice, a college student with average memory became capable of remembering strings of up to 80 numbers on a digit-span test (Ericsson et al., 1980).

How, then, did Rajan learn 31,811 digits of pi? Rajan said that he did not have a photographic memory, and psychologists Charles Thompson and coworkers (1993), who studied Rajan intensively, agreed. Instead, they found that Rajan used chunking; the mathematical tables of pi that he studied grouped digits in chunks of 10, so

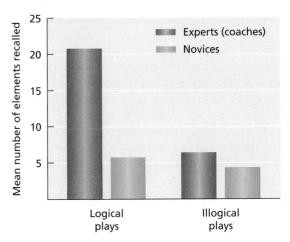

Figure 8.10

Schemas, expertise, and memory.
Diagrams of football plays were shown to football coaches (experts) and to people who had played football but were not coaches (novices). Given 5 seconds to see each play, coaches displayed excellent memory—but only when the plays were logical. Their well-developed football schemas were of little use when the patterns of Xs and Os were illogical. These findings are similar to those obtained when expert, intermediate, and novice chess players tried to reproduce meaningful and random arrangements of chess pieces. Source: Based on Garland & Barry, 1991.

Rajan did the same. But surprisingly, Rajan did not associate the chunks with meaningful material. Rather, beyond basic chunking, Rajan relied primarily on the brute force of rote memorization and extensive practice. How much practice? Thompson and coworkers estimated that it took Rajan over a year to learn the digits of pi.

Realize that just because rote memorization can transfer information into long-term memory, it's not necessarily the best way. Mnemonists (including the current record holder who recalled 67,890 digits of pi) often use elaborative rehearsal (Hu et al., 2009). Moreover, rote memorization is better suited to learning number strings than to learning material that has meaning. When Rajan applied his rote strategy to memory tasks that involved meaningful stimuli (e.g., written stories), he performed more poorly or no better than college students in a control group.

So, is exceptional memory a learned skill? After a year of practice, could the average person really remember 32,000 digits of pi? Thompson and coworkers (1993) believe that in memory, as in sports and music, endless skilled practice will not enable most people to rise to the top unless they also have the requisite innate ability. Yet Ericsson and coworkers (1993, 2004) disagree, arguing that "many characteristics once believed to reflect innate talent are actually the result of intense practice" (1993, p. 363).

? thinking **critically**

WOULD PERFECT MEMORY BE A GIFT OR A CURSE?

If you could have a perfect memory, would you want it? What might be the drawbacks? Think about it, then see page 291.

test yourself   Encoding

True or false?

1. According to the levels-of-processing model, semantic encoding represents deeper processing than structural encoding.
2. Rote memorization is an example of elaborative rehearsal.
3. Organizing information into hierarchies is an example of elaborative rehearsal.
4. It's easier to use dual coding with abstract rather than concrete concepts.
5. Researchers agree that exceptional memory is an innate ability, not a learned skill.

ANSWERS: 1-true, 2-false, 3-true, 4-false, 5-false

STORAGE: RETAINING INFORMATION

At a moment's notice you can recall an incredible wealth of information, from the name of Russia's capital to how you spent your most recent vacation. This ability to rapidly access diverse facts, concepts, and experiences has influenced many cognitive models of how information is stored and organized in memory.

Memory as a Network

We noted that memory is enhanced by forming associations between new information and other items already in memory. The general principle that memory involves associations goes to the heart of the *network* approach.

Associative Networks

One group of theories proposes that long-term memory can be represented as an **associative network,** *a massive network of associated ideas and concepts* (Collins & Loftus, 1975; Bower, 2008). Figure 8.11 shows what a tiny portion of such a

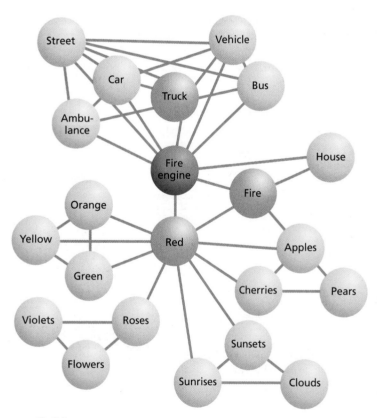

Figure 8.11

Semantic networks.
Each node in this semantic network represents a concept. The lines represent associations between concepts, with shorter lines indicating stronger associations. Source: Adapted from Collins & Loftus, 1975.

network might be like. In this network, each concept or unit of information—"fire engine," "red," and so on—is represented by a *node* somewhat akin to each knot in a huge fishing net. The lines in this network represent associations between concepts, with shorter lines indicating stronger associations. For simplicity, Figure 8.11 shows only a few connections extending from each node, but there could be hundreds or more. Notice that items within the same category—types of flowers, types of fruit, colors, and so on—generally have the strongest associations and therefore tend to be clustered closer together. In essence, an associative network is a type of schema; it is a mental framework that represents how we have organized information and how we understand the world.

Alan Collins and Elizabeth Loftus (1975) theorize that when people think about a concept, such as "fire engine," there is a *spreading activation* of related concepts throughout the network. For example, when you think about a "fire engine," related concepts such as "truck," "fire," and "red" should be partially activated as well. The term **priming** *refers to the activation of one concept (or one unit of information) by another.* Thus "fire engine" primes the node for "red," making it more likely that our memory for this color will be accessed (Chwilla & Kolk, 2002).

Neural Networks

Neural network models take a different approach to explain why spreading activation and priming occur (Chappell & Humphreys, 1994; Herd et al., 2006). Neural network models are computer models whose programming incorporates principles taken from the operation of the nervous system. A neural network has nodes (often called *units*) that are linked to each other, but unlike the nodes in associative network models, each node in a neural network model does not contain an individual unit of information. There is no single node for "red," no single node for "fire engine," and so on. Instead, each node in a neural network is more like a small information-processing unit. As an analogy, think of each neuron in your brain as a node. A neuron processes inputs and sends outputs to other neurons, but as far as we know, the concepts of "red" and "fire engine" are not stored within any single neuron.

Recall that in the brain, neurons have synaptic connections with many other neurons, receive and send signals that can be excitatory (increasing the likelihood that a neuron will fire) or inhibitory (decreasing the likelihood of firing), and will fire if the overall input they receive moves their electrical potential to a certain threshold point. Similarly, nodes in neural network models have connections with many other nodes, are programmed to receive and transmit excitatory or inhibitory signals, and become activated when the input they receive reaches a certain threshold strength. Just as learning experiences modify the brain's neural circuitry, in computer simulations neural networks "gain experience" by processing different bits of information, such as sounds or visual patterns. As they do, connections among various nodes become stronger or weaker (reflected by changes in the mathematical weight assigned to each connection) and the network learns to recognize and distinguish between different types of stimuli (e.g., images of faces, spoken words, and so on).

In trying to model how memory operates, if concepts such as "red" and "fire engine" are not stored in their own individual nodes, then where are they stored? In **neural network (connectionist) models,** *each memory is represented by a unique pattern of interconnected and simultaneously activated nodes.* When node 4 is activated simultaneously (i.e., in parallel) with nodes 95 and 423, the concept "red" comes to mind. But when node 4 is simultaneously activated with nodes 78 and 901, the concept of "fire engine" enters our thoughts.

As we look across the entire neural network, various nodes *distributed* throughout the network fire in parallel at each instant and simultaneously spread their activation to other nodes. In this manner, certain nodes prime other nodes, and concepts and information are retrieved. For this reason, *neural network (connectionist) models are often called* **parallel distributed processing (PDP) models** (Rumelhart et al., 1986). Scientists in many fields are using the neural network approach to model learning, memory, language disorders, and other cognitive processes (Joanisse, 2009).

Types of Long-Term Memory

Research with amnesia patients, brain-imaging studies, and animal experiments indicate that the brain houses several long-term memory systems (Park & Gutchess, 2005). Think back, for example, to H. M.'s amnesia. Once new facts or new personal experiences leave his immediate train of thought, he is unable to remember them consciously. Yet with practice, H. M. can retain the skills needed to perform new tasks even though

he cannot recall having seen the tasks before (Milner, 1965).

Declarative and Procedural Memory

Declarative memory *involves factual knowledge* and includes two subcategories (Figure 8.12). **Episodic memory** *is our store of knowledge concerning personal experiences: when, where, and what happened in the episodes of our lives.* Your recollections of childhood friends, a favorite movie, and what you ate this morning represent episodic memories. **Semantic memory** *represents general factual knowledge about the world and language, including memory for words and concepts.* You know that Mount Everest is the world's tallest peak and that $e = mc^2$. Episodic and semantic memories are called *declarative* because to demonstrate our knowledge, we typically have to declare it: we tell other people what we know.

H. M.'s brain damage impaired both components of his declarative memory. He could not remember new personal experiences, nor could he remember new general facts. For example, H. M. retained good memory for words that he had learned growing up (Kensinger et al., 2001). Yet no matter how many times he was told their definitions, he could not remember the meaning of new words (e.g., *Xerox, biodegradable*) that entered the English language in the years after his operation. In contrast, some brain-injured children cannot remember their daily personal experiences but can remember new factual knowledge, enabling them to learn language and attend mainstream schools (Vargha-Khadem et al., 1997).

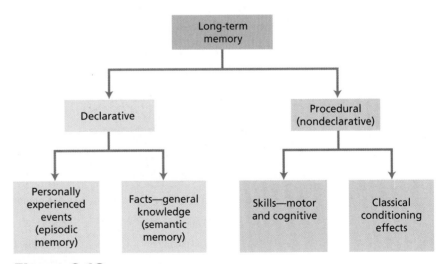

Figure 8.12

Multiple long-term memory systems.
Some theorists propose that we have separate but interacting declarative and procedural memory systems. Episodic and semantic memories are declarative; their contents can be verbalized. Procedural memory is demonstrated through skills and actions.

Procedural (nondeclarative) memory *is reflected in skills and actions* (Cohen et al., 2005). One component of procedural memory consists of skills that are expressed by doing things in particular situations, such as typing or riding a bicycle. H. M. formed a new procedural memory when he learned how to perform the mirror-tracing task.

Classically conditioned responses also reflect procedural memory. After a tone was repeatedly paired with a puff of air blown toward H. M.'s eye, he began to blink involuntarily to the tone alone (Woodruff-Pak, 1993). Although H. M. could not consciously remember undergoing this procedure (i.e., he did not form a declarative memory), his brain stored a memory for the tone–air puff association, and thus he blinked when subsequently exposed to the tone alone (i.e., he formed a procedural memory).

Explicit and Implicit Memory

Many researchers distinguish between *explicit* and *implicit memory*. **Explicit memory** *involves conscious or intentional memory retrieval, as when you consciously recognize or recall something. Recognition* requires us to decide whether a stimulus is familiar, as when an eyewitness is asked to pick out a suspect from a police lineup or when students take multiple-choice tests. In recognition tasks, the target stimuli (possible suspects or answers) are provided to you. *Recall* involves spontaneous memory retrieval, in the sense that you must retrieve the target stimuli or information on your own. This occurs when you are briefly shown a list of words and then asked to recall them. With *cued recall*, hints are given to stimulate memory. If you cannot recall the word *hat* from the list, we might say, "It rhymes with *bat*." As a student, you are no doubt familiar with test items that involve recall or cued recall, such as essay, short-answer, and fill-in-the-blank questions.

Implicit memory *occurs when memory influences our behavior without conscious awareness* (Mulligan & Dew, 2009). H. M. was able to form a procedural memory for performing the mirror-tracing task, although he had no conscious awareness of having learned it. His memory for the task (in this case, procedural memory) was implicit.

In less dramatic ways, each of us demonstrates memory without conscious awareness. Riding a bicycle, driving, and performing any well-learned skill are common examples. Bicycling to class, you may be consciously thinking about an upcoming exam while your implicit, procedural memory enables you to keep pedaling and maintain your balance.

Consider another example of implicit memory. Suppose that as part of an experiment you read a list of words (one word per second) that includes *kitchen, moon,* and *defend*. Days, weeks, or even a year later, you participate in another, seemingly unrelated study. The experimenter rapidly shows you many word stems, some of which might be <u>KIT—</u>, <u>MO—</u>, and <u>DE—</u>, and asks you to complete each stem to form a word. You are not aware that this is a memory test, but compared with people not given the original list of words, you will be more likely to complete the stems with words on the original list (e.g., <u>MOon</u>, rather than <u>MOther</u> or <u>MOney</u>). This represents one of many types of *priming tasks:* the word stems have activated, or primed, your stored mental representations of the original complete words. This suggests that information from the original list is still in your memory and is implicitly influencing your behavior even though you may have no explicit, conscious recall of the original words (Bruss & Mitchell, 2009).

---

test yourself   **Storage**

Match each numbered type of memory to one or more correct examples on the right.

1. episodic memory
2. procedural memory
3. semantic memory
4. declarative memory

a. a classically conditioned response
b. "Last Friday I went to the movies with friends."
c. "Galileo Galilei was an Italian astronomer."
d. a quarterback throwing a football

ANSWERS: 1-b, 2-a and d, 3-c, 4-b and c

RETRIEVAL: ACCESSING INFORMATION

Storing information is useless without the ability to retrieve it. A **retrieval cue** is *a stimulus, whether internal or external, that activates information stored in long-term memory.* If I ask you, "Have you seen Sonia today?" the word *Sonia* is intended to serve as a retrieval cue. Likewise, a yearbook picture can act as a retrieval cue that triggers memories of a classmate. Priming is another example of how a retrieval cue (*MO—*) can trigger associated elements (*MOon*) in memory, presumably via a process of spreading activation (Chwilla & Kolk, 2002).

The Value of Multiple Cues

Experiments by Timo Mäntylä (1986) vividly show the value of having multiple retrieval cues. In one, Swedish college students were presented with a list of 504 words. Some students were asked to think of and write down one association for each word, while others produced three associations per word. To illustrate, what three words come to your mind when I say *banana*? Perhaps you might think of *peel, fruit,* and *ice cream.*

The students had no idea that their memory would be tested, and after finishing the association task they were given an unexpected recall test for 252 of the original words. For some words, students were first shown the one or three associations they had just generated. As a control, for other words they were first shown one or three associations another participant had generated. Then they tried to recall the original word.

The results were remarkable. When the associations (i.e., retrieval cues) were self-generated, students shown one cue recalled 61 percent of the words and those shown three cues recalled 91 percent. In contrast, when students were shown cues that someone else had generated, recall with one cue dropped to 11 percent and with three cues to 55 percent. Further, when given another surprise recall test 1 week later on the remaining 252 words, students still remembered 65 percent of the words when they were first provided with three self-generated retrieval cues.

Why does having multiple, self-generated retrieval cues maximize recall? On the encoding side, generating your own associations involves deeper processing than does being presented with associations generated by someone else. Similarly, generating three associations involves deeper processing than generating only one. On the retrieval side, these self-generated associations become cues that have personal meaning. And with multiple cues, if one fails, another may activate the memory. The implication for studying academic material is clear. Think about the material you are studying, and draw one or (preferably) more links to ideas, knowledge, or experiences that have meaning for you.

The Value of Distinctiveness

To demonstrate a simple point, here is a brief self-test. A list of words appears below. Say each word to yourself (one per second); then when you see the word *WRITE,* look away and write down as many words as you can recall, in any order. Here's the list:

> sparrow, eagle, nest, owl, feather, goose, crow, artichoke, rooster, fly, robin, parrot, chirp, hawk, pigeon, WRITE

If you are like most of our own students, you probably recalled *artichoke* even though it appeared in the middle of the list. The other words all relate to birds, but *artichoke* is a food: it's distinctive. In general, distinctive stimuli are better remembered than nondistinctive ones (Bireta & Simels, 2009; Ghetti et al., 2002).

In school, when all the material starts looking the same, you can make it more distinctive by associating it with other information that is personally meaningful to you. According to Mäntylä (1986), this is one reason why students who generated their own three-word associations remembered almost all of the original 504 words. The associations formed a distinctive set of cues.

Distinctive events stand a greater chance of etching long-term memories that seem vivid and clear. In one study, college students listed their three clearest memories (Rubin & Kozin, 1984). Distinctive events such as weddings, romantic encounters, births and deaths, vacations, and accidents were among the most frequently recalled. In another study, college students watched a videotape of a guest lecturer who engaged in some distinctive, atypical behaviors (e.g., ate potato chips, burped) and some typical ones (e.g., sat down, took off jacket). On a memory test a week later, students correctly remembered about 80 percent of all the lecturer's behaviors, but they were more likely to report having a clear image of the distinctive ones (Neuschatz et al., 2002).

Arousal, Emotion, and Memory

Many experiences in our lives may be remembered better because they were distinctive and because they also stirred up our emotions and

Figure 8.13

A memory of an emotionally arousing, distinctive event can seem so vivid and clear that we feel we can picture it as if it were a snapshot of a moment in time. Researchers call this a *flashbulb memory*.

aroused us (Figure 8.13). In experiments, people shown arousing and neutral stimuli (e.g., pictures of happy, fearful, or neutral faces; violent or neutral film scenes) typically remember the arousing stimuli best, even when tested several weeks later (Putman et al., 2004).

Why do emotionally arousing stimuli wind their way more deeply into memory? By physiologically monitoring people, researchers have found that arousing stimuli trigger the release of stress hormones. This causes neurotransmitters to increase activation of the amygdala, a brain structure that helps encode the emotional aspects of experiences into longer-term memories (Chavez et al., 2009). Injecting rats with drugs that stimulate or inhibit stress-hormone activity will, respectively, boost or impair the rats' ability to remember responses that they are learning or have recently learned.

Outside the laboratory, researchers have found that emotional arousal enhances **autobiographical memories,** *recollections of personally experienced events that make up the stories of our lives* (Schaefer & Philippot, 2005). When people are asked to record their unique daily experiences in a diary and rate the emotional pleasantness and intensity of each event (e.g., say, on a 7-point scale ranging from "extremely unpleasant" to "extremely pleasant"), it typically is the more

intense events that they recall most vividly when tested days, months, or years later.

Over time, however, the emotionality of most pleasant and unpleasant memories may fade a bit (Walker et al., 1997). Interestingly, even though pleasant and unpleasant events may be equally arousing when they happen, the intensity of memories for pleasant events seems to fade little less rapidly over time. This slower emotional fading of positive memories, combined with cross-cultural findings that most people express positive life satisfaction, led Walker, Skowronski, and Thompson (2003) to proclaim that "life is pleasant—and memory helps to keep it that way!" (p. 203). Of course, as they emphasize, life surely is not pleasant for everyone, and some people don't exhibit these memory effects. Walker, Skowronski, Gibbons, and colleagues (2003) found that among mildly depressed students, the intensity of pleasant and unpleasant memories faded at the same rate. Moreover, some people's memories of traumatic experiences may remain emotionally intense for years.

Overall, then, distinctive and emotionally arousing events are recalled most easily or vividly over time. But just because a memory seems vivid, does this guarantee its accuracy? Let's take a look in the following "Myth or Reality?" segment.

Myth or Reality?
If You Can Confidently Recall Something, That Memory Is Accurate

Are vivid memories like "mental snapshots" of the past? If we recall an experience so confidently that we feel we "remember it just like yesterday," can we assume the memory is accurate? This confidence-accuracy assumption often plays out in the courtroom. As news reporter Leslie Stahl noted in a *60 Minutes* (2009, July 12) episode, "It's a cliché of courtroom dramas—that moment when the witness is asked 'Do you see the person who committed the crime here in this courtroom before you?' It happens in real courtrooms all the time, and to jurors, that point of the finger by a confident eyewitness is about as damning as evidence can get."

But as Stahl also noted, DNA testing has thus far revealed almost 200 cases in which misidentifications by crime victims or other eyewitnesses have helped send innocent defendants to prison. The *60 Minutes* episode told of a crime victim who carefully studied the perpetrator's face during a violent attack. In a police lineup and again in court, the victim was "absolutely certain" of correctly identifying the attacker. Informed 11 years later that DNA testing revealed the imprisoned man was innocent, the victim's stunned reaction was "That's not possible. . . . There's no question in my mind."

Such instances don't imply that crime victims and eyewitnesses usually are mistaken, but they do remind us that in the courtroom, high confidence and vivid recollections don't ensure memory accuracy. Is this also the case in other life contexts?

Consider research on **flashbulb memories**: *recollections that seem so vivid, so clear, that we picture them as if they were snapshots of moments in time.* They're most likely to occur for distinctive events—whether unexpected or expected—that evoke strong emotional reactions (Curci & Luminet, 2009). For example, even if you were a child at the time, perhaps you can still picture the moment on September 11, 2001, when you learned of the terrorist attacks on the United States. Positive events, such as opening a college-acceptance letter, also can produce flashbulb memories (Talarico, 2009).

Because flashbulb memories seem vivid and are easily recalled, we often feel confident of their accuracy. But are they accurate? In 1986 the space shuttle *Challenger* exploded moments after takeoff, killing all on board. It was a horrific event, watched live on TV by a shocked American public. The next day, researchers asked college students to describe how they learned of the disaster, where they were, who they were with, and so on (Neisser & Harsch, 1993). When interviewed again 3 years later, about half of the students remembered some of these autobiographical details correctly but recalled others inaccurately. One-fourth of the students completely misremembered all the major details and were astonished at how inaccurate their memories had become.

In 1997, people across the world were stunned when a car crash killed Princess Diana of Wales. A study in England found that 44 percent of participants said that they had seen a videotape on the TV news showing the crash take place. No such videotape was ever shown, yet they were as confident in their memory as people who said they never saw such a tape (Ost et al., 2002).

A day after the 9/11 terrorist attacks, researchers (Talarico & Rubin, 2003) asked college students to report autobiographical details (e.g., Where were you? Who were you with?) for two events: (1) the moment they learned about the attacks and (2) a typical college event of their choice that they had recently experienced (e.g., a party, sports event). A week, 6 weeks, and 32 weeks later, students' memories of 9/11 were no more accurate than those of the everyday event. For the everyday event, as time passed recall became less accurate, memories became less vivid, and memory confidence decreased. But for 9/11, despite a decrease over time in memory accuracy, students remained as confident and said their memories were as vivid as the day after the attacks. Similarly, examining a nationally representative sample of Americans, other researchers found that 2 years after the attacks, 55 percent of participants incorrectly recalled at least one major autobiographical detail about their experience of 9/11. Participants who had completely accurate recall were more confident of their memories than participants who made errors, but overall, even those who made errors said they were very confident to extremely confident of their memories (Conway et al., 2009).

Other studies of flashbulb memory, spanning different countries and world events, likewise indicate that confidently held, vivid memories can be inaccurate and are subject to various types of memory distortions that we'll discuss later in the chapter (Ost et al., 2008). Even more broadly, researchers have studied the confidence-accuracy relation with children and adults, inside and outside the laboratory, and for many types of events. Overall, memory confidence and accuracy are only weakly to moderately related (Bahrick et al., 2008; Busey et al., 2000). People accurately recall many events—even after years pass—and typically are very confident when they do. But people often swear by vivid, inaccurate memories as well. Vivid memories aren't mental snapshots that let us automatically recall experiences just as they happened, and confidence alone doesn't guarantee memory accuracy.

The Effects of Context, State, and Mood on Memory

Our ability to retrieve a memory is influenced not only by the nature of the original stimulus (such as its distinctiveness) but also by environmental, physiological, and psychological factors. Years ago, two Swedish researchers reported the case of a young woman who was raped while out for a jog (Christianson & Nilsson, 1989). When found by a passerby, she was in shock and could not remember the assault. Over the next 3 months, the police took her back to the crime scene several times. Although she could not recall the rape, she became emotionally aroused, suggesting implicit memory of the event. While jogging one day shortly thereafter, she consciously recalled the rape.

Why did her memory return? One possibility is based on the **encoding specificity principle,** *which states that memory is enhanced when conditions present during retrieval match those that were present during encoding* (Tulving & Thomson, 1973). When stimuli associated with an event become encoded as part of the memory, they may later serve as retrieval cues.

Context-Dependent Memory: Returning to the Scene

Applying the encoding specificity principle to *external* cues leads us to **context-dependent memory:** *it typically is easier to remember something in the same environment in which it was originally encoded.* Thus visiting your high school or old neighborhood may trigger memories of teachers, classmates, and friends. As with the Swedish jogger, police detectives may take an eyewitness or crime victim back to the crime scene, hoping to stimulate the person's memory.

In a classic experiment, Duncan Godden and Alan Baddeley (1975) asked scuba divers to learn some lists of words underwater and some on dry land. When the divers were later retested in both environments, lists learned underwater were recalled better underwater and those learned on land were better recalled on land (Figure 8.14). Other studies, spanning diverse environments, have replicated this finding (Smith & Vela, 2001).

Consider the relevance of context-dependent memory to college life. In one experiment, when randomly assigned college students studied material in either a quiet or noisy room, they later displayed better memory on short-answer and multiple-choice questions when tested in a similar (quiet or noisy) environment (Grant et al., 1998). Thus if you take exams in quiet environments, try to study in a quiet environment.

State-Dependent Memory: Arousal, Drugs, and Mood

Moving from external to internal cues, the concept of **state-dependent memory** *proposes that our ability to retrieve information is greater when our internal state at the time of retrieval matches our original state during learning.* The Swedish jogger who was raped consciously remembered her assault for the first time while jogging. In her case, both context-dependent cues (similar environment) and state-dependent cues (arousal while jogging) may have stimulated her memory.

Diverse experiments support this effect. Many students at the campus gym read course materials while exercising on a bicycle, treadmill, or stair-climber machine. Christopher Miles and Elinor Hardman (1998) found that material learned while we are aroused during aerobic exercise is later recalled more effectively if we are once again aerobically aroused, rather than at rest. Conversely, material learned at rest is better recalled at rest.

Many drugs produce physiological effects that directly impair memory, but state-dependent memory also explains why events experienced in a drugged state may be difficult to recall later

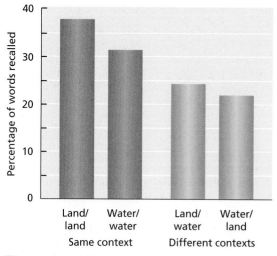

Figure 8.14

Context-dependent memory.
Scuba divers who learned lists of words while under water later recalled them best while under water, whereas words they learned on land were best recalled on land. Recall was poorer when the learning and testing environments were mismatched. Source: Adapted from Godden & Baddeley, 1975.

while in a drug-free state (Figure 8.15). Human and animal experiments examining alcohol, marijuana, amphetamines, and other drugs have often found that information recall is poorer when there is a mismatch between the person's states during learning and testing (Rezayof et al., 2008). This *does not* mean, by the way, that drugs improve memory relative to not taking drugs during initial learning.

Does state-dependent memory extend to mood states? Is material learned while we are in a happy mood or a sad mood better recalled when we are in that mood again? Inconsistent findings suggest that such *mood-dependent memory* is not a reliable phenomenon. Instead, there is more consistent evidence of **mood-congruent recall**: *we tend to recall information or events that are congruent with our current mood* (Fiedler et al., 2001). When happy, we are more likely to remember positive events, and when sad, we tend to remember negative events.

Thus far we have focused on how information is remembered. Now, in the next two sections, let's examine why we forget and why we sometimes remember events that never occurred.

Figure 8.15

State-dependent memory.

In the film *City Lights*, a drunken millionaire befriends and spends the evening partying with Charlie Chaplin after Chaplin saves his life. The next day, in a sober state, the millionaire doesn't remember Chaplin and considers him an unwanted pest. After getting drunk again, he remembers Chaplin and treats him like a good buddy.

test yourself   **Retrieval**

True or false?

1. Having multiple retrieval cues usually causes mental confusion and makes it harder to recall a memory.

2. Memories of highly distinctive, emotionally arousing events are almost always accurate, even many years later.

3. Context- and state-dependent memory both illustrate encoding specificity.

4. Police officers who take an eyewitness back to the scene of a crime to boost his memory are trying to apply the principle of context-dependent memory.

ANSWERS: 1-false, 2-false, 3-true, 4-true

FORGETTING

Some very bright people are legendary for their memory failures. The eminent French writer Voltaire began a passionate letter, "My Dear Hortense," and ended it, "Farewell, my dear Adele." The splendid absentmindedness of English nobleman Canon Sawyer once led him, while welcoming a visitor at a railroad station, to board the departing train and disappear (Bryan, 1986). Indeed, how we forget is as interesting a scientific question as how we remember.

The Course of Forgetting

The German psychologist Hermann Ebbinghaus (1885/1964) pioneered the study of forgetting by testing only one person—himself. He created more than 2,000 *nonsense syllables*, meaningless letter combinations (e.g., *biv, zaj, xew*), to study memory with minimal influence from prior learning, as would happen if he used actual words. In one study, Ebbinghaus performed more than 14,000 practice repetitions trying to memorize 420 lists of nonsense syllables.

Ebbinghaus typically measured memory by using a method called *relearning* and then computing a savings percentage. For example, if it initially took him 20 trials to learn a list but only half as many trials to relearn it a week later, then the savings percentage was 50 percent. In one series of studies, he retested his memory at various time intervals after mastering several lists of

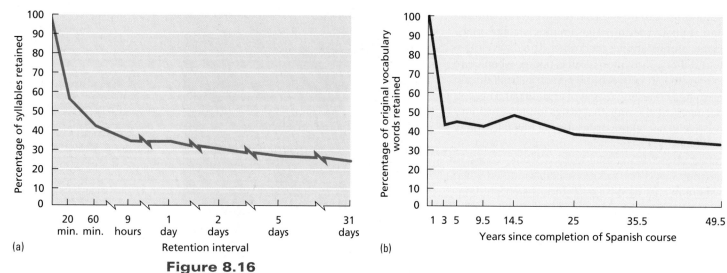

Figure 8.16

Forgetting over time.

(a) Hermann Ebbinghaus's forgetting curve shows a rapid loss of memory for nonsense syllables at first and then a more gradual decline. The rapid decline is probably due to the meaningless nature of the nonsense syllables. (b) The forgetting of vocabulary from high school Spanish language classes follows a similar curve, except that the time frame is in years, not days. Sources: Based on (a) Ebbinghaus, 1885/1964, and (b) Bahrick, 1984.

nonsense syllables. As Figure 8.16a shows, forgetting occurred rapidly at first and slowed noticeably thereafter.

Do we indeed forget most of what we learn so quickly? Ebbinghaus studied so many lists of nonsense syllables that his ability to distinguish among them undoubtedly suffered. If you learned just a few lists, the shape of your forgetting curve might resemble Ebbinghaus's, but the amount you forgot would likely be less. Moreover, when material is meaningful (unlike nonsense syllables), we are likely to retain more of it over time (Bahrick, 2005).

Consider the forgetting curve in Figure 8.16b, based on a study examining the vocabulary retention of people who had studied Spanish in school anywhere from 3 to 50 years earlier and then rarely used it (Bahrick, 1984). Once again, forgetting occurred more rapidly at first, but notice that the Spanish-retention study employed a time frame of years rather than hours and days as in Ebbinghaus's studies. Similarly, in the 3 years following the September 11, 2001, terrorist attacks in the U.S., the rate at which people forgot details about that day slowed after the first year (Conway et al., 2009).

Why Do We Forget?

If some memories last a lifetime, why do we forget so much? Explanations for normal memory loss emphasize difficulties in encoding, storage, and retrieval.

Encoding Failure

Many memory failures result not from forgetting information that we once knew, but from failing to encode the information into long-term memory in the first place (Daselaar et al., 2009). Much of what we sense simply is not processed deeply enough to commit to memory.

We noted earlier that few people can accurately depict a coin from memory. Even when the task is made easier by requiring only recognition, as in Figure 8.17, most people cannot identify the correct coin (Nickerson & Adams, 1979). Can

(a)   (b)   (c)   (d)

(e)   (f)   (g)   (h)

Figure 8.17

Which coin portrays a real penny?

Make your choice before reading further. Most people have difficulty choosing the correct one because they have never bothered to encode all of the features of a real penny. The correct penny is (d). Source: Adapted from Nickerson & Adams, 1979.

you? The details of a coin's appearance are not meaningful to most of us, and we may not notice them, no matter how often we see coins.

Even when we notice information, we may fail to encode it deeply because we turn our attention to something else. Brad Bushman and Angelica Bonacci (2002) randomly assigned 328 adults to watch either a sexually explicit, violent, or neutral TV program. Nine commercial advertisements (e.g., for snacks, cereal, laundry detergent) appeared during each program. Immediately afterward and again a day later, the researchers tested viewers' memory for the ads. At both times, viewers who watched the sexually explicit and violent programs remembered the fewest ads. Several factors might account for this, and as the researchers proposed, one of them is encoding failure: all the viewers clearly saw the ads, but those watching the sexually explicit and violent programs likely were the most preoccupied with thoughts about the content of the shows.

Decay of the Memory Trace

One early explanation for forgetting was **decay theory,** *which proposed that with time and disuse, the long-term physical memory trace in the nervous system fades away.* Decay theory soon fell into disfavor because scientists could not locate physical memory traces nor measure physical decay. In recent decades, however, scientists have begun to unravel how neural circuits change when a long-term memory is formed. This has sparked new interest in examining how these changes might decay over time (Villarreal et al., 2002).

Unfortunately, decay theory's prediction—the longer the time interval of disuse between learning and recall, the less should be recalled—is problematic. Some professional actors display perfect memory for words they last spoke on stage 2 years earlier—this despite having moved on to new acting roles and scripts (Noice & Noice, 2002b). Moreover, when research participants learn a list of words or a set of visual patterns and are retested at two different times, they sometimes recall material during the second testing that they could not remember during the first. This phenomenon, called *reminiscence,* seems inconsistent with the concept that a memory trace decays over time (Greene, 1992). In sum, scientists still debate the validity of decay theory (Brown et al., 2007).

Interference

According to *interference theory,* we forget information because other items in long-term memory impair our ability to retrieve it (Mayr, 2009;

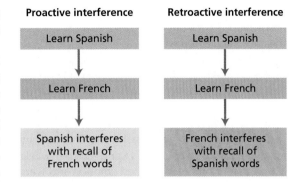

Figure 8.18

Interference and forgetting.
Interference is a major cause of forgetting. With proactive interference, older memories interfere with the retrieval of newer ones. With retroactive interference, newer memories interfere with the retrieval of older ones.

Postman & Underwood, 1973). Figure 8.18 illustrates two major types of interference. **Proactive interference** *occurs when material learned in the past interferes with recall of newer material.* Suppose that Kim changes residences, gets a new phone number, and memorizes it. That night, when a friend asks Kim for her new number, she can recall only three digits and instead keeps remembering her old phone number. Memory of her old phone number is interfering with her ability to retrieve the new one.

Retroactive interference *occurs when newly acquired information interferes with the ability to recall information learned at an earlier time.* Suppose Kim has now had her new phone number for two months and recalls it perfectly. If we ask her, "What was your old number?" Kim may have trouble recalling it, perhaps mixing up the digits with her new number. In general, the more similar two sets of information are, the more likely it is that interference will occur. Kim (or you) would probably experience little interference in recalling highly dissimilar material, such as her new phone number and French vocabulary.

Why does interference occur? It takes time for the brain to convert short-term memories into long-term memories, and some researchers propose that when new information is entered into the system, it can disrupt (i.e., retroactively interfere with) the conversion of older information into long-term memories (Wixted, 2005). Others believe that once long-term memories are formed, retroactive and proactive interference are caused by competition among retrieval cues (Anderson & Neely, 1996). When different memories become associated with similar or identical retrieval cues, confusion can result and accessing a cue may call up the wrong memory. Retrieval failure also can occur because we have too few retrieval cues or the cues may be too weak.

Almost all of us have experienced a retrieval problem called the **tip-of-the-tongue (TOT) state,** *in which we cannot recall something but feel that we are on the verge of remembering it.* When Bennett Schwartz (2002) asked 56 college students to record a diary for 4 weeks, he found that they averaged just over one TOT experience per week. Most often, TOT states aroused emotion and were triggered by the inability to remember the name of an acquaintance, famous person, or object. Sooner or later, the answer often popped into the mind spontaneously, but in many cases students had to consult a book or another person.

Motivated Forgetting

Psychodynamic and other psychologists propose that, at times, people are consciously or unconsciously motivated to forget (Knafo, 2009). Freud observed that during therapy, his patients remembered long-forgotten traumatic or anxiety-arousing events. One patient remembered with great shame that while standing beside her sister's coffin she had thought, "Now my brother-in-law is free to marry me." Freud concluded that the thought had been so shocking and anxiety arousing that the woman had *repressed* it—pushed it down into her unconscious mind, there to remain until it was uncovered years later during therapy. **Repression** *is a motivational process that protects us by blocking the conscious recall of anxiety-arousing memories.*

The concept of repression is controversial. Some evidence supports it, and other evidence does not (Follette & Davis, 2009; Karon, 2002). People certainly do forget unpleasant events— even traumatic ones—yet they also forget very pleasant events. If a person cannot remember a negative experience, is this due to a special psychological process called repression or to normal information-processing failures? Even more basically, if a person hasn't thought about an event for many years, does this necessarily indicate that the memory has been forgotten (McNally & Geraerts, 2009)? We will return to this topic shortly.

Forgetting to Do Things: Prospective Memory

Have you ever forgotten to mail a letter, turn off the oven, keep an appointment, or purchase something at the market? In contrast to *retrospective memory,* which refers to memory for past events, **prospective memory** *concerns remembering to perform an activity in the future.* That people forget to do things as often as they do is interesting, because prospective memories typically involve little content. Often we need only recall that we must perform some event-based task ("Remember, on your way out, mail the letter.") or time-based task ("Remember, take your medication at 4 P.M."). Successful prospective memory, however, draws on other cognitive abilities, such as planning and allocating attention while performing other tasks.

During adulthood, do we become increasingly absentminded about remembering to do things, as a common stereotype suggests? Numerous studies support this view (Logie & Maylor, 2009; Vogels et al., 2002). Typically, participants perform a task that requires their ongoing attention while trying to remember to signal the researcher at certain time intervals or whenever specific events take place. Older adults generally display poorer prospective memory, especially when signaling is time-based. However, when prospective memory is tested outside the laboratory using tasks such as simulated pill-taking, healthy adults in their 60s to 80s often perform as well as or better than adults in their 20s (Rendell & Thomson, 1999). Perhaps older adults are more motivated to remember in such situations, or they rely more on habit and setting up a standard routine (Anderson & Craik, 2000).

Amnesia

As H. M.'s case illustrates, the most dramatic instances of forgetting occur in amnesia. The term *amnesia* commonly refers to memory loss due to special conditions, such as brain injury, illness, or psychological trauma. However, as we'll see shortly, there is one type of amnesia that all of us experience.

Retrograde and Anterograde Amnesia

Amnesia takes several forms. **Retrograde amnesia** *represents memory loss for events that took place sometime in life before the onset of amnesia.* For example, H. M.'s brain operation, which took place at age 27, caused him to experience mild memory loss for events in his life that had occurred during the preceding year or two (i.e., when he was 25 to 26 years old). Football players experience retrograde amnesia when they are knocked out by a concussion, regain consciousness, and cannot remember the events just before being hit.

Anterograde amnesia *refers to memory loss for events that occur after the initial onset of amnesia.*

H. M.'s brain operation, and particularly the removal of much of his hippocampus, produced severe anterograde amnesia and robbed him of the ability to consciously remember new experiences and facts. Anterograde amnesia also can be produced by other conditions, such as *Korsakoff's syndrome*. This syndrome, which can result from chronic alcoholism, may also cause severe retrograde amnesia (Brand, 2007).

Dementia and Alzheimer's Disease

Dementia *refers to impaired memory and other cognitive deficits that accompany brain degeneration and interfere with normal functioning.* There are more than a dozen types and causes of dementia, and although it can occur at any point in life, dementia is most prevalent among elderly adults.

Alzheimer's disease (AD) *is a progressive brain disorder that is the most common cause of dementia among adults over the age of 65.* Estimates suggest that 5.3 million Americans have AD, and by 2050 the number of cases is predicted to rise to about 13.5 million (Mebane-Sims, 2009).

The early symptoms of AD, which worsen gradually over a period of years, include forgetfulness, poor judgment, confusion, and disorientation. Often, memory for recent events and new information is especially impaired. By itself, forgetfulness is not necessarily a sign that a person is developing AD. However, memory is the first psychological function affected, as AD initially attacks subcortical temporal lobe regions—areas near the hippocampus and then the hippocampus itself—that help convert short-term memories into long-term ones.

Alzheimer's disease spreads across the temporal lobes and to the frontal lobes and other cortical regions (Figure 8.19). As German physician Alois Alzheimer first noticed a century ago, patients with this disease have an abnormal amount of plaques and tangles in their brains. *Plaques* are clumps of protein fragments that build up on the outside of neurons, whereas *tangles* are fibers that get twisted and wound together within neurons (Shepherd et al., 2009). Neurons become damaged and die, brain tissue shrinks, and communication between neurons is impaired as AD disrupts several neurotransmitter systems, especially the acetylcholine system. Acetylcholine plays a key role in synaptic transmission in several brain areas involved in memory, and drugs that help maintain acetylcholine functioning have had some temporary success in improving AD patients' cognitive functioning (Ritchie et al., 2004).

Working memory and long-term memory worsen as AD progresses. If you read a list of just 3 words to healthy 80-year-old adults and then test their recall after a brief time delay, they will typically remember 2 or all 3 words. Patients with AD, however, typically recall either no words or 1 word (Chandler et al., 2004). Anterograde and retrograde amnesia become more severe, and procedural, semantic, episodic, and prospective memory can all be affected. Patients may lose the ability to learn new tasks or remember new information or experiences, forget how to perform familiar tasks, and have trouble recognizing even close family members.

What causes AD and its characteristic plaques and tangles? Scientists have identified several genes that contribute to early-onset AD, an inherited form of the disease that develops before the age of 65 (and as early as age 30) but accounts for only 5 to 10 percent of Alzheimer's cases (Belbin et al., 2009). For the more typical, late-onset AD, researchers have identified a gene called ApoE as a major risk factor (Yuan et al., 2009). This

The Progression of Alzheimer's Disease

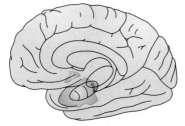
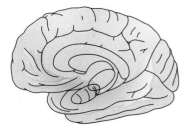

Preclinical AD   Mild to moderate AD   Severe AD

Blue indicates areas affected at various stages of AD.

Figure 8.19

The progression of Alzheimer's disease.

Source: National Institutes of Health, 2002.

gene helps direct the production of proteins that carry cholesterol in the blood plasma, and high cholesterol and other risk factors for cardiovascular disease may likewise increase the risk of developing AD.

If you know someone who has AD, then you're aware that it involves much more than memory loss. Patients experience language problems, disorganized thinking, and mood and personality changes. Ultimately, they may lose the ability to speak, walk, and control bladder and bowel functions. We'll have more to say about the psychological, physical, and social aspects of dementia and aging in Chapter 12.

Infantile (Childhood) Amnesia

There is one type of amnesia that almost all of us encounter: an inability to remember personal experiences from the first few years of our lives. Even though infants and preschoolers can form long-term memories of events in their lives (Peterson & Whalen, 2001), as adults we typically are unable to recall these events consciously. *This memory loss for early experiences is called* **infantile amnesia** (also known as *childhood amnesia*). Our memories of childhood typically do not include events that occurred before the age of 3 or 4, although some adults can partially recall major events (e.g., the birth of a sibling, hospitalization, or a death in the family) that happened before the age of 2 (Eacott & Crawley, 1998).

What causes infantile amnesia? One hypothesis is that brain regions that encode long-term episodic memories are still immature in the first years after birth. Another is that we do not encode our earliest experiences deeply and fail to form rich retrieval cues for them. Additionally, because infants lack a clear self-concept, they do not have a personal frame of reference around which to organize rich memories (Harley & Reese, 1999).

---

test yourself   Forgetting

Match each numbered concept to the correct item on the right.

1. retrograde amnesia
2. repression
3. anterograde amnesia
4. retroactive interference
5. proactive interference
6. encoding failure

a. motivated forgetting

b. a boy can't recall something because he wasn't paying enough attention

c. after brain trauma, a woman can't form new long-term memories

d. after brain trauma, a man can't remember his childhood years

e. after Amy learns a new gym lock code, she can't recall her old bike lock code

f. Bill tries to recall a new bank PIN code he memorized but mixes it up with the old code number

ANSWERS: 1-d, 2-a, 3-c, 4-e, 5-f, 6-b

MEMORY AS A CONSTRUCTIVE PROCESS

Retrieving information from long-term memory is not like viewing a digital replay. Our memories are often incomplete or sketchy. We may literally *construct* (or, as some say, *reconstruct*) a memory by piecing together bits of stored information in a way that seems real and accurate. Yet as our discussion of flashbulb memories illustrated, we may be highly confident of memories that in fact are inaccurate.

Memory construction can be amusing at times. Many of us have a tendency to recall the world through slightly rosy glasses, which helps us feel good about ourselves. For example, when college students in one study recalled their high school grades, the worse the grade was, the less often students remembered it accurately. Students correctly recalled almost all of their As, but only a third of their Ds (Figure 8.20). Most important, errors were positively biased; students usually misremembered their Bs as having been As, their Cs as Bs, and their Ds as Cs (Bahrick et al., 1996). Similarly, when college alumni were asked to recall

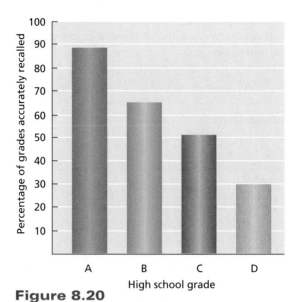

Figure 8.20

College students' rosy recall of high school grades.
The lower the grade, the less likely students were to accurately recall it. When students incorrectly recalled a grade, they almost always overestimated how well they did. SOURCE: Adapted from Bahrick et al., 1996.

their college grades, they erred 25 percent of the time, and 81 percent of these errors overestimated the actual course grade (Bahrick et al., 2008). As we will see, however, memory construction also can have serious personal and societal consequences.

Memory Distortion and Schemas

Almost a century ago, Sir Frederick Bartlett (1932) asked residents of Cambridge, England, to read stories and then retell them days or months later. One story, a Pacific Northwest Indian tale called "The War of the Ghosts," describes two young men who go down to a river to hunt seals. While there, warriors in canoes come up the river, and one of the young men agrees to join them for a raid on a town. During the raid, the man discovers that his companions are ghosts, and later he dies a mysterious death.

Bartlett's participants were 20th-century residents of England, not 18th-century Native Americans. When they retold the story, they partly reconstructed it in a way that made sense to them. A day after reading the story, one participant shortened it by almost half, described the hero as fishing rather than as hunting seals, and substituted the word *boat* for *canoe*. Bartlett found that the longer the time interval between the reading and retelling of the story, the more the story changed to fit English culture.

Bartlett, who coined the term *schema*, believed that people have generalized ideas (schemas) about how events happen, which they use to organize information and construct their memories. Recall, for example, the clothes-washing description. Schemas, however, can distort our memories by leading us to encode or retrieve information in ways that make sense and fit in with our preexisting assumptions about the world.

Memory construction also extends to how we visualize the world (Dickinson & Intraub, 2009). As Figure 8.21 illustrates, when college students in one study looked at photographs that had a main object within a scene and then drew what they saw from memory, they displayed *boundary extension;* they remembered the scene as wider-angled than it really was (Intraub et al., 1996). In real life, objects usually occur against an expansive background, creating a schema for how we

(a)

(b)

Figure 8.21

Boundary extension: what you see . . . what you remember.
Helene Intraub and her colleagues (1996) have found that when people (a) briefly look at a close-up picture, such as this one of a teddy bear, and then (b) draw the picture from memory, they unknowingly convert the image into a wide-angle scene in which the size of the main object shrinks. This effect is less likely to occur if the original picture is already a wide-angle scene. SOURCE: Images courtesy of Helene Intraub.

expect scenes to look. Thus when we remember close-up images, our schemas lead us to recall a broader scene than the one we saw. The following "Research Close-up" offers some insight into how schemas can lead us to remember things that never happened.

Research Close-up

Memory Illusions: Remembering Things That Never Occurred

STUDY 1: COLLEGE STUDENTS REMEMBERING WORD LISTS

SOURCE: HENRY L. ROEDIGER III and KATHLEEN MCDERMOTT (1995). Creating false memories: Remembering words not presented in lists. *Journal of Experimental Psychology: Learning, Memory, and Cognition, 21,* 803–814.

Introduction

In this famous experiment, Henry Roediger III and Kathleen McDermott examined how often false memories occurred while people performed a simple task: remembering lists of words. They also investigated whether people experience false memories as being vivid and clear.

Method

Building on previous research (Deese, 1959), the researchers created lists of 15 words. Each list contained words that, to varying degrees, were associated with a central organizing word. To illustrate, look at the following list:

> sour, candy, sugar, bitter, good, taste, tooth, nice, honey, soda, chocolate, heart, cake, tart, pie

The word *sweet* doesn't occur in the list, yet it is associated with these items. The central word (*sweet*) is called a *critical lure*.

Thirty-six college students each listened to 16 lists. For some lists, students' recall was measured as soon as each list ended. Then, after hearing all 16 lists, students performed a recognition task. They were given a sheet of paper with 96 words, half of which actually had been on the lists. The other words were critical lures and filler items. Students identified whether each word had been

on the lists they heard. If they selected a word, they also reported whether they had a vivid memory of having heard it or, instead, were sure that they had heard it but lacked a vivid memory.

Results

Students correctly recalled 62 percent of the real words but falsely recalled almost as many (55 percent) of the critical lures. On the recognition task, they correctly identified 62 percent of the actual words but falsely identified 72 percent of the critical lures. And in just over half of the cases in which students falsely recognized a critical lure, they reported having a vivid memory of it.

Discussion

Although critical lures were never presented, students falsely recalled them half of the time and falsely recognized them almost three-quarters of the time. Moreover, students often reported having a clear memory of the nonexistent critical lure. Many researchers have replicated this finding.

What causes these false memories? Roediger and McDermott (1995, 2000) argue that hearing the words activates an associative network—a schema—for the critical lure. For some people, the words *sour, candy, sugar,* etc. may consciously trigger a thought of "sweet." For others, spreading activation from the words unconsciously primes the concept of "sweet." Either way, the critical lure is activated, so that during retrieval people may misinterpret the source of activation and falsely remember the lure as being on the list (Figure 8.22).

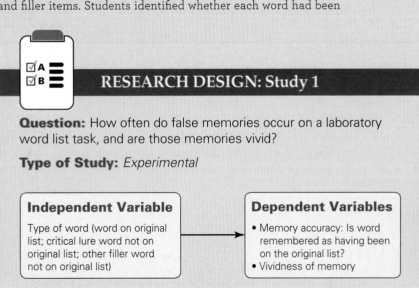

RESEARCH DESIGN: Study 1

Question: How often do false memories occur on a laboratory word list task, and are those memories vivid?

Type of Study: *Experimental*

Independent Variable	**Dependent Variables**
Type of word (word on original list; critical lure word not on original list; other filler word not on original list)	• Memory accuracy: Is word remembered as having been on the original list? • Vividness of memory

Figure 8.22

Memory illusion.
After listening to a list of related words, people often remember hearing a critical lure (*sweet*) that was never presented.

RESEARCH DESIGN: Study 2

Question: Is there a relation between displaying false memories in real life and in the laboratory?

Type of Study: *Repeats the basic experimental procedure of Study 1, and adds a correlational component that is shown below.*

Variable X

Naturally occurring false memory:
Have you been abducted by aliens?
Group 1: "No"
Group 2: "Yes," memory not explicit
Group 3: "Yes," memory is explicit

Variable Y

Memory accuracy on word list task (e.g., extent of false memories for critical lure words, accurate memories for words on original lists)

Introduction

Is there a relation between false memories on the word-list task in Study 1 and false memories for significant events in real life? To examine this question, Susan Clancy and coworkers recruited three groups of participants through newspaper advertisements: a control group of 13 people who said they had never been abducted by aliens, 9 people who were sure they had been abducted by aliens but who had no explicit memory of it, and 11 people who said that, for a time, they had forgotten that they had been abducted but then had a clear memory of the abduction gradually return to them. Why study people claiming to be alien abductees? Because, say the researchers, these individuals are reporting a major traumatic event that we can assume is unlikely to have occurred.

Method and Results

Participants listened to word lists of varying lengths, based on the lists used in Study 1. The three groups did not differ in how accurately they recalled and recognized words that actually had been on the lists. However, the two abductee groups falsely recalled and falsely recognized more critical lures than the control group, and those with explicit memories of abduction made the most recognition errors.

In your view, are these findings relevant to memory in the real world? Critics argue that the research context—college students learning word lists—may have little relevance to situations involving memory for important events. Yet Roediger and McDermott argue that this context makes the findings more impressive. Students knew it was a memory test and that inaccurate memories would be spotted. Further, memory was tested soon after hearing each list. If people can be confident of their false memories in this straightforward situation, then what might happen in real-world contexts in which conditions for remembering events are more complex and not as optimal?

Discussion

The results indicate a relation between how prone people are to display false memories both inside and outside the laboratory. This finding was replicated in a subsequent study involving people who reported memories of "past lives"—memories the researchers assumed were false (Meyersburg et al., 2009). Exposed to the same basic experimental procedure involving word lists and critical lures, people with past-life memories were just as accurate as control-group participants in remembering words that actually had been on the list, but they had more false memories of critical lures. Thus, in both studies, the authors found that a propensity to display false memories in real life (i.e., alien abduction, a past life) also manifests itself on a simple laboratory task.

STUDY 2: PEOPLE REPORTING ABDUCTION BY ALIENS

Source: Susan A. Clancy, Richard J. McNally, Daniel L. Schacter, Mark F. Lenzeweger, and Roger K. Pitman (2002). Memory distortion in people reporting abduction by aliens. *Journal of Abnormal Psychology, 111,* 455–461.

Misinformation Effects and Eyewitness Testimony

If memories are constructed, then information that occurs *after* an event may shape that construction process. This **misinformation effect,** *the distortion of a memory by misleading postevent information,* has been demonstrated in numerous studies (Porter et al., 2010). Misinformation effects have frequently been investigated in relation to mistaken eyewitness testimony. In one celebrated case, Father Bernard Pagano, a Roman Catholic priest, was positively identified by seven eyewitnesses as the perpetrator of a series of armed robberies in the Wilmington, Delaware, area. He was saved from almost certain conviction when the true robber, dubbed the "gentleman bandit" because of his politeness and concern for his victims, confessed to the crimes. You can see in Figure 8.23 that there was little physical resemblance between the two men.

Two key factors may have distorted the witnesses' memory. First, the polite manner of the robber is consistent with the schema many people

Figure 8.23

Seven eyewitnesses to armed robberies committed by Ronald Clouser (*left*) mistakenly identified Father Bernard Pagano (*right*) as the robber, probably as a result of information from police that influenced their memory reconstructions.

have of priests. Second, before presenting pictures of suspects to the eyewitnesses, the police let it be known that the suspect might be a priest. Father Pagano was the only suspect wearing a clerical collar (Tversky & Tuchin, 1989).

Even one or two words can produce a misinformation effect while questioning an eyewitness. Imagine that after witnessing a two-car crash, a police officer takes your statement and asks you, "About how fast were the cars going when they *contacted* each other?" In a classic experiment, college students viewed films of car accidents and then judged how fast the cars were going. As Figure 8.24 shows, the judged speed increased by up to 33 percent when the word *contacted* was changed to *hit, bumped into, collided with,* or *smashed into* (Loftus & Palmer, 1974).

Source Confusion

Misinformation effects also occur because of **source confusion** (also called *source monitoring error*), *our tendency to recall something or recognize*

it as familiar but to forget where we encountered it. Suppose an eyewitness to a crime looks through a series of mug shots and reports that none of the individuals is the perpetrator. Several days later, the eyewitness is brought back to view a live lineup and is asked to identify the person who committed the crime. In reality, none of the people in the lineup did, but one suspect was pictured in a mug shot that the eyewitness had seen days earlier. "That's the person," says the eyewitness. Source confusion occurs because the eyewitness recognizes the individual's face but fails to remember that this recognition stems from the mug shot. Instead, the witness mistakenly assumes that he or she saw the familiar-looking suspect committing the crime.

This scenario has been tested many times in experimental analogs. Participants who witness a staged event and later view mug shots are more likely to misidentify *innocent* suspects as having been involved in the event because of source confusion (Deffenbacher et al., 2006). Source confusion also occurs when people witness an event (e.g., a video of an unarmed home burglar) and then are exposed to misleading, suggestive statements about it (e.g., that the burglar had a gun). They may forget that the source of the misinformation was a question or statement made by someone else and then come to believe it was part of the event they had witnessed (Mitchell & Zaragoza, 2001).

Researchers have used brain-imaging to study the neural activity that occurs when false memories are created by misinformation (Okado & Stark, 2005), but the debate over whether misinformation permanently alters a witness's original memory is far from resolved. Still, researchers overwhelmingly agree that misinformation can distort eyewitness reports. This has raised concerns about the tainting of eyewitness testimony not only from adults but also from children in cases of alleged physical and sexual abuse (Bruck & Ceci, 2009).

The Child as Eyewitness

In cases of alleged child sexual abuse, there is often no conclusive corroborating medical evidence

Figure 8.24

A misinformation effect.
College students' memory of how fast two cars were moving just before an accident varied significantly depending on how the question was phrased. Source: Adapted from Loftus & Palmer, 1974.

How fast were the two cars going when they _____ each other?	
Words	**Perceived speed**
smashed into	41 mph
collided with	39 mph
bumped into	38 mph
hit	34 mph
contacted	31 mph

and the child is usually the only witness (London et al., 2008). If the charges are true, failing to convict the abuser and returning the child to an abusive environment is unthinkable. Conversely, if the charges are false, the consequences of convicting an innocent person are equally distressing.

Accuracy and Suggestibility

A single instance of suggestive questioning can distort some children's memory, but suggestive questioning most often leads to false memories when it is repeated (Bruck & Ceci, 2009).

In one experiment by Michelle Leichtman and Stephen Ceci (1995), 3- to 6-year-old children were told about a man named Sam Stone. Over several weeks, some children were repeatedly told stories that portrayed Sam as clumsy. Later Sam visited their classroom, was introduced, and behaved innocuously. The next day, the children were shown a ripped book and soiled teddy bear, things for which Sam was not responsible. Over the next 10 weeks they were interviewed several times, and some were asked suggestive questions about Sam (e.g., "When Sam Stone tore the book, did he do it on purpose, or was he being silly?"). Two weeks later a new interviewer asked all the children to describe Sam's visit to the classroom.

Children who had heard suggestive information about Sam—whether before, after, or especially before *and* after Sam's appearance—made more false reports about Sam's behavior than a control group that had never heard suggestive information. One child stated that after soaking the teddy bear in the bath, Sam smeared it with a crayon. These findings are troubling, because during many sexual-abuse investigations, the child initially denies being abused, but then after repeated suggestive questioning during therapy or police interviewing, the child acknowledges the abuse (Bruck & Ceci, 2009). Was the child understandably reluctant to open up at first, or did suggestive questions produce a false allegation?

Recall of Traumatic Events   How well do children remember traumatic events? In general, when children have been abused or have suffered other traumas, most seem to remember the events well, given their age (Goodman et al., 2010). Still, memory errors can occur for several reasons, including misinformation effects.

For example, Elaine Burgwyn-Bailes and co-workers (2001) interviewed 3- to 7-year-olds a few days, 6 weeks, and 1 year after the children underwent emergency plastic surgery for facial lacerations. At each interview, children accurately remembered most of the details of their operations, but they also mistakenly agreed with about 15 percent of leading questions ("Did the doctor's helper use any needles?") and suggestive questions ("The lady took off your watch, didn't she?") about events that never occurred. Compared to older children, younger children remembered fewer true details and agreed more often to leading and suggestive questions.

True versus False Reports: Can Professionals Tell Them Apart?

Can professionals reliably distinguish between children's accurate and false reports? The answer appears to be no, at least when false reports are caused by repeated, suggestive questioning. Mental health workers, social workers, prosecutors, and judges shown videotapes of children's reports in the Sam Stone experiment often rated false reports as highly credible. Perhaps many children who make false reports are credible because they are not intentionally lying; rather, they believe their memories are accurate. After suggestive questioning, children are as confident of their false memories as they are of their accurate ones (Roebers, 2002).

What should society do? Like adults, young children accurately remember a lot, but they also misremember and are susceptible to repeated suggestive questioning. Thanks to psychological research, law enforcement officials, mental health workers, and legal professionals are now paying more attention to how children's admissions of abuse are elicited, and training programs are helping practitioners minimize suggestive interviewing techniques (London et al., 2008). The goal is not to discredit children's allegations of abuse. To the contrary, the hope is that by minimizing the risk of false allegations, nonsuggestive interviewing will elicit allegations judged as even more compelling, thereby helping to ensure that justice is done.

The Recovered-Memory Controversy

In 1997, a woman from Illinois settled a lawsuit against two psychiatrists and their hospital for $10.6 million. She alleged that her psychiatrists used hypnosis, drugs, and other treatments that led her to develop false memories of having been a high priestess in a sexually abusive satanic cult (*APA Monitor*, 1997). Yet only years earlier, there had been a wave of cases in which adults—usually in the course of psychotherapy—began to remember

Figure 8.25

In a famous 1990 case, George Franklin was convicted for the 1969 murder of 8-year-old Susan Nason. Franklin's 28-year-old daughter Eileen (shown here) provided the key evidence: memories—recovered during therapy—of her father killing Susan. But the conviction was overturned because Eileen's memories were recovered under hypnosis. Details of the murder had been published in newspapers, possibly creating source confusion in Eileen's memory. She also had other recovered memories that were proven to be untrue.

long-forgotten childhood sexual abuse and sued their parents, other family members, and former teachers for the alleged trauma (Figure 8.25).

The scientific controversy over the validity of recovered memories of childhood trauma involves two issues. First, when a recovered memory of sexual abuse occurs, is it accurate? Second, if the abuse really happened, what caused the memory to be forgotten—repression or another psychological process? Let's briefly examine the second issue.

Many scientists and therapists question Freud's concept of repression. Repression implies a special psychological mechanism that actively pushes traumatic memories into the unconscious mind. Recovered memories of childhood sexual abuse or other traumas cannot be taken as automatic evidence of repression. Memory loss may have occurred because of ordinary sources of forgetting or because the victim reinterpreted the trauma to make it less upsetting or intentionally avoided thinking about the abuse (McNally & Geraerts, 2009). But beyond these factors, other researchers and many therapists believe that repression is a valid concept (Knafo, 2009). This controversy will not be resolved soon.

What about the more basic question? Can someone forget childhood sexual abuse,

by whatever psychological mechanism, and then recover that memory as an adult? Studies suggest that most adults who were abused in childhood remember the abuse (Goodman et al., 2010). Still, some survivors of natural disasters, children who witness the violent death of a parent, victims of rape, combat veterans, and victims of sexual and physical abuse have shown limited or no memory of their traumas (Epstein & Bottoms, 2002). Some victims of documented child sexual abuse cannot recall or do not think about their abuse for many years but have accurate memories return later (Kluft, 1999; McNally & Geraerts, 2009). Yet memory loss after psychological trauma is usually far shorter, with memory returning over weeks, months, or perhaps a few years. In many cases of trauma, the victim's primary problem is not memory loss but rather an *inability* to forget, which may involve involuntary nightmares or flashbacks (Berntsen, 2001).

Experiments reveal that when exposed to suggestive questioning, American college students developed memories of personal childhood events that never happened (e.g., being hospitalized overnight), and residents of Moscow developed memories for fictitious details (e.g., the presence of injured animals) of a terrorist bombing in their city (Nourkova et al., 2004). Such studies may not tap the intense trauma of directly experiencing sexual abuse, and for ethical reasons experimenters do not test whether false memories of sexual abuse can be implanted. Nevertheless, say many researchers and clinicians, add these findings to everything science has taught us about forgetting and constructive memory, and the conclusion is that we should not take the accuracy of recovered memories at face value (Wade et al., 2007). They are especially concerned that in recovered-memory therapy, therapists repeatedly suggest the possibility of abuse to people who are already emotionally vulnerable.

The message from science is not that all claims of recovered traumatic memories should be dismissed (Geraerts et al., 2007). Rather, it is to urge caution in unconditionally accepting those memories, particularly when suggestive techniques are used to recover the memories (Follette & Davis, 2009). Some day it may be scientifically possible to separate true memories from false ones; researchers have begun to establish that some types of true versus false memories are associated with different patterns of brain activity (Abe et al., 2008). But at present, these findings cannot be used to determine reliably whether any individual memory is true or false.

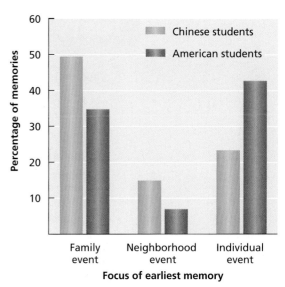

Figure 8.26

Culture and our earliest memories.
What is your earliest memory? In one study, Chinese students recalled events that, overall, were more family and neighborhood oriented than events recalled by American students. How else might our cultural upbringing and worldview influence memory? SOURCE: Based on Wang, 2001.

Culture and Memory Construction

Culture and memory have a reciprocal relation. On the one hand, cultural survival depends on transmitting knowledge and customs from one generation to the next. Without our capacity to remember events and information, culture simply could not exist (nor could we, as a species).

At the same time, culture influences memory. Our cultural upbringing shapes the schemas that we acquire and use to perceive ourselves and the world. For example, as we discussed in Chapter 1, most people living in northern Europe and North America learn to view the world through a relatively *individualistic* lens in which self-identity is based primarily on one's own attributes and achievements. People living in many Asian, African, and South American cultures tend to see the world through a more *collectivistic* framework in which personal identity is defined largely by ties to the extended family and other social groups. If cultural socialization influences our schemas and our schemas influence how we encode and reconstruct events, then people from different cultures may recall events in somewhat distinct ways.

Let's consider an example: our earliest memories. Compared to college students in Taiwan and China, and to Asian and Asian American college students in the U.S., Caucasion American college students report earlier childhood memories of both daytime events and nighttime dreams (Fiske & Pillemer, 2006; Wang, 2006). In one study, Qi Wang (2001) asked Caucasian American

students from Harvard University and Chinese students from Beijing University to describe their earliest memories (Figure 8.26). He predicted and found that the Americans were more likely than their Chinese counterparts to recall events that focused on individual experiences and self-determination (e.g., "I was sorting baseball cards when I dropped them. As I reached down to get them, I knocked over a jug of iced tea."). In contrast, Chinese students were more likely than American students to recall memories that involved family or neighborhood activities (e.g., "Dad taught me ancient poems. It was always when he was washing vegetables that he would explain a poem to me.").

Wang also found that American college students dated their earliest personal memory back to when they were, on average, $3\frac{1}{2}$ years old. Students in China, however, reported memories that, on average, dated to when they were almost 4 years old. Although the reason isn't clear, it may relate to American students' greater tendency to report earliest memories of single, distinctive events that involved greater emotionality, whereas Chinese students were more likely than Americans to report more routine events that involved collective activity.

Other researchers also have found cross-cultural differences in age of earliest memories. When Shelley MacDonald and coworkers (2000) studied New Zealand European, New Zealand Asian, New Zealand Maori, and Chinese adults, they found that Maori adults—whose traditional culture strongly values the past—recalled the earliest personal memories.

test yourself   Memory as a Constructive Process

True or false?

1. In one study, people who had memories of being abducted by aliens were especially prone to forming false memories on a laboratory task.

2. Children are susceptible to misinformation effects; adults are not susceptible.

3. Source confusion is one reason why misinformation effects occur.

4. Judges and prosecutors are highly accurate in telling when a child is reporting a false versus true memory.

ANSWERS: 1-true, 2-false, 3-true, 4-false

MEMORY AND THE BRAIN

Where in your brain are memories located? How were they formed? The quest for answers has taken some remarkable twists. Psychologist Karl Lashley spent decades searching for the *engram*—the physical trace that presumably was stored in the brain when a memory was formed. Lashley (1950) trained animals to perform tasks, such as running mazes, and later removed or damaged (lesioned) specific regions of their cortexes to see if they would forget how to perform the task. No matter what small area was lesioned, memories remained intact. Lashley never found the engram and concluded that a memory is stored throughout the brain.

Perhaps most striking was James McConnell's (1962) discovery of "memory transfer." He classically conditioned flatworms to a light that was paired with electric shock, eventually causing the worms to contract to the light alone. Next he chopped them up and fed the RNA (ribonucleic acid) from their cells to untrained worms. Amazingly, the untrained worms showed some conditioning to the light, suggesting that RNA might be a memory molecule that stores experiences. Some scientists replicated these findings, but others were unable to, and McConnell eventually gave up on the idea (Rilling, 1996). Yet despite the inevitable dead ends, scientists have learned a great deal about memory processes in the brain.

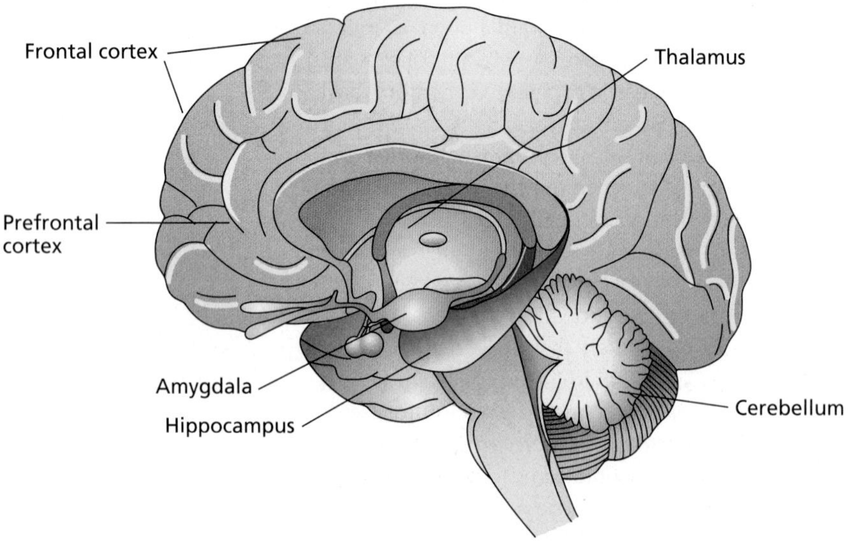

Where Are Memories Formed and Stored?

To answer this question, scientists examine how damage to different brain regions affects the memory of human patients and laboratory animals; they also peer into the healthy human brain as research participants perform various memory tasks. These lines of research reveal that memory involves many interacting brain regions. Figure 8.27 shows a few of the major regions.

Sensory and Working Memory

Sensory memory depends on our visual, auditory, and other sensory systems to detect stimulus information (e.g., the sounds of "Hi, my name is Carlos"), transform it into neural codes, and send it to the brain, where sensory areas of the cerebral cortex initially process it. As working memory becomes involved in different types of tasks—remembering a person's name and face, recalling a list of numbers, learning a concept in your textbook—cortical networks located in different lobes of the brain become more active (Lehmann et al., 2010). For example, using visuospatial working memory to form a mental image of an object will activate some of the same areas of the visual

Figure 8.27

Some brain regions involved in memory.

Many areas of the brain, such as the regions shown here, play key roles in memory.

cortex and other brain regions that become more active when looking at the actual object (Ganis et al., 2004).

The frontal lobes—especially the prefrontal cortex—play key roles in working memory (Christoff et al., 2009). The frontal lobes generally become more active during tasks that place greater demands on working memory. In one brain-imaging experiment, students paid attention to the meaning of words (i.e., deep, semantic encoding) or to whether the words were in capital or lowercase letters (i.e., shallow, perceptual encoding). Deeper encoding produced better memory for the words and greater activity in areas of the left prefrontal cortex, as Figure 8.28 shows (Gabrieli et al., 1996).

The frontal lobes seem to be particularly important in supporting central-executive functions, such as allocating attention to the other components of working memory. This does not mean, however, that the central executive resides exclusively within the frontal lobes. Frontal-lobe damage often—but not always—impairs central-executive functions of working memory. Moreover, patients with intact frontal lobes but damage in other brain areas may exhibit central-executive impairments (Adrés, 2003). Thus even the "master control" executive functions of working memory depend on a network of neural activity that connects regions across the brain.

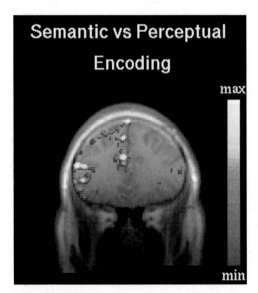

Figure 8.28

Depth of processing and the prefrontal lobes.

Four participants in one experiment performed shallow perceptual (i.e., structural) encoding and deep (semantic) encoding tasks while undergoing functional magnetic resonance imaging (fMRI). The results, shown here for one participant, revealed that semantic encoding was accompanied by greater neural activity in specific regions of the left prefrontal cortex. SOURCE: Photo courtesy of John Gabrieli.

Long-Term Memory

Where are long-term memories formed and stored? Once again, multiple brain areas are involved, but the hippocampus and its adjacent areas appear to play important roles in encoding certain types of long-term memories (Squire et al., 2004).

Declarative Memory Like H. M., many patients with extensive hippocampal damage retain the use of their short-term memory but cannot form new, explicit long-term declarative memories—memories for new personal experiences and facts. For example, one patient could recall the names of presidents elected before his brain injury occurred but not the names of presidents elected after his injury (Squire, 1987). The hippocampus does not seem to be the site where long-term declarative memories are permanently stored, which explains why H. M. retained his long-term memories acquired earlier in life. Rather, it helps to gradually convert short-term memories into permanent ones.

According to one view, the diverse components of an experience—where something happened, what the scene or people looked like, sounds we heard, the meaning of events or information, and so on—are processed initially in different regions of the cortex and then gradually bound together in the hippocampus. *This hypothetical and gradual binding process is called* **memory consolidation** (Hardt et al., 2010). Once a memory for a personal experience is consolidated, its various components appear to be stored across wide areas of the cortex, although we retrieve and reintegrate these components as a unified memory. Semantic memories (factual information) also appear to be stored across wide-ranging areas of the brain. As John Gabrieli (1998) notes, "knowledge in any domain [e.g., for pictures or words] . . . is distributed over a specific, but extensive, neural network that often extends over several lobes" (p. 94). Several brain regions, including portions of the prefrontal cortex and hippocampus, appear to be involved in consciously retrieving declarative memories (van Strien et al., 2009).

Although we have focused on the frontal lobes and hippocampus, memory formation also depends on other brain areas. For example, damage to the thalamus—the brain's major sensory relay station—can impair both the encoding of new memories and the retrieval of old ones (Hampstead & Koffler, 2009). In one famous case, a young U.S. Air Force technician named N. A. was injured in a freak accident (Squire, 1987). While his roommate was practicing thrusts with a miniature fencing foil, N. A. suddenly turned around in his seat and was stabbed through the right nostril, piercing his brain and damaging a portion of his thalamus. The damage permanently limited his ability to form new declarative memories. In many cases, thalamic damage also can cause permanent retrograde amnesia.

The amygdala encodes emotionally arousing aspects of stimuli and plays an important role in helping us form long-term memories for events that stir our emotions (LaBar & LeDoux, 2006). As we discussed earlier, in laboratory experiments, most people remember emotionally arousing stimuli (e.g., film clips, slides) better than neutral ones. Damage to the amygdala eliminates much of this "memory advantage" from arousing stimuli (LaBar & Phelps, 1998).

Procedural Memory   Along with other parts of the brain, the cerebellum plays an important role in forming procedural memories (Hubert et al., 2009). This helps explain why H. M., whose cerebellum was not damaged by the operation, showed improved performance at various hand-eye coordination tasks (e.g., mirror tracing) even though he was unable to consciously remember having performed the tasks.

Richard Thompson (1985) and coworkers have examined another type of procedural memory. Studying rabbits, they repeatedly paired a tone (CS) with a puff of air to the eyes (UCS), and soon the tone alone caused the rabbits to blink. As the rabbits learned this conditioned response, electrical recordings revealed increased activity in the cerebellum. Later Thompson found that removing a tiny portion of the cerebellum completely abolished the memory for the *conditioned* eyeblink but did not affect the rabbits' general (unconditioned) eyeblink response. Similarly, eyeblink conditioning fails to work with human patients who have a damaged cerebellum (Green & Woodruff-Pak, 2000).

How Are Memories Formed?

How does the nervous system form a memory? The answer appears to lie in chemical and physical changes that take place in the brain's neural circuitry.

Synaptic Change and Memory

Eric Kandel (2001) and his coworkers have studied a marine snail, *Aplysia californica,* for more than 25 years—work for which Kandel received a Nobel Prize in 2000. *Aplysia* is no mental giant, but it can learn, form memories, and has only about 20,000 neurons (compared with our 100 billion) that are larger and easier to study than ours. For example, *Aplysia* retracts its gill slightly in self-defense when a breathing organ atop the gill is gently squirted with water. But if a squirt is paired with electric shock to its tail, *Aplysia* covers up its gill with a protective flap of skin. After repeated pairings, *Aplysia* acquires a classically conditioned response and will cover its gill with the protective flap when the water is squirted alone. In other words, *Aplysia* forms a simple procedural memory.

Kandel and his coworkers have traced the formation of this procedural memory to a series of biochemical events that occur between and within various sensory neurons and motor neurons. How long these events last seems to be one key in determining whether short-term memories become long-term ones. If a single shock is paired with the squirt of water, certain chemical reactions shut off after a brief period and no permanent memory is formed. But with repeated pairings, these chemical reactions persist and a long-term memory forms. Days later, a squirt of water will still trigger a conditioned response.

During the conditioning procedure, various sensory neurons become densely packed with neurotransmitter release points, and postsynaptic motor neurons (which cause the protective flap to cover the gill) develop more receptor sites. These structural changes result in a greater ease of synaptic transmission that may be the basis for memory consolidation (Abel & Kandel, 1998).

Long-Term Potentiation

A different line of research, involving rats and other species with more complex nervous systems, supports the hypothesis that synaptic changes may be the basis for memory consolidation. Here, researchers try to mimic (albeit very crudely) a process of long-term memory formation by stimulating specific neural pathways with rapid bursts of electricity (say, 100 impulses per second for several seconds). They find that once this rapid stimulation ends, the neural pathway becomes stronger—synaptic connections are activated more easily—for days or even weeks (Wang & Morris, 2010). *This enduring increase in synaptic strength is called* **long-term potentiation (LTP).** LTP has been studied most extensively in regions of the hippocampus where neurons send and receive messages using glutamate, the most abundant neurotransmitter in the brain.

For LTP to occur, complex biochemical events must take place inside and between these neurons.

Administering drugs that inhibit these events will block LTP. Moreover, mice can be genetically bred to be deficient in certain proteins required for LTP. These mice not only have impaired long-term potentiation but also display memory deficits on a variety of learning tasks (Schimanski & Nguyen, 2005).

How does LTP occur? At least in some cases, when neural pathways are sufficiently stimulated, postsynaptic neurons alter their structure to become more responsive to glutamate. For example, postsynaptic neurons may change the shape of some receptor sites or may increase the number of receptor sites by developing additional tiny branches (spines) on their dendrites. Thus, in the future, presynaptic neurons will not need to release as much glutamate in order to stimulate postsynaptic neurons to fire. In sum, the formation of a long-term memory seems to involve long-lasting changes in synaptic efficiency that result from new or enhanced connections between presynaptic and postsynaptic neurons (Kandel, 2001; Wang & Morris, 2010).

In closing, we hope that this chapter has piqued your interest in understanding why we remember, forget, and sometimes misremember (see the Levels of Analysis feature below). We also hope that the chapter has applied value for you. To conclude the chapter, our "Applying Psychological Science" feature describes some ways to enhance your memory and academic learning.

Levels of Analysis | Memory

In this chapter we've explored remembering and forgetting and have seen that both processes can be examined at biological, psychological, and environmental levels. Let's use these levels of analysis to recap some of the main points we've covered.

ENVIRONMENTAL LEVEL
- Stimulus characteristics (e.g., distinctiveness, organization) influence encoding and retrieval.
- The position of an item in a series affects recall.
- The amount and rate of information affects our ability to recall it.
- Memory may be enhanced when encoding and retrieval take place in the same environment.
- Cultural upbringing influences our schemas and the age of earliest memories.
- Misinformation effects (postevent stimuli) can distort memories.

BIOLOGICAL LEVEL
- Our evolved memory capabilities display a balance between the adaptiveness of remembering and the adaptiveness of forgetting.
- Sensory memory depends on sensory systems that detect stimuli and output neural codes that are sent to the brain for processing.
- The frontal lobes, hippocampus, amygdala, thalamus, and cerebellum are among many brain regions that play key roles in working and/or long-term memory.
- Chemical and structural changes in neurons that increase synaptic transmission efficiency underlie long-term memory formation.
- Brain damage from disease, sudden brain injury, brain surgery, or other trauma can produce retrograde and anterograde amnesia.

PSYCHOLOGICAL LEVEL
- Memory codes are mental representations; and memory is a network of associated mental representations.
- Elaborative and maintenance rehearsal facilitate encoding.
- Memory confidence doesn't ensure memory accuracy.
- Mental schemas influence encoding and retrieval.
- Encoding failure and interference effects impair recall.
- Motivational biases (e.g., to feel good about oneself, to avoid anxiety-arousing information) may distort memories.

We noted in the chapter that memory is essential for survival. At the psychological and environmental levels of analysis, can you think of other functions that memory serves? Put differently, if you no longer had the ability to remember, what other psychological effects would this have for you, and how would it affect your ability to interact with the physical and social environment?

test yourself

Memory and the Brain

Match each numbered term to one item on the right to form the best overall set of matches.

1. amygdala
2. cerebellum
3. hippocampus
4. long-term potentiation
5. memory consolidation

a. plays a key role in forming procedural memories
b. plays a key role in declarative memory consolidation
c. gradual binding of various components of a memory
d. plays a key role in encoding emotional aspects of memories
e. enduring increase in synaptic strength as a memory forms

ANSWERS: 1-d, 2-a, 3-b, 4-e, 5-c

Applying Psychological Science

Improving Memory and Academic Learning

There are no magical or effortless ways to enhance memory, but psychological research offers many principles that you can put to your advantage. Memory-enhancement strategies fall into three broad categories:

- *external aids*, such as shopping lists, notes, and appointment calendars
- *general memory strategies*, such as organizing and rehearsing information
- *formal mnemonic techniques*, such as acronyms, the method of loci, and other systems that take practice to be used effectively

Memory researchers strongly recommend using external aids and general strategies to enhance memory. Of course, during closed-book college exams, external aids may land you in the dean's office! The following principles can enhance memory.

USE ELABORATIVE REHEARSAL

Elaborative rehearsal—focusing on the meaning of information—enhances deep processing and memory (Craik & Lockhart, 2008). Put simply, *if you are trying to commit information to memory, make sure that you understand what it means.* You may think we're daffy for stating such an obvious point, but many students try to learn material by rote memorization rather than by making an effort to understand it. Students who find material confusing sometimes try to bypass their confusion with rote memorization—an approach that often fails—whereas they should be seeking assistance to have the material explained. The learning objectives and practice tests that appear in the Online Learning Center (OLC) can help you process the course material more deeply by helping you focus on and think about key points.

LINK NEW INFORMATION TO EXISTING MEMORIES

Based on the principle that memory is a network of associated ideas (Bowers, 2008), once you understand the material, process it more deeply by associating it with information you already know. This

creates memory "hooks" onto which you can hang new information. Because you already have many memorable life experiences, *make new information personally meaningful by relating it to your life.*

ORGANIZE INFORMATION AND USE IMAGERY

Organizing information keeps you actively thinking about the material and makes it more meaningful (Herrmann et al., 2002). Before reading a chapter, look at its outline or headings to determine how the material is logically developed. When studying, take notes from a chapter and use outlining to organize the information. This hierarchical structure forces you to arrange main ideas above subordinate ones, and it becomes an additional retrieval cue that facilitates recall.

As dual coding theory predicts, images provide a splendid additional "cognitive hook" on which to hang and retrieve information (Paivio, 2006). Be creative. For example, to help you remember that flashbulb memories often are less accurate than people think, imagine a camera flashbulb with a big red X through it.

OVERLEARN THE MATERIAL

Overlearning *refers to continued rehearsal past the point of initial mastery.* At least in the short term, for about a week, overlearning improves memory and task performance (Rohrer et al., 2005). Just as elite athletes keep practicing their already-honed skills and professional actors continue to rehearse scripts they already know, before an exam, keep studying material after you have first learned it.

DISTRIBUTE LEARNING OVER TIME AND TEST YOURSELF

You have finished the readings and organized your notes for an upcoming test. Now it's time to study and review. Are you better off with *massed practice*, a marathon session of highly concentrated learning, or with *distributed practice*, several shorter sessions spread out over a few days? Research indicates that you will retain more information with distributed practice (Rohrer & Taylor, 2006).

Distributed practice can reduce fatigue and anxiety, both of which impair learning. Testing yourself ahead of time (e.g., using practice items, if available) helps you to further rehearse the material and to identify content that you don't understand.

MINIMIZE INTERFERENCE

Distributed practice is effective because rest periods between study sessions reduce interference from competing material. However, when you need to study for several exams on the same or consecutive days, there really are few rest periods. There is no simple solution to this problem. Suppose you have a psychology exam on Thursday and a sociology exam on Friday. Try to arrange several sessions of distributed practice for each exam over the preceding week. On Wednesday, limit your studying to psychology if possible. Once your psychology exam is over, return your attention to studying sociology. This way, the final study period for each course will occur as close as possible to test time and minimize interference from other cognitive activities. Studying before you go to sleep also may enhance retention by temporarily minimizing interference.

Chapter Summary

MEMORY AS INFORMATION PROCESSING

- Memory involves three main processes (encoding, storage, and retrieval) and three main components (sensory, working, and long-term memory).
- Sensory memory briefly holds incoming sensory information. Some information reaches working memory and long-term memory, where it is mentally represented by visual, phonological, semantic, or motor codes.
- Working memory processes a limited amount of information and supports other cognitive functions. It has phonological, visuospatial, episodic, and executive components.
- Long-term memory stores large amounts of information for up to a lifetime.

ENCODING: ENTERING INFORMATION

- Effortful processing involves intention and conscious attention. Automatic processing occurs without intention and requires minimal effort.
- Deep processing enhances memory. Elaborative rehearsal provides deeper processing than maintenance rehearsal. Hierarchies, chunking, dual coding that includes visual imagery, and other mnemonic devices facilitate deeper encoding.
- Schemas shape how we encode information and provide an important component of expertise. People who display exceptional memory take advantage of basic memory principles and mnemonic devices.

STORAGE: RETAINING INFORMATION

- Associative network models view long-term memory as a network of associated nodes, with each node representing a concept or unit of information.
- Neural network models propose that each piece of information in memory is represented by a unique pattern of multiple nodes that are simultaneously activated throughout the brain.
- Declarative long-term memories involve factual knowledge and include episodic and semantic memories. In contrast, procedural memory is reflected in skills and actions.

- Explicit memory involves conscious or intentional memory retrieval, whereas implicit memory influences our behavior without conscious awareness.

RETRIEVAL: ACCESSING INFORMATION

- Retrieval cues activate information stored in long-term memory. Retrieval is more likely when we have multiple, self-generated, and distinctive cues.
- We experience flashbulb memories as vivid snapshots of events and are confident of their accuracy. Over time, flashbulb memories may become inaccurate. Overall, memory accuracy and confidence are weakly to moderately related.
- The encoding specificity principle states that memory is enhanced when cues present during retrieval match the cues present during encoding. These cues may involve the same environment (context-dependent memory) or same internal state (state-dependent memory) present during original encoding. Mood states, however, provide an exception. Overall, we tend to recall stimuli that are congruent with our current mood.

FORGETTING

- We often cannot recall information because we never encoded it into long-term memory in the first place. Decay theory proposes that physical memory traces in long-term memory deteriorate with disuse over time.
- Proactive interference occurs when material learned in the past impairs recall of newer material. Retroactive interference occurs when newly acquired material impairs the ability to recall information learned at an earlier time.
- Psychodynamic theorists propose that we may forget anxiety-arousing material through repression, an unconscious process of motivated forgetting.
- Retrograde amnesia is memory loss for events that occurred before the onset of amnesia. Anterograde amnesia refers to memory loss for events that occur after the initial onset of amnesia. Alzheimer's disease produces both

types of amnesia and is the leading cause of dementia among elderly adults. Infantile amnesia is our inability to remember experiences from the first few years of our lives.

MEMORY AS A CONSTRUCTIVE PROCESS

- Our schemas may cause us to misremember events in ways that fit with our preexisting concepts and may lead us to recall events that never occurred.
- Misinformation effects occur when memory is distorted by misleading postevent information. This may occur because of source confusion: the tendency to recognize something as familiar but to forget where we encountered it.
- Vulnerability to misinformation effects is greater among younger than older children, and when suggestive questions are asked repeatedly. Experts cannot reliably tell when children are reporting accurate memories versus sincerely believed false memories.
- Psychologists debate whether recovered memories of child abuse are accurate and whether the abuse, if it occurred, was forgotten through repression or other psychological

processes. Concern about the possibility of false memory leads many experts to urge caution in unconditionally accepting the validity of recovered memories.

MEMORY AND THE BRAIN

- Memory involves numerous interacting brain regions. Sensory memory depends on input from our sensory systems and initial processing by cortical sensory areas.
- Working memory involves a network of brain regions. The frontal lobes play a key role in performing executive functions of working memory.
- The hippocampus helps consolidate long-term declarative memories. The cerebral cortex stores declarative memories across distributed sites. The amygdala encodes emotionally arousing aspects of events, and the cerebellum helps form procedural memories. Damage to the thalamus can produce severe amnesia.
- Studies of long-term potentiation in several species indicate that as memories form, complex chemical and structural changes that enhance synaptic efficiency occur in neurons.

KEY TERMS AND CONCEPTS

Each term has been boldfaced and defined in the chapter on the page indicated in parentheses.

Alzheimer's disease (AD) (p. 275)
anterograde amnesia (p. 274)
associative network (p. 264)
autobiographical memory (p. 268)
chunking (p. 256)
context-dependent memory (p. 270)
decay theory (p. 273)
declarative memory (p. 265)
dementia (p. 275)
dual coding theory (p. 261)
elaborative rehearsal (p. 260)
encoding (p. 254)
encoding specificity principle (p. 270)
episodic memory (p. 265)
explicit memory (p. 266)
flashbulb memories (p. 269)
implicit memory (p. 266)
infantile amnesia (p. 276)
levels of processing (p. 259)

long-term memory (p. 257)
long-term potentiation (LTP) (p. 286)
maintenance rehearsal (p. 260)
memory (p. 254)
memory codes (p. 255)
memory consolidation (p. 285)
method of loci (p. 261)
misinformation effect (p. 279)
mnemonic device (p. 261)
mnemonist (memorist) (p. 262)
mood-congruent recall (p. 271)
neural network (connectionist)
  model (p. 265)
overlearning (p. 288)
parallel distributed processing (PDP)
  model (p. 265)
priming (p. 264)
proactive interference (p. 273)

procedural (nondeclarative) memory
  (p. 266)
prospective memory (p. 274)
repression (p. 274)
retrieval (p. 254)
retrieval cue (p. 267)
retroactive interference (p. 273)
retrograde amnesia (p. 274)
schema (p. 261)
semantic memory (p. 265)
sensory memory (p. 254)
serial position effect (p. 257)
short-term memory (p. 255)
source confusion (p. 280)
state-dependent memory (p. 270)
storage (p. 254)
tip-of-the-tongue (TOT) state (p. 274)
working memory (p. 256)

? thinking **critically**

WOULD PERFECT MEMORY BE A GIFT OR A CURSE? (Page 263)

No doubt, perfect memory would have advantages, but were you able to think of any liabilities? Russian newspaper reporter S. V. Shereshevski—arguably the most famous mnemonist in history—had a remarkable capacity to remember numbers, poems in foreign languages, complex mathematical formulas, nonsense syllables, and sounds. Psychologist Aleksandr Luria (1968), who studied "S." for decades, describes how S. was tyrannized by his seeming inability to forget meaningless information. Almost any stimulus might unleash a flood of trivial memories that dominated his consciousness and made it difficult for him to concentrate or think abstractly.

S.'s experience may have been atypical, but perfect memory could indeed clutter up our thinking with trivial information. Moreover, perfect memory would deprive us of one of life's blessings: the ability to forget unpleasant experiences from our past. As illustrated in this chapter, imperfect memory allows us to view our past through slightly rosy glasses (Bahrick et al., 2008).

Would a perfect memory help you perform better on exams? On test questions calling only for definitions, formulas, or facts, probably so. But on questions asking you to apply concepts, synthesize ideas, analyze issues, and so forth, perfect memory might be of little benefit unless you also understood the material. In his graduate school classes,

Rajan had a tendency to try to commit the reading assignments to memory and reproduce them on tests. The strategy . . . is counterproductive in graduate courses where students are asked to apply their knowledge and understanding to new situations. . . . When taking tests, Rajan would write furiously . . . in hopes that the correct answer was somewhere in his response. . . . As he progressed in our graduate program, he tended to rely less on the strategy of memorizing everything and more on trying to understand and organize the information. (Thompson et al., 1993, p. 15)

Rajan's extraordinary memory for numbers did not extend to reading or visual tasks, but even if yours did, it still might tempt you to focus too heavily on sheer memorization and cause you to neglect paying attention to the meaning of the material. In sum, although imperfect memory can be frustrating and have serious consequences (as when eyewitnesses identify the wrong suspect), we should also appreciate how our memory system is balanced between the adaptiveness of remembering and the benefits of forgetting.

(By the way, in case you're curious, the current confirmed record for recalling pi is 67,890 digits, held by Chao Lu of China. To put this feat in perspective, imagine the next 19 pages of this textbook filled up with nothing but numbers!)

chapter nine

Language and Thinking

Myth or Reality?

Dyslexia Is a "Reading Backwards" Disorder
(page 307)

According to a popular stereotype, if you had dyslexia and read the sentence "It was a nice day," you might end up reading it as "It saw a nice bay" because reading letters or words backwards is the primary feature of dyslexia. Is it?

Figure 9.1

The "Miracle on the Hudson."
The successful ditching of U.S. Airways Flight 1549 in the Hudson River was a tribute to the power of human reasoning, language, and problem solving.

For the 150 passengers and 5 crew members aboard U.S. Airways Flight 1549 on January 15, 2009, their journey from New York City to Charlotte was about to become a dramatic test of human resourcefulness, with survival at stake. Ascending after takeoff from LaGuardia airport on that frigid afternoon, the Airbus collided with a flock of Canada geese, damaging both engines and causing them to lose thrust. Inside the cockpit, Captain Chesley Sullenberger and First Officer Jeff Skiles knew that the plane had little time to remain aloft. Quickly, they had to formulate a plan.

Sullenberger had to determine whether he or Skiles would pilot the crippled plane. "Typically what's done these days is for the first officer to be the pilot flying and for the captain to be the pilot monitoring, analyzing and managing the situation," Sullenberger later noted. "There wasn't time for that" (Shiner, 2009, para. 10). Although both pilots had similar total flying hours, Sullenberger knew that he was more experienced flying this aircraft. He also recognized that his side of the cockpit offered the better view of important flight path landmarks and that Skiles—due to more recent yearly flight-simulator training—would be faster at locating the proper emergency checklists from within a handbook kept in the cockpit. Sullenberger decided he would fly the plane and communicate with air traffic control; Skiles would focus on restarting the engines. The engines, however, wouldn't restart.

About 35 seconds after the bird strike, Sullenberger decided not to attempt a landing at LaGuardia or another nearby airport but instead to ditch the plane in the Hudson River.

> I could tell . . . that neither [airport] was a viable option. I also thought that I could not afford to choose wrongly. I could not afford to attempt to make it to a runway that in fact I could not make. Landing short, even by a little bit, can have catastrophic consequences. (Shiner, 2009, para. 16)

To increase the odds of a fast rescue, Sullenberger decided to ditch the plane where boats would be operating nearby. Flight attendants shouted emergency-landing instructions to the passengers, and the plane ditched merely 6 minutes after takeoff (Figure 9.1). As it slowly took on water, flight attendants communicated evacuation instructions. Eventually, all aboard were rescued alive. Two days after this "Miracle on the Hudson," a National Transportation Safety Board member called it "the most successful ditching in aviation history" (Olshan & Livingston, 2009).

Incidents like this one vividly illustrate the power of communication, reasoning, and problem solving—cognitive skills that underlie adaptive behavior. Whether it's a pilot talking with air traffic controllers, or flight attendants giving evacuation instructions to passengers, scientists would want to identify the building blocks of language and examine how people are able to understand what others say. Likewise, scientists would want to determine factors that contribute to or hinder effective reasoning and decision making. These are among the many topics we'll explore in this chapter.

We humans dominate our world because we communicate more effectively and think better than other animals do, skills that reflect our remarkable ability to create *mental representations* (Simon, 1990). **Mental representations** *include images, ideas, concepts, and principles.* At this very moment, through the printed words you are reading, mental representations are being transferred from our minds to yours. Indeed, the process of education is all about transferring mental representations from one mind to another.

LANGUAGE

Language has been called "the jewel in the crown of cognition" (Pinker, 2000) and "the human essence" (Chomsky, 1972). Much of our thinking, reasoning, and problem solving involves the use of **language:** *a system of symbols and rules for combining these symbols in ways that can generate an infinite number of possible messages and meanings.* To most of us, using our native language comes as naturally as breathing. Yet using language actually involves a host of complex skills. **Psycholinguistics** *is the scientific study of the psychological aspects of language,* such as how people understand, produce, and acquire language. Before delving into these topics, let's consider some functions of language.

Adaptive Functions of Language

According to anthropologists, the human brain probably achieved its present form some 50,000 years ago (Pilbeam, 1984). Yet it took another 35,000 years before lifelike paintings began to appear on cave walls and another 12,000 years before humans developed a way to store knowledge in the form of writing (Kottak, 2000). These time lags tell us that thought and language depend on more than the brain's physical structure; although the brain may not have physically evolved much over the past 50,000 years, human cognitive and linguistic skills clearly have.

Some evolutionary theorists believe that language use evolved as humans adopted a more socially oriented lifestyle and formed larger social units (Flinn, 1997). As the social environment became more complex, new survival problems emerged: the need to create divisions of labor and cooperative social systems, to develop social customs and communicate thoughts, and to pass on knowledge. Language made it easier for humans to adapt to these environmental demands (Bjorklund & Pellegrini, 2002).

"GOT IDEA. TALK BETTER. COMBINE WORDS. MAKE SENTENCES."

Figure 9.2

According to many theorists, the development of language was a major milestone in human evolution. Source: ScienceCartoonsPlus.com. Reprinted with permission.

It is no coincidence, then, that every human culture has developed language and that the human brain seems to have an inborn capacity to acquire any of the roughly 5,000 to 6,000 languages spoken across the globe. We have evolved into highly social creatures who need to communicate, and we have the physical characteristics (e.g., a highly developed brain, a vocal tract) to do so in the most flexible way known: through language (Figure 9.2).

Language underlies so much of what we do that it's almost impossible to imagine functioning without it. Conscious thinking often takes the form of inner speech. Through language, we can share our thoughts, feelings, goals, intentions, desires, needs, and memories with other people. Language also is a powerful learning mechanism. To get somewhere new, you don't have to drive or walk aimlessly. Instead, you ask for directions, Google a map, or listen to your GPS device. Through storytelling, books, instruction, mass media, and the Internet—language puts the knowledge accrued over generations at your fingertips.

Properties of Language

What captures your attention first when someone uses a foreign language that you don't speak: how different it sounds or looks when written, or simply how incomprehensible it seems? Yet what is striking about the world's languages is not their differences but their underlying similarities. Across the globe, there are four properties essential to any language: symbols, structure, meaning, and generativity. We will also describe a fifth property: displacement.

Language Is Symbolic and Structured

Language uses sounds, written characters, or some other system of symbols (e.g., hand signs) to represent objects, events, ideas, feelings, and actions. The symbols used in any given language are arbitrary. For example, the Spanish, French, and German words for *dog* are *perro, chien,* and *hund,* respectively. Nothing about how any one of these words looks or sounds makes it intrinsically correct for representing the concept of "dog." In English, *gerk, woof, professor,* or other words could be used to represent what we call a *dog.* But they aren't (even though "No Professors Allowed on the Lawn" has a certain ring to it). Regardless of how the word *dog* came into being, it has an agreed-on meaning. The same holds true for all the other words we use.

Language also has a rule-governed structure. A language's **grammar** *is the set of rules that dictates how symbols can be combined to create meaningful units of communication.* Thus if we ask you whether *zpflrovc* is an English word, you will almost certainly say "No." Why? Because it violates a rule of the English language: five consonants (*z, p, f, l, r*) cannot be put in an unbroken sequence. Likewise, if we ask you whether "Bananas have sale for I" is an appropriate English sentence, you will say "No. It should read: 'I have bananas for sale.'" In this case, "Bananas have sale for I" violates a portion of English grammar called **syntax,** *the rules that govern the order of words.* Even if you can't verbalize the grammatical rules violated in these examples, you know them implicitly.

The grammars of all languages share common functions, such as providing rules for how to change present tense ("I am walking the dog") into the past tense ("I walked the dog") or a negative ("I didn't walk the dog"). Yet just as symbols (e.g., words) vary across languages, so do grammatical rules. In English, for example, we say *green salad* and *big river,* which follow the rule that adjectives almost always come before the nouns they modify. In French and Spanish, however, adjectives often follow nouns (*salade verte, rio grande*). Although language changes over time, with new words and phrases appearing regularly,

they need to conform to the basic rules of that language.

Language Conveys Meaning

Once people learn the symbols and rules of a language, they can form and then transfer mental representations to other people. Thus you can tell a friend about your courses, favorite foods, feelings, and so on. Your friend will then extract meaning—hopefully, your intended meaning—from what you've said. But understanding **semantics,** *the meaning of words and sentences,* is a tricky business. For example, when you ask a friend "How did you do on the test?" and the reply is "I nailed it," you know that your friend is not saying "I hammered the test to the desk with a nail." Someone familiar with English knows not to interpret this expression literally; someone just beginning to learn English might find this expression perplexing.

Language Is Generative and Permits Displacement

Generativity *means that the symbols of language can be combined to generate an infinite number of messages that have novel meaning.* The English language, for example, has only 26 letters, but they can be combined into more than half a million words, which in turn can be combined to create a virtually limitless number of sentences. Thus you can create and understand a sentence like "Why is that sparrow standing underneath my pancake?" even though you are unlikely to have heard anything like it before.

Displacement *refers to the fact that language allows us to communicate about events and objects that are not physically present.* You can discuss the past and the future, as well as people, objects, and events that exist or take place elsewhere. You can even discuss imaginary situations, such as a sparrow standing underneath a pancake.

The Structure of Language

Psycholinguists describe language as having a *surface structure* and a *deep structure.* Language also has a hierarchical structure, in which smaller elements are combined into larger ones. Let's examine these issues.

Surface Structure and Deep Structure

When you read, listen to, or produce a sentence, its **surface structure** *consists of the symbols that are used and their order.* As noted earlier, syntax provides the rules for ordering words properly. In contrast, a sentence's **deep structure** *refers to the* *underlying meaning of the combined symbols*, which returns us to the issue of semantics.

Sentences can differ in surface structure but have the same deep structure. Consider:

1. Sam ate the cake.
2. The cake was eaten by Sam.
3. Eaten by Sam the cake was.

Each sentence conveys the same underlying meaning. Notice that the third has incorrect syntax. English isn't spoken this way, except perhaps by the fictional *Star Wars* character Yoda. Still, its meaning is clear enough.

Sometimes, a single surface structure gives rise to two deep structures, as occurs when people speak or write ambiguous sentences. Consider:

The police must stop drinking after midnight.

This sentence could mean that police officers need to enforce a curfew to prevent citizens from drinking alcohol after midnight. Or, it could mean that if police officers go out for drinks after work, they need to finish their drinking by midnight.

At times, people intentionally use words or phrases to create a *double entendre* (French for "double meaning") to convey two possible deep structures, one of which is often socially inappropriate. For example, in the movie *The Silence of the Lambs*, serial killer Hannibal Lecter tells FBI agent Clarice Starling "I do wish we could chat longer, but I'm having an old friend for dinner." The phrase "having an old friend for dinner" normally elicits only a single deep meaning, but because Lecter is "Hannibal the Cannibal," who eats his victims after killing them, the phrase was intentionally used to convey a second, more sinister deep structure.

In everyday life, when you read or hear speech, you are moving from the surface structure to deep structure—from the way a sentence looks or sounds to its deeper level of meaning. In contrast, when you express your thoughts to other people, you must transform deep structure (the meaning that you want to communicate) into a surface structure that others can understand.

 thinking **critically**

DISCERNING THE DEEP STRUCTURE OF LANGUAGE

Figure 9.3 shows a grave marker in the Boothill Graveyard in Tombstone, Arizona, where many notorious outlaws and gunfighters are buried. Analyze the marker carefully, and then identify two possible meanings for the inscription. Think about it, then see page 330.

Figure 9.3

This grave marker in Boothill Graveyard illustrates an interesting relation between surface structure and deep structure.

The Hierarchical Structure of Language

The most elementary building block of human language is the **phoneme,** *the smallest unit of speech sound in a language that can signal a difference in meaning.* Humans can produce about 100 phonemes, including the clicking sounds in some African languages, but no language uses them all. Some languages employ as few as 15 phonemes, and others more than 80. English uses about 40 phonemes, consisting of vowel and consonant sounds, as well as certain letter combinations such as *th* and *sh.* Thus sounds associated with *th, a,* and *t* can be combined to form the three-phoneme word *that.*

Phonemes have no inherent meaning, but they alter meaning when combined with other elements. For example, the phoneme *d* creates a different meaning from the phoneme *l* when it precedes *og* (i.e., *dog* versus *log*). At the next level of the hierarchy, phonemes are combined into **morphemes,** *the smallest units of meaning in a language.* Thus *dog, log,* and *ball* are all morphemes, as are prefixes and suffixes such as *pre-, un-, -ed,* and *-ous.* Notice in Figure 9.4 that morphemes are not always syllables. For example, in English *s* is not a syllable, but the final *s* on a noun is a morpheme that means "plural." Thus the word *fans* has one syllable but two morphemes. In every language, rules determine how phonemes can be combined into morphemes. English's 40 phonemes can be combined into more than 100,000 morphemes.

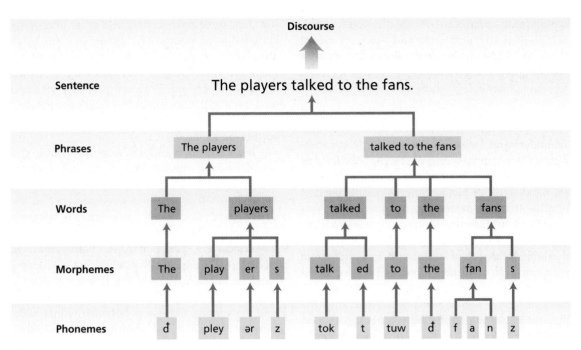

Figure 9.4

The hierarchical structure of language.
Human language is structured hierarchically, with phonemes being the most basic unit. The row of phonemes contains symbols used by linguists to denote particular sounds.

Morphemes, in turn, are the stuff of which words are formed. English morphemes can be combined into over 500,000 words, words into countless phrases, and phrases into an infinite number of sentences. Thus we have a five-step language hierarchy, beyond which lies the sixth and most comprehensive level, **discourse,** *in which sentences are combined into paragraphs, articles, books, conversations, and so forth.*

test yourself   Properties and Structure of Language

Match each numbered concept to the correct definition on the right.

1. grammar
2. phoneme
3. semantics
4. surface structure
5. displacement
6. morpheme

a. smallest unit of meaning in a language
b. the meaning of words and sentences
c. in a sentence, the symbols used and their order
d. rules for combining the symbols in a language
e. ability to communicate about things that aren't physically present
f. smallest unit of speech sound that signals a change in meaning

ANSWERS: 1-d, 2-f, 3-b, 4-c, 5-e, 6-a

Understanding and Producing Language

Here's a true story. A man answers a phone call, listens for 5 seconds, and hangs up. "It was a prerecorded telemarketing call," he tells his wife. "Some company called Pressgrits." "Pressgrits. That's a weird name," she says. Then it dawns on her. She is expecting an automated call from a company called Express Scripts to confirm an order. This was indeed the confirmation call.

How can a voice on the phone say "Express Scripts" and the husband hear it as "Pressgrits"? Did he need to clean out his ears? Hardly. He simply failed to perceive the morpheme *ex*, which left *press* for the first word. By saying "Press Scripts" rapidly, as the prerecorded voice did, you'll realize that phonetically, *pressscripts* and *pressgrits* are not far apart. Additionally, her husband had no context for interpreting the message. Context, as you'll see, plays a key role in understanding language.

The Role of Bottom-Up Processing

To understand language, your brain must recognize and interpret patterns of stimuli—the sounds of speech, shapes of letters, movements that create hand signs, or tactile patterns of dots used in Braille—that are detected by your sensory systems. And just like other perceptual tasks, extracting information from linguistic stimuli involves the joint influence of bottom-up and top-down processing. In **bottom-up processing,** *individual elements of a stimulus are analyzed and then combined to form a unified perception.* Analyzing the hierarchical structure of spoken language as a set of building blocks that uses phonemes to create morphemes and then morphemes to create words reflects a bottom-up approach.

Likewise, as you read this sentence, specialized cell groups in your brain are (1) analyzing the basic elements (e.g., contours, angles of lines) of the printed visual patterns that you see and (2) feeding this information to other cell groups that lead you to perceive these patterns as letters. We then recognize the words, which in turn become the building blocks for sentences, and sentences the building blocks for discourse. But at every step in this bottom-up sequence, including pattern recognition, our understanding of language also is influenced by top-down processing.

The Role of Top-Down Processing

In a Seattle farmers' market, there used to be a store called The Bead Store. The owners sold beads for making jewelry. Tourists would often walk by and ask "Where's the bread?" The store's sign said *Bead,* but many people perceived the word as *Bread,* a function perhaps of their perceptual set (i.e., a perceptual expectation) that they were in a farmers' market that sold food. Eventually, the owners put up a sign saying "We Don't Sell Bread."

In **top-down processing,** *sensory information is interpreted in light of existing knowledge, concepts, ideas, and expectations.* In Chapter 5 we discussed how people's unconscious expectations (i.e., perceptual sets) literally shape what they visually perceive. As the bead store example illustrates, people looked at a stimulus pattern on a store sign that said *Bead,* but *Bread* is what they saw.

Language by its very nature involves top-down processing, because the words you write, read, speak, or hear activate and draw upon your knowledge of vocabulary, grammar, and other linguistic rules that are stored in your long-term memory. That's why if we write "Bill g_ve th_ pe_cil to h_s fr__nd," you can probably interpret the words with little difficulty ("Bill gave the pencil to his friend"), despite the absence of several bottom-up elements.

Let's consider another example. Have you ever listened to someone speak a foreign language in which you aren't fluent and found that it was difficult to tell where one word ended and the next began? Conversely, non-English speakers would have the same problem listening to you speak. How is it, then, that in your native language this process of **speech segmentation**—*perceiving where each word within a spoken sentence begins and ends*—seems to occur automatically? When you read a sentence, the spaces between words make segmentation easy. But when people speak, they don't pause in between each pair of words. In fact, when people utter sentences, there is often more of a drop in sound energy between the segments within a word than between adjacent words. To illustrate, say "We hope you have a nice day" out loud. Did you distinctly segment each whole word, creating a sound energy break between each one? Or were your segments more like "We ho pew ha va nice day"? Moreover, in English about 40 percent of words consist of two or more syllables that are vocally stressed (i.e., emphasized) when spoken (Mattys, 2000). Thus in these and other words, the auditory breaks that we hear in speech often don't correspond well to the physical breaks produced by the spaces in written sentences.

Psycholinguists have discovered that we use several top-down cues to tell when one spoken word ends and another begins (Cunillera et al., 2006). For example, through experience we learn that certain sequences of phonemes are unlikely to occur within a single word, so when we hear these sounds in sequence we are more likely to perceive them as a word ending and the beginning of an adjacent word. We also use the context provided by the other words in a sentence to interpret the meaning of any individual word. Thus when people listen to a single spoken word (e.g., *ice*) and have to identify it based on its sound alone, they perform more poorly than when they listen to the same word spoken within two- to four-word segments (e.g., "covered in ice"; Pollack & Pickett, 1964).

Pragmatics: The Social Context of Language

Imagine that a passerby on the street asks you "Do you have the time?" You say "10:20" and part ways.

In this case, the question really is shorthand for "I'm not wearing a watch, so please tell me what time it is right now." You wouldn't respond to someone's request "Do you have the time?" merely by saying "Yes, I do" and then walking away. Likewise, if a friend says "I need you to explain this material to me. Do you have the time?" you wouldn't say "10:20" and walk away. In this context, you understand that "Do you have the time?" means "Can you take a few minutes to help me?"

These examples illustrate that it takes more than having a vocabulary and arranging words grammatically to understand language and communicate effectively. It also involves **pragmatics,** *a knowledge of the practical aspects of using language* (Cummings, 2005). Language occurs in a social context, and pragmatic knowledge not only helps you understand what other people are really saying, it helps you make sure that other people get the point of what you're communicating. Pragmatics is another example of how top-down processing influences language use.

Many social rules guide communication between people (Arundale, 2005; Grice, 1975). One rule states that messages should be as clear as possible (Figure 9.5). Depending on whether you're talking with an adult or a young child, you usually adjust your choice of words and sentence complexity. Pragmatics also depend on other aspects of the social context. When you write a term paper, you normally would use a more formal tone than when writing an e-mail to friends. Thus when a college student sent an e-mail to her instructor (it wasn't to one of us) that read "I can't find tomorrow's assignment could you pleeeeez send it to me pleeeeez, could ya, could ya?" the instructor sternly let the student know about her violation of pragmatics, namely, that the style of the message was inappropriate for the context.

? thinking **critically**

THE SLEEPING POLICEMAN

You're on vacation in England, driving to a countryside bed-and-breakfast to spend the night. You stop in a small town to get directions. A storekeeper tells you to take a left turn a mile up the road, drive "until you come to the sleeping policeman," and then take a right. What do you imagine "the sleeping policeman" (or "The Sleeping Policeman") might be? Think about it, then see page 331.

Language Functions, the Brain, and Sex Differences

Language functions are distributed in many areas of the brain, but the regions shown in Figure 9.6 are especially significant. As discussed in Chapter 4, Broca's area, located in the left hemisphere's frontal lobe, is most centrally involved in word production (lower-right brain scan). Wernicke's area, in the rear portion of the temporal lobe, is more centrally involved in speech comprehension (upper-left scan). People with damage in one or both areas typically suffer from **aphasia,** *an impairment in speech comprehension and/or production* that can be permanent or temporary (LaPointe, 2005). The visual area of the cortex is also involved in processing written words.

Years ago, scientists noted that men who suffer left-hemisphere strokes are more likely than women to show severe aphasic symptoms. In female stroke victims with left-hemisphere damage, language functions are more likely to be spared, suggesting that more of their language function is shared with the right hemisphere.

Brain-imaging research by Susan Rossell and coworkers (2002) supports this hypothesis.

Figure 9.5

A breakdown of pragmatics.

Although most of us might understand the underlying meaning of "Can I see you again?" it seems that in this case our suitor made an error in his choice of words. Source: Copyright © Jim Toomey. King Features Syndicate.

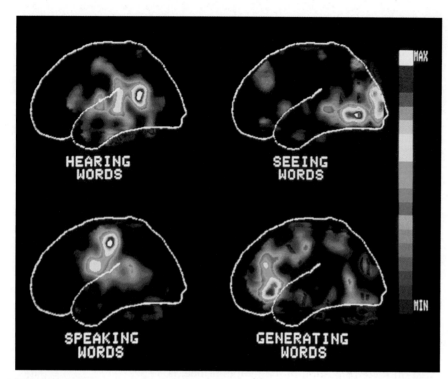

Figure 9.6

Brain areas involved in various aspects of language.
In these PET scans, regions of white, red, and yellow show the greatest activity. Notice in the upper-left image that Wernicke's area (in the temporal lobe) is especially active when we hear words, and in the lower-right image that Broca's area (located in the frontal lobe) is especially active when we generate words.

In their study, men and women engaged in a language task in which words and nonwords were presented on each side of a computer screen. Participants had to identify which was the real word as quickly as possible by pressing one of two computer keys. Functional MRIs (fMRIs) were recorded during the task and during a nonlanguage control task. Men exhibited greater left-hemisphere activation during the language task, whereas women's brain activation occurred in both the left and right hemispheres. Maximum activation occurred in regions corresponding to Broca's area and Wernicke's area.

Neural systems involved in several aspects of language may be organized differently in women than in men, but because this finding has been successfully replicated in some studies but not others, more research is needed to sort out why these inconsistencies occur (Démonet et al., 2005). Further, as a critical thinker, you should recognize that if men's and women's brains differ overall in some aspects of language processing, this finding does not establish by itself whether the source of those differences lies in our genes or possible gender-differences in language socialization (Kaiser et al., 2009).

Acquiring a First Language

Language acquisition is one of the most striking events in human cognitive development. It represents the joint influences of biology (nature) and environment (nurture). Many language experts believe that humans are born linguists, inheriting a biological readiness to recognize and eventually produce the sounds and structure of whatever language they are exposed to (Chomsky, 1986; Pinker, 2000).

Biological Foundations

Linguist Noam Chomsky proposes that from birth, our genetic endowment innately leads us to "interpret part of the environment as linguistic experience" (2005, p. 266). He has argued that we are born with a brain mechanism already "prewired" to understand general grammatical rules common to all languages (which he terms "universal grammar"), such as the principle that languages contain elements that are arranged in particular ways (Chomsky, 1986). Chomsky's views have generated much debate, including disagreements about whether we are born with brain systems specifically dedicated to language or instead have more general inborn cognitive capabilities (e.g., memory, learning) that by themselves can account for language acquisition (Valin, 2009).

Several facts suggest a biological basis for language acquisition. First, human children, despite their limited thinking skills, begin to master language early in life without any formal instruction. For example, whether born in Toledo, Taiwan, or Tanzania, young infants can perceive the entire range of phonemes found in the world's languages. Between 6 and 12 months of age, however, they begin to discriminate only those sounds that are specific to their native tongue. For example, Japanese children lose the ability to distinguish between the *r* and *l* sounds because their language does not make this phonetic distinction, but children exposed to English continue to discriminate these sounds as they mature. Likewise, Japanese-speaking children learn the syntactic rule to put the object before the verb ("Ichiro the ball hit"), whereas English-speaking children learn the syntactic rule that the verb comes before the object ("Ichiro hit the ball").

Moreover, despite their differences at the phoneme level, all adult languages throughout the world—including sign languages for the deaf, which developed independently in different parts of the world—seem to have common underlying structural characteristics. Language acquisition appears to represent the unfolding of a biologically primed process within a social learning environment (Aitchison, 1998; Chomsky, 2005).

Social Learning Processes

Given the required biological foundation, social learning plays a central role in acquiring a language (Pruden et al., 2006). Early on, caregivers attract children's attention and maintain their interest by conversing with them in what has been termed *child-directed speech,* a high-pitched intonation that seems to be used all over the world (Fernald et al., 1989). Caregivers also teach their children words by naming objects, reading aloud, and responding to the never-ending question "What dat?" (Figure 9.7).

The behaviorist B. F. Skinner (1957) developed an operant conditioning explanation for language acquisition. His basic premise was that children's language development is strongly governed by adults' positive reinforcement of appropriate language and nonreinforcement or correction of inappropriate verbalizations. Most modern psycholinguists doubt that operant learning principles alone can account for language development. For one thing, children learn so much so quickly. By grade 2 in elementary school, children have acquired about 5,000 to 6,000 words (Biemiller & Slonim, 2001). Observational studies also show that parents do *not* typically correct their children's grammar as language skills are developing. Rather, parents' corrections focus primarily on the "truth value" (or deep structure) of what the child is trying to communicate. They are less likely, for example, to correct a young child who says "I have two foots" than they are to correct one who says "I have four feet," even though the latter statement is grammatically correct (Brown, 1973). Further, much of children's language is different from that of their parents, and thus it can't be explained simply as an imitative process. Nonetheless, social learning is a crucial contributor to language acquisition, and language development reflects an interplay of biological and environmental factors.

Developmental Timetable

Language acquisition proceeds according to a developmental timetable that is common to all cultures. As Table 9.1 highlights, children progress from reflexive crying at birth through stages of cooing, babbling, and one-word utterances. By 2 years of age, children are uttering sentences, called *telegraphic speech,* that at first consist of a noun and a verb (e.g., "Want cookie"), with nonessential words left out. Soon, additional words may be added (e.g., "Daddy go car"). From that point on, speech development accelerates as vocabulary increases and sentences become more grammatically correct. In the short span of 5 years, an initially nonverbal creature has come to understand and produce a complex language.

In Chapter 5 we saw how normal perceptual development requires certain kinds of sensory input early in life. Many linguists believe there is also a critical period, or at least a sensitive period, from infancy to puberty during which the brain is optimally responsive to language input from the environment (Arshavsky, 2009; Long, 2005). If exposure to language is delayed beyond this period, then normal language acquisition either will not occur (the "critical period" hypothesis) or will still be possible but much more difficult to achieve (the "sensitive period" hypothesis). Support for at least a sensitive period comes from studies of children who lived by themselves in the wild or who were isolated from human contact by deranged parents. One such child, found when she was 6 years old, immediately received language training

Figure 9.7

Language development depends not only on the brain's biological programming device but also on exposure to one's language. Childhood is an important sensitive period for such exposure.

Table **9.1** | **Course of Normal Language Development in Children**

Age	Speech Characteristics
1–3 months	Infant can distinguish speech from nonspeech sounds and prefers speech sounds (phonemes). Undifferentiated crying gives way to cooing when happy.
4–6 months	Babbling sounds begin to occur. Child vocalizes in response to verbalizations of others.
7–11 months	Perception of phonemes narrows to include only the phonemes heard in the language spoken by others in the environment. Child moves tongue with vocalizations ("lalling"). Child discriminates between some words without understanding their meaning and begins to imitate word sounds heard from others.
12 months	First recognizable words typically spoken as one-word utterances to name familiar people and objects (e.g., *da-da* or *block*).
12–18 months	Child increases knowledge of word meanings and begins to use single words to express whole phrases or requests (e.g., *out* to express a desire to get out of the crib); primarily uses nouns.
18–24 months	Vocabulary expands to between 50 and 100 words. First rudimentary sentences appear, usually consisting of two words (e.g., *more milk*) with little or no use of articles (*the, a*), conjunctions (*and*), or auxiliary verbs (*can, will*). This condensed, or telegraphic, speech is characteristic of first sentences throughout the world.
2–4 years	Vocabulary expands rapidly at the rate of several hundred words every 6 months. Two-word sentences give way to longer sentences that, though often grammatically incorrect, exhibit basic language syntax. Child begins to express concepts with words and to use language to describe imaginary objects and ideas. Sentences become more correct syntactically.
4–5 years	Child has learned the basic grammatical rules for combining nouns, adjectives, articles, conjunctions, and verbs into meaningful sentences.

and seemed to develop normal language abilities (Brown, 1958). In contrast, language-deprived children who were found when they were past puberty acquired only limited language skills, despite extensive training (Clarke & Clarke, 2000; Curtiss, 1977).

The importance of early language exposure applies to any language, not just spoken language.

Because sign languages share the deep-structure characteristics of spoken languages, deaf children who learn sign language before puberty develop normal linguistic and cognitive abilities without having ever heard a spoken word (Marschark & Mayer, 1998). In contrast, deaf people who are not exposed to sign language before age 12 show language-learning deficits later in life (Morford, 2003).

test yourself   Understanding, Producing, and Acquiring Language

True or false?

1. Bottom-up processing occurs when our brain analyzes the visual patterns (e.g., contours) of written letters and words.

2. In English, we segment speech entirely by hearing the auditory breaks that occur when people speak.

3. Knowing when "it's cool" means "it's OK" rather than "it's a cool temperature" illustrates pragmatics.

4. Aphasia is an impairment in producing or understanding speech.

5. Social learning contributes to language development but can't fully explain it.

ANSWERS: 1-true, 2-false, 3-true, 4-true, 5-true

Bilingualism

For those of us trying to learn a second language, there are inspirational models. M. D. Berlitz, inventor of a well-known system for teaching foreign languages, spoke 58 of them. Sir John Bowring, a former British governor of Hong Kong who reputedly could speak 100 languages and read 100 more, noted that "it is scarcely more difficult to acquire five languages than one" (Bowring, 1877, p. 91).

Bilingualism, *the regular use of two languages,* is common throughout the world (Fabbro, 2001). Officially, Canada is a bilingual country. French is the official language of the province of Quebec, English is the official language elsewhere, and the federal government promotes both languages. But individually, only about 18 percent of Canadians (including 41 percent of those living in Quebec) speak both English and French (Statistics Canada, 2002). English is the sole official language in the United States, but as in Canada and other countries, a history of immigration means that many languages and bilingual combinations are spoken (Table 9.2).

Table **9.2** | **Most Commonly Spoken Languages at Home in the United States***

Language	Number of Homes
1. English	216,176,111
2. Spanish**	32,184,293
3. Chinese	2,300,467
4. French**	1,932,418
5. Tagalog***	1,376,632
6. Vietnamese	1,142,328
7. German	1,120,256
8. Korean	983,954
9. Russian	812,404
10. Italian	802,436
11. Arabic	686,986
12. Portuguese**	661,990
13. Polish	607,585
14. Hindi	462,371
15. Japanese	457,836

*Includes Americans who are at least 5 years old.

**Includes people who speak a Spanish, French, or Portuguese creole. A *creolized* language is a version of an original language (say, French) that has been blended with some characteristics of another language (say, English) and that evolves into the native language of people living in a certain area.

***Tagalog is native to the Philippines.

Source: U.S. Census Bureau, 2005c.

Does Bilingualism Affect Other Cognitive Abilities and First-Language Learning?

In childhood, does learning a second language influence the development of other cognitive abilities or affect acquisition of one's native language? Causation is difficult to establish, because researchers typically don't get to randomly assign children to bilingual or monolingual classrooms. Nevertheless, research suggests that bilingualism is associated with greater thinking flexibility, higher performance on nonverbal intelligence tests, and better performance on perceptual tasks that require people to inhibit attention to irrelevant information and pay attention to relevant information (Bialystok & Viswanathan, 2009; Kovacs, 2009).

For example, suppose you sit in front of a computer screen that displays an image like the one shown in Figure 9.8 (Bialystok & Martin, 2004). There's a box in the lower-left corner with a red square above it and a box in the lower-right corner with a blue circle above it. Next, a stimulus appears at the top of the screen—either a blue square or a red circle. At first, your task is to place the stimulus into the box that has the same color. If a blue square appears, you hit the letter O on the keyboard to drop it into the lower-right box. If a red circle appears, you hit the X key to drop it into the lower-left box. After several trials, however, we switch the rule. Now your task is to sort each stimulus by its shape, not by its color: drop blue squares into the left box and red circles into the right box. This new rule requires you to ignore the color of each stimulus, which just a moment ago was foremost in your mind, and instead to selectively focus your attention on the shape of the stimulus.

According to psychologist Ellen Bialystok (2009), one reason bilingual people perform better

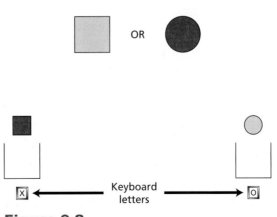

Figure 9.8

Measuring your ability to ignore irrelevant details.

This figure shows one of the attention-inhibition tasks used by Bialystok & Martin (2004).

than monolingual people on tasks like this is that in learning a second language, they gain continuous experience in using selective attention to focus on relevant information and ignore information that interferes with a task. For example, while speaking in their second language, bilinguals must ignore the more familiar words of their first language. Bilingual children also gain experience in frequently switching languages, which may contribute to their greater cognitive flexibility than monolingual children. Tasks like the one in Figure 9.8 require participants to switch decision-making strategies when the experimenter provides new instructions.

Bilingualism, however, may also have a linguistic cost. When children are raised learning two languages, they develop a somewhat smaller vocabulary in each language than do their monolingual age peers, and this vocabulary size difference also is found among bilingual adults (Bialystok & Feng, 2009; Portocarrero et al., 2007). At present, research suggests that in general, compared to monolinguals, bilinguals tend to perform more poorly on several linguistic tasks but display superior performance on other types of cognitive tasks (Bialystok, 2009; Kharkhurin, 2008).

The Bilingual Brain: Two Language Systems or One?

Is a second language represented in the same parts of the brain as the native language? One intriguing set of findings comes from studies of bilingual people who experience a brain trauma (e.g., from a tumor or stroke) and subsequently develop an aphasia. In some bilingual patients, the same linguistic ability—such as understanding the meaning of words—may be impaired to different degrees in each language or impaired in one language and not the other (Fabbro, 2001). Moreover, when brain damage produces similar impairments in both languages, patients may experience some simultaneous recovery in both languages or recovery in one language but not the other. These findings suggest that there is variability in how bilingual abilities are represented in the brain, and also that in some cases, each language is represented by at least partially distinct neural networks.

The question "Are there two language systems or one?" is far more complicated than it looks. The answer may depend on the aspect of language examined (e.g., word recognition, grammar), the age and proficiency of second-language learning, the degree of exposure, similarity of the two languages, and other factors. Still, brain-imaging

studies shed some interesting light on this issue. The most consistent finding is that when people acquire a second language early in life, both languages use a common neural network (Abutalebi, 2008; Bloch et al., 2009). In contrast, people who learn a second language only moderately well later in life, such as in adolescence or adulthood, typically show more variability in their neural activation patterns. At least for some language functions, their specific brain areas that process each language are partly distinct (Abutalebi, 2008; Bloch et al., 2009). Further, even for some cortical areas involved in processing both languages among older bilingual learners, greater activation tends to occur when the person uses the second language. This suggests that the person may have to exert more conscious effort to process the less dominant, second language.

Age and Second-Language Fluency

Many people start to learn a second language during high school or college or after emigrating to a foreign country during late adolescence or adulthood. Can these "late learners" achieve the fluency of native speakers? The answer is often tied to the hypothesis that there is a biologically based critical period for acquiring a second language—typically proposed to end by late childhood to the mid-teenage years—after which the capacity for true nativelike acquisition is essentially lost. In a nutshell, some psycholinguists believe the evidence supports a critical period hypothesis, others don't, and still others believe there are critical periods for acquiring some aspects of a second language (e.g., speaking without a "foreign" accent) but not other aspects (e.g., learning grammar; Rothman, 2008).

One finding is clear: overall, people who start learning a second language in late adolescence or adulthood achieve less proficiency than younger learners. Importantly, this occurs even when the various age groups have similar amounts of exposure to the second language. Figure 9.9a shows the results of two studies that examined people who had emigrated at various ages to the United States and whose native language was either Korean or Chinese (Johnson & Newport, 1989) or Spanish (Birdsong & Molis, 2001). In both studies, late-arriving immigrants (arrival after age 16) displayed the poorest grammar proficiency, despite having similar exposure to English as the earlier-arriving immigrants. Further, among the 55 late-arriving immigrants combined across both studies, only one achieved nativelike grammar proficiency, though a few others almost did. In

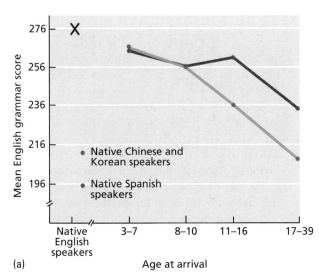

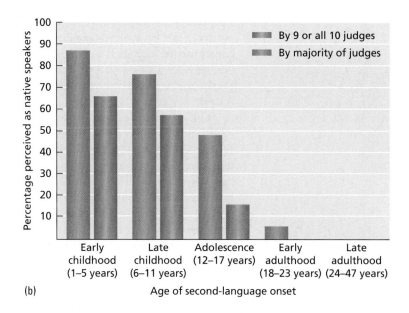

Figure 9.9

Age and proficiency of learning a second language.

(a) The X represents the average grammar score of native-born Americans. The blue line shows the grammar performance of Korean and Chinese individuals of various ages on a 276-item test of English grammar, The red line shows the grammar performance of native Spanish speakers of various ages on a 274-item version of the same grammar test. (b) Percentage of native Spanish speakers perceived to have nativelike Swedish fluency by native Swedish speakers. Sources: (a) Based on data from Johnson & Newport, 1989; Birdsong & Molis, 2001. (b) Abrahamsson & Hyltenstam, 2009.

contrast, most 3- to 7-year-olds achieved native-like grammar proficiency.

But how can we reconcile these and similar findings with those of other studies that generally report that about 5 to 20 percent of adult second-language learners achieve nativelike proficiency on various language tasks (Birdsong, 2005). Recent research by Niclas Abrahamsson and Kenneth Hyltenstam (2009) illustrates how answers to questions such as "Can adult second-language learners achieve nativelike proficiency?" depend strongly on how "nativelike proficiency" is defined and measured. First, they identified 195 native Spanish speakers who began learning Swedish at various ages and who considered themselves to have nativelike Swedish proficiency. Next, native Swedish speakers acted as judges and listened to speech samples from these participants and from a control group of native Swedish speakers. Based solely on the speech samples, 10 judges classified each participant as being a "nonnative" or "native Swedish speaker." Lastly, the researchers administered a battery of Swedish language tests to native Swedish speakers and to a sample of bilingual participants classified by a majority of judges as being native Swedish speakers.

The judges correctly identified all the native Swedish speakers. Figure 9.9b shows the percentage of native Spanish speakers identified as being native Swedish speakers either by a majority of judges (liberal criterion) or by 9 or 10 judges

(conservative criterion). Although all the bilingual participants believed they spoke Swedish with nativelike fluency, the judges thought otherwise, especially among the adolescent and adult participants. Further, only 7 percent of bilingual participants demonstrated nativelike proficiency on the entire battery of 10 language tests, and these all came from the childhood learner groups. Based on the test results, Abrahamsson and Kenneth Hyltenstam (2009) argue that to attain nativelike second-language proficiency, acquisition must start in childhood, and even that may not be sufficient. Other psycholinguists argue that criteria for judging nativelike proficiency can be too stringent, and thus the debate continues.

Reading

Typically, as long as we are exposed to an environment rich in spoken language, we will learn to produce and understand speech. Reading is a different animal: it requires extensive instruction (Carreiras et al., 2009). If written language came to humans as naturally as spoken language, there wouldn't be almost 759 million nonliterate adults across the globe (Watkins et al., 2008).

Learning to Read

Reading has been called "one of the most cognitively complex tasks that we will ever learn to do" (Pammer, 2009, p. 266). In the English language, for example, we must first learn to visually recognize a set of basic symbols—26 letters—that constitute the alphabet, as well as other visual elements such as punctuation marks and number symbols. We also learn names for these symbols (our "ABCs").

One of the most intricate steps in learning to read (and write) an alphabetic language such as English is making connections between how letters and letter combinations look when written and how they sound when spoken. For example, note how the letter *a* is voiced differently in each of the following five words: *mat, may, marble, mall,* and *mean* (in which the *a* is silent). Likewise, *e* is voiced differently in *met, meet,* and *ache,* as are various letter combinations such as *ch* in "*channel*" versus *ache*. If you are fluent in reading English, these phonological variations pose no problem. When learning to read, however, they frustrate attempts to apply simple rules such as "the letter *a* always sounds like *ay* and the letter *e* always sounds like *ee*."

This ability to translate print into sound—to have a mental map that connects written symbols to phonemes—is itself dependent on more basic understandings about the properties of language. As children acquire speech, they not only learn how to manipulate phonemes to produce different words, but also become aware that words are constructed from sequences of sounds and, thus, that words can be decoded into more basic sound elements. Psycholinguists use the term **phonological awareness** *to refer to this overall awareness of the sound structure of one's language,* and it is an important predictor of young children's subsequent reading ability (Furnes & Samuelsson, 2009).

Recognizing Written Words

Fluent reading involves rapid word recognition. In Chapter 1, we discussed a claim that

> . . . it deosn't mttaer waht oredr the ltteers in a wrod are, the olny iprmoatnt tihng is taht the frist and lsat ltteres are at the rghit pclae. . . . Tihs is bcuseae we do not raed ervey lteter by istlef but the wrod as a wlohe. (Anonymous, 2003)

We saw that the "letter ordering" claim, as an absolute conclusion, was false: words with interior jumbled letters can be very difficult to read. So, what's the validity of the claim that we don't read individual letters but instead read words "as a whole"?

One way we might recognize words as a "whole" is from their overall shape. The basic idea of the century-old *word shape hypothesis* is that

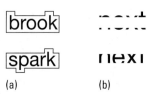

(a)   (b)

Figure 9.10

(a) Two words with a "shape envelop" drawn around each one. (b) Outer and inner portions of letters within words. SOURCE: Webb et al., 2006.

words have a holistic form, or "envelop," based on their pattern of letters (Cattell, 1886; Haber et al., 1983). For example, consider the different envelops created by *brook* and *spark* in Figure 9.10a.

Several types of evidence have been offered to support this hypothesis, including the iNtErEsTiNg finding that mixing lowercase and uppercase letters—which disrupts a word's typical shape—slows down word rEcOgNiTiOn. But mixed casing has other negative effects, such as making it more difficult to perceive some lowercase letters, and these—rather than overall shape disruption—appear to cause the reading impairment (Mayall et al., 1997). Overall, there is substantial evidence against this simple word-shape "envelop" hypothesis (Grainger, 2008), although visual information contained near the boundaries of letters—in the upper and lower portions of letters as illustrated in Figure 9.10b—may contribute more to word recognition than visual information in the middle portion (Beech & Mayall, 2005).

How then do fluent readers recognize written words? The issue isn't settled, but several lines of evidence point to at least one key component: the parallel processing of letter information within words (Beech & Mayall, 2005; Grainger, 2008). At a basic visual level, the brain simultaneously analyzes the features of multiple letters, acquiring information about individual letters and letter groupings, and coding their location. Some psycholinguists propose that our brain directly processes this visual information to determine the meaning of a word, while others contend that our brain also phonologically recodes printed text to help determine word meaning (Coltheart et al., 2001; Lee, 2009). But in any event, the notion that fluent reading does not involve visual processing at the level of individual letters appears to be wrong (Pelli et al., 2003).

Our brain also is processing other information as we read. Without conscious awareness, as in listening to speech, prior written words create top-down context effects that help prepare us for recognizing the words we're about to read. Additionally, our eye movements while reading are not smooth and continuous. We alternate between briefly fixating on a word, typically for a quarter second or less, and then making a rapid, distinct jump—called a *saccade*—to another word (and some of these saccades are backwards, e.g., right to left, when reading English). During fixations, our brain is receiving information from our visual periphery about the spacing of upcoming words, which helps to determine how large our next eye movement will be (Larson, 2004).

You can see that reading is a complex process. It depends on many brain areas, including ones specialized for detecting and recognizing visual features of objects, coding the identity of letters and their positions within words, processing the phonological aspects of language, and encoding the meaning of words (Pammer, 2009). For fluent readers, all this machinery exists under the radar screen. It seems effortless. Unfortunately, many children and adults struggle with reading, and as our "Myth or Reality?" feature discusses, this includes people diagnosed with *dyslexia*.

Myth or Reality?

Dyslexia Is a "Reading Backwards" Disorder

Harvey Hubbell V was diagnosed in the second grade as having dyslexia. Decades later, as director of *Dislecksia: The Movie*, Hubbell took to the streets of New York City and asked people, "What is dyslexia?" Most didn't know; some believed it was a sleep disorder or sexually transmitted disease (Hubbell, 2009).

Children and adults throughout the world have dyslexia, and about 5 to 17 percent of American schoolchildren are dyslexic (International Dyslexia Association, 2008; Shaywitz et al., 2008). You may know that dyslexia is a specific learning disability that affects people's ability to read, write, and spell. But what do you believe is its core feature? If your answer is along the lines of "reading backwards," or "seeing letters and words in reverse," you're not alone. This is a common belief that periodically gets reinforced in the popular media. Indeed, in 1984 an ABC television special (nominated for an Emmy Award) was titled *Backwards: The Riddle of Dyslexia*. And in a study of 250 faculty members, graduate students, and undergraduates in the education department at a large university, 70 percent believed that "word reversal is the major criterion in the identification of dyslexia" (Wadlington & Wadlington, 2005, p. 27).

It's a myth, however, that dyslexia is a "reading backwards" disorder. Dyslexics don't see or read everything in reverse when looking at a sentence. It's true that dyslexic individuals (children in particular) sometimes reverse letters, such as substituting *d* for *b* or *p* for *q*. They also may reverse individual words (e.g., *pat* for *tap*) or transpose letters within words (e.g., *wrap* for *warp*). But dyslexic children also make other linguistic errors that don't involve letter or word reversals, and importantly, children who are not dyslexic make letter and word reversal errors. Although dyslexic children make linguistic errors more frequently than other children, by late childhood some of these differences may shrink (Wolff & Melngailis, 1996). Older children, adolescents, and adults who have dyslexia may develop strategies that enable them to accurately read and spell individual words but still have trouble reading and writing fluently (Shaywitz et al., 2008). Thus letter and word reversals are not the hallmarks of dyslexia. They are only two among several manifestations of deeper language difficulties.

What are those difficulties? Most experts believe that dyslexia typically results from deficits in *phonological awareness* (Hanly & Vandenberg, 2010; Shaywitz et al., 2008). This may include difficulty in recognizing phonemes and poorer general awareness that words can be broken down into basic phonological elements. Perhaps most centrally, when it comes time to read, write, and spell, children and adults with dyslexia struggle more than their peers in making connections between the "look" and "sound" of letters and letter combinations (Goswami, 2008; Lyon et al., 2003).

Some studies have found that dyslexics are more likely than other people to display atypical eye movements on certain reading tasks, such as fixating longer on words or making more back-and-forth eye movements. However, these eye movement patterns appear to be the result of language processing deficits, not their cause (American Academy of Ophthalmology, 2009). An ongoing area of research—with mixed results thus far—is examining whether impaired coordination of the two eyes on reading tasks might contribute to causing some people's dyslexia (Kapoula et al., 2009; Kirby et al., 2008).

Two Other Myths and One Reality Related to Dyslexia

1. *Vision therapy is an effective treatment for dyslexia.* According to the American Academy of Ophthalmology, "scientific evidence does not support the efficacy of eye exercises, behavioral vision therapy, or special tinted filters or lenses for improving . . . long-term educational performance" (2009, para. 2).
2. *Most children with dyslexia eventually outgrow it.* Not so; dyslexia persists into adolescence and adulthood, and thus early diagnosis and intervention are important (Schatschneider & Torgesen, 2004).
3. *Dyslexia often has other negative psychological effects.* Sadly, this is true. For example, a British study found that overall, compared to other schoolchildren, children with dyslexia had more negative perceptions of how their peers and teachers felt about them, felt more stress about their academic performance, and had a poorer academic self-concept (Alexander-Passe, 2008). Hopefully, intervention programs designed to increase educators' awareness about dyslexia, coupled with greater investment in early diagnosis and treatment, will reduce the struggles and emotional pain felt by many people who have dyslexia (Shaywitz, 2008; Wadlington et al., 2008).

Can Other Animals Acquire Human Language?

Nonhuman species communicate in diverse ways. Chimpanzees grunt, bark, scream, and make gestures to other chimps. Dolphins make clicking sounds and high-pitched vocalizations (Figure 9.11). Many species use special calls to warn of predators and to attract mates (Alcock, 2005).

In some species, communication shows interesting parallels to human language. Just as humans have different languages, each songbird species has its own songs. And just as humans have a sensitive period in childhood for language acquisition, some songbirds will not sing normally in adulthood unless they hear the songs of their species while growing up (Wilbrecht & Nottebohm, 2003).

Although other species communicate, the capacity to use full-fledged language has long been regarded as the sole province of humans. Some scientists have attempted to challenge this assumption by teaching other species, such as apes and gray parrots, to use human language (Pepperberg, 2007). We'll focus here on the ape research, which has a more extensive history.

Washoe: Early Signs of Success

At first, investigators tried to teach chimpanzees to speak verbally, but chimps lack a vocal system that permits humanlike speech. A breakthrough came in 1966 when Allen Gardner and Beatrice Gardner (1969) took advantage of chimps' hand and finger dexterity and began teaching American Sign Language to a 10-month-old chimp named Washoe. They *cross-fostered* Washoe, raising her at home and treating her like a human child. By age 5,

"Although humans make sounds with their mouths and occasionally look at each other, there is no solid evidence that they actually communicate with each other."

Figure 9.11

Human scientists debate whether dolphins and other animals use language. Could the opposite also be occurring? Source: ScienceCartoonsPlus. com. Reprinted with permission.

Washoe had learned 160 signs. More important, at times she combined signs (e.g., "more fruit," "you tickle Washoe") in novel ways. Other researchers also had success. For example, a gorilla named Koko learned more than 600 signs (Bonvillian & Patterson, 1997).

Project Nim: Dissent from Within

At Columbia University, behaviorist Herbert Terrace (1979) taught sign language to a chimp he named Nim Chimpsky—a play on the name of linguist Noam Chomsky. But after years of work and videotape analysis of Nim's "conversations," Terrace concluded that when Nim combined symbols into longer sequences, he was either imitating his trainer's previous signs or "running on" with his hands until he got what he wanted. Moreover, Nim spontaneously signed only when he wanted something, which is not how humans use language. Terrace concluded that Nim had not learned language.

Some ape-language researchers disputed Terrace's conclusions. They agreed that although Washoe and other cross-fostered apes signed mainly to request things, other types of communication also occurred. At Central Washington University, Roger Fouts and Deborah Fouts continued working with Washoe and other cross-fostered chimps. They refrained from signing in front of Loulis, Washoe's adopted son, and found that Loulis acquired over 50 signs by observing other chimps communicate (Fouts et al., 1989). The chimps also signed with each other when humans weren't present, and signing occurred across various contexts, such as when they were playing and fighting (Cianelli & Fouts, 1998).

Kanzi: Chimp versus Child

Sue Savage-Rumbaugh of Georgia State University has worked extensively with a chimpanzee species called the *bonobo* (Figure 9.12). At age $1\frac{1}{2}$, a bonobo named Kanzi spontaneously showed an interest in using plastic geometric symbols that were associated with words. By age 4, with only informal training during social interactions, Kanzi had learned more than 80 symbols and produced a number of two- and three-word communications. Kanzi typically combined gestures and symbols that he pointed to on a laminated board or typed on a specially designed keyboard (see Figure 9.12a). For example, Kanzi created the combinations "Person chase Kanzi," "Kanzi chase person," and "Person chase person" to designate who should chase whom during play. Kanzi also responded to spoken English commands.

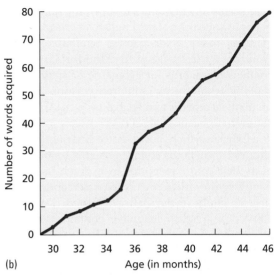

(a)   (b)

Figure 9.12

Can a chimpanzee acquire language?

(a) Using complex symbols, a bonobo communicates with psychologist Sue Savage-Rumbaugh. (b) This graph shows the rate of Kanzi's symbol acquisition over 17 months of informal training. Source: Adapted from Savage-Rumbaugh et al., 1986.

Savage-Rumbaugh and her coworkers (1993; Segerdahl et al., 2006) also tested Kanzi's ability to understand unfamiliar spoken sentences under controlled conditions. For example, when told "Give the doggie a shot," Kanzi picked up a toy dog, grabbed a toy hypodermic needle, and gave the dog a shot. For comparison, one of the researcher's daughters, Alia, was tested under the same conditions between the ages of 2 and $2\frac{1}{2}$. Kanzi correctly responded to 74 percent of the novel requests and Alia to 65 percent. In short, Kanzi was comprehending speech at the level of a human toddler.

Is It Language?

Recall that human language is symbolic and structured, conveys meaning, is generative, and permits displacement. Apes are capable of communicating with a small vocabulary of symbols and hand signs. They can convey meaning by using one- or two-symbol communications (e.g., "banana" or "give banana"), and have also produced some longer symbol strings that convey meaning. As for structure, there are examples of how apes follow—and violate—rules of grammar, but overall the evidence for "ape grammar" has been disappointing (Givón & Savage-Rumbaugh, 2009). Lastly, the evidence for generativity and displacement is limited and controversial.

Critics—even those impressed by Kanzi's feats—are not persuaded that apes are displaying language (Wynne, 2007). Some believe that ambiguous ape communications are interpreted as language because the researchers erroneously assume what must be going on inside the apes' minds. Conversely, proponents believe the data show that apes can acquire rudimentary language skills, a so-called "protolanguage" that lacks major qualities of true human language (Greenfield et al., 2008). If nothing else, this intriguing scientific work should remind us to appreciate something that we often take for granted, namely, the seemingly natural ease with which humans acquire full-blown language.

Language, Culture, and Thinking

Does the language we speak shape how we think? The linguist Benjamin Lee Whorf (1956) took an extreme position on this matter, contending in his **linguistic relativity hypothesis** *that language not only influences but also determines what we are capable of thinking.*

If the linguistic relativity hypothesis is correct, then people whose cultures have only a few words for colors should have greater difficulty in perceiving the spectrum of colors than do people whose languages have many color words. To test this proposition, Eleanor Rosch (1973) studied the Dani of New Guinea, who have only two color words in their language, one for bright warm colors and the other for dark cool ones. She found that contrary to what strict linguistic determinism would suggest, the Dani could discriminate among and remember a wide assortment of hues in much the same manner as can speakers of the English language, which contains many color names. Similarly, in the Amazon, the language of the Mundurukú people contains few words for geometric or spatial concepts, yet Mundurukú children perform as well on many geometric and spatial tasks as American children (Dehaene et al., 2006).

Other research, however, comparing English children and Himba children from Namibia, suggests that color categories in a given language have a greater influence on color perception than Rosch's study of the Dani suggested (Davidoff, 2004). The English language contains 11 basic color terms, whereas the Himba language has only 5. Himba children made fewer distinctions among colored tiles than did English children. For example, Himba children categorized under the color term *zoozu* a variety of dark colors, such as dark shades of blue, green, brown, purple, red, and the color black. English children distinguished among these colors and remembered the different hues better when retested on which ones they had seen earlier.

Still, most psycholinguists do not agree with Whorf's strong assertion that language *determines* how we think. They would say instead that language can *influence* how we think, categorize information, make decisions, and perceive our experiences (Newcombe & Uttal, 2006). Consider, for example, the ability of sexist language to evoke gender stereotypes (Figure 9.13). In one study, college students read one of the following statements:

> The psychologist believes in the dignity and worth of the individual human being. He is committed to increasing man's understanding of himself and others.

Figure 9.13

Sexist language influences our perceptions, our decisions, and the conclusions we draw. Which of these people would you assume is the chairperson of this committee? Might you consider the question differently if we said "Which of these people would you assume is the *chairman* of the committee?"

> Psychologists believe in the dignity and worth of the individual human being. They are committed to increasing people's understanding of themselves and others.

The students then were asked to rate the attractiveness of a career in psychology for men and women. Those who had read the first statement rated psychology as a less attractive profession for women than did the students who read the second statement, written in gender-neutral language (Briere & Lanktree, 1983). Apparently, the first statement implied that psychology is a male profession (when, actually, the majority of psychology doctorates awarded over the past decade went to women). In such ways, language can help create and maintain stereotypes.

test yourself   Bilingualism, Reading, and Language and Thought

True or False?

1. Bilingualism is associated with enhanced performance on some other cognitive tasks.
2. Typically, when people learn two languages proficiently at a young age, those languages share a common neural network.
3. Fluent readers recognize words by their overall shape, not by processing information about individual letters.
4. Seeing letters and words backwards is the primary cause of dyslexia.
5. Language influences how we categorize information and perceive our experiences.

ANSWERS: 1-true, 2-true, 3-false, 4-false, 5-true

Levels of **Analysis** — Language

We've seen that language is a complex cognitive activity jointly shaped by biology and the social environment. Let's consider how some of the factors we have discussed represent the biological, psychological, and environmental levels of analysis.

ENVIRONMENTAL LEVEL
- Social learning experiences guide language acquisition, beginning with early caretaker speech that exposes infants to the phonemes of a particular language.
- Formal educational experiences facilitate language development and are integral to learning to read.
- Extensive exposure to a bilingual environment influences the number of languages that children acquire.
- There are cultural variations in word use, such as in the number of words used to identify colors or the degree of sexist language.

BIOLOGICAL LEVEL
- Acquiring language depends on brain maturation and follows a similar developmental timetable across the globe.
- There appears to be a maturational critical or sensitive period for acquiring normal language capabilities.
- Using language involves a network of brain structures; among bilingual speakers, whether the two languages share the same network depends on age of acquisition and other factors.
- Hemispheric lateralization for language may differ between men and women.

PSYCHOLOGICAL LEVEL
- Cognitive processes (e.g., attention, memory) are involved in learning a language's symbols and grammatical rules.
- Bottom-up and top-down processes influence our ability to recognize speech and to read.
- Bilingualism appears to influence other cognitive abilities.
- Language influences how we think.

Consider this possible interaction among the three levels of analysis. Suppose a highly proficient bilingual speaker, raised from birth in a bilingual home, studies a third language in college and eventually learns it well. Would you expect all three languages to share a common brain network?

THINKING

Can pure thought move mountains? Perhaps not, but it can play a video game. Without speaking a word or lifting a finger, 19-year-old Tristan Lundemo looks at a video screen and makes a red electronic cursor (similar to the paddle in the video game *Pong*) move up, down, to the left, or to the right, merely by thinking it (Paulson, 2004). In this literal mind game, Lundemo tries to move the cursor quickly enough to strike rectangular targets that pop up and then disappear from random locations on the video screen.

Thought, Brain, and Mind

Lundemo is a patient with epilepsy who agreed to participate in a brain-computer interface study while undergoing diagnostic tests at Seattle's Harborview Medical Center (Figure 9.14). During a session, researchers attach 72 electrodes to Lundemo's scalp to record his brain's electrical activity. A computer analyzes the patterns and intensity of these brain signals and uses that information to control the movement of the cursor on the video screen. It's not that simple, however, as computer and human have to adapt to each other and learn the precise thought patterns that will

(a)

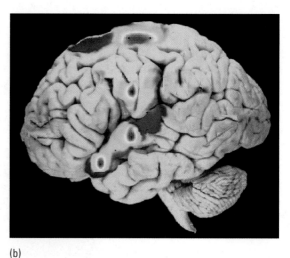

(b)

Figure 9.14

The power of pure thought.

(a) With electrodes attached to his scalp underneath the bandage, Tristan Lundemo uses his thoughts to control the movement of a cursor on a video screen. (b) Various brain regions become active when Lundemo moves the cursor in a particular direction.

make the cursor move. Lundemo is a fast study (as is the computer); he masters the task in two days. Electric mind over electronic matter.

Figure 9.14b shows that several brain regions become most active when Lundemo's thought moves the cursor in a particular direction. The pattern of brain activity changes when he has a thought that moves the cursor in a different direction. Researchers hope that this technology eventually will improve the lives of people who have lost limbs or are paralyzed.

Recall from Chapter 6 that according to some neuroscientists, conscious thought arises from the unified activity of different brain areas. In essence, of the many brain regions and circuits that are active at any instant, a particular subset joins in unified activity that is strong enough to become a conscious thought or perception (Koch, 2004). The specific brain activity pattern that composes this dominant subset varies from moment to moment as we experience different thoughts and respond

to changing stimuli. Even altering one's thought from "move up" to "move down" produces a different pattern of brain activity. Although we're still far from understanding exactly how the brain produces thought, from a biological level of analysis, thought exists as patterns of neural activity.

Subjectively, at the psychological level, thinking may seem to be the internal language of the mind—akin to "inner speech"—but it actually includes several mental activities. One mode of thought indeed takes the form of verbal statements that we "say in our minds." This is called **propositional thought** *because it expresses a proposition, or statement,* such as "I'm hungry" or "It's almost time for dinner." Another thought mode, **imaginal thought,** *consists of images that we can see, hear, or feel in our mind.* A third mode, **motoric thought,** *relates to mental representations of motor movements,* such as throwing an object. In this chapter, we'll focus on propositional and imaginal thought.

Concepts and Propositions

Much of our thinking occurs in the form of **propositions,** *statements that express ideas.* All propositions consist of concepts combined in a particular way. For example, "college students are intelligent people" is a proposition in which the concepts "college students" and "intelligent people" are linked by the verb *are* (Figure 9.15). **Concepts** *are basic units of semantic memory—mental categories into which we place objects, activities, abstractions* (such as "liberal" and "conservative"), *and events that have essential features in common.* Concepts

Concepts: College students   Intelligent people

Proposition: College students   —are—   Intelligent people

Figure 9.15

Concepts are building blocks of thinking and reasoning.

Concepts can be combined into propositions to create simple and complex thoughts, and the propositions can serve as the basis for reasoning and discourse.

can be acquired through explicit instruction or through our own observations of similarities and differences among various objects and events.

Many concepts are difficult to define explicitly. For example, although you might have difficulty defining what a vegetable is, you can quickly think of examples of vegetables, such as broccoli or carrots. According to Eleanor Rosch (1977), many concepts are defined by **prototypes,** *the most typical and familiar members of a category or class.* Rosch suggests that we often decide which category something belongs to by its degree of resemblance to the prototype.

Consider the following questions:

Is an eagle a bird?

Is a penguin a bird?

Is a bat a bird?

According to the prototype view, you should have come to a quicker decision on the first question than on the last two. Why? Because an eagle fits most people's "bird" prototype better than does a penguin (which is a bird, but cannot fly) or a bat (which is not a bird, but can fly). Experiments measuring how quickly participants responded yes or no to the preceding questions have found that it does indeed take most people longer to decide whether penguins or bats are birds (Rips, 1997).

Using prototypes is an elementary method of forming concepts. It requires only that we note similarities among objects. Thus children's early concepts are based on prototypes of the objects and people they encounter personally. They then decide if new objects are similar enough to the prototype to be a "Mommy," a "cookie," a "doggie," and so on (Smith & Zarate, 1992).

Reasoning

Reasoning is one aspect of intelligent thinking. It helps us acquire knowledge, make sound decisions, solve problems, and avoid the hazards and time-consuming efforts of trial and error. For example, people often solve problems by developing solutions in their minds before applying them in the external world.

Deductive Reasoning

Two types of reasoning underlie many of our attempts to make decisions and solve problems (Figure 9.16). In **deductive reasoning,** *we reason from the top down, that is, from general principles to a conclusion about a specific case.* When people reason deductively, they begin with a set of *premises*

(propositions assumed to be true) and determine what the premises imply about a specific situation. Deductive reasoning is the basis of formal mathematics and logic. Logicians regard it as the strongest and most valid form of reasoning because the conclusion *cannot be false* if the premises (factual statements) are true. More formally, the underlying deductive principle may be stated: given the general proposition "if X then Y," if X occurs, then you can infer Y. Thus, to use a classic deductive argument, or *syllogism,*

If all humans are mortal (first premise), and

if Socrates is a human (second premise),

then Socrates must be mortal (conclusion).

Inductive Reasoning

In **inductive reasoning,** *we reason from the bottom up, starting with specific facts and trying to develop a general principle.* Scientists use induction when they observe specific instances of a phenomenon and then form a general principle. After Ivan Pavlov observed repeatedly that the dogs in his laboratory began to salivate when approached by the experimenter who fed them, he began to think in terms of a general principle that eventually became the foundation of classical conditioning (repeated conditioned stimulus–unconditioned stimulus pairings produce a conditioned response).

A key difference between deductive and inductive reasoning lies in the certainty of the results. Deductive conclusions are certain to be true *if* the premises are true, but inductive reasoning leads to likelihood rather than certainty. Even if we reason inductively in a flawless manner, the possibility of error always remains because some

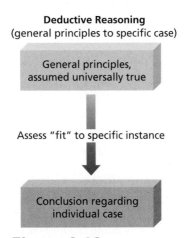
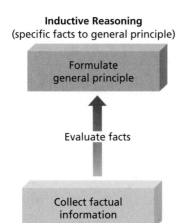

Deductive Reasoning
(general principles to specific case)

General principles, assumed universally true

Assess "fit" to specific instance

Conclusion regarding individual case

Inductive Reasoning
(specific facts to general principle)

Formulate general principle

Evaluate facts

Collect factual information

Figure 9.16

A comparison of deductive and inductive reasoning.

new observation may disprove our conclusion. Thus you may observe that every person named Jordan you have ever met has blue eyes, but it would obviously be inaccurate to reason that, therefore, all people named Jordan have blue eyes.

In daily life and in science, inductive and deductive reasoning may be used at different points in problem solving and decision making. For example, suppose you're ill and describe your symptoms to a physician. Based on specific facts from your description and an initial examination, the doctor uses inductive reasoning to formulate a tentative, general conclusion: "you have disease X." Of course, this inductive conclusion could be wrong. So, using deductive reasoning, the doctor may run further medical tests: "if you have disease X, then medical tests A and B should come back positive." If the test results don't come back positive, then the physician has to reconsider the diagnosis. Likewise, scientists use specific facts and findings to develop general explanations (e.g., theories). This represents inductive reasoning. Then they use those general explanations to derive new, specific predictions (e.g., hypotheses). This is deductive reasoning. If new research fails to support those predictions, then scientists—like the physician—need to reconsider the validity of their general explanations.

Stumbling Blocks in Reasoning

The ability to reason effectively is a key factor in critical thinking, making sound decisions, and solving problems. Unfortunately, several factors may impair effective reasoning.

Distraction by Irrelevant Information   Distinguishing relevant from irrelevant information can be challenging. Consider the following problem. As you solve it, analyze the mental steps you take, and do not read on until you have decided on an answer.

> Your drawer contains 19 black socks and 13 blue socks. Without turning on the light, how many socks do you have to pull out of the drawer to have a matching pair?

As you solved the problem, what information entered into your reasoning? Did you take into account the fact that there were 19 black socks and 13 blue ones? If so, you're like many students who do the same thing, thereby making the problem more difficult than it should be (Sternberg, 1988). All that matters is how many *colors* of socks there are. In this case, with two colors, once you have selected any three socks, you are bound to

have at least two of the same color. People often fail to solve problems because they focus on irrelevant information.

Belief Bias   Belief bias *is the tendency to abandon logical rules in favor of our own personal beliefs.* To illustrate, consider an experiment in which college students judged whether conclusions followed logically from syllogisms like the following:

> All things that are smoked are good for one's health.
>
> Cigarettes are smoked.
>
> Therefore cigarettes are good for one's health.

What do you think? Is the logic correct? Actually, it is. If we accept (for the moment) that the premises are true, then the conclusion *does* follow logically from the premises. Yet students in one study frequently claimed that the conclusion was not logically correct because they disagreed with the first premise that all things smoked are good for one's health. In this case, their beliefs about the harmful effects of smoking got in the way of their logic. When the same syllogism was presented with a nonsense word such as *ramadians* substituted for *cigarettes*, the errors in logic were markedly reduced (Markovits & Nantel, 1989). Incidentally, we agree that the conclusion that cigarettes are good for one's health is factually false. However, it is false because the first premise is false, not because the logic is faulty. Unfortunately, many people confuse factual correctness with logical correctness. The two are not the same.

Emotions and Framing   When evaluating problems or making decisions, we may abandon logical reasoning in favor of relying on our emotions— "trusting our gut"—to guide us (Slovic & Peters, 2006). Reasoning also can be affected by the particular way that information is presented to us, or "framed." **Framing** *refers to the idea that the same information, problem, or options can be structured and presented in different ways.* For example, in one classic study, college students who were told that a cancer treatment had a 50 percent success rate judged the treatment to be significantly more effective and expressed a greater willingness to have it administered to a family member than did participants who were told that the treatment had a 50 percent failure rate (Kahneman & Tversky, 1979).

Representing outcomes in terms of positives or negatives has this effect because people tend to assign greater costs to negative outcomes (such as losing $100) than they assign value to equivalent positive outcomes (finding $100). The proposition that "there is a 50 percent chance of failure" evokes thoughts about the patient's dying and causes the 50-50 treatment to appear riskier. Similarly, graphs or other visual displays can be designed to make identical information "look different" and thus influence people's judgments and decisions (Diacon & Hasseldine, 2007).

Framing can interfere with logical reasoning. This may be especially so when choices are framed to highlight potential positive or negative outcomes, thereby triggering emotions—such as fear, anger, or sadness—that may alter our perceptions of the risks associated with various choice options (Slovic & Peters, 2006). Framing also can enhance reasoning, as we'll now see.

Problem Solving and Decision Making

Humans have an unmatched ability to solve problems. Recalling the "Miracle on the Hudson," the cockpit crew's excellent problem-solving abilities enabled them to rapidly implement and execute a plan for successfully ditching U.S. Airways Flight 1549 and saving the terrified passengers' lives.

Steps in Problem Solving

In accomplishing that astonishing feat, the pilot and copilot had to rapidly gain an understanding of the problems they were facing (e.g., loss of thrust, airspeed, and altitude; too great a distance from the airport), generate solutions (e.g., maintain sufficient airspeed, restart engines, ditch the plane in the river), test those solutions (e.g., force the plane's nose downward to maintain sufficient airspeed; implement engine restart procedures), and then evaluate the results (e.g., engines won't restart; ditching successful). Problem solving typically proceeds through these four stages, and how well we carry out each stage affects our success (Figure 9.17).

Understanding, or Framing, the Problem   Have you ever been totally frustrated in attempting to solve a problem, then someone suggests a new way of looking at it, and the solution suddenly becomes obvious? How we mentally *frame* a problem can make a huge difference. Consider this example (Figure 9.18):

> Train A leaves Baltimore for its 50-mile trip to Washington, D.C., at a constant speed of 25 mph. At the same time, train B leaves Washington, bound for Baltimore at the same speed of 25 mph. The world's fastest crow leaves Baltimore at the same time as train A, flying above the tracks toward Washington at a speed of 60 mph. When

the crow encounters train B, it turns and flies back to train A, then instantly reverses its direction and flies back to train B. The supercharged bird continues this sequence until trains A and B meet midway between Baltimore and Washington. Try to solve this problem before reading on: what is the total distance the bird will have traveled in its excursions between trains A and B?

Many people approach this as a distance problem. That's natural, because the question is stated in terms of distance. They try to compute how far the bird will fly during each flight segment between trains A and B, sometimes filling up pages with frenzied computations. But suppose you approach the problem by asking not how far the bird will fly but *how long* it will take the trains to meet. The crow will have flown the same period of time at 60 mph. Now that you have reframed it as a time problem, the problem becomes easier to solve.

Our initial understanding of a problem is a key step toward solving it successfully. Framing a problem poorly can lead us into blind alleys and ineffective solutions. Framing it optimally gives us a chance to generate an effective solution. A knack for framing problems in effective ways that differ from conventional expectations has been called *outside-the-box thinking*.

Generating Potential Solutions   Once we have interpreted the problem, we can begin to formulate potential solutions. Ideally, we might proceed in the following fashion:

1. Determine the procedures and strategies that will be considered.

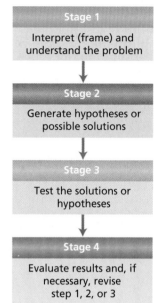

Figure 9.17

The stages of problem solving.

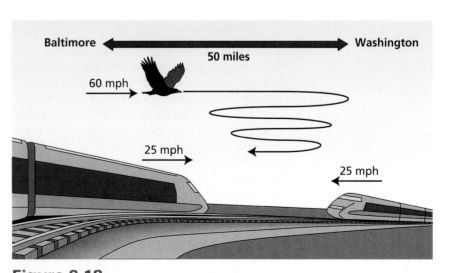

Figure 9.18

The crow-and-trains problem.
(The answer appears on page 331.)

Figure 9.19

Luchins's water jugs problems.
Using containers A, B, and C with the capacities shown in the table, how would you measure out the volumes indicated in the right-hand column? You may discover a general problem-solving schema that fits all seven problems.

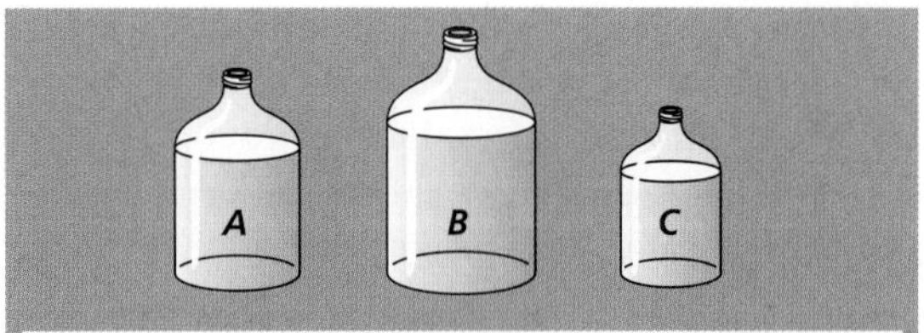

Problem	Given jugs of these sizes			Measure out this much water
	A	B	C	
1	21	127	3	100
2	14	46	5	22
3	18	43	10	5
4	7	42	6	23
5	20	57	4	29
6	23	49	3	20
7	15	39	3	18

2. Determine which solutions are consistent with the evidence that has been observed thus far. Rule out any solutions that do not fit the evidence.

Testing the Solutions   Consider the possible solutions that remain. If a solution requires you to choose between specific options, ask if there is any test that should give one result if one option is correct and another result if a different option is correct. If so, evaluate the options again in light of the new evidence from that test. In essence, this is what scientists do when they gather evidence.

Let's consider a common difficulty in discovering and applying solutions to problems. Consider problem 1 in Figure 9.19:

> You have a 21-cup jug, a 127-cup jug, and a 3-cup jug. Drawing and discarding as much water as you like, how will you measure out exactly 100 cups of water?

Try to solve all seven problems in Figure 9.19 in order, and write down your calculations for each one before reading on. Does a common solution emerge? If so, can you specify what it is?

As you worked the problems, you probably discovered that they are all solvable by the same formula, namely, $B - A - (2 \times C) =$ desired amount. In problem 1, for example, $127 - 21 - (2 \times 3) = 100$. If you discovered this, it gave you a logical formula that you could apply to the rest of the problems. And it worked, didn't it? However, by applying this successful formula to problems 6 and 7, you may have missed even easier solutions for these last two problems, namely, $A - C$ for problem 6 and $A + C$ for problem 7.

Abraham Luchins (1942) developed the water jugs problems to demonstrate how a **mental set**—

the tendency to stick to solutions that have worked in the past—can result in less effective problem solving. Luchins found that most people who worked on problems 6 and 7 were blinded by the mental set they had developed by working the first five problems. In contrast, people who had not worked on problems 1 through 5 almost always applied the simple solutions to problems 6 and 7. Sometimes, reliance on problem-solving concepts or solutions that have worked in the past can prevent us from exploring or recognizing solutions that are even better (Bilalić et al., 2008).

Evaluating Results   The final stage of problem solving is to evaluate the solutions. As we saw in the water jugs problems, even solutions that prove successful may not be the easiest or the best. Thus, after solving a problem, we should ask ourselves, "Would there have been an easier or more effective way to accomplish the same objective?" This can lead to the development of additional problem-solving principles that may be applicable to future problems.

Algorithms and Heuristics

Algorithms and *heuristics* are two broad approaches to solving problems. **Algorithms** *are formulas or precise sequences of procedures that automatically generate solutions* (Beilock & DeCaro, 2007). Mathematical formulas are algorithms, and if you use them properly, you will always get the correct answer. Consider another example, which illustrates a "brute force" algorithm. If the letters of a word are randomly scrambled to produce an anagram like *kabr*, we can always identify the word by rearranging the four letters in all 24 possible orders. Likewise, this algorithm will guarantee success with an eight-letter scrambled word, such as *rtyleibr*, but because there are 40,320 possible orders, using the "all possible orders" algorithm in this situation would be inefficient. Instead, you might use some rule-of-thumb strategy, such as trying out only consonants in the first and last positions, because you know that more words begin and end in consonants than in vowels. When we adopt rule-of-thumb approaches like this, we are using heuristics.

Heuristics *are general problem-solving strategies, similar to mental rules-of-thumb, that we apply to certain classes of situations.* One common heuristic, **means-ends analysis,** *involves identifying differences between the present situation and a desired goal, and then making changes that reduce these differences* (MacGregor & Omerand, 2001; Newell & Simon, 1972). Suppose that you have a 30-page paper due at the end of the term and have not begun working on it yet. The present situation is no pages written; the desired end goal is a 30-page paper. What, specifically, needs to be done to reduce that discrepancy, and how are you going to do it?

To answer these questions, you could use another heuristic called **subgoal analysis**: *formulating subgoals, or intermediate steps, toward a solution* (Houser-Marko & Sheldon, 2008). You would break down the task of writing a paper into subgoals, such as (1) choosing a topic, (2) doing library and Internet research to get the facts you need, (3) organizing the facts within a general outline of the paper, (4) writing a first draft of specific sections, (5) reorganizing and refining the first draft, and so on. In so doing, a huge task becomes a series of smaller and more manageable tasks, each with a subgoal that leads you toward the ultimate goal of a quality 30-page paper.

The Tower-of-Hanoi problem, explained in Figure 9.20, illustrates the value of setting subgoals. The first subgoal is to get ring C to the bottom of peg 3. The second subgoal is to get ring B over to peg 3. With these subgoals accomplished, the final subgoal of getting ring A to peg 3 is easy.

Uncertainty, Heuristics, and Decision Making

We use heuristics not only to solve problems but also to make a wide range of judgments and decisions, from judgments about our own health to decisions about purchases (Katapodi et al., 2005). In everyday life, our judgments and decisions typically involve outcome uncertainty. Often, the best we can hope for is that they will yield a high probability of a positive outcome. But because we seldom know what the exact probabilities are (for example, that a college course will be interesting or that a new dating relationship will become permanent), we often apply heuristics to form judgments about the likelihood of particular events or outcomes. Such heuristics often serve us very well, but they can also contribute to errors in judgment (Kahneman & Klein, 2009).

Many of our judgments and decisions focus on what other people are like. Suppose you receive the following description of a young woman:

> Linda is 31 years old, single, outspoken, and very bright. She majored in philosophy. As a student, she was deeply concerned with issues of discrimination and social justice, and she also participated in antinuclear demonstrations.

Now rate the likelihood that each of the following hypotheses is true. Use 1 to indicate the most likely statement, 8 to indicate the least likely statement,

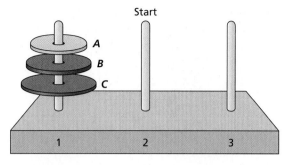

Start

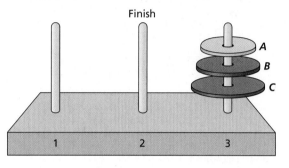

Finish

Figure 9.20

The Tower-of-Hanoi problem. The object is to move the rings one at a time from peg 1 to peg 3 in no more than seven moves. Only the top ring on a peg can be moved, and a larger ring can never be placed on top of a smaller one. (The answer appears on page 331.)

and any number between 2 and 7 to rate the likelihood of the second most likely statement.

__ Hypothesis A: Linda is active in the feminist movement.

__ Hypothesis B: Linda is a bank teller.

__ Hypothesis C: Linda is active in the feminist movement and is a bank teller.

Cognitive psychologists Amos Tversky and Daniel Kahneman (1982) used this problem in a series of classic experiments that studied the role of heuristics in judgment and decision making. They showed that certain heuristics underlie much of our inductive decision making (drawing conclusions from facts) and that misusing these heuristics results in many of our thinking errors. Let us examine how that occurs.

The Representativeness Heuristic "Will this be a good or bad course?" "Is this person nice or strange, geeky or cool?" Tversky, Kahneman, and their colleagues proposed that one way we judge the likelihood of something is by using the **representativeness heuristic**: *we think about how closely something fits our prototype for that particular concept, or class, and therefore how likely it is to be a member of that class* (Kahneman & Frederick, 2005; Tversky & Kahneman, 1982). In Linda's case, we ask "How closely does her description fit the prototype of a 'feminist' and of a 'bank teller'?" This is a reasonable question to ask, but sometimes our use of representativeness can cause us to make decisions that fly in the face of logic.

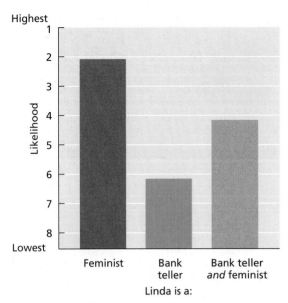

Figure 9.21

Illogical judgments.
This graph shows the mean likelihood judgments made by participants on the basis of the description of Linda (top left column). Overall, people judge it to be more likely that Linda is a bank teller and a feminist rather than just a bank teller. Logically, this is impossible.
SOURCE: Based on Tversky & Kahneman, 1982.

How did you order the three likelihood hypotheses? Figure 9.21 shows the mean likelihood estimates that college students attached to each statement. First, hypothesis A (Linda is a feminist) is rated as most likely. This is not surprising; the description does make her sound like a feminist. Second, the significant finding is that hypothesis C (Linda is a feminist bank teller) was favored over hypothesis B (Linda is a bank teller). But this cannot possibly be correct. Why not? Because (1) everyone who is both a feminist and a bank teller is also *simply* a bank teller, and (2) there are many bank tellers who are not feminists, and Linda could be one of them. Stated differently, any individual person is more likely to be simply a bank teller than to be a bank teller *and* a feminist— or, for that matter, a bank teller and anything else. People who say that hypothesis C is more likely than hypothesis B (and about 85 percent of people given this problem do so) violate the logical principle that the intersection of two events (e.g., at an ice cream parlor, the ice cream a customer orders is vanilla and is served on a cone) cannot be more likely than either event alone (the ice cream is vanilla; the ice cream is served on a cone). We equate the likelihood of something with how well it fits our prototype for that particular concept.

Tversky and Kahneman (1982) proposed that the reason people make this sort of error is that they confuse representativeness with probability.

Linda represents our prototype for a feminist bank teller better than she fits our prototype for a bank teller. Therefore, we erroneously think the former is more likely than the latter. In other words, if Linda is to be a bank teller at all, we think she must be a feminist bank teller.

The Availability Heuristic   Another heuristic that sometimes leads us astray is the **availability heuristic,** *in which people base judgments and decisions on how easily information is available in memory.* We tend to remember events that are most important and significant to us. Usually that principle serves us well, keeping important information at the forefront in our memories, ready to be applied. But if something easily comes to mind, we may exaggerate the likelihood that it could occur. For example, consider each of the following pairs and choose the more likely cause of death:

- murder or suicide?
- botulism or lightning?
- asthma or tornadoes?

When Paul Slovic and coworkers (1988) asked people to make these judgments, 80 percent chose murder over suicide as the more likely cause of death, 63 percent chose botulism over lightning, and 43 percent chose tornadoes over asthma. In actuality, public health statistics showed that people were 25 percent less likely to be murdered than to kill themselves, that lightning killed 53 times more people than botulism did, and that death by asthma was 21 times more likely than death as a result of a tornado. Yet murder, botulism, and tornadoes are more highly and dramatically publicized when they do occur and thus are more likely to come to mind.

Recent memorable events can increase people's belief that they may suffer a similar fate. After the terrorist hijackings of September 11, 2001, airline bookings and tourism declined dramatically within the United States for a significant period. Similarly, in the summer of 1975, when Steven Spielberg's movie *Jaws* burned into people's memories graphic images of a great white shark devouring swimmers at a New England seaside town, beach attendance all over the country decreased. The images available in memory—even though the movie was clearly fiction—increased people's perceived likelihood that they, too, could become shark bait.

Thus at times the representativeness and availability heuristics can lead us astray by distorting our estimates of how likely an event really is. In other words, they can blind us to the *base rates*, or actual frequencies, at which things occur.

In general, it's always best to find out what the actual probabilities are and make judgments on that basis; that's the strategy that allows insurance companies to flourish.

The availability heuristic also can influence the judgments we make about our own qualities. Suppose we ask you to recall two instances in which you behaved assertively; then we ask you to rate how assertive a person you are. Now imagine that we had asked you instead to recall eight such instances, rather than only two, and then rate your assertiveness. You might expect that thinking of eight instances when you behaved assertively would lead you to rate yourself as more assertive. After all, it's a larger amount of evidence. But when psychologist Eugene Caruso (2008) conducted such an experiment, the randomly assigned students who were asked to recall only two assertive instances rated themselves as significantly more assertive than students who were asked to recall eight instances. Why? Coming up with two assertive instances is an easier task (and was rated as easier by the students) than having to recall eight instances, and "Hey, if it was easy for me to think of examples when I was assertive, then it must be because I'm a relatively assertive person."

Confirmation Bias and Overconfidence

When we test a solution, idea, or hypothesis, what's the best type of evidence to gather? Here is a principle that may seem puzzling to you (it harkens back to the concept of *falsifiability* that we discussed in Chapter 2): the best thing we can do to test our ideas is to seek evidence that will *disconfirm* them, rather than only look for evidence that confirms them. Why? Disconfirming evidence has the potential to conclusively prove that our idea *cannot* be true in its current form. For example, consider the hypothesis "If a person waits until adulthood to start learning a second language, it will be impossible to achieve full native fluency." Because this statement is expressed in absolute terms, it could be proven untrue by finding people who became bilingual in adulthood and speak both languages with native fluency.

In contrast, confirming evidence doesn't establish absolute certainty. Even if we study 1 million adult bilingual learners and find that none speaks a second language with native fluency, we have obtained evidence that *supports* our hypothesis but doesn't *prove* it. Why doesn't this provide absolute proof? Because it is always possible that future studies may find adult bilingual learners who speak both languages with native fluency.

Following this disconfirmation principle is easier said than done, because people are often unwilling to challenge their cherished beliefs. Instead, they are prone to fall into a trap called **confirmation bias,** *tending to look for evidence that will confirm what they currently believe rather than looking for evidence that could disconfirm their beliefs* (Hart et al., 2009). Often, when people have strong beliefs about something, they are very selective in the kinds of information they expose themselves to. They seek out like-minded people, compatible mass media sources and Internet sites, and recall information that confirms their beliefs. Because they find it difficult to test and challenge their ideas, particularly those to which they are strongly committed, they often fail to get the evidence needed to make a correct decision.

Confirmation bias can contribute to **overconfidence,** *the tendency to overestimate one's correctness in factual knowledge, beliefs, and decisions.* Overconfidence, like confirmation bias, is widespread. In one study, college students were asked at the beginning of the academic year to make predictions about how likely it was (from 0 percent to 100 percent) that they would experience various personal events, such as dropping a course, breaking up with a romantic partner, or joining a fraternity or sorority. They also indicated how confident they were—how likely it was that they would be correct. Then, at the end of the academic year, they indicated which events had in fact occurred. Figure 9.22, shows that, overall, students' confidence exceeded their accuracy, and this overconfidence was equally great when the students were 100 percent sure of their predictions (Vallone et al., 1990). Studies of investment and business professionals, military strategists, weather forecasters, novice drivers, and other populations have found overconfidence effects (McKenzie et al., 2008; Mynttinen et al., 2009).

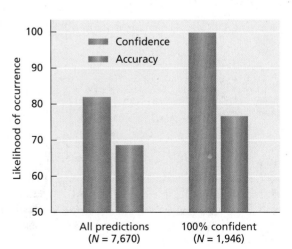

Figure 9.22

Displaying overconfidence. Overconfidence is illustrated in the discrepancy between the accuracy with which students predicted that specific events would occur to them during the coming academic year and the degree of confidence that they had in their predictions. Overall, accuracy was considerably lower than confidence level, even for those events for which the students expressed complete certainty. Source: Based on Vallone et al., 1990.

Overconfidence and confirmation bias can be potent adversaries in our search for correct predictions and decisions. When we're confident in the correctness of our views and reluctant to seek evidence that could prove them wrong, we can easily be blinded to the truth or to better and sometimes more creative ways of solving problems. Our "Applying Psychological Science" feature discusses some aspects of creative problem solving.

Applying Psychological Science

Guidelines for Creative Problem Solving

Creativity *is the ability to produce something that is both new and valuable* (Sternberg, 2006b). The product may be virtually anything, from a creative painting to a novel approach to solving a problem. Here, we'll be concerned with creative problem solving.

Research on reasoning offers insights into how effective and creative problem solvers think and how they approach problems. One component of creativity is the ability to break away from conventional approaches when the occasion demands it and to engage in **divergent thinking,** *the generation of novel ideas that depart from the norm* (Guilford, 1959; Silvia et al., 2009). In part, this means being able to apply concepts or propositions from one domain to another unrelated domain in a manner that produces a new insight. It also means refusing to be constrained by traditional approaches to a problem (Sternberg, 2006b). Creative people are, in this respect, intellectual rebels. The constraints created by the tried-and-true can be difficult to overcome.

Consider, for example, the nine-dot problem in Figure 9.23. Many people have difficulty solving this problem. Did you? If so, it may be because you imposed a traditional but unnecessary constraint on yourself and tried to stay within the boundary formed by the dots. But nothing in the statement of the problem forced you to do so. To solve the problem, try thinking outside the box.

Creative problem solvers are often able to ask themselves questions like the following to stimulate divergent thinking (Simonton, 1999):

- What would work instead?
- Are there new ways to use this? How else could it be used if I modified it in some way? By adding, subtracting, or rearranging parts, or by modifying the sequence in which things are done, could I make it more useful?

Figure 9.23

The nine-dot problem.
Without lifting your pencil from the paper, draw no more than four straight lines that will pass through all nine dots. (The answer appears on page 331.)

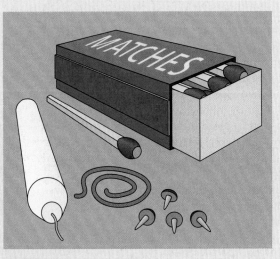

Figure 9.24

The candlestick problem.
Using these objects, find a way to mount the candle on a wall so it functions like a lamp. (The answer appears on page 331.)

- Do the elements remind me of anything else? What else is like this?

Use some of these questions when trying to solve the candlestick problem illustrated in Figure 9.24.

Solving the problem requires using some of the objects in unconventional ways. Many people, however, are prevented from doing so because of **functional fixedness,** *the tendency to be so fixed in their perception of the proper function of an object or procedure that they are blinded to new ways of using it.*

Sometimes creative solutions to problems seemingly appear out of the blue, suddenly popping into our mind in a flash of insight after we have temporarily given up and put the problem aside. This phenomenon is called **incubation:** *processing a problem, presumably at a subconscious level, while doing some other activity.* Experiments on incubation suggest that sometimes the best approach when we are stymied by a problem is indeed to put it aside for a while, focus on something else, and gain some psychological distance from it (Beeftink et al., 2008; Ellwood et al., 2009).

As you can see, creative problem solving involves many of the principles discussed earlier in the chapter. We see the operation of means-ends reasoning, the testing of hypotheses, and the need to overcome biases that may cause us to overestimate or underestimate the likelihood of certain outcomes. Here are some other general problem-solving guidelines:

1. When you encounter a new problem, ask yourself if it's similar to problems you've previously solved. Maybe the solution for solving a problem with similar features can be modified to solve this one. Take advantage of the storehouse of knowledge in long-term memory.

2. Make a true effort to test your ideas. Try to find evidence that would disconfirm your ideas, not only evidence that would confirm what you already believe. For example, if you are asked to accept statement X as true, see if you can imagine situations in which X would be false. Beware of the human tendency toward confirmation bias.

3. Make use of the means-ends problem-solving heuristic. Ask yourself what you are trying to accomplish, what the present state of affairs is, and what means you have for reducing the discrepancy.

4. Don't be afraid to use pencil and paper. Orderly notes and schematics can substitute for our rather limited working memory and allow us to have more information at hand to work with.

---

test yourself   Reasoning, Problem Solving, and Decision Making

Match each numbered concept to the correct definition on the right.

1. inductive reasoning

2. deductive reasoning

3. confirmation bias

4. availability heuristic

5. framing

6. belief bias

a. looking for evidence that supports rather than contradicts one's views

b. structuring or presenting the same information in different ways

c. using specific facts to come up with a general principle

d. information that's easily recalled disproportionately affects our judgments

e. using a general principle to draw conclusions about a specific case

f. relying on personal opinions rather than logical reasoning

ANSWERS: 1-c, 2-e, 3-a, 4-d, 5-b, 6-f

Knowledge, Expertise, and Wisdom

Each culture passes down knowledge from one generation to the next. This vast library of knowledge, combined with other learning experiences, forms the foundation for expertise and wisdom and supports the reasoning, decision-making, and problem-solving skills that we have been discussing in this chapter.

Acquiring Knowledge: Schemas and Scripts

One way to think about knowledge acquisition is as a process of building schemas. Most broadly, a **schema** is a *mental framework, an organized pattern of thought about some aspect of the world.* Concepts and categories represent types of schemas, and together they help you build a mental framework of your world, such as "interesting versus dull people" or "easy versus hard exams." Algorithms and heuristics also are types of schemas that provide you with mental frameworks for solving certain types of problems.

Another type of schema, called a **script,** *is a mental framework concerning a sequence of events that usually unfolds in a regular, almost standardized order.* For example, if we tell you that "John and Linda went to the movies," these mere seven words convey a lot of information because "going to the movies" is a fairly standardized (i.e., scripted) activity. You can reasonably assume that John and Linda got to the theater, waited in the ticket line and bought tickets (or bought them online), entered the theater where someone checked their tickets, bought a snack, found seats, and so on. The scripts that you learn—"attending class," "shopping," "driving," and so on—provide knowledge

Figure 9.25

(a) Chess master Gary Kasparov developed chess schemas that made him a worthy opponent for even the most sophisticated computers, including IBM's Deep Blue.
(b) Experienced snowboarders and skiers learn schemas for various types of snow, and the discriminations made possible by these schemas can affect planning and decision making. This boarder might approach a slope covered with "powder" differently than one covered with "corn" or "hardpack" because of their different effects on the board and potentially on the boarder's safety.

(a)

(b)

to guide and interpret actions. In sum, your knowledge grows as you acquire new scripts, concepts, and other types of schemas; as your existing schemas become more complex; and as you form connections between schemas.

The Nature of Expertise

Schemas help explain what it means to be an expert (Bilalić et al., 2008). Masters and grand masters in chess can glance at a chessboard and quickly plan strategies in the heat of competition. The world's best players can remember as many as 50,000 board configurations, including the locations of individual pieces (Chase & Simon, 1973). For years, world chess champion Gary Kasparov's sophisticated schemas enabled him to regularly defeat chess-playing computers that used logical rules, even those capable of logically analyzing up to 100,000 moves per second. It took Deep Blue, a 1.4-ton behemoth capable of calculating at a rate of 200 million positions and 200,000 moves per second, to finally defeat the schemas within Kasparov's 3-pound brain (Figure 9.25a).

Recall that when U.S. Airways Flight 1549 hit a flock of Canada geese shortly after takeoff and lost thrust in both engines, Captain Sullenberger rapidly had to make several critical decisions. This included the decision not to follow the procedure of letting the first officer pilot the plane while the captain monitors the situation. He also decided within 35 seconds of the collision to ditch the plane in the Hudson River rather than attempt an airport landing. Asked by an aviation magazine editor whether he was "calculating the distance" the plane could glide, Sullenberger replied, "It wasn't so much calculating as it was being acutely aware, based upon our energy state and by visually assessing the situation, of what was and what was not possible. There are several ways I used

my experience to do that" (Shiner, 2009, para. 15). Sullenberger also was able to instantly draw upon procedural schemas—scripts—to peform the difficult task of pushing the crippled jetliner's nose downward just enough to maintain optimal airspeed and control of plane.

Whether in aviation, chess, sports, medicine, science, or other fields, experts have developed many schemas to guide problem solving in their fields, and they are better than novices at recognizing when a schema should or should not be applied (Figure 9.25b; Montgomery et al., 2005). Further, as you learned in Chapter 8, schemas reside in long-term memory. Because experts rely on learned schemas, they take advantage of their spacious long-term memory. They can quickly analyze a problem deductively, pull the appropriate schema from memory, and apply the schema to solve the problem at hand (Horn & Masunaga, 2000). In contrast, novices who haven't yet learned specialized schemas must use general problem-solving methods that often tax working memory, the space-limited blackboard of the mind.

When people develop expertise, their brain functioning changes in ways that increase processing efficiency. This occurs even in animals. Thus, as macaque monkeys in one study became experts in categorizing objects, brain recordings revealed quicker and stronger activity in the specific neurons that responded to the important features used to categorize the stimuli (Sigala & Logothetis, 2002). Of course, efficient processing and expertise don't always guarantee an optimal decision or solution to a problem. Sometimes the schemas experts use may generate a good solution but inhibit further exploration of potentially better solutions (Bilalić et al., 2008). At other times, experts' reliance on familiar schemas to simplify a situation may lead to a poor or outright "wrong" decision (Kahneman & Klein, 2009).

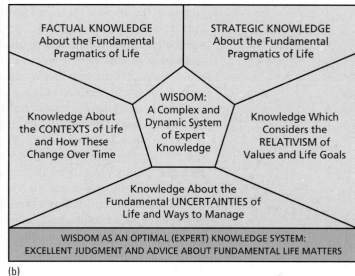

(a)   (b)

Figure 9.26

Wisdom.

(a) Among the Inuit of the Canadian Arctic, wisdom involves extensive cultural knowledge, involvement in community life, and teaching young people about cultural values. (b) Components of wisdom. Source: Baltes & Smith, 2008.

What Is Wisdom?

Anthropologist Peter Collings (2001) notes that, as in many cultures, the Inuit living in the Arctic of western Canada accord their elders special status and great respect (Figure 9.26). Young and old Inuit alike regard wisdom as a key component of aging successfully. To them, wisdom reflects "the individual's function as a repository of cultural knowledge and his or her involvement in community life by interacting with younger people and talking to them, teaching them about 'traditional' cultural values" (p. 146).

Does the Inuit conception of wisdom coincide with yours? If not, how would you define wisdom? To German psychologist Paul Baltes and his colleagues, **wisdom** *is a system of rich, expert knowledge about fundamental matters of life* (Baltes & Smith, 2008). After examining many cultural, historical, philosophical, religious, and psychological views of wisdom, they concluded that wisdom has five major components:

1. *Factual knowledge about life*, including knowledge about human nature, social relationships, and major life events

2. *Strategic knowledge about life*, including strategies for making decisions, handling conflict, and giving advice

3. *Knowledge about life-span contexts*, including awareness that life involves many contexts, such as family, friends, work, and leisure

4. *Knowledge of the relativism of values and goals*, including awareness that values and goals differ across people and societies

5. *Knowledge about life's uncertainties and how to manage them*, including awareness that the future cannot be fully known (see Figure 9.26)

Although this model links wisdom to expertise, realize that wisdom encompasses a breadth of expertise about life that goes well beyond being an expert in just one or a few areas. These combined qualities of extraordinary scope and truly superior knowledge and judgment make true wisdom hard to achieve (Baltes & Smith, 2008).

Metacognition: Knowing Your Own Cognitive Abilities

Have you ever had a friend or classmate say to you after an exam, "I don't understand why I got this question wrong" or "I don't understand how I got such a low grade—I thought I really knew this stuff"? Have you ever felt that way?

Recognizing What You Do and Don't Know

To cognitive psychologists, the term **metacognition** *refers to your awareness and understanding of your own cognitive abilities*. For example, *comprehension* has to do with understanding something, such as a concept that you just read about. You may *think* you understand the concept, but in actuality you may or may not understand it. Metacognition has to do with truly knowing whether you do or do not understand the concept. The particular component of metacognition that we're discussing in this case is *metacomprehension*. In other words, people who display good metacomprehension are accurate in judging what they do or don't know, whereas people with poor metacomprehension have difficulty judging what they actually do and don't understand. They may typically think they understand things that, in fact, they don't, or they may often think they don't understand things that they actually do.

Metacomprehension is only one aspect of metacognition. Another component, called *metamemory*, represents your awareness and knowledge of your memory capabilities. For example, suppose that you try to memorize a list of definitions or facts. Your ability to accurately judge how well you will be able to remember those items for an upcoming test reflects one aspect of metamemory. Unfortunately, some students may overestimate their ability to recall material in the future due to a belief that "if I can recall an item now, then I've learned it and don't need additional practice" (Karpicke, 2009).

As a student, your ability to effectively monitor what you do and don't know is an important ingredient in studying efficiently (Koriat & Bjork, 2005). Some students excel at this. Unfortunately, many studies have found that when it comes to reading text material, students overall are only mildly to moderately accurate in judging how well they understand what they are reading. Our "Research Close-up" examines one technique for improving students' metacomprehension.

Research Close-up

"Why Did I Get That Wrong?" Improving College Students' Awareness of Whether They Understand Text Material

SOURCE: KEITH W. THEIDE and MARY C. M. ANDERSON (2003). Summarizing can improve metacomprehension accuracy. *Contemporary Educational Psychology, 28*, 129–160.

INTRODUCTION

According to psychologists Keith Theide and Mary Anderson, this study is the first to examine whether students' metacomprehension for text material can be enhanced by requiring them to write summaries of that material. Theide and Anderson hypothesized that students who write delayed summaries of passages of text material will show better metacomprehension than students who write immediate summaries or no summaries. Presumably, the task of writing delayed rather than immediate summaries taps more powerfully into students' long-term memory and provides them with a better opportunity to assess whether they truly understand what they have read.

METHOD

Ethnically diverse samples of 75 and 90 college students taking introductory psychology participated, respectively, in Experiment 1 and Experiment 2. The students in each experiment read six passages of text material, with each passage focusing on a different topic (e.g., black holes, global warming, genetics, intelligence, Norse settlements). In Experiment 1, the passages were each about 220 words long, whereas in Experiment 2 they were much longer (1,100 to 1,600 words) and more similar in style to material presented in textbooks.

Students in each experiment were randomly assigned to one of three groups. In the no-summary group (control group), they read all six passages and then rated their comprehension of each passage ("How well do you think you understood the passage?") on a scale ranging from 1 ("very poorly") to 7 ("very well"). In the immediate-summary group, students summarized each passage immediately after they read it and then, after finishing all six summaries, rated

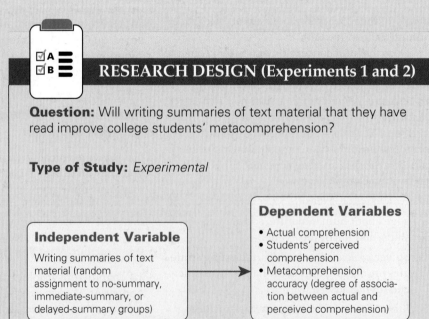

RESEARCH DESIGN (Experiments 1 and 2)

Question: Will writing summaries of text material that they have read improve college students' metacomprehension?

Type of Study: *Experimental*

Independent Variable

Writing summaries of text material (random assignment to no-summary, immediate-summary, or delayed-summary groups)

Dependent Variables

- Actual comprehension
- Students' perceived comprehension
- Metacomprehension accuracy (degree of association between actual and perceived comprehension)

their comprehension of each one. In the delayed-summary group, students read all six passages before summarizing each one and then rating their comprehension of each passage.

All students, after rating their comprehension, took a multiple-choice comprehension test for each passage that included both factual and conceptual questions. These tests enabled Theide and Anderson to measure how well students' *beliefs* about their comprehension (measured by the rating scales) correlated with their actual comprehension (measured by their test scores). The research design is summarized in the graphic on the preceding page.

RESULTS

The critical finding in both experiments was that students in the delayed-summary group were much more accurate than the other students in judging whether they knew or didn't know the material (Figure 9.27). In contrast, the three groups did not differ overall in their comprehension ratings or in their test performance. In other words, students in the delayed-summary group did not feel that they knew the material better, and in fact they didn't. Rather, summarizing the passages after a time delay helped them become more accurate in distinguishing the material they did know from the material they didn't.

DISCUSSION

As the researchers predicted, students' ability to accurately determine how well they understood text material improved greatly when they wrote delayed summaries. Because the delayed-summary group did not rate their comprehension higher or perform better on the comprehension tests than the other groups, we want to ensure that you do *not* reach the wrong conclusion of "So what if metacomprehension improved; the students didn't do better on the test."

Realize that the students in this experiment were not allowed to go back and study the text passages again before taking the

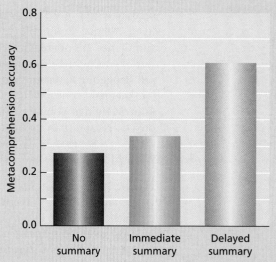

Figure 9.27

Writing summaries helps us recognize what we do and don't know.
Students who wrote delayed summaries of text material showed far better metacomprehension than did students who wrote immediate summaries or no summaries.

comprehension tests. Therefore, students in the delayed-summary group did not have the opportunity to act upon their superior metacognitive knowledge (i.e., to bone up on the material that they accurately felt they didn't know). But in real-world test situations, students who better recognize what they know and don't know can indeed put that information to use in preparing for a test. They can allocate more time to studying the material they have found difficult and less time to the material that they already understand. Students with poor metacomprehension may end up allocating their study time less efficiently, ignoring material that they think they know but truly don't.

Further Advice on Improving Metacognition

As a student, you want to be able to accurately assess how well you remember and understand course material *before* it's time to take a test. First, if you buy used textbooks to save money, try to buy copies that don't already contain highlighting or underlining. If that's not possible, ignore what the previous student has done and do your own highlighting or underlining. You don't know whether the prior book owner got an A, C, or F in the course. Some or much of that highlighting may be inappropriate, and research indicates that when students read text passages that are already inappropriately highlighted, this impairs accurate comprehension and leads students to overestimate how well they know the material (Gier et al., 2009).

Second, don't equate "I can recall material now" with "I've learned it and don't need to practice it more," which can impair metamemory (Karpicke, 2009). Keep practicing the material and

testing your ability to retrieve it. One way to do this is to take advantage of practice tests, such as those found in study guides. But don't try to memorize specific questions and answers from practice tests, as some students do. This does little to help you assess your broader understanding of the material. Instead, seriously study the material first, and then try to answer the practice questions. For each question, rate how confident you are that your answer is right; this may help you develop a better sense of whether your metacomprehension is good.

Finally, merely being able to recall definitions and facts won't necessarily let you know whether you understand the material on a deeper level. The "Research Close-up" study found that writing delayed summaries improved students' metacomprehension, and other research finds that writing summaries boosts actual comprehension of text material (Winne & Hadwin, 1998). Thus, try to write a brief delayed summary of each section within a chapter. Use the section titles (e.g., "Mental Rotation") to help structure your summaries. It's not magic. It takes time and effort. But in writing these summaries, if you find yourself struggling to remember the material or articulate the main concepts, then you have gained the knowledge that you need to restudy the material or seek assistance in trying to understand it.

Mental Imagery

Having spent most of this chapter discussing language and types of thought that we subjectively experience as inner speech, let's turn to another mode of thought: *mental imagery*. A **mental image** *is a representation of a stimulus that originates inside your brain, rather than from external sensory input.* Nighttime dreams are a common form of mental imagery. While awake, we may intentionally create and manipulate mental images to get a break from reality, relieve boredom, or help solve problems. Sir Isaac Newton and Albert Einstein used mental imagery to gain insights that led to the discovery of several laws of physics. In a daydream at age 16:

> Einstein imagined himself running alongside a light beam and asked himself the fateful question: what would the light beam look like? Like Newton visualizing throwing a rock until it orbited the earth like the moon, Einstein's attempt to imagine such a light beam would yield deep and surprising results. (Kaku, 2004, p. 43)

Mental images can represent different sensory modalities, as when we imagine the savory taste or enticing aroma of a favorite food. They can also represent motor movements, as when athletes or dancers use mental imagery to rehearse skills. Such mental images not only subjectively involve tastes, smells, sounds, and so on, but also activate sensorimotor circuits in the brain (Palmiero et al., 2009; Szameitat et al., 2007). Visual mental images are the most common and most thoroughly researched, and we'll focus on them here.

Mental Rotation

Look at the objects in Figure 9.28. In each pair, are the two objects different, or are they the same object that has been rotated to a different orientation? Typically, in this *mental-rotation task*, people rotate one object in their mind's eye until it lines up sufficiently with the other object to permit a same-different judgment.

In 1971, psychologists Roger Shepard and Jacqueline Metzler reported a landmark experiment that helped place the study of mental imagery on the scientific map. Their elegant experiment demonstrated that mental images could be studied by gathering objective data, rather than by relying exclusively on people's subjective self-reports. They presented each research participant with 1,600 pairs of rotated objects, including the objects shown in Figure 9.28. Upon seeing each pair, participants pulled one of two levers to signal whether the two objects were the same or different, and their speed of response was measured. For 800 pairs, the objects within the pair were identical and were rotated from each other

Figure 9.28

Mental rotation.

(a, b, c) These are three of the many pairs of objects used in Shepard and Metzler's (1971) mental-rotation study. (d) This graph shows the average number of seconds it took participants to decide that the two objects in each pair were similar, as a function of the initial angle of rotation. Factoring in the time that it took to make a physical response, participants' speed of mental rotation was approximately 60 degrees per second. In pairs (a) and (b) the objects are the same. In pair (c) they are different.

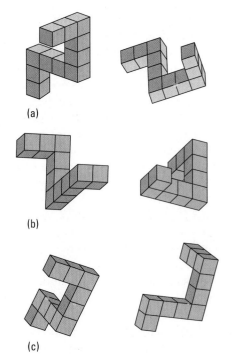

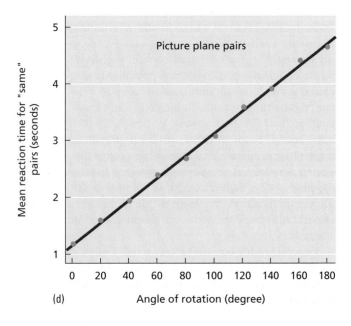

at an angle of either 0, 20, 40, 60, 80, 100, 120, 140, 160, or 180 degrees. The two objects within pair (a) and within pair (b) in Figure 9.28, for example, are the same and rotated 80 degrees from one another; those in pair (c) are different.

Subjectively, participants reported that they were able to mentally rotate the objects as if the objects existed in three-dimensional space but that the speed of this mental rotation process was limited. Shepard and Metzler's key finding concerned the pairs in which the two objects were the same. On these trials, the greater the difference in rotation between the two pictured objects, the longer it took participants to reach their decision (Figure 9.28d). Shepard and Metzler (1971) concluded that "if we can describe this process as some sort of 'mental rotation in three-dimensional space,' then . . . the average rate at which these particular objects can be thus 'rotated' is roughly 60° per second" (p. 703). Subsequent experiments, though not necessarily replicating the near-perfect linear relation found in Figure 9.28d, support the view that objects can be mentally rotated (Schendan & Lucia, 2009).

Are Mental Images Pictures in the Mind?

Many researchers believe that mental images, while not literally pictures in the mind, function in ways analogous to actual visual images and are represented in the brain as a type of perceptual code (Kosslyn et al., 2006). If this is the case, then mental images should have qualities similar to those that occur when we perceive objects and scenes in the real world. For example, if the objects portrayed in Figure 9.28 were real objects, you would be able to physically rotate them in three-dimensional space. Shepard and Metzler's (1971) experiment suggested that mental images likewise can be rotated within mental space.

Mental Imagery as Perception Let's consider an example that illustrates the perceptual nature of mental imagery. Look at the island in Figure 9.29. Notice that it contains seven landmarks (e.g., a hut, lake, hill, beach), each of which is marked by a red dot. Suppose that after giving you time to memorize this map, we ask you to close your eyes and focus on a mental image of the map. Next, we ask you to (1) focus on a particular landmark (say, the beach), (2) scan the map until you come to the hill, and (3) press a button (which measures your response time) when you find the hill. On another trial, we might ask you to start at the tree and scan the map until you come to the lake. In total, you will end up taking 21 of these mental trips as you scan once between every possible pair of locations.

In the real world, visually scanning between two objects takes longer when they are farther apart. Stephen Kosslyn and his colleagues (1978), who designed this "island" task, conducted an experiment and found that the greater the distance between two locations on the mental image of the map, the longer it took participants to scan and find the second location. This study and other research supports the view that mental images involve a spatial representation (Rinck & Denis, 2004).

Mental Imagery and the Brain

If mental imagery is rooted in perception, then people who experience brain damage that causes perceptual difficulties might also be expected to show similar impairments in forming mental images. In many instances this seems to be the case, but there are also exceptions. Some patients with brain damage have deficits in producing visual mental images, yet their visual perception is intact (Moro et al., 2008). Other cases involve the opposite pattern: the ability to produce mental images despite impaired visual perception (Bartolomeo, 2008). For example, some patients who have damage on one side of the brain (usually the right hemisphere) suffer from a condition called *visual neglect*: they fail to visually perceive objects on the other side (e.g., the left side) of their visual field. If you showed patients who have left-side visual neglect the picture of the island in Figure 9.29 and

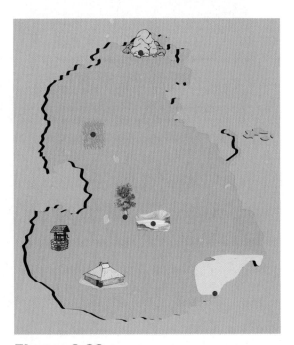

Figure 9.29

Imagine an island.

This island is similar to one used in Kosslyn et al.'s (1978) mental imagery scanning study.

asked them to draw a copy of it, they would draw the right side of the island but fail to copy the left side. However, in some cases, if you were to ask the patients to draw the picture from memory (by calling up a mental image of the picture of the island) rather than to copy it (which relies on direct visual perception), they would be able to draw the entire island (Halligan et al., 2003).

Brain-imaging studies of healthy people reveal that many brain regions that become more active when people visually perceive objects also become more active when people form mental images (Kaas et al., 2010). Moreover, researchers have found evidence of *imagery neurons*, which fire in response to a particular stimulus regardless of whether it is visual (a photo of a baseball) or imagined (a mental image of a baseball). Altogether, studies of impaired and healthy brain functioning suggest that while visual mental imagery and visual perception do not activate all of the same neural components, there is considerable overlap between these two processes (Stokes et al., 2009).

Levels of Analysis

Thinking Processes

We have now covered diverse aspects of human thought. The subjective experience of thinking fits squarely within the psychological level of analysis, but as we now recap, research on thinking spans the biological, psychological, and environmental levels of analysis.

ENVIRONMENTAL LEVEL
- Irrelevant information can impair reasoning.
- How a question is framed influences our ability to reason logically.
- The resemblance of a stimulus to a prototype can prompt the proper or improper use of the representativeness heuristic.
- Dramatic, vivid events may lead us to overestimate the likelihood of such future events.
- Cultural and educational experiences foster expertise and wisdom.
- Following instructions to write a delayed summary of textbook material increases students' metacomprehension.

BIOLOGICAL LEVEL
- Conscious thoughts exist as patterns of neural activity.
- Developing expertise changes brain functioning in ways that improve processing efficiency.
- In general, during mental imagery much of the brain's activity corresponds to that of visual perception.
- Often, brain damage that disrupts visual perception also impairs mental imagery.

PSYCHOLOGICAL LEVEL
- Much of our thinking involves concepts and takes the form of propositional thought.
- Belief bias can impair logical reasoning.
- We often rely on heuristics to solve problems and make decisions.
- At times the representativeness and availability heuristics, confirmation bias, and overconfidence may impair our decision making.
- To solve problems in their fields, experts make more effective use of schemas than do novices.
- In some ways, mental images function analogously to visual images.

Consider this possible interaction between the environmental and psychological levels of analysis. Do you think that educational experiences or training about thinking errors and biases would reduce people's future tendency to display such errors and biases?

test yourself

Knowledge, Expertise, Wisdom, Metacognition, and Mental Imagery

True or false?

1. The activity "Carl went to the library to study" is an example of a script.

2. Concepts, categories, algorithms, and heuristics are all examples of schemas.

3. Wisdom and expertise are the same thing.

4. The best way to increase metacomprehension of textbook material is to write a summary of it immediately after reading it.

5. Compared to novices, experts rely more on long-term memory in tasks related to their fields.

6. Mental imagery and visual perception activate entirely different brain areas.

ANSWERS: 1-true, 2-true, 3-false, 4-false, 5-true, 6-false

Chapter Summary

LANGUAGE

- Human language is symbolic and structured, conveys meaning, is generative, and permits displacement. Language facilitates cooperative social systems and knowledge transmission.

- A language's surface structure refers to how symbols are combined; the deep structure refers to the underlying meaning of the symbols. Language elements are hierarchically arranged: from phonemes to morphemes, words, phrases, and sentences.

- Understanding and producing language involves bottom-up and top-down processing.

- Scientists believe that humans have evolved an innate capacity for acquiring language. Infants can perceive all the phonemes that exist in all the languages of the world. Between 6 and 12 months of age, their speech discrimination narrows to include only the sounds specific to their native tongue. By ages 4 to 5, most children have learned basic grammatical rules for combining words into meaningful sentences.

- Language development depends on innate brain mechanisms that permit the learning and production of language, provided that the child is exposed to an appropriate linguistic environment during a sensitive period that extends from early childhood to puberty.

- Compared to monolingual children, bilingual children tend to perform better on cognitive tasks that involve inhibiting attention to irrelevant stimuli, but they develop a smaller vocabulary in each language. In general, when people acquire a second language early in life, both languages share a common neural network.

- Learning to read is more complex than acquiring speech. Poor phonological awareness is a major reason why people with dyslexia have difficulty learning to read.

- Apes have been taught to use hand signs or keyboard symbols to communicate in languagelike fashion. At best, they are capable of communicating with symbols at a level similar to that of a human toddler. Skeptics question whether apes can learn syntax and generate novel ideas.

- Language influences what people think and how effectively they think. Expansion of vocabulary allows people to encode and process information in more sophisticated ways.

THINKING

- Thoughts are propositional, imaginal, or motoric mental representations that exist as patterns of neural activity in the brain. Propositional thought involves the use of concepts in the form of statements. Concepts are mental categories, or classes, that share certain characteristics. Many concepts are based on prototypes.

- In deductive reasoning, we reason from general principles to a conclusion about a specific case. Inductive reasoning involves reasoning from a set of specific facts or observations to a general principle. Deductive conclusions cannot be false if appropriate logical rules are applied and the premises are true. Inductive reasoning cannot yield certainty. Unsuccessful reasoning can result from failure to select relevant information, belief bias, emotional reactions, and framing effects.

- Problem solving proceeds through several steps: (1) understanding the problem, (2) establishing initial hypotheses or potential solutions, (3) testing solutions against existing evidence, and (4) evaluating the results.

- People use several types of problem-solving schemas. Algorithms are formulas or procedures that guarantee correct solutions. Heuristics—such as means-ends analysis, subgoal analysis, the representativeness heuristic, and the availability heuristic—are general strategies that may or may not provide correct solutions.
- Humans exhibit confirmation bias, a tendency to look for facts to support hypotheses rather than to disprove them. They also suffer from overconfidence, a tendency to overestimate their knowledge and the correctness of their beliefs and decisions.
- In some situations, divergent thinking is needed for generating novel ideas. Functional fixedness can blind us to new ways of using an object or procedure, thereby interfering with creative problem solving. Sometimes, an incubation period permits problem solving to proceed subconsciously.
- Knowledge acquisition involves building mental frameworks, called schemas. One type of schema—scripts—provides a framework for understanding regular sequences of events. Compared with novices, experts have more schemas to guide

problem solving in their fields and more effective recognition of when each schema should be applied.
- Wisdom is a system of knowledge about the fundamental matters of life. It consists of rich factual knowledge, strategic knowledge, an understanding of life-span contexts, an awareness of the relativism of values and priorities, and the ability to recognize and manage uncertainty.
- Metacognition refers to a person's awareness of her or his own cognitive abilities. One aspect of metacognition, meta-comprehension, reflects how accurate people are at judging what they do and do not understand. After reading textbook material, writing summaries of that material after a time delay can increase metacomprehension.
- A mental image is a representation of a stimulus that originates inside the brain, rather than from external sensory input. Mental images of objects seem to have properties that are analogous to the properties of actual objects (e.g., you can rotate them, visually scan them). Brain research suggests that mental images are perceptual in nature.

KEY TERMS AND CONCEPTS

Each term has been boldfaced and defined in the chapter on the page indicated in parentheses.

algorithms (p. 316)
aphasia (p. 299)
availability heuristic (p. 318)
belief bias (p. 314)
bilingualism (p. 303)
bottom-up processing (p. 298)
concept (p. 312)
confirmation bias (p. 319)
creativity (p. 320)
deductive reasoning (p. 313)
deep structure (p. 295)
discourse (p. 297)
displacement (p. 295)
divergent thinking (p. 320)
framing (p. 314)
functional fixedness (p. 320)
generativity (p. 295)

grammar (p. 295)
heuristics (p. 316)
imaginal thought (p. 312)
incubation (p. 320)
inductive reasoning (p. 313)
language (p. 294)
linguistic relativity hypothesis (p. 309)
means-ends analysis (p. 316)
mental image (p. 326)
mental representations (p. 294)
mental set (p. 316)
metacognition (p. 323)
morpheme (p. 296)
motoric thought (p. 312)
overconfidence (p. 319)
phoneme (p. 296)
phonological awareness (p. 306)

pragmatics (p. 299)
proposition (p. 312)
propositional thought (p. 312)
prototype (p. 313)
psycholinguistics (p. 294)
representativeness heuristic (p. 317)
schema (p. 321)
script (p. 321)
semantics (p. 295)
speech segmentation (p. 298)
subgoal analysis (p. 317)
surface structure (p. 295)
syntax (p. 295)
top-down processing (p. 298)
wisdom (p. 323)

? thinking **critically**

DISCERNING THE DEEP STRUCTURES OF LANGUAGE (Page 296)

The final words on the grave marker ("No Les No More") consist of a single surface structure with two possible deep structures. First, given the preceding words on the tombstone, the phrase "No Les No More" could be a play on words, which in this case is meant to represent the

expression "No Less, No More." In other words, Lester Moore was killed by exactly 4 bullets, no less, no more. Or, the deep structure of "No Les No More" can be interpreted as meaning that Lester is no longer among the living. Thus, like the sentence "The police must stop drinking after midnight," the inscription on this tombstone has an ambiguous deep structure.

Sometimes, interpreting ambiguous sentences yields humorous results. For example, a newspaper headline that reads "Squad Helps Dog Bite Victim" is intended to mean that the squad helps the victim of a dog bite. But another deep structure is that the squad helped the dog to bite the victim!

THE SLEEPING POLICEMAN (Page 299)

This actual event illustrates how top-down processing and pragmatics affect our ability to understand language. First, I (your author, MP) didn't take the storekeeper's words literally; I did not expect to see a police officer sleeping on the side of the road!

Second, in England (and Ireland and Scotland), the taverns often have wonderfully colorful names: The Drunken Duck, The Black Swan, and so on. Given this knowledge, would it change your interpretation of "the sleeping policeman"? Indeed, I assumed that the storekeeper was referring to a pub or perhaps a restaurant—and I interpreted his spoken words as "The Sleeping Policeman."

Unfortunately, driving along the road, I saw nothing but farmland and homes. I returned to town and asked the storekeeper, "When you say 'Sleeping Policeman,' are you referring to a pub?" He chuckled and said, "Oh no, no. You know . . . it's that long thing in the road . . . the thing that slows you down." "Ah," I replied, "at home we call them speed bumps!"

My prior top-down knowledge about the names of English pubs shaped my assumption that "the sleeping policeman" referred to a pub. When I later asked English friends if they had heard of the term *sleeping policeman*, about half said no. Thus the storekeeper made an erroneous assumption as well, namely, that visitors would have the background to understand the meaning of the local idiom *sleeping policeman*. This reflects a breakdown in pragmatics: it violates the rule of clarity. Can you think of idioms (e.g., "give me a hand," "that's cool") that have obvious meaning to you but which may have a literal interpretation that could confuse a foreign visitor?

Answers to Problems in the Text

Figure 9.18 Baltimore and Washington are 50 miles apart. The trains are traveling at the same speed (25 mph). Hence they will meet at the halfway point, which is 25 miles, after 1 hour of travel time. Since the crow is flying at 60 mph, it will have flown a total of 60 miles when the trains meet.

Figure 9.20 Sequence of moves: A to 3, B to 2, A to 2, C to 3, A to 1, B to 3, A to 3.

Figure 9.23 Here are two solutions to the nine-dot problem. Both require you to think outside the box, literally.

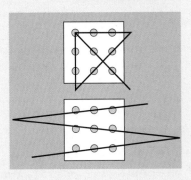

Figure 9.24 Solution to the candlestick problem:

chapter ten

Intelligence

CHAPTER OUTLINE

Myth or Reality?

Brains Are Like Engines: Bigger Means More Power (page 352)

For more than a century, psychologists have tried to determine whether intelligence depends on brain size. At one time, the issue seemed settled. But new research is suggesting a different conclusion.

We know that you highly esteem the kind of learning taught in those colleges. . . . But you, who are wise, must know that different nations have different conceptions of things: and you will not therefore take it amiss, if our ideas of this kind of education happen not to be the same with yours. We have had some experience of it; several of our young people were formerly brought up at the colleges of the Northern provinces; they were instructed in all your sciences; but, when they came back to us, they were bad runners, ignorant of every means of living in the woods, unable to bear either cold or hunger, knew neither how to build a cabin, take a deer, nor kill an enemy, spoke our language imperfectly, were therefore neither fit for hunters, warriors, nor counselors; they were totally good for nothing. . . .

We are, however not the less obligated by your kind offer, though we decline accepting it; and to show our grateful sense of it, if the gentlemen of Virginia will send us a dozen of their sons, we will take care of their education, instruct them in all we know, and make men of them. (A Native American leader quoted in Benjamin Franklin, *Remarks Concerning the Savage of North America* [1784])

This excerpt reveals cultural differences in how intelligence was measured and what knowledge was valued in colonial times. Can you think of any cultural or generational examples today that are similar to those mentioned in Franklin's anecdote? For example, how do your oldest relatives value your knowledge of e-mail, iTunes, Facebook, and Twitter?

This response to a well-intentioned offer by American colonists to provide Native American boys with access to European educational opportunities reminds us that people have different conceptions of what it means to be smart. In Western cultures, being smart is typically thought of as having good mental skills that are instrumental to succeeding in school and in higher-level jobs and occupations. As we shall see, people with good mental skills do indeed do better in school and on the job in our culture. But if we view intelligence in broader perspective as the ability to respond adaptively to the demands of a particular environment, we can understand why the Native American leader was less impressed with the products of Anglo-Saxon education than were the colonists. It's important to remember, then, that intelligence is not something that has concrete existence; it is, instead, a socially constructed concept (Sternberg, 2004; Figure 10.1).

In previous chapters, we have explored general principles of human learning, memory, thinking, reasoning, and problem solving. In all of these areas, we have seen that people differ widely in how effectively they learn, remember, think, and behave. Is it therefore the case that some people are generally more intelligent than others? Can we measure these differences and use the measures to predict success and failure in real-life settings? What is the nature of intelligence, and what factors account for the differences we observe in people's cognitive, emotional, and behavioral skills? Attempts to answer these questions have influenced our culture enormously. Today, there exists a multibillion-dollar intelligence-testing industry. Politicians and taxpayers demand that we assess the aptitudes and learning outcomes of children in a search for educational accountability. You yourself have undoubtedly taken mental ability tests for educational or occupational reasons. In fact, your results on one or more college-entrance examinations may have played an important role in your admission to college.

As we shall see, however, even after more than a century of research and theory development, there are still sharp disagreements about what intelligence is. In our discussion, we use the following definition, which accommodates most viewpoints: **Intelligence** *is the ability to acquire knowledge, to think and reason effectively, and to deal adaptively with the environment.*

Figure 10.1

The skills required to adapt successfully to environmental demands may differ from culture to culture, suggesting to some theorists that what constitutes intelligence may be somewhat culture-specific.

INTELLIGENCE IN HISTORICAL PERSPECTIVE

Historically, two scientists with entirely different agendas played seminal roles in the study and measurement of mental skills. The contributions of Sir Francis Galton and Alfred Binet set the stage for later attempts to measure intelligence and discover its causes.

Sir Francis Galton: Quantifying Mental Ability

Sir Francis Galton was a cousin of Charles Darwin and was strongly influenced by Darwin's theory of evolution. In his book *Hereditary Genius* (1869), Galton showed through the study of family trees that eminence and genius seemed to occur within certain families. No intellectual slouch himself, young Francis wrote a childhood letter to his sister that contained the following: "My dear Adele, I am 4 years old, and I can read any English book. I can say all of the Latin substantives and adjectives and active verbs besides 52 lines of Latin poetry."

Galton's research convinced him that eminent people had "inherited mental constitutions" that made them more fit for thinking than their less successful counterparts. Exhibiting his own belief bias, Galton dismissed the fact that the more successful people he studied almost invariably came from privileged environments.

Galton then attempted to demonstrate a biological basis for eminence by showing that people who were more socially and occupationally successful would also perform better on a variety of laboratory tasks thought to measure the "efficiency of the nervous system." He developed measures of reaction speed, hand strength, and sensory acuity. He even measured the size of people's skulls, believing that skull size reflected brain volume and hence intelligence.

In time, Galton's approach to mental-skills measurement fell into disfavor because his measures of nervous system efficiency proved unrelated to socially relevant measures of mental ability, such as academic and occupational success. Nonetheless, Galton's work created an interest in the measurement of mental abilities, setting the stage for the pioneering work of Alfred Binet.

Alfred Binet's Mental Tests

The modern intelligence-testing movement began at the turn of the 20th century, when the French psychologist Alfred Binet was commissioned by France's Ministry of Public Education to develop the test that was to become the forerunner of all modern intelligence tests. Unlike Galton, with whom he had trained, Binet was interested in solving a practical problem rather than supporting a theory. Certain children seemed unable to benefit from normal public schooling. Educators wanted an objective way to identify these children as early as possible so that some form of special education could be arranged for them.

In developing his tests, Binet made two assumptions about intelligence: First, mental abilities develop with age. Second, the rate at which people gain mental competence is a characteristic of the person and is fairly constant over time. In other words, a child who is less competent than expected at age 5 should also be lagging at age 10.

To develop a measure of mental skills, Binet asked experienced teachers what sorts of problems children could solve at ages 3, 4, 5, and so on, up through the school years. He then used their answers to develop a standardized interview in which an adult examiner posed a series of questions to a child to determine whether the child was performing at the correct mental level for his or her age (Table 10.1). The result of the testing was a score called the *mental age*. For instance, if an 8-year-old child could solve problems at the level of the average 10-year-old, the child would be said to have a mental age of 10. For the French school system, the practical implication was that educational attainment could be enhanced if placement in school were based at least in part on the child's mental age. An 8-year-old child with a mental age of 6 could hardly be expected to cope with the academic demands of a normal classroom for 8-year-olds.

The concept of mental age was subsequently expanded by the German psychologist William Stern to provide a relative score—a common yardstick of intellectual attainment—for people of different chronological ages. Stern's **intelligence quotient (IQ)** *was the ratio of mental age to chronological age, multiplied by 100: IQ = (mental age/chronological age) × 100*. Thus, a child who was performing at exactly his or her age level would have an IQ of 100. In our previous example, the child with a mental age of 10 and a chronological age of 8 would have an IQ of

$(10/8) \times 100 = 125$. A 16-year-old with a mental age of 20 would also have an IQ of 125, so the two would be comparable in intelligence even though their ages differed.

Today's tests no longer use the concept of mental age. Although the concept works pretty well for children, many of the basic skills measured by intelligence tests are acquired by about age 16 through normal life experiences and schooling, so that Stern's quotient is less useful for adults. Moreover, some intellectual skills show an actual decline at advanced ages. If we applied Stern's definition of IQ to a 20-year-old who performed at the typical level of an 80-year-old, we would have to say that the 20-year-old's IQ was 400! To deal with these problems, today's intelligence tests provide an "IQ" score that is not a quotient at all. Instead, it is based on a person's performance relative to the scores of other people the same age, with a score of

Table 10.1 | **Sample Problems from the Stanford-Binet Intelligence Test That Should Be Answered Correctly at Particular Ages**

Age 3—Child should be able to:	Point to objects that serve various functions such as "goes on your feet." Name pictures of objects such as *chair, flag*. Repeat a list of 2 words or digits such as *car, dog*.
Age 4—Child should be able to:	Discriminate visual forms such as squares, circles, and triangles. Define words such as *ball* and *bat*. Repeat 10-word sentences. Count up to 4 objects. Solve problems such as "In daytime it is light; at night it is . . . "
Age 6—Child should be able to:	State the differences between similar items such as *bird* and *dog*. Count up to 9 blocks. Solve analogies such as "An inch is short; a mile is . . . "
Age 9—Child should be able to:	Solve verbal problems such as "Tell me a number that rhymes with *tree*." Solve simple arithmetic problems such as "If I buy 4 cents' worth of candy and give the storekeeper 10 cents, how much money will I get back?" Repeat 4 digits in reverse order.
Age 12—Child should be able to:	Define words such as *muzzle*. Repeat 5 digits in reverse order. Solve verbal absurdities such as "Bill's feet are so big he has to pull his trousers over his head. What is foolish about that?"

Source: Terman & Merrill, 1972.

100 corresponding to the average performance of that age group.

Binet's Legacy: An Intelligence-Testing Industry Emerges

Lewis Terman, a professor at Stanford University, was intrigued by Binet's work. He revised Binet's test for use in the United States, translating it into English and rewriting some of its items to improve their relevance to American culture. Terman's revised test became known as the *Stanford-Binet*. By the mid-1920s, it had become widely accepted in North America as the gold standard for measuring mental aptitude. The Stanford-Binet contained mostly verbal items, and it yielded a single IQ score.

At about the time that the Stanford-Binet test was introduced in 1916, the United States entered World War I. One of Terman's students at Stanford, Arthur Otis, had been working on a group-administered test of intellectual ability. This test became the prototype for the *Army Alpha*, a verbally oriented test that was used to screen large numbers of U.S. Army recruits for intellectual fitness (Figure 10.2). Because some recruits were unable to read, a nonverbal instrument using mazes, picture-completion problems,

Figure 10.2

Since the beginning of World War I, millions of military recruits have taken the Army Alpha group intelligence test.

and digit-symbol tasks was also developed and given the name *Army Beta*. Before the war's end, more than 1.7 million men had been screened for intelligence using these tests.

Inspired by the success of the Army Alpha and Beta for measuring the intelligence of large numbers of people in a group setting, educators clamored for similar instruments to test groups of children. New group tests of intelligence, such as the Lorge-Thorndike Intelligence Test and the Otis-Lennon School Ability Test, soon appeared and became an important part of educational reform and policy. Many school districts use these or similar tests routinely, and you are likely to have taken one or more of them during your earlier school years.

Two decades after Terman introduced the American version of Binet's test, psychologist David Wechsler developed a major competitor to the Stanford-Binet. Wechsler believed that the Stanford-Binet relied too much on verbal skills. He thought that intelligence should be measured as a group of distinct but related verbal *and* nonverbal abilities. He therefore developed intelligence tests for adults and for children that measured both verbal and nonverbal intellectual skills. In 1939 the Wechsler Adult Intelligence Scale (WAIS) appeared, followed by the Wechsler Intelligence Scale for Children (WISC) in 1955 and the Wechsler Preschool and Primary Scale of Intelligence (WPPSI) in 1967. The Wechsler scales have undergone several revisions. Today, the Wechsler tests (WAIS-IV and WISC-IV) are the most popular individually administered intelligence tests in the United States (Coalson & Raiford, 2008). Following Wechsler's lead, the Stanford-Binet has also been revised to measure a wider range of mental abilities. Later in the chapter, we'll have a closer look at the Wechsler tests, as well as other measures that assess various classes of mental skills.

Intelligence has long been a major focus of psychological research, much of which has been inspired by questions that, even after a century of research, continue to evoke disagreement and controversy (Bartholomew, 2005). Should we regard intelligence as a single aptitude or as many specific abilities? Is intelligence an innate mental capacity, or is it a product of our upbringing? What kinds of brain processes underlie mental skills? Are there actually multiple intelligences, including some that may have little to do with mental skills? These and other questions have inspired a fascinating odyssey of scientific discovery. We begin with the most basic question of all: Just what is this attribute we call *intelligence*?

THE NATURE OF INTELLIGENCE

Psychologists have used two major approaches in the study of intelligence (Sternberg et al., 2003). The *psychometric approach* attempts to map the structure of intellect and to discover the kinds of mental competencies that underlie test performance. The *cognitive processes approach* studies the specific thought processes that underlie those mental competencies.

The Psychometric Approach: The Structure of Intellect

Psychometrics *is the statistical study of psychological tests.* The psychometric approach to intelligence tries to identify and measure the abilities that underlie individual differences in performance. In essence, it tries to provide a measurement-based map of the mind.

Factor Analysis: An Essential Tool

Psychometric researchers have long sought to identify the mental abilities of the human mind. How many are there? Are there dozens, or are there perhaps only one or a few basic abilities that underlie performance across diverse tasks? What is the nature of these abilities?

To answer questions like these, researchers administer diverse measures of mental abilities and then correlate them with one another. They reason that if certain tests are correlated highly with one another—if they "cluster" mathematically— then performance on these tests probably reflects the same underlying mental skill. Further, if the tests within a cluster correlate highly with one another but much less with tests in other clusters, then these various test clusters probably reflect different mental abilities. Thus researchers hope to determine the number of test clusters and to use this information to infer the nature of the underlying abilities.

When large numbers of tests are correlated with one another, many correlation coefficients result, and it is difficult to determine by visual examination the actual patterning of the test scores. Fortunately, a statistical technique called **factor analysis** *reduces a large number of measures to a smaller number of clusters, or factors, with each cluster containing variables that correlate highly with one another but less highly with variables in other clusters.* A factor allows us to infer the underlying characteristic that presumably accounts for the links among the variables in the cluster.

Table **10.2** | Correlations among Six Cognitive Ability Tests

Test	1	2	3	4	5	6
1	1.00	.84	.79	.46	.39	.43
2		1.00	.87	.51	.48	.54
3			1.00	.47	.50	.48
4				1.00	.88	.91
5					1.00	.82
6						1.00

To illustrate with a highly simplified example the kind of clustering of tests that we are interested in, consider the small correlation matrix in Table 10.2, based on only 6 different mental ability tests. (There might be as many as 10 to 15 tests in an actual study.) Examination of Table 10.2 reveals two clusters of tests. Tests 1, 2, and 3 correlate highly with one another. Tests 4, 5, and 6 also show high positive correlations with one another. But tests 1, 2, and 3 do not correlate highly with tests 4, 5, and 6. This indicates that the two sets of tests are measuring different abilities. A factor analysis would tell us that there are two different factors.

But what are these two sets of tests measuring? The factor analysis cannot answer this question; it can only identify the clusters for us. It's now up to us to examine the nature of the tests within each cluster and decide what the underlying factors might be. Suppose that test 1 is a measure of vocabulary, test 2 measures reading comprehension, and test 3 requires respondents to complete sentences with missing words. Because all three tasks involve the use of words, we might decide to call the underlying factor "verbal ability." Inspection of tests 4, 5, and 6 might reveal that all of them involve the use of numbers or mathematical word problems. We might therefore decide to name this factor "mathematical reasoning." What matters is that we have now reduced six variables to two variables, based on the correlations among them, and we have arrived at some idea of what the underlying abilities might be.

We should note, however, that the two clusters of tests we've identified are not totally unrelated to one another. The verbal and mathematical scores are also correlated with one another, though at a much lower level than within the clusters. This fact suggests that although the verbal and mathematical factors are clearly distinct from one another, they also share something in common, perhaps some more general mental ability that cuts across both verbal and mathematical abilities. This pattern of results anticipates one of the major controversies in the field of intelligence: is intelligence a general mental capacity, or does it consist of separate and specific mental abilities?

The *g* Factor: Intelligence as General Mental Capacity

The psychometric argument for intelligence as a general ability was first advanced by the British psychologist Charles Spearman (1923). He observed that school grades in different subjects, such as English and mathematics, were almost always positively correlated but not perfectly. Spearman found the same to be true for different types of Stanford-Binet intelligence test items, such as vocabulary questions, arithmetic reasoning problems, and the ability to solve puzzles. Were he to look at the correlation matrix in Table 10.2, he would be impressed by the fact that the verbal-ability cluster and mathematical-reasoning cluster are correlated with one another at about the .40 to .50 level. He would regard these correlations as evidence that verbal and mathematical abilities, while clearly different, also reflect a more basic or general mental capacity that contributes to them.

Spearman concluded that intellectual performance is determined partly by a *g* **factor,** *or general intelligence,* and partly by whatever special abilities might be required to perform that particular task. Spearman contended that because the general factor—the *g* factor—cuts across virtually all tasks, it constitutes the core of intelligence. Thus Spearman would argue that your performance in a mathematics course would depend mainly on your general intelligence but also on your specific ability to learn mathematics.

Today, many theorists continue to believe that the *g* factor is the core of what we call *intelligence.* Moreover, *g* matters a great deal as a predictor of both academic and job performance. Nathan Kuncel and coworkers (2004) performed a meta-analysis of 127 studies involving 20,352 participants in numerous educational and work settings. They concluded that the same general mental ability is significantly related to success in both areas of life. Taking this argument a step further, Frank Schmidt and John Hunter (2004) concluded that measures of the *g* factor predict job success even better than do measures of specific abilities tailored to individual jobs. Summarizing the research evidence, David Lubinski, a prominent intelligence researcher, concluded: "*g* is clearly the most important dimension uncovered in the study of cognitive abilities to date" (2004, p. 100).

Intelligence as Specific Mental Abilities

Spearman's conclusion about the centrality of the *g* factor was soon challenged by L. L. Thurstone of the University of Chicago. While Spearman had been impressed by the fact that scores on different mental tasks are correlated, Thurstone was impressed by the fact that the correlations are far from perfect. Thurstone therefore concluded that human mental performance depends not on a general factor but rather on seven distinct abilities, which he called *primary mental abilities* (Table 10.3). Thus Thurstone would focus on the two clusters of test scores shown in Table 10.2 and attach special significance to the high correlations within each cluster. He would expect that performance on a given verbal or mathematical task would be influenced more by the specific skills represented in the relevant cluster than by any *g* factor.

Following Thurstone's lead, other investigators claimed to have found many more specific cognitive factors. One prominent theorist maintained that there are more than 100 distinct and measurable mental abilities (Guilford, 1967). Other theorists suggest fewer abilities but maintain that intelligence is more complex than a single *g* factor.

For practical reasons, educators tend to find the specific-abilities notion of intelligence more attractive and useful than the general mental ability model (Mayer, 2000). They are more interested in identifying the specific mental skills involved in learning subjects such as reading, mathematics, and science. They are also interested in helping children increase the specific mental abilities that are needed for success in various subjects. For such purposes, general mental ability measures such as an overall IQ are less useful than are measures of specific cognitive abilities that can point to a student's areas of strength and weakness. Additionally, it may appear more feasible to

Table **10.3** | Thurstone's Primary Mental Abilities

Ability Name	Description
S–Space	Reasoning about visual scenes
V–Verbal comprehension	Understanding verbal statements
W–Word fluency	Producing verbal statements
N–Number facility	Dealing with numbers
P–Perceptual speed	Recognizing visual patterns
M–Rote memory	Memorization
R–Reasoning	Dealing with novel problems

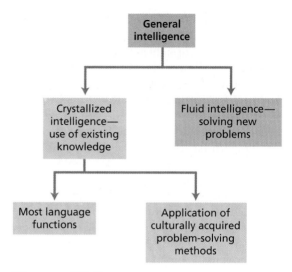

Figure 10.3

Crystallized and fluid intelligence.
Raymond Cattell and John Horn made an important distinction between crystallized and fluid intelligence. Crystallized intelligence is based more strongly on previous learning and experience, whereas fluid intelligence is a more creative type of intelligence.

enhance specific mental skills than to raise general intelligence.

Crystallized and Fluid Intelligence

Raymond Cattell (1971) and John Horn (1985) proposed a new model of intelligence (Figure 10.3). They broke down Spearman's general intelligence into two distinct but related subtypes of *g* (with a correlation of about .50). **Crystallized intelligence (g_c)** *is the ability to apply previously acquired knowledge to current problems.* Vocabulary and information tests are good measures of crystallized intelligence. Crystallized intelligence, which is the basis for expertise, depends on the ability to retrieve previously learned information and problem-solving schemas from long-term memory (Horn & Masunaga, 2000; Hunt, 1997). It is dependent on previous learning and practice (Figure 10.4).

Cattell and Horn's second general factor is **fluid intelligence (g_f),** *defined as the ability to deal with novel problem-solving situations for which personal experience does not provide a solution.* It involves inductive reasoning and creative problem-solving skills like those discussed in the previous chapter. Fluid intelligence is dependent primarily on the efficient functioning of the central nervous system rather than on prior experience and cultural context. People high in fluid intelligence can perceive relations among stimulus patterns and draw inferences from relationships. The tower-of-Hanoi and nine-dot problems you worked on in the previous chapter are fluid-intelligence tasks.

Figure 10.4

Crystallized intelligence is being expressed as this woman uses her acquired knowledge of mathematical concepts to solve this equation.

Fluid intelligence requires the abilities to reason abstractly, think logically, and manage information in working (short-term) memory so that new problems can be solved on "the blackboard of the mind" (Hunt, 1997). Thus long-term memory contributes strongly to crystallized intelligence, whereas fluid intelligence is particularly dependent on efficient working memory.

The g_c-g_f model is based in part on what has been learned about intellectual development in adulthood (Horn & Blankston, 2005). Cattell and Horn concluded that over our life span, we progress from using fluid intelligence to depending more on crystallized intelligence. Early in life, we encounter many problems for the first time, so we need fluid intelligence to figure out solutions. As experience makes us more knowledgeable, we have less need to approach each situation as a new problem. Instead, we simply call up appropriate information and schemas from long-term memory, thereby utilizing our crystallized intelligence. This is the essence of wisdom (Kunzman & Baltes, 2003).

Because long-term memory remains strong even as we age, performance on tests of crystallized intelligence improves during adulthood and remains stable well into late adulthood. In contrast, performance on tests of fluid intelligence begins to decline as people enter late adulthood (Daniels et al., 2006; Schaie, 1998). The fact that aging affects the two forms of intelligence differently is additional evidence that they represent different classes of mental abilities (Horn & Noll, 1997; Weinert & Hany, 2003).

Carroll's Three-Stratum Model: A Modern Synthesis

In their attempts to specify the nature of intellect, psychometric researchers have been administering measures of mental abilities for more than a century. The many tasks they have used have probably left no cognitive stone unturned. In an attempt to synthesize the results of prior research, John B. Carroll (2005) used factor analysis to reanalyze more than 460 different sets of data obtained by researchers around the world between 1935 and 1980. Carroll's analysis resulted in an integrative model of intelligence that contains elements of Spearman's, Thurstone's, and Cattell-Horn's models. The **three-stratum theory of cognitive abilities** *establishes three levels of mental skills— general, broad, and narrow—arranged in a hierarchical model.* As shown in Figure 10.5, at the top, or third stratum, of the model is a *g* factor thought to underlie most mental activity. Below *g* at the second stratum are eight broad intellectual factors arranged from left to right in terms of the extent to which they are influenced by (or correlated with) *g*. Fluid intelligence is most strongly related to (or "saturated with") *g*, and crystallized intelligence is next, indicating the importance of the Cattell-Horn factors. The other broad abilities at the second stratum involve basic cognitive functions, such as memory and learning, perceptual abilities, and speed of mental functioning, some of which resemble Thurstone's primary mental abilities. Finally, at the first stratum of the model are nearly 70 highly specific cognitive abilities that feed into the broader second-stratum factors. On average, these specific ability measures tend to correlate around .30 with one another, reflecting the common *g* factor at the top of the model. Carroll (2005) believes that the three-stratum model encompasses virtually all known cognitive abilities, and this model provides the most complete and detailed map of the human intellect derived from the psychometric approach to intelligence (McGrew, 2009).

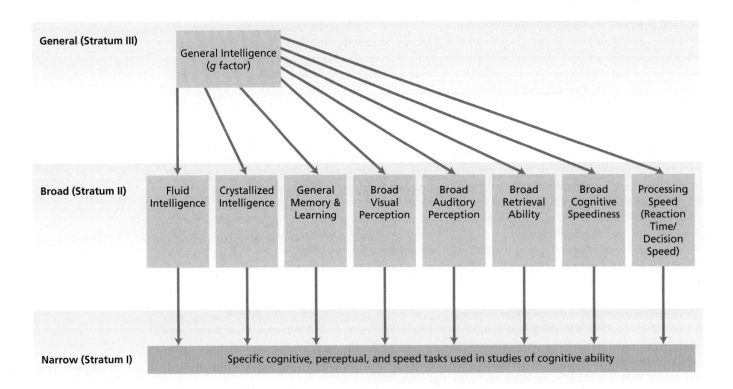

Figure 10.5

A modern model of intellect.

John B. Carroll's three-stratum model of cognitive skills is based on a reanalysis of more than 400 data sets. The model builds upward from specific skills to a *g* factor at its apex. The lengths of the arrows from Stratum III to Stratum II represent the contribution of the *g* factor to each Stratum II ability. Source: Adapted from Carroll, 2003.

Cognitive Process Approaches: The Nature of Intelligent Thinking

Psychometric theories of intelligence are statistically sophisticated ways of providing a map of the mind and describing *how* people differ from one another (Birney & Sternberg, 2006). What psychometric theories don't explain is *why* people vary in these mental skills. **Cognitive process theories** *explore the specific information-processing and cognitive processes that underlie intellectual ability.* Recall that this was the logic behind Galton's early attempts to relate thinking ability to speed of reaction and sensory acuity.

Robert Sternberg (1988, 2004) is a leading proponent of the cognitive processes approach to intelligence. His **triarchic theory of intelligence** *addresses both the psychological processes involved in intelligent behavior and the diverse forms that intelligence can take.* Sternberg's theory divides the cognitive processes that underlie intelligent behavior into three specific components (Figure 10.6).

Metacomponents *are the higher-order processes used to plan and regulate task performance.* They include problem-solving skills such as identifying problems, formulating hypotheses and strategies, testing them logically, and evaluating performance feedback. Sternberg believes that metacomponents are the fundamental sources of individual differences in fluid intelligence. He finds that intelligent people spend more time framing problems and developing strategies than do less intelligent people, who have a tendency to plunge right in without sufficient forethought.

Performance components *are the actual mental processes used to perform the task.* They include perceptual processing, retrieving appropriate memories and schemas from long-term memory, and generating responses. Finally, **knowledge-acquisition components** *allow us to learn from our experiences, store information in memory, and combine new insights with previously acquired information.* These abilities underlie individual differences in crystallized intelligence. Thus Sternberg's theory addresses the processes that underlie the distinction made by Cattell and Horn between fluid and crystallized intelligences.

Sternberg believes that there is more than one kind of intelligence. He suggests that environmental demands may call for three different classes of adaptive problem solving and that people differ in their intellectual strengths in these areas:

1. *Analytical intelligence* involves the kinds of academically oriented problem-solving skills measured by traditional intelligence tests.

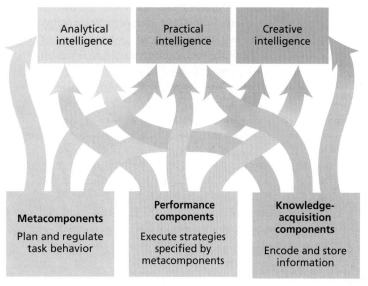

Types of Intellectual Competence

Analytical intelligence · Practical intelligence · Creative intelligence

Metacomponents — Plan and regulate task behavior

Performance components — Execute strategies specified by metacomponents

Knowledge-acquisition components — Encode and store information

Underlying Cognitive Processes

Figure 10.6

Sternberg's triarchic theory.
Sternberg's theory includes three different types of intelligence and three classes of cognitive processes that underlie each type of intelligence.

2. *Practical intelligence* refers to the skills needed to cope with everyday demands and to manage oneself and other people effectively.

3. *Creative intelligence* comprises the mental skills needed to deal adaptively with novel problems.

Sternberg has shown that these forms of intelligence, while having a modest underlying *g* factor, are also distinct from one another. Consider, for example, the relation between academic and practical skills. In one study, adolescents in Kenya were given one set of analytical tests measuring traditional academic knowledge and another set measuring their knowledge of natural herbal medicines used to treat illnesses, a kind of practical knowledge viewed by villagers as important to their survival. The results indicated that the practical intelligence measure of herbal knowledge was unrelated to (and sometimes negatively correlated with) the academic measures (Sternberg et al., 2001). Sternberg also found that Brazilian street children were very proficient at the math required to carry on their street businesses, despite the fact that many of them had failed mathematics in school (Sternberg, 2004).

Sternberg believes that educational programs should teach all three classes of skills, not just analytical-academic skills. In studies with elementary school children, he and his colleagues have shown that a curriculum that also teaches practical and creative skills results in greater mastery of course material than does a traditional analytic, memory-based approach to learning course content (Sternberg et al., 1998). As Sternberg's work illustrates, cognitive science is leading us to a focus on understanding and enhancing the mental processes that underlie intelligent behavior.

Broader Conceptions of Intelligence: Beyond Mental Competencies

Traditionally, intelligence has been viewed as *mental competence.* Some psychologists think this is too limited a definition to capture the range of human adaptations. They believe that intelligence may be more broadly conceived as relatively *independent intelligences* that relate to different adaptive demands.

Gardner's Multiple Intelligences

Harvard psychologist Howard Gardner (2003) is one of the strongest proponents of this view. Inspired by his observations of how specific human abilities are affected by brain damage, Gardner advanced a theory of multiple intelligences. The number of intelligences has varied as Gardner's work has progressed; he currently defines eight distinct varieties of adaptive abilities and a possible ninth variety (Gardner, 2000):

1. *Linguistic intelligence:* the ability to use language well, as writers do.

2. *Logical-mathematical intelligence:* the ability to reason mathematically and logically.

3. *Visuospatial intelligence:* the ability to solve spatial problems or to succeed in a field such as architecture.

4. *Musical intelligence:* the ability to perceive pitch and rhythm and to understand and produce music.

5. *Bodily-kinesthetic intelligence:* the ability to control body movements and skillfully manipulate objects, as demonstrated by a highly skilled dancer, athlete, or surgeon.

6. *Interpersonal intelligence:* the ability to understand and relate well to others.

7. *Intrapersonal intelligence:* the ability to understand oneself.

8. *Naturalistic intelligence:* the ability to detect and understand phenomena in the natural world, as a zoologist or meteorologist might.

In recent writings, Gardner (2000) has also speculated about a ninth possible intelligence, which he calls *existential intelligence,* a philosophically oriented ability to ponder questions about the meaning of one's existence, life, and death.

Gardner's first three intelligences are measured by existing intelligence tests, but the others are not. Indeed, some of Gardner's critics insist that these other abilities are not really part of the traditional concept of intelligence at all and that some of them are better regarded as talents. However, Gardner replies that the form of intelligence that is most highly valued within a given culture depends on the adaptive requirements of that culture. In Gardner's view, the abilities exhibited by Taylor Swift, Kobe Bryant, and Oprah Winfrey exemplify different forms of intelligence that are highly adaptive within their respective environments (Figure 10.7). Gardner further suggests that these different classes of abilities require the functioning of separate but interacting modules in the brain. Gardner's approach, though

Figure 10.7

According to Howard Gardner, these people's abilities exemplify forms of intelligence that are not measured by traditional intelligence tests. Taylor Swift possesses high musical intelligence, whereas Kobe Bryant and Oprah Winfrey exhibit high bodily-kinesthetic and interpersonal intelligence, respectively.

provocative, remains controversial because it goes far beyond traditional conceptions of intelligence as mental skills.

Personal and Emotional Intelligence

Building in part on Gardner's notions of *interpersonal* and *intrapersonal* intelligence, John Mayer (2008) has proposed that **personal intelligence,** *the ability to understand who one is and who one wants to be,* is a legitimate form of intelligence because, like other cognitive forms of intelligence, it involves the ability to carry out abstract reasoning in a valid and accurate manner. Mayer suggests that personal intelligence involves four key abilities:

1. The ability to process and reason about personally relevant information through introspection (looking within) and by observing yourself, other people, and the way others react to you.

2. The ability to incorporate the information gained through introspection and observation into an accurate self-knowledge of your traits, abilities, and values, as well as accurate models of others' personalities. This sort of knowledge helps enhance interpersonal relationships.

3. The ability to use personally relevant knowledge to guide your choices, such as a choice of occupation or marriage partner, when (or whether) to begin a family, and where to reside. Accurate compatibility choices enhance occupational success and personal well-being.

4. The ability to select goals that are consistent (rather than in conflict) with one another and that are realistic given your talents and resources. This may involve accurately deciding which competencies you need to increase to pursue your goals and how to increase them. The person high in personal intelligence also can draw on his or her personal memories and "life story" for self-direction and to recognize changes in goals and values as they occur over the life span.

Considerable evidence suggests that each of these abilities contributes to personal success and well-being (Chamorro-Premuzic & Furnham, 2006; Roberts et al., 2007). Like many cognitive competencies, these skills involve the executive functions of the frontal lobe, and proponents can make a strong case that they reflect intelligent thought. Compared with measurement of traditional mental skills, assessment of individual differences in personal intelligence is in its infancy, and further development of this concept will depend on the development of reliable and valid measures of the various skills.

Another form of adaptive ability, considered by some theorists to be a facet of personal intelligence, involves competence in the emotional domain (Mayer, 2008). **Emotional intelligence** *involves the abilities to read others' emotions accurately, to respond to them appropriately, to motivate oneself, to be aware of one's own emotions, and to regulate and control one's own emotional responses* (Mayer, 2008).

Emotional intelligence includes four components, or branches, as shown in Figure 10.8. The Mayer-Salovey-Caruso Emotional Intelligence Test (MSCEIT) includes specific tasks to measure each branch. *Perceiving emotions* is measured by people's accuracy in judging emotional expressions in facial photographs, as well as the emotional tones conveyed by different landscapes and designs. *Using emotions to facilitate thought* is measured by asking people to identify the emotions that would best enhance a particular type of thinking, such as how to deal with a distressed co-worker or plan a birthday party. To measure *understanding emotions,* people are asked to specify the conditions under which their emotions change in intensity or type; another task measures people's understanding of which basic emotions blend

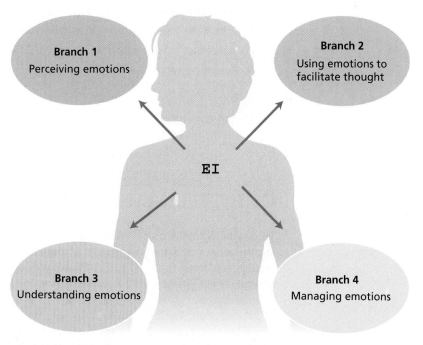

Figure 10.8

The structure of emotional intelligence (EI).

Four specific classes of emotion-detection and control abilities are assumed to underlie emotional intelligence. SOURCE: Based on Mayer, 2008.

together to create subtle emotions, such as envy or jealousy. Finally, *managing emotions* is measured by asking respondents to indicate how they can change their own or others' emotions to facilitate success or increase interpersonal harmony.

Proponents of emotional intelligence point to the important adaptive advantages of emotional skills in meeting the challenges of daily life, and they believe that the ability to read, respond to, and manage emotions has evolutionary roots. Emotionally intelligent people, they suggest, form stronger emotional bonds with others; enjoy greater success in careers, marriage, and child rearing; modulate their own emotions so as to avoid strong depression, anger, or anxiety; and work more effectively toward long-term goals by being able to control impulses for immediate gratification. In the end, some people who are high in emotional intelligence may enjoy more success in life than do others who surpass them in mental intelligence (Salovey & Pizzaro, 2003). They

also tend to use more effective coping strategies (Saklofske et al., 2007).

As is the case with Gardner's multiple intelligences, emotional intelligence has its critics. Some psychologists believe that the concept of intelligence is being stretched too far from its original focus on mental ability (e.g., Matthews et al., 2004). They would prefer a different term, such as *emotional competence*, to distinguish this concept from the traditional mental-skills concept of intelligence. But emotional-intelligence proponents respond that if we regard intelligence as adaptive abilities, we ought not limit ourselves to the purely cognitive realms of human ability, particularly since emotional intelligence, like personal intelligence, involves considerable thinking (Mayer, 2008). The debate concerning multiple intelligence continues to rage and promises to do so into the future.

So far we have explored the nature of intelligence. Let's now examine more closely how individual differences in intelligence are measured.

test yourself   The Nature of Intelligence

True or false?

1. Carroll's three-stratum model is an example of a cognitive processes approach.
2. There is strong scientific evidence for a *g* factor in intelligence.
3. Crystallized intelligence involves the use of existing knowledge to solve problems.
4. In Sternberg's theory, analytical intelligence is the one used to cope with everyday demands.
5. Emotional intelligence is one of Sternberg's triarchic intelligences.

ANSWERS: 1-false, 2-true, 3-true, 4-false, 5-false

THE MEASUREMENT OF INTELLIGENCE

Today, the Wechsler tests (WAIS-IV and WISC-IV) are the most popular individually administered intelligence tests in the United States (Groth-Marnat, 1999). They provide a good illustration of how intelligence is assessed.

Recall that Wechsler believed that intelligence tests should measure a wide array of mental abilities. His tests reflect that conviction. The WAIS-IV consists of a series of subtests that fall into four "index scales": Verbal Comprehension, Perceptual Reasoning, Working Memory, and

Processing Speed. A psychologist can therefore plot a profile based on the scores on each of the subtests to assess a person's pattern of intellectual strengths and weaknesses. The test yields five summary scores: one for each of the index scales and a Full-Scale Composite IQ based on all of the scales (Figure 10.9). For some purposes, it is useful to examine scoring differences between the index scales. For example, individuals from an impoverished environment with little formal schooling might score lower on the verbal subtests than on the others, suggesting that their overall IQ might be an underestimate of their intellectual potential. Sometimes, too, various types of brain damage are reflected in large

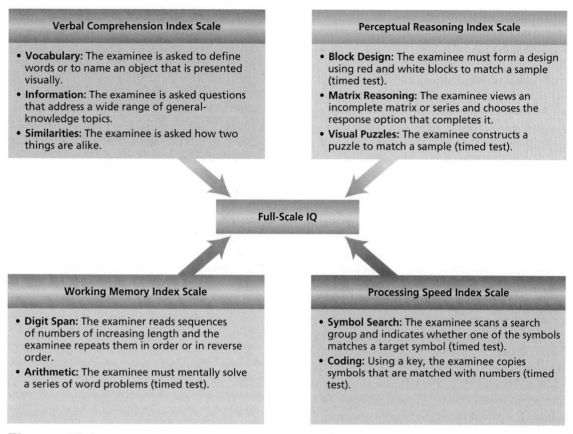

Verbal Comprehension Index Scale

- **Vocabulary:** The examinee is asked to define words or to name an object that is presented visually.
- **Information:** The examinee is asked questions that address a wide range of general-knowledge topics.
- **Similarities:** The examinee is asked how two things are alike.

Perceptual Reasoning Index Scale

- **Block Design:** The examinee must form a design using red and white blocks to match a sample (timed test).
- **Matrix Reasoning:** The examinee views an incomplete matrix or series and chooses the response option that completes it.
- **Visual Puzzles:** The examinee constructs a puzzle to match a sample (timed test).

Full-Scale IQ

Working Memory Index Scale

- **Digit Span:** The examiner reads sequences of numbers of increasing length and the examinee repeats them in order or in reverse order.
- **Arithmetic:** The examinee must mentally solve a series of word problems (timed test).

Processing Speed Index Scale

- **Symbol Search:** The examinee scans a search group and indicates whether one of the symbols matches a target symbol (timed test).
- **Coding:** Using a key, the examinee copies symbols that are matched with numbers (timed test).

Figure 10.9

Scales and subscales of the Wechsler Intelligence Scale for Adults IV (WAIS-IV).

Source: Based on Coalson & Raiford, 2008.

discrepancies between certain subtest scores (Goldstein, 2000; Strauss et al., 2006).

Increasing the Informational Yield from Intelligence Tests

Revisions of both the Stanford-Binet and the Wechsler scales have been responsive to advances in the understanding of the mental processes that underlie intelligence. The original Stanford-Binet yielded a single IQ score based mainly on verbal items, but today's test samples a wider range of abilities and provides, in addition to a composite IQ score, separate scores for Verbal Reasoning, Abstract/Visual Reasoning, Quantitative Reasoning, and Short-Term Memory. The WISC-IV, used to assess children between ages 6 and 11, provides, in addition to its Full-Scale IQ, separate scores for Verbal Comprehension, Perceptual Organization, Freedom from Distractibility, and Processing Speed. These scores make the tests more useful for understanding test takers' intellectual strengths and weaknesses and possibly planning educational interventions for them. Measurement

of specific abilities is also supported by the finding that as children mature, their general intelligence remains stable, but specific abilities become increasingly more differentiated (Kane & Brand, 2006).

Should We Test for Aptitude or Achievement?

Using written tests for selection purposes highlights an issue that Binet faced and that continues to plague test developers today: should we test a person's abstract "aptitude for learning," or should we test what a person already knows? Consider an example. In selecting applicants for college, we could give students either an **achievement test** *designed to find out how much they have learned so far in their lives,* or we could present them with an **aptitude test** *containing novel puzzle-like problems that presumably go beyond prior learning and are thought to measure applicants' potential for future learning and performance.*

The argument for achievement testing is that it is usually a good predictor of future performance in a similar situation. If a student learned a lot of academic material in high school (and therefore scored well on the test), he or she is likely to also learn a lot in college. The argument against achievement testing is that it assumes that everyone has had the same opportunity to learn the material being tested. In college selection, for example, a given applicant's test score could depend on whether that person went to a good school rather than on his or her ability to learn in college.

The argument for aptitude testing is that it is fairer because it supposedly depends less on prior knowledge than on a person's ability to react to the problems presented on the test. The argument against aptitude testing is that it is difficult to construct a test that is independent of prior learning. Further, such a test may require an ability to deal with puzzles that is not relevant to success in situations other than the test itself.

In fact, most intelligence tests measure a combination of aptitude and achievement, reflecting both native ability and previous learning (Lubinski, 2004). This has raised major scientific and social issues concerning the meaning of test scores, the extent to which improvement can be fostered by educational experiences, and the usefulness of the measures for describing mental competence and predicting performance in nontest situations.

Tests of mental skills have become a staple of Western societies. They are used to make important educational, occupational, and clinical decisions, as well as to set social policy. These measures also have become important scientific tools for cognitive psychologists who study the development, stability, operation, and modification of cognitive functions. We will now consider the scientific standards required for psychological tests.

Psychometric Standards for Intelligence Tests

A **psychological test** is a method for measuring individual differences related to some psychological concept, or construct, based on a sample of relevant behavior in a scientifically designed and controlled situation. In the case of intelligence testing, intelligence is the construct and scores obtained on the test are its operational definition. To design a test, we need to decide which specific behaviors serve as indicators of intellectual abilities. Then we need to devise test items that allow us to assess individual differences in those behaviors. We will, of course, need evidence that our sample of items (a sample, because we can't ask every conceivable question) actually measures the abilities we are assessing. As in designing an experiment (see Chapter 2), we want to collect a sample of relevant behavior under standardized conditions, attempting to control for other factors that could influence responses to the items. To understand how psychologists meet these requirements, we must examine three key measurement concepts: reliability, validity, and standardization. We should note that these standards apply to all psychological tests, not just intelligence measures.

Reliability

Reliability refers to consistency of measurement. As shown in Table 10.4, reliability can take several forms when applied to psychological tests. It can refer to consistency of measurement over time, consistency of measurement by the items within the test itself, or consistency in scores assigned by different examiners.

One of the most important is consistency over time. If you step on your bathroom scale five

Table **10.4** | Types of Reliability and Validity in Psychological Testing

Types of Reliability	Meaning and Critical Questions
Test-retest reliability	Are scores on the measure stable over time?
Internal consistency	Do all of the items on the measure seem to be measuring the same thing, as indicated by high correlations among them?
Interjudge reliability	Do different raters or scorers agree on their scoring or observations?
Types of Validity	
Construct validity	To what extent is the test actually measuring the construct of interest (e.g., intelligence)?
Content validity	Do the questions or test items relate to all aspects of the construct being measured?
Criterion-related validity	Do scores on the test predict some present or future behavior or outcome assumed to be affected by the construct being measured?

times in a row, you should expect it to register the same weight each time, unless you have a very unusual metabolism. Likewise, if we assume that intelligence is a relatively stable trait (and virtually all psychologists do), then scores on our measure should be stable, or consistent, over time. This type of measurement stability over time is defined as **test-retest reliability,** *which is assessed by administering the measure to the same group of participants on two (or more) separate occasions and correlating the two (or more) sets of scores.*

After about age 7, scores on intelligence tests show considerable stability, even over many years (Gregory, 1998). Over a short interval (2 to 12 weeks), the test-retest correlation of adult IQs on the WAIS-IV is .95, or nearly perfect (Coalson & Raiford, 2008). Correlations between IQs at age 9 and age 40 are in the .70 to .80 range (Plomin & Spinath, 2004), indicating a high degree of stability. In a Scottish national sample, scores on a test of general intelligence administered at age 11 correlated .66 with scores on the same test at age 80 (Deary et al., 2004). Thus, *relative to his or her age group,* a person who achieves an above-average IQ at age 9 or 11 is very likely to also be above the average for 40- or 80-year-olds when he or she reaches those ages. Even while children's cognitive skills are developing rapidly during middle childhood, IQs are quite stable, with test-retest coefficients around .90 (Canivez & Watkins, 1998).

Another form of reliability, **internal consistency,** *has to do with consistency of measurement within the test itself.* For example, if a Wechsler subtest is internally consistent, all of its items are measuring the same skill, as evidenced by high correlations among the items. In accord with this requirement, the individual items within the Wechsler subtests correlate substantially with one another (Gregory, 1998).

Finally, **interjudge reliability** *refers to consistency of measurement when different people observe the same event or score the same test.* Ideally, two psychologists who independently score the same test will assign exactly the same scores. To attain high interjudge reliability, the scoring instructions must be so explicit that trained professionals will use the scoring system in the same way.

Validity

As a general concept, **validity** *refers to how well a test actually measures what it is designed to measure.* As in the case of reliability, there are several types of validity (see Table 10.4).

As noted earlier, intelligence is a concept, or mental construct. **Construct validity** *exists when a test successfully measures the psychological construct it is designed to measure, as indicated by relations between test scores and other behaviors that it should be related to.* If an intelligence test had perfect construct validity, individual differences in IQs would be due to differences in intelligence and nothing else. In reality, this ideal is never attained, since other factors such as motivation and educational background also influence test scores.

Two other kinds of validity contribute to construct validity. **Content validity** *refers to whether the items on a test measure all the knowledge or skills that are assumed to underlie the construct of interest.* For example, if we want the Arithmetic subtest of the WAIS-IV to measure general mathematical reasoning skills, we would not want to have only addition problems; we would want the items to sample other relevant mathematical abilities as well, such as subtraction, division, and fractions.

If an intelligence test is measuring what it is assumed to measure, the IQ it yields should allow us to predict other behaviors that are assumed to be influenced by intelligence, such as school grades or job performance. These outcome measures are called *criterion measures,* and **criterion-related validity** *refers to the ability of test scores to correlate with meaningful criterion measures.* A critical issue for intelligence tests is the extent to which they predict the kinds of outcomes we would expect intelligence to influence, such as school and job performance. Let us examine this aspect of validity.

Intelligence and Academic Performance Intelligence tests were originally developed to predict academic and other forms of achievement. How valid are they for this purpose? Actually, they do fairly well and far better than personality factors do (Kaia et al., 2007). Correlations of IQ with school grades are in the .60 range for high school students and in the .30 to .50 range for college students (Kuncel et al., 2004). In general, then, people who score well on the tests tend to do well academically. Likewise, the college-entrance examination you took while in high school is designed to predict the criterion of grades in college by assessing verbal and mathematical abilities. In fact, SAT scores do predict college grades, with correlations slightly below .50 (Willingham et al., 1990). This correlation, which is about the same magnitude as the correlation between people's height and weight, is high enough to justify using the tests for screening purposes but low enough to necessitate the use of other predictors (such as high school grades) in combination with SAT scores.

Another measure of general intelligence used in selecting graduate students, the Miller Analogies Test, successfully predicts a variety of performance criteria, including grades, faculty ratings, comprehensive examination scores, and number of years required to attain the advanced degree, with validity coefficients ranging from .35 to .58 (Kuncel et al., 2004). There is little doubt that measures of intelligence successfully predict academic performance.

Job Performance, Income, and Longevity Intelligence test scores also predict military and job performance. General mental ability predicts both occupational level and performance within one's chosen occupation (Schmidt & Hunter, 2004). Intelligent individuals are far more likely to attain prestigious occupations. One study followed siblings raised together, thereby controlling for home background. When the siblings were in their late 20s, mental ability measures collected during young adulthood were related to their annual adult incomes. Siblings with IQs of 120 or more were, on average, earning $18,000 more than siblings of average intelligence (Murray, 1998). Intelligence correlates .50 to .70 with the level of socioeconomic status that people attain in adulthood (Lubinski, 2004).

People with higher intelligence perform better on their jobs, and the more complex the job, the more strongly intelligence is related to performance (Hunter & Hunter, 1984). The relation is particularly striking during the job-training period, when the superior learning ability of highly intelligent people helps them shine (Schmidt & Hunter, 2004). Furthermore, intelligence predicts job performance better than does job experience, specific abilities, or personality traits (Schmidt & Hunter, 2004). On a broader level, national IQ predicts technological achievement and national economic success (Gelade, 2008).

Intelligence predicts other life outcomes as well. People high in intelligence show better recovery from brain injuries (Stern, 2006). Moreover, intelligence literally predicts life and death. In 1932 every child in Scotland who had been born in 1921 was administered an intelligence test. These children and another similar-age cohort of children tested in 1947 were followed as their lives unfolded (Deary et al., 2004). Higher childhood intelligence was associated with significantly greater

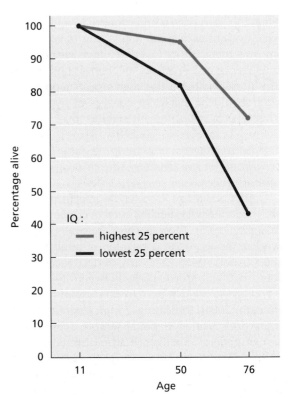

Figure 10.10

Does intelligence predict life span?
This graph shows the relation between IQ assessed at age 11 and survival at ages 50 and 76 in women followed in the Scottish Mental Survey. Source: Data from Whalley & Deary, 2001.

survival to age 76 in both men and women, but the results were particularly striking for women (Figure 10.10). Another sample of 11,603 Scots born in the 1950s shows a similar pattern (Leon et al., 2009).

How shall we account for these results? Is it possible that cognitive ability is a reflection of general fitness to survive (Der et al., 2009)? The researchers suggest the possibility that lower childhood intelligence may in some cases be influenced by prenatal or postnatal events that also impair later health. Or perhaps good brain development is related to optimal development of other bodily organs as well. But it is also possible that intelligent people are more likely to engage in healthy behaviors and to avoid unhealthy ones, or that higher intelligence allows people to live and work in safer physical environments or to enjoy better nutrition, thereby helping them live longer and healthier lives.

Standardization

The third measurement requirement, **standardization,** *has two meanings: (1) the development of* *norms and (2) rigorously controlled testing proce-dures.* The first meaning of standardization is especially important in providing a meaningful IQ score. It involves the collection of **norms,** *test scores derived from a large sample that represents particular age segments of the population.* These normative scores provide a basis for interpret-ing a given individual's score, just as the dis-tribution of scores in a course exam allows you to determine how well you did relative to your classmates. Normative data also allow us to re-calibrate the distribution of test scores so that an IQ of 100 will remain the "average" score even if the general population's test performance changes over time.

When norms are collected for mental skills (and for many other human characteristics), the scores usually form a **normal distribution,** *a bell-shaped curve with most scores clustering around the center of the curve.* On intelligence tests, the center of the distribution for each age group from childhood to late adulthood is assigned an IQ score of 100. Because the normal distribution has known statistical properties, we can specify what percentage of the population will score higher than a given score. Thus, as Figure 10.11 shows, an IQ score of 100 cuts the distribution in half, with an equal percentage of the popula-tion scoring above and below this midpoint. The farther we move from this average score of 100 in either direction, the fewer people attain the higher or lower scores. The figure also shows the percentage of people who score above cer-tain IQ levels. On modern intelligence tests, this method of assigning an IQ score has replaced the original formula of mental age divided by chronological age.

The Flynn Effect: Are We Getting Smarter?

The relative nature of the IQ allows its meaning to be preserved even if performance changes within the population. A notable discovery by New Zealand researcher James Flynn (1987, 1998) suggests that much of the world's population is scoring progressively higher on intelligence tests. This "rising-curve" phenomenon (also called the *Flynn effect*) has resulted in IQ increases of 28 points in the United States since 1910 and a similar increase in Britain since 1942. On average, IQs in the West have increased about 3 points per decade, meaning that today's average IQ would be about 115 if the tests were scored according to the norms used in 1955. The increase seems to be occurring to the same degree for both men and women and for different ethnic groups (Truscott & Frank, 2001).

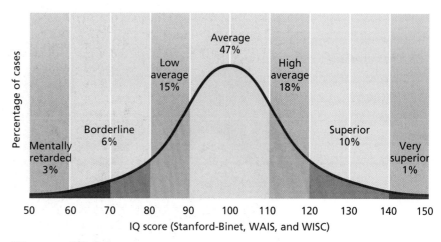

Figure 10.11

The bell curve of intelligence.

When administered to large groups of people, intelligence tests yield a normal, or bell-shaped, distribution of IQ scores that has known statistical properties. The mean of the distribution is set at 100. It is possible to specify for any given score which percentage of the standardization group achieved higher or lower scores. Common descriptive labels are shown relative to the bell-shaped distribution. The range of scores from 90 to 110 is labeled average and includes nearly half of the population.

The reasons underlying the Flynn effect are not clear, but several possibilities have been sug-gested (Flynn, 1998; Neisser et al., 1998). One possibility is that better nutrition has helped fuel the IQ increase. Height has also increased dramatically over the past century, and it, like increased brain functioning, may be due to nu-tritional gains (Lynn, 2009). Other explanations focus on the environment. Richer and more com-plex learning environments that require more complex coping may have increased mental abili-ties. Likewise, technological advances may have helped shape the kinds of analytical and abstract reasoning skills that boost performance on intel-ligence tests. Whatever the reasons, however, the rising-curve phenomenon means that the intel-ligence score distribution has to be recalibrated upward periodically if the average IQ is to re-main at 100, the traditional midpoint of the intel-ligence range.

Testing Conditions: Static and Dynamic Testing

Test instructions and procedures are designed to create a well-controlled, or standardized, en-vironment for administering the intelligence test so that other uncontrolled factors will not influ-ence scores. Tests like the Stanford-Binet and Wechsler scales have very detailed instructions that must be closely adhered to, even to the point of reading the instructions and items to the per-son being tested (Figure 10.12). The goal is to make sure that all testees are responding to as similar a stimulus situation as possible so that

Figure 10.12

When administering intelligence tests, psychologists use consistently applied instructions and procedures in order to create a standardized testing environment.

their scores will be solely a reflection of their ability. *This traditional approach to testing is called* **static testing.**

Some theorists suggest that the static approach to testing may reveal an incomplete picture of a person's abilities by measuring only the products of previous learning. In **dynamic testing,** *the standard testing is followed up with an interaction in which the examiner gives the respondent guided feedback on how to improve performance and observes how the person utilizes the information.* This part of the session provides a window to the individual's ability to profit from instruction and improve performance, and may disclose cognitive capacities not revealed by static testing.

Let's look in on a dynamic testing session with a 5-year-old child who is being tested for educational purposes. Daniel is impulsive in the classroom, and the teacher wants to know how best to instruct him. The child has been asked to draw a picture of a person (a task common to several

intelligence tests) and has hurriedly scribbled a poorly formed figure that merits a low score. The examiner wants to see how much Daniel can improve with feedback:

> Wow, Daniel. I can really tell that that's a boy. I see a head, two arms, and two legs. He even looks like he could be running, because his legs are kind of bent. Now we're going to work together to see if we can get this picture to look more like a boy. I think we need to think real hard about some more parts that people have and just where they need to go. I also noticed that you did this really fast, and that made this look kind of wobbly. So I'm going to help you slow down a bit so you can make this boy stand really straight. (Lidz, 1997, p. 283)

By testing the limits of Daniel's competencies and his ability to profit from various kinds of feedback, the dynamic tester may gain a fuller picture of his mental skills and may be able to make better educational recommendations. Dynamic testing can be particularly useful when people have not had equal learning opportunities, as occurs in disadvantaged groups. Equally important is the fact that dynamic feedback tends to improve test scores, and these new scores often relate more highly to educational outcomes than do the original test scores (Lidz, 1997). Dynamic testing can be particularly useful and revealing when testing people from cultures that are not accustomed to taking Western-style tests (Sternberg, 2004).

Assessing Intelligence in Non-Western Cultures

Special challenges await the psychologist who wants to assess intelligence in non-Western cultures. Traditional intelligence tests such as the WAIS and the Stanford-Binet draw heavily on the cognitive skills and learning that are needed to succeed in Western educational and occupational settings. They tend to have strong verbal content and to rely on the products of Western schooling. Taken into a cultural context where *smart* is defined in different ways and requires other kinds of adaptive behavior, such tests cannot hope to measure intelligence in a valid fashion. For example, the WAIS does not measure the ability to create herbal medicines, construct shelters, or navigate in the open sea. Robert Sternberg (2004) has advanced a *theory of successful intelligence* in which intelligence is whatever

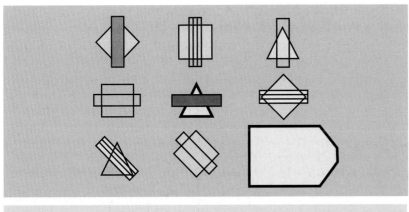

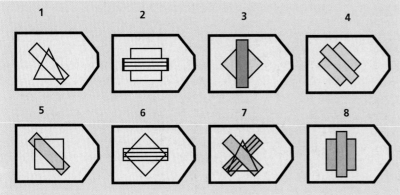

Figure 10.13

Culture-fair measurement?
This problem is similar to those on the Raven Progressive Matrices test. This nonverbal measure tests fluid-intelligence ability, requiring subjects to perceive relationships and decipher the rules underlying the pattern of drawings in the rows and columns of the upper figure and then to select the figure that is the missing entry from the eight alternatives below. (The answer appears on page 353.) SOURCE: Carpenter et al., 1990.

is required to meet the adaptive demands of a given culture. Sternberg believes that fundamental mental skills (the metacomponents described earlier) are required for successful behavior in any culture. These include the ability to mentally represent problems in a way that facilitates their solution, to develop potential solutions and to choose successfully among them, to utilize mental resources wisely, and to evaluate the effects of one's action plans. What differs is the kinds of problems to which these basic intellectual skills are applied. People from different cultures may think about the same problem in very different ways (Nisbett, 2003).

Two main approaches have been taken to meet the challenges of cross-cultural intelligence assessment. One is to choose reasoning problems that are not tied to the knowledge base of any culture but that reflect the ability to process and evaluate stimulus patterns. The problem shown in Figure 10.13 resembles one on the Raven Progressive Matrices, a test that is frequently used to measure fluid intelligence (Raven, 1962). On this nonverbal task, you must detect relationships and then decipher the rules underlying the pattern of drawings in the rows and columns of the upper figure. Finally, you must use this information to select the figure that is the missing entry from the eight alternatives below. The Raven test has been used in many cultures and measures a general mental capacity that is also measured by traditional intelligence tests in our culture (Jensen, 1998). Scores on the Raven correlate positively with measures of IQ derived from traditional tests, yet they seem to be more "culture fair." Can you solve Figure 10.13?

A second and more challenging approach is to create measures that are tailored to the kinds of knowledge and skills that are valued in the particular culture. Such tests may measure how smart an individual is in terms of the practical skills and adaptive behaviors within that culture. Scores may be unrelated or even negatively correlated with other measures of intelligence, yet they may predict successful functioning within that culture (Sternberg, 2004). If intelligence is defined as the ability to engage in culture-specific adaptive behavior, then who is to say that the culture-specific measure is not a valid measure of intelligence in that context?

Myth or Reality?

Brains Are Like Engines: Bigger Means More Power

If people with big heads have big brains, does that mean they are smarter than people with smaller heads? This question is not new. More than 100 years ago, Sir Francis Galton proposed a link between brain size and intellectual competency. Today, this notion continues to intrigue contemporary scientists.

In the animal kingdom, brain size and complexity is clearly related to mental capacity. We also know from evolutionary evidence that the brain size of humanoid species has increased over the ages. Particularly evident is growth in the parts of the brain involved in higher mental functions, especially the cerebral cortex and frontal lobes (Kolb & Whishaw, 2005). Considering the advances of modern civilization, one would conclude that today's humans are smarter than earlier, smaller-brained humanoids. But can we apply the correlation between brain size and intellectual competency to individual humans? Are you smarter than someone else because you wear a bigger baseball cap?

Historically, researchers, beginning with Galton, found that brain size is minimally related to intelligence. And other findings did not support a correlation between brain size and intellectual competency. For example:

- Neandertals, ancient humans hardly known for their intellectual brilliance, had slightly larger brains than we do (Kolb & Whishaw, 2005).
- Women and men have virtually identical mean IQs, but women's brains are smaller on average (Ankney, 1992).
- After Albert Einstein's death in 1955, a Missouri physician removed and preserved his brain. The brain has undergone several analyses by neuroscientists over the years. The examinations have shown that Einstein's brain was *not* larger than average overall; in fact, it was actually smaller than average in some regions (Witelson et al., 1999).

Historically, one of the problems that dogged researchers studying brain size was the difficulty of taking good measurements. Until the 1990s, researchers based estimates of brain size on size of the skull. Though skull size and brain volume are correlated, this is hardly a precise measure of brain size (Luders et al., 2009). Using this method, correlations of about .20 are typically found, suggesting a very modest relationship between brain volume and intelligence (Rushton & Davison, 2009).

With the advent of brain-imaging technology, particularly MRI-based methods, it is now possible to precisely measure overall brain size. In recent years, reviews of studies involving numerous independent samples have shown that the correlation between brain size and intelligence is substantially higher than previously assumed—in the .35 to .45 range, and as high as .60 when the most precise measures of general intelligence (*g* factor) are used (Haier et al., 2009; McDaniel, 2005; Rushton & Davison, 2009). Similar relations exist for all age and sex groups that have been studied.

So, Size Does Matter

But, as any car owner knows, power is not solely dependent on how big your engine is. Likewise, most modern neuroscientists believe that it's not only how large your brain is but also how efficiently it functions that matters. It's not just *quantity* but also *quality* that matters. For example, in addition to measuring brain size, MRI scans can show us the thickness of the cerebral cortex and concentrations of gray and white matter in specific areas of the brain. In a recent study, thickness of the cerebral cortex, particularly in the prefrontal, frontal, and parietal areas, was significantly correlated with both fluid and crystallized intelligence in a sample of young adults (Colom et al., 2008). There was some degree of specificity in the areas related to crystallized and fluid intellectual performance, as well as evidence for a *g* factor involving networks distributed throughout the brain. In the case of Albert Einstein's brain, histological examination showed that his parietal lobes were densely packed with both neurons and glial cells, which produce nutrients for neurons and support them. As a result, his parietal lobes were about 15 percent wider than normal. So densely was this brain area packed that some major fissures were no longer visible. Significantly, this area of the brain is involved in mathematical thinking and visuospatial functions—precisely the abilities that seemed to underlie Einstein's creative genius (Jung & Haier, 2007; Witelson et al., 1999).

But It's More Than Just Size

Most modern neuroscientists believe that both brain size *and* brain efficiency matter. For example, PET scan studies of brain metabolism taken while participants engaged in problem-solving tasks have shown lower levels of neuronal glucose consumption in people of high intelligence than in those of average or low intelligence, suggesting that intelligent brains work more efficiently and expend less energy (Haier et al., 1993). Intelligence also involves speed of processing, which relates to the efficiency of neural connections (Hunt, 2007).

Genetically influenced individual differences in brain *plasticity*—the ability of the brain to change by forming new connections among neurons in response to environmental input—may be a key neural factor underlying differences in intelligence (Luders et al., 2009; Rushton & Davison, 2009). The ability to quickly establish new neural networks would speed the learning process and increase processing speed and efficiency. People with brains capable of greater plasticity would therefore develop better intellectual skills. Recent evidence suggests that there may be a critical period for the growth of new neural circuits that ends at about age 16, the same age by which crystallized intelligence seems to achieve stability (Garlick, 2002).

We must remind ourselves, however, that we are talking about correlations between intellectual functioning and the newly developed measures of brain size and efficiency. Thus we face the familiar direction-of-causality question. Does larger brain mass cause higher intelligence, do lots of "intelligent" interactions with the environment facilitate brain growth, do they each influence one another as the brain and environment interact, or do other factors influence both brain mass and intelligence? The answers to these questions promise to expand our understanding of both intelligence and the brain.

The Measurement of Intelligence

Answer to the problem in Figure 10.13:

The correct choice is geometric form number 5. Can you specify why?

True or false?

1. Traditional intelligence tests measure both aptitude and achievement.
2. The Kaufman tests provide scores for both crystallized and fluid intelligence.
3. IQ scores show strong stability over many years.
4. IQ scores correlate about .60 with both high school and college grades.
5. Validity refers to consistency of measurement.
6. Brain size is moderately correlated with intelligence.

ANSWERS: 1-true, 2-true, 3-true, 4-false, 5-false, 6-true

HEREDITY, ENVIRONMENT, AND INTELLIGENCE

Genes and environment both influence intelligence, but they rarely operate independently of one another. The environment can influence how genes express themselves, as when prenatal factors or malnutrition retard gene-directed brain development. Likewise, genetic factors can influence the effects produced by the environment. For example, genetic factors influence which environments people select for themselves, how they respond to the environment, and how the environment responds to them (Plomin & Spinath, 2004; Scarr & McCartney, 1983).

As we saw in Chapter 3, intelligence clearly has a strong genetic component, with heritability coefficients between .50 and .70 being reported consistently in both twin and adoption studies (Plomin et al., 2007). This indicates that more than half, and perhaps more than two thirds, of the within-group variation in IQ is attributable to genetic factors. Overall, the pattern is quite clear: The more genes people have in common, the more similar they tend to be in IQ. In identical twins, the IQ correlation remains at about .80 from age 4 through adulthood. In adulthood, correlations for fraternal twins drop to around .40. Doubling this difference in correlations yields a heritability coefficient of .80 in adulthood, indicating that genetic factors become even more important as we age (Plomin & Spinath, 2004). One reason may be that new genes come on line to affect intelligence as more-advanced cognitive processes emerge during development. Another is that genetic influences snowball during development as people create and select environments that are compatible with their genetic characteristics.

Although genes are important foundations of the g factor (Plomin et al., 2007), there clearly is not a single "intelligence gene." The diverse abilities measured by intelligence tests are undoubtedly influenced by large numbers of interacting genes, and different combinations seem to underlie specific abilities (Lykken, 2006; Plomin & Spinath, 2004). The newly acquired ability to measure the genome directly has led to a search for specific genes and gene combinations that underlie intelligence. This brings us ever closer to an understanding of the neurological basis for human cognition, and a handful of candidate genes associated with intelligence have already been identified (Posthuma & de Geus, 2006).

Genes are not the whole story, however. As we noted in Chapter 3 (Table 3.2, page 77), IQ correlations for identical twins raised together are slightly higher than those for identical twins raised apart. The same is true for other types of siblings raised together and raised apart. This rules out an entirely genetic explanation. Although one's genotype is an important factor in determining intelligence test scores, environment seems to account for 30 to 50 percent of the IQ variation among people. Both shared and unshared environmental factors are involved. Behavior-genetic studies indicate that between a quarter and a third of the population variability in intelligence can be attributed to shared environmental factors, particularly the family environment (Figure 10.14). The importance of the home environment is also shown in studies of children who are removed from deprived

(a)

(b)

Figure 10.14

Shared family environment has a significant influence on intelligence, accounting for between a quarter and a third of IQ variation in children. The children in (a) are clearly in a more stimulating environment than those in (b).

environments and placed in middle- or upper-class adoptive homes. Typically, such children show a gradual increase in IQ on the order of 10 to 12 points (Scarr & Weinberg, 1977; Schiff & Lewontin, 1986). Conversely, when deprived children remain in their impoverished environments, either they show no improvement in IQ or they actually deteriorate intellectually over time (Serpell, 2000). Scores on general intelligence correlate around .40 with the socioeconomic status of the family in which a child is reared (Lubinski, 2004).

Recall also the Flynn effect, the notable IQ increases that have occurred in Western countries during the last century. It's highly unlikely that genetic changes can explain such gains. More likely, they are due to better and longer schooling over the past century, more-complex and stimulating environments provided by better-educated parents, technological advances (even television and video games), and better nutrition (Greenfield, 1998). Although the environment we live in may be more complex, fast-paced, and stressful than it was a century ago, it is also more conducive to learning the mental skills that are assessed on measures of intelligence.

As we might expect, educational experiences can have a significant positive impact on intelligence. Many studies have shown that school attendance can raise IQ and lack of attendance can lower scores (Ceci & Williams, 1997). It appears that the opportunity to practice mental skills like those assessed on cognitive tests is important in solidifying mental skills. Research on intelligence has had a strong impact on educational

curricula, and much has been learned about what, when, and how to teach. School-related gains in intelligence are most likely to be observed under the following conditions (Mayer, 2000; Nisbett, 2009):

- Rather than "teaching to" general mental ability, help students learn the specific cognitive skills and problem-solving approaches that underlie success in particular subjects. This is an outgrowth of education's increasing de-emphasis on the *g* factor and renewed emphasis on the development of specific mental skills.

- Replace the traditional emphasis on repetition and rote learning of facts with instruction in *how* to learn, critically think about, and apply course content. In this approach, teachers function as "mental coaches."

- Rather than waiting until low-level skills have been mastered before teaching learning tools such as memory-enhancement strategies, apply this "learning to learn" approach from the very beginning so that the skills are applied to even the most basic course content.

Many children begin their lives in conditions that are not conducive to developing intellectual skills. An important outgrowth of intelligence research is the attempt to intervene early in the lives of such children. Let us examine several of these programs and what they've accomplished.

Applying Psychological Science

Early-Childhood Interventions: A Means of Boosting Intelligence?

The belief that early-childhood education can influence the life success of poor children can be found in the 18th-century writings of the French social philosopher Jean Jacques Rousseau. In the United States today, that belief translates into the annual expenditure of more than $10 billion on early-intervention programs designed to reverse the downward course of cognitive and social development, school dropout rate, and joblessness that is so often seen in children from low-income families (Ramey et al., 1998).

In the 1960s, researchers and educators began to design early-childhood intervention programs such as Head Start in an attempt to compensate for the limited learning environments of disadvantaged children. Head Start began as a summer program and gradually increased in scope. But even when it was extended to a full school year, Head Start was only a half-day program that did not begin until age 4. The results were disappointing. Within 2 years, Head Start children were performing in school no better than children who had not attended Head Start (McKey et al., 1985).

What had gone wrong? Was the Head Start program too little, too late? How much might a more intensive program begun earlier in life help disadvantaged children? These questions inspired several notable intervention programs, namely, the Abecedarian Program and the High/Scope Perry Preschool Program.

Participants in the Abecedarian Program were healthy infants born to impoverished families in a southern U.S. community. Many were African American. The children were randomly assigned to an experimental preschool program or to a control group whose families received normal social services. The preschool group was given an intensive early-childhood educational program beginning when they were 6 months old and continuing until they began kindergarten at 5 years of age. Within an educational child-care setting, highly trained preschool personnel exposed the children to many stimulating learning experiences designed to foster the growth of cognitive skills (Figure 10.15). At age 5, the preschool program ended, but half of the preschool children and half of the control children were enrolled in a special home-and-school educational program during the first 3 years of school. This experimental design allowed the researchers to test the effects of early versus later intervention.

The long-term effects of the program have now been evaluated. By the time the children had been in the program for 1 year, they tested 18 IQ points higher than the control group. By age 15, the IQ advantage of the children in the preschool condition had decreased to about 5 points, but they also had higher scores on standardized tests of reading and mathematics than did the control-group children. Only about half as many had been held back a grade or placed in special education.

A particularly notable IQ effect was found for children in the preschool condition whose mothers were mentally retarded, having IQs below 70. In this sample, every one of the children who had the early intervention attained an IQ at least 20 points higher than their mother's, with an average difference of 32 IQ points. No such effect was found in the control group (Landesman & Ramey, 1989).

Figure 10.15

The Abecedarian program provided intensive preschool learning experiences for low-income high-risk children. Here a trainer in an early-intervention program teaches number concepts to a preschool child.

A difference of this magnitude is truly remarkable for children of mentally retarded parents, one reason being that such parents are unable to provide much in the way of intellectual stimulation for their children. Apparently, the preschool program provided the environmental stimulation needed for normal intellectual development to occur.

What of the control-group children who did not attend the preschool program but were exposed to the special program from 5 to 8 years of age? This delayed training had little effect on any of the outcome measures. Also, the later training had almost no added effects on the children who had been in the preschool program. It thus appears that early intervention has a much stronger effect than does later training. By the time disadvantaged children are in school, it may be too late to influence their future cognitive development to any great degree (Ramey & Ramey, 1998).

The Abecedarian Program showed positive intervention effects that were still apparent in adolescence. What effect does early intervention have on later adult functioning? Here, we turn to another program, the High/Scope Perry Preschool Program, carried out with African American children who lived in an impoverished area of Ypsilanti, Michigan. The participants were considered at high risk for educational and social problems. They were 2 or 3 years old when they were matched on IQ and family variables and randomly assigned either to an intensive preschool program or to a control group that did not receive the program. The intervention continued for 3 years.

Continued

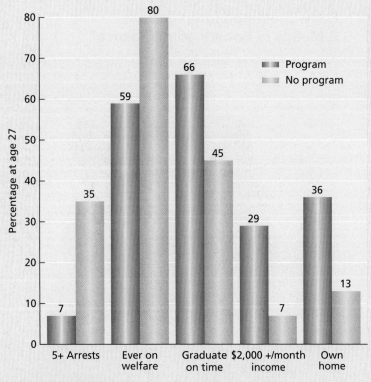

Figure 10.16

Effects of early intervention.
This graph shows the differences by age 27 between disadvantaged children who received the High/
Scope Perry Preschool Program and matched control children. Source: Schweinhart & Weikart, 1998.

The two groups of children have been followed up into adulthood, and the results are encouraging. Figure 10.16 compares what happened to the two groups in the 22 years after the program ended. The early-education group had lower crime rates, required less welfare assistance, exhibited better academic performance and progress, and had higher incomes and home ownership. A cost-benefit analysis showed that the early-intervention program provided taxpayers with a return of $7.16 for every dollar invested in the program (Schweinhart & Weikart, 1998).

Does early intervention work? The Abecedarian and High/Scope Perry programs suggest that it can provide social, intellectual, educational, and psychological dividends if the program is intensive enough and administered very early in life (Masten & Coatsworth, 1998; Reppucci et al., 1999). A more recent early-intervention program conducted with low-birth-weight children, also considered at risk for later cognitive impairment and academic failure, showed significant IQ gains of 7 to 10 points, but only for those children who had attended the program for at least 400 days between the ages of 2 and 3 (Hill et al., 2003). We should also note that the positive effects of early-intervention programs seem to occur only for disadvantaged children, for whom quality programs offer learning opportunities and support that the children would not experience at home. Such programs do little for middle- and upper-class children who already have those resources in their homes (Hetherington, 1998).

GROUP DIFFERENCES IN INTELLIGENCE

Some of the most controversial issues in the study of intelligence revolve around group differences. Ethnic and social-class differences exist, as do differences between men and women. The meaning of these differences—and their political, social, and educational implications—has often sparked bitter debate and, at times, discriminatory policies. It has also inspired stereotypes about certain groups and influenced the self-image of group members.

Ethnic Group Differences

Some of the most contentious debates in psychology have concerned the existence and meaning of ethnic and racial group differences in intelligence. Discussions of intellectual differences between ethnic groups and between men and women touch on deeply held notions of social equality. Because the questions under scrutiny are complex and the evidence does not warrant any simple conclusions, the debate is unlikely to be resolved any time soon.

In 1969, in the midst of the civil rights struggle, an article in the *Harvard Educational Review* by Arthur Jensen sparked debate and, in many quarters, outrage. Jensen concluded that because the heritability of intelligence is substantial, genetic differences are "strongly implicated" in ethnic group differences in intelligence. A quarter century later, in a *New York Times* best seller titled *The Bell Curve*, Richard Herrnstein and Charles Murray (1994) painted a pessimistic picture of the future for ethnic groups that lag behind in genetically influenced mental competencies. Like Jensen's article, *The Bell Curve* evoked considerable controversy.

Where ethnic groups are concerned, everyone agrees on certain facts. Today there are consistent differences in the average intelligence test scores of members of different racial and national groups. National comparisons indicate that Japanese children have the highest mean IQ in the world (Hunt, 1995). Their mean score of 111 places 77 percent of Japanese children above the mean scores of U.S. and European children. Within the United States, significant ethnic differences also exist. Asian Americans test slightly below White American norms on verbal skills but somewhat higher on tests related to spatial and mathematical reasoning. Hispanic people who have become U.S.-acculturated score at about the same level as

White Americans. African Americans score, on average, about 12 to 15 IQ points below the White American average (Jencks & Phillips, 1998).

This, of course, does not mean that all White Americans and Hispanic Americans test lower than Asian Americans or that all African Americans test lower than the other ethnic groups. There is great overlap among group IQ distributions, and in all groups, some individuals score at the highest levels. Nonetheless, the average group differences are large enough to have practical consequences, such as ethnic differences in academic achievement. The unanswered question is, where do these differences come from? Much work is currently underway to separate science from myth (Fish, 2002).

Are the Tests Biased?

Keep in mind that these group differences apply to test scores, which are the standard operational definition of the construct we call *intelligence.* Some have expressed concerns that these tests underestimate the mental competence of minority group members because the tests are based on Euro-American White culture and therefore are culturally biased.

Test bias can actually take two forms (Figure 10.17). **Outcome bias** *refers to the extent that a test underestimates a person's true intellectual ability.* **Predictive bias** *occurs if the test successfully predicts criterion measures, such as school or job performance, for some groups but not for others* (Serpell, 2000).

Defenders of intelligence tests dismiss both types of bias. They point out that ethnic group differences appear throughout intelligence tests, not just on those items that would, at face value, appear to be culturally biased (Jensen, 1980, 1998). They also point out that intelligence test scores predict the performance of minority group members as accurately as they predict White people's performance (Barrett & Depinet, 1991; Kuncel et al., 2004). For example, even though African Americans as a group score lower than White Americans, the tests predict academic and occupational performance with equal accuracy for both racial groups, indicating that they are measuring relevant mental skills (Hunt, 1995). Test critics remain unconvinced, asserting that current measures can be outcome-biased in underestimating the mental skills of ethnic minorities.

What Factors Underlie the Differences?

The next dispute about racial differences is a rather different one. The nature-nurture discussion tentatively accepts the differences in measures of mental abilities as being real and then asks why they exist. Consider the differences between White Americans

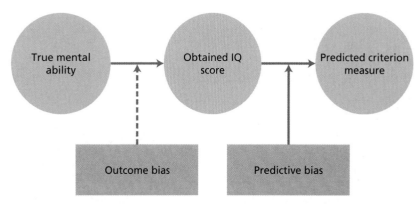

Figure 10.17

Test bias can take two forms. Outcome bias would occur if the nature of the test items significantly underestimated true mental ability because of factors such as cultural relevance. Predictive bias would occur if test scores predicted criterion measures accurately for one group but not for another.

and African Americans. On the nurture side, there is no question that a higher proportion of White American than African American children are raised and schooled in enriched environments that optimize the development of cognitive skills. However, social changes over the past 25 years have provided African Americans with greater access to educational and vocational opportunities and have coincided with an increase in African American IQs that has reduced the IQ difference between African Americans and White Americans by about a third (Barnett & Camilli, 2002). These shrinking ethnic differences also extend to reading and mathematics achievement tests in grades 1 through 12, as well as to SAT scores (Block, 2002).

People who are impressed by this decreasing test gap tend to attribute ethnic differences to environmental differences that could be changed, ranging from nutritional factors to educational opportunities (Grigorenko, 2003; Nisbett, 1998). Meredith Phillips and coworkers (1998) analyzed a wide range of family-environment factors in relation to intellectual differences between 5- and 6-year-old African American and White children. They concluded that family-environment factors alone could account for about two thirds of the test score gap. Figure 10.18 provides an agricultural analogy of how environmental factors (in this case, rich or poor soil) can produce group differences even for a genetically influenced variable.

The key role played by the social environment also may be illustrated by a historical example involving a different minority group. Early in the 20th century, the average Italian American child had an IQ of 87, about the same as the average score of African Americans today. Henry Goddard (1917), a leading hereditarian researcher of the time, concluded that 79 percent of Italian American immigrants were "feebleminded," posed a danger to the U.S. gene pool, and should not be allowed to emigrate to the United States. Today, the average Italian American student has an above-average IQ (Ceci, 1996). Obviously, genetic changes in Italian Americans could not produce

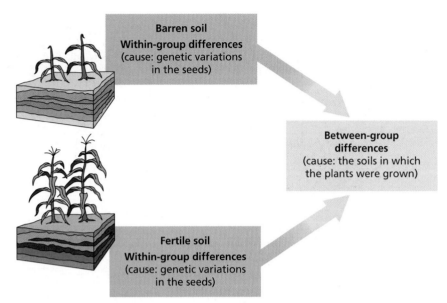

Figure 10.18

Heredity and environment.
The interaction of heredity and environment is shown in this agricultural analogy. Seeds planted in fertile soil will be, on average, larger than those planted in barren soil. This between-group variability is attributable to environment. Within each field, however, plants will also differ in size as a result of genetic factors. Applied to intelligence, this analogy indicates how between-group differences could result from environmental factors despite the fact that intelligence has a strong genetic component.

a gain of this size over such a short time. Cultural assimilation and educational and economic opportunity seem much more reasonable explanations for this pronounced increase in test scores.

Another factor worth noting is a tendency, even among some scientists, to overemphasize genetic differences between groups. Indeed, where measured directly, genetic differences, like test scores, tend to be greater *within* any given racial group than they are between racial groups (Block, 2002). For example, genetic variation is greater among African Americans and among White Americans than it is between the average African American and the average White American.

Do Blacks and Whites differ in their explanations for individual differences in mental skills? Recent research suggests that they do. In one study, 600 Blacks and 600 Whites were administered telephone interviews. During the interviews they were asked how important three sets of factors were in intelligence and mathematical aptitude: genetic ("someone's biological makeup that they get from their mother and father"), environmental ("the society in which they live, the people in their lives, and how they were raised"), and personal choice ("how much someone chooses to be one way or another"). As a group, Whites considered genetic factors most important and personal choice least important, whereas Blacks considered personal choice most important and genetic factors least important. Environmental factors were of intermediate and equal importance for both ethnic groups (Jayaratne et al., 2009). These findings suggest that Whites see mental skills as more fixed and less susceptible to change, whereas Blacks view them as more changeable. The latter result may provide a more fertile ground for messages of personal responsibility that have

been directed at the Black community by President Obama and other Black leaders in recent years and, possibly, for educational interventions directed at this minority population.

Sex Differences in Cognitive Abilities

Men and women differ in physical attributes and reproductive function. They also differ in their performance on certain types of intellectual tasks. The gender differences lie not in levels of general intelligence but rather in the patterns of cognitive skills that men and women exhibit. Men, on average, tend to outperform women slightly on certain spatial tasks, such as the ones shown in Figure 10.19. Men are more accurate in target-directed skills, such as throwing and catching objects, and they tend to perform slightly better on tests of mathematical reasoning. Women, on average, perform better on tests of perceptual speed, verbal fluency, and mathematical calculation and on precise manual tasks requiring fine motor coordination (Collins & Kimura, 1997; Lippa, 2005). Although typically small, these ability differences have been reported quite consistently by researchers (Halpern, 2004; Hines, 2005). Keep in mind, however, that men and women also vary considerably among themselves in all of these skills, and the performance distributions of males and females overlap considerably.

Psychologists have proposed explanations for these gender differences, citing both biological and environmental factors. The environmental explanations typically focus on the socialization experiences that males and females have as they grow up, especially the kinds of sex-typed activities that boys and girls are steered into (Crawford & Chaffin, 1997). Prior to the early 1980s, for example, boys were far more likely than girls to play sports that involve throwing and catching balls, which might help account for their general superiority in this ability. Evolutionary theorists have also weighed in on the differences, suggesting that sex-role specialization developed in ancestral environments. Men's roles, such as navigating and hunting, favored the development of the visuospatial abilities that show up in sex-difference research. Women's roles, such as child-rearing and tool-making activities, favored the development of verbal and manual-precision abilities (Joseph, 2000).

Biological explanations have increasingly focused on the effects of hormones on the developing brain (Halpern & Tan, 2001; Hines, 2005). These influences begin during a critical period shortly after conception, when the sex hormones establish sexual differentiation. The hormonal effects go far beyond reproductive characteristics, however. They also alter brain organization and appear to extend to a variety of behavioral differences between men and women, including aggression and problem-solving approaches (Hines, 2005; Lippa, 2005).

Do hormonal factors also influence cognitive performance later in life? Several studies have shown that fluctuations in women's hormonal levels during the menstrual cycle are related to fluctuations in task performance. When women have high levels of the female hormone estrogen, they perform better on some of the "feminine-ability" measures while showing declines in performance on some of the "male-ability" measures (Kimura, 1992; Moody, 1997). Testosterone levels are related to performance on "male" tasks (Hausmann et al., 2009). However, one study measured a wide range of sex hormones in men and women before they performed a variety of cognitive tasks. Men and women showed the typically reported differences in cognitive skills, but no relations were found between any of the measured hormones and cognitive performance (Halari et al., 2005). Thus the role of sex hormones in adulthood remains unclear. If hormones are involved, they may interact with other variables.

Beliefs, Expectations, and Cognitive Performance

Cognitive abilities are not the only mental determinants of how well people perform on intellectual and academic measures. Beliefs are also very important. Our beliefs about others' capabilities can affect how we respond to them. For example, many studies have shown that if teachers are told that a particular child has hidden potential or, alternatively, intellectual limitations, they increase or decrease the amount of attention and effort expended on that child, thereby influencing the child's development of cognitive skills (Rosenthal, 1985).

Even more important at times are our own self-beliefs, which tell us who we are and what we can and cannot do. Our self-concept is based on numerous experiences that convey to us who we are, how valued we are, and what we are capable of achieving in our lives. Some of this information comes from observing the consequences of our own behavior. But our self-concept can also be influenced by our membership in racial and gender groups. If certain stereotypes are widely associated with these groups, we may incorporate them into our self-concept. Once accepted, these self-beliefs may push us to behave in a way that is consistent with our self-concept. But beliefs also influence group behavior. Group members can experience

Problem-solving tasks favoring women

Women tend to perform better than men on tests of perceptual speed, in which people must rapidly identify matching items—for example, pairing the house on the far left with its twin.

On some tests of ideational fluency, for example those in which people must list objects that are the same color, and on tests of verbal fluency, for example those in which participants must list words that begin with the same letter, women also outperform men.

L _ _ _	Limp, Livery, Love, Laser, Liquid, Low, Like, Lag, Live, Lug, Light, Lift, Liver, Lime, Leg, Load, Lap, Lucid . . .

Problem-solving tasks favoring men

Men tend to perform better than women on certain spatial tasks. They do well on tests that involve mentally rotating an object or manipulating it in some fashion such as choosing which of the 3 objects at the right is the same as the one on the left.

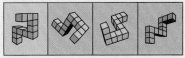

Men also are more accurate than women in target-directed motor skills, such as guiding or intercepting projectiles.

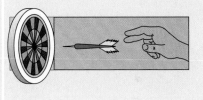

Figure 10.19

Male-female cognitive differences.

Some of the most consistent gender differences in cognitive abilities reported in the scientific literature occur on tasks like these. SOURCE: Adapted from Kimura, 1992.

stereotype threat *if they believe that certain behaviors on their part would confirm a negative stereotype in the minds of others.* Claude Steele (1997) believes that when stereotype threat occurs, it triggers achievement anxiety that undermines performance.

To test this hypothesis, Steele and Judson Aronson (1995) assessed the academic-performance effects of evoking one widely held stereotype: that African Americans have less intellectual ability than do White Americans. Participants were African American and White Stanford University students. In a laboratory setting, the students were administered the most difficult items from the Graduate Record Examination verbal test. There were two experimental conditions that varied the racial relevance of the test. In the experimental condition, the students were told that the test was a measure of intelligence (expected to activate the stereotype of African Americans as being less intelligent than White Americans). In the control condition, the students were told that the items were part of a laboratory task that was unrelated to general intellectual ability. If stereotype threat were activated, we should expect the African American students to perform more poorly relative to Whites in the experimental condition. And that's exactly what occurred. Even when the researchers controlled statistically for preexisting ethnic-group differences in verbal ability by using students' college-entrance SAT scores, the Black-White performance difference on

Figure 10.20

Effects of stereotype threat on cognitive performance.
Activating the stereotype that African Americans have less intellectual ability than White Americans resulted in African American students' poorer performance on a verbal test as compared with the performance by African American students in the control condition in which the stereotype was not activated. SOURCE: Steele, 1997.

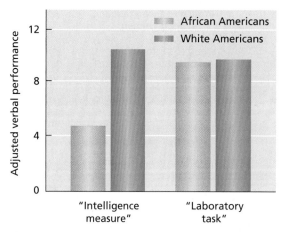

the experimental task was far greater if students thought that the task measured intelligence than if they were told it was unrelated to intelligence (Figure 10.20). Steele concluded that the fear of appearing less intelligent had aroused the anxiety of the Black students, thus lowering their performance. He suggested that stereotype threat could undermine the performance of any group for whom a task was stereotypically relevant, thus serving to actually reinforce the stereotype. More recent studies have shown that a drop in performance occurs only when the stereotype threat being manipulated arouses anxiety in the participants (Delgado & Prieto, 2009).

Earlier, we noted the role of sex hormones in male-female ability differences. We know that hormones can be activated by situational factors. Could such activation play a role in the effects of stereotype threat on performance? Our "Research Close-up" addresses this question.

Research Close-up

Sex Hormones, Gender Stereotypes, and Cognitive Performance

SOURCE: MARKUS HAUSMANN, DANIELA SCHOOFS, HARRIET E. S. ROSENTHAL, and KIRSTEN JORDAN (2009). Interactive effects of sex hormones and gender stereotypes on cognitive sex differences—A psychobiosocial approach. *Psychoneuroendocrinology, 34,* 389–401.

INTRODUCTION

Sex differences in verbal and spatial abilities arise at least in part because of the influence of sex hormones. During prenatal development, sex hormones have an *organizational* influence on physical development, including brain development, that can set the stage for sex differences in certain abilities. After birth, hormones can have *activational* effects on cognitive abilities that persist throughout the life span. Although the research is not entirely consistent, several studies indicate that levels of testosterone within the normal range are related to a male advantage on spatial tasks, particularly the mental-rotation task shown in Figure 10.19. Indeed, a single injection of testosterone can produce enhanced mental-rotation performance in men (Aleman et al., 2004). In women, task performance on female-superior verbal-ability tasks is best when female hormone levels are high.

This study was designed to determine if the activation of a stereotype that favored men over women on the mental-rotation task would enhance male performance (a phenomenon called *stereotype lift*) and depress that of women (*stereotype threat*). Additionally, the researchers wanted to determine whether this pattern of stereotype effects could be explained by the activating effects of testosterone, the male sex hormone that is present in both men and women.

METHOD

The participants were 55 men and 49 women with an average age of 24 years. A four-group design was used in which the men and women were randomly assigned to either an experimental or a control condition. Both groups were asked to imagine that they were about to meet a stranger. They were then given a list of personal descriptions of the stranger. In the experimental condition, designed to bring to mind gender stereotypes, the participants were asked to read each item on

RESEARCH DESIGN

Question: How do gender stereotypes and sex hormones interact to influence performance on a male-relevant cognitive task?

Type of Study: *Experimental/Correlational*

Independent Variables	Dependent Variables
Stereotype activation (manipulated and therefore experimental)	Mental-rotation scores
Sex of Participants (nonmanipulated and therefore correlational)	Testosterone levels

the list and then to indicate whether the stranger was a male or a female. The key item was "can imagine abstract objects and rotate them mentally in all directions." The control group was asked to indicate whether the person was a European or North American instead of whether the person was a man or woman.

Participants were then given several cognitive tests, the one of interest being a series of 24 mental-rotation problems similar to the one shown in Figure 10.19. Many studies have shown that men tend to perform better than women on this spatial-reasoning task. Each problem contained a target figure on the left and four stimulus figures on the right. Two of these stimulus figures were rotated versions of the target figure and two were not. The participant had 3 minutes to identify which figures matched the target figure, the score being based on how many figures were matched correctly. Immediately following the testing session, the participants supplied a saliva sample from which a testosterone reading

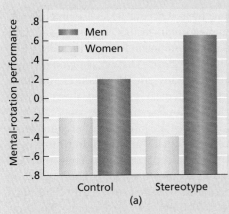
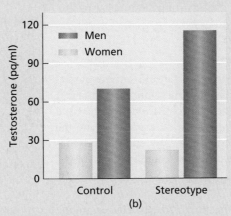

Figure 10.21

Activation of a gender stereotype that favors males resulted in both performance and testosterone-level effects. In (a), mental-rotation task performance was consistent with stereotype threat in women and stereotype lift in men. In (b), male and female testosterone levels closely paralleled the performance results. Source: Data from Hausmann et al., 2009.

was obtained. This design thus allowed the researchers to measure not only how the stereotype manipulation affected the performance of men and women, but also whether performance differences were accompanied by differences in testosterone level.

RESULTS

Both men and women in the experimental condition indicated that the stranger, described as doing well on the mental-rotation task, was more likely to be a male than a female (over 60 percent probability), demonstrating that the gender-stereotype manipulation was successful in evoking that stereotype.

Figure 10.21a shows the mean performance levels of the four groups. The zero point on the vertical axis in Figure 10.21a indicates the mean level of mental-rotation performance for all participants. Overall, males did better on the task, which would be expected. Of greater interest, the pattern of results in the stereotype-activation condition revealed a stereotype lift for men and a stereotype threat for women: the men in the experimental condition did better than their counterparts in the control condition, and the women in the experimental condition did worse than their counterparts in the control condition. In Figure 10.21b, we see the testosterone results, which directly parallel the performance results. Raising awareness of the gender stereotype was associated with higher levels of testosterone in the men in the experimental condition.

CRITICAL DISCUSSION

Previous research has shown that on spatial tasks like mental rotation, men show a performance advantage over women and that both men and women view males as being better at such tasks. Another line of research has shown that in both men and women, levels of the male hormone testosterone are related to performance on spatial tasks such as navigating a maze (Burkitt, 2007). In this study, the researchers investigated the combined roles of gender, gender stereotypes, and testosterone on performance. They found that men and women in their sample viewed the mental-rotation task as more male-relevant. Second, they found that in the control condition, there was no significant difference in performance between men and women. However, when the gender stereotype was activated in the experimental condition, men performed better and women less well than their counterparts in the control condition, a pattern consistent with stereotype lift in males and stereotype threat in females. Finally, they found that testosterone levels in the four conditions closely paralleled the mental-rotation results and that in men, testosterone level was highest in the experimental condition. Although these data are correlational in nature and don't allow us to make a definite causal interpretation, they are consistent with the notion that testosterone level may be a causal factor in stereotype lift and that levels of this sex hormone may increase in men when a gender stereotype favoring males is activated.

These results suggest the need for more research on relations between gender stereotypes, sex hormones, and performance on various cognitive tasks. Of particular interest would be a follow-up study in which a female-superior ability like verbal fluency was tested and measures of female sex hormones were measured in the four conditions. A finding that stereotype activation increased female sex hormone levels and resulted in performance differences suggesting stereotype lift in women and, possibly, stereotype threat in men would provide further evidence for an interacting causal pattern of gender stereotypes and hormones.

test yourself

Heredity, Environment, and Group Differences in Intelligence

True or false?

1. Intelligence exhibits high heritability in the .50 to .70 range.

2. Research has recently identified the gene associated with intelligence.

3. Adopted children from deprived backgrounds show IQ gains of 10 to 12 points in an enriched adoptive environment.

4. Early-intervention programs produce IQ gains only in disadvantaged children.

5. Ethnic group differences in intelligence can be attributed to biased tests that do not predict minority performance.

6. Males show a slight advantage over females on measures of mathematical reasoning.

ANSWERS: 1-true, 2-false, 3-true, 4-true, 5-false, 6-true

EXTREMES OF INTELLIGENCE

Because of the many genetic and environmental influences on intelligence, there are individuals at both ends of the intelligence distribution who have unusual mental abilities. At the upper end are the "intellectually gifted"; at the low end are those labeled "mentally retarded" or "cognitively disabled."

The Intellectually Gifted

At the top end of the intelligence bell curve are the intellectually gifted, whose IQs of 130 or higher place them in the top 10 percent of the population. Their high IQs do not mean that they are good at everything, however. As we might expect from the theories of multiple intelligences, many are enormously talented in one area of mental competence but quite average in other domains. Even with IQs over 150, large discrepancies are often found between verbal and spatial-mathematical skills (Achter et al., 1996). Thus a mathematical prodigy who figures out rules of algebra on his own at age 3 may have relatively unexceptional verbal skills.

What distinguishes the thought processes of the gifted? Some theorists believe that gifted children think in the same way as average children but simply do it much more efficiently (Jackson & Butterfield, 1986). Others disagree. When they see a child capable of memorizing an entire musical score after hearing it once, they conclude that this ability is based on a different quality of thinking that involves great intuition and a passion for the specific domain in which the child excels (Winner, 2000).

Only a small percentage of gifted children attain true eminence in later life. Eminence seems to be a special variety of giftedness. Joseph Renzulli (2002) has studied this rare group, and he believes that their success is a product of three interacting factors. The first is highly developed mental abilities—not only general intelligence but also specific mental abilities related to one's chosen field. Thus Einstein was blessed with unusual mathematical and spatial abilities (but not exceptional verbal skills). The second factor is the ability to engage in creative problem solving—that is, to come up with novel and unconventional ideas, to judge their potential value, and to apply them to challenging problems (Sternberg & Davidson, 2005). The third factor is motivation and dedication. Eminence involves a great deal of elbow grease and a determination to attain the highest levels of performance. Studies of eminent scientists, artists, musicians, writers, and athletes reveal that they tend to work much harder and to dedicate themselves more strongly to excellence than do their less eminent counterparts (Simonton, 2001). Given

that the person has the requisite level of intelligence, these nonintellectual factors become especially important. Many eminent figures, including Sigmund Freud and Charles Darwin, showed no signs of being exceptionally gifted as children, but their motivation and dedication helped them achieve greatness in their professions.

Like children at the low end of the competence continuum, intellectually gifted children often need special educational opportunities. They may become bored in regular classrooms and even drop out of school if they are not sufficiently challenged (Phillipson & McCann, 2007). Yet many school systems have de-emphasized programs for the gifted in the same spirit of egalitarianism that places cognitively challenged children in regular classrooms. Increasingly, parents of gifted children are enrolling their children in special camps and extracurricular programs to provide the needed intellectual stimulation and exposure to peer groups with common interests and abilities (Winner, 2000).

? thinking critically

ARE GIFTED CHILDREN MALADJUSTED?

The image of the introverted, socially awkward, and unhappy "nerd" is familiar to all of us. Gifted children are often depicted in the media as unathletic, interested in intellectual activities that do not excite most students, and socially inept. Is there truth in this stereotype? What would you expect research on gifted children to show? Think about your answer, then see page 366.

Mental Retardation

Approximately 3 to 5 percent of the U.S. population, or about 10 million people, are classified as having mental retardation, or a cognitive disability. The American Psychiatric Association has devised a four-level system that classifies mental retardation as mild, moderate, severe, or profound on the basis of IQ scores. Table 10.5 describes these classifications. As you can see, the vast majority have mild mental retardation, obtaining IQs between about 50 and 70. Most members of this largest group, given appropriate social and educational support, are capable of functioning adequately in mainstream society, holding jobs, and raising families. Progressively greater environmental support is needed as we move toward the profoundly disabled range, where institutional care is usually required.

Children with mild mental retardation can attend school, but they have difficulties in reading, writing, memory, and mathematical computation. Many of these difficulties result from

Table **10.5** | Adaptive Capabilities of Cognitively Challenged People over the Life Span

Category	Percentage of Retarded Population	Characteristics from Birth to Adulthood		
		Birth through Age 5	Age 6 through Age 20	Age 21 and Older
Mild: 50–70 IQ	85	Often not noticed as delayed by casual observer but is slower to walk, feed him- or herself, and talk than most children.	Can acquire practical skills and master reading and arithmetic to a third- to sixth-grade level with special education. Can be guided toward social conformity.	Can usually achieve adequate social, vocational, and self-maintenance skills. May need occasional guidance and support when under unusual social or economic stress.
Moderate: 35–50 IQ	10	Noticeable delays in motor development, especially in speech. Responds to training in various self-help activities.	Can learn simple communication, elementary health and safety habits, and simple manual skills. Does not progress in functional reading or arithmetic.	Can perform simple tasks under sheltered conditions, participate in simple recreation, and travel alone in familiar places. Usually incapable of self-maintenance.
Severe: 20–35 IQ	4	Marked delay in motor development. Little or no communication skill. May respond to training in elementary self-help, such as self-feeding.	Usually walks, barring specific disability. Has some understanding of speech and some response. Can profit from systematic habit training.	Can conform to daily routines and repetitive activities. Needs continuing direction and supervision in protective environment.
Profound: below 20 IQ	1	Gross disability. Minimal capacity for functioning in sensorimotor areas. Needs nursing care.	Obvious delays in all areas of development. Shows basic emotional responses. May respond to skillful training in use of legs, hands, and jaws. Needs close supervision.	May walk, need nursing care, have primitive speech. Usually benefits from regular physical activity. Incapable of self-maintenance.

Reprinted with permission from the *Diagnostic and Statistical Manual of Mental Disorders,* Text Revision. Copyright © 2000, American Psychiatric Association.

poorly developed problem-solving strategies. They often have deficiencies in the executive functions discussed in Chapter 4: reasoning, planning, and evaluating feedback from their efforts (Molfese & Molfese, 2002).

Cognitive disability has a variety of causes: some genetic, some due to other biological factors, and some due to environmental causes. Genetic abnormalities account for about 28 percent of all mental retardation cases (Winnepenninckx et al., 2003). More than 100 different genetic causes of retardation have been identified (Brown & Percy, 2007). For example, *Down syndrome* (formerly called *mongolism*), which is characterized by mild to severe mental disability, is caused by an abnormal division of the twenty-first chromosome pair.

Heritability plays a different role in mild retardation than it does in profound retardation (Plomin & Spinath, 2004). Cases of profound retardation are more likely to be caused by genetic accidents instead of an inherited genotype (Zechner et al., 2001). Therefore, profound retardation does not run in families. In one study of 17,000 children, about one half of 1 percent were profoundly retarded. None of these children's siblings had an IQ below 85, and their mean IQ was 103. In contrast, the siblings of the 1.2 percent who were mildly retarded had mean IQs of 85, and a third of the siblings had IQs below 75 (Nichols, 1984).

Mental disability can also be caused by accidents at birth, such as severe oxygen deprivation (anoxia); and by diseases experienced by the mother during pregnancy, such as rubella or syphilis. Likewise, drugs and alcohol taken by the mother—especially in the first weeks of pregnancy when a woman is often unaware she is pregnant—can cause neural damage and mental retardation. Despite this range of potential causes, in a significant majority (75 to 80 percent) of people with mental retardation, no clear biological cause can be found. Experts theorize that these cases may be due to undetectable brain damage, extreme environmental deprivation, or a combination of the two.

In the United States, federal law requires that children with a cognitive disability, who were formerly segregated into special education classes, be given individualized instruction in the "least restrictive environment." This has resulted in the practice of *mainstreaming,* or *inclusion programs,* which allows many children with cognitive disabilities to attend school in regular classrooms and experience a more normal peer environment (Figure 10.22). Many schools also provide for individualized instruction for such children so that they can receive the special attention they may require.

Figure 10.22

To an increasing extent, children of low intelligence have been included in normal classrooms rather than being confined to special education programs.

Levels of Analysis

Intellectual Functioning

In the preceding chapters, we have seen how humans learn, how they remember what they've learned, and how they think and solve problems. Language, thinking, and intelligent behavior are intimately related to one another and to the processes of learning and memory. As we have also seen, intelligent behavior has many causal factors. We now summarize the biological, psychological, and environmental factors we have discussed in this chapter.

ENVIRONMENTAL LEVEL

- Shared and unshared learning environments that interact with biological reaction range influence intellectual development.
- Cultural factors influence which behavioral capabilities are prized, adaptive, and defined as intelligent.
- Sex roles influence the development of stereotypes concerning sex differences in specific abilities.
- Administration of intelligence measures may place culturally different people at a disadvantage.

BIOLOGICAL LEVEL

- Genetic factors account for significant group variation in intelligence. They help establish a biological reaction range that sets limits on the impact of environmental factors.
- Brain size and neural efficiency are underlying factors for intellectual performance.
- Sex hormones play a role in certain types of mental abilities and appear to contribute to the modest sex differences that exist in certain cognitive abilities.

PSYCHOLOGICAL LEVEL

- There exists a general intelligence factor (*g* factor) that underlies other, more specific abilities.
- Specific cognitive and perceptual skills influence more specific task performance.
- Other cognitive skills underlie personal and emotional intelligence, as well as specific competencies described in Gardner's multiple intelligences and Sternberg's triarchic theory.
- Beliefs, anxieties, and expectations can affect cognitive performance in certain situations. Widely held stereotypes appear to contribute to the group performance differences seen in stereotype threat and stereotype lift.
- Motivational factors clearly influence intellectual outcomes.

Considering Sternberg's triarchic theory, can you formulate a hypothesis about how biological or environmental factors might be related to his definitions of analytical, practical, and creative intelligence?

Chapter Summary

INTELLIGENCE IN HISTORICAL PERSPECTIVE

- Intelligence is the ability to acquire knowledge, to think and reason effectively, and to deal adaptively with the environment.
- Because cultural environments differ in the skills most important for adaptation, cultural conceptions of intelligence may differ markedly.
- Galton's studies of hereditary genius and Binet's methods for measuring differences in children's mental skills were important historical milestones in the study of intelligence.

THE NATURE OF INTELLIGENCE

- The psychometric approach to intelligence attempts to map the structure of intellect and establish how many different classes of mental ability underlie test performance.
- Spearman believed that intelligence is determined both by specific cognitive abilities and by a general intelligence (g) factor that constitutes the core of intelligence. Thurstone disagreed, viewing intelligence as a set of specific abilities.
- Cattell and Horn differentiated between crystallized intelligence, the ability to apply previously learned knowledge to current problems, and fluid intelligence, the ability to deal with novel problem-solving situations for which personal experience does not provide a solution.
- Carroll's three-stratum model is based on reanalyses of hundreds of data sets. Mental abilities are represented at three levels, with general intelligence (g) at the apex and highly specific cognitive and perceptual skills at its base.
- Cognitive process theories of intelligence focus on the elementary information-processing abilities that contribute to intelligence. Sternberg's triarchic theory of intelligence includes a components subtheory that addresses the specific cognitive processes that underlie intelligent behavior.
- Sternberg and Gardner maintain that there are distinct forms of intelligence beyond the traditional concept. Sternberg differentiates between analytical, practical, and creative intelligence, and Gardner proposes nine different kinds of intelligence. More recently, personal and emotional intelligence have also been proposed as legitimate forms of intelligence.

THE MEASUREMENT OF INTELLIGENCE

- Most modern intelligence tests, such as the Wechsler scales, measure an array of mental abilities, including global IQ and verbal and performance IQs. Other scales provide separate scores for crystallized and fluid intelligence and for analytical, practical, and creative intelligence.
- Achievement tests measure what has already been learned, whereas aptitude tests are assumed to measure potential for future learning and performance. Most intelligence tests measure combinations of achievement and aptitude.
- Three important standards for psychological tests are reliability (consistency of measurement over time, within tests, and across scorers), validity (successful measurement of the construct and acceptable relations with relevant criterion measures), and standardization (development of norms and standard testing conditions).
- IQ scores successfully predict a range of academic, occupational, and life outcomes, including how long people live. Such findings indicate that intelligence tests are measuring important adaptational skills.
- The Flynn effect refers to the notable rise in intelligence test scores over the past century, possibly due to better living conditions, more schooling, or more complex environments.
- Dynamic testing provides information that static testing does not, and retest scores sometimes relate more strongly to criterion measures.
- Intelligence testing in non-Western cultures is a challenge. One approach is to use tests that are not tied to any culture's knowledge base. Another approach is to devise tests of the abilities that are important to adaptation in the particular culture. These culture-specific abilities may bear little relation to the mental skills assessed by Western intelligence tests.
- Recent physiological evidence suggests that the brains of intelligent people are larger in general and seem to function more efficiently. Differences in brain plasticity may underlie intelligence.

HEREDITY, ENVIRONMENT, AND INTELLIGENCE

- Intelligence is determined by interacting hereditary and environmental factors. Genes account for between 50 and 70 percent of population variation in IQ. Shared family environment accounts for perhaps one fourth to one third of the variance during childhood, but its effects seem to dissipate as people age. Educational experiences also influence mental skills. Heredity establishes a reaction range with upper and lower limits for intellectual potential.
- Heritability estimates of intelligence can vary, depending on sample characteristics. In impoverished families, shared environment has been found to be more important than genes, whereas the opposite has been found in affluent families. Twin studies have also shown that heritability effects on intelligence increase in adulthood.
- Intervention programs for disadvantaged children have positive effects on later achievement and life outcomes if they begin early in life and are applied intensively. They have little effect when applied after elementary school begins or with middle- or upper-class children.

GROUP DIFFERENCES IN INTELLIGENCE

- Cultural and ethnic differences in intelligence exist (though they may be narrowing), but the relative contributions of genetic and environmental factors are still in question. Evidence exists for both genetic and environmental determinants. Whether intelligence tests exhibit outcome bias in underestimating the mental abilities of minorities is a point of contention, but the tests do not appear to have predictive bias.
- Although the differences are not large, men tend as a group to score higher than women on certain spatial and mathematical reasoning tasks. Women perform slightly better than men on tests of perceptual speed, verbal fluency, mathematical calculation, and fine motor coordination. Both environmental and biological bases of sex differences (including sex hormones) have been suggested. Stereotype threat and stereotype lift are potential psychological factors for both sex-based and ethnic performance differences.

EXTREMES OF INTELLIGENCE

- Even people with IQs in the 150s often show discrepancies between specific skills. Those who achieve eminence tend to have, in addition to high IQs, high levels of interest and motivation in their chosen activities.
- Cognitive disability can range from mild to profound. The vast majority of disabled individuals are able to function in the mainstream of society, given appropriate support.

KEY TERMS AND CONCEPTS

Each term has been boldfaced and defined in the chapter on the page indicated in parentheses.

achievement test (p. 345)
aptitude test (p. 345)
cognitive process theories (p. 341)
construct validity (p. 347)
content validity (p. 347)
criterion-related validity (p. 347)
crystallized intelligence (g_c) (p. 339)
dynamic testing (p. 350)
emotional intelligence (p. 343)
factor analysis (p. 337)
fluid intelligence (g_f) (p. 339)
g factor (p. 338)

intelligence (p. 333)
intelligence quotient (IQ) (p. 335)
interjudge reliability (p. 347)
internal consistency (p. 347)
knowledge-acquisition components (p. 341)
metacomponents (p. 341)
normal distribution (p. 349)
norms (p. 349)
outcome bias (p. 357)
performance components (p. 341)
personal intelligence (p. 343)

predictive bias (p. 357)
psychological test (p. 346)
psychometrics (p. 337)
reliability (p. 346)
standardization (p. 348)
static testing (p. 350)
stereotype threat (p. 359)
test-retest reliability (p. 347)
three-stratum theory of cognitive abilities (p. 340)
triarchic theory of intelligence (p. 341)
validity (p. 347)

? thinking **critically**

ARE GIFTED CHILDREN MALADJUSTED?
(Page 362)

Like the cognitively disabled, the gifted are often the victims of stereotypes. Some characterize them as "geeks" and "nerds" who are eccentric and socially maladjusted. As is the case with many stereotypes, there is a grain of truth here. A review of the scientific literature on giftedness by Ellen Winner (2000) revealed that nearly a fourth of children with truly exceptional IQs at the high end of the gifted range (around 180) have social and psychological problems, about twice the rate found in nongifted children. Such children often have different interest patterns and encounter difficulty finding like-minded peers to relate to, resulting in solitude and loneliness. The research also revealed, however, that the vast majority of these highly intelligent children show adequate adjustment, providing evidence against any stereotype that would be applied to gifted children in general.

Consider also a project begun in the 1920s by Lewis Terman, the psychologist who developed the Stanford-Binet test. Terman identified 1,528 California children who had a mean IQ of 150 and began an extensive study of them that continued for over 70 years. Terman and the researchers who inherited the project found the "Termites," as they were called, to be above average not only in intelligence but also in height, weight, strength, physical health, emotional adjustment, and social maturity. They continued to exhibit high levels of adjustment throughout their adolescent and adult years. By midlife, the 1,528 Termites had authored 92 books, 2,200 scientific articles, and 235 patents. Their marriages tended to be happy and successful, and they seemed well adjusted psychologically (Sears, 1977). Nonetheless, some of the Termites underachieved and experienced social and psychological problems. These individuals tended to come from lower-socioeconomic backgrounds and to have parents who did not emphasize success or convey success expectations. The results were lowered motivation to achieve and a lack of confidence that they could accomplish their goals. Findings such as these show that capitalizing on one's high IQ requires an interest in some domain and the motivation to develop one's gifts.

Motivation and Emotion

CHAPTER OUTLINE

Myth or Reality?

The Lie Detector Can Tell if You're Guilty or Innocent (page 400)

The polygraph test is viewed by many as a nearly infallible means of establishing guilt or innocence. It is often said that an innocent person has nothing to fear from a lie detector test. Is that true?

Figure 11.1

Against great odds, Drs. Sampson Davis, Rameck Hunt, and George Jenkins realized their dreams. They now work to inspire other under-privileged youth. The Three Doctors received the Humanitarian Award at the 2009 BET Awards Show.

Sampson Davis, Rameck Hunt, and George Jenkins came from broken homes with absentee fathers and few positive role models. One had a drug-addicted mother. Crime, violence, drugs, and the specter of death pervaded the mean streets of their impoverished neighborhood of Newark, New Jersey—a place, says Hunt, "where the neighborhood either makes you or breaks you." By age 18, Davis and Hunt ran afoul of the law and spent time in juvenile detention. Like so many young men in that community, they seemed headed for a life of crime or poverty.

What the three teenagers did have going for them was above-average intelligence. A turning point in their lives was testing into one of Newark's three magnet high schools, where they became best friends. Throughout his teens, Jenkins had cherished the dream of becoming a dentist. During their senior year of high school, Jenkins, Davis, and Hunt made a pact: to attend a special prefreshman remedial program at Seton Hall University, to bear down academically, and to become doctors. For years to come, they studied together, supported each other, and inspired one another. At times the obstacles seemed insurmountable, but the pact kept them going. As Davis notes: "Strength comes from knowing that the power to overcome adversity and prevail lies within oneself. . . . When you've failed repeatedly and think you're done, that last try—the one that requires every ounce of will and strength you have—is often the one to pull you through" (Davis et al., 2002, p. 211).

Hunt, Davis, and Jenkins beat the odds. They graduated from college together and went on to medical and dental school. They all achieved their dreams (Figure 11.1). Today, Dr. Hunt is a specialist in internal medicine at Princeton University Medical Center. Dr. Davis is a Board-certified emergency medicine physician at St. Michaels Medical Center. Dr. Jenkins achieved his dream as well, and now serves as an assistant professor of clinical dentistry at Columbia University. The Three Doctors created an educational foundation that sponsors programs for poor inner-city families and wrote a best-selling book about their experiences to inspire others to achieve. Without doubt, theirs is a record of accomplishment that anyone would be proud of.

The remarkable story of the Three Doctors illustrates the power of human motivation. During the course of their striving, they experienced both success and adversity, and they often dealt with feelings of discouragement and anxiety about their futures. Motivation and emotion, two central concepts in psychology, are the focus of this chapter.

When our motives and goals are gratified, threatened, or thwarted, we often experience emotions. Psychologists are interested in the links between motives and emotions. What is the range of human motives and emotions? How do they develop, and what are the internal and external stimuli that arouse them? What consequences do they have on our behavior? As we shall see, answers to these questions require research at all three levels of analysis—biological, psychological, and environmental.

MOTIVATION

The concept of motivation is central in our attempt to understand behavior and its causes. The term itself comes from the Latin word *movere*, meaning "to move." Psychologists use the concept to help explain how internal factors seem to move animals and people toward certain goals. We therefore define **motivation** *as a process that influences the direction, persistence, and vigor of goal-directed behavior.*

Perspectives on Motivation

Because of its centrality as a scientific construct, every theoretical perspective has addressed the topic of motivation, and all of them have provided insights into the nature, functions, and consequences of motivation.

Evolution, Instincts, and Genes

Darwin's theory of evolution inspired early psychological views that instincts motivate much of our behavior. An **instinct** (also called a *fixed action pattern*) *is an inherited characteristic, common to all members of a species, that automatically produces a particular response when the organism is exposed to a particular stimulus.* By the 1920s, researchers had proposed thousands of human instincts (Atkinson, 1964).

Human instinct theories faded because little evidence supported them, and they often relied on circular reasoning: Why are people greedy? Because greed is an instinct. How do we know that greed is an instinct? Because people are greedy. As we have seen in earlier discussions of scientific thinking, circular reasoning explains nothing.

Scientists now study genetic contributions to motivation more productively. In gene knockout experiments done with animals (see Chapter 3), they disable specific genes and then examine the resulting effects on motivation. Researchers also conduct twin and adoption studies to examine how strongly heredity accounts for differences among people in many aspects of motivated behavior, such as the tendencies to be outgoing or to behave antisocially. Modern evolutionary psychologists also propose that many human motives have evolutionary underpinnings expressed through the actions of genes (Palmer & Palmer, 2002).

Homeostasis and Drives

Your body's biological systems are delicately balanced to ensure survival. For example, when you are hot, your body automatically tries to cool itself by perspiring. When you are cold, your body generates warmth by shivering. In 1932 Walter Cannon proposed the concept of **homeostasis,** *a state of internal physiological equilibrium that the body strives to maintain.*

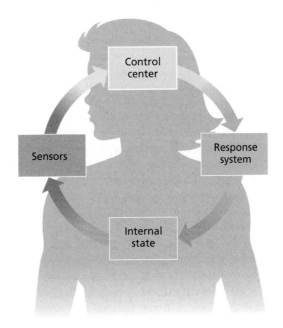

Figure 11.2

Homeostatic adaptation.

Your body's internal environment is regulated by homeostatic mechanisms. Sensors detect bodily changes and send this information to a control center, which in turn regulates a response system that restores bodily equilibrium.

Maintaining homeostasis requires a sensory mechanism for detecting changes in the internal environment, a response system that can restore equilibrium, and a control center that receives information from the sensors and activates the response system (Figure 11.2). The control center functions somewhat like the thermostat in a furnace or air-conditioning unit. Once the thermostat is set at a fixed temperature, or *set point*, sensors detect temperature changes in either direction. The control unit responds by turning on the furnace or air conditioner until the sensor indicates that the set point has been restored, and then turning it off.

According to Clark Hull's (1943) influential *drive theory of motivation*, physiological disruptions to homeostasis produce **drives,** *states of internal tension that motivate an organism to behave in ways that reduce this tension.* Drives such as hunger and thirst arise from tissue deficits (e.g., lack of food and water) and push an organism into action. Hull, a learning theorist, proposed that reducing drives is the ultimate goal of motivated behavior.

Homeostatic models are applied to many aspects of motivation, such as the regulation of hunger and thirst (Woods & Seeley, 2002). But drive concepts are less influential than in the past. For one thing, we often behave in ways that seem to increase rather than reduce states of arousal, as when we skip meals in order to diet or flock to tension-generating horror movies.

Approach and Avoidance Motivation: The BAS and BIS

Motivation impels us toward some things and away from others. We seek to maximize pleasure and minimize pain; we gravitate toward rewards and avoid punishment and deprivation. These seemingly universal tendencies reflect the activity of two distinct neural systems in the brain. According to Jeffrey Gray (1991), the **behavioral activation system (BAS)** *is roused to action by signals of potential reward and positive need gratification.* Activity in this neural system causes the person to begin or to increase movement toward positive goals (the things we want) in anticipation of pleasure. The BAS produces emotions of hope, elation, and happiness. Avoidance motivation reflects the activity of the **behavioral inhibition system (BIS),** *which responds to stimuli that signal potential pain, nonreinforcement, and punishment.* The BIS produces fear, inhibition of behavior (as when humans and other animals freeze in terror), as well as escape and avoidance behaviors (Figure 11.3). People high in BAS prefer change and novelty, whereas BIS fosters a preference for the familiar (Quilty et al., 2007).

Brain researchers are looking for the specific brain mechanisms underlying the pleasure-seeking and pain-minimizing functions of the BAS and the BIS. These mechanisms involve not only different neurotransmitter systems but also different brain regions. EEG and fMRI studies suggest that the prefrontal area in the left hemisphere, a region involved in goal-directed planning and self-regulation, is part of the BAS (Coan & Allen, 2003; Gray & Burgess, 2004). The BIS system is thought to involve several structures of the limbic system and the right frontal lobe (Sutton, 2002). However, there is still much to be learned about the neural underpinnings of the BAS and BIS.

The BAS and BIS are at the forefront of motivational research because they not only address the obviously important distinction between approach and avoidance motivation, but they also help organize the cognitive, physiological, and behavioral process involved in seeking pleasure and avoiding pain. These systems tie motivation and emotion together as well, for the BAS links approach motives and desired incentives with positive emotions, and the BIS links avoidance motives with negative emotions, such as fear, depression, and guilt.

Cognitive Processes: Incentives and Expectancies

Whereas drives are viewed as internal factors that push an organism into action, **incentives** *represent environmental stimuli that pull an organism toward a goal.* To a student, anticipating a good grade can be an incentive for studying, just as food can be an incentive for someone who is hungry (i.e., someone motivated by the hunger drive).

Why is it, however, that people often respond differently to the same incentive? Consider James, Lenora, and Harrison, students in a calculus class who have similar math aptitudes. James studies hard, but Lenora and Harrison put forth little effort. According to one cognitive approach, the **expectancy × value theory,** *goal-directed behavior is jointly determined by the strength of the person's expectation that particular behaviors will lead to a goal and by the incentive value the individual places on that goal* (Brehm & Self, 1989).

These two factors are multiplied, producing the following equation: Motivation = expectancy × incentive value. James works hard because he believes (expectancy) that the more he studies, the more likely it is he'll get an A (incentive), and he strongly desires an A. Lenora also believes that studying hard will lead to an A, but an A holds little incentive value for her in this course. In contrast, Harrison values an A but believes that studying hard is unlikely to produce a high grade for him. Therefore, Lenora and Harrison do not study as hard as James does.

Cognitive theorists also distinguish between **extrinsic motivation,** *performing an activity to obtain an external reward or avoid punishment,* and **intrinsic motivation,** *performing an activity for its*

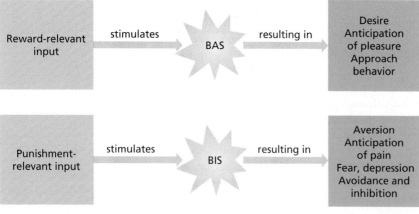

Figure 11.3

Approach and avoidance motivation.
Two neurological systems, the behavioral activation system (BAS) and the behavioral inhibition system (BIS), underlie the universal tendencies to maximize pleasure and minimize pain. The BAS regulates approach motivation, whereas the BIS regulates avoidance motivation. The systems also link approach and avoidance motivation with positive and aversive emotions.

own sake—because you find it enjoyable or challenging. In terms of incentives, a student who studies hard solely to get a good grade (rather than learn) is exhibiting extrinsic motivation.

Psychodynamic Views

The psychodynamic perspective views motivation within a broader context of personality development. Freud (1923) proposed that energy from unconscious motives—especially sexual and aggressive instincts—is often disguised and expressed through socially acceptable behaviors. Thus hidden aggressive impulses may fuel one's motivation to be a trial attorney or an athlete.

Research offers little support for Freud's "dual-instinct" model, but his work stimulated other psychodynamic theories that highlight motives such as people's desires for self-esteem and social belonging (Kohut, 1977). Modern psychodynamic theorists continue to emphasize that, along with conscious mental processes, unconscious motives guide how we act and feel (Westen, 1998). Cognitive psychologists hold a different (i.e., information-processing) view of the unconscious mind, but their research—along with studies of human social behavior—indicates that, indeed, people are not always aware of the factors that motivate them to act as they do (Chartrand & Bargh, 2002).

Maslow's Need Hierarchy

Abraham Maslow, a humanistic theorist, proposed a broad motivational model (1954). He believed that psychology's other perspectives ignore a key human motive: our striving for personal growth. He proposed the concept of a *need hierarchy*, a progression containing *deficiency needs* (needs concerned with physical and social survival) at the bottom and uniquely human *growth needs* at the top (Figure 11.4). After our basic physiological needs are satisfied, we focus on our need for safety and security. Once that is met, we then attend to needs at the next higher level, and so on. If situations change and lower-level needs are no longer met, we refocus our attention on them until they are satisfied.

To Maslow, **self-actualization,** *which represents the need to fulfill our potential,* is the ultimate human motive. It motivates us to perfect ourselves mentally, artistically, emotionally, and socially, to explore activities for their intrinsic satisfaction rather than to gain esteem and belongingness, and to live deep and meaningful lives dedicated to the betterment of all people, not just ourselves. Maslow believed that most people become so focused on attaining satisfaction of the

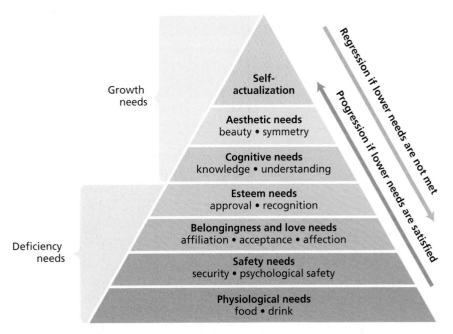

Figure 11.4

A motivational hierarchy.
Maslow proposed that needs are arranged in a hierarchy. After meeting our more basic needs, we experience need progression and focus on needs at the next level. If a need at a lower level is no longer satisfied, we experience need regression and focus once again on meeting that lower-level need.

needs lower in the hierarchy that they spend little time focused on becoming all they can be. Those rare people who approach self-actualization, such as Albert Einstein, Abraham Lincoln, Mahatma Gandhi, Mother Teresa, and Martin Luther King Jr., can make enormous contributions to our world. Some of these people achieve a state of *self-transcendence,* moving beyond a focus on self to commit themselves to the welfare of others, to spiritual fulfillment, and to causes higher than themselves (Koltko-Rivera, 2006).

Self-Determination Theory

A more recent humanistic theory of motivation has been advanced by Edward Deci and Richard Ryan (1985, 2009). **Self-determination theory** *focuses on three fundamental psychological needs—competence, autonomy, and relatedness—and on how they relate to intrinsic and extrinsic motivation.* These three needs are assumed to be just as basic and universal as biological needs like food and water. People are most fulfilled or self-actualized in their lives when they are able to satisfy these fundamental needs. When the needs are thwarted, there can be negative consequences to both psychological well-being and physical health (Deci & Ryan, 2009). Let's examine these needs more closely.

Competence motivation reflects a basic human need to experience oneself as capable, to master

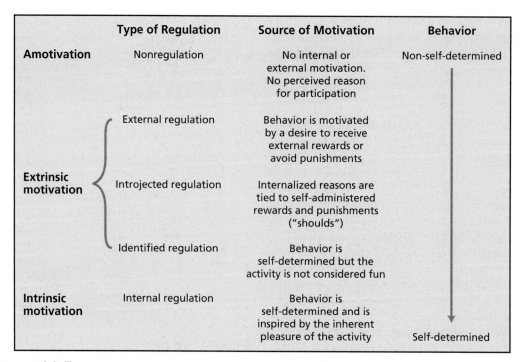

	Type of Regulation	Source of Motivation	Behavior
Amotivation	Nonregulation	No internal or external motivation. No perceived reason for participation	Non-self-determined
Extrinsic motivation	External regulation	Behavior is motivated by a desire to receive external rewards or avoid punishments	
	Introjected regulation	Internalized reasons are tied to self-administered rewards and punishments ("shoulds")	
	Identified regulation	Behavior is self-determined but the activity is not considered fun	
Intrinsic motivation	Internal regulation	Behavior is self-determined and is inspired by the inherent pleasure of the activity	Self-determined

Figure 11.5

Motivational regulation of behavior according to self-determination theory. Source: Deci & Ryan, 2009.

new challenges, and to perfect skills. This need motivates many exploratory and growth-inducing human behaviors. The need for *autonomy* (or self-determination) is satisfied when people experience their actions as a result of free choice without external interference. Autonomy leads to greater self-ownership of behaviors, feelings of personal control, and, in the view of self-determination theorists, self-actualization. *Relatedness* refers to our desire to form meaningful bonds with others—to care and to be cared for. At first glance, relatedness may seem opposed to autonomy, but the two can actually support one another. For example, when adolescents feel that their autonomy is acknowledged and supported by their parents, they feel a strong sense of relatedness to their parents (Roth et al., 2009; Ryan & Lynch, 1989). The same is true of workers who are given freedom by their bosses to develop their own plans for getting a job done (Tremblay et al., 2009). When true relatedness is achieved, people often feel freer to be themselves, and their relationships can improve and become more intimate.

Self-determination theory focuses strongly on distinctions between intrinsic and extrinsic control of motivated behavior. As noted earlier (page 370), intrinsically motivated behavior is done for its inherent ability to provide satisfaction and enjoyment, whereas extrinsically motivated behavior is done in the service of some external influence. Actually, this dichotomy is too simple,

and self-determination theorists have proposed a continuum that captures the degree to which behaviors are autonomous versus externally controlled (Figure 11.5). An absence of either extrinsic or intrinsic motivation occurs in the state of *amotivation,* shown at the top of Figure 11.5. Here, the behavior has no real motivational purpose, and people either discontinue the behavior or continue it out of pure routine.

The new model has three levels of extrinsic motivation. The least autonomous basis for action occurs in *external regulation,* where behavior is wholly under the external control of rewards, punishment, or deadlines imposed by others. Some students with no inherent interest in learning study only to achieve a degree that will earn them a higher-paying job after college. Some athletes are interested solely in personal awards and financial gain, with no real "love of the game." The next level of extrinsic motivation is *introjected regulation,* where some internalization of the reason for doing the behavior has occurred. Here, a student may study because she has internalized, or introjected, from her parents the notion that she "should" do so. The studying occurs not because of a love of learning more about the subject, but because not doing so would evoke guilt and doing well will enhance self-regard. Still more internalization of the motivation occurs at the level of *identified regulation,* where the behavior, though not inherently enjoyed, is done out of choice.

Here, an athlete who does not like lifting weights at 6:00 in the morning chooses to do so in order to become a better athlete. A student who does not enjoy studying statistics does so as a means to an internalized goal, becoming a better researcher.

The most autonomous form of motivation occurs in *internal regulation,* where the behavior is done for its own sake because it brings enjoyment, self-fulfillment, and stimulation. When a student finds a subject that provides such an outcome, it is like finding a "true love." For the athlete, it reflects a love of the sport regardless of any external incentives.

Relations between Intrinsic and Extrinsic Motivation   There is a story of an elderly woman who customarily took an afternoon nap. One day a group of children appeared at the vacant lot outside her bedroom window and began a noisy soccer match. The next day they returned. On the third day, the woman walked over to the lot as the children were about to begin their match. She called the children over and said, "I enjoy your matches so much that I'll give you each a quarter if you'll come and play every day." She then gave each of the children a quarter. With that, the delighted children played even more enthusiastically than before. The next day, the woman did the same thing, and the next as well. On the sixth day, she approached the children and said, "I can't afford to give you a quarter any more. From now on, I can give you only a nickel." One of the children replied, "I ain't doing this for a nickel. Let's get out of here." The children never returned, and the woman resumed her peaceful afternoon naps.

How can we account for the children's sudden loss of enthusiasm for the afternoon soccer matches? In terms of self-determination theory, the extrinsic reinforcer (money) undermined the children's intrinsic motivation to come to the lot and play soccer. Their play behavior had come under the reward control of the monetary reinforcer and was now externally regulated. When that reinforcer was reduced drastically, the motivation to engage in the behavior was likewise reduced. In one real-life example we know of, a 10-year-old champion swimmer now refuses to enter a meet until he determines that the first-place trophy is big enough.

This story has been acted out in numerous laboratories throughout the world. In many experiments, introducing extrinsic awards for the performance of intrinsically interesting behaviors has resulted in reduced motivation and performance if the external reinforcer was withdrawn. One meta-analysis of 128 studies resulted in the conclusion that extrinsic rewards can undermine self-determination and thereby reduce intrinsic motivation (Deci & Ryan, 2009). However, self-determination theory also postulates that under certain conditions, extrinsic rewards can enhance intrinsic motivation for a behavior. This is most likely to occur if the external reward is viewed as providing evidence of mastery and thereby satisfying the need for competence. This process causes an internalization of the activity into the self-system so that the activity becomes enjoyable in its own right (Duda & Treasure, 2010). Moreover, where intrinsic motivation is low to begin with, external rewards can provide a motivational boost until the person reaches a level of competence that allows enjoyment for its own sake.

The importance of self-determination theory's three basic needs has been strongly supported by research. The greater the extent to which behaviors help satisfy the basic needs of competence, autonomy, and relatedness, the more they become internalized and intrinsically motivating (Deci & Ryan, 2009). Satisfaction of the basic needs results in positive outcomes such as psychological well-being, happiness, enhanced worker performance and satisfaction, enhanced health-related behaviors (Mata et al., 2009), positive social relationships, and a sense of meaningfulness in life (Deci & Ryan, 2002, 2009; Sheldon et al., 2003). The most positive outcomes of all come from a balance among the three needs, which is associated with well-being and adaptive behavior in both adolescents and adults (Milyavskaya et al., 2009; Roth et al., 2009). A follow-up study of recent college graduates revealed that attainment of intrinsically motivated goals was associated with increases in well-being, whereas attainment of extrinsically motivated goals was not (and was sometimes associated with decreases in well-being). Moreover, the association between change in attainment of intrinsic aspirations and change in psychological health occurred as a result of satisfaction of the basic psychological needs for competence, autonomy, and relatedness (Niemiec et al., 2009). From a humanistic perspective, self-determination theory represents a new model for the elusive concept of self-actualization.

thinking **critically**

IS MASLOW'S NEED HIERARCHY VALID?

Does the concept of a need hierarchy, shown in Figure 11.4, make sense to you? How do you feel about the ordering of needs in Maslow's hierarchy? Think about it, then see page 412.

test yourself   Perspectives on Motivation

Match each numbered concept to the correct definition on the right.

1. instinct
2. behavioral activation system
3. incentive
4. self-actualization
5. intrinsic motivation

a. Maslow's highest need
b. fixed action pattern
c. self-determination theory
d. oriented toward rewards
e. environmental motivational trigger

ANSWERS: 1-b, 2-d, 3-e, 4-a, 5-c

Hunger and Weight Regulation

As we have seen in the previous section, psychology's diverse perspectives underscore the complexity of studying motivation. Let's now turn to one of our most basic motives: hunger. If you could give up all food forever and satisfy your nutritional needs with a daily pill, would you? Eating is a necessity, but for many people it also is one of life's delicious pleasures. Numerous biological, psychological, and environmental factors regulate our food intake, and hunger is being studied at all three levels of analysis.

The Physiology of Hunger

Eating and digestion supply the body with the fuel it needs to function and survive. **Metabolism** *is the body's rate of energy (or caloric) utilization*, and several physiological mechanisms keep your body in energy homeostasis by regulating how much you eat. For example, some physiological signals induce hunger and prompt eating, whereas others stop food intake by producing *satiety* (the state in which we no longer feel hungry).

However, it is not the case—as many people believe—that hunger and eating simply occur when we begin to run low on energy and that we feel full when immediate energy supplies are restored (Assanand et al., 1998). Your body monitors its energy supplies, but this information interacts with other factors (e.g., the amount and variety of food) to regulate food intake. Thus hunger and satiety are not necessarily linked to immediate energy needs (Woods & Seeley, 2002). Moreover, homeostatic mechanisms are designed to *prevent* us from running low on energy in the first place. In evolutionary terms, an organism that did not eat until its energy supply started to dissipate would be at a serious survival disadvantage.

Finally, many researchers believe that there is a **set point,** *a biologically determined standard around which body weight (or, more accurately, fat mass) is regulated* (Powley & Keesey, 1970). This view holds that if we overeat or undereat, homeostatic mechanisms alter our energy utilization and hunger so as to return us close to our original weight. Other researchers argue that set point theory has limitations. They propose that as we overeat or undereat, homeostatic mechanisms make it harder to keep gaining or losing weight but do not necessarily return us to our original weight. Over time we may settle in at a new weight. Stated differently, in this view "biology does not determine a fixed body weight, but rather a range or zone of body weight" (Levitsky, 2002, p. 147).

Signals That Start and Terminate a Meal Do the muscular contractions (hunger pangs) of an empty stomach produce hunger? In an early experiment, A. L. Washburn swallowed a balloon. When it reached his stomach, the balloon was inflated and hooked up to an amplifying device to record his stomach contractions (Figure 11.6). Washburn then pressed a key every time he felt hungry. The results: Washburn's stomach contractions did indeed correspond with his feelings of hunger (Cannon & Washburn, 1912). But did they *cause* the experience of hunger?

Subsequent research found that hunger does not depend on an empty or twitching stomach or, in fact, on any stomach at all! Animals display hunger and satiety even if all nerves from their stomachs to their brains are cut, and people who have had their stomachs surgically removed for medical reasons continue to feel hungry and satiated (Brown & Wallace, 1980). Thus other signals must help trigger hunger.

When you eat, digestive enzymes break food down into key nutrients, such as **glucose,**

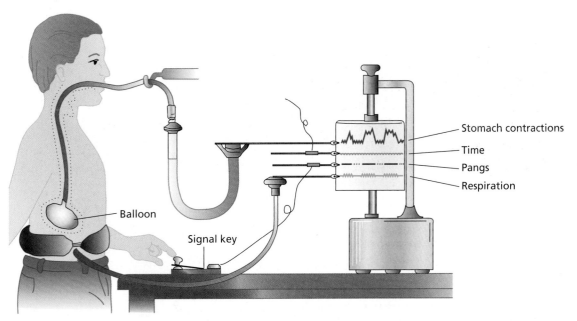

Figure 11.6

Do stomach sensations regulate hunger?

A. L. Washburn swallowed a balloon and inflated it in his stomach. A machine recorded stomach contractions by amplifying changes in the pressure on the balloon, and Washburn pressed a telegraph key every time he felt a hunger pang. Hunger pangs occurred when the stomach contracted.
Source: Based on Cannon & Washburn, 1912.

a simple sugar that is the body's (and especially the brain's) major source of immediately usable fuel. After a meal, some glucose is transported into cells to provide energy, but a large portion is transferred into your liver and fat cells, where it is converted into other nutrients and stored for later use. Sensors in the hypothalamus and liver monitor blood-glucose concentrations. When blood-glucose levels decrease slightly, the liver responds by converting stored nutrients back into glucose, causing blood-glucose levels to rise. Changes in the supply of glucose available to cells provide a signal that helps the brain regulate hunger (Campfield, 1997).

As you eat, several bodily signals cause you to end your meal. Stomach and intestinal distention are satiety signals (French & Cecil, 2001). The walls of these organs stretch as food fills them up, sending nerve signals to the brain. This does not mean, however, that your stomach has to be full for you to feel satiated. As we just noted, patients who have had their stomachs removed continue to experience satiety; this is due not only to intestinal distention but also to chemical signals. For example, **cholecystokinin (CCK)**—*a peptide (a type of hormone) that helps produce satiety*—and other peptides are released into the bloodstream by the small intestine as food arrives from the stomach. These peptides travel to the brain and stimulate receptors in several regions that decrease food intake (Degen et al., 2001).

Signals That Regulate General Appetite and Weight
Leptin *is a hormone secreted by fat cells.* It enters the bloodstream and reaches the brain, where it decreases appetite and increases energy expenditure.

Leptin is a long-term "background" signal. It does not make us feel full like CCK and other short-term satiety signals that respond directly to food intake during a meal. Instead, one way leptin may influence appetite is by increasing the potency of these other signals (Woods & Seeley, 2002). Thus, as we gain fat and secrete more leptin, we may tend to eat less because mealtime satiety factors make us feel full sooner. As we lose fat and secrete less leptin, it may take a greater accumulation of satiety signals and thus more food to make us feel full. In essence, lower leptin levels may tell the brain, "There isn't enough fat tissue, so it's time to eat more." Leptin levels, however, seem to fall more quickly when we lose fat (thus increasing appetite) than they rise when we gain fat. Some researchers suggest that this imbalance served a key adaptive function over the course of evolution; it tilted our ancestral scales in favor of maintaining an adequate fat mass when food was plentiful so that the odds of survival would be increased during times when food was scarce (Jéquier, 2002).

Evidence for leptin's important role grew out of research with genetically obese mice (Zhang et al., 1994). A gene called the *ob* gene (*ob* = obesity) normally directs fat cells to produce leptin, but mice

Figure 11.7

The mouse on the left has an *ob* gene mutation. Its fat cells fail to produce leptin, and it becomes obese. Leptin injections help such mice return to normal weight, as seen in the mouse on the right.

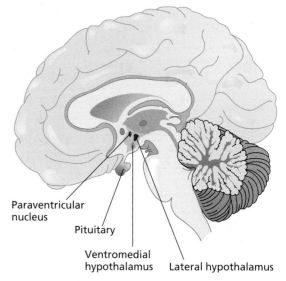

Paraventricular nucleus

Pituitary

Ventromedial hypothalamus   Lateral hypothalamus

Figure 11.8

Motivation and the hypothalamus.

Various structures within the hypothalamus play a role in regulating hunger, thirst, sexual arousal, and body temperature. The lateral hypothalamus (LH), ventromedial hypothalamus (VMH), and paraventricular nucleus (PVN) are involved in hunger regulation.

with an *ob* gene mutation lack leptin. As they gain weight, the brain does not receive this "curb your appetite" signal, and the mice overeat and become obese (Figure 11.7). Daily leptin injections reduce their appetite, and the mice become thinner. Another strain of obese mice produces ample leptin, but because of a mutation in a different gene (the *db* gene), their brain receptors are insensitive to leptin (Chen et al., 1996). The "curb your appetite" signal is there, but because they can't detect it they become obese. Even injecting these mice with additional leptin does not reduce their food intake and weight.

Are these specific *ob* and *db* gene mutations a major source of human obesity? Probably not, for these genetic conditions seem to be rare among humans. However, when these gene mutations do occur, they are associated with extreme obesity, suggesting the importance of normal leptin functioning in human weight regulation.

Might leptin injections be the magic bullet that helps most obese people lose weight? Unfortunately, probably not, because obese people already have ample leptin in their blood due to their fat mass, but their brain may be resistant to that information (Ravussin & Gautier, 1999).

Brain Mechanisms   Many brain regions—from the primitive brain stem to the lofty cerebral cortex—help regulate hunger and eating (Berthoud, 2002). But is there a master control center? Early experiments pointed to two regions in the hypothalamus. Areas near the side, called the *lateral hypothalamus (LH),* seemed to compose a "hunger-on" center (Figure 11.8). Electrically stimulating a rat's LH would cause it to start eating, and lesioning (damaging or destroying) the LH would cause it to refuse to eat, even to the point of starvation (Anand & Brobeck, 1951).

In contrast, structures in the lower-middle area, called the *ventromedial hypothalamus (VMH),* seemed to compose a "hunger-off" center. Electrically stimulating the VMH would cause even a hungry rat to stop eating, whereas lesioning the VMH would produce a glutton that ate frequently and doubled or tripled its body weight.

As scientists explored further, they learned that although the LH and VMH play a role in hunger regulation, they are not really hunger-on and hunger-off centers. For example, rats with LH damage stop eating and lose weight in part because they develop trouble swallowing and digesting, and they become generally unresponsive to external stimuli, not just to food. Moreover, axons from many brain areas funnel into the hypothalamus and then fan out again upon leaving it. Cutting these nerve tracts anywhere along their paths—not just within the hypothalamus—duplicates some of the effects of the LH and VMH lesions (Schwartz, 1984).

Researchers are examining how specific neural circuits within the hypothalamus regulate food intake. Many pathways involve the **paraventricular nucleus (PVN),** *a cluster of neurons packed with receptor sites for various transmitters that stimulate or reduce appetite.* The PVN appears to integrate several short-term and long-term signals that influence metabolic and digestive processes (Berthoud, 2002). One such signal, a chemical transmitter called *neuropeptide Y,* is a powerful appetite stimulant. Rats in one experiment quickly became obese when they received injections of neuropeptide Y into their PVN for 10 days. Their food intake doubled, and their body weight increased sixfold (Stanley et al., 1986).

Psychological Aspects of Hunger

Eating is positively reinforced by the good taste of food and negatively reinforced by hunger reduction. We develop an expectation that eating will be pleasurable, and this becomes an important motivator to seek and consume food. Indeed, even the mere thought of food can trigger hunger.

Attitudes, habits, and psychological needs also regulate food intake. Have you ever felt stuffed during a meal, yet finished it and even had dessert? Beliefs such as "don't leave food on your plate" and conditioned habits (autopilot snacking while watching TV) may lead us to eat even when we do not feel hungry. Conversely, countless dieters intentionally restrict their food intake even though they *are* hungry.

Especially for women, such food restriction often stems from social pressures to conform to cultural standards of beauty (Figure 11.9). Studies of *Playboy* centerfolds, Miss America contestants, and fashion models indicate a clear trend toward a thinner and increasingly unrealistic ideal female body shape from the 1950s into the 1990s (Owen & Laurel-Seller, 2000). Given the deluge of "thin = attractive" mass media messages in many parts of the globe, it's no wonder national surveys have revealed that

- although most young Australian women are of average, healthy weight, only a fifth are happy with their weight (Kenardy et al., 2001);
- among 12- to 19-year-old female Chinese students, 80 percent are concerned about their weight and feel fat at least some of the time (Huon et al., 2002);
- compared to male American high school students, female students are less likely to be overweight but much more likely to diet and think of themselves as overweight (Centers for Disease Control and Prevention [CDC], 2002b).

Indeed, relative to men, women became increasingly dissatisfied with their body image throughout the last half of the 20th century (Feingold & Mazzella, 1998).

A classic study by April Fallon and Paul Rozin (1985) suggests an additional reason why this is so. College women overestimated how

Figure 11.9

Throughout much of Western history, a full-bodied woman's figure was esteemed, as illustrated by (*left*) Peter Paul Rubens's 17th-century painting *The Three Graces* and by (*center*) actress Lillian Russell, who represented the American ideal of feminine beauty a century ago. In recent decades, the norm of "thin = beautiful" is illustrated (*right*) by this contemporary fashion model.

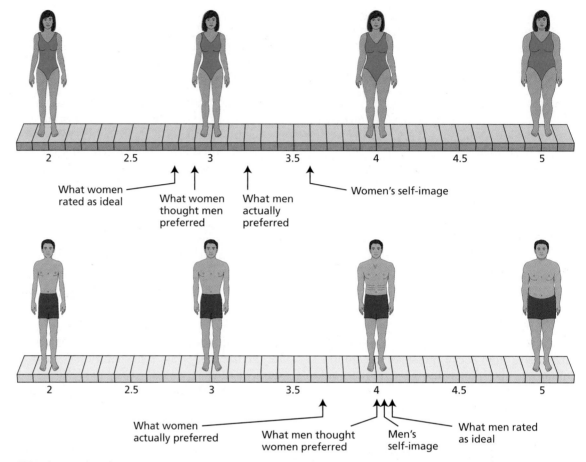

Figure 11.10

Preferred body shapes.

When making judgments while viewing body-size drawings, college women overestimated how thin they needed to be to conform to men's preferences, and they viewed their own body shape as heavier than ideal. Men overestimated how bulky or "buff" they needed to be to conform to women's preferences, but they viewed their body shape as close to ideal. Source: Based on Fallon & Rozin, 1985.

thin they needed to be to conform to men's preferences, whereas men overestimated how bulky they should be to conform to women's preferences (Figure 11.10). Women also perceived their body shape as heavier than ideal, whereas men viewed their body shape as close to ideal. These results were replicated in a more recent study of American and Spanish college men and women (Carlson & McAndrew, 2004). As Fallon and Rozin noted, "Overall, men's perceptions serve to keep them satisfied with their figures, whereas women's perceptions place pressure on them to lose weight" (1985, p. 102). Whether African American, Hispanic American, or Caucasian American, men seem more likely to have these ego-protective perceptions about their body shape than do women (Demarest & Allen, 2000).

Men too, however, may be influenced by cultural ideals. College men's satisfaction with their bodies decreases when they are exposed to a series of advertisements showing muscular males, but not when the advertisements contain men with average builds (Lorenzen et al., 2004). Male college athletes, who value muscle function, believe that women prefer a more muscular body type than their own, and most would prefer to be more muscular than they are (Raudenbush & Meyer, 2003). In general, it appears that women typically want to be thin; males who are overweight also want to be thinner, but those who are thin want to be heavier and more "buff" (Kostanski et al., 2004).

Environmental and Cultural Factors

Food availability is the most obvious environmental regulator of eating. For millions of people who live in poverty or famine-ravaged regions, food scarcity limits consumption. In contrast, abundant high-fat food in many countries contributes to a high rate of obesity (Wadden et al., 2002).

Food taste and variety also regulate eating. Good-tasting food increases food consumption, but during a meal and from meal to meal we can become tired of eating the same thing, causing us to terminate a meal more quickly (Rolls et al., 1981). In contrast, food variety increases consumption, which you may have observed when you eat at a buffet.

Through classical conditioning, we learn to associate the smell and sight of food with its taste, and these food cues can trigger hunger. Eating may be the last thing on your mind until your nose detects the sensuous aroma wafting from a bakery or popcorn machine. Similarly, rats who have recently eaten and do not appear to be hungry (e.g., they ignore available food) will eat again when presented with classically conditioned sounds and lights that they have learned to associate with food (Weingarten, 1983).

Many other environmental stimuli affect food intake. For example, we typically eat more when dining with other people than when we eat alone (deCastro, 2002). Cultural norms influence when, how, and what we eat. In Mediterranean countries such as Spain and Greece, people often begin dinner in the late evening (say, around 9 P.M.), by which time most North Americans have finished supper. And although we like variety, we usually feel most comfortable selecting familiar foods and often have difficulty overcoming our squeamish thoughts about unfamiliar dishes (Figure 11.11).

Figure 11.11

Cultural upbringing strongly affects food preferences. Would you like to eat these juicy insect larvae? Not interested? Perhaps you would prefer some other insects, reptiles, camel eyes, or dog—all delicacies in other cultures.

Obesity

The heaviest known man and woman in recorded history, both Americans, weighed 1,400 and 1,200 pounds, respectively (*Guinness Book*, 2000). Few people approach such extreme weight, but as measured by their *body mass index (BMI)*, which takes height and weight into account, a staggering 25 to 30 percent of American adults are obese and another 30 to 35 percent are overweight (Flegal et al., 2002). From Canada to the Palestinian West Bank, adult obesity rates of 20 to 50 percent have been reported in many studies (Abdul-Rahim et al., 2003).

Obesity places people at greater risk not only for many medical problems but also for being the target of stereotypes and prejudice (Teachman et al., 2003). Obesity is often blamed on a lack of willpower, a dysfunctional way of coping with stress, heightened sensitivity to external food cues (e.g., the sight and aroma of food), and emotional disturbances. Research, however, does not consistently find such psychological differences between obese and nonobese people (Faith et al., 2002; Leon & Roth, 1977).

Genes and Environment Do you know people who seem to gain weight easily and others who seem to eat as much as they want without adding pounds? Heredity influences one's basal metabolic rate and the tendency to store energy as either fat or lean tissue. Indeed, identical twins raised apart are about as similar in body mass as identical twins reared together. Overall, genetic factors appear to account for about 40 to 70 percent of the variation in BMI among women and among men (Maes et al., 1997).

More than 200 genes have been identified as possible contributors to human obesity (Comuzzie & Allison, 1998). However, although heredity affects our susceptibility to obesity, so does the environment. Genes have not changed much in recent decades, but obesity rates have increased significantly. According to some experts, the culprits are

- an abundance of inexpensive, tasty foods that are high in fat and/or carbohydrates;
- a cultural emphasis on getting the best value, which contributes to supersizing menu items;
- technological advances that decrease the need for daily physical activity (Wadden et al., 2002);
- high levels of dopamine in the brain's "reward pathways" that may make some people especially sensitive to the reinforcing properties of foods (Davis et al., 2007).

The Pima Indians of Arizona provide a striking example of how genes and environment interact to produce obesity. The Pimas are genetically predisposed to obesity and diabetes, but both conditions were rare among tribe members before the 20th century. Their native diet and physically active lifestyle prevented their genetic predisposition from expressing itself. But particularly among Pimas born after World War II, obesity rates increased dramatically as they adopted a Westernized diet and sedentary lifestyle. Today, Pimas living in Arizona have one of the highest rates of obesity (and diabetes) in the world. In contrast, Pimas living in northwest Mexico eat a more traditional diet and perform more physical labor, and their obesity rate is much lower than that of their Arizonan counterparts (Esparza et al., 2000).

Dieting and Weight Loss   Unfortunately for millions of overweight people, being fat primes them to stay fat, in part by altering body chemistry and energy expenditure (Logue, 1991). For example, obese people generally have higher levels of *insulin* (a hormone secreted by the pancreas that helps convert glucose into fat) than do people of normal weight. Substantial weight gain also makes it harder to exercise vigorously, and dieting slows basal metabolism because the body responds to food deprivation with decreased energy expenditure.

Does this mean that diets are doomed to fail? The common adage that "95 percent of people who lose weight regain it within a few years" evolved from just one study decades ago. According to Albert Stunkard, one of the researchers, 100 obesity patients were "just given a diet and sent on their way. That was state of the art in 1959" (quoted in Fritsch, 1999). In truth, we do not have good long-term estimates of weight-loss success rates, partly because we rarely hear from people who succeed (or fail) on their own without going to clinics or treatment programs.

We do know that about one third of Americans report that they are trying to lose weight, although not all are necessarily the ones who need to lose it. As Figure 11.12 shows, there are significant sex and ethnic differences in dieting that emerge even in adolescence (CDC, 2002b). Health concerns motivate some dieters, but psychological concerns and social pressures to be thin are the primary motivators for many others. Especially among women, what begins as a diet may unfortunately evolve into a health-threatening eating disorder.

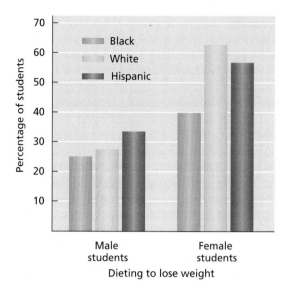

Figure 11.12

Ethnicity and dieting.
Whether Hispanic, Black, or White, female high school students are less likely than male students to actually be overweight or at risk for overweight, but as this graph shows, they are more likely to be dieting to lose weight. Especially among female students, Hispanics and Whites are most likely to diet. Source: Based on CDC, 2002b.

Eating Disorders: Anorexia and Bulimia

Victims of **anorexia nervosa** *have an intense fear of being fat and severely restrict their food intake to the point of self-starvation* (Figure 11.13). Despite looking emaciated and weighing less than 85 percent of what would be expected for their age and height, people with anorexia continue to view themselves as fat. Anorexia causes menstruation to stop, produces bone loss, stresses the heart, and increases the risk of death (Neumäker, 2000; Treasure, 2005).

People who suffer from **bulimia nervosa** *are also afraid of becoming fat, and they binge-eat and then purge the food,* usually by inducing vomiting or using laxatives. People with bulimia often consume 2,000 to 4,000 calories during binges and in some cases may consume 20,000 calories per day (Geracioti et al., 1995). Although most bulimics are of normal body weight, repeated purging can produce severe physical consequences, including gastric problems and badly eroded teeth. Whereas most anorexics do not see their food restriction as problematic, bulimics typically do. Nonetheless, they find it extremely difficult to alter their binge-purge pattern.

About 90 percent of people with anorexia and bulimia are women. About 7 percent of anorexics have a previous diagnosis of bulimia, and this group tends to exhibit higher levels of psychological disturbance (Santonastaso et al., 2006). Some surveys indicate that up to 10 percent of college women exhibit symptoms of bulimia, although its general prevalence among North American women is 1 to 3 percent—compared with 0.5 percent for anorexia (Becker et al., 1999).

Causes of Anorexia and Bulimia   What motivates such abnormal eating patterns? Researchers obviously can't do experiments to manipulate possible causes and see if people become anorexic or bulimic, but they can examine factors associated with the disorders and changes that occur in people when they are successfully treated. Such research suggests that a combination of environmental, psychological, and biological factors may be involved.

Anorexia and bulimia are more common in industrialized cultures where thinness is equated with beauty. However, cultural norms alone cannot account for eating disorders, because only a small percentage of women within a particular culture are anorexic or bulimic. Personality factors are another piece of the puzzle. People with anorexia often are perfectionists—high achievers who strive to live up to lofty self-standards, including strict ideals of an acceptably thin body (Tyrka et al., 2002). For them, losing weight becomes a battle for success and control: "It's me versus food, and I'm going to win." Their perfectionism and need for control may partly stem from their upbringing. They often describe their parents as disapproving and as setting abnormally high achievement standards. For some anorexic children and teens, food refusal may be reinforced by the distress they cause their parents to feel. In essence, self-starvation becomes a way to punish parents and gain some control (Chan & Ma, 2002). As one young anorexic teen said in a therapy session,

> It was, like, a power thing. I was like, look mom, I don't have to eat. I can piss you off. . . . That's the last thing your parents want is for you to die. . . . You can get back at anybody. And I guess . . . I need to find a way to forgive her . . . because . . . I'm killing myself. (*Dying to Be Thin*, 2000)

A different pattern emerges for people with bulimia, who tend to be depressed and anxious, exhibit low impulse control, and seem to lack a stable sense of personal identity (McElroy et al., 2006). Their food cravings are often triggered by stress and negative mood, and binging temporarily reduces their negative emotional state (Waters et al., 2001). But guilt, self-contempt, and anxiety

Figure 11.13

Anorexia nervosa is a potentially life-threatening disorder in which people virtually starve themselves to be thin. This anorexic woman returned to normal weight after therapy.

follow the binge, and purging may be a means of reducing these negative feelings.

On the biological side, genetic factors appear to predispose some people toward eating disorders. Concordance rates for eating disorders are higher among identical twins than fraternal twins and higher among first-degree relatives (parents and siblings) than second- or third-degree relatives (Kortegaard et al., 2001). Researchers are now searching for specific genes and combinations of genes that contribute to eating disorders.

Anorexics and bulimics also exhibit abnormal activity of serotonin, leptin, and other body chemicals (Kaye et al., 2002). Some researchers believe that neurotransmitter and hormonal imbalances help cause eating disorders. Others propose that such chemical changes initially are a *response* to abnormal eating patterns but that once started they *perpetuate* eating and digestive irregularities (Walsh & Devlin, 1998). Other bodily changes also help perpetuate eating disorders. For example, stomach acids expelled into the mouth during vomiting cause bulimics to lose taste sensitivity, making the normally unpleasant taste of vomit more tolerable (Rodin et al., 1990).

Treating eating disorders is difficult and may take years, but with professional help, about half of all anorexic and bulimic patients fully recover (Russell, 2006; Westen et al., 2004). Others are able to eat more normally but maintain their preoccupation with food and weight.

test yourself   Hunger and Weight Regulation

True or false?

1. Stomach contractions are the most important signal for hunger.
2. The peptide CCK is a signal for satiety.
3. Structures in the hypothalamus regulate food intake and satiety.
4. Most normal-weight women are satisfied with their bodies.
5. Genes play a major role in obesity.
6. Crash dieting is the best way to lose and keep off weight.
7. Binging and purging occurs in bulimia but not in anorexia.

ANSWERS: 1-false, 2-true, 3-true, 4-false, 5-true, 6-false, 7-true

Sexual Motivation

Why do people have sex? If you're thinking "Isn't it obvious?" let's take a look. Sex often is described as a biological reproductive motive, yet people usually do not have sex to conceive children. A drive to reproduce does not explain why people masturbate or why couples in their 70s and 80s have sex. Pleasure, then, must be the key. Evolution shaped our physiology so that sex feels good; periodically, having sex for pleasure leads to childbirth, through which our genes are passed on. But consider this:

- In a study asking adolescents why they have sex, both genders cited peer pressure more often than sexual gratification (Stark, 1989).

- In the 1920s, British sex researcher Helena Wright found that most women she surveyed viewed sex as an unenjoyable marital duty (Kelly, 2001).

- About 10 percent of American men and 20 percent of American women report that sex is not pleasurable (Laumann et al., 1994).

In reality, people engage in sex to reproduce, obtain and give sensual pleasure, express love, foster intimacy, fulfill a "duty," conform to peer pressure, and a host of other reasons.

Sexual Behavior: Patterns and Changes

Because most people don't care to let researchers into their bedrooms, scientists typically learn about people's sexual activities by conducting surveys. Alfred Kinsey and his colleagues (1948, 1953) conducted the first large-scale American sex surveys in the late 1930s, and many others have been conducted since then. One of the most thorough surveys, based on a nationally representative sample, found that about 70 percent of 18- to 59-year-old Americans have sex with a partner at least a few times per month (Figure 11.14; Laumann et al., 1994). In general, single adults who cohabit (are not married but live with a sexual partner) are the most sexually active, followed by married adults. Single adults who do not cohabit are the least active.

By their first year in American high school, 41 percent of male students and 29 percent of female students say they have had sexual intercourse (CDC, 2002b). Among unmarried American females in the early 1960s, 27 percent of 19-year-olds had engaged in sexual intercourse. By 1995, the corresponding figure was 72 percent (CDC, 1997). Changing social norms and a tendency to delay marriage have contributed to this rise in premarital sex. Premarital intercourse also became more common in a number of foreign countries during the last half of the 20th century. Findings over the past few years, however, suggest that this trend has leveled off and may be reversing (CDC, 2002b). This could be a response to an increased cultural emphasis on the depth of relationships and to the crisis concerning AIDS and other sexually transmitted diseases.

The Physiology of Sex

In 1953, William Masters and Virginia Johnson began a landmark study in which they examined the sexual responses of 694 men and women under laboratory conditions. In total, they physiologically monitored about 10,000 sexual episodes.

The Sexual Response Cycle   Masters and Johnson (1966) concluded that most people, when sexually

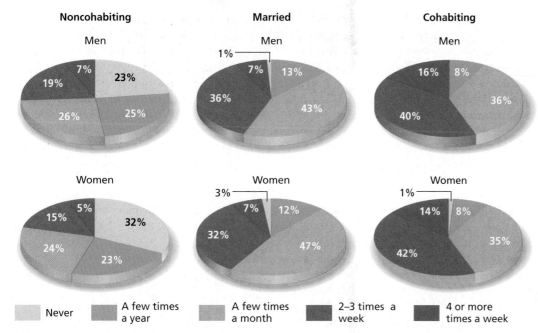

Figure 11.14

Sexual behavior patterns.

These graphs, based on a nationally representative sample of 18- to 59-year-old Americans, show frequency of sex in the past 12 months by gender and marital status. SOURCE: Adapted from Michael et al., 1994.

aroused, go through a four-stage **sexual response cycle** *of excitement, plateau, orgasm, and resolution* (Figure 11.15). During the *excitement phase*, arousal builds rapidly. Blood flow increases to arteries in and around the genital organs, nipples, and women's breasts, where it pools and causes these body areas to swell. The penis and clitoris begin to become erect, the vagina becomes lubricated, and muscle tension increases throughout the body. In the *plateau phase*, arousal continues

to build until there is enough muscle tension to trigger orgasm.

During the *orgasm phase* in males, rhythmic contractions of internal organs and muscle tissue surrounding the urethra project semen out of the penis. In females, orgasm involves rhythmic contractions of the outer third of the vagina, surrounding muscles, and the uterus. In males, orgasm is ordinarily followed by a *resolution phase*, during which physiological arousal decreases rapidly

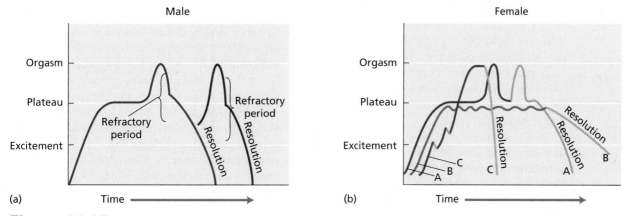

Figure 11.15

The human sexual response.

Masters and Johnson discovered a four-stage pattern of sexual response. (a) In males, there is a refractory period after orgasm during which no further response is possible. (b) In females, pattern A represents one or more orgasms followed by resolution, pattern B shows a plateau stage with no orgasm, and pattern C shows an orgasm with no preceding plateau stage. SOURCE: Based on Masters & Johnson, 1966.

and the genital organs return to their normal condition. During the resolution phase, males enter a *refractory period*, during which they are temporarily incapable of another orgasm. Females may have two or more successive orgasms before the onset of the resolution phase, but Masters and Johnson reported that most women experience only one. Of course, people may experience orgasm on some occasions but not others, and orgasm is not the only goal of all human sexual activity.

Hormonal Influences   As with hunger, the hypothalamus plays a key role in sexual motivation. It controls the pituitary gland, which regulates the secretion of hormones called *gonadotropins* into the bloodstream. In turn, these hormones affect the rate at which the *gonads* (testes in the male and ovaries in the female) secrete *androgens*, the so-called masculine sex hormones such as *testosterone,* and *estrogens,* the so-called feminine sex hormones such as *estradiol.* Realize that despite these labels, both men and women produce androgens and estrogens.

Sex hormones have *organizational effects* that direct the development of male and female sex characteristics (Byer et al., 2002). In the womb, male and female embryos form a primitive gonad that has the potential to develop into either testes or ovaries. If genetically male, the embryo forms testes about 8 weeks after conception. Then, as the testes release sex hormones during a key period of prenatal development, there typically is sufficient androgen activity to produce a male pattern of genital, reproductive, brain, and other organ development. Years later, as part of this pattern, the hypothalamus stimulates an increased release of sex hormones from the testes when the male reaches puberty. In contrast, a genetically female embryo does not form testes, and in the absence of sufficient androgen activity during this prenatal period, a female pattern of development ensues. As part of this pattern, at puberty the hypothalamus stimulates the release of sex hormones from the ovaries on a cyclical basis that regulates the female menstrual cycle.

Sex hormones also have *activational effects* that stimulate sexual desire and behavior. In nonhuman animals, mature males have a relatively constant secretion of sex hormones, and their readiness for sex is largely governed by the presence of environmental stimuli (e.g., a receptive female). In contrast, hormonal secretions in female animals follow an *estrus* cycle, and they are sexually receptive only during periods of high estrogen secretion (i.e., when they are in heat).

Sex hormones also influence human sexual desire. The natural hormonal surge of puberty increases sexual motivation, as would an artificial boost from receiving doses of testosterone (Tuiten et al., 2000). But in humans, normal short-term hormonal fluctuations have relatively little effect on sexual arousability (Morrell et al., 1984). Desire does not go up and down like a yo-yo as blood levels of sex hormones change, and women may experience high sexual desire at any time during their menstrual cycle. Moreover, in men and women, androgens—rather than estrogens—appear to have the primary influence on sexual desire (Hyde & DeLamater, 2003).

The Psychology of Sex

Sexual arousal involves more than physiological responses. It typically begins with desire and a sexual stimulus that is perceived positively (Walen & Roth, 1987). Such stimuli can even be imaginary.

Sexual fantasy is an important component of many people's lives, although studies in Europe, South America, and North America indicate that men sexually fantasize more often than women (Martinez & Raul, 2000). Among American adults, for example, about half of men and a fifth of women fantasize about sex at least once a day (Laumann et al., 1994). Fantasy nicely illustrates how mental processes can affect physiological functioning. Indeed, sexual fantasies alone may trigger genital erection and orgasm in some people and are often used to enhance arousal during masturbation.

Psychological factors can not only trigger sexual arousal but also inhibit it. A person may be engaged in sexual activity and then become turned off by something a partner does. About 1 in 3 American women and 1 in 6 men report that they simply lack an interest in sex (Laumann et al., 1994). Other people desire sex but have difficulty becoming or staying aroused. Stress, fatigue, and anger at one's partner can lead to temporary arousal problems. **Sexual dysfunction** *refers to chronic, impaired sexual functioning that distresses a person.* It may result from injuries, diseases, and drug effects, but some causes are psychological. Arousal difficulties also may stem from performance anxiety or may be a psychological consequence of sexual assault or childhood sexual abuse (Rumstein & Hunsley, 2001).

Cultural and Environmental Influences

Anyone who doubts culture's power to shape human behavior need only examine sexual customs around the globe. During sex, most Westerners probably do not poke a finger into their partner's ear, as do Trukese women of Micronesia, or bite off and then spit out hairs from their partner's eyebrows, as do South American Apinaye women (Hyde & DeLamater, 2003). You may find these practices unusual, but consider how some sexual techniques common in our culture—such as kissing—seem to members of other cultures: "There are a few societies . . . in which kissing is unknown. For example, when the Thonga of Africa first saw Europeans kissing, they laughed and said, 'Look at them; they eat each other's saliva and dirt'" (Hyde & DeLamater, 2003, pp. 10–11).

More important, the psychological meaning of sex itself depends on cultural contexts. Some societies and religions forbid premarital sex and may also prohibit public dress and behavior that arouse sexual desire (Figure 11.16). Many people who view themselves as very religious believe it is important to bring their sexual practices into harmony with their religious beliefs, which may condone sex only within marriage (Janus & Janus, 1993).

In contrast, some societies openly encourage premarital sex. Among Marquesan Islanders of eastern Polynesia, families sleep together in one room, and children have ample opportunity to observe sexual activity. When boys and girls reach adolescence, a middle-aged adult of the opposite sex instructs them in sexual techniques and has intercourse with them. Having other sexual partners prior to marriage is considered normal (Frayser, 1985). Clearly, what is regarded as proper, moral, and desirable varies enormously across cultures.

Environmental stimuli are pervasive and dependable elicitors of sexual desire and behavior. Such stimuli are prominently displayed both in everyday life and in the mass media. On a daily basis, TV shows present explicit scenes and sexual themes that would have been unthinkable half a century ago. The envelope is pushed even further by the ready availability of pornography, a multibillion-dollar industry whose primary consumers are men. Social commentators and psychologists have questioned whether pornography affects men's sexual attitudes and fosters sexual violence toward women.

Many pornographic materials model *rape myths*, suggesting that men are entitled to sex and that women enjoy being coerced into sex. Correlational studies paint an ambiguous picture of links between pornography and sexual violence against women. Some countries with high rates of rape have little pornography, whereas others have a great deal. Conversely, in some countries pornography is widely available but rates of rape are low (Bauserman, 1996). Similarly, research

Figure 11.16

Habits of dress that many people take for granted in Western societies, such as wearing tank tops, bare-midriff shirts, and short skirts, are unacceptable in other cultures because they are considered sexually provocative. A stark contrast is evident in these college students in the United States and in the Middle East.

with sex offenders shows that they do not differ from other men in amount or earliest age of exposure to pornography, and they are actually *less* aroused by nonviolent pornography. Yet they are more aroused by violent pornography and are also more likely to act sexually after viewing violent or even nonviolent pornography (Allen et al., 1995, 2000).

Controlled experiments paint a clearer causal picture. In some studies, male college students were randomly assigned to view material whose content was either neutral (i.e., nonsexual), sexually explicit but nonviolent (e.g., a couple having consensual sex), or sexually aggressive (e.g., a rape-myth depiction showing a woman who initially resists sexual assault but then becomes a willing participant). Later, the students interacted with another person (a female or male accomplice of the experimenter), who made errors on a learning task. Participants were instructed to punish the person with electric shock for each error, but they were free to choose the shock intensity and thus aggress by giving stronger shocks. (The confederate did not really receive any shock.)

The strongest experimental effects emerged when participants viewed violent pornography (Malamuth et al., 2000). At least temporarily, this increased men's tendency to aggress toward women but not toward other men. However, certain types of people, such as those who reported

the greatest attraction to sexual violence, were most strongly affected by viewing it. In addition to its connection with aggression, pornography also promotes a belief that sex is impersonal. An unwelcome side effect is that exposure to pornography decreases viewers' satisfaction with their own sexual partners (Donnerstein & Malamuth, 1997).

Sexual Orientation

Sexual orientation *refers to one's emotional and erotic preference for partners of a particular sex.* Determining one's sexual orientation seems simple: heterosexuals prefer opposite-sex partners, homosexuals prefer same-sex partners, and bisexuals are sexually attracted to members of both sexes. So how would you classify the sexual orientation of these two 25-year-olds?

- Susan feels sexually attracted to men and women, but she has had sex with men only and thinks of herself as heterosexual.

- Larry has had sex with other men twice since puberty, yet he isn't attracted to men and views himself as heterosexual.

Prevalence of Different Sexual Orientations   Some researchers view sexual orientation as a single dimension ranging from "exclusively heterosexual" to "exclusively homosexual," with "equally heterosexual and homosexual" at the midpoint. But others argue that sexual orientation has three dimensions: *self-identity, sexual attraction,* and *actual sexual behavior* (Kelly, 2001).

Figure 11.17 shows that about 2 to 3 percent of American men and 1 percent of American women identify themselves as homosexual or bisexual, but higher percentages report same-sex attraction and at least one same-sex sexual experience (Laumann et al., 1994). Overall, 10 percent of men and 9 percent of women answer affirmatively to at least one of the items in Figure 11.17. Rates of same-sex sexual activity seem to be slightly lower in England and France and slightly higher in Australia (Dunne et al., 2000; Johnson et al., 1992).

Determinants of Sexual Orientation   Theories about the origins of sexual orientation abound. An early and unsupported biological view proposed that homosexual and heterosexual males differ in their adult levels of sex hormones. Other early theories hypothesized that male homosexuality develops when boys grow up with a weak, ineffectual father and identify with a domineering mother, or that being sexually

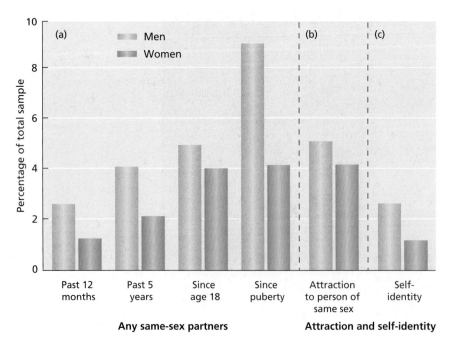

Figure 11.17

Behavior and self-perception.

More men and women report same-sex activity (a) and same-sex attraction (b) than view themselves as homosexual or bisexual (c). Source: Adapted from Laumann et al., 1994.

seduced by an adult homosexual causes children to divert their sex drive toward members of their own sex.

All of these theories have taken a scientific beating. In one study, Alan Bell and coworkers (1981) interviewed nearly 1,000 homosexual and more than 500 heterosexual men and women from the San Francisco area. They searched extensively for childhood or adolescent experiences that might predict adult sexual orientation, but only one consistent pattern emerged: even in childhood, homosexual men and women felt that they were somehow different from their same-sex peers and were more likely to engage in *gender-nonconforming behaviors*. Similarly, compared with heterosexual women, homosexual women in Brazil, Peru, the Philippines, and the United States were about twice as likely during childhood to be considered tomboys and to be interested in boys' clothes and toys (Whitam & Mathy, 1991). Study after study has obtained similar results (Cohen, 2002).

Still, why do such patterns arise? Highly publicized studies appeared in the early 1990s reporting anatomical differences in the brains of heterosexual versus homosexual men and identifying a genetic marker shared by some homosexual men. Subsequent research, however, has not consistently replicated these findings (Lasco et al., 2002). Nonetheless, there is growing evidence that heredity influences human sexual orientation. In one study, among gay men who had a brother, the concordance rates for sexual orientation (i.e., the brother was gay also) were 52 percent among identical twins, 22 percent among fraternal twins, and 11 percent among adoptive brothers (Bailey & Pillard, 1991). A later study of homosexual women yielded similar results (Bailey et al., 1993). Thus the closer the genetic relatedness, the higher the concordance rates for sexual orientation (Kirk et al., 2000).

According to another theory, the brain develops a neural pattern that predisposes an individual to prefer either female or male sex partners, depending on whether prenatal-sex-hormone activity follows a masculine or feminine path (Rahman, 2005). Experimentally altering animals' prenatal exposure to sex hormones can influence their sexual orientation. Moreover, in rare cases among humans, some genetically male fetuses are insensitive to their own androgen secretions and some female fetuses experience an atypical buildup of androgens. Studies of these individuals suggest a relation between prenatal-sex-hormone exposure and adulthood sexual orientation (Williams et al., 2000). Of course, the

human research is correlational and must be interpreted cautiously. For example, male fetuses who have androgen insensitivity develop the external anatomy of females and are typically raised as girls; socialization could account for their sexual orientation.

What about environmental influences? Even among identical twins, when one is homosexual, often the other is heterosexual. Thus a biological predisposition and socialization experiences may combine to determine sexual orientation. At present, scientists simply do not know what all the factors are. It is also possible, argues Daryl Bem (1996, 2001), that heredity affects sexual orientation only indirectly, by influencing children's basic personality style. He proposes that different personality styles then steer children toward gender-conforming or gender-nonconforming activities, causing them to feel similar to or different from same-sex peers. Ultimately, this affects their attraction to same-sex and opposite-sex peers. Bem's theory has mixed support and needs further testing (Bailey et al., 2000; Peplau et al., 1998).

Finally, there may be multiple paths toward developing a sexual orientation, and the paths for men and women may differ. Consider the intriguing finding shown in Figure 11.18. The greater the number of older brothers (but not older sisters) a newborn boy has, the greater the probability that he will develop a homosexual orientation.

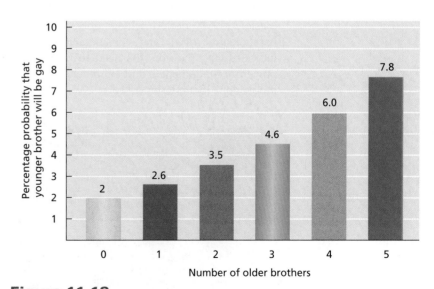

Figure 11.18

Homosexuality: the fraternal birth order effect.

The presence of each older brother increases by about one third the relative probability that a later-born male child will be gay. Thus, if there is a 2 percent probability that a man with no older brothers is gay, then the probability for a man with one older brother is about 2.6 to 2.7 percent, roughly a one-third relative increase.

SOURCE: Adapted from Blanchard & Bogaert, 1996.

In contrast, a woman's sexual orientation is not related to the number of older sisters or brothers in the family. Ray Blanchard (2001), the leading researcher of this *fraternal birth order effect*, has found it in 14 studies, involving more than 7,000 total participants.

? thinking **critically**

FRATERNAL BIRTH ORDER AND MALE HOMOSEXUALITY

Why might having older brothers increase the odds that a later-born male will have homosexual orientation? Think about possible explanations, then see page 413.

test yourself   Sexual Motivation

True or false?

1. Married couples have sex more often than cohabiting couples.
2. Since 1960, the proportion of 19-year-olds who have had sexual intercourse has nearly tripled.
3. Hormones have activational effects that govern the development of physical sex characteristics.
4. In humans, short-term fluctuations in hormones have little influence on sexual arousability.
5. Exposure to pornography decreases viewers' satisfaction with their own sexual partners.
6. Sex offenders have more and earlier exposure to pornography.

ANSWERS: 1-false, 2-true, 3-false, 4-true, 5-true, 6-false

Social Motivation

What makes your life most meaningful? To many people, close relationships are one key. The three doctors Sampson Davis, Rameck Hunt, and George Jenkins surely agree. Their deep friendship and mutual support sustained them through arduous years of college and medical school. Abraham Maslow (1954) viewed belongingness as a basic psychological need, and considerable research indicates that, indeed, "the need to belong is a powerful, fundamental, and extremely pervasive motivation" (Baumeister & Leary, 1995, p. 497).

Why Do We Affiliate?

Humans are social beings who affiliate in many ways (Figure 11.19). Some theorists propose that over the course of evolution, individuals whose biological makeup predisposed them to affiliate were more likely to survive and reproduce than those who were reclusive. By affording greater access to sexual mates, more protection from predators, an efficient division of labor, and the passing of knowledge across generations, a socially oriented lifestyle had considerable adaptive value (Kottak, 2000).

Figure 11.19

Affiliation brings us companionship, intimacy, love, support, and basic social contact. To satisfy these desires we form friendships, interact with family members, join groups, converse with strangers, and flock together in crowds.

In today's world, research has shown that positive social relationships are important contributors to life satisfaction (Diener et al., 2006; Haller & Hadler, 2006). Social relationships also help insulate us from stressors in our lives. One recent study showed that simply holding the hand of another person during a stressful event can lower physiological arousal (Coan et al., 2006).

Craig Hill (1987) suggests that we affiliate for four basic psychological reasons:

- To obtain positive stimulation
- To receive emotional support
- To gain attention
- To permit social comparison

Social comparison *involves comparing our beliefs, feelings, and behaviors with those of other people.* This helps us determine whether our responses are "normal" and enables us to judge the level of our cognitive and physical abilities (Festinger, 1954).

People differ in how strongly they desire to affiliate. In one study, college students who scored high on a personality test of "need for affiliation" made more friends during the semester than students who scored low (Byrne & Greendlinger, 1989). In another study, high school students wore beepers over a 1-week period. They were signaled approximately every 2 hours, at which time they recorded their thoughts and activities. Participants with a high need for affiliation were more likely than their peers to report that they were thinking about friends and wishing that they could be with people (Wong & Csikszentmihalyi, 1991). Still, even people with strong affiliation needs usually desire some time alone. Conversely, people with lower affiliation needs still seek periodic social contact. Some theorists, therefore, view affiliation needs within a homeostatic model (O'Connor & Rosenblood, 1996). They propose that each of us has our own optimal range of social contact. After periods when contact exceeds that range, we compensate by temporarily seeking more solitude. After periods when social contact falls below the optimal range, we increase our effort to be with others. Although some human and animal findings are consistent with this model, it needs much more testing.

Many studies have shown that situational factors influence our tendency to affiliate. For example, fear-inducing situations increase our desire to be with others. During emergencies, as in the aftermath of earthquakes, floods, and hurricanes, many people find themselves bonding with strangers. When afraid, we may prefer to be with others who face the same situation we do, which helps us gauge the normalcy of our reactions (Schachter, 1959).

When possible, we seem to desire most strongly to be with others who have already been through the same or similar situations (Kulik & Mahler, 2000). Doing so can provide us with information about what to expect. In one study, hospital patients awaiting open-heart surgery expressed a stronger desire to have roommates who already had been through surgery than preoperative roommates like themselves. In a later study, when patients were actually assigned postoperative rather than preoperative roommates, they became less anxious and later recovered from surgery more quickly (Kulik et al., 1996).

Being rejected or excluded from social relationships is a painful event for most people, and exclusion evokes a desire for social reconnection. In one set of experiments, threat of social exclusion caused college students to express greater interest in working with others and making new friends and to provide more rewards to their new interaction partners (Maner et al., 2007).

Achievement Motivation

In striving to become doctors, Sampson Davis, Rameck Hunt, and George Jenkins exemplified the desire to achieve. As a college student, you are keenly aware of society's emphasis on achievement, and you know that whether in school, sports, music, or other fields, some people seek out and thrive on challenges and others do not. In the 1950s, David McClelland, John Atkinson, and their coworkers (1953) began to explore individual differences in **need for achievement,** *a positive desire to accomplish tasks and compete successfully with standards of excellence.*

Motive for Success and Fear of Failure

McClelland and Atkinson proposed that achievement behavior can stem from a positively oriented *motive for success* and a negatively oriented motivation to avoid failure, more commonly called *fear of failure.* Need for achievement is the positive orientation toward success. In terms of the behavioral activation and behavioral inhibition systems discussed earlier, motive for success is the part of the BAS that relates to the achievement domain. Fear of failure is a BIS function.

McClelland and Atkinson measured the motive for success with a psychological test that asked participants to write stories in response to a number of pictures, such as the one in Figure 11.20. The stories were then analyzed for

Figure 11.20

Pictures like this are used to elicit stories that are scored for the motive to succeed. Which of the following two stories, written by different people, reflects a stronger motive to succeed? (1) This young man is sitting in school, but he is dreaming about the day when he will become a doctor. He will study and work harder than anyone else. He goes on to become one of the top medical researchers in the world. (2) The boy is daydreaming about how much he hates being in school. . . . He would like to run away from home and just take it easy on a tropical island. However, he is doomed to be in the rat race for the rest of his life.

achievement-relevant themes using a standardized coding system. The avoidance motive, fear of failure, was measured by psychological tests that asked people to report how much anxiety they experienced in achievement situations. McClelland and Atkinson found that their measures of need for achievement and fear of failure were independent (uncorrelated) dimensions, so that people could be high in both motives, low in both, or high in one and low in the other.

People who have a strong motive for success seek the thrill of victory, whereas those motivated by fear of failure seek to avoid the agony of defeat. Common sense suggests that a strong motive for success combined with a strong fear of failure might lead a person to perform better than someone who is motivated only by a desire for success. But this is not so. The anxiety associated with fear of failure can negate the impact of the need for achievement and can impair performance. In sports, the athlete with a high fear of failure is the one who tends to choke under pressure (Smith, 1996).

People high in achievement and low in fear of failure, called *high-need achievers*, don't necessarily outperform low-need achievers when conditions are relaxed and tasks are easy. However, when tasks are challenging or the importance of doing well is stressed, high-need achievers outshine low-need achievers. They perform at a higher level, and they are more persistent when they encounter barriers to achievement (McClelland, 1989). In general, high-need achievers are most likely to strive hard for success when

they perceive themselves as personally responsible for the outcome, when they perceive some risk of not succeeding, and when there is an opportunity to receive performance feedback (Koestner & McClelland, 1990).

When given a choice of performing a task that is very easy (a high probability of success), moderately difficult (a 40 to 60 percent probability of success), or very difficult (a low probability of success), which do you predict that high-need achievers will choose? Contrary to what you might expect, they prefer intermediate risks to extremely high or low risks because the outcome—success versus failure—*is most uncertain* (Atkinson & Birch, 1978). In contrast, low-need achievers are more likely to choose tasks that are easy (where success is almost assured) or very difficult (where success is not expected), so that nothing is on the line.

To understand this pattern, realize that it is the individual's *perception* of outcome uncertainty that counts. For most of us, the probability of successfully climbing Mt. Everest is virtually zero. But to highly trained mountaineers, the task is neither impossible nor easy. Decades ago, sociologist and mountain climber Dick Emerson (1966) joined a Mt. Everest expedition. As he predicted, the team members' communications with one another throughout the long climb struck a balance between optimistic and pessimistic comments about the chances of reaching their goal. This kept the climbers' perceived chance of success-failure close to 50-50 and maintained maximum motivation.

Achievement Goal Theory

Another way to understand achievement motivation is to examine the success goals that people seek to attain in task situations. **Achievement goal theory** *focuses on the manner in which success is defined both by the individual and within the achievement situation itself.* At the individual level, achievement goal theorists are interested in the achievement goal orientation that people have (Dweck, 1999). They differentiate between a **mastery orientation,** *in which the focus is on personal improvement, giving maximum effort, and perfecting new skills*, and an **ego orientation,** *in which the goal is to outperform others (hopefully, with as little effort as possible).* At the situational level the theory focuses on the **motivational climate** *that encourages or rewards either a mastery approach or an ego approach to defining success* (Figure 11.21).

Achievement Goal Orientations

Another way to understand achievement motivation is to examine the goals that people seek

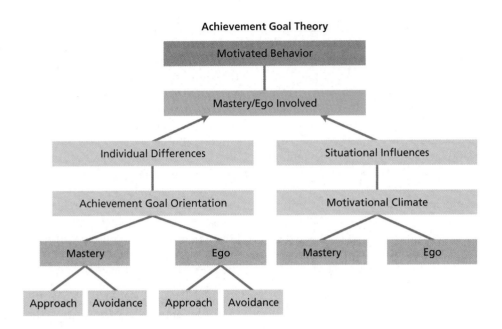

Achievement Goal Theory

Figure 11.21

Achievement goal theory.
Achievement goal theory focuses on the ways in which success is defined, both by individuals and within achievement environments. Individuals may have mastery or ego goal orientations, and the motivational climate created in achievement situations by significant others may emphasize and support mastery goals, such as effort and skill improvement, or ego definitions of success, such as outperforming others.

to attain in task situations. Think for a moment about a class you are taking. On a scale of 1 ("not at all true of me") to 7 ("very true of me"), rate these statements:

1. I want to learn as much as possible from this class.
2. I am motivated by the thought of outperforming the other students in this class.
3. My goal is to avoid learning too little in this class.
4. The main thing is to avoid doing more poorly than the others in this class.

These statements represent four different achievement goals, two of which are approach goals and two of which are avoidance or fear of failure goals (Curry et al., 2006; Elliot & McGregor, 2001). **Mastery-approach goals** (statement 1) *focus on the desire to master a task and learn new knowledge or skills,* whereas **ego-approach goals** (statement 2) *reflect a competitive orientation that focuses on outperforming other people.* On the avoidance side, **mastery-avoidance goals** (statement 3) *reflect a fear of not performing up to one's own standards,* whereas **ego-avoidance goals** (statement 4) *center on avoiding being outperformed by others.* These four goals are embodied in a 2 (definitions of success) × 2 (approach vs. avoidance) framework as different motivational approaches (see Figure 11.21). According to the **2 × 2 achievement goal theory,** *each of us can be described in terms of an "achievement motivation profile"* using statements like the four above. In one sample of college students, Nico

Van Yperen (2006) found that 34.4 percent were highest in mastery-approach, 13.7 percent in ego-approach, 33.6 percent in mastery-avoidance, and 18.3 percent in ego-avoidance. Men were twice as likely as women to report ego-avoidance goals and women were more likely than men to report mastery-avoidance goals. No sex differences were apparent in the two approach-goal orientations.

Although the 2 × 2 achievement goal framework is relatively new, preliminary results indicate that the four motives have different relations to other variables (Schunk et al., 2007). College students' achievement goals for a particular class, measured early in the academic term, help predict their psychological responses to the course as well as their course performance. Students with dominant mastery-approach motivation have higher intrinsic motivation to learn the material, perceive exams as a positive challenge, and rate the course as more interesting and enjoyable. Students with ego-avoidance motivation show exactly the opposite pattern. They lack intrinsic motivation, perceive exams as anxiety-provoking threats, report low levels of interest and enjoyment, and perform more poorly than any other motivational group. Interestingly, ego-approach motivation is most strongly associated with high performance but with less intrinsic motivation and enjoyment than mastery-approach motivation. Finally, in relation to intrinsic motivation, enjoyment, and feelings of competence, mastery-avoidance motivation seems more positive than ego-avoidance motivation and less positive than mastery-approach motivation, but it bears little relation to quality of performance (Curry et al., 2006; Van Yperen, 2006).

By incorporating both desire for success and fear of failure into one theory, the 2 × 2 framework represents a promising approach to understanding the various forms that achievement-related motives can take. Where performance in academic settings is concerned, the optimal motivational pattern may be a combination of mastery-approach and ego-approach goals. The mastery-approach goal enhances enjoyment and interest in the activity, and the ego-approach goal fosters higher performance within the competitive college environment, where grades are often determined by one's performance relative to others (Harackiewicz et al., 2002; McGregor & Elliot, 2002). The same may be true within competitive sports settings (McArdle & Duda, 2002).

Not all people are high on both mastery- and ego-approach orientations, however. If you are going to be high on one or the other, which would be preferable? Although both goal orientations contribute to success, research indicates that a mastery-goal orientation has several psychological advantages over an ego orientation (Dweck, 1999; McArdle & Duda, 2002). When success is defined as being one's best rather than competing with others, people can focus on and enjoy their own improvement and accomplishments. As shown above, they are more likely to experience intrinsic motivation and enjoyment of the activity. They also persist in the face of difficulties, select challenging goals, and exert maximum effort. Legendary basketball coach John Wooden captured the mastery orientation in his definition of success: "Success is peace of mind that comes from knowing that you did your best to become the best that you are capable of becoming. No one can do more."

For an ego-approach person, experiencing personal improvement or performing at his or her "best" would not in itself occasion feelings of success or competence. Indeed, knowing that one tried hard and failed to outperform others would cause an ego-oriented person to feel especially incompetent. If ego-oriented people begin to question their ability to compete successfully with others, they are more likely to reduce persistence and avoid the challenge at hand (Nicholls, 1989). Hall of Fame basketball coach Dean Smith captured one negative consequence of an ego-orientation: "If you make winning basketball games a life-or-death situation, you're going to have problems. For one thing, you'll be dead a lot."

Motivational Climate Besides individual differences in goal orientations, situational factors influence how success is defined. The motivational climate of an achievement setting is influenced by significant others, such as parents, teachers, coaches, and supervisors (Ames, 1992; Chi, 2004). In an ego-involving climate, performers are compared with one another, urged to compete to be the best, and those who perform best get special attention. In a mastery-involving climate, effort, enjoyment of the activity, and personal improvement are emphasized and rewarded. The assumption is that if people work to achieve their potential and give maximum effort, winning will take care of itself. These differing conceptions of success can have strong effects on participants. In children, they help shape the achievement goal orientations that are internalized.

Mastery-involving achievement environments have been linked to a variety of positive effects in school and sport settings. They foster higher intrinsic motivation and enjoyment of the setting, enhance perceptions of learning and mastery, and bolster self-esteem. Performance anxiety is also lower in such settings because the emphasis is on doing one's best (which is personally controllable) rather than on a win outcome that is dependent in part on how others perform. An ego-involving climate fosters the belief that ability, rather than hard work, leads to success, and satisfaction is gained by outperforming others rather than through skill improvement. At the level of task performance, mastery climates result in better skill development and higher performance levels, due in part to increased effort, greater enjoyment, and lowered anxiety (Dweck, 1999; McArdle & Duda, 2002).

Attempts to influence motivational climate have yielded encouraging results. When youth sport coaches were trained to create a mastery environment, their young athletes showed increased mastery-approach motivation and reduced fear of failure over the course of the sport season (Smith et al., 2007; Smoll et al., 2007).

Family, Culture, and Achievement Needs

How does achievement motivation develop? Providing a cognitively stimulating home environment fosters children's intrinsic motivation to perform academic tasks (Gottfried et al., 1998). And when parents or other key caregivers encourage and reward achievement but do not punish failure, they foster a strong motive for success (Koestner & McClelland, 1990). Conversely, fear of failure seems to develop when caregivers take successful achievement for granted but punish failure, thereby teaching the child to dread the possibility of failing (Weiner, 1992). Providing a mastery motivational climate in the home, the school, and the athletic setting also encourages the development of a mastery achievement orientation (Dweck, 1999; McArdle & Duda, 2002).

Cultural norms also shape achievement motivation. Individualistic cultures, such as those in North America and much of Europe, tend to stress personal achievement. In cultures that nurture collectivism, such as those in China and Japan, achievement motivation more strongly reflects a desire to fit into the family and social group, meet its expectations, and work for its goals (Markus & Kitayama, 1991). Chinese high school students, for example, typically care more about meeting their parents' expectations for academic success than do American students (Chen & Lan, 1998). In collectivistic Japan, business organizations have traditionally adopted the concept of *Kaizen* (continuous improvement), encouraging workers to develop skills and increase productivity (Elsey & Fujiwara, 2000). Such companies assume responsibility for their employees' welfare, promote them gradually, and are willing to retain them for life. In turn, the workers are more strongly motivated by loyalty to their managers and to the organization as the company becomes integral to their identities.

At the same time, the human desire to achieve transcends culture and can manifest itself in intriguing ways. Throughout history, some people have left their homelands to seek adventure or better lives elsewhere. Might achievement motivation relate to the desire to emigrate? To answer this question, researchers measured the achievement motivation of college students in Albania, the Czech Republic, and Slovenia and also asked students where they would like to live for most of their adult lives. In each sample, students who expressed a desire to emigrate had higher average achievement-motivation scores than students who said they wanted to remain in their homeland (Boneva et al., 1998).

Motivational Conflict

Motivational goals sometimes conflict with one another. Our desires to achieve success and to have fun may clash, for example, when we must choose between studying for an exam and attending a party. When something attracts us, we tend to approach it; when something repels us, we tend to avoid it. Different combinations of these tendencies can produce three basic types of conflict.

Approach-approach conflict *occurs when we face two attractive alternatives and selecting one means losing the other.* Conflict is greatest when both alternatives, such as a choice between two desirable careers, are equally attractive. In contrast, **avoidance-avoidance conflict** *occurs when we must choose between two undesirable alternatives.* Do I study boring material for an exam, or do I skip studying and fail? **Approach-avoidance conflict** *involves being attracted to and repelled by the same goal.* A squirrel being offered food by a person on a park bench is motivated by hunger to approach and by fear to keep its distance. A man desires an intimate relationship with a woman but fears the possibility of future rejection.

Approach and avoidance tendencies grow stronger as we get nearer to a desired goal (Miller, 1944). Usually, the avoidance tendency increases in strength faster than the approach tendency (Figure 11.22). Thus, at first we may be attracted to a goal and only slightly repelled by its drawbacks, but as we get closer to it the negative aspects become dominant. We may stop, retreat, approach again, and continue to vacillate in a state of conflict. However, the general strength of approach and avoidance tendencies differs across people. BAS-dominated individuals are more attuned to positive stimuli and the possibility of obtaining desired outcomes, whereas those with strong BIS tendencies are more sensitive to actual and anticipated negative outcomes (Elliot & Thrash, 2002; Sutton, 2002).

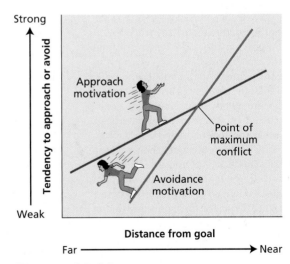

Figure 11.22

Approach-avoidance conflict.
According to Neal Miller (1944), the tendency to approach and the tendency to avoid grow stronger as one moves closer to a goal. However, the tendency to avoid increases faster than the tendency to approach. Maximum conflict is experienced where the two gradients cross, because at this point the opposing motives are equal in strength.

test yourself

Social Motivation, Achievement Motivation, and Motivational Conflict

True or false?

1. When people are afraid, their desire to affiliate increases.
2. Fear of social exclusion seems to be a basic human characteristic.
3. People who are high in need for achievement tend to choose tasks of high difficulty.
4. In general, a mastery goal orientation seems to have more positive consequences than an ego goal orientation.
5. In Eastern cultures, more emphasis is placed on individual than on group achievement.
6. In an approach-avoidance conflict, avoidance tendencies increase faster than approach tendencies as the goal is approached.

ANSWERS: 1-true, 2-true, 3-false, 4-true, 5-false, 6-true

Applying Psychological Science

Systematic Goal Setting: A Motivational Approach That Works

Motivation involves striving for definable goals, and it provides the impetus for goal-directed behavior. Goals can be set to satisfy virtually any need that we value. When such striving is organized, systematic, and based on sound psychological principles, success is maximized. Of all the approaches advanced by psychologists to enhance motivation and improve performance, none approaches systematic goal setting in its demonstrated effectiveness in a wide range of performance settings, from business to education, from science and medicine to sports (Latham & Locke, 2007). Stated simply, goal setting is a motivational technique that really works.

One of the mechanisms underlying the effectiveness of goal setting is **self-efficacy,** *the belief that one is capable of carrying out the specific behaviors needed to attain one's goals* (Bandura & Locke, 2003). Because positive self-efficacy beliefs are consistently related to success in behaving effectively and achieving goals, Albert Bandura (1997) and other social cognitive theorists have been strongly interested in practical measures for enhancing self-efficacy. When people are successful and when they attribute their success to their own competencies, their self-efficacy increases and assists them in subsequent goal-directed efforts. Moreover, successful people have usually mastered the skills involved in setting challenging and realistic goals, figuring out what they need to do on a day-to-day basis to achieve them and making the commitment to do what is required. As they achieve each goal they have set, they become more skillful and increase their sense of personal efficacy. Goal setting also helps meet the needs for competency and autonomy emphasized by self-determination theory, because it improves capabilities and the process is self-directed and in one's personal control.

Not all goal-setting procedures are created equal, and it is important to apply the principles that make goal-setting programs most effective (Locke & Latham, 2002). Here are some research-derived guidelines for effective goal setting:

- *Set specific, behavioral, and measurable goals.* The first step in changing some aspect of your life is to set a goal. The kind of goal you set is very important, because certain kinds of goals will encourage you to work harder, enjoy success, and increase self-efficacy. Studies show that specific and fairly narrow goals are far more effective than general "do your best" goals (Latham & Locke, 2006). A general goal like "improve my tennis game" is less helpful than "increase the number of serves I put in play by 10 percent." The latter goal refers to a specific behavior that you can focus on and measure.

- *Set behavioral, not outcome, goals.* Many of our goals relate to outcomes in the future, such as getting an A in this course. You are more likely to achieve such goals if you use the means-ends heuristic discussed in Chapter 9 and think about the specific things you must *do* to achieve that outcome goal. Behavioral goals (what one has to do) work better than outcome goals (getting the A) because they keep the focus on the necessary behaviors. A behavioral goal might be "read and outline the textbook and outline the lecture notes for 1 hour each day." Achieving this behavioral goal can also be measured quickly and repeatedly, giving you constant feedback. Many people focus on outcome goals and forget what has to be done day-to-day to achieve them. It has been said that there are three kinds of people in this world: those who make things happen, those who wait for things to happen, and those who wonder what happened. Make sure you're someone who makes things happen.

- *Set difficult but realistic goals.* Moderately difficult goals will challenge and motivate you and give you a sense of hope. When reached, they increase self-efficacy. Easy goals do not provide a sense of accomplishment, and extremely difficult or unattainable goals do not provide the success experiences you need to increase your self-efficacy. Instead, overly difficult goals destroy motivation.

- *Set positive, not negative, goals.* In Chapter 7 we discussed the advantages of positive reinforcement over punishment. Working toward positive goals, such as "study for 1 hour before dinner," is better than avoiding a negative consequence, as in "don't waste time." Again, positive goals keep you focused on the positive steps that you need to take to achieve them.
- *Set short-range and long-range goals.* Short-range goals are important because they provide the opportunity for immediate mastery experiences, and they keep you working positively. A long-range goal like "take all the courses for a double major" can easily be divided into a series of subgoals that you can be working toward right now. Short-range goals are like the steps on a staircase leading to the long-range goal. As each step is accomplished, you enjoy mastery experiences that also lead you toward your ultimate goal. In reaching any goal, "divide and conquer" is a cliché that works.
- *Set definite time spans for achievement.* To keep your goal-setting program on track, it is important to specify the dates by which you will meet specific performance goals or subgoals, as well as the behaviors needed to attain them in that time span.

One of the most important aspects of goal setting is systematically measuring progress toward the goal. This was shown in a study by Bandura and Daniel Cervone (1983) in which participants worked on a strenuous bicycle-pedaling task over a number of sessions. Two independent variables were manipulated in a four-group design: (1) whether the participants were given specific improvement goals before each session after the first one and (2) whether the participants were given feedback about their performance during the previous session. A control condition got neither goals nor feedback and provided a basis for evaluating the effects of goals and feedback, alone or in combination. The dependent variable was the electronically measured speed and power with which the participants pedaled.

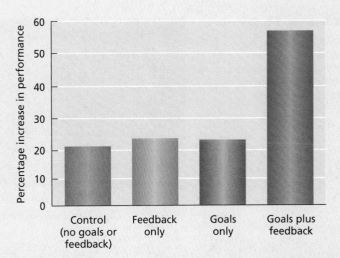

Figure 11.23

Goals are not enough.

This graph shows the effects of improvement goals and performance feedback on performance improvement on a grueling bicycling task. Clearly, the combination of explicit goals *and* performance feedback resulted in greater improvement in performance than did either element by itself. Source: Based on Bandura & Cervone, 1983.

As shown in Figure 11.23, simply having goals was not enough, nor was feedback effective by itself. But having both goals and feedback was a powerful combination. This shows how important it is to measure your progress toward your goal so that you get performance feedback and can see your improvement. Visible movement toward realistic goals builds self-efficacy.

Most of the preceding guidelines can be summarized in the acronym *SMART:* *S*pecific, *M*easurable, *A*ction-oriented, *R*ealistic, and *T*ime-based. And it is true that systematic goal setting is one of the smartest ways to work toward goals. None of the applications of science presented in this book has more potential value for helping you get the things you want in life.

EMOTION

Life without emotion would be bland and empty. Our experiences of love, anger, joy, fear, and other emotions energize and add color to our lives. **Emotions** *are feeling (or affect) states that involve a pattern of cognitive, physiological, and behavioral reactions to events.* Emotion theorist Richard Lazarus (2001) believed that motivation and emotions are always linked, because we react emotionally only when our motives and goals are gratified, threatened, or frustrated (Figure 11.24).

Emotions have important adaptive functions. Some emotions, such as fear and alarm, are part of an emergency arousal system that increases our chances of survival, as when we fight or flee when confronted by threat or danger. But positive emotions, such as interest, joy, excitement, contentment, and love, also have important adaptive functions. They help us form intimate relationships and broaden our thinking and behavior so that we explore, consider new ideas, try out new ways to achieve goals, play, and savor what we have (Fredrickson, 1998).

Emotions are also an important form of social communication. By providing clues about our internal states and intentions, emotions influence how other people behave toward us (Isaacs, 1998). Consider, for example, the effects of a baby's crying on adults, who generally respond with caretaking behaviors that have obvious survival value for the infant. Adults' expressions of sadness and distress also evoke concern, empathy, and helping behavior from others.

Figure 11.24

The intimate relations between motivation and emotion are seen in the strong emotional responses that occur when important goals are either attained or lost.

Positive emotional expressions also pay off. A smiling infant is likely to increase parents' feelings of affection and caring, thereby increasing the likelihood that the child's biological and emotional needs will be satisfied. Happy adults also tend to attract others and to have richer and more supportive relationships (Diener et al., 2006).

Positive emotions are an important part of life satisfaction, and negative emotions foster unhappiness (Diener et al., 2006). Negative emotions also are typically involved in normal stress reactions (Evans-Martin, 2007) and in many psychological disorders (Rottenberg & Johnson, 2007). The ability to self-regulate one's emotions is one mark of psychological adjustment (Denollet et al., 2007; Garber & Dodge, 2007).

The Nature of Emotions

Our emotional states share four common features:

1. Emotions are triggered by external or internal *eliciting stimuli.*

2. Emotional responses result from our *appraisals* of these stimuli, which give the situation its perceived meaning and significance.

3. Our *bodies respond physiologically* to our appraisals. We may become physically aroused, as when we feel fear, joy, or anger; or we may experience decreased arousal, as when we feel contentment or depression.

4. Emotions include *behavior tendencies.* Some are *expressive behaviors* (e.g., smiling with joy, crying). Others are *instrumental behaviors,* ways of doing something about the stimulus that evoked the emotion (e.g., studying for an anxiety-arousing test, fighting back in self-defense).

Figure 11.25 illustrates the general relations among these four emotional components. For example, an insulting remark from another person (eliciting stimulus) may evoke a cognitive appraisal that we have been unfairly demeaned, an increase in physiological arousal, a clenching of jaws and fists (expressive behavior), and a verbal attack on the other person (instrumental behavior). As the two-way arrows indicate, these emotional components can affect one another, so that our thoughts influence our feelings and our feelings influence our appraisals (Frijda et al., 2005). They exist in a larger associative network

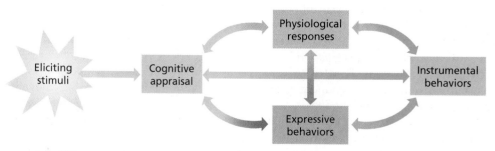

Figure 11.25

Components of emotion.

Emotion involves relations between eliciting stimuli, cognitive appraisal processes, physiological arousal, expressive behaviors, and instrumental behaviors. Note the reciprocal (two-way) causal relations that exist among the appraisal, physiological, and expressive and instrumental behavioral components. Appraisal influences arousal and expressive behaviors, and the latter affect ongoing appraisals.

that also includes links to motives, memories, ideas, and action tendencies. Stimulation of any of the network's components can trigger other elements, depending on the strengths of the associative links (Berkowitz & Harmon-Jones, 2004). For example, some people can generate strong anger and a tendency toward aggression just by recalling an event in which they were wronged. We'll discuss other linkages as well. Thus emotion is a dynamic, ongoing *process*, and any of its four elements can change rapidly in the course of an emotional episode.

Eliciting Stimuli

Emotions do not occur in a vacuum. They are responses to situations, people, objects, or events. We become angry *at* something or someone; fearful or proud *of* something; in love *with* someone. Moreover, the **eliciting stimuli** *that trigger cognitive appraisals and emotional responses* are not always external; they can be internal stimuli, such as a mental image of an upcoming vacation that makes us feel happy or a memory of an unpleasant encounter that arouses anger in us.

Innate biological factors help determine which stimuli have the greatest potential to arouse emotions (Panksepp, 2005). Newborn infants come equipped with the capacity to respond emotionally with either interest or distress to events in their environment (Galati & Lavelli, 1997). Adults, too, may be biologically primed to experience emotions in response to certain stimuli that have evolutionary significance. As we saw in Chapter 7, this may help explain why the majority of human phobias involve "primal" stimuli such as heights, water, sharks, snakes, or spiders, rather than modern threats such as guns, electrical transformers, and automobiles (Öhman & Wiens, 2005). A wide variety of aversive stimuli—pain, heat and cold, foul odors—can evoke anger and aggressive tendencies toward people who had nothing to do with creating the discomfort (Berkowitz & Harmon-Jones, 2004).

Learning also influences our emotions. Previous experiences can turn certain people or situations into eliciting stimuli. The mere sight of one's lover can evoke feelings of passion; the sight of a disliked person can trigger instantaneous revulsion that seems almost reflexive. On the broadest level, cultures have different standards for defining the good, the bad, and the ugly that affect how we appraise and respond to stimuli. Physical features that provoke sexual arousal and feelings of infatuation in one culture, such as ornamental facial scars or a bone through the nose, may elicit feelings of disgust in another.

The Cognitive Component

Cognitions (thoughts, images, memories, interpretations) are involved in virtually every aspect of emotion. Mental processes can evoke emotional responses. They are part of our inner experience of the emotion, and they influence how we express our emotions and act on them. A situation may evoke pleasure or distress, depending on how we appraise it. For example, a sexual advance may elicit anger, fear, or disgust instead of pleasure if it is unwanted or deemed inappropriate. **Cognitive appraisals** *are the interpretations and meanings that we attach to sensory stimuli.*

Both conscious and unconscious processes are involved in appraisals (Feldman-Barrett et al., 2007). Often we are not consciously aware of the appraisals that underlie emotional responses. Some appraisals seem to involve little more than an almost automatic interpretation of sensory input based on previous conditioning (Smith & Kirby, 2004). Indeed, most strong emotions are probably triggered initially in this automatic fashion, after which we may appraise the situation in a more reasoning manner. Even at this more "cognitive" level, however, our habitual ways of thinking can run off in a subconscious shorthand with little or no awareness on our part (Clore & Centerbar, 2004; Phelps, 2005). We often fail to appreciate how arbitrarily we interpret "the way things are."

The idea that emotional reactions are triggered by cognitive appraisals rather than external situations helps account for the fact that different people (or even the same person at different times) can have different emotional reactions to the same object, situation, or person (Figure 11.26).

Figure 11.26

Differences in appraisal can trigger entirely different emotional reactions, as in this instance, where some people are showing pleasure and others seem terrified. What kinds of appraisals are likely triggering these different emotional responses?

Culture and Appraisal   Cross-cultural researchers have asked people in various countries to recall events that triggered certain emotions and to answer questions about how they appraised or interpreted the situations. In one study conducted in 27 countries, people exhibited strong cross-cultural similarities in the types of appraisals that evoked joy, fear, anger, sadness, disgust, shame, and guilt (Wallbott & Scherer, 1988). Whenever any of these emotions occurred, similar appraisals were involved, regardless of the culture.

Despite these cross-cultural commonalities in appraisal, particular situations can evoke different appraisals and emotional reactions, depending on one's culture (Mesquita & Markus, 2005). Consider, for example, the circumstance of being alone. Tahitians often appraise being alone as an opportunity for bad spirits to bother a person, and fear is the most common emotional response. In the close-knit Utku Inuit, an Eskimo culture, being alone signifies social rejection and isolation, triggering sadness and loneliness. In Western cultures, being alone may at times represent a welcome respite from the frantic pace of daily life, evoking contentment and happiness (Mesquita et al., 1997). Thus, where appraisals are concerned, there seem to be certain universals but also some degree of cultural diversity in the more subtle aspects of interpreting situations.

The Physiological Component

When our feelings are stirred up, one of the first things we notice is bodily changes. Many parts of the body are involved in emotional arousal, but certain brain regions, the autonomic nervous system, and the endocrine system play especially significant roles.

Brain Structures and Neurotransmitters   Emotions involve important interactions between several brain areas, including the limbic system and cerebral cortex (Berridge, 2004; Damasio, 2005). If animals are electrically stimulated in specific areas of the limbic system, they will growl at and attack anything that approaches. Destroying the same sites produces an absence of aggression, even if the animal is provoked or attacked. Other limbic areas show the opposite pattern: lack of emotion when they are stimulated and unrestrained emotion when they are removed.

The cerebral cortex has many connections with the hypothalamus, amygdala, and other limbic system structures. Cognitive appraisal processes surely involve the cortex, where the mechanisms for language and complex thought reside.

Moreover, the ability to regulate emotion depends heavily on the executive functions of the prefrontal cortex, which lies immediately behind the forehead (Denollet et al., 2007; LeDoux & Phelps, 2000).

Groundbreaking research by psychologist Joseph LeDoux (2000) revealed that when the thalamus (the brain's sensory switchboard) receives input from the senses, it can send messages along two independent neural pathways, a "high road" traveling up to the cortex and a "low road" going directly to the nearby amygdala (Figure 11.27). The low road enables the amygdala to receive direct input from the senses and generate emotional reactions before the cerebral cortex has had time to fully interpret what is causing the reactions. LeDoux suggests that this primitive mechanism (which is the only emotional mechanism in species such as birds and reptiles) has survival value because it enables the organism to react with great speed before the cerebral cortex responds with a more carefully processed cognitive interpretation of the situation. This may be what occurs when a hiker sees what looks like a snake and jumps out of the way, only to realize an instant later that the object is actually a piece of rope.

The amygdala also seems to function as an early-warning system for threatening social stimuli. In one study, participants were asked to rate photos of people on how trustworthy they appeared to be. When the photos were presented later, brain scans using fMRI showed a burst of activity in the amygdala when people viewed those faces they had rated as untrustworthy, but participants showed no such response to faces they judged earlier as trustworthy (Winston et al., 2002). Another fMRI study showed that the amygdala also reacts to stimuli that evoke strong positive emotions (Hamann & Mao, 2002).

The existence of a dual system for emotional processing may help explain some puzzling aspects of our emotional lives. For example, most of us have had the experience of suddenly feeling a strong emotion without understanding why. LeDoux (2000) suggests that not all emotional responses register at the level of the cortex. He also suggests that people can have two simultaneous but different emotional reactions to the same event, a conscious one occurring as a result of cortical activity and an unconscious one triggered by the amygdala. This might help explain instances in which people are puzzled by behavioral reactions that seem to be at odds with the emotion they are consciously experiencing: "I don't know why I came across as being angry. I felt very warm and friendly." Some psychodynamic theorists are hailing these discoveries as support for the existence

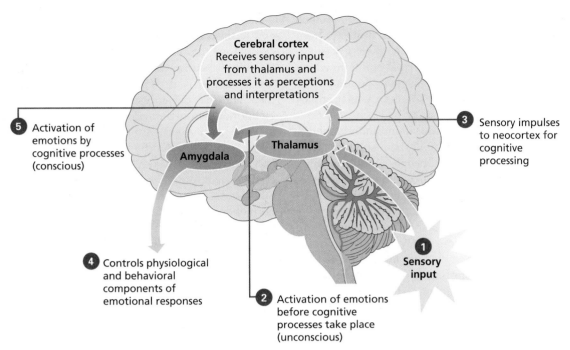

Figure 11.27

Dual emotional pathways.
Parallel neural processes may produce conscious and unconscious emotional responses at about the same time. LeDoux's research suggests that sensory input to the thalamus can be routed directly to the amygdala in the limbic system, producing an "unconscious" emotional response before cognitive responses evoked by the other pathway to the cortex can occur.

of unconscious emotional processes (Westen, 1998). Indeed, there is now little doubt that important aspects of emotional life can occur outside of conscious awareness (Bargh & Chartrand, 1999).

Brain activity is also involved in the regulation of emotional behavior. Of particular importance is the prefrontal cortex, the seat of executive functions involving reasoning, decision making, and control of impulsivity. Deficits in prefrontal functions cause emotions to be expressed in an unregulated manner that can have negative consequences (Boes et al., 2009).

Neuroscientist Candace Pert (1997) argues that because all of the neural structures involved in emotion operate biochemically, it is the ebb and flow of various neurotransmitter substances that activate the emotional programs residing in the brain. For example, dopamine and endorphin activity appears to underlie some pleasurable emotions, whereas serotonin and norepinephrine play a role in anger and in fear (Damasio, 2005; Depue & Collins, 1999). When the final story of the brain and emotion can at last be told, it will undoubtedly involve complex interactions between brain chemicals and neural structures (Frijda, 2006).

Hemispheric Activation and Emotion Decades ago in Italy, psychiatrists who were treating clinically depressed patients with electroshock treatments

to either the right or the left hemisphere observed a striking phenomenon. The electric current temporarily disrupted neural activity in the targeted hemisphere. With the left hemisphere knocked out (forcing the right hemisphere to take charge), patients had what physicians termed a "catastrophic" reaction, wailing and crying until the shock effects wore off. But when they applied shock to the right hemisphere, allowing the left hemisphere to dominate, the patients reacted much differently; they seemed unconcerned, happy, and sometimes even euphoric. Researchers noted a similar pattern of emotions in patients in whom one hemisphere had been damaged by lesions or strokes (Gainotti, 1972).

These findings suggest that left-hemisphere activation may underlie certain positive emotions and right-hemisphere functioning negative ones (Sutton, 2002). To test this proposition, Richard Davidson and Nathan Fox (1988) obtained EEG measures of frontal-lobe activity as people experienced positive and negative emotions. They found that when people felt positive emotions by recalling pleasurable experiences or watching a happy film, the left hemisphere was relatively more active than the right. But when sadness or other negative emotions were evoked by memories or watching a disgusting film, the right hemisphere became relatively more active. Moreover, this hemispheric pattern seems to be innate. Infants as young as 3 to 4 days old showed a similar pattern of hemispheric activation: left-hemisphere activation when given a sweet sucrose solution, which infants like, and right-hemisphere dominance in response to a citric acid solution, which apparently disgusts them.

Davidson and Fox also found individual differences in typical, or *resting,* hemispheric activation when they recorded people's EEG responses under emotionally neutral conditions. These resting differences predicted the tendency to experience positive or negative emotions. For example, human infants with resting right-hemisphere dominance were more likely to become upset and cry if their mothers later left the room than were those with resting left-hemisphere dominance. In adults, a higher resting level of right-hemisphere EEG activity may be a risk factor for the later development of adult depressive disorders (Tomarken & Keener, 1998).

Autonomic and Hormonal Processes You are afraid. Your heart starts to beat faster. Your body draws blood from your stomach to your muscles, and digestion slows to a crawl. You breathe harder and faster to get more energy-sustaining oxygen. Your blood-sugar level increases, producing more nutrients for your muscles. The pupils of your eyes dilate, admitting more light to increase your visual acuity. Your skin perspires to keep you cool and to flush out waste products created by extra exertion. Your muscles tense, ready for action.

Some theorists call this state of arousal the *fight-or-flight response.* It is produced by the sympathetic branch of the autonomic nervous system and by hormones from the endocrine system. The sympathetic nervous system produces arousal within a few seconds by directly stimulating the organs and muscles of the body. Meanwhile, the endocrine system pumps epinephrine, cortisol, and other stress hormones into the bloodstream. These hormones produce physiological effects like those triggered by the sympathetic nervous system, but their effects are longer lasting and can keep the body aroused for a considerable length of time.

Do different emotions produce different patterns of arousal? Only subtle autonomic differences occur among basic emotions as different as anger and fear (Cacioppo et al., 2000). Moreover, people differ from one another in their patterns of general arousal, so that we don't all show the same pattern of bodily arousal even when we're experiencing the same emotion. For example, when afraid, some of us might show marked changes in heart rate or blood pressure but only minor changes in muscle tension and respiration. Others would show different patterns. Thus there are no distinctive and universal physiological signatures for the basic emotions.

Myth or Reality?

The Lie Detector Can Tell if You're Guilty or Innocent

Given what you have learned so far about the physiology of emotion, do you think emotional arousal can tell us whether someone is telling the truth or lying? A scientific instrument known as a **polygraph** (Figure 11.28) *measures physiological responses, such as respiration, heart rate, and skin conductance (which increases in the presence of emotion due to sweat gland activity).* Because we have less control over physiological responses than over numerous other behaviors, many people regard the polygraph as a nearly infallible means of establishing whether someone is telling the truth. In one survey, two thirds of the general public believed that the polygraph is "reliable" or "useful" in detecting lying (Myers et al., 2006). However, this approach to detecting lying by increases in emotional arousal is highly controversial (Iacono & Patrick, 2006; Vrij, 2008).

Figure 11.28 shows a portion of a polygraph record. Polygraph examiners compare physiological responses to critical questions (e.g., "Were you present at the Jesse James National Bank when it was robbed the night of August 4, 2003?") with responses to control questions that make no reference to the crime or crime scene. In this case, note the changes that occurred on the autonomic measures after an emotionally loaded question was asked (point A to point B in Figure 11.28).

The issue, however, is whether this emotional response to a critical question means that the person was lying. Herein lies one major problem with polygraph tests. Innocent people may appear guilty when doubt, fear, or lack of confidence increases their autonomic activity (Iacono, 2008; Lilienfeld et al., 2010). Even a thought like "What if my answer makes me look guilty, even though I'm not?" in response to a critical question could send the polygraph pens into spasms that might suggest a lie. As David Lykken, a leading critic of the lie detector, has noted, "polygraph pens do no special dance when we are lying" (1981, p. 10).

Not only can innocent people appear guilty, but guilty people can also learn to beat the polygraph. For example, by biting their tongue, curling their toes, or contracting their anal sphincter when control questions are asked, people can produce an arousal response to those questions that looks similar to the arousal that occurs when they actually lie on critical questions. William Casey, former director of the U.S. Central Intelligence Agency, used to delight in his ability to fool the lie detector (Carlson & Hatfield, 1992).

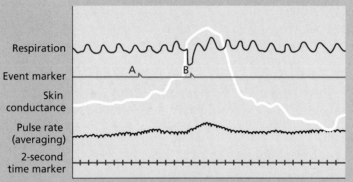

Respiration

Event marker

Skin conductance

Pulse rate (averaging)

2-second time marker

A   B

Figure 11.28

The lie detector.
The polygraph records physiological changes that are part of emotional responses. Between points A and B, an emotionally loaded question was asked. Within 2 seconds, the effects of the question were visible in the subject's respiration, skin conductance, and pulse rate. Does this mean he was lying?

Fred Fay, a prison convict who had been falsely convicted of murder partly on the basis of a polygraph test, also became an expert at defeating polygraph tests (too late, unfortunately, for his acquittal). On one occasion, Fay coached 27 fellow inmates who were scheduled for polygraph tests. All of the inmates told Fay they were guilty of the relevant crimes. Yet after only 20 minutes of instruction, 23 of the 27 inmates managed to beat the polygraph (Lykken, 1981). Such results sharply contradict the notion of an infallible lie detector.

Misgivings about the validity of polygraph tests are supported by studies in which experienced polygraph examiners were given the polygraph records of suspects known to be either innocent or guilty on the basis of other evidence. The experts were asked to judge the guilt or innocence of the suspects. They usually did quite well in identifying the guilty, attaining accuracy rates of 80 to 98 percent (Honts & Perry, 1992). However, they were less accurate in identifying the innocent, judging as many as 55 percent of the truly innocent suspects to be guilty in some studies

(Kleinmuntz & Szucko, 1984; Lykken, 1984). These error rates call into question the adage that an innocent person has nothing to fear from a polygraph test. On the other hand, guilty people who fail polygraph tests sometimes confess to the crime as a result (Ruscio, 2005).

Largely because of an unacceptably high likelihood that an innocent person might be judged guilty, the American Psychological Association has supported legal challenges to polygraph testing. Congressional testimony by psychologists strongly influenced passage of the Employee Polygraph Protection Act of 1988, which prohibits most nongovernmental polygraph testing. Moreover, polygraph results alone cannot be used to convict people of crimes in most jurisdictions (Daniels, 2002). Nonetheless, local and federal governments continue to use polygraph tests in internal criminal investigations and in police officer and national security screening, despite the weight of research evidence against their validity for these purposes (Cochrane et al., 2003; Kleiner, 2002).

The Behavioral Component

Although we can never directly experience another person's feelings, we often can infer that someone is angry, sad, fearful, or happy on the basis of **expressive behaviors,** *the person's observable emotional displays.* Indeed, others' emotional displays can even evoke similar responses in us, a process known as *empathy.* While watching a movie, have you ever experienced the same emotion as the central character? Professional actors sometimes become so immersed in the expressive behaviors of their characters that the boundaries between self and role begin to fade, as the late Kirk Douglas reported after filming the 1956 film *Lust for Life.* Douglas, having played the role of Vincent Van Gogh, the painter who on one occasion cut off an ear and offered it to a prostitute, said:

> I was close to getting lost in the character of Van Gogh. . . . I felt myself going over the line, into the skin of Van Gogh. . . . Sometimes I had to stop

myself from reaching my hand up and touching my ear to find out if it was actually there. It was a frightening experience. That way lies madness. . . . I could never play him again. (Lehmann-Haupt, 1988, p. 10)

Evolution and Emotional Expression Where do emotional expressions come from? In his classic work *The Expression of Emotions in Man and Animals* (1872/1965), Charles Darwin argued that emotional displays are products of evolution because they contribute to species survival. Darwin emphasized the basic similarity of emotional expression among animals and humans. For example, both wolves and humans bare their teeth when they are angry (Figure 11.29). As Darwin explained it, this behavior makes the animal look more ferocious and thus decreases its chances of being attacked and perhaps killed in a fight. Darwin did not maintain that all forms of emotional expression are innate, but he believed that many of them are.

Figure 11.29

Similarities among species in the expression of certain basic emotions convinced Darwin and other theorists that certain expressive behaviors have an evolutionary origin.

Like Darwin, modern evolutionary theorists stress the adaptive value of emotional expression (Izard, 1989; Plutchik, 1994). They believe that a set of **fundamental emotional patterns,** *or innate emotional reactions,* are wired into the nervous system (Panksepp, 2005). Their research shows that certain emotional expressions (e.g., rage and terror) are similar across all cultures, suggesting a universal biological basis for them. The fundamental emotional patterns proposed by three leading evolutionary theorists are shown in Table 11.1. Other emotions are based on some combination of these innate emotions. The evolutionary view does *not* assume that all emotional expressions are innate, nor does it deny that innate emotional expressions can be modified or inhibited as a result of social learning.

Facial Expression of Emotion Most of us are fairly confident in our ability to read the emotions of others. Although many parts of the body can communicate feelings, we tend to concentrate on what the face tells us. Most other species have relatively few facial muscles, so their facial expressions are limited. Only monkeys, apes, and humans have the well-developed facial muscles needed to produce a large number of expressions.

The development of sophisticated measuring procedures, such as Paul Ekman and Wallace Friesen's (1987) Facial Action Coding System (FACS), has permitted the precise study of facial expressions. FACS requires a trained observer to

Table **11.1**	Fundamental or Primary Innate Emotions Proposed by Three Leading Evolutionary Theorists		
Carroll Izard	**Silvan Tomkins**	**Robert Plutchik**
Anger	Anger	Anger
Fear	Fear	Fear
Joy	Joy	Enjoyment
Disgust	Disgust	Disgust
Interest	Interest	Anticipation
Surprise	Surprise	Surprise
Contempt	Contempt	
Shame	Shame	
	Sadness	Sadness
	Distress	
Guilt		
		Acceptance

Sources: Based on Izard, 1982; Tomkins, 1991; and Plutchik, 1994.

dissect an observed expression in terms of all the muscular actions that produced it. It takes about 100 minutes to score each minute of observed facial expression.

Although facial expressions can be valuable cues for judging emotion, even people within the same culture may learn to express the same emotions differently. For example, some people can appear very calm when they are angry or fearful, whereas others express even mild forms of

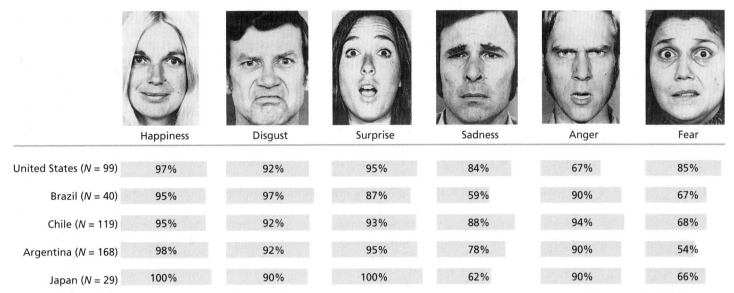

	Happiness	Disgust	Surprise	Sadness	Anger	Fear
United States (N = 99)	97%	92%	95%	84%	67%	85%
Brazil (N = 40)	95%	97%	87%	59%	90%	67%
Chile (N = 119)	95%	92%	93%	88%	94%	68%
Argentina (N = 168)	98%	92%	95%	78%	90%	54%
Japan (N = 29)	100%	90%	100%	62%	90%	66%

Figure 11.30

Culture and emotional expression.

Percentages of people from five different cultures who judged each face as expressing the emotions listed beneath the pictures.

Source: Ekman, 1973.

those same emotions in a highly expressive manner. Fortunately, we usually know something about the situation to which people are reacting, and this often helps us judge their emotions. Researchers have found that people's accuracy and agreement in labeling emotions from pictures are considerably higher when the pictures reveal situational cues (Keltner & Ekman, 2000). If a woman is crying, is she weeping because of sadness or because of happiness? A background showing her being declared the winner of a lottery will result in a different emotional judgment than one showing her standing at a graveside.

Across many different cultures, women have proven to be more accurate judges of emotional expressions than men (Zuckerman et al., 1976). Perhaps the ability to read emotions accurately has greater adaptive significance for women, whose traditional role within many cultures has been to care for others and attend to their needs (Buss, 1991). This ability may also result from cultural encouragement for women to be sensitive to others' emotions and to express their feelings openly (Taylor et al., 2000). However, it is worth noting that men who work in professions that emphasize these skills (such as psychotherapy, drama, and art) are as accurate as women in judging others' emotional expressions (Rosenthal et al., 1974).

What of Darwin's claim that certain facial expressions universally indicate specific emotions? Do people in different cultures agree on the emotions being expressed in facial photographs? Figure 11.30 shows the results of one study. You can see that there is generally high agreement on these photos of basic emotions, but there are also

some cultural variations. Other researchers have found levels of agreement ranging from 40 to 70 percent across a variety of cultures, well above chance but still far from perfect (Russell, 1994).

Cultural Display Rules Cultural display rules *dictate when and how particular emotions are to be expressed* (Yrizarry et al., 2001). Certain gestures, body postures, and physical movements can convey vastly different meanings in different cultures. For example, gesturing with an upright thumb while hitchhiking in certain regions of Greece could result in decidedly negative consequences, such as tire tracks on one's body. In those regions, an upright thumb is the equivalent of a raised middle finger in the United States (Morris et al., 1979). In most cultures, spitting on someone is a sign of contempt. Yet in the traditions of the Masai tribe of East Africa, being spat on is considered a great compliment, particularly if the person doing the spitting is a member of the opposite sex (Wierzbicka, 1986). One can only imagine what a Masai singles bar might be like.

More subtle differences exist as well. Nalini Ambady and colleagues have shown that people are generally more accurate at judging emotions when the emotions are expressed by members of their own cultural group rather than by members of a different cultural group (Elfenbein & Ambady, 2003). Just as people exhibit linguistic dialects, they also appear to have culturally based emotional behavior dialects.

An experiment by Paul Ekman, Wallace Friesen, and Phoebe Ellsworth (1972) nicely illustrates cultural commonalities and differences in emotional expression. Japanese and American students viewed a gory, stressful film in private. Unbeknownst to them, their facial expressions were being videotaped by a hidden camera. FACS codings of the students' facial displays showed no differences between the Japanese and American students; they expressed negative emotions of disgust and anxiety in the same way and with similar intensity as they watched the film. Afterward, the students were individually interviewed by a person of their ethnic group concerning their reactions to the film. The Japanese masked their earlier feelings of anxiety and disgust and presented a happy face throughout the interview, whereas the Americans' negative facial expressions closely mirrored those photographed while they watched the stressful movie. Based on such findings, many emotion theorists conclude that innate biological factors and cultural display rules *combine* to shape emotional expression across different cultures.

Instrumental Behaviors Emotional responses are often calls to action, requiring a response to the situation that aroused the emotion. A highly anxious student must find some way to cope with an impending test. A mother angered by her child's behavior must find a nondestructive way to get her point across. A person in love searches for ways to evoke affection from his or her partner. These are **instrumental behaviors,** *directed at achieving some emotion-relevant goal.*

People often assume that high emotional arousal enhances task performance, as when athletes try to psych themselves up for competition. Yet as students who have experienced extreme anxiety during exams could testify, high emotional arousal can also interfere with performance. In many situations, the relation between emotional arousal and performance seems to take the shape of an upside-down, or inverted, U. As physiological arousal increases up to some optimal level, performance improves. But beyond that optimal level, further increases in arousal impair performance. It is thus possible to be either too "flat" or too "high" to perform well.

The relation between arousal and performance depends not only on arousal level but also on how complicated the task is and how much precision it requires (Yerkes & Dodson, 1908). Generally speaking, the more complex the task, the lower the optimal arousal level. Thus even a moderate level of arousal can disrupt performance on a highly complex mental or motor task.

Figure 11.31 illustrates this principle and also shows that performance drops off less at high levels of arousal for the simplest task than for the others. In fact, even extreme arousal can enhance performance of very simple motor tasks, such as running or lifting something. This may account for seemingly superhuman feats we hear about occasionally. When a 110-pound New Hampshire woman was asked how she had managed to lift

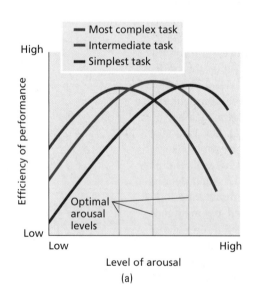
(a)

(b)

(c)

Figure 11.31

Arousal and performance.

(a) The relation between arousal and performance takes the form of an inverted U, with performance declining above and below an optimal arousal level. However, the more complex a task is, the lower the optimal level of arousal for performing it. For which of the tasks above, (b) or (c), should the optimal level be lower?

a 4,000-pound van that had rolled on top of her trapped husband, she answered, "I don't know how I did it. It didn't feel that heavy. I think it was the adrenaline" (*Newsweek,* 2002, March 11, p. 19).

In contrast, high emotionality can interfere with performance on complex mental and physical tasks. People may underachieve on intelligence tests if they are too anxious, and muscle tension can interfere with the skillful execution of complex physical movements (Landers & Arent, 2001). For example, the sport of golf requires precise and complex movements, so the optimal level of arousal is relatively low. Champion golfers often exhibit peak performance in high-pressure competition because they can control their level of arousal and keep it within the optimal range, whereas their opponents choke under the pressure of a putt worth hundreds of thousands of dollars.

Theories of Emotion

Where do emotional experiences come from? For more than 100 years, scientists have explored this question. Several classic theories have guided their efforts.

The James-Lange Somatic Theory

In 1890, the eminent psychologist William James ignited a controversy when he wrote:

> Common sense says . . . we meet a bear, are frightened, and run; we are insulted by a rival, are angry, and strike. The hypothesis here to be defended says that this order of sequence is incorrect and that the more rational statement is that we feel sorry *because* we cry, angry *because* we strike, afraid *because* we tremble. (James, 1890/1950, p. 451, italics added)

At about the same time, Danish psychologist Carl Lange reached a similar conclusion. According to the **James-Lange theory,** *our bodily reactions determine the subjective emotion we experience.* We know we are afraid or in love because our body's reactions tell us so. Today, this theory lives on as the *somatic theory of emotion* (Papanicolaou, 1989).

The Cannon-Bard Theory

It wasn't long before the James-Lange theory was challenged. In 1927, physiologist Walter Cannon fired back. He pointed out that people's bodies do *not* respond instantaneously to an emotional stimulus; several seconds may pass before signs of physiological arousal appear. Yet people typically experience the emotion immediately. This would be impossible according to the James-Lange theory. Cannon and his colleague L. L. Bard concluded that cognition must be involved as well.

The **Cannon-Bard theory** *proposed that the subjective experience of emotion and physiological arousal do not cause one another but instead are independent responses to an emotion-arousing situation.* When we encounter such a situation, sensory information is sent to the brain's thalamus, which simultaneously sends messages to the cerebral cortex and to the body's internal organs. The message to the cortex produces the experience of emotion, and the message to the internal organs produces physiological arousal. Figure 11.32 compares the James-Lange and Cannon-Bard theories.

The Role of Autonomic Feedback

The James-Lange and Cannon-Bard theories raised intriguing questions about how the various aspects of an emotional experience interact with one another. The theories differ on one crucial point. According to the James-Lange theory, feedback from the body's reactions to a situation tells the brain that we are experiencing an emotion. Without such bodily feedback, there would be no emotional response. In contrast, the Cannon-Bard theory maintains that emotional experiences result from signals sent directly from the thalamus to the cortex, not from bodily feedback. Is there any way to test whether bodily feedback is necessary?

In fact, there is. What if organisms were deprived of sensory feedback from their internal organs? Would they be devoid of emotional reactions? To answer this question, Cannon (1929) carried out experiments with animals in which he severed the nerves that provide feedback from the internal organs to the brain. He found that even after such surgery, the animals exhibited emotional responses, lending support to his theory that direct sensory messages to the brain are the emotional triggers. In like manner, people whose spinal cords have been severed in accidents and who receive no sensory feedback from body areas below the injury continue to feel intense emotions—sometimes more intense than those they experienced before their injuries. Moreover, people with upper and lower spinal cord injuries, who differ in the amount of bodily feedback they receive, do not differ in the intensity of their emotions (Chwalisz et al., 1988).

These results appear to cast doubt on the claim that arousal feedback from the body is

Figure 11.32

Two theories of emotion.
Two early theories of emotion continue to influence current research. The James-Lange theory holds that the experience of emotion is caused by somatic feedback and physiological arousal. According to the Cannon-Bard theory, the thalamus receives sensory input and simultaneously stimulates physiological responses and cognitive awareness.

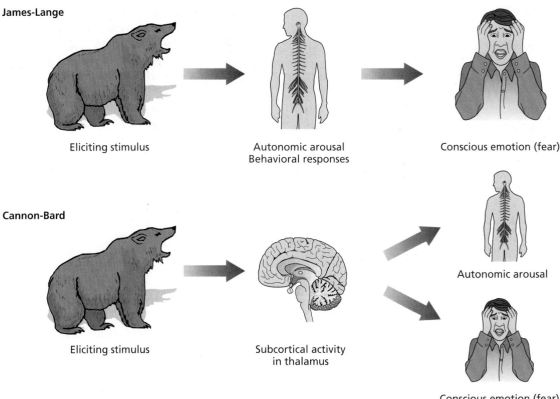

James-Lange

Eliciting stimulus → Autonomic arousal Behavioral responses → Conscious emotion (fear)

Cannon-Bard

Eliciting stimulus → Subcortical activity in thalamus → Autonomic arousal / Conscious emotion (fear)

absolutely necessary for people to experience intense emotions. But let's take this issue one step further.

The Role of Expressive Behaviors

Arousal feedback is not the only kind of bodily feedback considered important by the James-Lange somatic theory. Facial muscles involved in emotional displays also feed messages to the brain, and these muscles are active even in patients with spinal injuries who receive no sensory input from below the neck. According to the **facial feedback hypothesis,** *feedback from the facial muscles to the brain plays a key role in determining the nature and intensity of emotions that we experience*, as the James-Lange theory would suggest (Adelmann & Zajonc, 1989).

According to the theory, sensory input is first routed to the subcortical areas of the brain that control facial movements. These centers immediately send signals that activate the facial muscles. Sensory feedback from movement of facial muscles is then routed to the cerebral cortex, which produces our conscious experience of the emotion. To return to James's example of the bear, the facial feedback hypothesis says that we are frightened when the bear approaches partly because

an automatic expression of terror appears on our face and sends signals from our facial muscles to the cortex, where the subjective feelings of fear are produced.

In support of the facial feedback hypothesis, research shows that feedback from facial muscle patterns can arouse specific emotional reactions (Soussignan, 2002). In one study, Fritz Strack and coworkers (1988) found that when participants held pens in their teeth, activating muscles used in smiling (Figure 11.33a), they rated themselves as feeling more pleasant than when they held the pens with their lips, activating the muscles involved in frowning (Figure 11.33b). Participants also rated cartoons as funnier while holding pens in their teeth and activating the "happy muscles" than while holding pens with their lips (Figure 11.33c). In another study, researchers compared the subjective experiences of people who pronounced different sounds, such as *eee* and *ooh*. Saying *eee*, which activates muscles used in smiling, was associated with more pleasant feelings than saying *ooh*, which activates muscles involved in negative facial expressions (Zajonc et al., 1989). Perhaps portrait photographers should ask us to say *cheese* not only when they take our picture but also later, when they show us photo proofs that not even our mothers could love.

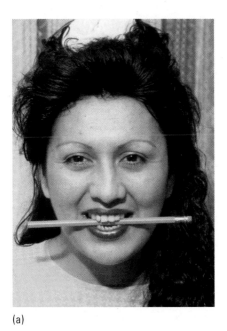

(a)

(b)

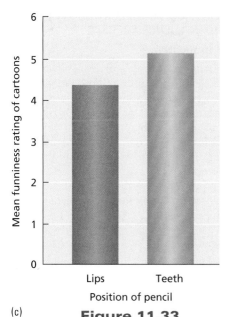

(c)

Figure 11.33

Facial feedback and emotional experience.
(a) Holding a pencil in the teeth, which activates the muscles used in smiling, evokes more pleasant feelings than (b) holding a pencil in one's lips, which activates muscles associated with negative emotions. (c) The findings shown in this graph provide support for the facial feedback hypothesis.
SOURCE: Based on Strack et al., 1988.

Cognitive-Affective Theories

Nowhere are mind-body interactions more obvious than in the emotions, where thinking and feeling are intimately connected. *Cognitive-affective theories* examine how cognitions and physiological responses interact (Clore & Centerbar, 2004; Smith & Kirby, 2004). Historically, Richard Lazarus and Stanley Schachter have been major figures in this approach.

Lazarus (2001) argued that all emotional responses require some sort of appraisal, whether we are aware of that appraisal or not. Schachter was intrigued with the factors that determine our emotional perceptions. According to Schachter's **two-factor theory of emotion,** *the intensity of physiological arousal tells us* how strongly *we are feeling something, but situational cues give us the information we need to label the arousal and tell ourselves* what *we are feeling*—fear, anger, love, or some other emotion (Schachter, 1966).

If appraisal and arousal affect one another in the ways these theories suggest, then by manipulating appraisals we should be able to influence physiological arousal. Moreover, if we can manipulate arousal, we should be able to influence cognitive appraisals of the situation. The "Research Close-up" examines two studies that test these propositions.

Cognition-Arousal Relations: Two Classic Experiments

SOURCES: JOSEPH SPEISMAN, RICHARD S. LAZARUS, ARNOLD MORDKOFF, & LES DAVISON (1964). Experimental reduction of stress based on ego-defense theory. *Journal of Abnormal and Social Psychology, 68,* 367–380.

STANLEY SCHACHTER & LADD WHEELER (1962). Epinephrine, chlorpromazine, and amusement. *Journal of Abnormal and Social Psychology, 65,* 121–128.

Two researchers who were at the forefront as appraisal-arousal theories of emotion were being developed in the 1960s were Richard Lazarus and Stanley Schachter. These two experiments are still considered classics in the field of emotion, and they gave impetus to the idea that appraisal and arousal influence one another.

Continued

LAZARUS: MANIPULATING APPRAISAL TO INFLUENCE AROUSAL

Introduction

Richard Lazarus and his University of California colleagues examined how differences in cognitive appraisal can influence physiological arousal. To do so, they needed to measure physiological arousal in response to eliciting stimuli, which were held constant for all participants, while influencing the manner in which the eliciting stimuli were appraised. If people in different appraisal conditions showed different arousal responses to the same eliciting stimuli, it would support the notion that arousal is influenced by appraisal.

Method

The researchers monitored college students' physiological responses while they watched an anthropology film, *Subincision in the Arunta*, which depicts in graphic detail an aboriginal puberty rite during which the penises of adolescent boys are cut with a jagged flint knife. The dependent variable, measured by recording electrodes attached to the participants' palms, was changes in electrical skin conductance caused by sweat gland activity.

To study the effects of participants' appraisal of the filmed visual stimuli on arousal, the researchers experimentally varied the film's sound track. Four different sound track conditions were used to manipulate the independent variable:

- A *trauma* sound track emphasized the pain suffered by the boys, the danger of infection, the jaggedness of the flint knife, and other unpleasant aspects of the operation.

- A *denial* sound track was just the opposite; it denied that the operation was excessively painful or traumatic and emphasized that the boys looked forward to entering adulthood by undergoing the rite and demonstrating their bravery.

- The *intellectualization* sound track, also designed to produce a more benign appraisal, ignored the emotional elements of the scenes altogether and focused on the traditions and history of the tribe.

- In a *silent* control condition, the film was shown without any sound track at all, leaving viewers to make their own appraisals.

Results

As shown in Figure 11.34, the sound tracks produced markedly different levels of arousal. As predicted, the trauma sound track resulted in the highest arousal, followed by the silent film condition, which likely evoked dire appraisals as well. The denial and intellectualization sound tracks, designed to create more benign appraisals, resulted in much lower levels of arousal. This classic study supported Lazarus's contention that appraisal can influence arousal.

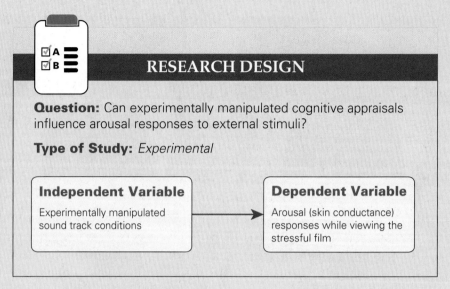

RESEARCH DESIGN

Question: Can experimentally manipulated cognitive appraisals influence arousal responses to external stimuli?

Type of Study: *Experimental*

Independent Variable	**Dependent Variable**
Experimentally manipulated sound track conditions	Arousal (skin conductance) responses while viewing the stressful film

SCHACHTER: MANIPULATING AROUSAL TO INFLUENCE APPRAISAL

Introduction

Is the reverse also true? Can level of arousal influence people's appraisal of an eliciting stimulus? To test this hypothesis, one must cause people to experience different levels of arousal without knowing the true reason. The level of arousal should then be attributed to whatever eliciting cues are present in the situation.

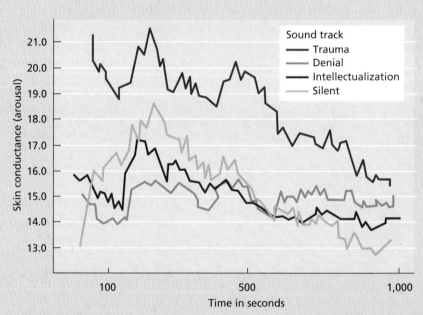

Figure 11.34

Does appraisal influence arousal?

Participants who viewed a film showing a painful tribal rite in vivid detail exhibited different levels of physiological arousal, depending on the sound track that accompanied the film. SOURCE: Speisman et al., 1964.

Method

In Stanley Schachter's laboratory at Columbia University, participants were told they were in a study involving the effects of a new vitamin called suproxin on visual perception. The researchers directly manipulated the level of physiological arousal by injecting participants with one of three different "suproxin" substances. In one condition, participants received epinephrine, a drug that increases arousal. In a second experimental condition, participants received a tranquilizer drug that would decrease arousal. A placebo control group received a saline injection that would have no effects on arousal. The experimenters told all participants that the suproxin injection would have no side effects (when, in fact, the epinephrine and tranquilizer would begin to have immediate—and opposite—effects on arousal). Then, while presumably waiting for the vitamin to take effect, the participants were shown a short movie "to provide continuous black and white stimulation to the eyes." The movie was a comedy film that included a slapstick chase scene. The experimenters hypothesized that the participants in the two drug conditions would attribute their heightened or lowered level of arousal to the funniness (or lack thereof) of the film, because they would know of no other reason why they should feel as they did.

Participants were observed from behind a one-way mirror while they watched the movie. The observers, who were unaware of which participants had received which injections, recorded how frequently the participants smiled, grinned, laughed, threw up their hands, slapped their legs, or doubled over with laughter. These behaviors were combined into an "amusement score" that served as the dependent variable measure of how funny the participants found the film to be.

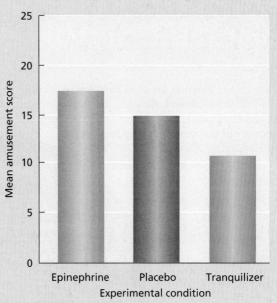

Figure 11.35

Does arousal influence appraisal?

Participants were injected with either epinephrine, a tranquilizer, or a placebo to affect arousal and then were shown a humorous film. The amount of amusement they displayed varied with their state of arousal. Source: Schachter & Wheeler, 1962.

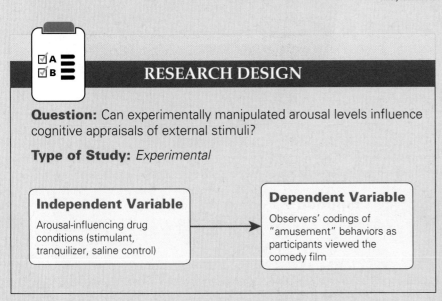

RESEARCH DESIGN

Question: Can experimentally manipulated arousal levels influence cognitive appraisals of external stimuli?

Type of Study: *Experimental*

Independent Variable	Dependent Variable
Arousal-influencing drug conditions (stimulant, tranquilizer, saline control)	Observers' codings of "amusement" behaviors as participants viewed the comedy film

Results

It appears that arousal cues can indeed influence one's appraisal of a situation. As Figure 11.35 shows, the results supported the hypothesis that level of arousal would influence participants' appraisal of the film. The aroused participants in the epinephrine group found the film funnier than the tranquilized participants did, and the placebo control group fell in the middle. Thus a person injected with epinephrine might think, "Here I am watching this film and getting all excited. This film's really funny!"

Critical Discussion

These two studies were among the first to experimentally manipulate appraisal and arousal so as to study their effects on one another. In the first study, even though it was not possible to completely control for participants' own tendencies to appraise situations in certain ways, the four sound track conditions did have effects on the arousal responses of participants as they watched the subincision film. When Schachter and Wheeler turned Lazarus's procedure around and manipulated arousal levels with the stimulant and tranquilizing drugs, they found the expected differences in appraisal of the funniness of a film, and they were able to measure these differences in terms of observable behavior rather than self-report. Thus these two studies show that appraisal influences arousal and that arousal can influence appraisals, demonstrating the two-way causal relation between cognition and arousal shown in the model of emotion originally presented in Figure 11.25 (page 396).

Levels of Analysis   Emotion

As we have seen, emotion involves complex interactions between mind, body, and the environment. As such, its study spans the biological, psychological, and environmental levels of analysis. Here is a summary of the factors that contribute to our understanding of emotion:

ENVIRONMENTAL LEVEL

- Many eliciting stimuli arise in the external environment.
- Individual and cultural learning experiences can affect emotional expression and experience.
- Some environmental stimuli are primed by evolutionary factors to be eliciting stimuli.

BIOLOGICAL LEVEL

- Genetic factors influence emotional reactivity from the moment of birth.
- Brain structures (especially the amygdala), other limbic structures, and the cortex are part of a two-component emotional system that can operate at both conscious and unconscious levels. The hemispheres differ in the emotions most strongly associated with them.
- Neurotransmitter systems play an important role in the neural activations and inhibitions that underlie emotion.

PSYCHOLOGICAL LEVEL

- Cognitive processes play an important role in the emotional response system, generating emotions and guiding instrumental and coping responses.
- Cognitive appraisals and physiological arousal influence one another.
- Knowledge of cultural norms for emotional expression influences both emotional experience and expression.

How might cognitive appraisal processes influence right/left hemisphere responses to environmental stimuli, and which emotions would be expected to result?

test yourself   Emotion

True or false?

1. Polygraph tests are more likely to make mistakes by suggesting guilt in innocent people than in correctly identifying guilty people.

2. Cultures differ widely in their facial expressions of basic emotions.

3. According to LeDoux's theory, sensory input to the amygdala may result in unconscious emotional responses.

4. Highly aroused people are especially likely to excel on very complex tasks.

5. The James-Lange theory states that, consistent with the facial feedback hypothesis, our emotional experiences are caused by our automatic bodily responses.

ANSWERS: 1-true, 2-false, 3-true, 4-false, 5-true

Chapter Summary

MOTIVATION

- Motivation influences the direction, vigor, and persistence of goal-directed behavior. Homeostatic models view motivation as an attempt to maintain equilibrium in bodily systems. Drive theories propose that tissue deficits create drives, such as hunger, that push an organism to reduce that deficit and restore homeostasis.

- Incentive theories emphasize environmental factors that pull people toward a goal. Expectancy × value theory explains why the same incentive may motivate some people but not others.

- Psychodynamic theories emphasize that unconscious motives guide much of our behavior. Abraham Maslow proposed that needs exist in a hierarchy, from basic biological needs to the ultimate need for self-actualization. Self-determination theory emphasizes the importance of three fundamental needs—competence, autonomy, and relatedness, as well as distinctions between intrinsic and extrinsic motivation.

- Physiological processes attempt to keep the body in energy homeostasis. Changes in the supply of glucose available to cells provide one signal that helps initiate hunger. During meals, hormones such as CCK are released into the bloodstream and help signal the brain to stop eating. Fat cells release leptin, which acts as a long-term signal that helps regulate appetite. The hypothalamus plays an important role in hunger regulation.

- Through classical conditioning, neutral stimuli can acquire the capacity to trigger hunger. Cultural norms affect our food preferences and eating habits. Heredity and the environment affect our susceptibility to becoming obese.

- Anorexia and bulimia occur more often in cultures that value thinness, and are associated with somewhat different psychological profiles. Heredity predisposes some people toward developing these eating disorders.

- The past half century has witnessed changing patterns of sexual activity, such as an increase in premarital sex, which now appears to have leveled off.

- During sexual intercourse, people often experience a four-stage physiological response pattern consisting of excitement, plateau, orgasm, and resolution.

- Environmental stimuli affect sexual desire. Viewing sexual violence reinforces men's belief in rape myths and generally increases men's aggression toward women.

- Sexual orientation involves dimensions of self-identity, sexual attraction, and actual sexual behavior. Scientists still do not completely understand the bases for sexual orientation.

- People differ in how strongly they need to affiliate, and some theorists view affiliative behavior as governed by homeostatic principles.

- Situations that induce fear often increase people's tendency to affiliate. When afraid, people often seek the company of others who have been through or are currently experiencing the same or a similar situation.

- Social exclusion is a painful experience for most people, and it often leads to attempts to reconnect socially in new relationships.

- High-need achievers have a strong motive for success and relatively low fear of failure. They tend to seek moderately difficult tasks that are challenging but attainable. Low-need achievers are more likely to choose easy tasks, where success is assured, or very difficult tasks, where success is not expected.

- Mastery-approach, ego-approach, mastery-avoidance, and ego-avoidance are four basic achievement goals. Compared with ego-involving environments, mastery-involving motivational climates foster more positive psychological and performance outcomes.

- Motivational goals may conflict with one another. Approach-approach conflict occurs when a person has to select between two attractive alternatives, whereas avoidance-avoidance conflict involves choosing between two undesirable alternatives. Approach-avoidance conflict occurs when we are attracted to and repelled by the same goal.

EMOTION

- The primary components of emotion are the eliciting stimuli, cognitive appraisals, physiological arousal, and expressive and instrumental behaviors. Innate factors and learning play important roles in determining the arousal properties of stimuli.

- The cognitive component of emotional experience involves the evaluative and personal appraisal of the eliciting stimuli. Cross-cultural research indicates considerable agreement across cultures in the appraisals that evoke basic emotions but also some degree of variation in more complex appraisals.

- Our physiological responses in emotion are produced by the hypothalamus, the limbic system, the cortex, and the autonomic and endocrine systems. There appear to be two systems for emotional behavior, one involving conscious processing by the cortex and the other involving unconscious processing by the amygdala.

- Negative emotions seem to reflect greater relative activation of the right hemisphere, whereas positive emotions are related to relatively greater activation in the left hemisphere.

- The validity of the polygraph as a lie detector has been questioned largely because of the difficulty of establishing the meaning of recorded physiological responses.

- The behavioral component of emotion includes expressive and instrumental behaviors. The accuracy of people's interpretation of these expressions is enhanced when situational cues are also available. Evolutionary theorists propose that certain fundamental emotional patterns are innate but agree that cultural learning can influence emotional expression.
- There is an optimal level of arousal for the performance of any task. This optimal level varies with the complexity of the task; complex tasks have lower optimal levels.

- The James-Lange theory maintains that we first become aroused and then judge what we are feeling. The Cannon-Bard theory proposes that arousal and cognition are independent and simultaneously triggered by the thalamus. According to Lazarus's cognitive-affective theory, appraisals trigger emotional arousal; in contrast, according to Schachter's two-factor theory of emotion, arousal tells us how strongly we are feeling while cognitions derived from situational cues help us label the specific emotion.

KEY TERMS AND CONCEPTS

Each term has been boldfaced and defined in the chapter on the page indicated in parentheses.

achievement goal theory (p. 390)
anorexia nervosa (p. 380)
approach-approach conflict (p. 393)
approach-avoidance conflict (p. 393)
avoidance-avoidance conflict (p. 393)
behavioral activation system (BAS) (p. 370)
behavioral inhibition system (BIS) (p. 370)
bulimia nervosa (p. 380)
Cannon-Bard theory (p. 405)
cholecystokinin (CCK) (p. 375)
cognitive appraisal (p. 397)
cultural display rules (p. 403)
drive (p. 369)
ego-approach goals (p. 391)
ego-avoidance goals (p. 391)
ego orientation (p. 390)
eliciting stimuli (p. 397)

emotion (p. 395)
expectancy × value theory (p. 370)
expressive behaviors (p. 401)
extrinsic motivation (p. 370)
facial feedback hypothesis (p. 406)
fundamental emotional patterns (p. 402)
glucose (p. 374)
homeostasis (p. 369)
incentive (p. 370)
instinct (p. 369)
instrumental behaviors (p. 404)
intrinsic motivation (p. 370)
James-Lange theory (p. 405)
leptin (p. 375)
mastery-approach goals (p. 391)
mastery-avoidance goals (p. 391)
mastery orientation (p. 390)

metabolism (p. 374)
motivation (p. 369)
motivational climate (p. 390)
need for achievement (p. 389)
paraventricular nucleus (PVN) (p. 376)
polygraph (p. 400)
self-actualization (p. 371)
self-determination theory (p. 371)
self-efficacy (p. 394)
set point (p. 374)
sexual dysfunction (p. 384)
sexual orientation (p. 386)
sexual response cycle (p. 383)
social comparison (p. 389)
2 × 2 achievement goal theory (p. 391)
two-factor theory of emotion (p. 407)

? thinking **critically**

IS MASLOW'S NEED HIERARCHY VALID?
(Page 373)

More than most psychological theories of motivation, Maslow's model appropriately emphasizes that diverse motives influence human behavior. The concepts of need progression and need regression seem to make intuitive sense. Motives do become stronger and weaker as circumstances change, and it seems logical that when people are starving, finding food becomes more important than contemplating beauty and truth.

Critics, however, have long questioned the validity of the need hierarchy and have argued that the concept of "self-actualization" is vague and hard to measure (Heylighen, 1992). The ordering of needs seems arbitrary, and the concepts of need progression and regression cannot account for important aspects

of motivated behavior. How does the hierarchy explain why prisoners of war endure torture rather than betray their comrades? why millions of women choose to live in constant hunger to be thin? why political protestors go on hunger strikes or risk their physical safety to defend principles they believe in? Does a need for knowledge and understanding really become prominent only after needs for social belonging and self-esteem are met? Throughout evolution, was seeking esteem and recognition more important and adaptive to our ancestors than acquiring knowledge to help them survive?

Finally, rather than viewing the journey toward self-actualization as a relatively independent striving to maximize one's potential, some modern humanists view the entire process as more relationship-oriented (Hanley & Abell, 2002). In their view, healthy social relationships not only satisfy deficiency needs for belonging and esteem but also are important for achieving and expressing self-actualization.

Despite these drawbacks, by calling attention to the human desire for growth and incorporating diverse motives, the intuitive appeal of Maslow's model has influenced thinking in fields such as philosophy, education, and business (Zinovieva, 2001).

FRATERNAL BIRTH ORDER AND MALE HOMOSEXUALITY (Page 388)

Blanchard (2001) estimates that the presence of each older brother increases by about one third the *relative probability* that a later-born male child will be gay. For example, if there is a 2 percent probability that a man with no older brothers is gay, then the probability for a man with one older brother is about 2.6 to 2.7 percent, roughly a one-third relative increase. As Blanchard (2001) notes, "the probability that a couple's son will be gay rises from 2 to 6 percent for their fifth son. That is a threefold increase. However, 94 percent of fifth sons will still be heterosexual" (p. 108).

So why does this effect occur? Perhaps you thought of one of these explanations: First, it may be that the greater the number of older brothers, the greater the possibility (however small) of having an incestuous sexual encounter with an older male while growing up. However, as Blanchard (2001) notes, evidence does not suggest that such incestuous experiences are linked to adulthood sexual orientation. Second, perhaps if an older brother has a homosexual orientation, awareness of this might influence a younger brother's sexual orientation. A study of gay men with gay brothers, however, found that most were aware of their own homosexual feelings before they became aware of their brother's homosexual orientation (Dawood et al., 2000).

Blanchard (2001) and his coworkers propose a biological explanation, called the *maternal immune hypothesis*. During pregnancy, male (but not female) fetuses contain substances that, as a group, are called *H-Y antigen,* which helps guide the fetal brain toward a male-typical pattern. Sometimes, H-Y antigen passes from the fetus to the mother's bloodstream, in which case it is a foreign substance to the mother. Thus the mother's immune system responds by producing antibodies (proteins) to combat the H-Y antigen. In turn, these antibodies pass from the mother to the fetus and reach the fetal brain. "When that happens, these antibodies partly prevent the fetal brain from developing in the male-typical pattern, so that the individual will later be attracted to men rather than women. The probability—or strength—of maternal immunization increases with each male fetus" (Blanchard, 2001, p. 110). Thus a mother with sons is more likely to carry and pass on these antibodies to any new male fetus, altering H-Y antigen's role in guiding fetal brain development toward a male-typical pattern. Blanchard estimates that for about one quarter of gay men, the development of their sexual orientation proceeded along this path. Of course, like other current theories, the maternal immune hypothesis needs much more testing.

chapter twelve

Development over the Life Span

Myth or Reality?

**The Aging Brain Is Like a Muscle: Use It or Lose It
(page 445)**

Does the "use it or lose it" principle of physical fitness also apply to our mental abilities? Do cognitive workouts help keep our brain "in shape" and fight off mental decline as we get older? What does science say about this "mental-exercise hypothesis"?

In 1799, three hunters discovered a remarkable child living in the forests of Aveyron, France. Most likely abandoned at a young age, he grew up isolated from human contact, foraging for food and surviving naked in the wild. About 12 years old, he easily climbed trees, ate nuts and roots, scratched and bit people who interfered with him, and made few sounds. He could walk upright yet ran quickly on all fours. Some regarded him as half-human, half-beast, and they called him the "Wild Boy of Aveyron" (Itard, 1894/1962).

Several medical experts concluded that the boy was incurably "mentally deficient," but others disagreed, noting that it took intelligence to survive in the wild. They argued that special education and care would enable the child to flower into a normal, civilized adult. In Paris, the boy was placed under the care of a prominent young physician, Jean-Marc Itard, who named him Victor and diligently supervised his training (Figure 12.1).

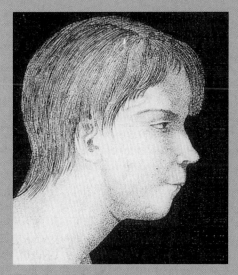

Figure 12.1

Victor, the "Wild Boy of Aveyron."

At first, Victor did not respond to stimuli that most people find aversive. Unfazed, he would stick his hand into boiling kitchen water to grab food or eagerly roll around half-naked on the cold winter ground. Eventually he learned to sense temperature differences, dress himself, and perform other self-care behaviors. Victor's emotional responses, which at first fluctuated without reason, began to fit the situation: He laughed in playful situations, shed tears over someone's death, and displayed some signs of affection toward Itard. Victor learned to read and write some words, communicate basic needs, and perform simple tasks.

Although Victor changed in important ways, as he grew older his progress slowed considerably. He never learned to speak, and after 5 years of education his cognitive, emotional, and social development remained limited. Pessimism over further progress grew, and Itard's "project" ended. Victor was moved to a nearby home, where a woman cared for him for the rest of his life.

A psychologist would ask whether Victor, had he been found and socialized at a younger age, could have shown greater progress or even a complete return to behavior typical of people his age. Is there an age beyond which intellectual and social recovery from such isolation becomes impossible? Further, was it social isolation that stunted Victor's development, or did illness, malnutrition, or other causes play a role?

In the early 1800s, people expected Victor's case to resolve an intense debate about the roles of nature versus nurture in shaping who we are. But it raised more questions than it answered. Was Victor a normal, inherently noble infant who became irreparably harmed by his childhood isolation, or as some claimed, was he born "mentally deficient"?

Some children exposed to extreme adversity are highly resilient and thrive later in life (Mersky & Topitzes, 2009). We cannot pinpoint why Victor failed to recover, but his famous case begs a fundamental question: Just how does the miracle of human development unfold, and what conditions are required for normal growth?

MAJOR ISSUES AND METHODS

Developmental psychology examines biological, physical, psychological, and behavioral changes that occur as we age. Four broad issues guide much developmental research.

- *Nature and nurture:* To what extent is our development the product of heredity (nature) and the product of environment (nurture)? How do nature and nurture interact?

- *Sensitive and critical periods:* Are some experiences especially important at particular ages? A **sensitive period** *is an optimal age range for certain experiences, but if those experiences occur at another time, normal development is still possible.* A **critical period** *is an age range during which certain experiences must occur for development to proceed normally or along a certain path* (Arshavsky, 2009).

- *Continuity versus discontinuity:* Is development continuous and gradual, as when a sapling slowly grows into a tree, or is it discontinuous, progressing through qualitatively distinct stages, as when a creeping caterpillar emerges from its cocoon as a soaring butterfly?

- *Stability versus change:* Do our characteristics remain consistent as we age?

Psychologists often use special research designs to investigate developmental questions (Figure 12.2). Suppose we want to study how intellectual abilities change from age 10 to age 60. Using a **cross-sectional design,** *we would compare people of different ages at the same point in time.* Thus in the next month we could administer intellectual tasks to 10-, 20-, 30-, 40-, 50-, and 60-year-olds. We would test each person only once and compare how well the different age groups performed. The cross-sectional design is widely used because data from many age groups can be collected relatively quickly, but a key drawback is that the different age groups, called *cohorts,* grew up in different historical periods. Thus, if 70-year-olds have poorer intellectual abilities than 30-year-olds, is this due to aging or to environmental differences (e.g., poorer nutrition or medical care) between growing up in the 1940s and 1950s versus the 1980s and 1990s?

To avoid this problem, a **longitudinal design** *repeatedly tests the same cohort as it grows older.* We could test a sample of 10-year-olds this month and then retest them every 10 years, up to age 60, thus ensuring that everyone is exposed to the same historical time frame. Unfortunately, a longitudinal design can be time-consuming, and as years pass, our sample may shrink as people move, drop out of the study, or die. Further, suppose we find that intelligence declines at age 60. Is this really due to aging or to developmental experiences unique to our particular cohort? Researchers can answer this question by using a **sequential design,** *which combines the cross-sectional and longitudinal approaches.* For example, we could test 10- through 60-year-olds now, retest them every 10 years, and then examine whether the various cohorts followed a similar developmental pattern. This design is the most comprehensive but also the costliest and most time-consuming.

Now let's turn to the process of human development. We begin with the *prenatal period,* approximately 266 days during which each of us developed from a single-celled organism barely larger than a pinhead into a wondrously complex newborn human.

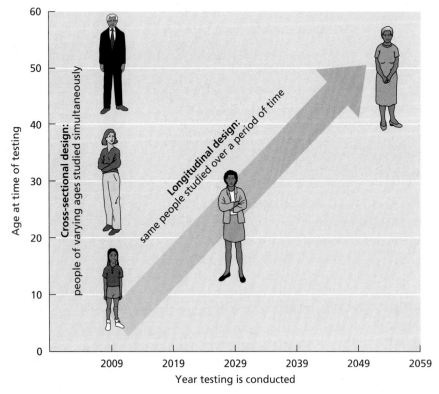

Figure 12.2

Developmental research designs.
Using a cross-sectional design, we would test different age groups in the year 2009 and compare their performance. Using a longitudinal design, we would test individuals of one age group and then retest them every 10 years until age 60. Using a sequential design, we would test 10- through 60-year-olds in the year 2009 and then retest them every 10 years until the youngest cohort reached age 60.

test yourself   **Major Issues and Methods**

True or False?

1. Researchers study 300 8-year-olds this year and study them again at ages 18 and 28. This is a cross-sectional design.

2. Researchers study 100 8-year-olds, 100 18-year-olds, and 100 28-year-olds now. Ten years later and ten years after that, they study the same participants again. This is a sequential design.

3. Dr. Piaget believes that children's development occurs in qualitatively distinct stages. This approach reflects a view that development is discontinuous.

ANSWERS: 1-false, 2-true, 3-true

PRENATAL DEVELOPMENT

Our genetic blueprint sets forth a path of prenatal development that consists of three stages (Figure 12.3). The *germinal stage* comprises approximately the first 2 weeks of development, beginning when a sperm fertilizes a female egg (*ovum*). *This fertilized egg is called a* **zygote,** and through repeated cell division it becomes a mass of cells that attaches to the mother's uterus about 10 to 14 days after conception.

The *embryonic stage* is next. The cell mass, now called an **embryo,** *develops from the end of week 2 through week 8 after conception.* Two life-support structures, the placenta and umbilical cord, develop at the start of this stage. Located on the uterine wall, the *placenta* contains membranes that allow nutrients to pass from the mother's blood to the umbilical cord. In turn, the *umbilical cord* contains blood vessels that carry these nutrients and oxygen to the embryo and transport waste products back from the embryo to the mother. Supplied with nutrients, embryonic cells rapidly divide and become specialized. Bodily organs and systems begin to form, and by week 8 the heart

of the inch-long embryo is beating, the brain is forming, and facial features such as eyes can be recognized.

Finally, during the *fetal stage,* the **fetus** *develops from week 9 after conception until birth.* Muscles strengthen and other bodily systems develop. At about 24 weeks the eyes open, and by 27 weeks (or several weeks younger, with top medical care) the fetus attains the *age of viability:* it is likely to survive outside the womb in case of premature birth (Tyson et al., 2008).

Genetics and Sex Determination

A female's egg cells and a male's sperm cells each have 23 chromosomes. At conception, an egg and sperm unite to form the zygote, which now contains the full set of 23 *pairs* of chromosomes found in other human cells. The 23rd pair of chromosomes determines the baby's sex. A genetic female's 23rd pair contains two X chromosomes (XX), so called because of their shape (Figure 12.4). Because women carry only X chromosomes, the 23rd chromosome in the egg is always an X. A genetic male's 23rd pair contains an X and a

Figure 12.3

These remarkable photos show (a) the moment of conception, as one of many sperm cells fertilizes the ovum, (b) the embryo at 6 to 7 weeks, and (c) the fetus at 3 months of age.

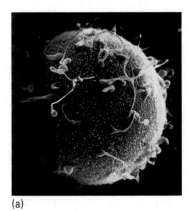

(a)

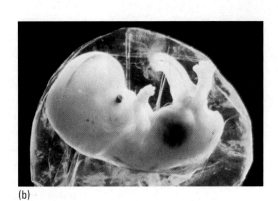

(b)

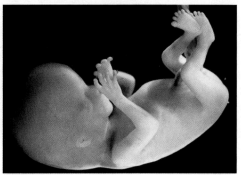

(c)

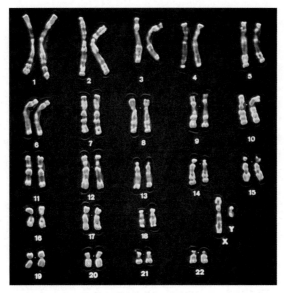

Figure 12.4

Most human cells contain 23 pairs of chromosomes. Each pair consists of one chromosome from each parent. The 23rd pair determines a person's sex. In males, the 23rd pair, which is shown in the lower right area of the photo, consists of an X chromosome and a Y chromosome. In females, the 23rd pair contains two X chromosomes.

Y chromosome (XY). Thus the 23rd chromosome in the sperm is an X in about half of the cases and a Y in the other half. The Y chromosome contains a specific gene, the *TDF (testis determining factor) gene,* that triggers male sexual development. The union of an egg with a sperm cell having a Y chromosome results in an XY combination and therefore a boy. A sperm containing an X chromosome produces an XX combination and therefore a girl.

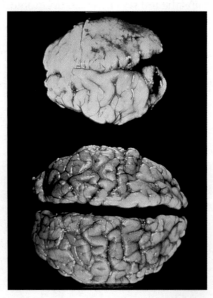

Figure 12.5

Children who suffer from fetal alcohol syndrome (FAS) not only look different but also have brains that are underdeveloped and smaller than those of normal children.

How does the Y chromosome determine male sex characteristics? At roughly 6 to 8 weeks after conception, the TDF gene initiates the development of testes. Once formed, the testes secrete sex hormones called *androgens* that continue to direct a male pattern of organ development. If the TDF gene is not present, as happens with an XX combination in the 23rd pair, testes do not form and—in the absence of sufficient androgen activity during this *prenatal critical period*—an inherent female pattern of organ development ensues.

Environmental Influences

Nature and nurture become intertwined even before we are born. **Teratogens** *are external agents that cause abnormal prenatal development.* The placenta prevents many dangerous substances from reaching the embryo and fetus, but some harmful chemicals and diseases can pass through. For example, if the mother contracts rubella (German measles)—especially when the embryo's eyes, ears, heart, and central nervous system are beginning to form early in pregnancy—it can cause blindness, deafness, heart defects, and mental retardation in the infant (Plotkin, 2006).

Sexually transmitted diseases can pass from mother to fetus and produce brain damage, blindness, and deafness, depending on the disease. Among pregnant women with untreated syphilis, about 25 percent of fetuses are born dead. Likewise, without treatment during pregnancy or delivery by cesarean section, about 25 percent of fetuses born to mothers with the human immunodeficiency virus (HIV) also are infected (Meleski & Damato, 2003).

Mercury, lead, radiation, and many other environmental toxins can produce birth defects, as can many drugs. **Fetal alcohol spectrum disorders (FASD)** *involve a range of mild to severe cognitive, behavioral, and/or physical deficits caused by prenatal exposure to alcohol* (Bjorkquist et al., 2010). One disorder within this spectrum, **fetal alcohol syndrome (FAS),** *involves a cluster of severe developmental abnormalities.* FAS children have facial abnormalities and small, malformed brains (Figure 12.5). Psychological and social impairments include mental retardation, attentional and perceptual deficits, impulsivity, and poor social skills (Murthy et al., 2009). Other children exposed to alcohol in the womb may display fewer or milder impairments.

The threshold levels of alcohol exposure needed to produce FASD, or FAS specifically, are not known. About one-third to one-half of infants born to alcoholic mothers have FAS, but even social drinking or a single episode of binge drinking can increase the risk of prenatal damage and long-term cognitive impairment. Because no amount of prenatal alcohol exposure has been confirmed to be absolutely safe, pregnant women and those trying to become pregnant are best advised to completely avoid drinking alcohol (Murthy et al., 2009).

Nicotine is another teratogen. Maternal smoking increases the risk of miscarriage, premature birth, and low birth weight (Kirchengast & Hartmann,

2003). Due to secondhand smoke, regular tobacco use by fathers also has been linked to low infant birth weight and increased risk of respiratory infections (Wakefield et al., 1998). Babies of pregnant mothers who regularly use heroin or cocaine are often born addicted and experience withdrawal symptoms after birth. Their cognitive functioning and ability to regulate their arousal and attention may also be impaired (Lewis et al., 2004).

test yourself   Prenatal Development

True or False?

1. In proper order, prenatal development passes through the germinal, embryonic, and fetal stages.
2. The 23rd chromosome in a woman's egg cell is either an X or a Y, and this is what determines a baby's sex.
3. Teratogens are environmental factors (e.g., a balanced diet) necessary for optimal prenatal development.

ANSWERS: 1-true, 2-false, 3-false

INFANCY AND CHILDHOOD

Studying infancy poses unique challenges. During research, infants may fuss, cry, soil their diapers, or simply fall asleep! Because infants cannot describe their experiences, psychologists must find clever ways to take advantage of responses that infants can make, such as sucking and moving their eyes, to draw inferences about their capabilities and preferences.

The Amazing Newborn

After emerging from the womb, does a newborn's world become a "buzzing, blooming confusion,"

as pioneering psychologist William James (1890/1950) proposed? Contrary to a long-held view of newborns as helpless and passive, research reveals that they are surprisingly sophisticated information processors.

Sensory Capabilities and Perceptual Preferences

Newborns' visual systems are immature. Their eye movements are not well coordinated, and they are very nearsighted (Figure 12.6). Still, infants scan their environment, and although objects look blurry to them, they can perceive some forms only a few days after birth. Newborns can reasonably see objects about 1 foot away, the typical distance

Figure 12.6

Seeing through an infant's eyes. These three images approximate the visual acuity of an infant at (a) 1 month, (b) 3 months, and (c) 12 months of age.

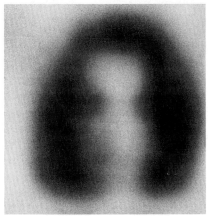
(a)

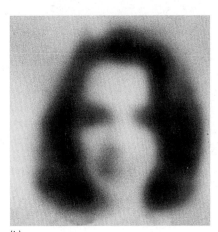
(b)

(c)

between their eyes and their mothers' eyes while nursing.

In a pioneering study, Robert Fantz (1961) used the *preferential looking procedure* to study infants' visual preferences. He placed infants on their backs, showed them two or more stimuli at the same time, and filmed their eyes to record how long they looked at each stimulus. Infants preferred complex patterns, such as realistic or scrambled drawings of a human face, to simple patterns and solid colors (Figure 12.7). Within hours after birth, newborns can distinguish the familiar face of their mother from that of a female stranger, and they prefer to gaze at the mother's face (Bushnell, 2001).

Just as you would make different facial expressions after tasting sweet, sour, or bitter substances, newborns' facial responses tell us that they have a reasonably well-developed sense of taste. Newborns also respond to touch and distinguish different odors. If exposed to pads taken from inside the bras of several nursing mothers, week-old infants will orient toward the scent of their own mother's pad. Newborns also can hear fairly well. They prefer human voices to other sounds and can distinguish their own mother's voice from that of a female stranger (Vouloumanos & Werker, 2007). As Figure 12.8 describes, newborns seem to prefer sounds that become familiar to them in their last weeks of fetal development, during which time they can hear sounds transmitted through the womb (DeCasper & Spence,

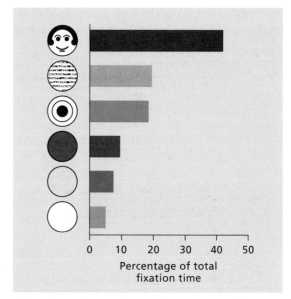

Figure 12.7

Infants' visual preferences.
Whether 2 days old or 2 to 3 months old (the data shown here), infants prefer to look at complex patterns more than simple patterns or solid colors. Source: Based on Fantz, 1961.

1986). Thus, in a rudimentary sense, simple forms of learning can occur inside the womb (Gruest et al., 2004).

Reflexes and Learning

Neonates are equipped with many **reflexes,** *automatic, inborn behaviors that occur in response to*

Figure 12.8

Can the fetus learn? Twice a day during their last 6 weeks of pregnancy, mothers in one study read out loud the same passage from Dr. Seuss's *The Cat in the Hat.* Two or 3 days after birth, their newborns were able to turn on a recording of their mother reading either *The Cat in the Hat* rhyme or an unfamiliar rhyme by sucking on a sensor-equipped nipple at different rates. Compared with infants in a control condition, these newborns more often altered their sucking rates in whichever direction (faster or slower) selected the familiar rhyme. Source: DeCasper & Spence, 1986.

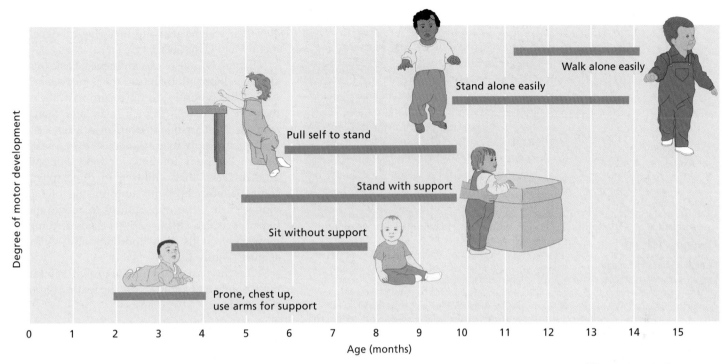

Figure 12.9

Infant motor development.

Infant motor development occurs in an orderly sequence, but the age at which abilities emerge varies across children. The left end of each bar represents the age by which 25 percent of children exhibit the skill; the right end represents the age by which 90 percent have mastered it.

specific stimuli. Some, including breathing, have obvious adaptive significance. Stroke a baby's cheek, and it will turn its head toward the direction it was touched and open its mouth—the *rooting reflex.* When something is placed in the infant's mouth, it will suck on it—the *sucking reflex.* Together, these reflexes increase the infant's ability to feed. In general, healthy reflexes indicate normal neurological maturity at birth.

Newborns learn in several ways. They habituate to repetitive, nonthreatening stimuli and can acquire classically conditioned responses. After a tone (CS) is repeatedly paired with a gentle puff of air to the eye (UCS), they will develop a conditioned eyeblink response to the tone alone (Lipsitt, 1990). Through operant conditioning, newborns learn that they can make things happen. Thus 3-day-old infants can learn to produce a specific pattern of bursts when they suck on a plastic nipple in order to activate a tape-recording of their mothers' voices (Moon & Fifer, 1990).

Within weeks or possibly days after birth, some newborns can reproduce a simple facial expression made by an adult model, providing evidence of a biologically based capacity for imitation (Meltzoff, 2002). By 9 months of age, infants who watch a model act in a novel way (e.g., pushing a button in a box to trigger a sound) can reproduce that action from memory a day later. In sum, infants are born with several mechanisms that help them respond to caretakers and learn important information.

Physical Development

Thanks to **maturation,** *the genetically programmed biological process that governs our growth,* our bodies and movement (motor) skills develop rapidly during infancy and childhood. As Figure 12.9 shows, infants vary in the age at which they acquire particular skills, but the sequence in which skills appear is typically the same across children.

Physical and motor development follow several biological principles. The **cephalocaudal principle** *reflects the tendency for development to proceed in a head-to-foot direction.* Thus, as you can see in Figure 12.3, the head of a fetus (and infant) is disproportionately large because physical growth concentrates first on the head. The **proximodistal principle** *states that development begins along the innermost parts of the body and continues toward the outermost parts.* Thus a fetus's arms develop before the hands and fingers.

The Young Brain

No organ develops more dramatically than the brain. At birth, the newborn's brain is far from mature and has reached only about 25 percent of its eventual adult weight. By age 6 months, however, the brain reaches 50 percent of its adult weight. As Figure 12.10 shows, neural networks that form the basis for cognitive and motor skills develop rapidly. The first brain areas to mature fully lie deep within the brain and regulate basic survival functions such as heartbeat and

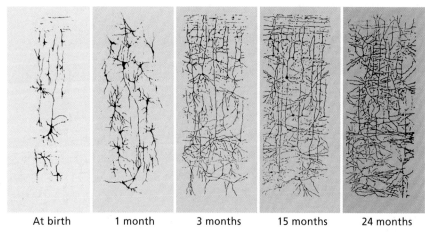

| At birth | 1 month | 3 months | 15 months | 24 months |

Figure 12.10

The brain matures and adapts.

Increases in the density of neural networks during early development are apparent in these drawings of tissue from the human cerebral cortex. Source: Reprinted by permission of the publisher from *The Postnatal Development of the Human Cerebral Cortex, Vols. I–VIII*, by Jesse LeRoy Conel, Cambridge, Mass.: Harvard University Press. Copyright © 1939, 1941, 1947, 1951, 1955, 1959, 1963, 1967 by the President and Fellows of Harvard College. Copyright © renewed 1967, 1969, 1975, 1979, 1983, 1987, 1991.

breathing. Among the last areas to mature is the frontal cortex, which is vital to our highest-level cognitive functions.

This rapid brain growth slows in later childhood (Sowell et al., 2001). Yet, although 5-year-olds' brains have reached almost 90 percent of their adult size, brain maturation continues. New synapses form, unnecessary synapses are pruned back and lost, association areas of the cortex mature, and the cerebral hemispheres become more highly specialized.

Environmental and Cultural Influences

Although guided by genetics, physical development is also influenced by experience. Diet is an obvious example. Chronic, severe malnutrition not only stunts general growth and brain development but also is a major source of infant death worldwide (Pelletier & Frongillo, 2003).

Babies thrive in an enriched environment—one in which the infant has the opportunity to interact with others and to manipulate suitable toys and other objects (Needham et al., 2002). Newborn rats (i.e., pups) raised in an enriched environment develop heavier brains, larger neurons, more synaptic connections, and greater amounts of brain neurotransmitters that enhance learning (Rosenzweig & Bennett, 1996).

Physical touch, too, affects growth in infancy. Depriving well-nourished rat pups of normal physical contact with their mothers stunts their development, whereas vigorously stroking the pups with a brush helps restore normal growth (Schanberg et al., 2003). Similarly, massaging

Figure 12.11

At the Parker Ranch in Hawaii, this 2-year-old is learning to ride a horse and use a lasso.

premature and full-term human infants accelerates their weight gain and neurological development (Field et al., 2006).

Experience also can influence basic motor skill development. Infants of the South American Ache tribe typically do not begin to walk until they are almost 2, about a year later than the average Western infant (Kaplan & Dove, 1987). The Ache people roam the dense rain forests of eastern Paraguay foraging for food. For safety, mothers keep their children in direct physical contact almost constantly until the age of 3, providing them little opportunity to move about. Experience also affects various types of complex movement skills that toddlers and children acquire (Figure 12.11).

Our discussion of physical growth reinforces three points that apply across the realm of human development:

- *Biology sets limits on environmental influences.* For example, no infant can be toilet-trained before the nerve fibers that help regulate bladder control have biologically matured.

- *Environmental influences can be powerful.* Nurturing environments foster physical and psychological growth, and impoverished environments can stunt growth.

- *Biological and environmental factors interact.* Enriched environments enhance brain development. In turn, brain development facilitates our ability to learn and benefit from environmental experiences.

Cognitive Development

How do the thought processes of a child develop? Swiss psychologist Jean Piaget (1926, 1977) spent more than 50 years exploring this question.

Piaget's Stage Model

Early in his career, Piaget worked for French psychologist Alfred Binet, a pioneer of intelligence testing. Piaget became intrigued when he noticed that children of the same age often made similar errors on test questions. To understand how children think, Piaget observed them and listened to them reason as they tried to solve problems. He proposed that children's thinking changes *qualitatively* with age and that it differs from the way adults think. Piaget believed that cognitive development results from an interaction of the brain's biological maturation and personal experiences. He viewed children as natural-born scientists who seek to understand their world.

To achieve this understanding, the brain builds **schemas,** *which are organized patterns of thought and action.* Think of a schema as a mental framework that guides our interaction with the world. For example, infants are born with a sucking reflex that provides a primitive schema for interacting with physical objects. In other words, sucking is a basic way in which the infant "knows" the world. When a child says "doggie" to describe a family pet, this word reflects a schema—a concept that the child is using to understand this particular experience.

Cognitive development occurs as we acquire new schemas and as our existing schemas become more complex. According to Piaget, two key processes are involved. **Assimilation** *is the process by which new experiences are incorporated into existing schemas.* When a young infant encounters a new object—a small plastic toy, a blanket, a doll—she will try to suck it. She tries to fit this new experience into a schema that she already has: objects are suckable. Similarly, a child who sees a skunk for the first time may exclaim "kitty!" After all, the skunk is about the size of a cat, is furry, and has four legs and a tail, so the child tries to make sense of this new experience by applying his familiar schema: "kitty."

Accommodation *is the process by which new experiences cause existing schemas to change.* As the infant tries to suck different objects, she will eventually encounter ones that are too big or that taste bad. Similarly, the child who calls a skunk a "kitty" may discover that this "kitty" exhibits some smelly behaviors not found in cats. This imbalance, or *disequilibrium,* between existing schemas and new experiences ultimately forces those schemas to change. Thus the infant's "suckability" schema will become more complex: some objects are suckable, some are not. The child's "kitty" schema also will change, and he will begin to develop new schemas for "doggie," "skunk," and so on.

Cognitive growth thus involves a give-and-take between trying to understand new experiences in terms of what we already know (assimilation) and having to modify our thinking when new experiences don't fit into our current schemas (accommodation). As Table 12.1 shows, Piaget charted four major stages of cognitive growth.

Sensorimotor Stage   From birth to about age 2, infants in the **sensorimotor stage** *understand their world primarily through sensory experiences and physical (motor) interactions with objects.* Reflexes are infants' earliest schemas, and as infants mature, they begin to explore their surroundings and realize

Table **12.1** | **Piaget's Stages of Cognitive Development**

Stage	Age (Years)	Major Characteristics
Sensorimotor	Birth to 2	• Infant understands world through sensory and motor experiences • Achieves object permanence • Exhibits emergence of symbolic thought
Preoperational	2 to 7	• Child uses symbolic thinking in the form of words and images to represent objects and experiences • Symbolic thinking enables child to engage in pretend play • Thinking displays egocentrism, irreversibility, and centration
Concrete operational	7 to 12	• Child can think logically about concrete events • Grasps concepts of conservation and serial ordering
Formal operational	12 on	• Adolescent can think more logically, abstractly, and flexibly • Can form hypotheses and systematically test them

that they can bang spoons, take objects apart, and make things happen.

For young infants, said Piaget, "out of sight" literally means "out of mind." If you hide 3-month-old Cindy's favorite toy from view, she will not search for it, as if the toy no longer exists (Figure 12.12). But around age 8 months, Cindy will search for and retrieve the hidden toy. She now grasps the concept of **object permanence,** *the understanding that an object continues to exist even when it no longer can be seen.*

Infants begin to acquire language after age 1, and toward the end of the sensorimotor period they increasingly use words to represent objects, needs, and actions. Thus, in the space of 2 years,

Figure 12.12

During the early sensorimotor period, a baby will reach for a visible toy (*left*) but not for one that has been hidden from view while the infant watches (*right*). According to Piaget, the child lacks the concept of object permanence; when something is out of sight, it ceases to exist.

(a)   Initial equality

(b)   Transformation

(c)   Which glass has more juice?

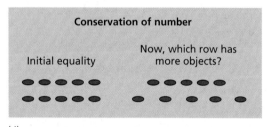

(d)

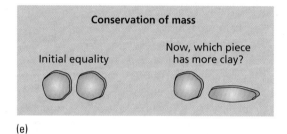

(e)

Figure 12.13

Conservation tasks.

(a, b, c) Conservation of volume: At the end of this sequence (*from left to right*), when the preoperational child is asked which beaker contains more liquid, he points to the taller one.

(d) Conservation of number: Two rows with an equal number of objects are aligned. After one row is spread out, preoperational children will say that it has more objects than the other row.

(e) Conservation of mass: Preoperational children watch as one of two identically sized clay balls is rolled into a new shape. They typically will say that the new shape now has more clay.

infants grow into planful thinkers who form simple concepts, solve some problems, and communicate their thoughts.

Preoperational Stage At about age 2, children enter a **preoperational stage,** *in which they represent the world symbolically through words and mental images but do not yet understand basic mental operations or rules.* Rapid language development helps children label objects and represent simple concepts, such as that two objects can be the "same" or "different." Children can think about the past ("yesterday") and future ("soon") and can better anticipate the consequences of their actions. Symbolic thinking enables them to engage in make-believe, or pretend play.

Despite these advances, children's cognitive abilities have major limitations. The preoperational child does not understand **conservation,** *the principle that basic properties of objects, such as their volume, mass, or quantity, stay the same (are "conserved") even though their outward appearance may change* (Figure 12.13). For example, 4-year-olds often say that the taller beaker in Figure 12.13c has more liquid than the shorter one. You understand that the liquid can be poured back into the short beaker to return to the original, equal state of affairs, but

children's thinking at this age displays *irreversibility:* it is difficult for them to reverse an action mentally. You also pay attention to height and width, recognizing that the liquid is "taller" because the beaker is narrower. But preoperational children exhibit *centration,* focusing (centering) on only one aspect of the situation, such as the height of the liquid.

Preoperational children's thinking also reflects **egocentrism,** *difficulty in viewing the world from someone else's perspective.* By *egocentrism* Piaget did not mean "selfishness" but rather that children at this stage believe that other people perceive things in the same way they do (Figure 12.14).

Concrete Operational Stage From about ages 7 to 12, said Piaget, children in the **concrete operational stage** *can perform basic mental operations concerning problems that involve tangible (i.e., "concrete") objects and situations.* They now grasp the concept of reversibility, display less centration, and easily solve conservation problems.

When concrete operational children confront problems that are hypothetical or require abstract reasoning, however, they often have difficulty or show rigid types of thinking. To demonstrate

Figure 12.14

The three-mountain problem.
Piaget used the three-mountain problem to illustrate the egocentrism of young children. Suppose that a preoperational child named Ted is looking at the mountains just as you are. Another child, Beth, is standing at the opposite (far) side of the table, and from her viewpoint she is unable to see the road winding down the steep slope of the mountain. Ted is asked what Beth sees. Because Ted is able to see the road, he will mistakenly say that Beth also can see it, indicating that he has failed to recognize Beth's perspective as different from his own.

this, ask a few 9-year-olds, "If you could have a third eye, where on your body would you put it? Draw a picture." Then ask them to explain their reasons. David Shaffer (1989) reports that 9-year-olds typically draw a face with a row of three eyes across it. Their thinking is concrete, bound by the reality that eyes appear on the face, and their justifications often are unsophisticated (e.g., "so I could see you better"). Many find the task silly because "Nobody has three eyes" (Shaffer, 1989, p. 324).

Formal Operational Stage   Piaget's model ends with the **formal operational stage**, *in which individuals can think logically about concrete and abstract problems, form hypotheses, and systematically test them.* Formal thinking begins around ages 11 to 12 and increases through adolescence (Ward & Overton, 1990).

Children entering this stage also begin to think more flexibly when tackling hypothetical problems, such as brainteasers, and typically enjoy the challenge. Shaffer (1989) reports that 11½- to 12-year-olds provide more creative answers and justifications to the third-eye problem than do 9-year-old concrete thinkers. One child placed the eye on the palm of his hands so that he could use it to "see around corners." Another placed it on top of his head, so that he could "revolve the eye to look in all directions."

Assessing Piaget's Theory: Stages, Ages, and Culture

Tests of Piaget's theory conducted around the world yield several general findings. First, it

appears that *the general cognitive abilities associated with Piaget's four stages occur in the same order across cultures* (Berry et al., 1992). For example, children understand object permanence before symbolic thinking blooms, and concrete reasoning emerges before abstract reasoning.

Second, children acquire many cognitive skills and concepts at an earlier age than Piaget believed (Wang et al., 2005). Even 3½- to 4½-month-olds display a basic grasp of object permanence when they are tested on special tasks that require them only to look at events rather than physically search for a hidden object.

Third, *cognitive development within each stage seems to proceed inconsistently.* A child may perform at the preoperational level on most tasks yet solve some tasks at a concrete operational level (Siegler, 1986). This challenges the idea that development proceeds in distinct stages: A child at a given stage should not show large inconsistencies in solving conceptually similar tasks.

Fourth, *culture influences cognitive development.* Piaget's Western perspective equated cognitive development with scientific-logical thinking, but "Many cultures . . . consider cognitive development to be more relational, involving the thinking skills and processes to engage in successful interpersonal contexts" (Matsumoto & Hull, 1994, p. 105). In Africa's Ivory Coast, the Baoulé people most strongly value a social intelligence that reflects the skills to get along with others and be respectful and responsible (Dasen et al., 1985).

Fifth, and most broadly, *cognitive development is more complex and variable than Piaget proposed* (Larivée et al., 2000). All children progress from simpler to more sophisticated thinking, but they don't necessarily follow the same developmental path.

Although research challenges many of Piaget's ideas, he revolutionized thinking about cognitive development. His work still guides many researchers, called *neo-Piagetians,* who have modified his theory to account for the issues discussed above (Becker, 2004).

The Social Context of Cognitive Development

Piaget acknowledged that social factors influence children's thinking, but he focused mainly on children's independent exploration of the physical world. In contrast, Russian psychologist Lev Vygotsky (1935/1978) highlighted how the sociocultural context of cognitive development interacts with the brain's biological maturation.

To illustrate, suppose that 5-year-olds Joshua and Juanita cannot solve Piaget's conservation problems. However, with guidance from a parent, teacher, or older sibling, Juanita can now solve these problems. Joshua, even with assistance, just doesn't understand. Are these two children really at the same cognitive level? Vygotsky says no, introducing a concept called the **zone of proximal development:** *the difference between what a child can do independently and what the child can do with assistance from adults or more-advanced peers.*

Why is the zone of proximal development important? For one thing, it helps us recognize what children may soon be able to do on their own. Second, it emphasizes that we can help move a child's cognitive development forward within limits (the "zone") dictated by the child's biological maturation. For example, parents who assist a child on scientific tasks may push the child's understanding further along by using age-appropriate but cognitively demanding speech (e.g., introducing scientific concepts) than by using only simpler speech (Tenenbaum & Leaper, 2003). Similarly, having older siblings around the house also may stimulate a younger child's cognitive development, as long as the child's brain is mature enough for the input (Ruffman et al., 1998).

Information-Processing Approaches

In contrast to Piaget's stage approach, many researchers view cognitive development as a continuous, gradual process in which the same set of information-processing abilities becomes more efficient over time. For example, as children age they acquire better information-search strategies, process information more quickly, and display better memory and metacognition. In turn, these qualities enable older children to reason and solve problems more effectively than younger children (Kail, 2007).

Information-Search Strategies Look at the two houses in Figure 12.15. Are they identical? This task is easy for you but not for young children. Elaine Vurpillot (1968) recorded the eye movements of 3- to 10-year-olds during tasks like this one. Preschoolers often failed to compare each window in the house on the left to the corresponding window in the house on the right; older children methodically scanned the houses. In short, older children are better able to search systematically for information (Merrill & Lookadoo, 2004).

Figure 12.15

A visual-search task.

Elaine Vurpillot used stimuli like these to assess visual inspection through filmed eye movements. Preschoolers fail to scan the pictures systematically, which often leads them to claim that the two houses are identical. SOURCE: Adapted from Vurpillot, 1968.

Processing Speed, Attention, and Response Inhibition As Robert Kail's (1991) review of 72 studies shows in Figure 12.16, the speed with which children process information becomes faster with age. Notice that processing speed improves continuously and that the relatively rapid rate of change between ages 8 and about 12 slows during adolescence. Children's attention span and ability to inhibit impulsive responses to distracting stimuli also improve with age. When performing tasks, older children are better able to focus their attention on relevant details and ignore irrelevant information (Luna et al., 2004).

Working Memory and Long-Term Memory Children's working memory improves with age (Gathercole et al., 2004). If you read older children a list of words or sentences of increasing length, they will be able to store more of that information in working memory and repeat more of it to you than will younger children. Older children also can retain and manipulate visuospatial information in working memory more effectively than younger children. For example, if you asked them to draw you a map to a friend's house several blocks and a few turns away, they would likely have little difficulty. A younger child might be able to lead you to the friend's house but would have difficulty drawing the route.

Older children are also more likely than younger children to use strategies to improve

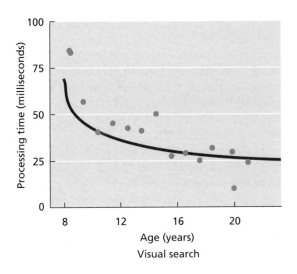

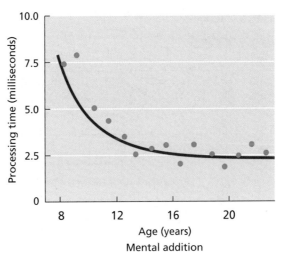

Figure 12.16

Information-processing speed quickens during childhood. These two graphs show how information-processing speed for visual-search and mental-addition tasks becomes faster with age. The relatively rapid rate of change between ages 8 and about 12 slows during adolescence. A similar non-linear pattern also occurs on name-retrieval, mental-rotation, and other cognitive tasks. SOURCE: Adapted from Kail, 1991.

memory (Schneider et al., 2004). In one study, when given lists of words or numbers to remember, preschoolers rarely used rehearsal spontaneously, whereas 8- to 10-year-olds could often be heard rehearsing words or numbers under their breath (Flavell, 1970). This helps older children to hold information in working memory and to process it into long-term memory. Given their more-advanced brain maturation and schooling, older children also can call upon a larger library of information stored in long-term memory when they need to solve problems or perform tasks.

Metacognition As we discussed in Chapter 9, metacognition refers to your awareness of your own cognitive processes. Compared to younger children, older children can better judge how well they understand material for a test. In turn, this helps them decide whether they need to study more or ask for help.

Despite the rise of information-processing approaches, the *discontinuity versus continuity* debate (gradual development versus the emergence of distinct stages) is still not resolved. Some psychologists propose that cognitive development involves both processes. Susan Gathercole (1998) suggests that memory capabilities change qualitatively (i.e., new abilities emerge) between infancy and age 7 but then undergo only gradual quantitative improvements through adolescence. Robbie Case (1987; Case et al., 2001) offered another view, proposing that gradual increases in information-processing capabilities within stages enable children to move qualitatively from one stage of cognitive development to the next.

Understanding the Physical World

Because infants cannot express their knowledge in words, developmental psychologists have created some ingenious approaches—such as the *violation-of-expectation experiment*—to examine infants' understanding of basic concepts (Baillargeon, 2004). This approach measures a basic aspect of infants' information processing: attention (i.e., time spent looking at a stimulus).

In these experiments, researchers begin with the hypothesis that young infants possess a certain concept—an expectation—about how the world works. For example, let's make the radical assumption that young infants have an expectation about the addition of very small numbers of objects, such as "one of a thing" plus "another one of the thing" equals "two of the things." Then researchers expose the infants to an "impossible event" that violates this expectation and a "possible event" that does not violate this expectation, as shown in Figure 12.17. If the infants stare longer at the impossible event, then the researchers take this as evidence that the infants understand the concept being tested. In other words, just as you would stare longer at a dropped pencil that suddenly stopped in midair than you would at one that fell to the ground, infants pay more attention to events that violate their understanding of the world.

These experiments suggest that young infants possess basic concepts about the physical properties of objects, such as that two solid objects cannot occupy the same space at the same time, and about the addition and subtraction of small numbers of objects, such as $1 + 1 = 2$, $2 + 1 = 3$, and $2 - 1 = 1$ (Spelke, 1994; Wynn, 1998). This approach is not without controversy, because as

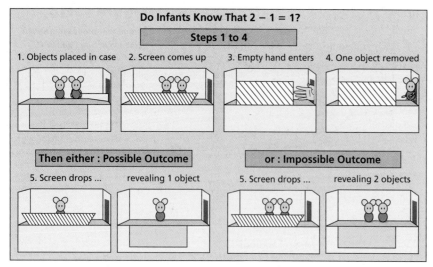

Figure 12.17

A violation-of-expectancy experiment.
Five-month-old infants watch the sequence of events shown in steps 1 through 4. Then, in step 5 they witness a "possible" or "impossible" event. Infants stare longer at the impossible event, suggesting that they were expecting only 1 object and are surprised to see 2 objects still there. In other words, they understand that 2 − 1 should equal 1. In another experiment, in steps 1 to 4, infants watch 1 object being added to another object. Then the screen is raised and lowered, revealing either 2 objects ("possible event") or just 1 object ("impossible event"). Once again, infants stare longer at the impossible event, suggesting that they understand that 1 + 1 should equal 2. Source: Wynn, 1992.

critics note, researchers are making large inferences about what must be going on inside the infant's head. Even so, as new research accumulates, it suggests that even 2½-month-olds understand more about how the physical world operates than was thought possible just two decades ago (Wang et al., 2005).

Theory of Mind: Understanding Mental States

The term **theory of mind** *refers to a person's beliefs about the "mind" and the ability to understand other people's mental states.* Piaget believed that children younger than 6 or 7 have trouble recognizing what other people are thinking. But consider the following story:

> Angela puts a candy bar inside a green box on the table, and then she goes away. Then her mother takes the candy bar out of the box and puts it inside a red bag on the bed. Angela doesn't see her mother do this. Later, Angela comes back and wants to get her candy because she is hungry. Where will Angela look for her candy bar?

On problems like this, most 2- and 3-year-olds indicate that Angela will look in the red bag, as if she had the same knowledge that they have. Piaget would not have been surprised. But many 4-year-olds say she will choose the green

box, recognizing that Angela does not have the information they do. Thus, at some level, they comprehend that Angela's mental state—her "mind"—is different from theirs (Ruffman et al., 1998). Studies of young children from African tribal societies, Canada, China, Japan, the United Kingdom, and the United States yield similar findings (Vinden, 2002).

Lying and deception also provide evidence of theory of mind. They imply an ability to recognize that one person can have information that another does not and, therefore, that a person can influence what other people think by withholding the truth. Researchers find that most 3-year-olds are capable of trying to deceive someone else and recognize the difference between lying and providing false information due to an innocent mistake (Carlson et al., 1998). Overall, it appears that children begin to understand some aspects of other people's thinking by age 3 to 4, well before Piaget proposed they could (Flavell, 2004).

Social-Emotional and Personality Development

Children grow not only physically and mentally but also emotionally and socially. They form attachments and develop social skills, and each child displays a unique personality—a distinctive yet somewhat consistent pattern of thinking, feeling, and behaving (McAdams & Olson, 2010).

Early Emotions and Emotion Regulation

Emotional responses communicate our inner states to other people and influence how others respond to us (Figure 12.18). Infants can't describe their feelings, but their facial expressions, vocalizations, and other behaviors provide a window into their emotional lives. By crying, they express distress. By focusing their gaze and staring at objects and people, they express interest. Around the world, within about 6 months after birth, infants begin to express joy and surprise ("peekaboo . . . I see you!"), and distress branches out into the separate emotions of disgust, anger, fear, and sadness (Lewis, 2000).

Around 18 months of age, infants begin to develop a sense of self, as illustrated by their ability to recognize themselves in a mirror. This growing self-awareness sets the stage for envy, embarrassment, and empathy to emerge. After age 2, as toddlers learn about performance standards and rules that they are supposed to follow, they begin to display pride and shame. Around the same age,

Figure 12.18

Emotional responses communicate our internal states, and they can influence how others respond to us, providing us with the aid and comfort we need.

they also display guilt—as evidenced by avoiding eye contact, shrugging shoulders, and making facial expressions (Kochanska et al., 1995).

Just as emotional reactions become more diverse with age, so does **emotion regulation,** *the processes by which we evaluate and modify our emotional reactions.* Young infants may suck their thumbs or a pacifier, turn their heads away from something unpleasant, or cling to a caretaker to soothe themselves. To reduce distress, toddlers may seek out a caretaker, cling to a doll or teddy bear, fling unpleasant objects away, or throw a tantrum to get what they want. Once they acquire language, children can reduce distress by talking to themselves and other people.

As children age, their emotional expressiveness and ability to regulate their emotions become part of their overall *emotional competence,* which in turn influences their social behavior and how well their peers and other people like them. Children who frequently display sadness or who can't control their anger are less likely to be popular, and emotional competence remains important for well-being as children develop (Eisenberg, 2002).

Social Skill Development

Children's success in making friends and getting along with peers depends not only on their emotional competence but also on skills such as initiating social contact, sharing, resolving conflict, and helping others. Daniel Berry and Erin O'Connor (2010) studied 1,168 children throughout elementary school and found that, overall, their social skills grew most rapidly between kindergarten and first grade and then again between third grade and fifth grade. Coupled with similar findings in other studies, this suggests that children's social skills grow in uneven spurts rather than in a constant fashion.

Berry and O'Connor (2010) also found that when teacher-child relations were more positive, children displayed greater growth in social skills. This was especially true for children who were experiencing emotional difficulties, such as anxiety or depression. Because this study was correlational, it's possible that children's growth in social skills contributed to greater positivity in their relations with teachers. Conversely, supportive relations with teachers may have facilitated children's social skill acquisition. Socialization influences children's social and emotional development, as teachers, peers, and especially parents serve as models and reinforce children for some types of social and emotional responses but not for others (Raval & Martini, 2009). As we'll now explore, heredity also contributes to children's basic emotional and behavioral style in social situations.

Temperament

From the moment of birth, infants differ from one another in **temperament,** *a biologically based general style of reacting emotionally and behaviorally to the environment.* Some infants are calm and happy; others are irritable and fussy. Some are outgoing and active; others are shy and inactive. Indeed, within any age group—children, adolescents, or adults—people differ in their general behavioral-emotional style (McAdams & Olson, 2010).

In a pioneering study, Alexander Thomas and Stella Chess (1977) had parents describe their babies' behavior. They found that most infants could be classified into three groups. "Easy infants" ate and slept on schedule, were playful, and accepted new situations with little fuss. "Difficult infants" were irritable, were fussy eaters and sleepers, and reacted negatively to new situations. "Slow-to-warm-up infants" were the least active, had mildly negative responses to new situations, but slowly adapted over time. Subsequently, the difficult infants were most likely to develop emotional and behavior problems during childhood.

This study was admired but also criticized for relying on parents' reports of their infants' behavior. Other researchers directly observed infants and identified temperamental styles that differed from those described by Thomas and Chess (1977). Moreover, researchers often found that temperament is only weakly to moderately stable during infancy (Carnicero et al., 2000). Some infants maintain a consistent temperament during their first 2 years of life, whereas others change.

Consider shyness, which forms part of a more general temperament style called *behavioral inhibition*. Inhibited infants are quiet and timid; they cry and withdraw when exposed to unfamiliar people, places, objects, and sounds. Uninhibited infants are more sociable, verbal, and spontaneous. Research by Jerome Kagan and coworkers (1988) found that about 20 to 25 percent of infants displayed this inhibited pattern, which remained moderately stable during infancy. They also studied these infants until age 7½. For the vast majority—those who were only mildly to moderately inhibited or uninhibited between the ages of 1 and 2 years—their temperament did not predict how shy or outgoing they would be as children. But for infants who were *highly* uninhibited or inhibited, the findings were different. Highly uninhibited infants tended to become sociable and talkative 7-year-olds, whereas highly inhibited infants developed into quiet, cautious, and shy 7-year-olds (Kagan, 1989).

thinking critically

SHY CHILD, SHY ADULT?

We have just seen that very shy or very outgoing infants tend to retain these traits into early childhood. Do you think that the very shy or outgoing child grows into a shy or outgoing adult? In general, does childhood temperament predict adult behavior? Think about it, then see page 457.

Erikson's Psychosocial Theory

Psychologist Erik Erikson (1968) believed that personality develops through confronting a series of eight **psychosocial stages,** *each involving a different "crisis" (i.e., conflict) over how we view ourselves in relation to other people and the world* (Table 12.2). Each crisis is present throughout life but takes on special importance during a particular age

Table 12.2 | Erikson's Psychosocial Stages

Age (Approximate Years)	Major Psychosocial Crisis
Infancy (first year)	Basic trust vs. basic mistrust
Toddlerhood (1–2)	Autonomy vs. shame and doubt
Early childhood (3–5)	Initiative vs. guilt
Middle childhood (6–12)	Industry vs. inferiority
Adolescence (12–19)	Identity vs. role confusion
Early adulthood (20–39)	Intimacy vs. isolation
Middle adulthood (40–64)	Generativity vs. stagnation
Late adulthood (65+)	Integrity vs. despair

period. Four of these crises occur in infancy and childhood:

1. *Basic trust versus basic mistrust:* Depending on how well our needs are met and how much love we receive during the first year of life, we develop a basic trust or mistrust of the world.

2. *Autonomy versus shame and doubt:* During the next 2 years, children begin to exercise their individuality. If parents unduly restrict children or make harsh toilet training demands, children develop shame and doubt about their abilities and later lack the courage to be independent.

3. *Initiative versus guilt:* From age 3 through age 5, children display great curiosity about the world. If they are allowed freedom to explore, they develop a sense of initiative. If they are held back or punished, they develop guilt about their desires and suppress their curiosity.

4. *Industry versus inferiority:* From age 6 until puberty, the child's life expands into school and peer activities. Children who experience pride and encouragement in mastering tasks develop *industry*—a striving to achieve. Repeated failure and lack of praise for trying leads to a sense of inferiority.

Although critics argue that Erikson's model lacks detail and question its stage approach, the model captures several major childhood issues. Some research supports Erikson's view that successfully resolving each crisis helps prepare us to meet the next one (McAdams & de St. Aubin, 1998). Because each stage of life creates new opportunities, possibilities for change are ever present. Yet like the early chapters of a novel, themes that emerge in childhood help set the stage for the unfolding story of our lives.

Attachment

Imagine a single-file procession of ducklings following you around campus and everywhere you went, as if you were their mother. For this to happen, we would only need to isolate the ducklings after they hatched and then expose them to you at a certain time. If they later encountered their real parents, the ducklings would ignore them and continue to follow you (Hess, 1959).

German ethologist Konrad Lorenz (1937) called this behavior **imprinting,** *a sudden, biologically primed form of attachment* (Figure 12.19). It occurs in some bird species, including ducks and geese, and in a few mammals, such as shrews. Imprinting involves a critical period. In mallard ducklings, the strongest imprinting occurs within 1 day after hatching, and by 2½ days the capacity to imprint is lost (Hess, 1959). Thus, in some species, offspring must be exposed to parents within hours or days after entering the world to attach to them.

In humans, **attachment** *refers to the strong emotional bond that develops between children and their primary caregivers.* Human infants do not automatically imprint on a caregiver, and there is not an immediate postbirth critical period during which contact is required for infant-caregiver bonding. Instead, the first few years of life seem to be a sensitive period when we can most easily form a secure bond with caregivers that enhances our adjustment later in life (Sroufe, 2002). Although it may be more difficult to form strong first attachments to caregivers later in childhood, it is still possible.

The Attachment Process   For decades, people assumed that infant-caregiver bonding resulted primarily from the mother's role in satisfying the infant's need for nourishment. Harry Harlow (1958) tested this notion by separating infant rhesus monkeys from their biological mothers shortly after birth. Each infant was raised in a cage with two artificial "surrogate mothers." One was a bare-wire cylinder with a feeding bottle attached to its "chest." The other was a wire cylinder covered with soft terry cloth without a feeding bottle.

Faced with this choice, the infant monkeys became attached to the cloth mother. When exposed to frightening situations, the infants ran to the cloth figure and clung tightly to it. They even maintained contact with the cloth mother while feeding from the wire mother's bottle (Figure 12.20). Thus Harlow showed that *contact comfort*—body contact with a comforting object— is more important in fostering attachment than is the provision of nourishment.

Around this time, other researchers studied human attachment in African, European, and North American societies. Based on this work, British psychoanalyst John Bowlby (1969) proposed that attachment in infancy develops in three phases:

1. *Indiscriminate attachment behavior:* Newborns cry, vocalize, and smile toward everyone, and these behaviors evoke caregiving from adults.

Figure 12.19

Canadian wildlife sculptor Bill Lishman imprinted Canada geese hatchlings to the sight of his ultralight airplane. Although the geese have now matured, the ultralight still represents "mother" to them, and they follow it in flight.

Figure 12.20

Infant monkeys, reared with a cloth-covered surrogate and a bare-wire surrogate from birth, preferred contact with the cloth "mother" even though the wire "mother" satisfied nutritional needs. Source: From Harlow, 1958.

2. *Discriminate attachment behavior:* Around 3 months of age, infants direct their attachment behaviors more toward familiar caregivers than toward strangers.

3. *Specific attachment behavior:* By 7 or 8 months of age, infants develop a meaningful attachment to specific caregivers. The caregiver becomes a secure base from which the infant can explore the environment.

As an infant's attachment becomes more focused, two types of anxiety occur. **Stranger anxiety,** *distress over contact with unfamiliar people,* often emerges around age 6 or 7 months and ends by age 18 months. When approached by, touched by, or handed over to a stranger, the infant becomes afraid, cries, and reaches for the caregiver. **Separation anxiety,** *distress over being separated from a primary caregiver,* typically begins a little later, peaks around age 12 to 16 months, and disappears between 2 and 3 years of age. Here the infant becomes anxious and cries when the caregiver is out of sight. Both forms of anxiety show a similar pattern across many cultures (Figure 12.21).

These responses, which coincide with infants' increasing cognitive and physical abilities, may be adaptive reactions shaped through evolution (Bowlby, 1973). At an age when infants master crawling and then learn to walk, fear of strangers and of separation may help prevent them from wandering beyond the sight of caretakers, especially in unfamiliar situations.

Around age 3 to 4, as children's cognitive and verbal skills grow, they develop a better understanding of their attachment relationships. According to Bowlby (1969), a stage of *goal-corrected partnership* emerges, in which children and caregivers can describe their feelings to each other and maintain their relationships whether they are together or apart.

Types of Attachment Infants develop different types of attachments with their caretakers. Psychologist Mary Ainsworth and coworkers (1978) developed the **strange situation,** *a standardized procedure for examining infant attachment.* The infant, typically a 12- to 18-month-old, first plays with toys in the mother's presence. Then a stranger enters the room and interacts with the child. Soon the mother departs, leaving the child with the stranger. Later the stranger departs, and the child is alone. Finally, the mother returns. The infant's behavior is observed throughout this procedure.

In the mother's presence, "securely attached" infants explore the playroom and react positively to the stranger (Ainsworth et al., 1978). They are distressed when the mother leaves and happily greet her when she returns. In contrast, there are two types of "insecurely attached" infants. "Anxious-resistant" infants are fearful when the

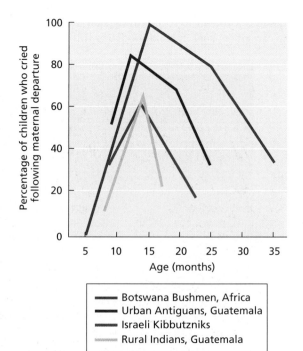

Figure 12.21

Separation anxiety across cultures.
The rise and fall of separation anxiety in infancy shows a similar pattern across cultures. Source: Based on Kagan et al., 1978.

mother is present, demand her attention, and are distressed when she leaves. They are not soothed when she returns and may angrily resist her attempts at contact. "Anxious-avoidant" infants show few signs of attachment, seldom cry when the mother leaves, and don't seek contact when she returns.

Across most cultures studied, about one-half to three-quarters of infants are securely attached. Mothers who are more sensitive to their babies' needs at home tend to have infants who are more securely attached in the strange situation (Posada et al., 2002). Moreover, securely attached infants seem to be better adjusted socially during childhood. Establishing a secure attachment early in life also may help foster a capacity for compassion and altruism that carries forward into adulthood (Mikulincer & Shaver, 2005).

Attachment Deprivation

If infants and young children are deprived of a stable attachment with a caregiver, how do they fare in the long run? Harry Harlow studied this issue under controlled conditions. After rearing "isolate" monkeys either alone or with artificial surrogate mothers, Harlow returned them to the monkey colony at 6 months of age. Exposed to other monkeys, the isolates were indifferent, terrified, or aggressive. When they became adults, some female isolates were artificially inseminated and gave birth, and they were highly abusive toward their firstborns (Harlow & Suomi, 1970). The conclusion: being raised without a secure attachment to a real, interactive caregiver produced long-term social impairment.

What of isolate human children? Victor, the "Wild Boy of Aveyron," was severely impaired after his isolation and showed only limited recovery after intensive remedial training. Did the lack of human contact stunt Victor's development, or was it brain damage, possibly present from birth?

In the 1960s, twin boys in Czechoslovakia were forced by their father and stepmother to live in extreme isolation beginning at 18 months of age. The twins were discovered at age 7, emotionally and socially retarded, with the cognitive development of a 3-year-old and speech skills of a 2-year-old. Jarmila Koluchova (1972, 1991) studied the boys for more than 20 years and found that they went on to become happy, sociable, and firmly attached to their foster family. Their IQs increased to normal levels, and they became well-adjusted adolescents and young adults.

Why the difference? Unlike Victor, the twins had each other's company, but in other cases even

Figure 12.22

In the 1980s, about 100,000 Romanian infants and children were warehoused in filthy, disease-ridden orphanages where they were often left unattended for days and had no opportunity to bond with caretakers. Studies of Romanian infants who were adopted into American homes before age 2 showed that about a third formed secure attachments, in contrast to the more typical 60 percent figure found in attachment studies. Still, that so many formed secure attachments is a testament to their resilience in bouncing back from extreme adversity.

"lone" isolate children have recovered. Perhaps most important, the twins' isolation ended and their rehabilitation began at a younger age, when the brain's neural plasticity is greater. They were 7; Victor was about 12.

In the 1980s, 100,000 Romanian infants and children were warehoused in orphanages under the most neglectful and squalid conditions imaginable (Figure 12.22). Despite this horrific neglect, after being adopted about a third of the Romanian infants studied had become securely attached to their adoptive parents (Wilson, 2003). Examining less extreme circumstances, Barbara Tizard and Jill Hodges (1978) studied children raised in orphanages where the nurses were attentive but high staff turnover prevented the children from forming a stable bond with any caretaker. Those adopted between ages 2 and 8 years typically formed healthy attachments with their adoptive parents, although in adolescence many had difficulty forming peer relationships because they were viewed as needing "too much attention" (Hodges & Tizard, 1989). Still, the vast majority of adopted children are normally adjusted and differ little from children raised by their biological parents (Miller et al., 2000).

In sum, infancy appears to be a sensitive, though not critical, period during which an initial attachment to caregivers forms most easily and facilitates subsequent development. Prolonged attachment deprivation creates developmental risks, but when deprived children are placed into a nurturing environment at a young enough age, many, if not most, become attached to their caretakers and grow into well-adjusted adults.

The Child-Care Controversy

When you were a young child, did someone other than a parent regularly care for you during the day? More than half of American preschoolers fall into this category, and the need for affordable, high-quality child care has been a pressing national concern for decades (Muenchow & Marsland, 2007). High-quality child care provides a stimulating environment with responsive caretakers, few children per caretaker, and low staff turnover, whereas poor day care does not (Marshall, 2004). In either case, many parents worry about how child care will affect their child's development. In the most comprehensive research project to date, psychologists working with the National Institute of Child Health and Human Development (NICHD) Early Child Care Research Network began studying approximately 1,400 American children from birth. Here are some major findings:

- *Attachment:* Overall, as measured by the strange-situation procedure, high-quality child care did not seem to disrupt infants' or very young children's attachment to their parents, even when they attended for many hours a week. When several negative factors combined—the child care was poor, the child spent many hours there, and parents were not sensitive to the child at home—the risk of insecure attachment increased (NICHD, 2001).

- *Social behavior:* Comparing the social development of children who experienced child care versus those raised exclusively by their mothers, virtually no significant differences emerged through age 4½ (NICHD, 2006). Among child-care children, spending a lot of time in child care was associated with more behavior problems by age 4½, but this relation disappeared by third grade (NICHD, 2002; Vandell et al., 2005).

- *Cognitive performance:* Overall, as with social development, children's cognitive development by age 4½ did not differ significantly whether they experienced child care or were raised exclusively by their mothers (NICHD, 2006). Among children in child care, exposure to higher-quality care was associated with better cognitive performance (NICHD, 2006).

Concerns about disrupted parent-child relations also surface when parents divorce. Our "Applying Psychological Science" feature examines this societally important issue.

Applying Psychological Science

Understanding How Divorce and Remarriage Affect Children

Divorce creates a stressful life transition for parents and their children. Because most divorced parents remarry, they and their children also experience a second major transition: becoming part of a stepfamily.

Decades ago, there was little scientific information on children of divorce and remarriage, but research now provides us with a better understanding of how these major transitions affect children. With this knowledge, local governments in more than 35 American states require soon-to-be-divorced parents to take classes on helping children cope with divorce.

HOW DOES DIVORCE AFFECT CHILDREN?

Many children report that parental divorce is one of the most painful experiences of their lives. In the short term, they may experience anxiety, fear, anger, confusion, depression, and behavior problems at school.

In the long term, children of divorce remain at greater risk for various difficulties, including academic problems, troubled relationships with family members and peers, low self-esteem, and depression (Dawson-McClure et al., 2004; Kushner, 2009). When

they become adolescents, children of divorced parents are more likely to drop out of school, be unemployed, use drugs, and become unmarried teen parents. In adulthood, they are more likely to experience conflict in relationships, unemployment, depression, and a higher divorce rate and to drink alcohol excessively (Huurre et al., 2006; Wauterickx et al., 2006).

Most of these problems, however, tend to cluster together into an overall pattern of maladjustment. Leading divorce researcher E. Mavis Hetherington and coworkers (1998) estimate that about 20 to 25 percent of children in divorced families, versus 10 percent of children in nondivorced families, experience this cluster of problems. This is a significantly elevated risk for maladjustment, but still, most children of divorced parents grow up to be normally adjusted adults.

SHOULD WE STAY TOGETHER FOR THE SAKE OF THE CHILD?

Many parents considering divorce wonder whether they should stay together for the child's sake. Reviewing 92 studies, Paul Amato and Bruce Keith (1991) found that when divorce ends a highly conflicted marriage, children's psychological adjustment typically benefits in the long run. High marital conflict can cause the children to feel "caught in the middle" in the battle between their parents, and decrease the children's feelings of well-being (Amato & Afifi, 2006). Children living with married but contentious parents display poorer school achievement, lower self-esteem, and more aggression and behavior problems than children from divorced families (Feldman et al., 2010). But many unhappy marriages do not involve extensive conflict, and in those cases divorce usually puts children at greater risk for maladjustment (Booth & Amato, 2001).

HOW CAN DIVORCED PARENTS HELP THEIR CHILDREN?

The major factor affecting a child's adjustment to divorce is the quality of life within the postdivorce family. The period during and after divorce can intensify parents' anger and conflicts. By fighting over their children or trying to enlist them in loyalty battles, parents can damage their children's well-being (Amato & Afifi, 2006). In contrast, cooperative and amicable parental behaviors can cushion the negative effects of divorce during this rocky transition (Hetherington & Stanley-Hagan, 2002). By remaining emotionally close to one's children and providing warmth, support, and clear rules, the parent who doesn't have custody can help them adjust to living with the custodial parent (Kushner, 2009). For children,

the lasting problems of divorce often lie in lingering parental conflicts, economic hardships that parents (especially mothers) often experience after divorce, and other factors that destabilize the parents' own lives.

HOW DO CHILDREN RESPOND TO REMARRIAGE AND STEPFAMILIES?

Forming a stepfamily temporarily disrupts children's relationships with the remarried custodial parent and typically increases children's short-term problem behaviors. In turn, such behavior can increase the risk of marital conflict between the stepparents (Jenkins et al., 2005). It can take several years for parents and children to adjust to their new roles within the stepfamily. In general, young adolescents seem to have the most difficulty coping with the transition into a stepfamily.

In remarriages, children may be hostile and reject the stepparent, especially when the stepparent attempts to be a strong disciplinarian. Children usually adjust better to living in a stepfamily when the custodial parent is warm but firm and has primary responsibility for discipline, and when the stepparent is warm but supports the custodial parent's authority (Bray & Berger, 1993).

Styles of Parenting

Beyond divorce and remarriage, how do different child-rearing practices affect children's development? After studying how parents interacted with their preschool children, Diana Baumrind (1967) identified two key dimensions of parental behavior. The first is *warmth versus hostility.* Warm parents communicate love and caring for the child, whereas hostile parents express rejection and behave as if they do not care about the child. The second dimension is *restrictiveness versus permissiveness.* Parents differ in the extent to which they make and enforce rules. As Figure 12.23 shows, combining these dimensions yields four parenting styles that are associated with different patterns of child development (Linver et al., 2002).

Authoritative parents *are controlling but warm.* They establish clear rules, consistently enforce them, and reward children's compliance with warmth and affection. They communicate high expectations, caring, and support. This style is associated with the most positive childhood outcomes. Children with authoritative parents tend to have higher self-esteem, are higher achievers in school, and have fewer conduct problems.

Authoritarian parents *also exert control but do so within a cold, unresponsive, or rejecting relationship.* Their children tend to have lower self-esteem, be less popular with peers, and perform more poorly in school than children with authoritative parents.

Indulgent parents *have warm, caring relationships with their children but do not provide the guidance and discipline that help children learn responsibility and concern for others.* Their children tend to be more immature and self-centered.

Neglectful parents *provide neither warmth nor rules nor guidance.* Their children are most likely to be insecurely attached, to have low achievement motivation and disturbed peer relationships, and to be impulsive and aggressive. Neglectful

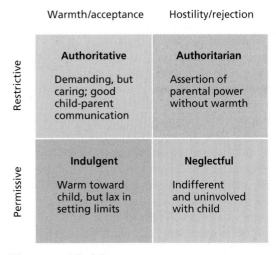

Figure 12.23

Four styles of child rearing.
Combining two basic dimensions of parental behavior (warmth-hostility and restrictiveness-permissiveness) yields four different styles of child rearing. SOURCE: Adapted from Maccoby & Martin, 1983.

parenting is associated with the most negative developmental outcomes.

Do these findings extend to adolescence? Laurence Steinberg and coworkers (1994) studied several thousand California and Wisconsin high school students. They found that overall, authoritative parenting and neglectful parenting were, respectively, associated with the most positive and negative developmental outcomes. Many of the findings held true across African American, Asian American, Caucasian American, and Hispanic American students (Lamborn et al., 1991).

Parenting-Heredity Interactions

Keep in mind that parent-child influences are bidirectional, illustrating once again the interaction of biology and environment in shaping behavior. Recall that children tend to display poorer cognitive, social, and emotional development when parents are not warm or responsive to the children's needs (NICHD, 2006). One example of bidirectional influence occurs when a child has a biologically based irritable temperament. This irritability causes parents to be emotionally cooler and less responsive to the child, and in turn these harsher parental responses further promote the child's difficult behavior. Also realize that parents do not mold their children's personality and behavior like lumps of clay. Parenting makes a difference, but the way children turn out depends on their heredity, peer and community influences, other experiences, and interactions among these factors (Mezulis et al., 2006).

Antisocial behavior provides another example of how the family environment and heredity interact. The child of a highly antisocial parent (i.e., a parent with high aggression, irritability, and a history of illegal activities) is at increased genetic risk for displaying antisocial behavior (e.g., lying, fighting, having a hot temper). This genetic risk is present, of course, even if the highly antisocial parent (usually the father) is completely absent from the home and the child is raised by the other parent. However, as Sara Jaffee and coworkers (2003) found, when high-antisocial fathers live at home and are involved in caretaking, this further increases children's antisocial behavior and risk of developing a conduct disorder. In contrast, when low-antisocial fathers live at home and participate in caretaking, this tends to decrease children's antisocial behavior. Jaffee and coworkers concluded that children of high-antisocial fathers who are involved in caretaking receive "a 'double whammy' of genetic and environmental risk for conduct problems" (p. 109).

Gender Identity and Socialization

Parenting also influences children's development in other ways, such as helping children develop a **gender identity,** *a sense of "femaleness" or "maleness" that becomes a central aspect of one's personal identity* (Gelman et al., 2004). Most children develop a basic gender identity between the ages of 2 and 3 and can label themselves (and others) as being either a boy or a girl, but their understanding of gender is still fragile. They may believe that a boy wearing a dress is a girl and that a girl can grow up to become a man. **Gender constancy,** *which is the understanding that being male or female is a permanent part of a person*, develops around age 6 to 7 (Szkrybalo & Ruble, 1999).

As gender identity develops, children also acquire *sex-role stereotypes*, which are beliefs about the characteristics and behaviors that are appropriate for boys and girls to possess. Every group, including family and cultural groups, has norms for expected and accepted gender behavior. Parents, siblings, friends, the mass media, and other socializing agents convey these norms to us as we grow up. Ultimately, as we internalize these norms, they become part of our identity (Martin & Ruble, 2004).

Sex-typing *involves treating others differently based on whether they are female or male.* From infancy onward, girls and boys are viewed and treated differently. Fathers use more physical and verbal prohibition with their 12-month-old sons than with their daughters, and they steer their sons away from activities that are considered stereotypically feminine (Snow et al., 1983). Even when their sons and daughters display equal interest and aptitude in science, fathers and mothers are more likely to believe that sons have the greater interest and will find science easier (Tenenbaum & Leaper, 2003). Indeed, as Figure 12.24 shows, when parents interact with their 1- to 8-year-olds at science exhibits in a children's museum, they are much more likely to explain the exhibits to their sons than to their daughters—even though the children rarely ask for such explanations (Crowley et al., 2001).

Sex-role stereotypes are also transmitted through observational learning and operant conditioning (Figure 12.25). Children observe and often attempt to emulate parents, other adults, peers, and television and movie characters (Bandura, 1965). In ways obvious and subtle, others approve of us and reinforce our behavior when we meet their expectations and disapprove of us when we don't. In turn, this influences the way children think about gender. Some children as young as 2 to 3 years of age display sex-role stereotypes in their ability to identify objects (such as

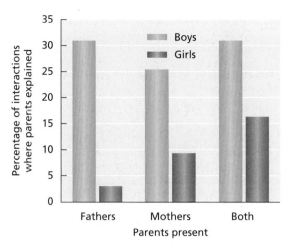

Figure 12.24

Do parents provide more scientific explanations to sons than to daughters?

Fathers and mothers provided more explanations to their 1- to 8-year-old sons than to their daughters while engaged with science exhibits at a children's museum. Similar results were obtained regardless of the children's ages. Source: Adapted from Crowley et al., 2001.

Figure 12.25

In subtle and not so subtle ways, cultures socialize most female and male children into gender-stereotypic activities.

hammers and brooms) and behaviors as "belonging with" one gender or the other (Campbell et al., 2004). By age 7 or 8, stereotyped thinking is firmly in place; children believe that boys and girls possess different personality traits and should hold different occupations as adults.

As children enter junior high school, they often display more flexible thinking about gender. Some come to believe that traditionally masculine and feminine traits can be blended within a single person—what is called an *androgynous gender identity*—as when a person is both assertive and compassionate. During junior high and high school, some adolescents maintain this view, but overall, gender stereotypes seem to become a little more rigid at this age, so that by early adulthood most people continue to adhere to relatively traditional beliefs (Alfieri et al., 1996).

Moral Development

All societies attempt to teach their members right from wrong. How does children's moral thinking change as they grow older?

Moral Thinking

Drawing on Piaget's cognitive stage model, Lawrence Kohlberg (1963, 1984) developed an influential theory of moral reasoning. He presented children, adolescents, and adults with hypothetical moral dilemmas such as the following:

Heinz's wife was dying from cancer. There was a rare drug that might save her, but the druggist who made the drug for $200 would not sell it for less than $2,000. Heinz tried hard, but he could only raise $1,000. The druggist refused to give Heinz the drug for that price even though Heinz promised to pay the rest later. So Heinz broke into the store to steal the drug. What do you think? Should Heinz have stolen the drug? Why or why not?

Kohlberg was interested not in whether people approved or disapproved of Heinz's behavior but rather in the *reasons for their judgments*. He analyzed responses to various moral dilemmas and identified three main levels of moral reasoning, with two substages within each level (Table 12.3).

Preconventional moral reasoning *is based on anticipated punishments or rewards.* Consider reasons given for stealing the drug. In stage 1, children focus on punishment: "Heinz should steal the drug because if he lets his wife die he'll get into trouble." In stage 2, morality is judged by anticipated rewards and doing what is in the person's own interest: "Heinz should steal the drug because that way he'll still have his wife with him."

Conventional moral reasoning *is based on conformity to social expectations, laws, and duties.* In stage 3, conformity stems from the desire to gain people's approval: "People will think that Heinz is bad if he doesn't steal the drug to save his wife." In stage 4, children believe that laws and duties must be obeyed simply because rules are meant to be followed. Thus "Heinz should steal the drug because it's his duty to take care of his wife."

Table **12.3** | Kohlberg's Stages of Moral Reasoning

Level of Moral Reasoning	Basis for Judging What Is Moral
Level 1: Preconventional Morality	**Actual or anticipated punishments or rewards, rather than internalized values**
Stage 1: Punishment-obedience orientation	Obeying rules and avoiding punishment
Stage 2: Instrumental-hedonistic orientation	Self-interest and gaining rewards
Level 2: Conventional Morality	**Conformity to the expectations of social groups; person adopts other people's values**
Stage 3: Good-child orientation	Gaining approval and maintaining good relationships with others
Stage 4: Law-and-order orientation	Doing one's duty, showing respect for authority, and maintaining social order
Level 3: Postconventional Morality	**Moral principles that have been internalized as part of one's belief and value system**
Stage 5: Social-contract orientation	General principles agreed on by society that foster community welfare and individual rights; recognition that society can decide to modify laws that lose their social utility
Stage 6: Universal ethical principles	Abstract ethical principles based on justice and equality; following one's conscience

Source: Adapted from Kohlberg, 1984.

Postconventional moral reasoning *is based on well-thought-out, general moral principles.* Stage 5 involves recognizing the importance of societal laws but also taking individual rights into account: "Stealing breaks the law, but what Heinz did was reasonable because he saved a life." In stage 6, morality is based on abstract, ethical principles of justice that are viewed as universal: "Saving life comes before financial gain, even if the person is a stranger."

Kohlberg believed that progress in moral reasoning depends on cognitive maturation and the opportunity to confront moral issues, particularly when such issues can be discussed with someone who is at a higher stage of development.

Culture, Gender, and Moral Reasoning

From North, Central, and South America to Africa, Asia, Europe, and India, studies of moral reasoning indicate that, overall:

- from childhood through adolescence, moral reasoning changes from preconventional to conventional levels;
- in adolescence and even in adulthood, postconventional reasoning is relatively uncommon;
- a person's moral judgments do not always reflect the same level or stage within levels (Eckensberger & Zimba, 1997).

Critics claim that Kohlberg's theory has a Western cultural bias. Fairness and justice are Kohlberg's postconventional ideals, but in many cultures the highest moral values focus on principles that do not fit easily into Kohlberg's model, such as respect for all animal life, collective harmony, and respect for the elderly (Iwasa, 2001).

Carol Gilligan (1982) argues that Kohlberg's emphasis on justice also reflects a male bias. She claims that highly moral women place greater value than men do on caring and responsibility for others' welfare. Overall, however, evidence of gender bias is mixed. Women use justice reasoning when the situation calls for it, and men use reasoning based on caring and relationships when appropriate. Nevertheless, Gilligan's analysis reinforces the key point that high-level moral reasoning can be based on values other than justice (Gump et al., 2000).

Moral Behavior and Conscience

Moral reasoning doesn't necessarily translate into moral behavior. B. F. Skinner (1971) proposed that we learn which behaviors are "good" and "bad" through their association with reinforcement and punishment. Other researchers propose that for children to conform to their culture's moral standards, they must understand that there are moral rules, be able to control their impulses to engage in forbidden behavior, and experience some negative emotion when they violate these rules (Figure 12.26).

By the age of 2, children come to understand that there are rules for behavior, and their emotional expressions suggest that they experience guilt when they break a known rule. Children's ability to stop themselves from engaging in forbidden behavior develops slowly, but even toddlers can do so at times. This internal regulatory mechanism, often referred to as *conscience,* tends to restrain individuals from acting in destructive or antisocial ways when they are not being monitored by parents or other adults (Kochanska et al., 2005).

Sigmund Freud (1935) believed that children develop a conscience by identifying with their parents. Few developmentalists believe in Freud's theory of how identification occurs (which we will discuss in Chapter 13), but they acknowledge that internalizing the societal values transmitted by parents or other caretakers provides the basis of a moral conscience. Children are most likely to internalize their parents' values when they have a positive relationship with them, when parents establish clear rules and provide explanations that facilitate children's awareness of parental values, and when discipline is firm but not harsh (Laible & Thompson, 2000).

Children's temperament also enters into the picture. Fearful, inhibited children tend to internalize parental values more easily and at an earlier age than less fearful children, particularly when their parents provide gentle discipline. For relatively fearless, uninhibited children, however, whether discipline is gentle or harsh is less important. A secure attachment with warm parents,

Figure 12.26

By firmly but not harshly signaling that this child's behavior was wrong and by explaining why it was wrong, this parent can help her child internalize moral values. The fact that the child experiences a negative emotion may be important to the internalization process.

rather than fear of punishment, appears to motivate fearless children to internalize their parents' standards. Thus the development of moral behavior is linked not only to children's moral thinking but also to their emotional development, attachment, and temperament (Kochanska et al., 2004).

test yourself   Infancy and Childhood

Match each concept on the left to the correct item on the right.

1. first psychosocial crisis
2. preoperational stage
3. concrete operational stage
4. temperament
5. strange situation
6. authoritative parenting style
7. zone of proximal development

a. a procedure used to assess infant attachment
b. difference between what a child can do alone and with help
c. limits and rules are set within a warm environment
d. basic trust versus mistrust
e. children understand conservation principles
f. biologically based general emotional and behavioral style
g. children display egocentrism

ANSWERS: 1-d, 2-g, 3-e, 4-f, 5-a, 6-c, 7-b

ADOLESCENCE AND ADULTHOOD

We call it Sunrise Dance. It's the biggest ceremony of the White Mountain Apache—when a girl passes from childhood to womanhood. . . .

On Friday evening Godmother dressed me . . . Saturday is like an endurance test. Men begin prayer chants at dawn. Godmother tells me to dance. . . . When the time comes for running, I go fast around a sacred cane. . . . Next, my father pours candies and corn kernels over me to protect me from famine. My Godfather directs

Figure 12.27

A White Mountain Apache girl participates in the Sunrise Dance, a four-day ceremony that initiates her into womanhood.

my dancing on Sunday. . . . Godfather paints me. . . . On Monday there is more visiting and blessing. (Quintero, 1980, pp. 262–271)

In some cultures, ceremonies like the Sunrise Dance represent *rites of passage* that mark a transition from childhood into adulthood status (Figure 12.27). But what of **adolescence,** *the period of development and gradual transition between childhood and adulthood?* Alice Schlegel and Herbert Barry (1991) found that among almost 200 nonindustrial societies worldwide, nearly all recognize some type of transition period between childhood and adulthood. Yet in many societies this period is brief and is not marked by a special term analogous to *adolescence.*

As we know it, the lengthy period called *adolescence* is largely an invention of 18th- to 20th-century Western culture (Valsiner & Lawrence, 1997). In preindustrial times, biological maturity was a major criterion for adult status. In many cultures, for example, girls were expected to marry once they became capable of bearing children. But as the Industrial Revolution brought new technology and a need for more schooling, recognition of adult status was delayed and the long transition period of adolescence evolved.

Adolescence differs from **puberty,** *a period of rapid maturation in which the person becomes capable of sexual reproduction.* These developmental periods overlap, but puberty is a biologically defined period, whereas adolescence is a broader social construction (Spear, 2000). Puberty is an important aspect of adolescence, but adolescence is also ushered in and out by changes in thinking, interests, social circumstances, and parental and societal expectations. In research studies, 12- to 18-year-olds—give or take a year at each end—are typically considered to be adolescents, but it's essential to keep in mind that the transitions into and through adolescence, and out of adolescence into adulthood, are gradual (Arnett, 2001).

Physical Development

We now explore some key developmental changes that occur in adolescence and adulthood, beginning with changes in the body's physical processes and capabilities. Note that when we talk about *young adulthood* (approximately 20 to 40 years of age), *middle adulthood* (roughly, one's 40s through early 60s), and *late adulthood* (approximately age 65 and older), these terms—like *adolescence*—represent social constructions rather than distinct biological stages.

Puberty

During adolescence, puberty ushers in important bodily changes as the brain's hypothalamus signals the pituitary gland to increase its hormonal secretions. Pituitary hormones stimulate other glands, speeding up maturation of the *primary sex characteristics* (the sex organs involved in reproduction). Hormonal changes also produce *secondary sex characteristics* (nonreproductive physical features, such as breasts in girls and facial hair in boys).

The pubertal landmark in girls is *menarche,* the first menstrual flow. For boys, it is the production of sperm and the first ejaculation. In North America and Europe, these events occur most often around age 11 to 13 for girls and 12 to 14 for boys (Kaltiala-Heino et al., 2003). Considerable variation, however, occurs among people and cultures. In parts of rural southern Mexico, for example, 50 percent of girls have their first menstrual period after the age of 13 (Malina et al., 2004).

The physical changes of puberty have psychological consequences. For one thing, hormones that steer puberty also can affect mood and behavior. Reactions to puberty are also influenced by whether it occurs early or late. Overall, early maturation tends to be associated with fewer negative outcomes for boys than for girls. Early-maturing boys and girls, for example, are at heightened risk for using drugs and smoking cigarettes (van Jaarsveld et al., 2007). For boys, however, the physical strength and size that they acquire often contribute to a positive body image, success in athletics, and popularity among peers.

In contrast, although some early-maturing girls welcome their changed appearance, the weight gain that comes with puberty results in a negative body image for others. Moreover, early maturation often exposes girls to greater social and sexual pressures from boys. Thus, compared to girls who mature later, early-maturing girls typically feel more self-conscious about their bodies and are more likely to eventually develop eating disorders, problems in school, major depression, and anxiety (Graber et al., 2004).

The Adolescent Brain

Compared to infancy and early childhood, overall brain growth slows from late childhood to adolescence. Still, the adolescent brain is in flux, establishing new neural connections while at the same time pruning away and losing a massive number of the overabundant synaptic connections formed during earlier years of explosive brain growth (Giorgio et al., 2010). This streamlining of neural networks permits more efficient communication between brain regions (Luciana, 2010).

Neural restructuring is especially prominent in the prefrontal cortex and the limbic system, regions that play a key role in planning and coordinating behaviors that satisfy motivational goals and emotional urges. Moreover, restructuring within the prefrontal cortex includes an upsurge in activity of dopamine, a neurotransmitter involved in regulating emotional arousal, pleasure and reward, and learning (Wahlstrom et al., 2010).

Psychologists are actively exploring how these brain changes provide a biological basis for the increase in drug use, risk taking, sensation seeking, and aggression displayed by many adolescents.

Physical Development in Adulthood

As maturation continues, people reach their peak of physical and perceptual functioning in young adulthood. The legs, arms, and other body parts typically reach maximum muscle strength at age 25 to 30. Vision, hearing, reaction time, and coordination peak in the early to mid-20s (Hayslip & Panek, 1989).

Although many physical capacities decline in the mid-30s, the changes aren't noticeable until years later. After age 40, muscles become weaker and less flexible, particularly in people with sedentary habits. *Basal metabolism,* the rate at which the resting body converts food into energy, also slows, resulting in a tendency to gain weight. Middle age is also the time when many people find their visual acuity declining, especially for close viewing. Women's fertility, which begins to decrease in early adulthood, now drops dramatically as the ovaries produce less estrogen; this process culminates in *menopause,* the cessation of menstruation, which occurs on average around age 50. Male fertility often persists throughout the life span, although it tends to decline after middle age. Despite these declines, many middle-aged adults remain in excellent health and are vigorously active. From climbing mountains to running marathons, they may achieve physical goals well beyond those attained by many younger adults.

Older adults are the fastest-growing segment of the population in many countries, and in the United States almost 1 in 5 people will be over 65 years of age by the year 2030 (U.S. Census Bureau, 2005c). By late adulthood, physical changes become more pronounced. By age 70, bones become more brittle and hardened ligaments make movements stiffer and slower. But with regular exercise and good nutrition, and barring major disease, many adults maintain physical vigor and an active lifestyle well into old age (Figure 12.28).

The Adult Brain

During the earliest years of adulthood, the brain's neural networks generally continue to become more efficiently integrated (Luna et al., 2004). But like other parts of the body, the brain declines later in adulthood. In a longitudinal study, psychologist Susan Resnick and her coworkers (2003) used magnetic resonance imaging to measure the loss of brain tissue among 92 men and women over a 4-year period. The participants were

Figure 12.28

Many older adults maintain a physically active lifestyle.

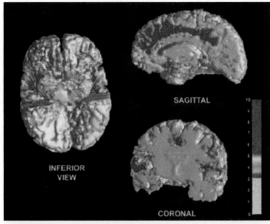

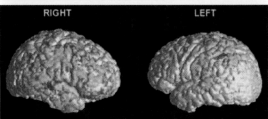

Figure 12.29

These photographs portray the average amount of brain-tissue loss that 92 men and women, ages 59 to 85 (who did not have brain disease), experienced over a 4-year period. Areas in red had the greatest loss. Source: Resnick et al., 2003.

59 to 85 years old at the start of the study, and none of them exhibited abnormal cognitive impairments. On average, over the next 4 years, they lost tissue at a rate of 5.4 percent per year in the brain regions studied, with the frontal and parietal lobes showing the greatest loss (Figure 12.29). Participants who were very healthy experienced less tissue loss than those who experienced medical problems, but still, even among physically and mentally healthy older adults, tissue loss is normal as the brain ages.

Cognitive Development

Supported by continuing brain maturation and learning experiences, cognitive changes during adolescence can be as dramatic as physical ones. Teenagers can spend a lot of time thinking about themselves and their social circumstances. Such thinking, argues David Elkind (1967), often reflects **adolescent egocentrism,** *a self-absorbed and distorted view of one's uniqueness and importance.* Elkind proposes that adolescent egocentrism has two main parts. First, adolescents often overestimate the uniqueness of their feelings and experiences, which Elkind calls the *personal fable.* Examples would be, "My parents can't possibly understand how I really feel" and "Nobody's ever felt love as deeply as ours." Second, many adolescents feel that they are always "on stage" and that "everybody's going to notice" how they look and what they do. Elkind calls this oversensitivity to social evaluation the *imaginary audience.*

Adolescents who think more egocentrically are somewhat more likely to engage in risky behaviors, due perhaps in part to a sense of invulnerability (Greene et al., 2000). At the same time, it's not clear that this self-consciousness truly reflects a thinking bias. Some theorists view teens' greater self-reflection as a natural outgrowth of the search for individuality and of realistic social consequences that teens face (Bell & Bromnick, 2003). They also suggest that young adults, overall, can be just as self-absorbed as adolescents.

Reasoning and Information Processing in Adolescence

Abstract reasoning abilities increase substantially during adolescence. Adolescents can more easily contemplate hypothetical issues, ranging from scientific problems to questions about social justice and the meaning of life (Figure 12.30a). They reason more flexibly than children and use both the deductive and inductive problem-solving methods described in Chapter 9. Recall that in Piaget's (1970) view, this signifies that adolescents have moved beyond concrete operational thinking and entered a new stage of cognitive development: formal operational thinking.

(a)

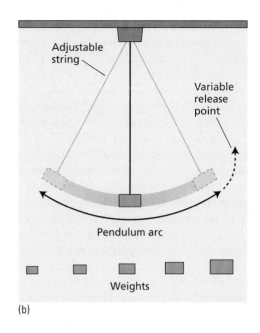

(b)

Figure 12.30

Adolescent thinking and the pendulum problem.

(a) When adolescents attain formal operational thought, they can use deductive reasoning to solve scientific problems systematically. (b) The materials for the pendulum problem used by Inhelder and Piaget include an adjustable string and a set of weights. The problem is to determine which factors influence how long it takes the pendulum to move through its arc. String length is the only relevant factor: The shorter the string, the less time it takes the pendulum to swing back and forth. Source: Adapted from Inhelder & Piaget, 1958.

Consider the pendulum problem in Figure 12.30b. Which variable(s)—length of the string, weight of the object, how hard it is pushed, and release point (height in the arc)—influence(s) how quickly the pendulum oscillates? This problem is best solved by forming and testing an organized set of deductive hypotheses (e.g., "*If* string length is a factor, *then* the swing time with a short versus long string should differ"). Concrete operational children struggle with this task (Inhelder & Piaget, 1958). For example, when they adjust the string length, they often adjust the weight as well, making it impossible to draw a conclusion about either variable. In contrast, adolescents think more systematically and manipulate one variable at a time while holding the others constant.

Continued improvements in information-processing capacities help abstract thinking to develop and foster better performance across a wide range of tasks. Although advancing more slowly than during childhood, the speed with which adolescents process information quickens, their working memory becomes more efficient, and they become better able to ignore distracting information, suppress irrelevant responses, and stay focused on the task at hand. In one recent study, information-processing speed and visuospatial working-memory abilities began to approach adultlike levels by middle adolescence, and the ability to suppress task-irrelevant responses did so by late adolescence (Luna et al., 2004).

Information Processing in Adulthood

In general, information-processing abilities decline during adulthood, but the age at which the decline begins can vary substantially (Charlton et al., 2009). For example, perceptual speed (reaction time) begins to decline steadily in early adulthood, perhaps as soon as one's early 20s (Salthouse, 2004). As adults age, it takes them longer to visually identify and evaluate stimuli, such as when looking at two patterns of lines and deciding whether they are the same. But a loss of perceptual speed may be only part of why older adults perform more slowly on such tasks. By late adulthood, people may process such information more conservatively, essentially trading off slower response times to gain greater accuracy in their judgments (Ratcliff et al., 2006).

Memory for new factual information also declines. With increasing age, adults generally find it harder to remember new series of numbers, names and faces of new people, and new map directions. On some tasks, such as recalling lists of unrelated words, performance worsens somewhat by the late 30s and then steadily declines after age 50 (Salthouse, 2004). Certain types of verbal memory, however, decline more slowly with age. Thus the ability to immediately repeat meaningful sentences decreases more slowly than the ability to repeat single, unrelated words. Even in late adulthood, healthy adults do well in recognizing familiar stimuli from long ago, such as the faces of high school classmates (Bahrick et al., 1975).

The effects of aging on prospective memory—the ability to remember to perform some action in the future—are less clear (McDaniel et al., 2003). By late adulthood, people generally display poorer prospective memory than young adults in time-based laboratory tasks (e.g., remembering to push a button every 15 minutes). On event-based tasks (e.g., remembering to push a button whenever a light comes on), age differences are less consistent. Moreover, when tested outside the laboratory, older adults may perform as well as young adults, even when the tasks (e.g., simulated pill taking) are time-based. However, when older people remember that they are supposed to execute a task ("Ah, I'm supposed to call Sylvia") and something temporarily delays them from performing it, they will be less likely to remember to perform the task immediately after the delay ends (McDaniel et al., 2003).

Intellectual Changes in Adulthood

How do intellectual abilities change in adulthood? The conclusion from early research seemed clear: after age 30, adults were over the

hill. When IQ scores of different age groups were compared in cross-sectional studies, a noticeable decline began between ages 30 and 40 (Doppelt & Wallace, 1955).

Researchers made a breakthrough by examining separate intellectual abilities rather than overall IQ. They studied *fluid intelligence*, which reflects the ability to perform mental operations (e.g., abstract and logical reasoning, solving spatial problems), and *crystallized intelligence*, which reflects the accumulation of verbal skills and factual knowledge (Horn & Cattell, 1966). Cross-sectional research typically found that fluid intelligence began to decline steadily in early adulthood, whereas crystallized intelligence peaked during middle adulthood and then began to decline in late adulthood (Figure 12.31a).

Was this early decline in fluid abilities really a function of aging or instead the result of different experiences encountered by the various generations? The older adults may have had less exposure to scientific problem solving in school or jobs that required less use of abstract intellectual skills. Such factors could have depressed their scores artificially.

To answer this question, K. Warner Schaie of Pennsylvania State University and coworkers (Schaie, 1994, 2005) began a study in 1956 that has now involved several thousand adults. This study uses a sequential design, incorporating

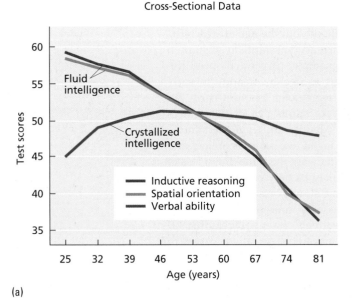

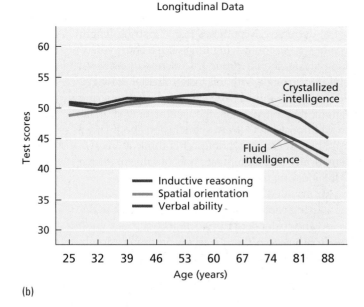

(a)   (b)

Figure 12.31

Intellectual abilities change during adulthood.

(a) Cross-sectional data (ages 25–81) indicate that fluid abilities (reasoning and spatial task performance) begin to decline in young adulthood, whereas crystallized intelligence (verbal ability) begins to decline in late adulthood. (b) However, longitudinal data (ages 25–88) from the same study indicate that both fluid and crystallized intelligence remain fairly stable through young and middle adulthood and do not decline significantly until late adulthood. The longitudinal and cross-sectional data are consistent in showing that crystallized abilities decline at a later age than fluid abilities. Source: Adapted from Schaie, 2005.

longitudinal and cross-sectional components. The longitudinal data do not support an early decline in either fluid or crystallized intelligence. Rather, most abilities are relatively stable throughout early and middle adulthood and do not reliably decline until late adulthood (Figure 12.31b). But both the cross-sectional and longitudinal data, along with findings from other studies, indicate that fluid intellectual abilities typically begin to decline at an earlier age than crystallized intelligence (Singer et al., 2003).

Is cognitive decline inevitable as we age? In the realm of physical fitness, experts tell us to "use it or lose it." Likewise, popular wisdom claims that the brain is like a muscle and that mental workouts and a cognitively stimulating lifestyle will keep the aging brain fit and combat cognitive decline. A related idea is that mental exercise and enrichment build up a "cognitive reserve"—extra brainpower in the mental tank—so that if decline occurs we can still function at a normal level (Petrosini et al., 2009). Is the mental-exercise hypothesis a myth, or is it reality?

Myth or Reality?

The Aging Brain Is Like a Muscle: Use It or Lose It

"The giant Nintendo store in Manhattan was swarming with silver-haired citizens," wrote *BusinessWeek* (2006, September, 25). They had come for a video game competition featuring *Brain Age*, a product designed to "give your brain the workout it needs" (Nintendo, 2007). *Brain Age* is one of many products in a mushrooming mental-exercise industry. Type "brainpower" or "mental exercise" into your Web browser, and you'll find numerous sites promoting mental-exercise advice and products that claim to enhance brain functioning and help fight cognitive declines of aging (Posit Science, 2010). Likewise, there's no shortage of self-help books—*Train Your Brain* (Winningham, 2010), *Brain Boot Camp* (Buzan, 2008), *Building Mental Muscle* (Gamon & Bragdon, 2003), and others—offering to boost your brainpower and keep your brain fit. Let's examine this so-called mental-exercise hypothesis.

In Schaie's (1994, 2005) longitudinal research, he found that adults who retained their level of cognitive functioning for a longer time tended to engage in more cognitively stimulating jobs and personal activities, such as reading and travel. These and similar findings from other studies are consistent with the mental-exercise hypothesis. But as a critical thinker, you should recognize that such findings are correlational and must be interpreted cautiously. Does engaging in cognitively stimulating activities cause people to retain more mental ability, does retaining more mental ability better allow people to keep engaging in cognitively demanding activities, or are there other factors—"third variables" relating to diet, lifestyle, heredity, and so forth—that may be the true cause of why mental exercise and mental ability are correlated?

Other evidence comes from numerous training experiments that find older adults' mental abilities can be improved by providing them with cognitively stimulating experiences. In one study of 70- to 91-year-olds, participants' performance at tasks requiring reasoning, visual attention, and perceptual-motor speed improved significantly after six 1-hour exposures to those tasks (Yang et al., 2006). In another study, Schaie and his coworkers found that 65- to 95-year-old adults' spatial and reasoning abilities could be improved by teaching them strategies for performing such tasks (Saczynski et al., 2002; Willis & Schaie, 1986). For many adults, this training restored their performance to the level it had been 14 years earlier. Moreover, compared to adults who didn't receive training, the trained adults were on average still performing better 14 years later.

Many training activities have been found to improve older adults' performance on specific cognitive tasks, including video games that require fast reaction times, computer-based memory and attention exercises, and regular participation in problem-solving groups to prepare for a community competition (Smith et al., 2009; Stine-Morrow et al., 2008).

So, on average, does mental exercise help to combat the cognitive declines of aging? Many scientists feel that the evidence is supportive (Delahunt et al., 2009; Petrosini et al., 2009). But some say not so fast (Koontz & Baskys, 2009), including psychologist Timothy Salthouse (2006). In Salthouse's view, training experiments show that stimulating activities can boost specific cognitive skills, but they have not reliably shown that mental exercise changes the *rate* (i.e., the slope) at which those skills decline with age. To illustrate, suppose that at the start of an experiment, adults in a training group and a no-training (control) group exhibit the same average score on a reasoning test. We then find that the training boosts reasoning performance by 10 points. For the next 5 years, we also find that each group's performance decreases on average by 1 point per year. Therefore, 5 years after our experiment, the trained group will still perform better than the untrained group by 10 points, but both groups will have declined cognitively and at the same rate. Of course, we could repeatedly expose people to the training each year to try to keep their skills up, but with advancing age in late adulthood, the same retraining will likely take longer or produce smaller improvements (Yang et al., 2006).

Salthouse (2006) believes that the mental-exercise hypothesis, at least in terms of slowing the rate of cognitive decline, is more a reflection of optimistic hope—a desire to feel that we can control how we age—than reality. But as he acknowledges, and as we and many other researchers emphasize, the finding that sustained cognitive stimulation can boost many adults' absolute level of particular mental skills is no trivial matter. In our view, there is reasonable support for this aspect of the mental-exercise hypothesis. In stating this, however, realize that we are not evaluating the claims of any particular mental-exercise product or program. Further, there is much that science doesn't yet know about mental exercise and aging, and it's important to avoid creating unrealistic expectations about the effectiveness of mental exercise as a sure-fire "treatment" to prevent cognitive decline or reverse existing dementia (Low & Anstey, 2009).

The Growth of Wisdom?

Even as various mental abilities begin to decline with age, people can still accumulate knowledge that leads to greater wisdom. Common sense says that as we age, we become "older but wiser," and a study of 26 cultures spanning the globe suggests that people generally believe this to be true (Löckenhoff et al., 2009). Is it?

Wisdom includes knowledge about human nature and social relationships, strategies for making decisions and handling conflict, and an ability to manage uncertainty (Baltes & Smith, 2008). To study the growth of wisdom, psychologists present people of different ages with hypothetical social problems or situations (e.g., a 15-year-old girl wants to get married right away) and ask them to provide solutions. Experts blind to the participants' ages then use specific criteria to judge the wisdom of the participants' answers.

Some findings suggest that wisdom rises steadily from age 13 to 25 and then remains relatively stable through age 75 (Baltes & Staudinger, 2000). Other studies, however, have found that adults in their 70s offer wiser solutions than young adults on some tasks (Happé et al., 1998).

Conservatively, from adolescence through one's mid-70s, it may be that "older but wiser" applies only up to a point, beyond which "older

but at least as wise" is more appropriate. Of course, these are averages, and to stereotype elderly adults as "wise" is just as inappropriate as to stereotype them as "senile."

Cognitive Impairment in Old Age

As we noted in Chapter 8, *dementia* is a gradual loss of cognitive abilities that accompanies abnormal brain deterioration and interferes with daily functioning. In people with dementia, an abnormal progressive degeneration of brain tissue occurs as a result of disease or injury.

Dementia is most common in late adulthood, and the term **senile dementia** *refers to dementia that begins after age 65.* Alzheimer's disease (AD), which we previously discussed in Chapter 8 in relation to memory loss, accounts for about two-thirds of senile dementia cases (Grossman et al., 2006). Overall, about 5 to 7 percent of adults aged 65 years and older have AD, but this percentage increases substantially with age (Hirtz et al., 2007). Parkinson's disease, Huntington's disease, and Creutzfeldt-Jakob disease are other common causes of senile dementia, and complications from high blood pressure and stroke may also be causes.

Impaired memory, particularly for very recent events, typically is one of the first symptoms of dementia to appear (Figure 12.32). Poor judgment, language problems, and disorientation may appear gradually or sporadically, and people who develop dementia typically have episodes of distress because they feel confused. Their behavior may become uninhibited, they may lose the ability to perform familiar tasks, and they may experience significant physical decline in addition to cognitive impairments.

Compared to other adults aged 65 years and older, those who more frequently engage in stimulating cognitive activity show a lower risk for subsequently developing Alzheimer's disease, but whether this truly reflects a causal relation remains to be seen (Wilson & Bennett, 2003). One thing is certain: as people live longer lives, finding a cure for Alzheimer's disease and other forms of senile dementia becomes more urgent. Until then, many of us can expect our own family members to become Alzheimer's patients.

Unfortunately, being a caregiver for a spouse or for one's elderly parent who has developed dementia often is a stressful and psychologically painful experience (Pinquart & Sörensen, 2003). More than half of the people diagnosed with senile dementia show combinations of depression,

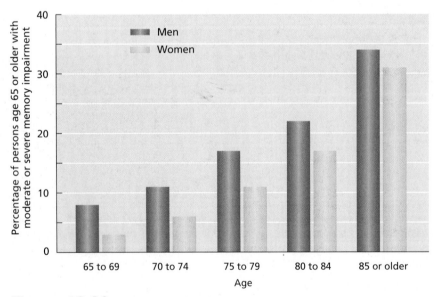

Figure 12.32

Impaired memory on a word-recall task.

Participants in this nationally representative sample of Americans were read a list of 20 words and asked to recall as many as they could. Most healthy adults were able to recall between 5 and 9 words. This graph shows that the percentage of people who recalled 4 or fewer words increased steadily during late adulthood. Source: Federal Interagency Forum on Aging-Related Statistics, 2006.

anxiety, agitation, paranoid reactions, and disordered thinking that may resemble schizophrenia. Ultimately, they may not even be able to walk, talk, or recognize close friends or family members.

In-depth studies in Finland, Germany, and the United States find that among adults over the age of 65 who do not suffer from dementia, 20 to 25 percent do have mild cognitive impairment (Unverzagt et al., 2001). Combining cases of mild impairment and dementia, some experts estimate that 79 percent of 65- to 74-year-olds and 45 percent of people age 85 and older remain "cognitively normal" (Unverzagt et al., 2001). Surely, these are not pleasant statistics, but they also make clear that even well into old age, cognitive impairment is not inevitable.

Social-Emotional Development

G. Stanley Hall (1904), the first psychologist to study adolescence, viewed it as a time of "storm and stress." Indeed, adolescents may grapple with difficult issues and experience substantial conflict, yet many find it to be a positive period of life. Thus Jeffrey Arnett proposes a modified view, noting that "not all adolescents experience storm and stress, but storm and stress is more likely during adolescence than at other ages" (1999, p. 317).

Adolescents' Search for Identity

"Who am I?" "What do I believe in?" Erik Erikson (1968) proposed that such questions reflect the pivotal crisis of adolescent personality development: *identity versus role confusion* (see Table 12.2 on page 430). Erikson believed that an adolescent's "identity crisis" (a term he coined) can be resolved positively, leading to a stable sense of identity, or it can end negatively, leading to confusion about one's identity and values.

Building on Erikson's work, James Marcia (1966, 2002) studied adolescents' and young adults' search for identity. Marcia classified the "identity status" of each person as follows:

- *Identity diffusion:* These teens and adults had not yet gone through an identity crisis. They seemed unconcerned or even cynical about identity issues and were not committed to a coherent set of values.

- *Foreclosure:* These individuals had not yet gone through an identity crisis either, but

for a different reason: they committed to an identity and set of values before experiencing a crisis. For example, some automatically adopted peer-group or parental values without giving these values much thought.

- *Moratorium:* These people wanted to establish a clear identity, were currently experiencing a crisis, but had not yet resolved it.

- *Identity achievement:* These individuals had gone through an identity crisis, successfully resolved it, and emerged with a coherent set of values.

Marcia found that most young adolescents are in identity diffusion or foreclosure; they have not experienced an identity crisis. But during the teen years, people typically begin to think more deeply about who they are, or they reconsider values they had adopted previously. This often leads to an identity crisis, and more than half successfully resolve it by early adulthood.

Identity, of course, is not a simple concept, and our sense of identity has multiple components (Camilleri & Malewska-Peyre, 1997). These include (1) our gender, ethnicity, and other attributes by which we define ourselves as members of social groups ("daughter," "student," "athlete"); (2) how we view our personal characteristics ("shy," "friendly"); and (3) our goals and values. Typically, we achieve a stable identity regarding some components before others, and changing situations may trigger new crises and cause us to reevaluate prior goals and values.

Culture plays a key role in identity formation, one that goes beyond the simple idea that we view ourselves as belonging to certain cultural groups. Our cultural upbringing influences the very way we view concepts such as "self" and "identity." Having grown up in an individualistic culture, my sense of identity assumes that I am an autonomous individual with clear boundaries separating me from other people. But in collectivistic cultures, the concept of "self" is traditionally based more strongly on the connectedness between people (Kagitçibasi, 1997). Thus the question "Who am I?" is more likely to be answered in ways that reflect a person's relationships with family members, friends, and others. Still, keep in mind that we are talking about relative differences. Across cultures, people's sense of identity incorporates elements that involve autonomy from—and interdependence with—other people (Mascolo & Li, 2004).

Relationships with Parents and Peers

When it comes to teenagers' relationships with their parents, is "storm and stress" the rule or the exception? In a national survey, about 80 percent of American teens living at home said that they thought highly of, and enjoyed spending time with, their parents (Moore et al., 2004). About two-thirds of the teens reported an overall positive relationship with their parents.

Likewise, research in China and the Netherlands, and with various American ethnic groups, suggests that teen-parent conflict is not as severe as often assumed (Chen et al., 1998). For example, Andrew Fuligni (1998) studied 1,341 female and male American students in 6th, 8th, and 10th grades. The students came from immigrant and native-born families of Mexican, Chinese, Filipino, and European ancestry. He found that among both sexes and all four ethnic groups, teenagers' level of conflict with mothers and fathers was low.

Most adolescents also state that if they face a serious problem, they can confide in one or both parents (National Center on Addiction and Substance Abuse, 2005). Yet many adolescents also feel that for various reasons, including the right to preserve their independence, it is acceptable to lie to their parents at times. As Figure 12.33 shows, in one study most high school students said that they had lied to their parents on several issues in the past year (Jensen et al., 2004).

Some parents and teenagers do struggle a lot, and parent-teen conflict is correlated with other signs of distress. For example, among American, Chinese, and Taiwanese teens, those who report more conflict with parents also display higher levels of school misconduct (e.g., skipping school), more antisocial behavior (e.g., getting into fistfights), lower self-esteem, more drug use, and less life satisfaction (Caughlin & Malis, 2004; Chen et al., 1998). Recalling the principle that correlation does not equal causation, we must consider that although parent-teen conflict may be a cause of teens' psychological problems, it also is likely to be caused *by* such problems.

From Alabama to the Arctic, teens like to spend time hanging out with friends. Peer relationships increase in importance during adolescence, and some studies find that teenagers spend more time with peers than doing almost anything else. But this pattern may be stronger in North America than in Europe or Asia, where people of all ages, teens included, generally place a relatively strong emphasis on family relationships (Chen et al., 1998).

Adolescent friendships are typically more intimate than those at previous ages and involve a greater sharing of problems. Peers can strongly influence a teenager's values and behaviors, thereby facilitating the process of separating from parents and establishing one's own identity. For some adolescents, however, experiences with peers increase the risk

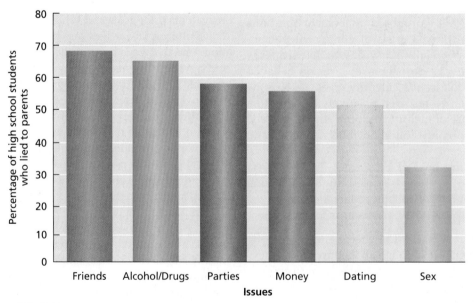

Figure 12.33

Issues about Which Teens Lie to Their Parents

In one study, 229 students attending a public high school were asked how often they lied to their parents about six issues. For each issue, this graph shows the percentage of students who reported lying to their parents at least once during the past year. Source: Jensen et al., 2004.

of misconduct, such as skipping school, damaging property, or using drugs (Larson et al., 2006). Fortunately, peer pressure *against* misconduct typically has an even stronger effect, and closeness to parents is an added buffer that helps many teenagers resist peer pressure to do misdeeds (Chen et al., 1998). Despite increased peer influence during adolescence, parental influence remains high on political, religious, moral, and career issues. In many ways, the so-called generation gap is narrower than is often assumed.

Emotional Changes in Adolescence

As you progressed from childhood through your teenage years, did you generally become a more or less happy person? Reed Larson and coworkers (2002) examined changes in teenage emotionality in a creative and powerful way. They randomly selected 328 5th- through 8th-graders (ages 10 to 14) from working- and middle-class suburban families living near Chicago. Students carried electronic pagers and paper booklets with them for 1 week, and the time of year that each student did this was randomly determined. From morning through evening, each student was beeped at random times. On a questionnaire, the students rated how happy or unhappy, cheerful or irritable, and friendly or angry they felt at that moment. The researchers also measured students' self-esteem, depression, and the number of major stressful events experienced during the last 6 months. This procedure was repeated with the same students 4 years later, when the students were in 9th through 12th grade.

Overall, girls' and boys' daily emotional experiences were more positive than negative. Still, teens' daily emotionality became less positive as they moved into and through early adolescence, with changes leveling off and emotions becoming more stable during late adolescence. As they aged, 34 percent of the teens showed a major downward change (less-positive emotions), and 16 percent showed a major upward change (more-positive emotions). The remaining half of the students showed a smaller amount of change in emotions, although once again, downward changes were twice as common as upward changes. The study also revealed that students who reported less-positive emotions tended to have lower self-esteem and more frequent major stressful events during the preceding 6 months.

The Transition to Adulthood

In many traditional cultures, marriage is the key transitional event into adulthood (Arnett, 2001). Through socialization, males develop skills that will enable them to provide for a family of their own, and females learn skills needed to care for children and run a household. Marriage signifies that each partner has acquired these skills and is capable of raising a family.

In industrialized societies, how do we know when someone has become an adult? Our "Research Close-up" examines this question.

Research Close-up

What Does It Take to Become an Adult?

SOURCE: JEFFREY J. ARNETT (2001). Conceptions of the transition to adulthood: Perspectives from adolescence through midlife. *Journal of Adult Development, 8,* 133–143.

INTRODUCTION

How would you answer if we asked you, "Have you reached adulthood?" And in your view, just what does it take to be considered an adult? Jeffrey Arnett examined how Americans in various age groups viewed the transition to adulthood. Whereas previous research focused on the viewpoints of adolescents and people in their 20s, this study also examined the viewpoints of older adults.

METHOD

Men and women from a midsized, Midwestern American community were recruited to participate. There were 519 participants, representing three age groups: 13- to 19-year-olds, 20- to 29-year-olds, and 30- to 55-year-olds. Participants rated ("yes" or "no") whether each of 38 specific characteristics "must be achieved before a person can be considered an adult." These characteristics were presented in random order and represented six general categories of criteria for judging adult status. These categories and some sample items appear in Table 12.4.

Continued

Table **12.4** | **Possible Criteria for Attaining Adulthood**

General Category	Sample of Specific Characteristics
Individualism	Be responsible for one's actions; determine own values/beliefs; attain financial freedom
Family Capacities	Be capable of caring for and financially supporting a family
Norm Compliance	Refrain from crime, irresponsible sex, drunk driving, illegal drug use
Biological Transitions	Be capable of fathering/bearing children
Legal/Chronological Transitions	Reach age 18; reach age 21; obtain driver's license
Role Transitions	Full-time employment; establish career; finish education, get married

Each participant also was asked, "Do you think that you have reached adulthood?" The answer options were "yes," "no," and "in some respects yes, in some respects no." The Research Design diagram summarizes key aspects of the method.

RESULTS

What qualities were judged as necessary to be considered an adult? Regardless of age group, about 90 percent of participants endorsed the importance of accepting responsibility for one's actions. Establishing one's own values and beliefs, seeing oneself as an equal with one's parents, and attaining financial independence were the next most frequently chosen qualities among all age groups. Items such as "reaching age 18," "employed full-time," and "marriage" were endorsed by only 47, 32, and 13 percent of participants, respectively. In fact, if you look at the six general categories shown in Table 12.4, they are listed in the overall order of importance, as determined by the average ratings of all the items in each category. Overall, there was strong consistency in how the various age groups viewed the importance of these characteristics.

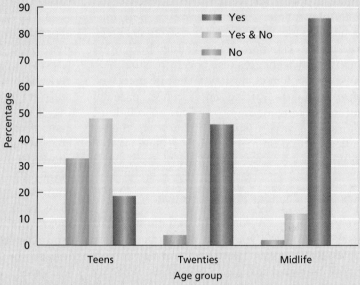

Figure 12.34

Have you reached adulthood?

This graph shows the percentage of people in their teens, 20s, and 30s to mid-50s (midlife) who felt that they had not, partially, or fully reached adulthood. Source: Arnett, 2001.

In contrast, substantial age differences emerged in whether participants viewed themselves as having reached adulthood. As Figure 12.34 shows, among adolescents (average age 16 years), fewer than a fifth said that they had reached adulthood. Among people in their 20s (average age 24 years), almost half said that they had reached adulthood. Still, in both of these age groups, the transitional "yes and no" response was most common. Only among people in midlife (average age 42 years) did most view themselves as having fully attained adulthood.

DISCUSSION

Along with other research conducted across the United States, this study reveals that on the psychological road to adulthood, biological, legal, chronological, and role transitions take a backseat. *Individualism*—becoming a responsible, independent person—was judged to be the single most important general criterion. Still, in making the transition from adolescence to adulthood, multiple factors appear to come into play for most people.

This study had strengths and limitations. The 38 characteristics for judging adulthood status were carefully chosen on the basis of prior research, and the participants represented a broad age range. However, as a critical thinker you should recognize that this study used a cross-sectional design. The findings tell us, at a given point in time, how various age groups view the transition to adulthood. It would be interesting to study the same participants using a longitudinal design and thus examine more precisely how people's views of "becoming an adult" change as they grow older.

RESEARCH DESIGN

Question: How do people of various ages view the transition to adulthood?

Type of Study: *Correlational*

Variable X

Age
(Three age groups: 13 to 19, 20 to 29, and 30 to 55 years)

Variable Y

View of transition to adulthood (e.g., Is this characteristic necessary to be considered an adult? Are you an adult?)

Emerging Adulthood Beliefs across Cultures

What criteria do people from other cultures view as necessary to be considered an adult? Studies in Argentina, Canada, China, Israel, and Romania provide some answers (Nelson, 2009). First, there are many cross-cultural differences. For example, in one study, aboriginal Canadian college students (i.e., Inuit, Métis, North American Indian) rated role transitions and biological transitions as more important criteria than did Caucasian Canadian students (Cheah & Nelson, 2004). In another study, most Chinese students at a university in Beijing felt that to be considered an adult, one had to be able to take care of one's parents financially, a view that only a relatively small minority of American college students share (Nelson et al., 2004).

Second, across studies, there also are striking similarities. Whether American, aboriginal or Caucasian Canadian, Chinese, or Romanian, accepting responsibility for one's actions typically is ranked as the most important single criterion overall. Moreover, although some cultural groups view role, biological, and legal transitions to be more important than other groups, across studies such transitions are viewed as less important overall than criteria that focus on independence and maturity in relationships, taking care of one's own family (one's partner and children), and norm compliance (Nelson, 2009).

Stages versus Critical Events in Adulthood

Many researchers view adult social development as a progression through age-related stages (Levinson, 1990). According to Erik Erikson (1959/1980; see Table 12.2 on page 430), *intimacy versus isolation* is the major developmental challenge of early adulthood (ages 20 to 39). Intimacy is the ability to open oneself to another person and to form close relationships. This is the period of adulthood in which many people form close adult friendships, fall in love, and marry.

Middle adulthood (ages 40 to 64) brings with it the issue of *generativity versus stagnation*. Through their careers, raising children, or involvement in other activities, people achieve generativity by doing things for others and making the world a better place. Certainly, many young adults make such contributions, but generativity typically becomes a more central issue later in adulthood (Slater, 2003).

Late adulthood (age 65 and older) accentuates the final crisis, *integrity versus despair*. Older adults review their life and evaluate its meaning. If the major crises of earlier stages have been successfully resolved, the person experiences integrity: a sense of completeness and fulfillment. Older adults who have not achieved positive outcomes at earlier stages may experience despair, regretting that they had not lived their lives in a more fulfilling way.

Consistent with Erikson's model, many goals increase in importance as people age, and successfully resolving certain life tasks contributes to mastering others (McAdams & de St. Aubin, 1998). But critics caution that we should avoid viewing early, middle, and late adulthood as strict stages in which one life task takes over while others fade away. Although older adults are more concerned about generativity and integrity than are younger adults, they remain highly concerned about intimacy (Sheldon & Kasser, 2001).

Another way to view adult social development is through the major life events that people experience. Sigmund Freud (1935) once defined psychological adjustment as "the ability to love and work," and many key life events revolve around these two themes.

Marriage and Family

Around the world, most people marry or form another type of family union at some point in their lives, and family structures can vary widely both across and within various cultures (Figure 12.35). The "average" family in America and some other countries has changed in several ways over recent generations. For example, Baby Boomers were

Figure 12.35

These children, from a family of herders in the Republic of Mongolia, are living in an extended family unit that includes parents, grandparents, great-grandparents, and other relatives. In the United States in 2001, one-third of all children lived in single-parent households. Source: U.S. Census Bureau, 2002.

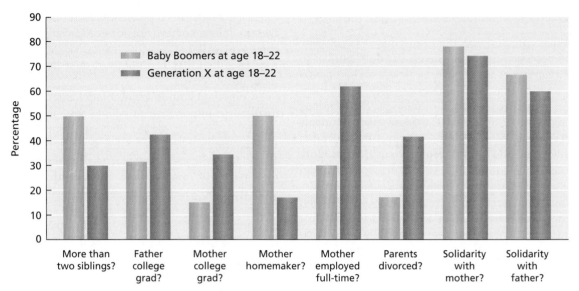

Figure 12.36

Growing up in different generations.

Baby Boomers were surveyed when they were 18 to 22 years old and asked to identify various characteristics of the families in which they had grown up. A generation later, when the Baby Boomers' children (Generation X) had turned 18 to 22 years old, they answered the same survey questions as their parents had. Source: Bengtson, 2001.

born a few years after the end of World War II, and their children (born in the 1960s through the early 1980s) became known as Generation X. As Figure 12.36 shows, compared to the families that Baby Boomers grew up in, members of Generation X are more likely to have experienced parental divorce, had two working parents, had a smaller number of siblings, and yet maintained a similar level of closeness to their parents (Bengtson, 2001).

A high divorce rate in many countries indicates that marital happiness is by no means automatic. Successful marriages are characterized by emotional closeness and support, positive communication and problem solving, and a willingness to accept and support changes in the partner (Brock & Lawrence, 2009). On average, marital satisfaction declines over the first few years after the knot is tied (McNulty & Karney, 2004). This does not mean, however, that most couples are unhappy. They are still satisfied, just less so than they were. In a sense, the honeymoon is over.

The birth of a first baby dramatically alters the way couples spend their time. For many couples, marital satisfaction decreases in the year or two after their first child is born (Lawrence et al., 2010). Compared with husbands, wives are more likely to leave their outside jobs, spend more time parenting, and feel that their spouses are not helping enough. Disagreements over the division of labor and parenting are a major contributor to the drop in marital satisfaction (Frisco & Williams, 2003).

Over a broader age period, cross-sectional studies suggest a U-shaped relation between marital satisfaction and progression through major life events. The percentage of couples reporting that they are "very satisfied" in their marriage typically is highest before or just as the first child is born, drops during child-rearing years, and increases after all the children have left home (Orbuch et al., 1996). Contrary to the popular "empty nest" stereotype, most middle-aged couples do not become significantly depressed or suffer a crisis when their children leave home (Chiriboga, 1989). Couples maintain meaningful relationships with their children but have more time to spend with each other and pursue leisure activities.

Despite the stresses that accompany marriage and parenthood, studies around the globe find that married people experience greater subjective well-being than unmarried adults (Keyes & Waterman, 2003). They tend to be happier and live longer. Although raising children is demanding, parents often report that having children is one of the best things that has happened in their lives.

Some couples in committed relationships *cohabit*—that is, live together without being married. In 1960, the ratio of married to cohabiting households in the United States was about 95 to 1. By 2000, that ratio had shrunk to 10 to 1, representing almost 5.5 million cohabiting households (U.S. Census Bureau, 2003). Some couples cohabit as a permanent alternative to marriage, but many do so as a "trial marriage" to determine if they are compatible before tying the knot. In Sweden, premarital cohabitation appears to be the norm (Duvander, 1999).

thinking critically

COHABITATION AS A "TRIAL MARRIAGE"
What would you predict? Do couples who live together before getting married have a lower, higher, or similar rate of divorce compared to couples who do not live together before they get married? Why? Think about it, then see page 457.

Establishing a Career

In the adult world, one of the first questions a new acquaintance typically asks is "So, what do you do?" A career helps us earn a living and defines part of our identity. Work provides an outlet for achievement, gives us structure, and is a significant source of social interactions. Having satisfying relationships at work is especially important in collectivistic countries (Siu, 2003).

According to Donald Super (1957), a pioneer in the field of vocational psychology, from childhood through our mid-20s, we first enter a *growth stage* of career interests in which we form initial impressions about the types of jobs we like or dislike. This is followed by a more earnest *exploration stage* in which we form tentative ideas about a preferred career and pursue the necessary education or training.

From the mid-20s to mid-40s, people often enter an *establishment phase* during which they begin to make their mark. Initially, they may experience some job instability. After college, for example, many people are likely to change careers at least once. Eventually, careers tend to become more stable, and people enter a *maintenance stage* that continues into late adulthood. Finally, during the *decline stage,* people's investment in work tends to decrease, and they eventually retire.

Although this general model is useful, people's career paths vary quite a bit, and this is especially true for women. Overall, compared to their fathers and mothers at the same age, today's young women hold higher career aspirations (Bengtson, 2001). Still, family responsibilities, which fall disproportionately on women even when their married partners have similar job status, are a major cause of women's work gaps outside the home, reductions to part-time work status, or delayed entry into the workforce (Smithson et al., 2004). After raising a family, many women enter the workforce for the first time, reinvigorate an earlier career, or return to college to prepare for a new one. Career gaps also occur when adults must temporarily leave the workforce to care for their elderly parents. As in raising children, women disproportionately fill this elder-care role.

Midlife Crisis: Fact or Fiction?

Popular wisdom holds that along the developmental path of career and family, people hit a massive pothole called the *midlife crisis.* Is it a reality? Daniel Levinson and his coworkers (1978, 1986) studied 85 men and women longitudinally and found that many experienced a turbulent midlife transition between the ages of 40 and 45. They began to focus on their mortality and realized that some of their life's dreams pertaining to career, family, and relationships would not come true.

Critics note that Levinson's sample was small and nonrepresentative. In fact, considerable evidence suggests that the notion of an inevitable, full-blown midlife crisis is a myth (Lachman, 2004). Research conducted around the world shows that happiness and life satisfaction generally do not decrease throughout adulthood (Diener et al., 1999). In one study of adolescents and people in early, middle, and late adulthood from eight western European countries, about 80 percent of each age group reported they were "satisfied" or "very satisfied" with their lives (Ingelhart & Rabier, 1986). Moreover, people in their 40s do *not* have the highest rates of divorce, suicide, depression, feelings of meaninglessness, or emotional instability (Kessler et al., 2004).

In sum, middle-aged adults surely experience important conflicts, disappointments, and worries—and some indeed experience major crises—but so do people of all ages (Wethington, 2000). As Erikson emphasized, there are major goals to achieve, crises to resolve, and rewards to experience in every phase of life.

Retirement and the "Golden Years"

Retirement is an important milestone. Some adults view it as a reminder that they are growing older, but many look forward to leisure and other opportunities they were unable to pursue during their careers. Most retired people do not become anxious, depressed, or dissatisfied with life due to retirement itself, although those who have strong work values are most apt to miss their jobs (Hyde et al., 2004).

The decision to retire or keep working typically involves many factors, such as one's feelings about the job, leisure interests, physical health, and family relationships. Family income, leisure time, and family roles change with retirement, and married couples often experience increased marital stress after a spouse retires, especially if the other spouse is still working. Over time, however, they typically adjust to their new circumstances and marital quality is enhanced (Moen et al., 2001).

Some people, of course, do not have the luxury to choose their work status. They may be forced into retirement by job layoffs or mandatory retirement ages, or feel compelled to keep working for economic reasons. These circumstances can have a significant impact on well-being, trigger depression, and produce long-lasting anger (Blau, 2008). Whether in their 50s, 60s, or 70s, adults who are working or retired because this is what *they* prefer report higher life satisfaction and better physical and mental health than adults who are involuntarily working or retired (Shultz et al., 1998). Of course, declining physical and mental health also may be factors that lead people to retire in the first place.

Death and Dying

Jeanne Louise Calment was born in France 10 years after the American Civil War. By age 60, she had lived through World War I and the invention of the radio, telephone, motion picture, automobile, and airplane. Still to come was World War II, television, space flight, computers, and the Internet. Calment rode a bicycle until age 100, and when she died in 1997 at the verified age of 122, she had lived longer than any human in recorded history.

Part of being human is the fact that we are mortal. Like other aspects of life-span development, death can be viewed at several levels. It is an inevitable biological process, but one with important psychological and environmental components.

In her pioneering work on dying, Elisabeth Kübler-Ross (1969) found that terminally ill patients often experienced five stages as they coped with impending death. *Denial* typically came first, as the person refused to accept that the illness was terminal. Next, denial often gave way to *anger* and then to *bargaining,* such as "Lord, please let me live long enough to see my grandchild." *Depression* ushered in the fourth stage, as patients began to grieve. Finally, many experienced *acceptance* and a resigned sense of peacefulness.

It is essential to keep in mind that these stages do not represent a "normal" or "correct" way to face death and that terminally ill patients' reactions may not typify those of people facing death under other circumstances (Doka, 1995). Even among terminally ill patients, some move back and forth between stages, do not experience all the stages, or look forward to death. Indeed, some scientists question whether people's psychological responses to their impending death are stagelike at all (Kastenbaum, 2000). Nevertheless, Kübler-Ross's work spurred great interest in understanding and helping people cope with death.

As Figure 12.37 illustrates, beliefs and customs concerning death vary across cultures and among individuals (Morgan et al., 2009). To some, death means the complete end of one's existence. Others believe in reincarnation or an afterlife. Death also means different things to people of different ages. By late and even middle adulthood, people typically have lost more friends and loved ones and have thought more about their own eventual death than have younger people. As one 80-year-old put it, "More of the people I know are in heaven now than on earth."

Understandably, the elderly are more accepting of their own death than any other age group. In the midst of a fatal heart attack, an 81-year-old man we knew reassuringly told his family, "It's my time. It's been a good life." We should all wish for this blessing of a fulfilled life's journey.

Figure 12.37

Many cultures honor a person's death with a ceremony that involves family, friends, and the wider community. In some cultures, this traditionally is a somber occasion; in others, it is a more joyous celebration.

Levels of **Analysis**

Life Span Development

We've seen in this chapter that aging is biological process intertwined with psychological and environmental components. Using these three levels of analysis, let's highlight some of the main points we've covered.

BIOLOGICAL LEVEL

- Our genetic blueprint guides the aging process.
- Critical and sensitive periods occur during prenatal development and childhood.
- A surge in pituitary hormones during puberty speeds maturation of sex organs and produces secondary sex characteristics.
- Brain maturation is especially rapid during infancy and childhood. Many neural circuits are rewired during adolescence.
- People generally achieve their physical and perceptual peak and greatest brain efficiency in young adulthood.
- Abnormal degeneration of brain tissue causes dementia.

ENVIRONMENTAL LEVEL

- Teratogens cause abnormal prenatal development.
- Different parenting styles are associated with different child development outcomes.
- Prolonged social isolation poses developmental risks.
- Development occurs in a sociocultural context.
- Peer relations take on increased importance during adolescence.
- Some cultures mark a transition into adulthood by a formal rite of passage.
- Exposure to cognitively stimulating environments can improve intellectual functioning.

PSYCHOLOGICAL LEVEL

- Newborns have perceptual preferences and basic learning capabilities.
- The acquisition of schemas and improved information-processing underlie cognitive development.
- Infant-caregiver attachment in humans involves periods of stranger and separation anxiety.
- Children's ability to express and regulate their emotions improves with age; they acquire a gender identity.
- The capacity for abstract thinking and a focus on one's identity increase during adolescence.
- People vary greatly in the age at which they feel they have attained adulthood.
- Achieving intimacy, generativity, and integrity are major challenges of adulthood.

Consider this possible interaction between environmental and psychological levels of analysis. In Arnett's research on the psychological transition to adulthood among American students, "individualism" emerged as a key factor. In cultures that are relatively more collectivistic, do you think that people would place greater weight on other characteristics in judging whether they have reached adulthood?

test yourself

Adolescence and Adulthood

True or False?

1. Puberty is a biological concept; adolescence is a sociocultural concept.
2. Overall, early maturation has more positive consequences for girls than for boys.
3. Information-processing abilities improve during adolescence, but more slowly than in childhood.
4. Most teens say they have very negative relations with their parents that last throughout adolescence.
5. In adulthood, fluid mental abilities typically begin to decline before crystallized mental abilities.
6. Erikson proposed that the main psychosocial crisis of early adulthood is intimacy versus isolation.

ANSWERS: 1-true, 2-false, 3-true, 4-false, 5-true, 6-true

Chapter Summary

MAJOR ISSUES AND METHODS

- Developmental psychologists study the aging process. Questions about the influence of nature and nurture, critical and sensitive periods, continuity versus discontinuity, and stability versus change have guided much developmental research.
- Cross-sectional designs compare different age groups at one point in time. A longitudinal design repeatedly tests the same age group as it grows older. Sequential designs test several groups at one point in time and then again as they grow older.

PRENATAL DEVELOPMENT

- Prenatal development involves the germinal, embryonic, and fetal stages.
- The 23rd chromosome in a mother's egg cell is always an X chromosome. If the 23rd chromosome in the father's sperm cell is an X, the child will be genetically female (XX); if it is a Y, the child will be genetically male (XY).
- Teratogens such as maternal illnesses, environmental toxins, and drugs can cause abnormal prenatal development.

INFANCY AND CHILDHOOD

- Newborns distinguish between different visual patterns, sounds, odors, and tastes. They display perceptual preferences and learn through classical and operant conditioning. Biology and environment (e.g., deprivation and enrichment) jointly steer children's physical and psychological development.
- According to Piaget, cognitive development depends on processes of assimilation and accommodation and proceeds through sensorimotor, preoperational, concrete operational, and formal operational stages. Vygotsky emphasized the sociocultural context of cognitive development. Each child has a zone of proximal development, reflecting the difference between what the child can do independently and what she or he can do with assistance from others.
- Information-processing capacities improve with age. Older children search for information more systematically, process it more quickly, and display better memory.
- Children's emotions and emotion-regulation strategies become more varied and complex with age. Extreme temperamental styles in infancy and childhood can predict some aspects of functioning years later.
- Erikson believed that personality development proceeds through eight major psychosocial stages. Each stage involves a major crisis, and how we resolve it affects our ability to meet the challenges of the next stage.
- Infant-caretaker attachment develops in phases, and infants experience periods of stranger and separation anxiety. Secure attachment is associated with better developmental outcomes than is insecure attachment. For most children, day care does not disrupt attachment. Divorce typically disrupts children's short-term psychological adjustment, and for some it is associated with long-term maladjustment.
- Parenting styles vary along dimensions of warmth-hostility and restrictiveness-permissiveness. Children of authoritative parents generally display the best developmental outcomes. Gender identity begins to form early in childhood, and socialization influences children's acquisition of sex-role stereotypes.
- Kohlberg proposed that moral reasoning proceeds through preconventional, conventional, and postconventional levels. The development of moral behavior is linked to children's cognitive, emotional, and social development.

ADOLESCENCE AND ADULTHOOD

- Adolescence is a socially constructed transition period between childhood and adulthood. In contrast, puberty is a biologically based period of rapid maturation. Physical and perceptual functioning typically peak in young adulthood.
- Adolescents may show egocentric social thinking. Their abstract thinking blossoms, and information-processing abilities improve. Beginning in early adulthood information-processing speed slows, but many intellectual abilities do not begin to decline reliably until late adulthood.
- The search for identity is a key task of adolescence. During adolescence, peer relationships become more important. Most teens maintain good relationships with their parents. Overall, for most teens daily emotional experience becomes less positive as they move into and through early adolescence.
- The age at which people think that they have become adults varies widely. Among Americans, it depends strongly on viewing oneself as a responsible, independent person. Erikson proposed that intimacy versus isolation, generativity versus stagnation, and integrity versus despair are the main crises of early, middle, and late adulthood, respectively.
- For many couples, marital satisfaction tends to decline in the years following the birth of children but increases later in adulthood. In the workplace, women typically experience more career gaps and more variable career paths than men do. Most adults do not experience a full-blown midlife crisis. Similarly, most retired people do not become more anxious, depressed, or lonely due to voluntary retirement.
- Many terminally ill patients experience similar psychological reactions as they cope with impending death, but beliefs and feelings about death vary with culture and age, and there is no "normal" way to approach death.

KEY TERMS AND CONCEPTS

Each term has been boldfaced and defined in the chapter on the page indicated in parentheses.

accommodation (p. 423)
adolescence (p. 440)
adolescent egocentrism (p. 442)
assimilation (p. 423)
attachment (p. 431)
authoritarian parents (p. 435)
authoritative parents (p. 435)
cephalocaudal principle (p. 421)
concrete operational stage (p. 424)
conservation (p. 424)
conventional moral reasoning
  (p. 437)
critical period (p. 416)
cross-sectional design (p. 416)
egocentrism (p. 424)
embryo (p. 417)
emotion regulation (p. 429)

fetal alcohol spectrum disorders (FASD)
  (p. 418)
fetal alcohol syndrome (FAS) (p. 418)
fetus (p. 417)
formal operational stage (p. 425)
gender constancy (p. 436)
gender identity (p. 436)
imprinting (p. 431)
indulgent parents (p. 435)
longitudinal design (p. 416)
maturation (p. 421)
neglectful parents (p. 435)
object permanence (p. 423)
postconventional moral reasoning (p. 438)
preconventional moral reasoning (p. 437)
preoperational stage (p. 424)
proximodistal principle (p. 421)

psychosocial stages (p. 430)
puberty (p. 440)
reflexes (p. 420)
schema (p. 423)
senile dementia (p. 446)
sensitive period (p. 416)
sensorimotor stage (p. 423)
separation anxiety (p. 432)
sequential design (p. 416)
sex-typing (p. 436)
stranger anxiety (p. 432)
strange situation (p. 432)
temperament (p. 429)
teratogens (p. 418)
theory of mind (p. 428)
zone of proximal development (p. 426)
zygote (p. 417)

 thinking **critically**

SHY CHILD, SHY ADULT? (Page 430)

To answer this question, psychologists patiently conduct longitudinal research, measuring people's temperament in childhood and then examining whether it correlates with people's traits or behaviors in adulthood. For example, in America and Sweden, shy, behaviorally inhibited 8- to 12-year-old boys are more likely than non-shy peers to delay marriage and fatherhood when they grow up, possibly reflecting their reluctance to enter new social relationships (Caspi et al., 1988; Kerr et al., 1996). Shy American girls are more likely as adults to quit work after marriage and become homemakers, whereas shy Swedish girls are less likely to complete college than are non-shy girls.

What about temperament in early childhood? Denise Newman and co-workers (1997) measured the temperament of 961 New Zealanders at age 3, based on a 90-minute observation of each child. At age 21, participants were studied again. Compared with 3-year-olds with a "well-adjusted temperament," those who were "undercontrolled" (i.e., irritable, impulsive, inattentive) reported more antisocial behavior in adulthood and greater conflict in family and romantic relationships, and they were more likely to have been fired from a job. In contrast, children with an "inhibited temperament" (i.e., socially shy and fearful) reported having less overall companionship in adulthood.

Most young children are well adjusted and display only mild to moderately strong temperamental traits. Differences in temperament among these children only weakly predict how they will function as adults. But for the remaining children, their strong temperamental traits can provide better insight

into adulthood functioning. Still, predicting how any individual child will turn out as an adult is difficult. Many factors influence development, and even during childhood, strong temperaments often mellow (Pfeifer et al., 2002). Even so, it is remarkable that a mere 90-minute observation of children at age 3 can modestly predict different patterns of adjustment 18 years later.

COHABITATION AS A "TRIAL MARRIAGE" (Page 453)

Large national surveys in several countries, including Canada, Germany, Sweden, and the United States, have found that premarital cohabitation is associated with a *higher* risk of subsequent divorce (Heaton, 2002). Many researchers, however, believe that the cohabitation-divorce relation does not reflect cause and effect. Rather, couples who choose to cohabit before marriage appear to differ psychologically from couples who don't cohabit first. They tend to be less religious and less committed to their partners and to marriage as an institution (Stanley et al., 2004). Taken together, these preexisting factors would increase the risk of divorce even if these couples had not cohabited before tying the knot. In some studies, when researchers focus on cohabiting couples who start out with a strong orientation toward marriage, they find that the risk of divorce is no higher and the quality of marital relations is no poorer than among couples who did not cohabit prior to marriage (Bruederl et al., 1997). Still, research does *not* support the view that, overall, cohabitation reduces the risk of subsequent divorce.

chapter thirteen

Personality

CHAPTER OUTLINE

Myth or Reality?

Criminal Profiling Is a Useful Investigative Tool (page 499)

Media productions like *Criminal Minds*, *Profiler*, and *The Silence of the Lambs* depict federal agents and psychologists who help solve crimes by creating personality profiles of likely perpetrators. But what's the scientific verdict on the usefulness of criminal profiling? Does it really help solve crimes?

On a hot summer evening in 1966, a University of Texas student wrote the following letter:

> I don't really understand myself these days. I am supposed to be an average, reasonable, and intelligent young man. However, lately (I can't recall when it started) I have been the victim of many unusual and irrational thoughts. These thoughts constantly recur, and it requires a tremendous mental effort to concentrate on useful and progressive tasks. In March when my parents made a physical break I noticed a great deal of stress. I consulted a Dr. Cochrum at the University Health Center and asked him to recommend some-one that I could consult with about some psychiatric disorders I felt I had. I talked with a doctor once for about two hours and tried to convey to him my fears that I felt overcome by overwhelming violent impulses. After one session I never saw the doctor again, and since then I have been fighting my mental turmoil alone, and seemingly to no avail. After my death I wish that an autopsy would be performed on me to see if there is any visible physical disorder. I have had some tremendous headaches in the past and have consumed two large bottles of Excedrin in the past three months. (Lavergne, 1997, p. 8)

(a)

(b)

Figure 13.1

(a) Charles Whitman with his wife, whom he later murdered. Few thought this exemplary citizen capable of the heinous acts of violence he committed. (b) Whitman (arrow) fires from the University of Texas tower onto the campus below.

Later that night, Charles Whitman killed his wife and mother, both of whom were lovingly supportive of him. The next morning, he carried a high-powered hunting rifle to the top of a 307-foot tower on the busy University of Texas campus in Austin and opened fire on all those passing by below. Within 90 horrifying minutes, he killed 16 people and wounded 30 others before he himself was killed by police.

On the surface, Charles Whitman (Figure 13.1) seemed as solid and upstanding as the University of Texas tower from which he rained death on unsuspecting strangers. He came from a wealthy, prominent Florida family and was an outstanding student, an accomplished pianist, one of the youngest Eagle Scouts in state history, and a former U.S. Marine who had been awarded a Good Conduct Medal and the Marine Corps Expeditionary Medal. He married the woman of his dreams, and the two were seen as an ideal couple. Whitman became a University of Texas student when he was selected by the Marines for a prestigious engineering scholarship. In his spare time, he served as a scoutmaster in Austin.

A psychological scientist who specializes in personality would want to know what could have caused this exemplary citizen to commit such extraordinary acts of violence. On December 18, 2001, the Austin History Center opened its records on Charles Whitman to public scrutiny. These records provide important insights into the complexities of Whitman's personality and the turmoil that existed within him. Although the Whitman incident occurred decades ago, it is sadly reminiscent of more recent acts of violence in schools, communities, and workplaces across the United States. In this chapter's "Applying Psychological Science" feature (page 490), we will analyze Whitman's personality from the various perspectives on personality, applying their theoretical concepts and research findings. Such analysis helps us paint a more complete portrait of Whitman and may further our understanding not only of him but also of others who commit acts of violence and terrorism.

WHAT IS PERSONALITY?

The concept of personality arises from the fascinating spectrum of human individuality. We observe that people differ meaningfully in the ways they customarily think, feel, and act. These distinctive behavior patterns help define one's identity as a person. As one group of theorists noted, each of us is in certain respects like *all other* people, like *some other* people, and like *no other* person who has lived in the past or will exist in the future (Kluckhohn & Murray, 1953).

The concept of personality also rests on the observation that a given person seems to behave somewhat consistently over time and across different situations. From this perceived consistency comes the notion of *personality traits* that characterize an individual's customary ways of responding to his or her world. Although only modest stability is found from childhood personality to adult personality, personality becomes more stable as we enter adulthood (Caspi & Roberts, 1999; Terracciano et al., 2006). Nonetheless, even in adulthood, a capacity for meaningful personality change remains (Lewis, 1999; Roberts et al., 2002).

Combining these notions of individuality and consistency, we can define **personality** as the *distinctive and relatively enduring ways of thinking, feeling, and acting that characterize a person's responses to life situations*. Note that this definition refers not only to personal characteristics but also to situations. Personality psychologists are therefore interested in studying "person-by-situation" interactions in their efforts to understand the distinctive behaviors of individuals (Robins et al., 2007).

The thoughts, feelings, and actions that are seen as reflecting an individual's personality typically have three characteristics. First, they are seen as *behavioral components of identity* that distinguish that person from other people. Second, the behaviors are viewed as being caused primarily by *internal rather than environmental factors*. Third, the person's behaviors seem to have *organization and structure*; they seem to fit together in a meaningful fashion, suggesting an inner personality that guides and directs behavior (Figure 13.2).

The study of personality has been guided by the psychodynamic, humanistic, biological, behavioral, cognitive, and sociocultural perspectives. These perspectives provide different conceptions of what personality is and how it functions. As one pair of observers noted,

> It seems hard to believe that all the theorists are talking about the same creature, who is now angelic and now depraved, now a black-box robot shaped by reinforcers and now a shaper of its own destiny, now devious . . . and now hardheadedly oriented to solid reality. (Stone & Church, 1968, p. 4)

Yet this very diversity of viewpoints arises from the fact that the theorists have their own personalities that influence how they perceive and understand themselves and their world. No doubt, you will find some of their theories more in accord with your own life views than you will find others.

For personality psychologists, the subjective truth of a theory is less important than its *usefulness*. As discussed in Chapter 2, a scientific theory is useful to the extent that it (1) provides a comprehensive framework within which known facts can be incorporated, (2) allows us to predict future events with some precision, and (3) stimulates the discovery of new knowledge. We will evaluate each of the theories we describe in terms of these scientific standards. We will consider a number of approaches to the study of personality, beginning with the seminal work of Sigmund Freud, whose psychodynamic theory set the stage for a century of progress in the study of personality.

THE PSYCHODYNAMIC PERSPECTIVE

The first formal theory of personality was advanced by Sigmund Freud in the early years of the 20th century, and it is the prototype of the psychodynamic approach. Psychodynamic theorists look for the causes of behavior in a dynamic interplay of inner forces that often conflict with one another. They also focus on unconscious determinants of behavior. Sigmund Freud's psychoanalytic theory is one of the great intellectual contributions of

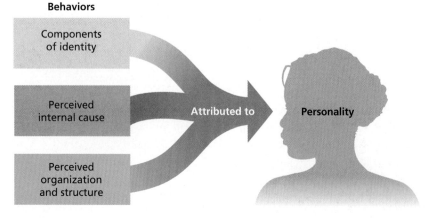

Figure 13.2

The behaviors of personality.
Certain perceived characteristics of behavior are seen as reflecting an individual's personality.

modern times, and it continues to influence Western thought today. Opposition to Freud's ideas was a stimulus for most of the other theories discussed in this chapter.

Freud's Psychoanalytic Theory

Freud (1856–1939) spent most of his life in Vienna, where he attended medical school with the intention of becoming a medical researcher (Figure 13.3). He was particularly interested in brain functioning. A pivotal event in his life occurred when he was awarded a fellowship to study in Paris with the famous French neurologist Jean Charcot. Charcot was treating patients who suffered from a disorder called *conversion hysteria*, in which physical symptoms such as paralysis and blindness appear suddenly and with no apparent physical cause. Freud's experiences in treating these patients convinced him that their symptoms were related to painful memories and feelings that seemed to have been *repressed*, or pushed out of awareness. When his patients were able to reexperience these traumatic memories and unacceptable feelings, which were often sexual or aggressive in nature, their physical symptoms often disappeared or improved markedly.

These observations convinced Freud that an unconscious part of the mind exerts great influence on behavior. He began to experiment with various techniques to unearth the buried contents of the unconscious mind, including hypnosis, *free association* (saying whatever comes to mind, no matter how trivial or embarrassing), and dream analysis. In an attempt to relieve his own painful bouts of depression, Freud also conducted an extensive self-analysis based on his own dreams.

In 1900, Freud published *The Interpretation of Dreams*. The book sold only 600 copies in the first six years after its publication, but his revolutionary ideas began to attract followers. His theory also evoked scathing criticism from a Victorian society that was not ready to regard the human being as a seething cauldron of sexual and aggressive impulses. In the words of one commentator,

> It is a shattering experience for anyone seriously committed to the Western tradition of morality and rationality to take a steadfast, unflinching look at what Freud has to say. It is humiliating to be compelled to admit the grossly seamy side of so many grand ideals. . . . To experience Freud is to partake a second time of the forbidden fruit. (Brown, 1959, p. xi)

Freud based his theory on careful clinical observation and constantly sought to expand it. Over

Figure 13.3

Sigmund Freud is shown here with his daughter Anna, who herself became an influential psychoanalytic theorist.

time, psychoanalysis became (1) a theory of personality, (2) an approach to studying the mind, and (3) a method for treating psychological disorders.

Psychic Energy and Mental Events

Inspired by the hydraulic models of 19th-century physics, which emphasized exchanges and releases of physical energy, Freud considered personality to be an energy system, somewhat like the steam engines of his day. According to Freud, instinctual drives generate *psychic energy*, which powers the mind and constantly presses for either direct or indirect release. For example, a buildup of energy from sexual drives might be discharged directly in the form of sexual activity or indirectly through such diverse behaviors as sexual fantasies, farming, or painting.

Mental events may be conscious, preconscious, or unconscious. The *conscious mind* consists of mental events in current awareness. The *preconscious mind* contains memories, feelings, thoughts, and images that we are unaware of at the moment but that can be recalled, such as a friend's telephone number or memories of your 16th birthday.

Because we can be aware of their contents, we are likely to see the conscious and preconscious areas of the mind as the most prominent ones. But Freud believed that these areas are dwarfed in both size and importance by the *unconscious mind*, a dynamic realm of wishes, feelings, and impulses that lies beyond our awareness. He wrote, "The (conscious) mind is an iceberg—it floats with only one-seventh of its bulk above water." Only when impulses from the unconscious are discharged in one way or another, such as in dreams, slips of the tongue, or some disguised behavior, does the unconscious reveal itself, sometimes with unfortunate consequences. In the throes of passion, a young man proclaimed his love for his fiancée by gasping, "I love you, Marcia." The only problem was that his fiancée's name was Amy. Marcia was a former girlfriend. Freud would probably have concluded (as did Amy) that the slip of the tongue was a sign that erotic feelings for Marcia, which the man vehemently denied, were still bubbling within his subconscious mind. Psychoanalysts believe that such verbal slips are holes in our armor of conscious control and expressions of our true feelings.

The Structure of Personality

Freud divided personality into three separate but interacting structures: *id, ego,* and *superego*. The **id** *is the innermost core of the personality, the only structure present at birth, and the source of all psychic energy.* It exists totally within the unconscious mind (Figure 13.4). Freud described the id as "a chaos, a cauldron of seething excitations" (Freud, 1900/1965, p. 73). The id has no direct contact with reality and functions in a totally irrational manner. Operating according to the **pleasure principle,** *it seeks immediate gratification or release, regardless of rational considerations and environmental realities.* Its dictum: "Want . . . take!"

The id cannot directly satisfy itself by obtaining what it needs from the environment because it has no contact with the outer world. In the course of development, a new structure therefore develops. The **ego** *has direct contact with reality and functions primarily at a conscious level.* It operates according to the **reality principle,** *testing reality to decide when and under what conditions the id can safely discharge its impulses and satisfy its needs.* For example, the ego would seek sexual gratification within a consenting relationship rather than allow the pleasure principle to dictate an impulsive sexual assault on the first person who happened by. Freud wrote, "In popular language, we may say that the ego stands for reason and sanity, in contrast to the id which contains untamed passions" (Freud, 1900/1965, p. 238).

The last personality structure to develop is the **superego,** *the moral arm of the personality.* Developing by the age of 4 or 5, the superego contains the traditional values and ideals of family and society. These ideals are internalized by the child through identification with his or her parents, who also use reinforcement and punishment to teach the child what is "right," what is "wrong," and how the child "should" be. With the development of the superego, self-control is substituted for external control. Like the ego, the superego strives to control the instincts of the id, particularly the sexual and aggressive impulses that are condemned by society. In a sense the id says "I want!" and the superego replies "Don't you dare! That would be evil!" Whereas the ego simply tries to postpone instinctual gratification until conditions are safe and appropriate, the superego, in its blind quest for perfection, tries to

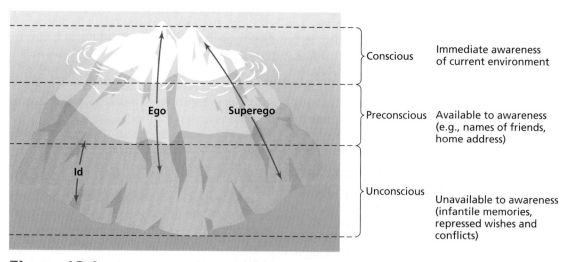

Figure 13.4

Freud's model of personality.

Freud's own representation of his three-part conception of personality shows the relation of the id, ego, and superego to the unconscious, preconscious, and conscious areas of the mind. Note how relatively small the conscious portion of the mind is compared with the unconscious. Source: Adapted from Smith, 1998.

block gratification permanently. For the superego, moralistic goals take precedence over realistic ones, regardless of the potential cost to the individual. Thus the superego might cause a person to experience intense guilt over sexual activity even within marriage because it has internalized the idea that "sex is dirty."

With the development of the superego, the ego sits squarely in the eye of a psychic storm. It must achieve compromises between the demands of the id, the constraints of the superego, and the demands of reality. This balancing act has earned the ego the title "executive of the personality."

Conflict, Anxiety, and Defense

The dynamics of personality involve a never-ending struggle between instincts and drives in the id striving for release and counterforces generated by the ego and superego to contain them. Observable behavior often represents compromises between motives, needs, impulses, and defenses. When the ego confronts impulses that threaten to get out of control or is faced with dangers from the environment, anxiety results. Like physical pain, anxiety serves as a danger signal and motivates the ego to deal with the problem at hand. In many instances, the anxiety can be reduced through realistic coping behaviors, as when a person who is extremely angry at someone works out the problem through rational discussion instead of murderous assault. However, when realistic strategies are ineffective in reducing anxiety, the ego may resort to **defense mechanisms,** *unconscious mental operations that deny or distort reality.* Some of the defense mechanisms permit the release of impulses from the id in disguised forms that will not conflict with forces in the external world or with the prohibitions of the superego. The major defense mechanisms are described in Table 13.1.

Psychoanalysts believe that repression is the primary means by which the ego keeps the lid on the id. In **repression,** *the ego uses some of its energy to prevent anxiety-arousing memories, feelings, and impulses from entering consciousness.* Repressed thoughts and wishes remain in the unconscious, striving for release, but they may be expressed indirectly, as in slips of the tongue or in dreams. Through the defense mechanism of **sublimation,** *taboo impulses may even be channeled into socially desirable and admirable behaviors, completely masking the sinister underlying impulses.* For example, hostile impulses may find expression in becoming a bounty hunter or a trial lawyer. Although Freud described several defense mechanisms, his

Table **13.1** | **Psychoanalytic Ego Defense Mechanisms**

Defense Mechanism	Description	Example
Repression	An active defensive process pushes anxiety-arousing impulses or memories into the unconscious mind.	A person who was sexually abused in childhood develops amnesia for the event.
Denial	A person refuses to acknowledge anxiety-arousing aspects of the environment. The denial may involve either the emotions connected with the event or the event itself.	A man who is told he has terminal cancer refuses to consider the possibility that he will not recover.
Displacement	An unacceptable or dangerous impulse is repressed, then directed at a safer substitute target.	A man who is harassed by his boss experiences no anger at work but then goes home and abuses his wife and children.
Intellectualization	The emotion connected with an upsetting event is repressed, and the situation is dealt with as an intellectually interesting event.	A person who has been rejected in an important relationship talks in a highly rational manner about the "interesting unpredictability of love relationships."
Projection	An unacceptable impulse is repressed, then attributed to (projected onto) other people.	A woman with strong repressed desires to have an affair continually accuses her husband of being unfaithful to her.
Rationalization	A person constructs a false but plausible explanation or excuse for an anxiety-arousing behavior or event that has already occurred.	A student caught cheating on an exam justifies the act by pointing out that the professor's tests are unfair and, besides, everybody else was cheating too.
Reaction formation	An anxiety-arousing impulse is repressed, and its psychic energy finds release in an exaggerated expression of the opposite behavior.	A mother who harbors feelings of resentment toward her child represses them and becomes overprotective of the child.
Sublimation	A repressed impulse is released in the form of a socially acceptable or even admired behavior.	A man with strong hostile impulses becomes an investigative reporter who ruins political careers with his stories.

primary interest was in repression. His daughter Anna Freud, also a psychoanalyst, extended his ideas and described many of the defense mechanisms shown in Table 13.1.

Defense mechanisms operate unconsciously, so people are usually unaware that they are using self-deception to ward off anxiety. Almost everyone uses defense mechanisms at times, but maladjusted people use them excessively in place of more-realistic approaches to dealing with problems.

Psychosexual Development

Freud's clinical experiences convinced him that adult personality traits are powerfully influenced by experiences in the first years of life. He proposed that children pass through a series of **psychosexual stages** *during which the id's pleasure-seeking tendencies are focused on specific pleasure-sensitive areas of the body—the erogenous zones.* Potential deprivations or overindulgences can arise during any of these stages, resulting in **fixation,** *a state of arrested psychosexual development in which instincts are focused on a particular psychic theme.* **Regression,** *a psychological retreat to an earlier psychosexual stage,* can occur in the face of stressful demands that exceed one's coping capabilities.

The first of these stages is the *oral stage,* which occurs during infancy. Infants gain primary satisfaction from taking in food and from sucking on a breast, a thumb, or some other object. Freud proposed that either excessive gratification or frustration of oral needs can result in fixation on oral themes of self-indulgence or dependency as an adult.

In the second and third years of life, children enter the *anal stage,* and pleasure becomes focused on the process of elimination. During toilet training, the child is faced with society's first attempt to control a biological urge. According to Freud, harsh toilet training can produce compulsions, overemphasis on cleanliness, obsessive concerns with orderliness, and insistence on rigid rules and rituals. In contrast, Freud speculated that extremely lax toilet training results in a messy, negative, and dominant adult personality.

The most controversial of Freud's stages is the *phallic stage,* which begins at 4 to 5 years of age. This is the time when children begin to derive pleasure from their sexual organs. Freud believed that during this stage of early sexual awakenings, the male child experiences erotic feelings toward his mother, desires to possess her sexually, and views his father as a rival. At the same time, however, these feelings arouse strong guilt and a fear that the father might find out and castrate him,

hence the term *castration anxiety. This conflictual situation involving love for the mother and hostility toward the father is the* **Oedipus complex,** named for the Greek character Oedipus, who unknowingly killed his father and married his mother. Girls, meanwhile, discover that they lack a penis, blame the mother for their lack of what Freud considered the more desirable sex organ, and wish to bear their father's child as a substitute for the penis they lack. *The female counterpart of the Oedipus complex was termed the* **Electra complex.**

Freud believed that the phallic stage is a major milestone in the development of gender identity, for children normally resolve these conflicts by repressing their sexual impulses and moving from a sexual attachment to the opposite-sex parent to *identification* with the same-sex parent. Boys take on the traits of their fathers and girls those of their mothers. Identification allows the child to possess the opposite-sex parent indirectly, or vicariously, and also helps form the superego as the child internalizes the parent's values and moral beliefs.

As the phallic stage draws to a close at about 6 years of age, children enter the *latency stage,* during which sexuality becomes dormant for about six years. Sexuality normally reemerges in adolescence as the beginning of a lifelong *genital stage,* in which erotic impulses find direct expression in sexual relationships.

Neoanalytic and Object Relations Approaches

Freud's ideas were so revolutionary that they generated disagreement even within his circle of disciples. **Neoanalytic theorists** *were psychoanalysts who disagreed with certain aspects of Freud's thinking and developed their own theories.* Among them were Alfred Adler, Karen Horney, Erik Erikson, and Carl Jung. The neoanalysts believed that Freud did not give social and cultural factors a sufficiently important role in the development and dynamics of personality. In particular, they believed that he stressed infantile sexuality too much (Kurzweil, 1989). The second major criticism was that Freud laid too much emphasis on the events of childhood as determinants of adult personality. Neoanalytic theorists agreed that childhood experiences are important, but some theorists, such as Erikson, believed that personality development continues throughout the life span as individuals confront challenges that are specific to particular phases in their lives.

In contrast to Freud's assertion that behavior is motivated by inborn sexual and aggressive instincts and drives, Alfred Adler (1870–1937) insisted that humans are inherently social beings who are motivated by *social interest*, the desire to advance the welfare of others. They care about others, cooperate with them, and place general social welfare above selfish personal interests (Figure 13.5). In contrast, Freud seemed to view people as savage animals caged by the bars of civilization. Perhaps influenced by his own struggles to overcome childhood illnesses and accidents, Adler also postulated a general motive of *striving for superiority*, which drives people to compensate for real or imagined defects in themselves (the *inferiority complex*) and to strive to be ever more competent in life.

Like Adler, Carl Jung (1875–1961) was Freud's friend and associate before he broke away and developed his own theory. Jung expanded Freud's notion of the unconscious in unique directions. For example, he believed that humans possess not only a **personal unconscious** *based on their life experiences* but also a **collective unconscious** *that consists of memories accumulated throughout the entire history of the human race.* These memories are represented by **archetypes,** *inherited tendencies to interpret experiences in certain ways.* Archetypes find expression in symbols, myths, and beliefs that appear across many cultures, such as the image of a god, an evil force, the hero, the good mother, and the quest for self-unity and completeness (Figure 13.6). Jung's ideas bear some similarities to those of contemporary evolutionary theorists who emphasize innate cognitive processes.

Following Freud's death in 1939, Melanie Klein (1975), Otto Kernberg (1984), Margaret Mahler (1968), and Heinz Kohut (1971) developed a new psychodynamic emphasis. **Object relations theories** *focus on the images or mental representations that people form of themselves and other people as a result of early experiences with caregivers.* Whether realistic or distorted, these internal representations of important adults—for example, of the mother as kind or malevolent, the father as protective or abusive—become lenses, or working models, through which later social interactions are viewed, and these relational themes exert an unconscious influence on a person's relationships throughout life (Shaver & Mikulincer, 2009). People who have difficulties forming and maintaining intimate relationships tend to mentally represent themselves and others in negative ways, expecting painful interactions and attributing malevolence or rejection to others (Kernberg, 1984; Nigg et al., 1992). These working models often create self-fulfilling prophesies, influencing the recurring relationships people form with others (Fraley & Shaver, 2008).

Figure 13.5

In Alfred Adler's theory, people have an inborn social interest that can cause them to put society's welfare above their interests. Mother Teresa's selfless service to the poor and oppressed is one striking example.

Figure 13.6

Shown here is the famous neoanalyst Carl Jung. Behind him is a *mandala* (Sanskrit for "circle"), which symbolizes wholeness and completion. The mandala symbol occurs within numerous cultures and religions of the world, suggesting to Jung that it is a reflection of the collective unconscious.

Adult Attachment Styles

John Bowlby's (1969) attachment theory, discussed in Chapter 12, is an outgrowth of the object relations approach. Correlational research relating early attachment experiences to later adult relationships is yielding provocative results. For example, college students with a history of positive early attachments tend to have longer and more satisfying romances (Shaver & Clark, 1996). In contrast, child-abusing parents often have mental representations of their own parents as punitive, rejecting, and abusive (van Ijzendoorn, 1995). Table 13.2 shows descriptive statements that characterize people who manifest "secure," "avoidant," and "anxious-ambivalent" adult attachment styles. These attachment styles are associated with adjustment and well-being. Three studies by Benjamin Hankin and coworkers (2005) examined the relation between adult attachment dimensions and symptoms of emotional distress (anxiety and depression). Across all three studies, avoidant and anxious-ambivalent attachment predicted depressive symptoms, and anxious attachment was associated with anxiety symptoms. When people with these attachment styles seek treatment for their problems, anxious and avoidant attachment patterns also predict poorer response to psychotherapy because issues involving fear of abandonment and trust complicate the therapeutic relationship (Shorey & Snyder, 2006). Finally, attachment styles affect parenting. In one study, parents with avoidant attachment style reported that they found parenthood more

Table **13.2** | **Attachment Styles in Adult Relationships**

> **Question:** Which of the following best describes your feelings?*
>
> 1. I find it relatively easy to get close to others and am comfortable depending on them and having them depend on me. I don't often worry about being abandoned or about someone getting too close to me.
>
> 2. I am somewhat uncomfortable being close to others; I find it difficult to trust them completely, difficult to allow myself to depend on them. I am nervous when anyone gets too close, and often, love partners want me to be more intimate than I feel comfortable being.
>
> 3. I find that others are reluctant to get as close as I would like. I often worry that my partner doesn't really love me or won't want to stay with me. I want to merge completely with another person, and this desire sometimes scares people away.
>
> *The first type of attachment style is described as "secure," the second as "avoidant," and the third as "anxious."
> Source: Based on Shaver et al., 1988.

stressful and less satisfying and personally meaningful because of difficulties in developing close and emotionally supportive relationships with their children (Rholes et al., 2006). Such difficulties may also help create an avoidant or anxious attachment style in their children.

Today, many psychodynamic therapists say that they rely more heavily on object relations concepts than on classical psychoanalytic theory (Jurist et al., 2008; Westen, 1998). The concepts in object relations theories are also easier to define and measure operationally, making them more amenable to research.

Attachment theory predicts that once attachment styles are set down by childhood experiences, they continue to play themselves out in adult relationships. Our "Research Close-up" explores the possibility that this can result in abusive romantic relationships.

Evaluating the Psychodynamic Approach

Freud was committed to testing his ideas through case studies and clinical observations. He believed that careful observations of everyday behavior and clinical phenomena were the best source of evidence. He opposed experimental research, believing that the complex phenomena he had identified could not be studied under controlled conditions (Rosenzweig, 1992). Most modern psychologists do not believe that clinical observations are sufficient proof, but they do acknowledge the difficulty of studying psychoanalytic concepts under controlled laboratory conditions (Carver & Scheier, 2003; Mischel et al., 2004). Indeed, a major shortcoming of psychoanalytic theory is that many of its concepts are ambiguous and difficult to measure or even to define operationally. How, for example, can we measure the strength of an individual's id impulses and unconscious ego defenses or study processes that are by definition unconscious and inaccessible to the person?

Although psychoanalytic theory has profoundly influenced psychology, psychiatry, and other fields, it has often been criticized on scientific grounds. One reason is that many of its specific propositions have not held up under the scrutiny of research (Fisher & Greenberg, 1996). To some critics, psychoanalytic theory seems to be more science fiction than science. A great drawback of the theory is that it is hard to test, not because it doesn't explain enough but because it often explains too much to allow clear-cut behavioral predictions (Meehl, 1995). For example, suppose we predict on the basis of psychoanalytic theory that participants in an experimental condition will behave

Research Close-up

Attachment Style and Abusive Romantic Relationships

SOURCE: VIVIAN ZAYAS and YUICHI SHODA (2007). Predicting preferences for dating partners from past experiences of psychological abuse: Identifying the psychological ingredients of situations. *Personality and Social Psychology Bulletin, 33*, 123–138.

INTRODUCTION

Researchers who study abusive romantic relationships have noted that involvement in such relationships tends to repeat itself over time, and that such experiences are more common in women with an anxious attachment style (Dutton, 2006). Does this occur by chance, or is it possible that people with particular personality patterns somehow seek out one another to re-create destructive relationships marked by psychological abuse? One possibility is that adult attachment styles predispose people to prefer romantic partners who fit their working models of intimate relationships. To test this hypothesis, Vivian Zayas and Yuichi Shoda studied the romantic partner preferences of women with a history of victimization and of men with a history of abusing women in romantic relationships (Figure 13.7).

METHOD

From students in large introductory psychology classes, two groups of women were identified. One group consisted of 32 women who reported being victims of frequent psychological abuse in their most recent long-term romantic relationship. On a 60-item measure of abusive behaviors, these women reported that experiences like the following had often occurred with their romantic partner during a 12-month period: *isolation and emotional control* (e.g., "My partner tried to keep me from seeing or talking to my family"); *undermining self-esteem* (e.g., "My partner treated me like I was stupid"); *jealousy* (e.g., "My partner was jealous of my friends"); *verbal abuse* (e.g., "My partner swore at me"); and *emotional withdrawal* (e.g., "My partner sulked and refused to talk about a problem"). A comparison group of 33 low-abuse women reported that such experiences occurred seldom or never in their most recent relationship. The women in each group also completed a self-report measure of attachment style, including a scale of attachment anxiety that included items such as "I worry a lot about my relationships."

To create a real-life situation to assess romantic partner preference, the women participated in a computer dating procedure in which they indicated how much they would like to date each of 16 different men who provided descriptions of themselves. The self-descriptions of these 16 men were compiled from actual self-descriptions provided by a group of college men. These statements were rated by a separate sample of women on desirability in a dating partner and potential for being abusive. Statements rated as high in potential for abusiveness reflected a predisposition toward anger (e.g., "Warning ahead, I do have a very bad temper"), jealousy ("I do admit that I will get jealous if you are always going over to

Figure 13.7

Do adult attachment styles lead some women into abusive relationships?

one of your guy friends' houses"), themes regarding trust and emotional control (e.g., "I will treat you like God until you break my trust and then you are just another person"), and possessiveness. The ratings of desirability and abuse potential were used to create potential male dating partners who fell into three categories: (a) potentially abusive (4 ads); (b) undesirable as a dating partner but not abusive (8 ads); and (c) desirable as a dating partner and not abusive (4 ads).

The high-abuse and low-abuse women viewed each of the 16 personal ads on an experimenter-constructed Web site, where each male's ad had a separate Web page with his description of himself but no picture. They made four rounds of forced-choice selections. In the first round, they selected eight of the 16 ads that were most preferable to them. In the second round, they selected four of the eight, in the third round, two of the four, and in the final round, they selected the person they were most interested in getting to know better.

In a second part of the study, college men were administered the psychological-abuse questionnaire that the women had completed and were asked how often they had engaged in the abusive behaviors in their previous romantic relationship. The researchers identified 46 men who were abusive and 47 who reported inflicting little or no abuse. These two groups of men engaged in an identical Internet dating procedure as the women, except that the personal ads of the women were designed to either express high or low levels of attachment anxiety. Eight of the descriptions suggested high attachment anxiety and eight did not. The attachment anxiety

Continued

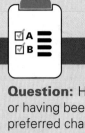

RESEARCH DESIGN

Question: How is a history of having been psychologically abused or having been the perpetrator of psychological abuse related to preferred characteristics of future dating partners?

Type of Study: *Correlational*

Variable X	**Variable Y**
Abused vs. non-abused women	Characteristics of most-preferred dating partner
Abusing vs. non-abusing men	

statements in the personal ads were drawn from the measure used to assess attachment anxiety in the women's portion of the study, and an independent sample of men rated the descriptions of these potential dating partners as indicating higher relationship anxiety.

RESULTS

The researchers first examined the relations between attachment anxiety and past abuse. In agreement with previous research, they found that the high-abuse women were significantly more anxious about their close relationships and fearful of losing them.

Of major interest were the dating preferences of the two groups of women. Table 13.3a shows the percentages of high-abuse and low-abuse women whose top choice from among the 16 was either a desirable, an undesirable, or an abusive partner. The low-abuse women overwhelmingly preferred a desirable partner, and very few of them chose one of the potentially abusive men. In striking contrast, the high-abuse women were three times as likely to choose one of the four potentially abusive dating partners and less likely than low-abuse women to choose a desirable one.

The men's dating preferences are shown in Table 13.3b. Here again, we see a notable contrast. The vast majority of the non-abusive men preferred a woman who was low in attachment anxiety. In contrast, a majority of the abusive men chose a potential dating partner who was high in the characteristic of attachment anxiety, which this and other studies have shown to be common in women who are victimized by abuse.

DISCUSSION

This study illustrates the potential usefulness of concepts derived from object relations theory in understanding human relationships. The notion that early experiences in intimate relationships produce working models of what is to be expected in future relationships has received considerable research support

(Mikulincer & Shaver, 2009). In this study, we see evidence that people may perpetuate self-injurious and destructive relationship patterns. Women with histories of abuse in romantic relationships might be expected to steer clear of future relationships of this kind. Instead, they are as likely to choose a dating partner who has been judged by others to be impulsive, possessive, jealous, aggressive, hostile, degrading, and potentially violent as they are to choose a desirable and non-abusive partner.

Men's personality characteristics also influence their choice of potential romantic partners. Men without a history of abusing women show little desire to relate to insecure, relationship-anxious women. In contrast, abusive men are drawn to these women who are more likely to become dependent on them and therefore tolerate their behavior as they act out their hostile impulses within the relationship. Clearly, the choices of both men and women are based on "psychological ingredients" of the situation, which include the stimulus characteristics of the potential partner.

This study also raises several interesting questions that deserve research attention. The focus here was on psychological abuse, which probably occurs more often than physical abuse. Do these findings generalize to physically abusive relationships? Likewise, this investigation addressed relationships in which men abused women. What are the "active ingredients" of partners in relationships in which men are psychologically abused by women? Answers to questions like these would increase our understanding of how personality and situational factors interact in destructive interpersonal relationships.

Table 13.3 | **Percentages of Women and Men Who Chose Each Type of Dating Partner**

(a) Women's Choices

Abuse Group	Preferred Male Dating Partner		
	Desirable	**Undesirable**	**Abusive**
Low-Abuse Women	66.7	21.2	12.1
High-Abuse Women	40.6	21.9	37.5

(b) Men's Choices

Abuse Group	Preferred Female Dating Partner	
	Low Attachment Anxiety	**High Attachment Anxiety**
Non-Abusing Men	72.3	27.7
Abusing Men	39.1	60.9

aggressively but they behave instead in a loving manner. Is the theory wrong, or is the aggression being masked by the operation of a defense mechanism such as reaction formation (which produces exaggerated behaviors that are the opposite of the impulse)? The difficulty in making clear-cut behavioral predictions means that some psychoanalytic hypotheses cannot be disproved, and this detracts greatly from the theory's scientific usefulness.

Freud's emphasis on the unconscious was scorned by a Victorian society that emphasized rationality, and later generations of personality psychologists with a behaviorist orientation condemned it as unscientific. However, research during the past 20 years has vindicated Freud's belief in unconscious psychic events by showing that nonconscious mental and emotional phenomena do indeed occur and can affect our behavior (Chartrand & Bargh, 2002; Erdelyi, 2001).

On the other hand, the unconscious processes that have been demonstrated experimentally are by no means as exotic as the seething cauldron of forbidden wishes and desires described by Freud (Kihlstrom, 1999). Rather, current research has unearthed what one theorist describes as "a kinder, gentler unconscious" (Greenwald, 1992).

Freud's ideas about psychosexual development are the most controversial feature of his theory. Although many theorists reject Freud's assertions about childhood sexuality and the notion of specific psychosexual stages, there is strong evidence that childhood experiences do indeed influence the development of personality (Westen et al., 2008). The previously wide gulf between psychodynamic theories and other psychological perspectives is starting to narrow, due largely to the development of new methods for studying unconscious mental processes.

test yourself — Personality and the Psychodynamic Perspective

True or false?

1. According to Freud, the id is the only structure of the personality present at birth.
2. The ego supplies the psychic energy for the operation of the personality.
3. The superego is the moral arm of the personality.
4. The defense mechanisms are ego functions.
5. Archetypes reside in the personal unconscious.
6. Research shows that toleration of abusive romantic partners by women is related to an anxious attachment style.

ANSWERS: 1-true, 2-false, 3-true, 4-true, 5-false, 6-true

THE PHENOMENOLOGICAL-HUMANISTIC PERSPECTIVE

The approaches we will describe next were in part a reaction to Freud's conception of people as driven by "those half-tamed demons that inhabit the human beast" (Freud, 1900/1965, p. 202). In contrast to Freud, these theorists believed that our behavior is not a reaction to unconscious drives and conflicts but rather a response to our immediate conscious experience of self and environment (Kelly, 1955; Rogers, 1951). This *emphasis on the primacy of immediate experience is known as* **phenomenology,** and it focuses our attention on the present instead of the past. These theorists also regarded themselves as humanists. They embraced a positive view that affirms the inherent dignity and goodness of the human spirit, as well as the individual's creative potential and inborn striving toward personal growth (Figure 13.8).

George Kelly's Personal Construct Theory

> To the humanist every man is a scientist by disposition as well as by right, every subject is an incipient experimenter, and every person is by daily necessity a fellow psychologist. (Kelly, 1966, quoted in Maher, 1979, p. 205)

A theory developed by George Kelly (1905–1967) in the 1950s has had a strong and pervasive influence on many other theorists. According to Kelly, people's primary goal is to make sense out of the world, to find personal meaning in it. When they are unable to do so, they experience uncertainty and anxiety. To achieve understanding, they try

Figure 13.8

The motivations underlying behavior are much different for humanistic theorists than they are for Freudians. In the view of humanistic theorists like Abraham Maslow and Carl Rogers, creative and artistic accomplishments like this artist's sculpture are not a product of intrapsychiatric conflict and sublimation but rather an expression of an innate tendency toward self-actualization.

to explain and understand the events of their lives, and they test this understanding in the same way scientists do: by attempting to anticipate, to predict.

Kelly's primary interest was how people construct reality. They do so by their individual system of **personal constructs,** *cognitive categories into which they sort the people and events in their lives.* In Kelly's theory, the personal construct system was the primary basis for individual differences in personality.

As noted in our discussion of concept formation in Chapter 9, all perception involves categorizing. From birth onward, Kelly maintained, stimuli are categorized, given meaning, and reacted to in terms of the categories, or personal constructs, into which they are placed. Every person has her or his own pattern of preferred personal constructs (such as "good," "bad," "successful," "powerful," and so on), which vary in personal importance. By understanding these constructs, the rules an individual uses to assign events to categories, and her or his hypotheses about how the categories relate to one another, Kelly believed that we can understand the person's psychological world. If we can understand the individual's internal world, then we can understand and predict that person's behavior.

The same event can be categorized, or perceived, in entirely different ways by different people. For example, suppose that two lovers break up. One observer may construe the event as "simple incompatibility"; another may think

that one person was "jilted" by the other; another might describe the breakup as the "result of parental meddling"; another might call it "a terrible development"; and a fifth might see it as "a blessing in disguise."

Rather than evaluating alternative constructions according to whether or not they are true (which we cannot know), Kelly examined the consequences of construing in particular ways. For example, if one of the people in the broken relationship interpreted what happened as "being rejected," Kelly would try to discover the consequences for the person of construing the situation in that way. If the construction led to bad outcomes, such as feelings of worthlessness or the conclusion that "no one will ever love me, and I'll never get involved again," then the task would be to find a more useful alternative (for example, "I am someone who hasn't found the right person yet but who will if I keep trying."). Kelly, a clinical psychologist, saw psychotherapy as a way of demonstrating to clients that their constructions are *hypotheses* rather than facts. Once clients realize this, they can be encouraged to test the hypotheses that govern their lives, just as scientists do, and to replace maladaptive ones with more useful ones.

As people seek to understand events within the world, they develop habitual tendencies related to categorization of people and events. Such tendencies can be measured by tasks that determine the extent to which particular categories are used in making such distinctions (Robinson et al., 2004). Kelly developed a measure called the **Role Construct Repertory Test,** or **Rep Test,** *to assess individuals' personal construct systems.* In taking the Rep Test, you are asked to consider people or events in your life that are important to you. You then consider them in groups of three (for example, father, best friend, romantic partner) and indicate how any two of them are similar to one another and different from the third. In this way, the basic dimensions of similarity and difference that you use to categorize people and events—your personal constructs—will begin to emerge. The Rep Test can also assess other aspects of your construct system, such as the number of different constructs that you use.

In order to help clients experiment with new viewpoints and behaviors, Kelly developed a therapeutic technique called *fixed-role therapy.* He wrote role descriptions and behavioral scripts for his clients that differed from their typical views of themselves. For example, a shy person might be asked to play the role of a more confident and assertive person for two or three days, to think and act like a confident person. Kelly and the client would practice the role within the therapy setting to be certain that the client had a command of the required behaviors and the view of the world that a confident individual would have. Kelly hoped that by trying out the new role, the client might gain a firsthand appreciation for the ways in which different constructions and behaviors could lead to more satisfying life outcomes. Kelly suggested that a willingness to experiment with new roles and ways of thinking can help all of us develop in ways that enhance our lives.

Carl Rogers's Theory of the Self

Carl Rogers (1902–1987), a colleague of George Kelly's on the Ohio State University faculty in the 1950s, was one of the most influential humanistic theorists. As a humanist, Rogers believed that the forces that direct behavior are within us and that when they are not distorted or blocked by our environment, they can be trusted to direct us toward **self-actualization,** *the highest realization of human potential.*

The Self

The central concept in Rogers's theory is the **self,** *an organized, consistent set of perceptions of and beliefs about oneself* (Rogers, 1959). Once formed, the self plays a powerful role in guiding our perceptions and directing our behavior. The self thus has two facets: it is an object of perception (the self-concept) and an internal entity that directs behavior.

Rogers theorized that at the beginning of their lives, children cannot distinguish between themselves and their environment. As they interact with their world, children begin to distinguish between the "me" and the "not-me." The self-concept continues to develop in response to our life experiences, though many aspects of it remain quite stable over time.

Once the self-concept is established, there is a tendency to maintain it, for it helps us understand our relationship to the world around us. We therefore have needs for **self-consistency,** *an absence of conflict among self-perceptions,* and **congruence,** *consistency between self-perceptions and experience.* Any experience we have that is inconsistent, or incongruous, with our self-concept, including our perceptions of our own behavior, evokes **threat,** *or anxiety.* Well-adjusted individuals can respond to threat adaptively by modifying the self-concept so that the experiences are congruent with the self. But other people choose to deny or distort their experiences to remove the incongruence, a strategy that can lead to what Rogers termed "problems in living." Thus a person who always attributes

"I can't say I like the looks of that bunch."

Figure 13.9

Tendencies to behave in accordance with one's self-concept can at times have ominous implications.
SOURCE: Copyright © Dana Fradon/The New Yorker Collection/www.cartoonbank.com.

interpersonal difficulties to shortcomings in another person will be unlikely to consider the possibility that he or she may have some self-defeating behavior patterns that deserve attention.

To preserve their self-concepts, people not only interpret situations in self-congruent ways, but they also behave in ways that will lead others to respond to them in a self-confirming fashion (Swann & Bosson, 2008). If Camille has an image of herself as unlovable and certain to be rejected if she lets people get close enough to hurt her, she may behave in ways that distance others. When her behavior is successful, others pull away from her, confirming in her mind that she is indeed unlovable. As Rogers frequently noted, people are pushed by self-consistency needs to behave in accord with their self-concept (Figure 13.9).

According to Rogers, the degree of congruence between self-concept and experience helps define one's level of adjustment. The more rigid and inflexible people's self-concepts are, the less open they will be to their experiences and the more maladjusted they will become (Figure 13.10a). If there is a significant degree of incongruence between self and experience and if the experiences are forceful enough, the defenses used to deny and distort reality may collapse, resulting in extreme anxiety and a temporary disorganization of the self-concept.

The Need for Positive Regard

Rogers believed that we are born with an innate **need for positive regard**—*for acceptance, sympathy,*

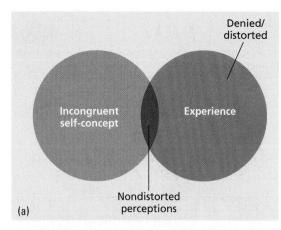

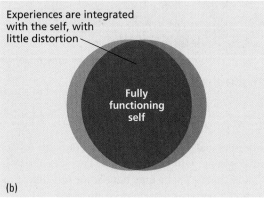

Figure 13.10

Degree of congruence between self-concept and experience.
(a) Maladjustment occurs when a person faced with incongruities between self and experience distorts or denies reality to make it consistent with the self-concept. (b) In contrast, extremely well-adjusted, or fully functioning, people integrate experiences into the self with minimal distortion, so that they are able to profit fully from their experiences.

and love from others. Rogers viewed positive regard as essential for healthy development. Ideally, positive regard received from the parents is unconditional—that is, independent of how the child behaves. **Unconditional positive regard** *communicates that the person is inherently worthy of love, regardless of accomplishments or behavior*. In contrast, *conditional positive regard* is dependent on how the child behaves; in the extreme case, love and acceptance are given to the child *only* when the child behaves as the parents want. A study by Avi Assor and coworkers (2004) suggests long-term negative consequences of this child-rearing approach. College students who reported that their mothers and fathers used conditional regard in four domains (emotion control, prosocial behavior, academics, and sports performance) also experienced up-and-down fluctuations in their self-esteem, and they resented their parents as young adults.

People need positive regard not only from others but also from themselves. Thus a **need for positive self-regard,** *the desire to feel good about*

ourselves, also develops. Lack of unconditional positive regard from parents and other significant people in the past teaches people that they are worthy of approval and love only when they meet certain standards. This fosters the development of **conditions of worth** *that dictate the circumstances under which we approve or disapprove of ourselves.* A child who experiences parental approval when behaving in a friendly fashion but disapproval whenever she becomes angry or aggressive may come to disapprove of her own angry feelings, even when they are justified. As an adult, she may deny in herself all feelings of anger and struggle to preserve a self-image of being totally loving. Rogers believed that conditions of worth can tyrannize people and cause major incongruence between self and experience, as well as a need to deny or distort important aspects of experience. Conditions of worth are similar to the "shoulds" and "musts" that populate the Freudian superego.

Fully Functioning Persons

Toward the end of his career, Rogers became particularly interested in **fully functioning persons,** *individuals who were close to achieving self-actualization.* As Rogers viewed them, such people do not hide behind masks or adopt artificial roles. They feel a sense of inner freedom, self-determination, and choice in the direction of their growth. They have no fear of behaving spontaneously, freely, and creatively. Because they are fairly free of conditions of worth, they can accept inner and outer experiences as they are, without modifying them defensively to suit a rigid self-concept or the expectations of others. Thus a fully functioning unmarried woman would be able to (1) state quite frankly that her career is more important to her than a role as wife and mother (*if* she truly felt that way), even if others did not approve of her choice, and (2) act comfortably on those feelings. In this sense, she could be true to herself (see Figure 13.10b).

thinking critically

IS SELF-ACTUALIZATION A USEFUL SCIENTIFIC CONSTRUCT?

Self-actualization is a central concept for humanistic theorists such as Maslow and Rogers. Consider what you have learned about formulating a psychological construct and evaluating a theory according to scientific principles. Can you see any problems with establishing the existence of this core motivation from a scientific perspective? Think about it, then see page 503 for a discussion.

| Table **13.4** | Items Similar to Those Found on Self-Esteem Scales* |

1. I believe I am a worthwhile person.
2. There are many things I would change about myself if I could. (reverse scored)
3. I approve of myself as a person.
4. I have many positive traits.
5. I like who I am.
6. There are many things I don't like about myself. (reverse scored)

*Items are scored on a scale ranging from −3 ("strongly disagree") to +3 ("strongly agree").

Research on the Self

By giving the self a central place in his theory, Rogers helped stimulate a great deal of research on the self-concept. Two topics at the forefront are (1) the development of self-esteem and its effects on behavior, and (2) the roles played by self-verification and self-enhancement motives.

Self-Esteem

Self-esteem, *how positively or negatively we feel about ourselves,* is a very important aspect of personal well-being, happiness, and adjustment (Diener, 2000; Lilienfeld et al., 2010). Table 13.4 shows the types of test items that are used to measure differences in self-esteem. Adult men and women do not differ much in overall level of self-esteem on such measures (Brown, 1998; Larsen & Buss, 2010). The largest sex differences occur from age 15 to age 18, when males report higher self-esteem than females (Kling et al., 1999).

Level of self-esteem is quite stable over the life span, with correlations of .50 to .70 from childhood to old age (Trzesniewski et al., 2003). High self-esteem is related to many positive behaviors and life outcomes. People with high self-esteem are happier with their lives, have fewer interpersonal problems, achieve at a higher and more consistent level, are less susceptible to social pressure, and are more capable of forming satisfying love relationships (Brown, 1998). In contrast, people with poor self-images are less likely to try to make themselves feel better when they experience negative moods in response to perceived failures in their lives (Heimpel et al., 2002). This may be one reason why they are more prone to psychological problems such as anxiety and depression, to physical illness, and to poor social relationships and underachievement (Brown, 1998).

People who are low in self-esteem are more reactive to the ups and downs of everyday life. In one study, 15 working couples completed a daily diary and mood ratings during a three-week period. Low self-esteem men and women felt more loved and accepted by their spouses on days when they enjoyed professional successes, but less loved on days when they experienced professional failures. People high in self-esteem were not affected in this manner (Murray et al., 2006).

What conditions foster the development of high self-esteem? Children develop higher self-esteem when their parents communicate unconditional acceptance and love, establish clear guidelines for behavior, and reinforce compliance while giving the child freedom to make decisions and express opinions within those guidelines (Brown, 1998; Coopersmith, 1967). Beginning in early childhood, success in achieving positive outcomes builds a sense that one is an effective person (Hawley & Little, 2002). Feedback received from other people also has an impact on the child's sense of self. One study showed that when low-self-esteem children were exposed to highly supportive youth sport coaches who gave them large amounts of positive reinforcement and encouragement, the children's self-esteem increased significantly over the course of the sports season (Smoll et al., 1993). Apparently, the positive feedback caused the children to revise their self-concepts in a positive direction.

Self-Verification and Self-Enhancement Motives

Rogers proposed that people are motivated to preserve their self-concepts by maintaining self-consistency and congruence. **Self-verification** *refers to this need to confirm the self-concept.* In one study, researchers asked college students to describe themselves in order to measure their self-concepts. In a later and supposedly unrelated experiment, the students interacted with other participants and received fake feedback from them in the form of adjectives that were either consistent or inconsistent with their self-concepts. Later, when the students were asked to recall and identify the adjectives that had been attributed to them, they showed greater recall for the consistent adjectives, suggesting that people selectively attend to and recall self-consistent information (Suinn et al., 1962).

Self-verification needs are also expressed in people's tendency to seek out self-confirming relationships. One study found that if people with firmly held negative self-views marry spouses who appraise them favorably, they tend to eventually withdraw from the marriage. Such people are more likely to remain with spouses who agree with the negative image they have of themselves. In contrast, people with positive self-concepts prefer spouses who share their positive views of themselves (Swann et al., 1992).

Rogers (1959) also suggested that people have a need to regard themselves positively, and research confirms the existence of **self-enhancement,** *a strong and pervasive tendency to gain and preserve a positive self-image.* Self-enhancement needs have been demonstrated across many cultures (Sedikides et al., 2003), and several self-enhancement strategies have been identified. For example, people show a marked tendency to attribute their successes to their own abilities and effort but to attribute their failures to environmental factors. Furthermore, most people rate themselves as better than average on virtually any socially desirable characteristic that is subjective in nature (Leary, 2004). The vast majority of businesspeople and politicians rate themselves as more ethical than the average. In defiance of mathematical possibility, about 80 percent of high school students rate themselves in the top 10 percent in their ability to get along with others. Even people who have been hospitalized after causing auto accidents rate themselves as more skillful than the average driver (Greenberg et al., 1997). People generally view themselves as improving over time, relative to their peers (Ross & Wilson, 2003). Indeed, as evidence on self-serving biases in self-perception continues to accumulate, researchers are concluding that positive illusions of this sort are the rule rather than the exception in well-adjusted people and that these self-enhancement tendencies contribute to people's psychological well-being (Taylor & Brown, 1988; Taylor et al., 2003).

For people who are low in self-esteem, self-enhancement needs sometimes override self-verification tendencies (Tesser, 2004). In a series of experimental studies, Tiffiny Bernichon and coworkers (2003) found that low-self-esteem individuals have a strong tendency to seek out positive feedback about themselves even when it is not self-verifying. The pervasiveness of self-enhancement tendencies makes one wonder why so many people have low self-esteem. One answer is that although they desire positive self-enhancing feedback from others, low-self-esteem people don't provide much internal positive feedback to themselves. One experiment showed that when people low in self-esteem showed the same level of improvement on a laboratory task as did high-self-esteem individuals, they viewed themselves as improving far less. They also judged themselves more harshly when their performance decreased (Josephs et al., 2003). If one has trouble saying nice things about oneself, the kind of positive input that builds or repairs self-esteem is hard to come by.

Evaluating the Phenomenological-Humanistic Approach

What matters most in phenomenological-humanistic approaches is how people view themselves and the world. Some critics believe that the humanistic view relies too heavily on individuals' reports of their personal experiences. For example, psychoanalytic critics maintain that accepting what a person says at face value can easily lead to erroneous conclusions because of the always-present influence of unconscious defenses.

Although humanism may indeed seem nonscientific to some, Rogers (1959) dedicated himself to developing a theory whose concepts could be measured and its laws tested. One of his most notable contributions was a series of groundbreaking studies on the process of self-growth that can occur in psychotherapy. To assess the effectiveness of psychotherapy, Rogers and his coworkers measured the discrepancy between clients' *ideal selves* (how they would like to be) and their *perceived selves* (their perceptions of what they were actually like). The studies revealed that when clients first entered therapy, the discrepancy was typically large but that it got smaller as therapy proceeded, suggesting that therapy may help the client become more self-accepting and perhaps also more realistic. Rogers and his coworkers also discovered important therapist characteristics that either aid or impede the process of self-actualization in therapy. We will describe this research in Chapter 16.

Several recent developments have put humanistic concepts back into the scientific spotlight. Deci and Ryan's (2009) self-determination theory, described in Chapter 11, has focused new scientific attention on humanistic concepts such as autonomy, competence, and relatedness. New methods for measuring brain activation are enabling psychologists to study self-processes as they occur at a biological level (Heatherton et al., 2004). Additionally, the positive psychology movement, described in Chapter 1, has redirected many psychologists to the study of human strengths, happiness, virtue, and other humanistic concerns (Peterson & Seligman, 2004; Snyder & Lopez, 2007).

THE TRAIT PERSPECTIVE: MAPPING THE STRUCTURE OF PERSONALITY

What are the ways in which people differ in personality? People have described others' traits from time immemorial. So have personality psychologists known as *trait theorists.* The goals of trait theorists are to describe the basic classes of behavior that define personality, to devise ways of measuring individual differences in personality traits, and to use these measures to understand and predict a person's behavior.

Personality traits *are relatively stable cognitive, emotional, and behavioral characteristics of people that help establish their individual identities and distinguish them from others.* The starting point for the trait researcher is identifying the behaviors that define a particular trait. But here we have an embarrassment of riches. Years ago, the trait theorist Gordon Allport went through the English dictionary and painstakingly recorded all of the words that could be used to describe personal traits. The result: a gigantic list of 17,953 words (Allport & Odbert, 1936). Obviously, it would be impractical, if not impossible, to describe people in terms of where they fall on roughly 18,000 dimensions. The trait theorist's goal is to condense all of these behavioral descriptors into a manageable number of basic traits that can capture personal individuality.

Factor Analytic Approaches

Psychologists have taken two major approaches to discover and define personality traits. One approach is to propose traits (e.g., "dominance," "friendliness," "self-esteem") on the basis of words or concepts from everyday discourse or from concepts in existing personality theories. This is referred to as the *lexical approach.* A more systematic approach uses the statistical tool of *factor analysis,* the approach described in Chapter 10 that has been used to identify distinct mental abilities. In personality research, **factor analysis** *is used to identify clusters of behaviors that are highly correlated (positively or negatively) with one another, but not with behaviors in other clusters.* Such behavior clusters can be viewed as reflecting a basic dimension, or trait, on which people vary. For example, you might find that most people who are socially reserved also avoid parties, enjoy quiet activities, and like being alone. At the other end of the spectrum are people who are very talkative and sociable, like parties and excitement, dislike solitary activities such as reading, and constantly seek out new acquaintances. These behavioral patterns define a general factor, or dimension, that we might label *introversion-extraversion* (or simply *extraversion*). At one end of the dimension are highly introverted behaviors, and at the other end are highly extraverted behaviors (Figure 13.11). Presumably, each of us could be placed at some point along this dimension in terms of our customary behavior patterns. In fact, as we will see, factor analytic studies have shown introversion-extraversion to be a major dimension of personality.

Cattell's Sixteen Personality Factors

If you were asked to describe and compare every person you know, how many different traits would it take to do the job? This is where trait

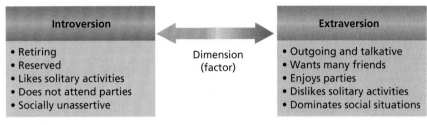

Figure 13.11

Describing personality through factor analysis.
Factor analysis allows researchers to reduce many behaviors to a smaller number of basic dimensions, or factors, that are relatively independent of one another. A factor comprises behaviors that are highly correlated with one another (either positively or negatively) and are therefore assumed to have common psychological meaning. Here we see the kinds of behaviors that might fall on the two ends of an introversion-extraversion dimension.

theorists begin to part company. Because factor analysis can be used and interpreted in different ways, trait theorists have cut up the personality pie into smaller or larger pieces. For example, the pioneering trait theorist Raymond B. Cattell (1965) asked thousands of participants to rate themselves on numerous behavioral characteristics; he also obtained ratings from people who knew the participants well. When he subjected this mass of data to factor analysis, he identified 16 basic behavior clusters, or factors (Figure 13.12). Using this information, Cattell developed a widely used personality test called the *16 Personality Factor Questionnaire (16PF)* to measure individual differences on each of the

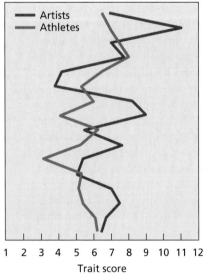

Figure 13.12

Cattell's 16 personality factors.
Raymond B. Cattell identified 16 basic personality traits through factor analysis. Here we see personality profiles (mean scores) for Olympic athletes and creative artists on the 16PF, the test developed by Cattell to measure the traits. Source: Cattell, 1965.

dimensions and provide a comprehensive personality description. He was able to develop personality profiles not only for individuals but also for groups of people. For example, Figure 13.12 compares average scores obtained by creative artists and Olympic athletes.

The Five Factor Model

Other trait researchers believe that Cattell's 16 dimensions are more than we need. Their factor analytic studies suggest that five higher-order factors, each including several of Cattell's more specific factors, are all that we need to capture the basic structure of personality (McCrae & Costa, 2003). These theorists also propose that these "Big Five" factors may be universal to the human species, for the same five factors have been found consistently in trait ratings within diverse North American, Asian, Hispanic, and European cultures (John & Srivastava, 1999; Trull & Geary, 1997).

The Big Five factors are shown in Table 13.5. (The acronym OCEAN—for Openness, Conscientiousness, Extraversion, Agreeableness, and Neuroticism—may help you remember them.) Proponents of the *Five Factor Model* believe that when a person is placed at a specific point on each of these five dimensions by means of a psychological test, behavior ratings, or direct observations of behavior, the essence of her or his personality has been captured (McCrae & Costa, 2008).

What do you think about that conclusion? Your reaction may be one of skepticism, since it seems that there *must* be more to individuality than can be captured by only five dimensions. However, we should remember that, as discussed in Chapter 5, the incredible number of colors that the human visual system can distinguish is based on the activity patterns of only *three* types of cones. Thus the blending of five personality dimensions could account for enormous variation in personality patterns.

Trait theorists not only try to describe the basic structure of personality but also attempt to predict real-life behavior on the basis of a person's traits. Even if a few general traits such as the Big Five seem adequate to describe important features of personality, it is entirely possible that a larger number of specific traits such as Cattell's would capture nuances of behavior within particular situations and would therefore be better for predictive purposes. Measures of the global Big Five factors seldom correlate above .20 to .30 with real-life behavioral outcomes (e.g., Paunonen, 2003). In recognition of this fact, the Big Five Model now includes six subcategories, or *facets* (see Table 13.5), under each of the five major factors, and the personality test used to measure the Big Five (the *NEO Personality Inventory*, or *NEO-PI*) now provides scores on each of these facets as well as on the corresponding major factor. For example, scores are obtained not only for the main factor of Extraversion, but also for facets such as Activity and Positive Emotions. These more specific dimensions permit sharper behavioral predictions (McCrae & Costa, 2008). For example, the Positive Emotions facet of Extraversion is more highly related to life satisfaction than is the total Extraversion score based on all six facets (Schimmack et al., 2004).

Stability of Personality Traits over Time

Because traits are viewed as enduring behavioral predispositions, they should show some degree of stability over time. Yet they should not be unchangeable. As we might expect, the research literature shows evidence for both stability and change (Caspi & Roberts, 1999; Helson et al., 2002). Some personality dimensions tend to be more stable than others. On the one hand, introversion/extraversion, as well as more basic traits such as emotionality and activity level, tend to be quite stable from childhood into adulthood and across the adult years (Eysenck, 1990; Zuckerman, 2005). Self-esteem also shows strong stability (Trzesniewski et al., 2003). On the other hand, both cross-sectional and longitudinal studies indicate that among the Big Five, Neuroticism, Openness, and Extraversion exhibit average declines from the late teens to the early 30s, whereas Agreeableness and Conscientiousness tend to increase (Costa & McCrae, 2008). Likewise, individuals can show developmental changes in many aspects of personality given influential life experiences, including involvement in counseling and psychotherapy (Roberts et al., 2008).

Certain habits of thought may also be fairly stable. One is our tendency to think optimistically or pessimistically. Melanie Burns and Martin Seligman (1991) coded diaries and letters that elderly people had written approximately 50 years earlier for the tendency to respond either optimistically or pessimistically to life events. The elderly people also completed a personality test that measured their current

| Table **13.5** | The Big Five Personality Factors and the Behavioral Facets They Include |

	Big Five Factors	Behaviors (facets)
O	Openness versus closedness to experience	Ideas (curious)
		Fantasy (imaginative)
		Aesthetics (artistic)
		Actions (wide interests)
		Feelings (excitable)
		Values (unconventional)
C	Conscientiousness versus lack of direction	Competence (efficient)
		Order (organized)
		Dutifulness (not careless)
		Achievement striving (thorough)
		Self-discipline (not lazy)
		Deliberation (not impulsive)
E	Extraversion versus introversion	Gregariousness (sociable)
		Assertiveness (forceful)
		Activity (energetic)
		Excitement-seeking (adventurous)
		Positive emotions (enthusiastic)
		Warmth (outgoing)
A	Agreeableness versus antagonism	Trust (forgiving)
		Straightforwardness (not demanding)
		Altruism (warm)
		Compliance (not stubborn)
		Modesty (not show-off)
		Tender-mindedness (sympathetic)
N	Neuroticism versus emotional stability	Anxiety (tense)
		Angry hostility (irritable)
		Depression (not contented)
		Self-consciousness (shy)
		Impulsiveness (moody)
		Vulnerability (not self-confident)

Source: Based on McCrae & Costa, 2008.

optimistic-pessimistic tendencies. Although little consistency over time was shown for dealing optimistically or pessimistically with positive events, Burns and Seligman found a stable tendency to respond with optimism or pessimism to negative life events. The authors suggested that the tendency to be pessimistic might constitute an enduring risk factor for depression, low achievement, and physical illness, and they

Table **13.6**	Sample Items from a Trait Measure of Optimism-Pessimism*

1. In uncertain times, I usually expect the best.
2. Overall, I expect more good things to happen to me than bad.
3. If something can go wrong for me, it will.
4. I rarely count on good things happening to me.

*Items on the Life Orientation Test are answered on a 5-point scale ranging from "strongly disagree" to "strongly agree."
Source: Adapted from Scheier et al., 1994.

are now studying such linkages. Table 13.6 contains items from the *Life Orientation Test* (Scheier & Carver, 1985), used by personality researchers to measure the trait of optimism-pessimism.

Consistency across Situations

As noted at the beginning of the chapter, one of the reasons we have a concept of personality is that we view people as behaving consistently across situations. Is that assumption of consistency warranted by the data? When Walter Mischel reviewed the evidence in 1968, he came to a surprising conclusion: there was more evidence for inconsistency than for consistency. Even on a trait as central as honesty, people can show considerable behavioral variability across situations. In a classic study done 40 years earlier, Hugh Hartshorne and Mark May (1928) tested the honesty of thousands of children. The children were given opportunities to lie, steal, and cheat in a number of different settings: at home, in school, at a party, and in an athletic contest. The rather surprising finding was that "lying, cheating and stealing as measured by the test situations in this study are only very loosely related. . . . Most children will deceive in certain situations but not in others" (p. 411). More than a half century later, Mischel (1984) reported similar findings for college students on the trait of conscientiousness. A student might be highly conscientious in one situation (e.g., coming to work on time) without being conscientious in another (e.g., turning in class assignments on time). Many other studies revealed similar behavioral inconsistency across situations.

To some, this called the very concept of personality traits into question. They reasoned that if behavior is so inconsistent, maybe only the situation is important and we don't need an internal concept called "personality" to account for behavior. This conclusion triggered a lively debate that continued for nearly two decades. Let's consider some of the insights that have arisen from the consistency debate.

Three factors make it difficult to predict on the basis of personality traits how people will behave in particular situations. First, personality traits interact with other traits, as well as with characteristics of different situations. This melding accounts for the incredible richness we see in personality, but it also poses a challenge to psychologists who want to predict behavior. If several different traits, such as honesty, dominance, and agreeableness, influence a behavior in a particular situation, our ability to predict on the basis of only one of the traits is bound to be quite limited (Ahadi & Diener, 1989).

Second, the degree of consistency across situations is influenced by how important a given trait is for the person. A person for whom honesty is a cornerstone of the self-concept may show considerable stability in honest behaviors across situations because her or his feelings of self-worth may be linked to living up to moral standards regardless of the circumstances (Kenrick & Funder, 1988).

Third, people differ in their tendency to tailor their behavior to what is called for by the situation. This personality trait is called *self-monitoring* (Table 13.7). People who are high in **self-monitoring** *are very attentive to situational cues and adapt their behavior to what they think would be most appropriate.* Extreme self-monitors are behavioral chameleons who act very differently in various situations because of their ability to "read" situations, know the appropriate behaviors, and develop effective behavioral plans (Ickes et al., 2006). Low self-monitors, on the other hand, tend to act primarily in terms of their internal beliefs and attitudes rather than

Table **13.7**	Sample Items from the Self-Monitoring Scale*

1. In different situations and with different people, I often act like very different persons.
2. I am not always the person I appear to be.
3. I have trouble changing my behavior to suit different people and different situations.
4. I would not change my opinion (or the way I do things) in order to please someone or win their favor.

*Items 1 and 2 are keyed "true" and items 3 and 4 "false" for self-monitoring.
Source: Based on Snyder, 1987.

the demands of the situation. The saying "What you see is what you get" applies well to low self-monitors, and such people show greater consistency across situations than do high self-monitors (Snyder, 1987).

According to some trait theorists, the stability and distinctiveness that we see in personality does not come from the fact that we behave the same way in every situation. Rather, people exhibit different *average* amounts of extraversion, emotional stability, agreeableness, honesty, and other traits across many different situations (Epstein, 1983; Kenrick & Funder, 1988). Nonetheless, if they want to understand more about these interactions between personality traits, situations, and behavior, personality researchers need to define the relevant characteristics of both the person and the situation (Shoda & Mischel, 2000; Zayas & Shoda, 2007).

Evaluating the Trait Approach

Despite differences of opinion concerning the nature and number of basic personality dimensions, trait theorists have made an important contribution by focusing attention on the value of identifying, classifying, and measuring stable, enduring personality dispositions. Several challenges confront trait theorists, however. If we are to capture the true complexities of personality, we must pay more attention to how traits combine with one another to affect various behaviors (Ahadi & Diener, 1989; Smith et al., 1990). All too often, researchers try to make specific predictions on the basis of a single measured personality trait without taking into account other personality factors that might also influence the behavior in question. This approach sells short the complexity of personality.

In evaluating the trait perspective, we must remember the distinction between description and explanation. To say that someone is outgoing and fun-loving *because* she is high in extraversion is merely to describe the behavior with a trait name, not to explain the inner disposition and how it operates. Traditionally, the trait perspective has been more concerned with describing the structure of personality, measuring individual differences in personality traits, and predicting behavior than with understanding the psychological processes that underlie the traits. For example, a shortcoming of the Five Factor Model is its lack of explanatory power; it tells us nothing about the causal factors that produce extraverted, neurotic, or agreeable people's experiences and actions (Cervone, 1999).

BIOLOGICAL FOUNDATIONS OF PERSONALITY

Both nature and nurture influence the development of personality traits, but their contributions differ according to the trait in question (Plomin & Caspi, 1999). Biological explanations for personality differences focus on three levels. As we saw in Chapter 3, one group of theorists uses evolutionary principles to explain why particular traits exist in the human species (e.g., Buss, 1999). Others seek the genetic bases for trait inheritance (Plomin, 1997). And still others search for differences in the functioning of the nervous system (Heatherton et al., 2004; Pickering & Gray, 1999). Having discussed evolutionary personality theory in Chapter 3, we will focus here on genetic and neuroscience approaches.

Genetics and Personality

Have you ever been told that you share a personality trait with a parent or relative? Perhaps you wondered where the presumed similarity originated. Could it possibly have been inherited? Twin studies are particularly informative for studying the role of genetic factors because they compare the degree of personality resemblance between monozygotic twins, who have identical genetic makeup, and dizygotic twins, who do not (Lykken, 2006; Munafo, 2009). On a great many psychological characteristics, identical twins are more similar to each other than are fraternal twins, suggesting a role for genetics. However, the issue is clouded by the possibility that identical twins may also have more similar environments than fraternal twins because others are inclined to treat them more similarly (Krueger & Johnson, 2008).

The ideal solution to this problem would be to compare personality traits in identical and fraternal twins who were raised together and those who were separated early in life and raised apart. If the identical twins who were reared in different families were as similar as those reared together, a more powerful argument could be made for the role of genetic factors. Moreover, this research design would allow us to divide the total variation among individuals on each personality trait into three components: (1) variation attributable to genetic factors; (2) variation due to a shared family environment in those raised together; and (3) variation attributable to other factors, including unique individual life experiences. The

Table **13.8** | Estimates of the Percentages of Group Variance in 14 Personality Traits Attributable to Genetic and Environmental Factors

Trait	Genetic	Familial Environment	Unique Environment
Well-being	.48	.13	.39
Social potency	.54	.10	.36
Achievement	.39	.11	.50
Social closeness	.40	.19	.41
Stress reaction	.53	.00	.47
Alienation	.45	.11	.54
Aggression	.44	.00	.56
Control	.44	.00	.56
Harm avoidance	.55	.00	.45
Traditionalism	.45	.12	.43
Absorption	.50	.03	.47
Positive emotionality	.40	.22	.38
Negative emotionality	.55	.02	.43
Constraint	.58	.00	.42

NOTE: The variance estimates are based on a comparison of the degree of personality similarity in identical and fraternal twins who were reared together or apart.
SOURCE: Adapted from Tellegen et al., 1988.

relative influence of these sources of variation can be estimated by comparing personality test correlations in identical and fraternal twins who were raised together or apart.

The most comprehensive study (which included the Jim twins described at the beginning of Chapter 3) was conducted by Auke Tellegen and his colleagues at the University of Minnesota. The four groups of twin pairs were administered measures of 14 different personality traits, and the personality variation attributable to genetic, familial environment, and unique environment was calculated for each personality characteristic.

As shown in Table 13.8, genetic factors accounted for approximately 40 to 50 percent of the variance among people in trait scores. In contrast, the degree of resemblance did not differ much whether the twin pairs were reared together or apart, showing that general features of the family environment, such as its emotional climate and degree of affluence, accounted for little variance in any of the traits. The same result occurred in a recent study of self-esteem in Japanese twins (Kamakura et al., 2007). However, this does not mean that experience is not important. Rather

than the family environment, it is the individual's unique environmental experiences, such as his or her school experiences and interactions with peers, that account for considerable personality variance. Even within the same family, therefore, individual children have different experiences while growing up, and it is these unique experiences together with their genes that help shape personality development.

Personality and the Nervous System

One logical place to look for biological underpinnings of personality is in individual differences in brain functioning (Canli, 2006; Zuckerman, 2005). Two examples are Hans Eysenck's research and theorizing on extraversion and emotional stability and more recent work on temperament.

Eysenck's Extraversion-Stability Model

We've now seen that among trait theorists, there are "splitters," such as Cattell, who posit a large number of basic traits, and "lumpers," such as the Big Five theorists, who favor a smaller number. Hans J. Eysenck (1916–1997), one of Britain's leading psychologists, was the ultimate lumper (Figure 13.13a). He maintained that normal personality can be understood in terms of only *two* basic dimensions. These dimensions of Introversion-Extraversion and Stability-Instability (sometimes, as in the Big Five, called Neuroticism) blend together to form all of the more specific traits. Eysenck's two "supertraits" are comparable to the Big Five traits of Extraversion and Neuroticism.

Eysenck's Extraversion-Stability model is shown in Figure 13.13b. Note that the two basic dimensions intersect at right angles, meaning that they are statistically independent, or uncorrelated. The secondary traits shown in the circle reflect varying combinations, or mixtures, of the two primary dimensions. Thus we can see that the emotionally stable extravert is a carefree, lively person who tends to be well adjusted and to seek out leadership roles. In contrast, unstable extraverts tend to be touchy, aggressive, and restless. The stable introvert is calm, reliable, and eventempered, but the unstable introvert tends to be rigid, anxious, and moody. Different combinations of the two basic personality dimensions can thus produce very diverse personality patterns.

Eysenck (1967) was one of the first modern theorists to suggest a biological basis for major personality traits. He linked Introversion-Extraversion and Stability-Instability to differences

(a)

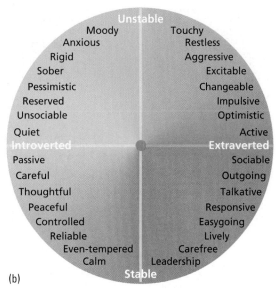

(b)

Figure 13.13

A two-factor model.
According to Hans Eysenck (a), various combinations of two major dimensions of personality, Introversion-Extraversion and Stability-Instability (or Neuroticism), combine to form more specific traits (b).
SOURCE: Eysenck, 1967.

in individuals' normal patterns of arousal within the brain. He started with the notion that there is an optimal, or preferred, level of biological arousal in the brain. Eysenck believed that extreme introverts are chronically *overaroused*; their brains are too electrically active, so they try to minimize stimulation and reduce arousal to get down to their optimal arousal level, or comfort zone. In contrast, the brains of extreme extraverts are chronically *underaroused,* so they need powerful or frequent stimulation to achieve an optimal level of cortical arousal and excitation. The extravert thus seeks social contact and physical arousal, likes parties, takes chances, is assertive, and suffers boredom easily.

Whereas Introversion-Extraversion reflects a person's *customary* level of arousal, Stability-Instability represents the suddenness with which *shifts* in arousal occur. Unstable people have hair-trigger nervous systems that show large and sudden shifts in arousal, whereas stable people show smaller and more gradual shifts (Pickering & Gray, 1999). Eysenck also called this stability dimension *Neuroticism* because he found that people with extremely unstable nervous systems are more likely to experience emotional problems that require clinical attention.

Eysenck proposed that the arousal patterns underlying Introversion-Extraversion and Stability-Instability have genetic bases. A growing body of evidence from twin studies supports his view. Identical twins are much more alike on these traits than are fraternal twins, and about half of the variance among people can be attributed to hereditary factors (Loehlin et al., 1988;

Plomin, 1997). Eysenck believed that although personality is strongly influenced by life experiences, the ways people respond to those experiences may be at least partly programmed by biological factors. Contemporary research using brain imaging continues to find brain activation patterns related to Extraversion and Stability. These studies show that the neural bases of these factors go beyond general arousal, involving specific brain structures (Canli, 2004; De Young & Gray, 2009).

Temperament: Building Blocks of Personality

Temperament *refers to individual differences in emotional and behavioral styles that appear so early in life that they are assumed to have a biological basis.* Such temperamental factors as emotionality, activity level, sociability, and impulsivity are visible even in infancy (Buss & Plomin, 1975, 1984). Temperamental factors are not assumed to be personality traits in their own right, but they are viewed as biological building blocks that influence the subsequent development of personality. The fact that these temperamental factors are more highly correlated in identical than in fraternal twins suggests a genetic link (Rothbart et al., 2009).

Recent research has focused on biological differences in inhibited and uninhibited people. First identified by Jerome Kagan (1999) on the basis of behavioral observations and biological functioning, inhibited infants and children are shy, restrained in their behavior, and react to unfamiliar people and situations with distress and avoidance

(a)

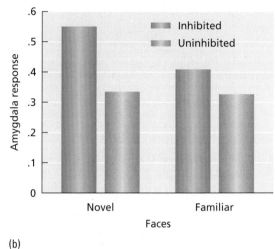

(b)

Figure 13.14

Does childhood temperament predict adult personality?

(a) Inhibited temperament expresses itself as shyness and negative reactions to novel situations and people (even Santa) early in life and is assumed to have a biological basis. (b) Adults who were identified as inhibited in childhood showed elevated reactions in the amygdala (a brain region known to initiate and organize fear responses) when exposed to faces they had not seen before, suggesting stability of this temperamental factor into adulthood. Source: Data from Schwartz et al., 2003.

(Figure 13.14a). In contrast, uninhibited children respond positively to new situations and people and seem to enjoy novelty. About 20 percent of infants are inhibited, and about 40 percent are uninhibited. Kagan (1999) found that these temperamental patterns can be identified in the first 4 months of life and that they persist into later childhood in many (but not all) children. These two groups of children also differ physiologically, with the inhibited children showing higher levels of physiological arousal and stress-hormone secretion in response to unfamiliar situations and people.

Recent research sheds light on brain regions that contribute to inhibited and uninhibited tendencies. One important region is the amygdala, the structure in the limbic system that organizes fear responses. Kagan suggested that the amygdala was involved in the physiological overreactivity he measured in inhibited children. In a more recent study, fMRI brain recordings were taken in young adults who had been categorized either as highly inhibited or as uninhibited when they were 2 years old (Schwartz et al., 2003). Of interest was how the amygdala would react to pictures of familiar and unfamiliar human faces. As shown in Figure 13.14b, those adults who had been uninhibited as children showed relatively low amygdala reactivity to both familiar and novel faces, whereas the formerly inhibited participants showed particularly high reactivity to the novel faces. This study thereby demonstrated a negative response to novel stimuli in inhibited

people that extended from childhood to adulthood, as well as a possible biological basis for this tendency.

We should note that temperament is not destiny. Although biological factors are clearly involved, the environment also can bring about some degree of change in temperamental characteristics. We should remember that temperamentally based behavior patterns help create environments that can perpetuate the behavior patterns. For example, people are unlikely to gravitate toward shy, inhibited individuals, thereby depriving them of positive experiences that might counteract their shyness. Likewise, temperamental traits may need particular kinds of environments to express themselves. Elaine Aron and coworkers (2005) found that adult shyness occurred most predictably when the underlying temperamental characteristic was paired with an adverse childhood environment. Although the link between child temperament and adult personality is far from perfect, there is little doubt that temperament is one building block in personality development.

Evaluating the Biological Approach

Biological research, spurred by technical advances in measuring nervous system activity and in evaluating genetic influences, is forging new frontiers in personality science. As we learn more about how biological functions are affected by developmental experiences and how they interact with situational factors, new insights about personality development will be achieved.

Behavior genetics research on personality is moving in some exciting new directions. In the past, twin studies of personality typically have examined degrees of similarity on self-report measures of personality traits. Yet, as we have emphasized, personality characteristics act in combination with situational factors. In a landmark study in Germany, Peter Borkenau and coworkers (2006) studied the role of genes and environment on person-by-situation interaction patterns. The behaviors of 168 identical and 132 fraternal twins were carefully observed and coded as each person reacted to 15 different situations, some involving social encounters and others requiring problem solving. By comparing the degree of similarity in person-by-situation behavioral profiles across the 15 situations in the two types of twin pairs, the researchers established that about 25 percent of the variation in behavioral profiles could be attributed to genetic factors. As in previous studies, shared-environment effects were negligible. This study shows that genetic factors influence not only what people say about their personality, but also how they adjust their behavior to different situations.

test yourself   Trait and Biological Perspectives on Personality

True or false?

1. The Big Five traits are strong predictors of many behaviors.
2. Introversion/extraversion exhibits high stability over time.
3. The trait perspective is supported by high levels of cross-situational consistency in behavior.
4. Unique environmental experiences account for more group variance in personality than does shared family environment.
5. Inhibited individuals exhibit elevated reactivity in the amygdala when presented with novel stimuli.

ANSWERS: 1-false, 2-true, 3-false, 4-true, 5-true

THE SOCIAL-COGNITIVE PERSPECTIVE

To understand behavior, psychodynamic, humanistic, and trait theorists emphasize internal personal causes of behavior, such as unconscious conflicts, self-actualization tendencies, and personality traits. In a sense, they account for behavior from the inside out. In contrast, behaviorists emphasize environmental causes and view humans as reactors to external events (Parker et al., 1998). To them, behavior is to be explained from the outside in. Behaviorists such as Ivan Pavlov, John Watson, and B. F. Skinner were more interested in discovering universal laws of learning than in identifying individual differences in behavior, and they rejected the notion of an "internal personality" that directs behavior. Nonetheless, the laws of learning that they discovered have great relevance for understanding personality. Many behaviors ascribed to personality are acquired through classical and operant conditioning, and the role of life experiences is undeniable.

Despite the power of the environment, however, some behaviorists believed that a purely behavioral account could not fully capture the workings of human personality. They believed that the learner is not simply a passive reactor to environmental forces and that internal processes could not be excluded from an understanding of personality. They viewed the human as perceiver, a thinker and a planner who mentally interprets events, thinks about the past, anticipates the future, and decides how to behave. Environmental effects are filtered through these cognitive processes and are influenced—even changed—by them. **Social-cognitive theories** *combine the behavioral and cognitive perspectives into an approach to personality that stresses the interaction of a thinking human with a social environment that provides learning experiences.* Social-cognitive theorists believe that the debate on whether behavior is more strongly influenced by personal factors or by the person's environment is basically a meaningless one (Fleeson, 2004; Smith & Shoda, 2009). Instead, according to the social-cognitive principle of **reciprocal determinism,** *the person, the person's*

Reciprocal Determinism

Environment	Person
• Stimuli from social or physical environment • Reinforcement contingencies	• Personality characteristics • Cognitive processes • Self-regulation skills

Behavior

• Type
• Frequency
• Intensity

Figure 13.15

Reciprocal determinism.

A key concept in social-cognitive theory is reciprocal determinism, in which characteristics of the person, the person's behavior, and the environment all affect one another in reciprocal, or two-way, causal relations.

behavior, and the environment all influence one another in a pattern of two-way causal links (Bandura, 1986; Figure 13.15).

As an example, let us consider how these interactions or linkages might operate in the case of a hostile and disagreeable man we'll call Tom. Tom's disagreeableness trait manifests

Figure 13.16

Research shows that people with an internal locus of control are more likely to take an active role in social-change movements.

itself in an irritable, cynical, and uncooperative behavior pattern (his personality influences his behavior). Tom's disagreeable behaviors tend to evoke negative responses from others (his behavior causes his social environment to respond to him in kind). These negative social consequences reinforce and strengthen still further his personality trait (including his expectations that others will eventually reject him), and they also strengthen his disagreeable behavior tendencies (his environment influences both his personality trait and his social behavior). Thus Tom's personality, his behavior, and his environment all influence one another, much to his detriment.

Julian Rotter: Expectancy, Reinforcement Value, and Locus of Control

In 1954, Julian Rotter (whose name rhymes with *motor*) laid the foundation for today's social-cognitive approaches. According to Rotter, the likelihood that we will engage in a particular behavior in a given situation is influenced by two factors: *expectancy* and *reinforcement value*. Expectancy is our perception of how likely it is that certain consequences will occur if we engage in a particular behavior within a specific situation. Reinforcement value is basically how much we desire or dread the outcome that we expect the behavior to produce. Thus a student who strongly values academic success and also expects that studying will result in high grades is likely to study (Rotter, 1954). Note that this approach makes use of reinforcement, a central behaviorist concept, but views its effects within a cognitive framework that emphasizes how we think about our behavior and its expected outcomes.

Locus of Control

One of Rotter's most influential expectancy concepts is **internal-external locus of control,** *an expectancy concerning the degree of personal control we have in our lives.* People with an *internal* locus of control believe that life outcomes are largely under personal control and depend on their own behavior (Figure 13.16). In contrast, people with an *external* locus of control believe that their fate has less to do with their own efforts than with the influence of external factors, such as luck, chance, and powerful others. Table 13.9 contains items from Rotter's (1966) *Internal-External (I-E) Scale,* used to measure individual differences in locus of control. Locus of control is called a *generalized expectancy* because it applies across many life domains as a general worldview.

Locus of control is a highly researched personality variable. Quite consistently, people with an internal locus of control behave in a more self-determined fashion (Pervin et al., 2005). In the 1960s, African Americans who actively participated in the civil rights movement were more internal on the I-E Scale than were those who did not (Rotter, 1966). "Internal" college students achieve better grades than do "external" students of equal academic ability, probably because they link their studying to degree of success and work harder. Internals are more likely to actively seek out the information needed to succeed in a given situation (Ingold, 1989). Interpersonally, internals are more resistant to social influence, whereas externals tend to give in to high-status people they see as powerful.

Internal locus of control is positively related to self-esteem and feelings of personal effectiveness, and internals tend to cope with stress in a more active and problem-focused manner than do externals (Jennings, 1990). They are also less likely to experience psychological maladjustment in the form of depression or anxiety (Hoffart & Martinson, 1991). Workers with an internal locus of control have fewer workplace accidents because they follow safety procedures (Stuhlmacher et al., 2009).

Albert Bandura: Social Learning and Self-Efficacy

Albert Bandura has made major contributions to the development of the social-cognitive approach. His early studies of modeling, described in Chapter 7, helped combine the psychology of learning with the cognitive perspective. Bandura's social learning analyses of aggression, moral behavior, and behavioral self-control demonstrated the wide applicability of the social-cognitive approach (Bandura, 1986). Perhaps his most influential contribution, however, is his theory and research on self-efficacy.

Self-Efficacy

According to Bandura (1997), a key factor in how people regulate their lives is their sense of **self-efficacy,** *their beliefs concerning their ability to perform the behaviors needed to achieve desired outcomes.*

Table 13.9 | **Sample Items from Rotter's Internal-External Scale**

Choose statement (a) or (b) from each numbered choice.

1. (a) Many times I feel that I have little influence over the things that happen to me.
   (b) It is impossible for me to believe that chance or luck plays an important part in my life.
2. (a) The average citizen can have an influence in government decisions.
   (b) The world is run by the few people in power, and there isn't much the little guy can do about it.
3. (a) In the long run, people get the respect they deserve in this world.
   (b) Unfortunately, an individual's worth often passes unrecognized no matter how hard one tries.

NOTE: 1b, 2a, and 3a are the internal alternatives.
SOURCE: Adapted from Rotter, 1966.

People whose self-efficacy is high have confidence in their ability to do what it takes to overcome obstacles and achieve their goals.

A good deal of research has been done on the factors that create differences in self-efficacy (Figure 13.17). Four important determinants have been identified (Bandura, 1997). First and most important is our previous *performance experiences* in similar situations. Such experiences shape our beliefs about our capabilities. For example, as shown in Figure 13.18, college women who felt that they had mastered the martial arts and emotional-control skills taught in a physical self-defense training program showed dramatic increases in

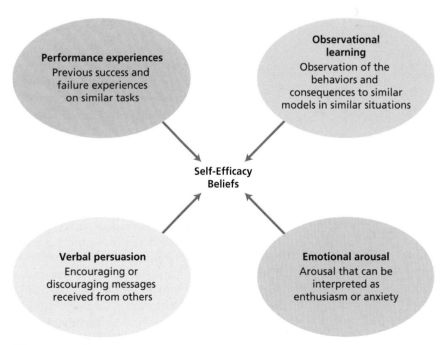

Figure 13.17

Self-efficacy beliefs.
Four classes of information affect self-efficacy beliefs. SOURCE: Based on Bandura, 1997.

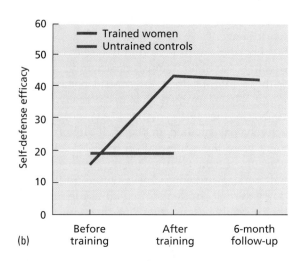

(a)   (b)

Figure 13.18

Effects of self-defense training.

(a) Physical self-defense training has dramatic effects on women's self-efficacy to perform the behaviors needed to defend themselves.
(b) The physical defense self-efficacy scores in this study could extend from 6 to 60. Source: Based on Weitlauf et al., 2000.

their belief that they could escape from or disable a potential assailant or rapist (Weitlauf et al., 2000).

Bandura stresses that self-efficacy beliefs are always specific to particular situations. Thus we may have high self-efficacy in some situations and low self-efficacy in others. For example, the women who mastered the physical self-defense skills did not feel more capable in all areas of their lives, despite their enhanced self-defense efficacy.

A second determinant of self-efficacy is *observational learning*—that is, observing others' behaviors and their outcomes. If you observe a person similar to yourself accomplish a particular goal, then you are likely to believe that if you perform those same behaviors you will also succeed. A striking example of how powerful such expectations can be comes from the world of sports. At one time, physiologists insisted that it was physically impossible for a human being to run a mile in less than 4 minutes, and no one in the history of track and field had ever done it. When the Englishman Roger Bannister broke the 4-minute barrier in 1954, that limiting belief was shattered. The impact on other runners' performance was immediate and dramatic. In the year following Bannister's accomplishment, 37 other runners broke the barrier, and in the year after that, nearly 300 runners did the "impossible." Apparently, a great many people came to believe that "if he can do it, so can I," and their new sense of self-efficacy enhanced their performance.

Third, self-efficacy can be increased or decreased by *verbal persuasion*. The messages we get from other people who affirm our abilities or downgrade them affect our efficacy beliefs. Thus inspirational teachers who convey high standards and a "you can do it" conviction can inspire their students to great accomplishments, as exemplified in the true-life story of Jaime Escalante, the mathematics teacher featured in the movie *Stand and Deliver* (Figure 13.19). By convincing inner-city minority students who had trouble doing simple arithmetic that they were capable of much more, and by helping them prove their hidden competencies to themselves, Escalante helped them achieve award-winning success in calculus.

Fourth, high *emotional arousal* that is interpreted as anxiety or fatigue tends to decrease self-efficacy. However, if we find ourselves able to control such arousal, it may enhance efficacy beliefs and subsequent performance. For example, test-anxious college students who were given training in stress-management relaxation techniques showed increases in their belief that they could remain relaxed and focused during tests, and their test performance and grade point averages improved significantly as they controlled anxious arousal (Smith, 1989).

Efficacy beliefs are strong predictors of future performance and accomplishment (Bandura, 1997). They become a kind of self-fulfilling prophecy. In the words of Henry Ford, "Whether you believe you can do something or you believe you can't, you're probably right."

Figure 13.19

The film *Stand and Deliver* depicted the extraordinary accomplishments of math teacher Jaime Escalante, who inspired his inner-city students to exceptional achievement in calculus. His stated faith in their potential and their own performance accomplishments enhanced their sense of self-efficacy.

Walter Mischel and Yuichi Shoda: The Cognitive-Affective Personality System

Walter Mischel, who studied under George Kelly and Julian Rotter at Ohio State and was a colleague of Albert Bandura's at Stanford, is a third key figure in social-cognitive theory. Bandura and Mischel became part of the "cognitive revolution" that occurred among behaviorists during the 1960s. They believed that a more cognitive approach to personality was required, one that takes into account not only the power of situational learning factors but also how people characteristically deal mentally and emotionally with experiences. Mischel set out to identify the important "person variables" that could help account for individual differences in personality.

In the most recent formulation of social-cognitive theory, Mischel and Yuichi Shoda (1999) describe a **cognitive-affective personality system (CAPS)**, *an organized system of five person variables that interact continuously with one another and with the environment, generating the distinctive patterns of behavior that characterize the person* (Mischel, 1999). The dynamic interplay among these five variables (encoding strategies, expectancies and beliefs, goals and values, affects, and competencies and

self-regulatory processes), together with the characteristics of the situation, accounts for individual differences among people, as well as differences in people's behavior across different situations. Let us examine these five personality variables, previewed in Table 13.10.

Encodings and Personal Constructs

We respond to the world as perceived. As Kelly proposed in his theory of personal constructs, discussed earlier in this chapter, people differ greatly in how they customarily *encode* (mentally represent, categorize, interpret) situations. Our encodings determine how we respond emotionally and behaviorally to situations. For example, studies of highly aggressive youth reveal that they have a strong tendency to perceive others as having disrespect and hostile intent toward them. Thus they are primed to interpret ambiguous acts by others, such as being unintentionally brushed against on a stairway at school, as an aggressive act and to react with a violent response (Dodge, 1986). Other individuals tend to encode ambiguous interpersonal events, such as not being greeted by a fellow student, as instances of personal rejection and to become depressed as a result (Downey & Feldman, 1996). As object relations theorists have suggested, the mental representations or working models we have of relationships influence how we perceive (encode) and respond to others in our later relationships. This is an example of how the CAPS can incorporate concepts and insights from other theories, including psychodynamic ones.

Expectancies and Beliefs

As Rotter emphasized, what we expect will happen if we behave in a particular way is a strong

Table **13.10** | **Person Variables in the Cognitive-Affective Personality System (CAPS)**

1. What is my perception of the situation? *Encoding strategies* help us to categorize and understand events.

2. How likely is it that certain outcomes will occur if I behave in manner X? in manner Y? How likely am I to succeed/How much personal control do I have? These are the person's *expectancies and beliefs*.

3. How much do I want to experience, or to avoid, those outcomes? This relates to the person's *goals and values*, or the person's motivational structure.

4. How do I feel about this? These emotional responses constitute the person's *affects*, or feelings.

5. Do I have the behavioral skills needed to deal with this situation? What should I do? *Personal competencies* and *self-regulation processes* affect behavior as well.

Source: After Mischel, 1999.

determinant of our behavioral choices. **Behavior-outcome expectancies** *represent the "if-then" links between alternative behaviors and possible outcomes. If I take that course in organic chemistry, then what will happen to my grade point average? How likely is it that I'll be forgiven if I apologize?* Different people may have different answers to such questions and therefore vary in their response to the same situation.

In addition to behavior-outcome expectancies, beliefs about our competencies and about the degree of personal control we have influence our actions. Thus the CAPS model also includes Bandura's self-efficacy and Rotter's locus of control as important expectancy variables.

Goals and Values

Motivation plays a central role in attempts to understand behavior, and it is represented in the CAPS as goals and values that guide our behavior, cause us to persist in the face of barriers, and determine the outcomes and situations we seek and our reactions to them (Higgins, 1996). People differ in the goals that are important to them and the values that guide their lives. These differences can cause people to behave very differently in situations that are relevant to these important personality factors.

Affects (Emotions)

Anything that implies important consequences for us, whether beneficial or harmful, can trigger an emotional response (Lazarus, 2001). Once aroused, emotions color our perceptions and influence our behavior. For example, if you are already feeling bad due to an argument with a friend and you then get negative feedback in the form of a poor grade on a test, you may feel demoralized for a time. Emotions also affect other CAPS components. Anxiety, for example, can significantly lower outcome expectancies in performance situations (Shepperd et al., 2005).

Competencies and Self-Regulation Processes

Social-cognitive theorists stress that people extensively control, or regulate, their own behavior. People's ability to control their own behavior is a distinguishing aspect of personality, as are the competencies they develop that allow them to adapt to life successfully and pursue important goals. Some of these competencies are cognitive problem-solving methods (such as systematic goal setting) that allow them to plan successful strategies, whereas others involve the ability to exert personal control over thoughts, emotions, and behaviors.

One important way people regulate their own behavior is through self-administered consequences. **Self-regulation processes** *refer to internal, self-administered rewards and punishments* (Bandura, 1999; Mischel, 1999). In response to our own behaviors, we generate positive evaluations and emotions such as pride, self-approval, and the conviction that we did "the right thing." In contrast, we may respond with negative responses such as self-reproach, shame, and guilt when we violate our personal standards. Self-reinforcement processes often override external consequences, making us more autonomous and self-directed.

Figure 13.20 shows how the CAPS system (represented inside the circle) responds to situations and generates behaviors. Features of the present situation are perceived and encoded as a first step. In this case, assume that the four relevant features are of a potential male dating partner. In this case, Feature 2 (a statement by the person that he has a very bad temper) is encoded as a warning sign. This encoding evokes an expectancy that this man might be potentially abusive and the woman experiences a negative emotional response and another expectancy that this would not be a good relationship to get into. Together, these two expectancies and the anxiety they arouse about getting into a relationship with this man evoke a competent behavioral script for gracefully declining the date (Behavior 1). This behavior should effectively end the encounter

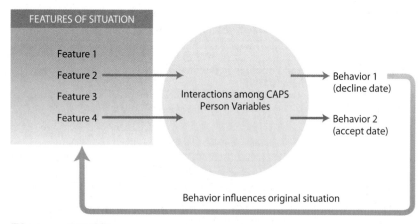

Figure 13.20

The Cognitive-Affective Personality System (CAPS).
Within the circle are the CAPS variables described in the text, connected in a stable network of relations that characterize the individual's personality functioning. Different features of the situation can be processed, resulting in different behaviors. In line with social-cognitive theory's principle of reciprocal determinism, output behaviors can, in turn, influence the situation.

(path from Behavior 1 back to the situation). It is worth noting that if the woman had encoded a different feature of the man (for example, Feature 4, how handsome he is), the cognitive-affective processes might have led to Behavior 2 (accept the date) because she highly values a handsome dating partner, thereby leading to a different situation (involvement in the relationship). We see, therefore, that it is the dynamic relations among the components of the CAPS that account for the links between the "active ingredients" of situations, personality processes, and behavior, and that our ongoing behaviors feed back into and influence the situation in accordance with the social-cognitive concept of reciprocal determinism. In this manner, the CAPS ties together situations, personality, behaviors, and their consequences.

Reconciling Personality Coherence with Behavioral Inconsistency

As noted in our earlier discussion of the trait perspective, people's behavior often shows a notable lack of consistency across situations, a fact that has caused some to question the traditional concept of personality. How can we have a coherent and stable personality yet show such inconsistency across different situations? Does personality really matter? Recent social-cognitive research and theoretical advances may provide the answer to this paradox of personality coherence and inconsistent behavior by focusing on person-by-situation interactions.

In CAPS theory, personality is defined in terms of the cognitive-affective person variables and the interactions among them. The CAPS system is assumed to be stable and consistent, although it can surely be modified by significant experiences. Behavior, however, need not be consistent. How a person behaves depends on many factors, including the features of the situation, how these features are encoded, the expectancies and beliefs that are activated, the goals that are relevant, the emotions that might occur, and the plans and self-regulatory processes that help determine the behavior. Thus it is entirely possible for people to behave inconsistently across situations that seem very similar to an outside observer. People will behave similarly in situations that, *to them,* have important characteristics in common, but they may behave inconsistently in situations that differ in ways that evoke different responses from the CAPS (Shoda & Mischel, 2000).

As a result of interactions between situations and the personality system, people exhibit distinctive **behavioral signatures,** *consistent ways of*

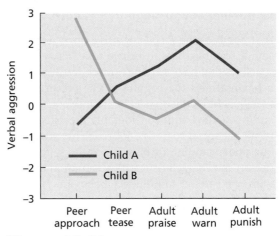

Figure 13.21

Stable situation-behavior patterns.
This chart shows the aggressive responses of two children, A and B, in five different summer camp situations. These data show the children's distinctive behavioral signatures for aggressive responding, even though their aggression scores averaged across the five settings were quite similar. The zero point on the vertical axis represents the average amount of verbal aggression shown in each situation by all the children in the study. SOURCE: Adapted from Shoda et al., 1994.

responding in particular classes of situations. These behavioral signatures are the outward manifestation of personality that establish a person's unique identity (Mischel et al., 2002). Research shows that people can have very distinctive behavioral signatures. For example, Figure 13.21 shows the behavioral patterns of two verbally aggressive children in a residential summer camp (Shoda et al., 1994). The children's behaviors were systematically observed and coded for more than 150 hours per child. Overall, these two children were quite similar in the overall number of verbally aggressive responses they made. However, inspection of the *situational patterns* of aggression reveals that child A reacted very aggressively toward adults, whether they were behaving toward the child in a warm or a punitive fashion. In contrast, this child consistently showed relatively little aggression toward peers. Child B showed quite a different pattern, consistently reacting with low levels of aggression toward adults or when being teased by peers but showing a consistently high level of aggression when peers approached him in a friendly manner.

The important lesson here is that if we simply averaged the aggressive behavior counts across the five situations, the two children would look equally aggressive. But in so doing, we would mask the distinctive and consistent behavioral signatures that define each child's individuality. Thus the coherence of personality is shown not at the level of individual behaviors but at the level of behavioral signatures (situation-by-behavior patterns).

Evaluating Social-Cognitive Theories

A strength of the social-cognitive approach is its sound scientific base. It brings together two perspectives that have strong research traditions: the behavioral and the cognitive. The constructs of social-cognitive theory can be defined, measured, and researched with considerable precision. As a result, the social-cognitive approach has advanced our understanding of how processes within the person and characteristics of the situation interact with one another to influence behavior. Another strength is its ability to translate insights derived from other perspectives into cognitive-behavioral concepts (Mischel et al., 2004).

Social-cognitive theory also helps resolve an apparent contradiction between the central assumption that personality produces stability in behavior and research findings that people's behavior is not very consistent across different situations (Funder, 2008). Mischel and Shoda's CAPS theory suggests that the inconsistency of a person's behavior across situations is actually a manifestation of a stable underlying cognitive-affective personality structure that reacts to certain features of situations. However, the ability of the CAPS to predict specific behavior needs further examination, and it will be challenging to measure the numerous interactions among the CAPS components. Much more needs to be learned about how the CAPS operates, but this question is being explored by many current researchers (Cervone & Shoda, 1999; Mischel et al., 2004). Another major challenge will be to find out what active ingredients of situations cause people to encode them in similar ways, thereby producing the consistencies in behavior that constitute behavioral signatures (Ten-Berge et al., 2002). The study of abused women and abusive men (Zayas & Shoda, 2007) in this chapter's "Research Close-up" (page 467) is one attempt to identify the active stimulus ingredients of a situation.

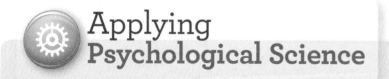

Applying Psychological Science

Understanding Charles Whitman: What Can the Personality Perspectives Tell Us?

We began this chapter with a description of Charles Whitman's murderous rampage. In the preceding pages, we have discussed five major perspectives on personality—psychodynamic, phenomenological-humanistic, trait, biological, and social-cognitive. Each perspective contributes different theoretical constructs and views behavior through a slightly different lens. We now apply these perspectives to try to achieve a fuller understanding of who Charles Whitman was and the factors that resulted in the tragedy at the University of Texas.

THE PSYCHODYNAMIC PERSPECTIVE

Though born into a family of means and showered with material goods, Whitman grew up within a chaotic home environment. His father was a self-made but brutal man who ruled his house with an iron fist and frequently beat his wife. He tolerated no weakness from his sons and viciously belittled them for any perceived failures. Whitman was very close to his mother and deeply resented his father's treatment of her, which, according to Freud, would only enhance any unresolved Oedipal hostility toward the father. In his suicide note, he wrote, "The intense hatred I feel for my father is beyond description" (Lavergne, 1997, p. 168). Lacking a good paternal model with whom to identify, Whitman seemed to have a poorly developed superego and was a walking time bomb held in check by tenuous defenses. On the night he killed his mother, under the burden of his stress, he may have regressed into an infantile state of rage. Later, neighbors told police that the only sounds they heard were that of a "child crying and whimpering," which they found puzzling since no children lived in the condominiums.

Object relations theories also have applicability to Whitman. Despite his hatred for his father, his own family experiences caused him to enter his marriage with an internal working model of "abusive husband" and "submissive wife." To his later regret, he beat his own wife on two occasions in the early years of his marriage. He was determined not to repeat this behavior and kept a journal in which he constantly wrote self-instructions about how to be a good husband. For the most part, these external constraints were effective in keeping his intense hostility in check—until the accumulation of severe life stressors caused his controls to disintegrate. "Unusual and irrational thoughts" began to intrude into consciousness as his defenses were strained to the breaking point, and he eventually exploded into violence. The psychiatrist at the student health center who interviewed him several months before the tower incident reported that although he "had something about him that expressed the all-American boy," he "seemed to be oozing with hostility." Whitman told the psychiatrist that he had frequent fantasies about "going up on the tower with a deer rifle and shooting people," but the psychiatrist did not take these fantasies seriously because of his nonviolent history (Lavergne, 1997, p. 137).

THE PHENOMENOLOGICAL-HUMANISTIC PERSPECTIVE

What kinds of insights can the phenomenological-humanistic perspective contribute to the Charles Whitman case? The obvious starting point is Whitman's self-concept. Despite the successful facade of achievement and exemplary behavior erected during his childhood and adolescent years, the abuse and denigration Whitman received from his father took a heavy toll on his self-concept. After years of being belittled, he was eager to prove himself as a man when he enlisted in the Marines. He worked hard and successfully at being a good soldier, but things began to deteriorate after he enrolled at the University of Texas on a Marine Corps scholarship. In the absence of the disciplinary structure provided first by his father and then by the Marines, he began to get into trouble, and his grades suffered to the point that his scholarship was withdrawn. He was ordered to return to his former Marine unit, where he now found military life oppressive. His conduct deteriorated, and he was court-martialed for gambling and for threatening the life of a fellow Marine with a pistol. This proved to be an early indication of his potential for violence.

Eventually, thanks to his father's political influence, Whitman was honorably discharged and returned to the University of Texas. Academic difficulties there left him riddled with self-doubt, and he struggled desperately to reduce the discrepancy between his ideal self and his perceived self. Soon he began to despair of ever being the person he wanted to be, and failure to live up to his conditions of worth undermined his self-esteem even further. After he killed his wife while she slept, Whitman left a letter on her body in which he professed his love for her and his desire to relieve her of the shame she would surely experience as his wife.

THE TRAIT PERSPECTIVE

Personality psychologists with a trait orientation would be interested in where Whitman fell on a number of relevant personality dimensions. On the Big Five, he likely would have scored high on Extraversion and Agreeableness (with some notable departures from agreeableness when frustrated), inconsistent on Conscientiousness, and high on Neuroticism. If Whitman had been given a battery of personality tests shortly before the incident, would he have exhibited a profile showing a low level of self-esteem, poor stress-management skills, high hostility, and poor impulse control? How would his scores have changed from the period when he was functioning well in adolescence to the period after he was in the Marines? Unfortunately, we will never know the answers to these questions because, to our knowledge, Whitman never took a personality test. It's quite possible that had Whitman been tested in the days preceding his murderous acts, his test results might have warned professionals about his potential for violent behavior.

THE BIOLOGICAL PERSPECTIVE

In Whitman's suicide letter, we find references to "tremendous headaches" for which he had been medicating himself and a request that an autopsy be done after his death to see if a "visible physical disorder" existed. In fact, a postmortem examination of his brain detected a fast-growing glioblastoma multiforme tumor affecting the thalamus, hypothalamus, and amygdala, major parts of the aggression circuitry of the brain, including an area where electrical stimulation can induce rage responses in animals (Raine et al., 2000). Medical authorities evaluating Whitman's case differed on the importance of the tumor, but it was consistent with several of his behavior patterns, including the incessant writing of notes and letters in his final weeks. The tumor could have been a predisposing factor that lowered his inhibitions against violent behavior.

A second potential biological factor could be the genes Whitman inherited from his father, who had a penchant for violent behavior and frequently beat his wife and children. Aggression has a genetic basis (Malouf et al., 2008; Wasserman & Wachbroit, 2001), and it is possible that a biological predisposition interacted with environmental factors to increase Whitman's potential for violent behavior.

THE SOCIAL-COGNITIVE PERSPECTIVE

The behavioral aspect of the social-cognitive perspective would focus on past learning experiences that predisposed him to violence. These are not hard to find in his history. His father provided an aggressive model during his formative years, controlling his wife and children with physical abuse. His father was also a gun enthusiast, and there were guns hanging in virtually every room of the Whitman home. Family photos show young Charles holding guns when he was only 2 years old, and his father made sure he received plenty of training in using them. Long before he enlisted in the Marines, Whitman was an expert marksman, and the Marines built on this expertise with sniper training that earned him a sharpshooter's badge. As other aspects of his life were crumbling, Whitman's marksmanship was a continuing and positive part of his personal self-identity, and he told several University of Texas acquaintances how easy it would be to pick off people from the tower. His expertise made him a deadly killer as he fired from the tower with stunning accuracy, killing people up to a half mile away.

How might Charles Whitman be represented within the CAPS model? At the level of *encoding processes*, Mischel and Shoda would focus on how he viewed himself and his world. Aggression is fueled by perceptions that we have been wronged and that the provocation was intentional (Lazarus, 2001). Clearly, Whitman felt victimized both by his father and by the Marines, and he saw the world as so malevolent that he regarded killing his wife and mother as acts of mercy. Moreover, his view of himself became increasingly negative as his life's fortunes declined. His outcome and self-efficacy *expectancies* became increasingly negative. One source of self-efficacy that remained unchanged was his exceptional marksmanship, and this competency became the medium for the expression of his rage, as well as his entree to the death he desired.

Whitman's *values* involved success in his career, in academics, and as a husband. Success was nowhere in sight in any of these areas, producing feelings of frustration and creating unbearable stress in his life. He felt unworthy of his wife and deeply regretted the two incidents early in their marriage when he had beaten her.

At the level of *affect*, what also stands out is Whitman's internal rage. In the words of the psychiatrist who saw him shortly before his outburst, he was "fairly oozing" with generalized hostility. Whitman tried to achieve his goals and exercise self-control with elaborate manuals filled with specific self-instructions about how to act, what to say, and how to inhibit his hostility. Eventually, though, in the absence of adequate *self-regulation skills*, these external controls failed, with tragic consequences.

Applying the concept of *behavioral signatures* to Charles Whitman, it is clear that Whitman's behavior differed dramatically across situations. Most of the time, he was an all-American boy, charming, witty, agreeable, and a loving husband. However, when under stress, his defenses against his inner rage began to crumble and he became hostile and aggressive, capable of abusing his wife and threatening to shoot a fellow Marine. When stress reached a sufficiently severe level, his controls broke down completely and he committed the murderous acts. In the if-then language of behavioral signatures, we might summarize this aspect of his personality as: *if* not under stress, *then* friendly and well controlled; but *if* under stress and facing severe failure, *then* hostile and impulsive.

Having now described the various perspectives on personality, we have seen that each presents us with a different picture of human nature and that each focuses on particular determinants of human individuality. Moreover, each perspective provides us with different pieces of the complex puzzle that was Charles Whitman.

test yourself   The Social-Cognitive Perspective

Match each numbered social-cognitive concept to the correct definition on the right.

1. self-efficacy
2. locus of control
3. encodings
4. behavioral signatures

a. mental representations of situations and oneself
b. situation-specific behavior patterns
c. belief in one's own ability to achieve goals
d. belief in internal/external controls over one's life

ANSWERS: 1-c, 2-d, 3-a, 4-b

CULTURE, GENDER, AND PERSONALITY

As we have seen, personality is a product of interacting biological and environmental influences. Children inherit different biologies that influence how their environment, including culture, affects them (Kagan & Fox, 2006).

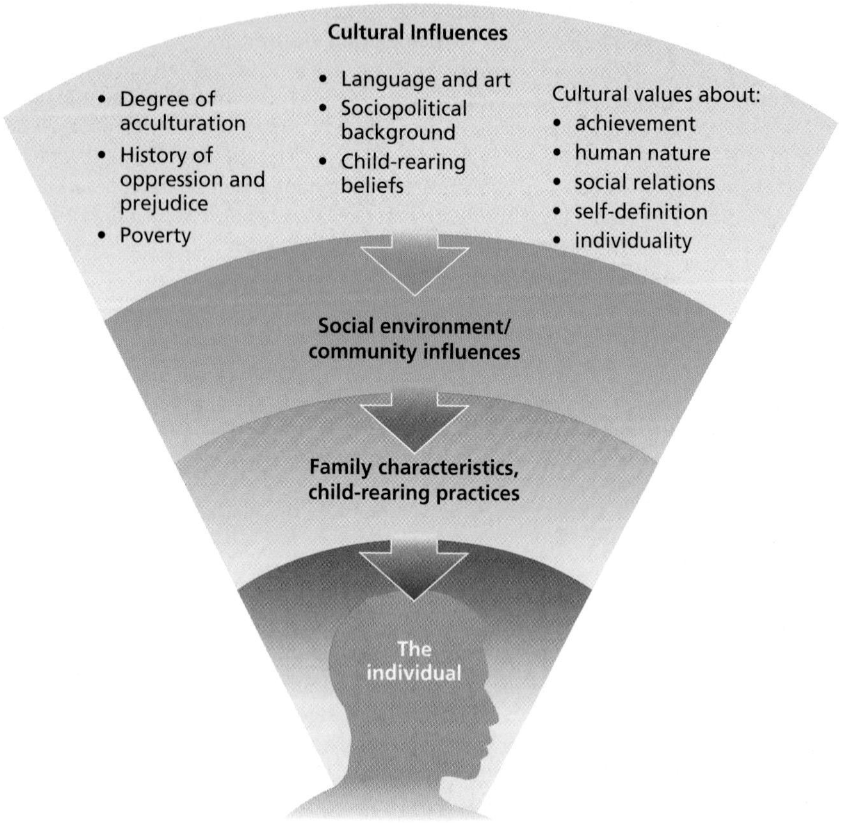

Cultural Influences

- Degree of acculturation
- History of oppression and prejudice
- Poverty

- Language and art
- Sociopolitical background
- Child-rearing beliefs

Cultural values about:
- achievement
- human nature
- social relations
- self-definition
- individuality

Social environment/ community influences

Family characteristics, child-rearing practices

The individual

Figure 13.22

Culture and personality.

This model shows how cultural elements are transmitted to the individual through the medium of social environment and family influences. Source: Based on factors cited by Locke, 1992, and Sue & Sue, 1990.

Environment exists at many different levels, ranging from the physical surroundings in which we develop to the increasingly global social contexts shown in Figure 13.22. Among the most important, yet unappreciated, environmental influences is the culture in which we develop. We are often unaware of these influences because they serve as an amorphous background against which the specific events of our lives unfold. Culture encompasses unstated assumptions (including assumptions about the very nature of reality), norms, values, sex roles, and habitual ways of behaving that are shared by members of a social group. It influences what we perceive, how we perceive, how we relate to ourselves and others, and how we behave (Benet-Martinez & Oishi, 2008).

Culture Differences

Cultures differ along a number of dimensions that can affect personality development (Draguns, 2009; Triandis & Suh, 2002). One is *complexity*. Consider how much more complex a Western information-age culture is than a hunter-gatherer culture in a remote region of an undeveloped country. Consider also how much more potential for diversity and conflict of values and behavioral norms exists in a highly complex culture.

A second cultural dimension is *tightness*. In tight cultures, there are many rules about behavior, and those who deviate from the cultural norms, even in minor ways, are likely to be punished. In Singapore, for example, adolescents are expected to adhere strictly to social norms that forbid experimenting with alcohol, tobacco, or sexual intercourse (Ball & Mosselle, 1995). As a result of explicit norms, people tend to differ less from one another in tight cultures than they do in loose cultures, where diversity in beliefs, values, and "doing your own thing" is permitted or even encouraged. Loose cultures are most likely to occur where people within a social group are not highly dependent on one another and where diversity is tolerated or even encouraged. Thus we would expect American adolescents to show greater diversity and feelings of individuality than those in Singapore. They might also experience more conflicts in deciding which values to embrace and what type of person they want to be.

Important personality differences have been found between people in *individualistic* and *collectivistic* cultures, although we should emphasize that significant variation can be found within any given culture. On average, only about 40 percent of people within a particular culture strongly embrace either individualistic or collectivistic goals (Triandis & Suh, 2002). In one study, American and Japanese college students were given a self-concept questionnaire on which they listed their five most important attributes. The researchers then classified each statement according to whether it referred to a personal attribute (e.g., "I am honest," "I am smart"), a social identity (e.g., "I am an oldest son," "I am a student"), or something else, such as a physical trait. As Figure 13.23 shows, the Americans were far more likely than the Japanese to list personal traits, abilities, or dispositions, whereas the Japanese more frequently described themselves in social identity

terms. Thus the social embeddedness of the collectivistic Japanese culture was reflected in their self-perceptions, as was cultural individualism in the Americans' self-concepts (Cousins, 1989). Interestingly, personality trait measures do not predict behavior as well in collectivistic cultures as they do in individualistic cultures, possibly because environmental factors play a stronger role in the behavior of collectivistic individuals (Church & Katigbak, 2000).

Self-enhancement needs are equally strong in individualistic and collectivistic cultures, but they are satisfied in different ways. Individualists enhance the self through personal successes, whereas collectivists feel better about themselves when their group succeeds (Sedikides et al., 2003). In individualistic cultures, personal success also serves to increase people's motivation, whereas in collectivistic cultures, motivation increases after failure, as the person attempts to change the self and conform to the demands of the situation (Heine et al., 2000). Even emotional lives differ. In a study of cultural differences in experienced emotions, Americans reported more self-oriented positive emotions, such as self-pride and personal happiness, whereas Japanese reported more interpersonally oriented positive emotions, such as closeness, friendliness, and respect (Kitayama et al., 2000). On self-esteem measures, Japanese score lower than Americans. Shinobu Kitayama and Hazel Markus (1999) explain that in Japanese culture, self-criticism is not bad, for it serves the valuable function of encouraging self-improvement that can benefit the individual and society. In Western cultures, self-criticism is predictive of depression, but this is not the case in Japan.

Gender Schemas

Gender-role socialization provides us with **gender schemas,** *organized mental structures that contain our understanding of the attributes and behaviors that are appropriate and expected for males and females* (Bem, 1981). Within a given culture, gender schemas tell us what the typical man or woman should be like. In Western cultures, men tend to prize attributes related to achievement, emotional strength, athleticism, and self-sufficiency, whereas women prize interpersonal competencies, kindness, and helpfulness to others (Beyer, 1990; Marsh, 1990). In this sense, men in Western cultures tend to develop more of an individualistic self-concept, emphasizing achievement and separateness from others, whereas women's self-concepts tend to be more collectivistic, emphasizing their social connectedness with others (Kashima et al., 1995). Nonetheless, we should keep in mind that significant individual

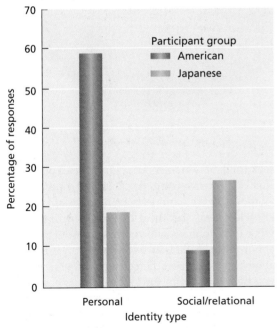

Figure 13.23

Cultural differences in the self-concept.

This graph shows the percentages of personal identity and social/relational self-attributes given by Japanese and American college students as key aspects of their self-concepts. SOURCE: Adapted from Cousins, 1989.

Levels of Analysis

Conceptions of Personality

As we have now seen, diverse conceptions of personality have focused on different aspects and mechanisms of personality functioning. An understanding of how personality accounts for individual differences in behavior requires analysis at the biological, psychological, and environmental levels of analysis.

BIOLOGICAL LEVEL

- Global personality dispositions are shaped by evolutionary forces, and individual differences in these dispositions occur because of environmental forces that require particular adaptations (evolutionary personality theory).
- Genetic factors account for significant heritability of most personality variables (behavior genetics).
- Individual differences exist in customary levels of cortical arousal and speed of arousal shifts (Eysenck).
- Temperamental differences present from birth influence personality development.

PSYCHOLOGICAL LEVEL

- Psychodynamic processes involving impulse, defenses, unconscious conflicts, and psychosexual developmental factors shape adult personality (Freud).
- Object relations and attachment styles develop during childhood.
- Personal constructs influence how the world is understood and responded to (Kelly).
- Behavior is influenced by self-actualization, the self-concept, self-verification, and self-enhancement processes (Rogers).
- Individual differences in behavior are attributed to presumably stable personality traits (trait theorists).
- Cognitive-affective person factors interact with situational and social learning factors to create behavioral signatures (social-cognitive theorists).

ENVIRONMENTAL LEVEL

- Early relationships with parents and other significant figures underlie personality differences and working models of the world (psychoanalytic, neoanalytic, and object relations theorists).
- Environmental factors can support or interfere with the natural tendency toward self-actualization (humanistic theorists).
- Shared and (especially) unshared environments interact with genetic predispositions, including temperament (behavior genetics).
- Past social learning experiences, cultural learning, and current situational factors help create behavioral signatures (social cognitive theorists).

How would we expect a physically abusive childhood environment to affect children who are high and low in Eysenck's dimension of Stability?

differences exist within each gender group, with many women being individualists and many men collectivists (Triandis & Suh, 2002). As noted earlier, men and women do not differ significantly in self-esteem in United States samples, suggesting that there are numerous behavioral routes to feeling good about oneself.

PERSONALITY ASSESSMENT

If you were to be introduced to Jennifer, a woman you had never met before, and given one week to provide a complete personality description of her, what would you do? Chances are, you would

seek information in a variety of ways. You might start by interviewing Jennifer and finding out as much as you could about her. Based on your knowledge of the theories we have discussed, what questions would you ask? Would you ask about early-childhood experiences and dreams? about how she sees herself and others? Would you be interested in the kinds of traits embodied in the Big Five Model or in Eysenck's dimension of Introversion-Extraversion? Would you want to know how Jennifer customarily feels and responds in various situations? Your answers to these questions and your other assessment decisions would in some sense reflect your own theory of what is important in describing personality.

You probably would not be content simply to interview Jennifer. You might also decide to interview other people who know her well and get their views of what she is like. You might even ask them to rate her on a variety of traits, and you could ask Jennifer to rate herself on the same measures to see if her self-concept agrees with how others see her.

Finally, you might decide that it would be useful to actually observe how Jennifer behaves in a variety of situations. You would want to observe her in a way that would allow you to get as natural and characteristic a sample of her behavior as possible. This information, together with that obtained from Jennifer and from those who know her best, might provide a reasonable basis for a personality description.

Figure 13.24 shows the major methods that psychologists use to assess personality characteristics (Boyle & Helmes, 2009). As you can see, they use some of the same methods you might have chosen: the interview, trait ratings, and behavior reports, as well as behavioral assessment, or direct observation and measurement of the subject's behavior. In addition, psychologists have developed several types of tests, including objective self-report measures and projective tests that ask respondents to interpret ambiguous stimuli, such as inkblots or pictures. Finally, physiological measures can be used to measure various aspects of personality, such as emotional reactivity or levels of cortical arousal.

The task of devising valid and useful personality measures is anything but simple, and it has taxed the ingenuity of psychologists for nearly a century. To be useful from either a scientific or a practical perspective, personality tests must conform to the standards of reliability and validity discussed in Chapter 10. *Reliability*, or consistency of measurement, takes several forms. A test that measures a stable personality trait should yield similar scores when administered to the same individuals at different times (test-retest reliability). Another aspect of reliability is that different professionals should score and interpret the test in the same way (interjudge reliability).

Validity refers to the most important question of all: Is the test actually measuring the personality variable that it is intended to measure? A valid test allows us to predict behavior that is influenced by the personality variable being measured. Research on test reliability and validity is an important activity of personality psychologists, and good measures of personality are an absolute must for scientific research on personality and for ethical clinical application (Chamorro-Premuzic, 2007; Domino, 2000).

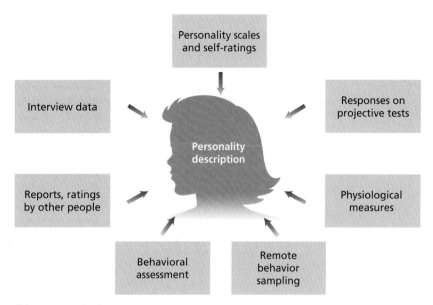

Figure 13.24

Measurement approaches used to assess personality.

In general, current personality assessment tests perform as well as measures in a variety of other health service areas, as shown in the findings of 125 meta-analyses and 800 comparative studies (Meyer et al., 2001). These include electrocardiograms, mammography, Pap smears, serum cholesterol tests, PET scans, and MRIs. That's the good news. The bad news is that neither the psychological nor the medical tests have as much validity as one would like.

Interviews

Interviews are one of the oldest methods of assessment. Long before the invention of writing, people undoubtedly made judgments about others by observing them and talking with them. Interviewers can obtain information about a person's thoughts, feelings, and other internal states, as well as information about current and past relationships, experiences, and behavior. This assessment method is particularly popular among psychodynamic and phenomenological-humanistic workers.

Structured interviews *contain a set of specific questions that are administered to every participant.* An attempt is made to create a standardized situation so that interviewees' responses to more-or-less identical stimuli can be interpreted and compared. Such interviews are frequently used to collect research data or to make a psychiatric diagnosis. Other interviews are unstructured, with interviewers tailoring their questions to the particular individual and situation.

Good interviewers do not limit their attention to what an interviewee says; they also look at how she or he says it. They note interviewees' general appearance and grooming, their voice and speech patterns, the content of their statements, and their facial expressions and posture. Sometimes, attitudes that are not expressed verbally can be inferred from behavior, as in this instance:

> During the interview she held her small son on her lap. The child began to play with his genitals. The mother, without looking directly at the child, moved his hand away and held it securely for a while. . . . Later in the interview the mother was asked what she ordinarily did when the child masturbated. She replied that he never did this— he was a very "good" boy. She was evidently entirely unconscious of what had transpired in the very presence of the interviewer. (Maccoby & Maccoby, 1954, p. 484)

The interview is valuable for the direct personal contact it provides, but it has some limitations. First, characteristics of the interviewer may influence how the interviewee responds and thus affect the validity of the information. In addition, the validity of information obtained depends on the interviewee's desire to cooperate, to respond honestly, and to report accurately what the interviewer is trying to assess.

Despite its limitations, the face-to-face interview is essential for certain purposes. For example, a clinical psychologist needs to observe and converse with a person who is being considered for admission to a mental hospital. Interviews are often used in research as well. The challenge is to design and conduct interviews in ways that maximize the validity of the data obtained from the respondent.

Behavioral Assessment

Personality psychologists can sometimes observe the behaviors they are interested in rather than asking people about them. In **behavioral assessment,** *psychologists devise an explicit coding system that contains the behavioral categories of interest.* Then they train observers until they show high levels of agreement (interjudge reliability) in using the coding categories to record behavior. Assessors may code the behavior in live settings, or they may code videotaped behavior sequences. A staple of behaviorists, behavioral assessment can provide valuable information about how frequently and under what conditions certain classes of behavior occur (Hersen, 2006). Social-cognitive researchers used this method to measure the behavioral signatures of the verbally aggressive children in the summer camp environment discussed earlier.

Behavioral assessment requires precision in defining the behaviors of interest and the conditions under which they occur. For example, observers studying a young child who is having problems in school do not simply say, "Jerry is disruptive." Instead, they try to answer the question "What, specifically, does Jerry *do* that causes disruption?" Once they have identified Jerry's specific behaviors, the next questions are "How often and under what conditions does the disruptive behavior occur?" and "What kinds of outcomes do the behaviors produce?" Answers to these questions can be particularly important not only in measuring differences in people's personality characteristics but also in identifying potential situational causes of their behavior and in devising behavior-change interventions (Greene & Ollendick, 2000; Haynes, 2000).

Remote Behavior Sampling

It is not practical or possible for behavioral assessors to follow people around from situation to situation on a daily basis. In addition, assessors are frequently interested in unobservable events, such as emotional reactions and thinking patterns, that may shed considerable light on personality functioning. Through **remote behavior sampling,** *researchers and clinicians can collect self-reported samples of behavior from respondents as they live their daily lives.* A tiny computerized device resembling a cell phone is used. The device pages respondents at randomly determined times of the day (Figure 13.25). When the beeper sounds, respondents rate or record their current thoughts, feelings, or behaviors, depending on what the researcher or therapist is assessing (Stone et al., 2000). Respondents may also report on aspects of the situation they are in so that situation-behavior interactions can be examined. Remote sampling procedures can be used over weeks or even months to collect a large behavior sample across many situations. This approach to personality assessment holds great promise, for it enables researchers and clinicians to detect patterns of personal functioning that might not be revealed by other methods.

Personality Scales

Personality scales, or inventories, are widely used for assessing personality in both research and clinical work. They are considered *objective* measures because they include standard sets of questions, usually in a true-false or rating-scale format, that are scored using an agreed-on scoring key (Nezami & Butcher, 2000). Their advantages include (1) the ability to collect data from many people at the same time, (2) the fact that all people respond to the same items, and (3) ease of scoring.

A different approach to developing personality scales is the **empirical approach,** *in which items are chosen not because their content seems relevant to the trait on rational grounds, but because each item has been answered differently by groups of people* (for example, introverts and extraverts) *known to differ in the personality characteristic of interest.* The **Minnesota Multiphasic Personality Inventory-2 (MMPI-2)** *is a widely used personality test developed according to the empirical approach.* The MMPI was originally designed to provide an objective basis for psychiatric diagnosis. Its 567 true-false items consist of statements that were answered differently by groups of patients diagnosed with specific psychiatric disorders (e.g., hysteria, paranoia, and schizophrenia) than by respondents in a nonpsychiatric comparison sample. It did not matter what the item said. If paranoids responded differently than nonpatients to "I like basketball better than baseball," that item would go onto the Paranoia scale. The items vary widely in content; some are concerned with attitudes and emotions, others relate to overt behavior and symptoms, and still others refer to the person's life history.

The MMPI-2 has 3 validity scales and 10 clinical scales (Table 13.11). The validity scales are used to detect tendencies to present either an overly positive picture or to exaggerate the degree of psychological disturbance. Although the scales were originally intended to measure severe

Figure 13.25

In remote behavior sampling, a computerized device resembling a cell phone is used to collect responses from participants—such as ratings of their mood at a certain time—as they live their daily lives.

Their major disadvantage is the possibility that some people will choose not to answer the items truthfully, in which case their scores will not be valid reflections of the trait being measured. To combat this threat to validity, some widely used tests have special *validity scales* that detect tendencies to respond in a socially desirable manner or to present an overly negative image of oneself.

The items on personality scales are developed in two major ways. In the **rational-theoretical approach,** *items are based on the theorist's conception of the personality trait to be measured.* For example, to develop a measure of introversion-extraversion, we would ask ourselves what introverts and extraverts often say about themselves, and then we would write items that captured those kinds of self-descriptions (e.g., "I love to be at large social gatherings" or "I'm very content to spend time by myself"). One frequently used measure of this kind is the **NEO Personality Inventory (NEO-PI),** *which measures the Big Five personality traits of Openness, Conscientiousness, Extraversion, Agreeableness, and Neuroticism* (Costa & McCrae, 1992). Other scales developed according to the rational-theoretical approach are the measures of optimism-pessimism, self-monitoring, and locus of control shown in Tables 13.6, 13.7, and 13.9.

Table 13.11 | The Validity and Clinical Scales of the Minnesota Multiphasic Personality Inventory-2 (MMPI-2) and the Behavioral Characteristics Associated with High Scores on the Scales

Scale	Abbreviation	Behavioral Correlates
Validity scales		
Lie	L	Lies or is highly conventional
Frequency	F	Exaggerates complaints, answers haphazardly
Correction	K	Denies problems
Clinical scales		
Hypochondriasis	Hs	Expresses bodily concerns and complaints
Depression	D	Is depressed, pessimistic, guilty
Hysteria	Hy	Reacts to stress with physical symptoms, lacks insight into negative feelings
Psychopathic deviate	Pd	Is impulsive, in conflict with the law, involved in stormy relationships
Masculinity, femininity	Mf	Has interests characteristic of the opposite sex
Paranoia	Pa	Is suspicious, resentful
Psychasthenia	Pt	Is anxious, worried, high-strung
Schizophrenia	Sc	Is confused, disorganized, disoriented, and withdrawn from others
Hypomania	Ma	Is energetic, active, restless
Social introversion	Si	Is introverted, with little social contact

personality deviations such as schizophrenia, depression, and psychopathic personality, the *profile* of scores obtained on the various scales also reveals important aspects of personality functioning even in people who do not display such disorders (Graham, 2006). Thus the MMPI-2 is used not only as an aid to psychiatric diagnosis but also for personality description and as a screening device in industrial and military settings.

Projective Tests

Freud and other psychodynamic theorists emphasized the importance of unconscious factors in understanding behavior. By definition, however, people are unaware of unconscious dynamics, so they cannot report them to interviewers or on self-report tests like the NEO-PI or the MMPI-2. Other methods were therefore needed to assess them.

Projective tests *present subjects with ambiguous stimuli and ask for some interpretation of them.* The assumption is that because the meaning of the stimulus is unclear, the subject's interpretation will have to come from within, reflecting the projection of inner needs, feelings, and ways of viewing the world onto the stimulus. The following fictional story helps illustrate the rationale for projective techniques:

> During the administration of a set of Rorschach inkblots, the man being tested saw every one of the inkblots as either sex organs or people engaging in sexual acts. After the last inkblot, the psychologist declared, "I've never in my entire career

seen anyone as obsessed with sex as you seem to be." The man responded indignantly, "What do you mean, *I'm* obsessed with sex? *You're* the one with all the dirty pictures!"

The stimuli that people are asked to respond to include inkblots and pictures. The **Rorschach test** *consists of 10 inkblots.* The person being tested is shown each one in succession and asked, "What does this look like? What might it be?" (Figure 13.26). After responding, the person is asked to explain what specific feature of the inkblot (e.g., its shape or its color) makes it seem that way. Examiners categorize and score responses in terms of the kinds of objects reported, the features attended to (e.g., the whole blot, colored portions, tiny details), and the emotional tone of particular types of responses (Erdberg, 2000).

Interpretations made by Rorschach examiners are often based on what the responses seem to symbolize. For example, people who see peering eyes and threatening figures in the inkblots are likely to be viewed as projecting their own paranoid fears and suspicions onto the stimuli. One drawback of the Rorschach is that different examiners may interpret the same response very differently, producing unreliability among examiners. In an attempt to minimize clinician subjectivity in interpreting Rorschach responses, John Exner (1991) developed a scoring system with specific coding categories and scoring criteria. Although this system created greater uniformity in scoring, many of the personality interpretations derived from the Rorschach lack research support (Lilienfeld et al., 2000). Nonetheless, many psychodynamic clinicians maintain their faith in the Rorschach, insisting that they find it useful for gaining insight into unconscious processes, and the test seems to be especially valuable in detecting psychotic thought disorders (Society for Personality Assessment, 2005).

The **Thematic Apperception Test (TAT)** *consists of a series of pictures derived from paintings, drawings, and magazine illustrations.* In general, the pictures are less ambiguous than the Rorschach inkblots, but they still require an interpretation. To illustrate, look at the picture in Figure 13.27, and then write a story that addresses the following questions:

- What is happening? Who are the people involved?

- What has led up to this situation?

- What is being thought, felt, and wanted, and by whom?

- What will happen? How will the story turn out?

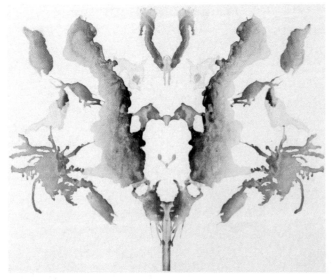

Figure 13.26

During a Rorschach test administration, the person being tested is shown a series of inkblots similar to this one and is asked to indicate what each resembles and what feature of the stimulus (for example, its shape or its color) makes it appear that way.

Figure 13.27

A picture from the Thematic Apperception Test.
Subjects are asked to make up a story about the picture, covering specific points, such as those listed in the text. The stories are analyzed for recurrent themes that are assumed to reflect significant aspects of personality. Source: Reprinted by permission of the publisher from *Thematic Apperception Test*, by Henry A. Murray, Card 12F, Cambridge, MA: Harvard University Press. Copyright © 1943 by the President and Fellows of Harvard College. Copyright © renewed 1971 by Henry A. Murray.

The stories told in response to a set of 10 to 20 pictures are analyzed for recurrent themes that are assumed to reflect important aspects of the respondent's personality. These might include the kinds of personal relationships depicted in the stories, the types of motives and feelings that are attributed to the characters, whether positive or negative outcomes occur, and factors that produce these outcomes such as personal weaknesses or forces in the environment (Langan-Fox & Grant, 2006).

The TAT, like the Rorschach, typically relies on the subjective interpretation of test responses, which can result in different interpretations of the same stories. Since not everyone can be right, the possibility of erroneous interpretations is obvious. Where specific systems have been developed to score stories, however, the TAT has proven to be a useful and valid test (Atkinson, 1958). As discussed in Chapter 11, scoring of stories told to TAT pictures is used by researchers to measure achievement motivation. The TAT appears to provide a more valid measure of this and other motives, such as power, than do objective self-report measures of the same motives, showing stronger relations with motivated behavior (Ferguson, 2000). Despite such exceptions, however, objective measures of personality have generally been found to have better reliability and validity than projective measures (Lilienfeld et al., 2000; Nezami & Butcher, 2000).

Myth or Reality?

Criminal Profiling Is a Useful Investigative Tool

Among the new media darlings are psychological profilers, often some of the first experts to appear on crime shows hosted by entertainers like Nancy Grace and Greta Van Susteren after a notable crime occurs. Their gifts for analyzing the criminal mind based on crime-scene data, such as detective reports, photographs, and autopsy results, have been dramatized in movies like *The Silence of the Lambs* (1991) and *Copycat* (1995), and on television series such as *Profiler, Criminal Minds*, and *CSI: Crime Scene Investigation*. In the United States, trained Federal Bureau of Investigation (FBI) profilers provide assistance in more than 1,000 cases per year, and profilers are being used in many other countries as well (Snook et al., 2008). Survey results show that a large majority of police officials and mental health professionals (over 80 percent in some studies) believe that personality profiles generated by experienced profilers provide unique insights that assist in solving crimes (Snook et al., 2008; Torres et al., 2006).

What's the Evidence?

An accumulating body of research suggests a far more modest conclusion concerning the reliability, validity, and usefulness of profilers' input than that suggested in the survey results above. In these studies, professional profilers are compared with nonprofessionals who also make specific predictions after reviewing detailed information from previous cases in which the "truth" about the offender and all aspects of the criminal act are known. Brent Snook and coworkers (2007) reviewed the results of four well-controlled studies and found that the expert profilers did only slightly better than college students and psychologists without forensic experience in overall accuracy of their predictions (but that both groups were so far from perfect that major investigative errors could have resulted from the information they provided). Even more significant was the finding that the expert profilers were actually *less* accurate than the nonexperts in predicting offenders' (1) physical characteristics (e.g., sex, race, and age), (2) personality-related characteristics such as motives, thought processes, and guilt, and (3) personal characteristics such as education, social class, and marital status.

After analyzing more than 130 criminal profiling articles, Snook and coworkers (2007) found that profilers were prone to

Continued

use subjective, intuitive, and impressionistic bases for predictions rather than scientifically derived information on offender characteristics that could be the basis for more accurate predictions. Numerous studies across many prediction settings have shown the same results—that clinical intuition is decidedly inferior to the use of simple mathematical formulas incorporating scientifically established predictor variables in predicting outcomes (Meehl, 1997). This *actuarial* or statistical approach, similar to the mathematical approach used by insurance companies to maximize their predictions of who should be insured and at what level of premium, is superior to the intuitive-impressionistic approach because the actuarial formula (1) makes use of variables that actually predict the outcome and (2) weights these variables appropriately, attaching greater importance to variables having higher predictive value. Intuitive predictors often base predictions on variables that make sense to them but are invalid, and they also fail to weight even valid predictors in terms of their actual importance. In one comprehensive review of 136 studies in which expert interpretations were pitted against actuarial formulas across many settings, the impressionistic/intuitive approach did better than the formula in only 8 instances, whereas the actuarial approach achieved greater accuracy 64 times (Grove & Meehl, 1996).

Snook and coworkers also found that many profilers base their descriptions on outmoded trait models such as a distinction between "organized" and "disorganized" criminals, a typology that has been proven inadequate in describing crime patterns (Canter et al., 2004). Profilers also embrace the false assumption that people behave consistently across situations, assuming that a particular trait will express itself in all areas of the criminal's life, including crime-related behavior. They therefore do not place enough weight on situational factors. We've already seen that people do not exhibit high behavioral consistency, and the same applies to criminal behavior. Contrary to popular belief, for example, a recent study revealed no evidence for consistency across the crimes committed by serial killers (Bateman & Salfati, 2007). This seems a particularly meaningful finding given the frequent use of profilers in such cases.

Why the "Illusion" Persists

Based on their extensive review of 130 studies of criminal profiling, one set of reviewers labeled the practice an investigative "illusion" (Snook et al., 2008, p. 1257). Given the lack of scientific evidence for profiling, why does it continue to enjoy such a high level of credibility among police and the media? One reason is that sometimes profilers hit the mark with their predictions in a spectacular fashion, and these infrequent "hits" are widely reported because they are newsworthy. But even correct profiler predictions are usually mixed with a large number of other statements that turn out not to apply. Moreover, profilers and their promoters often provide information only on the *number* of correct predictions they have made that helped solve cases and not on the *percentage* of correct predictions. This can present a distorted picture of their successes. Studies that have examined all predictions bear this out. For example, it might impress you that in 21 well-publicized criminal cases, expert profilers made a total of 158 correct descriptions of the criminals' personal characteristics—if that's all you were told. However, in these 21 cases the profilers actually made 880 descriptive statements, 82 percent of which were unsubstantiated by later evidence

(Alison et al., 2003). Knowing that 722 of their predictions were wrong, you might come away less impressed, particularly since any one of the incorrect predictions could have led police investigators astray.

Another factor favoring profilers is what is known as the *expert heuristic*. People, quite appropriately, tend to give great credibility to someone who is labeled an expert because it is generally a good idea to depend on such people and believe what they say. And what could be more credible than a "veteran FBI profiler"? Research has shown that offender descriptions are rated by police officers as more valid and useful if attributed to an "expert profiler" than if that label is not applied (Kocsis & Hayes, 2004).

Circus owner P. T. Barnum used to say that he liked to "give a little something to everyone" who attended the circus. In personality assessment, the **Barnum effect** *refers to our ability to find vague and general personality descriptions believable because they seem to apply to us.* The problem is that they also apply to almost everyone else, too. If we told you on the basis of a personality test you took that "you sometimes have doubts about some of your abilities," "you have a short attention span when dealing with boring people," "you have a desire to be liked and admired by others," and "you are strongly committed to a successful future," you might think we had a pretty good test. But if we gave those statements to 50 of your classmates, they would probably think the same thing, even though they might differ from you in important ways. Snook and coworkers (2007) found that many of the statements put out by profilers are Barnum-type statements, such as "the person has sexual concerns, has had conflicts with his family, and has trouble controlling his impulses when stress becomes overwhelming or things get very boring," or (in the case of a serial ax murderer), "the perpetrator has mental health issues." The problem is that such statements are likely to apply to a very large proportion of the criminal (as well as noncriminal) population. When such statements are later found to apply to the perpetrator of the crime, police and media may be impressed with the accuracy of the statements. Barnum-type statements can be generated by anyone who has studied criminals in general, but they do not typically provide the precision that is needed to find the needle in the haystack who committed the crime.

Some of the human reasoning fallacies described in Chapter 9 are also at work (Lilienfeld et al., 2010; Snook et al., 2008). One is *confirmation bias,* the common tendency to look for or selectively focus on information that is consistent with one's beliefs or wishes. Thus people who believe in the usefulness of profiling may selectively attend to the successful cases and ignore or fail to remember the more frequent instances in which profilers provided false descriptions of criminals. Profilers themselves may selectively remember their successes (*self-enhancement bias*) and become more confident in their ability to make correct predictions than they should be (the phenomenon of *overconfidence*).

So, what's the scientific verdict on criminal profiling? Particularly where traditional "clinical intuition" methods are concerned, there is little evidence that profiling provides consistently useful descriptions of criminals' personality characteristics. It is possible that new approaches that use more scientifically based statistical methods could improve the currently unimpressive picture (Goodwill et al., 2009). However, such methods will also bear the burden of demonstrating "beyond a reasonable doubt" that profiling greatly improves on what police already do to identify and apprehend criminals.

test yourself — Culture, Gender, and Personality Assessment

True or False?

1. People from an individualistic culture are more likely than those from a collectivistic culture to describe themselves in terms of stable personality traits.
2. In Western cultures, the female gender schema emphasizes emotional strength and self-sufficiency more than the male schema does.
3. Interjudge reliability is more important on projective tests than on personality scales.
4. The MMPI-2 was developed using the rational-theoretical approach.
5. Projective tests include the Rorschach and the Thematic Apperception Test.

ANSWERS: 1-true, 2-false, 3-true, 4-false, 5-true

Chapter Summary

WHAT IS PERSONALITY?

- Personality refers to the distinctive and relatively enduring ways of thinking, feeling, and acting that characterize a person's responses to life situations. Behaviors attributed to personality are viewed as establishing an individual's personal identity, having an internal cause, and having a meaningful organization and structure.
- Scientifically useful personality theories organize existing knowledge, allow the prediction of future events, and stimulate the discovery of new knowledge.

THE PSYCHODYNAMIC PERSPECTIVE

- The dynamics of personality involve continuous conflict between impulses of the id and counterforces of the ego and superego. To deal with threat, the ego may develop defense mechanisms to ward off anxiety and permit instinctual gratification in disguised forms.
- Freud believed that adult personality traits are molded by how children deal with instinctual urges and social reality during the oral, anal, and phallic stages.
- Neoanalytic theorists modified and extended Freud's ideas in important ways, stressing social and cultural factors in personality development. Object relations theorists focus on the mental representations that people form of themselves and other people.

THE PHENOMENOLOGICAL-HUMANISTIC PERSPECTIVE

- Humanistic theories emphasize the subjective experiences of the individual and thus deal with perceptual and cognitive processes. George Kelly's theory addresses the manner in which people differ in their constructions of reality by the personal constructs they use to categorize their experiences.

- Rogers's theory attaches central importance to the role of the self and an innate drive toward self-actualization. Experiences that are incongruous with the established self-concept produce threat and may result in a denial or distortion of reality. Conditional positive regard may result in unrealistic conditions of worth that can conflict with self-actualization. Rogers described a number of characteristics of the fully functioning person.
- Rogers's theory helped stimulate a great deal of research on the self-concept, including studies on the origins and effects of differences in self-esteem, self-enhancement and self-verification motives, and self-concept change. Recent humanistic developments include self-determination theory and the study of character strengths and virtues.

THE TRAIT PERSPECTIVE: MAPPING THE STRUCTURE OF PERSONALITY

- Trait theorists try to identify and measure the basic dimensions of personality, often employing factor analysis to find dimensions of personality. Cattell suggested 16 basic traits; other theorists insist that 5 (or even fewer) may be adequate. Prediction studies indicate that a larger number of more-specific traits may be superior for predicting behavior in specific situations.
- Traits have not proved to be highly consistent across situations, and they also vary in stability over time. Individual differences in self-monitoring tendencies influence the amount of cross-situational consistency people exhibit in social situations. Traits produce inconsistency by interacting not only with situations but also with one another.

BIOLOGICAL FOUNDATIONS OF PERSONALITY

- Genetic factors account for as much as half of the group variance in personality test scores, with individual experiences accounting for most of the remainder. Evolutionary theories of personality attribute some personality dispositions to genetically controlled mechanisms based on natural selection.
- In Eysenck's theory, Introversion-Extraversion reflects a person's customary level of arousal, whereas Stability-Instability represents the suddenness with which shifts in arousal occur.
- Differences in temperament appear early in life and are assumed to have a biological basis. Temperament is stable during childhood and into adulthood. Inhibited children and adults appear to have highly reactive amygdalas that trigger fear responses to unfamiliar people and situations.

THE SOCIAL-COGNITIVE PERSPECTIVE

- Social-cognitive theories are concerned with how social relationships, learning experiences, and cognitive processes jointly contribute to behavior. A key concept is reciprocal determinism, relating to two-way causal relations between people, their behavior, and the environment.
- Rotter viewed behavior as influenced by expectancies and the reinforcement value of potential outcomes. Locus of control is a generalized belief in the extent to which we can control the outcomes in our life.
- Bandura's concept of self-efficacy relates to our self-perceived ability to carry out the behaviors necessary to achieve goals in a particular situation. It is influenced by past performance attainments, verbal persuasion, observation of others' attainments, and perceived emotional arousal. Self-efficacy can be enhanced through the application of systematic goal-setting procedures.
- According to Mischel and Shoda, situational features activate the person's cognitive-affective personality system (CAPS). The CAPS involves individual differences in encoding strategies, expectancies and beliefs, goals

and values, affects, and competencies and self-regulation processes. The CAPS interacts with features of the environment, helping to explain why people have specific behavioral signatures and do not behave consistently across situations

CULTURE, GENDER, AND PERSONALITY

- Cultures differ along several important dimensions, including complexity, tightness, and individualism-collectivism, all of which can affect personality development.
- People from individualistic cultures tend to describe themselves in terms of personal traits, abilities, or dispositions, whereas those from collectivistic cultures are more likely to describe themselves in social identity terms.
- Gender schemas are organized mental structures that contain our understanding of the attributes and behaviors that are appropriate and expected for males and females. In Western cultures, men tend to value achievement, emotional strength, and self-sufficiency, whereas women prize interpersonal skills, kindness, and helpfulness to others.

PERSONALITY ASSESSMENT

- Methods used by psychologists to assess personality include the interview, behavioral assessment, remote behavior sampling, personality scales, and projective tests.
- The major approaches to constructing personality scales are the rational-theoretical approach, in which items are written on an intuitive basis, and the empirical approach, in which items discriminate between groups known to differ on the trait of interest.
- Projective tests present ambiguous stimuli to people. It is assumed that interpretations of such stimuli give clues to important internal processes. The Rorschach inkblot test and the Thematic Apperception Test are the most commonly used projective tests.
- Despite widespread belief in the value of criminal profiling, research reveals high levels of inaccuracy.

KEY TERMS AND CONCEPTS

Each term has been boldfaced and defined in the chapter on the page indicated in parentheses.

archetypes (p. 465)

Barnum effect (p. 500)

behavioral assessment (p. 496)

behavioral signatures (p. 489)

behavior-outcome expectancy (p. 488)

cognitive-affective personality system (CAPS) (p. 487)

collective unconscious (p. 465)

conditions of worth (p. 472)

congruence (p. 471)

defense mechanisms (p. 463)

ego (p. 462)

Electra complex (p. 464)

empirical approach (p. 497)

factor analysis (p. 475)

fixation (p. 464)

fully functioning persons (p. 472)

gender schemas (p. 493)

id (p. 462)

internal-external locus of control (p. 484)

Minnesota Multiphasic Personality Inventory-2 (MMPI-2) (p. 497)

need for positive regard (p. 471)

need for positive self-regard (p. 472)

neoanalytic theorists (p. 464)

NEO Personality Inventory (NEO-PI) (p. 497)

thinking **critically**

IS SELF-ACTUALIZATION A USEFUL SCIENTIFIC CONSTRUCT? (Page 472)

Self-actualization is a centerpiece of some humanistic theories, but it is troublesome from a scientific perspective. Some critics believe that it is impossible to define an individual's actualizing tendency except in terms of the behavior that it supposedly produces. This would be an example of circular reasoning: Why did the person achieve such success? Because of self-actualization. How do we know self-actualization was at work? Because the person achieved great success.

Unless a construct can be operationally defined in a manner independent of the phenomenon it is supposed to cause, it is not scientifically useful. A construct must also be measurable. While it is true that concepts related to the self-actualization motive (such as people's beliefs that they are fulfilling their potential) could potentially be measured, most psychologists suggest that rather than being a scientific construct, self-actualization is better considered a philosophical concept.

14

Health and Well-Being

CHAPTER OUTLINE

Myth or Reality?

College Binge Drinking Is Harmless Fun
(page 514)

Heavy drinking among college students is commonplace. Is binging a harmless aspect of college life, as most students believe, or is it dangerous behavior? Scientific studies help reveal the facts.

Priscilla, now 18, had anything but an idyllic childhood. She grew up in an impoverished inner-city home with an alcoholic father who physically and sexually abused her and her younger sister. Priscilla's mother, too helpless and fearful to protect her children, was hospitalized twice for "nervous breakdowns." When Priscilla was 8 years old, a neighbor who suspected the sexual abuse reported the father to Child Protective Services. Upon being notified of the impending investigation, Priscilla's father called his family together in the living room and told them, "You drove me to this." He then put a gun to his head and committed suicide as his wife and children watched in horror. From that point on, Priscilla had to work after school to help support her family. For a time, the family was homeless and lived in a shelter. Her mother became increasingly disturbed and sometimes beat her.

Given her life circumstances, how could Priscilla become anything except an unhappy, maladjusted person, her emotional life dominated by anxiety, anger, and depression? Instead, she grew into a delightful and popular young woman who was emotionally well adjusted, president of her high school class, a talented singer, and an honor student who was awarded a scholarship to an Ivy League university.

*   *   *

In his book *Persuasion and Healing,* psychiatrist Jerome Frank (1961) described a treatment performed by the German physician Hans Rehder on three bedridden patients. One patient had an inflamed gallbladder and chronic gallstones. The second was having difficulty recovering from pancreatic surgery and had experienced such severe weight loss that Rehder described her as "skeletal." The third patient was dying from a painful uterine cancer that had spread throughout her body.

Conventional medicine had done all that was possible for the women, so Rehder decided to try the unconventional. He told the women that he had discovered a powerful faith healer who could cure with remarkable success simply by directing his healing power to a particular place. Rehder told each woman that he had arranged for this healing power to be projected to her room at a specific time and date. In truth, he had already tried the healer without telling the women, and there had been no change in their conditions.

To Rehder's astonishment, within a few days after the appointed healing date, the patient with gallstones lost all of her symptoms, returned home, and remained symptom-free for a year. The woman who had been wasting away began to eat and subsequently gained 30 pounds. The patient with cancer was already a terminal case, but her bloated body soon excreted excess fluids, she gained strength, and her blood count improved. She was able to return home and lived for 3 months in relative comfort.

From a scientific perspective, the first story raises these questions: How common is the resilience seen in Priscilla also found in other children? What factors are responsible for such resilience? And can we increase resilience in people? A scientist would find the second story fascinating but would want to know whether the "mind over body" results Rehder reported can be replicated under controlled scientific conditions and, if so, what the biological processes are that produce such startling effects. We'll address the questions about resilience beginning on page 525 and about pain and illness starting on page 535.

These cases illustrate some of the intriguing phenomena studied in the field of *health psychology*. Children like Priscilla have been termed "invulnerable" or "resilient" youngsters because they somehow develop normally or even exceptionally in the face of great adversity (Garmezy, 1983; Masten, 2001). What allows resilient people to rise above extraordinarily stressful environments while other individuals, blessed with more benign life histories, collapse under the weight of relatively minor stresses? And what are we to think of the dramatic physical changes that followed Rehder's invocation of the faith healer's curative powers? How can mind triumph over body to such a degree? Can a simple belief that one will be healed stop illness in its tracks? The answers to these questions will show us that adapting to the demands and challenges in our lives involves complex interactions between the person, the environment, and behavior. Figure 14.1 previews some of the biological, psychological, and environmental factors that influence our health and well-being.

Health psychology *addresses factors that influence well-being and illness, as well as measures that can be taken to promote health and prevent illness.* It therefore confronts many of the leading problems of our times. For example, because stress has negative effects on both physical and psychological well-being, the study of stress and coping is a central focus of health psychology (Elovainio

& Kivimaki, 2009; Hampson & Friedman, 2008). Pain is another important topic because it is a central feature of many illnesses and a major stressor. Health psychologists explore factors that influence pain perceptions and develop psychological interventions to reduce people's suffering. As we shall see, they also develop and evaluate health-promotion and disease-prevention programs.

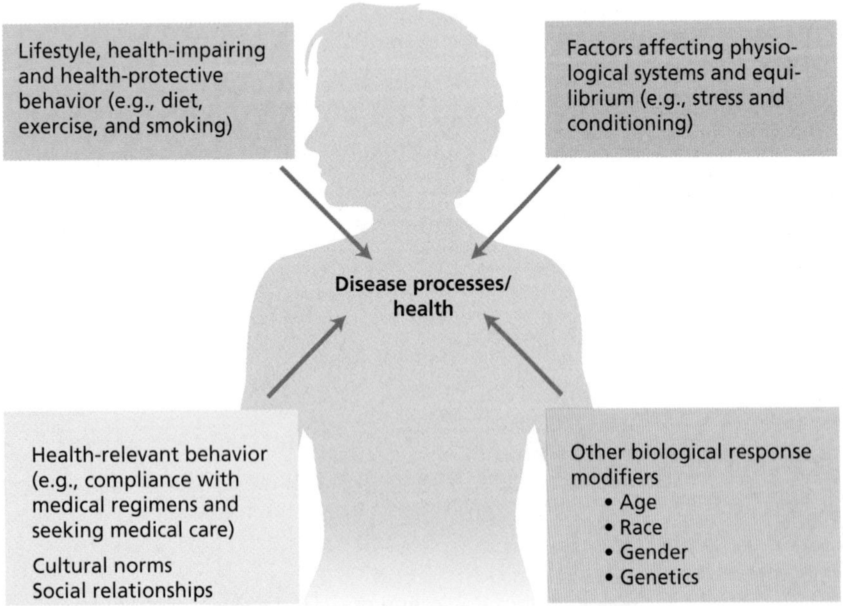

BEHAVIORAL FOUNDATIONS OF HEALTH

In 1979, the Surgeon General of the United States issued a landmark report titled *Healthy People* (U.S. Public Health Service, 1979). The report concluded that improvements in the health of Americans are more likely to result from efforts to prevent disease and promote healthy behaviors than from new drugs and medical technologies. Two recent U.S. government reports, *Healthy People 2010* and *Health, United States 2008*, provide strong evidence for that assertion.

Consider today's leading causes of death in the United States and Europe in comparison with the leading killers in 1900. As Figure 14.2 shows, the leading culprits have changed from influenza, pneumonia, tuberculosis, and gastroenteritis to heart disease, cancer, and stroke. The major killers of the early 1900s have been largely controlled by medical advances. In contrast, the death rate has almost doubled for heart disease and tripled for cancer since 1900. As shown in Table 14.1, these diseases and today's other killers are strongly influenced by behavioral factors. Health authorities estimate that half of all cases of early mortality (deaths occurring prior to the life-expectancy age within a culture) from the 10 leading causes of death can be traced to risky behaviors, such as cigarette smoking, excessive alcohol consumption, insufficient exercise, poor dietary habits, use of illicit drugs, failure to adhere to doctors' instructions, unsafe sex practices, and failure to wear automobile seat belts (Mokdad et al., 2004).

Recognition of the crucial role that behavior plays in health maintenance has prompted much research in the field of health psychology. Psychologists have helped identify many of the psychological and social causes for risky health behaviors, and the clear need for lifestyle interventions has spurred attempts around the world to promote positive changes in such behaviors (Suls & Wallston, 2003; Taylor, 2009). Modifying

Figure 14.1

Biological, psychological, and environmental factors that contribute to disease processes and health.

Source: Adapted from Baum, 1994.

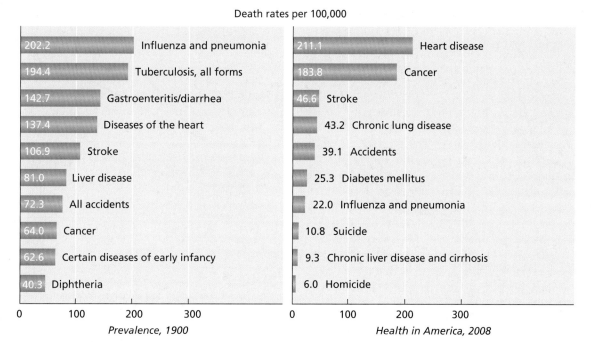

Death rates per 100,000

Prevalence, 1900
- 202.2 Influenza and pneumonia
- 194.4 Tuberculosis, all forms
- 142.7 Gastroenteritis/diarrhea
- 137.4 Diseases of the heart
- 106.9 Stroke
- 81.0 Liver disease
- 72.3 All accidents
- 64.0 Cancer
- 62.6 Certain diseases of early infancy
- 40.3 Diphtheria

Health in America, 2008
- 211.1 Heart disease
- 183.8 Cancer
- 46.6 Stroke
- 43.2 Chronic lung disease
- 39.1 Accidents
- 25.3 Diabetes mellitus
- 22.0 Influenza and pneumonia
- 10.8 Suicide
- 9.3 Chronic liver disease and cirrhosis
- 6.0 Homicide

Figure 14.2

Causes of death, 1900 versus 2008.
Modern causes of death are far more attributable to health-endangering behaviors. Sources: Based on Murphy, 2000; Sexton, 1979; and National Center for Health Statistics, 2008.

people's health behaviors as a form of illness prevention can reduce medical costs and avert the physical and psychological distress that illness produces.

Health-related behaviors fall into two main categories. *Health-enhancing behaviors* serve to maintain or increase health. Such behaviors include exercise, healthy dietary habits, safe sexual practices, regular medical checkups, and breast and testicular self-examination. *Health-threatening behaviors* promote the development of illness. They include tobacco use, fatty diets, a sedentary lifestyle, and unprotected sexual activity. Behavioral health-promotion efforts involve increasing health-enhancing behaviors and reducing health-threatening ones. As we shall see, psychologists have developed programs that focus on both classes of behavior.

Health-Enhancing Behaviors

During the 1970s, the role of behavior in maintaining health and living longer became evident as researchers began to study the effects of lifestyle. Figure 14.3 shows the results of one longitudinal study of nearly 7,000 adults. The researchers studied the relation of seven good-health practices to life expectancy. These included

Table 14.1 | **Behavioral Risk Factors for the Five Leading Causes of Death in the United States**

Disease	Risk Factors
Heart disease	Tobacco, obesity, elevated blood pressure, cholesterol, sedentary lifestyle
Cancer	Tobacco, improper diet, alcohol, environmental exposure
Cerebrovascular disease (stroke)	Tobacco, elevated blood pressure, cholesterol, sedentary lifestyle
Chronic lung disease	Tobacco, environmental exposure
Accidental injuries	Safety belt nonuse, alcohol, home hazards

Source: Based on McGinnis, 1994.

7 to 8 hours of sleep per day, eating breakfast, not smoking, rarely eating between meals, being at or near one's prescribed body weight, engaging in regular physical activity, and drinking only small to moderate amounts of alcohol. For men and women alike, these behaviors predicted a longer life. A higher mortality rate among those with poor health practices began to appear in men between the ages of 45 and 64 and in women between 55 and 64 (Belloc, 1973). Let's examine some of these health-enhancing behaviors and what can be done to increase them.

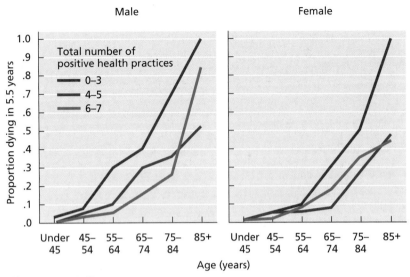

Figure 14.3

Healthy habits and longevity.

These data show the relation between the number of positive health practices and longevity in men and women. Those who adhered to few of the health practices experienced earlier mortality, with the pattern appearing earlier in men than in women. Source: Adapted from Belloc, 1973.

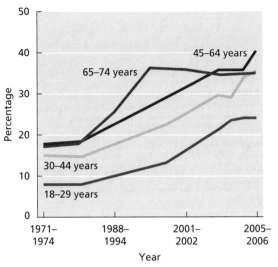

Figure 14.4

Among all American age groups, obesity has increased dramatically in the past 40 years. Source: National Center for Health Statistics, 2008.

Exercise

The couch potato lives! (But apparently not as long.) A sedentary lifestyle is a significant risk factor for health problems, including coronary heart disease and obesity (National Center for Health Statistics, 2008; Taylor, 2009). *Health, United States, 2008,* produced by the U.S. Centers for Disease Control and the National Center for Health Statistics, provides some telling statistics. Despite the widely publicized warnings about physical inactivity, only a third of Americans over age 18 engage in regular physical activity, and only one in five does strength or resistance training. As fewer people now engage in vigorous manual labor, inactivity has helped double the rate of obesity since 1900, despite a 10 percent decrease in daily caloric intake over the same period. Figure 14.4 shows the progressive increase in obesity among Americans of all age groups since 1971.

Aerobic exercise *is sustained activity, such as jogging, swimming, and bicycling, that elevates the heart rate and increases the body's need for oxygen.* This kind of exercise has many physical benefits. In a body that is well conditioned by regular aerobic exercise, the heart beats more slowly and efficiently, oxygen is better utilized, slow-wave sleep increases, cholesterol levels may be reduced, physiological adaptation to stressors is enhanced, and more calories are burned (deGeus, 2000).

Exercise is associated with physical health and longevity (Figure 14.5). A study that followed 17,000 Harvard undergraduates into middle age revealed that death rates were one-quarter to

one-third lower among moderate exercisers than among those in a less active group of the same age. Surprisingly, extremely high levels of exercise were not associated with enhanced health; instead, moderate exercise (burning 2,000 to 3,500 calories per week) on a regular basis produced the best health benefits (Paffenbarger et al., 1986). Performing at 70 to 85 percent of maximal heart

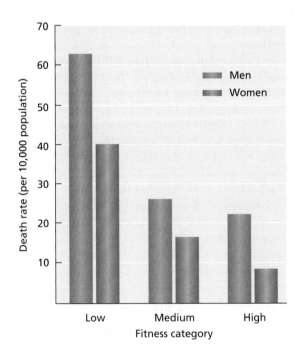

Figure 14.5

Aerobic exercise and health.

Aerobic exercise is an important health-enhancing behavior, contributing to physical well-being. Significantly higher death rates occur for both men and women who are low in physical fitness. Source: Data from Blair et al., 1989.

rate nonstop for 15 minutes three times a week significantly reduces risk for coronary heart disease (Dishman, 1982; National Center for Health Statistics, 2008). Such exercise also has positive psychological effects, reducing depression and anxiety (Morgan, 1997).

Despite the demonstrated benefits of regular exercise, people in developed countries have a strong tendency to either avoid or discontinue it after a short period. In the United States, for example, only one fourth of the adult population exercises at levels high enough to maintain cardiorespiratory fitness and reduce the risk of premature death (Ehrman, 2003). When employers offer exercise programs to their employees, it is uncommon for more than 30 percent to participate, and dropout rates of 50 percent within 6 months are found in virtually all exercise programs that have been studied (Chenoweth, 2002; Dishman, 1994). On the other hand, people who are able to persist for 3 to 6 months are likely to continue as exercise becomes a healthy habit (McAuley, 1992).

What factors predict dropout? This is an important research question, for if we can identify the risk factors, we can take measures to counteract them. Research has shown that general attitudes toward physical fitness do *not* predict adherence or dropout. The exercise-related attitudes of dropouts and people who adhere to their exercise programs are equally favorable (Suls & Wallston, 2003). However, low self-efficacy for success in exercising regularly ("I can't do this"), Type A behavior pattern ("Sorry, too busy to exercise"), inflated estimates of current physical fitness ("I'm already in great shape from walking from my couch to the refrigerator"), and inactive leisure-time pursuits (such as watching television and walking to the refrigerator) all predict dropout (Martin & Dubbert, 1985; Wilcox & Storandt, 1996). The strongest social-environmental factor related to dropout is lack of social support from friends, family, or other exercisers (Ehrman, 2003).

Psychologists have been able to increase compliance by helping exercisers identify these impediments and prepare specific strategies to deal with them before they occur (Rosen, 2000; Simkin & Gross, 1994). These include setting specific goals and writing contracts that promise adherence. A person who anticipates feeling too tired to work out at the end of the day might prepare a set of self-statements about how much better she will feel after exercising. If she is not receiving social support and encouragement from others, she could also arrange for a pleasurable activity after her workout to positively reinforce her exercising (Courneya, 1995).

Diet and Weight Control

Obesity (being more than 20 percent overweight) is becoming an increasingly urgent problem. Since 1960, the incidence of obesity among American adults has increased from 13 percent to 34 percent. Today, 19 percent of children 6 to 11 years of age are overweight, compared with only 7 percent in 1980, and the corresponding figure among 12- to 19-year-olds has more than tripled, from 5 percent to 17 percent (National Center for Health Statistics, 2008). If current trends continue, obesity's death toll will soon exceed 500,000 each year in the United States alone (Mokdad et al., 2004). *Health, United States, 2008,* reported that 16 percent of Americans have dangerously high serum cholesterol and 10 percent have developed diabetes, which can result in blindness, amputations, and early death. Both are related to obesity and dietary habits.

Obesity is a risk factor for a variety of chronic diseases, such as cardiovascular disease, kidney disease, and diabetes. Women who are 30 percent overweight are more than 3 times more likely to develop heart disease than normal-weight women (Manson et al., 1990). For reasons yet unknown, fat that is localized in the abdomen is a far greater risk factor for cardiovascular disease, diabetes, and cancer than is excessive fat in the hips, thighs, or buttocks (Taylor, 2009). Accumulation of abdominal fat is increased by yo-yo dieting, which results in big weight fluctuations (Figure 14.6). Such dieting markedly increases the risk of dying from cardiovascular disease, an excellent reason to avoid this practice (Hafen & Hoeger, 1998; Rodin et al., 1990).

Psychologists have developed intervention programs for weight control. Were you to enroll in a behavioral program for weight loss, here is what would happen: The program would begin with a period of self-monitoring, during which you would keep careful records of what, how much, and under what circumstances you eat. This is designed to make you more aware of your eating habits and to identify situational factors (antecedents) that affect your food intake. You would then learn to take control over those antecedents. For example, you would learn to make low-calorie foods, such as raw vegetables, freely available and to limit high-calorie foods in the house. You would then learn stimulus-control techniques, such as confining your eating to one location in the house and eating only at certain times of the day. Because overeaters tend to wolf down their food and overload their stomachs, you would also learn to slow down your eating

Figure 14.6

Extreme dieting, coupled with difficulty in maintaining weight-reduction behaviors, can result in large weight fluctuations that can endanger health.

by putting down eating utensils until each bite is chewed and swallowed, and you would learn to pause between mouthfuls. These behaviors reduce food intake and help you learn to pay attention to how full you are. You would also be told to savor each mouthful of food. The goal is to eat less but enjoy it more. Finally, you would learn to chart the amount of food you eat to provide constant feedback, and you would arrange to positively reinforce yourself for successful performance. These behavioral practices would be combined with nutritional guidelines to help you eat a healthier diet. Table 14.2 shows specific

guidelines from a highly successful weight-reduction program developed by Yale psychologist Kelly Brownell (1994).

Research shows that the addition of an exercise program increases the positive effects of behavioral eating-control programs (Avenell et al., 2004; Wadden et al., 1997). High levels of physical activity are associated with initial weight loss and its maintenance, and exercise adds to the effectiveness of other weight-loss methods, such as dietary change. Research indicates that many overweight people are able to attain gradual weight loss of about 2 pounds per week for up to 20 weeks and to keep the weight off for 2 years and beyond (Jackson et al., 1999; Taylor, 2009).

Health-Threatening Behaviors

We now turn our attention to several types of health-impairing behaviors. We begin with a class of behavior that two decades ago was not considered a major health threat. Next, we discuss risky sexual behaviors that threaten people's physical and psychological well-being, as well as a number of serious sexually transmitted diseases, including one that mysteriously emerged in the early 1980s. Following that, we will examine the persistent personal and societal problem of substance abuse.

Table **14.2** | **A Sample of Effective Behavioral Weight-Control Techniques**

Keep an eating diary	Keep problem foods out of sight
Examine your eating patterns	Serve and eat one portion at a time
Prevent automatic eating	Use gradual shaping for behavior change
Examine triggers for eating	Distinguish hunger from cravings
Do nothing else while eating	Focus on behavior, not weight loss
Eat in one place	Cope positively with slips, lapses
Put your fork down between bites	Keep an exercise diary
Pause during the meal	Understand the benefits of exercise
Shop on a full stomach	Know calorie values of various exercise activities
Buy foods that require preparation	Program exercise activity

Source: Based on Brownell, 1994.

Type A Behavior Pattern

The Type A behavior pattern was discovered by an upholsterer working on the office chairs of a physician who specialized in treating heart attack victims. The upholsterer noticed an unusual wear pattern at the front of the seats, not the back, indicating that the patients were constantly sitting on the edges of their seats and moving about.

This edge-of-the-seat pattern typifies the behaviors seen in people with the **Type A behavior pattern,** *who tend to live under great pressure and demand much of themselves and others.* Many Type A people are workaholics, continually striving to get more done in less time. Type A people are also characterized by high levels of competitiveness and ambition, which can foster aggressiveness and hostility when things get in their way (Figure 14.7). In contrast, people labeled Type B show the opposite pattern of patience, serenity, and lack of time urgency.

Several large-scale studies suggest that even when other physical risk factors, such as obesity and smoking, are taken into account, Type A men and women have about double the risk for coronary heart disease (CHD) compared with less driven people (Hampson & Friedman, 2008; Rosenman et al., 1975). However, research indicates that not all components of the Type A pattern increase vulnerability to CHD. The Type A person's fast-paced, time-conscious lifestyle and high ambition apparently are not the culprits. Rather, the crucial component seems to be negative emotions, particularly anger. The Type A behavior pattern virtually guarantees that these people will encounter many stressful situations, such as time pressures of their own making and frustrations that anger them. A cynical hostility marked by suspiciousness, resentment, frequent anger, distrust, and antagonism is likely to alienate others, produce interpersonal stress and conflict, and reduce the amount of social support the person receives. In addition, Type A people tend to overreact physiologically to stressful events and take longer to recover, a biological factor that may contribute to their tendency to develop heart disease (Taylor, 2009). John Hunter, a combative 18th-century pioneer in cardiovascular medicine, recognized his own vulnerability when he said, "My life is in the hands of any rascal who chooses to put me in a passion." Hunter's statement proved to be prophetic; he died of a heart attack during an angry debate at a hospital board meeting.

Risky Sexual Behaviors

For many people, sexual behavior is an important source of relationship satisfaction and pleasure. It

Figure 14.7

Studies of the hard-driving Type A behavior pattern have shown that the most damaging aspect is the negative emotions, particularly anger and hostility, that Type A people experience.

also has important implications for both psychological and physical well-being. On the negative side, unsafe sexual practices can result in unwanted pregnancies in mothers who are not prepared or mature enough to care for their offspring properly. In the United States, approximately 750,000 adolescents become pregnant each year, most of them unintended (National Center for Health Statistics, 2008). Unintended teen pregnancies have major negative implications for the educational and financial prospects of the teen mother, as the father frequently relinquishes the care of the child to the mother.

Unsafe sexual behaviors are also a source of sexually transmitted diseases (STDs), which now afflict one in six American adults (National Center for Health Statistics, 2008). These include syphilis, gonorrhea, and genital herpes, all of which can have major negative social and health implications. Some of these infections are on the rise. The incidence of *chlamydia* infections, a major cause of various genital and eye diseases that can cause serious damage to the reproductive systems of both males and females if left untreated, has tripled since 1990 and is the most frequently seen STD. Public health officials know that the most effective safeguard against STDs (aside from abstinence) is the use of condoms. Intervention studies have shown that fear appeals are relatively ineffective means of increasing condom use. The most effective programs emphasize putting on condoms as part of foreplay, role-playing the importance of always using condoms, and building self-efficacy in practicing safe sex (Albarracin et al., 2006).

On June 5, 1981, the Centers for Disease Control reported the first case of *acquired immune deficiency syndrome (AIDS)*. In the decades that followed, AIDS grew from an unknown disease into a devastating worldwide epidemic for which no medical cure has been found. According to the World Health Organization (2004), about 16,000 new infections occur each day. Worldwide, 1 in every 100 adults between the ages of 15 and 49 is infected with the HIV virus that causes AIDS, and the disease has so far claimed the lives of nearly 20 million people. Of the 3.1 million people who died from AIDS in 2004, 37 percent were women and 20 percent were children. In some countries of southern Africa, 25 to 40 percent of the population is infected, including a third of all pregnant women. Globally, only 5 to 10 percent of the cases now occur in homosexual men (the population typically identified with the affliction), and by the early 2000s, women comprised half of all HIV cases (United Nations, 2002). After 2000, rates of infection began to rise again among homosexual men in North America, Europe, and Australia due to increases in risky sexual behavior and a false sense of security due to new medications. On a global level, the AIDS epidemic threatens to overwhelm the world's health-care financing and delivery systems.

AIDS is caused by the *human immunodeficiency virus (HIV)*, which cripples the immune system. The patient then becomes vulnerable to invading viruses, bacteria, and tumors, which are the actual killers. Because the HIV virus evolves rapidly, vaccines are at present ineffective in preventing its spread. Moreover, the incubation period between initial HIV infection and the appearance of AIDS symptoms may be as long as 10 years, meaning that an infected person may unknowingly pass the virus on to many other people. The major modes of transmission are direct exposure to infected semen, vaginal fluids, and blood through either heterosexual or homosexual contact; the sharing of infected needles in intravenous drug use; and exposure to infected blood through transfusion or in the womb. Breast milk is also a major means of transmission through which many women have unknowingly transmitted the HIV virus to their children.

In the absence of a vaccine or cure, the only existing means of controlling the AIDS epidemic is by changing the high-risk behaviors that transmit the virus. In this respect, AIDS is as much a psychological problem as a medical one. Prevention programs are typically designed to (1) educate people concerning the risks that attend certain behaviors, such as unprotected sex; (2) motivate people to change their behavior and convince them that they can do so; (3) provide specific guidelines for changing the risky behaviors and teach the skills needed for change; and (4) give support and encouragement for the desired changes.

Early AIDS interventions were directed at homosexual men, who were originally the major at-risk group. In this population, a primary mechanism of HIV transmission is anal intercourse without the use of a condom. In one successful prevention study (Kelly et al., 1989), 42 homosexual men went through a program that instructed them on the risks accompanying unprotected intercourse, helped them develop and rehearse strategies for avoiding high-risk situations (such as sexual relations with strangers), and taught them how to be more assertive in refusing to engage in high-risk behaviors. Another group of 43 homosexual men also completed the program after initially serving as an untreated control group.

Both groups were assessed before and after the first group went through the program and then were followed for 8 months after completing the program to assess long-term behavior changes. As Figure 14.8 shows, the intervention program resulted in a substantial and lasting increase in the use of condoms during sexual activity. A more recent study of homeless HIV-positive adults resulted in treated patients (as compared to an

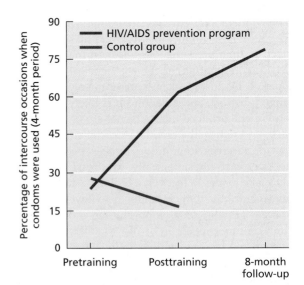

Figure 14.8

Effects of an AIDS prevention program.

An AIDS prevention program for homosexual men increased their use of condoms during sexual activity. The program educated the men on the risks involved in sexual behaviors (especially unprotected sex), promoted the use of condoms, and taught them coping skills to deal with high-risk situations. Source: Based on Kelly et al., 1989.

untreated control group) engaging in 34 percent fewer risky sexual acts and 72 percent fewer sexual encounters with partners who were HIV-negative or of unknown status (Rotheram-Borus et al., 2008). Another target for interventions is heterosexual women, who not only are the fastest-growing segment of the HIV population but who also have the potential to infect their babies if they become pregnant.

A combination of increased sense of vulnerability to HIV infection and confidence in one's ability to use condoms produces the highest levels of protection motivation and intention to use condoms. However, threat appeals should be combined with feasible and effective coping strategies, take into account the listeners' readiness for change, and address the common complaint that condom use decreases sexual pleasure (Sturges et al., 2009).

Even when something as urgent as AIDS prevention is involved, the success of prevention programs depends on the extent to which the social system supports the desired changes. When sexual abstinence or the use of condoms runs contrary to the values of an individual or cultural group, people may continue to engage in high-risk behaviors even though they have been informed of the dangers involved (Morales, 2009). Likewise, within both homosexual and heterosexual populations, and particularly among adolescents and young adults, many individuals continue to have an irrational sense of invulnerability to infection, and this belief contributes to a failure to abstain from sex or to engage in protected sexual practices (Kelly, 2001). Counteracting these barriers to safe sexual behavior is a major challenge for health psychologists. One successful approach to this problem was a program described in the Chapter 7 "Research Close-up," in which modeling procedures were transmitted through an engaging radio drama to promote safe sex in Tanzania (Bandura, 2000).

Substance Abuse

Substance abuse exacts a fearsome toll on society. Tobacco use harms smokers and those who breathe their secondhand smoke. Smoking ranks as the single largest cause of preventable death, killing nearly half a million Americans each year (Mokdad et al., 2004). Currently, 23 percent of U.S. men and 19 percent of U.S. women are smokers (National Center for Health Statistics, 2008). Although tobacco use has leveled off in the United States since 1985, tobacco products have been aggressively marketed in other countries, and sales have nearly doubled over the past 15 years. The coming decades will

therefore witness an increase in the diseases caused by smoking, particularly in developing countries that are ill equipped to provide good prevention programs and medical treatment.

Alcohol abuse also contributes enormously to human suffering. In the United States alone, alcohol abuse costs more than $100 billion a year in decreased work productivity and treatment costs and $13.8 billion in alcohol-related automobile accidents (National Center for Health Statistics, 2008). Alcohol is implicated in half of all fatal automobile accidents and is a leading factor in industrial and farm accidents (Figure 14.9). Alcohol abuse is also highly damaging to one's health. Death rates among those who abuse alcohol are 2 to 4 times higher for men and 3 to 7 times higher for women, depending on the disease in question. Life expectancy is reduced by 10 to 12 years (National Center for Health Statistics, 2008). Alcohol affects the welfare of others as well. Some children are born with fetal alcohol syndrome, and others are subjected to disruptive family relationships, including domestic violence. For every person who has a problem with alcohol, an average of four other people's lives are adversely affected on a daily basis (Levinthal, 1996).

Other varieties of substance abuse also have adverse effects. Many crimes are committed by users of illicit drugs in order to support their habit (Kendall, 1998). Moreover, substance abuse is highly associated with psychological disorders, often being part of a larger pattern of maladjustment in both adolescents and adults (Miller & Brown, 1997).

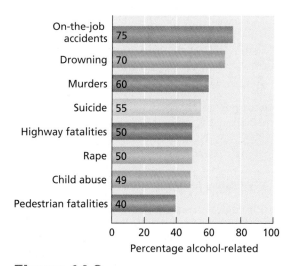

Figure 14.9

Societal costs of alcohol abuse.
This graph shows the percentage of common negative events that are alcohol-related. Source: Based on Carroll, 1993.

Myth or Reality?

College Binge Drinking Is Harmless Fun

Drinking may be a popular way to blow off steam after a grueling week of classes or to celebrate the victory of a sports team. The consumption of beer and mixed drinks is commonplace in social settings on and off campus. Many students view heavy-drinking parties as a natural part of college life, like going to classes or athletic events. Studies have found that many heavy-drinking students, who average 40 to 50 drinks per week, do not view their behavior as either abnormal or problematic (Mitka, 2009).

And why should they? Hasn't college always been this way? The 1978 film *Animal House* chronicled wild college parties of the early 1960s. The parents of many of today's college students may well have participated in the same alcohol-induced rites of passage as college students themselves. Sure, some people get into trouble with the law or get injured, but that would happen whether or not students were drinking heavily, right?

Students themselves don't think it's an issue. In one national study by the Harvard School of Public Health, binge drinking was defined as having more than 4 (for women) or 5 (for men) drinks at a time on at least three occasions during the previous 2 weeks (Wechsler et al., 2000, 2002). Data from 14,000 students at 119 U.S.

colleges revealed that 50 percent of the men and 40 percent of the women met this binging criterion. Although 36 percent of the men and 25 percent of the women reported being drunk 3 or more times in the past month, fewer than 1 percent of them saw themselves as having an alcohol problem.

Binge drinking in college is harmless. That's the myth. In reality, heavy-drinking students are placing themselves at considerable risk. As the Harvard study showed, the dangerous consequences of their drinking became clear when binge drinkers were asked about alcohol-related problems (Table 14.3).

Frequent binge drinkers were 7 to 10 times more likely than moderate drinkers to engage in unplanned and unprotected sexual intercourse, to suffer injuries, to drive under the influence of alcohol, to damage property, and to get into trouble with the law. At schools with the highest alcohol-consumption rates, nondrinkers and moderate drinkers were 2 to 3 times more likely to report physical assault, sexual harassment, destruction of their property, and interruption of their sleep and studying by heavy drinkers. So, while common belief may have it that heavy drinking is harmless fun, scientific findings suggest otherwise.

Table **14.3** | Percentage of College Students Reporting Drinking-Related Problems

Drinking-Related Problem	Nonbinge Drinkers N = 5,063	Occasional Binge Drinkers N = 2,962	Frequent Binge Drinkers N = 3,135
Get behind in schoolwork	9.8	26.0	46.3
Did something I regret	18.0	39.6	62.0
Forgot where I was or what I did	10.0	27.2	54.0
Arguments or fights	9.7	23.0	42.6
Had unplanned sex	7.8	22.3	41.5
Had unprotected sex	3.7	9.8	20.4
Damaged property	2.3	8.9	22.7
Trouble with police	1.4	5.2	12.7
Get hurt or injured	3.9	10.9	26.6
Drove after drinking	18.6	39.7	56.7
Reported 5 or more alcohol-related problems	3.5	16.6	48.0

NOTE: Occasional binge drinkers binged 1 to 2 times in the past 2 weeks; frequent binge drinkers binged more than 3 times in the same period.
SOURCE: Data from Wechsler et al., 2000, 2002.

Interventions for Substance Abuse

Psychological principles discussed in earlier chapters have been successfully applied to the treatment of smoking, problem drinking, and drug use (Taylor, 2009). Several approaches have proven effective in facilitating positive behavior change.

Motivational Interviewing If smokers, problem drinkers, drug abusers, and others who practice self-defeating behaviors are to change, they must increase their awareness of their problems, have a desire to take action, and believe that they can change (Miller & Rose, 2009). Rather than confronting the person with his or her problem (which often drives away people who need help), the technique of **motivational interviewing** *leads the person to his or her own conclusion by asking questions that focus on discrepancies between the current* *state of affairs and the individual's ideal self-image, desired behaviors, and desired outcomes.* Focusing on these discrepancies may help motivate change. Consider the following exchange:

> *Client:* I really don't believe I have a drinking problem.
>
> *Counselor:* You're the best judge of that. May I ask how many drinks you have a day?
>
> *Client:* Oh, it varies. Probably 5 or 6.
>
> *Counselor:* Is that about what you'd like to be drinking?
>
> *Client:* Well, I'd probably be better off if I cut down a little—maybe to 3 or 4.
>
> *Counselor:* How would that be helpful to you?
>
> *Client:* Well, I could study better and reduce the arguments with my roommate. I can get pretty nasty when I'm buzzed. I hate being nasty. I'm not that kind of person. Our relationship is going downhill, and I'd hate to lose a friend.
>
> *Counselor:* Well, you know, you don't have to have a big problem in order to want to make a change. I'm sure you could do so if you really want to.
>
> *Client:* I can see that I'd be more the person I want to be if I worked on this.
>
> *Counselor:* And I'd be happy to help you make your change.

Following a client's decision to pursue behavior change, the counselor helps the client set specific goals and select from a menu of behavior-change strategies the ones he or she would like to employ. Thereafter, the counselor provides feedback and support for the client's efforts.

Motivational interviewing has proven to be an effective and low-cost treatment approach for substance abusers (Miller & Rollnick, 2002). In one large-scale study of alcohol-abuse patients, a 4-session motivational interviewing intervention proved to be as effective as a 12-session program modeled on Alcoholics Anonymous (Project MATCH Research Group, 1997). More than 20 other studies have demonstrated the effectiveness of motivational interviewing with problem drinkers (Vasilaki et al., 2006).

Multimodal Treatments   All substance-abuse behaviors are resistant to change—and for good reason. Some people may be more vulnerable than others because of genetic factors, which may account for 50 percent of the population variance in alcoholism vulnerability (Ducci & Goldman, 2008). Craving, caused by either psychological need or physical dependence, is a huge barrier to overcome. Negative emotions, such as anxiety, irritability, or depression, are temporary results of abstinence that cause many who quit successfully to have relapses. Past conditioning may create stimuli that trigger the behavior in certain common situations. For example, coffee drinking or social situations are linked with smoking for many individuals, thus encouraging lapses in behavioral control when those stimuli are present. The numerous factors that encourage smoking, drinking, or drug abuse make these behaviors very hard to change. Psychologists are therefore willing to combine anything that has proven effective into what they hope will be a more powerful behavior-change package to apply when people are ready to make a change. These **multimodal treatments** *often combine biological measures* (e.g., the use of nicotine patches to help smokers quit), *with psychological measures* such as the following:

- Aversion therapy, in which the undesired behavior is associated with an aversive stimulus, such as electric shock or a nausea-producing drug, in an attempt to create a negative emotional response to the currently pleasurable substance

- Relaxation and stress-management training, which help the person adapt to and deal with stressful situations, including a procedure called mindfulness meditation, which has become an important tool in the treatment of addictive behaviors (McCown & Reibel, 2010)

- Self-monitoring procedures that help the person identify the antecedents and consequences of the abuse behaviors

- Coping and social-skills training for dealing with high-risk situations that trigger abuse

- Marital and family counseling to reduce conflicts and increase social support for change

- Positive-reinforcement procedures to strengthen change

This broad-based multimodal approach appears to produce favorable outcomes for many people who have substance addictions. Despite some encouraging results, however, typical treatment results are less favorable: long-term maintenance of behavior changes often occurs in fewer than 30 percent of treated individuals, whether the target behavior is smoking, drinking, or some other substance abuse (Ockene et al., 2001). The goal of many researchers is therefore to develop more effective treatment packages.

Harm-Reduction Approaches Substance abuse not only has negative effects on physical well-being but often results in other severe consequences, such as self-defeating sexual and aggressive behaviors. **Harm reduction** *is a prevention strategy that is designed not to eliminate a problem behavior but rather to reduce the harmful effects of that behavior when it occurs* (MacCoun, 1998; Weingardt & Marlatt, 1998). In the area of drug abuse, harm-reduction approaches include needle and syringe exchange programs to reduce the spread of HIV infections. Another example is methadone maintenance programs for heroin addicts, which are targeted at reducing addicts' need to engage in criminal activity to feed their heroin habits. The reasoning is that even if an addictive behavior cannot be eliminated, it is possible to modify how often and under what conditions it occurs and thereby minimize its harmful effects on the person and society. Harm-reduction programs have enjoyed considerable success in several European countries. Making drugs available to addicts as part of a required treatment process reduces criminal behavior performed to obtain money for drugs and undermines the drug trade in general (Heather, 2006). Harm-reduction proponents (e.g., MacCoun, 1998) view their approach as a viable alternative to the current "war on drugs," which they consider an abject failure that has done little more than swell the profits of drug cartels and the number of people in our prisons.

The harm that can befall college students who abuse alcohol has inspired a new generation of intervention programs focused on helping problem drinkers control how much and under what circumstances they drink. The goal is to reduce harmful consequences to the problem drinkers and others (Marlatt et al., 2001). In one harm-reduction project, 115 college women who had been charged with violating campus alcohol policies participated in the study. The two-hour group intervention focused on female-specific reasons for drinking and included decisional balance (benefits versus costs of heavy drinking), goal setting, and other exercises designed to enhance controlled drinking skills. The brief intervention proved to be effective. Alcohol use was reduced by 29.9 percent and negative consequences were reduced by 35.87 percent between the preintervention and a 3-month follow-up. Further, the intervention appeared to successfully initiate change in the heaviest drinkers, as women who drank at risky levels reduced alcohol consumption to a greater extent than women who drank at moderate levels.

How People Change: The Transtheoretical Model

In order to increase health-enhancing behaviors and reduce health-threatening ones, we need to understand the processes that underlie behavior change in general. Psychologists James Prochaska and Carlo DiClemente began to study the process that occurs as people modify their thoughts, feelings, and behaviors in positive ways, either on their own or with professional help. Their research resulted in a **transtheoretical model** *that identified six major stages in the change process* (DiClemente, 2003; Prochaska & DiClemente, 1984).

1. *Precontemplation:* The person does not perceive a health-related problem, denies that it is something that endangers well-being, or feels powerless to change.

2. *Contemplation:* The person perceives a problem or the desirability of a behavior change but has not yet decided to take action. Thus some smokers are well aware of the health risks of their habit, yet they are not ready to make a decision to quit. Until the perceived benefits of changing outweigh the costs or effort involved, contemplators will not take action.

3. *Preparation:* The person has decided to change the behavior, is making preliminary plans to do so, and may be taking preliminary steps, such as cutting down on the number of cigarettes per day (Figure 14.10).

4. *Action:* The person actively begins to engage in behavior change, perhaps stopping smoking altogether. Success at this stage hinges on the behavior-control skills necessary to carry out the plan of action. The action stage requires the greatest commitment of effort and energy.

5. *Maintenance:* The person has been successful in avoiding relapse and has controlled the target behavior for at least 6 months. This does not mean that the struggle is over. Many people lapse back into their former behavior patterns at various times, but they reinstate their change efforts, as would

Figure 14.10

The transtheoretical model identifies a series of stages through which a smoker would pass before successfully quitting.

The transtheoretical model helps us understand how people change, and it has important applied implications. For example, we know that different intervention procedures are needed for people at various stages. Psychologists have therefore developed ways of determining what stage a person is in so that they can apply *stage-matched interventions* designed to move the person toward the action, maintenance, and termination stages. Precontemplators need consciousness-raising information that finally convinces them that there is a problem, as well as social support to change (De Vries et al., 1998). Contemplators often need a wake-up emotional experience that increases their motivation to change or causes them to re-evaluate themselves in relation to the behavior. For example, a serious auto accident while intoxicated may finally convince a problem drinker that her or his behavior has to change. In the preparation stage, the person needs to develop a specific plan (ideally based on the goal-setting procedures described in Chapter 11) and have the skills to carry it out before action is likely to be successful. Only when the person is ready for the action stage are change techniques, however powerful, likely to have their intended effect.

Maintaining Positive Change: Relapse Prevention

Despite the availability of effective methods for changing behavior, high dropout rates and failure to maintain positive behavior changes are a major problem in every health-relevant behavior we've discussed, from exercise maintenance to weight control to ending substance abuse. Why do people relapse into their problem behaviors, or abandon health-promoting practices, and what can be done to prevent this? Research on these questions has led to a better understanding of the relapse process and an intervention known as **relapse prevention** *that is designed to reduce the risk of relapse* (Marlatt & Gordon, 1985). Research with substance abusers shows that most *relapses* (a full-fledged return to the undesirable behavior pattern) tend to occur after the person has suffered one or more *lapses* (occasional "slips") in response to high-risk situations. *High-risk situations* include stressful events, interpersonal conflicts, social pressure to perform the undesirable behavior, being in the company of other individuals using the substance, and experiencing negative emotions (Marlatt, 1996).

be expected when one is trying to change deeply ingrained habits. It typically takes smokers three to five cycles through the action stage before they finally beat the habit, and New Year's resolutions are typically made for 5 or more consecutive years before they are finally carried out successfully (Prochaska et al., 1994; Schachter, 1982).

6. *Termination:* The change in behavior is so ingrained and under personal control that the original problem behavior will never return.

The transtheoretical model does not assume that people go through the stages in a smooth sequence. Longitudinal studies have shown that many people move forward and backward through the stages as they try to change their behavior over time, and many people make repeated efforts to change before they finally succeed (Davidson, 1998; Evers et al., 1998). However, failure at a given stage is likely to occur if the previous stages have not been mastered.

The path to substance-related relapse is shown in the bottom portion of Figure 14.11

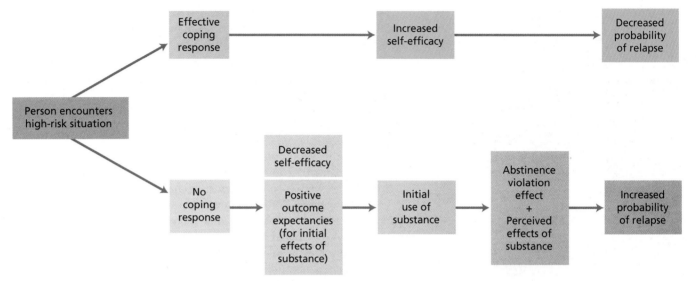

Figure 14.11

Relapse and relapse prevention.
Relapse is most likely to occur as a result of inadequate coping skills for dealing with high-risk situations, a focus on anticipated positive effects of engaging in the behavior, and a resulting abstinence violation effect that causes the person to feel incapable of successful change and to abandon attempts at behavior control. Source: Marlatt & Gordon, 1985.

(although the model can also be applied to *not* engaging in a health-enhancing behavior, such as exercise). Increased likelihood of relapse occurs when people have not developed strong enough coping skills to deal successfully with the high-risk situations. As a result, they experience low self-efficacy, believing that they are not strong enough to resist the temptations, or they allow expected positive benefits (such as enjoyment of the substance or anticipated stress reduction) to influence their decisions to perform the undesirable behaviors. A lapse then occurs, followed by a critically important reaction called the **abstinence violation effect,** *in which the person becomes upset and self-blaming over the lapse and views it as proof that he or she will never be strong enough to resist temptation.* This sense of hopelessness places people at great risk to abandon all attempts to change, and in many cases a total relapse will occur. In one study of relapses in dieting, the abstinence violation effect was more strongly associated with relapse episodes than were culinary temptations (Carels et al., 2004).

Relapse resistance is shown in the upper portion of Figure 14.11. When confronting high-risk situations, people who have effective coping skills feel confident in their ability to handle them and are far less likely to relapse, even if they slip (lapse) once in a while. To develop this adaptive process, relapse-prevention specialists tell people that a lapse means only that they've encountered

a situation that exceeded their current coping skills. Moreover, the lapse has given them valuable information about the specific situational, cognitive, and emotional antecedents that they must learn to handle more effectively. When they master the needed skills, they will be better able to resist high-risk situations. They can then direct their attention to learning and practicing the required skills so that self-efficacy improves. The continuing focus is on "progress, not perfection."

Relapse-prevention training is increasingly being incorporated into many behavior-change programs. It has proven effective in changing many problematic behaviors, including overeating, smoking, cocaine and marijuana abuse, and sexual offending (Witkiewicz & Marlatt, 2004). More recently, a meditation technique has been incorporated into relapse prevention to help people deal with aversive emotions related to their problem behaviors and to improve their self-awareness (McCown & Reibel, 2010). Relapse prevention is also an important complement to the transtheoretical model, which tells us that many people regress from the action and even maintenance stages back into a previous stage because they are not prepared to deal with the lapses that almost inevitably occur as they try to alter ingrained behavior patterns. Being prepared for occasional lapses helps people move more smoothly from the preparation stage to the action and maintenance stages (DiClemente, 2003).

STRESS AND WELL-BEING

The term *stress* appears regularly in our everyday discourse. It is also a leading topic of study in psychology. What, exactly, is stress?

Psychologists have conceived of stress in three different ways: as a stimulus, as a response, and as an ongoing interaction between an organism and its environment. Some scientists define stress as events that place strong demands on us. These *demanding or threatening situations are* **stressors.** We refer to stress as a *stimulus* when we make statements such as, "I've got a lot of stress in my life right now. I have three exams next week, I lost my class notes, my fiancé just announced a vow of eternal celibacy, and my car broke down."

Stress can also be a *response* that has cognitive, physiological, and behavioral components. Thus a person might say, "I'm feeling all stressed out. I'm tensed up, I'm having trouble concentrating on things, I can't sleep, and I've been irritable all week." The presence of negative emotions is an important feature of the stress response and links the study of stress with the field of emotion (Zautra, 2003).

A third way of thinking about stress combines the stimulus and response definitions into a more inclusive model. Here stress is viewed as a *person-situation interaction,* or more formally, as an ongoing transaction between the organism and its environment (Lazarus, 1991, 1998). This conception of stress is the basis for the model shown in Figure 14.12, and it will guide our discussion of stress. From this perspective, **stress** can be defined

Figure 14.12

The nature of stress.
Stress involves complex interactions among situational (stressor) characteristics, cognitive appraisal processes, physiological responses, and behavioral attempts to cope with the situational demands. Stressor characteristics that influence stress responses are shown. The lower "Effects" panels show potential cognitive, physiological, and behavioral stress responses that can interfere with well-being.

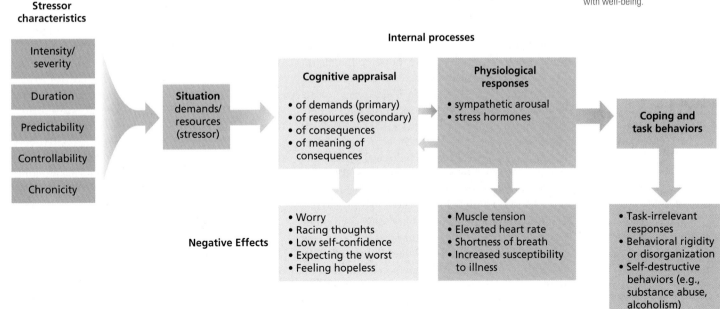

Stressor characteristics

- Intensity/severity
- Duration
- Predictability
- Controllability
- Chronicity

Internal processes

Situation demands/resources (stressor)

Cognitive appraisal
- of demands (primary)
- of resources (secondary)
- of consequences
- of meaning of consequences

Physiological responses
- sympathetic arousal
- stress hormones

Coping and task behaviors

Negative Effects

- Worry
- Racing thoughts
- Low self-confidence
- Expecting the worst
- Feeling hopeless

- Muscle tension
- Elevated heart rate
- Shortness of breath
- Increased susceptibility to illness

- Task-irrelevant responses
- Behavioral rigidity or disorganization
- Self-destructive behaviors (e.g., substance abuse, alcoholism)

(a)

(b)

Figure 14.13

Stressful life events can vary from (a) catastrophic ones, such as 2010's earthquake in Haiti, to (b) microstressors, or daily hassles. Both classes of stressor take their toll on physical and psychological well-being.

as *a pattern of cognitive appraisals, physiological responses, and behavioral tendencies that occurs in response to a perceived imbalance between situational demands and the resources needed to cope with them.*

Stressors

Let's begin with the situational component of stress. Stressors are specific kinds of stimuli. Whether physical or psychological, they place demands on us that threaten our well-being and require us to adapt in some manner. The more the demands of a situation outweigh the resources we have to deal with them, the more stressful a situation is likely to be.

Stressors differ in their severity (Figure 14.13). They can range from *microstressors*—the daily hassles and minor annoyances, such as difficult co-workers, traffic jams, and academic deadlines—to more severe stressors. *Major negative events,* such as the death or loss of a loved one, an academic or career failure, a serious illness, or being the victim of a serious crime, place strong demands on us and require major efforts to cope. *Catastrophic events* tend to occur unexpectedly and typically affect large numbers of people (Resick, 2005). They include traumatic natural disasters, acts of war or terrorism, and physical or psychological torture. As we shall see, all three classes of stressors can have significant negative effects on psychological and physical well-being (Aldwin, 2007; Zautra, 2003).

In addition to intensity or severity, other characteristics that make situations more or less stressful are listed at the far left of Figure 14.12. In general, events over which a person has little or no control, which occur suddenly and unpredictably, and which impact a person over a long period of time seem to take the greatest toll on physical and psychological well-being (Taylor, 2009).

Measuring Stressful Life Events

Researchers have taken a number of approaches to study the relation between life events and well-being. Some studies involve participants who are known to have lived through a natural disaster or lost a loved one to death. In other cases, researchers may have to rely on people's self-reports, using **life event scales** to *quantify the amount of life stress that a person has experienced over a given period of time* (e.g., the past 3 months, 6 months, or year). Such scales consist of lists of life events (up to 200 of them) that a person may have experienced (for example, "death of a family member," "new job," "financial problems," or "new romantic relationship"). They also indicate whether the events were positive or negative and whether they had a major or minor impact on the respondent's life. Researchers can score the scale for the number of specific kinds of events that occurred (for example, "minor negative," "major negative," "major positive"). They can obtain additional information by asking respondents to rate the predictability, controllability, and duration of each event they experienced, permitting an analysis of these factors as well. Life event scales have been widely used in life-stress research.

The Stress Response: A Mind-Body Link

Let's now consider how people respond to stressors. Like the emotional responses discussed in Chapter 11, the **stress response** *has cognitive, physiological, and behavioral components.*

Cognitive Appraisals

We respond to situations as we perceive them. The starting point for the stress response is therefore our cognitive appraisal of the situation and its implications for us. As Figure 14.12 indicates, four aspects of the appraisal process are particularly significant:

- Appraisal of the *nature and demands* of the situation. Is it benign or neutral, or does it threaten your well-being?

- Appraisal of the *resources* available to cope with it. Coping resources include your knowledge and abilities, your verbal skills, and your social resources, such as people who will give you emotional support and encouragement. Do you have what it takes?

- Appraisal of the *consequences* of the situation. Appraising the consequences as very costly and very likely to occur increases the perceived stressfulness of the situation.

- Appraisal of the *personal meaning;* that is, what the outcome might imply about you. For example, if your feelings of self-worth depend on how successful you are in a given situation, you may regard doing poorly as evidence that you are a worthless failure.

Our appraisals may or may not be realistic. Distortions and mistaken appraisals can occur at any of the four points in the appraisal process, causing inappropriate stress responses. People may overestimate the difficulty of the demands, they may underestimate their own resources, they may exaggerate the seriousness of the consequences and the likelihood that they will occur, or they may have irrational self-beliefs (for example, that a rejection means you're unlovable). The fact that appraisal patterns can differ so greatly from person to person helps us understand why different perceptions of the same event or situation vary among people and why some people are particularly vulnerable to certain types of demands.

Physiological Responses

As soon as we make appraisals, the body responds to them (Kemeny, 2004; Steckler et al., 2005). Although appraisals begin the process, appraisals and physiological responses affect one another (Sun, 2005). Sensory feedback from our body's response can cause us to reappraise how stressful a situation is and whether our resources are sufficient to cope with it. Thus, if you find yourself trembling and your heart pounding as you sit down to take a test, you may appraise the situation as even more threatening than you did initially. The two-way arrows between the cognitive and physiological elements in Figure 14.12 illustrate this.

Endocrinologist Hans Selye (1976) was a pioneer in studying the body's response to stress. He described a physiological response pattern to strong and prolonged stressors. The **general adaptation syndrome (GAS)** *consists of three phases: alarm, resistance, and exhaustion* (Figure 14.14).

In response to a physical or psychological stressor, organisms exhibit an immediate increase in physiological arousal as the body mobilizes itself to respond to the threat. This *alarm reaction* occurs because of the sudden activation of the sympathetic nervous system and the release of stress hormones by the endocrine system. The alarm stage cannot last indefinitely, however, and the body's natural tendency to maintain the balanced internal state of homeostasis causes activity in the parasympathetic nervous system, which reduces arousal. The body continues to remain on

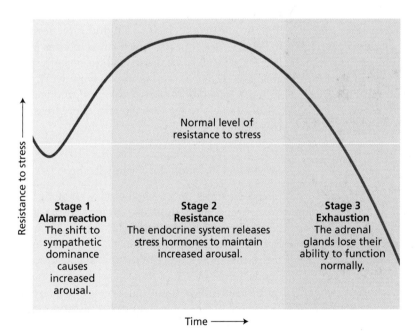

Figure 14.14

Hans Selye's general adaptation syndrome.

When a person is exposed to a stressor, the body's resistance is temporarily reduced by a state of shock until the alarm reaction mobilizes the body's resources. During the stage of resistance, stress hormones maintain the body's defensive changes, and the bodily reactions characteristic of the alarm reaction virtually disappear. But if the stress persists over a long time, the body's resources become depleted, and exhaustion occurs; the organism can no longer cope and is highly vulnerable to breakdown. Source: Selye, 1976.

red alert, however, responding with the second stage, resistance.

During *resistance,* the body's resources are mobilized by the continued outpouring of stress hormones by the endocrine system, particularly the adrenal glands. Resistance can last for a relatively long time, but the body's resources are being depleted and immune system functioning is being partially suppressed by the stress hormones (Chiappelli, 2000). If the stressor is intense and persists too long, the body will eventually reach a stage of *exhaustion,* in which there is increased vulnerability to disease and, in some extreme cases, collapse and death. Selye theorized that whichever body system is weakest (e.g., cardiovascular, respiratory, gastrointestinal) will be the one most affected.

Effects of Stress on Well-Being

From a biological perspective, it seems that a high-arousal fight-or-flight biological mechanism sculpted by evolution to help us survive life-threatening *physical* stressors may be maladaptive for dealing with the *psychological* stressors of modern life. In terms of survival, taking a final exam or sitting in rush-hour traffic is not equivalent to an attack by a hungry saber-toothed tiger, where high arousal could facilitate fighting or fleeing. In Selye's view, our physiological responses may thereby take an unnecessary toll on our physical and psychological well-being. Selye's work inspired a generation of psychological and medical researchers to explore the effects of stress on psychological and physical well-being.

Stress and Psychological Well-Being

Effects of stress on psychological well-being are clearest and most dramatic among people who have experienced catastrophic life events. Anthony Rubonis and Leonard Bickman (1991) surveyed the results of 52 studies of victims of catastrophic floods, hurricanes, and fires. In the wake of natural disasters, they found an average increase of 17 percent in rates of psychological disorders such as anxiety and depression.

Some stressors are so traumatic that they can have a strong and long-lasting psychological impact (Resick, 2005). More than 50 years after the horrors of the Holocaust, psychological scars remained for Jewish survivors of Nazi concentration camps (Nadler & Ben-Slushan, 1989; Valent, 2000). Many survivors were still troubled by high levels of anxiety and recurrent nightmares about their traumatic experiences. Depression and crying spells were also common, as were feelings of insecurity and difficulties in forming close relationships. As one researcher reported, "child survivors (now in their 50s and 60s), despite their outward normalcy, remain entrapped in this survival mode" (Valent, 1998, p. 751).

Long-lasting psychological symptoms have also been found among soldiers who experienced the trauma of combat. Twenty years after the 1982 Lebanon war, Israeli soldiers who had seen combat reported more psychological, social, and health problems than did a matched group of veterans who had not experienced combat (Zahava et al., 2006).

The trauma of being raped can leave psychological scars that are painful and long-lasting. In one long-term study, one fourth of the women felt that they had not recovered psychologically 6 years after being raped (Meyer & Taylor, 1986). More-common severe stressors, such as unemployment, also leave scars. In a 15-year longitudinal study of German workers, losing employment was followed by significant declines in subjective well-being. Even after regaining employment, some workers never returned to their previous levels of life satisfaction (Lucas et al., 2004).

Many researchers have examined relations between self-reported negative life events and measures of psychological well-being. Findings consistently show that the more negative life events people report, the more likely they are to also report symptoms of anxiety, depression, and unhappiness (Holahan & Moos, 1990; Monroe & Peterman, 1988). Many medical and psychological researchers have therefore concluded that stress causes distress, and this conclusion has been widely accepted among the general public and in the mass media.

thinking critically

DO STRESSFUL EVENTS CAUSE PSYCHOLOGICAL DISTRESS?

A consistent statistical relation has been shown between stressful life events and psychological distress; the greater the number of stressful events people have experienced, the more distress they are likely to report. Based on these results, are you willing to accept the conclusion that life stress causes distress, or can you think of other possible reasons for this relation? Think about it, then see page 545.

Stress and Illness

Stress can combine with other physical and psychological factors to influence the entire spectrum of physical illnesses, from the common cold to cancer, heart disease, diabetes, and sudden death (Lovallo, 2005; Suls & Wallston, 2003). Sometimes the effects are immediate. On the day of the 1994 earthquake in Northridge, California, the number of sudden deaths due to heart attacks in the greater Los Angeles area nearly tripled from an average of 35.7 per day during the previous seven days to 101 (Leor et al., 1996).

Other effects of major stressors on physical well-being are less immediate but no less severe. Within 1 month following the death of a spouse, bereaved widowers and widows begin to show a higher mortality rate than married people of the same age who have not lost a spouse (Kaprio et al., 1987), and within 1 year after spousal death, about two-thirds of bereaved people decline in health (Irwin et al., 1987). A notably increased rate of mortality is found in men, who tend to respond to the death of a spouse with relatively greater distress and health declines than do women (Stroebe et al., 2001). Stressful life events have also been linked to a higher risk of developing cancer (Sklar & Anisman, 1981). People who experience the chronic stress that attends caring for a spouse with Alzheimer's disease have significantly increased risk for health problems (Vitaliano et al., 2004).

Linkages between long-term stress and illness are not surprising, for physiological responses to stressors can directly harm other body systems. For example, the secretion of stress hormones, such as epinephrine, norepinephrine, and cortisol, is a major part of the stress response (Miller et al., 2007). These hormones affect the activity of the heart, and excessive secretions can damage the lining of the arteries. By reducing fat metabolism, the stress hormones also can contribute to the fatty blockages in arteries that cause heart attacks and strokes (Lovallo & Gerin, 2003; Willenberg et al., 2000).

Stress also can contribute to health breakdowns by causing people to behave in ways that increase the risk of illness. For example, people with diabetes frequently can control their disease through medication, exercise, and diet; when under stress, however, they are less likely to regulate their diets and take their medications, resulting in an increased risk of serious medical consequences (Brantley & Garrett, 1993). People are also more likely to quit exercising when under stress, even if the primary reason they began exercising in the first place was to reduce stress

(Stetson et al., 1997). Stress may also lead to smoking, alcohol and drug use, sleep loss, undereating or overeating, and other health-threatening behaviors. Poor dietary and sleep patterns in students studying for final exams may increase the risk of illness and a ruined semester break.

Stress and the Immune System

At this moment, microscopic soldiers patrol every part of your body, including your brain. They are on a search-and-destroy mission, seeking out biological invaders that could disable or kill you. Programmed into this legion of tiny defenders is an innate ability to recognize which substances belong to the body and which are foreign and must be destroyed. Such recognition occurs because *foreign substances known as* **antigens** (meaning *anti*body *gen*erators) *trigger a biochemical response from the immune system.* Bacteria, viruses, abnormal cells, and many chemical molecules with antigenic properties start the wars that rage inside our bodies every moment of every day (Figure 14.15).

A normal, healthy immune system is a wonder of nature. Like the nervous system, the immune system has an exquisite capacity to receive, interpret, and respond to specific forms of

Figure 14.15

An immune system cell reaches out to capture bacteria, shown here in yellow. The bacteria that have already been pulled to the surface of the cell will be engulfed and devoured.

stimulation. It senses, learns, remembers, and reacts; in other words, it behaves. It has a remarkable memory. Once it has encountered one of the millions of different antigens that enter the body, it will recognize the antigen immediately in the future and produce the biochemical weapons, or *antibodies,* needed to destroy it (Nossal & Hall, 1995). This memory is the basis for developing vaccines to protect people and animals from some diseases; it is also the reason we normally catch diseases such as mumps and chicken pox only once in our lives. Unfortunately, although the immune system's memory may be perfect, our body's defenses may not be. Some bacteria and viruses evolve so rapidly that they can change just enough over time to slip past the sentinels in our immune system and give us this year's cold or flu.

The importance of the immune system to our health and well-being cannot be overstated. Considerable evidence suggests that life stress can weaken immune functioning (Suls & Wallston, 2003; Taylor, 2009). Research by Ronald Glaser, Janet Kiecolt-Glaser, and their coworkers at Ohio State University has shown that reduced immune system effectiveness is one possible reason for increased risk of illness (Kiecolt-Glaser et al., 2002; Marsland et al., 2001). In one study, researchers closely followed medical students over a 1-year period. They collected blood samples from the students during three stressful academic examination periods in order to measure immune cell activity. The researchers found that immune system effectiveness was reduced during the stressful exam periods and that this reduction was linked to the likelihood of becoming ill. Other studies have shown that stress hormones released into the bloodstream by the adrenal glands can suppress the activity of specific immune system cells, increasing the likelihood of illness (Cohen & Herbert, 1996; Maier & Watkins, 1999).

Research has shown that external stressors can "get into" the immune system in several ways. Fibers extending from the brain into lymph tissues can release a wide variety of chemicals that bind to receptors on white blood cells, thus influencing immune functions. As noted earlier, stress hormones such as cortisol and epinephrine also bind to cells in the immune system and influence their functions. Third, people's attempts to cope with stressors sometimes lead them to behave in ways (e.g., substance use or not sleeping enough) that impair immunity (Taylor, 2009).

There are two kinds of immune reactions. *Natural immunity* occurs quickly (often within minutes) of an immune challenge and is relatively nonspecific in nature. One type of natural immunity is inflammation, in which certain immune cells congregate at the site of an infection and release toxic substances that kill invaders. *Natural killer (NK) cells* attack tumors and help keep invaders at bay during the early stages of infection. From an evolutionary perspective, natural immunity is an adaptive feature of the fight-or-flight response to an acute physical stressor that could produce injury and the entry of pathogens into the body through wounds.

Specific immunity is a much more targeted process and takes longer to occur, sometimes up to several days. The immune system analyzes the specific properties of the invader and then forms specific antibodies that can neutralize bacteria, kill cancerous cells, or bind to viruses to prevent their entry into healthy cells.

Like immune reactions, stressors can differ in a number of ways, including how they occur and how long they last. Acute, time-limited stressors, such as participating in a stressful job interview, actually enhance the fast-acting natural immunity process (Segerstrom and Miller, 2004). The number of natural killer cells in the blood increases, and the immune system readies itself for a protective-infection response. Specific immunity does not increase, however, probably because the stressor is very brief. But longer-lasting stressors (e.g., weeklong preparation for an important examination), and chronic stressors (e.g., caring for a spouse with Alzheimer's disease, severe marital conflict, or unemployment), are the most damaging to health because they have suppressive effects on both types of immunity. Hundreds of studies support a *biphasic model* in which acute stress temporarily enhances the immune response, whereas chronic stress suppresses it over time (Dhabhar & McEwen, 2001; Segerstrom & Miller, 2004).

Two types of stress hormones, catecholamines and cortisol, are important links between physiological reactivity and health. Both mobilize the body's fight-or-flight response in the face of stressors, but they have somewhat different effects on the body. Cortisol's arousal effects last much longer and seem to be more damaging than those produced by the catecholamines (unless the catecholamines are secreted at high levels over a long period of time). Cortisol reduces immune system functioning and helps create fatty deposits in the arteries that lead to heart disease. In contrast, catecholamine secretion increases immune system functioning (Taylor, 2009). The fact that physical exercise creates catecholamine-produced arousal may help account for its health-enhancing effects and its ability to promote stress resistance (Ehrman, 2003; Morgan, 1997).

True or false?

1. Exhaustion is the third stage of Selye's general adaptation syndrome.

2. Relations between life stress measures and distress show that stress causes psychological distress.

3. Short-term acute stressors increase both natural and specific immunity, whereas chronic stressors increase only natural immunity.

4. Of the adrenal stress hormones, cortisol has more damaging effects on the body than catecholamines.

ANSWERS: 1-true, 2-false, 3-false, 4-true

RESILIENCE: FACING DOWN ADVERSITY

At the beginning of this chapter you met Priscilla, a child who grew up in a terrible home environment with a father who abused her and committed suicide in her presence. Somehow, despite these experiences, Priscilla grew into a highly successful young woman. Since the 1970s, psychologists such as Emmy Werner have been studying children who exhibit **resilience,** *the ability to tolerate, and even thrive in, highly stressful circumstances* (Hass & Graydon, 2009; Werner & Smith, 1982).

What factors matter in the lives of resilient children like Priscilla, who rise far above what their environments would predict for them? Are they "superkids," as a *New York Times* writer referred to them? After reviewing many studies of unusually resilient children and adolescents, Keith Burt and Ann Masten (2010) concluded that such children are monuments to the ordinary adaptive processes that occur in the lives of most children, factors Masten (2001) has termed "ordinary magic." Resilient children have certain characteristics that contribute to a positive outcome even in the face of stressful life events (Table 14.4). These characteristics include adequate intellectual functioning, social skills, self-efficacy, and faith (optimism and hope), as well as environmental factors, such as a relationship with at least one caring, prosocial adult.

To be resilient, a child need not have all of the characteristics listed in Table 14.4, but he or she must have some of them. Good intellectual functioning and a supportive relationship with a caring adult seem to be the most important (Masten & Coatsworth, 1998). In Priscilla's case, this positive adult relationship did not exist with either parent. Instead, the critical relationship was provided by a loving elementary school teacher who befriended, encouraged, and guided her during the critical formative period of middle childhood. This key relationship, combined with Priscilla's obvious intelligence, allowed her to develop self-esteem, a belief in her own capabilities, and the will to nurture her talents.

In Priscilla, then, we have an example of what can happen even in the face of great adversity when certain critical protective factors are present. As Masten (2001) concluded,

> What began as a quest for the extraordinary has revealed the power of the ordinary. Resilience does not come from rare and special qualities, but from the everyday magic of ordinary, normative human resources in the minds, brains, and bodies of children, in their families and relationships, and in their communities. (p. 235)

Even as adults, some individuals seem to tolerate extremely demanding stressors over a long

Table **14.4** | **Personal and Environmental Factors That Contribute to Stress-Resilience in Children**

Source	Characteristic
Individual	Good intellectual functioning
	Appealing, sociable, easygoing disposition
	Self-efficacy, self-confidence, high self-esteem
	Talents
	Faith
Family	Close relationship to caring parent figure
	Authoritative parenting: warmth, structure, high expectations
	Socioeconomic advantages
	Connections to extended supportive family networks
Extrafamilial context	Bonds to prosocial adults outside the family
	Connections to prosocial organizations
	Attending effective schools

Source: Masten & Coatsworth, 1998.

Figure 14.16

Between 2004 and 2005, Israeli Jews and Arabs were subjected to deadly and unpredictable rocket attacks. They reacted psychologically in various ways, with some exhibiting increased distress and others demonstrating resilience. Source: Hobfoll et al., 2009.

period of time without negative effects. Stevan Hobfoll and coworkers (2009) studied a national sample of 709 Israeli Jews and Arabs during the Second Intifada, a period of terrorist and rocket attacks on the civilian population that caused significant casualties in 2004–2005 (Figure 14.16). By administering measures of psychological distress at the beginning and end of this period, they were able to assess differing patterns of change in psychological symptoms. The researchers identified four distinct patterns. Most common (54 percent)

Figure 14.17

Social support is one of the strongest protective factors against stress.

was chronic distress, with high symptoms of distress at both assessment points. A second pattern (10.3 percent) was characterized by increased psychological stress over time. Other people, however, exhibited resilience, the "ability to maintain relatively stable, healthy levels of psychological functioning" in the face of highly disruptive and threatening events (Bonanno, 2005, p. 265). Of the terrorism victims, 22 percent reported low symptoms of distress at both assessment points, and another 13.5 percent showed a significant decrease in distress over time, even as the attacks became more frequent and deadly.

The fact that people differ so dramatically in their responses to stressful events has prompted many health psychologists to search for personal and environmental factors that make people less reactive to stressful events. So-called **protective factors** *are environmental or personal resources that create resilience, helping people cope more effectively with stressful events.* They include physiological reactivity, social support, effective coping skills, and personality factors such as hardiness, coping self-efficacy, optimism, emotional expressiveness, and an ability to find meaning in stressful events.

Social Support

Social support is one of the most important environmental resources (Suls & Wallston, 2003). The knowledge that we can rely on others for help and support in a time of crisis helps blunt the impact of stress (Figure 14.17). In contrast, lack of social support is a significant vulnerability factor. Studies carried out in the United States, Finland, and Sweden carefully tracked the well-being of some 37,000 people for up to 12 years. Even after taking into account medical risk factors such as age, smoking, high blood pressure, high cholesterol levels, obesity, and lack of physical exercise, the researchers found that people with weak social ties were twice as likely to die during the period of the study as those with strong ties to others (House et al., 1988). The relation between social isolation and poor health was stronger for men than for women.

One way that social support protects against stress is by enhancing immune system functioning. Robert Baron and his coworkers (1990) studied distressed people whose spouses were being treated for cancer. When they were exposed to an antigen, those who rated themselves as high in social support produced more immune cells, particularly at high levels of the antigen, than did those who indicated lower social support in their lives. These results may help explain why people who have high levels of social support are more disease-resistant when they are under stress (Hampson & Friedman, 2008).

Besides enhancing immune system functioning, social support has a number of other stress-buffering benefits. First, people who feel that they are part of a social system experience a greater sense of identity and meaning in their lives, which in turn results in greater psychological well-being (Cohen, 1988; Rodin & Salovey, 1989). Second, social networks reduce exposure to other risk factors, such as loneliness. Third, having the backing of others can increase one's sense of control over stressors. Finally, true friends can apply social pressure to prevent people from coping with stressors in maladaptive ways (e.g., through alcohol or drug use).

Coping Self-Efficacy and Perceived Control

When confronted by a stressor, one of the most significant appraisals we make is whether we have sufficient resources to cope with the demands (Bandura, 1997). Small wonder, then, that **coping self-efficacy**—*the belief that we can perform the behaviors necessary to cope successfully*—is an important protective factor (Bandura, 1989). Even events that are appraised as extremely demanding may generate little stress if we believe that we have the skills to deal with them.

Self-efficacy is always specific to the particular situation: "Can I handle *these* demands?" As noted in Chapter 13, previous successes in similar situations increase efficacy; failures undermine it (Bandura, 1997). People can also increase efficacy expectancies by observing others cope successfully and through social persuasion and encouragement from others. The teacher who befriended Priscilla constantly gave her the message "I believe in you. You can do it!" Finally, experiencing a low level of physiological arousal in the face of a stressor can convey a sense of control and ability to cope, demonstrating another way in which arousal can affect appraisal.

Optimism and Positive Attitudes

Our beliefs about how things are likely to turn out also play an important role in dealing with stressors. Recent research indicates that optimistic people are at lowered risk for anxiety and depression when they confront stressful events. Optimistic people tend to interpret their troubles as temporary, controllable, and specific to one situation, whereas pessimists view their problems as uncontrollable, long-lasting, and generalized to many life domains (Seligman, 2002).

To see if optimism predicts physical well-being, researchers at the Mayo Clinic in Minnesota followed up with 839 patients who referred themselves for medical treatment in 1960. Among the tests that the patients had taken was a measure of general optimism. By the year 2000, 200 of these patients had died. On average, the optimists had lived 19 percent longer than the pessimists (Marata et al., 2000). In another study, researchers followed women who came to the National Cancer Institute for breast cancer treatment for 5 years. On average, women who were optimistic about their recovery lived significantly longer than pessimists, even when the physical severity of the disease was the same at the beginning of the 5-year period (Levy et al., 1988).

Attitudes also matter, as a study of aging people demonstrated. The process of aging is a background stressor in many people's lives. People's reactions differ considerably as their hair thins, wrinkles deepen, physical and sexual capacity diminishes, health declines, acquaintances begin to die, and a sense of mortality becomes more salient. Some dread the aging process, whereas others accept or even find value in it. Over a 23-year period, researchers assessed attitudes toward aging in a large community sample of men and women who were over 50 years of age. Statistically controlling for age, physical health, and loneliness, the researchers found that participants' attitudes toward aging predicted longevity even better than their physical health did (Figure 14.18). On average, people with positive attitudes toward their aging lived an average of 7.6 years

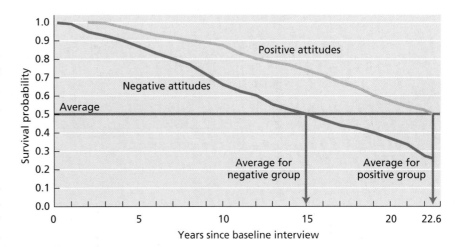

Figure 14.18

Aging attitudes and longevity.
Research has shown a relation between positive or negative self-perceptions of one's aging and subsequent longevity. These survival curves show the likelihood that a randomly selected group member will still be alive in a given year after the beginning of the study. The median number of years until death was 15 in the group with negative self-attitudes and 22.6 among positive-attitude participants. Source: Adapted from Levy et al., 2002.

longer than did their counterparts with negative attitudes (Levy et al., 2002). This survival advantage existed whether the positive-attitude people were in their 50s, 60s, 70s, or 80s when the study began. Clearly, attitude makes a difference—and perhaps a life-or-death difference.

Trauma Disclosure and Emotional Expressiveness

Is there any truth to the popular belief that when we are stressed out and upset, it's good to talk with someone about it? Denise Sloan and Brian Marx (2004) studied college students who had experienced a traumatic event in their lives. The students completed measures of stress symptoms, depression, and number of days they had been sick since the beginning of the school term. In an experimental condition, participants were then asked to write about the traumatic event, whereas those in the control condition did an unrelated task. Physiological arousal was recorded as the participants performed the tasks.

One month later, the students again completed the measures of psychological symptoms and sick days. The students had not differed on any of these measures at baseline, but they differed strongly afterward (Figure 14.19). Those who had written about their traumas showed lowered stress and depression scores. They also reported fewer sick days at the follow-up. The more physiologically aroused the participants in the written-disclosure group became while they wrote about their traumatic events, the healthier they looked physically and psychologically a month later. The researchers concluded that writing or talking

about a traumatic event affords exposure to the situational cues that accompanied the trauma and now function as conditioned stimuli that trigger distress. Exposure allows extinction to occur, thus reducing the stimuli's emotional impact.

How lasting are the effects of trauma disclosure? Do they last longer than the 1 month found in this study? To find out, Sloan and colleagues (2009) repeated the study and performed follow-ups at 2, 4, and 6 months after the writing exercise. Compared with a no-writing control group, reductions in distress were found at 2 months, but no group differences were evident beyond that point. This illustrates the importance of replication and studying the long-term effects of interventions. While trauma disclosure and emotional venting seem to produce short-term positive effects, dealing effectively with the consequences of trauma may be a process that needs to occur periodically over an extended time frame.

If expressing feelings can have at least short-term beneficial effects, what are the consequences of bottling up emotions? While constantly venting strong negative feelings may not be a good way to make friends and influence people, an inability to express negative feelings can also have its costs. Some studies have reported relations between cancer development and the use of denial or repressive coping strategies, but others have not (McKenna et al., 1999; Hampson & Friedman, 2008).

So, is it better to purge one's feelings or bottle them up? As in the earlier discussion of coping strategies, the best outcomes may occur if we have the flexibility to do either, depending on the situation. George Bonanno and coworkers (2004) studied New York City college students shortly

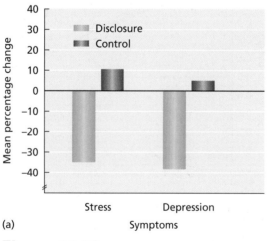

(a)

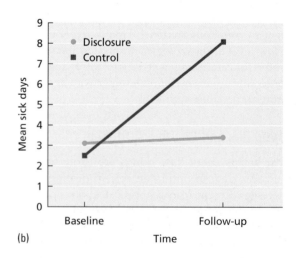

(b)

Figure 14.19

Does trauma disclosure help?

These data show the effects of written disclosure concerning a previous traumatic life event on (a) subsequent stress symptoms, depression, and (b) number of self-reported sick days. Source: Based on Sloan & Marx, 2004.

after the September 11, 2001, terrorist attacks. In a series of laboratory tasks, participants were required alternately to openly express emotional responses and to suppress them. The researchers found that the students who were most able to engage in *both* emotional expression and suppression reported less distress about the terrorist attacks and less general life distress 2 years later than did participants who were less flexible in their emotional responses. We should note, however, that the hostile, explosive expression of anger is not a recommended type of emotional expressiveness.

Finding Meaning in Stressful Life Events

Humanistic theorists emphasize the human need to find meaning in one's life and the psychological benefits of doing so (May, 1961; McKnight & Kashdan, 2009). Some people find personal meaning through spiritual beliefs, which can be a great comfort in the face of crises (Mascaro & Rosen, 2006). Daniel McIntosh and coworkers (1993) studied 124 parents who had lost their babies to sudden infant death syndrome. They found that grieving parents whose religious beliefs provided some higher meaning to their loss experienced greater well-being and less distress 18 months later. In another study, researchers found that people who were able to find meaning in the death of a family member experienced less distress during the year following the loss. Finding a sense of meaning from their own process of coping with the loss (e.g., the sense that the event helped them grow spiritually) had even longer-term positive effects (Davis et al., 1998). Other evidence also suggests that religious service and religious strength and comfort are significant predictors of well-being. Among the 92,395 participants in the 8-year longitudinal Women's Health Initiative Observational Study, these religious variables were related to a 10 to 20 percent reduction in all causes of mortality (Schnall et al., 2008).

Religious beliefs can be a two-edged sword, however: they can either decrease or increase stress, depending on their nature and the type of stressor to which they are applied. In one study of elderly people with medical problems, poorer physical and psychological adjustment occurred in patients who viewed God as punishing them; saw themselves as the victims of demonic forces; expressed anger toward God, clergy, or church members; or questioned their faith (Koenig et al., 1998). Religious beliefs may have positive effects in dealing with some types of stressors but not with others. Such beliefs seem to help people cope

more effectively with losses, illnesses, and personal setbacks. In contrast, they can increase the negative impact of other stressors such as marital problems and abuse, perhaps by inducing guilt or creating internal pressures to remain in the stressful relationship (Strawbridge et al., 1998).

Coping Strategies

> My courage sank, and with each succeeding minute it became less possible to resist this horror. My cue came, and on I went to that stage where I knew with grim certainty I would not be capable of remaining more than a few minutes.... I took one pace forward and stopped abruptly. My voice had started to fade, my throat closed up and the audience was beginning to go giddily round.
> (Aaron, 1986, p. 24)

This account of stage fright was given not by a novice actor in his first play but by Sir Laurence Olivier, considered by many the greatest actor of his generation. Few people were aware that for most of his career, Olivier experienced a private hell before every appearance. His audiences saw only what happened once he stepped onto the stage: another flawless performance. Olivier had a remarkable ability to purge the terror from his mind, relax his body, and concentrate fully on his role once showtime arrived (Aaron, 1986).

Although people might respond to a stressor in many ways, coping strategies can be divided into the three broad classes shown in Figure 14.20. **Problem-focused coping** *strategies attempt to confront and directly deal with the demands of the situation or to change the situation so that it is no longer*

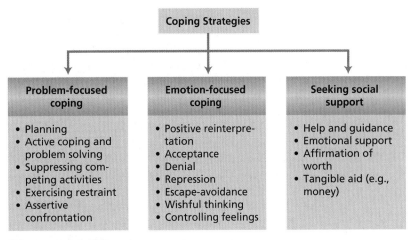

Figure 14.20

Ways of coping.
Coping strategies fall into three general categories: (1) problem-focused coping, actively attempting to respond to situational demands; (2) emotion-focused coping, directed at minimizing emotional distress; and (3) seeking or accepting social support.

stressful. Examples of problem-focused strategies might include studying for a test, going directly to another person to work out a misunderstanding, or signing up for a course to improve one's time-management skills.

Rather than dealing directly with the stressful situation, **emotion-focused coping** *strategies attempt to manage the emotional responses that result from it.* Olivier was obviously able to control his paralyzing fear once he stepped onstage, relaxing his body to reduce arousal. Some forms of emotion-focused coping involve appraising the situation in a manner that minimizes its emotional impact. A person might deal with the stress from an interpersonal conflict by denying that any problem exists. Other forms involve avoidance or acceptance of the stressful situation. Thus a student might decide to deal with anxiety about an upcoming test by going to a party and forgetting about it. Informed that he has a terminal illness, a man might decide that nothing can be done about the situation and simply accept this unwelcome reality—or he might use the avoidance strategy of discontinuing medical treatment and keeping the illness a secret, even from close family members.

A third class of coping strategies involves **seeking social support,** *that is, turning to others for assistance and emotional support in times of stress.* Thus the student might seek the help of a classmate in preparing for the test, and the man with the terminal illness might choose to join a support group for the terminally ill. Priscilla accepted and benefited from the social support provided by the teacher who befriended her.

Gender, Culture, and Coping

Many factors, including gender roles and culture, influence our tendency to favor one coping strategy over another. Although men and women both use problem-focused coping, men are more likely to use it as the first strategy when they confront a stressor (Ptacek et al., 1992). Women, who tend to have larger support networks and higher needs for affiliation than men, are more likely than men to seek social support (Billings & Moos, 1984; Schwarzer, 1998). Women also are somewhat more likely than men to use emotion-focused coping (Carver et al., 1989; Pearlin & Schooler, 1978).

This general pattern of coping preferences is consistent with the socialization that boys and girls traditionally experience. In most cultures, boys are pushed to be more independent, assertive, and self-sufficient, whereas girls are expected

to be more emotionally expressive, supportive, and dependent (Eccles, 1991; Lytton & Romney, 1991). In the words of stress researcher Shelley Taylor (2009), the common male response is "fight or flight," whereas women are more likely than men to "tend and befriend." *Tending* involves nurturant activities designed to protect the self, offspring, and significant others. These behaviors promote safety and reduce distress. *Befriending* is the creation and maintenance of social networks that may aid in this process.

Taylor (2006) speculates that the tend-and-befriend pattern is a product of biological mechanisms that underlie attachment and caregiving behavioral tendencies in women. The female hormone oxytocin, acting in conjunction with female reproductive hormones and endorphin mechanisms, may be a key player in this biological system.

Researchers have also found cultural differences in coping. North Americans and Europeans show a tendency to use problem-focused coping more than do Asian and Hispanic people, who tend to favor emotion-focused coping and social support (Essau & Trommsdorff, 1996; Jung, 1995). Asians also show a greater tendency to avoid stressful situations involving interpersonal conflict, perhaps reflecting their culture's emphasis on interpersonal harmony (Chang, 1996). In a study of how American married couples deal with marital stress, African Americans reported a greater tendency than Caucasian Americans to seek social support (Sistler & Moore, 1996). The manner in which particular coping strategies affect well-being under differing cultural conditions is an important topic for future research.

Effectiveness of Coping Strategies

Which of the three general classes of coping strategies would you expect to be most generally effective? Whenever we ask this question in our classes, the majority of our students vote for problem-focused coping. This response is understandable, because many people, particularly in Western cultures, approach problems with the attitude that if something needs fixing, we should fix it.

What does the research literature say? Charles Holahan and Rudolf Moos (1990) studied coping patterns and psychological outcomes in more than 400 California adults over a 1-year period. Although people often used several coping methods in dealing with a stressor, problem-focused coping methods and seeking social support were most often associated with favorable adjustment to stressors. In contrast, emotion-focused strategies that involved avoiding feelings or taking things out on other people predicted depression and poorer adjustment. Other studies have yielded similar results. In children and adults and across many different types of stressors, emotion-focused strategies that involve avoidance, denial, and wishful thinking seem to be related to less effective adaptation (Aldwin, 2007; Ben-Zur, 2009). On the other hand, there are adaptive emotion-focused strategies, such as identifying and changing irrational negative appraisals and learning relaxation skills to control arousal. Physical exercise also has well-established stress-reduction effects (Aldwin, 2007). These are effective methods for reducing stress responses without avoiding or distorting reality, and their use in a structured stress-reduction program has been shown to have positive effects (Chiauzzi et al., 2008).

Despite the evidence generally favoring problem-focused coping, attempting to change the situation is not always the most adaptive way to cope with a stressor. Problem-focused coping works best in situations where there is some prospect of controlling the stressor (Park et al., 2004). However, there are situations that we cannot influence or modify, and in those cases problem-focused coping may do more harm than good (Figure 14.21). Instead, emotion-focused coping may be the most adaptive approach we can take, for although we cannot master the situation, we may be able to prevent or control maladaptive emotional responses to it. Of course, reliance on emotion-focused coping is likely to be maladaptive if it prevents us from acting to change situations in which we actually *do* have control.

No coping strategy or technique is equally effective in all situations. Instead, effectiveness depends on the characteristics of the situation, the appropriateness of the technique, and the skill with which it is carried out. People are likely to adapt well to the stresses of life if they have mastered a variety of coping techniques and know how and when to apply them most effectively. The importance of controllability in the choice of techniques recalls the wisdom in theologian Reinhold Niebuhr's famous prayer that asks for the courage to change those things that can be changed, the forbearance to accept those that cannot be changed, and the wisdom to discern the difference.

How do coping patterns relate to resilience in the face of stress? The study in the "Research Close-up" addressed this question.

Figure 14.21

In response to situations like this, where one has little control over the stressor, emotion-focused coping that reduces distress is more useful than problem-focused coping.

Beyond Resilience: Posttraumatic Growth

Some of the most inspirational stories we hear are of people whose response to a tragic event or life crisis is personal growth. Despite the suffering they endure, they change in fundamental ways that make them better people. Some report finding new meaning in their lives, increased self-esteem stemming from an appreciation of their own strengths and resilience, increased self-reliance, strengthened relationships and increased intimacy in their relationships, greater compassion and altruism, and important changes in personal philosophies, including increased spirituality. Many report a new appreciation of life, increased feelings of happiness, and a determination to make their remaining days count for themselves and others (Lechner et al., 2009; Tedeschi & Calhoun, 1995). *This experience of major positive change following a crisis* is called **posttraumatic growth (PTG).**

How do college students like yourself respond to a traumatic event? In a recent study of 1,281 college students, researchers administered PTG-relevant measures of positive relationships, meaning in life, life satisfaction, gratitude for life's blessings, religious commitment and spirituality, and feelings of personal growth. Two months later, they readministered the same scales and

Research Close-up

Stress Resilience, Coping, and Illness

SOURCE: JOYCE P. YI, RONALD E. SMITH, and PETER P. VITALIANO (2005). Stress-resilience, illness, and coping: A person-focused investigation of young women athletes. *Journal of Behavioral Medicine, 28,* 257–265.

INTRODUCTION

Some people are resilient in the face of stress, failing to show its expected negative effects on well-being. What psychological characteristics contribute to their ability to weather life's storms? This study tested the hypothesis that preferred coping strategies are one component of the resilient person's psychological makeup. It involved a large-scale study of the effects of life stress on the physical well-being of healthy high school students.

METHOD

The participants were 404 female athletes from 52 varsity sports teams (basketball, soccer, gymnastics, and track) at 13 high schools. Before the season started, the athletes completed a life events measure that asked them to identify which of 198 events they had experienced in the past 6 months, and they rated how positive or negative, major or minor, the events were. The researchers then selected 127 athletes who reported many major negative life events (an average of 24 such events), identifying them as a high-stress at-risk group.

The athletes also completed a measure of preferred coping strategies in response to the most stressful event they had experienced. They indicated the extent to which they had employed each of the following strategies in dealing with the event:

- Problem-focused coping (e.g., "made a plan of action and followed it"; "changed something about myself so I could deal with the situation better")
- Social-support seeking ("talked to someone about how I was feeling"; "accepted sympathy and understanding from someone")
- Rational threat appraisal ("didn't let it get to me"; "accepted it, since nothing could be done")
- Wishful thinking ("hoped a miracle would happen to solve the problem"; "wished the situation would go away")
- Blaming others ("took it out on others"; "found out what other person was responsible")
- Avoidance ("refused to believe it had happened"; "tried to forget the whole thing")

The investigators hired each of the 52 teams' coaches as research assistants. Each day from the beginning of preseason practice to the end of the sport season, the coaches filed reports of which athletes on their teams were unable to participate in practices or contests because of injury or illness. In this study, the focus was on illness.

Based on the life stress and illness-absenteeism data (corrected for different number of participation days in the various sports), resilient and non-resilient groups of athletes were selected for comparison. High-stress athletes who missed no practices or games during the course of the sport season were designated as the "resilient" group. Those designated as "non-resilient" were athletes from the upper third of the time-loss distribution who missed a median of 8 participation days because of physical illness.

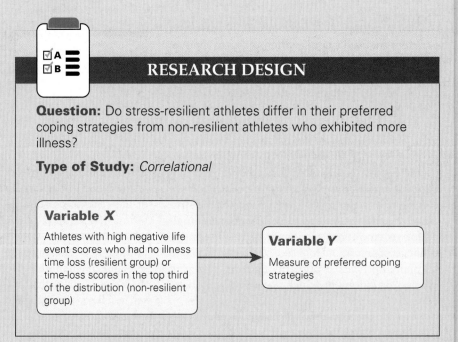

RESEARCH DESIGN

Question: Do stress-resilient athletes differ in their preferred coping strategies from non-resilient athletes who exhibited more illness?

Type of Study: *Correlational*

Variable X

Athletes with high negative life event scores who had no illness time loss (resilient group) or time-loss scores in the top third of the distribution (non-resilient group)

Variable Y

Measure of preferred coping strategies

RESULTS

The researchers constructed coping-strategy profiles based on the athletes' coping scale scores. On the basis of previous research on the adaptiveness of the coping strategies they measured, they designated problem-focused coping, social-support seeking, and rational threat appraisal as generally adaptive strategies. Wishful thinking, blaming others, and avoidance were considered nonadaptive strategies. If coping strategies contributed to resilience, the researchers hypothesized that the resilient athletes would be more likely to favor the adaptive coping strategies.

The mean profiles for the resilient and non-resilient athletes are shown in Figure 14.22. As you can see, in accordance with expectations, the groups differed on a number of the coping strategy

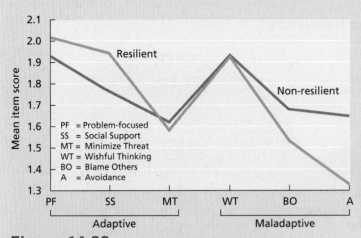

Figure 14.22

Coping strategies reported by stress-resilient and non-resilient athletes.
Source: Yi et al., 2005.

scales. Compared with the non-resilient athletes, the stress-resilient group showed a stronger tendency to use problem-focused coping and to seek social support and a lower tendency to blame others and use avoidance. Fifty-one percent of the resilient athletes had their highest use scores on the two adaptive strategies, whereas 58 percent of the non-resilient athletes had their highest scores on avoidance and blaming others.

DISCUSSION

This study, conducted in a real-world environment with healthy young people, showed clear coping-strategy differences between resilient and non-resilient groups. The resilient athletes were more likely to favor the adaptive strategies. They tended to tackle the problem in a problem-focused manner and/or to seek and accept social support. Most notably, they did not employ the strategies of avoidance and blaming others, both of which have been found to be maladaptive in other research (Aldwin, 2007; Ben-Zur, 2009).

Several limitations of the study should be noted. As in many previous studies of coping, the measure of coping asked about how the athletes coped with a single negative life event, and we do not know how much that measure reflects how the women typically deal with stressors. Second, the researchers focused on what the athletes reported as major stressful events, but they didn't take into account other characteristics of the stressor, such as controllability and chronicity, that could affect both the coping strategies selected and the possible biological impact of the stressful event. Finally, because these results are correlational in nature (since illness was not experimentally manipulated), there could be other unmeasured variables involved, such as emotional expressivity or hostility, that influence both coping and illness and therefore account for the differences between the two groups. Despite these reservations, however, the study does strengthen the research-based link between coping and resilience, and it points to future research that can examine more closely the role of coping in illness, as well as the biological processes that make people more or less resilient in the face of stressors.

also asked students if they had experienced any traumatic events that caused them intense fear, grief, helplessness, or horror since the first testing. Such an event was reported by 120 students. The majority of events involved sudden death of a close friend or loved one, a life-threatening accident, assault, illness, rape, or an accident that killed someone.

Table 14.5 shows the percentages of students who showed significant positive and negative changes on the PTG measures. Although the majority of the students did not change following the traumatic event, some of them reported positive changes. Such growth was associated with lower levels of depression and anxiety (Frazier et al., 2009). This study involved a relatively brief time interval, and other investigators have found that PTG effects tend to become stronger over time as the process of coping and cognitive processing of the event and oneself unfold (Gangstad et al., 2009). One review of 103 studies of PTG in a variety of populations concluded that optimism, social support, positive appraisal, and religious coping were the strongest predictors of growth (Prati & Pietrantoni, 2009).

Nothing can shelter us completely from traumatic life experiences. The good news is that despite the pain they cause us, tragedies, if handled appropriately, can be stepping stones to personal transformation and growth.

Table **14.5** | Percentages of College Students Who Reported Increases or Decreases in Various Experiences Relevant to Posttraumatic Growth

Measure	Increase %	Decrease %
Positive relationships	14	8
Meaning in life	12	5
Life satisfaction	25	7
Gratitude for blessings	8	12
Spiritual/religious growth	7	11
Feelings of personal growth	14	8

Source: Data from Frazier et al., 2009, Table 1, p. 915.

Levels of Analysis

Stress and Resilience

Stress involves complex interactions among environmental, cognitive, physiological, and behavioral processes. As such, its study occurs at all of the levels of analysis that characterize psychological research.

ENVIRONMENTAL LEVEL

- Situational events that exceed an individual's resources become stressors.
- Situational factors that influence how stressful an event is likely to be are severity, predictability, duration, controllability, and chronicity.
- Social support can increase the ability to withstand stressors.
- Stressor controllability influences how effective particular coping strategies will be.

BIOLOGICAL LEVEL

- Evolutionary processes have shaped a fight-or-flight biological response that contributed to survival.
- The autonomic and endocrine systems respond to situational stressors.
- Part of the physiological response to stressors involves the immune system, which may either enhance or depress immunity.

PSYCHOLOGICAL LEVEL

- Cognitive appraisal of demands, resources, potential consequences, and personal meaning determines whether a life event becomes a stressor.
- Personality factors such as coping self-efficacy, optimism, emotional expressiveness, and a sense of personal meaning influence how resilient to stress a person is.
- Some people show important psychological growth in response to a traumatic event.
- Problem-focused coping is more adaptive for controllable stressors; emotion-focused strategies and support-seeking is more adaptive for uncontrollable ones.

Consider a possible interaction between the psychological factor of optimism and the environmental factor of an uncontrollable stressor, such as a natural disaster. How would the interaction of these two factors influence how the person would respond when the disaster occurred?

test yourself

Resilience

True or false?

1. Research on resilient children showed that authoritative parenting was the most important protective factor.
2. In Hofboll et al.'s study, about 35 percent of the Israelis subjected to terrorist and rocket attacks showed resilience.
3. Social support is a powerful buffer against stress, and it has been shown to enhance immune system functioning.
4. Optimism has been shown to be a major stress-protective factor that also is linked to longevity.
5. Religious beliefs can sometimes have negative effects in coping with stressors.
6. The "tend and befriend" response to stress that is characteristic in males has been linked to testosterone.

ANSWERS: 1-false, 2-true, 3-true, 4-true, 5-true, 6-false

PAIN AND ILLNESS

Physical pain surely is one of the most unpleasant realities of life, and most of us do our best to avoid this stressor. Hundreds of thousands seek relief from unbearable pain, and one-third of all people experience pain that requires medical attention at some time in their lives. One in 4 American adults say that in the past month they suffered a bout of pain that lasted at least one day, and 1 in 10 say that it lasted a year or more (National Center for Health Statistics, 2008). Pain is a significant feature of many illnesses, and some form of pain is responsible for 80 percent of all medical complaints in North America and Europe (Hunter et al., 2009).

Cultural and Psychological Influences on Pain

As a complex perception, pain is influenced by numerous factors. Cultural learning, meanings attributed to pain, beliefs, and personality factors all affect our experiences of pain.

Cultural Factors

Our interpretation of pain impulses sent to the brain depends in part on our experiences and beliefs, and both of these factors are influenced by the culture in which we develop (Rollman, 1998). Consider, for example, the experience of childbirth. This event is widely perceived as a painful ordeal in Western cultures, and many women express considerable anxiety about going through it (Blechman & Brownell, 1998). Yet in some cultures, women show virtually no distress during childbirth. Indeed, in one culture studied by anthropologists, it was customary for the woman's husband to get into bed and groan as if he were in great pain while the woman calmly gave birth to the child. The husband stayed in bed with the baby to recover from his terrible ordeal while the mother returned to work in the fields almost immediately (Kroeber, 1948).

Certain societies in India practice an unusual hook-hanging ritual. A holy person, chosen to bless children and crops, travels from village to village on a special ceremonial cart. Large steel hooks, attached by ropes to the top of the cart, are shoved under the skin and muscles on each side of the holy person's back. At the climax of the ceremony, he leaps from the cart and swings free, hanging only by the hooks embedded in his back (Figure 14.23). Incredibly, though hanging from the hooks with his entire body weight,

Figure 14.23

Cultural beliefs and pain tolerance.
Illustrated here is a hook-hanging ceremony practiced in remote villages in India. After blessing all the children and farm fields in a village, the celebrant leaps from the cart and hangs suspended by the hooks embedded in his back in a state of ecstasy, showing no sign of pain. Source: Adapted from Kosambi, 1967.

the celebrant shows no evidence of pain during the ritual; on the contrary, he appears to be in a state of ecstasy. When the hooks are removed, the wounds heal rapidly and are scarcely visible within two weeks (Kosambi, 1967).

Meanings and Beliefs

While different cultural groups do not appear to differ in their ability to discriminate among pain stimuli, they do differ greatly in their interpretation of pain and the amount of suffering they experience (Rollman, 1998; Zatzick & Dimsdale, 1990). In the Indian hook-hanging ceremony, for example, the religious meanings attached to the act seem to transform the interpretations and meaning of the sensory input from the hooks. Likewise, childbearing mothers in cultures where the pain of childbirth is not feared do not attach strong negative emotions to the associated sensations, and they therefore suffer far less.

Differences exist not only among cultural groups but also within them, as physician Henry Beecher (1959) observed while working at Anzio Beachhead in World War II and later at Massachusetts General Hospital. At Anzio, Beecher found that only about 25 percent of the severely wounded soldiers he observed required pain medication, compared with 80 percent of civilian men who had received similarly serious "wounds" from surgeons at Massachusetts

Figure 14.24

The amount of pain a wounded soldier experiences may be influenced by the meaning it has for him. Does the wound represent a ticket home to his loved ones, or does it herald a lifetime of pain and disability?

General. Why the difference? Beecher concluded that for the soldiers, the battle wounds meant evacuation from the war zone and a socially acceptable ticket back home to their loved ones. For the civilian surgical patients, on the other hand, the operation wounds meant a major life disruption and possible complications. The different meanings attributed to the pain stimuli resulted in very different levels of suffering and, consequently, different needs for pain relief (Figure 14.24).

Perhaps nowhere is the influence of belief on pain perception more evident than in the effects of **placebos,** *physiologically inert substances that have no medicinal value but are thought by the patient to be helpful* (Shapiro & Shapiro, 1997). At the beginning of this chapter, we described the observations made by German physician Hans Rehder, whose female patients responded with startling improvements in their symptoms to the news that he had invoked the healing powers of a faith healer. Similar observations have been made in pain research. In one classic study by Beecher (1959), either a placebo or a morphine injection was given to 122 surgical patients who were suffering postoperative pain. All were told they were receiving pain medication. Of those who received morphine, 67 percent reported relief, but 42 percent of those given placebos reported equal relief. More recent medical studies of placebo effects have yielded even higher rates of pain relief—as high as 100 percent in some studies (Hunter et al., 2009; Turner et al., 1994). However, it is also clear that placebos work only

if people *believe* they are going to work. Research using PET-scan technology at the Karolinska Institute in Sweden indicates that given a positive belief in the placebo's effectiveness, the brain sends messages that result in the release of **endorphins,** *opiate substances in the brain that reduce pain* (Petrovic et al., 2002).

Where pain is concerned, the statement "I can control it" may be more than an idle boast or an empty reassurance. In one experiment, patients suffering from the prolonged pain of a bone-marrow transplant were randomly assigned to one of two conditions. One group was allowed to directly control the amount of pain medication they received intravenously. The other patients were given prescribed amounts of the same medication by the hospital staff (and told they could request additional medication if needed). The patients who had direct control over their medication not only rated their pain as less intense but also gave themselves less pain medication (Zucker et al., 1998).

Personality Factors

People who have the personality trait of neuroticism—the tendency to appraise things negatively and to experience negative emotions such as anxiety, anger, and depression—report higher levels of physical pain, both in relation to medical conditions and in controlled laboratory administrations of painful stimuli such as heat, cold, electrical shock, or pressure (Edwards et al., 2006; Lahey, 2009). In contrast, personality styles that include optimism and a sense of personal control over one's life are associated with lower pain perception and less suffering (Eloviano & Kivimaki, 2009). Moreover, patients with chronic pain conditions who are able to simply accept the pain rather than bemoaning their fate and responding emotionally to it have less disability, better social adjustment, and higher work performance (McCracken, 1998).

The fact that psychological processes are so central to the experience of pain has stimulated research on methods that can be used to control or reduce pain and suffering. The following discussion highlights this important area of application.

Controlling Pain and Suffering

We all occasionally experience physical pain, and for some people, pain is a never-ending nightmare. Psychological pain-control strategies have received increasing attention from health psychologists (Gatchel, 2005; Turk & Winter, 2006).

Cognitive Strategies

Recent attention has focused on two classes of cognitive strategies known as *dissociation* and *association*. A *dissociative strategy* involves dissociating, or distracting, oneself from the painful sensory input. This can be done in a variety of ways: by directing your attention to some other feature of the external situation, by vividly imagining a pleasurable experience, or by repeating a word or thought to yourself. Research has shown that dissociative strategies are most effective when they require a great deal of concentration or mental activity, thereby directing attention away from the painful stimuli.

If you are a recreational jogger or a long-distance runner, you may be familiar with the discomfort of extending yourself. Endurance running seems an ideal real-life task to use in the study of cognitive strategies. William Morgan and coworkers (1983) gave this simple dissociative strategy to participants who were running on a treadmill to exhaustion: "Focus your attention on a spot in front of you on the treadmill, and say 'down' each time your right foot comes down on the treadmill." A control group also ran the treadmill but did not receive the strategy. Although the two groups did not differ physiologically while running on the treadmill, the mental-strategy group was able to tolerate the discomfort of treadmill running 32 percent longer than the control group.

A more dramatic, high-tech dissociative strategy is being used in the burn center at the Harborview Medical Center in Seattle, Washington. There, children and adults with burns covering up to 60 percent of their bodies are donning virtual-reality (VR) goggles during the often agonizing processes of wound cleansing and physical therapy. The goggles take patients into a visually compelling world of shapes and colors. Pain ratings are significantly lower when these patients are immersed in virtual reality than when they are in a nondistracted condition (Hoffman et al., 2001). In controlled laboratory research, VR has proven highly effective in reducing pain (Magora et al., 2006).

Associative strategies are just the opposite of dissociative ones. Here you focus your attention on the physical sensations and study them in a detached and unemotional fashion, taking care not to label them as painful or difficult to tolerate. It appears that when pain is intense, associative strategies become more effective than dissociative ones (McCaul & Malott, 1984). There seems to be a point at which pain stimuli become too intense to

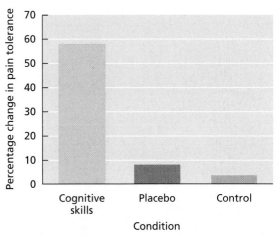

Figure 14.25

Coping strategies and pain tolerance.

These data show the increases in pain tolerance in an ice-water/hand-immersion task exhibited by a cognitive-skills training group, a placebo condition, and a control group that repeated the task with no intervention. SOURCE: Based on Bandura et al., 1987.

ignore and dissociative strategies become ineffective. Thus one strategy is to use dissociation as long as possible and then shift to an associative mode.

Combined dissociative and associative strategies can be quite effective in dealing with acute pain. In one study, participants' pain tolerance was tested by measuring how long they could keep one of their hands immersed in ice water. One group of participants was then trained and practiced a number of dissociative coping strategies (such as attention diversion and the use of distracting imagery) and associative strategies (such as imagining that the hand immersed in the ice water was detached from the body and focusing nonemotionally on the pain sensations). Two control groups equated in initial pain tolerance were given either no strategies or a placebo pain reducer. Then their ice-water pain tolerance was tested a second time. As shown in Figure 14.25, the cognitive-skills training resulted in a large increase in pain tolerance (Bandura et al., 1987).

Hospital Interventions: Giving Patients Informational Control

Having relevant information about a challenging environment and event is also a kind of cognitive control, since it tells us what to expect (Taylor, 2009). In the medical setting of the past, doctors typically gave patients no more information than needed about a specific medical procedure and its aftermath. However, psychological research on how certain types of information reduce anxiety

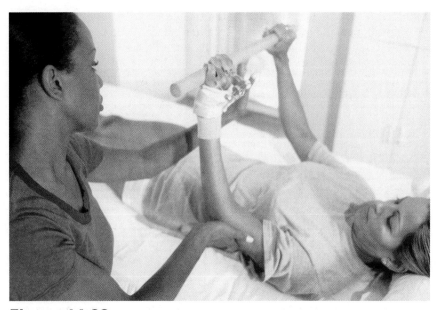

Figure 14.26

A key to preventing chronic pain and disability is to begin physical activity again as soon as possible.

and contribute to positive medical outcomes has ushered in a new era in many medical settings. Imagine that you're in the hospital for major surgery. You know that this surgical procedure entails risk and that your recovery will be painful. What kinds of information would help you cope and recuperate more easily?

You might profit from *sensory information* about what you will feel after the operation. Knowing, for example, that patients often have shooting pains in the stomach after the surgery could prevent surprise or fear if it occurred to you. You would see the pain as a normal consequence of the surgery and the recovery process rather than as a sign of danger.

Second, *procedural information* on the surgery itself would help you understand what exactly is going to be done and why. You might be shown a model of the body part to demonstrate what will be done in the surgery, or you might see a video describing the procedure (Auerbach et al., 2004). This kind of information would give you a sense of predictability and control and reassure you that precautions were being taken to anticipate and reduce possible hazards.

Third, you could profit from *coping guidance* about handling the pain or other complications from the surgery. For example, you might learn breathing exercises designed to reduce pain by helping you relax (Tollison et al., 2002). You also might be taught some of the cognitive strategies previously described to get through sieges of acute pain during the recovery process.

Informational interventions have proved helpful in many medical settings. Surgical patients show a better course of recovery and require less pain medication than those treated in a traditional fashion (Faust, 1991). Such interventions have proven remarkably successful in decreasing distress in hospitalized children, who are likely to find major medical procedures particularly frightening (Christopherson & Mortweet, 2001).

A Key Behavioral Strategy: Stay Active

Recovering patients who avoid activity and become overly protective of an injured body part are at risk for developing a chronic pain condition (Hunter et al., 2009; Turk, 2001). It is important to return to activity after an injury as soon as the healing process will allow (Figure 14.26). A key to successfully treating chronic-pain patients who have "shut themselves down" is to decrease their guarding and resting behaviors and to modify their belief that their pain signals body damage. Such interventions produce significant decreases in patient disability (Jensen et al., 2001). Wilbert Fordyce (1988), a leader in the behavioral treatment of pain, emphasizes the negative effects that unnecessary rest and disuse of a body part can have on recovery:

> The lavish prescription of rest virtually ensures adverse disuse effects. With disuse in the musculoskeletal system, movement then becomes painful. But pain from disuse risks being interpreted by patient and professional as an indication of lack of healing. The result may become more prescribed rest or practical disuse and yet more pain with movement. . . . Pain problems originating in tissue injury but in which healing has occurred are made better by use. Patients must be helped to understand the dictum "To make it better, use it.". . . People who have something better to do don't suffer as much. (p. 282)

Lifestyle Changes and Medical Recovery

Teaching people how to control their health-related behaviors can have dramatic benefits even for those who are already afflicted with serious illnesses. William Haskell and coworkers (1994) randomly divided a sample of patients suffering from coronary artery disease into two groups. Both groups received the usual high-quality medical care from their physicians at Stanford University Medical School. In addition, the experimental group received a behavioral self-regulation program that targeted health factors such as smoking, exercise, weight, nutrition, and medication adherence.

A 4-year follow-up revealed dramatic results. Those receiving the usual medical care showed either no improvement or a worsening of their conditions, and their health habits had not improved. In contrast, those who also received the behavioral self-regulation program showed significant positive changes in their health habits. They reduced their intake of dietary fat, lowered their bad (LDL) cholesterol and raised their good (HDL) cholesterol, increased their exercise, and raised their cardiovascular capacity. The program also influenced the progression of the disease; the self-management group, as compared with the control group, had 47 percent less buildup of blockage material on artery walls. During the 4-year follow-up period, 45 percent of the control patients either died or had nonfatal heart attacks or other cardiac emergencies, compared with only 24 percent in the behavior self-regulation group. Lifestyle-change procedures that increase self-efficacy may be especially useful. A recent study of patients suffering from coronary heart disease showed that self-efficacy for maintaining health predicted subsequent hospitalization and mortality as well as medical tests of cardiac function (Sarkar et al., 2009).

test yourself — Pain and Illness

True or false?

1. Some form of pain is responsible for up to 80 percent of all medical complaints in North America.

2. Regardless of culture, people experience suffering when their pain receptors are stimulated.

3. As Beecher observed, fewer World War II soldiers required pain medication for their wounds than civilian surgical patients with similar wounds.

4. Placebos are often as effective as pain medications in relieving pain.

5. Anxious and depressed people report higher levels of pain.

6. In response to intense pain, dissociative strategies are more effective than associative strategies.

7. For patients recovering from an injury, it is best to remain inactive.

ANSWERS: 1-true, 2-false, 3-true, 4-true, 5-true, 6-false, 7-false

HAPPINESS

For many years, researchers focused primarily on negative emotions such as anxiety, depression, and anger. More recently, however, attention has turned to the positive emotions (Aspinwall & Staudinger, 2003; Eid & Larson, 2008). Among psychological researchers, there currently is growing interest in the topic of happiness, or its more technical term **subjective well-being (SWB):** *people's emotional responses and their degree of satisfaction with various aspects of their life* (Diener, 2009; Seligman, 2002).

SWB is typically assessed by self-report ratings of contentment, happiness, and satisfaction. Before reading on, please see Table 14.6.

How Happy Are People?

Ed and Carol Diener (1996) reviewed findings from nearly 1,000 representative samples in 43 Westernized and developing nations. Across all countries, on the scale ranging from 0 to 10 shown in Table 14.6, the mean rating of personal happiness was 6.33, indicating mild happiness.

Table **14.6** | How Happy Are You?

Here are two measures of subjective well-being. Answer the following questions, then see the text to compare yourself with others.

First, how would you rate your own general life satisfaction on the following scale?

| 0 | 1 | 2 | 3 | 4 | 5 | 6 | 7 | 8 | 9 | 10 |

Most unhappy   *Most happy*

Next, answer the following questions:

What percentage of the time are you happy? _____

What percentage of the time are you neutral? _____

What percentage of the time are you unhappy? _____

(Make sure your percentages add up to 100.)

In only two economically poor nations, India and the Dominican Republic, did average SWB fall into the unhappy range of the scale. In the United States, all ethnic groups scored well above the neutral point on the happiness scale (Andrews, 1991). Nonetheless, countries differed in their levels of SWB, with the United States, Canada, Britain, and the Scandinavian countries ranked in the top 10 of the 43 countries.

On the second scale in Table 14.6, college students on average reported being happy 65 percent of the time, neutral 15 percent of the time, and unhappy 20 percent of the time (Larsen & Diener, 1985). Thus it appears that across many populations, people report living lives that are more happy than unhappy.

Who's happier, men or women? Research shows that the sexes are about equal in global happiness, but there is an important qualifier: women on average experience *both* positive and negative emotions more intensely than men do (Wood et al., 1989). The more extreme emotional responses of women balance out, resulting in an average level of happiness similar to that produced by men's less extreme highs and lows.

What Makes People Happy?

To answer this question, some researchers have examined the *resources* that might contribute to happiness, such as attractiveness, intelligence, wealth, and health. Others have studied internal *psychological processes* that underlie our experiences of happiness.

Personal Resources

Healthy?   Is health required for happiness? Not necessarily. On average, individuals with severe and disabling medical conditions such as paralyses do report lower levels of life satisfaction than nondisabled people, yet about two-thirds of disabled people rate their lives as somewhat or very satisfying (Mehnert et al., 1990).

Wealthy?   The actress Sophie Tucker once remarked, "I've been rich and I've been poor. Rich is better." Most people would probably agree with her statement. If you had more money, you'd be happier, correct? The media (especially those late-night infomercials) are filled with assertions that when you get that big house, fancy car, yacht, and vacation home, life will be absolutely blissful.

Well, perhaps not. Although people in affluent countries are happier on average than people who live in abject poverty, countries differ in many ways besides wealth (e.g., in terms of social and political turmoil) that could also affect SWB. When wealth and SWB are correlated within the same country, whether the country is poor or affluent, wealth is only weakly related to happiness (Diener et al., 1999). Even extreme changes in wealth, such as a big inheritance or winning a lottery, have only a temporary positive impact on SWB (Brickman et al., 1978). Thus, where health and wealth are concerned, not having enough of these resources may create unhappiness because important basic needs can't be met, but once adequate levels are attained, further increases seem to do little to promote lasting happiness. In the United States, wealth and happiness are moderately related if household income dips below $50,000, at which level families are struggling to pay the bills and put food on the table. But above $50,000, the wealth-happiness relation pretty much disappears (Helliwell & Putnam, 2004). The disconnect is graphically illustrated by the fact that on a 7-point scale of happiness (with 1 being "not a very happy person" and 7 being "a very happy person") the average score of *Forbes* magazine's 400 richest Americans was 5.8. But so was the average for a sample of Pennsylvania Amish, despite the fact that the average Amish person is poorer by several billion dollars. So, where money is concerned, the take-home message is "enough is enough."

Wise?   What about being smart? Overall, intelligence bears little relation to happiness (Seligman, 2002). Educational level does have a weak positive relation to SWB, probably because it helps people avoid poverty and compete for satisfying jobs. Unemployment is one of the strongest predictors of life dissatisfaction, and an adequate educational level can help people avoid this fate (Clark, 1998).

Relationships?   If being healthy, wealthy, and wise won't guarantee happiness, perhaps intimate relationships will. Here researchers consistently find that happy people have more satisfying social relationships (Diener et al., 2006). Additionally, married men and women are significantly happier on average than are single and divorced people. Still, the meaning of these correlational results is not clear. Do social relationships promote greater life satisfaction, or are happier, better-adjusted people more able to establish and sustain good social relationships and stable marriages? Or is there some third variable, such as a personality factor like being more extraverted (i.e., more outgoing), that promotes both happiness and the ability to develop satisfying social relations?

Biological and Psychological Processes

Overall, personal resources and external circumstances account for only about 15 to 20 percent of the total variability among people in happiness ratings (Argyle, 1999). Perhaps psychological processes, rather than resources, are the keys to happiness.

A Happiness Set Point? Increasing evidence points to a biologically based *set point* for positive affect, much like the one we described for body weight in Chapter 11. Gloomy Gus's baseline level of happiness may be attributable as much to the genes he inherited from his parents as to his life circumstances. A study of 2,310 identical and fraternal twins revealed that the identical twins were far more similar in SWB, regardless of their life circumstances (Lykken & Tellegen, 1996). Perhaps genetic factors contribute in some way to the individual differences in right- and left-hemisphere activation discussed earlier, or maybe they influence neurotransmitter systems that underlie positive and negative emotions (Hamer & Copeland, 1998).

The Hedonic Treadmill A biological set point for happiness would help account for what has been termed the **hedonic treadmill,** *our capacity to adapt to both good and bad*. Just as people adapt their walking speed to the speed of a treadmill, so people adapt to the positive and negative events of life. The hedonic treadmill may help account for some of the findings we reviewed about personal resources. For example, lottery winners experience ecstatic positive feelings at first, but in less than 3 months, they return to being no more happy than they were before. People who suffer paralysis are in the pits at first, then typically and gradually return to being more happy. This adaptation has limits. Certain major negative events, such as the death of a spouse or child, we never get used to or adapt to very slowly (Bonnano et al., 2008).

Cognitive Processes Having a sense of meaning in life also is correlated with happiness. Many people report that their spiritual or religious beliefs contribute to a sense of meaning, and some—though not all—studies find a positive correlation

between religiosity and happiness (Diener et al., 1999; Diener & Seligman, 2002). Giving of oneself, such as helping others as a volunteer, contributes to a sense of meaning and life satisfaction (Snyder et al., 2000). But again, causality is difficult to infer. Does a greater sense of meaning promote happiness? Does happiness lead people to feel that their life is more meaningful? Or does some third factor cause both?

"How well off are you?" we might ask. "Compared to whom?" you might reply. That's a very good answer. Research reveals that feelings of life satisfaction are based on how we compare ourselves and our circumstances with other people and their circumstances and with past conditions we have experienced (Buunk & Gibbons, 1997). When we engage in **downward comparison,** *seeing ourselves as better off than the standard for comparison,* we experience increased satisfaction. In contrast, **upward comparison,** *when we view ourselves as worse off than the standard for comparison*, produces dissatisfaction. In one study, college students kept a written record of every time they compared their appearance, grades, abilities, possessions, or personality with someone else's over a 2-week period. At the same time, they recorded their current mood. Downward comparisons with less fortunate or less talented people were consistently associated with positive moods, and upward comparisons were associated with negative emotional reactions (Wheeler & Miyake, 1992). Thus, depending on what or whom you compare yourself with, you can be an eagle among starlings or a moth among butterflies.

Personality and Cultural Factors Personality factors clearly predispose some people to be happier than others. Individuals who are sociable, optimistic, altruistic, curious, and open to new experiences report higher levels of happiness and are rated by others as happier than are those who have the opposite traits (Diener & Seligman, 2002; Larsen & Buss, 2010).

One's culture may also influence the factors that contribute to happiness. Eunkook Suh and coworkers (1998) found that in the individualistic "me" societies of North America and Europe, successes that people can attribute to their own skill and effort contribute to happiness. In collectivistic cultures of Southeast Asia, however, the well-being of the group seems to be a more important factor in personal happiness than one's own emotional life, and people derive more pleasure from accomplishments achieved as part of a group effort (Kitayama et al., 2000).

As we have seen, happiness is more than just a positive feeling. It also involves a more enduring component of life satisfaction and purpose. We are happiest when we use our attributes to pursue and achieve meaningful goals, and when these goals serve a higher purpose than ourselves, we achieve a contentment that transcends momentary pleasures. The building blocks of happiness are the positive emotions, and by their important role in helping us build personal resources and resilience, they form the link between happiness and desirable life outcomes (Cohn et al., 2009).

Applying Psychological Science

How to Be Happy: Guidelines from Psychological Research

As research has accumulated on factors that relate to happiness, psychologists have been able to offer advice based on data rather than intuition (Seligman, 2002; Snyder & Lopez, 2007). Most psychologists believe that happiness, like a good marriage, is something that one must work at (Diener & Biswas-Diener, 2008). Here, then, are some science-derived suggestions that may help you maintain and enhance personal happiness. (See also the "Research Close-up" "Very Happy People" on page 46.)

- *Spend time with other people, and work to develop close relationships.* Research consistently suggests that good relationships provide the strongest basis for life satisfaction. Even if you tend to be introverted, form at least a few close relationships, and nurture them. Make time for social interactions.
- *Look for ways to be helpful to others, and reach out to the less fortunate.* Try to make a positive difference in the lives of others. Doing so will increase your sense of self-worth, add meaning to your life, and deepen relationships with those whose lives you touch. It will also help put your own problems in perspective and direct your energies away from self-absorption. There's a lot to be said for the proposition that we receive by giving. In one 5-year longitudinal study of elderly people, Stephanie Brown and coworkers (2003) found that those who gave help and support to friends, relatives, and family members had lower mortality rates than those who did not, even when health and other quality-of-life variables were statistically controlled. Likewise, highly sociable people are more resistant to infectious diseases, despite their greater exposure to other people who might be contagious (Cohen et al., 2003). Martin Seligman (2002) believes that truly authentic and lasting happiness awaits those who utilize their virtues and strengths (i.e., your kindness, integrity, enthusiasm, perseverance) "in the service of something larger to obtain meaning" (p. 263).
- *Seek meaning and challenge in work.* Enjoying one's work is a prime ingredient of happiness. If you feel stuck doing something that provides little gratification, be it your job or your major, consider looking for something more satisfying. Everyone has to make a living, but many people spend their lives doing things they don't derive satisfaction or meaning from—hardly a recipe for a happy life. Even if you love your work, strive for balance between work and personal pursuits. People on their deathbeds rarely, if ever, express the wish that they had spent more time at the office.
- *Set meaningful personal goals for yourself, and make progress toward them.* Whether in work, school, or relationships, engaging in goal-directed activity and seeing yourself moving toward your goals will provide a basis for life satisfaction and foster feelings of being in greater control of your life. Many people find that spiritual development (religiously based or not) confers meaning in their lives.
- *Make time for enjoyable activities.* One of the benefits of time-management skills is the ability to schedule everyday activities that provide pleasure around school, work, and other obligations. Make time for a hobby, reading, and recreational activities.
- *Nurture physical well-being.* Many studies show that even moderate physical exercise contributes to emotional well-being (Morgan, 1997). Exercise provides a temporary respite from life's stressors. When done in a social context, it adds the benefits of social interaction as well. People who exercise, get sufficient sleep, and practice good dietary habits tend to be more stress resistant and satisfied with themselves and their lives (Taylor, 2009).
- *Be open to new experiences.* Some of our most pleasurable experiences can occur when we try new things. It's easy to fall into a rut, so whether it's traveling, developing a new hobby, or taking a college course on a new subject, be open to doing something you haven't done before.
- *Cultivate optimism, and count your blessings.* As we've seen, cognitive appraisals influence emotions, and an upbeat, optimistic approach to life is linked with subjective well-being. Try to look on the positive side of things, to see demanding events as challenges and opportunities rather than threats. Learn to appreciate and be grateful for even the mundane, average day in which nothing bad happens to you. There is a Buddhist saying: "Happiness is a day without a toothache." All of us are gifted in ways that we may take for granted. Perhaps we should focus more often on these typically ignored aspects of good fortune.

test yourself   **Happiness**

True or false?

1. College students report feeling happy about 30 percent of the time.
2. Wealthy people are happier in general than destitute people.
3. Health and intelligence are only weakly related to happiness.
4. Religiosity is generally found to be related to happiness.
5. Genetic factors may contribute to one's level of happiness.
6. Upward comparison tends to increase life satisfaction.
7. Personal success contributes more to happiness in collectivistic cultures than it does in individualistic cultures.

ANSWERS: 1-false, 2-true, 3-true, 4-true, 5-true, 6-false, 7-false

Chapter Summary

BEHAVIORAL FOUNDATIONS OF HEALTH

- Behavioral processes are important contributors to physical well-being. The field of health psychology studies factors that influence well-being as well as measures that might be taken to enhance well-being.
- Exercise affects both physical and psychological well-being. Numerous behavioral interventions have been developed to promote exercise, but many people fail to adhere to exercise programs. One factor that influences adherence is social support. People who are able to stick with an exercise program for 3 to 6 months have a better chance of adhering to it thereafter.
- About a third of the American population is obese, as are nearly 1 in 5 children and adolescents. Behavioral weight-control programs feature self-monitoring, stimulus-control procedures, and eating procedures designed to help people eat less but enjoy their food more. The addition of an exercise program to weight-control procedures enhances weight loss.
- Type A behavior pattern increases vulnerability to coronary heart disease. The anger/hostility component appears to be the most damaging facet of the Type A pattern.
- Because HIV infection is caused by high-risk sexual and drug-abuse behaviors (e.g., sharing needles), a prevention approach is essential. Cultural factors sometimes conflict with safe-sex practices, increasing the challenges of reducing health-endangering behaviors.
- Substance abuse is highly associated with other disorders and is often part of a larger pattern of maladjustment. A promising intervention technique is motivational interviewing, a nonconfrontational procedure designed to engage the person's own motivation to change self-defeating behaviors. Multimodal treatments combine a number of techniques,

including aversion therapy, stress-management and coping-skills training, and positive reinforcement for change.
- Harm-reduction approaches attempt to reduce the negative consequences that a behavior produces rather than to focus on stopping the behavior itself. Examples include needle exchange programs for drug addicts and programs designed to reduce the destructive consequences of binge drinking in college students.
- The transtheoretical model identifies six stages through which people may move during the process of successful long-term behavioral change: precontemplation, contemplation, preparation, action, maintenance, and termination.
- Relapse prevention is designed to keep lapses from becoming relapses by building effective coping skills to deal with high-risk situations and countering the abstinence violation effect when lapses occur. This approach enhances the effects of many behavior-change programs.

STRESS AND WELL-BEING

- Various theorists view stress as a stimulus; as a response having cognitive, physiological, and behavioral components; or as an interaction (i.e., transaction) between the person and the environment. The last view incorporates the stimulus and response conceptions into a more dynamic model.
- Stressors are events that place physical or psychological demands on organisms. The stressfulness of a situation is defined by the balance between demands and resources. Life events vary in terms of how positive or negative they are and how intense they are. Other dimensions that affect their impact include duration, predictability, controllability, and chronicity.

- Cognitive appraisal processes play an essential role in people's responses to stressors. People appraise the nature of the demands, the resources available to deal with them, the possible consequences of the situation, and the personal meaning of these consequences. Distortions at any of these levels can result in inappropriate stress responses.
- The physiological response to stressors is mediated by the autonomic and endocrine systems and involves a pattern of arousal that mobilizes the body to deal with the stressor. Selye described a general adaptation syndrome (GAS), which involves the stages of alarm, resistance, and exhaustion.
- Measures of both major negative life events and micro-stressors are associated with negative psychological outcomes, such as anxiety and depression. Life stress also is related to negative health changes. It can worsen preexisting medical conditions and increase the risk of illness and death. Reduced immune system functioning produces some of the negative health effects caused by stress.
- Individual differences in physiological reactivity also affect well-being. People who exhibit strong and prolonged arousal responses are more susceptible to negative psychological and health effects. Physiological reactivity can predispose people to health problems, particularly if they respond with high levels of cortisol.

RESILIENCE: FACING DOWN ADVERSITY

- Studies of highly resilient children reveal important characteristics that contribute to positive outcomes as children mature, such as good intellectual functioning, social skills, self-efficacy, and hope, usually nurtured by social support from at least one caring adult in the child's life.
- Vulnerability and protective factors make people more or less susceptible to stressors. Social support is an important protective factor, having both direct and buffering effects that help people cope with stress.
- Coping self-efficacy and optimism are cognitive protective factors. Trauma disclosure has shown at least short-term positive effects on physical and psychological well-being. Severe emotional constraint may be a health risk factor. Flexibility in emotional expression and suppression seems desirable. Spiritual beliefs often help people cope more effectively with stressful life events, but certain religious beliefs seem capable of increasing stress.

- Three major ways of coping with stressors are problem-focused coping, emotion-focused coping, and seeking social support. Problem-focused coping and seeking social support generally relate to better adjustment than emotion-focused coping. However, in situations involving low personal control, emotion-focused coping may be the most appropriate and effective strategy.
- Posttraumatic growth has been reported by some people who have endured major traumatic events.

PAIN AND ILLNESS

- Pain is a complex perception influenced by biological, psychological, and sociocultural factors.
- Cultural factors influence the appraisal and response to painful stimuli, as do beliefs. Expectations of relief produced by placebos can markedly reduce medical symptoms and pain. Negative emotional states increase suffering and decrease pain tolerance.
- Psychological techniques for pain control include (1) cognitive strategies, such as dissociative and associative techniques; (2) providing medical patients with sensory and procedural information to increase cognitive control and support; and (3) increasing activity level to counter chronic pain.

HAPPINESS

- In most countries, the average person is mildly happy. Psychological processes are more consistently related to subjective well-being than are resources such as health, wealth, and high intelligence.
- Evidence exists for a genetically based set point for subjective well-being. The hedonic treadmill reflects the tendency of people to return to this set point following positive or negative life events. Having a sense of meaning in life is correlated with happiness, as are downward comparisons, when we see ourselves as better off than the standard for comparison.
- Cultural differences exist in the bases for happiness. Success linked to individual skill and effort is more strongly linked with subjective well-being in individualistic cultures, whereas group welfare evokes happiness in collectivistic cultures.

KEY TERMS AND CONCEPTS

Each term has been boldfaced and defined in the chapter on the page indicated in parentheses.

abstinence violation effect (p. 518)
aerobic exercise (p. 508)
antigens (p. 523)
coping self-efficacy (p. 527)

downward comparison (p. 541)
emotion-focused coping
 (p. 530)
endorphins (p. 536)

general adaptation syndrome
 (GAS) (p. 521)
harm reduction (p. 516)
health psychology (p. 506)

thinking critically

DO STRESSFUL EVENTS CAUSE PSYCHOLOGICAL DISTRESS? (Page 522)

As we noted, the relation between stress and distress is correlational. Now let's think critically and challenge the causal interpretation. Certainly, it's possible that life stress causes psychological distress—and there are various kinds of evidence to suggest that it does. But it is also possible that distress may be the causal factor instead of the effect. That is, distressed people may be more likely than nondistressed people to remember and report negative things that have happened to them. Or they may tend to view more events as negative, resulting in higher negative life-change scores. Moreover, psychological distress could actually cause people to behave in ways that produce more negative events. For example, research has shown that anxious and depressed people often evoke negative reactions from others because of their gloomy outlook and their tendency to frustrate others' attempts to help them feel better.

And that's not all: a third possibility is that some other variable causes both negative life events *and* psychological distress to go up or down, thus creating the relation between them. The Big Five personality trait of Neuroticism, discussed in Chapter 13, might be such a third variable. We know that people who are high in neuroticism have a tendency to experience lots of negative emotions *and* to get themselves into stressful situations through their self-defeating behaviors (Lahey, 2009). Differences in neuroticism could thus cause the relation between stress and distress. These different causal possibilities remind us that stressful life events are part of a network of causal relations and that stressful life events can function as either a cause or an effect.

chapter fifteen

Psychological Disorders

CHAPTER OUTLINE

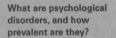

Myth or Reality?

People with Psychological Disorders Are Dangerous (page 575)

We often hear about violent crimes committed by mentally disturbed perpetrators. Are people with psychological disorders more dangerous than the average person? What do we know about the link between mental illness and violence?

In the early 1970s, one of your authors (RES) was a brand-new professor at the University of Washington. I remember well a most impressive young man who took my introductory psychology and personality courses. Even in those large classes, he stood out as one of the top students. He did very well on tests, made insightful comments in class, and seemed mature beyond his years. When he came to my office hours, impeccably dressed, to discuss his interest in a psychology major, I encouraged him to apply for the honors program. I learned that he was working at a local crisis clinic, manning a telephone hotline. I also saw him several times at UW basketball games, carrying a young child around on his shoulders, and I pointed him out to my wife as a model student.

At the time, I was doing research on psychological factors that influence jury decisions, and I was pleased when the young man came to me and asked me to be the advisor for his psychology honors thesis. He was interested in the role of a defendant's history of mental illness on judgments made by students acting on a mock jury, and he had a nice experimental study already in the planning stages. I met with him for several sessions to plan the study. One day he announced that he was going to postpone the study for a while because he was going to work for the governor's reelection committee. Six months later, he returned to tell me that he had decided to get his psychology degree without the honor's thesis so that he could apply to law school. He asked me to write a letter of recommendation. I gladly agreed to do so and wrote a glowing endorsement of his application. He was accepted to a good law school in another state, and I never saw him again.

Two years later, however, I received an unexpected visit from two homicide detectives from the Seattle Police Department. They said they had established my student, Ted Bundy, as a prime suspect in a string of murders of young women and wondered if I had any psychological insights that would assist them in their investigation.

As a well-trained clinical psychologist who was teaching a graduate course in clinical personality assessment, I wondered how I, like virtually everyone who knew Bundy, could have been so far off track in my glowing evaluation of a serial killer.

As a scientist, I wondered what kinds of causal factors could have combined to produce a charismatic, cold-blooded psychopathic murderer like Ted Bundy. As we'll examine in this chapter's discussion of personality disorders, researchers are piecing together the answers to this question, and all three levels of analysis—biological, psychological, and environmental—are involved.

THE SCOPE AND NATURE OF PSYCHOLOGICAL DISORDERS

Fortunately, there aren't many Ted Bundys among us. But that doesn't mean that psychological disorders do not have a major impact on individual and societal well-being. According to U.S. government statistics (National Institute of Mental Health, 2008):

- An estimated 26.2 percent of Americans ages 18 and older—about 57.7 million people—suffer from a diagnosable mental disorder in any given year.

- Nearly half of all Americans between the ages of 15 and 54 will experience a psychological disorder at some point in their lives.

- Psychological disorders are now the leading cause of disability, exceeding physical illnesses and accidents.

- Medications used to treat anxiety and depression are among the most frequently prescribed drugs in the United States.

- One American attempts suicide every 45 seconds, and 33,300 people end their lives each year.

- Each year, more than a million students withdraw from college because of emotional problems.

- One in 4 Americans will have a substance-abuse disorder during his or her lifetime, and alcohol abuse alone costs the U.S. economy about $117 billion a year in lost productivity.

- In developed economies like the United States, psychological disorders account for over 15 percent of the financial burden of illness, more than the burden caused by all cancers.

These cold statistics, startling though they may be, cannot possibly capture the intense suffering that they reflect. They cannot communicate the confusion and alienation felt by the schizophrenic person whose psychological world is disintegrating, the intense personal misery of a depressed person who is sinking into a quagmire of hopelessness, the terror experienced by someone with a panic disorder, or the frustration endured by the families and friends of those who have psychological disorders.

This chapter is therefore not just about the problems of "someone else." Even if you are fortunate enough to be in the 50 percent of people who will not experience a psychological disorder in your lifetime, statistics suggest that you'll almost surely have a family member, friend, or acquaintance who will.

Your college undoubtedly offers a course that deals with psychological disorders. At many schools, the course is titled "abnormal psychology." This title reflects a core notion that the thoughts, feelings, and behaviors of people who are diagnosed with a psychological disorder, or "mental illness," are different in some way. But what does "abnormal" mean?

What Is "Abnormal"?

Defining what is normal and what is abnormal is no easy matter, as there are many yardsticks we could apply. Here are a few possibilities (Leising et al., 2009; Wakefield, 2006):

1. The personal values of a given diagnostician

2. The expectations of the culture in which a person currently lives

3. The expectations of the person's culture of origin

4. General assumptions about human nature

5. Statistical deviation from the norm

6. Harmfulness, suffering, and impairment

Most people would not find criteria 1 and 5 satisfactory bases for judging a person to be disordered. Where criterion 1 is concerned, the diagnosis could depend on arbitrary and unusual beliefs of the person making the judgments, such as a conviction that women should never work. Where deviation from the norm (criterion 5) is concerned, an extremely well adjusted or highly intelligent person would be judged abnormal.

Criteria 2 through 4 do reflect cultural or even more widespread beliefs about what is appropriate, so that judgments about what is normal and what is abnormal can differ depending on the time and the culture. For example, cannibalism has been practiced in many cultures around the world (Walker, 2001). In contemporary Western culture, however, such behavior would be viewed as extraordinarily pathological. To cite a more realistic example, until December 15, 1973, homosexuality was officially considered a form of mental illness. On that day, however, the trustees of the American Psychiatric Association voted to remove homosexuality from the psychiatric classification system—surely the quickest and most widespread cure in the history of psychiatry. Despite this formal change in the psychiatric status of this sexual orientation, some people in our society continue to view homosexuality as an indicator of psychological disturbance, illustrating to some the arbitrary nature of abnormality judgments (Herek, 2002).

Despite the arbitrariness of time, place, and value judgments, three criteria inherent in criterion 6—distress, dysfunction, and deviance—seem to govern decisions about abnormality, and one or more of them seem to apply to virtually any behavior regarded as abnormal (Wakefield, 2006). As shown in Figure 15.1, we are likely to

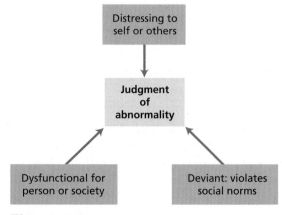

Figure 15.1

Abnormality as a social construct.
Whether a behavior is considered abnormal involves a social judgment made on the basis of the three Ds: distress, dysfunction, and deviance.

label behaviors as abnormal if they are intensely *distressing* to the individual. People who are excessively anxious, depressed, dissatisfied, or otherwise seriously upset about themselves or about life circumstances may be viewed as disturbed, particularly if they seem to have little control over these reactions. On the other hand, personal distress is neither necessary nor sufficient to define abnormality. Some seriously disturbed mental patients are so out of touch with reality that they seem to experience little distress, and yet their bizarre thought processes and behaviors are considered very abnormal. And although all of us experience suffering as a part of our lives, our distress is not likely to be judged abnormal unless it is disproportionately intense or long-lasting relative to the situation.

Second, most behaviors judged abnormal are *dysfunctional* either for the individual or for society. Behaviors that interfere with a person's ability to work or to experience satisfying relationships with other people are likely to be seen as maladaptive and self-defeating, especially if the person seems unable to control such behaviors. Some behaviors are labeled as abnormal because they interfere with the well-being of society. But even here, the standards are not cut-and-dried. For example, is a suicide bomber who detonates a bomb in a public market a psychologically disturbed individual, a criminal, or a patriot?

The third criterion for abnormality is society's judgments concerning the *deviance* of a given behavior. Conduct within every society is regulated by *norms*, behavioral rules that specify how people are expected to think, feel, and behave. Some norms are explicitly codified as laws, and violation of these norms defines criminal behavior. Other norms, however, are far less explicit. For example, it is generally expected in our culture that one should not carry on animated conversations with people who are not present, nor should one face the rear of an elevator and stare intently into the eyes of a fellow passenger (don't try this unless you want to see an elevator empty out quickly). People are likely to be viewed as psychologically disturbed if they violate these unstated norms, especially if the violations make others uncomfortable and cannot be attributed to environmental causes.

To summarize, both personal and social judgments of behavior enter into considerations of what is abnormal. Thus we may define **abnormal behavior** *as behavior that is personally distressing, personally dysfunctional, and/or so culturally deviant that other people judge it to be inappropriate or maladaptive.* There is great variety in the behaviors that are judged to be abnormal in contemporary society. Indeed, no less than 374 disorders are included in the current manual of the American Psychiatric Association—the DSM-IV-TR (*Diagnostic and Statistical Manual of Mental Disorders, Fourth Edition, Textual Revision*). Table 15.1 shows some of the major categories.

Table **15.1** | **A Sample of Major Diagnostic Categories in the DSM-IV-TR**

1. *Anxiety disorders:* Intense, frequent, or inappropriate anxiety, but no loss of reality contact: includes phobias, generalized anxiety reactions, panic disorders, obsessive-compulsive disorders, and posttraumatic stress disorders
2. *Mood (affective) disorders:* Marked disturbances of mood, including depression and mania (extreme elation and excitement)
3. *Somatoform disorders:* Physical symptoms, such as blindness, paralysis, or pain, that have no physical basis and are assumed to be caused by psychological factors; also, excessive preoccupations and worry about health (hypochondriasis)
4. *Dissociative disorders:* Psychologically caused problems of consciousness and self-identification, including amnesia and multiple personalities (dissociative identity disorder)
5. *Schizophrenic and other psychotic disorders:* Severe disorders of thinking, perception, and emotion that involve loss of contact with reality and disordered behavior
6. *Substance-abuse disorders:* Personal and social problems associated with the use of psychoactive substances, such as alcohol, heroin, or other drugs
7. *Sexual and gender identity disorders:* Inability to function sexually or enjoy sexuality (sexual dysfunctions): deviant sexual behaviors, such as child molestation and arousal by inappropriate objects (fetishes); strong discomfort with one's gender accompanied by the desire to be a member of the other sex
8. *Eating disorders:* Includes anorexia nervosa (self-starvation) and bulimia nervosa (patterns of binging and purging)
9. *Personality disorders:* Rigid, stable, and maladaptive personality patterns, such as antisocial, dependent, paranoid, and narcissistic disorders

Source: Based on American Psychiatric Association, 2000.

HISTORICAL PERSPECTIVES ON DEVIANT BEHAVIOR

Psychological disorders are not just a modern problem. The pages of history are filled with accounts of prominent people who suffered from psychological disorders (Figure 15.2). The Bible describes King Saul's mad rages and terrors. Tamerlane, the 14th-century Mongol conqueror of much of Europe and Asia, delighted in constructing pyramids made up of as many as 40,000 human skulls. The composer Mozart developed marked paranoid symptoms and was convinced he was being poisoned during the time he was composing his *Requiem.* Abraham Lincoln suffered recurrent bouts of depression throughout his life and was, on one occasion, so depressed that he failed to show up for his own wedding. Winston Churchill also periodically suffered from severe depression, referring to it as his "black dog." Contemporary celebrities Donald Trump and Cameron Diaz both have publicly discussed their obsession with germs, which causes Trump to avoid pushing elevator buttons or shaking hands and compelled Diaz to wash her hands many times a day and open doors with her elbows.

Throughout history, human societies have explained and responded to abnormal behavior in different ways at different times, based on their values and assumptions about human life and behavior. The belief that abnormal behavior is caused by supernatural forces goes back to the ancient Chinese, Egyptians, and Hebrews, all of whom attributed deviance to the work of the devil. One ancient treatment was based on the notion that bizarre behavior reflected an evil spirit's attempt to escape from a person's body. In order

Figure 15.3

An early treatment for disordered behavior was trephination, in which a hole was chiseled through the skull to release the evil spirit thought to be causing the abnormal behavior. Some people survived the operation, but many died from it.

to release the spirit, a procedure called *trephination* was carried out. A sharp tool was used to chisel a hole about 2 centimeters in diameter in the skull (Figure 15.3). It seems likely that in many cases trephination successfully eliminated abnormal behavior by putting an end to the patient's life.

In medieval Europe, the demonological model of abnormality held that disturbed people either were possessed involuntarily by the devil or had voluntarily made a pact with the forces of darkness (Figure 15.4). The killing of witches was justified on theological grounds, and various "diagnostic" tests were devised. One was to bind a woman's hands and feet and throw her into a lake or pond. Based on the notion that impurities float to the surface, a woman who sank and drowned could be posthumously declared pure

Figure 15.2

Abraham Lincoln and Winston Churchill suffered from severe depression during their lifetimes. Celebrities Cameron Diaz and Donald Trump have reported obsessive-compulsive issues involving germ contamination.

Figure 15.4

This painting by Francisco de Goya reflects the widespread belief that disordered people were possessed by the devil. *Sabbath* portrays the weekly gathering of Satan and the witches he possessed.

(a pronouncement that must have been enormously comforting to her loved ones). Of course, a woman who floated was in *real* trouble. During the 16th and 17th centuries, more than 100,000 people with psychological disorders were identified as witches, hunted down, and executed.

Centuries earlier, about the 5th century B.C., the Greek physician Hippocrates suggested that mental illnesses were diseases just like physical disorders. Anticipating the modern viewpoint, Hippocrates believed that the site of mental illness was the brain. By the 1800s, Western medicine had returned to viewing mental disorders as biologically based and was attempting to extend medical diagnoses to them. The biological emphasis was given impetus by the discovery that *general paresis*, a disorder characterized in its advanced stages by mental deterioration and bizarre behavior, resulted from massive brain deterioration caused by the sexually transmitted disease syphilis. This was a breakthrough—the first demonstration that a psychological disorder was caused by an underlying physical malady.

In the early 1900s, Sigmund Freud's theory of psychoanalysis ushered in psychological interpretations of disordered behavior. As we shall see, psychodynamic theories of abnormal behavior were soon joined by other models based on behavioral, cognitive, and humanistic concepts. These various conceptions focus on different classes of causal factors and help capture the complex determinants of abnormal behavior. The importance of cultural factors has also received increasing attention. Although many questions remain, these perspectives have given us a deeper understanding of how biological, psychological, and environmental factors can combine to cause psychological disorders.

Today, many psychologists find it useful to incorporate these factors into a more general framework. According to the **vulnerability-stress model** (sometimes called the *diathesis-stress model;* Figure 15.5), *each of us has some degree of vulnerability (ranging from very low to very high) for developing a psychological disorder, given sufficient stress.* The *vulnerability*, or predisposition, can have a biological basis, such as our genotype, over- or underactivity of a neurotransmitter system in the brain, a hair-trigger autonomic nervous system, or a hormonal factor. It could also be due to a personality factor, such as low self-esteem or extreme pessimism, or to previous environmental factors, such as poverty or a severe trauma or loss earlier in life. Likewise, cultural factors can create vulnerability to certain kinds of disorders (Tinsley-Li & Jenkins, 2007).

But vulnerability is only part of the equation. In most instances, a predisposition creates a disorder only when a *stressor*—some recent or current event that requires a person to cope—combines with the vulnerability to trigger the disorder (van Praag, 2004). Thus a person who has a genetic predisposition to depression or who suffered a traumatic loss of a parent early in life may be primed

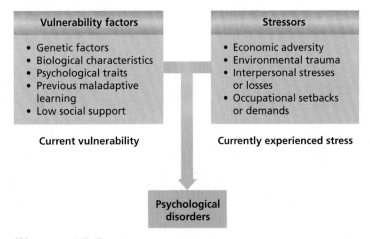

Figure 15.5

The vulnerability-stress model.
This popular conception attributes behavior disorders to interactions between personal vulnerability factors and life stressors. Personal vulnerability factors contribute to maladaptive efforts to cope with life's challenges.

to develop a depressive disorder *if* faced with the stress of a significant loss later in life. As we shall see, the biological, psychological, and environmental levels of analysis have all contributed to the vulnerability-stress model and to our understanding of behavior disorders and how they develop.

? thinking **critically**

"DO I HAVE THAT DISORDER?"

When people read descriptions of disorders, whether physical or psychological, they often see some of those symptoms or characteristics in themselves. In medical education, this is sometimes termed "medical students' disease." If you experience such concerns as you read about the various psychological disorders in this chapter, how should you decide whether you have a problem worthy of professional attention? After thinking about this, compare your standards with those discussed on page 590.

We now discuss the major psychological disorders, as well as the causal factors that have been identified by researchers. Later, we discuss scientific and societal issues relating to the process of psychiatric diagnosis. We begin with disorders that are characterized by distressing and maladaptive emotions, namely, anxiety and depression.

ANXIETY DISORDERS

Naomi was walking across campus the first time it happened. Her heart began pounding and skipping beats. She grew weak and shaky, began sweating profusely, and felt an indescribable sense of impending doom. She was sure she was either going insane or was about to die on the spot. Gathering all her strength, she made it to her dormitory room and began to feel better. Now, after several such incidents while on campus, she is afraid to leave her dorm.

We have all experienced **anxiety,** *the state of tension and apprehension that is a natural response to perceived threat.* In **anxiety disorders,** *the frequency and intensity of anxiety responses are out of proportion to the situations that trigger them, and the anxiety interferes with daily life.*

Anxiety responses have four components: (1) a *subjective-emotional* component, including feelings of tension and apprehension; (2) a *cognitive* component, including worrisome thoughts and a sense of inability to cope; (3) *physiological* responses, including increased heart rate and blood pressure, muscle tension, rapid breathing, nausea, dry mouth, diarrhea, and frequent urination; and (4) *behavioral* responses, such as avoidance of certain situations and impaired task performance (Barlow, 2002; Figure 15.6). Anxiety disorders take a number of different forms, including phobic disorder, generalized anxiety disorder, panic disorder, obsessive-compulsive disorder, and posttraumatic stress disorder.

Two statistics are commonly used in epidemiological research. *Incidence* refers to the number of *new* cases that occur during a given period. *Prevalence* refers to the number of people who have a disorder during a specified period of time (i.e., both new and previously existing cases). Large-scale population studies indicate that anxiety disorders are the most prevalent psychological disorders in the United States, affecting 18.6 percent of adult Americans in a given year (Kessler et al., 2005b; National Institute of Mental Health, 2008).

Anxiety disorders can express themselves in a variety of ways. Figure 15.7 shows prevalence rates for the various anxiety disorders, each of which occurs more frequently in females than in males. In more than 70 percent of cases, anxiety disorders interfere significantly with life functions or cause the person to seek medical or psychological treatment (Narrow et al., 2002).

Phobic Disorder

Phobias *are strong and irrational fears of certain objects or situations.* The word *phobia* is derived from *Phobos,* the Greek god of fear, whose likeness was painted on masks and shields to frighten enemies in battle. Today's phobic individual fights a different kind of battle, with fears of a less realistic but no less intense nature.

Figure 15.6

Components of anxiety. Anxiety consists of subjective-emotional, cognitive, physiological, and behavioral components.

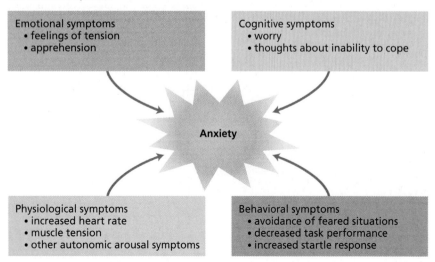

Emotional symptoms
• feelings of tension
• apprehension

Cognitive symptoms
• worry
• thoughts about inability to cope

Anxiety

Physiological symptoms
• increased heart rate
• muscle tension
• other autonomic arousal symptoms

Behavioral symptoms
• avoidance of feared situations
• decreased task performance
• increased startle response

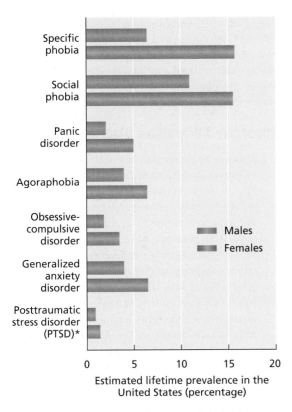

Figure 15.7

Prevalence rates for anxiety disorders.
This graph shows the lifetime prevalence rates for anxiety disorders in American men and women. All of the anxiety disorders occur more frequently in women. Sources: Based on Kessler et al., 2005a.

People with phobias realize that their fears are out of proportion to the danger involved, but they feel helpless to deal with these fears. Instead, they make strenuous efforts to avoid the phobic situation or object. Among the most common phobias in Western society are **agoraphobia,** *a fear of open or public places from which escape would be difficult;* **social phobias,** *excessive fear of situations in which the person might be evaluated and possibly embarrassed;* and **specific phobias,** *such as a fear of dogs, snakes, spiders, airplanes, elevators, enclosed spaces, water, injections, or germs.* Animal fears are common among women; fear of heights, among men (Curtis et al., 1998). Phobias can develop at any point in life, but some of them arise during childhood. Many social phobias evolve out of extreme shyness during childhood (Beidel & Turner, 2007). Phobias may also begin in adolescence or early adulthood. Once phobias develop, they seldom go away on their own, and they may broaden and intensify over time (Stein & Hollander, 2002).

The degree of impairment caused by a phobia depends in part on how often the phobic stimulus

Figure 15.8

People who suffer from phobic disorders cope in different ways. One woman's acrophobia (fear of heights) has not prevented her from operating the glass-walled elevator to the top of Seattle's 600-foot Space Needle for more than 20 years. She never looks out the window or through the narrow crack between her elevator door and the observation deck. Away from her job, the woman is afraid to climb a ladder or stand on a chair.

is encountered in the individual's normal activities. For example, fear of flying is a common phobia that occurs in some 25 million Americans (Kessler et al., 2005b). An airplane phobia may be a relatively minor inconvenience for a person who never needs to fly, but it would be a serious handicap for a sales representative whose job requires extensive travel. Some people, however, are able to develop job-saving strategies to keep their anxiety manageable (Figure 15.8).

Generalized Anxiety Disorder

As its name implies, **generalized anxiety disorder** *is a chronic (ongoing) state of diffuse, or free-floating, anxiety that is not attached to specific situations or objects.* The anxiety may last for months, with the signs almost continually present.

> Emotionally, John feels jittery, tense, and constantly on edge. Cognitively, he expects something awful to happen but doesn't know what.

Physically, John sweats constantly under his arms, his stomach is usually upset, he has diarrhea, and he is unable to attain a refreshing level of sleep.

As we might expect, this disorder can markedly interfere with daily functioning, even if the symptoms are not continually present for the 6 months required for a formal diagnosis (Kessler & Wittchen, 2002). The person may find it hard to concentrate, to make decisions, and to remember commitments. Onset tends to occur in childhood and adolescence (Kessler et al., 2005a).

Panic Disorder

In contrast to generalized anxiety disorder, which involves chronic tension and anxiety, **panic disorders** *occur suddenly and unpredictably, and they are much more intense.* The symptoms of panic attacks can be terrifying. As in the case of Naomi, the college student described above, it is not unusual for victims to believe that they are dying (Ballenger, 2000).

As in Naomi's case, panic attacks usually occur out of the blue and in the absence of any identifiable stimulus. It is this unpredictable quality that makes panic attacks so mysterious and terrifying to their victims. About 60 percent of people with daytime panic disorders also experience attacks during their sleep. Their symptoms awaken them, and they fear that they are dying (Craske & Rowe, 1997).

Many people who suffer recurrent panic attacks develop agoraphobia (an aversion to public places) because they fear that they will have an attack in public. In extreme cases, they may fear leaving the familiar setting of the home, and some have been known to remain housebound for years at a time because of their "fear of fear."

As the attacks continued, Ms. Watson began to dread going out of the house alone. She feared that while out she would have an attack and would be stranded and helpless. She stopped riding the subway to work out of fear she might be trapped in a car between stops when an attack struck, preferring instead to walk the 20 blocks between her home and work. Social and recreational activities, previously frequent and enjoyed, were severely curtailed because an attack might occur. (Spitzer et al., 1983, p. 8)

Formal diagnosis of a panic disorder requires recurrent attacks that do not seem tied to environmental stimuli, followed by psychological or behavioral problems. These typically involve persistent fear of future attacks or agoraphobic responses. Panic disorders with or without agoraphobia tend to appear in late adolescence or early adulthood and affect about 6 percent of the population over

their lifetimes (Kessler et al., 2005a). Even more common are occasional panic attacks. In one survey of Canadian students, 34 percent reported having had at least one unexpected panic attack within the previous year, usually during periods of extreme stress (Norton et al., 1985).

Obsessive-Compulsive Disorder

A 38-year-old mother of one child had been obsessed by fears of contamination during her entire adult life. Literally hundreds of times a day, thoughts of being infected by germs would occur to her. Once she began to think that either she or her child might become infected, she could not dismiss the thought. The constant concern about infection resulted in a series of washing and cleaning rituals that took up most of her day. Her child was confined to one room only, which the woman tried to keep entirely free of germs by scrubbing it—floor to ceiling—several times a day. Moreover, she opened and closed all doors with her feet, in order to avoid contaminating her own hands. (Rachman & Hodgson, 1980)

This woman was diagnosed as having an *obsessive-compulsive disorder.* Such disorders usually consist of two components—one cognitive, the other behavioral—although either can occur alone. **Obsessions** *are repetitive and unwelcome thoughts, images, or impulses that invade consciousness, are often abhorrent to the person, and are very difficult to dismiss or control.* This mother was tyrannized by thoughts and images of contamination. **Compulsions** *are repetitive behavioral responses*—like the woman's cleaning rituals—*that can be resisted only with great difficulty.* Compulsions are often responses that function to reduce the anxiety associated with the intrusive thoughts (Clark & O'Connor, 2005; De Silva & Rachman, 1998). Once the mother performed her compulsive cleaning acts, she was relatively free from anxiety, at least until the thoughts of contamination intruded once more.

In this case, the woman's germ obsession clearly interfered with her life, as well as her daughter's. One man's obsession resulted in a far more favorable outcome: Louis Pasteur's discovery of a process for eliminating destructive microorganisms and limiting fermentation in milk, beer, and other liquids. His tireless work on this invention was fueled in part by his own obsession about contamination and infection. Pasteur refused to shake hands with others and had a ritual of vigorously wiping his plate and glass before dining (Asimov, 1997).

Behavioral compulsions are extremely difficult to control. They often involve checking things repeatedly (for example, whether the door was locked or the gas burners on the stove were turned off), cleaning or hand washing, and repeating tasks endlessly. If the person does not perform the compulsive act, he or she may experience strong anxiety, perhaps even a panic attack. Like phobic avoidance responses, compulsions are strengthened through a process of negative reinforcement, because they allow the person to avoid anxiety (Jenike, 1998).

Recent studies have found the lifetime prevalence of obsessive-compulsive disorder in the United States to be about 1.6 per 100 people. Onset typically occurs in the 20s (Kessler et al., 2005a).

Posttraumatic Stress Disorder

Posttraumatic stress disorder (PTSD) *is a severe anxiety disorder that can occur in people who have been exposed to traumatic life events* (Figure 15.9). Four major symptoms commonly occur in this anxiety disorder (Falsetti et al., 2005; Wilson & Keane, 2004):

1. The person experiences severe symptoms of anxiety, arousal, and distress that were not present before the trauma.

2. The victim relives the trauma recurrently in flashbacks, in dreams, and in fantasy.

3. The person becomes numb to the world and avoids stimuli that serve as reminders of the trauma.

4. The individual experiences intense survivor guilt in instances where others were killed and the individual was somehow spared.

The PTSD category arose in part from studies of soldiers who had been subjected to the horrors of war. One study found the incidence of PTSD to be 7 times more likely for Vietnam veterans who spent significant time in combat and were wounded than for other Vietnam-era veterans (Centers for Disease Control [CDC], 1988). Another study reported a 12-month PTSD rate of 27.8 percent following combat exposure (Prigerson et al., 2002). Civilian war victims may be even more vulnerable than soldiers. Amy Ai and coworkers (2002) found a PTSD rate of 60.5 percent in a sample of refugees from the bloody civil war in Kosovo. On average, the refugees reported having experienced 15 war-related traumatic events. Traumas caused by human actions, such as war, rape, and torture, are 5 to 10 times more likely to precipitate PTSD than are natural disasters, such as hurricanes and earthquakes (Bracha, 2006; Corales, 2005). Compared with men, women exhibit twice the rate of PTSD following exposure to traumatic events (Kimerling et al., 2003).

Figure 15.9

The devastation and loss of life caused by natural disasters like this one can have long-lasting psychological consequences.

Terrorist acts can exact a heavy toll in PTSD. Interviews with 1,008 adult residents of Manhattan revealed that 7.5 percent experienced symptoms consistent with a PTSD diagnosis in the 5 to 8 weeks following the attacks of September 11, 2001. In those living closest to the World Trade Center, the PTSD rate was 20 percent (Galea et al., 2002).

The psychological wreckage caused by PTSD may increase vulnerability to the later development of other disorders. One study found that women who experienced PTSD had twice the risk of developing a depressive disorder and 3 times the risk of developing alcohol-related problems in the future (Bresalau et al., 1997). A meta-analysis of 39 studies showed sharp increases in anger, hostility, and aggression after trauma exposure (Orth & Wieland, 2006). Such findings highlight the importance of posttrauma intervention aimed at preventing the development of PTSD (Litz, 2004).

Causal Factors in Anxiety Disorders

Anxiety is a complex phenomenon having biological, psychological, and environmental causes, and all three levels of analysis have provided major insights into the development and maintenance of anxiety disorders. Within the vulnerability-stress model presented earlier, any of these factors can create predispositions to respond to stressors with an anxiety disorder (Beidel et al., 2007; Velotis, 2006).

Biological Factors

Genetic factors may create a vulnerability to anxiety disorders (Jang, 2005). Where clinical levels of anxiety are concerned, identical twins have a concordance rate (i.e., if one twin has it, so does the other) of about 40 percent for anxiety disorders, compared with a 4 percent concordance rate in fraternal twins (Carey & Gottesman, 1981). Recent research indicates that as much as 61 percent of the population variance in panic disorder and 44 percent of the agoraphobia variance is genetically influenced (Gelernter & Stein, 2009). Although such findings indicate a genetic predisposition, the concordance rate even in identical twins is far from 100 percent, indicating the significance of psychological and environmental factors.

Psychologist David Barlow (2002), a leading expert on anxiety disorders, suggests that the genetically caused vulnerability may take the form of an autonomic nervous system that overreacts to perceived threat, creating high levels of physiological arousal. Hereditary factors may also cause overreactivity of neurotransmitter systems involved in emotional responses (Brown & Barlow, 2009; Mineka et al., 1998). One such transmitter is GABA (gamma-aminobutyric acid), an inhibitory transmitter that reduces neural activity in the amygdala and other brain structures that trigger emotional arousal. Some researchers believe that abnormally low levels of inhibitory GABA activity in these arousal areas may cause some people to have highly reactive nervous systems that quickly produce anxiety responses to stressors (Bremner, 2000). In support of this hypothesis, brain scans show that patients with a history of panic attacks have a 22 percent lower concentration of GABA in the occipital cortex than age-matched controls without panic disorder (Goddard et al., 2001). Such people also could be more susceptible to classically conditioned phobias because they already have a strong unconditioned arousal response in place, ready to be conditioned to new stimuli. Other transmitter systems, particularly serotonin, also are involved in the anxiety disorders (Akimova et al., 2009).

As noted earlier, women exhibit anxiety disorders more often than men do. In a large-scale study of adolescents, Peter Lewinsohn and coworkers (1998) found that this sex difference emerges as early as 7 years of age. Even when the researchers applied statistical methods to control for sex differences in 11 psychosocial factors (including negative life events, self-esteem, and social support), a large sex difference in anxiety disorders remained. Such findings suggest a sex-linked biological predisposition for anxiety disorders, but social conditions that give women less power and personal control may also contribute (Craske, 2003). As in other instances of sex differences, it seems likely that biological, psychological, and environmental factors combine in complex ways.

Psychological Factors

Psychodynamic Theories   Anxiety is a central concept in psychoanalytic conceptions of abnormal behavior. Freud referred to anxiety-based disorders as *neuroses*. According to Freud, **neurotic anxiety** *occurs when unacceptable impulses threaten to overwhelm the ego's defenses and explode into consciousness or action.* How the ego's defense mechanisms deal with neurotic anxiety determines the form of the anxiety disorder. Freud believed that in phobic disorders, neurotic anxiety is displaced onto some external stimulus that has symbolic significance in relation to the underlying conflict. For example, in one of Freud's most celebrated cases, a 5-year-old boy named Hans suddenly developed a fear of horses and the possibility of being bitten. Seeing a horse fall down near his home worsened his fear, and little Hans began to dread leaving his home. To Freud, the phobia resulted from the boy's unresolved Oedipus complex. The powerful horse represented Hans's father, and the fear of being bitten symbolized Hans's unconscious fear of being castrated by his father if he acted on his sexual desire for his mother; the falling horse symbolized Hans's forbidden triumph over his father.

Psychoanalysts believe that obsessions and compulsions are also ways of handling anxiety. According to Freud, the obsession is symbolically related to, but less terrifying than, the underlying impulse. A compulsion is a way of taking back, or undoing, one's unacceptable urges, as when obsessive thoughts about dirt and compulsive hand washing are used to deal with one's "dirty" sexual impulses. Finally, generalized anxiety and panic attacks are thought to occur when one's defenses are not strong enough to control or contain neurotic anxiety but are strong enough to hide the underlying conflict.

Cognitive Factors   Cognitive theorists stress the role of maladaptive thought patterns and beliefs in anxiety disorders (Brown & Barlow, 2009). People with anxiety disorders catastrophize about demands and magnify them into threats. They anticipate that the worst will happen and feel powerless to cope effectively (Clark, 1988). Attentional processes are especially sensitive to threatening stimuli (Bar-Haim et al., 2007). Intrusive thoughts about the previous traumatic event are a central feature of posttraumatic stress disorder, and the presence of such thoughts after the trauma predicts the later development of PTSD (Falsetti et al., 2005).

Cognitive processes also play an important role in panic disorders. According to David Barlow (2002), panic attacks can be triggered by exaggerated misinterpretations of normal anxiety symptoms, such as heart palpitations, dizziness, and breathlessness. The person appraises these as signs that a heart attack or a psychological loss of control is about to occur, and these catastrophic appraisals create even more anxiety until the process spirals out of control, producing a full-blown state of panic (Figure 15.10). Helping panic patients replace such mortal-danger appraisals with more benign interpretations of their bodily symptoms (e.g., "It's only a bit of anxiety, not a heart attack") results in a marked reduction in panic attacks (Barlow, 1997; Craske, 1999).

The Role of Learning From the behavioral perspective, classical conditioning, observational learning, or operant conditioning can contribute to the development of an anxiety disorder. Some fears are acquired as a result of traumatic experiences that produce a classically conditioned fear response (Waters et al., 2009). For example, a person who has suffered a traumatic fall from a high place may develop a fear of heights (CR) because the high place (CS) was associated with the pain and trauma of the fall (UCS).

Classical conditioning cannot be the whole story, however, because many phobic people have never had a traumatic experience with the phobic object or situation that they now fear (Bruce & Sanderson, 1998; Menzies & Clarke, 1995). Most people who are afraid to fly have never been in an airplane crash. So how did they learn their fear? Clearly, phobias also can be acquired through observational learning. For example, televised images of airplane crashes evoke high levels of fear in some people. Yet most people do not develop phobias under these conditions, so there must be still more going on. It may be that biological dispositions and cognitive factors help determine whether a person develops a phobia from observing or even hearing about a traumatic event. Thus, if a person has a biological disposition toward intense fear, experiences traumatic scenes vicariously, and comes to believe that "the same thing could happen to me," the likelihood of developing a phobia on the basis of observational learning may increase.

Once anxiety is learned, either through classical or vicarious conditioning, it may be triggered either by cues from the environment or by internal cues, such as thoughts and images (Pitman et al., 2000). In phobic reactions, the cues tend to be

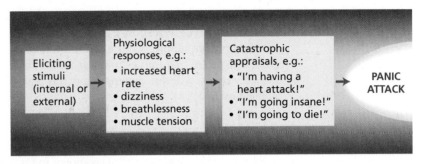

Figure 15.10

What causes panic attacks?
Cognitive explanations of panic attacks describe a process in which normal manifestations of anxiety are appraised catastrophically, increasing anxiety to a level that ultimately results in a full-blown panic attack.

external ones relating to the feared object or situation. In panic disorders, the anxiety-arousing cues tend to be internal ones, such as bodily sensations (e.g., heart palpitations) or mental images, such as the image of collapsing and having a seizure in a public place (Craske, 1999).

In addition to classical conditioning and observational learning, operant conditioning also plays a role. People are highly motivated to avoid or escape anxiety because it is such an unpleasant emotional state. As you'll recall from Chapter 7, negative reinforcement is the process whereby behaviors that are successful in reducing an undesirable consequence (such as anxiety) are strengthened. Thus the obsessive-compulsive mother's scrubbing ritual reduces anxiety about contamination and prevents her from experiencing anxiety. In the case of agoraphobia, remaining at home also serves as a *safety signal,* a place where the person is unlikely to experience a panic attack (Brown & Barlow, 2009). Again, anxiety reduction reinforces the response of staying at home (Figure 15.11). Unfortunately, successful avoidance, while producing an immediate positive benefit,

Figure 15.11

Panic and agoraphobia.
This diagram illustrates how panic disorders contribute to the development of agoraphobia. Negative reinforcement through anxiety reduction fosters avoidance of feared situations (a), as well as an attraction to safety signals, such as one's own home (b), where panic does not occur.

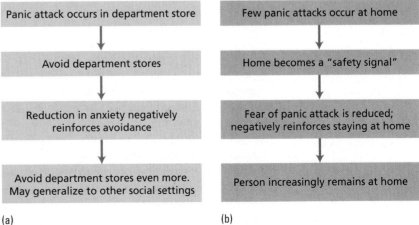

prolongs the problem in the long run. It prevents the learned anxiety response from being extinguished, which would occur eventually if these people exposed themselves to the feared stimuli enough times without experiencing the feared consequences.

Sociocultural Factors

Social and cultural factors also play a role in the development of anxiety disorders (Lopez & Guarnaccia, 2000). The role of culture is most dramatically shown in **culture-bound disorders,** *which occur only in certain locales.* One such disorder found in Japan is a social phobia called *Taijin Kyofushu* (Tanaka-Matsumi, 1979). People with this disorder are pathologically fearful of offending others by emitting offensive odors, blushing, staring inappropriately, or having a blemish or improper facial expression. Taijin Kyofushu has been attributed to the Japanese cultural value of extreme interpersonal sensitivity and to cultural prohibitions against expressing negative emotions or causing discomfort in others (Kleinknecht et al., 1997). Another culture-bound disorder is *koro,* a Southeast Asian anxiety disorder in which a man fears that his penis is going to retract into his abdomen and kill him.

Western culture also spawns culture-specific anxiety reactions. Although formally classified as an eating disorder, anorexia nervosa has a strong phobic component, namely, the fear of getting fat. It also has obsessive-compulsive elements. This eating disorder is found almost exclusively in developed countries, where being thin has become a cultural obsession (Becker et al., 1999).

test yourself   Anxiety Disorders

True or false?

1. The most prevalent anxiety disorders are specific and social phobias.
2. The highest levels of anxiety are experienced in panic disorder.
3. Unpredictable natural disasters are more likely to precipitate PTSD than are human actions.
4. Women have a higher incidence of anxiety disorders than do men.
5. Biological factors are the main determinants of panic disorders.
6. Agoraphobia can be explained in part by negative-reinforcement processes.

ANSWERS: 1-true, 2-true, 3-false, 4-true, 5-false, 6-true

SOMATOFORM AND DISSOCIATIVE DISORDERS: ANXIETY INFERRED

The anxiety disorders just considered involve anxiety and stress reactions that are vividly experienced by the sufferer and, often, are externally observable. In some other disorders, however, underlying anxiety is largely inferred, or assumed to be present, rather than outwardly expressed. In somatoform and dissociative disorders, for example, the person may not consciously feel any anxiety because the function of the disorders is to protect the person from strong psychological conflict (Rosenhan & Seligman, 1989). Psychodynamic theorists believe that whatever distress the person may experience in such disorders is less stressful than the underlying anxiety that is being defended against.

Somatoform Disorders

Somatoform disorders *involve physical complaints or disabilities that suggest a medical problem but that have no known biological cause and are not produced voluntarily by the person* (Kirmayer & Looper, 2007). In **hypochondriasis,** *people become unduly alarmed about any physical symptom they detect and are convinced that they have or are about to have a serious illness.* They are unduly preoccupied with their health and imagine that virtually any physical change indicates a serious illness, often to the consternation of acquaintances and physicians. One person with hypochondriasis reportedly had inscribed on his tombstone, "I told you I wasn't feeling well."

People with **pain disorder** *experience intense pain that is either out of proportion to whatever medical condition they might have or for which no physical basis can be found.* In such people, a minor injury may be experienced as intensely painful.

Impairments resulting from the pain response may include inability to work or attend school, substantial use (and, sometimes, misuse) of pain-relieving medications, frequent use of the health-care system, and interpersonal and marital disruption.

Somatoform disorders differ from *psychophysiological disorders,* in which psychological factors cause or contribute to a real medical condition, such as migraine headaches, asthma, hypertension (chronic high blood pressure), or cardiac problems. In peptic ulcers, for example, stress-produced outpouring of peptic acid into the stomach produces an actual lesion in the stomach wall. The resulting pain is therefore caused by the actual physical damage. In a somatoform disorder, no physical basis for the pain would be found.

Perhaps the most fascinating of the somatoform disorders is **conversion disorder,** *in which serious neurological symptoms, such as paralysis, loss of sensation, or blindness, suddenly occur.* In such cases, electrophysiological recordings and brain imaging indicate that sensory and motor pathways in the brain are intact (Black et al., 2004). People with conversion disorders often exhibit *la belle indifference,* a strange lack of concern about their symptoms and their implications (Pajer, 2000). In some cases, the complaint itself is physiologically impossible. An example is *glove anesthesia,* in which a person loses all sensation below the wrist. As Figure 15.12 shows, the hand is served by nerves that also provide sensory input to the wrist and arm, making glove anesthesia anatomically impossible.

Although *psychogenic blindness* is rare in the general population, researchers discovered the

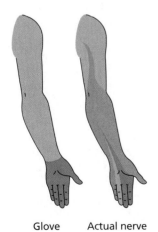

Glove   Actual nerve
anesthesia innervation

Figure 15.12

An impossible conversion disorder symptom.
Glove anesthesia is a conversion disorder in which all feeling is lost below the wrist. The skin areas served by nerves in the arm make this symptom physiologically impossible.

Figure 15.13

A physician examines a Cambodian refugee who appears to be suffering from psychologically induced blindness. There is nothing wrong with his eyes, but he cannot see.

largest known civilian group of people in the world with trauma-induced blindness. They were Cambodian refugees who escaped from their country and settled in southern California. These survivors of the "killing fields" of Cambodia were subjected to unspeakable horror at the hands of the Khmer Rouge in the years following the Vietnam War (Cooke, 1991). More than 150 of them became functionally blind, even though their eyes appeared intact and electrophysiological monitoring showed that visual stimuli registered in their visual cortex (Figure 15.13). Many of the victims reported that their blindness came on suddenly after they witnessed traumatic scenes of murder. Were the sights from the outer world so painful that the visual system involuntarily shut down? An intriguing but as yet unanswered question is how cultural factors might have affected the development of this response to trauma.

A predisposition to somatoform disorders may involve a combination of biological and psychological vulnerabilities. Somatoform disorders tend to run in families, though it is not clear whether this reflects the role of genetic factors, environmental learning and social reinforcement for bodily symptoms, or both (Trimble, 2003). Additionally, some people may experience internal sensations more vividly than others, or they may focus more attention on them. Somatoform patients are also very suggestible. One study found them to be far more responsive to hypnotic suggestions than were matched controls, and conversion patients' hypnotic susceptibility scores were significantly correlated with the number of conversion symptoms they reported (Roelofs et al., 2002).

The incidence of somatoform disorders tends to be much higher in cultures that discourage open discussion of emotions or that stigmatize psychological disorders (Tanaka-Matsumi & Draguns, 1997). Within Western cultures, there are subgroups, such as the police and military, in which open discussion of feelings and self-disclosure of psychological problems are frowned on. In such settings, somatic symptoms may be the only acceptable outlet for emotional distress. The same may occur in people who are so emotionally constricted that they cannot acknowledge their emotions or verbally communicate them to others (Dell & O'Neil, 2009).

Dissociative Disorders

Ordinarily, personality has unity and coherence, and the many facets of the self are integrated so that people act, think, and feel with some degree of consistency. Memory plays a critical role in this integration, for it connects past with present and provides a sense of personal identity that extends over time. **Dissociative disorders** *involve a breakdown of normal personality integration, resulting in significant alterations in memory or identity.* Three forms that such disorders can take are *psychogenic amnesia, psychogenic fugue,* and *dissociative identity disorder* (van der Hart & Nijenhuis, 2009).

In **psychogenic amnesia,** *a person responds to a stressful event with extensive but selective memory loss.* Some people can remember nothing about their past. Others can no longer recall specific events, people, or places, although other contents of memory, such as cognitive, language, and motor skills remain intact.

Psychogenic fugue *is a more profound dissociative disorder in which a person loses all sense of personal identity, gives up her or his customary life, wanders to a new faraway location, and establishes a new identity.* Usually the fugue (derived from the Latin word *fugere,* "to flee") is triggered by a highly stressful event or trauma, and it may last from a few hours or days to several years. Some adolescent runaways have been found to be in a fugue state, and married fugue victims may wed someone else and start a new career (Loewenstein, 1991). Typically, the fugue ends when the person suddenly recovers his or her original identity and "wakes up," mystified and distressed at being in a strange place under strange circumstances.

Dissociative Identity (Multiple Personality) Disorder

In **dissociative identity disorder (DID)** (formerly called *multiple personality disorder), two or more separate personalities coexist in the same person.* DID is the most striking and widely publicized of the dissociative disorders, and several celebrated cases have been the topic of books and movies,

Figure 15.14

In one celebrated depiction of dissociative identity disorder, motel clerk Norman Bates is shocked to discover the body of a woman murdered in her shower by his mother (actually his alter personality) in the movie *Psycho.*

such as *Sybil, The Three Faces of Eve,* and *Psycho* (Figure 15.14). In DID, a primary personality, or *host personality,* appears more often than the others (called *alters*), but each personality has its own integrated set of memories and behaviors. The personalities may or may not know about the existence of the others. They can differ in age and gender, and they can differ not only mentally and behaviorally but also physiologically.

Mental health workers and researchers have reported dramatic differences among the alternate personalities of DID patients, including physical health differences, voice changes, and even changes in right- and left-handedness. Some patients have severe allergies when one personality is present but no allergies when the others are active. One patient nearly died of a violent allergic reaction to a bee sting. A week later, when an alternate personality was active, another sting produced no reaction. Female patients frequently have different menstrual cycles for each female personality; one patient had three periods per month. Other patients need eyeglasses with different prescriptions for different personalities; one may be farsighted, another nearsighted (Miller et al., 1991). Epileptic patients with DID often have their seizures in one personality but not another (Drake et al., 1988).

What Causes DID?

According to Frank Putnam's **trauma-dissociation theory,** *the development of new personalities occurs in response to severe stress.* For the vast majority of patients, this begins in early childhood, frequently in response to physical or sexual abuse. Putnam (1989) studied the life histories of 100 diagnosed DID cases and found that 97 of them reported severe abuse and trauma in early and middle childhood, a time when children's identities are not well established and it is quite easy for them to dissociate. Putnam believes that in response to the trauma and their helplessness to resist it, children may engage in something akin to self-hypnosis and dissociate from reality. They create an alternate identity to detach themselves from the trauma, to transfer what is happening to someone else who can handle it, and to blunt the pain. Over time, it is theorized, the protective functions served by the new personality remain separate in the form of an alternate personality rather than being integrated into the host personality (Meyer & Osborne, 1987; Putnam, 2000).

DID has become a controversial diagnosis. Some critics question how often it actually occurs, and others question its very existence (Piper & Merskey, 2004; Spanos, 1994). Prior to 1970, only about 100 cases had been reported worldwide, and even today DID is virtually unknown in many cultures, including Japan (Takahashi, 1990). But after the disorder was highly publicized in popular books and movies, many additional cases appeared, numbering in the tens of thousands by the mid-1990s. The number of alternate personalities also had increased from 2 or 3 to an average of about 15 (Spanos, 1994). Could this dramatic increase in the prevalence of DID and number of alters be the result of publicity and patient or therapist expectations? Additionally, critics wonder why children with DID are rarely reported. Is it because children do not yet have adult conceptions of DID (Piper & Merskey, 2004)? As we noted in our discussion of hypnosis in Chapter 6, people can become so immersed in an imagined role (such as an alter personality) that it becomes quite real to them, and they act accordingly (Spanos, 1996). Proponents of the trauma-dissociation theory reject this criticism of DID, insisting that it is a valid psychiatric disorder (Ross, 2009). The controversy that swirls around DID is inspiring research that may advance our understanding of factors that can produce alterations in memory, physiological responses, and behavior.

MOOD DISORDERS: DEPRESSION AND MANIA

Another set of emotion-based disorders are **mood disorders,** *which include depression and mania (excessive excitement).* Together with anxiety disorders, mood disorders are the most frequently experienced psychological disorders. There is high *comorbidity* (co-occurrence) involving anxiety and mood disorders. About half of all depressed people also experience an anxiety disorder (National Institute of Mental Health, 2008).

Depression

Jeremy has been depressed for several years, but things are even worse now. He feels totally inadequate and inferior. The future looks hopeless, and he cannot sleep at night. During the day, he can barely function, and his moods alternate between deadening depression and intense anxiety. A friend has suggested that he seek professional counseling, but Jeremy is convinced that he has slipped too deeply into the black hole of despair to ever feel good again. He wonders how long he wants to go on living in his private hell.

Almost everyone has experienced depression, at least in its milder and more temporary forms. Loss and pain are inevitable parts of life, and when they occur, most of us feel blue, sad, discouraged, apathetic, and passive. The future looks bleak, and some of the zest goes out of living. Such reactions are normal; at any point in time, 25 to 30 percent of college undergraduates experience mild depression (Seligman, 1991). These feelings usually fade after the event has passed or as the person becomes accustomed to the new situation.

In clinical depression, however, the frequency, intensity, and duration of depressive symptoms are out of proportion to the person's life situation. Some people may respond to a minor setback or loss with **major depression,** *an intense depressed state that leaves them unable to function effectively in their lives.* This disorder occurs in 16.6 percent of Americans during their lifetimes (Kessler et al., 2005a). Jeremy, the young man described above, suffers from a major depression. Other people exhibit **dysthymia,** *a less intense form of depression that has less dramatic effects on personal and occupational functioning.* Dysthymia, though less intense, is a more chronic and longer-lasting form of misery, occurring for years on end with some intervals of normal mood that never last more than a few weeks or months. About 2.5 percent of Americans suffer from dysthymia during their lives (Kessler et al., 2005a).

The *negative mood state* is the core feature of depression. When depressed people are asked how they feel, they most commonly report sadness, misery, and loneliness. Whereas people with anxiety disorders retain their capacity to experience pleasure, depressed people lose it (Ruscio et al., 2007). Activities that used to bring satisfaction and

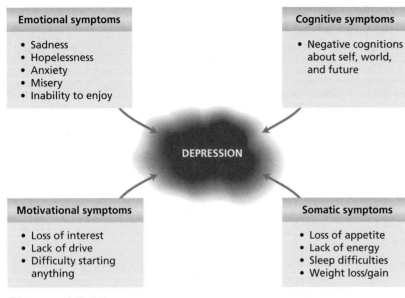

Figure 15.15

Facets of depression.

Depression includes emotional, cognitive, motivational, and somatic features.

happiness feel dull and flat. Even biological pleasures, such as eating and sex, lose their appeal.

Although depression is primarily a disorder of emotion or mood, there are three other types of symptoms: cognitive, motivational, and somatic (Figure 15.15). *Cognitive symptoms* are a central part of depression. Depressed people have difficulty concentrating and making decisions. They usually have low self-esteem, believing that they are inferior, inadequate, and incompetent. When setbacks occur in their lives, depressed people tend to blame themselves; they await failure that will be caused by their own inadequacies. Depressed people almost always view the future with great pessimism and hopelessness (Clark et al., 1999).

Motivational symptoms in depression involve an inability to get started and to perform behaviors that might produce pleasure or accomplishment. A depressed student may be unable to get out of bed in the morning, let alone go to class or study. Everything seems too much of an effort. In extreme depressive reactions, the person may have to be prodded out of bed, clothed, and fed. In some cases of severe depression, the person's movements slow down and she or he walks or talks slowly and with excruciating effort.

Somatic (bodily) *symptoms* often include loss of appetite and weight loss in moderate and severe depression, whereas in mild depression, weight gain sometimes occurs as a person eats compulsively. Sleep disturbances, particularly insomnia, are common. Sleep disturbance and weight loss lead to fatigue and weakness, which tend to add

to the depressed feelings. Depressed people also may lose sexual desire and responsiveness.

Bipolar Disorder

When a person experiences only depression, the disorder is called *unipolar depression.* In a **bipolar disorder,** *depression (which is usually the dominant state) alternates with periods of* **mania,** *a state of highly excited mood and behavior that is quite the opposite of depression.* In a manic state, mood is euphoric and cognitions are grandiose. The person sees no limits to what he or she can accomplish and fails to consider negative consequences that may ensue if grandiose plans are acted on. At a motivational level, manic behavior is hyperactive. The manic person engages in frenetic activity, be it in work, in sexual relationships, or in other areas of life. The 19th-century composer Robert Schumann produced 27 works during a one-year manic phase, but his productivity ground to a halt when he sank back into the depressive phase of his bipolar disorder (Jamison, 1995). Manic people can become very irritable and aggressive when their momentary goals are frustrated in any way (Miklowitz, 2007).

In a manic state, speech is often rapid or pressured, as if the person must say as many words as possible in the time allotted. With this flurry of activity comes a greatly lessened need for sleep. A person may go for several days without sleeping, until exhaustion inevitably sets in and the mania slows down.

A case described by Benjamin Kleinmuntz (1980) illustrates the poor judgment and hyperexcitability that attend a manic state. A 56-year-old dentist awoke one morning convinced that because he was the most gifted dental surgeon in his part of the country, he had an obligation to share his skill with as many people as possible. He therefore decided to convert his two-chair practice to 20 booths so that he could see more patients. That morning, he drew up plans for the remodel and called a number of contractors for bids. But by the end of the day, he became irritated with the "interminable delays" and decided to do the work himself. After he finished with his last patient, he began to knock down the walls of his office with a sledgehammer. He also smashed all of his dental equipment, saying, "This junk is not suitable for the likes of me." Alarmed tenants of his building called the police, and he was taken to a mental hospital. There, he was in perpetual motion. He could not sit still, and his speech was described as "overexcited." He paced the room like a caged animal.

Prevalence and Course of Mood Disorders

Epidemiological studies in the United States suggest that at this moment, about 1 in 20 Americans is severely depressed (Narrow et al., 2002; National Institute of Mental Health, 2008). Statistically, the chances are that nearly 1 in 5 Americans will have a depressive episode of clinical proportions at least once in her or his lifetime (Kessler et al., 2005a). No age group is exempt from depression. It appears in infants as young as 6 months who have been separated from their mothers for prolonged periods. The rate of depressive symptoms in children and adolescents is as high as that in adults (Essau & Petermann, 1999).

Data from numerous studies indicate that depression is on the rise among young people, with the onset of depression increasing dramatically in 15- to 19-year-olds (Burke et al., 1991; Lebrun, 2007). Figure 15.16 shows that the lifetime prevalence of major depression in the United States has increased in every decade since the 1930s, and the steepness of the curve indicates an earlier onset in those born after 1966.

Prevalence of depressive disorders is similar across socioeconomic and ethnic groups, but there is a major sex difference in our culture. Although men and women do not differ in prevalence of bipolar disorder, women appear to be about twice as likely as men to suffer unipolar depression (Figure 15.17). Women are most likely to suffer

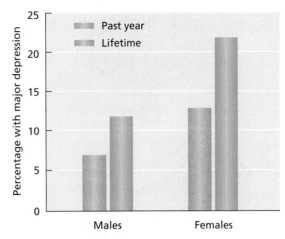

Figure 15.17

Sex differences in depression.
Prevalence rates for major depression in men and women. Source: Based on Kessler et al., 2005a.

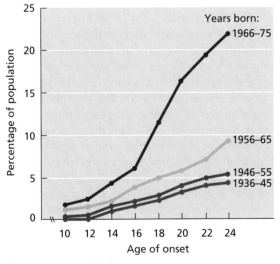

Figure 15.16

The rising incidence of depression.
Depression rates in the United States have increased every decade from the 1930s to the 1990s. Some theorists think that the "me" generation, with its emphasis on individual attainment and reduced commitment to traditional values of family, religion, and the common good, has sowed the seeds of its own depression. Source: U.S. Department of Health and Human Services, 2002.

their first episode of depression in their 20s, men in their 40s (Keyes & Goodman, 2006).

Many people who suffer depressive episodes never seek treatment. What is likely to happen to such people? Perhaps the one positive thing that can be said about depression is that it usually dissipates over time. After the initial episode, which typically comes on suddenly after a stressful experience, depression typically lasts an average of 5 to 10 months when untreated (Tollefson, 1993).

Once a depressive episode has occurred, one of three patterns may follow. In perhaps 40 percent of all cases, clinical depression will not recur following recovery. Many other cases show a second pattern: recovery with recurrence. On average, these people will remain symptom-free for perhaps 3 years before experiencing another depressive episode of about the same severity and duration. The interval between subsequent episodes of depression tends to become shorter over the years (Rubin, 2000). Finally, about 10 percent of people who have a major depressive episode will not recover and will remain chronically depressed (Figure 15.18).

Manic episodes, though less common than depressive reactions, are far more likely to recur. Fewer than 1 percent of the population experiences mania, but more than 90 percent of those who do have a recurrence (American Psychiatric Association, 2000; Noll, 2007).

Causal Factors in Mood Disorders

As in the case of anxiety disorders, the mood disorders are a product of interacting biological, psychological, and environmental factors.

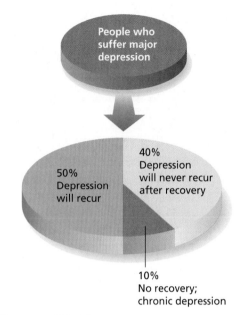

Figure 15.18

What follows major depression?

One of three outcomes may follow a major depressive episode. About 40 percent never have a recurrence, perhaps 50 percent have a recurrence, and about 10 percent suffer chronic (ever present) depression.

All three levels of analysis have provided key insights into how these disorders develop and are maintained.

Biological Factors

Both genetic and neurochemical factors have been linked to depression. Genetic factors surface in both twin and adoption studies (McGuffin et al., 2005). Identical twins have a concordance rate of about 67 percent for experiencing clinical depression, compared with a rate of only 15 percent for fraternal twins (Gershon et al., 1989). Among adopted people who develop depression, biological relatives are about 8 times more likely than adoptive relatives to also suffer from depression (Wender et al., 1986). What is likely to be inherited is a predisposition to develop a depressive disorder, given certain kinds of environmental factors such as significant losses and low social support (Brown & Barlow, 2009; Jang, 2005).

Two genetically based temperament systems discussed in Chapter 11 (page 370), the behavioral inhibition system (neuroticism) and the behavioral activation system (extraversion) are heavily involved in the development of mood disorders (Brown, 2007). You'll recall that the behavioral activation system (BAS) is reward oriented and activated by cues that predict future pleasure, whereas the behavioral inhibition system (BIS)

is pain-avoidant and generates fear and anxiety. Depression is predicted by high BIS sensitivity and low BAS activity. Mania, on the other hand, is linked to high reward-oriented BAS functioning, and scores on the personality variable of extraversion (tied heavily to the BAS) predict the future development of bipolar mania (Lonnqvist et al., 2009). Cues connoting potential reward, achievement gratification, and goal attainment trigger BAS activation, leading to the manic person's elevated positive emotions and expectations, high activity level, and self-confidence. With clear failure, however, BAS deactivation can cause a flip-flop into feelings of depression (Alloy et al., 2009).

Increasingly, biological research has focused on the possible role of brain chemistry in depression. One influential theory holds that depression is a disorder of motivation caused by underactivity in a family of neurotransmitters that include norepinephrine, dopamine, and serotonin. These transmitters, which are involved in the BAS, play important roles in brain circuits that produce reward and pleasure. When neural transmission decreases in these brain regions, the result is the lack of pleasure and loss of motivation that characterize depression (Areán, 2007). Also in support of this theory, several highly effective antidepressant drugs operate by increasing the activity of these neurotransmitters, thereby further stimulating the neural systems that underlie positive mood and goal-directed behavior. A study by Lescia Tremblay and coworkers (2002) tested the amount of reward experienced by depressed patients when these centers were activated by a stimulant drug that produces pleasure. Severely depressed individuals showed a much stronger pleasure response to the drug than did nondepressed people, supporting the hypothesis of a "pleasure deficit" in the brain (see Figure 15.19). Later research by Ian Gotlib and coworkers (2004a) using fMRI readings of emotion areas of the brain showed low levels of neuron responsiveness to both happy and sad scenes, as if the emotion response systems had shut down. This may account for the lack of positive emotionality and the "emptiness" of the depressive emotional experience.

Bipolar disorder, in which depression alternates with less frequent periods of mania, has been studied primarily at the biological level because it appears to have a stronger genetic basis than does unipolar depression (Young & Joffe, 1997). Among both men and women, the lifetime risk of developing a bipolar disorder is just below 1 percent. Yet about 50 percent of patients with

Figure 15.19

Women who suffer from postpartum depression can lose the capacity to experience pleasure while interacting with their babies. Reductions in depression can restore the brain's capacity to generate normal levels of pleasure during maternal interactions.

Figure 15.20

Psychoanalysts believe that early catastrophic losses increase vulnerability to later depressive disorders.

bipolar disorder have a parent, grandparent, or child with the disorder (Barondes, 1999; Rubin, 2000). The concordance rate for bipolar disorder is 5 times higher in identical twins than in fraternal twins, suggesting a genetic link.

Manic disorders may stem from an over-production of the same BAS-related neurotransmitters that are underactive in depression. This might explain the symptom picture that is quite the opposite of that seen in depression. Significantly, lithium chloride, the drug most frequently used to calm manic disorders, works by decreasing the activity of these transmitters in the brain's motivational/pleasure activation system (LeMoal, 1999; Robinson, 1997).

Psychological Factors

Biological factors seem to increase vulnerability to certain types of psychological and environmental events that can then trigger mood disorders. Other perspectives specify what those events might be.

Personality-Based Vulnerability Psychoanalysts Karl Abraham (1911) and Sigmund Freud (1957) believed that early traumatic losses or rejections create vulnerability for later depression by triggering a grieving and rage process that becomes part of the individual's personality (Figure 15.20). Subsequent losses and rejection reactivate the original loss and cause a reaction not only to the current event but also to the unresolved loss from the past.

Were he alive today, Freud would surely point to research by the British sociologists George Brown and Terrill Harris (1978) to support his theory of early loss. Brown and Harris interviewed women in London and found that the rate of depression among women who had lost their mothers before age 11 and who had also experienced a severe recent loss was almost 3 times higher than that among women who had experienced a similar recent loss but had not lost their mothers before age 11. Experiencing the death of a father during childhood is also associated with increased risk of later depression (Barnes & Prosen, 1985; Bowlby, 2000).

Cognitive Processes According to Aaron Beck (1976), depressed people victimize themselves through their own beliefs that they are defective, worthless, and inadequate. They also believe that whatever happens to them is bad and that negative things will continue happening because of their personal defects (Clark et al., 1989). This **depressive cognitive triad** *involves negative thoughts concerning (1) the world, (2) oneself, and (3) the future* that seem to pop into consciousness automatically, and many depressed people report that they cannot control or suppress the negative thoughts (Wenzlaff et al., 1988). Depressed people also tend to recall most of their failures and few of their successes, and they tend to focus much of their attention on their perceived inadequacies (Clark et al., 1999; Haaga et al., 1991). Depressed people also detect pictures of sad faces at lower exposure times and remember them better than do nondepressed people (Gotlib et al., 2004b), indicating a perceptual and memory sensitivity to the negative, and they are more likely to distort their memories of negative events.

As noted in the discussion of self-enhancement tendencies in Chapter 13, most people tend to take personal credit for the good outcomes in their lives and to blame their misfortunes on factors outside themselves, thereby maintaining and enhancing their self-esteem. According to Beck, depressed people do exactly the opposite: they exhibit a **depressive attributional pattern,** *attributing successes or other positive events to factors outside the self while attributing negative outcomes to personal factors* (Figure 15.21). Beck believes that taking no credit for successes but blaming themselves for failures helps depressed people maintain low self-esteem and their belief that they are worthless failures. Quite literally, they can't win, even when they do!

Not surprisingly, low self-esteem operates as a significant risk factor for later depression. This was established in two large-scale longitudinal studies in which over 4,000 adults ranging in age from 18 to 88 years were followed for 4 to 9 years. At all age levels, low self-esteem predicted later depressive episodes (Orth et al., 2009).

Another prominent cognitive account of depression, **learned helplessness theory,** *holds that depression occurs when people expect that bad events will occur and that there is nothing they can do to prevent them or cope with them* (Abramson et al., 1978; Seligman & Isaacowitz, 2000). The depressive attributional pattern plays a central role in the learned helplessness model, but learned helplessness theorists take it a step further by specifying what the negative attributions for failures are like. They suggest that chronic and intense depression occurs as the result of negative attributions for failures that are personal ("It's all *my* fault"), stable ("I'll *always* be this way"), and global ("I'm

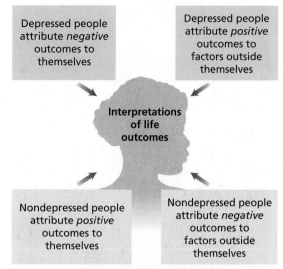

Depressive attributional pattern

Depressed people attribute *negative* outcomes to themselves

Depressed people attribute *positive* outcomes to factors outside themselves

Interpretations of life outcomes

Nondepressed people attribute *positive* outcomes to themselves

Nondepressed people attribute *negative* outcomes to factors outside themselves

Self-enhancement attributional pattern (nondepressed people)

Figure 15.21

The depressive attributional pattern.
Cognitive theorists believe that the attributional patterns of depressed people are the opposite of the self-enhancing patterns that characterize nondepressed people. In the depressive attributional pattern, people attribute negative outcomes to themselves and positive outcomes to factors outside themselves.

a *total* loser"). Thus people who attribute negative events in their lives to factors such as low intelligence, physical repulsiveness, or an unlovable personality tend to believe that their personal defects will render them helpless to avoid negative events in the future, and their sense of hopelessness places them at significantly greater risk for depression.

Mania is dominated by quite another pattern of thinking. The person in a manic state is expansive, optimistic, and excited—all emotions linked with the behavioral activation system. In a longitudinal study, Lauren Alloy and coworkers (2009) compared 195 people with bipolar disorder with a demographically matched group of persons without bipolar disorder. They found that cognitions involving autonomy (a focus on individualistic achievement and self-sufficiency), high performance standards ("A person should do well at everything"), and a tendency toward self-criticism when goals are not obtained predicted not only bipolar group membership but also the occurrence of future hypomanic episodes.

Learning and Environmental Factors   The behavioral perspective also has important things to say about depression. Peter Lewinsohn and his colleagues (1985) believe that depression is usually triggered by a loss, by some other punishing event, or by a drastic decrease in the amount of positive reinforcement that the person receives from her or his environment. As the depression begins to take hold, people stop performing behaviors that previously provided reinforcement, such as hobbies and socializing. Depressed people also tend to generate additional negative life events through their negative moods, pessimism, and reduced functioning (Harkness & Stewart, 2009). Moreover, they tend to make others feel anxious, depressed, and hostile (Joiner & Coyne, 1999). Eventually, these other people (including friends and family members) begin to lose patience, failing to understand why the person doesn't snap out of it. This diminishes social support still further and may eventually cause depressed people to be abandoned by those who are most important to them (Nezlek et al., 2000). Longitudinal studies show that reductions in social support are a good predictor of subsequent depression (Burton et al., 2004). Figure 15.22 shows the cyclical course of depression.

Behavioral theorists believe that to begin feeling better, depressed people must break this vicious cycle by initially setting positive goals and forcing themselves to engage in behaviors that are likely to produce some degree of pleasure. Eventually, positive reinforcement produced by this process of *behavioral activation* will begin to counteract the depressive affect, undermine the sense of hopelessness that characterizes depression, and increase feelings of personal control over the environment (Martell et al., 2004).

Environmental factors may also help explain why depression tends to run in families. Constance Hammen (1991) studied the family histories of depressed people and concluded that children of depressed parents often experience poor parenting and many stressful experiences as they grow up. As a result, they may fail to develop good coping skills and a positive self-concept, making them more vulnerable later in life to stressful events that can trigger depressive reactions. This conclusion is supported by findings that children of depressed parents exhibit a significantly higher incidence of depression and other disorders as adolescents and young adults (Lieb et al., 2002).

Sociocultural Factors

Although depression exists in virtually all cultures, its prevalence, symptom pattern, and causes reflect cultural variation (Lopez & Guarnaccia, 2000). For example, the prevalence of depressive

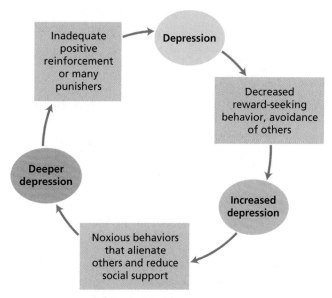

Figure 15.22

Lewinsohn's behavioral model of depression.
Behaviorists focus on the environmental causes and effects of depression. Depression results from loss of positive reinforcement and produces further declines in reinforcement and social support in a vicious-cycle fashion.

disorders is far lower in Hong Kong and Taiwan than in Western nations. People in these societies tend to have strong social support from family and other groups, which helps reduce the negative impact of loss and disappointments when they occur (Tseng et al., 1990).

Cultural factors also can affect the ways in which depression is manifested. Feelings of guilt and personal inadequacy seem to predominate in North American and western European countries, whereas somatic symptoms of fatigue, loss of appetite, and sleep difficulties are more often reported in Latin, Chinese, and African cultures (Manson, 1994).

Finally, cultural factors may influence who develops depression. As noted earlier, women are about twice as likely as men to report feeling depressed in technologically advanced countries such as Canada, the United States, and other Western nations (Keyes & Goodman, 2006). Yet this sex difference is not found in developing countries (Culbertson, 1997; Nolen-Hoeksema, 1990). At present, we do not know why this pattern occurs, but attempts are under way to learn more about how the cultural environment influences the development of depression.

At one time or another, many depressed people consider suicide as a way to escape from the unhappiness of their lives. We now examine suicide, its causes, and what can be done to prevent this tragic event.

Applying Psychological Science

Understanding and Preventing Suicide

Suicide *is the willful taking of one's own life.* The World Health Organization estimates that worldwide, nearly 500,000 people commit suicide each year—almost 1 per minute. Twelve to 25 times that number engage in nonfatal suicide attempts (National Institute of Mental Health, 2009). In the United States, suicide is the second most frequent cause of death (after accidents) among high school and college students, and suicide rates among 15- to 24-year-olds more than doubled between 1957 and 2008 (National Center for Health Statistics, 2009; Figure 15.23). Contrary to the belief of many, suicide is far more common than homicide. Nearly twice as many suicides (30,622) as homicides (16,611) occurred in the United States in 2004 (National Center for Health Statistics, 2009).

Women attempt suicide about 3 times more often than men, but men are 4 times more likely to actually kill themselves (National Institute of Mental Health, 2009). These differences may be due to (1) a higher incidence of depression in women and (2) men's choice of more-lethal methods, such as shooting themselves or jumping off buildings. The suicide rates for both men and women are higher among those who have been divorced or widowed. Women's suicides are more likely to be triggered by failures in love relationships, whereas career failure more often prompts men's suicides (Shneidman, 1998). A history of sexual or physical abuse significantly increases the likelihood of later suicide attempts (Garnefski & Arends, 1998).

Depression, whether unipolar or bipolar, is one of the strongest predictors of suicide (Goldston et al., 2006; Ostacher & Eidelman, 2006). About 15 percent of clinically depressed individuals will eventually kill themselves, a rate that is 22 to 36 times higher than the suicide rate for the general population. An estimated 80 percent of suicidal people are significantly depressed (Yen et al., 2003). It is noteworthy, however, that suicides do not usually occur when depression is deepest. Instead, suicide often occurs unexpectedly as a depressed (or bipolar) person seems to be emerging from depression and feeling better. The lifting of depression may provide the energy needed to complete the suicidal act but not reduce the person's underlying sense of hopelessness and despair.

MOTIVES FOR SUICIDE

There appear to be two fundamental motivations for suicide: the desire to end one's life and the desire to manipulate and coerce other people into doing what the suicidal person wants (Beck et al., 1979; Shneidman, 1998). Those who want to end their lives have basically given up. They see no other way to deal with intolerable emotional distress, and in death they see an end to their problems. In one study, 56 percent of suicide attempts were classified as having been motivated by the desire to die (Beck, 1976). These attempts were accompanied by high levels of depression and hopelessness, and they tended to be more lethal than other suicide attempts.

The second primary motivation for suicide is manipulation of others. Many *parasuicides* (suicide attempts that do not end in death) are cries for help or attempts to coerce people to meet one's needs. Trying to prevent a lover from ending a relationship, inducing guilt in others, or dramatizing one's suffering are manipulative motives. Manipulative suicide attempters tend to use less lethal means (such as drug overdose or wrist slashing) and to make sure help is available. In the study cited earlier (Beck, 1976), 13 percent of the suicide attempts were classified as manipulative. The remaining 31 percent combined the two types of motivation.

Other contributors to suicidal ideation and behavior are a desire to no longer be a burden to others and a sense of social alienation (Joiner et al., 2009). A small minority of suicides result from altruistic decisions to sacrifice one's life for the survival of others; examples include the soldier who dives on a hand grenade to save his comrades' lives or the mother who elects to give birth rather than aborting her baby, knowing that she will die in the process.

WARNING SIGNS FOR SUICIDE

The best predictor of suicide attempts in both men and women is a verbal or behavioral threat to commit suicide, and such threats should always be taken seriously. One of the most destructive myths about suicide is that people who talk openly about suicide are just seeking attention and don't actually intend to carry out the act. Yet research shows that a high proportion of suicide attempts— perhaps 80 percent—are preceded by some kind of warning (Bagley & Ramsay, 1997). Sometimes the warning is an explicit statement of intent, such as "I don't want to go on living" or "I won't be a burden much longer." Other times the warnings are more subtle, as when a person expresses hopelessness about the future, withdraws from others or from favorite activities, gives away treasured possessions, or takes unusual risks. Other important risk factors are a history of previous suicide attempts and a detailed plan that involves a lethal method (Chiles & Strossahl, 1995; Shneidman, 1998). Substance use and abuse also increase suicide risk (Yen et al., 2003).

SUICIDE PREVENTION: WHAT YOU CAN DO

Scientific research has taught us much about the dynamics and prevention of suicide. These findings provide the following guidelines for preventing this tragic answer to life's problems and for helping potentially suicidal people:

1. Another myth about suicide is that broaching the topic with a potentially suicidal person may prompt the person

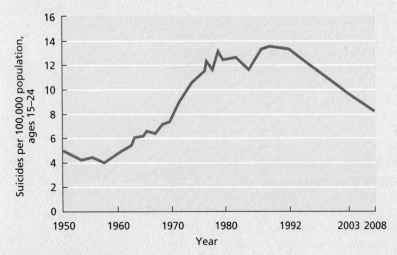

Figure 15.23

The rising suicide rate in young people.
This graph illustrates the suicide rate per 100,000 persons ages 15 to 24, from 1950 to 2008.
SOURCE: Based on National Center for Health Statistics, 2009.

to carry out the act. In truth, the best first step if you suspect that someone may be suicidal is to ask the person directly whether he or she is considering suicide: "Have you thought about hurting yourself or ending your life?" If the person responds affirmatively, try to find out if he or she has a plan or a time frame in mind. Do not be hesitant to approach the person. *Diffusion of responsibility* (discussed in Chapters 2 and 17) could result in your assuming that someone else is helping the person when in fact no one is (Goldsmith, 2003). Your ultimate goal should be to help the person receive assistance from a qualified professional as soon as possible, not to treat the person yourself. Nonetheless, you can take some immediate steps that may be helpful.

2. Many suicidal people feel alone in their misery. It is important to provide social support and empathy at this critical juncture. An expression of genuine concern can pave the way for other potentially helpful interventions (Barnett & Porter, 1998). For example, a frank discussion of the problem that is foremost in the person's life can be helpful. Suicidal people often feel totally overwhelmed by life, and focusing on a specific problem may help the person realize that it is not unsolvable and need not cloud his or her total perception of life.

3. When people are distressed and hopeless, their time orientation tends to narrow, and they have difficulty seeing beyond their current distress. Try to help the person see his or her present situation within a wider time perspective and to consider positive possibilities that might exist in the future. In particular, discuss reasons for continuing to live, and focus on any doubts the person might have about electing suicide. For example, if the person indicates that his or her family will suffer greatly from the suicide, adopt this as one of your arguments for finding a different solution to the problem. Many suicidal people would like to feel that they do not have to commit suicide. Capitalize on such feelings.

4. If a person is suicidal, stay with him or her and seek professional assistance. Most cities have suicide-prevention centers that offer 24-hour services, including telephone and direct counseling. These centers are usually listed under *suicide* or *crisis* in the phone book.

Levels of Analysis

Anxiety and Mood Disorders

Although the core emotions in the anxiety and mood disorders seem quite different, they tend to co-occur in many people. Typical results were obtained in a study of 1,127 outpatients who had either anxiety or mood disorder diagnoses. Incidence results indicated that 55 percent of the patients had both anxiety and depression symptoms at the time of assessment, a figure that rose to 76 percent when lifetime prevalence was studied (Brown et al., 2001). This high level of comorbidity has led some clinical scientists to suspect that common causal factors underlie both disorders, with different combinations resulting in either anxiety, depression, or both. One such theory has been proposed by David Barlow (Barlow, 2002; Suarez et al., 2009). Termed the **triple vulnerability model of emotional disorders,** *it draws on the biological, psychological, and environmental levels of analysis.*

ENVIRONMENTAL LEVEL
- Environmental life events that involve traumatic conditioning of fear and anxiety and severe losses that trigger depression prime people for later episodes of anxiety and depression.
- Another environmental vulnerability factor is growing up with depressed parents or with parents who indoctrinate in children the message that the world is a dangerous place that one is powerless to cope with.
- Negative life events that might not overwhelm a person without the triple vulnerability factors can trigger an anxiety or affective disorder in a vulnerable person.

BIOLOGICAL LEVEL
- Biological vulnerability comes from genetic factors that favor ascendancy of the BIS over the BAS. There is a well-established heritability of 30 to 50 percent in BIS sensitivity, priming BIS-sensitive people to experience anxiety and depression in response to threat or loss.
- An additional (and probably related) factor is a highly reactive sympathetic nervous system that overreacts to threat and increases the ease with which conditioned anxiety responses can be established.

PSYCHOLOGICAL LEVEL
- Psychological vulnerability is related to cognitive factors and coping strategies. The development of irrational ideas that generate depression or anxiety creates a psychological world that primes people for emotional disorders.
- Likewise, ineffective coping strategies such as avoidance, blaming others, and wishful thinking, combined with low levels of self-efficacy that inhibits use of more adaptive problem-focused and social support coping, help create negative life events and interfere with acting adaptively.

The triple vulnerability model is promising because it accounts for much of what we know about the causal factors in anxiety. What implications does it have for treating anxiety disorders? We will describe treatment approaches to anxiety in Chapter 16.

SCHIZOPHRENIA

Of all the psychological disorders, schizophrenia is the most bizarre and, in many ways, the most puzzling. It is also one of the most challenging disorders to treat effectively (McKenna, 2007). Despite many theories of schizophrenia and thousands of research studies, a complete understanding of this disorder continues to elude us. **Schizophrenia** *includes severe disturbances in thinking, speech, perception, emotion, and behavior* (Herz & Marder, 2002). Schizophrenia is one of a family of *psychotic* disorders, all of which involve some loss of contact with reality, as well as bizarre behaviors and experiences.

The term *schizophrenia* was introduced by the Swiss psychiatrist Eugen Bleuler in 1911. Literally, the term means "split mind," which has often led people to confuse schizophrenia with dissociative identity disorder ("split personality") or with a Dr. Jekyll–Mr. Hyde phenomenon. But multiple personalities are not what Bleuler had in mind when he coined the term. Instead, he intended to suggest that certain psychological functions, such as thought, language, and emotion, which are normally integrated with one another, are somehow split apart or disconnected in schizophrenia.

Characteristics of Schizophrenia

A diagnosis of schizophrenia requires evidence that a person misinterprets reality and exhibits disordered attention, thought, or perception. In addition, she or he typically withdraws from social interactions, communicates in strange or inappropriate ways, neglects personal grooming, and behaves in a disorganized fashion (American Psychiatric Association, 2000).

The schizophrenic thought disorder sometimes entails **delusions,** *false beliefs that are sustained in the face of evidence that normally would be sufficient to destroy them.* A schizophrenic person may believe that his brain is being turned to glass by ray guns operated by his enemies from outer space (a *delusion of persecution*) or that Jesus Christ is one of his special agents (a *delusion of grandeur*). Several aspects of thought disorder were described by a schizophrenic patient during a period of recovery:

> The most wearing aspect of schizophrenia is the fierce battle that goes on inside my head in which conflicts become irresolvable. I am so ambivalent that my mind can divide on a subject, and those two parts subdivide over and over until my mind feels like it is in pieces, and I am totally disorganized. At other times, I feel like I am trapped inside my head, banging against its walls, trying desperately to escape while my lips can utter only nonsense. (*New York Times*, 1986, March 18, p. C12)

Perceptual disorganization and disordered thought become more pronounced as people progress into a schizophrenic condition (McKenna & Oh, 2003). Unwanted thoughts constantly intrude into consciousness (Morrison, 2005). What the world might come to look like from inside the schizophrenic mind is illustrated in art created by schizophrenic patients during periods of disturbance (Figure 15.24). Some experience **hallucinations,** *false perceptions that have a compelling sense of reality.* Auditory hallucinations (typically voices speaking to the patient) are most common, although visual and tactile hallucinations may also occur. This person describes his hallucinations:

> Recently, my mind has played tricks on me, creating The People inside my head who sometimes come

(a)

(b)

Figure 15.24

(a) Patients diagnosed with schizo-phrenia are tormented by bizarre and intrusive thoughts and images. (b) This picture, drawn by a patient diagnosed with schizophrenia, may offer insights into his subjective world.

out to haunt me and torment me. They surround me in rooms, hide behind trees and under the snow outside. They taunt me and scream at me and de-vise plans to break my spirit. The voices come and go, but The People are always there, always real. (*New York Times,* 1986, March 18, p. C12)

The language of people with schizophrenia is often disorganized, and it may contain strange words.

> I am here from a foreign university . . . and you have to have a "plausity" of all acts of amendment to go through for the children's code . . . and it is no mental disturbance or "putenance" . . . it is an "amorition" law . . . it is like their "privatilinia." (Vetter, 1969, p. 189)

Patients' language sometimes contains words that are based on rhymes or other associations rather than meaning. Consider the following conversa-tion between a psychologist and a hospitalized schizophrenic patient:

> After two weeks, the psychologist said to him: "As you say, you are wired precisely wrong. But why won't you let me see the diagram?" Carl answered: "Never, ever will you find the lever, the eternalever that will sever me forever with my real, seal, deal, heel. It is not on my shoe, not even on the sole. It walks away." (Rosenhan & Selig-man, 1989, p. 369)

Schizophrenia can affect emotions in a num-ber of ways. Many people with schizophrenia have *blunted affect,* manifesting less sadness, joy, and anger than most people. Others have *flat*

affect, showing almost no emotions at all. Their voices are monotonous and their faces impassive. *Inappropriate affect* can also occur, as in the follow-ing case:

> The psychologist noted that Carl "smiles when he is uncomfortable, and smiles more when in pain. He cries during television comedies. He seems angry when justice is done, frightened when someone compliments him, and roars with laugh-ter on reading that a young child was burned in a tragic fire." (Rosenhan & Seligman, 1989, p. 369)

Subtypes of Schizophrenia

Schizophrenia has cognitive, emotional, and behav-ioral facets that can vary widely from case to case. There are four major subtypes of schizophrenia:

- **Paranoid schizophrenia,** *whose most promi-nent features are delusions of persecution, in which people believe that others mean to harm them, and delusions of grandeur, in which they believe they are enormously important.* Suspi-cion, anxiety, or anger may accompany the delusions, and hallucinations also may occur in this subtype.

- **Disorganized schizophrenia,** *whose central features are confusion and incoherence, together with severe deterioration of adaptive behavior, such as personal hygiene, social skills, and self-care.* Thought disorganization is often so extreme that it is difficult to communi-cate with these individuals. Their behavior often appears silly and childlike, and their

Figure 15.25

The woman pictured here exhibits catatonic rigidity. She might hold this position for several hours. If someone were to move her limbs into another position, she would maintain that position, a phenomenon known as *waxy flexibility*.

emotional responses are highly inappropriate. People with disorganized schizophrenia are usually unable to function on their own.

- **Catatonic schizophrenia,** *characterized by striking motor disturbances ranging from muscular rigidity to random or repetitive movements.* People with catatonic schizophrenia sometimes alternate between stuporous states, in which they seem oblivious to reality, and agitated excitement, during which they can be dangerous to others. While in a stuporous state, they may exhibit *waxy flexibility*, in which their limbs can be molded by another person into grotesque positions that they will then maintain for hours (Figure 15.25).

- **Undifferentiated schizophrenia,** *a category assigned to people who exhibit some of the symptoms and thought disorders of the above categories but who do not have enough of the specific criteria to be diagnosed in those categories.*

In addition to these formal DSM-IV-TR categories, many mental health workers and researchers divide schizophrenic reactions into two main categories on the basis of two classes of symptoms. One type is characterized by a predominance of **positive symptoms,** *bizarre behaviors such as delusions, hallucinations, and disordered speech and thinking.* These symptoms are called *positive* because they represent pathological extremes of

normal processes. The second type features **negative symptoms**—*an absence of normal reactions, such as lack of emotional expression, loss of motivation, and an absence of speech* (Herz & Marder, 2002).

The distinction between positive-symptom and negative-symptom subtypes seems to be an important one. Researchers have found differences in brain function between schizophrenics having positive symptoms and those with primarily negative symptoms (Gur et al., 1998; Zakzanis, 1998). The subtypes also show differences in life history and prognosis. Negative symptoms are likely to be associated with a long history of poor functioning prior to diagnosis and with a poor outcome following treatment (McGlashan & Fenton, 1992). In contrast, positive symptoms, especially those associated with a diagnosis of paranoid schizophrenia, are associated with good functioning prior to breakdown and a better prognosis for eventual recovery, particularly if the symptoms came on suddenly and were preceded by a history of relatively good adjustment (Fenton & McGlashan, 1991a, 1991b).

Schizophrenia afflicts only 1 to 2 percent of the population, yet schizophrenic patients occupy about half of all psychiatric hospital beds in the United States. Many who are not hospitalized barely function as homeless street people in large cities (Herman et al., 1998). About 10 percent of people with schizophrenia remain permanently impaired, and 65 percent show intermittent periods of normal functioning. The other 25 percent recover from the disorder (American Psychiatric Association, 2000).

Causal Factors in Schizophrenia

Because of the seriousness of the disorder and the many years of anguish and incapacitation that its victims are likely to experience, schizophrenia has long been a focus of research. There is a growing consensus that schizophrenia results from a biologically based vulnerability factor that is set into motion by psychological and environmental events (Herz & Marder, 2002; McGuffin et al., 2005).

Biological Factors

Biological factors are prominently involved in schizophrenia (Abi-Dargham & Guillin, 2007). Genetic, biochemical, and brain factors have been investigated.

Genetic Predisposition   Strong evidence exists for a genetic predisposition to schizophrenia, although the specific genes involved and their roles in creating the disposition are still unknown

(Hall et al., 2007; McGuffin et al., 2005). As Figure 15.26 shows, the more closely one is related to a person diagnosed with schizophrenia, the greater the likelihood of developing the disorder during one's lifetime. Twin studies show that identical twins have higher concordance rates than fraternal twins, and adoption studies show much higher concordance with biological parents than with adoptive parents (Jang, 2005; Kety, 1988). But, again, genetics do not by themselves account for the development of schizophrenia. If they did, the concordance rate in identical twins would be 100 percent, not 48 percent.

Brain Abnormalities Brain scans have indicated a number of structural abnormalities in the brains of schizophrenic patients. According to the *neuro-degenerative hypothesis*, destruction of neural tissue can cause schizophrenia (Weinberger & McClure, 2002). MRI studies have shown mild to moderate *brain atrophy*, a general loss or deterioration of neurons in the cerebral cortex and limbic system, together with enlarged ventricles (cavities that contain cerebrospinal fluid; Figure 15.27). The atrophy is centered in brain regions that influence cognitive processes and emotion, which may help explain the thought disorders and inappropriate emotions that are seen in such patients. Likewise, MRI images of the thalamus, which collects and routes sensory input to various parts of the brain, reveal abnormalities (Williamson, 2006). This may help account for the disordered attention and perception reported by schizophrenic patients whose cerebral cortex may be getting garbled or unfiltered information from the thalamus (Andreason et al., 1994). All of these structural differences are more common in patients who exhibit the negative-symptom pattern (Herz & Marder, 2002). As we have seen, these patients have a poorer chance of recovery than those with the positive-symptom pattern.

Biochemical Factors Dopamine, a major excitatory neurotransmitter, may play a key role in schizophrenia. According to the **dopamine hypothesis**, *the symptoms of schizophrenia— particularly positive symptoms—are produced by overactivity of the dopamine system in areas of the brain that regulate emotional expression, motivated behavior, and cognitive functioning* (Heinrichs, 2001). People diagnosed with schizophrenia have more dopamine receptors on neuron membranes than do nonschizophrenics, and these receptors seem to be overreactive to dopamine stimulation. Additional support comes from the finding that the effectiveness of antipsychotic drugs used to treat

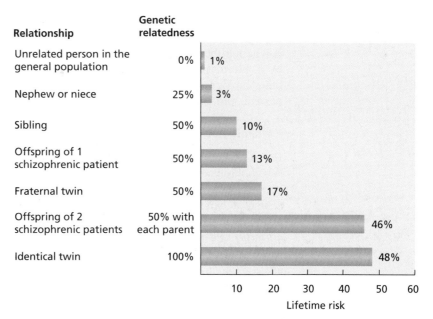

Relationship	Genetic relatedness	Lifetime risk (%)
Unrelated person in the general population	0%	1%
Nephew or niece	25%	3%
Sibling	50%	10%
Offspring of 1 schizophrenic patient	50%	13%
Fraternal twin	50%	17%
Offspring of 2 schizophrenic patients	50% with each parent	46%
Identical twin	100%	48%

Figure 15.26

Genes and schizophrenia.
The degree of risk for developing schizophrenia in one's lifetime correlates highly with the degree of genetic relationship with someone who has that disorder. These data summarize the results of 40 concordance studies conducted in many countries. SOURCE: Based on Gottesman, 1991.

schizophrenia is positively related to their ability to reduce dopamine-produced synaptic activity (Creese et al., 1976; Green, 1997). Other neurotransmitter systems are probably involved in this complex disorder as well. But dopamine is not the whole story, and recent research has shown that the dopamine system is part of a much larger and complex network in which a deficiency of neural input from cortical areas also plays a role (Benes, 2009).

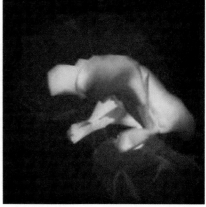

Figure 15.27

Schizophrenia and the brain.
One difference between the brains of schizophrenics and nonschizophrenics is enlarged ventricles (the grayish structures seen in the MRIs) in the schizophrenic brain (*right*). Findings like these support the position that brain abnormalities play a role in schizophrenia.

The biochemical and brain findings concerning schizophrenia are intriguing. What is not clear is whether they cause the disorder or are caused by it. Future research is almost certain to reveal other biological bases for the complex disorders of schizophrenia.

Psychological Factors

Freud and other psychoanalytic thinkers viewed schizophrenia as a retreat from unbearable stress and conflict. For Freud, schizophrenia represented an extreme example of the defense mechanism of **regression,** *in which a person retreats to an earlier and more secure (even infantile) stage of psychosocial development in the face of overwhelming anxiety.* Other psychodynamic thinkers, focusing on the interpersonal withdrawal that is an important feature of schizophrenia, view the disorder as a retreat from an interpersonal world that has become too stressful to deal with. Although Freud's regression explanation has not received much direct research support (Fisher & Greenberg, 1996), the belief that life stress is a causal factor is generally accepted today (Airey & Sodhi, 2007).

Some cognitive theorists believe that people with schizophrenia have a defect in the attentional mechanism that filters out irrelevant stimuli, so that they are overwhelmed by both internal and external stimuli. Sensory input thus becomes a chaotic flood, and irrelevant thoughts and images flash into consciousness. The stimulus overload produces distractibility, thought disorganization, and the sense of being overwhelmed by disconnected thoughts and ideas. As one schizophrenic patient noted, "Everything seems to come pouring in at once . . . I can't seem to keep anything out" (Carson et al., 1988, p. 329). The recent MRI findings of thalamic abnormalities described earlier may help explain how this stimulus overload could occur through a malfunction of the brain's switchboard.

Environmental Factors

Stressful life events seem to play an important role in the emergence of schizophrenic behavior (McKenna, 2007). These events tend to cluster in the 2 or 3 weeks preceding the "psychotic break," when the acute signs of the disorder appear (Day et al., 1987). Stressful life events seem to interact with biological or personality vulnerability factors. A highly vulnerable person may require little in the way of life stress to reach the breaking point (van Praag, 2004). In one study, psychotic and nonpsychotic people rated their emotional responses as they encountered stressful events in their daily lives. Psychotic individuals reacted to their stressors with more intense negative emotions, suggesting that emotional overreactivity may be a vulnerability factor (Myin-Germeys et al., 2001). In a longitudinal study, Nancy Docherty and co-workers (2009) tested schizophrenic patients and matched normal controls for emotional reactivity, then followed the two groups for 9 months. They found that as a group, the schizophrenic patients were more emotionally reactive and that the more reactive the patients were, the more likely they were to respond to stressful life events with an increase in psychotic symptoms.

Family dynamics have long been a prime suspect in the origins of schizophrenia, but the search for parent or family characteristics that might cause the disorder has been largely unsuccessful. Significantly, children of biologically normal parents who are raised by schizophrenic adoptive parents do *not* show an increased risk of developing schizophrenia (Kety, 1988). Although people with schizophrenia often come from families with problems, the nature and seriousness of those problems are not different from those of families in which nonschizophrenics are raised. This does not mean that family dynamics are not important; rather, it may mean that an individual must have a biological vulnerability factor in order to be damaged by stressful family events to such a degree. Indeed, there is evidence that this vulnerability factor may appear early in life. In one study, researchers analyzed home movies showing preschizophrenic children (those who were later to develop schizophrenic behaviors) and their nonschizophrenic brothers and sisters. Even at these early ages—sometimes as young as 2 years of age—preschizophrenic children tended to show more odd and uncoordinated movements and less emotional expressiveness, especially for positive emotions (Grimes & Walker, 1994). These behavioral oddities may not only reflect a vulnerability factor, but they may also help create environmental stress by evoking negative reactions from others.

Sociocultural Factors

Sociocultural factors are undoubtedly linked to schizophrenia (Murray et al., 2003). Many studies have found that the prevalence of schizophrenia is highest in lower-socioeconomic populations (Figure 15.28). Why is this? Is poverty a cause of schizophrenia, or is it an effect of the disorder? Two views give opposite answers. The **social causation hypothesis** *attributes the higher prevalence of schizophrenia to the higher levels of stress that low-income people experience,* particularly within urban

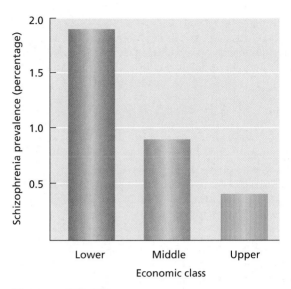

Figure 15.28

Social class and schizophrenia.
This graph shows the relation between economic status and prevalence of schizophrenia. Is economic status a cause or an effect of schizophrenia? Or does some other factor cause both? Source: Based on Keith et al., 1991.

environments. In contrast, the **social drift hypothesis** *proposes that as people develop schizophrenia, their personal and occupational functioning deteriorates, so that they drift down the socioeconomic ladder* into poverty and migrate to economically depressed urban environments. Perhaps social causation and social drift are both at work, for the factors that link poverty, social and environmental stressors, and schizophrenia are undoubtedly complex.

In contrast to most of the disorders we have described so far, schizophrenia may be a culture-free disorder. A worldwide epidemiological study sponsored by the World Health Organization indicated that the prevalence of schizophrenia is not dramatically different throughout the world (Jablensky et al., 1992). However, researchers have found that the likelihood of recovery is greater in developing countries than in the developed nations of North America and western Europe. This may reflect a stronger community orientation and greater social support extended to disturbed people in developing countries (Tanaka-Matsumi & Draguns, 1997).

Myth or Reality?

People with Psychological Disorders Are Dangerous

Would you mind living next door to a person who had just returned home from a mental hospital? Would you worry that this person is potentially a danger to you? If you answered yes to these questions, you are not alone. A widely shared stereotype of the mentally ill is that they are dangerous. One survey revealed that 80 percent of Americans believe that the mentally ill are prone to violence (Ganguli, 2000).

When they occur, violent acts committed by mentally ill people or former mental patients often are sensationalized in the media. Fictional depictions of psychologically disturbed individuals often involve violent behavior. Prime-time television shows mentally ill people committing violent acts 10 times more often than normal characters (Stout et al., 2004). Movies like *Psycho, Cape Fear, Fatal Attraction,* and *Misery* depict violent perpetrators with obvious psychological problems. Vivid media depictions of violence by disturbed individuals, such as Andrea Yates (diagnosed with psychotic depression), who drowned her four children, and Seung-Hui Cho (described as having schizophrenic characteristics), who committed a massacre at Virginia Tech University, are almost guaranteed to activate the *availability heuristic,* which causes people to overestimate the true likelihood of vividly recalled events (see Chapter 9).

As is true of many stereotypes, there's a grain of truth to the belief that mentally ill people are dangerous. Several groups of psychological disorders produce potentially violent individuals. Serial killers like Ted Bundy, John Muhammad (the D.C. Sniper), and Charles Manson represent extreme examples of how destructive some psychopathic (but not legally insane) individuals can be. People suffering from paranoid schizophrenia (especially those with delusions of persecution and/or "command" hallucinations in which a voice tells them to commit violence) are also at heightened risk for violence, as are catatonic schizophrenics who have stopped taking their medications and some bipolar individuals in a manic state (Torrey & Zdanowicz, 2001). The fact is, however, that the vast majority of people with psychological disorders do not fall into these categories. The two largest diagnostic groups, people with anxiety disorders and depression, are likely to be no more dangerous than the average person, and severely depressed people in particular are of greater danger to themselves than they are to others. Even schizophrenic people off their medications are more likely to be victims than perpetrators of street violence because their cognitive impairment makes them vulnerable to exploitation by others (Teplin et al., 2005).

As we've seen, severe disorders such as schizophrenia are more common in lower socioeconomic groups, and violent behavior is also more common at lower socioeconomic levels. In a study designed to control for this factor, people with mental disorders were followed for one year following their discharge from psychiatric hospitals (Steadman et al., 1998). The frequency with which they, family members, or police records revealed violent acts was compared with the frequency of similar acts in "normal" people from the same lower-socioeconomic neighborhoods where the former patients lived.

Continued

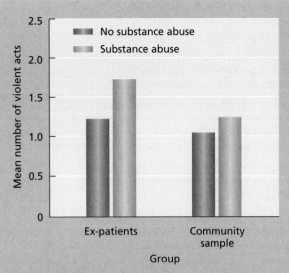

Figure 15.29

Challenging a popular stereotype.

This graph shows the mean number of violent acts committed by former psychiatric inpatients during the year following their discharge, as compared with similar acts committed by nonpatients living in their lower-socioeconomic neighborhoods. No difference was found between former patients and other community members when neither group engaged in substance abuse; however, when substance abuse was a factor, it was associated with more violence in both ex-patient and nonpatient samples. Source: Based on Steadman et al., 1998.

As shown in Figure 15.29, former inpatients without substance-abuse problems differed little in violence rates from nonpatients without substance-abuse problems during the yearlong period. However, substance abuse (which occurred more often among the former patients) was associated with a significant increase in the mean number of violent acts in both groups, but particularly the ex-patients. Substance abuse by ex-patients was associated with later violence in a more recent study as well (Mulvey et al., 2006). The researchers also found that violent acts by the former mental patients were most frequently directed toward family members and acquaintances. Indeed, nonpatients were actually more likely than former patients to commit the kinds of violent acts outside of the home that most frighten the public.

Based on this and other research, the following conclusion by two prominent mental health researchers appears reasonable:

> To date, nearly every modern study indicates that public fears are way out of proportion to the empirical reality. The magnitude of the violence risk associated with mental illness is comparable to that associated with age, educational attainment, and gender and is limited to only some disorders and symptom constellations. Furthermore, because serious mental illness is relatively rare and the excess risk modest, the contribution of mental illness to overall levels of violence in our society is miniscule. (Link & Steuve, 1998, p. 403)

test yourself   Schizophrenia

True or false?

1. The dopamine hypothesis states that schizophrenia is produced by an undersupply of this neurotransmitter.

2. Adoption studies show that the biological parents of schizophrenic people are more likely than their adoptive parents to have the disorder.

3. Schizophrenic patients with positive symptoms have a better prognosis for recovery than do those with negative symptoms.

4. Freudians attribute schizophrenia to a process of repression.

5. Schizophrenia is equally prevalent in all social classes.

ANSWERS: 1-false, 2-true, 3-true, 4-false, 5-false

PERSONALITY DISORDERS

People diagnosed with **personality disorders** *exhibit stable, ingrained, inflexible, and maladaptive ways of thinking, feeling, and behaving.* When they encounter situations in which their typical behavior patterns do not work, they are likely to intensify their inappropriate ways of coping, their emotional controls may break down, and unresolved conflicts tend to reemerge (Lenzenweger & Clarkin, 2005; Millon et al., 2004).

Table 15.2 briefly describes the 10 personality disorders in the current psychiatric diagnostic codes. The disorders are divided into three clusters that capture important commonalities: *dramatic and impulsive* behaviors, *anxious and fearful*

Table **15.2** | **DSM-IV-TR Personality Disorders and Their Major Features**

Dramatic/Impulsive Cluster
Antisocial personality disorder: Severe irresponsible and antisocial behavior beginning in childhood and continuing past age 18; impulsive need gratification and lack of empathy for others; often highly manipulative and seem to lack conscience
Histrionic personality disorder: Excessive, dramatic emotional reactions and attention seeking; often sexually provocative; highly impressionable and suggestible; out of touch with negative feelings
Narcissistic personality disorder: Grandiose self-concept; lack of empathy, and oversensitivity to evaluation; constant need for admiration from others; proud self-display
Borderline personality disorder: Pattern of severe instability of self-image, interpersonal relationships, and emotions, often expressing alternating extremes of love and hatred toward the same person; high frequency of manipulative suicidal behavior
Anxious/Fearful Cluster
Avoidant personality disorder: Extreme social discomfort and timidity; feelings of inadequacy and fearfulness of being negatively evaluated
Dependent personality disorder: Extreme submissive and dependent behavior; fears of separation from those who satisfy dependency needs
Obsessive-compulsive personality disorder: Extreme perfectionism, orderliness, and inflexibility; preoccupied with mental and interpersonal control
Odd/Eccentric Cluster
Schizoid personality disorder: Indifference to social relationships and a restricted range of experiencing and expressing emotions
Schizotypal personality disorder: Odd thoughts, appearance, and behavior, and extreme discomfort in social situations
Paranoid personality disorder: An unwarranted tendency to interpret the behavior of other people as threatening, exploiting, or harmful
SOURCE: Based on DSM-IV-TR, American Psychiatric Association, 2000.

behaviors, and *odd and eccentric* behaviors. As many as 10 to 15 percent of adults in the United States and European countries may have personality disorders. A study in Norway found a prevalence rate of 13.4 percent, equally distributed among men and women. The most frequently encountered were avoidant, paranoid, histrionic, and obsessive-compulsive personality disorders (Torgerson et al., 2001).

Among the personality disorders, the most destructive to society is the *antisocial personality disorder* (Livesley, 2003). This personality disorder has received by far the greatest attention from clinicians and researchers over the years (Reich, 2006). A second personality disorder that is attracting a great deal of current attention is the *borderline personality disorder*. We will focus on these two disorders.

Antisocial Personality Disorder (Psychopathy)

People with **antisocial personality disorder (APD)** *seem to lack a conscience; they exhibit little anxiety or guilt and tend to be impulsive and unable to delay gratification of their needs.* People with APD are among the most interpersonally destructive and emotionally harmful individuals. Males outnumber females 3 to 1 in this diagnostic group (American Psychiatric Association, 2000).

In the past, individuals with APD were referred to as *psychopaths* or *sociopaths*. Many theorists and clinicians still prefer the more traditional term *psychopathy*, for it represents a more general personality dimension. Actual antisocial behavior occurs in only a portion of psychopathic individuals. Many subclinical psychopaths flourish in settings, including politics and business, where their charisma, manipulativeness, false sincerity, and ability to deceive others can pay off. Spectacular political scandals and business schemes attest to what happens when psychopathic tendencies are not sufficiently self-regulated (Millon & Davis, 2000).

Research shows that there are two behavioral clusters of behaviors associated with psychopathy. The first cluster consists of selfishness, callousness, and interpersonal manipulation, and the second represents impulsivity, instability, and social deviance (Raine, 2008). A diagnosis of antisocial personality disorder is likely to require both behavior clusters. Many subclinical psychopaths

Figure 15.30

Violent psychopaths have frequently been represented on the screen. A recent example is the cold-blooded hit man chillingly portrayed by Javier Bardem in the film, *No Country for Old Men* (2007).

have only the first cluster (plus impulsivity, to varying degrees). Nonetheless, they can cause considerable harm because of their loose moral standards, ability to deceive others, and lack of empathy.

Psychopaths often exhibit a lack of emotional attachment to other people, as suggested in this report by a man diagnosed as having an antisocial personality disorder:

> When I was in high school my best friend got leukemia and died and I went to his funeral. Everybody else was crying . . . (but) . . . I suddenly realized I wasn't feeling anything at all. . . . That night I thought about it some more and found I wouldn't miss my mother and father if they died and that I wasn't too nuts about my brothers and sisters for that matter. I figured there wasn't anybody I really cared for but, then, I didn't need any of them anyway so I rolled over and went to sleep. (McNeil, 1967, p. 87)

A lack of capacity to care about others can make antisocial individuals a danger to society (Figure 15.30). For example, serial killers Charles Manson, Ted Bundy, and Jeffrey Dahmer failed to show any remorse for their crimes or sympathy for their victims. Although antisocial individuals often verbalize feelings and commitments with great sincerity, their behaviors indicate otherwise. They often appear very intelligent and charming, and they have the ability to rationalize their

inappropriate behavior so that it appears reasonable and justifiable. Consequently, they are often virtuosos at manipulating others and talking their way out of trouble.

To be diagnosed with APD, a person must be at least 18 years of age. However, the diagnostic criteria also require substantial evidence of antisocial behavior before the age of 15, including such acts as habitual lying, early and aggressive sexual behavior, excessive drinking, theft, vandalism, and chronic rule violations at home and school. Thus APD is the culmination of a deviant behavior pattern that typically begins in childhood (Kernberg, 2000).

Causal Factors

Biological, psychological, and environmental factors are all implicated in the development of psychopathy.

Biological Factors   Biological research on antisocial personality disorder has focused on both genetic and physiological factors. Evidence for a genetic predisposition is shown in consistently higher rates of concordance for antisocial behavior in identical twins than in fraternal twins (Airey & Sodhi, 2007). Heritability is between .40 and .50 for antisocial behavior in children, adolescents, and adults (Bouchard, 2004). Adoption studies suggest a similar conclusion. When researchers compared the criminal records of men who had been adopted early in life with those of their biological fathers and their adoptive fathers, they found that the criminality rate was nearly twice as high if the biological father had a criminal record and the adoptive father did not, clearly suggesting the operation of genetic factors (Cloninger & Gottesman, 1989).

How might genetic factors predispose individuals to engage in antisocial behavior? One clue might lie in the relative absence of anxiety and guilt that seems to characterize APD. Many researchers have suggested that the physiological basis for the disorder might be some dysfunction in brain structures that govern emotional arousal and behavioral self-control, particularly the amygdala and the prefrontal cortex (Blair, 2005; Raine, 2008). Dysfunction in these two areas would result in behavioral impulsiveness and a chronically underaroused state that impairs avoidance learning, causes boredom, and encourages a search for excitement (Arnett, 1997; Ishikawa et al., 2001). In support of a physiological basis, both children and adults with antisocial behavior patterns have lower heart rates, particularly when under stress (Ortiz & Raine, 2004). MRIs also reveal that antisocial individuals have subtle neurological deficits in the prefrontal lobes—the seat of executive functions such as planning, reasoning, and behavioral inhibition; these neurological deficits are associated with reduced autonomic activity (Raine et al., 2000). It thus appears, as long suspected, that severely antisocial individuals may indeed be wired differently at a neurological level, responding with less arousal and greater impulsiveness to both pleasurable and unpleasant stimuli (Raine, 2008).

Psychological and Environmental Factors Psychodynamic theorists regard antisocial people as lacking a conscience. Psychoanalytic theorists suggest that such people lack anxiety and guilt because they did not develop an adequate superego (Gabbard, 1990). In the absence of a well-developed superego, the restraints on the id are reduced, resulting in impulsive and hedonistic behavior. The failure to develop a strong superego is thought to result from inadequate identification with appropriate adult figures because these figures were either physically or psychologically unavailable to the child (Kernberg, 2000). In support of this position, the absence of the father from the home is related to a higher incidence of antisocial symptoms in children, even when socioeconomic status is equated (Pfiffner et al., 2001).

Cognitive theorists believe that an important feature in antisocial individuals is their consistent failure to think about or anticipate the long-term negative consequences of their acts. As a result, they behave impulsively, thinking only of what they want at that moment (Bandura, 1997). From this perspective, a key to preventing psychopaths from getting into trouble is to help them develop the cognitive controls (i.e., the executive functions) needed to think before acting impulsively.

Learning through modeling may also play an important role. Antisocial individuals often come from homes in which parents exhibit a good deal of aggression and are inattentive to their children's needs (Rutter, 1997). Such parents provide role models for both aggressive behavior and disregard for the needs of others. Another important environmental factor is exposure to deviant peers. Children who become antisocial often learn some of their deviant behaviors from peer groups that both model antisocial behavior and reinforce it with social approval (Bandura, 1997). It is easy to see how such environmental factors, combined with a possible genetic predisposition for antisocial behavior, would encourage the development of deviant behavior patterns (van Goozen et al., 2007).

Like some biological theories, learning explanations suggest that people with antisocial personality disorder lack impulse control. Learning theorists believe that poor impulse control occurs in these individuals because of an impaired ability to develop conditioned fear responses when punished, which would correspond with the lower physiological arousal and amygdala activity identified with brain recordings (Raine, 2008). This results in a deficit in avoidance learning. Hans Eysenck (1964) maintained that developing a conscience depends on the ability to learn fear and inhibitory avoidance responses, and people who fail to do so will be less able to inhibit their behavior. In accord with this hypothesis, Adrian Raine and coworkers (1996) did a 14-year follow-up of males who had been subjected at age 15 to a classical conditioning procedure in which a soft tone was used as the CS and a loud, aversive tone as the UCS. Conditioned fear was measured by the participants' skin-conductance response when the CS occurred after a number of pairings with the loud UCS. The researchers found that men who accumulated a criminal record by age 29 had shown much poorer fear conditioning at age 15 than had those with no criminal record.

SOURCE: YALING YANG, ADRIAN RAINE, TODD LENCZ, SUSAN BIHRLE, LORI LaCASSE, and PATRICK COLLETTI (2005). Volume reduction in prefrontal gray matter in unsuccessful criminal psychopaths. *Biological Psychiatry, 57,* 1103–1108.

INTRODUCTION

The impulsive, poorly planned behavior of many psychopaths, together with their seeming inability to profit from punishment, has intrigued clinical researchers for more than 150 years. Some have drawn parallels with the case of Phineas Gage, described at the beginning of Chapter 4, whose severe frontal-lobe damage from the railroad spike that was propelled through his brain resulted in poorly controlled behavior. We now know that the prefrontal cortex is the site of executive functions, such as planning, reasoning, rule adherence, and self-control. The prefrontal cortex also has important connections with structures that govern autonomic arousal, which, as we have seen, is deficient in psychopaths.

This study was designed to assess possible structural deficits in two groups of psychopaths: "unsuccessful" ones with a history of arrests and "successful" ones with no previous arrests or convictions. A second goal was to relate any structural differences that might be found in the prefrontal cortex with scores on a psychological test that measures the various aspects of psychopathy. Reasoning that successful psychopaths planned their crimes more carefully so that they would not be caught, the researchers expected that the prefrontal areas of the unsuccessful psychopaths should differ more from the controls than would those of the successful psychopaths.

METHOD

Three groups of participants were compared on MRI and psychological test measures. They were drawn from five Los Angeles temporary-employment agencies. On the basis of diagnostic interviews, a psychological test that measures psychopathy (the Psychopathy Checklist-Revised; Hare, 1991), self-reports of criminal activity (obtained with a legal guarantee of confidentiality), and official criminal records of arrests and convictions, the researchers identified 16 unsuccessful psychopaths who had an average of 4.06 criminal convictions and 13 successful psychopaths who had no convictions. These groups were compared with 23 control subjects with no evidence of psychopathy and no criminal arrests. The prefrontal-lobe volume scores measured by MRI were corrected for total brain mass.

RESULTS

The two groups of psychopaths both reported significantly more antisocial activities than did the controls, and although the successful psychopaths were somewhat lower on the antisocial lifestyle score than the unsuccessful ones, the major difference was that the successful ones did not get caught.

MRI recordings of the volume of frontal-lobe gray matter (neuron bodies) were compared in the three groups. The results are shown in Figure 15.31. As expected, the groups differed in prefrontal gray matter. Unsuccessful psychopaths had a 22 percent reduction in prefrontal gray-matter volume compared with the control subjects, perhaps reflecting their self-control deficiencies. Successful psychopaths, though having somewhat less prefrontal volume, did not differ from the normal controls. Further, for the entire sample, gray-matter volume in the prefrontal area was negatively correlated with scores on Hare's psychopathy test ($r = -.39$).

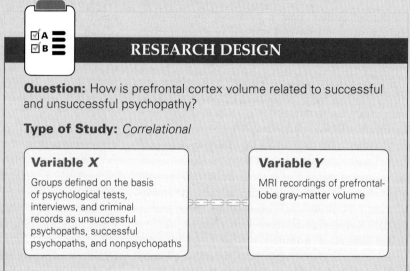

RESEARCH DESIGN

Question: How is prefrontal cortex volume related to successful and unsuccessful psychopathy?

Type of Study: *Correlational*

Variable X

Groups defined on the basis of psychological tests, interviews, and criminal records as unsuccessful psychopaths, successful psychopaths, and nonpsychopaths

Variable Y

MRI recordings of prefrontal-lobe gray-matter volume

DISCUSSION

As noted above, psychopathy is a dimension that reflects varying degrees of maladjustment and societal destructiveness. Some psychopaths engage in poorly planned impulsive antisocial behaviors, whereas others with similar tendencies have enough self-control, judgment, fear, or guilt to avoid crossing paths with the legal system. The intact prefrontal structure may provide successful psychopaths with the cognitive resources to manipulate and con others and avoid capture.

This is the first study to compare relevant brain areas (in this case, the prefrontal cortex) of unsuccessful and successful psychopaths. The results strengthen the link between prefrontal-lobe deficits and antisocial behavior. It seems likely that the prefrontal cortex is not the sole source of psychopathic behavior, for it has extensive connections with other brain areas. Whatever the case, evidence increases that psychopathy has a strong biological basis.

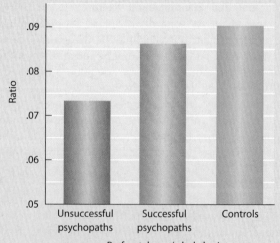

Figure 15.31

This graph shows the relative amount of prefrontal cortex gray matter in normal controls compared with successful and unsuccessful psychopaths. SOURCE: Yang et al., 2005, Fig. 1, p. 1106.

Borderline Personality Disorder

The borderline personality disorder has become the focus of intense interest among clinical researchers because of its chaotic effects on those who suffer from the disorder, their families, and their therapists. The disorder may occur in 3 to 5 percent of the general population (Clarkin et al., 1992; Selby & Joiner, 2009). About two thirds of those diagnosed are women.

Before 1980, the term *borderline* referred to an intermediate level of disturbance between neurotic and psychotic. Now, however, **borderline personality disorder (BPD)** *refers to a collection of symptoms characterized primarily by serious instability in behavior, emotion, identity, and interpersonal relationships.* A central feature of BPD is *emotional dysregulation,* an inability to control negative emotions in response to stressful life events, many of which borderline individuals themselves cause (Linehan & Dexter-Mazza, 2008; Selby et al., 2009).

Borderline individuals have intense and unstable personal relationships, and they experience chronic feelings of extreme anger, loneliness, and emptiness, as well as momentary losses of personal identity (Kuo & Linehan, 2009). They are inclined to engage in impulsive behavior such as running away, promiscuity, binge eating, and drug abuse, and their lives are often marked by repetitive self-destructive behaviors, such as self-mutilation and suicide attempts that seem designed to call forth a "saving" response from other people in their lives (McMurran et al., 2007).

BPD is highly associated with a number of other disorders, including mood disorders, PTSD, and substance-abuse disorders. In one study, the BPD symptoms of emotional instability and impulsivity predicted recurrent problems in academic achievement and social relationships 2 years later (Bagge et al., 2004). One intensive study of 57 people diagnosed with BPD revealed a total of 42 suicide threats, 40 drug overdoses, 36 instances of self-mutilation and cutting, 38 episodes of drug abuse, 36 instances of promiscuity with near-strangers, and 14 accidents, mainly caused by reckless driving (Linehan, 1993).

The chaos that marks the lives of borderline patients extends to their relationships with their psychotherapists. Borderline patients are considered to be among the most difficult clients to treat because of their clinging dependency, their irrational anger, and their tendency to engage in manipulative suicide threats and gestures as efforts to control the therapist (Linehan, 1993). Many

borderline individuals, 6 to 10 percent in various large-scale studies, eventually do kill themselves, either by miscalculation or by design (Davis et al., 1999; Pompili et al., 2009).

Causal Factors

Borderline people tend to have chaotic personal histories marked by interpersonal strife, sexual and physical abuse, and inconsistent parenting. This history is sometimes reflected in their earliest memories. In one study, borderline and normal participants were asked to describe their earliest memories in life. When the researchers analyzed the content of the memory reports, they found that the borderline respondents reported 6 times more events in which someone had treated them in a malevolent manner or had injured them emotionally or physically. Borderline individuals also viewed potential helpers as far less helpful to them (Nigg et al., 1992). Parents of many borderline individuals are described as abusive, rejecting, and nonaffirming, and some theorists suggest that an early lack of acceptance by parents may cripple self-esteem and lead to clinging dependency and an inability to cope with separation (Cardasis et al., 1997). As borderline individuals mature, their behaviors tend to evoke negative reactions and rejection from others, affirming their sense of worthlessness and their view of the world as malevolent.

Psychoanalyst Otto Kernberg has focused on the dramatic changes that borderline people exhibit in their relationships with others (Kernberg, 1984; Kernberg & Caligor, 2005). Their sudden and vitriolic shifts from extreme love and clinging dependence to intense hatred or feelings of abandonment reflect a cognitive process that he calls **splitting,** *the failure to integrate positive and negative aspects of another's behavior* (e.g., a parent who is usually accepting but sometimes voices disapproval) *into a coherent whole.* As a result, the borderline individual may react as if the other person had two separate identities, one deserving of love and the other of hatred. Whichever of these seemingly independent images the borderline individual is reacting to at the moment totally determines how she or he relates or feels (Figure 15.32). Together with severe problems in emotional control, splitting makes for chaotic and unpredictable relationships.

Biological factors also seem to be at work (Depue & Lenzenweger, 2005). Close relatives of those with BPD are 5 times more likely than those in the general population to also have the disorder (Torgerson, 2000). The emotional explosiveness

Figure 15.32

Actress Glenn Close's portrayal of Alex in the movie *Fatal Attraction* illustrates the tendency of people with borderline personality disorder to show dramatic shifts in their relationships. During her affair with Dan, played by Michael Douglas, Alex goes from consuming love to a homicidal rage in which she tries to murder her lover with a butcher knife when he tries to end the relationship.

and impulsivity of borderline individuals may also reflect some biological abnormality in neurotransmitter systems or areas of the brain that contribute to emotional self-regulation (Gurvitz et al., 2000). It seems entirely possible that BPD reflects an interaction between biological factors and an early history of trauma, rejection,

and psychological if not physical abandonment. Finally, sociocultural factors may also contribute to this disorder. Cases of BPD seem to increase in societies that are unstable and rapidly changing, leaving some of their members with a sense of emptiness, problems of identity, and fears of abandonment (Paris, 1993).

test yourself   **Personality Disorders**

True or false?

1. Personality disorders are pathological extensions of normal personality functioning.
2. Psychopaths have a highly overactive emotional arousal system that triggers violence.
3. There are no sex differences in the incidence of either antisocial or borderline disorders.
4. Many borderline people report having parents who were abusive and did not affirm their feelings.
5. Antisocial emotional and behavioral characteristics have been linked to deficits in the prefrontal cortex.

ANSWERS: 1-true, 2-false, 3-false, 4-true, 5-true

CHILDHOOD DISORDERS

Psychological disorders can occur at any point in the life span. Mental health professionals have observed symptoms resembling clinical depression in infants, and older children exhibit a wide range of problem behaviors (Mash & Barkley, 2003). In one study of several thousand children between the ages of 2 and 5, researchers diagnosed more than 20 percent of the children with a DSM-IV disorder and considered half of these to be significantly impaired by their symptoms (Lavigne et al., 1996). Similar levels of incidence and

impairment exist in children between the ages of 9 and 17 (Satcher, 1999).

Other studies show that only about 40 percent of children with psychological disorders receive professional attention, and only half of this group is seen by qualified mental health professionals (Satcher, 1999). In contrast, 74 percent of children with physical handicaps receive professional treatment (U.S. Office of Behavior Technology, 1990). Failure to treat childhood behavior disorders not only results in needless distress for children and families, but such disorders tend to continue into adulthood as psychological problems. In one New Zealand study, 4 in 5 adults with diagnosed DSM disorders had histories of childhood or adolescent problems that also met DSM criteria (Newman et al., 1996).

Although many childhood disorders are the subject of current research, two are receiving particular attention. *Attention deficit/hyperactivity disorder* is of interest because it is the most frequently diagnosed childhood disorder. *Autism* is being scrutinized because it is becoming more common and is one of the most baffling disorders.

Attention Deficit/Hyperactivity Disorder

In **attention deficit/hyperactivity disorder (ADHD),** *problems may take the form of inattention, hyperactivity/impulsivity, or a combination of the two.* Ratings by teachers and parents indicate that 7 to 10 percent of American children meet DSM-IV-TR criteria for the disorder, making ADHD the most common childhood disorder. The disorder occurs at least 4 times more frequently in boys than in girls. Boys are more likely to exhibit aggressive and impulsive behaviors, whereas girls are more likely to be primarily inattentive (Poremba & Poremba, 2007). Some professionals believe that the ADHD diagnosis is applied too liberally, since normal children also exhibit the behaviors in question. They worry that some children may be labeled and medicated inappropriately (Carlson, 2000).

It may be tempting to assume that children routinely outgrow ADHD, but follow-up studies of individuals diagnosed with the disorder suggest that for 50 to 80 percent, the problems persist into adolescence and, for 30 to 50 percent, into adulthood (Biederman, 1998). Overall, adults with ADHD have more occupational, family, emotional, and interpersonal problems.

Despite many years of research, the precise causes of ADHD are unknown. Genetic factors are probably involved, as concordance rates are higher in identical than in fraternal twins. In adoption studies of ADHD children, the children's biological parents are more likely to have ADHD than the adoptive parents (Smalley et al., 2000). Experts have long suspected that the disorder has a biological basis, but EEG studies of electrical brain activity and imaging studies of brain structures and neurotransmitters have failed to reveal consistent differences between people with ADHD and control groups (Green, 1999). This may be due to the fact that ADHD is a multifaceted disorder with several subcategories of biological patterns. Environmental factors such as inconsistent parenting are also involved, perhaps in complex combinations with biological factors.

Autistic Disorder

One of the most mysterious and perplexing of all disorders is autism. First identified by the American psychiatrist Leo Kanner in 1943, **autistic disorder** *is a long-term disorder characterized by extreme unresponsiveness to others, poor communication skills, and highly repetitive and rigid behavior patterns.* Autism affects one in every 110 American children (Centers for Disease Control, 2009). Typically appearing in the first three years of life in the form of unresponsiveness and lack of interest in others, autism tends to be a lifelong disorder. Approximately 70 percent remain severely disabled into adulthood and cannot lead independent lives. More than two thirds have mental retardation, with IQs below 70 and frequently below 35. The rest have normal to above-average intelligence. But even the highest-functioning adults with autism have problems in communication, restricted interests and activities, and difficulty relating to others (Hillman et al., 2007).

Lack of social responsiveness to others is a central feature of autism. Autistic infants typically do not reach out to or even make eye contact with their parents. They seem not to recognize or care who is around them. Autistic children do not engage in normal play with either adults or peers and often do not even acknowledge their presence.

Language and communication difficulties are also common, with half of autistic children not developing language. The language that does develop is often strange, involving repetition of words or phrases with little recognition of meaning. Many engage in *echolalia,* the exact echoing of phrases spoken by others.

Sameness and routine are very important, and autistic children become extremely upset at even minute changes. The movement of a piece of furniture even slightly or the change of one word in a song may evoke a tantrum. Some theorists believe that sameness is an attempt to avoid overstimulation, but nobody knows for sure.

Autistic individuals have repetitive and stereotyped behavior patterns and interests (Figure 15.33). They may spend their time spinning objects, playing with objects like jar tops, flicking their fingers, or rocking their bodies. Some engage in self-injurious behaviors, such as banging their heads against sharp objects or biting chunks of flesh out of their bodies, and these children may have to be physically restrained.

Figure 15.33

People with autism often engage in odd and repetitive stereotyped behaviors. For example, an autistic child may manipulate an object for hours at a time, showing no interest in playing with other children or relating to adults.

A few autistic people, such as the man portrayed by Dustin Hoffman in *Rain Man*, exhibit extraordinary *savant* (from the French word for "wise," or "learned") abilities. A common savant skill is calendar calculation. An autistic person with this ability could tell you in an instant what day of the week your birthday will fall on in 2039. Others can perfectly reproduce any song or commercial after hearing it once. Sometimes these skills give the impression of superior intelligence, even in people who have mental retardation.

Causal Factors

Leo Kanner (1943), who first described childhood autism, offered a psychodynamic explanation. He speculated that these children had been driven into their own worlds by a cold and ungiving family environment during infancy. Parents (particularly the mother) were described as "refrigerator parents" who had thawed out just long enough to conceive a child. These were purely theoretical statements, and no evidence for such a family pattern has ever existed, but generations of parents who were exposed to this hypothesis suffered the agony of thinking they had caused their child's autistic disorder.

Today, it is widely accepted that autism has a biological basis (Vaccarino & Smith, 2009). What that might be remains undetermined, however. Widespread anomalies in the structures and

functioning of the brain have been found in autistic children. For example, brain-imaging studies show that the brains of autistic children are 5 to 10 percent larger than average at 18 months to 4 years of age. There is also evidence of accelerated pruning of neural connections during early life, and prefrontal-cortex development is also abnormal. Finally, brain scans of autistic individuals reveal abnormal development in the cerebellum, which coordinates movement and is involved in shifting attention (Courchesne et al., 2003). The precise manner in which these brain differences are related to autism is the subject of extensive current research.

Genetic factors have been linked to autism. Recent molecular-genetics studies suggest that there may be 4 to 6 major genes and 20 to 30 others that contribute to a lesser degree. It also appears that different genes may be involved for boys than for girls (Schellenberg et al., 2006). Siblings of autistic children are 200 times more likely to have the disorder than are children in the general population, and concordance is highest in identical twins (Piven et al., 1997). No single gene seems involved; instead, there may be multiple interacting genes. One notable finding is that many relatives of autistic children, though not manifesting the disorder themselves, have unusual personality characteristics that parallel autism, including aloofness and very narrow and specialized interests (Rutter, 2000).

Another line of research is examining autism from the *theory of mind* perspective. As discussed in Chapter 12, theory of mind refers to an awareness of what others are thinking and how they may be reacting internally. Normal children become aware of some characteristics of other people's thinking by age 3 or 4 (Ritblatt, 2000). Autistic people seem to have poorly developed skills in this area, making it difficult for them to communicate with others or understand how other people might be internally reacting to them (Heerey et al., 2003). Autistic children also show poor comprehension of others' emotional responses, such as expressions of distress (Dawson et al., 2004). Theory of mind deficits could severely impair language and social development, and they are a strong focus of current research on autism.

Finally, a significant controversy has arisen concerning the possible role of children's vaccinations as a cause of autism. The controversy has stimulated a significant amount of research. A recent review of the scientific evidence led to the following conclusion:

> The parents should not be apprehensive about the fact that immunization is likely to risk the protection of the child. There is no evidence that *autism*

is caused by any vaccine or any additive or preservative ever used in one. There have been large, well-controlled studies done all over the Western world that have confirmed this finding over and over again. A comparison of the risk factors, such as death or disabilities, as a result of not vaccinating a child is significantly larger than the risk of causing an autism spectrum disorder by immunizing. (Rhea, 2009, p. 962)

SCIENTIFIC AND SOCIAL ISSUES IN DIAGNOSIS

Classification is a necessary first step toward introducing order into discussions of the nature, causes, and treatment of psychological disorders. To be scientifically and practically useful, a classification system must meet standards of diagnostic reliability and validity. **Reliability** *means that clinicians using the system should show high levels of agreement in their diagnostic decisions.* Because professionals with different types and amounts of training—including psychologists, psychiatrists, social workers, and physicians—make diagnostic decisions, the system should be couched in terms of observable behaviors that can be reliably detected in order to minimize subjective judgments (American Psychiatric Association, 2000). **Validity** *means that the diagnostic categories should accurately capture the essential features of the various disorders.* Thus, if research and clinical observations show that a given disorder has four behavioral characteristics, the diagnostic category for that disorder should also have those four features. Moreover, the diagnostic categories should allow us to differentiate one psychological disorder from another.

The Diagnostic and Statistical Manual of Mental Disorders, Fourth Edition, Text Revision (DSM-IV-TR; American Psychiatric Association, 2000), is the most widely used diagnostic classification system in the United States. For each of its more than 350 diagnostic categories, the manual contains detailed lists of observable behaviors that must be present in order for a diagnosis to be made.

Reflecting an awareness of interacting personal and environmental factors, the DSM allows diagnostic information to be represented along five dimensions, or *axes,* that take both the person and her or his life situation into account (Segal & Coolidge, 2007). Axis I represents current clinical symptoms, that is, the deviant behaviors or thought processes that are occurring at the present time. Axis II reflects long-standing personality disorders or mental retardation, both of which

can influence the person's behavior and response to treatment. Axis III notes any medical conditions that might be relevant, such as high blood pressure or a recent concussion. Reflecting the vulnerability-stress model discussed earlier, the clinician also rates the intensity of psychosocial or environmental problems in the person's recent life on Axis IV and the person's coping resources, as reflected in recent adaptive functioning, on Axis V.

DSM-V: Integrating Categorical and Dimensional Approaches

The American Psychiatric Association is in the process of revising the diagnostic system, which is due to appear as DSM-V in 2013. Panels of experts on each disorder are studying the research literature in order to suggest revisions to the system (American Psychiatric Association, 2010).

The current classification system is a *categorical* system, in which people are placed within specific diagnostic categories. The highly specific behavioral criteria in the DSM-IV-TR diagnostic categories clearly have improved Axis I reliability over earlier versions (Brown et al., 2001; Nathan & Lagenbucher, 1999). One trade-off, however, is that the criteria are so detailed and specific, many people—as many as 50 percent—don't fit neatly into the categories (Westen et al., 2004). Moreover, people who receive the same diagnosis may share only certain symptoms and look very different from one another. Finally, the categorical system does not provide a way of capturing the severity of the person's disorder, nor can it capture symptoms that are adaptively important but not severe enough to meet the behavioral criteria for the disorder.

An alternative (or supplement) to the categorical system is a *dimensional* system, in which relevant behaviors are rated along a severity yardstick. Such a system is based on the assumption that psychological disorders are extensions different in degree, rather than kind, from normal personality functioning. As an example, consider the dimension of behavior that extends from normal, adaptive conscientiousness to the maladaptive extremes seen in a person with a compulsive disorder (Table 15.3). The maladaptive exaggeration of what is a normally adaptive personality style, or inability to engage in the adaptive behaviors, can be applied to virtually all disorders (Brown & Barlow, 2009). Likewise, it appears that much of the comorbidity that exists among current diagnostic categories, such as anxiety and depression, reflects variations in

Table **15.3** | From Conscientious Personality to Obsessive-Compulsive Disorder: A Dimensional View

Adaptive Conscientiousness	Subclinical	Disordered	Severely Disordered
"I do what I'm supposed to do. I have a strong work ethic, and I take pride in my work. I like to take my time and do things right."	"I feel as if I need to work on things until I get them right so that others will not disapprove of me if they find even one small mistake."	"I can't put something aside until it's perfect, even if it's plenty good enough to meet my obligations and needs."	"I check and recheck my work until I'm sure that no one could find fault with what I've done. I can't stop worrying that it's not perfect."

SOURCE: After Millon and Davis, 2000.

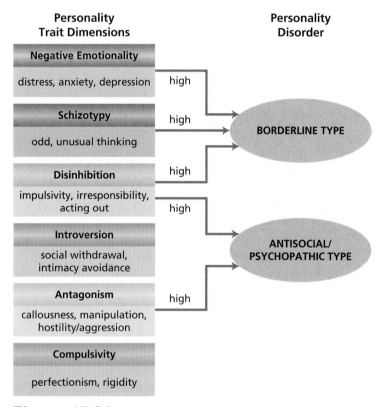

Figure 15.34

From personality to personality disorder.
The DSM-V Task Force has proposed six basic personality dimensions, with high ratings indicating greater psychological impairment. Here we see which of these personality trait dimensions are most prominently involved in borderline and antisocial/psychopathic personality disorder types.

the same underlying factors, such as activity in the behavioral inhibition system, or the personality trait of neuroticism (Brown, 2007; Widiger & Smith, 2008). Representing individuals along basic personality or symptom dimensions is attractive to a growing number of experts on the DSM-V revision panels because they believe that such a system may better represent the uniqueness of each individual and avoid the one-size-fits-all disadvantages of being assigned to a particular diagnostic category (American Psychiatric Association, 2010).

In February 2010, the American Psychiatric Association released its DSM-V revision proposals for professional comment. Although diagnostic categories are retained, the proposed system incorporates, as mentioned, dimensional scales that are used to rate the presence and severity of specific symptoms and personality characteristics. A prime example is in the personality disorders, where six basic dimensions of disordered personality functioning—Negative Emotionality, Introversion, Antagonism, Disinhibition, Compulsivity, and Schizotypy (odd thinking and behavior)—are rated by clinicians in order to define a set of six personality disorders. Figure 15.34 shows how different combinations of the personality dimensions (and their more specific behavioral facets) give rise the antisocial and borderline personality disorders described earlier. Some of the basic personality dimensions clearly reflect the maladaptive extremes of the traits in the Five Factor Model of normal personality described in Chapter 13 (Widiger et al., 2009). These factors—Extraversion, Agreeableness, Conscientiousness, Neuroticism, and Openness to experience—are thought by proponents to be universal dimensions of personality. One beneficial consequence of the proposed DSM-V approach to the diagnosis of personality disorders is that it helps to link normal and abnormal personality functioning. Moreover, the dimensional severity ratings that clinicians will give to the behaviors involved in each diagnostic category in the DSM-V will result in a fine-grained description that better reflects each person's individuality while also helping clinicians develop an effective treatment strategy (Skodol & Bender, 2009).

Consequences of Diagnostic Labeling

Beyond their clinical and scientific utility, diagnostic labels can have important personal, social, and legal consequences for people who receive them.

Social and Personal Consequences

Once a diagnostic label is attached to a person, it becomes all too easy to accept the label as an accurate description of the *individual* rather than of the *behavior*. It then becomes difficult to look at the person's behavior objectively, without preconceptions about how he or she will act. It also is likely to affect how others will interact with that person. Consider how you might react if you were told that your new next-door neighbor had been diagnosed as a pedophile. It would be surprising indeed if this label did not influence your perceptions and interactions with that person, whether or not the label was accurate.

In one famous and controversial study, eight normal individuals, including psychologist David Rosenhan (1973), got themselves admitted to psychiatric hospitals in five different states by telling mental health workers that they were hearing strange voices. Not surprisingly, they received diagnoses of schizophrenia upon admission. Once in the hospitals, however, they acted completely normal for the duration of their stays. When they were discharged after intervals ranging from 7 to 52 days, they typically received the diagnosis "schizophrenia, in remission." This label means that even in the absence of deviant behavior, the disorder was still presumed to be present, though not currently active. Once attached (understandably in this case, given participants' reports of hearing strange voices), diagnostic labels were not easily shed even when the disordered behaviors were no longer present.

Diagnostic labels may also add to the burden of psychological disorders if the person with the disorder or others react negatively to the labels (Corrigan, 2005). When people become aware that a psychiatric label has been applied to them, they may accept the new identity implied by the label and develop the expected role and outlook. Because psychiatric labels often carry degrading and stigmatizing implications, the effects on morale and self-esteem can be devastating. Moreover, a person may despair of ever changing and therefore give up trying to deal with life circumstances that may be responsible for the problems. In this way, the expectations that accompany a label may result in a self-fulfilling prophecy, in which expectation becomes reality. Because of the stigma attached to "mental illness," many people with psychological disorders do not seek treatment. Of course, a psychiatric label can be a two-edged sword, and the other side of this stigmatizing concern is that the label will evoke sympathy, understanding, and support from others (Lilienfeld et al., 2010).

Legal Consequences

Psychiatric diagnoses also have important legal consequences (Schlesinger, 2007). Individuals judged to be dangerous to themselves or others may be involuntarily committed to mental institutions under certain circumstances. When so committed, they lose some of their civil rights and may be detained indefinitely if their behavior does not improve.

The law tries to take into account the mental status of individuals accused of crimes. Two particularly important legal concepts are *competency* and *insanity*. **Competency** *refers to a defendant's state of mind at the time of a judicial hearing* (not at the time the crime was committed). A defendant deemed too disturbed to understand the nature of the legal proceedings may be labeled "not competent to stand trial" and institutionalized until judged competent.

Insanity *relates to the presumed state of mind of the defendant at the time the crime was committed.* Defendants may be declared "not guilty by reason of insanity" if they are judged to have been so severely impaired during the commission of a crime that they lacked the capacity either to appreciate the wrongfulness of their acts or to control their conduct. It is important to understand that insanity is a legal term, not a psychological one.

The insanity defense has long been hotly debated. Despite the fact that the insanity plea is entered in only 1 of every 500 felony cases and that in 85 percent of those cases the prosecution agrees that the person was indeed insane, it has become more difficult to plead insanity successfully. Until two decades ago, the prosecution was required to prove that the defendant was *not* insane when the crime was committed. Today, the burden has shifted to the defense to prove that the client was too impaired at the time of the crime to be held accountable for it. A recent U.S. Supreme Court decision (*Clark v. Arizona*, 2006) gave the option of not considering mental illness as evidence in criminal trials, increasing further the difficulty of mounting an insanity defense.

To balance punishment for crimes with concerns about a defendant's mental status and possible need for treatment, Canada and an increasing number of U.S. jurisdictions have adopted a verdict of "guilty but mentally ill." This verdict imposes a normal sentence for a crime but sends the defendant to a mental hospital for treatment. Defendants who are considered to have recovered before serving out their time are then sent to prison for the remainder of the sentence.

test yourself

Childhood Disorders and Scientific and Social Diagnostic Issues

True or false?

1. ADHD in childhood seldom persists into adulthood.

2. The traditional view that autism is caused by parental behaviors is no longer held.

3. The current DSM is a categorical system of diagnosis.

4. The legal term *insanity* refers to the mental capacity of the suspect to stand trial.

5. Today, the burden for proving the insanity of a defendant falls on the defense.

ANSWERS: 1-false, 2-true, 3-true, 4-false, 5-true

A Closing Thought

All of us do the best we can to adapt to the many demands we face during the course of our lives. In this chapter, we have seen the intense personal and societal suffering that occurs when biologically and experientially produced vulnerabilities combine with stressful demands to create psychological disorders. It is our hope that this discussion has increased your understanding of and compassion for those who suffer from these disorders. No one wants to be dysfunctional and miserable, and everyone deserves the opportunity to live a meaningful and fulfilling life. In the next chapter, we will focus on what can be done through psychological and biological treatments to ease the suffering that results from psychological disorders.

Chapter Summary

THE SCOPE AND NATURE OF PSYCHOLOGICAL DISORDERS

- Behavior that is judged to reflect a psychological disorder typically is (1) distressing to the person or to other people; (2) dysfunctional, maladaptive, or self-defeating; and/or (3) socially deviant in a way that arouses discomfort in others and cannot be attributed to environmental causes.

HISTORICAL PERSPECTIVES ON DEVIANT BEHAVIOR

- At various times in history, deviant behavior has been attributed to supernatural sources, biological causes, and psychodynamic factors.
- The vulnerability-stress model is currently a popular way to understand the interacting personal, biological, and environmental causes of behavior.

ANXIETY DISORDERS

- Anxiety involves four components: (1) subjective-emotional feelings of tension and apprehension; (2) cognitive processes involving worry, perceptions of threat, and lack of control; (3) excessive physiological arousal; and (4) behaviors that reflect the anxious state and others that are designed to escape or avoid the feared object or situation.

- Anxiety disorders include phobic disorder (an irrational fear of a specific object or situation), generalized anxiety disorder (recurrent anxiety reactions that are difficult to link to specific environmental stimuli), panic disorder, obsessive-compulsive disorder (which involves uncontrollable and unwelcome thoughts and repetitive behaviors), and posttraumatic stress disorder.

- Biological factors in anxiety disorders include both genetic and biochemical processes, possibly involving the action of neurotransmitters, such as GABA, within parts of the brain that control emotional arousal. The greater prevalence of anxiety disorders in women has been explained in both biological and sociocultural terms.

- Psychoanalytic theorists believe that neurotic anxiety results from the inability of the ego's defenses to deal with internal psychological conflicts. The cognitive perspective stresses the role of cognitive distortions, including the tendency to magnify the degree of threat and danger and, in the case of panic disorder, to misinterpret normal anxiety symptoms in ways that can evoke panic.

- The behavioral perspective views anxiety as a learned response established through classical conditioning or vicarious learning. The avoidance responses in phobias and compulsive disorders are seen as operant responses that are negatively reinforced through anxiety reduction.

- Sociocultural factors are also involved in anxiety disorders, as illustrated by certain culture-bound anxiety disorders.

SOMATOFORM AND DISSOCIATIVE DISORDERS: ANXIETY INFERRED

- Somatoform disorders involve physical complaints that do not have a physiological explanation. They include hypochondriasis, pain disorder, and conversion disorder.
- Familial similarities in somatoform disorders may have a biological basis, or they may be the result of environmental shaping through attention and sympathy. Such disorders tend to occur with greater frequency in cultures that discourage open expression of negative emotions.
- Dissociative disorders involve alterations in memory and personal identity. The major dissociative disorders are psychogenic amnesia, psychogenic fugue, and dissociative identity disorder (DID). Trauma-dissociation and role theories have been invoked to explain the causes of DID.

MOOD DISORDERS: DEPRESSION AND MANIA

- Mood disorders comprise several depressive disorders and bipolar disorder, in which intermittent periods of mania (intense mood and behavior activation) occur. Depression has four sets of symptoms: emotional, cognitive, motivational, and somatic. The symptoms of negative emotions and thoughts, loss of motivation, and behavioral slowness are reversed in mania.
- Both genetic and neurochemical factors have been linked to depression. One prominent biochemical theory links depression to an underactivity of neurotransmitters (norepinephrine, dopamine, and serotonin) that activate brain areas involved in pleasure and positive motivation. Bipolar disorder seems to have an even stronger genetic component than unipolar depression does.
- Psychoanalytic theorists view depression as a long-term consequence of traumatic losses or rejections early in life that create a personality vulnerability pattern.
- Cognitive theorists emphasize the role of negative beliefs about the self, the world, and the future (the depressive cognitive triad) and describe a depressive attributional pattern, in which negative outcomes are attributed to personal causes and successes to situational causes. Seligman's theory of learned helplessness suggests that attributing negative outcomes to personal, stable, and global causes fosters chronic depression.
- The behavioral approach focuses on the vicious cycle in which depression-induced inactivity and aversive behaviors reduce reinforcement from the environment and thereby increase depression still further.
- Manipulation and a desire to escape distress are the two major motives for suicide. The risk for suicide increases if the person is depressed and has a lethal plan and a past history of parasuicide.
- The widespread belief that one should not ask a depressed person about suicide is a myth.

SCHIZOPHRENIA

- Schizophrenia features disordered thinking and language; poor contact with reality; flat, blunted, or inappropriate emotion; and disordered behavior. The cognitive portion of the disorder can involve delusions (false beliefs) or hallucinations (false perceptions).
- Schizophrenia includes four subtypes: paranoid, disorganized, catatonic, and undifferentiated. Another categorization is based on the nature of the symptoms: positive versus negative.
- Strong evidence suggests that a genetic predisposition to schizophrenia makes some people particularly vulnerable to stressful life events. The dopamine hypothesis states that schizophrenia involves overactivity of the dopamine system, resulting in too much stimulation.
- Psychoanalytic theorists regard schizophrenia as a profound regression to a primitive stage of psychosocial development in response to unbearable stress. Cognitive theorists focus on the thought disorder that is central to schizophrenia. One idea is that people with schizophrenia have a defect in their attentional filters. Deficiencies also may exist in the executive functions needed to organize behavior.
- Stressful life events often precede a schizophrenic episode, but researchers have not been successful in identifying a family pattern related to the onset of schizophrenia.
- Sociocultural accounts of the higher incidence of schizophrenia at lower socioeconomic levels include the social causation hypothesis, which attributes schizophrenia to the higher levels of life stress that poor people experience, and the competing social drift hypothesis, which attributes the downward drift into poverty to the progression of the disorder. Schizophrenia does not appear to differ in prevalence across cultures.

PERSONALITY DISORDERS

- Personality disorders are rigid, maladaptive patterns of behavior that persist over a long time.
- Antisocial personality disorder (psychopathy) is characterized by an egocentric and manipulative tendency toward immediate self-gratification, a lack of empathy for others, a tendency to act out impulsively, and a failure to profit from punishment.
- Research on antisocial personality disorder suggests that genetic and physiological factors that result in emotional underarousal, poor reasoning, and self-control contribute to the disorder's causes. Psychoanalysts view the disorder as a failure to develop the superego. Learning explanations focus on exposure to aggressive, uncaring models and on the failure of punishment to inhibit maladaptive behaviors.
- Borderline personality disorder is characterized by serious instability in behavior, emotion, interpersonal relationships, and personal identity, as well as impulsive and self-destructive behaviors. The disorder is associated with abusive parenting.

CHILDHOOD DISORDERS

- Psychological disorders can occur at any point in the life span, and epidemiological data show that both children and adolescents exhibit a variety of disorders. Moreover, many childhood disorders are precursors for psychological disorders in adulthood.
- Attention deficit/hyperactivity disorder (ADHD) and autistic disorder originate in childhood and often persist into adulthood. ADHD can involve inattention, hyperactivity, or a combination of the two.
- Autistic disorder is a severe disorder that involves extreme unresponsiveness to others, poor communication skills, and highly repetitive and rigid behavior. Both disorders appear to have biological underpinnings, but the nature of these causal factors is not fully understood.

SCIENTIFIC AND SOCIAL ISSUES IN DIAGNOSIS

- The DSM-IV-TR describes the current status of the individual using five different dimensions, or axes, that capture personal and environmental factors. Reliability (diagnostic agreement) and validity are important issues in diagnostic classification systems. The DSM-IV-TR is a categorical classification system, and dimensional elements will be featured in the DSM-V.
- Among the important issues in psychiatric diagnosis are the potential negative effects of labeling on social perceptions and self-perceptions. Legal implications of competency and insanity judgments are also receiving attention. Competency to stand trial means that the individual is in sufficient contact with reality to understand the legal proceedings. Insanity refers to an inability to appreciate the wrongfulness of one's act or to control one's behavior at the time the crime was committed.

KEY TERMS AND CONCEPTS

Each term has been boldfaced and defined in the chapter on the page indicated in parentheses.

abnormal behavior (p. 549)
agoraphobia (p. 553)
antisocial personality disorder (APD) (p. 577)
anxiety (p. 552)
anxiety disorders (p. 552)
attention deficit/hyperactivity disorder (ADHD) (p. 583)
autistic disorder (p. 583)
bipolar disorder (p. 562)
borderline personality disorder (BPD) (p. 581)
catatonic schizophrenia (p. 572)
competency (p. 587)
compulsion (p. 554)
conversion disorder (p. 559)
culture-bound disorders (p. 558)
delusions (p. 570)
depressive attributional pattern (p. 566)
depressive cognitive triad (p. 566)
disorganized schizophrenia (p. 571)

dissociative disorders (p. 560)
dissociative identity disorder (DID) (p. 560)
dopamine hypothesis (p. 573)
dysthymia (p. 561)
generalized anxiety disorder (p. 553)
hallucinations (p. 570)
hypochondriasis (p. 558)
insanity (p. 587)
learned helplessness theory (p. 566)
major depression (p. 561)
mania (p. 562)
mood disorders (p. 561)
negative symptoms (p. 572)
neurotic anxiety (p. 556)
obsession (p. 554)
pain disorder (p. 558)
panic disorder (p. 554)
paranoid schizophrenia (p. 571)
personality disorder (p. 576)
phobia (p. 552)

positive symptoms (p. 572)
posttraumatic stress disorder (PTSD) (p. 555)
psychogenic amnesia (p. 560)
psychogenic fugue (p. 560)
regression (p. 574)
reliability (p. 585)
schizophrenia (p. 570)
social causation hypothesis (p. 574)
social drift hypothesis (p. 575)
social phobia (p. 553)
somatoform disorder (p. 558)
specific phobia (p. 553)
splitting (p. 581)
suicide (p. 568)
trauma-dissociation theory (p. 560)
triple vulnerability model of emotional disorders (p. 569)
undifferentiated schizophrenia (p. 572)
validity (p. 585)
vulnerability-stress model (p. 551)

? thinking critically

"DO I HAVE THAT DISORDER?" (Page 552)

Wondering if you have a psychological disorder when reading a description of it is quite understandable. We all experience problems in living at various times, and we may react in ways that bear similarities to the disorders described in this chapter. Logically, seeing such a similarity does not necessarily mean that you have the disorder at a clinically significant level. On the other hand, if you find that maladaptive behaviors such as those described in this chapter are interfering with your happiness or personal effectiveness, then you should not hesitate

to seek professional assistance in changing these behaviors. In addition to the three Ds discussed earlier (distress, dysfunction, and deviance), you will want to consider the frequency with which the particular behaviors or experiences occur, as well as their intensity and their duration. When problem behaviors occur frequently, are intense, and/or last for a long time, they are more likely to be clinically significant. In such a case, it is important not to let any stigma you might attach to having a psychological problem keep you from acting in your best interest and discussing your problem with a mental health professional.

chapter sixteen

Treatment of Psychological Disorders

Myth or Reality?

Antidepressant Drugs Are Safe and Effective (page 614)

Depressed? There's a pill for that, and antidepressants like Cymbalta, Lexapro, Paxil, and Zoloft are among the most frequently prescribed of all drugs. But how safe and effective are these drugs? The answer may surprise you.

I fought my way through Harvard in the midst of psychosis and "spaciness." . . . There is no doubt in my mind that therapy helped me get through school. . . . For so long I wondered why my therapist insisted on talking about my relationship with him. He was not my problem; the problem was my life— my past, my fears, what I was going to do tomorrow, how I would handle things, sometimes just how to survive. . . . It took a long time, but finally I saw why it was important to explore my relationship with my therapist—it was the first real relationship I had ever had: that is, the first I felt safe enough to invest myself in. I rationalized that it was all right because I would learn from this relationship how to relate to other people and maybe even one day leave behind the isolation of my own world. . . . I often felt at odds with my therapist until I could see that he was a real person and he related to me and I to him, not only as patient and therapist, but as human beings. Eventually I began to feel that I too was a person, not just an outsider looking in on the world.

Medication or superficial support is not a substitute for the feeling that one is understood by another human being. For me, the greatest gift came the day I realized that my therapist really had stood by me for years and that he would continue to stand by me and help me achieve what I wanted to achieve. With that realization, my viability as a person began to grow. ("A Recovering Patient," 1986, pp. 68–70)

In this poignant account, written by a person who had suffered from schizophrenia for much of her life, we see that even in this most serious of behavior disorders, humans can reach out and help one another. As clinical scientists, we would want to know about the type of therapeutic approach used, how effective it was as compared to another approach, and what causal factors—biological, environmental, and psychological—shaped how this patient viewed the world before and after therapy.

This chapter explores the many approaches that are being taken to treat psychological disorders, as well as the critical issue of their effectiveness. Although first-person reports, like the one above, suggest that many people derive considerable benefit from psychotherapy, psychologists demand much more in the way of evidence. Nearly 60 years of research on psychological treatments has taught us that the question of efficacy, or treatment outcome, is a tremendously complex one that has no simple answers. Yet as we shall see, much has been learned about the effectiveness of these various therapeutic approaches and about the factors that influence treatment outcome.

PSYCHOLOGICAL TREATMENTS

The basic goal of all psychotherapy, whatever the approach, is to help people change maladaptive thoughts, feelings, and behavior patterns so that they can live happier and more productive lives. As the remarks of the "recovering patient" suggest, the relationship between the client and the person providing help is a prime ingredient of psychotherapeutic success (Binder & Strupp, 1997; Gabbard et al., 2005). Within that helping relationship, therapists use a variety of treatment techniques to promote positive changes in the client. These techniques vary widely, depending on the therapists' own theories of cause and change, and they may range from biomedical approaches (such as administering psychoactive drugs) to a wide variety of psychological treatments. Both of these elements— relationship and techniques—are important to the success of the treatment enterprise (Figure 16.1).

A number of professional groups provide psychological treatments. *Clinical and counseling psychologists* make up one group. These psychologists, who typically hold a PhD (Doctor of Philosophy) or PsyD (Doctor of Psychology), have received 5 or more years of intensive training and supervision in a variety of psychotherapeutic techniques, as well as training in research and psychological assessment techniques. The PhD, typically conferred by university psychology departments, is a more science-oriented degree. The PsyD degree, usually conferred by professional schools, is more professionally than scientifically oriented. Another major group of psychotherapists, *psychiatrists,* are medical doctors who specialize in psychotherapy and in biomedical treatments, such as drug therapy.

In addition to psychologists and psychiatrists, a number of other professionals provide treatment. These professionals typically receive a master's degree based on 2 years of highly focused and practical training. They include *psychiatric social workers,* who often work in community agencies; *marriage and family counselors,* who specialize in problems arising from family relationships; *pastoral counselors,* who tend to focus on spiritual issues; and *substance-abuse counselors,* who work with substance and sexual abusers and their victims.

Having previewed the nature of therapy and those who provide it, we will now consider the major therapeutic approaches that have developed within the perspectives on human behavior (Figure 16.2). We should note, however, that broadly trained therapists combine elements of

Figure 16.1

The process of therapy involves a relationship between a client and a therapist, who applies the techniques dictated by his or her approach to treatment. The quality of the therapeutic relationship, the therapy techniques used, and the client's commitment to change all influence the outcome.

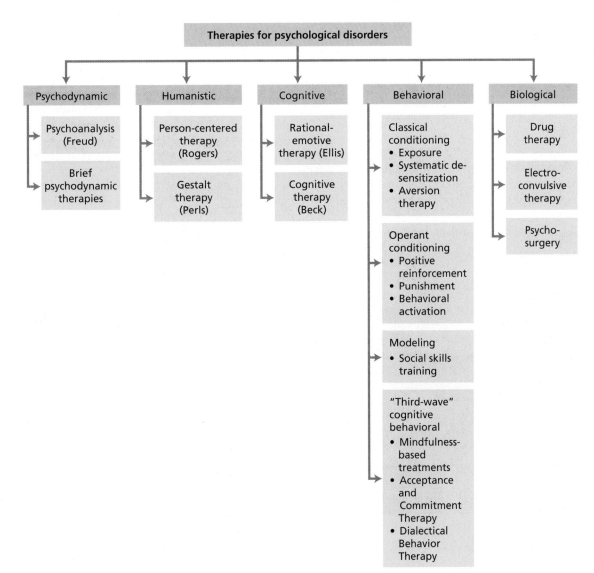

Figure 16.2

Major approaches to treatment. This diagram gives an overview of the major treatment approaches to behavior disorders.

the various therapeutic approaches in order to tailor treatment to the specific needs of the client (O'Leary & Murphy, 2006).

PSYCHODYNAMIC THERAPIES

Of the many psychotherapeutic approaches, psychodynamic treatments have the longest tradition. Their historical roots lie in Sigmund Freud's psychoanalytic theory. Although both the theory and the techniques of therapy were later modified by his followers and by those who defected to pursue rival approaches, the psychodynamic principles underlying Freud's approach continue to exert a major influence today (Alexander, 2004). Psychodynamic approaches have in common a focus on internal conflicts and unconscious factors that underlie maladaptive behavior.

Psychoanalysis

The term *psychoanalysis* refers not only to Freud's theory of personality but also to the specific approach to treatment that he developed. The goal of psychoanalysis is to help clients achieve **insight,** *the conscious awareness of the psychodynamics that underlie their problems.* Such awareness permits clients to adjust their behavior to their current life situations, rather than repeating the maladaptive routines learned in childhood. Analysts believe that as the client repeatedly encounters and deals with

long-buried emotions, motives, and conflicts within and outside of therapy, the psychic energy that was previously devoted to keeping unconscious conflicts under control can be released and redirected to more adaptive ways of living (Gabbard, 2004). We now consider the methods and concepts that Freud developed to achieve the end product of successful therapy: "Where there was id, there shall ego be" (Freud, 1923, p. 148).

Free Association

Freud believed that mental events are meaningfully associated with one another, so that clues to the contents of the unconscious can be found in the ongoing stream of thoughts, memories, images, and feelings that we experience. In the technique of **free association,** *clients verbally report without censorship any thoughts, feelings, or images that enter their awareness.* Analysts sit out of sight behind the client so that the client's thought processes will be determined primarily by internal factors (Figure 16.3).

The analyst does not expect that free association will necessarily lead directly to unconscious material but rather that it will provide clues concerning important themes or issues (Hoffer & Youngren, 2004). For example, a client's stream of thoughts may suddenly stop after she mentions her father, suggesting that she was approaching a loaded topic that activated repressive defenses.

Dream Interpretation

Psychoanalysts believe that dreams express impulses, fantasies, and wishes that the client's defenses keep bottled up in the unconscious during waking hours (Glucksman, 2001). Even in dreams, which Freud termed "the royal road to the unconscious," defensive processes usually disguise the threatening material to protect the dreamer from the anxiety that the material might evoke. In dream interpretation, the analyst helps the client search for the unconscious material contained in the dreams. One means of doing so is to ask the client to free-associate to each element of the dream. The analyst then helps the client arrive at an understanding of what the symbols in the dream might really represent.

Resistance

Although clients come to therapists for help, they also have an unconscious investment in maintaining the status quo. After all, underlying their problems are unconscious conflicts so threatening and painful that the ego has resorted

Figure 16.3

In classical Freudian psychoanalysis, the client reclines on a couch while the analyst sits out of view to minimize external stimuli that might influence the client's thought processes.

to maladaptive defensive strategies to deal with them. These avoidance patterns emerge in the course of therapy as **resistance,** *defensive maneuvers that hinder the process of therapy.* Resistance can appear in many different forms. A client may suddenly avoid talking about certain topics. Resistance is a sign that anxiety-arousing material is being approached. An important task of analysis is to explore the reasons for resistance, both to promote insight and to guard against the ultimate resistance: the client's decision to drop out of therapy prematurely.

Transference

As noted earlier, the analyst sits out of view of the client and reveals nothing to the client about herself or himself. Eventually, Freud discovered, clients begin to project onto the "blank screen" of the therapist important perceptions and feelings related to their underlying conflicts. **Transference** *occurs when the client responds irrationally to the analyst as if she or he were an important figure from the client's past.* Transference is considered a most important process in psychoanalysis, for it brings into the open repressed feelings and maladaptive behavior patterns that both the therapist and client can discover and explore (Murdin & Scott, 2007).

Transference takes two basic forms. *Positive transference* occurs when a client transfers feelings of intense affection, dependency, or love to the analyst, based on past relationships. The therapist may become, for example, the parent who never provided the love the client yearned for. *Negative transference* involves irrational expressions of anger, hatred, fear, or disappointment transferred onto the therapist from important past relationships. Analysts believe that until transference reactions are analyzed and resolved, there can be no full resolution of the client's problems. In the following excerpt from a psychoanalytic session, a client traces her transference reaction to its source and then recognizes the operation of similar reactions in other relationships.

> *Client:* My brother Harry, the one I had the sex experiences with when I was little. He made me do things I didn't want to. . . . I'm afraid of you taking advantage of me. If I tell you I like you, that means you'll make me do what you want.
>
> *Therapist:* Just like Harry made you do what he wanted.
>
> *Client:* Yes. I didn't want to let him do what he did, but I couldn't help myself. I hated myself. That's why. I know it now

because there is no reason why I should feel you are the same way. That's why I act that way with other people too. . . . I don't like to have people get too close to me. The whole thing is the same as happens with you. It's all so silly and wrong. You aren't my brother and the other people aren't my brother. I never saw the connection until now. (Wolberg, 1967, pp. 660–661)

In this interchange, we see both positive and negative transference reactions based on an important past relationship. The client's feelings about her brother continue to play out in her fear of getting close to others, including the analyst, and being exploited once again.

Interpretation

How can analysts help clients detect and understand resistances, the meaning of dream symbols, and transference reactions? The analyst's chief therapeutic technique for these purposes is **interpretation,** *any statement by the therapist that is intended to provide the client with insight into his or her behavior or dynamics.* An interpretative statement confronts clients with something that they have not previously admitted into consciousness, for example, "It's almost as if you're angry with me without realizing it."

A general rule in psychoanalytic treatment is to interpret what is already near the surface and just beyond the client's current awareness (McWilliams, 2004). Offering "deep" interpretations of strongly defended unconscious dynamics is considered poor technique because, even if they are correct, such interpretations are so far removed from the client's current awareness that they cannot be informative or helpful.

Brief Psychodynamic and Interpersonal Therapies

Classical psychoanalysis as practiced by Freud (and by a declining number of contemporary analysts) is an expensive and time-consuming process, for the goal is no less than rebuilding the client's personality. In classical psychoanalysis, it is not uncommon for a client to be seen 5 times a week for 5 years or more. Today, however, many therapists consider this level of client and therapist commitment both impractical and unnecessary. Their conclusion is supported by psychotherapy studies that measured the degree of improvement that occurred over the course of therapy. One early study (Howard et al., 1986) showed that about half of the clients improved markedly within 8 sessions, and most therapeutic effects as rated by researchers occurred within 26 sessions. The results of a more recent study involving 4,676 clients and 204 therapists in a university counseling center measured improvement using the Outcome Questionnaire-45, a measure of psychological symptoms and unhappiness. As Figure 16.4 shows, by the tenth session, most of the improvement had occurred. The researchers also found that regardless of the total number of sessions the clients received, the rate of improvement was highest at the beginning and decreased over time (Baldwin et al., 2009). A study of more than 4,000 clients seen in therapy in the United Kingdom also found that clinically significant change did not increase in clients seen beyond 10 sessions (Stiles et al., 2008).

To an increasing extent, psychodynamic therapists are adopting briefer and more economical approaches (Levenson, 2010). Like psychoanalysis, brief psychodynamic psychotherapies focus on understanding the maladaptive influences of the past and relating them to current patterns of self-defeating behavior. Many of these brief therapies utilize basic concepts from psychoanalysis, such as the importance of insight and the use of interpretation, but they employ them in a more focused and active fashion (Binder, 2004). The therapist and client are likely to sit facing each other, and conversation typically replaces free association. Clients are seen 1 or 2 times a week rather than daily, and the goal is typically limited to helping the client deal with specific life problems rather than attempting a complete rebuilding of the client's personality. Therapy is therefore more likely to focus on the client's current life situations than on past childhood experiences and may involve teaching the client specific interpersonal and emotion-control skills (Benjamin, 2003).

One recently developed brief therapy, **interpersonal therapy,** *focuses almost exclusively on clients' current relationships with important people in their lives* (Weissman et al., 2007). This therapy, designed in part for research on the treatment of depression, is highly structured and seldom takes longer than 15 to 20 sessions. Therapeutic goals include resolving role disputes such as marital conflict, adjusting to the loss of a relationship or to a changed relationship, and identifying and correcting deficits in social skills that make it difficult for the client to initiate or maintain satisfying relationships. The therapist collaborates very actively with the client in finding solutions to these problems and may invite the client to link issues in current relationships with those in important past relationships, thereby showing that what happened in the past need not be carried into the present. In controlled outcome studies, interpersonal therapy has proven effective for several disorders, particularly depression (Chambless & Hollon, 1998; Coren, 2010).

HUMANISTIC PSYCHOTHERAPIES

In contrast to psychodynamic theorists, who view behavior as a product of unconscious processes, humanistic theorists view humans as capable of consciously controlling their actions and taking responsibility for their choices and behavior. These theorists also believe that everyone possesses inner resources for self-healing and personal growth and that disordered behavior reflects a blocking of the natural growth process. This blocking is brought about by distorted perceptions, lack of awareness about feelings, or a negative self-image. The therapist's goal is to create an environment in which clients can engage in self-exploration and remove the barriers that block their natural tendencies toward personal growth (Greenberg & Rice, 1997). These barriers often result from childhood experiences that fostered unrealistic or maladaptive standards for self-worth. When people try to live their lives according to the expectations of others, rather than their own desires and feelings, they often feel unfulfilled and empty and unsure about who they really are.

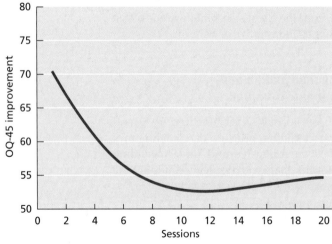

Figure 16.4

Decrease in psychological symptoms as a function of number of sessions seen in psychotherapy. The highest rate of improvement is seen early in treatment. Results like these have helped stimulate the development of short-term treatments. Source: Baldwin et al., 2009.

In contrast to classical psychoanalytic therapy, humanistic approaches focus primarily on the present and future instead of the past. Therapy is directed at helping clients to become aware of feelings as they occur, rather than to achieve insights into the childhood origins of those feelings.

Person-Centered Therapy

The best-known and most widely used humanistic therapy is the *person-centered* (formerly called *client-centered*) approach (Cain, 2010). Carl Rogers (1959, 1980; Figure 16.5), who developed the approach, became convinced that the important active ingredient in therapy is the relationship that develops between client and therapist, and he began to focus his attention on the kind of therapeutic environment that seemed most effective in fostering self-exploration and personal growth (Bozarth et al., 2002). Rogers's research and experiences as a therapist identified three important and interrelated therapist attributes:

- **Unconditional positive regard** *is communicated when the therapist shows that he or she genuinely cares about and accepts the client, without judgment or evaluation.* The therapist also communicates a sense of trust in the client's ability to work through her or his problems. In part, this sense of trust is communicated in the therapist's refusal to offer advice or guidance.

- **Empathy,** *the willingness and ability to view the world through the client's eyes,* is a second vital factor (Blackstone, 2007). In a good relationship, the therapist comes to sense the feelings and meanings experienced by the client and

communicates this understanding to the client. The therapist does this by *reflecting* back to the client what she or he is communicating—perhaps by rephrasing something the client has just said in a way that captures the meaning and emotion involved.

- **Genuineness** *refers to consistency between the way the therapist feels and the way he or she behaves.* The therapist must be open enough to express his or her own feelings honestly, whether positive or negative. In the case of negative feelings, this may seem to be contradictory to the attribute of unconditional positive regard, but that is not necessarily the case. Indeed, the most striking demonstrations of both attributes occur when a therapist can express displeasure with a client's behavior and at the same time communicate acceptance of the client as a person. For example, a therapist might say, "I feel frustrated with the way you handled that situation because I want things to work out better than that for you."

Rogers believed that when therapists can express these three key therapeutic attributes, they create a climate in which the client feels accepted, understood, and free to explore basic attitudes and feelings without fear of being judged or rejected. Within such a climate, the client experiences the courage and freedom to grow. These therapeutic attitudes are exhibited in the following excerpt from one of Rogers's therapy sessions (Rogers, 1951, p. 49):

Client: I cannot be the kind of person I want to be. I guess maybe I haven't the guts or the strength to kill myself, and if someone else would relieve me of the responsibility or I would be in an accident, I— just don't want to live.

Rogers: At the present time things look so black that you can't see much point in living. (Note the use of empathic reflection and the absence of any criticism.)

Client: Yes, I wish I'd never started this therapy. I was happy when I was living in my dream world. There I could be the kind of person I wanted to be. But now there is such a wide, wide gap between my ideal and what I am. . . . (Notice how the client responds to reflection with more information.)

Rogers: It's really tough digging into this like you are and at times the shelter of your dream world looks more attractive and comfortable. (Reflection.)

Figure 16.5

"Psychotherapy is the releasing of an already existing capacity in a potentially competent individual, not the expert manipulation of a more or less passive personality."—Carl Rogers

Client: My dream world or suicide. . . . So I don't see why I should waste your time coming in twice a week—I'm not worth it—what do you think?

Rogers: It's up to you. . . . It isn't wasting my time. I'd be glad to see you whenever you come, but it's how you feel about it. . . . (Note the genuineness in stating an honest desire to see the client and the unconditional positive regard in trusting her capacity and responsibility for choice.)

Rogers believed that as clients experience a constructive therapeutic relationship, they exhibit increased self-acceptance, greater self-awareness, enhanced self-reliance, increased comfort with other relationships, and improved life functioning (Rogers, 1959). Research does indicate that therapists' characteristics have a strong effect on the outcome of psychotherapy. Therapy is most likely to be successful when the therapist is perceived as genuine, warm, and empathic (Sachse & Elliott, 2002). Two decades after Rogers's death, the person-centered approach remains an influential force (Cain, 2010; Tudor & Worral, 2006).

Gestalt Therapy

Frederick S. (Fritz) Perls, a European psychoanalyst who was trained in Gestalt psychology, developed another humanistic approach to treatment that he called Gestalt therapy. As noted in Chapter 5, the term *gestalt* ("organized whole") refers to perceptual principles through which people actively organize stimulus elements into meaningful "whole" patterns. Ordinarily, whatever we perceive, whether external stimuli, ideas, or emotions, we concentrate on only part of our whole experience—the figure—while largely ignoring the background against which the figure appears. For people who have psychological difficulties, that background includes important feelings, wishes, and thoughts that are blocked from ordinary awareness because they would evoke anxiety. Gestalt therapy's goal is to bring them into immediate awareness so that the client can be whole once again.

Gestalt therapy, often carried out in groups, utilizes a variety of imaginative techniques to help clients "get in touch with their inner selves." These methods are much more active and dramatic than person-centered approaches and are sometimes even confrontational. Therapists often ask clients to role-play different aspects of themselves so that they may directly experience their inner dynamics. In the *empty-chair technique,* a client may be asked to imagine his mother sitting in the chair and then carry on a conversation in which he alternately role-plays his mother and himself, changing chairs for each role and honestly telling her how he feels about important issues in their relationship. These techniques can evoke powerful feelings and make clients aware of unresolved issues that affect other relationships in their lives as well. Recent research on the empty-chair technique indicates that it does indeed help clients resolve "unfinished business" with significant individuals from their pasts (Greenberg & Malcolm, 2002). Although Perls died in 1970, Gestalt therapy remains a vital force, and its principles and techniques are being incorporated into nonhumanistic therapies as well (Burley & Freier, 2004; Cain & Seeman, 2002).

test yourself   Psychodynamic and Humanistic Therapies

Match each numbered term to the correct definition on the right.

1. insight
2. resistance
3. interpersonal therapy
4. interpretations
5. Gestalt therapy
6. unconditional positive regard
7. transference

a. irrational responses to the therapist
b. brief psychodynamic treatment
c. empty-chair technique
d. key person-centered therapist attribute
e. analyst's statements about the client's behavior or dynamics
f. client's understanding of his or her own psychodynamics
g. defensive response to anxiety-arousing material

ANSWERS: 1-f, 2-g, 3-b, 4-e, 5-c, 6-d, 7-a

COGNITIVE THERAPIES

We now consider two important thought-changing approaches. Although originally labeled as "cognitive" therapies, they eventually became integral parts of today's "cognitive-behavior therapy" movement (Dobson, 2009).

As we saw in the previous chapter, many behavior disorders, including anxiety, mood, and schizophrenic disorders, involve maladaptive ways of thinking about oneself and the world. Cognitive approaches to psychotherapy focus on the role of irrational and self-defeating thought patterns, and therapists who employ this approach try to help clients discover and change the cognitions that underlie their problems.

In contrast to psychoanalysts, cognitive therapists do not emphasize the importance of unconscious psychodynamic processes. They do, however, point out that because our habitual thought patterns are so well-practiced and ingrained, they tend to "run off" almost automatically, so that we may be only minimally aware of them and may simply accept them as reflecting reality (Clark et al., 1999). Consequently, clients often need help in identifying the beliefs, ideas, and self-statements that trigger maladaptive emotions and behaviors. Once identified, these cognitions can be challenged and, with practice and effort, changed. Albert Ellis and Aaron Beck have been influential figures in the cognitive approach to therapy.

Ellis's Rational-Emotive Therapy

Albert Ellis, originally trained as a psychoanalytic therapist, became convinced that irrational thoughts, rather than unconscious dynamics, were the most immediate cause of self-defeating emotions. In the 1960s, his new approach of *rational-emotive therapy* helped launch the cognitive revolution in clinical psychology.

Ellis's theory of emotional disturbance and his rational-emotive therapy are embodied in his ABCD model (Figure 16.6).

- *A* stands for the *activating event* that seems to trigger the emotion.

- *B* stands for the *belief system* that underlies the way in which a person appraises the event.

- *C* stands for the emotional and behavioral *consequences* of that appraisal.

- *D* is the key to changing maladaptive emotions and behaviors: *disputing,* or challenging, an erroneous belief system.

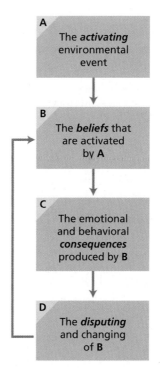

Figure 16.6

Ellis's ABCD model.
Albert Ellis's ABCD model describes his theory of the cause—and remediation—of maladaptive emotional responses and behaviors. In rational-emotive therapy, the goal is to discover, dispute, and change the client's maladaptive beliefs.

Ellis pointed out that people are accustomed to viewing their emotions (C) as being caused directly by events (A). Thus a young man who is turned down for a date may feel rejected and depressed. However, Ellis would insist that the woman's refusal is *not* the true reason for the emotional reaction. Rather, the young man's depression is caused by his irrational belief that "because she doesn't want to be with me, I'm worthless, and no one will ever want me." If the young man does not want to feel depressed and rejected, this belief must be countered and replaced by a more rational interpretation (e.g., "It would have been nice if she had accepted my invitation, but I don't need to turn it into a catastrophe. It doesn't mean other women will never care about me.").

Rational-emotive therapists introduce clients to commonly held irrational beliefs (Table 16.1) and then train them to ferret out the particular ideas that underlie their maladaptive emotional responses (Figure 16.7). In the behavioral aspect of rational-emotive therapy, clients are given homework assignments to help them analyze and change self-statements. They may be asked to place themselves in challenging situations and practice control over their emotions by using new self-statements. For example, a shy person might

Table **16.1**	Irrational Ideas That Cause Disturbance and Alternatives That Might Be Offered by a Rational-Emotive Therapist

Irrational Belief	Rational Alternative
It is a dire necessity that I be loved and approved of by virtually everyone for everything I do.	Although we might prefer approval to disapproval, our self-worth need not depend on the love and approval of others. Self-respect is more important than giving up one's individuality to buy the approval of others.
I must be thoroughly competent and achieving to be worthwhile. To fail is to be a *failure*.	As imperfect and fallible human beings, we are bound to fail from time to time. We can control only effort; we have incomplete control over outcome. We are better off focusing on the process of doing rather than on demands that we do well.
It is terrible, awful, and catastrophic when things are not the way I demand that they be.	Stop catastrophizing and turning an annoyance or irritation into a major crisis. Who are we to demand that things be different from what they are? When we turn our preferences into dire necessities, we set ourselves up for needless distress. We had best learn to change those things we can control and accept those that we can't control (and be wise enough to know the difference).
Human misery is externally caused and forced on us by other people and events.	Human misery is produced not by external factors but rather by what we tell ourselves about those events. We feel as we think, and most of our misery is needlessly self-inflicted by irrational habits of thinking.
Because something deeply affected me in the past, it must continue to do so.	We hold ourselves prisoner to the past because we continue to believe philosophies and ideas learned in the past. If they are still troubling us today, it is because we are still propagandizing ourselves with irrational nonsense. We *can* control how we think in the present and thereby liberate ourselves from the "scars" of the past.

be required to go to a party and practice rational thoughts that counteract social anxiety. Ellis reports that he overcame his own fears of women's rejections by going to Central Park in New York, practicing anxiety-reducing self-statements and striking up conversations with more than 100 different women. He reports that he got only one

Figure 16.7

"The essence of effective therapy according to rational-emotive therapy is full tolerance of people as individuals combined with a ruthless campaign against their self-defeating ideas. . . . These can be easily elicited and demolished by any scientist worth his or her salt; and the rational-emotive therapist is exactly that: an exposing and nonsense-annihilating scientist."—Albert Ellis

date, but he overcame his anxiety without being either assaulted or arrested. By learning and practicing cognitive coping responses, clients can eventually modify underlying belief systems in ways that enhance well-being (Dryden, 2002).

Beck's Cognitive Therapy

Like Ellis, Aaron Beck's goal is to point out errors of thinking and logic that underlie emotional disturbance and to help clients identify and reprogram their overlearned automatic thought patterns (Figure 16.8). In treating depressed clients, a first step is to help clients realize that their thoughts, and not the situation, cause their maladaptive emotional reactions. This sets the stage for identifying and changing the self-defeating thoughts:

> *Beck:* So failing a test means a lot to you. But if failing a test could drive people into clinical depression, wouldn't you expect everyone who failed a test to have a depression? Did everyone who failed get depressed enough to require treatment?
>
> *Client:* No, but it depends on how important the test was to the person.
>
> *Beck:* Right, and who decides the importance?
>
> *Client:* I do.
>
> *Beck:* Now what did failing mean?
>
> *Client:* (Tearful) That I couldn't get into law school.

Figure 16.8

"The formula for treatment may be stated in simple terms: The therapist helps the patient to identify his warped thinking and to learn more realistic ways to formulate his experience."—Aaron Beck

Beck: And what does that mean to you?

Client: That I'm just not smart enough.

Beck: Anything else?

Client: That I can never be happy.

Beck: And how do those thoughts make you feel?

Client: Very unhappy.

Beck: So it is the *meaning* of failing a test that makes you very unhappy. In fact, believing that you can never be happy is a powerful factor in producing unhappiness. So you get yourself into a trap—by definition, failure to get into law school equals "I can never be happy." (Beck et al., 1979, pp. 145–146, italics added)

Beck's contributions to understanding and treating depression have made his cognitive therapy a psychological treatment of choice for that disorder. In one study, cognitive therapy with booster sessions after depression decreased resulted in improvement maintenance in 97 percent of depressed clients, with nonrecurrence of depression in 75 percent of them (Vittengl et al., 2009). Cognitive therapy also has been applied to the treatment of anxiety and personality disorders (Beck et al., 2004; Clark, 2004). As we shall see, cognitive therapy also is being combined with other therapeutic techniques to form highly effective treatment packages for certain disorders.

BEHAVIOR THERAPIES

In the 1960s, behavioral approaches emerged as a dramatic departure from the assumptions and methods that characterized psychoanalytic and humanistic therapies. The new practitioners of behavior therapy denied the importance of inner dynamics. Instead, they insisted that (1) maladaptive behaviors are not merely symptoms of underlying problems: rather, they *are* the problem; (2) problem behaviors are learned in the same ways normal behaviors are; and (3) maladaptive behaviors can be unlearned by applying principles derived from research on classical conditioning, operant conditioning, and modeling. Behaviorists demonstrated that these learning procedures could be applied effectively to change the behaviors of schizophrenia, to treat anxiety disorders, and to modify many child and adult behavior problems that seemed resistant to traditional therapy approaches (Hersen, 2002).

Classical conditioning procedures have been used in two major ways. First, they have been used to reduce, or decondition, anxiety responses. Second, they have been used in attempts to condition aversive emotional responses to a particular class of stimuli, such as alcohol or inappropriate sexual objects. The most commonly used classical conditioning procedures are *exposure therapies, systematic desensitization,* and *aversion therapy.*

Exposure: An Extinction Approach

From a behavioral point of view, phobias and other fears result from classically conditioned emotional responses. The conditioning experience is assumed to involve a pairing of the phobic object (the neutral stimulus) with an aversive unconditioned stimulus (UCS). As a result, the phobic stimulus becomes a conditioned stimulus (CS) that elicits the conditioned response (CR) of anxiety. According to the two-factor learning theory discussed in Chapters 7 and 11, avoidance responses to the phobic situation are then reinforced by anxiety reduction (operant conditioning based on negative reinforcement). Thus a man who is bitten by a dog may subsequently be afraid of dogs. Moreover, each time he avoids a dog, his avoidance response is strengthened through anxiety reduction.

According to this formulation, the most direct way to reduce the fear is through a process of classical extinction of the anxiety response. This requires **exposure** *to the feared CS in the absence of the UCS* while using **response prevention** *to keep the operant avoidance response from occurring.* This is the theoretical basis for the exposure approach (Marks, 1991; Zinbarg et al., 1992). The client may be exposed to a real-life dog or asked to imagine scenes involving interactions with dogs. These stimuli will, of course, evoke considerable anxiety, but the anxiety will extinguish in time if the person remains in the presence of the CS and the UCS does not occur (Rosqvist & Hersen, 2006).

Some critics of exposure treatment are concerned that the intense anxiety created by the treatment may worsen the problem or cause clients to flee from treatment (Bruce & Sanderson, 1998). In a study of women being treated for posttraumatic stress disorder with exposure created by imaging the traumatic event, 15.4 percent of the women did indeed show a temporary increase in PTSD symptom intensity when exposure began. However, this increase did not impair treatment effectiveness or increase the likelihood of withdrawal from treatment (Foa et al., 2002).

Exposure has proved to be a highly effective technique for extinguishing anxiety responses in both animals and humans (Roth & Fonagy, 2005; Spiegler & Guevremont, 2003). It is considered a treatment of choice for posttraumatic stress disorder (Massad & Hulsey, 2006; Zoellner et al., 2009). A one-session exposure treatment successfully extinguished clinical phobias in children (Ollendick et al., 2009). Both real-life (*in vivo*) and imaginal exposure are effective. An additional advantage is that clients can administer exposure treatment to themselves under a therapist's direction with high success rates (Marks, 1991).

Computer technology has provided a new method for delivering exposure treatments by bringing the external environment into the therapy room. **Virtual reality (VR)** *involves the use of computer technology to create highly realistic virtual environments that simulate actual experience so vividly that they evoke many of the same reactions that a comparable real-world environment would.* Observers typically wear helmets containing two small video monitors (one for each eye) attached to a high-speed computer. The image to each eye is slightly different, producing binocular depth-perception cues that result in a 3-D image. With the aid of position-tracking devices, the computer monitors the person's physical movements and adjusts the images and sounds accordingly (Figure 16.9). Observers thus have a vivid sense of being "present" in a different place when navigating through the virtual world. VR is increasingly being applied to the treatment of anxiety disorders, particularly phobias (Wiederhold & Wiederhold, 2005). Once software for a particular fear has been developed, many therapists can apply the treatment in their offices, repeatedly exposing the client to the feared stimuli, which may be difficult to find in the real world.

Systematic Desensitization: A Counterconditioning Approach

In 1958, Joseph Wolpe helped launch the behavior therapy movement with his introduction of **systematic desensitization,** *a learning-based treatment for anxiety disorders.* Wolpe also presented impressive outcome data for 100 phobic patients he had treated with the technique. Systematic desensitization remains a widely used treatment today. In many controlled studies, its success rate in treating a wide range of phobic disorders has been 80 percent or better (Rachman, 1998; Spiegler & Guevremont, 2003).

Wolpe viewed anxiety as a classically conditioned emotional response. His goal was to eliminate the anxiety by using a procedure called **counterconditioning,** *in which a new response that is incompatible with anxiety is conditioned to the anxiety-arousing CS.* The difference between extinction and counterconditioning is that extinction requires only exposure to the CS; it does not require a substitute response to counter the anxiety response.

The first step in systematic desensitization is to train the client in the skill of voluntary muscle relaxation, using an approach of tensing, then relaxing the muscles. Next the client is helped to construct a **stimulus hierarchy** *of 10 to 20 scenes arranged in roughly equal steps from low-anxiety scenes*

Figure 16.9

This woman with a spider phobia views a virtual "spider world" inside the helmet. She also handles a realistic toy spider whose movements inside the virtual environment are linked to her manipulation of the toy. The monitor shows the scene being experienced by the client in this exposure treatment.

to high-anxiety ones. Table 16.2 shows a stimulus hierarchy that was used in treating a college student with high test anxiety.

In the desensitization sessions, the therapist deeply relaxes the client and then asks the client to vividly imagine the first scene in the hierarchy (the least anxiety-arousing one) for several seconds. The client can't be both relaxed and anxious at the same time, so if the relaxation is strong enough, it replaces anxiety as the CR to that stimulus—the counterconditioning process. When the client can imagine that scene for increasingly longer periods without experiencing anxiety, the therapist proceeds to the next scene. When low-arousal scenes have been deconditioned, some of the total anxiety has been reduced and the person is now ready to imagine more anxiety-arousing scenes without becoming anxious. Therapists can also accomplish desensitization through carefully controlled exposure to a hierarchy of real-life situations (e.g., having a person with a phobia of heights actually stand on a step stool and, eventually, walk across a suspension bridge while voluntarily relaxing). Both imaginal and real-life desensitization approaches are highly effective in reducing anxiety (Hersen, 2003).

Although both exposure therapy based on extinction and systematic desensitization are very effective in reducing fear responses, there are practical trade-offs. Systematic desensitization is sometimes preferred over exposure therapy because it produces far less anxiety for the client during the treatment. Exposure, however, often achieves the desired reduction in anxiety with a briefer course of therapy than does systematic desensitization (Bruce & Sanderson, 1998).

Aversion Therapy

For some clients, the therapeutic goal is not to reduce anxiety but actually to condition anxiety to a particular stimulus that triggers deviant behavior. In **aversion therapy,** *the therapist pairs a stimulus that is attractive to the client (the CS) with a noxious UCS in an attempt to condition an aversion to the CS.* For example, aversion treatment for alcoholics may involve injecting the client with a nausea-producing drug and then having him or her drink alcohol (the CS) as nausea (the UCS) develops. Electric shock may also be paired with alcohol ingestion. Similarly, pedophiles (child molesters) have undergone treatment in which strong electric shocks are paired with slides showing children similar to those the offenders sexually abused (Figure 16.10). To measure the effects of the treatment for males, therapists can use a

Table **16.2**	A Stimulus Hierarchy Used in the Systematic Desensitization Treatment of a Test-Anxious College Student
Scene	**Hierarchy of Anxiety-Arousing Scenes**
1	Hearing about someone else who has a test
2	Instructor announcing that a test will be given in 3 weeks
3	Instructor reminding class that there will be a test in 2 weeks
4	Overhearing classmates talk about studying for the test, which will occur in 1 week
5	Instructor reminding class of what it will be tested on in 2 days
6	Leaving class the day before the exam
7	Studying the night before the exam
8	Getting up the morning of the exam
9	Walking toward the building where the exam will be given
10	Walking into the testing room
11	Instructor walking into the room with the tests
12	Tests being passed out
13	Reading the test questions
14	Watching others finish the test
15	Seeing a question I can't answer
16	Instructor waiting for me to finish the test

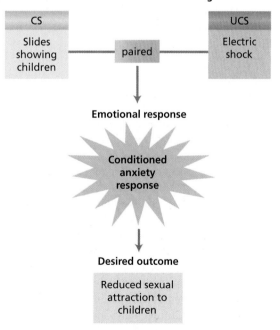

Figure 16.10

Aversion therapy.
The classical conditioning that occurs in aversion therapy is illustrated in the treatment of pedophiles who receive electric shocks as they view pictures of children. The goal of the treatment is the development of a conditioned aversion in order to reduce sexual attraction to children.

physiological recording device that measures penile blood-volume responses to the slides; the therapists can then compare the readings before and after treatment (Sandler, 1986).

Aversion therapies have been applied to a range of disorders, with variable results. In one study of 278 alcoholics who underwent aversion therapy, 190 (63 percent) were still abstinent a year after treatment had ended. Three years later, a third of the patients were still abstinent, an impressive result given the traditionally high relapse rate in chronic alcoholic individuals (Wiens & Menustik, 1983). Unfortunately, treatment gains from aversion therapies often fail to generalize from the treatment setting to the real world. A recovering alcoholic or drug addict who goes to a party where friends abuse the substance is likely to have difficulty resisting the temptation to relapse. Some experts believe that aversion therapy is most likely to succeed if it is part of a more comprehensive treatment program in which the client also learns specific coping skills for avoiding relapses (Marlatt & Gordon, 1985).

Operant Conditioning Treatments

The term **behavior modification** *refers to treatment techniques that apply operant conditioning procedures in an attempt to increase or decrease a specific behavior.* These techniques may use any of the operant procedures for manipulating the environment that we discussed in Chapter 7: positive reinforcement, extinction, negative reinforcement, or punishment.

The focus in behavior modification is on externally observable behaviors. The behaviors targeted for change are measured throughout the treatment program, allowing the therapist to track the progress of the treatment program and to make modifications if behavior change begins to lag.

Behavior modification techniques have been successfully applied to many different behavior disorders. They have yielded particularly impressive results when used in populations that are difficult to treat with more traditional therapies, such as hospitalized schizophrenic patients, profoundly disturbed children, and individuals with mental retardation (Ayllon & Azrin, 1968; Lovaas, 1977; Martin & Pear, 2010). We now consider the use of positive reinforcement and punishment in two of these populations.

Positive Reinforcement Techniques

One of the dangers of long-term psychiatric hospitalization is the gradual loss of social, personal-care, and occupational skills needed to survive outside the hospital. Such deterioration is common among chronic schizophrenic patients who have been hospitalized for an extended period. Verbal psychotherapies have very limited success in rebuilding such skills.

In the 1960s, Teodoro Ayllon and Nathan Azrin (1968) introduced a revolutionary approach to the treatment of hospitalized schizophrenic patients. The **token economy** *involves the systematic application of positive reinforcement to strengthen desired behaviors*—such as personal grooming, appropriate social responses, housekeeping behaviors, working on assigned jobs, and participation in vocational training programs. Rather than being given reinforcers such as food or grounds privileges directly, patients earn a specified number of plastic tokens for the performance of each desired behavior listed on a kind of menu. Patients can then redeem the tokens for a wide range of tangible reinforcers, such as a private room, exclusive rental of a radio or TV set, selection of personal furniture, freedom to leave the ward and walk around the grounds, recreational activities, and items from the hospital commissary. The long-term goal of token-economy programs is to jump-start the behaviors that the patient will need to get along in the world outside the hospital. The tangible reinforcers used in these programs eventually come under the control of social reinforcers and self-reinforcement processes (such as self-pride). When this begins to occur, the tokens can be phased out and the desired behaviors will continue (Kazdin, 2003). Using this technique, Ayllon and Azrin reported remarkable increases in adaptive behavior in patients for whom change seemed hopeless.

Token-economy programs have proven to be highly effective with some of the most challenging populations. In one study, a token-economy program was carried out over a 4-year period with severely disturbed schizophrenic patients who had been hospitalized an average of more than 17 years. During the course of the program, 98 percent of the patients from the behavioral treatment program were able to be released from the hospital (most to shelter-care facilities in the community), compared with only 45 percent of a control group that received the normal hospital treatments (Paul & Lentz, 1977). Token economies have also been applied successfully within business, school, prison, and home environments to increase desirable behaviors (Martin & Pear, 2010).

Therapeutic Application of Punishment

As we saw in Chapter 7, punishment is the quickest way to stop a behavior from occurring, but most psychologists regard it as the least preferred way to control behavior because of its aversive qualities and potential negative side effects. Therefore, before deciding to use punishment as a therapy technique, therapists ask themselves two important questions: (1) Are there alternative, less painful approaches that might be effective? (2) Is the behavior to be eliminated sufficiently injurious to the individual or to society to justify the severity of the punishment?

Sometimes the answers to these questions lead to a decision to use punishment. For example, some of the most startling self-destructive behaviors occur in certain severely disturbed autistic children. Such children may strike themselves repeatedly, bang their heads on sharp objects, bite or tear pieces of flesh from their bodies, or engage in other self-mutilating behaviors. O. Ivar Lovaas (1977), a UCLA psychologist who pioneered the use of operant conditioning techniques in the treatment of such children, successfully eliminated such behaviors with a limited number of contingent electric shocks. One 7-year-old boy had been self-injurious for 5 years and had to be kept in physical restraints. During one 90-minute period when his restraints were removed, he struck himself more than 3,000 times. With the consent of his parents, shock electrodes were attached to the boy, and he was given a painful electric shock each time he struck himself. Only 12 shocks were needed to virtually eliminate the self-destructive behavior. In another case, 15 shocks eliminated self-destructive behavior in a severely disturbed girl with a history of banging her head against objects. Punishment is never employed without the consent of the client or the client's legal guardian in cases when the client is a minor or is mentally incompetent to give consent.

Behavioral Activation Therapy for Depression

As described in Chapter 15, the behavioral perspective views depression as caused and maintained by a decrease in positive reinforcement. According to Peter Lewinsohn and his colleagues (1985), depression is usually triggered by a loss, a personal setback, or some other punishing events that drastically reduce the amount of positive reinforcement that the person receives from the environment. As the depression begins to take hold, people stop performing behaviors that previously provided reinforcement, such as hobbies, physical activity, sexual behavior, and socializing. From this perspective, the key to stopping the downward spiral of depression and subsequent declines in reinforcement is to induce clients to behave in ways that will produce pleasure (or at least counter feeling depressed).

Based on an earlier behavioral treatment developed by Lewinsohn (1974), **behavioral activation** *is a behavioral treatment for depression that increases positively reinforcing behaviors* (Kanter et al., 2009; Martell et al., 2010). Rather than trying to change cognitions, as in cognitive therapy for depression, the behavioral activation therapist works with the client to change behaviors that will increase reinforcement and thereby reduce depression. This involves identifying behaviors that in the past have provided pleasure but are no longer occurring, or new behaviors that have a chance of being pleasurable. The therapist and client work together to set behavioral goals, develop daily routines that contain potentially reinforcing activities, and draw up behavioral contracts that increase the chances that the client will follow through. The treatment also teaches skills for problem solving, emotional control, and social interaction if needed. For example, clients are taught to counter depressive thoughts not by challenging and trying to change them, as in cognitive therapy, but by simply turning their attention outward and concentrating on stimuli in the external environment or on whatever activity they are performing. By activating positive behaviors that produce positive reinforcement, the goal is to counter depression and increase life satisfaction. Later in this chapter, the "Research Close-up" will describe a recent clinical trial that pitted behavioral activation against cognitive therapy and antidepressant drug treatment.

Modeling and Social Skills Training

Modeling is one of the most important and effective learning processes in humans, and modeling procedures have been used to treat a variety of behavioral problems. One of the most widely used applications is designed to teach clients social skills that they lack.

In **social skills training,** *clients learn new skills by observing and then imitating a model who performs a socially skillful behavior.* In the following example, a therapist served as a model for his client, a socially anxious college student who had great difficulty asking women for dates. The client began by pretending to ask for a date over the telephone:

> *Client:* By the way (pause), I don't suppose you want to go out Saturday night?
>
> *Therapist:* Up to actually asking for the date you were very good. However, if I were the girl, I might have been

offended when you said, "By the way." It's like asking her out is pretty casual. Also, the way you posed the question, you are kind of suggesting to her that she doesn't want to go out with you. Pretend for the moment I'm you. Now, how does this sound: "There's a movie at the Varsity Theater that I want to see. If you don't have other plans, I'd very much like to take you."

Client: That sounded good. Like you were sure of yourself and like the girl, too.

Therapist: Why don't you try it? (Rimm & Masters, 1979, p. 74).

Social skills training has been used with many populations, including individuals who have minor deficits in social skills, delinquents who need to learn how to resist negative peer pressures, and even hospitalized schizophrenic patients who need to learn social skills in order to function adaptively outside the hospital (Bellack et al., 2004). It often is used in conjunction with other psychological or biological treatments to jump-start new adaptive behaviors that can then be strengthened by natural reinforcers in the client's everyday environment.

Research demonstrates that increased self-efficacy is a key factor in the effectiveness of social skills training. When clients come to believe that they are capable of performing the desired behaviors, they are more likely to be successful in doing so (Bandura, 1997; Maddux, 1999). Observing successful models also increases self-efficacy by encouraging the view "If she can do that, so can I."

"Third-Wave" Cognitive-Behavioral Therapies

Since the 1950s, behavior therapies have developed through three phases. The first phase of treatments was based on animal models of classical and operant conditioning and explicitly excluded cognitive principles. The second wave, beginning in the 1960s, was the emergence of cognitive-behavioral approaches like rational-emotive behavior therapy (Ellis), cognitive therapy (Beck), and modeling and role-playing approaches (Bandura). Collectively, these were called cognitive-behavioral therapies.

The past decade has seen the emergence of so-called *third-wave cognitive-behavioral therapies* (Hayes et al., 2006; Ost, 2008). These therapies all incorporate the concept of mindfulness as a central objective of behavior change, and they represent the addition of humanistic concepts and Eastern methods to behavior therapy (Koons, 2007). They include a variety of mindfulness-based approaches to various problems, as well as Acceptance and Commitment Therapy and Dialectical Behavior Therapy.

Mindfulness-Based Treatments

Mindfulness *is a mental state of awareness, focus, openness, and acceptance of immediate experience.* It also involves a nonjudgmental appraisal, so that in a state of mindfulness, difficult thoughts and feelings have much less impact. In some ways, mindfulness is like the *association cognitive techniques* (focusing nonjudgmentally on the sensations rather than trying to distract oneself) that increase the ability to tolerate painful stimuli (Chapter 14, p. 537).

An important tool for learning mindfulness is a meditation technique in which people develop a tranquil state and focus closely on their sensations, thoughts, and feelings, allowing them to come and go without a struggle. The meditation technique is being incorporated into a variety of cognitive-behavioral treatments, including mindfulness-based stress reduction (MBSR; McCown & Riebel, 2010; Kabat-Zinn et al., 1992) and mindfulness-based relapse prevention (MBRP; Bowen et al., 2009). As a stress-management approach, mindfulness meditation reduces physiological arousal, and the detached cognitive outlook helps free people from emotion-escalating emotional processes. It is being successfully applied to treat a variety of stress-related medical conditions and psychological disorders, including anxiety and depression (Grossman et al., 2004; McCown & Riebel, 2010).

Mindfulness meditation has also been added to the relapse-prevention techniques discussed in Chapter 14 (p. 517). Here, it is used to prevent relapse by increasing awareness of thoughts and emotions that trigger lapses, thereby interrupting the previous cycle of automatic substance-abuse behaviors. It also helps abusers deal with lapses by helping to neutralize self-blame and thoughts of hopelessness, which often turns lapses into complete relapses by producing the abstinence violation effect. In a study by Sarah Bowen and coworkers (2009), MBRP was applied to substance abusers who had completed intensive inpatient or outpatient treatment. As shown in Figure 16.11, compared with the control group that got traditional community aftercare, the MBRP group had less than half the number of days of alcohol or drug use in the 2 months following treatment. However, the group difference was no longer evident at 4 months after treatment, suggesting the need for booster sessions. MBRP, though promising, needs to be compared with relapse-prevention treatment without the mindfulness procedure to see if it adds to the traditional procedures.

Acceptance and Commitment Therapy

Developed by Steven Hayes (Hayes et al., 2006), **Acceptance and Commitment Therapy (ACT)** also *focuses on the process of mindfulness as a vehicle for change.* An important difference in emphasis from traditional cognitive therapy is that instead of teaching people to exert control over their thoughts and feelings, the ACT therapist teaches clients to "just notice," accept, and embrace them, even previously unwanted ones. This matter-of-fact acceptance of a thought (e.g., "I am thinking that he doesn't like me" by a social phobic) helps reduce the emotional impact of the thought and helps defuse the anxiety it would ordinarily evoke. Even if anxiety were to be aroused, it would simply be examined and accepted as a temporary experience. This helps to strip away its emotional impact.

The "commitment" part of the treatment lies in examining one's life, deciding what is most important to one's true self, and setting life goals in accordance with those values. The therapist then helps the client develop strategies to work toward those goals and to remain committed to them. Although solid randomized clinical trials of ACT are rare, more than 30 efficacy studies have been reported, with moderate therapeutic effect sizes. The American Psychological Association has listed it as an empirically supported treatment "with modest research support."

Dialectical Behavior Therapy

Dialectical Behavior Therapy (DBT) *is a treatment developed specifically for the treatment of borderline personality disorder.* As described in Chapter 15, this complex disorder is characterized by chaotic interpersonal relationships, poor emotional control, self-destructive behaviors, and low self-esteem. As many as 70 to 80 percent of borderline individuals attempt suicide, and about 10 percent eventually kill themselves (Chapman, 2010). Other self-destructive behaviors, such as cutting themselves, also occur when under stress. Borderline clients are among the most challenging to treat because of the severity and diversity of their symptoms, the potential for suicide, and their tendency to have stormy relationships with therapists and to drop out of therapy.

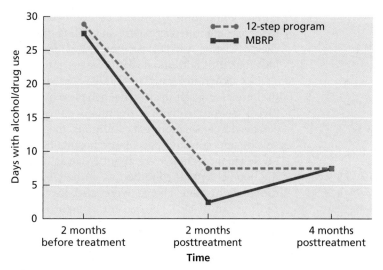

Figure 16.11

This graph shows the number of days of alcohol or drug use reported by clients receiving either MBRB treatment or a 12-step program. Reports were made 2 months before treatment as well as 2 and 4 months after treatment. Source: Data from Bowen et al., 2009.

Treating clients with such a diversity of problems requires a variety of techniques. Therefore, DBT, developed by Marsha Linehan (1993), includes a "package" of elements from cognitive, behavioral, humanistic, and psychodynamic therapies. Behavioral techniques are used to help clients learn interpersonal, problem-solving, and emotion-control skills. Cognitive approaches are employed to help clients learn more adaptive thinking about the world, relationships, and themselves. A psychodynamic element traces the history of early deprivation and rejection that created many of the problems. Finally, a humanistic emphasis on acceptance of thoughts and feelings has been added to help clients better tolerate unhappiness and negative emotions as they occur. Mindfulness procedures are a foundation for the other skills taught in DBT, because they help clients accept and tolerate the powerful emotions they experience in their lives. The goal is to become capable of calmly recognizing situations, thoughts, and their impact, rather than being overwhelmed or avoiding them. DBT is intensive in nature, with clients seen in both individual and group sessions by multiple therapists for up to 150 hours. Because of the diversity of skill-building techniques that it contains, DBT is increasingly being applied to many other types of disorders as well (Galietta et al., 2010).

A major goal of treatment is to bring self-destructive behaviors, such as suicide attempts and self-mutilation, under control. DBT seems to be uniquely effective in this regard. In a comprehensive clinical trial (Linehan et al., 2006), 101 borderline clients were randomly assigned to either

DBT or community treatment by non-behavioral therapists identified as experts in treating difficult clients. Clients were treated for 1 year, then followed up for 1 additional year to assess outcomes.

As shown in Figure 16.12, DBT was successful in reducing self-destructive behavior over the 2-year period. Although treatment gains were achieved in both treatment conditions, the rate of suicide attempts and psychiatric hospitalizations for suicidal ideation were about twice as high in the non-behavioral condition as in the DBT condition. Borderline clients were also less likely to drop out of DBT (19 percent, compared with 41 percent in the community therapy condition).

Third-wave therapies have yielded promising results in initial studies, but they do not yet have the extensive research base that older cognitive-behavioral treatments have. Additional well-designed clinical trials are needed to determine their overall effectiveness, the range of disorders that can be treated with them, and the specific contribution of mindfulness procedures (Ost, 2008).

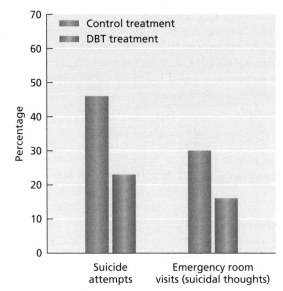

Figure 16.12

This graph shows the percentages of borderline personality disorder clients treated with dialectical behavior therapy or non-behavioral therapy who made suicide attempts or visits to hospital emergency rooms because of suicidal thoughts. Source: Data from Linehan et al., 2006.

test yourself   **Cognitive and Behavioral Approaches**

True or false?

1. The cognitive therapy developed by Albert Ellis is called rational-emotive therapy.
2. Exposure is based on the learning principle of counterconditioning.
3. A classical conditioning procedure used to treat alcoholics and pedophiles is aversive conditioning.
4. A technique used to shape adaptive behavior in schizophrenic patients is negative reinforcement.
5. A behavioral treatment used to counter depression is behavioral activation.
6. Dialectical Behavior Therapy was developed to treat borderline personality disorder.

ANSWERS: 1-true, 2-false, 3-true, 4-false, 5-true, 6-true

GROUP, FAMILY, AND MARITAL THERAPIES

Most of the therapeutic approaches we have discussed so far can be carried out with groups of clients as well as with individuals (Brabender et al., 2004). Indeed, group training in coping skills is an integral part of DBT (Linehan, 1993). Therapy groups typically include 6 to 8 clients and a single therapist. Within a group, clients can experience acceptance, support, and a sense of belonging. They soon see that other people also struggle with problems, a realization that helps counter feelings of isolation and deviance. Clients also can observe how others approach problems, and the interpersonal relations that develop within the group can be a training ground for learning new interpersonal skills. Furthermore, clients can gain insight into how they are perceived by others (Erford, 2010).

Family Therapy

Sometimes the group being treated is a family. Family therapy arose from the clinical observation that many clients who had shown marked improvement in individual therapy—often in institutional settings—suffered relapses when they returned home and began interacting with their families. This observation led to an important concept in the field of psychotherapy, namely, that the disorder shown by the "identified patient" may reflect dysfunctional relationships within the family system and that permanent change in the client may require that the entire family system be the focus of therapy (Nichols & Schwartz, 2010). Family therapists therefore help the family understand how it functions and how its unique patterns of interaction contribute to conflicts and to the problems of one or more members (Figure 16.13):

> In one family, Jessica, an anorexic 14-year-old girl, was the identified patient. However, as the therapist worked with the family, he saw a competitive struggle for the father's attention and observed that the girl was able to compete and get "cuddly" affection from her father only when she presented herself to him as a "sick" person. To bring the hidden dynamics out into the open, the therapist worked at getting the family members to express their desires more directly—in words instead of through hidden behavioral messages. In time, Jessica became capable of expressing her need for affection directly to her father, and her anorexia disappeared. (Based on Aponte & Hoffman, 1973)

Figure 16.13

Family therapists focus on the total pattern of family interactions, and they include the entire family in treatment.

Marital Therapy

Today's soaring divorce rate is a stark reflection of the difficulties that exist in many marriages. Nearly half of all first marriages end in divorce, and the divorce rate is even higher among people who remarry (Hetherington, 1998). Couples frequently seek marital therapy because they are troubled by their relationship or because they are contemplating separation or divorce. Typically, the therapist works with both partners together, and therapy focuses on clarifying and improving the interactions between them (Harway, 2005).

Research has shown that happily married couples differ from distressed couples in that they talk more to one another, keep channels of communication open, show more sensitivity to each other's feelings and needs, and are more skilled at solving problems (Gottman & Levenson, 1992). Marital therapy targets improvement in these areas.

Distressed couples frequently have faulty communication patterns, as demonstrated in the following case:

> *Husband:* She never comes up to me and kisses me. I am always the one to make the overtures.
>
> *Therapist:* Have you told your wife you would like this from her—more demonstration of affection?
>
> *Husband:* Well, no. You'd think she'd know.
>
> *Wife:* No, how would I know? You always said you didn't like aggressive women.
>
> *Husband:* I don't, I don't like dominating women.
>
> *Wife:* Well, I thought you meant women who make the overtures. How am I to know what you want?
>
> *Therapist:* You'd have a better idea if he had been able to tell you. (Satir, 1967, pp. 72–73)

An important recent addition to marital therapy is a focus on *acceptance* (Jacobson & Christensen, 1996). This addition was based on findings that in well-functioning couples, as well as in those who profit from treatment, partners make a decision to accept those aspects of the partner's behavior that probably are too ingrained to change. For example, it makes little sense to demand that a person with a highly introverted personality style suddenly become a social gadfly and life of the party. The therapeutic emphasis is on helping couples work toward change in those areas where change is possible and helping them learn to accept aspects of the partner and the relationship that seem unlikely to change. Doing so reduces frustration, lessens demands on the other spouse, and allows the couple to focus on and enjoy the positive aspects of their relationship. The addition of acceptance training to the other elements of marital therapy has improved treatment outcomes (Christensen et al., 2006).

CULTURAL AND GENDER ISSUES IN PSYCHOTHERAPY

Psychological treatments reflect the cultural context in which they develop. Within the dominant cultures of western Europe and North America, personal problems are seen as originating within people in the form of dysfunctional thinking, conflict, and stress responses. People are assumed to be capable of expressing their feelings and taking personal responsibility for improving themselves. We can easily see these values and assumptions reflected in the therapies we have discussed. Psychodynamic, humanistic, cognitive, and behavioral treatments all focus on changing these internal factors.

These values are not shared by all cultures and ethnic groups, however. For example, people from some Asian cultures might view the "therapeutic" expression of hostility toward one's parents as unthinkable (Hall & Okazaki, 2003). Likewise, the suggestion that assertiveness training would be helpful in competing more successfully with others and standing up for one's rights might be appalling to a person from a collectivistic culture (Cooper & Denner, 1998). Given diverse cultural norms and values, we should not be surprised that some individuals from non-Western cultures view psychotherapy as a totally inappropriate, and even shameful, option for the solution of their problems in living (Foulks et al., 1995).

Cultural Factors in Treatment Utilization

Recent large-scale epidemiological studies suggest that rates of mental illness differ among ethnic groups. Summarizing the results, Stanley Sue and June Chu (2003) concluded that African Americans appear to have low rates despite a history of prejudice, discrimination, and the resulting stress. American Indians and Alaska Natives have high rates, and Mexican Americans and Asian American and Pacific Islanders show slightly lower or very similar rates compared to non-Hispanic Whites. Even more clear, however, is the fact that members of minority groups use mental health services far less than the majority White population does (Wang et al., 2002). Even

when minority group members seek out mental health services, they often fail to stay in treatment. As a result, many problems that could benefit from psychological treatment go untreated (Ivey et al., 2006; Wang et al., 2002).

Psychologists Derald Sue and David Sue (1990) have identified several barriers to treatment among minority groups. One of them is a cultural norm against turning to professionals outside one's own culture for help. Instead, these individuals turn to family, clergy, acupuncturists, herbalists, and folk healers for assistance. Moreover, for many minority group members, a history of frustrating experiences with White bureaucracies makes them unwilling to approach a hospital or mental health center. There may also be language barriers.

Sometimes access to treatment is a major problem. Because many minority groups suffer high rates of unemployment and poverty, they may lack health insurance and be unable to afford therapy. Likewise, many community mental health agencies and professional therapists are located outside the areas where the underserved populations live. But even within health systems like Medicare, minorities do not receive equal treatment. In one study of individuals 65 years or older in Medicare+Choice plans, researchers assessed the percentage of members receiving mental health services, rates of follow-up after hospitalization for mental illness, the number of practitioner contacts for antidepressant medication management, and the number of referrals to effective treatments. On all of these measures, elderly members of minority groups received poorer treatment than did Whites (Virnig et al., 2004).

But according to Stanley Sue and Nolan Zane (1987), the biggest problem of all is the shortage of skilled counselors who can provide culturally responsive forms of treatment. Therapists often have little familiarity with the cultural backgrounds and personal characteristics of ethnic groups other than their own. For example, a therapeutic goal that emphasizes the direct and assertive expression of negative feelings may conflict with the cultural norms of a client from an Asian culture. Sometimes, as well, therapists operate on the basis of inaccurate stereotypes that result in unrealistic and possibly inappropriate goals and expectations, as well as great difficulty in establishing the positive client-therapist relationship that has been shown to be a powerful factor in therapeutic success (Ivey et al., 2006).

What can be done to increase access of culturally diverse groups to psychological treatment?

One answer is to take therapy to the people. Studies have shown that establishing mental health service agencies in minority population areas increases utilization of mental health services, particularly if agencies are staffed by culturally skilled counselors (Sue, 1998). Another solution might be to train more therapists from these ethnic groups. Stanley Sue and his coworkers (1991) found that dropout rates fell and the number of therapy sessions increased when clients saw ethnically similar therapists. However, for clients who elect to remain in therapy, it has *not* been demonstrated that treatment outcomes are better for clients who work with therapists from their own ethnic group. What seems more important than an ethnic match is for the therapist and client to form a good relationship and to share similar viewpoints regarding goals for treatment and preferred means for resolving problems (Figure 16.14). Giuseppe Costantino and coworkers (2009) found that **cultural congruence**—*treatment that is consistent with cultural beliefs and expectations*—predicted good therapy outcomes for elderly Hispanic clients.

Stanley Sue (1998) suggests that **culturally competent therapists** *are able to use knowledge about the client's culture to achieve a broad understanding of the client.* At the same time, they are attentive to how the client may differ from the cultural stereotype, thereby balancing cultural understanding with the individual characteristics and needs of the client. They also are able to introduce *culture-specific elements* into the therapy. Thus a therapist might draw on some of the techniques used by folk healers within that culture (e.g., prayer or a specific ritual) to effect changes in the client. Obviously, this would require a good working knowledge of the client's culture, plus a willingness to take advantage of what is therapeutically effective for promoting positive changes in that culture (Mishne, 2002). When therapists receive cultural competence training, they are able to work more effectively with members of other cultures, and clients are more likely to remain in treatment (Wade & Bernstein, 1991).

Gender Issues in Therapy

Even within the same culture, the lives of men and women can differ in many ways, as can the life demands they must cope with. As we saw in Chapter 15, psychological disorders, particularly those involving anxiety and depression, occur more frequently among women in Western cultures. This may reflect the impact of specific stressors that women face, such as poverty (women are overrepresented at the poverty level); lack of

Figure 16.14

Research suggests that the outcome of therapy with minority populations is affected more by the cultural sensitivity and competency of the therapist than it is by the ethnic similarity of therapist and client.

opportunity fostered by sexism; strains created by the demanding multiple roles of mother, worker, and spouse among married women; and the violence and histories of abuse that many women experience. In many instances, psychological problems arise not so much from internal problems and conflicts but from oppressive elements in the family, social, and political worlds. As women strive for more egalitarian relationships with men and for equal opportunity to develop their potential, they often meet external barriers that are deeply embedded in their culture's traditional sex roles and, in some cultures, religious traditions.

Feminist therapy *focuses on women's issues and strives to help women achieve greater personal freedom and self-determination* (Brown, 1994; Worell & Remer, 2003). It is not a specific therapeutic technique but rather an orientation that takes into account issues that affect women's lives. In the eyes of many therapists, it may be more important to focus on what can be done to change women's life circumstances than to help them adapt to sex-role expectations that constrain them (Brown, 1994).

It is important for therapists to support people in making choices that meet their needs, whether it be a man who wants to stay at home and care for children or a woman who wants a career in the military. Whether the therapist is a man or a woman, what seems most important is the therapist's sensitivity to gender issues.

BIOLOGICAL APPROACHES TO TREATMENT

In the previous chapter, we found that biological factors play an important role in many psychological disorders. Thus a medical approach designed to alter the brain's functioning is an alternative (or an addition) to psychological treatment.

Drug Therapies

Drug therapies are the most commonly used biological interventions. Discoveries in the field of *psychopharmacology* (the study of how drugs affect cognitions, emotions, and behavior) have revolutionized the treatment of the entire range of behavior disorders. Drugs that affect mood, thought, and behavior are now the most frequently prescribed medications in the United States (National Institute of Mental Health, 2008). The most commonly prescribed drugs fall into three major categories: antipsychotic drugs, antianxiety drugs, and antidepressant drugs. Effective drugs (e.g., lithium) also exist for the treatment of mania.

Antipsychotic Drugs

Perhaps the most dramatic effects of drug therapy have occurred in the treatment of severely disordered people, permitting many of them to function outside of the hospital setting (Shorter, 1998). As shown in Figure 16.15, a sharp decline in the number of inpatients in public mental hospitals occurred after 1955, when antipsychotic drugs were first introduced on a wide scale.

The revolution in drug therapy for severe psychological disorders began in the early 1950s, when it was accidentally discovered that *reserpine*, a drug derived from the snakeroot plant, calmed psychotic patients. This discovery resulted in the development of synthetic *antipsychotic drugs* (also called *major tranquilizers*), used today to treat schizophrenic disorders. The primary effect of the major tranquilizers is to decrease the action of dopamine, the neurotransmitter whose overactivity is thought to be involved in schizophrenia (Schatzberg et al., 2010). These drugs dramatically reduce positive symptoms, such as hallucinations and delusions. However, they have little effect on negative symptoms, such as apathy and withdrawal, and 20 to 40 percent of people with schizophrenia get little or no relief from them (Rosenbaum et al., 2009).

Antipsychotic drugs are now so widely used that nearly all schizophrenic patients living in the United States, Canada, and western Europe have received them at one time or another. Because patients often relapse very quickly if they stop taking the drugs, it is common practice to continue the medication indefinitely once the individual has returned to the community.

Antipsychotic drugs have reduced the need for padded cells, straitjackets, and other restraints that were formerly used to control the disordered behavior of hospitalized patients. Although they allow many patients to be released from hospitals, these drugs can produce **tardive dyskinesia,** *a severe movement disorder*. Uncontrollable and grotesque movements of the face and tongue are especially prominent in this disorder, and sometimes the patient's arms and legs flail uncontrollably. Tardive dyskinesia can be more debilitating than the psychotic symptoms that prompted the drug treatment, and it appears to be irreversible once it develops. Within 4 years of beginning antipsychotic medications, about 20 percent of young adults and 30 percent of those over 55 develop tardive dyskinesia symptoms (Schatzberg et al., 2010).

Researchers are working to develop new drugs that can control schizophrenic symptoms without producing side effects, such as the devastating symptoms of tardive dyskinesia. A newer drug called *clozapine* (Clozaril) reduces not only positive symptoms but negative ones as well, and it appears not to produce tardive dyskinesia (Marangell, 2002). Unfortunately, it produces a fatal blood disease (agranulocytosis) in 1 to 2 percent of people who take it, requiring

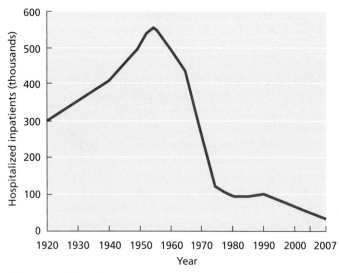

Figure 16.15

Effects of antipsychotic drugs.

Antipsychotic drugs have revolutionized the treatment of severely disturbed individuals, allowing many of them to leave mental hospitals. Note the decline that occurred following the introduction of antipsychotic drugs in the mid-1950s. Source: National Institute of Mental Health, 2008.

expensive weekly blood tests for patients who use the medication.

Antipsychotic drugs can often be used effectively in conjunction with psychotherapy. For example, drugs may be used to bring psychotic symptoms under control so that the patient can benefit from other approaches such as social skills training, family therapy, and group therapy.

Antianxiety Drugs

Surveys have shown that more than 15 percent of Americans between the ages of 18 and 74 use antianxiety or tranquilizing drugs such as the brand names Valium, Xanax, and BuSpar (Schatzberg et al., 2010). These drugs are designed to reduce anxiety as much as possible without affecting alertness or concentration. Sometimes antianxiety drugs are used in combination with psychotherapy to help clients cope successfully with problematic situations. A temporary reduction in anxiety from the use of a drug may allow a client to enter anxiety-arousing situations and learn to cope more effectively with them.

Antianxiety drugs work by slowing down excitatory synaptic activity in the nervous system. For example, *buspirone* (BuSpar) functions by blocking receptors of the excitatory transmitter serotonin and by enhancing the postsynaptic activity of GABA, an inhibitory transmitter that reduces neural activity in areas of the brain associated with emotional arousal (Gorman, 2002; Rosenbaum et al., 2009).

Antianxiety drugs can have a variety of undesirable side effects, such as drowsiness, lethargy, and concentration difficulties. A more serious drawback is psychological and physical dependence that can result from their long-term use. People who have developed physiological dependence can experience characteristic withdrawal symptoms, such as intense anxiety, nausea, and restlessness when they stop taking the drug (Lieberman, 1998). In addition, anxiety symptoms often return when people stop taking the drugs.

Antidepressant Drugs

Antidepressant drugs fall into three major categories: *tricyclics* (e.g., Elavil, Tofranil), *monoamine oxidase (MAO) inhibitors* (e.g., Nardil, Parnate), and *selective serotonin reuptake inhibitors*, or *SSRIs* (e.g., Prozac, Zoloft, Paxil). The first two classes increase the activity of the excitatory neurotransmitters norepinephrine and serotonin, whose lowered level of activity in brain regions involved in positive emotion and motivation is related to depression. The tricyclics work by preventing reuptake of the excitatory transmitters into the presynaptic neurons, allowing them to continue stimulating postsynaptic neurons. The MAO inhibitors reduce the activity of monoamine oxidase, an enzyme that breaks down the neurotransmitters in the synapse.

MAO inhibitors have more severe side effects than the tricyclics. They can cause dangerous elevations in blood pressure when taken with certain foods, such as cheeses and some types of wine. Many patients abandon their antidepressant medications because of severe side effects (Pompili et al., 2009). The SSRIs were designed to decrease side effects by increasing the activity of just one transmitter, serotonin (Marangell, 2002). Like the other antidepressants, however, SSRIs do have side effects. For example, about 30 percent of patients on Prozac report nervousness, insomnia, sweating, joint pain, or sexual dysfunction (Hellerstein et al., 1993). Nonetheless, the SSRIs are gradually replacing the tricyclics because, in addition to milder side effects, they reduce depressive symptoms more rapidly and also reduce anxiety symptoms that often accompany depression (Schatzberg et al., 2010). Figure 16.16 shows how the SSRIs produce their effects.

Increasingly, depression researchers are studying the effects of combining drugs and psychotherapy. A meta-analysis of such studies revealed that recovery rates for psychotherapy and the combined treatments did not differ, but that both were superior to drug therapy alone (Furukawa et al., 2006). Moreover, relapse rates are lower for psychotherapy than for drugs, particularly if patients stop taking their medication (Kazdin, 2008). Following successful drug therapy, about half of all patients soon relapse (Rush et al., 2009).

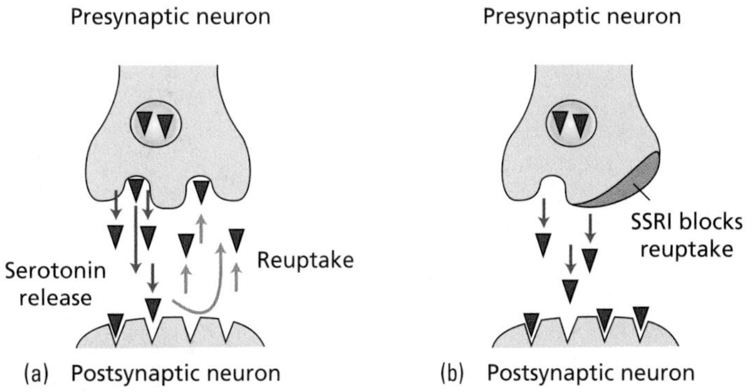

Presynaptic neuron   Presynaptic neuron

Serotonin release   Reuptake   SSRI blocks reuptake

(a)   Postsynaptic neuron   (b)   Postsynaptic neuron

Figure 16.16

SSRI mechanisms.

(a) When a presynaptic neuron releases serotonin into the synaptic space, a reuptake mechanism begins to pull neurotransmitter molecules back into the "sending" neuron, limiting the stimulation of the postsynaptic neuron. (b) Selective serotonin reuptake inhibitors (SSRIs) allow serotonin, whose activity is reduced in depressed clients, to continue its stimulation of postsynaptic neurons by inhibiting the reuptake of serotonin into the presynaptic neuron.

Myth or Reality?

Antidepressant Drugs Are Safe and Effective

Antidepressant drugs have become a treatment of choice for depression in both adults and children. As a less expensive form of treatment than psychotherapy, they are especially attractive to insurers and managed-care providers, and with good reason. Clinicians often observe dramatic improvements in people given SSRIs and other antidepressants. A recent clinical trial involving 4,041 depressed patients revealed that after a sequence of treatment with one to four different antidepressants, 67 percent showed remission of depression, and half of those patients did not relapse (Rush et al., 2009). In recent years, however, increasing concerns have been raised about antidepressants' efficacy and potential side effects (Ghaemi, 2008; Schweitzer et al., 2009).

Placebo Effects

When compared with no-treatment control conditions, antidepressant medication (ADM) effects are quite impressive. But when placebo controls are introduced in randomized clinical trials, the picture can change dramatically. If placebo patients simply believe they are receiving an antidepressant, they frequently show improvement that rivals drug effects. By dividing the amount of change shown in the placebo group by the magnitude of change shown by the drug group, one can estimate how much of the drug effect is truly attributable to the pharmacological effects of the drug. For example, in two clinical trials of the SSRI Zoloft in depressed children and adolescents, placebo patients showed 85 percent as much improvement as those who received Zoloft. Both groups showed notable decreases in self-reported depression, but the difference between Zoloft and placebo groups was so small as to be of no practical significance (Wagner et al., 2003).

Typical placebo results for adults are shown in a reanalysis of data from 38 clinical trials submitted to the U.S. Food and Drug Administration (FDA). The outcome measure in these studies was based on ratings of depression symptoms by clinicians who were blind to the experimental condition. As shown in Figure 16.17, improvement rates in the placebo conditions ranged from 68 to 89 percent of those shown in the antidepressant medication conditions, suggesting that expectancies and beliefs account for much of the drugs' effects and that the actual pharmacological effects of the drugs are quite small. Indeed, the data on Paxil, Zoloft, and Celexa actually underestimate placebo effects because in 9 other trials where no significant differences were found between the drugs and placebos, the investigators did not provide depression change scores (Kirsch et al., 2002). In such studies, the placebo effect could account for as much as 100 percent of patient improvement, so that the placebo effect means for those drugs would be even higher than the ones shown in Figure 16.17. Even where statistically significant differences were found between drug and placebo conditions on depression ratings, the actual differences were typically too small to be of any clinical significance. Finally, a reanalysis of the data from several major clinical trials revealed that antidepressant drug effects exceeded placebo effects only for the most severely depressed 13 percent of patients (Fournier et al., 2010). For the vast majority of patients, the drugs were no better than a placebo.

The strength of placebo effects may also be underestimated in many studies because of the practice of dropping from clinical trials any patient in the placebo condition who shows 20 percent or more improvement in the first week or two of the trial. Such patients are called *placebo washouts*. In contrast, patients in the drug condition who show similar levels of improvement are retained in the study. Obviously, this practice loads the dice in favor of the drug condition. Another factor favoring drug effects is the selective publication of results. Although the drug companies (who conduct or sponsor much of the research on their drugs) are required to submit the raw data from all trials to the FDA, studies that do not show significant drug effects may not find their way into the published literature (Antonuccio et al., 2003).

Do the Benefits Outweigh the Dangers?

Given the small treatment effects that can be attributed to pharmacological factors, some researchers are questioning whether the benefits achieved through antidepressant drug treatment outweigh possible costs. Despite the fact that SSRIs have less severe side effects than older antidepressants, such side effects do exist. Even when patients have shown improvement on the drugs, they sometimes abandon them because of these effects. In a study of 161 SSRI

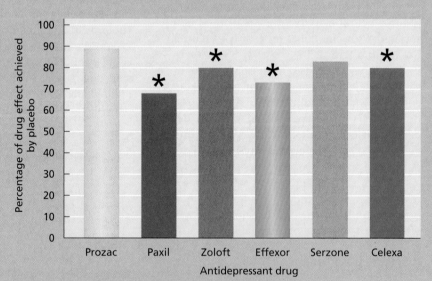

Figure 16.17

Placebo effects and antidepressant (SSRI) drugs.

These data were derived by dividing the magnitude of improvement shown by placebo controls by the magnitude of change shown by the drug group. They suggest that, on average, around 79 percent of the drug effects may be attributable to patient expectations that they will be helped by the drug, rather than to pharmacological effects. SOURCE: Adapted from Kirsch et al., 2002.

The asterisks indicate drugs for which depression improvement scores were not submitted because the drug and placebo groups did not differ significantly, suggesting even stronger placebo effects for those drugs.

quitters conducted by Madelon Bolling and Robert Kohlenberg (2004), 46 percent complained of having experienced a narrowed range of emotions, 32.9 percent of "not feeling like myself," 24 percent of a loss of creativity, 18 percent of apathy, 17 percent of concentration difficulties, and 13 percent of increased anger. When people stop taking SSRIs, about 25 percent experience a *discontinuation syndrome*, which can include severe sensory, somatic, gastrointestinal, and sleep problems, as well as irritability and anxiety (Robinson, 2006). Some patients report that these discontinuation symptoms are worse than the original depression. Finally, reports of suicidal thoughts and behaviors in patients on SSRIs have raised concerns (Stone et al., 2009). One study compared suicide attempts and suicides of adults in randomized clinical trials comparing SSRIs with placebos (Healy, 2004). Overall, 1 in 80 of all SSRI recipients attempted or committed suicide, compared with 1 in 200 of all placebo patients. In children, the risk may be even greater (Jureidini et al., 2004). At the urging of the British Medical Society, the United Kingdom Committee on Safety in Medicines has banned the use of all SSRIs with the exception of Prozac for patients under 18 years of age. In the United States, new clinical guidelines recommend the use of psychological interventions, such as cognitive-behavioral and interpersonal therapy, over antidepressants for treating children except in the most extreme cases of danger to the patient and nonresponsiveness to other forms of treatment, and then only with the informed consent of parents (Potter, 2009; Wong et al., 2004). The link between SSRIs and suicide risk is still a subject of debate, but in May 2007, the FDA declared that antidepressants pose a risk of increased suicidal thoughts among young adults, as they do in children. This followed an earlier FDA Public Health Advisory suggesting caution in using antidepressants in treating both adults and children.

Clearly, the results of ongoing studies of the efficacy, side effects, and cost/benefit aspects of antidepressants have enormous clinical and economic implications. As the limitations of current drugs become more apparent, research continues on the development of new drugs that are more effective and have fewer side effects (Marks et al., 2008; Thase, 2009).

Electroconvulsive Therapy

Another biologically based treatment, *electroconvulsive therapy (ECT)*, was based on the observation by a Hungarian physician that schizophrenia and epilepsy rarely occur in the same person. (Apparently, he didn't stop to consider the fact that the probability of epilepsy and *any* other disorder occurring together is very low.) The physician therefore suggested that seizure induction might be useful in the treatment of schizophrenia. In 1938, two Italian physicians, Ugo Cerletti and Lucio Bini, began to treat schizophrenic patients by attaching electrodes to their skulls and inducing a seizure by means of an electric current administered to the brain. In early applications of ECT, a wide-awake patient was strapped to a table, electrodes were attached to the patient's scalp, and a current of roughly 100 volts was applied to the brain, producing violent convulsions and loss of consciousness. Sometimes the seizures were so violent that patients fractured their arms or legs.

Today the procedure is quite different (Figure 16.18). A patient is first given a sedative and a muscle relaxant to prevent injuries from the convulsions. The patient is then placed on a well-padded mattress, and electrodes are attached to his or her scalp. A modified procedure in which electrodes are placed on only one side of the head is often used. The duration of the shock is less than a second, causing a seizure of the central nervous system. There is little observable movement in the patient, other than a twitching of the toes and a slight facial grimace. The patient wakes up 10 to 20 minutes after ECT, possibly with a headache, sore muscles, and some confusion. Recently, scientists have been able to calibrate the amount of electric current a patient needs so that treatments can be individualized, and research is being carried out to determine whether certain drugs can further reduce seizure-induced confusion and amnesia.

When ECT was first introduced in the 1930s, it was applied to a wide range of disorders, but later research revealed that it cannot relieve anxiety disorders and is of questionable value for schizophrenic patients (Herrington & Lader, 1996).

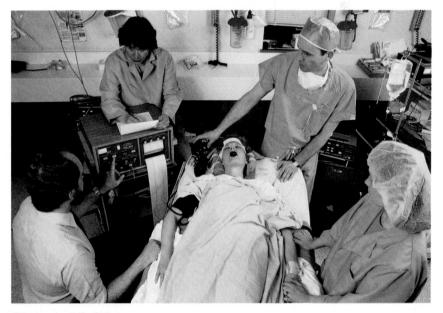

Figure 16.18

A severely depressed and possibly suicidal patient is prepared for an ECT session. The patient has been sedated and given a muscle relaxant to minimize limb movements during the brief electrical stimulation of the brain. The rubber object in her mouth prevents her from biting her tongue or damaging her teeth during the convulsion.

However, ECT can be useful in treating severe depression, particularly if there is a high risk of suicide. In such cases, the use of antidepressant drugs may be impractical because they will likely take several weeks to begin reducing the depression. In contrast, the effects of ECT can be immediate. Controlled studies indicate that 60 to 70 percent of severely depressed people given ECT improve, but no one knows why ECT works (Rey & Walter, 1997).

ECT has many critics. Some note that even when the effects are dramatically positive, the possibility of a depressive relapse is high, perhaps 85 percent (Swartz, 1995). Although current methods prevent the physical injuries that occurred in earlier times, other concerns have been raised about the safety of ECT. In some instances permanent memory loss has been reported, and there are also concerns about the possibility of permanent brain damage when ECT is used repeatedly. Today the number of ECT treatments is limited to fewer than 10, and scientific evidence suggests that today's ECT is a safer treatment than previous forms were. For example, MRI studies of patients who received brief pulse treatment to both sides of the brain revealed no evidence of brain damage (Coffey et al., 1991). After reviewing both sides of the issue, the American Psychiatric Association (1990) concluded that this therapy should be regarded as a useful procedure for major depression in patients who cannot take or do not respond to medication.

Psychosurgery

Psychosurgery *refers to surgical procedures that remove or destroy brain tissue in an attempt to change disordered behavior.* It is the least used of the biomedical procedures, but such was not always the case. In the 1930s, before the advent of antipsychotic drugs, Portuguese surgeon Egas Moniz reported that cutting the nerve tracts that connect the frontal lobes with subcortical areas of the brain involved in emotion resulted in a calming of psychotic and uncontrollably violent patients. The operation eliminated emotional input from the limbic system into the areas of the brain connected with executive functions of planning and reasoning. Walter Freeman developed a 10-minute *lobotomy* operation performed by inserting an ice pick–like instrument with sharp edges through the eye socket into the brain, then wiggling it back and forth to sever the targeted nerve tracts. During the 1930s and 1940s, tens of thousands of patients—50,000 in the United States alone—underwent the operation. Moniz received a Nobel Prize for his discovery.

Initial enthusiasm for lobotomy was soon replaced by a sober recognition that the massive neural damage it caused had severe side effects on mental and emotional functioning. Seizures, stupor, memory and reasoning impairments, and listlessness occurred frequently. With the development of antipsychotic drugs in the 1950s, the frequency of lobotomies decreased, and they are hardly ever used today. However, more precise and limited psychosurgery procedures are sometimes used in the most extreme cases and when every other avenue has been tried. One procedure, called *cingulotomy*, involves cutting a small fiber bundle near the corpus callosum that connects the frontal lobes with the limbic system. Cingulotomy has been used successfully in treating severe depressive and obsessive-compulsive disorders that have failed to improve with drug treatment or psychotherapy. However, this more limited procedure can also produce side effects, including seizures (Pressman, 1998). Appropriately, cingulotomy and other forms of psychosurgery are considered to be last-resort procedures.

Mind, Body, and Therapeutic Interventions

The impact of drug and electroconvulsive therapies on psychological disorders illustrates once again the important interactions between biological and psychological phenomena. In the final analysis, both psychological and biological treatments affect brain functioning in ways that can change disordered thoughts, emotions, and behavior. Moreover, they may constitute different routes to the same changes, as illustrated in a study by Tomas Furmark and coworkers (2002) at Uppsala University in Sweden. The researchers randomly assigned patients with social phobia to 9-week treatments that involved either drug therapy with an SSRI or a course of cognitive and behavioral psychotherapy involving exposure to feared social situations and cognitive modification of anxiety-arousing thoughts. Before and after treatment, the participants received PET scans while they gave a hastily prepared speech to a group of 6 to 8 people standing around the scanner bed. They also provided subjective ratings of their anxiety during the procedure. Uniformly high anxiety scores were reported by all participants prior to treatment.

Both treatments were effective, although overall, the psychological treatment produced a stronger reduction in fear and social phobia symptoms than did the drug treatment. Nonetheless, when the researchers compared the pre- and posttreatment PET scans of those participants who responded to the two treatments with reduced social anxiety, the psychotherapy and drug groups showed basically the same changes in neural blood flow from the first speech situation to the second. These changes involved reduced neural activity in an "anxiety circuit" involving the amygdala, the hippocampus, and areas of the temporal cerebral cortex (Figure 16.19). Treatment nonresponders did not show these brain changes. Thus different forms of therapy, whether psychological or biological, may result in similar changes at a neurological level and, ultimately, at a behavioral level. One suggestion is that medications can help prime the neural network changes needed for recovery, thus allowing psychotherapies to work move effectively (Cozolino, 2010).

An important factor to keep in mind is that drug treatments, however effective they may be in modifying some disordered behaviors in the short term, do not cure the disorder. They suppress symptoms but do not teach the client coping

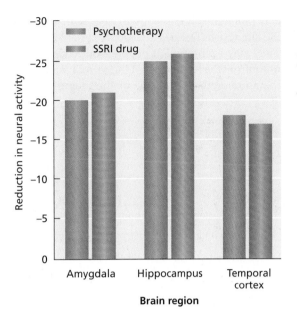

Figure 16.19

Drug and therapy effects on the brain.
Clients treated for social phobia received either psychotherapy or drug therapy. Those clients who responded to their respective treatments with reduced anxiety showed nearly identical changes in PET-scan recordings of neural activity in three areas of the brain whose activation is thought to underlie anxiety.
Source: Based on Furmark et al., 2002.

Levels of Analysis

Therapeutic Change

Interacting biological, psychological, and environmental factors are involved in the positive changes produced by the psychological and biological therapies we have described. Here are some of the factors identified in scientific research:

ENVIRONMENTAL LEVEL
- Psychotherapies create a therapeutic environment for unlearning maladaptive cognitive and behavioral patterns and acquiring adaptive ones.
- Quality of the therapeutic relationship partially underlies the effectiveness of any therapeutic approach.
- Cultural congruence and exposure to culturally competent therapists are important factors in therapeutic change in minority clients.

BIOLOGICAL LEVEL
- All changes, whether produced by psychotherapy, a biological therapy, or a combination of the two, result in structural changes in brain circuitry and synaptic networks.
- Changes in neurotransmitter, autonomic, or hormonal factors underlie positive changes in response to treatments.
- Research on current drugs and the development of new ones are an important focus of current research.

PSYCHOLOGICAL LEVEL
- Insights into the psychodynamic and unconscious factors in maladaptive behavior are the focus of psychodynamic approaches.
- Humanistic therapies produce self-concept changes and encourage self-exploration.
- Some behavior therapies attempt to modify conditioned emotional responses. Other behavioral approaches use operant techniques to directly modify behavior.
- Changes in maladaptive cognitions that trigger maladaptive emotions and behavior are brought about by cognitive therapy. Mindfulness meditation, which increases self-awareness, reduces stress, and encourages the acceptance of immediate experience, is increasingly being incorporated into treatments.

If behavior is ultimately governed by the brain, how would you respond to the position that, therefore, we should be developing only biological treatments?

and problem-solving skills to deal with stressful life situations (DeLongis, 2000; Nezu et al., 2000). They may even prevent people from taking steps to confront the real causes of their problems. Many therapists believe that one of the major benefits of psychological treatments is their potential not only to help clients deal with current problems but also to increase their personal resources so that they might enjoy a higher level of adjustment and life satisfaction in the future (Hollon, 1996).

---

test yourself

Family Therapy, Cultural-Gender Issues, and Biological Treatments

True or false?

1. Family therapy focuses on the most maladjusted member of the family.
2. Encouraging acceptance of spouses' objectionable behavior increases the effectiveness of marital therapy.
3. Antipsychotic drugs have drastically reduced the number of hospitalized psychotic patients.
4. Antianxiety drugs can produce psychological but not physical dependence.
5. SSRIs produce their antidepressant effects by decreasing the activity of serotonin.
6. SSRIs increase the risk of suicide in children.
7. Patients treated with ECT rarely relapse.

ANSWERS: 1-false, 2-true, 3-true, 4-false, 5-false, 6-true, 7-false

---

EVALUATING TREATMENTS

Given the human suffering created by psychological disorders, the effects of biological and psychological therapies have both personal and societal implications. Practicing clinicians and clinical researchers want to know which approaches are most effective against which kinds of problems and what the effective active ingredients of each treatment are. Following a long-standing tradition in medicine, the impetus today is toward *evidence-based practice* (American Psychological Association Task Force, 2006; Freeman & Power, 2007).

Today the basic question "Does therapy work?" is viewed as a gross oversimplification of a much more involved question known as the **specificity question:** *Which types of therapy administered by which kinds of therapists to which kinds of clients having which kinds of problems produce which kinds of effects?* After nearly a half century of research involving many hundreds of studies, this complex question still is not fully answered (Kazdin, 2008). Nonetheless, for many reasons, this question demands answers. Selecting and administering the most appropriate kind of intervention is vital in human terms. It is also important for economic reasons. Billions of dollars are spent each year on psychological treatments, with an increasing share of these costs paid by so-called third parties such as insurance companies, health maintenance organizations, and government agencies. As the costs rise, those who bear the financial burden increase their demands for accountability and for demonstrations that the treatments are useful.

Psychotherapy Research Methods

Conducting good psychotherapy research is one of the most challenging tasks in all of psychology, because there are so many variables that cannot be completely controlled. In contrast to laboratory studies, in which the experimental conditions can be highly standardized, therapist-client interactions are by their nature infinitely varied. Another difficulty involves measuring the effects of psychotherapy. Figure 16.20 shows some of the typical ways of measuring change. These measures differ in the outcome variable assessed (thoughts, emotions, or behaviors) and in the source of the data (the therapist, the client, or other informants). Which measures of change are most important or valid? What if one set of measures indicates improvement, another indicates no change, and a third suggests that the client is worse off than before treatment? How should we evaluate the effects of the therapy? These are just a few of the vexing issues that can arise in psychotherapy research.

A variety of methods have been used to assess the effects of psychotherapy. The individual case study can provide useful information, particularly if objective data are collected throughout

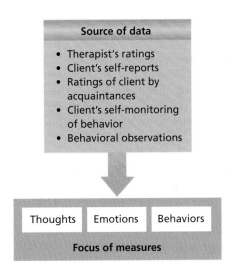

Source of data

- Therapist's ratings
- Client's self-reports
- Ratings of client by acquaintances
- Client's self-monitoring of behavior
- Behavioral observations

| Thoughts | Emotions | Behaviors |

Focus of measures

Figure 16.20

Psychotherapy outcome measures.
The measures used to assess the outcome of psychotherapy may come from a variety of data sources, and they may measure different aspects of the client's functioning.

and following therapy. However, it can be difficult to generalize conclusions from the individual case. One remedy to this problem is to present multiple case studies of people who have received similar treatment (Kazdin, 2008).

A second approach is to survey large numbers of people who have been in therapy and measure their reactions to their experience. This provides us with information about what is happening in the world of clinical practice. A third method is the experimental approach as embodied in the **randomized clinical trial (RCT)**, *in which clients are randomly assigned to treatment or control conditions, and the treatment and control groups are compared on outcome measures.*

Randomized Clinical Trials

For many of the reasons mentioned in Chapter 2, where we discussed the value of experimental methods for drawing conclusions about causality, psychotherapy researchers favor the randomized clinical trial. In this "gold standard" method for evaluating treatments, participants who have well-defined psychological disorders and are similar on other variables that might affect response to treatment (e.g., age and ethnic status) are randomly assigned either to an experimental condition that gets treatment or to a control condition (Kazdin, 2003). The control group may be either a no-treatment condition (typically, a waiting-list condition), a **placebo control group** *that gets an intervention that is not expected to work,* or an already-proven alternative treatment. The placebo condition is designed to control for client

expectations of improvement and for being seen by a therapist. (For ethical reasons, clients in the control group, whether it be a no-treatment or placebo condition, are given the option of receiving the real treatment later.)

Another research design, which avoids the ethical dilemma of withholding or delaying treatment for some participants, involves randomly assigning participants either to the treatment being studied or to another kind of treatment that has proven effective for that disorder. If the new treatment being tested in the experimental condition is found to be at least as effective as the established treatment, then its value is supported. Sometimes, the design of a study involves a group in which the treatment is combined with another intervention such as a drug treatment. It is then possible to see if the group that received the drug *plus* psychotherapy does better than the groups that got only the drug or only the therapy (Hollon, 1996; Pull, 2007).

To standardize a research treatment, much as one would do in a laboratory experiment, one American Psychological Association (APA) treatment-evaluation committee recommended issuing a manual containing procedures that therapists have to follow exactly and evaluating therapists' adherence to these procedures by observing them or taping their sessions (Chambless & Hollon, 1998). These recommendations aim to ensure that participants in a particular treatment condition are truly receiving the same kind of therapy. The committee also recommended that at least some of the measures of improvement be behavioral in nature. Further, to minimize experimenter bias in evaluating change during interviews or behavioral observations following treatment, interviewers and observers should not know whether a given client was in the control group or the experimental group.

Finally, the committee recommended that therapists collect follow-up data. This is extremely important, for we want to know not only how the treatment conditions differ at the end of the clinical trial but also how long-lasting the effects are. For example, in some studies comparing psychotherapy for depression with the effects of antidepressant drugs, the drug treatment effects occurred more quickly and were stronger at the end of the treatment period, suggesting a superiority for drug therapy. But follow-up data showed psychotherapy to be more effective in the long term. Because clients had learned specific psychological skills that they could apply after therapy ended, there were fewer relapses into depression (Hollon & Beck, 1994; Weissman & Markowitz, 1994).

Figure 16.21 summarizes in schematic form the procedures used in conducting an RCT to evaluate a treatment. It also shows how many factors must be taken into account to ensure meaningful scientific results.

Empirically Supported Treatments In the late 1990s, an APA task force surveyed the results of randomized clinical trials that met the rigorous criteria described above. The goal was to identify **empirically supported treatments (ESTs),** *treatments that had been demonstrated in several independent studies to be efficacious for treating specific disorders.* Most of the therapies identified by the task force were cognitive or behavioral in nature. As examples, cognitive therapy and interpersonal therapies were deemed efficacious for depression. Exposure procedures and systematic desensitization were treatments of choice for anxiety disorders, and dialectical behavior therapy was the most effective treatment for borderline personality disorder. Efficacious treatments for other disorders were also identified.

Although the EST approach can provide useful guidelines for both clinical practice and for the training of therapists, concerns have been raised by critics of this approach. They point out that only cognitive and behavioral treatments are "manualized," so that longer-term, more flexible psychodynamic and humanistic treatments are being left out. Critics also point out that in real-world clinical practice, therapists do not rigorously follow a treatment manual, preferring to structure the treatment approach to the individual client. Another problem is the requirement that the patients in the clinical trials have only one DSM-diagnosed clinical disorder. Unfortunately, however, 30 to 50 percent of clinical cases do not fit into a DSM category, and many have more than one disorder. In some randomized clinical trials with certain disorders, up to 70 percent of the potential clients had to be excluded because they had additional disorders (Westen et al., 2004). It is therefore possible that results from such studies may not apply to the general population of clinical cases. Finally, critics fear that a premature adherence to today's empirically supported treatments will stifle the development of new therapies that could be even more effective (Goldfried & Eubanks-Carter, 2004; Levant, 2004).

The Search for Therapeutic Principles The EST approach focuses on the efficacy of particular treatment packages. A suggested alternative is to broaden the inquiry to identify *empirically supported principles* that predict therapeutic outcomes (Castonguay & Beutler, 2005; Goldfried & Eubanks-Carter, 2004). Another APA task force has been formed to explore empirically supported treatment *principles* (Castonguay & Beutler, 2005). Principles are general statements of strategies or variables that promote change (for example, "The therapist helps the patient appraise and increase the accuracy of self- and other perceptions" or "The therapist focuses on and builds upon the patient's strengths"). These principles could be about patient variables, therapist variables, diagnostic type, or treatment strategies. Although

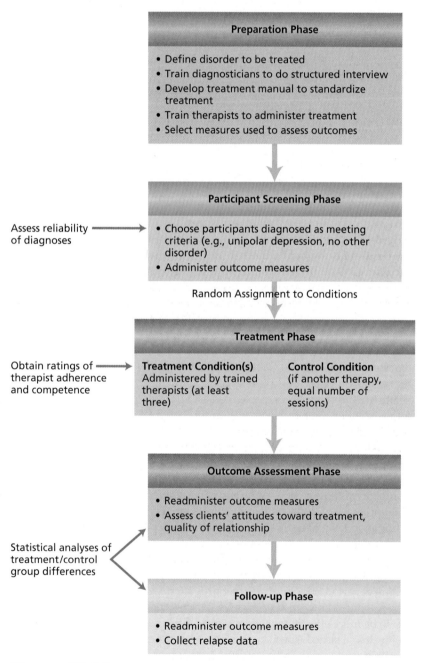

Figure 16.21

Phases and procedures in a well-designed randomized clinical trial.

priority would be given to results derived from randomized clinical trials, other types of research, including data-oriented case studies and survey studies, would also be surveyed.

Meta-Analysis: A Look at the Big Picture

As discussed in Chapter 2, the technique of **meta-analysis** *allows researchers to combine the statistical results of many studies to arrive at an overall conclusion.* In the psychotherapy research literature, they can compute an effect size statistic that represents a common measure of treatment effectiveness. The **effect size** *tells researchers what percentage of clients who received therapy had a more favorable outcome than that of the average control client who did not receive the treatment.*

In 1977, Mary Ann Smith and Gene Glass used meta-analysis to combine the effects of 375 studies of psychotherapy involving 25,000 clients and 25,000 control participants. These studies differed in many ways, but they all compared a treatment condition with a control condition. The results indicated that the average therapy client had a more favorable outcome than 75 percent of the untreated cases. These results prompted Smith and Glass to conclude that therapy does indeed have positive effects beyond spontaneous remission. More recent therapy meta-analyses support this conclusion.

Glass and Smith also concluded that psychodynamic, person-centered, and behavioral approaches were quite similar in their effectiveness. *This finding of similar efficacy for widely differing therapies has been termed the* **dodo bird verdict,** after the dodo bird's statement in *Alice in Wonderland* that "everybody has won and all must have prizes" (Luborsky et al., 2002). Other researchers challenge this conclusion, maintaining that lumping together studies involving different kinds of clinical problems may mask *differential effectiveness,* i.e., the fact that specific therapies might be highly effective for treating some clinical disorders but not others (Kazdin, 2008; Westen & Morrison, 2001). Later meta-analyses have tended to focus on specific disorders and the treatments that are most effective for them. Table 16.3 shows the results of recent meta-analyses of EST studies for the treatment of several disorders (Westen et al., 2004).

In evaluating the results of meta-analyses, we should remember that the studies lumped together in a meta-analysis can differ in many ways, including the nature and severity of the problems that were treated, the outcome measures that were used, and the quality of the methodology. Psychotherapy researchers point out that combining good studies with less adequate ones can

Table **16.3**	Meta-Analyses of Improvement and Recovery Rates for Empirically Supported Treatments Applied to Various Adult Disorders
Disorder	**Percentage Improved or Recovered***
Obsessive-compulsive disorder	66.7
Panic disorder	63.3
Generalized anxiety disorder	52.1
Major depression	50.8
Bulimia	50.0

*Note: *Improvement* typically means at least a 30 to 50 percent reduction in symptoms; *recovery* means total symptom reduction. The data for bulimia are for recovery only. The number of randomized clinical trials summarized range from 7 to 26 for the various disorders.

Sources: Adapted from Thompson-Brenner et al., 2003; Westen et al., 2004; Westen & Morrison, 2001.

produce misleading results (Kazdin, 2003). When studies that meet rigorous research standards are compared in meta-analyses with less rigorous studies, the rigorous studies tend to yield more favorable outcomes for therapy conditions (Matt & Navarro, 1997). Apparently, the rigorous methods used in such studies allow effective therapies to show their true effects.

Survey Research

A good example of the survey approach is a study carried out by the periodical *Consumer Reports* (*CR*; Seligman, 1995). One form of *CR*'s 1994 annual survey, mailed to 184,000 randomly selected subscribers, contained a section on stress and mental health. Readers were asked to complete the mental health section if they had sought help for emotional problems in the past 3 years. A total of 22,000 readers responded to the questionnaire—a 13 percent response rate that is typical of *CR* surveys. Of these, 35 percent reported that they had a mental health problem, and 40 percent (approximately 2,900 respondents) of this group reported that they had sought professional help from a psychologist, psychiatrist, social worker, or marriage counselor. The respondents were asked to indicate how much they improved as a result of treatment and how satisfied they were with the treatment they received.

Forty-two percent of the respondents said that they had been helped "a lot," and 44 percent "somewhat." Eighty-nine percent were "somewhat satisfied" or "very satisfied" with the treatment they received. *CR* consultant Martin Seligman concluded that "*CR* has provided empirical validation of the effectiveness of therapy" (1995, p. 974). Further, he concluded that the survey method used in this study might actually have provided data that are more representative of real-life outcomes than data yielded by highly controlled clinical trials.

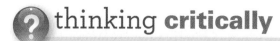

thinking **critically**

DO SURVEY RESULTS PROVIDE AN ACCURATE PICTURE OF TREATMENT EFFECTIVENESS?

Based on what you've already learned about research methods, do you agree with Seligman's conclusion that the *CR* data may be a more valid reflection of therapy success than data from randomized clinical trials? Can you think of any aspects of the *CR* methods that might limit your ability to conclude how effective psychotherapy is? Compare your thoughts with the issues discussed on page 632.

Factors Affecting the Outcome of Therapy

Clearly, not everyone who enters therapy profits from it. There is even evidence that some clients—perhaps 10 percent—may get worse as a result of treatment (Castonguay et al., 2010; Lambert et al., 1986). What, then, are the factors that influence treatment outcome? Research to answer this question has focused on three sets of variables: client variables, therapist variables, and technique variables (Figure 16.22). The APA task force on empirically supported principles has identified variables that make a difference within each of these categories (Castonguay & Beutler, 2005).

Client Variables

Where client variables are concerned, three important factors are the client's openness to therapy, self-relatedness, and the nature of the problem (Castonguay & Beutler, 2005). **Openness** *involves clients' general willingness to invest themselves in therapy and take the risks required to change themselves.*

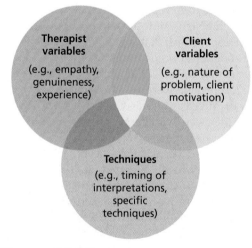

Figure 16.22

Determinants of therapy outcome.
Research on factors that influence therapy outcome has focused on three sets of interacting variables: client variables, therapist variables, and technique variables.

Self-relatedness *refers to their ability to experience and understand internal states such as thoughts and emotions, to be attuned to the processes that go on in their relationships with their therapists, and to apply what they learn in therapy to their lives outside of treatment* (Howard et al., 1993). A third important client factor is the nature of the problem and its degree of fit with the therapy being used, i.e., the EST for that disorder. For example, specific problems such as phobias may respond best to a behavioral anxiety-reduction treatment such as systematic desensitization or exposure, whereas a more global problem, such as a search for self-discovery and greater meaning in life, may respond better to a psychodynamic, cognitive, or humanistic approach. Much more research is needed on client characteristics that influence response to particular therapies.

Therapist and Technique Variables

Therapist variables are important, too. In one analysis of therapy outcomes for 1,198 clients who were treated by 60 different therapists, 17 percent of patient outcome variation was attributable to therapist behaviors (Lutz et al., 2007).

Among therapist variables, perhaps the most important is the quality of the relationship that the therapist is able to establish with the client (Castonguay & Beutler, 2005; Zuroff & Blatt, 2006). Carl Rogers's emphasis on the importance of therapist qualities such as empathy, unconditional acceptance of the client as a person, and genuineness has been borne out in a great many studies. An empathic, trusting, and caring relationship forms the foundation on which the specific techniques employed by the therapist can have their most beneficial effects (Blackstone, 2007). Quality of the therapeutic relationship accounts for about 30 percent of the variance in treatment outcome (Kazdin, 2008).

When therapists do not manifest these behaviors, the effects of therapy are not simply null; clients actually can get worse. For example, hostile interchanges between therapist and client can contribute to a *deterioration effect* in therapy (Binder & Strupp, 1997).

Assuming the therapy relationship is a positive one, there is still the consideration of technique variables. A therapist needs to be skilled and knowledgeable in selecting and implementing the appropriate techniques for each client and situation. For example, a large-scale study at the University of Pennsylvania revealed that the correctness of the interpretations made by psychoanalytic therapists, as measured by expert ratings, was related to more positive treatment outcome (Crits-Christoph et al., 1988). Likewise, in a detailed analysis of the audiotaped therapy sessions of 21 psychotherapists, Enrico Jones and coworkers (1988) found that the most effective therapists adjusted their techniques to the specific needs of their clients. They concluded that "general relationship factors, such as therapeutic alliance, are closely bound with the skillful selection and application of psychotherapeutic techniques" (p. 55).

Common Factors

Despite dramatic differences in the techniques they employ, various therapies tend to enjoy similar success rates, perhaps because people who differ on the client variables are lumped together within studies. This finding has led many experts to search for **common factors,** *characteristics shared by these diverse forms of therapy that might contribute to their success.* These common factors include:

- Clients' faith in the therapist and a belief that they are receiving help

- A plausible explanation for clients' problems and an alternative way of helping them look at themselves and their problems

- A protective setting in which clients can experience and express their deepest feelings within a supportive relationship

- An opportunity for clients to practice new behaviors

- Clients' achieving increased optimism and self-efficacy

How important these common factors are in comparison with specific therapeutic techniques is currently unknown, and the dodo bird verdict described earlier may reflect a failure to identify specific factors that underlie therapeutic success (Beutler, 2002). The complexities of psychotherapy pose a formidable challenge for clinical researchers. Despite decades of research on the efficacy of psychotherapy techniques, there is still much to learn. We know that some techniques are very effective for certain problems. Yet in the words of the eminent British psychotherapy researcher Isaac Marks, "Little is known about which treatment components produce improvement, how they do so, and why they do not help all sufferers" (Marks, 2002, p. 200).

Research Close-up

Drug versus Psychological Treatments for Depression: A Randomized Clinical Trial

SOURCE: SONA DIMIDJIAN, STEVEN D. HOLLON, KEITH S. DOBSON, KAREN B. SCHMALING, ROBERT J. KOHLENBERG, MICHAEL E. ADDIS, et al. (2006). Randomized trial of behavioral activation, cognitive therapy, and antidepressant medication in the acute treatment of adults with major depression. *Journal of Consulting and Clinical Psychology, 74,* 658–670.

INTRODUCTION

Depression is one of the most prevalent psychological disorders, and its successful treatment is a major mental health priority. As noted in previous sections of this chapter, the most widely used treatments during the past decade have been cognitive therapy, interpersonal psychotherapy, and drug treatments, all of which have proven effective in 30 to 50 percent of treated cases. Although antidepressant drug treatment has outperformed cognitive therapy in some studies, at the end of the clinical trial, many clients do not want to continue to take drugs, experience severe side effects if they do take them, or discontinue their use, resulting in poor maintenance of positive effects. Moreover, drug treatments do not teach clients effective coping skills that may help them counter depression in the future.

The new treatment tested in this study was behavioral activation therapy. As described earlier, the treatment is derived from

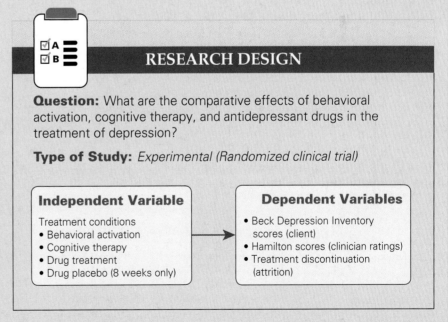

RESEARCH DESIGN

Question: What are the comparative effects of behavioral activation, cognitive therapy, and antidepressant drugs in the treatment of depression?

Type of Study: *Experimental (Randomized clinical trial)*

Independent Variable

Treatment conditions
- Behavioral activation
- Cognitive therapy
- Drug treatment
- Drug placebo (8 weeks only)

Dependent Variables

- Beck Depression Inventory scores (client)
- Hamilton scores (clinician ratings)
- Treatment discontinuation (attrition)

a behavioral theory of depression that focuses on the spiraling loss of positive reinforcement that occurs in depression as clients stop engaging in positive behaviors and alienate others with their

Continued

inertia and depressed moods (Lewinsohn et al., 1985). The goal is to increase behaviors that will increase positive reinforcement that counters depression and help clients regain enjoyment in their lives. This study is the first to compare the effects of behavioral activation therapy with the effects produced by cognitive therapy and antidepressant drug treatment.

METHOD

A total of 241 people between the ages of 18 and 60 years who met DSM criteria for major depressive disorder were randomly assigned to one of four conditions: behavioral activation therapy, cognitive therapy, drug treatment, or a drug placebo condition. The clients underwent treatment for 16 weeks. Those in the antidepressant medication condition received the SSRI drug paroxetine (Paxil). A set of outcome measures was administered before treatment, after 8 weeks, and after 16 weeks. These included the Beck Depression Inventory, a self-report measure of depression, and the Hamilton Rating Scale for Depression, which was based on a clinical interview by a psychologist or psychiatrist who was unaware of which condition the client was in.

Behavioral activation treatment seeks to identify and engage clients in activities that are reinforcing and consistent with life goals. Clients monitor their moods and behaviors and work with their therapist to design and schedule daily routines designed to get them engaged with their social and physical environment in productive ways. This may include forcing themselves to participate in social or physical-exercise activities that they formerly enjoyed. They also learn and practice ways to avoid negative thinking by redirecting their attention toward their immediate experiences in the real world. In the cognitive therapy condition, clients focused on identifying and changing automatic thought patterns that create depression, as described earlier in the chapter.

In accordance with empirically supported treatment principles, therapists closely followed manuals prepared for each therapy in order to standardize treatment. To make sure that the therapists in the treatment conditions were conducting the treatments as designed, outside experts in each treatment rated videotaped sessions for "treatment adherence." These ratings indicated that all of the treatments were appropriately delivered.

For ethical reasons, the placebo condition was only maintained for 8 weeks, after which members of that condition were given the option of receiving any of the other treatments. (Their data were not included in the assessment of the three treatment conditions described below.)

RESULTS

As in previous research, the highest treatment dropout (attrition) rate was in the drug therapy condition, where 44 percent of the clients either refused the treatment or dropped out during the study. By comparison, the attrition rates were only 16 percent in the behavioral activation condition and 13 percent in the cognitive therapy condition.

Two levels of improvement were assessed on the Beck self-report and Hamilton clinical ratings of depression. *Response to treatment* was defined as a clinically significant decrease of at least 50 percent in depression scores. *Remission* was declared when a client's scores dropped below the clinical depression cutoff point into the normal range for nondepressed people.

On the basis of the pretreatment scores that were used to match the treatment groups for severity of depression, the clinical researchers divided the clients into low- and high-severity groups and compared the treatments within the two severity groups. In the low-severity group, all of the treatments resulted in improvement (including the placebo condition at 8 weeks). There was no statistical difference between the groups, although cognitive therapy had the highest overall response and remission rates (65 percent and 55 percent, respectively).

Table 16.4 shows the response and remission results for the severely depressed clients. Here, behavioral activation showed a superiority to the other treatments, with the drug group doing generally more poorly than the cognitive therapy group. Clients who had been treated with behavioral activation indicated that they felt less depressed than the other treatment groups, and clinical interviewer ratings also indicated a better outcome.

DISCUSSION

This is a highly significant and exceptionally well-controlled randomized clinical trial. The investigators made certain that the treatments were being delivered as intended. Clinicians who conducted the clinical interviews and provided Hamilton ratings of depression were blind to the experimental conditions. The groups were equivalent in depression at the beginning of treatment so that it was possible to plot improvement in a meaningful fashion.

This study reflects the scientific strategy of comparing new treatments with already-established ones. Based on the results of this study and an earlier one (Jacobson et al., 2001), behavioral activation therapy appears to be a highly promising treatment, particularly for severely depressed people. In particular, its superiority over

---

Table 16.4 | **Percentage of Severely Depressed Clients Who Showed Response (Improvement) and Remission (Normalization) after Behavioral Activation (BA), Cognitive Therapy (CT), and Antidepressant Drug (ADM) Treatments**

| Condition | Outcome Measure | | | |
| | Beck Depression Inventory (Client Self-Report) | | Hamilton Depression Rating Scale (Clinician Rating) | |
	Percent Response*	Percent Remission**	Percent Response*	Percent Remission**
Behavioral Activation	76	52	60	54
Cognitive Therapy	48	40	56	35
Drug Treatment	49	42	40	23

*At least 50 percent decrease in depression scores
**Depression decrease into normal range
SOURCE: Data from Dimidjian et al., 2006.

drug treatment provides an alternative to antidepressants, which many people refuse to take or discontinue as unpleasant side effects arise. For severely depressed clients, behavioral activation was also superior to cognitive therapy, which has been the favored psychological treatment for depression. It appears that cognitive therapy may still be the treatment of choice for less depressed individuals, however. The different effects of the two psychological treatments as a function of severity of depression is an important finding, for it helps to answer the practical question of which treatment is most effective for which clinical populations.

The results of this study were measured at the end of the 16-week treatment period. A follow-up study is needed to examine how long-lasting the positive treatment effects are. Typically, psychological treatments have done better at follow-up, because many people in drug conditions discontinue their drugs or become dissatisfied and seek alternate treatments. Behavioral activation may be especially effective in the longer run because it helps clients to make lifestyle changes that should provide them with continuing positive reinforcement. It remains to be seen if future research supports this expectation.

PSYCHOLOGICAL DISORDERS AND SOCIETY

Since the days of insane asylums, first established in the 16th century to segregate the mentally ill from society, severe behavior disorders have been treated in institutional settings. Across the United States, nearly 300 state-funded mental hospitals were built between 1845 and 1945. Many private facilities were also built. The number of patients being treated in public mental hospitals increased steadily from about 250,000 in 1920 to more than 500,000 in 1950. By 1955 psychiatric patients occupied half of all hospital beds in the United States. However, it was readily apparent to mental health experts that although there were some high-quality institutions, many public mental hospitals were not fulfilling their intended role as treatment facilities. They were overcrowded, understaffed, and underfinanced. Many of them could provide little more than minimal custodial care and a haven from the stresses and demands of the outside world. Moreover, people who were admitted to such hospitals often sank into a chronic "sick" role in which passive dependence and "crazy" behavior were not only tolerated but expected (Goffman, 1961; Scheff, 1966). They lost the self-confidence, motivation, and skills needed to return and adapt to the outside world and had little chance of surviving outside the hospital.

Deinstitutionalization

By the 1960s, the stage was set for a new approach to the treatment of behavior disorders. Concerns about the inadequacies of mental hospitals, together with the ability of antipsychotic drugs to normalize patients' behavior, resulted in a **deinstitutionalization movement** *to transfer the primary focus of treatment from the hospital to the community.*

In 1963, Congress passed the Community Mental Health Centers Act, which provided for the establishment of one mental health center for every 50,000 people. Community mental health centers are designed to provide outpatient psychotherapy and drug treatment so that clients can remain in their normal social and work environments. The centers also can arrange for short-term inpatient care, usually at a local general hospital, when clients are acutely disturbed, and many have crisis centers and telephone hotlines to respond to emergency situations. Finally, community mental health centers provide education and consultation. For example, staff members may provide drug education programs to local schools or educate police officers on how to deal with seriously disturbed people they might encounter in the line of duty.

Combined with the development of effective drug treatments, the impact of deinstitutionalization on the treatment of behavior disorders has been dramatic. According to the National Institute of Mental Health, 77.4 percent of all patients were being treated as inpatients in public and private hospitals in 1955. By 1990, the inpatient figure had shrunk to 27.1 percent.

The concept of community treatment is a good one, for it allows people to remain in their social and work environments and to be treated with minimal disruption of their lives. However, it requires the availability of high-quality mental health care in community clinics, halfway houses, sheltered workshops, and other community facilities. When these facilities are available, deinstitutionalization can work. Unfortunately, many communities have never been able to fund the needed facilities, and the 1980s saw sharp cutbacks in federal funding of community mental health centers. As a result, many patients are being released into communities that are ill prepared to care for their needs. The result is a *revolving door phenomenon* involving repeated rehospitalizations. Nearly three-fourths of all hospital admissions involve formerly hospitalized

Figure 16.23

The revolving door phenomenon created by inadequate funding of community-based treatment facilities has produced a large population of severely disturbed homeless people who live on our nation's streets.

patients. While in the hospital, they respond well to medication and are soon released back into a community that cannot offer them the care they require. Following their release, they may stop taking their medication, their condition deteriorates to the point that they must be rehospitalized, and the cycle begins again.

This revolving door has produced a growing population of disturbed and homeless people who have nowhere to go for help (Figure 16.23). In some states with large urban populations, the largest mental wards exist not in hospitals but on city streets. There are as many as 1 million homeless people in the United States, and approximately one-third have a severe mental disorder, typically schizophrenia (Torrey, 1997). One large-scale public health survey study revealed that only 15.3 percent of people with serious mental disorders had received minimally adequate treatment during the previous year (Wang et al., 2002).

Mental Health Treatment in Today's Health-Care Environment

Rising medical and insurance costs have swelled the rolls of health maintenance organizations (HMOs), and managed care has altered the mental health treatment landscape dramatically. The desire of HMOs and insurance providers to contain health costs translates into a strong preference for drug treatments and short-term versus more costly long-term forms of psychotherapy, as well as the use of masters-level counselors who

charge lower fees. Third-party providers are also demanding evidence that the treatments they are paying for are effective. These pressures have had some positive results, including the stimulation of research on treatment outcomes and the development of some effective short-term therapies.

There are, however, some negative effects as well. To many psychologists, the most serious is that many decisions about the type and duration of therapy are being made by untrained representatives of insurers or HMOs, rather than by the client or a mental health professional. In some instances, the number of sessions permitted may be woefully inadequate to treat a serious disorder (Figure 16.24). Although many psychologists concede that some of the more effective treatments are short-term cognitive-behavioral and interpersonal therapies, they do not believe that these treatments are best for every problem and client. Current data suggest that about 12 to 18 sessions are required to achieve a 50 percent recovery rate for most disorders (Hansen et al., 2002). Managed-care plans frequently limit payment to fewer sessions than this, so that many managed-care subscribers do not receive the level of care that they need. Likewise, the preference for drug treatments that require minimal contact between the patient and a professional may provide short-term improvement at the cost of a more satisfactory long-term result that could occur with psychological treatments that allow the development of better coping skills. Moreover, as we have

"It's your insurance company, they say you're cured."

Figure 16.24

In today's managed-care environment, treatment decisions may be made by untrained representatives of an insurance company instead of a health-care professional. SOURCE: From *The Wall Street Journal* by permission of Cartoon Features Syndicate.

seen in this chapter's "Myth or Reality?" feature, drug therapy has its own negative consequences.

Preventive Mental Health

Up to now, we have focused entirely on what can be done to help people once they have developed a behavior disorder. Successful treatment is one way to reduce the toll of human suffering produced by failures to adapt. Another way is to try to *prevent* the development of disorders through psychological intervention. In terms of economic, personal, and societal costs, it may indeed be the case that "an ounce of prevention is worth a pound of cure." If current efforts to enhance personal well-being and to slow the rise of health-care costs are to be successful, the prevention of behavior disorders must be a focal point of social policy. In some cases, this may involve treating psychological disorders during childhood in an attempt to prevent their continuation into adult life. School-based intervention programs have proven effective in preventing and reducing aggressive behaviors in children (Wilson et al., 2003). In addition, anxiety, depression, conduct disorders, and attention-deficit/hyperactivity disorder have responded positively to interventions applied in childhood (Compton et al., 2002; Farmer et al., 2002), but additional research is needed to see if the positive treatment effects persist into adulthood.

People may become vulnerable to psychological disorders as the result of situational factors, personal factors, or both. Thus prevention can be approached from two perspectives (Figure 16.25). **Situation-focused prevention** *is directed at either reducing or eliminating the environmental causes of behavior disorders or enhancing situational factors that help prevent the development of disorders.* Programs designed to enhance the functioning of families, reduce stress within organizations, provide better educational opportunities for children, and develop a sense of connection to other people and the community at large all have the potential to help prevent the development of behavior disorders (Albee, 1997; Taylor & Wang, 2000). One community intervention program was designed to prevent the development of antisocial personality disorder in a high-risk inner-city environment. Between the ages of 3 and 5 years, children randomly assigned to the experimental group participated in an intensive nutritional, physical-exercise, and educational program. Children exposed to this program had lower scores on measures of antisocial personality disorder at age 17 and lower criminal records at age 23 than did those in the control group (Raine et al., 2003).

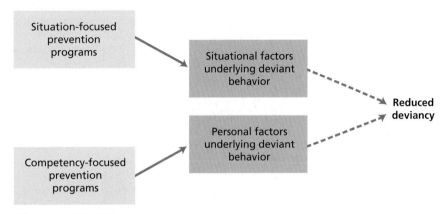

Figure 16.25

Preventive mental health.

Two approaches to the prevention of psychological disorders are based on the principle that deviant behavior represents the interaction of personal and situational factors. Situation-focused approaches increase situational protective factors or reduce vulnerability factors in the environment. Competency-focused approaches reduce personal vulnerability factors or strengthen personal competencies and coping skills.

The personal side of the equation is addressed by **competency-focused prevention,** *designed to increase personal resources and coping skills.* Such programs may focus on strengthening resistance to stress, improving social and vocational competencies, enhancing self-esteem, and helping people gain the skills needed to build stronger social support systems. One illustrative program, developed by Edna Foa and her coworkers (1995), focused on preventing posttraumatic stress disorder (PTSD) in women who had recently been raped or assaulted.

The victims were randomly assigned either to a treatment condition or to an untreated control condition. In hourly sessions over a 4-week period, the women in the treatment group learned about the common psychological reactions to being raped, helping them to realize that their responses were understandable, given what they had experienced. They relived their trauma through guided imagery to help defuse their lingering fears through exposure. The women also learned stress-management coping skills such as relaxation, and they went through a cognitive therapy procedure to replace stress-producing cognitions with more realistic appraisals.

The results of the prevention program are shown in Figure 16.26. The women exposed to the prevention treatment had less severe symptoms at both the 2-month and 5.5-month assessments. Moreover, 2 months after their trauma, diagnostic interviews with the women in the two groups revealed that 70 percent of the women in the control condition met the DSM-IV criteria for PTSD, compared with only 10 percent of the women who had received the prevention program. Thus, for

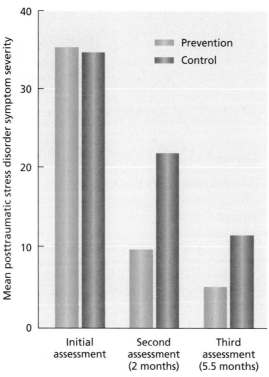

Figure 16.26

Preventing PTSD.
A competency-based prevention project was designed to prevent PTSD in women who were victims of rape and assault. The program, which combined a number of behavioral and cognitive therapy techniques to increase stress-management coping skills, sharply reduced the likelihood of developing PTSD. SOURCE: Foa et al., 1995.

many of the women, an efficient 4-week program prevented what might have been a PTSD disorder that would have created tremendous personal misery and required a far more expensive and time-consuming course of therapy.

To help counter the high incidence of psychological disorders (20 to 30 percent) in soldiers who return from combat in Iraq and Afghanistan, the

U.S. Army has developed an intervention called Battlemind. It involves a debriefing phase and an emphasis on adapting combat skills soldiers have learned to their home environment. For example, the same skills that helped create close bonds with fellow soldiers can be applied to enhance family cohesion. They also learn how to decrease hypervigilance, startle, and irritability. A clinical trial revealed fewer PTSD symptoms, fewer sleep problems, and less depression in Battlemind recipients (Adler et al., 2009).

Although many mental health experts believe that more resources need to be focused on the prevention of maladaptive behavior, they also recognize that prevention presents its own challenges. For one, we cannot develop an intervention program until we understand the causes of the disorder we want to reduce. Even when causal factors are known, we also need to understand what kinds of interventions will be successful in modifying them. This requires careful research into which types of programs are most effective in preventing which types of problems in which types of people—our old specificity question.

Another practical problem is that the effects of prevention are usually not immediately obvious. It may take years for their effects to become evident. Moreover, their effects (which usually involve the *absence* of a disorder) can be hard to measure. For these reasons, prevention programs can be difficult to justify when funding priorities are being set, even though the programs may, in the long run, have greater positive impact than programs that focus on treating disorders that have already developed.

Having described the nature and benefits of treatments, we end this chapter with some research-derived guidelines for seeking and profiting from therapy.

Applying Psychological Science

When and Where to Seek Therapy

No one is immune to the problems of living. Every day, each of us does the best we can to balance our personal and social resources against the demands created by our life circumstances. We all have certain vulnerabilities, and if environmental demands and our vulnerabilities combine to overrun our resources, we may experience psychological problems for which professional assistance would be helpful. Here are some general guidelines for seeking such help and profiting from it.

WHEN TO SEEK HELP

First is the issue of when to seek help. In general terms, you should consider seeking professional assistance if any of the following applies:

- You are experiencing serious emotional discomfort, such as feelings of depression or anxiety, that are adversely affecting your personal, work, or family life.

- You are encountering a serious problem or life transition that you feel unable to handle on your own.
- A problem that has interfered with your life or personal happiness in the past is worsening or has suddenly resurfaced.
- You have experienced some traumatic event, either in the past or recently, that you find yourself frequently thinking about, dreaming about, or responding to with negative emotions.
- You are preoccupied with your weight or body image, and are taking extreme steps, such as not eating or purging yourself by vomiting or taking laxatives.
- You have severe and recurring conflicts with other people.
- You hear voices telling you what to do, or you feel that others are controlling your thoughts.

WHERE TO SEEK HELP

How does one go about getting help in dealing with psychological problems? Help may be sought at a college counseling center, at a community agency, at an HMO, or from a professional in private practice. The campus counseling center is often a good place for a college student to start, for it can provide direct help or an appropriate referral to a reputable mental health professional. If you are at a larger university that has a graduate program in clinical or counseling psychology, there also may be an on-campus psychology training clinic administered by that program. There you would typically work with a graduate student who is being closely supervised by a licensed clinician.

How expensive is treatment? For college students it is often offered free or at a nominal fee at a campus facility or HMO. Community agencies typically have a sliding-fee scale based on the client's income, so financial considerations need not be a barrier to seeking professional assistance. A private practitioner may charge as much as medical doctors, dentists, and attorneys do, often exceeding $100 per 50-minute session. As a prospective client, you should always ask beforehand about the fee. You also should check into the mental health benefits provided by your health insurance policy, including what kinds of treatments and the number of sessions it covers and whether it will reimburse your chosen treatment provider. Student insurance plans usually cover on-campus treatment.

WHAT TO LOOK FOR IN A THERAPIST

In choosing a therapist, what should you look for? It is important that your therapist be well trained and competent. Ask the therapist about her or his degree, license, training, therapeutic orientation, and the problems in which she or he specializes. This chapter has provided an overview of the major theoretical orientations, and one or more of them may seem especially attractive to you or suited to the problems you want to address.

As we've seen, the relationship between client and therapist is of the utmost importance. You will want a therapist who can create a good working relationship with you. The degree of "value similarity" between you and the therapist can be important. Timothy Kelly and Hans Strupp (1992) found that the most positive therapeutic outcomes were achieved when the client and therapist were neither very similar nor very dissimilar in values. High similarity may result in a failure to explore value-related issues, whereas too much dissimilarity may interfere with building a good therapeutic relationship. One exception to this general rule may occur in the area of religious values. Clients who have strong and committed religious values may profit most from a therapy that supports those values and uses them to help change problem behaviors (Probst et al., 1992).

Some clients prefer to work with either a male or female therapist, or one who is heterosexual or gay or lesbian, depending in part on the nature of the personal issues that have caused them to seek counseling. As we have seen, research has shown that personal warmth, sincere concern, and empathy are important therapist characteristics. You should like and feel comfortable with your therapist, and you should feel at ease with the methods the therapist uses. Under no circumstances should your therapeutic relationship involve physical intimacy of any kind (even hugging). If a therapist should ever engage in such behavior, you should immediately terminate treatment with that therapist and notify the appropriate professional organization, such as the state psychological or medical association. Such conduct is a serious breach of professional ethics and cannot be condoned under any circumstances.

WHAT CAN YOU EXPECT?

You and your therapist should have explicit, agreed-on goals for the treatment program. If therapy proceeds well, you will experience beneficial changes that indicate movement toward your goals. It may take some time for these changes to occur, however, since long-standing personal vulnerabilities are not easily changed, and significant change seldom occurs overnight. If you do not see any progress after several months or if you seem to be functioning less well than before, you should discuss your progress with the therapist. The therapist may be more satisfied with your progress than you are. However, if you continue to be dissatisfied with your progress or with the therapeutic relationship, you may at some point decide to terminate it. This should not prevent you from seeking help from another therapist.

Entering a helping relationship is a courageous step, and resolving problems in living may involve taking risks and experiencing pain. However, many clients look back on the pain and risks and feel that the process was a valuable one that enabled them to live happier lives than they otherwise could have. Here is a reflection by Dr. Sandra L. Harris, a prominent clinical psychologist, on the course of therapy she undertook as a college student:

> When I think about the girl I was in my freshman year at the University of Maryland and the young woman I was when I graduated four years later, it is clear that it was not only the issues Jim and I discussed, but how we talked that made the difference. The intangibles of trust, respect, and caring were at least as important as the active problem solving that transpired in our weekly meetings. It was not a dramatic transformation, rather it was a slight shifting of a path by a few degrees on the compass. Over the years that shift has had a cumulative effect and I walk a very different road than I would have without him. (Harris, 1981, p. 3)

test yourself

Treatment Evaluation and Community-Based Approaches

True or false?

1. RCTs are regarded as the gold standard in psychotherapy research.

2. Most empirically supported treatments are psychodynamic or humanistic.

3. At least one well-designed study is required to establish a treatment as empirically supported.

4. Meta-analyses support the dodo bird verdict that a variety of psychodynamic, humanistic, cognitive, and behavioral therapies are similar in general efficacy.

5. The quality of the therapeutic relationship accounts for about 30 percent of the variation in outcome.

6. Health-care reform would be an example of a competency-focused prevention program.

ANSWERS: 1-true, 2-false, 3-false, 4-true, 5-true, 6-false

Chapter Summary

PSYCHOLOGICAL TREATMENTS

- Each of the major perspectives—psychodynamic, humanistic, cognitive, behavioral, and biological—have inspired effective treatments for behavior disorders.

- Treatments are administered by a variety of practitioners, including psychologists, psychiatrists, social workers, and counselors.

PSYCHODYNAMIC THERAPIES

- The goal of Freudian psychoanalysis is to help clients achieve insight into the unconscious dynamics that underlie their behavior disorders so that they can deal adaptively with the current environment.

- The chief means for promoting insight in psychoanalysis are the therapist's interpretations of free associations, dream content, resistance, and transference reactions.

- Brief psychodynamic psychotherapies tend to focus more on current life events. Interpersonal therapy is a structured therapy that focuses on current interpersonal problems and the development of needed interpersonal skills.

HUMANISTIC PSYCHOTHERAPIES

- Humanistic psychotherapies attempt to liberate the client's natural tendency toward self-actualization by establishing a growth-inducing therapeutic relationship.

- Rogers's person-centered therapy emphasizes the importance of three therapist characteristics: unconditional positive regard, empathy, and genuineness.

- The goal of Gestalt therapy is to remove blockages to clients' awareness of the wholeness of immediate experience by making them more aware of their feelings and the ways in which they interact with others.

COGNITIVE THERAPIES

- Ellis's rational-emotive therapy and Beck's cognitive therapy focus on discovering and changing maladaptive beliefs and logical errors of thinking that underlie maladaptive emotional responses and behaviors.

BEHAVIOR THERAPIES

- Behavioral treatments based on classical conditioning are directed at modifying emotional responses. Exposure is designed to extinguish anxiety reactions by exposing clients to anxiety-arousing stimuli and preventing an avoidance response from occurring. Systematic desensitization is designed to countercondition a response that is incompatible with anxiety, such as relaxation, to anxiety-arousing stimuli. Aversion therapy is used to establish a conditioned aversion response to an inappropriate stimulus that attracts the client.

- Operant procedures have been applied successfully in many behavior modification programs. The token economy is a positive-reinforcement program designed to strengthen adaptive behaviors in hospitalized patients. Punishment has been used to reduce self-destructive behaviors in disturbed children.

- Modeling is an important component of social skills training programs, which help clients learn and rehearse more effective social behaviors.

- "Third-wave" cognitive-behavioral therapies have adopted mindfulness techniques as a tool for therapeutic change through increased focus on the moment and acceptance of negative thoughts and emotions. They include Acceptance and Commitment Therapy and Dialectical Behavior Therapy.

GROUP, FAMILY, AND MARITAL THERAPIES

- Group approaches offer clients a number of advantages, including opportunities to form close relationships with others, to gain insights into how they interact with others and are perceived by them, and to observe how others approach problems.
- Family therapy is based on the notion that individuals' problems are often reflections of dysfunctional family systems. Such systems should be treated as a unit.
- Marital therapies help couples improve their communication patterns and resolve difficulties in their relationships. In behavioral marital therapies, couples receive communication and relationship skills training to increase positive interactions in their marriages. The recent addition of acceptance training has improved outcomes.

CULTURAL AND GENDER ISSUES IN PSYCHOTHERAPY

- Research has shown that members of minority groups underutilize mental health services. Barriers include lack of access to therapists who can provide culturally responsive forms of treatment. More important to outcome than a cultural match is a therapist who can understand the client's cultural background and share similar viewpoints on therapy goals and the means to achieve them.
- Culturally competent therapists develop and test hypotheses within therapy rather than operate on stereotypes, take into account both cultural and individual factors in understanding the client, and are willing to introduce culture-specific elements into therapy.
- Awareness of oppressive environmental conditions that adversely affect women and a willingness to support life goals that do not necessarily conform to gender expectations can increase therapeutic outcomes. Whether the therapist is a man or a woman seems less important to outcome than gender sensitivity.

BIOLOGICAL APPROACHES TO TREATMENT

- Drugs have revolutionized the treatment of many behavior disorders and have permitted many hospitalized patients to function outside of institutions.
- Effective drug treatments exist for anxiety, schizophrenia, and depression. Some of these drugs have undesirable side effects and can be addictive. All of them affect specific classes of neurotransmitters within the brain. Antidepressants may be less safe and effective than previously assumed.
- Modern electroconvulsive therapy is much safer and used less frequently than in the past. It is used primarily to treat severe depression, particularly when a threat of suicide exists.

- Psychosurgery techniques have become more precise, but they are still generally used only after all other treatment options have failed.
- Drugs and psychotherapy may be combined to hasten the relief of a client's symptoms while establishing more effective coping responses to deal with the sources of the disorder.

EVALUATING TREATMENTS

- Randomized clinical trials (RCTs) are the gold standard of treatment evaluation methods. They employ experimental techniques to maximize control and draw scientifically sound conclusions.
- Survey studies of therapy outcomes lack experimental controls and may exaggerate the effectiveness of treatments.
- Meta-analysis is a method for combining the results of many studies into an effect size statistic. One large-scale meta-analysis of treatment outcome studies indicated that therapy subjects improved more than about 75 percent of control subjects and that various therapies seemed to differ little in effectiveness.
- Three sets of interacting factors affect the outcome of treatment: client characteristics (including the nature of the problem), therapist characteristics, and therapy techniques.
- Many therapy researchers have concluded that the most important common factor in the success of various therapies is the quality of the relationship that the therapist establishes with the client. The three characteristics suggested by Rogers—empathy, unconditional positive regard, and genuineness—seem to be particularly important.

PSYCHOLOGICAL DISORDERS AND SOCIETY

- The introduction of drug therapies that normalize disturbed behavior, as well as concerns about the hospitalization syndrome, have helped stimulate a move toward deinstitutionalization—the treatment of people in their communities.
- Research has shown that deinstitutionalization can work when adequate community treatment is provided. Unfortunately, many communities have been unable to fund the needed facilities, resulting in the revolving door phenomenon of release and rehospitalization, as well as a new generation of homeless people who live on the streets and do not receive needed treatment.
- Prevention programs may be classified as either situation-focused or competency-focused, depending on whether they are directed at changing environmental conditions or personal factors.

KEY TERMS AND CONCEPTS

Each term has been boldfaced and defined in the chapter on the page indicated in parentheses.

Acceptance and Commitment
  Therapy (ACT) (p. 607)
aversion therapy (p. 603)
behavioral activation (p. 605)
behavior modification (p. 604)
common factors (p. 623)
competency-focused prevention (p. 627)
counterconditioning (p. 602)
cultural congruence (p. 611)
culturally competent therapist (p. 611)
deinstitutionalization movement (p. 625)
Dialectical Behavior Therapy
  (DBT) (p. 607)
dodo bird verdict (p. 621)
effect size (p. 621)

empathy (p. 597)
empirically supported treatments
  (ESTs) (p. 620)
exposure (p. 601)
feminist therapy (p. 611)
free association (p. 594)
genuineness (p. 597)
insight (p. 594)
interpersonal therapy (p. 596)
interpretation (p. 595)
meta-analysis (p. 621)
mindfulness (p. 606)
openness (p. 622)
placebo control group (p. 619)
psychosurgery (p. 616)

randomized clinical trial (RCT) (p. 619)
resistance (p. 595)
response prevention (p. 601)
self-relatedness (p. 622)
situation-focused prevention (p. 627)
social skills training (p. 605)
specificity question (p. 618)
stimulus hierarchy (p. 602)
systematic desensitization (p. 602)
tardive dyskinesia (p. 612)
token economy (p. 604)
transference (p. 595)
unconditional positive regard (p. 597)
virtual reality (VR) (p. 602)

 thinking **critically**

DO SURVEY RESULTS PROVIDE AN ACCURATE PICTURE OF TREATMENT EFFECTIVENESS? (Page 622)

Seligman's conclusion that the *CR* survey provides a realistic appraisal of treatment effects is thought-provoking, but before you accept this conclusion, you should consider some of the survey's shortcomings. First, consider the nature of the *CR* sample. Only 1.6 percent of the original 184,000 people contacted described their therapy experience. Is it possible that among the other 98.4 percent are a significant number of people who had been in therapy with unfavorable results and chose not to share their experiences? If so, the effectiveness of therapy could be exaggerated in this self-selected sample.

Second, what about the nature and quality of the data? We have only global, after-the-fact reports from clients. There is no way to corroborate respondents' reports with other sources of data. How do we know that they are not biased by memory distortions or by rationalizing their investment ("If I spent that much time and money, I must have gotten better")? Rationalization could also account for the apparent superiority of long-term therapy, where more time and money were expended, as well as the tendency to return the questionnaire and share the success story.

Third, what has the *CR* study told us about the more important specificity question? We don't know if some matches of clinical problems with specific forms of therapy yielded better outcomes than others. In fact, we can't even be sure about what kinds of therapy were administered, because respondents didn't describe their treatments in detail.

Fourth, how about the absence of a control group? Can we rule out spontaneous remission of symptoms? As we saw in Chapter 15, many mental health problems (e.g., depression and anxiety) fluctuate or improve with time. People who are assessed at their low points, when they are most likely to seek therapy, are almost certain to improve, with or without therapy (Mintz et al., 1996). Could this factor alone explain the respondents' perceptions that they had improved? As Seligman himself conceded, "Because there are no control groups, the *CR* . . . study cannot tell us directly whether talking to sympathetic friends or merely letting time pass would have produced just as much improvement as treatment by a mental-health professional" (1995, p. 972).

Despite the interpretive challenges that attend community studies like this, psychotherapy researchers agree that it is critically important to see how well the treatment principles and techniques identified in controlled studies work in the real world (Westen et al., 2004). One way to accomplish this is by systematically measuring the variables of interest within individual cases being seen by practicing therapists in the community. A large number of single-client case studies containing such measurement can provide important data on the effectiveness of specific therapies and the factors that influence those outcomes (Goldfried & Eubanks-Carter, 2004).

chapter seventeen

Social Thinking and Behavior

CHAPTER OUTLINE

Myth or Reality?

Violent Video Games Promote Aggression (page 669)

Does playing violent video games increase the risk that people will act aggressively in other situations, or does it generally reduce players' aggressive tendencies by giving them an opportunity to "blow off steam" in a safe fantasy environment? Which perspective is best supported by scientific research?

Figure 17.1

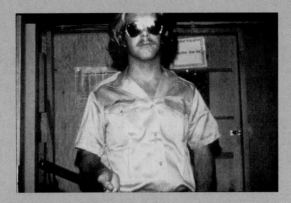

The prison had become a living hell. Hidden behind their mirrored sunglasses, the guards asserted their total authority over the prisoners. They made the prisoners ask permission to do virtually anything, including going to the toilet. The guards conducted roll calls in the middle of the night to assert their power and disrupt the prisoners' sleep, and they forced prisoners to do push-ups, sometimes with a foot pushing down on the prisoner's back. For their part, the prisoners became increasingly passive and depressed. They hated the guards but were powerless against them. After a few days, one prisoner cracked emotionally. Soon another broke down. Before long, the demoralized prisoners became nothing more than what the guards expected them to be: piteous objects of scorn and abuse (Figure 17.1).

This prison was not in some brutal dictatorship, the prisoners were not hardened criminals, nor were the guards sadistic psychopaths. Instead, this prison was in the basement of the psychology building at Stanford University, and the guards and prisoners were college students who had volunteered for a study of "prison life." Before the study, screening questionnaires, interviews, and psychological tests showed the participants to be well adjusted.

Philip Zimbardo, the social psychologist who designed the study, watched in disbelief as scenes of callous inhumanity unfolded before him. As one guard recalled, "I made them . . . clean out the toilets with their bare hands. I practically considered the prisoners cattle. . . ." (Zimbardo et al., 1973, p. 42). What began as a 2-week simulation of prison life had to be halted after only 6 days. Afterward, Zimbardo and his associates held several sessions with the participants to help them work through their powerful emotional reactions, and they maintained contact during the following year to minimize the risk that participants would experience lasting negative effects.

Decades later, the Stanford Prison Experiment remains a landmark for dramatically illustrating a basic concept: behavior is determined not only by our biological endowment and past learning experiences but also by the power of the immediate social situation (Haney & Zimbardo, 2009).

Scientists would want to determine the psychological processes and key characteristics of the prison simulation that transformed normal college students into such callous people. They also would ask whether principles learned from the simulation generalize to other social settings.

As social creatures, we spend our days in an ever changing series of social environments that profoundly shape how we behave, think, and feel. This chapter explores the field of social psychology, which studies how we think about our social world (*social thinking*), how other people influence our behavior (*social influence*), and how we relate toward other people (*social relations*).

SOCIAL THINKING

In your judgment, why did some guards in the Stanford prison study act so brutally? Did you form any impressions of the guards or prisoners as you read about the study? Do you feel that the study was worthwhile? These questions focus on three key aspects of social thinking: *attributions, impressions,* and *attitudes.*

Attribution: Perceiving the Causes of Behavior

In everyday life we often make **attributions,** *judgments about the causes of our own and other people's behavior and outcomes* (Figure 17.2). Was my A on the midterm due to hard work and ability, or was it just an easy test? Did Bill criticize Linda because he is a rude person, or was he provoked? Did the guards' brutal behavior reflect their personalities or some aspect of the situation? In the courtroom, jurors' attributions about a defendant's behavior influence their decisions about guilt versus innocence.

Personal versus Situational Attributions

Our attempts to understand why people behave as they do typically involve either personal attributions or situational attributions (Heider, 1958; Stewart et al., 2010). *Personal (internal) attributions* infer that people's characteristics cause their behavior: "Bill insulted Linda because he is rude." "My A on the midterm exam reflects my high ability." *Situational (external) attributions* infer that aspects of the situation cause a behavior: "Bill was provoked into insulting Linda." "I received an A because the test was easy."

How do we decide whether a behavior is caused by personal or situational factors? Suppose you ask Kim for advice on whether to take a particular course, Art 391, and she tells you that the course is terrible. Is Art 391 really poor (a situational attribution), or is it something about Kim (a personal attribution) that led to this response? According to Harold Kelley (1973), three types of information determine the attribution we make:

Figure 17.2

"He's been under a lot of stress lately." "He only thinks about himself. What a jerk!" Depending on which attribution she makes for her husband's outburst, this woman may respond with understanding or anger.

consistency, distinctiveness, and *consensus.* First, is Kim's response consistent over time? If you ask Kim again two weeks later and she still says that Art 391 is terrible, then consistency is high. Second, is her response distinctive? If Kim dislikes only Art 391, then distinctiveness is high; if she thinks that most of her courses are terrible, then distinctiveness is low. Finally, how do other people respond? If other students agree with Kim that Art 391 is poor, then consensus is high, but if they disagree with her, then consensus is low.

As Figure 17.3 illustrates, when consistency, distinctiveness, and consensus are all high, we are likely to make a situational attribution: "The course is bad." But when consistency is high and the other two factors are low, we make a personal attribution: "Perhaps Kim is overly critical." Humans, however, are often not so logical. We often take mental shortcuts and make snap judgments that bias our attributions.

Attributional Biases

Social psychology teaches us that the immediate social environment profoundly influences behavior, yet at times we ignore this when making attributions. Instead, we commit a bias called the **fundamental attribution error:** *we underestimate the impact of the situation and overestimate the role of personal factors when explaining other people's behavior* (Ross, 2001). This thinking bias has been found in real-world situations and laboratory experiments (Neuschatz et al., 2008).

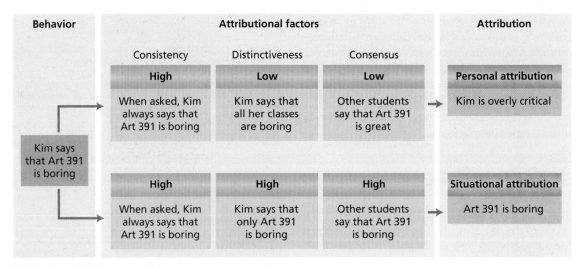

Figure 17.3

Forming personal and situational attributions.

Consistency, distinctiveness, and consensus information help us determine whether to make personal or situational attributions for someone else's behavior. Note that in both examples consistency is high. If Kim's behavior has low consistency (sometimes she says Art 391 is boring, and other times she says it's interesting), we typically attribute the behavior to transient conditions (e.g., changes in Kim's mood) rather than to stable personal or situational factors. Source: Based on Kelley, 1973.

Imagine that as part of a course assignment you write an essay on whether physicians should be allowed to help terminally ill patients commit suicide. The professor gives you the choice of writing in favor of or against physician-assisted suicide. Your classmates read the essay, and because they know you had a choice, they logically assume that the essay's content reflects your personal views. Thus, if the essay opposes physician-assisted suicide, your classmates will conclude that you are against this practice.

But suppose instead that the professor assigns you to write a supportive essay or assigns you to write an opposing essay. Your classmates know that you were not given a choice. Logically, the content of the essay reflects the situation to which you were assigned. After all, perhaps you are against physician-assisted suicide but were told to write an essay in favor of it, or vice versa. Yet experiments indicate that the content of the essay will still influence your classmates' perception of whether you support or oppose the issue (Jones & Harris, 1967). Similarly, people make the fundamental attribution error when—solely on the basis of actors' professional roles—they expect TV and movie stars to have the same personal traits as the characters they play (Tal-Or & Papirman, 2007).

Psychologists debate what causes the fundamental attribution error, but they agree that it's not inevitable (Stewart et al., 2010). When people have time to reflect on their judgments or are highly motivated to be careful, the fundamental attribution error is reduced. Moreover, keep in mind that the fundamental attribution error applies to how we perceive other people's behavior rather than our own. As comedian George Carlin noted, the slow driver ahead of us is a "moron," and the fast driver trying to pass us is a "maniac." Yet we don't think of ourselves as a moron or a maniac when we do these things, perhaps because we are more aware of situational factors (e.g., an unfamiliar road) impinging on us. After the Stanford prison study ended, guards who had treated prisoners cruelly were quick to attribute their behavior to the role that they had been in rather than to their personal qualities.

Indeed, when it comes to explaining our own behavior, we often make attributions that protect or enhance our self-esteem by displaying a **self-serving bias,** *the tendency to make personal attributions for successes and situational attributions for failures* (Ross & Nisbett, 1991). The strength of this bias, however, depends on many factors. For example, a meta-analysis of 266 studies by Amy Mezulis and her coworkers (2004) found that depressed individuals are much less likely than most people to display a self-serving bias. Indeed, depressed people often display the opposite pattern—taking too little credit for successes and too much credit for failures—which helps keep them depressed.

Culture and Attribution

Culture influences how we perceive our social world. Consider the fundamental attribution error. Many studies suggest that the tendency to attribute other people's behavior to personal factors reflects a Westernized emphasis on individualism (Triandis, 2001). In one study, participants of varying ages from India and the United States attributed causality for other people's behavior (Miller, 1984). As Figure 17.4 shows, with increasing age, Indians made more situational attributions, whereas Americans made more personal attributions. Culture also influences attributions for our own behavior. Asians living in their homelands are less likely to display a self-serving attributional bias than are Americans or other Westerners (Mezulis et al., 2004). Modesty, for example, is highly valued in China's collectivistic culture, and Chinese college students take less personal credit for successful social interactions and accept more responsibility for their failures than do American students.

Beyond influencing the types of attributions that we make, our cultural background also affects how we go about making attributions. Consider that East Asians tend to hold a more holistic view of the universe than Westerners (Nisbett et al., 2008). This view, reflected in the belief that all events are interconnected, leads East Asians to develop more complex views about the causes of behavior. Accordingly, Incheol Choi and coworkers (2003) predicted and found that compared to European American college students, Korean college students scored higher on measures of holistic thinking and also took more information into account when making causal attributions for other people's behavior.

Forming and Maintaining Impressions

As social beings, we constantly form impressions of other people, just as they form impressions of us. Attributions play a key role: Do you attribute the guards' behavior in the Stanford prison study to the role they were placed in or to their personal characteristics? Other factors, however, also affect how we form and maintain impressions.

How Important Are First Impressions?

Try this exercise. Tell a few people that you know someone who is "intelligent, industrious, impulsive, critical, stubborn, and envious," and ask them how much they "like" this person. Repeat the process with a few others, only describe the person as "envious, stubborn, critical, impulsive, industrious, and intelligent." In a famous study, Solomon Asch (1946) found that the person in the first description is perceived more positively—as more sociable and happier—than

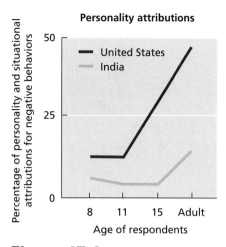
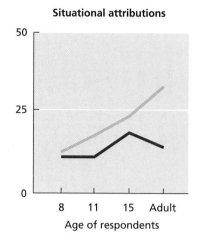

Figure 17.4

Culture influences attributions.

In this classic study, with increasing age from childhood to adulthood, Americans showed a greater tendency to make personality attributions for other people's behaviors. In contrast, participants from India showed an increased tendency to make situational attributions. Source: Adapted from Miller, 1984.

the person in the second description, even though both groups received identical information but in reverse order.

When forming impressions, the **primacy effect** *refers to our tendency to attach more importance to the initial information that we learn about a person.* New information can change our opinion, but it has to "work harder" for two reasons. First, we tend to be most alert to information we receive first. Second, initial information may shape how we perceive subsequent information. Imagine an athlete who gets off to a great start in training camp. The coach attributes high ability to the athlete. But as time goes on, the athlete's performance declines. To maintain this positive initial impression, the coach may attribute the performance decline to fatigue or a string of bad breaks. First impressions also carry extra weight because they influence our desire to make further contact with a person (Sunnafrank et al., 2004). It's difficult to overcome someone's negative first impression of you if that person subsequently avoids or ignores you.

Primacy is the rule of thumb in impression formation, especially for people who dislike ambiguity and uncertainty (Kruglanski, 2004). We seem to have a remarkable capacity for forming snap judgments based on small amounts of initial information (Ambady & Skowronski, 2008). Some evolutionary psychologists propose that evaluating stimuli quickly (such as rapidly distinguishing friend from foe) was adaptive for our survival (Krebs & Denton, 1997). But we are not slaves to primacy. Primacy effects decrease—and *recency effects* (giving greater weight to the most recent

(a)

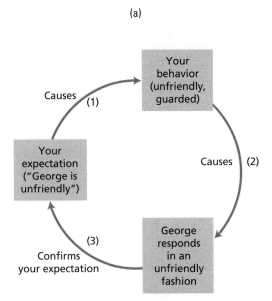

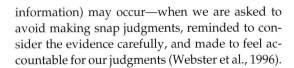

(b)

Figure 17.5

A self-fulfilling prophecy.

(a) Your expectation concerning George may influence your behavior and his response to you. (b) What first impressions will these people form of each other? How might these impressions influence their behavior and possibly create a self-fulfilling prophecy?

information) may occur—when we are asked to avoid making snap judgments, reminded to consider the evidence carefully, and made to feel accountable for our judgments (Webster et al., 1996).

Seeing What We Expect to See

Imagine that we are going to a party and I tell you that the host, George, is a distant, aloof, cold person. You meet him and try to make conversation, but George doesn't say much and avoids eye contact. A bit later, you say to me, "You were right, he's really a cold fish." Now let's roll back this scene. Suppose I describe George as nice but extremely shy. Later, when you try to make conversation, he doesn't say much and avoids eye contact. You say to me, "You were right, he's really shy." Same behavior, different impression. This example reminds us of a basic perceptual principle highlighted in Chapter 5. Whether perceiving objects or people, our *perceptual set*, which is a readiness to perceive the world in a particular way, powerfully shapes how we interpret a stimulus.

What creates our perceptual sets? One factor that we have discussed throughout the book is *schemas*, mental frameworks that help us organize and interpret information. By telling you that our host is "cold" or "shy," I activate a set of concepts and expectations (your schema) for how such a person is likely to behave. The host's behavior can

be interpreted in many ways, but you fit his behavior into the schema that is already activated.

A **stereotype**, *which is a generalized belief about a group or category of people,* represents a powerful type of schema. In one study, participants watched a videotape of a 9-year-old girl named Hannah and then judged her academic potential (Darley & Gross, 1983). They were told either that Hannah came from an upper-middle-class environment and had parents with white-collar careers or that she came from a poor neighborhood and had parents who were blue-collar workers. On the videotape, Hannah displayed average performance, answering some questions correctly and missing others. All participants saw the same performance, but those who thought Hannah came from a poor background rated her as having less ability. This study illustrates how our stereotypes (e.g., about social class) can bias the way we perceive other people's behavior.

Creating What We Expect to See

Seeing what we expect to see is only one way we confirm our initial impressions. Usually without conscious awareness, a **self-fulfilling prophecy** *occurs when people's erroneous expectations lead them to act toward others in a way that brings about the expected behaviors, thereby confirming their original impression.* Returning to our party example, if you expect George to be cold and aloof, then perhaps when you meet him you smile less and stand farther away than you would have if I had told you that George was a great guy. Perhaps when he looks at you, you avert your gaze, leading him to perceive you as less likable (Mason et al., 2005). In any case, his reserved response, in part, could be a reaction to *your* behavior (Figure 17.5a).

Self-fulfilling prophecies have been demonstrated in hundreds of studies across different settings, including schools, businesses, sports, close relationships, and interactions with strangers (Madon et al., 2006; Shapiro et al., 2007). When we interact with other people, our initially unfounded expectations can influence how we behave toward them, shaping their behavior in a way that confirms our expectations (Figure 17.5b).

Attitudes and Attitude Change

Beyond attributions and impressions, much of our social thinking involves the attitudes that we hold. Indeed, from political elections and war to the latest fashion craze, attitudes help steer the course of world events. An **attitude** *is a positive or negative evaluative reaction toward a stimulus, such as a person, action, object, or concept* (Crano & Prislin, 2006). Whether agreeing or disagreeing with a political policy or a friend's opinion of a movie, you are displaying an evaluative reaction (Figure 17.6). Our attitudes help define our identity, guide our actions, and influence how we judge people (Fazio & Roskos-Ewoldsen, 2005).

Do Our Attitudes Influence Our Behavior?

If we tell you that, according to research, people's attitudes strongly guide their behavior, you might reply "So what? That's just common sense." But consider a classic study by Richard LaPiere (1934). In the 1930s, he toured the United States with a young Chinese couple, stopping at 251 restaurants, hotels, and other establishments. At the time, prejudice against Asians was widespread, yet the couple—who often entered the establishment before LaPiere did—were refused service only once. Later LaPiere wrote to all of these establishments, asking if they would provide service to Chinese patrons. More than 90 percent of those who responded stated that they would not.

We cannot be sure that the people who expressed negative attitudes in the survey were the same ones who, months earlier, had served the Chinese couple. Yet the discrepancy between prejudicial attitudes and nondiscriminatory behavior seemed overwhelming and called the

Figure 17.6

Attitudes represent an important form of social thinking. They help define who we are, and they affect the way people judge one another. Do the attitudes expressed by these protestors influence your impression of them?

"commonsense" assumption of attitude-behavior consistency into question. Decades of better-controlled research, however, indicate that attitudes do predict behavior (Hunecke et al., 2010). Three factors help explain why the attitude-behavior relationship is strong in some cases but weak in others.

First, *attitudes influence behavior more strongly when situational factors that contradict our attitudes are weak.* For example, conformity pressures may lead us to behave in ways that are at odds with our inner convictions. According to the **theory of planned behavior** and similar models (Ajzen, 1991), *our intention to engage in a behavior is strongest when we have a positive attitude toward that behavior, when subjective norms (our perceptions of what other people think we should do) support our attitudes, and when we believe that the behavior is under our control.* Researchers have successfully used this theory to predict whether people will become smokers, exercise regularly, drive safely, donate blood, undergo cancer screening, and perform many other behaviors (Sieverding et al., 2010).

Second, *attitudes have a greater influence on behavior when we are aware of them and when they are strongly held.* Sometimes we seem to act without thinking, out of impulse or habit. Attitude-behavior consistency increases when people consciously think about or are reminded of their attitudes before acting (White et al., 2002).

Third, *general attitudes best predict general classes of behavior, and specific attitudes best predict specific behaviors.* For example, Martin Fishbein and Icek Ajzen (1974) found almost no relation between people's general attitudes toward religion and 70 specific religious behaviors (such as the frequency of attending services). But when they combined the 70 specific behaviors into a single global index of religious behavior, the relation between general religious attitudes and overall religious behavior was substantial.

Does Our Behavior Influence Our Attitudes?

Under the proper conditions, our attitudes guide our behavior. But attitude-behavior consistency is not a one-way street: We also may come to develop attitudes that are consistent with how we behave (McKimmie et al., 2009). In the Stanford prison study, as the guards slipped into their roles and began mistreating the prisoners, they began to view the prisoners as little more than animals. Why should this be?

Cognitive Dissonance   Imagine that you volunteer for an experiment, arrive at the laboratory, and repeatedly perform two extremely boring tasks: emptying and filling a tray with spools and turning 48 pegs stuck into holes. After you endure 60 minutes of sheer boredom, the experimenter enters, thanks you for participating, and asks for your help: it is important for the next student to begin the study with a positive attitude about the tasks, and all you have to do is tell the student that the boring tasks are interesting. Depending on the condition to which you have been randomly assigned, the experimenter offers to pay you either $1 or $20 for, essentially, lying to the next participant. You agree to do so. Afterward, you go to the psychology department's main office to collect your money and fill out a "routine form" that asks how much you enjoyed the tasks in the experiment.

Make a prediction: Comparing participants who lied for $1 and who lied for $20 with a control group that simply rated the boring tasks without telling any lie beforehand, which of the three groups rated the task most positively? Why?

Common sense might suggest that participants paid $20 would feel happiest about the

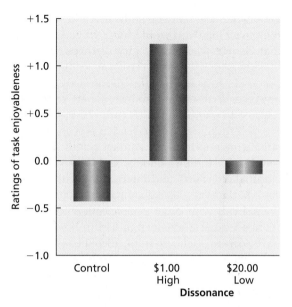

Figure 17.7

Cognitive dissonance and external justification.
In a classic study, participants lied to a fellow student by saying that a boring task was interesting. Those offered $1 to lie later rated the task most positively. Presumably, they reduced their cognitive dissonance about lying by convincing themselves that the task was interesting after all. Participants offered $20 had an external justification to lie, experienced little dissonance, and therefore did not need to convince themselves that the task was enjoyable. They and control participants who had not lied rated the boring task less favorably than the $1 group. Source: Based on Festinger & Carlsmith, 1959.

experiment and rate the tasks most highly. However, as Leon Festinger and J. Merrill Carlsmith (1959) predicted in a classic experiment, participants who were paid $1 gave the most positive ratings. Indeed, they actually rated the boring tasks as "somewhat enjoyable" (Figure 17.7)!

According to Festinger's (1957) **theory of cognitive dissonance,** *people strive for consistency in their cognitions.* When two or more cognitions contradict one another (such as "I am a truthful person" and "I just told another student that those boring tasks were interesting"), the person experiences an uncomfortable state of tension, which Festinger calls *cognitive dissonance,* and becomes motivated to reduce this dissonance. The theory predicts that to reduce dissonance and restore a state of cognitive consistency, people will change one of their cognitions or add new cognitions. Participants who received $20 could justify their behavior by adding a new cognition—"Who wouldn't tell a little lie for $20?"—and there was little reason for them to change their attitude toward the boring tasks. Those who had lied for only $1 could not use this trivial monetary gain to justify their behavior. But if they could convince themselves that the tasks actually were enjoyable, then they wouldn't have been lying after all. Thus they changed their attitude about the task to bring it more in line with how they had behaved.

Behavior that is inconsistent with one's attitude is called *counterattitudinal behavior,* and it produces dissonance only if we perceive that our actions were freely chosen rather than coerced. Freely chosen behaviors that produce foreseeable negative consequences or that threaten our sense of self-worth are especially likely to arouse dissonance. Once the behavior occurs, people start to consider the meaning of what they have done, and this produces dissonance (Cooper et al., 2005). Recall the statement by one of the guards in the Stanford prison study regarding his treatment of the prisoners: "I was surprised at myself." If the guard thought of himself as a good, moral person, then his callous behavior toward the prisoners should have created dissonance. Changing his attitude toward the prisoners—essentially coming to see them as "cattle" who did not have the same rights as humans—would have reduced dissonance.

Dissonance, however, does not always lead to attitude change. People can reduce dissonance by finding external justifications, by noting that other people also have behaved counterattitudinally, or by making other excuses (McKimmie et al., 2009). In Scandinavian surveys, among people who drank alcohol despite having negative attitudes toward drinking, one rationalization seemed to be "I may not be perfect, but other people are still worse" (Mäkelä, 1997).

Self-Perception   If we see someone campaigning for a political candidate, we will likely assume that this person has a positive attitude toward the candidate. If we see someone exerting great effort to achieve a goal, we will logically judge that the goal is important to that person. In short, we infer what other people's attitudes must be by watching how they behave. According to Daryl Bem's (1972) **self-perception theory,** *we make inferences about our own attitudes in much the same way: by observing how we behave.* Knowing that for very little external justification ($1) you have told a fellow student that the boring experimental tasks are enjoyable, you logically conclude that deep down you must feel that the tasks were at least somewhat enjoyable. In Bem's view, your attitude is not produced by a mysterious concept called *cognitive dissonance;* rather, you simply observe how you have acted and infer how you must have felt to have behaved in this fashion.

Self-perception theory and cognitive dissonance theory both predict that counterattitudinal behavior produces attitude change. One key difference, however, is that only dissonance theory assumes that we experience heightened physiological arousal (tension produced by dissonance) when we engage in counterattitudinal behavior. Do we? At least in some instances it appears that this does happen (Harmon-Jones et al., 1996).

In general, dissonance theory best explains why people change their views after behaving in ways that openly contradict their clearly defined attitudes, especially when such behaviors threaten their self-image (Stone & Cooper, 2003). Lying to someone for a measly dollar threatens our self-image of honesty, and acting inhumanely toward prisoners threatens our self-image of being a good, decent person—unless we can somehow justify those actions to ourselves. However, when counterattitudinal behavior does not threaten self-worth and we have weak attitudes to begin with, such behavior is less likely to create significant arousal—yet people still may alter their attitudes to be more consistent with how they have behaved. In this case, self-perception theory may provide the better explanation. Thus both dissonance theory and self-perception theory appear to be correct, but under different circumstances (Tesser & Shaffer, 1990). Both theories, however, agree that *our behaviors can influence our attitudes.*

Persuasion

Persuasion is a fact of everyday life, and it represents the intersection of social thinking and our next topic: social influence. Persuaders try to influence our beliefs and attitudes so that we will vote for them, buy their products, do them favors, or otherwise behave as they want us to. Here we examine three aspects of the persuasion process.

The Communicator   Communicator credibility— *how believable we perceive the communicator to be*—is often a key to effective persuasion. In fact, audience members who do not enjoy thinking deeply about issues may pay little attention to the content of a message and simply go along with the opinions of a highly credible source. Credibility has two major components: *expertise* and *trustworthiness* (Schul et al., 2004; Tobin & Raymundo, 2009). The most effective persuader is one who appears to be an expert and to be presenting the truth in an unbiased manner. We are especially likely to perceive communicators as trustworthy when they advocate a point of view that is contrary to their own self-interest (Petty et al., 2001). Communicators who are physically attractive, likable, and similar to us (such as in interests or goals) may also gain a persuasive edge, which is why

Figure 17.8

Fear appeals are a common approach to persuasion. They are most effective when people believe that a feared event could occur ("Driving after drinking can increase my risk of an accident"), that the consequences would be aversive ("I could lose my license or be killed"), that there is an effective way to reduce the risk ("If I drink, I won't drive"), and that they can carry out this behavior without great cost ("Have a designated driver; call a friend").

advertisers around the world spend millions of dollars hiring attractive, likable stars to promote their products (Messner et al., 2008).

The Message   In trying to persuade someone, is it more effective to present only your side of the issue or to also present the opposition's arguments and then refute them? Overall, research indicates that the *two-sided refutational approach* is most effective (Allen, 1991). Especially if an audience initially disagrees with the communicator's viewpoint or is aware that there are two sides to the issue, a two-sided message will be perceived as less biased.

Many messages, such as the one in Figure 17.8, attempt to persuade by arousing fear.

Does it work? Or do people reduce their fear simply by denying the credibility of the message or the communicator? Overall, fear arousal seems to work best when the message evokes moderate to strong fear and also provides people with effective, feasible (i.e., low-cost) ways to reduce the threat (Dillard & Anderson, 2004). High-fear messages accompanied by inadequate information about "what to do" typically lead to denial.

The Audience   A message loaded with logical arguments and facts may prove highly persuasive to some people yet fall flat on its face with others. One reason is that people differ in their *need for cognition*. Some enjoy analyzing issues; others prefer not to spend much mental effort.

According to Richard Petty and John Cacioppo, there are two basic routes to persuasion (Petty & Cacioppo 1986; Petty et al., 2005). The **central route to persuasion** *occurs when people think carefully about the message and are influenced because they find the arguments compelling.* The **peripheral route to persuasion** *occurs when people do not scrutinize the message but are influenced mostly by other factors such as a speaker's attractiveness or a message's emotional appeal.* Attitude change that results from the central route tends to last longer and to predict future behavior more successfully.

People who have a high need for cognition tend to follow the central route to persuasion. In forming attitudes about consumer services and products, for example, they pay attention to information about the service and product (Wood & Swait, 2002). In contrast, people with a low need for cognition are more strongly influenced by peripheral cues, such as the attractiveness of the person who endorses the product.

test yourself   Social Thinking

True or False?

1. When making attributions for other people's behavior, we typically overestimate the role of situational factors.
2. Cross-cultural differences exist in people's tendency to make situational versus personal attributions for other people's behavior.
3. The idea that first impressions are especially important is a myth.
4. A self-fulfilling prophecy begins with a false belief or expectation.
5. According to cognitive dissonance theory, attitudes influence behavior, but behavior doesn't influence attitudes.
6. In persuasion, fear arousal works best when the message arouses only a small amount of fear.

ANSWERS: 1-false, 2-true, 3-false, 4-true, 5-false, 6-false

SOCIAL INFLUENCE

Brad, a guard in the Stanford prison study, starts treating prisoners harshly after witnessing several of his fellow guards do the same. Jenna, a college sophomore, picks up the slack on a class project because other members of her group aren't pulling their weight. These diverse situations share a basic ingredient: they involve social influence.

Norms, Conformity, and Obedience

Years ago, a professor on our campus gave his class an unusual assignment: without doing anything illegal, each student was to violate some unspoken rule of social behavior and observe how others reacted. One student licked her plate clean at a formal dinner, receiving cold stares from the other guests. Another boarded a nearly empty city bus, sat down next to the only other passenger, and said "Hi!" The passenger sat up stiffly and stared out the window.

Social norms *are shared expectations about how people should think, feel, and behave,* and they are the glue that binds social systems together (Schaller & Crandall, 2004). Some norms are formal laws, but many—as illustrated by the preceding examples—are implicit and unspoken. Such norms often regulate daily behavior without our conscious awareness; we take them for granted until they are violated.

A **social role** *consists of a set of norms that characterizes how people in a given social position ought to behave.* The social roles of "college student," "professor," "police officer," and "spouse" carry different sets of behavior expectations. Because we may wear many hats in our daily life, *role conflict* can occur when the norms accompanying different roles clash. College students who hold jobs and have children often experience role conflict as they try to juggle the competing demands of school, work, and parenthood.

Norms and roles can influence behavior so strongly that they compel a person to act uncharacteristically. The guards in the Stanford prison study were well-adjusted students, yet norms related to the role of "guard" seemed to override their values, leading to their dehumanizing treatment of the prisoners.

Norm Formation and Culture

Social norms lose invisibility not only when they are violated but also when we examine behavior across cultures and historical periods (Figure 17.9a). In doing so, we see that many social customs that we take for granted as "normal"—from gender roles and children's peer relations to views about love, marriage, and what constitutes an attractive

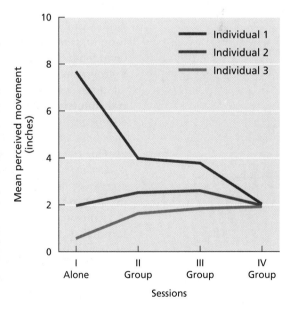

Figure 17.9

The evolution of norms across time and cultures.

(*left*) The Academy Award–winning movie *Million Dollar Baby* portrayed an aspiring American professional female boxer—an activity that women would be barred from in many countries, and that women were barred from decades ago in America. (*right*) Even randomly created groups spontaneously form norms. In Sherif's experiments, individuals' autokinetic judgments made alone (session I) began to converge when they were made in the presence of two other participants (sessions II, III, and IV). Each mean is based on 100 judgments per session. These data are from one of the three-person groups. Notice that the final norm is not simply the average of the original judgments that the group members made while alone. Source: Based on Sherif, 1935.

body shape—are not "normal" when judged from other cultural perspectives (Rubin et al., 2010).

It is difficult to imagine any society, organization, or social group functioning well without norms. In a pioneering experiment, Muzafer Sherif (1935) found that even randomly created groups develop norms. The task involved an optical illusion called the *autokinetic effect:* when people stare at a dot of light projected on a screen in a dark room, they begin to perceive the dot as moving, even though it really is stationary. When Sherif tested college students individually over several trials, each student perceived the light to move a different amount, from an inch or two to almost a foot.

Later the students were randomly placed into groups of 3 and made further judgments. As group members heard one another's judgments over several sessions, their judgments converged and a group norm evolved. The participants did not say "Hey, let's develop a group norm." It just happened. And, just as norms vary across cultures, the evolved norm for the autokinetic effect varied from group to group (Figure 17.9b).

Sherif's finding has been replicated in other countries and with different tasks. Whether at a cultural level or in small random groups, humans develop common standards for behavior and judgment (Arrow & Burns, 2004).

Why Do People Conform?

Norms can influence behavior only if people conform to them. Without *conformity*—the adjustment of individual behaviors, attitudes, and beliefs to a group standard—we would have social chaos. At times we conform due to **informational social influence,** *following the opinions or behavior of other people because we believe that they have accurate knowledge and that what they are doing is right.* We also may succumb to **normative social influence,** *conforming to obtain the rewards that come from being accepted by other people while at the same time avoiding their rejection* (Bond, 2005).

Solomon Asch's (1951, 1956) landmark conformity experiments illustrated both types of influence. In the experimental condition, groups of college students performed several trials of a simple visual task (Figure 17.10) in which they were asked—for various sets of lines—which of 3 comparison lines was the same length as a standard line (line A). Only one member of the group, however, actually was a participant. The rest were accomplices of the experimenter. Group members sat around a table and were called on in order. The real participant sat next to last. According to plan, every accomplice intentionally gave the

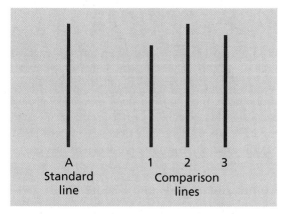

Figure 17.10

Asch's classic conformity experiment.
In Asch's (1956) conformity experiments, students were asked to judge which of three comparison lines was the same length as the standard line. They performed this task for multiple trials, using a different set of standard and comparison lines each time.

same wrong answer on some trials. Imagine yourself hearing the first group member choose line 1. (You think to yourself, "Huh?") Then the next four members also choose line 1. (You're wondering, "Can this really be?") Now it is your turn.

Would anybody conform to the group's incorrect judgments? Asch found that overall, participants conformed 37 percent of the time, compared with a mere 1 percent error rate in a control condition where people judged the lines by themselves. This finding stunned many scientists because the task was so easy and the confederates did not overtly pressure participants to conform.

After the task was over, some participants told the experimenter that they felt the group was wrong but went along to avoid making waves and suffering possible rejection. This reflects normative social influence. After several trials, other participants yielded to informational social influence and began to doubt their eyesight and judgment.

Factors That Affect Conformity

Asch showed that complex social behavior could be studied under controlled conditions. In other experiments, he manipulated different variables and measured their effects on conformity. Consider two examples:

- *Group size:* Conformity increased as group size increased from 1 to about 4 or 5 confederates, but further increases in group size did not increase conformity. Other studies using Asch's procedure likewise fail to support the commonsense assumption that pressures to conform will keep increasing as group size becomes larger and larger (Bond, 2005).

- *Presence of a dissenter:* According to plan, one confederate disagreed with the others (e.g., the majority said "line 3"; the dissenter said "line 2" or even "line 1"). This greatly reduced participants' conformity. When someone dissents, this serves as a model for remaining independent from the group.

Around the globe, conformity in face-to-face situations tends to be greater among research participants from collectivistic cultures, where group harmony is valued more highly than in individualistic cultures (Bond & Smith, 1996; Cinnerella & Green, 2007).

Minority Influence

Although majority influence is powerful, in political, business, and other real-world contexts dissenting information presented by the minority may cause majority members to change their view (Butera & Levine, 2009). Dissenting opinions are more likely to sway the majority when they come from several minority members rather than just one (Clark, 2001). Serge Moscovici (1985) proposes that to maximize its influence, the minority must be highly committed to its point of view, remain independent in the face of majority pressure, yet appear to keep an open mind. Indeed, reviewing almost 100 studies, Wendy Wood and coworkers (1994) found that minority influence is strongest when the minority maintains a highly consistent position over time.

However, if the minority appears too unreasonable, deviant, or negative, it may cause the majority to become entrenched.

Obedience to Authority

Like conformity to a group, obedience to an authority figure is inherently neither good nor bad. As an airplane passenger, you would not be amused if the copilot disregarded the pilot's commands simply because he or she didn't feel like obeying, putting the flight and your life at risk. Without obedience, society would face chaos. But obedience can also produce tragic results. After World War II, the famous Nuremberg trials were held to judge Nazi war criminals who had slaughtered millions of innocent people in concentration camps. In many instances, the defendants argued that they had only followed orders. In the massacre of men, women, and children at My Lai during the Vietnam War, American soldiers accused of atrocities gave the same explanation. No doubt we will continue to hear the cry "I was just following orders" as accountability is judged for more recent mass atrocities around the globe.

Just as the Nuremberg court did, many of us reject justifications based on obedience to authority as mere rationalizations, secure in our conviction that we would behave more humanely in such situations. But would we? Our "Research Close-up"—part of the most famous series of studies ever conducted in social psychology—suggests some provocative answers.

 **Research Close-up**

The Dilemma of Obedience: When Conscience Confronts Malevolent Authority

SOURCE: STANLEY MILGRAM (1974). *Obedience to Authority.* New York: Harper & Row.

INTRODUCTION

Fueled by a scientific interest in social influence and a desire to understand the horrors of the Holocaust, psychologist Stanley Milgram (1974) asked a disturbing question: Would ordinary citizens obey the orders of an authority figure if those orders meant physically harming an innocent person? He conducted 18 studies between 1960 and 1963 to answer this question.

Collectively, this famous research is known as the "Milgram experiments," or "obedience experiments." Yet each study was not an experiment but rather a descriptive study in which all participants were exposed to the same situation and observed under

controlled laboratory conditions. Milgram, however, carefully changed (i.e., manipulated) different aspects of the situation from one study to another in order to identify factors that increased or decreased people's obedience. In this sense, his overall research program reflects the experimental method. Let's examine one study.

METHOD

Forty men, ranging in age from 20 to 50 and representing a cross section of occupations and educational backgrounds, participated in the study. At the laboratory, each participant met a middle-aged man who was introduced as another participant but who was actually a confederate. Participants were told that the experiment examined the effects of punishment on memory. Then, through a

Continued

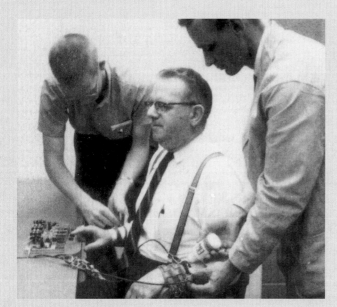

Figure 17.11

The participant (teacher) saw the learner (a confederate) being strapped into the chair.

supposedly random draw (it was rigged), the real participant became the "teacher" and the confederate became the "learner." The teacher presented a series of memory problems to the learner through a two-way intercom system. Each time the learner made an error, the teacher was instructed to administer an electric shock using a machine that had 30 switches, beginning with 15 volts and increasing step-by-step to 450 volts. As the teacher watched, the experimenter strapped the learner into a chair in an adjoining room and hooked him up to wires from the shock generator (Figure 17.11). The learner expressed concern about the shocks and mentioned that he had a slight heart problem.

RESEARCH DESIGN

Question: Will "ordinary citizens" obey a researcher's orders to inflict painful electric shocks upon a person, against that person's will? What factors influence obedience?

Type of Study:

Overall research program   *Experimental. The situation is systematically changed from study to study and effects on behavior are observed.*

Independent Variable

Variables are manipulated, one at a time (e.g., Teacher can or cannot see the Learner; Experimenter gives orders in person or by phone)

Dependent Variable

Level of obedience (as measured by the highest intensity of shock delivered by the Teacher to the Learner)

Returning to the main room, the experimenter gave the teacher a sample shock (45 volts) and then ordered the experiment to begin. Unbeknownst to the teacher, the learner intentionally committed many errors, and he did *not* actually receive any shock. The learner made verbal protests that were standardized on a tape recorder, so that they were the same for all participants.

As the learner's errors mounted, the teacher increased the shock. If the teacher balked at continuing, the experimenter issued one or more escalating commands, such as "Please continue," "You must continue," and "You have no other choice." At 75 volts, the learner moaned when the teacher threw the switch. At 150 volts, he moaned again and said, "Experimenter! That's all. Get me out of here. I told you I had heart trouble. My heart's starting to bother me now. Get me out of here, please. . . . I refuse to go on. Let me out." Beyond 200 volts, he emitted agonized screams every time a shock was delivered, yelling "Let me out! Let me out!" At 300 volts, the learner refused to answer and continued screaming to be let out. At 345 volts and beyond, there was only silence. Full obedience was operationally defined as continuing to the maximum shock level of 450 volts. The research design diagram highlights the design of the featured study and of Milgram's overall research program.

RESULTS

Participants wrestled with a dilemma. Should they continue to hurt this innocent person, as the experimenter commanded, or should they stop the learner's pain by openly disobeying? Most participants became distressed. Some trembled, sweated, laughed nervously, or, in a few cases, experienced convulsions. But would they obey? Make a prediction: What percentage of people obeyed to 450 volts?

Before the study, Milgram had asked psychiatrists, professors, university students, and middle-class adults to predict the outcome. They said that virtually no one (1 percent) would obey fully. Indeed, most participants balked or protested at one time or another and said they would not continue. But ultimately, 26 of the 40 men (65 percent) obeyed all the way to the end (Figure 17.12).

DISCUSSION

Milgram's research has generated controversy for decades (Blass, 2004; Miller, 2004). Its ethics were harshly criticized because participants were deceived, were exposed to substantial stress, and risked long-lasting negative effects to their self-image (Baumrind, 1964). Milgram countered that the research was so socially significant as to warrant the deception, that participants were carefully debriefed afterward, and that psychiatric follow-ups of a sample of obedient participants suggested no long-term ill effects. Weighing the costs and benefits, do you believe that this research was justified?

Researchers also debate why obedience was high, but many agree with Milgram's view that participants psychologically transferred much of the responsibility for the learner's fate to the experimenter. Participants viewed the experimenter as an expert, legitimate authority figure

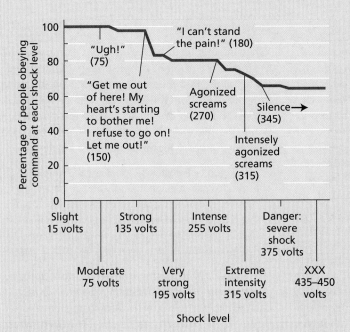

Figure 17.12

You must obey.

This graph shows the percentage of male participants who continued to shock the learner through various voltage levels. Source: Based on Milgram, 1974.

(Blass & Schmitt, 2001). While administering the shock, some participants stated that they "were not responsible" for what happened. Others asked, "Who is responsible if something happens to the learner?" When the experimenter replied, "I am responsible," participants felt greater freedom to continue. Yet they were the ones flipping the switch.

How would you have responded in Milgram's experiment? Almost all of our students say that they would have disobeyed either before or when the victim began protesting at the 150-volt level. Indeed, in one study, students in psychology classes—whether familiar with Milgram's results or not—said that they would stop at around 150 volts (Geher et al., 2002). So suppose we conduct an obedience study today but with real electric shocks and with you as the learner. The teacher will be a randomly selected student from your class. Are you confident that this student will disobey the experimenter and stop giving you shocks when you start yelling in protest? Few of our students or other students express such confidence (Geher et al., 2002). In short, virtually all of us are confident that *we* would disobey early on, but we are less sure about *other* people—and they in turn are not so sure about *us*.

Factors That Influence Obedience

By manipulating the following aspects of the laboratory situation, Milgram and other researchers obtained obedience rates ranging from 0 to more than 90 percent:

- *Remoteness of the victim:* Obedience was greatest when the learner was out of sight. When the teacher and learner were placed in the same room, obedience dropped to 40 percent. Further, when the teacher had to make physical contact and force the learner's hand onto a "shock plate," obedience dropped to 30 percent (Figure 17.13).

- *Closeness and legitimacy of the authority figure:* Obedience was highest when the authority figure was close by and perceived as legitimate. When the experimenter left the scene and gave orders by phone or when an "ordinary person" (a confederate) took over and gave the orders, obedience dropped to about 20 percent.

- *Diffusion of responsibility:* When another "participant" (actually a confederate) flipped the shock switch and the real participants only had to perform another aspect of the task, 93 percent obeyed. In short, *obedience increases when someone else does the dirty work.*

In contrast, when Harvey Tilker (1970) made participants feel fully responsible for the learner's welfare, not a single person obeyed to the end.

- *Personal characteristics:* Milgram compared the political orientations, religious affiliations, occupations, education, length of military service, and psychological characteristics of obedient versus disobedient participants. Differences were weak or nonexistent.

Figure 17.13

In one of Milgram's studies (touch proximity), the teacher was ordered to physically force the learner's hand onto a "shock plate" after the learner refused to continue. Here, 30 percent of participants obeyed fully to 450 volts. Although touch proximity strongly reduced obedience, that a significant minority still obeyed raises considerable concern.

Would People Obey Today?

Our students often ask us, "If Milgram's obedience study were conducted today, would the results be similar?" And for years we've been answering, "We suspect so," and here's why. For 25 years after Milgram's research, experiments were conducted in different countries, in "real-world" settings and laboratories, using a similar "electric shock" procedure and different obedience procedures, and with children, adolescents, and adults as participants. Overall, the findings revealed levels of obedience that were depressingly consistent with Milgram's results (Meeus & Raaijmakers, 1986). Then, for ethical reasons, obedience studies like Milgram's were discontinued.

Recently, however, social psychologist Jerry Burger (2009) conducted an interesting obedience study. Burger's procedures were reviewed by the American Psychological Association and paralleled Milgram's original approach, but only up to the 150-volt shock level: the point at which the learner protested vigorously, complained of a heart condition, and demanded to be released. To avoid exposing participants to too much stress, this was the highest shock level used in Burger's study. The 150-volt level also was a logical point to stop, because Milgram had found that participants who continued past this level were very likely to obey all the way to the maximum 450-volt level. Thus, in Burger's study, full obedience meant that after hearing the learner's protests at 150 volts (and if necessary, being ordered to continue by the experimenter), the participant continued with the task of reading the words to the learner, after which the procedure was stopped. Burger found that 65 percent of the 18 men tested obeyed fully, a high obedience rate consistent with the findings of Milgram's research.

Women also participated in the study. To learn about their results, see the following "Thinking Critically" feature.

 thinking critically

DO WOMEN DIFFER FROM MEN IN OBEDIENCE?
Suppose that the participants in Milgram's featured study had been women. Keeping everything else constant (i.e., the same male experimenter and male learner), would you expect women to be more or less obedient than the men or equally obedient? Why? Think about it, then see page 673.

Lessons Learned

What lessons shall we draw from this research? Certainly, it is *not* that people are apathetic or evil. Participants became stressed precisely because they did care about the learner's welfare. Neither is the lesson that we are sheep. If we were, obedience would be high across all situations, which is not the case. Rather, Milgram sums up a key lesson:

> It would be a mistake . . . to make the simple-minded statement that kindly and good persons disobey while those who are cruel do not . . . often, it is not so much the kind of person a man is as the kind of situation in which he finds himself that determines how he will act. (Milgram, 1974, p. 205)

Thus, by arranging the situation appropriately, most people—ordinary, decent citizens—can be induced to follow orders from an authority figure they perceive as legitimate, even when doing so contributes to harming an innocent person. The applicability of this principle to the Holocaust and other atrocities seems clear (Blass, 2008). During the Holocaust, obedience was made easier because most of the personnel working at the concentration camps were cogs in a horrendous wheel: they didn't pull the switch to flood the chambers with gas but instead performed other tasks. Their victims also were "remote" at the moment of their murder. Further, to lessen concentration camp workers' feelings of responsibility, Hitler's subordinate Heinrich Himmler told them in manipulative speeches that only he and Hitler were personally responsible for what took place (Dawidowicz, 1975).

Does obedience research suggest that we are not responsible for following orders? This is a moral and legal question, not a scientific one. But if anything, this research should heighten our responsibility for being aware of the pitfalls of blind obedience and prevent us from being so smug or naive as to feel that such events "could never happen here." Beyond obedience, Milgram's research provides yet another powerful example of how social contexts can induce people to behave in ways that they never would have imagined possible (Figure 17.14).

Detecting and Resisting Compliance Techniques

From telemarketers and salespeople to TV and Internet advertisements, would-be persuaders often come armed with special *compliance techniques:* strategies that may manipulate you into saying yes when you really want to say no. By learning

Figure 17.14

In 2005, this photograph shocked the world. U.S. Army reservist Lynndie England faced a court-martial for assaulting prisoners in the 2003 Abu Ghraib Iraqi prisoner scandal. Her family said it couldn't be the same loving person that they knew. Army reservist Charles Graner, the presumed ringleader of the guards, claimed that they were following orders. The military jury rejected the claim. The mass media turned to the lessons of Milgram's research and the Stanford prison study to try to make sense of the guards' behavior.

to identify these techniques, you will be in a better position to resist them.

The powerful **norm of reciprocity** *involves the expectation that when others treat us well, we should respond in kind.* Thus, to get you to comply with a request, I can do something nice for you now—such as an unsolicited favor—in hopes that you will feel pressure to reciprocate later when I present you with my request (Cialdini, 2008).

Now consider the **door-in-the-face technique:** *a persuader makes a large request, expecting you to reject it* (you "slam the door" in the persuader's face), *and then presents a smaller request.* Telemarketers feast on this technique. Rather than ask you directly for a modest monetary donation to some organization, they first ask for a much larger contribution, knowing that you will say no. After you politely refuse, they ask for the smaller contribution. In one experiment, after people declined an initial request to donate $25 to a charity, they were more likely to donate $2 than were participants who were directly asked for $2 (Wang et al., 1989). To be effective, the same persuader must make both requests. The persuader "compromises" by making the second, smaller request, so we feel pressure to reciprocate by complying (Lecat et al., 2009). Refusing the first request also may produce guilt, and complying with the smaller request may help us reduce guilt or feel socially responsible (Tusing & Dillard, 2000).

Using the **foot-in-the-door technique,** *a persuader gets you to comply with a small request first* (getting the "foot in the door") *and later presents a larger request* (Eastwick & Gardner, 2009). Imagine receiving an e-mail from a stranger who asks for simple advice about a word processing program. It takes less than 1 minute to reply, and you do—as did all the participants in an actual experiment (Guéguen, 2002). After you comply, the person sends a second e-mail asking you to help with a class project by filling out a 20-minute online questionnaire. In the experiment, 76 percent of college students complied, compared to merely 44 percent in a control group that received only the class-project request.

With a final technique, **lowballing,** *a persuader gets you to commit to some action and then—before you actually perform the behavior—he or she increases the "cost" of that same behavior* (Cialdini, 2008). Imagine negotiating to buy a used car for $8,000, a "great price." The salesperson says, "I need to confirm this with my manager," comes back shortly, and states, "I'm afraid my manager says the price is too low. But you can have the car for only $400 more. It's still a great price." At this point, you are more likely to go through with the deal than you would have been, had the "real" $8,400 price been quoted at the outset.

Both lowballing and the foot-in-the-door technique involve moving from a smaller request to a larger, more costly one. With lowballing, however, the stakes for the *same behavior* are raised after you commit to it but *before* you consummate the behavior. Having made a commitment, you may find it easier to rationalize the added costs or may feel obligated to the person to whom you made the commitment.

By recognizing when compliance techniques are being used to manipulate your behavior, you are in a better position to resist them. For example, consider the norm of reciprocity. Robert Cialdini (2008), an expert on influence techniques, suggests that the key is not to resist the initial gift or favor; instead, accept the unsolicited "favor," but if the person then asks you for a favor in return, recognize this as a manipulative trick. Of course, you can still choose to comply if you believe it's the right thing to do. The goal is not to automatically reject every social influence attempt but to avoid feeling coerced into doing something you don't want to do.

Behavior in Groups

Much of human behavior occurs in groups. People often form groups to share interests and activities and to perform tasks and achieve goals that are too complex or demanding to be accomplished by one person.

Social Loafing

Social loafing *is the tendency for people to expend less individual effort when working in a group than when working alone.* Social loafing involves collective performance, that is, situations in which group members pool their efforts with one another. It can occur on physical tasks and on cognitive tasks, as when groups have to evaluate written materials or make decisions. Why does social loafing occur? Steven Karau and Kipling Williams (1993, 2001) propose a *collective effort model:* on a collective task, people will put forth only as much effort as they expect is needed to attain a valued goal. In support of this model, studies reveal that social loafing is *more* likely to occur when

- the person believes that individual performance within the group is not being monitored;
- the task (goal) or the group has less value or meaning to the person;
- the person generally displays low motivation to strive for success and expects that coworkers will display high effort (Hart et al., 2004).

Social loafing also depends on gender and culture. It occurs more strongly in all-male groups than in all-female or mixed-sex groups, possibly because women may be more concerned about group outcomes than are men. Participants from individualistic cultures (e.g., Canada and the United States) exhibit more social loafing than people from collectivistic cultures (e.g., China, Japan, Taiwan), in which group goals are especially valued.

Social loafing suggests that in terms of group performance, the whole is less than the sum of its parts. But this is not always the case. Social loafing may disappear when members highly value their group or the task goal. In fact, to achieve a highly desired goal, some people may engage in **social compensation,** *working harder in a group than when alone to compensate for other members' lower output* (Hart et al., 2001; Todd et al., 2006).

Moreover, when it's possible to monitor individuals' performance within the group, social loafing may be reduced by structuring rewards to simultaneously acknowledge team and individual performance. Group rewards keep each member focused on the importance of teamwork, and individual rewards keep each member focused on executing her or his particular subtasks (Pearsall et al., 2010).

Group Polarization

Key decisions are often entrusted to groups, such as committees, because groups are assumed to be more conservative than individuals and less likely to go off the deep end. Is this assumption correct? It is, as long as the group is generally conservative to begin with. In such cases, the group's final opinion or attitude will likely be even *more conservative.* But if the group members lean toward a liberal or risky viewpoint to begin with, the group's decision will tend to become *more liberal or riskier.* This principle is called **group polarization:** *when a group of like-minded people discuss an issue, the "average" opinion of group members tends to become more extreme* (Krizan & Baron, 2007).

Why does group polarization occur? One reason, reflecting normative social influence, is that individuals who are attracted to a group may be motivated to adopt a more extreme position to gain the group's approval. A second reason, reflecting informational social influence, is that during group discussions people hear arguments supporting their positions that they had not previously considered (Sia et al., 2002).

Groupthink

After the U.S. military ignored warning signs of imminent attack by Japan in 1941, the fleet at Pearl Harbor was destroyed in a "surprise" attack. In 1961, President Kennedy and his advisors launched the hopelessly doomed Bay of Pigs invasion of Cuba. After analyzing these and other historical accounts of disastrous group decisions, Irving Janis (1982) concluded that in each case the decision makers fell victim to a process that he named **groupthink,** *the tendency of group members to suspend critical thinking because they are striving to seek agreement.*

As Figure 17.15 shows, Janis proposed that groupthink is most likely to occur when a group

- is under *high stress* to reach a decision;
- is *insulated* from outside input;
- has a *directive leader* who promotes a personal agenda;
- has *high cohesiveness*, reflecting a spirit of closeness and ability to work well together.

Under these conditions, the group is so committed to reaching consensus and remaining loyal that members suspend their critical judgment. Particularly when facing a collective threat, the group's desire to maintain a positive view of itself may lead members to reach agreement without carefully weighing opposing views (Turner et al., 2007).

Antecedent conditions

1. High stress to reach a decision
2. Insulation of the group
3. Directive leadership
4. High cohesiveness

↓

Some symptoms of groupthink

1. Illusion of invulnerability
   (group overestimates itself)
2. Direct pressure on dissenters
3. Self-censorship
4. Illusion of unanimity
5. Self-appointed mind guards

↓

**Groupthink increases risk of
defective decision making**

1. Incomplete survey of alternatives
2. Incomplete survey of objectives
3. Failure to examine risks of
   preferred choice
4. Poor information search
5. Failure to reappraise alternatives

Figure 17.15

Groupthink.
This diagram illustrates the antecedents, symptoms, and negative effects of groupthink on decision making. SOURCE: Adapted from Janis, 1982.

to the fatal launch of the space shuttle *Challenger* in 1986 (Esser & Lindoerfer, 1989). The engineers who designed the rocket boosters opposed the launch, fearing that freezing weather would make the rocket's rubber seals too brittle to contain hot gasses. But NASA was under high stress, and leadership was directive. This mission was carrying America's first civilian into space, there had been several delays, and NASA didn't want another. To foster an illusion of unanimity, a key NASA executive excluded the engineers from the final decision-making process (Magnuson, 1986). Thanks to mind guarding, the NASA official who gave the final go-ahead never knew of the engineers' concerns.

In 2003, in the days leading up to the fiery disintegration of the space shuttle *Columbia* as it reentered earth's atmosphere, engineers, supervisors, and some NASA officials debated whether *Columbia*'s left wing had been damaged during launch (Figure 17.16). But as the Columbia Accident Investigation Board found, tragically, "dangerous aspects of NASA's 1986 culture . . . remained unchanged," such as a "need to produce consensus at each level" that filtered out dissenting information on safety risks (2003, p. 198).

Can groupthink be prevented? Janis suggested that it might, if the leader remains impartial during discussions, encourages critical thinking,

Various symptoms signal that groupthink is at work. Group members who express doubt get *direct pressure* to stop rocking the boat. Some members serve as *mind guards* and prevent negative information from reaching the group. Ultimately, members display *self-censorship* and withhold their doubts, creating an *illusion of unanimity* in which each member comes to believe that everyone else seems to agree with the decision. Overall, the group leader and members who favor the leader's position will have their confidence in the decision reinforced, whereas members who have doubts will feel pressure to go along with the group (Henningsen et al., 2006).

Groupthink principles have been applied to diverse situations. In the business world, groupthink can contribute to poor management decisions that adversely affect the financial value and public reputation of a company (Eaton, 2001). In crime investigations, groupthink may lead the investigative team to prematurely reach agreement on a particular interpretation of the case without adequately considering other alternatives (Kerstholt & Eikelboom, 2007).

Many aspects of groupthink were present during the decision-making process leading up

Figure 17.16

On February 1, 2003, the space shuttle *Columbia* disintegrated as it reentered earth's atmosphere, killing all of the crew members on board.

Figure 17.17

Deindividuation can lead to a loss of restraint that causes people to engage in uncharacteristic behaviors.

(1981) analyzed newspaper reports of incidents in which crowds were present when a person threatened to jump off a building, in 10 of 21 cases the crowd had encouraged the person to jump. Why would people in crowds act this way?

In crowds, people may experience **deindividuation,** *a loss of individuality that leads to disinhibited behavior* (Festinger et al., 1952; Zimbardo, 2004). But what is the primary aspect of deindividuation that disinhibits behavior? Tom Postmes and Russell Spears (1998) meta-analyzed 60 deindividuation studies and determined that *anonymity to outsiders* was the key. Conditions that make an individual feel less identifiable to people *outside* the group reduce feelings of accountability and, slightly but consistently, increase the risk of antisocial actions (Figure 17.17). Postmes and Spears suggest that being anonymous to outsiders enhances the individual's tendency to focus on her or his identity with the group and makes the person more responsive to emerging group norms.

During the Stanford prison study, no names were used and prisoners had to address guards as "Mr. Correctional Officer." All guards wore identical uniforms and reflecting sunglasses that prevented the prisoners from making direct eye contact. The guards were unaware that their behavior was being monitored by the experimenters, and antisocial norms evolved from the role of "tough prison guard" adopted by participants who spontaneously took over leadership roles (Zimbardo et al., 1973). These factors led Zimbardo to conclude that deindividuation was a key factor in the cruelty exhibited by the guards. Reducing anonymity—and thereby increasing public accountability—may be the most basic approach to counteracting deindividuation.

brings in outsiders to offer their opinions, and divides the larger group into subgroups—to see if each subgroup independently reaches the same decision. Requiring group members to critique each other's ideas—rather than criticize the person whose idea is being considered—may reduce groupthink by fostering more creative problem solving (Troyer & Youngreen, 2009).

Deindividuation

Years ago in New York City, a man sat perched on the ledge of an upper-story window for an hour while a crowd of nearly 500 people below shouted at him to jump. Fortunately, police rescued him. Yet New York is hardly alone. When Leon Mann

test yourself   Social Influence

Match each concept on the left to the best example on the right.

1. lowballing
2. normative social influence
3. door-in-the-face technique
4. foot-in-the-door technique
5. informational social influence

a. Craig conforms to a group to gain the members' approval.

b. To get Roberto to comply with a large request, Todd first makes a small request.

c. Nate asks his mom for $250, knowing she'll say no. After she refuses, he asks for $50.

d. Amy offers Helen a sweater for $25. After Helen agrees, Amy says, "On second thought, I just can't sell it for less than $30."

e. Jill conforms to a group's decision because she believes it to be correct.

ANSWERS: 1-d, 2-a, 3-c, 4-b, 5-e

SOCIAL RELATIONS

People like and love, and dislike and hate. They help one another and harm one another. As we now explore, social relations take many forms.

Attraction: Liking and Loving Others

Commenting on friendship and love, humorist Mason Cooley once quipped, "Friendship is love minus sex and plus reason. Love is friendship plus sex and minus reason" (Columbia, 1996). Alas, the difference between *liking* and *loving* may not be so simple, but attraction is indeed the first phase of most friendships and romantic relationships. What causes us to connect with some people but not others?

Initial Attraction: Proximity, Mere Exposure, and Similarity

People cannot develop a relationship unless they first meet, and proximity (nearness) is the best predictor of who will cross paths with whom. In today's increasingly wired world, friendships and romances sometimes develop after strangers make initial contact through Internet chat rooms or e-mail. Still, *physical proximity* matters. We tend to interact most with people who are physically closer. Residents in married-student apartments are most likely to form friendships with other residents who live close by, and students assigned specific classroom seats are most likely to become friends with students seated nearby (Back et al., 2008).

Proximity increases the chance of frequent encounters, and more than 200 experiments in different countries provide evidence of a **mere exposure effect:** *repeated exposure to a stimulus typically increases our liking for it.* No matter the stimuli—college classmates, photographs of faces, novel brand names, and so on—exposure generally enhances liking, and this occurs even when we are not consciously aware of those repeated exposures (Hansen & Wänke, 2009).

After two people meet, then what? When it comes to attraction, folk wisdom covers all the bases. On the one hand, "opposites attract." On the other hand, "birds of a feather flock together." So which is it? Cross-cultural evidence overwhelmingly supports the role of *similarity:* people most often are attracted to others who are similar to themselves. For psychological attributes, similarity of attitudes and values seems to matter the most (Buss, 1985).

In the laboratory, college students' degree of liking for a stranger can be predicted very accurately simply by knowing the proportion of similar attitudes that they share (Byrne, 1997). Outside the laboratory, researchers matched college students on a brief 30-minute date, pairing people with partners who had either highly similar or dissimilar attitudes (Byrne et al., 1970). Students were more attracted to similar partners and had a stronger desire to date them. One reason we like people with similar attitudes is that they validate our view of the world. Yet even trivial or chance similarities between people also boost attraction (J. Jones et al., 2004).

Like mismatched roommates Felix Unger (an uptight neatnik) and Oscar Madison (a carefree slob) in the classic movie *The Odd Couple,* do opposites ever attract? At times, of course. But more often, opposites repel. When choosing potential friends or mates, we typically screen out people who are dissimilar to us. And when dissimilar people do form relationships, they tend not to last as long. Often, when we initially find a dissimilar characteristic of another person appealing, we come to dislike it over time (Felmlee, 1998).

Spellbound by Beauty

It may be shallow and unfair, but most people seem drawn to beauty like moths to a flame. Indeed, throughout the animal kingdom, species have evolved distinct physical features to attract mates (Figure 17.18).

In many studies, when men and women rate the desirability of short-term dating partners, their judgments are influenced most strongly by how good-looking the person is. Consider the heterosexual college students who participated in a recent speed-dating study at a U.S. public university (Luo & Zhang, 2009). Prior to the actual

Figure 17.18

Hey good lookin'! Many species, such as these frigate birds (male on the left), have evolved distinct features and ritualized mating displays to attract a potential mate's attention.

speed-dating sessions, the researchers measured each student's interests, values, personality characteristics, and other personal factors. Eight research team members also rated each student's physical attractiveness based on a photograph of the student taken moments prior to their particular speed-dating session. During the sessions, each speed date lasted 5 minutes, and immediately afterward participants rated their desire to see that person again. The results: for men and women, their desire to date a partner they met depended far more strongly on the partner's physical attractiveness than on any other characteristic the researchers measured.

In other research, psychologists have measured people's physical attractiveness and personal characteristics and then randomly paired them on actual blind dates. In one classic study with university students, a partner's physical attractiveness was the only factor that predicted students' attraction (Walster et al., 1966). Women and men with physically attractive partners liked them more and had a stronger desire to date them again. Similarly, among 100 gay men whom researchers paired together for a date, men's liking for a partner and desire to date him again were most strongly influenced by the partner's physical attractiveness (Sergios & Cody, 1985–1986).

Facial Attractiveness: Is "Average" Beautiful?
Given beauty's power, what makes a face

physically attractive? Beauty may be in the eye of the beholder, but within and across cultures, people are seeing through similar eyes; their ratings of facial attractiveness agree strongly (Langlois et al., 2000).

Look at face 3 and face 5 in Figure 17.19. The first thing you need to know is that these people don't exist. These photos are composites, "averaged" male and female faces created digitally by blending 16 photographs of young men and 16 photographs of young women (Johnston et al., 2001). Using different sets of photographs, studies in North America, Europe, and Asia consistently find that people typically rate "averaged" male and female faces as more attractive than almost all of the individual faces used to create the composites (Langlois & Roggman, 1990). Moreover, people perceive individual faces as more attractive when those faces are digitally modified to look more like the "averaged" face (Rhodes et al., 2001). One reason that averaged faces seem more attractive is that they are more symmetrical, and people prefer facial symmetry (B. Jones et al., 2004). However, even when viewing faces from the side, where symmetry is not an issue, averaged faces are still rated as more attractive.

As Gestalt psychologists noted, in visual perception, the whole is more than the sum of its parts. As individual facial features—noses, eyes, lips, and so on—conform more to an "averaged"

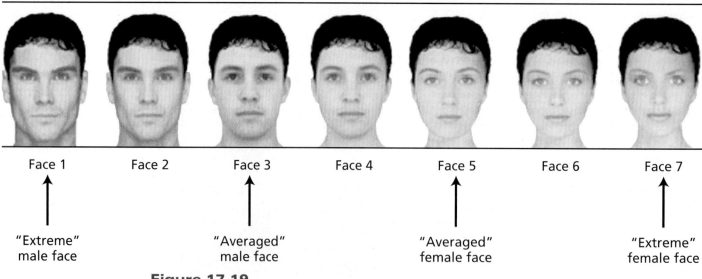

Face 1   Face 2   Face 3   Face 4   Face 5   Face 6   Face 7

"Extreme" male face   "Averaged" male face   "Averaged" female face   "Extreme" female face

Figure 17.19

Judging beauty.
Which male face do you find most attractive? Which female face? Face 3 and face 5 are "averaged" composite photographs digitally created by blending photos of 16 men and 16 women, respectively. These averaged composites were then digitally altered to accentuate either masculine or feminine features. Faces 1 and 7 are extremely masculinized and feminized, respectively; faces 2 and 6, moderately so. Face 4 blends the masculine and feminine features. In actual experiments, masculinization-feminization changes typically are done very gradually, creating many more choices than you see here. SOURCE: From Johnston et al., 2001, Figure 1. Adapted with permission.

norm, we perceive the "whole face" as more attractive. But keep in mind that some individual faces, which deviate from their composite, are rated the most attractive of all. Moreover, as Figure 17.19 shows, some researchers have taken composite faces and digitally altered them to appear progressively more masculine (e.g., larger jaw and brow ridges) or more feminine (e.g., fuller lips, a narrower jaw). Consistently, people perceive moderately feminized composite faces as the most attractive (Johnston et al., 2001; Perret et al., 1998). In contrast, depending on the study, male faces that have been somewhat masculinized or feminized are rated as the most attractive.

Affiliating with Beautiful People   What motivates the desire to affiliate with attractive people? One factor may be the widespread stereotype that "what is beautiful is good"; we often assume that attractive people have more positive personality characteristics than unattractive people. The popular media reinforce this stereotype. Analyzing 5 decades of top-grossing U.S. movies, Stephen Smith and coworkers (1999) found that good-looking male and female characters were portrayed as more intelligent, moral, and sociable than less attractive characters. Because we are often judged by the company we keep, we also may prefer to associate with attractive people to buttress our self-esteem (Richardson, 1991). Evolutionary psychologists propose that we are biologically predisposed to be drawn to attractive people. They point to research showing that newborns prefer to look at attractive faces and that 6-month-olds can categorize faces as attractive or unattractive (Ramsey et al., 2004).

Although we are attracted to "beautiful people," romantic relationships typically reveal a **matching effect:** *we are most likely to have a partner whose level of physical attractiveness is similar to our own* (Takeuchi, 2006). In this case, "birds of equally attractive feathers flock together." One reason for this is that the most attractive people may match up first and are "taken," then the next most attractive people match up, and so on. Another factor is that people may refrain from approaching potential dating partners who are more attractive than they are to lessen the risk of rejection.

As Attraction Deepens: Close Relationships

Budding relationships grow closer as people share more diverse and meaningful experiences (Altman & Taylor, 1973). *Self-disclosure*—the sharing of innermost thoughts and feelings—plays a key role (Dindia, 2002). In friendships, dating relationships, and marriages, more extensive and intimate self-disclosure is associated with greater emotional involvement and relationship satisfaction. This relation is reciprocal. Self-disclosure fosters intimacy and trust, and intimacy and trust encourage self-disclosure.

Social exchange theory *proposes that the course of a relationship is governed by rewards and costs that the partners experience* (Thibaut & Kelley, 1959). Rewards include companionship, emotional support, and the satisfaction of other needs (van de Rijt & Macy, 2006). Costs may include the effort spent to maintain the relationship, arguments, conflicting goals, and so forth. The overall *outcome* (rewards minus costs) in a relationship can be positive or negative.

Outcomes are evaluated against two standards (Figure 17.20). The first, called the *comparison level*, is the outcome that a person has grown to expect in relationships, and it influences the person's *satisfaction* with the present relationship. Outcomes that meet or exceed the comparison level are satisfying; those that fall below this standard are dissatisfying. The second standard, called the *comparison level for alternatives*, focuses on potential alternatives to the relationship, and it influences the person's degree of *commitment*. Even when a relationship is satisfying, partners may feel low commitment if they perceive that something better is available. In turn, the partners' sense of commitment helps predict whether they will remain together or end their relationship in the future (Sprecher, 2001).

Sociocultural and Evolutionary Views

According to social exchange theory, a partner's desirable characteristics can be viewed as rewards, whereas undesirable characteristics

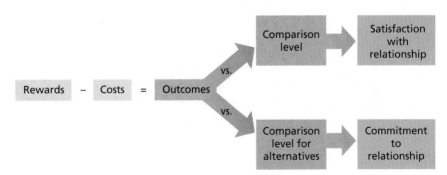

Figure 17.20

Social relationships: Are you satisfied and committed?

According to Thibaut and Kelley's (1959) social exchange theory, rewards minus costs equal the outcome of a relationship. Comparing our outcomes with two standards, the comparison level and the comparison level for alternatives, determines our satisfaction and commitment to the relationship, respectively.

represent costs. But what specific characteristics do people desire in a partner? In a massive study involving 10,000 men and women from 37 cultures around the world, evolutionary psychologist David Buss and coworkers asked people to identify the qualities they sought in an ideal long-term mate (Buss, 1989; Buss et al., 1990). Overall, for both sexes, mutual attraction/love, dependable character, emotional stability, and a pleasing disposition emerged (in that order) as the most highly rated of the 18 characteristics evaluated.

The importance attached to many qualities, however, varied considerably across cultures. For example, whereas American men and women viewed refinement/neatness as having only modest importance, Iranian men and women viewed it as the most important quality they desired in a mate. In many cultures, a mate's chastity (no previous experience in sexual intercourse) was viewed as last or near-last in importance, but in China and India, men and women viewed chastity as an important quality in a mate.

There also are remarkably consistent sex differences in mate preferences across cultures. Men tend to place greater value on a potential mate's physical attractiveness and domestic skills, whereas women place greater value on a potential mate's earning potential, status, and ambitiousness. Men tend to desire a mate who is a few years younger, whereas young and middle-aged women tend to desire a mate who is a few years older (Alterovitz & Mendelsohn, 2009). Men also are more likely to desire and pursue a greater number of short-term romantic encounters than are women (Schmitt et al., 2001).

As we discussed in detail in Chapter 3, some evolutionary psychologists argue that these sex differences reflect inherited predispositions, shaped by natural selection in response to different adaptive problems that men and women have faced over the ages (Gangestad et al., 2006). According to the *sexual strategies theory,* ancestral men who were predisposed to have sex with more partners increased the likelihood of fathering more children and passing on their genes. Such men may have perceived a woman's youth and attractive appearance as signs that she was fertile and had many years left to bear children (Buss, 1989). Ancestral women, however, maximized their reproductive success by selecting a mate who was willing and able to commit time, energy, and other resources (e.g., food, shelter, protection) to the family (Buss, 1989).

Do men and women have different biological wiring when it comes to romantic attraction and relationships? *Social structure theory* proposes that most of these sex differences in mating strategies and preferences occur because society directs men into more advantaged social and economic roles (Eagly & Wood, 1999, 2006). As this theory predicts, in cultures with more gender equality, many of the sex differences in mate preferences shrink. Women place less emphasis, for example, on a mate's earning power and status, and men and women seek mates more similar in age. Men's tendency to place more emphasis on a mate's physical attractiveness, however, does not decrease in such cultures. But it is still a leap, say critics, to conclude that sex differences in mating preferences reflect a hereditary predisposition rather than some other aspect of gender socialization that may be consistent across cultures.

This issue is far from settled, but perhaps the most important point for you to realize is that the notion that men and women come from "different planets" when it comes to attraction, romance, and close relationships is more pop psychology than reliable science (Hazan & Diamond, 2000). Sex differences exist, but cross-cultural differences tend to be stronger. That is, men and women within the same culture are typically more similar to one another than are men from different cultures or women from different cultures (Buss et al., 1990).

Love

Love must be powerful, for as a common adage says, "it makes the world go round." Indeed, Buss and coworkers (1990) found that mutual attraction/love was highly valued in a mate across cultures. But what is love?

When it comes to romantic relationships, many psychologists identify two basic types of love: *passionate* and *companionate* (Hatfield, 1988). **Passionate love** *involves intense emotion, arousal, and yearning for the partner.* We may ride an emotional roller coaster that ranges from ecstasy when the partner is present to heartsickness when the person is absent. **Companionate love** *involves affection and deep caring about the partner's well-being.* At least when studied in Westernized countries, both types of love contribute to satisfaction in long-term romantic relationships (Sprecher & Regan, 1998). In general, passionate love is less stable and declines more quickly over time than companionate love, but this does not mean that the flames of passionate love inevitably extinguish.

However, psychologist Robert Sternberg (1988, 2006a) views love as more complex. His theory, best known as the **triangular theory of love,** *proposes that love involves three major components: passion, intimacy, and commitment. Passion* refers to feelings of physical attraction and sexual desire; *intimacy* involves closeness, sharing, and valuing one's partner; and *commitment* represents a decision to remain in the relationship. Taken one at a time, each component is associated with greater satisfaction and happiness among the partners in a relationship (Sternberg, 2006a), but it is the combination of components that defines various types of love.

Figure 17.21 shows that different combinations characterize seven types of love (plus *nonlove*, which is the absence of all three). Sternberg proposes that the ultimate form of love between people—*consummate love*—occurs when intimacy, passion, and commitment are all present. Clearly, for close relationships to develop and endure, they need more than passion alone. Intimacy and commitment provide a basis for the friendship and trust that sustain and increase love. As our "Applying Psychological Science" feature highlights, other behaviors also help make close relationships successful.

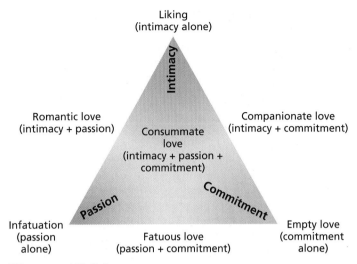

Figure 17.21

The complexity of love.

According to Sternberg, different types of love involve varying combinations of intimacy, commitment, and passion. Consummate love involves the presence of all three factors, whereas nonlove represents the absence of all three.

Applying Psychological Science

Making Close Relationships Work: Lessons from Psychological Research

Close relationships go through good times and bad, persisting or dissolving over time. Consider marriage. Although highly intimate, this union is often fragile, and many marriages end in divorce. How can people make their close relationships more satisfying and stable? Research on marriage suggests several answers that also can be applied to dating relationships and friendships.

For decades, most marital research simply asked people about their marriages. But as Figure 17.22 shows, researchers are now bringing couples into laboratories to videotape their interactions and chart their facial reactions, stress hormones, and other physiological responses as they discuss emotionally charged issues (Robles et al., 2006). Rather than focusing only on unhappy couples to find out what is going wrong in their relationships, researchers also are studying happy couples to discover the secrets of their success.

Using these methods, psychologists have predicted with impressive accuracy whether marriages will last or dissolve. In one

Rolled eyes

Dimpled cheeks

Contempt: If prolonged, this expression is a red alert. Especially when accompanied by sarcasm and insults, it suggests a marriage in serious trouble.

Figure 17.22

The "love lab."

In Gottman's "love lab," married couples (husband shown in rear) are filmed while interacting. Researchers record facial expressions, physiological arousal, fidgeting, and other responses.

Continued

laboratory study, John Gottman and coworkers (1998) collected behavioral and physiological data from 130 newlywed couples as they discussed areas of marital conflict (e.g., in-laws, finances, sex) during the first 6 months of their marriages. Six years later, participants reported whether they were happily married, unhappily married, or divorced. Using data collected while the couples were newlyweds, the researchers predicted marital happiness/unhappiness and divorce with 80 percent accuracy.

Surprisingly, the amount of anger expressed by husbands and wives in their laboratory interactions was not the predictor. Instead, the crucial factor was the manner in which couples dealt with their anger. Four behaviors were particularly important: *criticism, contempt, defensiveness,* and *stonewalling* (listener withdrawal and nonresponsiveness).

Couples headed for unhappiness or divorce often exhibit these behaviors while discussing conflict, thereby escalating their conflict and negative emotions. When the wife criticizes the husband, he often responds defensively or stonewalls and withdraws from her attempts to reach some resolution. Her resulting frustration leads to stronger emotional displays and criticism, and the interaction degenerates into exchanges of contempt in which the partners tear each other down. Once this negative cycle develops, even positive overtures by one spouse are likely to evoke a negative response from the other.

Happily married couples also experience conflict and anger but keep the spiral of negativity from getting out of control. Instead, they make frequent "repair attempts" to resolve their differences in a spirit of mutual respect and support. In happy marriages, the wife often introduces the conflict topic gently, rather than with criticism and strong emotion. Next a key factor occurs: the husband responds to the wife's issues with concern and respect, which de-escalates negative emotion. A husband who turns off the TV and listens to his wife or who says, "I can see you're upset, so let's work this out," demonstrates that her concerns are important to him. In happy marriages, after the husbands' responsiveness de-escalates the conflict, couples soothe one another with positive comments and humor, resulting in more emotionally positive interchanges and lowered physiological arousal.

Happily married couples maintain a much higher ratio of positive to negative interactions than couples headed for divorce, and this history provides a positive "emotional bank account" that helps them repair and recover from their immediate anger and conflict (Wilson & Gottman, 2002). They also strive to get to know each other deeply—their fears, dreams, attitudes, and values—and they continually update their knowledge. This allows each partner to be more responsive to the other's needs and to navigate around relationship roadblocks (Gottman et al., 2006). Such behavior contributes to an essential aspect of happy marriages: an intimate friendship between the partners. The lessons of happy marriages can be applied to other types of close relationships.

Ostracism: Rejection Hurts

We've been focusing on close relationships, but obviously, many relationships never get off the ground. All of us risk rejection when we try to initiate a new friendship or romantic relationship, join an established group (e.g., a social club), or simply participate with people in some temporary activity. Even after initial acceptance, social tides may change and people may reject or ignore us out of newfound disinterest, dislike, or anger.

Research on *ostracism* (ignoring or excluding someone) suggests that there is more truth to the phrase "rejection hurts" than you might think. Psychologist Naomi Eisenberger and coworkers (2003) measured the brain activity of research participants who played an interactive computer game with, presumably, two other unseen players. In reality, there were no other players and the game was computer-controlled. The game, *Cyberball*, involved tossing a virtual ball back and forth among the three players. After a period during which all three players interacted online, the other two players suddenly ignored the participant by tossing the ball back and forth only to each other. The real participants felt excluded and distressed, and neural activity patterns in their cerebral cortex were "very similar to those found in studies of physical pain . . . providing evidence that the experience . . . of social and physical pain share a common neuroanatomical basis" (p. 291).

Ostracism, whether it occurs while playing online video games, participating in online chat rooms, or participating in face-to-face interactions, exerts a psychological cost (van Beest & Williams, 2006). In experiments, being ignored and excluded dampens people's moods, decreases their sense of belonging, and—perhaps by heightening their fear of further rejection—makes them more likely to conform to the clearly incorrect judgments of a group. Especially when it occurs face-to-face, social exclusion reduces people's self-esteem and feelings of control.

If ostracism can produce these effects in the laboratory, then it's no wonder that it is used so frequently and powerfully to influence people in everyday life. One common example: the infamous silent treatment. According to one survey, two-thirds of Americans say that they have even used the silent treatment on someone they love (Faulkner et al., as cited in Williams et al., 2000). And keeping in mind that most people, when ostracized, don't retaliate physically, it's worth noting that social rejection has repeatedly cropped up as a potential contributing factor in cases of extreme school violence. Mark Leary and coworkers (2003) examined 15 highly publicized cases (e.g., Littleton, Colorado; Jonesboro, Arkansas) in which students had shot other students during school hours. In all but two cases, the shooters had experienced either prolonged social rejection (e.g., ostracism, teasing) or more immediate romantic rejection. Combined with other factors, such as existing psychological problems (e.g., depression, sadistic tendencies), painful social rejection may have created a deadly mix.

Prejudice: Bias against Others

Walk into a party, classroom, job interview—any social situation—and just by looking at your body build and facial attractiveness, people will start to form an impression of you (Crandall et al., 2001). Children and adults tend to form less favorable impressions of people who are less attractive. They expect them to have less desirable personality traits and to achieve less success and happiness in life, even though these factors actually are unrelated or only weakly related to attractiveness and other facial features (Zebrowitz et al., 1996).

Perhaps above all characteristics, ethnicity and gender matter the most in impression formation. They are likely to be the first characteristics someone notices about you and, like so many other personal qualities, can be the basis for prejudice and discrimination (van Laar & Levin, 2006). **Prejudice** *refers to a negative attitude toward people based on their membership in a group.* Thus we *prejudge* people—dislike them or hold negative beliefs about them—simply because they are female or male, belong to one ethnic group or religion rather than to another, are gay or straight, and so on. **Discrimination** *refers to overt behavior that involves treating people unfairly based on the group to which they belong.*

Explicit and Implicit Prejudice

Even in this day and age, examples of overt prejudice and discrimination are abundant. Armed conflicts based on ethnic or religious divisions continue across the globe; hate crimes persist; and people's race, gender, religion, and sexual orientation spark unfair treatment (Herek, 2000). In some ways, however, the most blatant forms of prejudice and discrimination have decreased in many countries. Racial segregation is no longer sanctioned by government policy in the United States or South Africa, and opinion polls indicate that fewer people express prejudiced attitudes toward other ethnic groups than was the case decades ago.

Although prejudiced attitudes may have faded a bit, in many ways modern racism, sexism, and other forms of prejudice have gone underground and are more difficult to detect. In contrast to **explicit prejudice**, *which people express publicly,* **implicit prejudice** *is hidden from public view.* Many people intentionally hide their prejudices, expressing them only when they feel it is safe or socially appropriate. In other cases, people may honestly believe that they are not prejudiced but still show unconscious biases when tested in sophisticated ways (Fazio et al., 1995).

We can use questionnaires to measure explicit prejudice, but how can we measure implicit prejudice? Some researchers have found that subtle movements of facial muscles involved in smiling (and in some studies, in frowning) can be used to predict people's biases toward members of another ethnic group (Vanman et al., 2004). But most often, measures of implicit prejudice assess people's reaction times at special cognitive tasks (Greenwald et al., 1998; Olson & Fazio, 2003).

To give you a general idea of how an implicit prejudice test might work (they're actually more complicated than this), suppose that a series of word pairs, such as "black-pleasant" and "white-pleasant" are flashed on a computer screen. As soon as you see each pair, your task is to press a computer key as quickly as you can, and this represents your reaction time. The principle underlying this task is that people react more quickly when they perceive that the concepts (i.e., the two words in each pair) "fit" together than when the concepts don't. Thus, *without conscious control,* a person prejudiced against Blacks will react more slowly to the "black-pleasant" pair than to the "white-pleasant" pair. Again, this example is simplified. The actual tests measure how quickly people make judgments about concepts and groups.

Psychologists have found that implicit measures, such as the *Implicit Association Test (IAT)*, can reveal many types of unconscious prejudice (Greenwald et al., 2006). These tests also can predict other types of biased responses that explicit measures—which can be easily distorted by people unaware of or trying to hide their prejudice—fail to predict. For example, Kurt Hugenberg and Galen Bodenhausen (2003) used the IAT to measure White college students' implicit prejudice toward Blacks; they also used a self-report rating scale to measure explicit prejudice. Finally, they showed the students short, computer-generated movie clips that portrayed the faces of either White or Black males making a range of angry, ambiguous, and happy expressions. Compared to students who had lower implicit prejudice, those who had higher implicit prejudice were more likely to perceive the ambiguous facial expressions of Black males as expressing anger. In contrast, students' reactions to the facial expressions were not related to their explicit prejudice scores.

Cognitive Roots of Prejudice

Whether overt or subtle, prejudice and discrimination are caused by a constellation of factors. These include historical and cultural norms that legitimize differential treatment of various groups and socialization processes through which parents and other adults transmit values and beliefs to children. Let's examine several cognitive and motivational causes of prejudice.

Categorization and "Us-Them" Thinking   To organize and simplify our world, we have a tendency to categorize people and objects. At times, this helps us predict other people's behavior and react quickly to environmental stimuli (Ito & Cacioppo, 2000). But our tendency to categorize people also helps lay a foundation for prejudice.

Categorization leads to the perception of in-groups and out-groups, groups to which we do and do not belong, respectively. In turn, in-group versus out-group distinctions spawn several common biases. *In-group favoritism* represents the tendency to favor in-group members and attribute more positive qualities to "us" than to "them," whereas *out-group derogation* reflects a tendency to attribute more negative qualities to "them" than to "us." Although people may display both biases, especially when they feel threatened, in-group favoritism is usually the stronger of the two (Hewstone et al., 2002).

People also display an *out-group homogeneity bias*. They generally view members of out-groups as being more similar to one another than are members of in-groups (Brauer, 2001). In other words, we perceive that "they are all alike" but recognize that "we are diverse." The mere fact that we identify people as "Asian," "Hispanic," "Black," and "White" reflects such a bias, because each of these ethnic categories contains many subgroups. In one study, Anglo-American college students were less likely to distinguish among "Hispanic" subgroups than were Cuban American, Mexican American, and Puerto Rican American college students (Huddy & Virtanen, 1995). But just like the Anglo-American students, the Cuban American, Mexican American, and Puerto Rican American students also engaged in us-them thinking: they saw their own subgroup as distinct from the others but did not differentiate between the other two Hispanic subgroups.

Stereotypes and Attributional Distortions   Categorization and in-group biases enhance the tendency to judge other people based on their perceived group membership rather than their individual characteristics. Whether at a conscious or unconscious level, category labels pertaining to people's race, gender, and other attributes seem to activate stereotypes about them (Wheeler & Fiske, 2005). Figure 17.23 illustrates two ways in which racial categorization and gender categorization activate stereotypes and affect our perceptions.

What happens when we encounter individual members of out-groups whose behavior clearly contradicts our stereotypes? One possibility is that we may change our stereotype; but if we are motivated to hold on to our prejudiced belief, we may explain away discrepant behavior in several ways. For example, the out-group member may be seen as an exceptional case or as having succeeded at a task not because of high ability but because of good luck, special advantage, or some other situational factor (Stewart et al., 2010).

Motivational Roots of Prejudice

People's ingrained ways of perceiving the world—categorizing, forming in-groups and out-groups, and so forth—prepare the wheels of prejudice to go into motion, but motivational factors affect how fast those wheels spin. For example, prejudice and stereotyping increase when social motives squarely focus our attention on the fact that people belong to in-groups or out-groups (Wheeler & Fiske, 2005).

Competition and Conflict   According to **realistic conflict theory,** *competition for limited resources fosters prejudice.* In the United States and Europe, hostility toward minority groups increases when economic conditions worsen (Pettigrew & Meertens, 1995). Originally, it was believed that a threat to one's personal welfare (as in the fear of losing one's job to a minority worker) was the prime motivator of prejudice, but research suggests that prejudice is triggered more strongly by a *perceived threat to one's in-group*. Among Whites, prejudice against Blacks is not related to personal resource gains and losses but to the belief that White people as a group are in danger of being "overtaken" (Bobo, 1988). Indeed, even when people are angry and know that an out-group did not cause that anger, their implicit prejudice still increases toward the out-group. David DeSteno and coworkers (2004) suggest that the emotion of anger is so closely linked to conflict

(a)

(b)

Figure 17.23

Classic experiments on prejudice.

(a) Who is holding the razor knife? Allport and Postman (1947) showed this picture to one person, who then described it while looking at it. A second person listened to this description and was asked to repeat it "as exactly as possible" to another person, who repeated this description to another person, and so on (up to six or seven tellings). In more than half of the trials following this procedure, at some point the Black man was erroneously described as holding the knife. (b) Which person contributes most strongly to this research team? When the drawing showed an all-male group, an all-female group, or a mixed-gender group with a man at the head of the table (seat 3), participants said that the person in seat 3 was the strongest member. But in this mixed-gender drawing with a woman in seat 3, most male and female participants picked one of the two men. Source: (a) Allport & Postman, 1947; (b) based on Porter & Geis, 1981.

and competition between groups that it automatically activates feelings of prejudice toward out-groups.

Enhancing Self-Esteem   According to **social identity theory,** *prejudice stems from a need to enhance our self-esteem.* Some experiments find that people express more prejudice after their self-esteem is threatened (e.g., receiving negative feedback about their abilities) and that the opportunity to derogate others helps restore self-esteem (Fein & Spencer, 1997). Self-esteem, however, is based on two components: a personal identity and a group identity (Tajfel & Turner, 1986). We can raise self-esteem not only by acknowledging our own virtues but also by associating ourselves with our in-group's accomplishments. Conversely, threats to our in-group threaten our self-esteem and may prompt us to derogate the out-group that constitutes the threat (Perdue et al., 1990).

How Prejudice Confirms Itself

Self-fulfilling prophecies are one of the most invisible yet damaging ways of maintaining prejudiced beliefs. An experiment by Carl Word and

his colleagues (1974) illustrates this point. The researchers began with the premise—supported by research at the time—that Whites held several negative stereotypes of Blacks. In the experiment, White male college students interviewed White and Black high school students who were seeking admission into a special group. The college students used a fixed set of interview questions provided by the experimenter, and unknown to them, each applicant was an accomplice who had been trained to respond in a standard way to the questions. The findings indicated that these White participants sat farther away, conducted shorter interviews, and made more speech errors when the applicants were Black. In short, their behavior was discriminatory.

But this is only half the picture. In a second experiment—a job interview simulation—White male undergraduates served as *job applicants.* Through random assignment, they were treated either as the White applicants had been treated in the first experiment or as the Black applicants had been treated. Thus, for half the participants, the interviewer sat farther away, held a shorter interview, and made more speech errors. The findings revealed that White participants who were treated more negatively performed worse during the job interview, were less composed, made more speech errors, and rated the interviewer as less friendly. In short, these experiments suggest that an interviewer's negative stereotypes can lead to discriminatory treatment during a job interview, and this discriminatory behavior can cause the applicant to perform more poorly—ultimately confirming the interviewer's initial stereotype.

Stanford psychologist Claude Steele (Nussbaum & Steele, 2007) has demonstrated another debilitating way that prejudice ends up confirming itself. As described in Chapter 10, his concept of **stereotype threat** *proposes that stereotypes create self-consciousness among stereotyped group members and a fear that they will live up to other people's stereotypes.* For example, in a study comparing female and male college students who major in various fields, women majoring in the traditionally "male" fields of math, science, and engineering reported the highest level of stereotype threat (Steele et al., 2002). They were more likely to feel that they (as well as other women in their major) had been targets of sex discrimination and that because of their gender, other people (including their professors) expected them to have less ability and do more poorly.

Stereotype threat can occur even if group members do not accept the stereotype themselves, and experiments reveal its debilitating consequences. Given the stereotype that "Blacks are not as intelligent as Whites," Black college students who take a difficult verbal ability test perform more poorly when it is described as an "intelligence test" than when it is described merely as a "laboratory task." In contrast, the intelligence-test description does not decrease White students' performance. Similar results were found for other stereotypes relating to mathematical ability, namely, "Whites are inferior to Asians," "Latinos are inferior to Whites," and "women are inferior to men." When a difficult standardized math test is given in situations that activate these stereotypes, Whites, Latinos, and women perform more poorly than when the test is presented in a more neutral way (Aronson et al., 1999; Gonzales et al., 2002).

Reducing Prejudice

Psychologists do more than just study the causes of prejudice; they also develop and examine ways to reduce prejudice and its harmful effects. For example, stereotype threat's negative effects on women's math performance can

be reduced by allowing them to take math tests without men present and by exposing them to female role models who succeed at such tasks (McIntyre et al., 2003). Similarly, among Black schoolchildren, presenting math tests as "challenges" and "learning opportunities" rather than as "tests of math ability" has eliminated the negative performance effects of stereotype threat (Alter et al., 2010). Might a direct educational approach also work?

An Educational Approach to Reducing Stereotype Threat Michael Johns and his coworkers (2005) asked male and female college students to take a difficult math test. To minimize stereotype threat, one group of randomly assigned students was told that the test was merely an exercise in problem solving. To maximize stereotype threat, a second group and a third group were told that the test assessed mathematical aptitude and that women's and men's scores would be compared. The third group, however, also received educational information about stereotype threat, and the women in this group were told that if they felt anxious during the test, stereotype threat might be the cause.

Would teaching women about stereotype threat make them even more anxious and further impair their math performance, or would it improve their performance by letting them know what to expect and allowing them to make an external attribution (i.e., to the societal stereotype) for their anxiety? As Figure 17.24 shows, compared to the "math test" condition, the teaching intervention boosted women's performance.

Promoting Equal Status Contact to Reduce Prejudice What about reducing people's prejudice toward one another? The best-known approaches to prejudice reduction are based on a principle called **equal status contact:** *prejudice between people is most likely to be reduced when they (1) engage in sustained close contact, (2) have equal status, (3) work to achieve a common goal that requires cooperation, and (4) are supported by broader social norms* (Allport, 1954; Figure 17.25).

In 1954, the United States Supreme Court handed down a momentous decision in the case of *Brown v. Board of Education,* ruling that school segregation based solely on race violates the constitutional rights of racial minorities. Providing key testimony, several psychologists stated that segregation contributed to racial prejudice and hostility. Unfortunately, decades later, when Walter Stephan (1990) reviewed more than 80

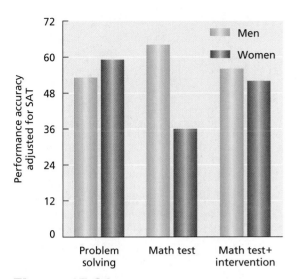

Figure 17.24

Reducing stereotype threat.

This graph shows the results of Johns and coworkers' (2005) study of stereotype threat. In the "math test + intervention" condition, women were told that the task was a math test, but they also were given educational information about stereotype threat. Thus armed, they ended up performing significantly better than the women who were told only that the task was a math test. Moreover, their performance was not significantly poorer than that of the women who were told that the task was merely a problem-solving exercise.

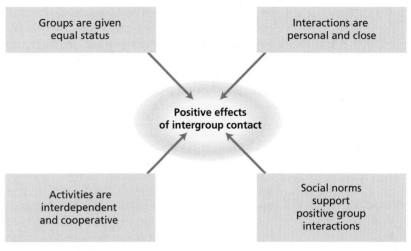

Figure 17.25

Reducing prejudice: equal status contact.

Prejudice between two people or groups is most likely to decrease when contact between them occurs under these four conditions.

evaluation studies of desegregation programs, he concluded that desegregation did not consistently reduce racial prejudice.

Why weren't the results more positive? First, the condition of equal-status contact was often not met, and contact when status is unequal serves only to perpetuate both groups' negative stereotypes of one another. Second, in many integrated school situations, close and personal contact between group members did not occur. Black and White students were sometimes placed in different learning tracks that minimized in-class contact, and they tended to associate only with members of their own ethnic group outside of class. Third, classroom experiences focused on individual rather than cooperative learning. And finally, intergroup contact was often not supported by broader social norms; in the early years of desegregation, many White politicians, parents, teachers, and school officials militantly opposed school integration.

When intergroup contact takes place under proper conditions, however, prejudice often decreases (Krahé & Altwasser, 2006). In school settings, *cooperative learning programs* place children into multiracial learning groups. Contact is close and sustained, each child is accorded equal status, and each has responsibility for learning and then teaching other group members one piece of

the information that is needed for the group to succeed in its assignment (Aronson & Patnoe, 1997). The children also can forge a common group identity, much as athletes on a team or members of a military unit form a group identity. Overall, such programs reduce prejudice and promote appreciation of ethnic group differences (McKown, 2005).

Using Simulations to Reduce "Shooter Bias"
Finally, let's examine another type of racial bias. In several highly publicized cases during the past decade, police officers investigating a crime have shot and killed unarmed Black men. The officers, faced with a split-second decision about whether to shoot, mistakenly perceived that these men were either reaching for or holding a weapon. Was the victims' race a factor in these shootings? Social psychologists devised experiments in which college students and other adults quickly had to decide whether to shoot armed and unarmed White and Black suspects who appeared on a computer screen during a video simulation. The results revealed a "shooter bias" in which participants—both White and Black participants in some studies—were more likely to shoot unarmed suspects who were Black (Correll et al., 2002).

Subsequently, in separate computer simulation experiments with college students and police officers, E. Ashby Plant and coworkers have been able to reduce this shooter bias (Plant & Peruche, 2005; Plant et al., 2005). The shooting simulation program, like those used in other experiments, was designed so that White and Black criminal suspects were equally likely to be armed or unarmed. Over time, with repeated exposure to the simulation program, the shooter bias that students and police officers displayed on the earlier trials disappeared. As the researchers note, these findings are only a promising first step that await further testing in more rigorous police academy training programs.

Prosocial Behavior: Helping Others

Helping, or *prosocial behavior*, comes in many forms, from performing heroic acts of bravery to tutoring a classmate. Acts of violence often dominate the headlines, but we should not lose sight of the mountains of good deeds performed around the world each day.

Why Do People Help?

Biological, psychological, and environmental factors all play a role in motivating prosocial behavior (Dovidio et al., 2006). Let's examine a few of these factors.

Evolution and Prosocial Behavior Prosocial behavior occurs throughout the animal kingdom. Evolutionary psychologists and sociobiologists (biologists who study species' social behavior) propose that helping has a genetic basis, shaped by evolution (Hamilton, 1964). According to the principle of **kin selection**, *organisms are most likely to help others with whom they share the most genes, namely, their offspring and genetic relatives* (Figure 17.26). By protecting their kin, prosocial individuals increase the odds that their genes will survive across successive generations, and the gene pool of the species increasingly represents the genes of its prosocial members (West et al., 2002). In this manner, over the course of evolution, helping became a biologically predisposed response to certain situations. Sociobiologists note that identical twins are more similar in the trait of helpfulness than are fraternal twins or nontwin siblings (Rushton, 1989).

But what accounts for the abundant helping that humans display toward friends and strangers, and that some animal species display toward non-kin (Clutton-Brock, 2002)? Sociobiologists propose the concept of *reciprocal altruism:* helping others increases the odds that they will help us or our kin in return, thereby enhancing the survival of our genes (Trivers, 1971).

Critics question sociobiologists' generalizations from nonhumans to humans, and in some cases kin selection and reciprocal altruism do not adequately explain why people or animals

Figure 17.26

Spotting a predator, this female ground squirrel may sound an alarm call that warns other squirrels. Is the call truly a prosocial act, much like a human yelling "Look out!"? Perhaps it simply indicates the squirrel's own sense of alarm, much as we might scream out of fear for our own safety. But if this is the case, why is she more likely to sound this call when her own kin—rather than other squirrels—are nearby?

cooperate (Clutton-Brock, 2002). Sociobiologists counter that genetic factors only predispose us to act in certain ways. Experience also shapes helping behavior.

Social Learning and Cultural Influences Beginning in childhood, we are exposed to helpful models and taught prosocial norms. The *norm of reciprocity* states that we should reciprocate when others treat us kindly, and the *norm of social responsibility* states that people should help others and contribute to the welfare of society (De Cremer & van Lange, 2001). We receive approval for adhering to these norms, receive disapproval for violating them, and observe other people receiving praise for following these norms. Eventually, we internalize prosocial norms and values as our own.

Studies in Europe, Asia, and North America confirm that socialization matters (Eisenberg, 2004). Children are more likely to act prosocially when they have been raised by parents who have high moral standards, who are warm and supportive, and who encourage their children to develop empathy and "put themselves in other people's shoes" (Krevans & Gibbs, 1996). However, there also are cross-cultural differences in beliefs about when and why we should help. For example, Joan Miller and coworkers (1990) found that Hindu children and adults in India believe that one has a moral obligation to help friends and strangers, whether their need is serious or mild. In contrast, when a person's need for assistance is mild, American children and adults view helping as more of a choice than an obligation.

Empathy and Altruism   C. Daniel Batson (2006) proposes that prosocial behavior can be motivated by altruistic as well as egoistic goals. *Altruism* refers to unselfishness, or helping another for the ultimate purpose of enhancing that person's welfare. In contrast, *egoistic goals* involve helping others to improve our own welfare, such as to increase our self-esteem, avoid feeling guilty for not helping, obtain praise, or alleviate the distress we feel when seeing someone suffer. Do humans truly have a capacity to help others without any concern for themselves? Batson believes that true altruism exists, and according to his **empathy-altruism hypothesis,** *altruism is produced by empathy—the ability to put oneself in the place of another and to share what that person is experiencing* (Batson, 1991, 2006).

Figure 17.27

Why do bystanders sometimes fail to assist a person in need?

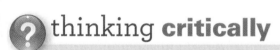

thinking **critically**

DOES PURE ALTRUISM REALLY EXIST?

Do you believe that people ever help one another for purely altruistic reasons? Or is even a small degree of egoism always involved? Think about it, then see page 673.

When Do People Help?

Ordinary citizens often go to great lengths to help strangers yet at times fail to assist people who are clearly in distress (Figure 17.27). What, then, influences whether a bystander will intervene? Many situational and personal factors, such as not being in a hurry, recently observing a prosocial role model, and being in a good mood, increase the odds that we will help someone in need (Eisenberg, 2000).

Bibb Latané and John Darley (1970) view bystander intervention as a 5-step process (Figure 17.28). First, a bystander will not help unless she or he notices the situation. So imagine that as you walk along a street, you hear two people yelling and then hear a scream coming from inside a house. Now what? Many social situations are ambiguous, and step 2 involves deciding

whether this really is an emergency. To answer this question, we often engage in *social comparison:* we look around to see how other people are responding. You might say to yourself, "No one else seems concerned, so it mustn't be serious."

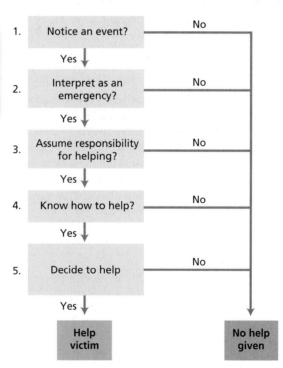

Figure 17.28

When will a bystander intervene?
Bystander intervention in an emergency situation can be viewed as a 5-step process. If the answer at each step is yes, help is given.
SOURCE: Based on Latané & Darley, 1970.

In Kitty Genovese's murder, discussed in Chapter 2, some bystanders mistakenly thought that, because nobody else intervened, they were merely witnessing a "lovers' quarrel" (Darley & Latané, 1968).

If you conclude that the situation is an emergency, then you move to step 3: assuming responsibility to intervene. If you are the only person to hear someone screaming, then responsibility for helping falls squarely on you. But if others are present, there may be a *diffusion of responsibility*—"If I don't help, someone else will"—and if each bystander has this thought, the victim won't receive help. In the Kitty Genovese murder, many bystanders who *did* interpret the incident as an emergency failed to intervene because they assumed that someone else had already done so (Darley & Latané, 1968).

If you do take responsibility, then in step 4 your self-efficacy (confidence in dealing with the situation) comes into play. Sometimes, we fail to help because we don't know how to or we believe our help will be ineffective. But even if self-efficacy is high, in step 5 you still may decide not to intervene. For example, you may perceive that the costs of helping outweigh the benefits (Fritzsche et al., 2000).

As this model indicates, the commonsense adage "there is safety in numbers" is not always true when it comes to receiving help. Many experiments find a **bystander effect:** *the presence of multiple bystanders inhibits each person's tendency to help, largely due to social comparison* (at step 2) *or diffusion of responsibility* (at step 3). This inhibition is more likely to occur when the bystanders are strangers rather than friends; it even occurs when communicating over the Internet. During a 30-day period, P. M. Markey (2000) sent a general request for help ("Can anyone tell me how to look at someone's profile?") to 200 chat groups. Assistance came more slowly from larger chat groups than from smaller ones.

Whom Do People Help?

Some people are more likely to receive help than others, for the following reasons:

- *Similarity:* Whether in attitudes, nationality, or other characteristics, perceiving that a person is similar to us increases our willingness to provide help (Dovidio, 1984).
- *Gender:* Male bystanders are more likely to help a woman than a man in need, whereas female bystanders are equally likely to help women and men (Eagly & Crowley, 1986).

- *Perceived fairness and responsibility:* Beliefs about fairness influence people's willingness to help others (Blader & Tyler, 2002). For example, people are more likely to help someone if they perceive that the person is not responsible for causing his or her own misfortune.

Increasing Prosocial Behavior

Can prosocial behavior be increased? One approach, consistent with social learning theory, is to expose people to prosocial models. Psychologists have used prosocial modeling as part of a nationwide program to increase blood donations (Sarason et al., 1991). Students in 66 high schools watched an audiovisual program showing high school donors giving blood. Compared with a control condition presented with a standard appeal from the local blood bank, the prosocial video increased blood donations by 17 percent.

Research suggests that developing feelings of empathy and connectedness with others also may make people more likely to help (Eisenberg, 2000), and simply learning about factors that hinder bystander intervention may increase the tendency to help someone in distress. Arthur Beaman and coworkers (1978) exposed some college students to information about the bystander effect. Control participants did not receive this information. Two weeks later, more than half of the students who had learned about the bystander effect provided aid to the victim of an accident (staged by the researchers), compared with only about one-fourth of the control-group participants.

Aggression: Harming Others

We love. We nurture. We help. But as current events and the history of humankind attest, we also harm. In humans, *aggression* represents any form of behavior that is intended to harm another person. What causes people to aggress?

Biological Factors in Aggression

From barnyard bulls to laboratory mice, animals can be selectively bred to be more or less aggressive (Nyberg et al., 2003). In some species, certain aggressive behaviors are reflexively triggered by specific environmental stimuli (Figure 17.29). Humans don't display such rigid, inborn aggressive responses, but heredity influences why some people are more aggressive than others. Even when raised in different homes, identical twins display more similar

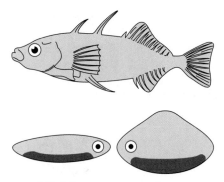

Figure 17.29

Sex and the stickleback: triggers for aggression.
During the mating season, the male stickleback fish develops a red belly. The sight of another red-bellied male—a potential rival for a mate—reflexively triggers an attack by the first male. The key releaser stimulus for this fixed action pattern is the red marking. A male stickleback will not attack a realistic-looking male model that has no red belly, but it will attack unrealistic fish models that have this red marking.
Source: Based on Tinbergen, 1951.

patterns of aggression than do fraternal twins (Beatty et al., 2002).

Some theorists propose that, as in other species, a genetic predisposition toward aggression can be traced to evolutionary adaptation. Aggression at the proper time, they argue, helped our ancestors to compete successfully for mates, food, and shelter and to survive against attack. This increased the odds that individuals who were predisposed to such aggression would pass their genes on to the next generation (Rushton, 1989).

There is no single brain center for aggression, nor one "aggression chemical." Electrically stimulate certain neural pathways in a cat's hypothalamus, and it will arch its back and attack. Surgically destroy areas of the amygdala—an approach that has been used with some violent human criminals—and in many species, defensive aggression will decrease (Aggleton, 1993). Especially in humans, aggression also involves activity in the frontal lobes—the seat of reasoning and impulse control. Deficient frontal-lobe activity makes it more difficult to regulate aggressive impulses generated by deeper brain regions (Kim, 2004; Raine, 2002).

Atypically low levels of serotonin activity appear to play a role in impulsive aggression, as when people lash out from emotional rage (Moore et al., 2002). In many species of mammals, higher levels of the sex hormone testosterone (found in males and females) contribute to greater *social aggression,* acts that establish a dominance hierarchy among members of a species. But in humans and other primates, the association between testosterone and aggression is weaker (O'Connor et al., 2002).

Environmental Stimuli and Learning

Our present environment and past learning experiences also influence aggression. *Frustration,* which occurs when some event interferes with our progress toward a goal, increases the risk of verbal and physical aggression, as do aversive events such as extreme heat, provocation, painful stimuli, and crowding. But we do not always respond to frustration by acting aggressively. Inhibited by our internal moral standards, we may simply control ourselves and find nonaggressive ways of dealing with conflict (Anderson & Bushman, 2002).

Aggression, like other behaviors, is influenced by learning. Nonaggressive animals can be trained to become vicious aggressors if reinforcement is arranged so that they are consistently victorious in fights with weaker animals. Such operant conditioning also affects human aggression. Preschool children become increasingly aggressive when their aggressive behavior produces positive outcomes for them, such as when they successfully force another child to give up a desired toy (Patterson et al., 1967).

As Albert Bandura's (1965) classic "Bobo doll" experiments (see Chapter 7) clearly demonstrated, aggression also can be learned by observing others. Children learn how to aggress even when they witness an aggressive model being punished. Later, if the punishing agent is not present or if rewards are available for aggressing, children are likely to reproduce the model's actions. Correlational studies, while not establishing cause and effect, find that aggressive and delinquent children tend to have parents who often behave aggressively (Duman & Margolin, 2007; Stormshak et al., 2000).

Psychological Factors in Aggression

Many psychological factors affect whether we behave aggressively in specific situations. From face-to-face and cyber (e.g., e-mail) aggression among schoolmates, to gang violence, rape, and war, people may employ several types of *self-justification* to make it psychologically easier to harm other people (Pornari & Wood, 2010). Aggressors may blame the victim for imagined wrongs or otherwise convince themselves that the victim "deserves it." They may also dehumanize their victims, as the guard in the Stanford prison study did when he began to view the prisoners as "cattle."

Our *attribution of intentionality* and degree of empathy also affect how we respond to provocation. When we believe that someone's negative behavior toward us was intentional, we are more likely to become angry and retaliate

(Graham et al., 1992). And when someone offends us and then apologizes, whether we forgive the person partly depends on how well we empathize with his or her viewpoint (McCullough et al., 1997).

Sigmund Freud believed that impulses from aggressive instincts build up inside us over time, have to be released, and then build up again in a never-ending cycle. His principle of **catharsis** *stated that performing an act of aggression discharges aggressive energy and temporarily reduces our impulse to aggress.* But how does one do this in a world where violence is punished? Freud proposed that we can channel aggressive impulses into socially acceptable behaviors (such as sports) and discharge aggressive impulses *vicariously* by watching and identifying with other people who behave aggressively.

If people can't express their aggressive impulses, will the pressures build up and explode? Sometimes, meek or unassertive people do commit shocking and brutal crimes. These people, whom Edwin Megargee (1966) describes as having *overcontrolled hostility,* show little immediate reaction to provocations. Instead, they bottle up their anger and, after provocations accumulate, suddenly erupt into violence. The final provocation that triggers their outburst is often trivial. One 10-year-old boy with no prior history of aggression stabbed his sister more than 80 times with an ice pick after she changed the channel during his favorite TV show. After the aggressive outburst, such people typically revert to their former passive, unassertive state. Female prison inmates who score high on tests measuring overcontrolled hostility are more likely to have committed a one-time violent crime than repeated violent crimes or a nonviolent crime (Verona & Carbonell, 2000; Figure 17.30).

Cases of overcontrolled hostility seem to be consistent with the concept of catharsis, but much research is not. For example, hitting a punching bag while thinking about someone who has just angered them increases—not decreases—people's subsequent aggressive behavior toward that person (Bushman, 2002). And what about watching violent movies and TV programs? Do these activities help people blow off steam, as some stars in the entertainment industry claim?

Media Violence and Aggression

Many movies and TV programs are saturated with violence. To psychodynamic theorists, media violence should be a cathartic pot of gold that decreases viewers' aggression. In contrast, social-cognitive theorists believe that viewing

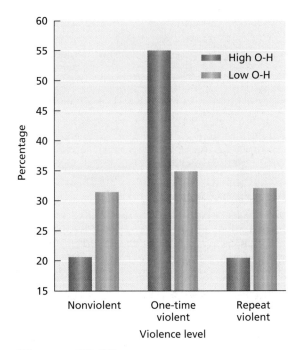

Figure 17.30

Overcontrolled hostility: behind prison bars.

Female inmates at a state prison completed psychological tests that identified whether they had high overcontrolled hostility (High O-H) or low overcontrolled hostility (Low O-H). Inmates with high overcontrolled hostility—but not inmates with low overcontrolled hostility—were much more likely to have committed a one-time violent crime than a nonviolent crime or multiple violent crimes. Source: Adapted from Verona & Carbonell, 2000.

media violence is more likely to increase than to decrease people's aggression (Anderson et al., 2010; Huesmann & Taylor, 2006). They argue that

- viewers may learn new aggressive behaviors through modeling (i.e., social learning);
- viewers' beliefs, attitudes, and expectations about aggression may change, such as coming to believe that aggression usually will "pay off";
- viewers' immediate arousal and hostile emotion may increase;
- viewers may become desensitized to the sight of violence and to the suffering of victims;
- repeated exposure to media violence may make viewers' personalities more aggressive.

To many researchers and professional organizations, including the American Psychological Association, the evidence clearly favors the social-cognitive view (Huesmann, 2010; Murray, 2008). We agree. Overall, laboratory experiments demonstrate a causal link between short-term violent media exposure and increased immediate aggression, and several longitudinal correlational studies suggest a more lasting association (Eron, 1987). In one study, boys and girls were assessed during elementary school and again in their early 20s. Those who watched greater amounts of TV violence in childhood were more likely than their peers to display physical aggression when they became adults (Huesmann et al., 2003). This association was not simply due to the fact that children who watched the most TV violence were more aggressive to begin with. Moreover, boys and girls who perceived TV violence to be highly realistic and identified strongly with same-sex aggressive TV characters were most likely to act aggressively as adults.

Some researchers argue that the link between exposure to media violence and subseqent aggression is weak at best and that research has not clearly established that media violence promotes serious aggression, such as violent criminal behavior (Ferguson, 2009; Savage & Yancy, 2008). Other scientists view the link as strong, and some point out that even a weak causal relation would be important because a huge number of children and adults are exposed to media violence and because aggression has potentially severe consequences when it occurs (Huesmann & Taylor, 2006; Murray, 2008).

Figure 17.31

Do children who play graphically violent video games become desensitized to violence and more likely to behave aggressively toward other people? See the "Myth or Reality?" discussion below.

Beyond TV and the movies, many video games contain violent content (Figure 17.31). Do such games also increase people's aggression? Let's explore whether this is myth or reality.

Myth or Reality?

Violent Video Games Promote Aggression

On a summer's eve in 2008, four bored teenagers from New Hyde Park, New York, decided to go on a crime spree. Seeking to emulate the behavior of the lead character in the violent video game *Grand Theft Auto IV*, they beat and robbed a victim, broke into garages, attempted a carjacking, and tried to rob a man driving a van before they were finally arrested by the police (Crowley, 2008, June 27). Almost a decade earlier, in April 1999, two students in Colorado went on a shooting rampage at Columbine High School, killing a teacher and 12 students and wounding others. The killers were avid players of many violent video games, most notably the "first-person shooter" games *Doom* and *Doom 2* (Block, 2007).

In North America and Europe, crimes like these reinforce public, political, and scientific concerns about the effects of violent video games (Glock & Kneer, 2009). Yet such tragic cases cannot, by themselves, provide clear answers. Many factors play a role in aggression, and trying after the fact to isolate how any single factor contributed to a crime typically involves much speculation. Had the four bored teens or the two Columbine shooters never played a violent video game (or watched a violent movie), would they still have committed those crimes?

Keep in mind that in other school shootings, the killers have had little if any experience with violent video games (Ferguson,

2008). Moreover, many millions of people play violent video games (and watch violent media) and don't commit violent crimes. So, in an interview on the TV station CNN, was the president of the Interactive Digital Software Association correct when he stated, "I think the issue has been vastly overblown.... There is absolutely no evidence, none, that playing a violent video game leads to aggressive behavior" (Lowenstein, 2000, May 12; quoted in Anderson & Bushman, 2001, p. 353)?

Not quite. Even before 2000, experiments in which researchers directly manipulated people's exposure to violent video games provided some causal evidence. In what remains one of the better experiments to this date, Roland Irwin and Alan Gross (1995) randomly assigned sixty 7- and 8-year-old boys to play either a violent or nonviolent video game for 20 minutes. Afterward, each participant engaged in a 10-minute "free-play" period with another boy (an accomplice). Next, as each participant competed against this boy on a task for a prize, the boy (according to plan) cheated. Compared with participants who had played the nonviolent game, those who had played the violent game displayed more physical and verbal aggression toward inanimate objects (e.g., toys), more verbal aggression toward the other boy during the free-play period, and more physical aggression toward the boy during the competition.

Continued

Thinking Critically about Causality

Let's think critically about these results. Did the violent content of the video game increase the children's aggression, or was it simply a more exciting game?' Heart-rate measures recorded before and during video game play indicated that the violent game was not more arousing, strengthening the conclusion that the game's content was the key factor. Other experiments with college students have found that briefly playing violent video games, at least in the short-term, increases subsequent aggressive behavior and physiologically desensitizes students to scenes of real-world violence (Carnagey & Anderson, 2005; Carnagey et al., 2007).

Some correlational studies also suggest a possible link between playing violent video games and getting into physical fights (Gentile et al., 2004; Rudatsikira et al., 2008). But as a critical thinker, remember that correlation doesn't establish causation. Recall the bidirectionality problem: perhaps getting into fights produces consequences (e.g., anger, frustration) that prompt people to play violent video games. Also consider the third-variable problem: perhaps people who have a more hostile personality to begin with play more violent video games and also get into more fights. Indeed, in one study, adolescents exposed to more violent video games did score higher on personality tests of hostility (Gentile et al., 2004). So the researchers adjusted their statistical analyses to take this possible confounding factor into account. They found that violent video game exposure was still correlated—albeit weakly—with a tendency to get into more physical fights.

Several longitudinal studies have examined the effects of video game violence. For example, a 1-month longitudinal American study involving older participants (average age 28 years) found no link between playing an online violent video game and subsequent aggression (Williams & Skoric, 2005). In contrast, three longer-term studies, two of adolescents in Germany and one of adolescents and children in Finland, found that exposure to violent video games helped to predict physical aggression or delinquency 24 to 30 months later (Hopf et al., 2008; Möller & Krahé, 2009; Wallenius & Punamäki, 2008).

The Big Picture

Based on the most comprehensive meta-analysis of violent video game research to date—covering 136 studies and 130,296 participants in Western countries and Japan—Craig Anderson and his colleagues (2010a) concluded that playing violent video games increases people's aggressive behavior, cognition, and emotions and also desensitizes them to violence. Most of these associations are weak, but they all support social-cognitive models of aggression. As for practical importance, Anderson and his colleagues note that, "When effects accumulate across time, or when large portions of the population are exposed to the risk, or when consequences are severe, statistically small effects become much more important" (2010a, p. 170). As an analogy, think of some factor (e.g., shoe or ski design, anxiety) that impairs a sprinter's or downhill skier's time in a competition by only two-tenths of a second. In many circumstances, this might be trivial, but in the Olympics it could mean the difference between a gold medal and no medal at all.

As in the case of mass media research, debate about violent video games still exists. Based on their own smaller meta-analysis and concerns about the methods used in many studies, Christopher Ferguson and John Kilburn (2009) believe that it's premature to conclude that violent video games cause aggression. Researchers have also swapped critiques about whose meta-analysis approach is more appropriate (Anderson et al., 2010b; Ferguson & Kilburn, 2010).

We agree that more research, and especially more complete longitudinal research, is needed. But based on the evidence available now, the conclusion that exposure to video game violence increases the risk of aggression is more reality than myth (Huesmann, 2010). This doesn't mean that everyone who plays violent video games becomes more aggressive, angrier, or desensitized. After Australian researchers exposed adolescents to a violent video game for 20 minutes, 72 percent showed no significant change in feelings of anger. But among those who changed, almost 3 times as many experienced increased (20.6 percent) rather than decreased (7.4 percent) anger (Unsworth et al., 2007). And certainly, the overwhelming majority of children, teens, and adults who play violent video games don't go out and assault or kill people. But aggression comes in many forms—physical and verbal, obvious and subtle—and even the potential for a small increased risk of aggression among some people can have important consequences.

A Final Word

In Chapter 1 we began a shared journey through the sprawling domain of modern-day psychology. That journey has taken us from the inner recesses of the mind to our social world. We have examined how the brain's intricate workings underlie our thoughts, feelings, and behaviors. We also have explored the learning mechanisms that enable us to profit from our experiences and adapt to our environment. We have seen how the environment in which we live, including our culture, exerts powerful influences over who we become and how we behave. We have achieved greater understanding of the cognitive processes that help define our humanity. We have also gained insights into the processes by which we develop from a single cell into the most psychologically complex creature on our planet, and we have explored the personality processes that help make each of us unique. We have learned about the many ways in which people cope, both adaptively and maladaptively, with the demands of living, as well as the many interventions that help people live happier and more fulfilling lives. As we have found in every area of psychological study, the brain, mind, and environment interact in complex ways to influence our behavior.

We are privileged to have been your guides in this psychological journey. We hope that your introductory psychology course has influenced your conception of human nature, your understanding of yourself and others, your capacity to think critically about your world, and your ability to utilize psychological principles to enrich your life.

Levels of Analysis

Aggression

We've just seen that biological, psychological, and environmental factors all contribute to aggressive behavior. Let's recap some of these factors.

ENVIRONMENTAL LEVEL

- Stimuli that produce frustration (i.e., that block goal accomplishment) increase the risk of aggression.
- Painful stimuli, extreme heat, and crowding increase the risk of aggression.
- Past and present reinforcement for aggression affects the likelihood of current aggressive behavior.
- Exposure to live models and media models who display aggression can promote the social learning of aggression.

BIOLOGICAL LEVEL

- Within a species, heredity partly accounts for individual differences in aggressiveness.
- The frontal lobes, amygdala, hypothalamus, and other brain regions play key roles in regulating aggression.
- Serotonin is among the major neurotransmitters that regulate aggression.
- Higher testosterone levels contribute to greater social aggression in many mammalian species.

PSYCHOLOGICAL LEVEL

- Aggression is more likely when another person's harmful behavior is perceived as intentional.
- A lack of empathy for a potential target increases the risk of aggression toward that person.
- People denigrate and dehumanize potential targets to self-justify acts of aggression.
- Impaired reasoning may decrease the ability to regulate hostile feelings.

In the section of this chapter on social influence, we discussed how norms, conformity, obedience, and group processes affect behavior. Think about the relevance of these social influence factors in accounting for human aggression. For example, in what contexts do these factors promote or inhibit aggression, and how do they shape the form that aggression takes?

test yourself

Social Relations

True or False?

1. In initial romantic attraction, the general rule is "opposites attract."
2. Scientific attempts to predict marital divorce have succeeded much better than chance guessing.
3. According to realistic conflict theory, prejudice stems from a need to enhance one's self-esteem.
4. Teaching people about stereotype threat usually worsens their performance.
5. The kin selection principle explains prosocial behavior from an evolutionary perspective.
6. As more bystanders witness an emergency, their confidence grows and they are more likely to intervene.
7. The brain does not have a single, master "aggression-on" center.
8. Overall, media-violence research supports the catharsis hypothesis.

ANSWERS: 1-false, 2-true, 3-false, 4-false, 5-true, 6-false, 7-true, 8-false

Chapter Summary

SOCIAL THINKING

- Consistency, distinctiveness, and consensus information jointly influence whether we make personal or situational attributions for behavior. We often underestimate the role of situational factors when making attributions for other people's behavior, and we display a self-serving bias when making attributions for our own successes and failures.

- First impressions generally carry extra weight. Stereotypes and schemas create perceptual sets that shape our impressions. Through self-fulfilling prophecies, our initially false expectations shape the way we act toward someone. In turn, this person responds to our behavior in ways that confirm our expectations.

- Attitudes predict behavior best when situational influences are weak, when the attitude is strong, and when we consciously think about our attitude. Behavior also influences attitudes. Counterattitudinal behavior is most likely to create cognitive dissonance when the behavior is freely chosen and threatens our self-worth or produces foreseeable negative consequences. To reduce dissonance, we may change our attitude to become more consistent with how we have acted.

- In persuasion, communicator credibility is highest when the communicator is perceived as expert and trustworthy. Fear-arousing communications may be effective if they arouse moderate to strong fear and suggest how to avoid the feared result. The central route to persuasion works best with listeners who have a high need for cognition; for those with a low cognition need, the peripheral route works better.

SOCIAL INFLUENCE

- Social norms are shared expectations about how group members should behave. People conform because of informational and normative social influence. The majority's size and presence of a dissenter influence people's degree of conformity. Milgram's research found unexpectedly high percentages of people willing to obey destructive orders. Such obedience is stronger when the victim is remote and when the authority figure is close by, legitimate, and assumes responsibility for what happens.

- People use the norm of reciprocity and the door-in-the-face, foot-in-the-door, and lowballing techniques to increase others' compliance with their requests.

- Social loafing occurs when people exert less individual effort when working as a group than when working alone. Loafing decreases when the goal is valued highly and individual performance within the group is monitored.

- When the members of a decision-making group share the same conservative or liberal viewpoint, the group's final decision often becomes more extreme than the average initial opinion of the individual members. Cohesive decision-making groups that have directive leaders, are under high stress, and are insulated from outside input may display groupthink.

- Deindividuation is a temporary lowering of restraints that can occur when a person is immersed in a group or crowd. Anonymity to outsiders appears to be the key factor in producing deindividuation.

SOCIAL RELATIONS

- Proximity, mere exposure, similarity of attitudes, and physical attractiveness typically enhance our attraction toward someone. Social exchange theory analyzes relationships in terms of the rewards and costs experienced by each partner. Evolutionary theorists propose that gender differences in mate preferences reflect inherited tendencies. Sociocultural theorists believe that these differences result from socialization and economic gender inequities.

- Ostracism produces negative psychological consequences and activates many of the same brain regions that underlie physical pain.

- Prejudice stems partly from our tendency to perceive in-groups and out-groups. People typically display in-group favoritism and an out-group homogeneity bias. Perceived threats to one's in-group and a need to enhance one's self-esteem can motivate prejudice. Prejudice often is reduced when in-group and out-group members work closely together, with equal status, on tasks involving common goals and under conditions of broader institutional support.

- Some theorists propose that through kin selection and reciprocal altruism, human evolution has shaped a genetic predisposition toward prosocial behavior. Social learning theorists emphasize how norms, modeling, and reinforcement shape prosocial behavior. The presence of multiple bystanders may decrease bystander intervention through social comparison processes and a diffusion of responsibility for helping. Prosocial behavior can be increased by enhancing people's feelings of empathy for victims and providing prosocial models.

- Heredity influences an organism's tendency to aggress. The hypothalamus, amygdala, and frontal lobes play central roles in aggression. Provocation, extreme heat, crowding, and stimuli that cause frustration or pain increase the risk of aggression. People are more likely to aggress when they find ways to justify and rationalize their aggressive behavior, perceive provocation as intentional, and have little empathy for others. Although some experts disagree, research generally supports the prediction of social-cognitive theory that exposure to media violence increases the risk that people will act aggressively.

KEY TERMS AND CONCEPTS

Each term has been boldfaced and defined in the chapter on the page indicated in parentheses.

attitude (p. 639)
attribution (p. 635)
bystander effect (p. 666)
catharsis (p. 668)
central route to persuasion (p. 642)
communicator credibility (p. 641)
companionate love (p. 656)
deindividuation (p. 652)
discrimination (p. 659)
door-in-the-face technique (p. 649)
empathy-altruism hypothesis (p. 665)
equal status contact (p. 662)
explicit prejudice (p. 659)
foot-in-the-door technique (p. 649)
fundamental attribution error (p. 635)

group polarization (p. 650)
groupthink (p. 650)
implicit prejudice (p. 659)
informational social influence (p. 644)
kin selection (p. 664)
lowballing (p. 649)
matching effect (p. 655)
mere exposure effect (p. 653)
normative social influence (p. 644)
norm of reciprocity (p. 649)
passionate love (p. 656)
peripheral route to persuasion (p. 642)
prejudice (p. 659)
primacy effect (p. 637)
realistic conflict theory (p. 660)

self-fulfilling prophecy (p. 638)
self-perception theory (p. 641)
self-serving bias (p. 636)
social compensation (p. 650)
social exchange theory (p. 655)
social identity theory (p. 661)
social loafing (p. 650)
social norms (p. 643)
social role (p. 643)
stereotype (p. 638)
stereotype threat (p. 662)
theory of cognitive dissonance (p. 640)
theory of planned behavior (p. 639)
triangular theory of love (p. 656)

? thinking critically

DO WOMEN DIFFER FROM MEN IN OBEDIENCE? (Page 648)

What was your hypothesis about sex differences in obedience? About half of our students predict that women would be more likely to keep obeying the experimenter's orders. Their rationale: given traditional sex-role expectations that men are more dominant than women (especially at the time of Milgram's research), women would be less likely to defy the authority of a male experimenter. About half of our students disagree, hypothesizing that women have more empathy than men and thus would be more likely to disobey once they hear the learner screaming and pleading to stop. Finally, a few students expect no sex difference, believing the previous factors would "cancel each other out." All three hypotheses sound plausible, highlighting a key problem with relying solely on common sense: different people have different "common sense," leading to diverse predictions that cover all the bases.

Milgram conducted one obedience study with 40 women, using the identical procedures described in the "Research Close-up." In the study with men, 65 percent obeyed fully. Among the women, the results were identical: 65 percent obeyed fully. Other researchers, including Burger (2009) in his recent study, have failed to find consistent sex differences in obedience rates. Another study, conducted in Jordan, examined 6- to 8-year-old, 10- to 12-year-old, and 14- to 16-year-old boys and girls placed in the role of "teacher" (Shanab & Yahya, 1977). The experimenter was female, and the "learner" was a confederate matched in age and sex to each participant (e.g., 10- to 12-year-old girls administered fake shocks to a similarly aged girl). Overall, 73 percent of participants fully obeyed, and neither their sex nor age significantly influenced this rate. In sum, the most reasonable conclusion is that there are no consistent sex differences in obedience rates in studies like those conducted by Milgram.

DOES PURE ALTRUISM REALLY EXIST? (Page 665)

Do you believe that people ever help others for purely altruistic reasons? Perhaps your response is "Sure. Some Good Samaritans care only about the victim's welfare and even help people at a cost to themselves." Certainly, people make anonymous donations to charities and help strangers when no one (including the recipient) is taking note of their good deeds. In such cases, we can seemingly rule out motives for helping based on gaining recognition or others' approval. But still, doesn't helping someone make us feel good about ourselves?

Moreover, by helping someone, don't we feel better knowing that the person's plight has been reduced? According to the *negative state relief model*, high empathy causes us to feel distress when we learn of others' suffering, so by helping them we reduce our own personal distress—a self-focused, egoistic goal, not an altruistic one (Cialdini et al., 1987).

Batson and many psychologists believe that while egoistic motives account for some prosocial behavior, at times people do help others for purely altruistic reasons (Batson, 2006). Yet other psychologists remain unconvinced, arguing that some negative state relief is always involved (Cialdini et al., 1997).

Recent brain-imaging findings add some provocative fuel to this debate. Empathizing with someone else's pain does not produce the same sensations (i.e., somatosensory cortex activation) that we experience when we are in pain, but it does activate many of the brain areas (e.g., other parts of the cortex, brain stem, thalamus, and cerebellum) that process emotional aspects of our own pain (Singer et al., 2004). Moreover, people who feel greater empathy for another's pain experience greater activation in these brain areas. So what do you think? Does this suggest that when helping behavior stems from empathy, it does indeed involve negative state relief and therefore is not purely altruistic?

Appendix: Statistics in Psychology

At various points throughout the text, we have briefly described statistical procedures to help you understand the information being presented. This appendix discusses statistics in greater detail and focuses on the concepts underlying these procedures. Our goal is to help you understand how psychologists use statistics in their research.

For some students, the prospect of studying statistics evokes visions of complex higher mathematics. You will find, however, that if you can add, subtract, multiply, and divide, you can easily perform basic statistical operations.

DESCRIPTIVE STATISTICS

Psychological research often involves a large number of measurements. Typically, it is difficult to make sense of the data merely by examining the individual scores of each participant. **Descriptive statistics** *summarize and describe the characteristics of a set* (also called a *distribution*) *of scores.*

To summarize a set of scores, we might first construct a **frequency distribution,** *which shows how many participants received each score.* For example, suppose that 50 college students took a 32-item psychological test that measured their level of self-esteem. The frequency distribution in Table A.1 tells us that two participants had scores of 30, 31, or 32; one had a score of 27, 28, or 29; eleven had scores of 15, 16, or 17, and so on. Note that the researcher chose to use *intervals* of three points (e.g., 30–32) rather than to show the number

Table **A.1** | Frequency Distribution of Self-Esteem Scores

Self-Esteem Scores	Frequency
30–32	2
27–29	1
24–26	4
21–23	6
18–20	9
15–17	11
12–14	8
9–11	3
6–8	4
3–5	1
0–2	1

(frequency) of participants who obtained each of the 33 possible (0–32) scores. She could have done the latter if she had wished to break down the scores even further. The number of intervals chosen is somewhat arbitrary, but frequency distributions often contain 10 to 12 categories.

This frequency distribution tells us at a glance about certain characteristics of the data, such as whether scores tend to cluster in one region of the distribution or are scattered throughout. We can easily convert these data into a **histogram,** *which is a graph of a frequency distribution.* Typically, the scores (or, in this case, score intervals) are plotted along the horizontal axis (i.e., *X-axis,* or *abscissa*), and the frequencies are plotted on the vertical axis (i.e., *Y-axis,* or *ordinate*). This produces a column or bar above each score or score interval that shows how frequently the score occurred. Figure A.1 represents a histogram of the self-esteem scores for our sample of 50 college students.

Measures of Central Tendency

Frequency distributions and histograms give us a general picture of how scores are distributed. As we briefly discussed in Chapter 2, **measures of central tendency** *describe a distribution in terms of a single statistic that is in some way "typical" of the sample as a whole.* There are three commonly used measures of central tendency: the *mode,* the *mean,* and the *median.* For example, Table A.2 shows how 10 hypothetical college seniors performed on the midterm exam in an advanced psychology class. In this class, the instructor assigns grades such that a score of 90 equals an A; 80, a B; and 70, a C. Our task is to arrive at a single number that somehow typifies the exam scores of the group as a whole.

The **mode** *is the most frequently occurring score in a distribution.* In this class, 88 is the mode because it is the only score obtained by more than one person (Rowe and Miyamoto). Although the mode is easy to identify in a distribution, it is not always the most representative score, particularly if it falls far from the center of the distribution. For example, suppose that Rowe's exam grade had been 94, rather than 88. In this case, the most frequent score—the mode—would now be 94 (Wilson and Rowe). But if we told you that on this exam the typical score was 94, it would provide you with an overly optimistic view of how the class performed.

The most commonly used measure of central tendency, the **mean,** *represents the arithmetic average of a set of scores.* The mean is calculated by adding up all the scores and dividing by the number of scores. The statistical formula for computing the mean is:

$$M = \frac{\Sigma X}{N}$$

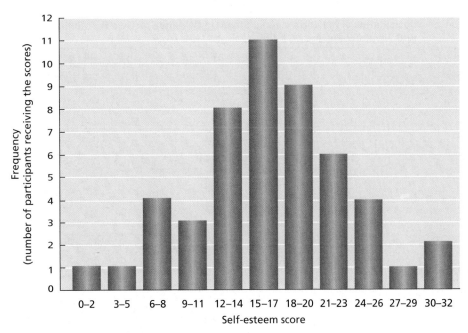

Figure A.1

A histogram of the self-esteem distribution shown in Table A.1.

Table **A.2**	**Midterm Exam Scores of 10 College Seniors**
Student	**Score**
1. Wilson	94
2. Ibanez	91
3. Rowe	88
4. Miyamoto	88
5. Stein	83
6. Diaz	82
7. Anderson	81
8. Bradford	80
9. Kruger	73
10. Thompson	70
$N = 10$	$\Sigma X = 830$

Mode = The score that occurs most often—in this case, 88.

Mean = The arithmetic average, computed by the following formula:

$$M = \frac{\Sigma X}{N} = \frac{830}{10} = 83$$

Median = The point above and below which there is an equal number of scores. In this case, because there is an even number of scores, the median is midway between the 5th and 6th scores—that is, 82.5.

X is the symbol for an individual score, N denotes the number of scores, and M is the symbol for the mean of the individual scores. The Greek letter Σ (sigma) means "the sum." Thus, to compute the mean score on this exam, we simply add the individual scores and divide the total by 10, the number of scores. As Table A.2 shows, the mean score is 83.

As we noted in Chapter 2, one shortcoming of the mean is that it can be strongly affected by one or more extremely high or low scores that are not representative of the group as a whole. Suppose, for example, that Kruger and Thompson, rather than getting scores of 73 and 70, hadn't studied for this test at all and completely bombed it, getting scores of 30 and 23, respectively. This would change the mean from 83 to 74, giving you the impression that the typical score was a C+ when in fact the other 8 students all had scores ranging between A and B.

Our third measure of central tendency, the **median,** *is the point that divides the distribution in half when the individual scores are arranged in order from lowest to highest.* In other words, half of the scores lie above the median and half below it. If there is an odd number of scores, there will be one score that is exactly in the middle. If there were 11 exam scores in Table A.2, the sixth-ranked score would be the median, because 5 scores would fall above and 5 below. In a distribution having an even number of scores, such as in Table A.2, the median is halfway between the 2 middle scores. In our exam score distribution, the median is the point halfway between student 5 (83 points) and student 6 (82 points), or 82.5 points.

The median has an important property that the mean does not have: it is unaffected by extreme scores. Whether Kruger and Thompson respectively have scores of 73 and 70 or scores of 30 and 23, the median remains the same. Therefore, the median is more representative of the group as a whole in instances when there are very extreme scores. The median, however, can fail to capture important information. For example, suppose that the top four students on this test had achieved perfect scores of 100.

Table **A.3** | **Computation of the Variance and Standard Deviation for Two Distributions of Scores with Identical Means ($M = 10$)**

	Distribution A			Distribution B	
X (score)	**X − M = x**	**x²**	**X (score)**	**X − M = x**	**x²**
12	+2	4	18	+8	64
12	+2	4	18	+8	64
11	+1	1	15	+5	25
11	+1	1	15	+5	25
10	0	0	10	0	0
10	0	0	10	0	0
9	−1	1	5	−5	25
9	−1	1	5	−5	25
8	−2	4	2	−8	64
8	−2	4	2	−8	64
$\Sigma X = 100$	$\Sigma x = 0$	$\Sigma x^2 = 20$	$\Sigma x = 100$	$\Sigma x = 0$	$\Sigma x^2 = 356$

$N = 10$

$M = 10.00$

x (deviation) $= X - M$

$\text{variance} = \dfrac{\Sigma x^2}{N} = \dfrac{20}{10} = 2.00$

SD (standard deviation) $= \sqrt{2.00} = 1.414$

$N = 10$

$M = 10.00$

$\text{variance} = \dfrac{\Sigma x^2}{N} = \dfrac{356}{10} = 35.60$

$SD = \sqrt{35.60} = 5.967$

In this case the median would not change, because the "middle score" would still be the midpoint between student 5 and student 6. The mean, however, would increase from 83 to almost 87 (869 points/10 = 86.9 points) and reflect the higher scores obtained by these four students.

Measures of Variability

Measures of central tendency provide us with a single score that typifies the distribution. But to describe a distribution adequately, we need to know more. One key question concerns the amount of variability, or spread, that exists among scores. Do they tend to cluster closely about the mean, or do they vary widely? **Measures of variability** *provide information about the spread of scores in a distribution.*

The **range**, *which is the difference between the highest and the lowest score in a distribution*, is the simplest but least informative measure of variability. On the midterm exam in Table A.2, the range is 94 − 70 = 24 points. But suppose that, in Table A.2, all the other students (student 2 through student 9) had scores of 85. If we knew only the range of scores, we might be led to believe that the scores in this distribution varied far more from one another than they actually do. Thus it would be more useful to know how much, on average, each score varies or deviates from the mean of the distribution.

To do this we first create a *deviation score* (represented by a lowercase x) that measures the distance between each score (X) and the mean (M). To provide a simple example, suppose we have two distributions, A and B, each composed of 10 scores. Looking at the "X (score)" column in Table A.3 for each distribution, you can see that although each distribution has a mean of 10, the scores in distribution B are more spread out than in distribution A. Now for each score we compute how much it differs from the mean (i.e., $x = X - M$). At this stage, you might think that to measure the variability of each distribution we need only add up its deviation scores and then compute the average deviation. But we have a problem. Even though distribution B is more spread out than distribution A, adding up the deviation scores for each distribution yields a sum of zero ($\Sigma x = 0$). In fact, the sum of deviation scores for any distribution will always add up to zero.

To avoid this problem, we must get rid of the plus and minus signs that end up canceling each other out. As the rightmost column (i.e., the "x^2" column) under each distribution in Table A.3 shows, we achieve this goal by taking each deviation score, squaring it, and then adding up these squared deviation scores. This produces a sum of 20 for distribution A and 356 for distribution B. Now we divide by 10 (i.e., the number of scores in each distribution) to find the average squared deviation. This statistic, called the **variance,** *is the average of the squared deviation scores about the mean.* You can see that the variance for distribution B (35.60) is considerably greater than the variance for distribution A (2.00), reflecting the greater spread of the scores in B.

The most popular measure of variability, the **standard deviation (SD),** *is the square root of the variance.* Because we had to square the deviation scores to compute the variance, we now return to the original scale of measurement by taking the square root of the variance. Thus the standard deviation describes variability in the same units of measurement as the original data. You can see in Table A.3 that the standard deviation from the mean of distribution B (5.967) is more than four times greater than the standard deviation from the mean of distribution A (1.414).

THE NORMAL CURVE

The **normal curve** *is a symmetrical bell-shaped curve that represents a theoretical distribution of scores in the population.* In the normal curve, 50 percent of the cases fall on each side of the mean, and the median and mode have the same value as the mean. Figure A.2 shows that in a normal curve, as we move away from the mean, the frequency of each score steadily decreases. The normal curve is important because many variables in the population—weight, height, IQ, and anxiety, to name a few—are distributed in a way that approximates the normal curve. Thus a few people are extremely tall or short, a greater number of people are moderately tall or short, and most are close to average in height.

The normal curve has several key properties. The most important of these is that the standard deviation can be used to divide the normal curve into areas containing known percentages of the population. In a normal curve, about two-thirds of the scores fall within plus or minus 1 standard deviation of the mean; about 95 percent of cases fall within plus or minus 2 standard deviations; and nearly all of the cases fall between 3 standard deviations above and 3 standard deviations below the mean. Therefore, if we know that a psychological characteristic or any other variable is normally distributed, then we can deduce more information about it. For example, IQ scores as measured by the Wechsler intelligence tests (see Chapter 10) are normally distributed with a mean of 100 and a standard deviation of 15. Knowing this, we can use our knowledge of the normal curve to answer questions like these:

1. What percentage of people have IQs between 70 and 130? (Approximately 95 percent. These scores are −2 SD and +2 SD from the mean, respectively. As Figure A.2 shows, this area below the curve includes 13.59 + 34.13 + 34.13 + 13.59 percent of the cases, or 95.44 percent.)

2. My IQ is 115, so where does that place me? (115 is +1 SD above the mean, so as Figure A.2 shows, about 16 percent of the population will have a higher IQ, and 84 percent will have a lower IQ. That is, the area to the right of +1 SD represents 13.59 + 2.14 + 0.13 percent of the cases, or 15.86 percent.)

3. What is the probability that a person selected at random from the population will have an IQ of 145 or more? (About one-eighth of 1 percent. This probability corresponds to the area under the curve beyond +3 SD, or 0.13 percent.)

These examples point to a major use of the normal curve: it allows us to estimate the probability that a given event will occur. Indeed, the statistical tests we describe next are methods for arriving at probability statements based on the assumption that the variables being investigated are normally distributed.

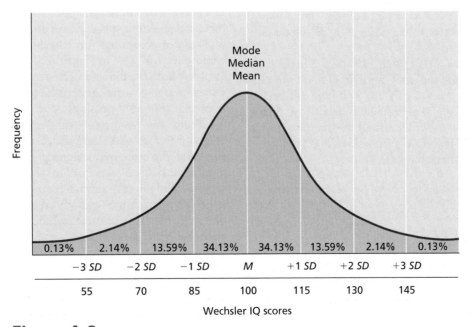

Figure A.2

The normal curve, showing the percentage of cases falling within each area of the normal distribution and also showing Wechsler IQ scores that correspond to standard deviation (SD) units.

STATISTICAL METHODS FOR DATA ANALYSIS

Given a set of data for any single variable, such as the scores of a sample of people on a self-esteem test, we use descriptive statistics to summarize the characteristics of those data. But psychologists do more than describe variables individually. They seek to explain and predict behavior by examining how variables are *related* to one another. The following statistical methods are used to analyze relations among variables and draw inferences about the meaning of those relations.

Accounting for Variance in Behavior

Behavior varies. It varies between individuals (e.g., some people are more aggressive or helpful than others), and it varies for the same individual across time and situations (a person may perform a task well under some conditions but more poorly under other circumstances). Explaining why variations in behavior occur (i.e., accounting for variance) is a central goal of psychological science.

As an example, suppose we want to examine how the number of bystanders present during an emergency influences the speed with which they assist a person in distress. In this instance, the number of bystanders is the independent variable, and the speed of helping is the dependent variable. We conduct an experiment, randomly assign participants to different conditions (one, two, or four bystanders present), and find that, overall, bystanders who were alone responded most quickly and groups of four responded most slowly. We also find that the speed of response varied even within each condition; for example, among those bystanders who were alone, some simply responded more quickly than others. Maybe they were in a better mood, had more altruistic personalities, and so on.

In any experiment, the total amount of variation in people's behavior (e.g., speed of helping) may be divided into two components: the amount of *variance accounted for* by the differences in the independent variable(s) being manipulated (e.g., being placed alone or with other bystanders) and the amount of variance that is left over and therefore must be due to other factors (e.g., participants' mood, personalities). Thus,

Total variance	=	Variance accounted for (due to independent variables)	+	Variance not accounted for (due to random, unmeasured, or uncontrolled factors)

In our experiment, suppose a statistical analysis reveals that 20 percent of the total variance in the speed with which participants helped a person in distress can be accounted for by our independent variable—the number of other bystanders present. Figure A.3 shows this schematically. The other 80 percent of the variance in speed of helping is due to other factors that were not controlled in the experiment. Some of these other factors, which are random and beyond the control of the experimenter,

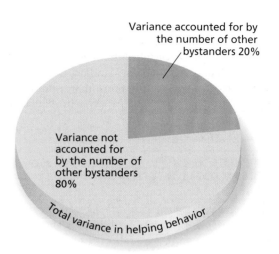

Figure A.3

The total amount of variation in the dependent variable (speed of responding to another person in distress) is represented within the circle. The total variance may be divided into one portion accounted for by the independent variable (number of bystanders) and another portion not accounted for by the independent variable.

produce what is called *error variance*. For example, some participants may have been momentarily preoccupied with personal problems and thus responded more slowly than they otherwise would have. The rest of the unexplained variance results from factors that systematically affect the speed of helping but that the researcher either does not know about or were not examined in the experiment. Such variables may include the participants' personality characteristics or mood, the victim's gender, the nature of the emergency, and so forth. In future research, we might introduce additional independent variables, such as manipulating (i.e., creating) an environment that puts bystanders in a good or bad mood just prior to the emergency. By studying other independent variables, we attempt to increase the amount of variance accounted for, thereby increasing the size of the "accounted for" area in Figure A.3. Perhaps we will find that by knowing both the number of bystanders present and the participants' mood, we can now account for 35 percent of the variance in people's speed of helping.

From this perspective, understanding and/or predicting behavior involves isolating factors that account for behavioral variance. The more important a particular variable is, the more variance it helps us account for. To be sure, we can never completely eliminate the random factors that produce error variance. But as scientific research proceeds, the goal is to discover new variables that account for additional portions of the total variance in people's behavior.

Correlational Methods

The concept of "variance accounted for" applies not only to experiments but also to correlational studies. As discussed in Chapter 2, correlational research does not involve manipulating independent variables. Rather, it involves measuring two or more variables and determining whether changes in one variable are associated with changes in the other. Suppose that we administer two psychological tests—one measuring self-esteem and the other measuring depression—to 200 adults. On each test we will find that the scores vary: some people will have higher self-esteem than others, and some will be more depressed than others. The question is this: Is there a relation between the variance in self-esteem scores and the variance in depression scores? Stated differently, as self-esteem scores (variable X) become higher or lower (i.e., as they move further away from the mean of X), do depression scores (variable Y) tend to become either higher or lower (i.e., move away from the mean of Y) in a systematic manner?

The Correlation Coefficient

Relations between variables can differ in *direction* (positive or negative) and in *strength*. To illustrate, imagine that we have a sample of six people, with scores on two variables (X and Y) for each person. Table A.4 shows five hypothetical sets of X and Y scores for these six people. In set A, the relation between variables X and Y is positive in direction. That is, higher scores on variable X are associated with higher scores on Y, and lower scores on X are associated with lower scores on Y. In contrast, set E reveals a negative relation. Here, higher scores on X are associated with lower Y scores, and vice versa. In set C, the pairs of X and Y scores bear no clear relation to each other: they are not correlated. As scores on X change, scores on Y do not change in any consistent manner. Thus in sets A, C, and E, we see three different types of relations—positive, none, and negative.

To illustrate how relations between variables differ in strength, let us compare set A with set B. In set A, there is a perfect positive relation between X and Y: as each X score increases by a constant amount (in this case, by 1), each Y score also increases by a constant amount (in this case, by 2). In set B, individuals having higher X scores also tend to have higher Y scores, but this positive relation is not as consistent as in set A. For example, in set B, participant 3 has a higher X score than participant 2 yet a lower Y score. Likewise, compare set E with set D. Set E displays a perfect negative relation: as each X score increases by a constant amount, each Y score decreases by a constant amount. In set D, the negative relation between X and Y is not as consistent and thus is not as strong.

The **Pearson product-moment correlation coefficient** *is a statistic that reflects the direction and strength of the relation between two variables.* The correlation coefficient (designated *r*) can range in magnitude from −1.00 to +1.00. If *r* = +1.00, this reflects a perfect positive relation between X and Y scores, as in set A of Table A.4. A correlation coefficient of −1.00 signifies a perfect negative relation, as in set E. Correlations close to 0.00 indicate no systematic relation between the variables, as in set C.

In actual research, a correlation of −1.00 or +1.00 is rare; psychological variables tend to be imperfectly correlated with one another. More typically, correlation coefficients might resemble those in sets B (*r* = +.58) and D (*r* = −.75). Remember that it is the magnitude of the correlation coefficient and not its sign (direction) that indicates the degree to which two variables are related to one another. Thus, X and Y are more strongly related in set D (*r* = −.75) than in set B (*r* = +.58), even though the correlation in set D is negative.

How shall we interpret a correlation coefficient? A correlation of +.50, for example, does *not* mean that X and Y are 50 percent related. Rather, squaring the correlation coefficient (r^2) indicates the amount of variance that the two variables share or have in common. Stated another way, r^2 tells us how much

Table **A.4** | **Five Data Sets Illustrating Various Relations That May Exist between Two Variables**

Participant	Set A		Set B		Set C		Set D		Set E	
	X	Y	X	Y	X	Y	X	Y	X	Y
1	1	2	1	4	1	5	1	6	1	12
2	2	4	2	5	2	8	2	8	2	10
3	3	6	3	2	3	6	3	10	3	8
4	4	8	4	10	4	2	4	4	4	6
5	5	10	5	6	5	6	5	2	5	4
6	6	12	6	8	6	7	6	1	6	2
N = 6	*r* = +1.00		*r* = +.58		*r* = .00		*r* = −.75		*r* = −1.00	

Each set consists of the scores of 6 people on two variables, X and Y. The Pearson product-moment correlation coefficient (*r*) has been computed for each set. The computational formula for *r* is as follows:

$$r = \frac{N(\Sigma X_i Y_i) - (\Sigma X_i)(\Sigma Y_i)}{\sqrt{[N(\Sigma X_i^2) - (\Sigma X_i)^2][N(\Sigma Y_i^2) - (\Sigma Y_i)^2]}}$$

Where X_i = Each person's score on variable X; ΣX_i = sum of Xs
Y_i = Each person's score on variable Y; ΣY_i = sum of Ys
N = Total number of people

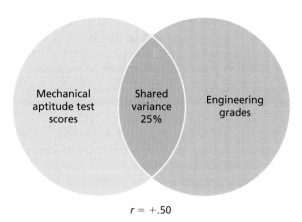

$$r = +.50$$

Figure A.4

Squaring the correlation coefficient provides an estimate of the amount of variance shared by two variables. In this instance, $r = +.50$, indicating that 25 percent of the variance in engineering grades in this sample can be accounted for by individual differences in mechanical aptitude.

of the variance in one measure can be accounted for by differences in the other measure. For example, suppose we obtain a correlation of $+.50$ between scores on a mechanical aptitude test and grades in a college engineering course. As illustrated in Figure A.4, squaring the correlation coefficient ($+.50^2 = .25$) tells us that 25 percent of the total variance in course grades can be accounted for by differences in mechanical aptitude scores. Obviously, the more highly two variables are correlated, the more common variance they share. If the two variables in Figure A.4 correlated .70, the area of overlap would include about half of each circle, because $(+.70)^2 = .49$. Finally, if two variables are perfectly correlated, the two circles in Figure A.4 would overlap completely.

Recall from Chapter 2 that a correlation between two variables does not allow us to conclude that one caused the other. We know only that they are statistically related to one another. If variables X and Y are correlated, it is possible that X causes Y or that Y causes X—or that both X and Y are caused by some third variable, Z (for example, spatial reasoning ability).

Correlation and Prediction

If two variables are correlated and we know an individual's score on one variable, then this information will help us estimate his or her score on the other variable. *The more highly two variables are correlated, the more accurate our predictions will be.* In fact, if two variables are perfectly correlated—if their variance overlaps completely—we can make precise predictions. For example, in set A of Table A.4, once we know a person's score on X, we can accurately predict that $Y = 2X$. (Conversely, if we know Y, we can predict that $X = .5Y$.) In statistical prediction based on correlation, we are thus taking advantage of lawful relations among variables to predict to the individual case.

There are many practical applications for predictions based on correlational analysis. Industrial-organizational psychologists, for example, often help organizations develop aptitude tests that correlate with on-the-job performance.

Personnel managers can therefore use job applicants' test scores to predict which applicants are most likely to perform well, just as colleges use high school students' scores on standardized tests (e.g., the SAT) to help estimate potential college performance. The more highly a *predictor variable* (e.g., aptitude test scores) is correlated with the *criterion variable* (e.g., job performance or college grades), the more accurate the selection decisions will be.

Factor Analysis

Researchers often measure many variables and examine the correlations among them. For example, suppose we want to develop a psychological test to measure individual differences in anxiety. Let us assume that we write 40 items that we think would be answered differently by people who are high and low in anxiety. We then administer these items to a large sample of people. For each item, the person responds on the following scale: 0 ("not at all like me"); 1 ("a little like me"); 2 ("somewhat like me"); and 3 ("very much like me"). We then correlate scores on each of the 40 items with one another. We reason that if test items are correlated highly with one another—if scores on these items "cluster," or "hang together"—then these items are probably measuring the same underlying aspect of anxiety. Further, if the items within one cluster correlate highly with one another but are not correlated highly with items in other clusters, then these various item clusters probably reflect different aspects of people's experiences of anxiety. Thus we also hope to determine the number of item clusters and to use this information to infer the nature of anxiety.

When the sets of scores for the 40 items are correlated with one another (N = the number of items), we will end up with 780 correlations—that is, $[N \times (N - 1)]/2$, or $[40 \times 39]/2$ correlations—to examine. Obviously, with so many correlations, trying to determine visually which items cluster together (while not clustering with other items) is a hopeless task. Fortunately, a statistical technique called **factor analysis** *reduces a large number of correlations among many measures to a smaller number of clusters, with each cluster containing variables that correlate highly with one another.* Today, computers can analyze the patterns of correlations and perform a factor analysis in a few seconds. The term *factor* refers to the underlying characteristic that presumably accounts for why the measures within each cluster are linked.

Factor analysis is complex, and for purposes of this discussion, we need not be concerned with its mathematical basis. Our interest is in how psychologists use it as a research tool, so consider a simple example. Let us assume that the factor analysis indicates that there are two distinct clusters of items that include 38 of the 40 items. Table A.5 shows the correlations among only 6 of those 38 items. Such a table is called a *correlation matrix*. The correlation coefficients of 1.00 along the diagonal of the matrix reflect the obvious fact that each variable correlates perfectly with itself. Because the bottom half of the matrix contains the same correlations as the top, we need concern ourselves with only the upper half.

Table **A.5** | **Intercorrelations among Six Items from an Anxiety Scale**

Test	1	2	3	4	5	6
1	1.00	.84	.76	.47	.53	.42
2		1.00	.79	.44	.39	.51
3			1.00	.50	.38	.46
4				1.00	.82	.74
5					1.00	.92
6						1.00

Table A.5 shows that items 1, 2, and 3 correlate highly with one another. Likewise, items 4, 5, and 6 correlate strongly with one another. Notice also that items 1, 2, and 3 have much lower correlations with items 4, 5, and 6, indicating that the two clusters are measuring different things. But just what do these two clusters of items measure? Factor analysis cannot answer this question directly; it can only identify the clusters for us. Now it is up to us to examine the nature of the items in each cluster and decide what the underlying factors might be.

Suppose that item 1 says "My body feels tense much of the time," item 2 reads "My heart often pounds in my chest," and item 3 says "My underarms are often wet with perspiration." Because all three items relate to bodily arousal responses, we might decide to call this first factor *physiological arousal* or *somatic anxiety*. Now, let's take a look at items 4, 5, and 6 and see if we can figure out what they're measuring. Item 4 reads "I worry that something bad is going to happen," item 5 says "I have great difficulty concentrating because of worrisome thoughts," and item 6 says "I worry that I will not be able to handle important situations." These items seem to capture mental aspects of anxiety rather than physiological responses, so we might decide to call our second factor *worry* or *cognitive anxiety*. And, in fact, this factor structure is what typically is found when anxiety items are subjected to factor analysis. Indeed, consistent findings that the somatic and cognitive components are distinct aspects of anxiety (and other emotions) have stimulated and supported the models of emotion and stress described in Chapters 11 and 14 of this book. From a practical perspective, we now have a scientific basis for constructing two subscales from our anxiety measure so that, in addition to a total score, we can also measure differences between people in both somatic and cognitive anxiety. We can see, therefore, why factor analysis is a valuable tool within psychology, where researchers often attempt to identify basic dimensions of behavior and experience.

Inferential Statistics and Hypothesis Testing

Regardless of the type of research, psychologists rarely have access to the entire population of people they are interested in. Instead, they must be satisfied with studying relatively small samples of participants. Thus, 80 introductory psychology students might participate in an experiment on bystander helping, and 400 adults recruited through newspaper advertisements

might participate in a correlational study examining the relation between self-esteem and depression. On the basis of the results obtained from such samples, researchers seek to generalize their conclusions to the population as a whole.

In experiments, we are typically interested in overall differences between the various conditions. Suppose we find that participants randomly assigned to be alone help a victim more quickly than participants assigned to groups of two or four bystanders. Before concluding that the independent variable (number of bystanders) truly influenced the dependent variable (speed of helping), we first must ask whether this difference is "real" or is merely a "chance" finding. In other words, because our data are based only on a particular sample of people in each condition, how do we know that similar results would have occurred if we had tested other samples? Perhaps for one reason or another the participants we tested were not truly representative of the populations from which they were drawn. Perhaps, despite random assignment, participants assigned to be alone happened by chance to have more highly altruistic personalities than participants in the other conditions, and this (rather than being alone) is the reason they helped more quickly.

Inferential statistics *tell us how confident we can be in drawing conclusions or inferences about a population based on findings obtained from a sample.* Thus, if we observe differences in an experiment between experimental and control groups or find that there is a correlation between two variables, we use inferential statistics to determine the likelihood that these results occurred by chance alone and thus do not reflect a genuine difference in the population from which the sample was drawn. When researchers analyze their data and conclude that a correlation or a difference in behavior between groups in an experiment is "statistically significant," the term **statistical significance** *means that it is unlikely that the particular finding occurred by chance alone.* Psychologists typically consider a result to be statistically significant only if it could have occurred by chance alone less than 5 times in 100.

The logic underlying tests of statistical significance is related to our previous discussion of the normal curve and its statistical properties. Determining statistical significance is in many ways similar to the IQ problem presented earlier in the Appendix: If IQ is normally distributed with a mean of 100 and a standard deviation of 15, what is the likelihood of randomly selecting a person with an IQ of 145? To answer that question, all we had to do was to determine what proportion of cases are 3 standard deviations above the mean in a normal distribution. We found that proportion to be about one-eighth of 1 percent. Thus we would expect to randomly select a person with an IQ that high about 1 in 1,000 times—pretty small odds. With this example in mind, let us consider the logic of statistical inference in greater detail.

Suppose we are interested in the effects of a stress-management program on the academic performance of freshman college students who are high in test anxiety. We hypothesize that learning to control anxiety during tests will result in better performance. We randomly assign 40 students who have received high scores on a self-report measure of test anxiety to either an experimental group (20 participants) that participates in a stress-management program for test anxiety, or to a control group (20 participants) that receives no guidance or treatment. All of the students take the same required courses, and at the end of the academic year we compare the mean grade point averages of the two groups. On a 0.0 (F) to 4.0 (A) scale, we find that the experimental group (training program condition) obtains a mean grade point of 3.17 and the control group has a mean grade point of 2.61. Thus the difference between the two groups is $3.17 - 2.61 = +0.56$ grade point. How can we decide whether this difference between the two samples reflects a difference in the respective populations (i.e., all high-test-anxious students who might participate in a stress-management program and all who do not)?

If we repeated our experiment several times with different high-anxiety participants, we would find that the means for the two samples would vary in each experiment. For example, the next three times we performed the study the means might be 2.94 (experimental) versus 2.77 (control), 3.34 versus 2.31, and 2.89 versus 2.83, yielding differences between the groups of 0.17, 1.03, and 0.06, respectively. By repeating the experiment a great many times, we could create a distribution of experimental versus control difference scores, and mathematical theory tells us that this distribution would be a *normal* distribution. This gives us the key. Because we have a normal distribution, just as we previously assessed the exact likelihood of randomly selecting a person with an IQ of 145, we can now determine the likelihood of randomly obtaining a difference of any particular size between our sample means. But to do this, we must first know what the mean and standard deviation of our distribution of differences are. As we've seen, one way to determine these values would be to perform our experiment a large number of times. But, fortunately, we can estimate these values on the basis of a single experiment and thereby avoid the need for many replications.

To do this, we use an approach to statistical analysis that involves testing the **null hypothesis,** *which states that any observed differences between the samples are due to chance.* We begin by assuming that the null hypothesis is true—that there is no real difference, for example, in grade point average between the populations of trained and untrained test-anxious students. If

the null hypothesis is true, then if we repeated our experiment a great many times, we would expect the mean of our distribution of difference scores to be zero. Therefore, the normal distribution of difference scores would cluster around this mean of zero. The standard deviation of this normal distribution can be estimated from the standard deviations of the two samples, although the mathematics need not concern us here.

In our hypothetical experiment, we obtained grade point means of 3.17 for the experimental group and 2.61 for the control group, a difference of +0.56. Let us now suppose that the standard deviation of our distribution of differences between means was estimated on the basis of our samples to be .25. Thus our obtained difference of +0.56 is slightly more than 2 SD above the mean (0) of the null hypothesis distribution. From the properties of the normal curve, we know that more than 95 percent of the cases fall in the area of the curve between −2 SD and +2 SD. Thus, *if the null hypothesis were true,* we would expect a difference in means as large as .56 (either above or below zero) less than 5 percent of the time on the basis of chance factors. This probability level meets the criterion for statistical significance described earlier. In view of this fact, we would reject the null hypothesis and conclude that there is a real difference in grade point average in the two populations. Thus our experimental hypothesis that the stress-management program resulted in a higher level of academic performance would be supported.

Note that we used the term *supported,* not *proven,* because we are making an inference based on a probability statement. There is, after all, some possibility (though less than 5 percent) that the null hypothesis is true and this really was a chance finding. Note also that this statistical analysis does not tell us why the stress-management group performed better (e.g., Did they perform better due to the program's content or the mere attention they received?). This is one reason why repeating, or replicating, research studies is so valuable. If another study—particularly one with more control groups—also yields statistically significant results, we can have more confidence that the difference we obtained reflects a real relation between the independent and dependent variables. But no matter how many times we repeat the experiment, we shall never move from the world of probability into the world of absolute truth.

Appendix Summary

- Descriptive statistics summarize the characteristics of a set of data. A frequency distribution shows how many participants received each score. Histograms are graphs of frequency distributions.
- The mean, median, and mode are measures of central tendency, and each describes a distribution in terms of a single "typical" score. The range, variance, and standard deviation are measures of variability, and each describes how much variation there is within a set of scores.

- A normal curve is a theoretical, symmetrical bell-shaped curve. Fifty percent of the cases fall on each side of the mean, and the mean, median, and mode all have the same value. The standard deviation can be used to make probability estimates by dividing the normal distribution into areas containing known percentages of a population.
- Researchers seek to determine how much behavioral variance can be accounted for by relations between variables,

including experimental manipulations, and how much is due to random, unmeasured, or uncontrolled factors.

• Two variables are correlated when changes in the scores of one variable correspond reliably with changes in the scores of the other variable. Correlations may be positive, negative, or zero, as well as weak or strong. Squaring the correlation coefficient tells us how much of the variance in one measure can be accounted for by differences in the other measure. Correlation does not allow us to assume causality, but it often gives us the basis for predictions.

• Factor analysis reduces a large number of measures to a smaller number of clusters. The measures within each cluster are highly intercorrelated and reflect the same underlying dimension.

• Inferential statistics tell us how likely it is that differences between groups or correlations among variables are the result of chance alone. We need inferential statistics because most research is done with samples, and such statistics allow us to generalize conclusions to the population from which the sample was drawn.

• Typically, a result is considered statistically significant only if it could have occurred by chance alone less than 5 times in 100. Statistical analysis often involves testing the null hypothesis, which assumes that any observed difference between group means or correlation among variables is due to chance. Inferential statistics yield probability statements, not absolute proof.

KEY TERMS AND CONCEPTS

descriptive statistics (A-1)
factor analysis (A-7)
frequency distribution (A-1)
histogram (A-1)
inferential statistics (A-8)
mean (A-1)

measures of central tendency (A-1)
measures of variability (A-3)
median (A-2)
mode (A-1)
normal curve (A-4)
null hypothesis (A-9)

Pearson product-moment correlation
  coefficient (A-6)
range (A-3)
standard deviation (SD) (A-3)
statistical significance (A-8)
variance (A-3)

Glossary

A

abnormal behavior Behavior that is personally distressful, personally dysfunctional, and/or so culturally deviant that other people judge it to be inappropriate or maladaptive.

absolute refractory period The brief time interval following an action potential when a neuron is incapable of being stimulated to fire another impulse.

absolute threshold The lowest intensity at which a stimulus can be detected 50 percent of the time.

abstinence violation effect A response to a lapse in which a person blames himself or herself and concludes that he or she is incapable of resisting high-risk situations.

Acceptance and Commitment Therapy (ACT) A recently developed "third wave" behavior therapy that focuses on mindfulness, accepting negative feelings, and identifying core values.

accommodation In cognitive development, the process by which new experiences cause existing schemas to change.

acetylcholine (ACh) An excitatory neurotransmitter that operates at synapses with muscles and is also the transmitter in some neural networks involved in memory.

achievement goal theory A theory of achievement motivation that stresses the goals (ego versus mastery) and motivational climates that influence achievement strivings.

achievement test A measure of an individual's degree of accomplishment in a particular subject or task based on a relatively standardized set of experiences.

action potential A nerve impulse resulting from the depolarization of an axon's cell membrane.

activation-synthesis theory Maintains that dreams represent the brain's attempt to interpret random patterns of neural activation triggered by the brain stem during sleep.

adaptations Biological and behavioral changes that allow organisms to meet recurring environmental challenges to their survival, thereby increasing their reproductive ability.

adaptive significance The manner in which a particular behavior enhances an organism's chances of survival and reproduction in its natural environment.

adolescence The period of development that involves a gradual transition between childhood and adulthood.

adolescent egocentrism Highly self-focused thinking, particularly in the early teenage years.

adoption study A research method in behavior genetics in which adopted people are compared on some characteristic with both their biological and adoptive parents in an attempt to determine the strength of the characteristic's genetic component.

adrenal glands Endocrine glands that release stress hormones, including catecholamines and corticosteroids.

aerobic exercise Sustained activity that elevates the heart rate and increases the body's need for oxygen.

agonist A drug that increases or mimics the activity of a neurotransmitter.

agoraphobia A fear of being in places or situations (e.g., on a bridge or a bus, in crowds or wide open spaces) from which escape might be difficult in the event of sudden incapacitation.

alcohol myopia When intoxicated, a "short-sightedness" in thinking (a failure to consider consequences) caused by an inability to pay attention to as much information as when sober.

algorithms Procedures, such as mathematical formulas, that automatically generate correct solutions to problems.

alleles Alternate forms of a gene that produce different characteristics.

all-or-none law States that an action potential is not proportional to the intensity of stimulation; either a neuron fires with maximum intensity or it does not fire (compare with *graded potential*).

alpha waves A brain-wave pattern of 8 to 12 cycles per second that is characteristic of humans in a relaxed, drowsy state.

Alzheimer's disease (AD) A brain disorder, typically but not always occurring in old age, whose prominent features are memory loss and confused thinking.

amplitude The vertical size of the sound wave, which gives rise to the perception of loudness and is measured in terms of decibels.

amygdala A limbic system structure that helps organize emotional response patterns.

anorexia nervosa An eating disorder involving a severe and sometimes fatal restriction of food intake.

antagonist A drug that inhibits or decreases the action of a neurotransmitter.

anterograde amnesia Memory loss for events that occur after the initial onset of amnesia.

anticipatory nausea and vomiting (ANV) Classically conditioned nausea and vomiting that occur when cancer patients are exposed to stimuli associated with their treatment.

antigens Literally, antibody generators, or foreign substances that activate the cells of the immune system.

antisocial personality disorder (APD) A long-term stable disorder characterized by a lack of conscience, defects in empathy, and a tendency to act out in an impulsive manner that disregards future consequences.

anxiety An emotional state characterized by apprehension accompanied by physiological arousal and fearful behavior.

anxiety disorders A group of behavior disorders in which anxiety and associated maladaptive behaviors are the core of the disturbance.

aphasia The partial or total loss of ability to understand speech (receptive aphasia) or to produce it (productive aphasia).

applied behavior analysis A process in which operant conditioning is combined with scientific data collection to solve individual and societal problems.

applied research Research that is designed to solve or examine specific, practical problems.

approach-approach conflict A conflict in which an individual is simultaneously attracted to two incompatible positive goals.

approach-avoidance conflict A conflict in which an individual is simultaneously attracted to and repelled by the same goal.

aptitude test A measure of a person's ability to profit from further training or experience in an occupation or skill; usually based on a measure of skills gained over a person's lifetime rather than during a specific course of study.

archetypes   In Jung's theory, innate concepts and memories (e.g., God, the hero, the good mother); memories that reside in the collective unconscious.

archival measures   Records or past documents that contain information about some type of behavior.

assimilation   In cognitive development, the process by which new experiences are incorporated into existing schemas.

association cortex   The areas of the cerebral cortex that do not have sensory or motor functions but are involved in the integration of neural activity that underlies perception, language, and other higher-order mental processes.

associative network   The view that long-term memory is organized as a massive network of associated ideas and concepts.

attachment   The strong emotional bond that develops between two people; developmentally, the bond between children and their primary caregivers.

attention deficit/hyperactivity disorder (ADHD)   A disorder, usually originating in childhood, that may take the form of attentional difficulties, hyperactivity/impulsivity, or a combination of the two that results in impaired functioning.

attitude   A positive or negative evaluative reaction toward a stimulus (e.g., toward a person, action, object, or concept).

attribution   A judgment about the causes of our own and other people's behavior.

authoritarian parents   Caregivers who exert control over their children within a cold, unresponsive, or rejecting relationship.

authoritative parents   Caregivers who are controlling but warm; they establish and enforce clear rules within a caring, supportive atmosphere.

autistic disorder   A severe developmental disorder characterized by extreme unresponsiveness to others, poor communication skills, and highly repetitive and rigid behavior patterns.

autobiographical memories   Recollections of personally experienced events that make up the "story of our life."

automatic (unconscious) processing   Mental activities that occur with minimal or no conscious control or awareness.

autonomic nervous system   The branch of the peripheral nervous system that activates the body's involuntary muscles (e.g., heart) and internal organs.

availability heuristic   A rule of thumb used to make likelihood judgments based on how easily examples of that category of events come to mind or are "available" in memory.

aversion therapy   A form of therapy in which a conditioned stimulus that currently evokes a positive but maladaptive response is paired with a noxious, unpleasant unconditioned stimulus, in an attempt to condition a repulsion toward the conditioned stimulus.

aversive punishment (positive punishment, punishment by application)   A type of punishment in which an operant response is weakened by the subsequent presentation of a noxious stimulus.

avoidance-avoidance conflict   A conflict in which an individual must choose between two undesirable alternatives.

avoidance conditioning   A form of learning in which an organism learns a response to avoid an undesirable consequence.

axon   An extension from one side of the neuron cell body that conducts nerve impulses to other neurons, muscles, or glands.

B

Barnum effect   The tendency for people to see descriptive statements that apply to most people as uniquely descriptive of themselves.

basic research   Research designed to obtain knowledge for its own sake.

basilar membrane   A membrane that runs the length of the cochlea and contains the organ of Corti and its sound receptor hair cells.

behavioral activation   A treatment for depression that engages clients in life activities designed to increase positive reinforcement in their lives.

behavioral activation system (BAS)   A neural system that is activated by cues indicating potential reward and positive need gratification. Activity in this neural system causes the person to begin or to increase movement toward positive goals in anticipation of pleasure.

behavioral assessment   The measurement of behavior through direct observation and application of a coding system.

behavioral inhibition system (BIS)   A neural system that is activated by cues indicating potential pain, nonreinforcement, and punishment. Activity in this neural system produces fear, inhibition of behavior, as well as escape and avoidance behaviors.

behavioral neuroscience   A subfield of psychology that examines brain processes and other physiological functions that underlie our behavior, sensory experiences, emotions, and thoughts.

behavioral perspective   A view that emphasizes how the environment and learning experiences shape and control behavior.

behavioral signatures   Individually consistent ways of responding in particular classes of situations.

behavior genetics   The scientific study of the role of genetic inheritance in behavior.

behaviorism   A school of psychology that emphasizes the effects of learning and environmental control on behavior and maintains that the proper subject matter of psychology is observable behavior.

behavior modification   Therapeutic procedures based on operant conditioning principles, such as positive reinforcement, operant extinction, and punishment.

behavior-outcome expectancy   The subjective likelihood that a particular consequence will follow a particular behavior in a given situation.

belief bias   The tendency to abandon logical rules and to form a conclusion based on one's existing beliefs.

beta waves   A brain-wave pattern of 15 to 30 cycles per second that is characteristic of humans who are in an alert waking state.

bilingualism   The use of two languages in daily life.

binocular depth cues   Depth cues that require the use of both eyes.

binocular disparity   The binocular depth cue produced by the projection of slightly different images of an object on the retinas of the two eyes.

biologically based mechanisms   Evolved biological structures that receive input from the environment, process the information, and respond to it.

biological perspective   A view that focuses on the role of biological factors in behavior, including biochemical and brain processes, as well as genetic and evolutionary factors.

biopsychology   A subfield of psychology that focuses on the biological underpinnings of behavior, thought, and emotion.

bipolar disorder   A mood disorder in which intermittent mania appears against a background of depression.

blindsight   A disorder in which people are blind in part of their visual field yet, in special tests, respond to stimuli in that field despite reporting that they cannot see those stimuli.

blood-brain barrier   A specialized lining of cells in the brain's blood vessels that screens out foreign substances while letting nutrients pass through to neurons.

borderline personality disorder (BPD)   A serious personality disorder characterized by severe instability in behavior, emotion, identity, and interpersonal relationships.

bottom-up processing   Perceptual processes that begin with the analysis of individual elements of the stimulus and work up to the brain's integration of them into a unified perception.

brain stem   The portion of the brain formed by the swelling of the spinal cord as it enters the skull; its structures regulate basic survival functions of the body, such as heart rate and respiration.

British empiricism   A 17th-century school of philosophy championed by Locke, according to which all the contents of the mind are gained experientially through the senses.

Broca's area   A region of the left frontal lobe involved in speech production.

bulimia nervosa   An eating disorder that involves a repeated cycle of binge eating followed by purging of the food.

bystander effect   The principle that the presence of multiple bystanders inhibits each person's tendency to help, largely due to social comparison or diffusion of responsibility.

C

Cannon-Bard theory   A theory of emotion that proposed that the thalamus sends simultaneous messages to the cortex (producing our experience of emotion) and to the viscera and skeletal muscles, producing actions and physiological responses.

case study   An in-depth analysis of an individual, group, or event.

catatonic schizophrenia   A schizophrenic reaction characterized by alternating stuporous states and agitated excitement, during which the person can be quite dangerous.

catharsis   The idea that performing an act of aggression discharges aggressive energy and temporarily reduces our impulse to aggress.

central nervous system   The portion of the nervous system that includes the brain and the spinal cord.

central route to persuasion   Occurs when people think carefully about a message and are influenced because they find the arguments compelling.

cephalocaudal principle   The tendency for physical development to proceed in a head-to-foot direction.

cerebellum   A convoluted hindbrain structure involved in motor coordination and some aspects of learning and memory.

cerebral cortex   The gray, convoluted outer covering of the brain that is the seat of higher-order sensory, motor, perceptual, and mental processes.

cerebrum   The most advanced portion of the brain, containing the cerebral cortex and underlying structures.

chaining   An operant conditioning procedure used to develop a sequence (chain) of responses by reinforcing each response with the opportunity to perform the next response.

cholecystokinin (CCK)   A peptide (hormone) that helps produce satiety and cessation of eating.

chromosomes   Tightly coiled strands of deoxyribonucleic acid (DNA) and protein that contain the genes.

chunking   Combining individual items into larger units of meaning.

circadian rhythms   Biological cycles within the body that occur on an approximately 24-hour cycle.

classical conditioning   A procedure in which a formerly neutral stimulus (the conditioned stimulus) comes to elicit a conditioned response by virtue of being paired with an unconditioned stimulus that naturally elicits a similar response (the unconditioned response).

clinical psychology   A subfield of psychology that focuses on the study and treatment of mental disorders.

cochlea   A small coil-shaped structure of the inner ear that contains the receptors for sound.

cognitive-affective personality system (CAPS)   A model that organizes five "person variables" that account for how a person might respond to a particular situation; the dynamic interplay among these five factors, together with the characteristics of the situation, accounts for individual differences between people, as well as differences in people's behavior across different situations.

cognitive appraisal   The process of making judgments about situations, personal capabilities, likely consequences, and personal meaning of consequences.

cognitive behaviorism   A behavioral approach that incorporates cognitive concepts, suggesting that the environment influences our behavior by affecting our thoughts and giving us information.

cognitive map   A mental representation of the spatial layout of an area.

cognitive neuroscience   An area of psychology that intersects the subfields of cognitive psychology and physiological psychology and examines brain processes that underlie mental activity.

cognitive perspective   A view that emphasizes humans as information processors and problem solvers, and that focuses on the mental processes that influence behavior.

cognitive-process dream theories   Approaches that focus on how (rather than why) we dream, and propose that dreaming and

waking thought are produced by the same mental systems in the brain.

cognitive process theories   Approaches to intelligence that analyze the mental processes that underlie intelligent thinking.

cognitive psychology   An area of psychology that specializes in studying mental processes such as thinking, memory, planning, reasoning, attention, and perception.

collective unconscious   Jung's notion of an unconscious that consists of innate ancestral memories.

common factors   Therapeutic elements that are possessed by virtually any type of therapy and that may contribute to the similar positive effects shown by many different treatment approaches.

communicator credibility   The degree to which an audience views a communicator as believable, largely based on the communicator's expertise and trustworthiness.

companionate love   An affectionate relationship characterized by commitment and caring about the partner's well-being; sometimes contrasted with passionate love, which is more intensely emotional.

compensatory response   A bodily response that opposes a drug's effects and occurs in an attempt to restore homeostasis.

competency   A legal decision that a defendant is mentally capable of understanding the nature of the charges, participating meaningfully in the trial, and consulting with his or her attorney.

competency-focused intervention   Prevention programs that are designed to enhance personal resources needed to cope with situations that might otherwise cause psychological disorders.

compulsion   A repetitive act that the person feels compelled to carry out, often in response to an obsessive thought or image.

computerized axial tomography (CT, or CAT) scan   A method of scanning the brain with narrow beams of X rays that are then analyzed and combined by a computer to provide pictures of brain structures from many different angles.

concept   A mental category containing similiar objects, people, and events.

concordance   The likelihood that two people share a particular characteristic.

concrete operational stage   In Piaget's theory, the stage of cognitive development during which children can perform basic mental operations concerning problems that involve tangible (i.e., "concrete") objects and situations.

conditioned response (CR)   In classical conditioning, a response to a conditioned stimulus; the conditioned response is established by pairing a conditioned stimulus with an unconditioned stimulus that evokes a similar response.

conditioned stimulus (CS)   A stimulus that comes to evoke a conditioned response after being paired with an unconditioned stimulus.

conditioned taste aversion   A learned repulsion to a food that formerly was neutral or desired, by virtue of pairing the food with an aversive unconditioned stimulus.

conditions of worth   Internalized standards for self-worth fostered by conditional positive regard from others.

conduction deafness   Hearing loss caused by damage to the mechanical system that conducts sound waves to the cochlea.

cones   Photoreceptors in the retina that function best in bright light and are differentially sensitive to red, green, or blue wavelengths.

confirmation bias   The tendency to seek and favor information that reinforces our beliefs rather than to be open to disconfirming information.

confounding of variables   In an experiment, a situation in which the independent variable is intertwined or mixed up with another, uncontrolled variable; thus we cannot tell which variable is responsible for changes in the behavior of interest (i.e., in the dependent variable).

congruence   Consistency between self-perceptions and experience.

consciousness   Our moment-to-moment awareness of ourselves and our environment; consciousness involves selective attention to ongoing thoughts, perceptions, and feelings.

conservation   The principle that basic properties of objects, such as their mass or quantity, stay the same (are "conserved") even though their outward appearance may change.

construct validity   The extent to which a test measures the psychological construct (e.g., intelligence, anxiety) that it is purported to measure.

content validity   The extent to which test items adequately sample the domain that the test is supposed to measure (e.g., intelligence, mathematical reasoning).

context-dependent memory   The phenomenon that it is typically easier to remember something in the same environment in which it was originally learned or experienced.

continuous reinforcement   A reinforcement schedule in which each response of a particular type is followed by reinforcement.

control group   In an experiment, the group that either is not exposed to the treatment or receives a zero level of the independent variable.

controlled (conscious) processing   Mental processing that requires volitional control and attentiveness.

conventional moral reasoning   According to Kohlberg, the stage at which moral judgments are based on conformity to social expectations, laws, and duties.

convergence   A binocular depth cue produced by the muscles that rotate the eyes as they focus on nearby objects.

conversion disorder   A disorder in which serious neurological symptoms, such as paralysis, loss of sensation, or blindness, suddenly occur without physical cause.

coping self-efficacy   Beliefs relating to our ability to deal effectively with a stressful stimulus or situation, including pain.

corpus callosum   A broad band of white, myelinated fibers that connects the left and right cerebral hemispheres and allows the two hemispheres to communicate with one another.

correlational research   Research that measures two or more naturally occurring variables and examines whether they are statistically related.

correlation coefficient   A statistic that indicates the direction and strength of a relation between two variables; values can range from $+1.00$ to -1.00.

counterbalancing   In experiments, a procedure in which each participant engages in all of the conditions. The order of the conditions is altered for different participants so that, overall, no condition has an order advantage relative to the other conditions.

counterconditioning   The process of conditioning an incompatible response to a particular stimulus to eliminate a maladaptive response (e.g., anxiety), as occurs in systematic desensitization.

creativity   The ability to produce something that is both new and valuable.

criterion-related validity   The ability of psychological test scores to correlate with some present or future behavior assumed to be influenced by the construct measured by the test.

critical periods   Limited time periods during which plasticity can occur as a result of experience or in response to injury; in development, a time period in which exposure to particular kinds of stimulation is required for normal growth to occur.

cross-sectional design   A research design that simultaneously compares people of different ages at a particular point in time.

crystallized intelligence (g_c)   Intellectual abilities that depend on a store of information and the acquisition of particular skills (compare with *fluid intelligence*).

cultural congruence   The extent to which a form of treatment is consistent with the culture of a particular ethnic group.

cultural display rules   Cultural norms that regulate when and how emotions are expressed.

culturally competent therapists   Practitioners who have a set of therapeutic skills, including scientific mindedness, the ability to consider both cultural and individual factors, and the capacity to introduce culture-specific elements into therapy with people from minority cultures.

cultural psychology (cross-cultural psychology)   A subfield of psychology that explores how culture is transmitted to its members and examines psychological similarities and differences that occur between people from diverse cultures.

culture-bound disorders   Behavior disorders whose specific forms are restricted to one particular cultural context.

D

dark adaptation   The progressive increase in brightness sensitivity that occurs over time as photopigments regenerate themselves during exposure to low levels of illumination.

decay theory   Maintains that with time and disuse, the physical memory trace in the nervous system fades away.

decibel   A logarithmic measure of sound intensity.

decision criterion   In signal detection theory, the potentially changing standard of how certain a person must be that a stimulus is present in order to report its presence.

declarative memory   Our memory for factual knowledge, which comprises two subcategories: knowledge pertaining to personal experiences (episodic memory) and knowledge of general facts and language (semantic memory).

deductive reasoning   Reasoning from a general principle to a specific case.

deep structure   A linguistic term that refers to the underlying meaning of a spoken or written sentence; the meanings that make up deep structure are stored as concepts and rules in long-term memory.

defense mechanisms   Unconscious processes that help us cope with anxiety and the pain of traumatic experiences. Defense mechanisms prevent the expression of anxiety-arousing impulses or allow them to appear in disguised forms.

deindividuation   A state of increased anonymity in which a person, often as part of a group or crowd, engages in disinhibited behavior.

deinstitutionalization movement   The attempt to move the primary locus of treatment from mental hospitals to the community.

delta waves   Low-frequency, high-amplitude brain waves that occur in stage 3 sleep and predominate in stage 4 sleep.

delusions   False beliefs, often involving themes of persecution or grandeur, that are sustained in the face of evidence that normally would be sufficient to destroy them.

dementia   The gradual loss of cognitive abilities that accompanies brain deterioration and interferes with normal functioning.

dendrites   Small branching fibers that extend from the soma of a neuron and receive messages from adjacent neurons.

dependent variable   In an experiment, the factor measured by the researcher that presumably is influenced by the independent variable.

depressants   Drugs—including alcohol, barbiturates, and tranquilizers—that reduce neural activity and can decrease feelings of tension and anxiety.

depressive attributional pattern   The tendency of depressed people to attribute negative outcomes to their own inadequacies and positive outcomes to factors outside of themselves.

descriptive research   Research in which the main goal is to carefully describe how organisms behave, particularly in natural settings.

descriptive statistics   Statistics that summarize and describe the characteristics of a set of scores.

developmental psychology   A subfield of psychology that examines human physical, psychological, and social development across the life span.

Dialectical Behavior Therapy (DBT)   A recently developed cognitive-behavioral treatment for borderline personality disorder.

difference threshold   The smallest difference between two similar stimuli that people can detect; also called the *just noticeable difference (jnd)*.

discourse   The combining of sentences into larger language units, such as paragraphs, articles, novels, and so on.

discrimination (classical conditioning)   The occurrence of a conditioned response to one stimulus but not to another stimulus.

discrimination (social behavior)   Treating people unfairly based on the group to which they belong.

discriminative stimulus   An antecedent stimulus that signals the likelihood of certain consequences if a response is made.

disorganized schizophrenia   A schizophrenic disorder marked by verbal incoherence, disordered thought processes, disorganized behavior, and inappropriate emotional responses.

displacement   The capacity of language to represent objects and conditions that are not physically present.

dissociation theories (of hypnosis)   Views that focus on hypnosis as an altered state involving a division ("dissociation") of consciousness; one theory proposes that the hypnotized person simultaneously experiences two streams of consciousness that are cut off from one another.

dissociative disorders   Disorders that involve a major dissociation of personal identity or memory.

dissociative identity disorder (DID)   A dissociative disorder in which two or more separate identities or personalities coexist within an individual.

divergent thinking   A creative form of thinking that involves generating novel ideas that diverge from the normal ways of thinking about something.

divided attention   The ability to perform more than one activity at the same time.

dodo bird verdict   The conclusion reached by some psychotherapy researchers that virtually all treatment approaches have similar success rates.

dominant gene   A gene that will produce a particular effect by overriding the influence of a recessive gene for the same characteristic.

door-in-the-face technique   A manipulation technique in which a persuader makes a large request, expecting you to reject it, and then presents a smaller request.

dopamine hypothesis   States that the symptoms of schizophrenia are produced by overactivity of the dopamine system in areas of the brain that regulate emotional expression, motivated behavior, and cognitive functioning.

double-blind procedure   A procedure in which both the participant and the experimenter are kept unaware of the research condition to which the participant has been assigned.

downward comparison   Seeing oneself or one's situation as more positive than a standard of comparison, thereby increasing one's sense of well-being.

drive   A state of internal tension that motivates an organism to behave in ways that reduce this tension.

dual coding theory   Maintains that if we encode information using both verbal and imagery codes, the chances improve that at least one of the two codes will be available later to support recall.

dual-process theory   A modern theory of color vision that combines the trichromatic and opponent-process theories. Light waves are coded by red-, blue-, and green-sensitive cones in the retina and by opponent processes thereafter in the visual system.

dynamic testing   A procedure in which static (standardized testing) is followed up with an interaction in which the examiner gives the subject guided feedback on how to improve performance and observes how the subject utilizes the information.

dysthymia   A depressive mood disorder of moderate intensity that occurs over a long period of time but does not disrupt functioning, as a major depression does.

E

effect size   In meta-analysis, a measure of treatment effectiveness that indicates what percentage of treated clients improve more than the average untreated client.

ego   The "executive" of the personality that is partly conscious and that mediates between the impulses of the id, the prohibitions of the superego, and the dictates of reality.

ego-approach goals   An achievement orientation that focuses on being judged successful as a result of outperforming others.

ego-avoidance goals   An achievement orientation that focuses on avoiding negative judgments by self or others due to failing to outperform others.

egocentrism   Difficulty in viewing the world from someone else's perspective.

ego orientation   An achievement goal orientation in which success is defined in terms of how well one compares with others and "wins out."

elaborative rehearsal   Focusing on the meaning of information or relating it to other things we already know.

Electra complex   The female version of the Oedipus complex in which the female child experiences erotic feelings toward her father, desires to possess him sexually, and views her mother as a rival.

electroencephalograph (EEG)   A device used to record the simultaneous activity of many thousands of neurons through electrodes attached to the scalp.

eliciting stimuli   Internal or external cues that evoke an emotional response.

embryo   A scientific term for the prenatal organism during the 2nd week through the 8th week after conception.

emotion   A pattern of cognitive, physiological, and behavioral responses to situations and events that have relevance to important goals or motives.

emotional intelligence   The ability to respond adaptively in the emotional realm by reading and responding appropriately to others' emotions and to be aware of and have the ability to control one's own emotions.

emotion-focused coping   Coping strategies directed at minimizing or reducing emotional responses to a stressor.

emotion regulation   The processes by which we evaluate and modify our emotional reactions.

empathy   The capacity for experiencing the same emotional response being exhibited by another person; in therapy, the ability of a therapist to view the world through the client's eyes and to understand the client's emotions.

empathy-altruism hypothesis   The view that pure altruism does exist and that it is produced by the capacity to empathize with the person in need of aid.

empirical approach   An approach to test construction in which items (regardless of their content) are chosen that differentiate between two groups that are known to differ on a particular personality variable.

empirically supported therapies (ESTs)   Psychotherapy and behavior-change techniques that have been shown to be efficacious in controlled clinical trials.

encoding   Getting information into the memory system by translating it into a neural code that the brain processes and stores.

encoding specificity principle   States that memory is enhanced when conditions present during retrieval match those that were present during encoding.

endocrine system   The body's system of glands that secrete hormones into the bloodstream and thereby affect many bodily functions.

endorphins   Natural opiate-like substances that are involved in pain reduction.

epigenetics   Changes in gene expression that are independent of the DNA itself and are caused instead by environmental factors.

episodic memory   Our store of factual knowledge concerning personal experiences—when, where, and what happened in the episodes of our lives.

equal status contact   The principle that prejudice between people is most likely to be reduced when they engage in sustained close contact, have equal status within the context of their interaction, work to achieve a common goal that requires cooperation, and are supported by broader social norms that encourage prejudice reduction.

escape conditioning   A form of learning in which the organism learns to perform a behavior to terminate an aversive stimulus.

evocative influence   The tendency of a genetically influenced characteristic (e.g., agreeableness) to evoke a particular response from others.

evoked culture   The notion that cultures may themselves be the product of biological mechanisms that evolved to meet specific adaptational challenges.

evolution   A change over time in the frequency with which particular genes, and the characteristics they produce, occur within an interbreeding population.

evolutionary/circadian sleep models   The view that in the course of evolution, each species developed an adaptive circadian sleep-wake pattern that increased its chances of survival in relation to its environmental demands.

evolutionary psychology   A field of study that focuses on the role of evolutionary processes (especially natural selection) in the development of adaptive psychological mechanisms and social behavior in humans.

expectancy × value theory   A cognitive theory stating that goal-directed behavior is jointly influenced by (1) the person's expectancy that a particular behavior will contribute to reaching the goal and (2) how positively or negatively the person values the goal.

experiment   A research method in which the researcher manipulates an independent variable under controlled conditions and measures whether this produces changes in a dependent variable.

experimental group   In an experiment, the group that receives a treatment or is exposed to an active level of the independent variable.

experimental psychology   A subfield of psychology that focuses on basic processes such as learning, sensory systems (e.g., vision), perception, and motivational states (e.g., hunger).

experimenter expectancy effects   Subtle and unintentional ways in which an experimenter influences participants to behave in a way that will confirm the experimenter's hypothesis.

explicit memory   Conscious or intentional memory retrieval.

explicit prejudice   Prejudice that is expressed publicly, as when talking with someone or responding to a questionnaire.

exposure   A behavior therapy treatment in which clients are presented, either in vivo or in their imagination, with fear-inducing stimuli, thus allowing extinction to occur.

exposure therapies   Therapeutic techniques designed to extinguish anxiety responses by exposing clients to anxiety-arousing stimuli or situations while preventing escape or avoidance.

expressive behavior   Observable behavior that accompanies subjectively experienced emotions.

external validity   The degree to which the results of a study can be generalized to other people, settings, and conditions.

extinction (classical conditioning)   Occurs when a conditioned stimulus is presented without the unconditioned stimulus, causing the conditioned response to weaken and eventually stop occurring.

extinction (operant conditioning)   See *operant extinction.*

extrinsic motivation   Motivation to perform a behavior to obtain external rewards and reinforcers, such as money, status, attention, and praise.

F

facial feedback hypothesis   States that somatic feedback from facial muscles to the brain influences emotional experience.

factor analysis   A statistical technique that permits a researcher to reduce a large number of measures to a small number of clusters or factors; it identifies the clusters of behavior or test scores that are highly correlated with one another.

family study   The study of people who are related to one another to determine whether degree of genetic similarity is related to similarity on a particular trait.

feature detectors   Sensory neurons that respond to particular features of a stimulus, such as its shape, angle, or color.

feminist therapy   An orientation that focuses on women's issues and strives to help female clients achieve greater self-determination.

fetal alcohol spectrum disorders (FASD)   A range of mild to severe developmental abnormalities produced by prenatal exposure to alcohol.

fetal alcohol syndrome (FAS)   A severe group of abnormalities resulting from prenatal exposure to alcohol.

fetus   A scientific term for the prenatal organism from the 9th week after conception until birth.

figure-ground relations   Perceptual organization in which a focal stimulus is perceived as a figure against a background of other stimuli.

fixation   A state of arrested development due to unresolved conflicts at a particular earlier psychosexual stage.

fixed action pattern   An unlearned response that is automatically triggered by a simple (releaser) stimulus.

fixed-interval (FI) schedule   A reinforcement schedule in which the first response of a particular type is reinforced after a constant time interval.

fixed-ratio (FR) schedule   A reinforcement schedule in which reinforcement is given after a constant number of responses of a particular type.

flashbulb memories   Recollections that seem so vivid and clear that we can picture them as if they were snapshots of moments in time.

fluid intelligence (g_f)   The ability to deal with novel problem-solving situations for which personal experience does not supply a solution (compare with *crystallized intelligence*).

foot-in-the-door technique   A manipulation technique in which the persuader gets you to comply with a small request first and later presents a larger request.

forebrain   Brain structures above the midbrain, including the thalamus, hypothalamus, limbic system, and the cerebral hemispheres; involved in higher-order sensory, motor, and cognitive functions.

formal operational stage   In Piaget's theory, the period in which individuals are able to think logically and systematically about both concrete and abstract problems, form hypotheses, and test them in a thoughtful way.

fovea   A small area in the center of the retina that contains only cones and where visual acuity is greatest.

framing   The idea that the same information, problem, or choice options can be structured, presented, and thought about in different ways.

free association   In psychoanalysis, the procedure of verbalizing all thoughts that enter consciousness without censorship.

frequency   In audition, the number of cycles per second in a sound wave that is responsible for the pitch of the sound; the measure of frequency is the hertz (Hz), which equals one cycle per second.

frequency distribution   For a set of data, a table that shows how frequently each score value has occurred for a particular variable.

frequency theory of pitch perception   Maintains that the number of nerve impulses sent to the brain by the hair cells of the cochlea corresponds to the frequency of the sound wave; this theory is accurate at low frequencies.

fully functioning persons   Rogers's term for self-actualized people who are free from unrealistic conditions of worth and who exhibit congruence, spontaneity, creativity, and a desire to develop still further.

functional fixedness   A phenomenon often found in problem-solving tasks in which the customary use of an object interferes with its use in a novel situation.

functionalism   An early school of American psychology that focused on the functions of consciousness and behavior in helping organisms adapt to their environment and satisfy their needs.

functional MRI (fMRI)   A brain-scanning procedure that produces pictures of blood flow in the brain taken less than a second apart.

fundamental attribution error   The tendency to underestimate the impact of the situation and overestimate the role of personal factors when explaining other people's behavior.

fundamental emotional patterns   Basic emotional response patterns that are believed to be innate.

G

gate control theory   A theory of pain that postulates the existence of gating mechanisms in the spinal cord and brain that can increase or decrease the experience of pain by regulating the flow of pain impulses to the brain.

gender constancy   The understanding that being male or female is a permanent part of a person.

gender identity   The sense of "femaleness" or "maleness" that is an integral part of our identity.

gender schemas   Organized mental structures that contain our understanding of the attributes and behaviors that are appropriate and expected for males and females.

general adaptation syndrome (GAS)   Selye's description of the body's responses to a stressor, which includes successive phases of alarm, resistance, and exhaustion.

generalized anxiety disorder   A chronic state of diffuse, or "free-floating," anxiety that is not attached to specific situations or objects.

generativity   The principle that, in any given language, symbols can be combined to generate an infinite number of messages that have novel meaning.

genes   The biological units of heredity, located on the chromosomes.

genetic determinism   The notion that genes produce invariant and unavoidable effects that cannot be altered.

genotype   The specific genetic makeup of the individual, which may or may not be expressed in the observable phenotype.

genuineness   The ability of a therapist to honestly express her or his feelings to a client.

Gestalt laws of perceptual organization   The notion that people group and interpret stimuli in accordance with similarity, proximity, closure, and continuity.

g factor   A general intellectual capacity that underlies more specific intellectual abilities.

glucose   A simple sugar that is the body's (and especially the brain's) major source of immediately usable fuel.

graded potential   A change in the electrical potential of a neuron that is proportional to the intensity of the incoming stimulation but not sufficient to produce an action potential.

grammar   In any given language, the set of rules that dictates how symbols can be combined to create meaningful units of communication.

group polarization   When a group of like-minded people discusses an issue, the "average" opinion of group members tends to become more extreme.

groupthink   The tendency of group members to suspend critical thinking because they are motivated to seek agreement.

gustation   The sense of taste.

H

habituation   A decrease in the strength of a response to a repeated stimulus.

hallucinations   False perceptions that have a compelling sense of reality.

hallucinogens   Drugs, such as LSD and PCP, that distort or intensify sensory experiences and evoke hallucinations and disordered thought processes.

harm reduction   A prevention strategy that is designed not to eliminate a problem behavior but to reduce its harmful consequences.

health psychology   The study of psychological and behavioral factors in the prevention and treatment of illness and the enhancement of health.

hedonic treadmill   The tendency of people to return to a less extreme level of pleasure or pain with the passage of time following a very positive or very negative life change.

Hering's opponent-process theory   The color vision theory stating that the retina contains three sets of color receptors that respond differentially to red-green, blue-yellow, and black-white; the opponent processes that result can produce a perception of any hue.

heritability coefficient   A numerical estimate of the percentage of group variability in a particular characteristic that can be attributed to genetic factors.

hertz (Hz)   The measure of sound-wave frequency as cycles per second.

heuristics   A method of problem solving characterized by quick and easy search procedures similar to rules of thumb.

higher-order conditioning   In classical conditioning, a neutral stimulus becomes a conditioned stimulus after it is paired with another conditioned stimulus (rather than with the original unconditioned stimulus).

hindbrain   The part of the brain situated immediately above the spinal cord that contains the brain stem and cerebellum.

hippocampus   A structure of the limbic system that plays a key role in the formation and storage of memories.

histogram   A graph of a frequency distribution.

homeostasis   The maintenance of biological equilibrium, or balance, within the body.

hormones   Chemical substances secreted by the glands of the endocrine system that travel in the bloodstream and affect bodily organs, psychological functions, and development.

humanistic perspective (humanism)   A psychological view that emphasizes personal freedom, choice, and self-actualization.

hypnosis   A condition of enhanced suggestibility in which some people are able to experience imagined situations as if they were real.

hypnotic susceptibility scale   A set of induction procedures and test questions that enable researchers to measure a person's responsiveness to hypnotic suggestions.

hypochondriasis   A somatoform disorder characterized by an overreaction to physical symptoms and a conviction that one has or is on the verge of a serious illness.

hypothalamus   A forebrain structure located below the thalamus and above the pituitary gland that controls autonomic and hormonal processes and plays a major role in many aspects of motivation and emotional behavior.

hypothesis   A tentative explanation or a prediction about some phenomenon.

I

id   The primitive and unconscious part of the personality that contains the instincts.

illusions   Incorrect perceptions based on false perceptual hypotheses that often result from constancies that do not apply to the stimuli in question.

imaginal thought   A form of thinking that uses images that can be from any sense modality.

implicit memory   Occurs when memory influences our behavior without conscious awareness.

implicit prejudice   Prejudice that is hidden from public view, either intentionally or

because the person is not aware that he or she is prejudiced.

imprinting   In some species, a sudden, biologically primed form of attachment.

inattentional blindness   The failure of unattended stimuli to register in consciousness.

incentive   An environmental stimulus or condition that motivates behavior.

incremental theorist   An individual who believes that people's characteristics are changeable, not fixed.

incubation   A phenomenon in which the solution to a problem suddenly appears in consciousness after a problem solver has stopped thinking about it for a while.

independent variable   In an experiment, the factor that is manipulated by the researcher.

inductive reasoning   Reasoning that proceeds from a set of specific facts to a general conclusion or principle.

indulgent parents   Caregivers who have warm and caring relationships with their children but do not provide much guidance or discipline.

industrial-organizational (I/O) psychology   A subfield of psychology that focuses on people's behavior in the workplace.

infantile amnesia   An inability to remember personal experiences from the first few years of our lives.

inferential statistics   Statistics that tell us how confident we can be in drawing conclusions or inferences about a population based on findings obtained from a sample.

informational social influence   Following the opinions or behavior of other people because we believe that they have accurate knowledge and that what they are doing is "right."

informed consent   The principle that prior to agreeing to participate in research, a person should be fully informed about the procedures, the benefits, the risks involved, the right to withdraw at any time without penalty, and matters of confidentiality and privacy.

insanity   A legal decision that a defendant was so severely impaired at the time a crime was committed that he or she was incapable of appreciating the wrongfulness of the act or controlling his or her behavior.

insight   In Gestalt psychology, the sudden perception of a useful relation or solution to a problem; in psychoanalysis, the conscious awareness of unconscious dynamics that underlie psychological problems.

insomnia   A sleep disorder involving chronic difficulty in falling asleep, staying asleep, or experiencing restful sleep.

instinct   An inherited characteristic, common to all members of a species, that automatically produces a particular response when

the organism is exposed to a particular stimulus.

instinctive drift   The tendency for instinctive behaviors to override a conditioning procedure, thus making it difficult to create or maintain a conditioned response.

instrumental behaviors   In emotion, coping behaviors that are directed at achieving the goal or performing the task that is relevant to the emotion.

intelligence   The ability to acquire knowledge, to think and reason effectively, and to deal adaptively with the environment.

intelligence quotient (IQ)   Originally defined as mental age (MA) divided by chronological age (CA) multiplied by 100 (IQ = [MA/CA] × 100); an IQ of 100 indicates that an individual is average for his or her age group. IQ scores today are based on norms derived from people of various ages.

interaction   An interaction occurs (i.e., two factors "interact") when the way in which one factor influences behavior depends on the presence of the other factor.

interjudge reliability   The extent to which different observers or scorers agree in their scoring of a particular test or observed behavior.

internal consistency   The extent to which items within a psychological test correlate with one another, indicating that they are measuring a common characteristic.

internal-external locus of control   In Rotter's theory, a generalized expectancy that one's outcomes are under personal versus external control.

internal validity   The degree to which an experiment produces clear causal conclusions; internal validity is high when there is no confounding of variables.

interneurons   Neurons that are neither sensory nor motor neurons but that perform associative or integrative functions within the nervous system.

interpersonal therapy   A form of brief therapy that focuses on the client's interpersonal problems and seeks to develop new interpersonal skills.

interpretation   In psychoanalysis, a statement made by the analyst that is intended to promote insight in the client.

intrinsic motivation   The motivation to perform a task simply because one finds it interesting or enjoyable for its own sake.

J

James-Lange theory   A theory of emotion that proposed that emotional experience is based on a person's perception of her or his bodily responses.

K

kin selection   The view that organisms are most likely to help others with whom they share the most genes—namely, their offspring and genetic relatives.

kinesthesis   The body sense that provides feedback on the position and movements of our body parts.

knock-in procedure   A genetic manipulation procedure in which the function of a gene is disabled so that the effects on behavior or physical functions can be studied.

knockout procedure   A genetic manipulation procedure in which a new gene is inserted into an organism so that its effect on behavior or physical functions can be studied.

knowledge-acquisition components   In Sternberg's triarchic model of intelligence, the mental capabilities that allow us to learn from our experiences, store information in memory, and combine new insights with previously acquired information.

L

language   A system of symbols and rules for combining them that can produce an infinite number of possible messages and meanings.

latent learning   Learning that occurs in the absence of reinforcement but is not displayed until reinforcement is later introduced into the situation.

lateralization   The degree of localization of a function in either the right or the left cerebral hemisphere.

law of effect   Thorndike's concept that a response followed by satisfying consequences will become more likely to occur, whereas a response followed by unsatisfying consequences will become less likely to occur.

learned helplessness theory   A theory of depression maintaining that if people are unable to control life events, they develop a state of helplessness that leads to depressive symptoms.

learning   A relatively enduring change in an organism's behavior or performance capabilities that occurs as a result of experience.

lens   The transparent structure behind the pupil that changes its shape to focus images on the retina.

leptin   A hormone secreted by fat cells that decreases general appetite.

levels of processing   The concept that the more deeply we process information, the better it will be remembered.

life event scale   A measure in which respondents select from a list those life changes they have experienced over a specific period of time. Such measures are used to assess life stressors as well as positive events.

limbic system   A group of subcortical structures, including the hippocampus and amygdala, that are involved in organizing many goal-directed and emotional behaviors.

linguistic relativity hypothesis   The idea, suggested by Whorf, that people's language determines the ways in which they perceive and think about their world.

longitudinal design   A research approach in which the same people are repeatedly tested as they grow older.

long-term memory   Our vast library of more durable stored memories.

long-term potentiation   An enduring increase in synaptic strength that occurs after a neural circuit is rapidly stimulated.

lowballing   A manipulation technique in which a persuader gets you to commit to some action and then—before you actually perform the behavior—she or he increases the "cost" of that same behavior.

M

magnetic resonance imaging (MRI)   A brain-scanning procedure that produces a highly detailed image of living tissue based on the tissue's response to a magnetic field; can be used to study both structure and, in the case of functional MRI (fMRI), brain functions as they occur.

maintenance rehearsal   The simple rote repetition of information.

major depression   A mood disorder characterized by intense depression that interferes markedly with functioning.

mania   A state of intense emotional and behavioral excitement in which a person feels very optimistic and energized.

mastery-approach goals   Goals related to the desire to master a task and learn new knowledge and skills.

mastery-avoidance goals   Goals that reflect a fear of not performing up to one's own standards.

mastery orientation   An achievement goal orientation in which success is defined in terms of personal improvement and enjoyment rather than in terms of comparisons with the performance of others.

matching effect   In romantic relationships, the tendency for partners to have a similar level of physical attractiveness.

maturation   A genetically programmed biological process that governs our growth.

mean   A statistic that represents the arithmetic average of a set of scores.

means-ends analysis   A heuristic problem-solving device in which people first define a subgoal that they hope to achieve (an "end"), compare that subgoal with their present state of knowledge, and, if there is a discrepancy between them, try to find the means to reduce the difference.

measures of central tendency   Statistics that describe a distribution (a set of data) in terms of a single number that is in some way "typical" of the distribution as a whole.

measures of variability   Statistics that provide information about the spread of scores in a distribution.

median   In a set of data, the point that divides the distribution in half when the individual scores are arranged in order from lowest to highest.

medulla   A brain stem structure that controls vital functions, including heartbeat and respiration.

melatonin   A hormone, secreted by the pineal gland, that has a relaxing effect on the body and promotes a readiness for sleep.

memory   The processes that allow us to record, store, and later retrieve experiences and information.

memory codes   Mental representations of some type of information or stimulus.

memory consolidation   The creation and binding together of neural codes that allow information to be transferred from working memory into long-term memory.

menstrual synchrony   The tendency for some women who live together or are close friends to become more similar to one another in the timing of their menstrual cycles over time.

mental image   A representation of a stimulus that originates inside your brain, rather than from external sensory input.

mental representations   Cognitive representations of the world, including images, ideas, concepts, and principles, that are the foundations of thinking and problem solving.

mental set   The tendency to stick to problem-solving strategies or solutions that have worked in the past.

mere exposure effect   The tendency to evaluate a stimulus more favorably after repeated exposure to it.

meta-analysis   A statistical procedure for combining the results of different studies that examine the same topic.

metabolism   The rate of energy expenditure by the body.

metacognition   Your awareness and understanding of your own cognitive abilities.

metacomponents   In Sternberg's triarchic model of intelligence, the higher-level intellectual abilities used to plan and regulate task performance.

method of loci A memory aid in which pieces of information (e.g., items in a list) are each associated with a mental image of a different physical location.

midbrain Brain structures above the hindbrain that are involved in sensory and motor functions and in attention and states of consciousness.

mindfulness A mental state of awareness, focus, openness, and acceptance of immediate experience.

Minnesota Multiphasic Personality Inventory-2 (MMPI-2) A widely used personality test whose items were developed using the empirical approach of comparing various kinds of psychiatric patients with a nonpsychiatric sample.

misinformation effect The distortion of a memory by misleading postevent information.

mnemonic device A strategy or technique that aids memory.

mnemonist (memorist) A person who displays extraordinary memory skills.

mode A statistic that represents the most frequently occurring score in a distribution of data.

monocular depth cues Depth cues that require only one eye; include linear perspective, decreasing size, height in the horizontal plane, texture, clarity, light and shadow, motion parallax, and interposition.

mood-congruent recall The tendency to recall information or events that are congruent with our current mood.

mood disorders Psychological disorders whose core conditions involve maladaptive mood states, such as depression or mania.

morpheme The smallest unit of meaning in a given language; English morphemes include whole words, prefixes, and suffixes. There are over 100,000 English morphemes.

motivation A process that influences the direction, persistence, and vigor of goal-directed behavior.

motivational climate The achievement context created by adults. In an ego-involving climate, performers are compared with one another and urged to compete to be the best; those who perform best get special attention. In a mastery-involving climate, effort, enjoyment of the activity, and personal improvement are emphasized and rewarded.

motivational interviewing A treatment approach that avoids confrontation and leads clients to their own realization of a problem and increases their motivation to change.

motor cortex The cortical area in the rear portion of the frontal lobes that controls voluntary movements on the opposite sides of the body.

motoric thought Mental representations of motor movements, such as throwing an object.

motor neurons Specialized neurons that carry neural messages from the brain and spinal cord to the muscles and glands.

multimodal treatments Substance-abuse interventions that combine a number of treatments, such as aversion therapy and coping skills training.

mutation Random errors occurring during gene replication that can result in a new phenotypic effect.

myelin sheath A fatty insulating substance on the axon of some neurons that increases the speed of neural transmission.

N

narcolepsy A sleep disorder that involves extreme daytime sleepiness and sudden, uncontrollable sleep attacks during waking hours.

naturalistic observation A method in which the researcher observes behavior in a natural setting and tries to avoid influencing the participants being observed.

natural selection The evolutionary process through which characteristics that increase the likelihood of survival and reproduction are preserved in the gene pool and thereby become more common in a species over time.

need for achievement The desire to accomplish tasks and attain standards of excellence.

need for positive regard In Rogers's personality theory, an innate need to be positively evaluated by significant others, which enhances survival potential and need satisfaction.

need for positive self-regard In Rogers's personality theory, the psychological need to feel positively about oneself that underlies self-enhancement behaviors.

negative correlation A relation between two variables in which higher scores on one variable are associated with lower scores on the other variable.

negative reinforcement A response is strengthened by the subsequent removal of an aversive stimulus.

negative symptoms Schizophrenic symptoms that reflect a lack of normal reactions, such as emotions, speech, or social behaviors.

neglectful parents Caregivers who provide neither warmth nor rules or guidance.

neoanalytic theorists Former followers of Freud, such as Adler and Jung, who developed their own psychodynamic theories that generally de-emphasized psychosexual factors in favor of social ones and gave increased emphasis to ego functioning.

NEO Personality Inventory (NEO-PI) An objective personality test that measures the Big Five personality factors of extraversion, agreeableness, neuroticism, conscientiousness, and openness to experience.

nerve deafness Hearing loss caused by damage to the cochlear receptor cells or to the auditory nerve.

neural network (connectionist) model States that each concept stored in memory is represented by a unique pattern of distributed and simultaneously activated nodes that process information in parallel; also known as a *parallel distributed processing model.*

neural plasticity The ability of neurons to modify their structure and function in response to experiential factors or injury.

neural stem cells Immature "uncommitted" cells that can mature into any type of neuron or glial cell needed by the brain.

neurogenesis The production of new neurons in the nervous system, sometimes to replace neurons that have died or been damaged.

neuromodulators Neurotransmitter substances that are released by neurons and circulate within the nervous system to affect the sensitivity of many neurons to their natural transmitter substances.

neurons Nerve cells that constitute the basic building blocks of the nervous system.

neurotic anxiety In psychoanalytic theory, a state of anxiety that arises when impulses from the id threaten to break through into awareness or behavior.

neurotransmitters Chemical substances that are released from the axons of one neuron, travel across the synaptic space, and bind to specially keyed receptors in another neuron, where they produce a chemical reaction that is either excitatory or inhibitory.

night terrors A disorder in which a sleeper—often feeling a strong sense of dread or danger—becomes aroused to a near panic state.

normal curve A symmetrical bell-shaped curve that represents a theoretical distribution of scores in the population.

normal distribution A frequency distribution in the shape of a symmetrical or bell-shaped curve that satisfies certain mathematical conditions deduced from the theory of probability.

normative social influence Conformity motivated by gaining social acceptance and avoiding social rejection.

norm of reciprocity The tendency to respond in kind when other people treat us well or poorly.

norms (cultural or group) Rules (often unwritten) that specify what behavior is acceptable and expected for members of a particular culture or group.

null hypothesis   The hypothesis that any observed differences between samples on the variable(s) of interest are due to chance (i.e., in an experiment, the hypothesis that the independent variable had no effect on the dependent variable).

O

object permanence   The recognition that an object continues to exist even when it no longer can be seen.

object relations theories   The view that people form images or mental representations of themselves and other people as a result of early experiences with caregivers.

observational learning   Learning through observing the behavior of a model.

obsession   An unwanted and disturbing thought or image that invades consciousness and is very difficult to control.

Oedipus complex   The male child experiences erotic feelings toward his mother, desires to possess her sexually, and views his father as a rival.

olfaction   The sense of smell.

olfactory bulb   A forebrain structure that receives input from the receptors for the sense of smell.

openness   The client's willingness to become personally invested in the process of therapy that predicts favorable therapeutic outcomes.

operant conditioning   A type of learning in which behavior is modified by its consequences, such as by reinforcement and punishment.

operant discrimination   An operant response occurs when a particular antecedent stimulus is present but not when another antecedent stimulus is present.

operant extinction   Occurs when the absence of reinforcement for a previously reinforced response causes that response to weaken and eventually stop.

operant generalization   An operant response occurs to a new antecedent stimulus that is similar to the original antecedent stimulus.

operational definition   Defining a concept or variable in terms of the specific procedures used to produce or measure it.

opiates   A category of drugs consisting of opium and drugs derived from it, such as morphine, codeine, and heroin.

optic nerve   The bundle of ganglion cell axons that carries information from the visual receptors to the visual area of the thalamus.

organ of Corti   Structures embedded in the basilar membrane that contain the hair cell receptors for sound.

outcome bias   Occurs when an intelligence test score underestimates a person's true intellectual ability.

overconfidence   The pervasive tendency to overestimate one's degree of knowledge and predictive ability.

overlearning   Continued rehearsal past the point of initial learning that significantly improves performance on memory tasks.

P

pain disorder   A somatoform disorder in which the person's complaints of pain cannot be accounted for in terms of degree of physical damage.

panic disorder   An anxiety disorder characterized by unpredictable panic attacks and a pervasive fear that another will occur; may also result in agoraphobia.

parallel distributed processing (PDP) model   A computer model in which each item in memory is represented by a particular pattern of distributed yet interconnected nodes that are activated simultaneously (i.e., that operate in parallel); also known as a *neural network model*.

paranoid schizophrenia   A schizophrenic disorder marked by delusional thinking and suspiciousness.

parasympathetic nervous system   The branch of the autonomic nervous system that slows down bodily processes to conserve energy and reduce arousal.

paraventricular nucleus (PVN)   A cluster of neurons in the hypothalamus packed with receptor sites for transmitters that stimulate or reduce appetite.

partial (intermittent) reinforcement   A reinforcement schedule in which only a portion of the responses of a particular type are followed by a reinforcer.

passionate love   A form of love that involves intense emotional arousal and yearning for one's partner.

Pearson product-moment correlation coefficient   A statistic that reflects the direction and strength of the relation between two variables; can range in magnitude from -1.00 to $+1.00$.

perception   The process of organizing stimulus input and giving it meaning.

perceptual constancies   The ability to recognize stimulus characteristics—size, color, and so on—under varying conditions.

perceptual schemas   Internal representations that contain the essential features of an object of perception.

perceptual set   A readiness to perceive a stimulus in a particular way based on expectations, motives, emotions, or beliefs.

performance components   In Sternberg's triarchic model of intelligence, the specific mental processes used to perform a task.

peripheral nervous system   All of the neurons that connect the central nervous system with the sensory receptors, the muscles, and the glands.

peripheral route to persuasion   Occurs when people do not scrutinize a message but are influenced mostly by other factors such as a speaker's attractiveness or a message's emotional appeal.

personal constructs   In George Kelly's personality theory, the cognitive categories used to sort events and make comparisons among people and events.

personal intelligence   A proposed form of intelligence involving the degree of insight into oneself and one's behaviors and their consequences.

personality   Those biologically and environmentally determined characteristics within the person that account for distinctive and relatively enduring patterns of thinking, feeling, and acting.

personality disorders   Stable, inflexible, and maladaptive ways of thinking, feeling, and acting.

personality psychology   A subfield of psychology that focuses on the nature of human personality.

personality traits   Relatively stable cognitive, emotional, and behavioral characteristics that help establish people's individual identities.

personal unconscious   According to Jung, those aspects of the unconscious that arise from the individual's life experiences.

phenomenology   A philosophical approach that focuses on immediate subjective experience.

phenotype   The observable characteristics produced by one's genetic endowment.

pheromones   Chemical signals found in natural body scents.

phobias   Strong and irrational fears of particular objects or circumstances.

phoneme   The smallest unit of speech sound in a language that can signal a difference in meaning. English has 40 phonemes.

phonological awareness   A person's overall awareness of the sound structure of one's language.

photopigments   Protein molecules within the rods and cones whose chemical reactions when absorbing light result in the generation of nerve impulses.

placebo   An inactive or inert substance.

placebo control group   A control group that receives an intervention that is assumed to have no therapeutic value.

placebo effect A change in behavior that occurs because of the expectation or belief that one is receiving a treatment.

place theory of pitch perception States that sound frequencies are coded in terms of the portion of the basilar membrane where the fluid wave in the cochlea peaks; this theory accounts for perception of frequencies above 4,000 hertz.

pleasure principle The drive for instant need gratification that is characteristic of the id.

polygenic transmission A number of genes working together to create a particular phenotypic characteristic.

polygraph A research and clinical instrument that measures a wide array of physiological responses.

pons A brain stem structure having sensory and motor tracts whose functions are involved in sleep and dreaming.

population In a survey, the entire set of individuals about whom we wish to draw a conclusion.

positive correlation A relation between two variables in which higher scores on one variable are associated with higher scores on the other variable.

positive psychology movement A view that emphasizes the study of human strengths, fulfillment, and optimal living.

positive reinforcement A response is strengthened by the subsequent presentation of a stimulus.

positive symptoms Schizophrenic symptoms such as delusions, hallucinations, and disordered speech and thinking.

positron-emission tomography (PET) scan A procedure that provides a visual display of the absorption of a radioactive substance by neurons, indicating how actively they are involved as the brain performs a task.

postconventional moral reasoning According to Kohlberg, the stage at which moral judgments are based on a system of internalized, well-thought-out moral principles.

posttraumatic growth (PTG) The experience of positive psychological changes reported by some individuals following a major life crisis or traumatic event.

posttraumatic stress disorder (PTSD) A pattern of distressing symptoms, such as flashbacks, nightmares, avoidance, and anxiety responses that recur after a traumatic experience.

pragmatics A knowledge of the practical aspects of using language, such as how our choice of words depends on the social context.

preconventional moral reasoning According to Kohlberg, the stage at which moral judgments are based on anticipated punishments or rewards.

predictive bias Occurs when an intelligence test successfully predicts criterion measures, such as school or job performance, for some groups but not for others.

prefrontal cortex The area of the frontal lobe just behind the eyes and forehead that is involved in the executive functions of planning, self-awareness, and responsibility.

prejudice A negative attitude toward people based on their membership in a group.

preoperational stage In Piaget's theory, the stage of cognitive development in which children represent the world symbolically through words and mental images but do not yet understand basic mental operations or rules.

preparedness The notion that, through evolution, animals have become biologically predisposed to learn some associations more readily than other associations.

primacy effect In impression formation, our tendency to attach more importance to the initial information that we learn about a person.

primary reinforcer A positive reinforcer that satisfies a biological need, such as food or water.

priming Occurs when exposure to a stimulus influences how you subsequently respond to that same or another stimulus; in long-term memory, refers to the activation of one concept by another.

proactive interference Occurs when material learned in the past interferes with the recall of newer material.

problem-focused coping Coping strategies that involve direct attempts to confront and master a stressful situation.

problem-solving dream models The view that dreams can help us find creative solutions to our problems and conflicts because they are not constrained by reality.

procedural (nondeclarative) memory Memory that is reflected in learned skills and actions.

projective tests Tests, such as the Rorschach and the Thematic Apperception Test, that present ambiguous stimuli to the subject; the responses are assumed to be based on a projection of internal characteristics of the person onto the stimuli.

proposition A statement that expresses an idea.

propositional thought A thought that expresses an idea in linguistic form, as when we seem to hear or say a sentence in our mind.

prospective memory Remembering to perform an activity in the future.

protective factors Environmental or personal resources that help people fare better in the face of stress.

prototype The most typical and familiar member of a class that defines a concept.

proximodistal principle The tendency for physical development to begin along the innermost parts of the body and continue toward the outermost parts.

psychoactive drugs Chemicals that produce alterations in consciousness, emotion, and behavior.

psychoanalysis A psychological theory, developed by Freud, that emphasizes internal and primarily unconscious causes of behavior.

psychodynamic perspective A psychological perspective that focuses on how personality processes—including unconscious impulses, defenses, and conflicts—influence behavior.

psychogenic amnesia An extensive but selective memory loss that occurs after a traumatic event.

psychogenic fugue A dissociative phenomenon in which a person loses all sense of personal identity and wanders to another place and establishes a new identity.

psycholinguistics The scientific field that studies psychological aspects of language.

psychological test A method for measuring individual differences related to some psychological construct, based on a sample of relevant behavior obtained under standardized conditions.

psychology The scientific study of behavior and the mind.

psychometrics The statistical study of psychological tests; the psychometric approach to intelligence focuses on the number and nature of abilities that define intelligence.

psychophysics The study of relations between the physical characteristics of stimuli and the sensory experiences they evoke.

psychosexual stages Stages of development in which psychic energy is focused on certain body parts. The major childhood stages are the oral, anal, and phallic stages; experiences during these stages are assumed to shape personality development.

psychosocial stages A sequence of eight developmental stages proposed by Erikson, each of which involves a different "crisis" (i.e., conflict) over how we view ourselves in relation to other people and the world.

psychosurgery Surgical procedures, such as lobotomy or cingulotomy, in which brain tissue involved in a behavior disorder is removed or destroyed.

puberty A period of rapid biological maturation in which the person becomes capable of sexual reproduction.

punishment A response is weakened by an outcome that follows it.

R

random assignment A procedure in which each participant has an equal likelihood of being assigned to any one group within an experiment.

randomized clinical trial (RCT) A treatment research design that involves the random assignment of clients having specific problems to an experimental (therapy) group or to a control condition so as to draw sound causal conclusions about the therapy's efficacy.

random sampling In survey research, a method of choosing a sample in which each member of the population has an equal probability of being included in the sample.

range A statistic that represents the difference between the highest and the lowest scores in a distribution.

rational-theoretical approach An approach to test construction in which test items are made up on the basis of a theorist's conception of a construct.

reaction range The genetically influenced limits within which environmental factors can exert their effects on an organism.

realistic conflict theory Maintains that competition for limited resources fosters prejudice.

reality principle The ego's tendency to take reality factors into account and to act in a rational fashion in need satisfaction.

receptor sites Protein molecules on neurons' dendrites or soma that are specially shaped to accommodate a specific neurotransmitter molecule.

recessive gene A gene whose influence on the phenotypic expression of a characteristic is masked by a dominant gene.

reciprocal determinism Bandura's model of two-way causal relations between the person, behavior, and the environment.

reflexes Automatic, inborn behaviors triggered by specific stimuli.

regression A psychoanalytic defense mechanism in which a person retreats to an earlier stage of development in response to stress.

reinforcement A response is strengthened by an outcome that follows it.

relapse prevention A treatment approach designed to teach coping skills, increase self-efficacy, and counter the abstinence violation effect, thus reducing the likelihood of relapse.

reliability In psychological testing, the consistency with which a measure assesses a given characteristic or different observers agree on a given score. Diagnostic reliability refers to agreement among clinicians making diagnostic judgments.

remote behavior sampling A method of collecting samples of behavior from respondents as they live their daily lives.

REM sleep A recurring sleep stage characterized by rapid eye movements, increased physiological arousal, paralysis of the voluntary muscles, and a high rate of dreaming.

REM-sleep behavior disorder (RBD) A sleep disorder in which the loss of muscle tone that causes normal REM-sleep paralysis is absent, thereby enabling sleepers to move about—sometimes violently—and seemingly act out their dreams.

replication The process of repeating a study to determine whether the original findings can be duplicated.

representativeness heuristic A rule of thumb in estimating the probability that an object or event belongs to a certain category based on the extent to which it represents a prototype of that category.

representative sample A sample that accurately reflects the important characteristics of the population.

repression The basic defense mechanism that actively keeps anxiety-arousing material in the unconscious.

resilience The ability to withstand psychological stress.

resistance Largely unconscious maneuvers that protect clients from dealing with anxiety-arousing material in therapy.

response cost (negative punishment, punishment by removal) A type of punishment in which an operant response is weakened by the subsequent removal of a stimulus that was not the cause of the original response (e.g., TV privileges are taken away from a child who is misbehaving in order to gain attention).

response prevention The prevention of escape or avoidance responses during exposure to an anxiety-arousing conditioned stimulus so that extinction can occur.

resting potential The voltage differential between the inside and outside of a neuron (about −70 mv) caused by the unequal distribution of ions inside the neuron's membrane and outside in the fluid surrounding the neuron when the neuron is at rest.

restoration model The theory that sleep recharges our run-down bodies and allows us to recover from physical and mental fatigue.

reticular formation A structure extending from the hindbrain into the lower forebrain that plays a central role in consciousness, sleep, and attention, in part by alerting and activating higher brain centers (ascending portion) and by selectively blocking some inputs to higher regions in the brain (descending portion).

retina The light-sensitive tissue at the back of the eye that contains the visual receptors.

retrieval The process of accessing information in long-term memory.

retrieval cue Any stimulus, whether internal or external, that triggers the activation of information stored in long-term memory.

retroactive interference Occurs when newly acquired information interferes with the ability to recall information learned at an earlier time.

retrograde amnesia Memory loss for events that occurred prior to the onset of amnesia.

reuptake The process whereby transmitter substances are taken back into the presynaptic neuron so that they do not continue to stimulate postsynaptic neurons.

rods Photoreceptors in the retina that function under low levels of illumination and do not give rise to color sensations.

Role Construct Repertory (Rep) Test The technique developed by personality psychologist Kelly to assess people's personal constructs by asking them to describe the ways in which people resemble and differ from one another.

Rorschach test A projective technique involving the interpretation of inkblots that is used by psychodynamic psychologists to assess perceptual and psychodynamic aspects of personality.

S

sample In a survey, a subset of individuals drawn from the population.

scatterplot A graph commonly used to examine correlational data; each pair of scores on variable X and variable Y is plotted as a single point.

schema A mental framework; an organized pattern of thought about some aspect of the world, such as a class of people, events, situations, or objects.

schizophrenia A psychotic disorder involving serious impairments of attention, thought, language, emotion, and behavior.

script A specialized schema that represents a sequence of events (e.g., "going to the movies") that unfolds in a regular, almost standardized order.

seasonal affective disorder (SAD) A disorder in which depressive symptoms appear or worsen during certain seasons of the year (most typically, fall and winter) and then improve during the other seasons.

secondary (conditioned) reinforcer A stimulus that acquires reinforcing qualities by being associated with a primary reinforcer.

seeking social support Turning to others for assistance or emotional support in times of stress.

selective attention   A cognitive process that focuses awareness on some stimuli to the exclusion of others.

self   In Rogers's theory, an organized, consistent set of perceptions and beliefs about oneself.

self-actualization   In humanistic theories, an inborn tendency to strive toward the realization of one's full potential.

self-consistency   An absence of conflict among self-perceptions.

self-determination theory   A humanistic theory formulated by Deci and Ryan that focuses on three fundamental psychological needs: competence, autonomy, and relatedness.

self-efficacy   The conviction that we can perform the behaviors necessary to produce a desired outcome.

self-enhancement   Processes whereby one enhances positive self-regard.

self-esteem   How positively or negatively we feel about ourselves.

self-fulfilling prophecy   Occurs when people's erroneous expectations lead them to act toward others in a way that brings about the expected behaviors, thereby confirming the original impression.

self-monitoring   A personality trait that reflects people's tendencies to regulate their social behavior in accord with situational cues, as opposed to internal values, attitudes, and needs.

self-perception theory   Maintains that we make inferences about our own attitudes by observing how we behave.

self-regulation processes   In social-cognitive theory, skills that allow for personal control over one's thoughts, feelings, or behaviors.

self-relatedness   A client's ability to be flexible to change, to listen carefully to the therapist, and to constructively use what is learned in therapy.

self-serving bias   The tendency to make relatively more personal attributions for success and situational attributions for failures.

self-verification   The tendency to try to verify or validate one's existing self-concept (i.e., to satisfy congruence needs).

semantic memory   General factual knowledge about the world and language, including memory for words and concepts.

semantics   The linguistic rules for connecting symbols in language to what they represent.

senile dementia   Dementia (a gradual loss of cognitive abilities due to normal brain deterioration) that begins after age 65.

sensation   The process by which stimuli are detected, transduced into nerve impulses, and sent to the brain.

sensitive period   An optimal age range for certain experiences, but if those experiences occur at another time, normal development will still be possible.

sensorimotor stage   In Piaget's theory, the stage of cognitive development in which children understand their world primarily through sensory experiences and physical (motor) interactions with objects.

sensory adaptation   Diminishing sensitivity to an unchanging stimulus with the passage of time as sensory neurons habituate to the stimulation.

sensory memory   Memory processes that retain incoming sensory information just long enough for it to be recognized.

sensory neurons   Specialized neurons that carry messages from the sense organs to the spinal cord and brain.

sensory prosthetic device   A device for providing sensory input that can, to some extent, substitute for what cannot be supplied by the person's own sensory receptors.

separation anxiety   Distress experienced by infants when they are separated from a primary caregiver, peaking between ages 12 and 16 months and disappearing between ages 2 and 3 years.

sequential design   A research approach that involves repeatedly testing several age cohorts as they grow older.

serial position effect   The finding that recall is influenced by an item's position in a series.

set point   A biologically determined standard around which body weight (or, more specifically, our fat mass) is regulated.

sex-typing   Treating other people differently based on whether they are female or male.

sexual dysfunction   Chronic, impaired sexual functioning that distresses a person.

sexual orientation   A person's emotional and erotic preference for partners of a particular sex.

sexual response cycle   A physiological response to sexual stimulation that involves stages of excitement, plateau, orgasm, and resolution.

sexual strategies (parental investment) theory   Maintains that sex differences in mating strategies and mating preferences reflect inherited biological predispositions that have been shaped in women and men over the course of evolution.

shaping   An operant conditioning procedure in which reinforcement begins with a behavior that the organism can already perform and then is made contingent on behaviors that increasingly approximate the final desired behavior.

shared environment   The environmental conditions shared by a family or other social group over a period of time.

short-term memory   A memory store that temporarily holds a limited amount of information.

signal detection theory   A theory that assumes that stimulus detection is not based on a fixed absolute threshold but rather is affected by rewards, punishments, expectations, and motivational factors.

situation-focused prevention   Prevention efforts that focus on altering environmental conditions that are known to promote the development of psychological disorders.

Skinner box   An experimental chamber in which animals learn to perform operant responses, such as pressing a bar or pecking, so that the learning process can be studied.

sleep apnea   A disorder characterized by a repeated cycle in which the sleeper stops breathing, momentarily awakens gasping for air, and then returns to sleep.

slow-wave sleep   Stages 3 and 4 of sleep, in which the EEG pattern shows large, slow brain waves called delta waves.

social causation hypothesis   The proposition that attributes the higher prevalence of schizophrenia in low-income people to the greater stress they experience.

social-cognitive theories (of hypnosis)   The view that hypnotic experiences occur because people are highly motivated to assume the role of being hypnotized; the person develops a readiness to perceive hypnotic experiences as real and involuntary.

social-cognitive theory (social-learning theory)   A cognitive behavioral approach to personality developed by Bandura and Mischel that emphasizes the role of social learning, cognitive processes, and self-regulation.

social comparison   The act of comparing one's personal attributes, abilities, and opinions with those of other people.

social compensation   Working harder when in a group than when alone to compensate for other members' lower output.

social desirability bias   A tendency to self-report or behave in a way that presents oneself in a favorable light, rather than respond as one truly feels.

social drift hypothesis   The notion that as people develop schizophrenia, their personal and occupational functioning deteriorates, so that they drift down the socioeconomic ladder.

social exchange theory   A theory proposing that a social relationship can best be described in terms of exchanges of rewards and costs between the two partners.

social identity theory   Maintains that prejudice stems from a need to enhance our self-esteem.

social learning theory   Bandura's former name for *social-cognitive theory*.

social loafing   The tendency for people to expend less individual effort when working collectively in a group than when working alone.

social norms   Shared expectations about how people should think, feel, and behave.

social phobia   An excessive and inappropriate fear of social situations in which a person might be evaluated and possibly embarrassed.

social psychology   A subfield of psychology that examines people's thoughts, feelings, and behavior in relation to the social world.

social role   A set of norms that characterizes how people in a given social position (e.g., "the college student," "the police officer") ought to behave.

social skills training   A technique in which a client learns more effective social behaviors by observing and imitating a skillful model.

social structure theory   Maintains that men and women behave differently, such as expressing different mate preferences, because society directs them into different social and economic roles.

sociocultural perspective   A view that emphasizes the role of culture and the social environment in influencing our behavior, thoughts, and emotions.

somatic nervous system   The branch of the peripheral nervous system that provides input from the sensory receptors and output to the voluntary muscles of the body.

somatic sensory cortex   Cortical strips in the front portions of the parietal lobes that receive sensory input from the opposite side of the body.

somatoform disorder   A disorder in which a person complains of bodily symptoms that cannot be accounted for in terms of actual physical damage or dysfunction.

source confusion   The tendency to recall something or recognize it as familiar but to forget where it was encountered. Also called *source monitoring error.*

specificity question   The ultimate question of psychotherapy research: "Which types of therapy administered by which kinds of therapists to which kinds of clients having which kinds of problems produce which kinds of effects?"

specific phobia   An irrational and excessive fear of specific objects or situations that pose little or no actual threat.

speech segmentation   The task of perceiving where each word within a spoken sentence begins and ends.

splitting   A tendency, often found in people with borderline personality disorder, to not integrate the positive and negative aspects of

another's behavior into a coherent cognitive representation of the person.

spontaneous recovery   In classical conditioning, the reappearance of a previously extinguished conditioned response after a period of time has passed following extinction.

standard deviation (SD)   A measure of variability that takes into account how much each score in a distribution deviates from the average score. Statistically, the square root of the variance of a set of scores.

standardization   In psychological testing, refers to (1) creating a standard set of procedures for administering a test or making observations and (2) deriving norms with which an individual's performance can be compared.

state-dependent memory   The enhanced ability to retrieve information when our internal state at the time of retrieval matches our original state during learning.

static testing   The traditional approach to testing, in which the test is administered under highly standardized conditions.

statistical significance   In research, a term that means it is unlikely that a particular finding occurred by chance alone. Psychologists typically consider a result to be statistically significant only if it could have occurred by chance less than 5 times in 100.

stereotype   A generalized belief about a group or category of people.

stereotype threat   The anxiety created by the perceived possibility that one's behavior or performance will confirm a negative stereotype about one's group.

stimulants   Drugs that stimulate neural activity, resulting in a state of excitement or aroused euphoria.

stimulus control   The occurrence of an operant behavior in response to a discriminative stimulus.

stimulus generalization   A conditioned response occurs to stimuli other than the original conditioned stimulus, based on the similarity of these stimuli to the conditioned stimulus.

stimulus hierarchy   In systematic desensitization, the creation of a series of anxiety-arousing stimuli that are ranked in terms of the amount of anxiety they evoke.

storage   The retention of information in memory over time.

stranger anxiety   Distress over contact with strangers that typically develops in the first year of infancy and dissipates in the second year.

strange situation   A standardized procedure used to determine the type of emotional attachment between an infant and a caregiver.

strategic pluralism   The notion that multiple—even contradictory—behavioral strategies

(e.g., introversion and extraversion) might be adaptive in certain environments and would therefore be maintained through natural selection.

stress   A term variously used to refer to (1) situations that place strong demands on an organism, (2) the cognitive, physiological, and behavioral responses to such situations, and (3) the ongoing transaction between individuals and demanding situations.

stressors   Situations that place demands on organisms that tax or exceed their resources.

stress response   The pattern of cognitive, physiological, and behavioral reactions to demands that exceed a person's resources.

stroboscopic movement   The illusory movement produced when adjacent lights are illuminated and extinguished at specific time intervals.

structuralism   An early German school of psychology established by Wundt that attempted to study the structure of the mind by breaking it down into its basic components, which were believed to be sensations.

structured interview   A standardized interview protocol in which specific questions are asked.

subgoal analysis   A problem-solving heuristic in which people attack a large problem by formulating subgoals, or intermediate steps toward a solution.

subjective well-being (SWB)   Happiness; the overall degree of satisfaction with one's life.

sublimation   The channeling of unacceptable impulses into socially accepted behaviors, as when aggressive drives are expressed in violent sports.

subliminal stimuli   Weak stimuli below the perceptual threshold that are not consciously perceived.

substance dependence   A maladaptive pattern of substance use that causes a person significant distress or substantially impairs that person's life; substance dependence is diagnosed as occurring "with physiological dependence" if drug tolerance or withdrawal symptoms have developed.

suicide   The willful taking of one's own life.

superego   In psychonalysis, the moral arm of the personality that internalizes the standards and values of society and serves as the person's conscience.

suprachiasmatic nuclei (SCN)   The brain's master "biological clock," located in the hypothalamus, that regulates most circadian rhythms.

surface structure   A linguistic term for the words and organization of a spoken or written sentence. Two sentences may have quite different surface structure but still mean the same thing.

survey research   A method using question-naires or interviews to obtain information about many people.

sympathetic nervous system   The branch of the autonomic nervous system that has an arousal function on the body's internal organs, speeding up bodily processes and mobilizing the body.

synaptic space   The microscopic space between the axons of one neuron and the dendrites or cell body of another over which the nerve impulse is transmitted.

synaptic vesicles   Chambers within the axon that contain the neurotransmitter substance.

synesthesia   A condition in which stimuli are experienced not only in the normal sensory modality but in others as well.

syntax   The rules for the combination of symbols within a given language.

systematic desensitization   A procedure used to eliminate anxiety using counter-conditioning, in which a new response that is incompatible with anxiety is condi-tioned to the anxiety-arousing conditioned stimulus.

T

tardive dyskinesia   An irreversible motor dis-order that can occur as a side effect of certain antipsychotic drugs.

taste buds   Chemical receptors for taste in the tongue and in the roof and back of the mouth that are sensitive to the qualities of sweet, sour, salty, and bitter.

temperament   A biologically based general style of reacting emotionally and behavior-ally to the environment.

teratogens   Environmental (nongenetic) agents that cause abnormal prenatal development.

test-retest reliability   The extent to which scores on a presumably stable characteristic are consistent over time.

thalamus   A major sensory integration and relay center in the forebrain, sometimes re-ferred to as the brain's sensory switchboard.

THC (tetrahydrocannabinol)   The major active ingredient in marijuana.

Thematic Apperception Test (TAT)   A projec-tive personality test in which people make up stories in response to pictures.

theory   A set of formal statements that explains how and why certain events or phenomena are related to one another.

theory of cognitive dissonance   States that people strive to maintain consistency in their beliefs and actions and that inconsistency creates dissonance (i.e., unpleasant arousal) that motivates people to restore balance by changing their cognitions or behavior.

theory of mind   A person's beliefs about the "mind" and the ability to understand other people's mental states.

theory of planned behavior   Maintains that our intention to engage in a behavior is strongest when we have a positive attitude toward that behavior, when subjective norms (our perceptions of what other people think we should do) support our attitudes, and when we believe that the behavior is under our control.

threat   In Rogers's theory, any experience we have that is inconsistent with our self-concept, including our perceptions of our own behavior. Threat evokes anxiety.

three-stratum theory of cognitive abilities   A model of intelligence based on factor analy-sis that contains three hierarchical levels of ability, from specific skills to a general intel-lectual (g) factor.

tip-of-the-tongue (TOT) state   The experience of being unable to recall something but feel-ing that you are on the verge of remember-ing it.

token economy   A procedure in which desir-able behaviors are reinforced with tokens or points that can later be redeemed for other reinforcers.

tolerance   A condition in which increasingly larger doses of a drug are required to pro-duce the same level of bodily responses; caused by the body's compensatory re-sponses, which counter the effects of the drug.

top-down processing   Perceptual processing in which existing knowledge, concepts, ideas, or expectations are applied in order to make sense of incoming stimulation.

transduction   The conversion of one form of energy into another; in sensation, the process whereby physical stimuli are translated into nerve impulses.

transference   The psychoanalytic phenomenon in which a client responds irrationally to the analyst as if the latter were an important person from the client's past who plays a sig-nificant role in the client's dynamics.

transtheoretical model   A model of behavior change that includes the phases of precon-templation, contemplation, preparation, ac-tion, maintenance, and termination.

trauma-dissociation theory   Accounts for the development of dissociative identity disor-der as a defense against severe childhood abuse or trauma.

triangular theory of love   Maintains that various types of love result from different combinations of three core factors: intimacy, commitment, and passion.

triarchic theory of intelligence   Sternberg's theory of intelligence that distinguishes between analytical, practical, and creative forms of mental ability.

triple vulnerability model of emotional disorders   A theoretical model of psycho-pathology that there are common biological, psychological, and environmental vulner-ability factors that foster the development of anxiety and depressive disorders.

twin study   A research method in behavior genetics in which identical (monozygotic) and fraternal (dizygotic) twins are compared on some characteristic; this method is par-ticularly informative if the twins have been raised in different environments.

2 × 2 achievement goal theory   A model of motivation in which each person can be described in terms of an achievement motivation profile involving four types of goals: mastery-approach, ego-approach, mastery-avoidance, and ego-avoidance goals.

two-factor theory of avoidance learning   Main-tains that avoidance learning first involves the classical conditioning of fear, followed by learning operant responses that avoid an anticipated aversive stimulus and thus are reinforced by anxiety reduction.

two-factor theory of emotion   Schachter's theory stating that intensity of physiologi-cal arousal determines perceived intensity of emotion, whereas appraisal of environ-mental cues tells us which emotion we are experiencing.

Type A behavior pattern   A sense of time ur-gency, pressured behavior, and hostility that appears to be a risk factor in coronary heart disease.

U

unconditional positive regard   A communi-cated attitude of total and unconditional acceptance of another person that conveys the person's intrinsic worth.

unconditioned response (UCR)   A response (usually reflexive or innate) that is elicited by a specific stimulus (the unconditioned stimulus) without prior learning.

unconditioned stimulus (UCS)   A stimulus that elicits a particular reflexive or innate response (the unconditioned response) without prior learning.

undifferentiated schizophrenia   A residual category of schizophrenia for people who show some of the symptoms of paranoid, disorganized, and catatonic types but not enough to be placed in one of those diagnostic categories.

unobtrusive measures   Techniques for mea-suring behavior in which participants are kept unaware that their behavior is being recorded or observed.

unshared environment   The unique experiences of each individual within a family—as opposed to the common experiences of the whole family.

upward comparison   Seeing oneself or one's situation as worse off than the standard for comparison.

V

validity   The extent to which a test actually measures what it is supposed to measure; the degree to which a diagnostic system's categories contain the core features of the behavior disorders and permit differentiation among the disorders.

variable   Any characteristic of an organism or situation that can vary.

variable-interval (VI) schedule   A reinforcement schedule in which reinforcement follows the first response of a particular type that occurs after an average but variable time interval following the last reinforced response.

variable-ratio (VR) schedule   A reinforcement schedule in which reinforcement is based on an average but variable number of responses of a particular type.

variance   A statistic that measures the average of the squared deviation scores about the mean of a distribution.

vestibular sense   The sense of body orientation, or equilibrium.

virtual reality (VR)   Computer-produced virtual environments that immerse an individual and produce experiences similar to those of a corresponding real environment.

visual acuity   The ability to see fine detail.

visual agnosia   A disorder in which an individual is unable to visually recognize objects.

vulnerability-stress model   Explains behavior disorders as resulting from predisposing biological or psychological vulnerability factors that are triggered by a stressor.

W

Weber's law   States that to perceive a difference between two stimuli, the stimuli must differ by a constant percentage or ratio.

Wernicke's area   An area of the left temporal lobe that is involved in speech comprehension.

wisdom   A system of knowledge about the meaning and conduct of life.

wish fulfillment   In Freudian theory, the partial or complete satisfaction of a psychological need through dreaming or waking fantasy.

withdrawal   The occurrence of compensatory responses after drug use is discontinued, causing the person to experience physiological reactions opposite to those that had been produced by the drug.

working memory   A mental workspace that temporarily stores information, actively processes it, and supports other cognitive functions.

Y

Young-Helmholtz trichromatic theory   The color vision theory stating that there are three types of color receptors in the retina—one for red, one for blue, and one for green—and that combinations of activation of these receptors can produce perception of any hue in the visible spectrum.

Z

zone of proximal development   The difference between what a child can do independently and what the child can do with assistance from adults or more advanced peers.

zygote   The fertilized egg.

References

Aaron, S. (1986). *Stage fright*. Chicago: University of Chicago Press.

Abdul-Rahim, H. F., Holmboe-Ottesen, G., Stene, L. C. M., Husseini, A., Giacaman, R., Jervell, J., & Bjertness, E. (2003). Obesity in a rural and an urban Palestinian West Bank population. *International Journal of Obesity, 27*, 140–146.

Abe, N., Okuda, J., Suzuki, M., Sasaki, H., Matsuda, T., Mori, E., et al. (2008). Neural correlates of true memory, false memory, and deception. *Cerebral Cortex, 18*, 2811–2819.

Abel, T., & Kandel, E. (1998). Positive and negative regulatory mechanisms that mediate long-term memory storage. *Brain Research Reviews, 26*, 360–378.

Abi-Dargham, A., & Guillin, A. (Eds.). (2007). *Integrating the neurobiology of schizophrenia*. New York: Elsevier Science.

Abraham, K. (1911). Notes on the psychoanalytic investigation and treatment of manic-depressive insanity and allied conditions. In *Selected papers of Karl Abraham*. New York: Basic Books, 1968.

Abrahamsson, N., & Hyltenstam, K. (2009). Age of onset and nativelikeness in a second language: Listener perception versus linguistic scrutiny. *Language Learning, 59*, 249–306.

Abramowitz, A. J., & Caron, M. L. (2010). Psychological and neuropsychological testing. In M. K. Dulcan (Ed.), *Dulcan's textbook of child and adolescent psychiatry*. Arlington, VA: American Psychiatric Publishing.

Abramson, L. Y., Seligman, M. E. P., & Teasdale, J. D. (1978). Learned helplessness in humans: Critique and reformulation. *Journal of Abnormal Psychology, 87*, 49–74.

Abutalebi, J. (2008). Neural aspects of second language representation and language control. *ActaPsychologica, 128*, 466–478.

Achter, J., Lubinski, D., & Benbow, C. P. (1996). Multipotentiality among the intellectually gifted: "It was never there and already it's vanishing." *Journal of Counseling Psychology, 43*, 65–76.

Adair, R. K. (1990). *The physics of baseball*. New York: Harper & Row.

Adam, J. J., Hommel, B., & Umilta, C. (2005). Preparing for perception and action (II): Automatic and effortful processes in response cueing. *Visual Cognition, 12*, 1444–1473.

Adams, P. R., & Cox, K. J. A. (2002). Synaptic Darwinism and neocortical function. *Neurocomputing, 42*, 197–214.

Adelmann, P. K., & Zajonc, R. B. (1989). Facial efference and the experience of emotion. *Annual Review of Psychology, 40*, 249–280.

Ader, R. (2003). Conditioned immunomodulation: Research needs and directions. *Brain, Behavior and Immunity, 17*(Suppl. 1), S51–S57.

Ader, R., & Cohen, N. (1975). Behaviorally conditioned immunosuppression. *Psychosomatic Medicine, 37*, 333–340.

Ader, R., & Cohen, N. (1982). Behaviorally conditioned immunosuppression and murine systemic lupus erythematosus. *Science, 215*(4539), 1534–1536.

Adler, A. B., Bliese, P. D., McGurk, D., et al. (2009). Battlemind debriefing and battlemind training as early interventions with soldiers returning from Iraq: Randomization by platoon. *Journal of Consulting and Clinical Psychology, 77*, 928–940.

Adrés, P. (2003). Frontal cortex as the central executive of working memory: Time to revise our view. *Cortex, 39*, 871–895.

Aggleton, J. P. (1993). The contribution of the amygdala to normal and abnormal emotional states. *Trends in Neurosciences, 16*, 328–333.

Ahadi, S., & Diener, E. (1989). Multiple determinants and effect size. *Journal of Personality and Social Psychology, 56*, 398–406.

Ahn, H. J. (2005). Child care teachers' strategies in children's socialization of emotion. *Early Child Development & Care, 175*, 49–61.

Ai, A. K., Peterson, C., & Ubelhor, D. (2002). War-related trauma and symptoms of posttraumatic stress disorder among adult Kosovar refugees. *Journal of Traumatic Stress, 15*, 157–160.

Aiello, R. (Ed.). (1994). *Musical perceptions*. London: Oxford University Press.

Ainsworth, M., Blehar, M. C., Waters, E., & Wall, S. (1978). *Patterns of attachment: A psychological study of the strange situation*. Hillsdale, NJ: Erlbaum.

Airey, D., & Sodhi, M. (2007). *Schizophrenia*. New York: Chelsea House.

Aitchison, J. (1998). *The articulate mammal: An introduction to psycholinguistics*. Florence, KY: Taylor & Francis/Routledge.

Aitken, S., & Bower, T. G. (1982). Intersensory substitution in the blind. *Journal of Experimental Child Psychology, 33*, 309–323.

Ajzen, I. (1991). The theory of planned behavior. *Organizational Behavior and Human Decision Processes, 50*, 179–211.

Akerstedt, T., Kecklund, G., & Hoerte, L. G. (2001). Night driving, season and the risk of highway accidents. *Sleep: Journal of Sleep and Sleep Disorders Research, 24*, 401–406.

Akimova, S., Lanzenberger, R., & Kasper, S. (2009). The serotonin-1A receptor in anxiety disorders. *Biological Psychology, 66*, 627–635.

Alam, N., Kumar, S., Rai, S., Methippara, M., Szymusiak, R., & McGinty, D. (2009). Role of adenosine A$_1$ receptor in the perifornical-lateral hypothalamic area in sleep-wake regulation in rats. *Brain Research, 1304*, 96–104.

Albarracin, D., Durantini, M. R., & Earl, A. (2006). Empirical and theoretical conclusions of an analysis of outcomes of HIV prevention interventions. *Psychological Science, 15*, 73–78.

Albee, G. W. (1997). Speak no evil? *American Psychologist, 52*, 1143–1144.

Alcock, J. (2005). *Animal behavior: An evolutionary approach* (8th ed.). New York: Sinauer.

Alcock, J. E. (2010). The parapsychologist's lament. In S. Krippner & H. L. Harris (Eds.), *The neurobiology of psychics, mediums, and other extraordinary people*. Santa Barbara, CA: Praeger/ABC-CLIO.

Aldwin, C. M. (2007). *Stress, coping, and development: An integrative perspective*. New York: Guilford Press.

Aleman, A., Bronk, E., Kessels, R. P. C., et al. (2004). A single administration of testosterone improves visuospatial ability in young women. *Psychoneuroendocrinology, 29*, 612–617.

Alexander-Passe, N. (2008). The sources and manifestations of stress amongst school-aged dyslexics, compared with sibling controls. *Dyslexia: An International Journal of Research and Practice, 14*, 291–313.

Alfieri, T., Ruble, D. N., & Higgins, E. T. (1996). Gender stereotypes during adolescence: Developmental changes and the transition to junior high school. *Developmental Psychology, 32*, 1129–1137.

Alison, L. J., Smith, M. D., Eastman, O., & Rainbow, L. (2003). Toulmin's philosophy of argument and its relevance to offender profiling. *Psychology, Crime, and Law, 9*, 173–183.

Allen, J. (2010). *Cystic fibrosis*. New York: Taylor and Francis.

Allen, M. (1991). Meta-analysis comparing the persuasiveness of one-sided and two-sided messages. *Western Journal of Speech Communication, 55*, 390–404.

Allen, M., D'Alessio, D., & Brezgel, K. (1995). A meta-analysis summarizing the effects of pornography: II. Aggression after exposure. *Human Communication Research, 22*, 258–283.

Allen, M., D'Alessio, D., & Emmers-Sommer, T. M. (2000). Reactions of criminal sexual offenders to pornography: A meta-analytic summary. In M. Roloff (Ed.), *Communication Yearbook 22*. Thousand Oaks, CA: Sage.

Alloy, L. B., Abramson, L. Y., Walshaw, P. D., Gerstein, P. D., et al. (2009). Behavioral approach system (BAS)–relevant cognitive styles and bipolar spectrum disorders: Concurrent and prospective associations. *Journal of Abnormal Psychology, 118*, 459–471.

Allport, G. W. (1954). *The nature of prejudice*. Reading, MA: Addison-Wesley.

Allport, G. W., & Odbert, H. S. (1936). Trait names: A psycho-lexical study. *Psychological Monographs, 47*(Whole No. 211).

Allport, G. W., & Postman, L. J. (1947). *The psychology of rumor*. New York: Holt.

Alter, A. L., Aronson, J., Darley, J. M., Rodriguez, C., & Ruble, D. N. (2010). Rising to the threat: Reducing stereotype threat by reframing the threat as a challenge. *Journal of Experimental Social Psychology, 46,* 166–171.

Alterovitz, S. S. R., & Mendelsohn, G. A. (2009). Partner preferences across the life span: Online dating by older adults. *Psychology and Aging, 24,* 513–517.

Altman, I., & Taylor, D. A. (1973). *Social penetration: The development of interpersonal relationships.* New York: Holt, Rinehart & Winston.

Altman, J., & Bayer, S. A. (1996). *Development of the cerebellar system: In relation to its evolution, structure and functions.* Boca Raton, FL: CRC-Press.

Amato, P. R, & Afifi, T. D. (2006). Feeling caught between parents: Adult children's relations with parents and subjective well-being. *Journal of Marriage and Family, 68,* 222–235.

Amato, P. R., & Keith, B. (1991). Parental divorce and the well-being of children: A meta-analysis. *Psychological Bulletin, 110,* 26–46.

Ambady, N., & Skowronski, J. J. (Eds.). (2008). *First impressions.* New York: Guilford Press.

American Academy of Ophthalmology. (2009). Policy Statement: Learning disabilities, dyslexia, and vision. San Francisco: Author. Retrieved December 10, 2009, from http://www.aao.org/about/policy/upload/Learning-Disabilities-Dyslexia-Vision-2009.pdf

American Psychiatric Association. (1990). *The practice of ECT: Recommendations for treatment, training, and privileging.* Washington, DC: American Psychiatric Press.

American Psychiatric Association. (2000). *The diagnostic and statistical manual of mental disorders, fourth edition, text revision (DSM-IV).* Washington, DC: Author.

American Psychiatric Association (2010). *Work group proposals for DSM-V disorders.* Retrieved February 18, 2010, from http://www.DSM5.org

American Psychological Association. (2002). Ethical principles of psychologists and code of conduct. *American Psychologist, 57,* 1060–1073.

American Psychological Association. (2005). *New Definition: Hypnosis.* Retrieved December 14, 2009, from http://www.apa.org/divisions/div30/define_hypnosis.html

American Psychological Association. (2010). *ACT/ Parents raising safe kids program.* Retrieved February 5, 2010, from http://www.apa.org/pi/prevent-violence/programs/act.aspx

American Psychological Association Research Office. (2001). Employment characteristics of APA members by membership status, 2000 (Table 4). In *2000 APA Directory Survey.* Washington, DC: American Psychological Association.

American Psychological Association Task Force. (2006). Evidence-based practice in psychology. *American Psychologist, 61,* 271–285.

Ames, C. (1992). Achievement goals and adaptive motivation patterns: The role of the environment. In G. Roberts (Ed.), *Motivation in sport and exercise.* Champaign, IL: Human Kinetics.

Anand, B. K., & Brobeck, J. R. (1951). Hypothalamic control of food intake in rats and cats. *Yale Journal of Biology and Medicine, 24,* 123–140.

Anderson, C. A., & Bushman, B. J. (2001). Effects of violent video games on aggressive behavior, aggressive cognition, aggressive affect, physiological arousal, and prosocial behavior: A meta-analytic review of the scientific literature. *Psychological Science, 12,* 353–359.

Anderson, C. A., & Bushman, B. J. (2002). Human aggression. *Annual Review of Psychology, 53,* 27–51.

Anderson, C. A., Shibuya, A., Ihori, N., Swing, E. L., Bushman, B. J., Sakamoto, A., et al. (2010). Violent video game effects on aggression, empathy, and prosocial behavior in Eastern and Western countries: A meta-analytic review. *Psychological Bulletin, 136,* 151–173.

Anderson, M. C., & Neely, J. H. (1996). Interference and inhibition in memory retrieval. In E. L. Bjork & R. A. Bjork (Eds.), *Memory: Handbook of perception and cognition* (2nd ed.). San Diego, CA: Academic Press.

Anderson, N. D., & Craik, F. I. M. (2000). Memory in the aging brain. In E. Tulving & F. I. M. Craik (Eds.), *The Oxford handbook of memory.* New York: Oxford University Press.

Ando, Y. (2009). *Auditory and visual perception.* New York: Springer.

Andreason, N. C., Arndt, S., Swayze, V., Cizadlo, T., et al. (1994). Thalamic abnormalities in schizophrenia visualized through magnetic resonance image averaging. *Science, 266,* 294–298.

Andrews, F. M. (1991). Stability and change in levels and structure of subjective well-being: USA 1972 and 1988. *Social Indicators Research, 25,* 1–30.

Ankney, C. D. (1992). Sex differences in relative brain size: The mismeasure of women, too? *Intelligence, 16,* 329–336.

Anthony, J. C. (2006). The epidemiology of cannabis dependence. In R. A. Roffman & R. S. Stephens (Eds.), *Cannabis dependence: Its nature, consequences and treatment.* Cambridge, England: Cambridge.

Antonuccio, D. O., Danton, W. G., et al. (2003). Psychology in the prescription era: Building a firewall between marketing and science. *American Psychologist, 58,* 1028–1043.

Antrobus, J. (1991). Dreaming: Cognitive processes during cortical activation and high afferent thresholds. *Psychological Review, 98,* 96–121.

APA Monitor. (1997, December). *Author, 28*(12).

Aponte, H., & Hoffman, L. (1973). The open door. A structural approach to a family with an anorectic child. *Family Process, 12,* 1–44.

Areán, P. (2007). Mood disorders: Depressive disorders. In M. Hersen, S. M. Turner, & D. C. Beidel (Eds.), *Adult psychopathology and diagnosis.* Hoboken, NJ: Wiley.

"A Recovering Patient." (1986). "Can we talk?" The schizophrenic patient in psychotherapy. *American Journal of Psychiatry, 143,* 68–70.

Arendt, J. (2009). Managing jet lag: Some of the problems and possible new solutions. *Sleep Medicine Reviews, 13,* 249–256.

Argyle, M. (1999). Causes and correlates of happiness. In D. Kahneman, E. Diener, & N. Schwarz (Eds.), *Well-being: The foundations of hedonic psychology.* New York: Russell Sage Foundation.

Arnett, J. J. (1999). Adolescent storm and stress, reconsidered. *American Psychologist, 54,* 317–326.

Arnett, J. J. (2001). Conceptions of the transition to adulthood: Perspectives from adolescence through midlife. *Journal of Adult Development, 8,* 133–143.

Arnett, P. A. (1997). Autonomic responsivity in psychopaths: A critical review and theoretical proposal. *Clinical Psychology Review, 17,* 903–936.

Aron, E., Aron, A., & Davies, K. M. (2005). Adult shyness: The interaction of temperamental sensitivity and an adverse childhood environment. *Personality and Social Psychology Bulletin, 31,* 181–197.

Aronson, E., & Patnoe, S. (1997). *The jigsaw classroom: Building cooperation in the classroom* (2nd ed.). New York: Longman.

Aronson, J., Lustina, M. J., Good, C., Keough, K., Steele, C. M., & Brown, J. (1999). When White men can't do math: Necessary and sufficient factors in stereotype threat. *Journal of Experimental Social Psychology, 35,* 29–46.

Arrow, H., & Burns, K. L. (2004). Self-organizing culture: How norms emerge in small groups. In M. Schaller & C. S. Crandall (Eds.), *The psychological foundations of culture.* Mahwah, NJ: Erlbaum.

Arshavsky, Y. I. (2009). Two functions of early language experience. *Brain Research Reviews, 60,* 327–340.

Arundale, R. B. (2005). Pragmatics, conversational implicature, and conversation. In K. L. Fitch & R. E. Sanders (Eds.), *Handbook of language and social interaction.* Mahwah, NJ: Erlbaum.

Asch, S. E. (1946). Forming impressions of personality. *Journal of Abnormal and Social Psychology, 41,* 258–290.

Asch, S. E. (1951). Effects of group pressure upon the modification and distortion of judgment. In H. Guetzkow (Ed.), *Groups, leadership, and men.* Pittsburgh: Carnegie Press.

Asch, S. E. (1956). Studies of independence and conformity: A minority of one against a unanimous majority. *Psychological Monographs, 70,* 416.

Asimov, I. (1997). *Isaac Asimov's book of facts.* New York: Random House/Wings Books.

Aspinwall, L. G., & Staudinger, U. M. (Eds.). (2003). *A psychology of human strengths: Fundamental questions and future directions for a positive psychology.* Washington, DC: American Psychological Association.

Assanand, S. P., John, P. J., & Lehman, D. R. (1998). Teaching theories of hunger and eating: Overcoming students' misconceptions. *Teaching of Psychology, 25,* 44–46.

Assor, A., Roth, G., & Deci, E. L. (2004). The emotional costs of parents' conditional regard: A self-determination theory analysis. *Journal of Personality, 72,* 47–88.

Athens, E. S., Vollmer, T. R., & Pipkin, C. C. S. P. (2007). Shaping academic task engagement with percentile schedules. *Journal of Applied Behavior Analysis, 40,* 475–488.

Atkinson, J. W. (Ed.). (1958). *Motives in fantasy, action, and society.* Princeton, NJ: Van Nostrand.

Atkinson, J. W. (1964). *An introduction to motivation.* Princeton, NJ: Van Nostrand.

Atkinson, J. W., & Birch, D. (1978). *An introduction to motivation.* New York: Van Nostrand.

Atkinson, R. C., & Shiffrin, R. M. (1968). Human memory: A proposed system and its control processes. In K. W. Spence & J. T. Spence (Eds.), *Advances in the psychology of learning and motivation: Research and theory* (Vol. 2). New York: Academic Press.

Auerbach, S. M., Penberthy, A. R., & Kiesler, D. J. (2004). Opportunity for control, interpersonal impacts, and adjustment to a long-term invasive health care procedure. *Journal of Behavioral Medicine, 27*, 11–29.

Avenell, A., Brown, T. J., Mc Gee, M. A., Campbell, M. K., et al. (2004). What interventions should we add to weight reducing diets in adults with obesity? A systematic review of randomized controlled trials of adding drug therapy, exercise, behaviour therapy or a combination of these interventions. *Journal of Human Nutrition and Dietetics, 17*, 293–316.

Ayllon, T., & Azrin, N. H. (1968). *The token economy: A motivational system for therapy and rehabilitation.* New York: Appleton-Century-Crofts.

Baars, B. J. (1997). In the theatre of consciousness: Global workspace theory, a rigorous scientific theory of consciousness. *Journal of Consciousness Studies, 4*, 292–309.

Baars, B. J. (2007). The global workspace theory of consciousness. In M. Velmans & S. Schneider (Eds.), *The Blackwell companion to consciousness.* Malden, MA: Blackwell.

Bach-y-Rita, P. (2004). Tactile sensory substitution studies. In M. C. Roco & C. D. Montemagno (Eds.), *The coevolution of human potential and converging technologies.* New York: New York Academy of Sciences.

Back, M. D., Schmukle, S. C., & Egloff, B. (2008). Becoming friends by chance. *Psychological Science, 19*, 439–440.

Backhaus, W. G., Kliegl, R., & Werner, J. S. (Eds.). (1998). *Color vision: Perspectives from different disciplines.* New York: Walter de Gruyter.

Baddeley, A. (2007). *Working memory, thought, and action.* London: Oxford University Press.

Baddeley, A. (2010). Long-term and working memory: How do they interact? In L. Bäckman & L. Nyberg (Eds.), *Memory, aging and the brain: A Festschrift in honour of Lars-Göran Nilsson.* New York: Psychology.

Baddeley, A. D. (2002). Is working memory still working? *European Psychologist, 7*, 85–97.

Baddeley, A. D., & Hitch, G. J. (1974). Working memory. In G. H. Bower (Ed.), *The psychology of learning and motivation* (Vol. 8). New York: Academic Press.

Baehr, E. K. (2001). Circadian phase-delaying effects of nocturnal exercise in older and young adults. *Dissertation Abstracts International: Section B: The Sciences and Engineering, 62*(4-B), 2105.

Bagge, C., Nickell, A., Stepp, S., Durrett, C., Jackson, K., & Trull, T. J. (2004). Borderline personality disorder features predict negative outcomes 2 years later. *Journal of Abnormal Psychology, 113*, 279–288.

Bagley, C., & Ramsay, R. (1997). *Suicidal behaviour in adolescents and adults: Research, taxonomy and prevention.* Ashgate, England: Ashgate Publishing.

Bahrick, H. P. (1984). Semantic memory content in permastore: Fifty years of memory for Spanish learned in school. *Journal of Experimental Psychology: General, 113*, 1–29.

Bahrick, H. P. (2005). The long-term neglect of long-term memory: Reasons and remedies. In A. F. Healy (Ed.), *Experimental cognitive psychology and its applications: Decade of behavior.* Washington, DC: American Psychological Association.

Bahrick, H. P., Bahrick, P. O., & Wittlinger, R. P. (1975). Fifty years of memory for names and faces: A cross-sectional approach. *Journal of Experimental Psychology: General, 104*, 54–75.

Bahrick, H. P., Hall, L. K., & Berger, S. A. (1996). Accuracy and distortion in memory for high school grades. *Psychological Science, 7*, 265–271.

Bailey, J. M., Dunne, M. P., & Martin, N. G. (2000). Genetic and environmental influences on sexual orientation and its correlates in an Australian twin sample. *Journal of Personality and Social Psychology, 78*, 524–536.

Bailey, J. M., & Pillard, R. C. (1991). A genetic study of male sexual orientation. *Archives of General Psychiatry, 48*, 1089–1096.

Bailey, J. M., Pillard, R. C., Neale, M. C., & Agyei, Y. (1993). Heritable factors influence sexual orientation in women. *Archives of General Psychiatry, 50*, 217–223.

Baillargeon, R. (2004). Infants' physical world. *Current Directions in Psychological Science, 13*, 89–94.

Baldwin, S. A., Berkeljon, A., Atkins, D. C., Olsen, J. A., & Nielsen, S. L. (2009). Rates of change in naturalistic psychotherapy: Contrasting dose–effect and good-enough level models of change. *Journal of Consulting and Clinical Psychology, 77*, 203–211.

Ball, J., & Mosselle, K. (1995). Health risk behaviors of adolescents in Singapore. *Asian Journal of Psychology, 1*, 54–62.

Ballard, C. (2001). *Understanding the senses.* New York: Rosen.

Ballenger, J. C. (2000). Panic disorder and agoraphobia. In G. Fink (Ed.), *Encyclopedia of stress.* San Diego, CA: Academic Press.

Baltes, P. B., & Smith, J. (2008). The fascination of wisdom: Its nature, ontogeny, and function. *Perspectives on Psychological Science, 3*, 56–64.

Baltes, P., & Staudinger, U. M. (2000). Wisdom: A metaheuristic (pragmatic) to orchestrate mind and virtue toward excellence. *American Psychologist, 55*, 122–136.

Bandura, A. (1965). Influence of models' reinforcement contingencies on the acquisition of imitated responses. *Journal of Personality and Social Psychology, 1*, 589–595.

Bandura, A. (1969). *Principles of behavior modification.* New York: Holt, Rinehart & Winston.

Bandura, A. (1986). *Social foundations of thought and action: A social-cognitive theory.* Englewood Cliffs, NJ: Prentice Hall.

Bandura, A. (1989). Social cognitive theory. *Annals of Child Development, 6*, 3–58.

Bandura, A. (1997). *Self-efficacy: The exercise of control.* New York: W. H. Freeman.

Bandura, A. (1999). Social cognitive theory of personality. In D. Cervone & Y. Shoda (Eds.), *The coherence of personality.* New York: Guilford Press.

Bandura, A. (2000). Health promotion from the perspective of social cognitive theory. In P. Norman, C. Abraham, & M. Conner (Eds.), *Understanding and changing health behaviour.* Reading, England: Harwood.

Bandura, A. (2002). Environmental sustainability by sociocognitive deceleration of population growth. In P. Schmuck & W. P. Schultz (Eds.), *Psychology of sustainable development.* Dordrecht, Netherlands: Kluwer.

Bandura, A. (2008). Reconstrual of "free will" from the agentic perspective of social cognitive theory. In J. Baer, J. C. Kaufman, & R. F. Baumeister (Eds.), *Are we free? Psychology and free will.* New York: Oxford University Press.

Bandura, A., & Cervone, D. (1983). Self-evaluative and self-efficacy mechanisms governing the motivational effects of goal systems. *Journal of Personality and Social Psychology, 45*, 1017–1028.

Bandura, A., & Locke, E. (2003). Negative self efficacy and goal effects revisited. *Journal of Applied Psychology, 88*, 87–99.

Bandura, A., O'Leary, A., Taylor, C., et al. (1987). Perceived self-efficacy and pain control: Opioid and nonopioid mechanisms. *Journal of Personality and Social Psychology, 53*, 563–571.

Bannerman, R. L., Milders, M., de Gelder, B. D., & Sahraie, A. (2009). Orienting to threat: Faster localization of fearful facial expressions and body postures revealed by saccadic eye movements. *Proceedings in Biological Science, 276*, 1635–1641.

Barber, J. (1998). The mysterious persistence of hypnotic analgesia. *International Journal of Clinical and Experimental Hypnosis, 46*, 28–43.

Bargh, J. A., & Chartrand, T. L. (1999). The unbearable automaticity of being. *American Psychologist, 54*, 462–479.

Bargh, J. A., & Morsella, E. (2010). Unconscious behavioral guidance systems. In C. R. Agnew, D. E. Carlston, W. G. Graziano, & J. R. Kelly (Eds.), *Then a miracle occurs: Focusing on behavior in social psychological theory and research.* New York: Oxford University Press.

Bar-Haim, Y., Lamy, D., Pergamin, L., Bakermans-Kranenburg, M., & van Ijzendoorn, M. H. (2007). Threat-related attentional bias in anxious and non-anxious individuals: A meta-analytic study. *Psychological Bulletin, 133*, 1–24.

Barlow, D. H. (1997). Cognitive-behavioral therapy for panic disorder: Current status. *Journal of Clinical Psychiatry, 58*(Suppl. 2), 32–36.

Barlow, D. H. (2002). *Anxiety and its disorders.* New York: Guilford Press.

Barlow, D. H. (2008). *Clinical handbook of psychological disorders: A step-by-step treatment manual* (3rd ed.). New York: Guilford Press.

Barnes, G. E., & Prosen, H. (1985). Parental death and depression. *Journal of Abnormal Psychology, 94*, 64–69.

Barnett, J. E., & Porter, J. E. (1998). The suicidal patient: Clinical and risk management strategies. In L. VandeCreek & S. Knapp (Eds.), *Innovations in clinical practice: A source book* (Vol. 16). Sarasota, FL: Professional Resource Press.

Barnett, W. S., & Camilli, G. (2002). Compensatory preschool education, cognitive development, and "race." In J. Fish (Ed.), *Race and intelligence: Separating science from myth.* Mahwah, NJ: Erlbaum.

Baron, R. S., Cutrona, C. E., Hicklin, D., Russell, D. W., & Lubaroff, D. M. (1990). Social support and immune responses among spouses of cancer patients. *Journal of Personality and Social Psychology, 59*, 344–352.

Barondes, S. H. (1999). *Mood genes: Hunting for origins of mania and depression.* New York: Oxford University Press.

Barrett, G. V., & Depinet, R. L. (1991). A reconsideration of testing for competence rather than intelligence. *American Psychologist, 46*, 1012–1024.

Barrow, C. J. (2003). *Environmental change and human development: The place of environmental change in human evolution.* New York: Oxford University Press.

Bartholomew, D. L. (2005). *Measuring intelligence: Facts and fallacies.* New York: Cambridge University Press.

Bartlett, D. J., Marshall, N. S., Williams, A., & Grunstein, R. R. (2008). Predictors of primary medical care consultation for sleep disorders. *Sleep Medicine, 9,* 857–864.

Bartlett, F. C. (1932). *Remembering: A study in experimental and social psychology.* New York: Cambridge University Press.

Bartolomeo, P. (2002). The relationship between visual perception and visual mental imagery: A reappraisal of the neuropsychological evidence. *Cortex, 38,* 357–378.

Bateman, A. L., & Salfati, C. G. (2007). An examination of behavioral consistency using individual behaviors or groups of behaviors in serial homicide. *Behavioral Sciences & the Law, 25,* 527–544.

Batson, C. D. (1991). *The altruism question: Toward a social-psychological answer.* Hillsdale, NJ: Erlbaum.

Batson, C. D. (2006). "Not all self-interest after all": Economics of empathy-induced altruism. In D. De Cremer, D. M. Zeelenberg, & J. K. Murnighan (Eds.), *Social psychology and economics.* Mahwah, NJ: Erlbaum.

Battista, S. R., Stewart, S. H., Fulton, H. G., Steeves, D., Darredeau, C., & Gavric, D. (2008). A further investigation of the relations of anxiety sensitivity to smoking motives. *Addictive Behaviors, 33,* 1402–1408.

Baum, A. (1994). Disease processes: Behavioral, biological, and environmental interactions in disease processes. In S. J. Blumenthal, K. Matthews, & S. M. Weiss (Eds.), *New research frontiers in behavioral medicine: Proceedings of the national conference.* Washington, DC: NIH Publications.

Baumeister, R. (Ed.). (1993). *Self-esteem: The puzzle of low self regard.* New York: Plenum.

Baumeister, R. F., Catanese, K. R., & Vohs, K. D. (2001). Is there a gender difference in strength of sex drive? Theoretical views, conceptual distinctions, and a review of relevant evidence. *Personality and Social Psychology Review, 5,* 242–273.

Baumeister, R. F., & Leary, M. R. (1995). The need to belong: Desire for interpersonal attachments as a fundamental human motivation. *Psychological Bulletin, 117,* 497–529.

Baumeister, R. F., & Tice, D. M. (1990). Anxiety and social exclusion. *Journal of Social and Clinical Psychology, 9,* 165–195.

Baumrind, D. (1964). Some thoughts on ethics of research: After reading Milgram's behavioral study of "obedience." *American Psychologist, 19,* 421–423.

Baumrind, D. (1967). Child care practices anteceding three patterns of preschool behavior. *Genetic Psychology Monographs, 75,* 43–88.

Bauserman, R. (1996). Sexual aggression and pornography: A review of correlational research. *Basic and Applied Social Psychology, 18,* 405–427.

Bayley, T. M., Dye, L., Jones, S., DeBono, M., & Hill, A. J. (2002). Food cravings and aversions during pregnancy: Relationships with nausea and vomiting. *Appetite, 38,* 45–51.

Bazzett, T. (2008). An introduction to behavior genetics.

Beaman, A. L., Barnes, P. J., Klentz, B., & McQuirk, B. (1978). Increasing helping rates through information dissemination: Teaching pays. *Personality and Social Psychology Bulletin, 4,* 406–411.

Beatty, M. J., Heisel, A. D., Hall, A. E., Levine, T. R., & La France, B. H. (2002). What can we learn from the study of twins about genetic and environmental influences on interpersonal affiliation, aggressiveness, and social anxiety? A meta-analytic study. *Communication Monographs, 69,* 1–18.

Beauchamp, G. K., & Bartoshuk, L. (Eds.). (1997). *Tasting and smelling.* Philadelphia: Academic Press.

Beck, A. T. (1976). *Cognitive therapy and the emotional disorders.* New York: International Universities Press.

Beck, A. T., Freeman, A., & Davis, D. D. (2004). *Cognitive therapy of personality disorders* (2nd ed.). New York: Guilford Press.

Beck, A. T., Rush, A. J., Shaw, B. F., & Emery, G. (1979). *Cognitive therapy of depression.* New York: Guilford Press.

Becker, A. E., Grinspoon, S. K., Klibanski, A., & Herzog, D. B. (1999). Current concepts: Eating disorders. *New England Journal of Medicine, 340,* 1092–1098.

Becker, J. (2004). Reconsidering the role of overcoming perturbations in cognitive development: Constructivism and consciousness. *Human Development, 47,* 77–93.

Beech, J. R., & Mayall, K. A. (2005). The word shape hypothesis re-examined: Evidence for an external feature advantage in visual word recognition. *Journal of Research in Reading, 28,* 302–319.

Beecher, H. K. (1959). Generalization from pain of various types and diverse origins. *Science, 130,* 267–268.

Beeftink, F., van Eerde, W., & Rutte, C. G. (2008). The effect of interruptions and breaks on insight and impasses: Do you need a break right now? *Creativity Research Journal, 20,* 358–364.

Beidel, D. C., & Turner, S. M. (2007). *Shy children, phobic adults: Nature and treatment of social anxiety disorders.* Washington, DC: American Psychological Association.

Beidel, D. C., Turner, S. M., & Stipelman, B. (2007). Anxiety disorders. In M. Hersen, S. M. Turner, & D. C. Beidel (Eds.), *Adult psychopathology and diagnosis.* Hoboken, NJ: Wiley.

Beilock, S. L., & Carr, T. H. (2001). On the fragility of skilled performance: What governs choking under pressure? *Journal of Experimental Psychology: General, 130,* 701–725.

Beilock, S. L., & DeCaro, M. S. (2007). From poor performance to success under stress: Working memory, strategy selection, and mathematical problem solving under pressure. *Journal of Experimental Psychology: Learning, Memory, and Cognition, 33,* 983–998.

Bekesy, G. von. (1957). The ear. *Scientific American, 230,* 66–78.

Belbin, O., Beaumont, H., Warden, D., Smith, A. D., Kalsheker, N., & Morgan, K. (2009). PSEN polymorphisms alter the rate of cognitive decline in sporadic Alzheimer's disease patients. *Neurobiology of Aging, 30,* 1992–1999.

Bell, A. P., Weinberg, M. S., & Hammersmith, S. K. (1981). *Sexual preference: Its development in men and women.* Bloomington: Indiana University Press.

Bell, J. H., & Bromnick, R. D. (2003). The social reality of the imaginary audience: A ground theory approach. *Adolescence, 38,* 205–219.

Bellack, A. S., Mueser, K. T., Gingerich, S., & Agresta, J. (2004). *Social skills training for schizophrenia* (2nd ed.). New York: Guilford Press.

Belloc, N. B. (1973). Relationship of health practices and mortality. *Preventive Medicine, 2,* 67–81.

Bem, D. J. (1972). Self-perception theory. In L. Berkowitz (Ed.), *Advances in experimental social psychology* (Vol. 6). New York: Academic Press.

Bem, D. J. (1996). Exotic becomes erotic: A developmental theory of sexual orientation. *Psychological Review, 103,* 320–335.

Bem, D. J. (2001). Exotic becomes erotic: Integrating biological and experiential antecedents of sexual orientation. In A. R. D'Augelli & C. J. Patterson (Eds.), *Lesbian, gay, and bisexual identities and youth: Psychological perspectives.* London: Oxford University Press.

Bem, D. J., & Honorton, C. (1994). Does psi exist? Replicable evidence for an anomalous process of information transfer. *Psychological Bulletin, 115,* 4–18.

Bem, S. L. (1981). Gender schema theory: A cognitive account of sex typing. *Psychological Review, 88,* 354–364.

Benedito-Silva, A. A., Menna-Barreto, I. S., Cipolla-Neto, J., Marques, N., & Tenreiro, S. (1989). A self-evaluation questionnaire for the determination of morningness-eveningness types in Brazil. *Chronobiologia, 16,* 311.

Benes, F. M. (2009). Neural circuitry models of schizophrenia: Is it dopamine, GABA, glutamate, or something else? *Biological Psychiatry, 65,* 1003–1005.

Benet-Martinez, V., & Oishi, S. (2008). Culture and personality. In O. P. John, R. W. Robins, & L. A. Pervin (Eds.), *Handbook of personality theory and research* (3rd ed.). New York: Guilford Press.

Bengtson, V. L. (2001). Beyond the nuclear family: The increasing importance of multigenerational bonds. *Journal of Marriage and the Family, 63,* 1–16.

Benjamin, A. S., & Bjork, R. A. (2000). On the relationship between recognition speed and accuracy for words rehearsed via rote versus elaborative rehearsal. *Journal of Experimental Psychology: Learning, Memory, and Cognition, 26,* 638–648.

Benjamin, L. S. (2003). *Interpersonal reconstructive therapy: Promoting change in nonresponders.* New York: Guilford Press.

Ben-Zur, H. (2009). Coping styles and affect. *International Journal of Stress Management, 16,* 87–101.

Berkowitz, L., & Harmon-Jones, E. (2004). Toward an understanding of the determinants of anger. *Emotion, 4,* 107–130.

Berlin, L. J., Ispa, J. M., Fine, M. A., Malone, P. S., Brooks-Gunn, J., Brady-Smith, C., et al. (2009). Correlates and consequences of spanking and verbal punishment for low-income White, African American, and Mexican American toddlers. *Child Development, 80,* 1403–1420.

Bernichon, T., Cook, K. E., & Brown, J. D. (2003). Seeking self-evaluative feedback: The interactive role of global self-esteem and specific self-views. *Journal of Personality and Social Psychology, 84,* 194–204.

Berntsen, D. (2001). Involuntary memories of emotional events: Do memories of traumas and extremely happy events differ? *Applied Cognitive Psychology, 5,* S135–S158.

Berridge, K. C. (2004). Motivation concepts in behavioral neuroscience. *Physiology and Behavior, 81,* 179–209.

Berry, D., & O'Connor, E. (2010). Behavioral risk, teacher–child relationships, and social skill development across middle childhood: A child-by-environment analysis of change. *Journal of Applied Developmental Psychology, 31,* 1–14.

Berry, J. W., Poortinga, Y. H., Segall, M. H., & Dasen, P. (1992). *Cross-cultural psychology: Research and application.* New York: Cambridge University Press.

Berthoud, H. R. (2002). Multiple neural systems controlling food intake and body weight. *Neuroscience and Biobehavioral Reviews, 26,* 393–428.

Best, S. J., Krueger, B., Hubbard, C., & Smith, A. (2001). An assessment of the generalizability of Internet surveys. *Social Science Computer Review, 19,* 131–145.

Beutler, L. E. (2002). The dodo bird is extinct. *Clinical Psychology: Science and Practice, 9,* 30–34.

Beyer, S. (1990). Gender differences in the accuracy of self-evaluations of performance. *Journal of Personality and Social Psychology, 59,* 960–970.

Bialystok, E. (2009). Bilingualism: The good, the bad, and the indifferent. *Bilingualism: Language and Cognition, 12,* 3–11.

Bialystok, E., & Feng, X. (2009). Language proficiency and executive control in proactive interference: Evidence from monolingual and bilingual children and adults. *Brain and Language, 109,* 93–100.

Bialystok, E., & Martin, M. M. (2004). Attention and inhibition in bilingual children: Evidence from the dimensional change card sort task. *Developmental Science, 7,* 325–339.

Bialystok, E., & Viswanathan, M. (2009). Components of executive control with advantages for bilingual children in two cultures. *Cognition, 112,* 494–500.

Biederman, J. (1998). Attention-deficit/hyperactive disorder: A life-span perspective. *Journal of Clinical Psychology, 59,* 1–13.

Bieling, P. J., Israeli, A. L., & Antony, M. M. (2004). Is perfectionism good, bad, or both? Examining models of the perfectionism construct. *Personality and Individual Differences, 36,* 1373–1385.

Biemiller, A., & Slonim, N. (2001). Estimating root word vocabulary growth in normative and advantaged populations: Evidence for a common sequence of vocabulary acquisition. *Journal of Educational Psychology, 93,* 498–520.

Bilalic, M., McLeod, P., & Gobet, F. (2008). Why good thoughts block better ones: The mechanism of the pernicious Einstellung (set) effect. *Cognition, 9,* 652–661.

Biller, J., Brazis, P., & Masdeu, J. C. (2006). *Localization in clinical neurology.* Philadelphia: Lippincott, Williams, & Wilkins.

Billings, A. G., & Moos, R. H. (1984). Coping, stress, and social resources among adults with unipolar depression. *Journal of Personality and Social Psychology, 46,* 877–891.

Binder, J. L. (2004). *Key competencies in brief dynamic psychotherapy.* New York: Guilford Press.

Binder, J. L., & Strupp, H. H. (1997). "Negative process": A recurrently discovered and underestimated facet of therapeutic process and outcome in the individual psychotherapy of adults. *Clinical Psychology: Science and Practice, 4,* 121–139.

Birdsong, D. (2005). Interpreting age effects in second language acquisition. In J. F. Kroll & A. M. B. deGroot (Eds.), *Handbook of bilingualism: Psycholinguistic approaches.* New York: Oxford University Press.

Birdsong, D., & Molis, M. (2001). On the evidence for maturational constraints in second-language acquisition. *Journal of Memory and Language, 44,* 235–249.

Bireta, T. J., & Simels, B. A. (2009). The isolation effect and advertising: Are unusual advertisements remembered better? In M. R. Kelley (Ed.), *Applied Memory.* Hauppauge, NY: Nova Science.

Birney, D. P., & Sternberg, R. J. (2006). Intelligence and cognitive abilities as competencies in development. In E. Bialystok & F. I. M. Craik (Eds.), *Lifespan cognition: Mechanisms of change.* New York: Oxford University Press.

Bjorklund, D. F., & Pellegrini, A. D. (2002). Evolutionary perspectives on social development. In P. K. Smith & C. H. Hart (Eds.), *Blackwell handbook of childhood social development.* Malden, MA: Blackwell.

Bjorkquist, O. A., Fryer, S. L., Reiss, A. L., Mattson, S. N., & Riley, E. P. (2010). Cingulate gyrus morphology in children and adolescents with fetal alcohol spectrum disorders. *Psychiatry Research: Neuroimaging, 181,* 101–107.

Black, D. N., Seritan, A. L., Taber, K. H., & Hurley, R. A. (2004). Conversion hysteria: Lessons from functional imaging. *Journal of Neuropsychiatry & Clinical Neurosciences, 16,* 245–251.

Black, D. W. (1999). *Bad boys, bad men: Confronting antisocial personality disorder.* New York: Oxford University Press.

Blackstone, J. (2007). *The empathic ground: Intersubjectivity and nonduality in the psychotherapeutic process.* Albany, NY: State University of New York Press.

Blader, S. L., & Tyler, T. R. (2002). Justice and empathy: What motivates people to help others? In M. Ross & D. T. Miller (Eds.), *The justice motive in everyday life.* New York: Cambridge University Press.

Blair, J. (2005). *Development of the psychopath: Emotion and the brain.* St. Louis, MO: Blackwell.

Blair, S. N., Kohl, H. W., III, Paffenbarger, R. S., et al. (1989). Physical fitness and all-cause mortality: A prospective study of healthy men and women. *Journal of the American Medical Association, 262,* 2395–2401.

Blakemore, C., & Cooper, G. G. (1970). Development of the brain depends on visual environment. *Nature, 228,* 477–478.

Blanchard, R. (2001). Fraternal birth order and the maternal immune hypothesis of male homosexuality. *Hormones and Behavior, 40,* 105–114.

Blanchard, R., & Bogaert, A. F. (1996). Homosexuality in men and number of older brothers. *American Journal of Psychiatry, 153,* 27–31.

Blanke, O., Ortigue, S., Landis, T., & Seeck, M. (2002). Stimulating illusory own-body perceptions. *Nature, 419*(6904), 269–270.

Blass, T. (2004). *The man who shocked the world: The life and legacy of Stanley Milgram.* New York: Basic Books.

Blass, T. (2008). What can Milgram's obedience experiments contribute to our understanding of followership? In R. E. Riggio, I. Chaleff, & J. Lipman-Blumen (Eds.), *The art of followership: How great followers create great leaders and organizations.* San Francisco: Jossey-Bass.

Blass, T., & Schmitt, C. (2001). The nature of perceived authority in the Milgram paradigm: Two replications. *Current Psychology: Developmental, Learning, Personality, Social, 20,* 115–121.

Blau, G. (2008). Exploring antecedents of individual grieving stages during an anticipated worksite closure. *Journal of Occupational and Organizational Psychology, 81,* 529–550.

Blechman, E., & Brownell, K. D. (1998). *Behavioral medicine and women: A comprehensive handbook.* New York: Guilford Press.

Blessing, W. W. (1997). *The lower brainstem and bodily homeostasis.* New York: Oxford University Press.

Bloch, C., Kaiser, A., Kuenzli, E., Zappatore, D., Haller, S., Franceschini, R., et al. (2009). The age of second language in Broca's and Wernicke's area. *Neuropsychologia, 47,* 625–633.

Block, J. J. (2007). Lessons from Columbine: Virtual and real rage. *American Journal of Forensic Psychiatry, 28*(2), 1–27.

Block, N. (2002). How heritability misleads about race. In J. M. Fish (Ed.), *Race and intelligence: Separating science from myth.* Mahwah, NJ: Erlbaum.

Blodgett, H. C. (1929). The effect of the introduction of reward on the maze performance of rats. *University of California Publications in Psychology, 4*(8), 114–126.

Bloomfield, K., Greenfield, T. K., Kraus, L., & Augustin, R. (2002). A comparison of drinking patterns and alcohol-related problems in the United States and Germany, 1995. *Substance Use and Misuse, 37,* 399–428.

Bobo, L. (1988). Attitudes toward the Black political movement: Trends, meaning, and effects of racial policy preferences. *Social Psychology Quarterly, 51,* 287–302.

Bolles, R. C., & Beecher, M. D. (Eds.). (1988). *Evolution and learning.* Hillsdale, NJ: Erlbaum.

Bolling, M. Y., & Kohlenberg, R. J. (2004). Reasons for quitting serotonin reuptake inhibitor therapy: Paradoxical psychological side effects and patient satisfaction. *Psychotherapy and Psychosomatics, 73*(6), 380–385.

Bonanno, G. A. (2005). Clarifying and extending the construct of adult resilience. *American Psychologist, 60,* 265–267.

Bonanno, G. A., Boerner, K., & Wortman, C. B. (2008). Trajectories of grieving. In M. S. Stroebe, R. O. Hansson, et al. (Eds.), *Handbook of bereavement research and practice: Advances in theory and intervention.* Washington, DC: American Psychological Association.

Bonanno, G. A., Papa, A., Lalande, K., Westphal, M., & Coifman, K. (2004). The importance of being flexible. *Psychological Science, 15,* 482–487.

Bond, R. (2005). Group size and conformity. *Group Processes & Intergroup Relations, 8,* 331–354.

Bond, R., & Smith, P. B. (1996). Culture and conformity: A meta-analysis of studies using Asch's

(1952b, 1956) line judgment task. *Psychological Bulletin, 119,* 111–137.

Boneva, B., Frieze, I. H., Ferligoj, A., Pauknerova, D., & Orgocka, A. (1998). Achievement, power, and affiliation motives as clues to (e)migration desires: A four-countries comparison. *European Psychologist, 3,* 247–254.

Bonnel, A. M., & Hafter, E. R. (1998). Divided attention between simultaneous auditory and visual signals. *Perception & Psychophysics, 60,* 179–190.

Bonvillian, J. D., & Patterson, F. G. P. (1997). Sign language acquisition and the development of meaning in a lowland gorilla. In C. Mandell & A. McCabe (Eds.), *The problem of meaning: Behavioral and cognitive perspectives.* Amsterdam: North-Holland/Elsevier Science.

Booth, A., & Amato, P. R. (2001). Parental pre-divorce relations and offspring postdivorce well-being. *Journal of Marriage and the Family, 63,* 197–212.

Bootzin, R. R. (2002). Cognitive-behavioral treatment of insomnia: Knitting up the ravell'd sleeve of care. In D. T. Kenny, J. G. Carlson, F. J. McGuigan, & J. L. Sheppard (Eds.), *Stress and health: Research and clinical applications.* Amsterdam: Harwood.

Borkenau, P., Riemann, R., Spinath, F. M., & Angleitner, A. (2006). Genetic and environmental influences on person x situation profiles. *Journal of Personality, 74,* 1451–1480.

Borod, J. C. (2000). *The neuropsychology of emotion.* New York: Oxford University Press.

Boschker, M. S., Baker, F. C., & Michaels, C. F. (2002). Memory for the functional characteristics of climbing walls: Perceiving affordances. *Journal of Motor Behavior, 34,* 25–36.

Bouchard, T. J. (2004). Genetic influence on human psychological traits. *Current Directions in Psychological Science, 13,* 148–151.

Bouchard, T. J., Lykken, D. T., McGue, M., Segal, N. L., & Tellegen, A. (1990). Sources of human psychological differences: The Minnesota study of twins reared apart. *Science, 250,* 223–228.

Bouchard, T. J., & McGue, M. (1981). Familial studies of intelligence: A review. *Science, 212,* 1055–1059.

Boulos, Z. (1998). Bright light treatment for jet lag and shift work. In R. Lam & W. Raymond (Eds.), *Seasonal affective disorder and beyond: Light treatment for SAD and non-SAD conditions.* Washington, DC: American Psychiatric Press.

Bowen, S., Chawla, N., Collins, S. E., Witkiewits, K., et al. (2009). Mindfulness-based relapse prevention for substance use disorders: A pilot efficacy trial. *Substance Abuse, 30,* 295–305.

Bower, B. (2009). Males, females swap sex stereotypes. *Science News, 175*(11), 5–6.

Bowlby, J. (1969). *Attachment and loss: Vol. 1. Attachment.* New York: Basic Books.

Bowlby, J. (1973). *Attachment and loss: Vol. 2. Separation: Anxiety and anger.* London: Hogarth.

Bowlby, J. (2000). *Loss: Sadness and depression.* New York: Basic Books.

Bowring, J. (1877). *Autobiographical recollections of Sir John Bowring.* London: H. S. King.

Boyd, R., & Richerson, P. J. (2005). *The origin and evolution of cultures.* New York: Oxford University Press.

Boyle, G. J., & Helmes, E. (2009). Methods of personality assessment. In P. J. Corr & G. Matthews

(Eds.), *The Cambridge handbook of personality psychology.* Cambridge, England: Cambridge University Press.

Bozarth, J. D., Zimring, F. M., & Tausch, R. (2002). Client-centered therapy: The evolution of a revolution. In D. J. Cain (Ed.), *Humanistic psychotherapies: Handbook of research and practice.* Washington, DC: American Psychological Association.

Brabender, V., Fallon, A. E., & Smolar, A. I. (2004). *Essentials of group therapy.* New York: Wiley.

Bracha, H. S. (2006). Human brain evolution and the "neuroevolutionary time-depth principle": Implications for the reclassification of fear-circuitry-related traits in DSM-V and for studying resilience to warzone-related posttraumatic stress disorder. *Progress in Neuro-Pharmacology & Biological Psychiatry, 30,* 827–853.

Bradizza, C. M., & Stasiewkz, P. R. (2009). Alcohol and drug use disorders. In K. Salzinger & M. R. Serper (Eds.), *Behavioral mechanisms and psychopathology: Advancing the explanation of its nature, cause, and treatment.* Washington, DC: American Psychological Association.

Brand, M. (2007). Cognitive profile of patients with alcoholic Korsakoff's syndrome. *International Journal on Disability and Human Development, 6,* 161–170.

Bransford, J. D., & Johnson, M. K. (1972). Contextual prerequisites for understanding: Some investigations of comprehension and recall. *Journal of Verbal Learning & Verbal Behavior, 11,* 717–726.

Brantley, P., & Garrett, V. D. (1993). Psychobiological approaches to health and disease. In B. Sutker & H. E. Adams (Eds.), *Comprehensive handbook of psychopathology* (2nd ed.). New York: Plenum.

Brauer, M. (2001). Intergroup perception in the social context: The effects of social status and group membership on perceived out-group homogeneity and ethnocentrism. *Journal of Experimental Social Psychology, 37,* 15–31.

Bray, J. H., & Berger, S. H. (1993). Developmental issues in Step Families Research Project: Family relationships and parent-child interactions. *Journal of Family Psychology, 7,* 76–90.

Brazel, C. Y., & Rao, M. S. (2004). Aging and neuronal replacement. *Ageing Research Reviews, 3,* 465–483.

Brehm, J. W., & Self, E. A. (1989). The intensity of motivation. *Annual Review of Psychology, 40,* 109–131.

Breland, K., & Breland, M. (1961). The misbehavior of organisms. *American Psychologist, 16,* 681–684.

Breland, K., & Breland, M. (1966). *Animal behavior.* New York: Macmillan.

Bremner, J. D. (2000). Neurobiology of posttraumatic stress disorder. In G. Fink (Ed.), *Encyclopedia of stress.* San Diego, CA: Academic Press.

Bremner, J. D. (2005). *Brain imaging handbook.* New York: Norton.

Breslau, N. S., Davis, G. C., Andreski, P., Peterson, E. L., & Schultz, L. R. (1997). Sex differences in post-traumatic stress disorder. *Archives of General Psychiatry, 54,* 1044–1048.

Brickman, P., Coates, D., & Janoff-Bulman, R. (1978). Lottery winners and accident victims: Is happiness relative? *Journal of Personality and Social Psychology, 36,* 917–927.

Briere, J., & Lanktree, C. (1983). Sex role-related effects of sex bias in language. *Sex Roles, 9,* 625–632.

Broadbent, D. E. (1958). *Perception and communication.* London: Pergamon Press.

Broberg, D. J., & Bernstein, I. L. (1987). Candy as a scapegoat in the prevention of food aversions in children receiving chemotherapy. *Cancer, 60,* 2344–2347.

Brock, R. L., & Lawrence, E. (2009). Too much of a good thing: Underprovision versus overprovision of partner support. *Journal of Family Psychology, 23,* 181–192.

Brogdal, P. (2010). *The central nervous system: Structure and function.* New York: Oxford University Press.

Brown, G. D. A., Neath, I., & Chater, N. (2007). A temporal ratio model of memory. *Psychological Review, 114,* 539–576.

Brown, G. W., & Harris, T. O. (1978). *Social origins of depression.* London: Tavistock Press.

Brown, I., & Percy, M. (Eds.). (2007). *A comprehensive guide to intellectual and developmental disabilities.* Baltimore, MD: Paul H. Brookes Publishing Company.

Brown, J. A. (1958). Some tests of the decay theory of immediate memory. *Quarterly Journal of Experimental Psychology, 10,* 12–21.

Brown, J. D. (1998). *The self.* Boston: McGraw-Hill.

Brown, L. S. (1994). *Subversive dialogues: Theory in feminist therapy.* New York: Basic Books.

Brown, N. O. (1959). *Life against death.* New York: Random House.

Brown, R. (1973). *A first language: The early stages.* Cambridge, MA: Harvard University Press.

Brown, T. A. (2007). Temporal course and structural relations among dimensions of temperament and DSM-IV anxiety and mood disorder constructs. *Journal of Abnormal Psychology, 116,* 313–328.

Brown, T. A., & Barlow, D. H. (2009). A proposal for a dimensional classification system based on the shared features of the DSM-IV anxiety and mood disorders: Implications for assessment and treatment. *Psychological Assessment, 21,* 256–271.

Brown, T. A., Di-Nardo, P. A., Lehman, C. L., & Campbell, L. A. (2001). Reliability of DSM-IV anxiety and mood disorders: Implications for the classification of emotional disorders. *Journal of Abnormal Psychology, 110,* 49–58.

Brown, T. S., & Wallace, P. (1980). *Physiological psychology.* New York: Academic Press.

Brownell, K. D. (1994). *The LEARN program for weight control.* Dallas, TX: American Health.

Bruce, T. J., & Sanderson, W. C. (1998). *Specific phobias: Clinical applications of evidence-based psychotherapy.* Northvale, NJ: Aronson.

Bruck, M., & Ceci, S. J. (2009). Reliability of child witnesses' reports. In K. S. Douglas, J. L. Skeem, & S. O. Lilienfeld, (Eds.), *Psychological science in the courtroom: Consensus and controversy.* New York: Guilford Press.

Bruederl, J., Diekmann, A., & Engelhardt, H. (1997). Erhoeht eine Probeehe das Scheidungrisiko? Eine empirische Untersuchung mit dem Familiensurvey [Does a trial marriage increase divorce risk? Empirical study of the Families Survey]. *Koelner Zeitschrift fuer Soziologie und Sozialpsychologie, 49,* 205–222.

Bruss, P. J., & Mitchell, D. B. (2009). Memory systems, processes, and tasks: Taxonomic clarification via factor analysis. *American Journal of Psychology, 122,* 175–189.

Buck, L., & Axel, R. (1991). A novel multigene family may encode odorant receptors: A molecular basis for odor recognition. *Cell, 65,* 175–187.

Bulkeley, K., & Kahan, T. L. (2008). The impact of September 11 on dreaming. *Consciousness and Cognition: An International Journal, 17,* 1248–1256.

Bullier, J. (2002). Neural basis of vision. In H. Pashler & S. Yantis (Eds.), *Steven's handbook of experimental psychology: Vol. 1. Sensation and perception* (3rd ed.). New York: Wiley.

Burger, J. M. (2009). Replicating Milgram: Would people still obey today? *American Psychologist, 64,* 1–11.

Burgess, C. A., & Kirsch, I. (1999). Expectancy information as a moderator of the effects of hypnosis on memory. *Contemporary Hypnosis, 16,* 22–31.

Burgwyn-Bailes, E., Baker-Ward, L., Gordon, B. N., & Ornstein, P. A. (2001). Children's memory for emergency medical treatment after one year: The impact of individual difference variables on recall and suggestibility. *Applied Cognitive Psychology, 15,* S25–S48.

Burke, K. C., Burke, J. D., Rae, D. S., & Regier, D. A. (1991). Comparing age at onset of major depression and other psychiatric disorders by birth cohorts in five U.S. community populations. *Archives of General Psychiatry, 48,* 789–795.

Burkitt, J., Widman, D., & Saucier, D. M. (2007). Evidence for the influence of testosterone in the performance of spatial navigation in a virtual water maze in women but not in men. *Hormones and Behavior, 51,* 649–654.

Burley, T., & Freier, M. C. (2004). Character structure: A gestalt-cognitive theory. *Psychotherapy: Theory, Research, Practice, Training, 41,* 321–331.

Burns, M. O., & Seligman, M. E. P. (1991). Explanatory style, helplessness, and depression. In C. R. Snyder & D. R. Forsyth (Eds.), *Handbook of social and clinical psychology: The health perspective.* New York: Pergamon Press.

Burnstein, E., Crandall, C., & Kitayama, S. (1994). Some neo-Darwinian decision rules for altruism: Weighing cues for inclusive fitness as a function of the biological importance of the decision. *Journal of Personality and Social Psychology, 67,* 773–789.

Burt, K. B., & Masten, A. S. (2010). Development in the transition to adulthood. In J. E. Grant & M. N. Potenza (Eds.), *Young adult mental health.* New York: Oxford University Press.

Burton, E., Stice, E., & Seeley, J. R (2004). A prospective test of the stress-buffering model of depression in adolescent girls: No support once again. *Journal of Consulting and Clinical Psychology, 72,* 689–697.

Busey, T. A., Tunnicliff, J. J., Loftus, G. R., & Loftus, E. F. (2000). Accounts of the confidence-accuracy relation in recognition memory. *Psychonomic Bulletin and Review, 7,* 26–48.

Bushman, B. J. (2002). Does venting anger feed or extinguish the flame? Catharsis, rumination, distraction, anger and aggressive responding. *Personality and Social Psychology, 28,* 724–731.

Bushman, B. J., & Bonacci, A. M. (2002). Violence and sex impair memory for television ads. *Journal of Applied Psychology, 87,* 557–564.

Bushman, B. J., Rothstein, H. R., & Anderson, C. A. (2010). Much ado about something: Violent video game effects and a school of red herring: Reply to Ferguson and Kilburn (2010). *Psychological Bulletin, 136,* 182–187.

Bushnell, I. W. R. (2001). Mother's face recognition in newborn infants: Learning and memory. *Infant and Child Development, 10,* 67–74.

BusinessWeek (2006, September 25). *Chicken soup for the aging brain.* Author. Retrieved January 7, 2010, from http://www.businessweek.com/magazine/content/06_39/b4002100.htm?chan=tc&campaign_id=rss_tech.rss091506a

Buske-Kirschbaum, A., Kirschbaum, C., & Hellhammer, D. H. (1994). Conditioned modulation of NK cells in humans: Alteration of cell activity and cell number by conditioning protocols. *Psychologische Beitraege, 36,* 100–111.

Buske-Kirschbaum, A., Kirschbaum, C., Stierle, H., & Lehnert, H. (1992). Conditioned increase of natural killer cell activity (NKCA) in humans. *Psychosomatic Medicine, 54,* 123–132.

Buss, A., & Plomin, R. (1975). *A temperament theory of personality development.* New York: Wiley.

Buss, A., & Plomin, R. (1984). *Temperament: Early developing personality traits.* Hillsdale, NJ: Erlbaum.

Buss, D. M. (1985). Human mate selection. *American Scientist, 73,* 47–51.

Buss, D. M. (1989). Sex differences in human mate preferences: Evolutionary hypotheses tested in 37 cultures. *Behavioral and Brain Sciences, 12,* 1–49.

Buss, D. M. (1991). Evolutionary personality theory. *Annual Review of Psychology, 42,* 459–491.

Buss, D. M. (1995). Evolutionary psychology: A new paradigm for psychological science. *Psychological Inquiry, 6,* 1–30.

Buss, D. M. (1999). Human nature and individual differences: The evolution of human personality. In L. A. Pervin & O. P. John (Eds.), *Handbook of personality: Theory and research.* New York: Guilford Press.

Buss, D. M. (2007). *Evolutionary psychology. The new science of the mind.* Boston: Allyn & Bacon.

Buss, D. M., Abbott, M., Angleitner, A., Asherian, A., Biaggio, A., Blanco-Villasenor, A., et al. (1990). International preferences in selecting mates: A study of 37 cultures. *Journal of Cross-Cultural Psychology, 21,* 5–47.

Buss, D. M., & Schmitt, D. P. (1993). Sexual strategies theory: An evolutionary perspective on human mating. *Psychological Review, 100,* 204–232.

Butera, F., & Levine, J. (2009). *Coping with minority status: Responses to exclusion and inclusion.* New York: Cambridge University Press.

Buunk, B., & Gibbons, F. X. (Eds.). (1997). *Health, coping, and well-being: Perspectives from social comparison theory.* Mahwah, NJ: Erlbaum.

Buzan, T. (2008). *Brain boot camp.* New York: Metro.

Byer, C. O., Shainberg, L. W., & Galliano, G. (2002). *Dimensions of human sexuality* (6th ed.). Boston: McGraw-Hill.

Byrd, M. R., Richards, D. F., Hove, G., & Frima, P. C. (2002). Treatment of early onset hair pulling as a simple habit. *Behavior Modification, 26,* 400–411.

Byrne, D. (1997). An overview (and underview) of research and theory within the attraction paradigm. *Journal of Social and Personal Relationships, 14,* 417–431.

Byrne, D., Ervin, C. R., & Lamberth, J. (1970). Continuity between the experimental study of attraction and real-life computer dating. *Journal of Personality and Social Psychology, 16,* 157–165.

Byrne, D., & Greendlinger, V. (1989). *Need for affiliation as a predictor of classroom friendships.* Unpublished manuscript, State University of New York at Albany.

Cabeza, R., Nyberg, L., & Park, D. C. (2005). *Cognitive neuroscience of aging: Linking cognitive and cerebral aging.* New York: Oxford University Press.

Cacioppo, J. T., Berntson, J. T., Poehlmann, K. M., & Ito, T. A. (2000). The psychophysiology of emotion. In M. Lewis & J. M. Haviland-Jones (Eds.), *Handbook of emotions* (2nd ed.). New York: Guilford Press.

Cain, D. J. (2010). *Person-centered psychotherapies.* Washington, DC: American Psychological Association.

Cain, D. J., & Seeman, J. (Eds.). (2002). *Humanistic psychotherapies: Handbook of research and practice.* Washington, DC: American Psychological Association.

Cairns, H. (1952). Disturbances of consciousness in lesions of the mid-brain and diencephalon. *Brain, 75,* 107–114.

Camilleri, C., & Malewska-Peyre, H. (1997). Socialization and identity strategies. In J. W. Berry, P. R. Dasen & T. S. Saraswathi (Eds.), *Handbook of cross-cultural psychology: Basic processes and human development: Vol. 2. Handbook of cross-cultural psychology* (2nd ed.). Boston: Allyn & Bacon.

Campbell, A., Shirley, L., & Candy, J. (2004). A longitudinal study of gender-related cognition and behaviour. *Developmental Science, 7,* 1–9.

Campfield, L. A. (1997). Metabolic and hormonal controls of food intake: Highlights of the last 25 years: 1972–1997. *Appetite, 29,* 135–152.

Canivez, G. L., & Watkins, M. W. (1998). Long-term stability of the Wechsler Intelligence Scale for Children—Third Edition. *Psychological Assessment, 10,* 285–291.

Canli, T. (2004). Functional brain mapping of extraversion and neuroticism: Learning from individual differences in emotion processing. *Journal of Personality, 72,* 1105–1132.

Canli, T. (Ed.). (2006). *Biology of personality and individual differences.* New York: Guilford Press.

Cannon, W. B. (1942). "Voodoo" death. *American Anthropologist, 44,* 169–181.

Cannon, W. B., & Washburn, A. L. (1912). An explanation of hunger. *American Journal of Physiology, 29,* 441–454.

Canter, D. V., Alison, L. J., & Wentink, N. (2004). The organized/disorganized typology of serial murder: Myth or model? *Psychology, Public Policy, and Law, 10,* 293–320.

Cardasis, W., Hochman, J. A., & Silk, K. R. (1997). Transitional objects and borderline personality disorder. *American Journal of Psychiatry, 154,* 250–255.

Carels, R. A., Douglass, O. M., & Cacciapaglia, H. M. (2004). An ecological momentary assessment of relapse crises in dieting. *Journal of Consulting and Clinical Psychology, 72,* 341–348.

Carey, G., & Gottesman, I. I. (1981). Twin and family studies of anxiety, phobic, and obsession disorders. In D. F. Klein & J. Rabkin (Eds.), *Anxiety: New research and changing concepts.* New York: Raven Press.

Carlson, C. (2000). ADHD is overdiagnosed. In R. L. Atkinson, R. C. Atkinson, E. E. Smith, D. J. Bem, & S. Nolen-Hoeksema, *Hilgard's introduction to psychology* (13th ed.). Ft. Worth, TX: Harcourt Brace.

Carlson, E. A., & McAndrew, F. T. (2004). Body shape ideals and perceptions of body shape in Spanish and American college students. *Perceptual and Motor Skills, 99,* 1071–1074.

Carlson, J. G., & Hatfield, E. (1992). *Psychology of emotion.* Ft. Worth, TX: Harcourt Brace Jovanovich.

Carlson, S. M., Moses, L. J., & Hix, H. R. (1998). The role of inhibitory processes in young children's difficulties with deception and false belief. *Child Development, 69,* 672–691.

Carnagey, N. L., & Anderson, C. A. (2005). The effects of reward and punishment in violent video games on aggressive affect, cognition, and behavior. *Psychological Science, 16,* 882–889.

Carnagey, N. L., Anderson, C. A., & Bushman, B. J. (2007). The effect of video game violence on physiological desensitization to real-life violence. *Journal of Experimental Social Psychology, 43,* 489–496.

Carnahan, T., & McFarland, S. (2007). Revisiting the Stanford prison experiment: Could participant self-selection have led to the cruelty? *Personality and Social Psychology Bulletin, 33,* 603–614.

Carney, L. H. (2002). Neural basis of audition. In H. Pashler & S. Yantis (Eds.), *Steven's handbook of experimental psychology: Vol. 1. Sensation and perception* (3rd ed.). New York: Wiley.

Carnicero, J. A. C., Perez-Lopez, J., Salinas, M. D. C. G., & Martinez-Fuentes, M. T. (2000). A longitudinal study of temperament in infancy: Stability and convergence of measures. *European Journal of Personality, 14,* 21–37.

Carpenter, P. A., Just, M. A., & Shell, P. (1990). What one intelligence test measures: A theoretical account of the processing in the Raven Progressive Matrices Test. *Psychological Review, 97,* 404–431.

Carpenter, R., & Robson, J. (Eds.). (1999). *Vision research: A practical guide to laboratory methods.* New York: Oxford University Press.

Carreiras, M., Seghier, M. L., Baquero, S., Estévez, A., Lozano, A., Devlin, J. T., et al. (2009). An anatomical signature for literacy. *Nature, 461,* 983–986.

Carroll, C. R. (1993). *Drugs in modern society.* Madison, WI: Brown & Benchmark.

Carroll, J. B. (2005). The three-stratum theory of cognitive skills. In D. P. Flanagan & P. L. Harrison (Eds.), *Contemporary intellectual assessment: Theories, tests, and issues* (2nd ed.). New York: Guilford Press.

Carson, R. C., Butcher, J. N., & Coleman, J. C. (1988). *Abnormal psychology and modern life* (8th ed.). Glenview, IL: Scott, Foresman.

Cartwright, R. D. (1977). *Night life: Explorations in dreaming.* Englewood Cliffs, NJ: Prentice Hall.

Caruso, E. M. (2008). Use of experienced retrieval ease in self and social judgments. *Journal of Experimental Social Psychology, 44,* 148–155.

Carver, C. S., & Scheier, M. F. (2003). *Perspectives on personality* (5th ed.). Boston: Allyn & Bacon.

Carver, C. S., Scheier, M. F., & Weintraub, J. K. (1989). Assessing coping strategies: A theoretically based approach. *Journal of Personality and Social Psychology, 56,* 267–283.

Case, R. (1987). The structure and process of intellectual development. *International Journal of Psychology, 22,* 571–607.

Case, R., Demetriou, A., Platsidou, M., & Kazi, S. (2001). Integrating concepts and tests of intelligence from the differential and developmental traditions. *Intelligence, 29,* 307–336.

Casner, S. M. (2009). Perceived vs. measured effects of advanced cockpit systems on pilot workload and error: Are pilots' beliefs misaligned with reality? *Applied Ergonomics, 40,* 448–456.

Caspi, A., Elder, G. H., & Bem, D. J. (1988). Moving away from the world: Life course patterns of shy children. *Developmental Psychology, 24,* 824–831.

Caspi, A., & Roberts, B. W. (1999). Personality continuity and change across the life course. In L. A. Pervin & O. P. John (Eds.), *Handbook of personality: Theory and research.* New York: Guilford Press.

Castonguay, L. G., & Beutler, L. E. (2005). *Principles of therapeutic change that work.* New York: Oxford University Press.

Castonguay, L. G., Boswell, J. F., Constantino, M. J., Goldfried, M. R., & Hill, C. E. (2010). Training implications of harmful effects of psychological treatments. *American Psychologist, 65,* 34–49.

Castrén, E. (2009). Neural plasticity and recovery from depression. *Duodecim, 125,* 1781–1786.

Catania, A. C. (2001). Positive psychology and positive reinforcement. *American Psychologist, 56,* 86–87.

Cattell, J. (1886). The time taken up by cerebral operations. *Mind, 11,* 377–392. Retrieved February 27, 2010, from http://psychclassics.yorku.ca/Cattell/Time/part3.htm

Cattell, R. B. (1965). *The scientific analysis of personality.* Chicago: Aldine.

Cattell, R. B. (1971). *Abilities: Their growth, structure, and action.* Boston: Houghton Mifflin.

Caughlin, J. P., & Malis, R. S. (2004). Demand/withdraw communication between parents and adolescents: Connections with self-esteem and substance use. *Journal of Social and Personal Relationships, 21,* 125–148.

Ceci, S. J. (1996). *On intelligence: A bioecological treatise on intellectual development.* Cambridge, MA: Harvard University Press.

Ceci, S. J., & Williams, W. M. (1997). Schooling, intelligence, and income. *American Psychologist, 52,* 1051–1058.

Centers for Disease Control and Prevention. (1988). *Posttraumatic stress disorders.* Atlanta, GA: Author.

Centers for Disease Control and Prevention. (1997). *Fertility, family planning, and women's health: New data from the 1995 National Survey on Family Growth* (Series 23, No. 19). Washington, DC: Author.

Centers for Disease Control and Prevention. (2002a). *Causes of death in the United States.* Atlanta, GA: Author.

Centers for Disease Control and Prevention. (2002b). Youth risk behavior surveillance—United States, 2001. *Morbidity and Mortality Weekly Report, 51*(SS04), 1–64. Washington, DC: Author.

Cervone, D. (1999). Bottom-up explanation in personality psychology: The case of cross-situational consistency. In D. Cervone & Y. Shoda (Eds.), *The coherence of personality.* New York: Guilford Press.

Cervone, D., & Shoda, Y. (1999). *The coherence of personality: Social-cognitive bases of consistency, variability, and organization.* New York: Guilford Press.

Chalmers, D. J. (1995). The puzzle of conscious experience. *Scientific American, 273*(6), 80–86.

Chambless, D. L., & Hollon, S. D. (1998). Defining empirically supported therapies. *Journal of Consulting and Clinical Psychology, 66,* 7–18.

Chamorro-Premuzic, T. (2007). *Personality and individual differences.* London: Blackwell.

Chamorro-Premuzic, T., & Furnham, A. (2006). Intellectual competence and intelligent personality: A third way in differential psychology. *Review of General Psychology, 10,* 251–267.

Chan, Z. C. Y., & Ma, J. L. C. (2002). Family themes of food refusal: Disciplining the body and punishing the family. *Health Care for Women International, 23,* 49–58.

Chandler, M. J., Lacritz, L. H., Cicerello, A. R., Chapman, S. B., Honig, L. S., Weiner, M. F., & Cullum, C. M. (2004). Three-word recall in normal aging. *Journal of Clinical and Experimental Neuropsychology, 26,* 1128–1133.

Chang, E. C. (1996). Cultural differences in optimism, pessimism, and coping: Predictors of subsequent adjustment in American and Caucasian American college students. *Journal of Counseling Psychology, 43,* 113–123.

Chang, I. J., Pettit, R. W., & Katsurada, E. (2006). Where and when to spank: A comparison between U.S. and Japanese college students. *Journal of Family Violence, 21,* 281–286.

Chapell, M. S., Blanding, Z. B., Silverstein, M. E., Takahashi, M., Newman, B., Gubi, A., & McCann, N. (2005). Test anxiety and academic performance in undergraduate and graduate students. *Journal of Educational Psychology, 97,* 268–274.

Chapman, A. L. (2010). Borderline personality disorder. In D. McKay, J. S. Abramowitz, & S. Taylor (Eds.), *Cognitive-behavioral therapy for refractory cases: Turning failure into success.* Washington, DC: American Psychological Association.

Chappell, M., & Humphreys, M. S. (1994). An auto-associative neural network for sparse representations: Analysis and application to models of recognition and cued recall. *Psychological Review, 101,* 103–128.

Charlton, R. A., Barrick, T. R., Markus, H. S., & Morris, R. G. (2009). Theory of mind associations with other cognitive functions and brain imaging in normal aging. *Psychology and Aging, 24,* 338–348.

Chartrand, T. L., & Bargh, J. A. (2002). Nonconscious motivations: Their activation, operation, and consequences. In A. Tesser, D. A. Stapel, & J. V. Wood (Eds.), *Self and motivation: Emerging psychological perspectives.* Washington, DC: American Psychological Association.

Chartrand, T. L., Bargh, J. A., & van Baaren, R. (2002). *Consequences of automatic evaluation for mood.* Manuscript submitted for publication.

Chase, W. G., & Simon, H. A. (1973). Perception in chess. *Cognitive Psychology, 4*, 55–81.

Chavez, C. M., McGaugh, J. L., & Weinberger, N. M. (2009). The basolateral amygdala modulates specific sensory memory representations in the cerebral cortex. *Neurobiology of Learning and Memory, 91*, 382–392.

Cheah, C. S. L., & Nelson, L. J. (2004). The role of acculturation in the emerging adulthood of Aboriginal college students. *International Journal of Behavioral Development, 28*, 495–507.

Chen, C., Greenberger, E., Lester, J., Dong, Q., & Guo, M. S. (1998). A cross-cultural study of family and peer correlates of adolescent misconduct. *Developmental Psychology, 34*, 770–781.

Chen, H., Charlat, O., Tartaglia, L. A., Woolf, E. A., Weng, X., & Ellis, S. J. (1996). Evidence that the diabetes gene encodes the leptin receptor: Identification of a mutation in the leptin receptor gene in db/db mice. *Cell, 84*, 491–495.

Chen, H., & Lan, W. (1998). Adolescents' perceptions of their parents' academic expectations: Comparison of American, Chinese-American, and Chinese high school students. *Adolescence, 33*, 385–390.

Chen, S., English, T., & Peng, K. (2006). Self-verification and contextualized self-views. *Personality and Social Psychology Bulletin, 32*, 930–942.

Chenoweth, D. (2002). *Evaluating worksite health promotion.* Champaign, IL: Human Kinetics.

Chi, L. (2004). Achievement goal theory. In T. Morris & J. Summers (Eds.), *Sport psychology: Theories, applications, and issues* (2nd ed.). Sydney, Australia: Wiley.

Chiappe, D., & MacDonald, K. (2005). The evolution of domain-general mechanisms in intelligence and learning. *Journal of General Psychology, 132*, 5–40.

Chiappelli, F. (2000). Immune suppression. In G. Fink (Ed.), *Encyclopedia of stress.* San Diego, CA: Academic Press.

Chiauzzi, E., Brevard, J., Thurn, C., et al. (2008). MyStudentBody-Stress: An online stress management intervention for college students. *Journal of Health Communication, 13*, 555–572.

Chiles, J. A., & Strossahl, K. D. (1995). *The suicidal patient: Principles of assessment, treatment, and case management.* Washington, DC: American Psychiatric Press.

Chiriboga, D. A. (1989). Mental health at the midpoint: Crisis, challenge, or relief? In S. Hunter & M. Sundel (Eds.), *Midlife myths: Issues, findings, and practice implications.* Newbury Park, CA: Sage.

Choi, I., Dalal, R., Kim Prieto, C., & Park, H. (2003). Culture and judgement of causal relevance. *Journal of Personality and Social Psychology, 84*, 46–59.

Chomsky, N. (1972). *Language and mind.* New York: Harcourt.

Chomsky, N. (1986). *Knowledge of language: Its nature, origin and use.* New York: Praeger.

Chomsky, N. (2005). Universals of human nature. *Psychotherapy and Psychosomatics, 74*, 263–268.

Christensen, A., Atkins, D. C., Yi, J., Baucom, D. H., & George, W. H. (2006). Couple and individual adjustment for 2 years following a randomized clinical trial comparing traditional versus integrative behavioral couple therapy. *Journal of Consulting and Clinical Psychology, 74*, 1180–1191.

Christianson, S. A., & Nilsson, L. G. (1989). Hysterical amnesia: A case of aversively motivated isolation of memory. In T. Archer & L. G. Nilsson (Eds.), *Aversion, avoidance, and anxiety: Perspectives on aversively motivated behavior.* Hillsdale, NJ: Erlbaum.

Christoff, K., Keramatian, K., Gordon, A. M., Smith, R., & Mädler, B. (2009). Prefrontal organization of cognitive control according to levels of abstraction. *Brain Research, 1286*, 94–105.

Christopherson, E. R., & Mortweet, S. L. (2001). *Treatments that work with children: Empirically supported strategies for managing childhood problems.* Washington, DC: American Psychological Association.

Church, A. T., & Katigbak, M. S. (2000). Trait psychology in the Philippines. *American Behavioral Scientist, 44*, 73–94.

Chwalisz, K., Diener, E., & Gallagher, D. (1988). Autonomic arousal feedback and emotional experience: Evidence from the spinal cord injured. *Journal of Personality and Social Psychology, 54*, 820–828.

Chwilla, D. J., & Kolk, H. H. J. (2002). Three step priming in lexical decision. *Memory and Cognition, 30*, 217–225.

Cialdini, R. B. (2008). *Influence: Science and practice* (5th ed.). Boston: Allyn & Bacon.

Cialdini, R. B., Brown, S. L., Lewis, B. P., & Luce, C. (1997). Reinterpreting the empathy-altruism relationship: When one into one equals oneness. *Journal of Personality and Social Psychology, 73*, 481–494.

Cialdini, R. B., Schaller, M., Hoolihan, D., Arps, K., Fultz, J., & Beaman, A. L. (1987). Empathy-based helping: Is it selflessly or selfishly motivated? *Journal of Personality and Social Psychology, 52*, 749–758.

Cianelli, S. N., & Fouts, R. S. (1998). Chimpanzee to chimpanzee American Sign Language. *Human Evolution, 13*, 147–159.

Ciarello, C., Welcome, S. E., Halderman, L. K., et al. (2009). A large scale investigation of lateralization in cortical anatomy and word reading: Are there sex differences? *Neuropsychology, 23*, 210–222.

Cigales, M., Field, T., Lundy, B., Cuadra, A., & Hart, S. (1997). Massage enhances recovery from habituation in normal infants. *Infant Behavior and Development, 20*, 29–34.

Cinnirella, M., & Green, B. (2007). Does "cyber-conformity" vary cross-culturally? Exploring the effect of culture and communication medium on social conformity. *Computers in Human Behavior, 23*, 2011–2025.

Clancy, S. A., McNally, R. J., Schacter, D. L., Lenzeweger, M. F., & Pitman, R. K. (2002). Memory distortion in people reporting abduction by aliens. *Journal of Abnormal Psychology, 111*, 455–461.

Clark, A. E. (1998). *The positive externalities of higher unemployment: Evidence from household data.* Working paper, Université d'Orléans, Orléans, France.

Clark, D. A. (2004). *Cognitive-behavioral therapy for OCD.* New York: Guilford Press.

Clark, D. A., Beck, A. T., & Alford, B. A. (1999). *Scientific foundations of cognitive theory and therapy of depression.* New York: Wiley.

Clark, D. A., Beck, A. T., & Brown, G. (1989). Cognitive mediation in general psychiatric outpatients: A test of the content-specificity hypothesis. *Journal of Personality and Social Psychology, 56*, 958–964.

Clark, D. A., & O'Connor, K. (2005). Thinking is believing: Ego-dystonic intrusive thoughts in obsessive-compulsive disorder. In D. A. Clark (Ed.), *Intrusive thoughts in clinical disorders: Theory, research, and treatment.* New York: Guilford Press.

Clark, D. M. (1988). A cognitive model of panic attacks. In S. Rachman & J. D. Maser (Eds.), *Panic: Psychological perspectives.* Hillsdale, NJ: Erlbaum.

Clark, K. B., & Clark, M. P. (1947). Racial identification and preference in Negro children. In T. N. Newcomb & E. L. Hartley (Eds.), *Readings in Social Psychology.* New York: Holt.

Clark, R. D. (1990). The impact of AIDS on gender differences in willingness to engage in casual sex. *Journal of Applied Social Psychology, 20*, 771–782.

Clark, R. D., III. (2001). Effects of majority defection and multiple minority sources on minority influence. *Group Dynamics, 5*, 57–62.

Clark, R. D., III, & Hatfield, E. (1989). Gender differences in willingness to engage in casual sex. *Journal of Psychology and Human Sexuality, 2*, 39–55.

Clark, W. R., & Grunstein, M. (2005). *Are we hardwired? The role of genes in human behavior.* New York: Oxford University Press.

Clarke, A. M., & Clarke, A. D. B. (2000). *Early experience and the life path.* London: Kingsley.

Clarkin, J. F., Marziali, E., & Munroe-Blum, H. (1992). *Borderline personality disorder: Clinical and empirical perspectives.* New York: Guilford Press.

Clay, R. A. (2002). Advertising as science. *Monitor on Psychology, 33*(9), 38–41.

Clements, A. M., Rimrodt, S. L., Abel, J. R., Blankner, J. G., et al. (2006). Sex differences in cerebral laterality of language and visuospatial processing. *Brain and Language, 98*, 150–158.

Clifasefi, S. L., Takarangi, M. K., & Bergman, J. S. (2006). Blind drunk: The effects of alcohol on inattentional blindness. *Applied Cognitive Psychology, 20*, 697–704.

Cloninger, C. R., & Gottesman, I. I. (1989). Genetic and environmental factors in antisocial behavior disorders. In S. Mednick, T. Moffitt, & S. Strack (Eds.), *The causes of crime: New biological approaches.* Cambridge, England: Cambridge University Press.

Clore, G. L., & Centerbar, D. (2004). Analyzing anger: How to make people mad. *Emotion, 4*, 139–144.

Clutton-Brock, T. (2002). Breeding together: Kin selection and mutualism in cooperative vertebrates. *Science, 296*, 69–72.

Coalson, D. L., & Raiford, S. E. (2008). *WAIS-IV: Technical and interpretive manual.* San Antonio, TX: Pearson.

Coan, J. A., & Allen, J. (2003). Frontal EEG asymmetry and the behavioral activation and inhibition systems. *Psychophysiology, 40*, 106–114.

Coan, J. A., Schaefer, H. S., & Davidson, R. J. (2006). Lending a hand: Social regulation of the neural response to threat. *Psychological Science, 17*, 1032–1039.

Cochrane, R. E., Tett, R. P., & Vandecreek, L. (2003). Psychological testing and the selection of police officers: A national survey. *Criminal Justice and Behavior, 30*, 115–120.

Coelho, C. M., & Purkis, H. (2009). The origins of specific phobias: Influential theories and current perspectives. *Review of General Psychology, 13,* 335–348.

Coffey, C. E., Weiner, R. D., Djang, W. T., et al. (1991). Brain anatomic effects of electroconvulsive therapy: A prospective magnetic resonance imaging study. *Archives of General Psychiatry, 48,* 1013–1020.

Cohen, D. A., Pascual-Leone, A., Press, D. Z., & Robertson, E. M. (2005). Off-line learning of motor skill memory: A double dissociation of goal and movement. *Proceedings of the National Academy of Sciences of the United States of America, 102,* 18237–41.

Cohen, K. M. (2002). Relationships among childhood sex-atypical behavior, spatial ability, handedness, and sexual orientation in men. *Archives of Sexual Behavior, 31,* 129–143.

Cohen, S. (1988). Psychosocial models of the role of social support in the etiology of physical disease. *Health Psychology, 7,* 269–297.

Cohen, S., Doyle, W. J., Turner, R., Alper, C. M., & Skoner, D. P. (2003). Sociability and susceptibility to the common cold. *Psychological Science, 14,* 389–395.

Cohen, S., & Herbert, T. B. (1996). Health psychology: Psychological factors and physical disease from the perspective of human psychoneuroimmunology. *Annual Review of Psychology, 47,* 113–142.

Cohn, M. A., Fredrickson, B. L. Brown, S. L., et al. (2009). Happiness unpacked: Positive emotions increase life satisfaction by building resilience. *Emotion, 9,* 361–368.

Collings, P. (2001). If you got everything, it's good enough: Perspectives on successful aging in a Canadian Inuit community. *Journal of Cross-Cultural Gerontology, 16,* 127–155.

Collins, A. M., & Loftus, E. F. (1975). A spreading activation theory of semantic processing. *Psychological Review, 82,* 407–428.

Collins, D. W., & Kimura, D. (1997). A large sex difference on a two-dimensional mental rotation task. *Behavioral Neuroscience, 111,* 845–849.

Colom, R., Haier, R. J., Head, K., et al. (2008). Gray matter correlates of fluid, crystallized, and spatial intelligence: Testing the P-FIT model. *Intelligence, 36,* 124–135.

Colonius, H., & Dzhafarov, E. N. (2006). *Measurement and representation of sensation.* Mahwah, NJ: Erlbaum.

Coltheart, M., Rastle, K., Perry, C., Langdon, R., & Ziegler, J. (2001). DRC: A dual route cascaded model of visual word recognition and reading aloud. *Psychological Review, 108,* 204–256.

Columbia. (1996). *The Columbia world of quotations.* Retrieved March 21, 2003, from http://www.bartleby.com

Columbia Accident Investigation Board. (2003). *Report* (Vol. 1). Retrieved October 2, 2003, from http://www.nasa.gov/columbia/home/index.html

Committee on Animal Research and Ethics (CARE). (2005). Research with animals in psychology. American Psychological Association. Retrieved March 14, 2005, from http://www.apa.org/science/animal2.html

Compton, S., Burns, B. J., Egger, H. L., & Robertson, E. (2002). Review of the evidence base for treatment of childhood psychopathology: Internalizing disorders. *Journal of Consulting and Clinical Psychology, 71,* 1240–1266.

Comuzzie, A. G., & Allison, D. B. (1998). The search for human obesity genes. *Science, 280,* 1374–1377.

Conlan, R. (1999). *States of mind: New discoveries about how our brains make us who we are.* New York: Dane Press.

Conway, A. R., Skitka, L. J., Hemmerich, J. A., & Kershaw, T. C. (2009). Flashbulb memory for 11 September 2001. *Applied Cognitive Psychology, 23,* 605–623.

Cooke, P. (1991, June 23). They cried until they couldn't see. *New York Times Magazine, 25,* 43.

Cooper, C. R., & Denner, J. (1998). Theories linking culture and psychology: Universal and community-specific processes. *Annual Review of Psychology, 49,* 559–584.

Cooper, J., Mirabile, R., & Scher, S. J. (2005). Actions and attitudes: The theory of cognitive dissonance. In T. C. Brock & M. C. Green (Eds.), *Persuasion: Psychological insights and perspectives* (2nd ed.). Thousand Oaks, CA: Sage.

Coopersmith, S. (1967). *The antecedents of self-esteem.* San Francisco: Freeman.

Corales, T. A. (Ed.). (2005). *Focus on posttraumatic stress disorder research.* Hauppauge, NY: Nova Science.

Cordova, J. V., Gee, C. B., & Warren, L. Z. (2005). Emotional skillfulness in marriage: Intimacy as a mediator of the relationship between emotional skillfulness and marital satisfaction. *Journal of Social and Clinical Psychology, 24,* 218–235.

Core Institute. (2002). *Statistics on substance use by college students.* Carbondale, IL: Author.

Coren, A., & Frosh, S. (Eds.). (2010). *Short-term psychotherapy: A psychodynamic approach.* Washington, DC: American Psychological Association.

Correll, J., Park, B., Judd, C. M., & Wittenbrink, B. (2002). The police officer's dilemma: Using ethnicity to disambiguate potentially threatening individuals. *Journal of Personality and Social Psychology, 83,* 1314–1329.

Corrigan, P. W. (2005). *On the stigma of mental illness: Practical strategies for research and social change.* Washington, DC: American Psychological Association.

Cosmides, L., & Tooby, J. (2002). Unraveling the enigma of human intelligence: Evolutionary psychology and the multimodular mind. In R. J. Sternberg & J. C. Kaufman (Eds.), *The evolution of intelligence.* Mahwah, NJ: Erlbaum.

Costantino, G., Malgady, R. G., & Primavera, L. H. (2009). Congruence between culturally competent treatment and cultural needs of older Latinos. *Journal of Consulting and Clinical Psychology, 77,* 941–949.

Courchesne, E., Carper, R., & Aksboomoff, N. (2003). Evidence of brain overgrowth in the first year of life. *Journal of the American Medical Association, 290,* 337–344.

Courneya, K. S. (1995). Understanding readiness for regular physical activity in older individuals: An application of the theory of planned behavior. *Health Psychology, 14,* 80–87.

Cousins, S. D. (1989). Culture and self-perception in the United States and Japan. *Journal of Personality and Social Psychology, 56,* 124–131.

Cowan, C. P., & Cowan, P. A. (2000). *When partners become parents: The big life change for couples.* Mahwah, NJ: Erlbaum.

Cozolino, L. (2010). *The neuroscience of psychotherapy: Healing the social brain.* New York: Routledge.

Craik, F. I. M., & Lockhart, R. S. (1972). Levels of processing: A framework for memory research. *Journal of Verbal Learning and Verbal Behavior, 11,* 671–684.

Craik, F. I. M., & Lockhart, R. S. (2008). Levels of processing and Zinchenko's approach to memory research. *Journal of Russian & East European Psychology, 46,* 52–60.

Craik, F. I. M., & Tulving, E. (1975). Depth of processing and the retention of words in episodic memory. *Journal of Experimental Psychology: General, 104,* 268–294.

Crandall, C. S., D'Anello, S., Sakalli, N., Lazarus, E., Wieczorkowska, G., & Feather, N. T. (2001). An attribution-value model of prejudice: Anti-fat attitudes in six nations. *Personality and Social Psychology Bulletin, 27,* 30–37.

Crano, W. D., & Prislin, R. (2006). Attitudes and persuasion. *Annual Review of Psychology, 57,* 345–374.

Craske, M. (1999). *Anxiety disorders: Psychological approaches to theory and treatment.* Boulder, CO: Westview Press.

Craske, M. (2003). *Origins of phobias and anxiety disorders: Why more women than men?* New York: Elsevier Science.

Craske, M. G., & Rowe, M. K. (1997). Nocturnal panic. *Clinical Psychology: Science and Practice, 4,* 153–174.

Crawford, M., & Chaffin, R. (1997). The meanings of difference: Cognition in social and cultural context. In P. J. Caplan & M. Crawford (Eds.), *Gender differences in human cognition. Counterpoints: Cognition, memory, and language.* New York: Oxford University Press.

Creese, I., Burd, D. R., & Snyder, S. H. (1976). Dopamine receptor binding predicts clinical and pharmacological potencies of antischizophrenic drugs. *Science, 192,* 481–483.

Crits-Christoph, P., Cooper, A., & Luborsky, L. (1988). The accuracy of therapists' interpretations and the outcome of dynamic psychotherapy. *Journal of Consulting and Clinical Psychology, 56,* 490–495.

Crowley, K. (2008, June 27). "Game Boy" havoc on LI—teens busted in "grand theft auto" spree. *New York Post.* Retrieved February 12, 2010, from http://proquest.umi.com/pqdweb?index=2&did=1501482521&SrchMode=1&sid=1&Fmt=3&VInst=PROD&VType=PDQ&RQT=309&VName=PQD&TS=1267587664&clientId=8991

Crowley, K., Callanan, M. A., Tenenbaum, H. R., & Allen, E. (2001). Parents explain more often to boys than to girls during shared scientific thinking. *Psychological Science, 12,* 258–261.

Culbertson, F. M. (1997). Depression and gender: An international review. *American Psychologist, 52,* 25–31.

Cummings, L. (2005). *Pragmatics: A multidisciplinary perspective.* Mahwah, NJ: Erlbaum.

Cunillera, T., Toro, J. M., Sebastian-Galles, N., & Rodriguez-Fornells, A. (2006). The effects of stress and statistical cues on continuous speech segmentation: An event-related brain potential study. *Brain Research, 1123,* 168–178.

Curci A., & Luminet, O. (2009). Flashbulb memories for expected events: A test of the emotional-integrative model. *Applied Cognitive Psychology, 23,* 98–114.

Curry, F., Elliot, A. J., Fonseca, D. D., & Moller, A. C. (2006). The social-cognitive model of achievement motivation and the 2 × 2 achievement goal framework. *Journal of Personality and Social Psychology, 90,* 666–679.

Curtis, G. C., Magee, W. J., Eaton, W. W., Wittchen, H.-U., & Kessler, R. C. (1998). Specific fears and phobias: Epidemiology and classification. *British Journal of Psychiatry, 173,* 112–117.

Curtiss, S. (1977). *Genie: A psychological study of a modern day "wild child."* New York: Academic Press.

Cytowic, R. E. (2002). *Synesthesia: A union of the senses* (2nd ed.). Boston: MIT Press.

Cytowic, R. E., & Eagleman, D. M. (2009). *Wednesday is indigo blue: Discovering the brain of synesthesia.* Cambridge, MA: MIT Press.

Daily Telegraph. (2009, April 1). *Can people read sentences in which the letters are jumbled?* Retrieved February 5, 2010, from http://www.dailytelegraph.com.au/news/wacky/can-people-read-sentences-in-which-the-letters-are-jumbled/story-e6frev20-1225693235558

Dalgarno, P. (2007). Subjective effects of *Salvia divinorum? Journal of Psychoactive Drugs, 39,* 143–149.

Dalton, P. (2002). Olfaction. In H. Pashler & S. Yantis (Eds.), *Steven's handbook of experimental psychology: Vol. 1. Sensation and perception* (3rd ed.). New York: Wiley.

Daly, M., & Wilson, M. (1988). *Homicide.* New York: Aldine de Gruyter.

Damasio, A. R. (2005). Emotions and feelings: A neurobiological perspective. In A. S. R. Manstead, N. H. Frijda, A. H. Fischer, & K. Oatley (Eds.), *Feelings and Emotions: The Amsterdam Symposium.* New York: Cambridge University Press.

Daniels, C. W. (2002). Legal aspects of polygraph admissibility in the United States. In M. Kleiner (Ed.), *Handbook of polygraph testing.* San Diego, CA: Academic Press.

Daniels, K., Toth, J., & Jacoby, J. (2006). The aging of executive functions. In E. Bialystok & F. I. M. Craik (Eds.), *Lifespan cognition: Mechanisms of change.* New York: Oxford University Press.

Daniels, P., Gura, T., & Stein, L. (2007). *Body: The complete human.* Washington, DC: National Geographic.

Darley, J. M., & Gross, P. H. (1983). A hypothesis-confirming bias in labeling effects. *Journal of Personality and Social Psychology, 44,* 20–33.

Darley, J. M., & Latané, B. (1968). Bystander intervention in emergencies: Diffusion of responsibility. *Journal of Personality and Social Psychology, 8,* 377–383.

Daselaar, S. M., Prince, S. E., Dennis, N. A., Hayes, S. M., Kim, H., & Cabeza, R. (2009). Posterior midline and ventral parietal activity is associated with retrieval success and encoding failure. *Frontiers in Human Neuroscience, 3*(13), doi:10.3389/neuro.09.013.2009

Dasen, P. R., Barthélémy, D., Kan, E., Kouamé, K., Daouda, K., Adjéi, K. K., & Assandé, N.

(1985). N'glouele, l'intelligence chez les Baoulé [N'glouele, intelligence according to the Baoulé]. *Archives de Psychologie, 53,* 293–324.

Davidoff, J. (2004). Coloured thinking. *Psychologist, 17,* 570–572.

Davidson, R. J. (1998). *Neuropsychological perspectives on affective and anxiety disorders.* Chicago: Psychology Press.

Davidson, R. J., & Fox, N. A. (1988). Cerebral asymmetry and emotion: Developmental and individual differences. In D. L. Molfese & S. J. Segalowitz (Eds.), *Brain lateralization in children: Developmental implications.* New York: Guilford Press.

Davis, C., Patte, K., Levitan, R., Reid, C., Tweed, S., & Curtis, C. (2007). From motivation to behaviour: A model of reward sensitivity, overeating, and food preferences in the risk profile for obesity. *Appetite, 48,* 12–19.

Davis, C. G., Nolen, H. S., & Larson, J. (1998). Making sense of loss and benefiting from the experience: Two construals of meaning. *Journal of Personality and Social Psychology, 75,* 561–574.

Davis, K. C., Hendershot, C. S., George, W. H., Norris, J., & Heiman, J. R. (2007). Alcohol's effects on sexual decision making: An integration of alcohol myopia and individual differences. *Journal of Studies on Alcohol and Drugs, 68,* 843–851.

Davis, M. (2003). *MRC Cognition and Brain Sciences Unit. Cambridge University.* Retrieved December 18, 2009, from http://www.mrccbu.cam.ac.uk/people/matt.davis/Cmabrigde/

Davis, T., Gunderson, J. G., & Myers, M. (1999). Borderline personality disorder. In D. G. Jacobs (Ed.), *The Harvard Medical School Guide to suicide assessment and intervention.* San Francisco: Jossey-Bass.

Dawidowicz, L. S. (1975). *The war against the Jews, 1933–1945.* New York: Holt, Rinehart & Winston.

Dawkins, R. (2006). *The selfish gene* (revised edition). New York: Oxford University Press.

Dawood, K., Pillar, R. C., Horvath, C., Revelle, W., & Bailey, J. M. (2000). Familial aspects of male homosexuality. *Archives of Sexual Behavior, 29,* 155–163.

Dawson, G., Toth, K., Abbott, R., Osterling, J., Munson, J., Estes, A., & Liaw, J. (2004). Early social attention impairments in autism: Social orienting, joint attention, and attention to distress. *Developmental Psychology, 40,* 271–283.

Dawson-McClure, S. R., Sandler, I. N., Wolchik, S. A., & Millsap, R. E. (2004). Risk as a moderator of the effects of prevention programs for children from divorced families: A six-year longitudinal study. *Journal of Abnormal Child Psychology, 32,* 175–190.

Day, R., Nielsen, J. A., Korten, A., et al. (1987). Stressful life events preceding the acute onset of schizophrenia. *Culture, Medicine, and Psychiatry, 11,* 123–205.

Deary, I. J., Whiteman, M. C., Starr, J. M., Whalley, L. J., & Fox, H. (2004). The impact of childhood intelligence on later life: Following up the Scottish Medical Surveys of 1932 and 1947. *Journal of Personality and Social Psychology, 86,* 130–147.

Dębiec, J., & LeDoux, J. E. (2009). The amygdala networks of fear: From animal models to human psychopathology. In D. McKay, J. S. Abramowitz, S. Jonathan, S. Taylor, &

G. J. G. Asmundson (Eds.), *Current perspectives on the anxiety disorders; Implications for DSM-V and beyond.* New York: Springer.

DeCasper, A. J., & Spence, M. J. (1986). Prenatal maternal speech influences newborns' perceptions of speech sounds. *Infant Behavior and Development, 9,* 133–150.

deCastro, J. M. (2002). Age-related changes in the social, psychological, and temporal influences on food intake in free-living, healthy, adult humans. *Journals of Gerontology: Series A. Biological Sciences and Medical Sciences, 57A,* 368–377.

Deci, E. L., & Ryan, R. M. (1985). *Intrinsic motivation and self-determination in human behavior.* New York: Plenum Press.

Deci, E. L., & Ryan, R. M. (2002). *Handbook of self-determination theory research.* Rochester, NY: University of Rochester Press.

Deci, E. L., & Ryan, R. M. (2009). Self determination theory: A consideration of human motivational universals. In P. J. Corr & G. Matthews (Eds.), *The Cambridge handbook of personality psychology.* Cambridge, England: Cambridge University Press.

De Cremer, D., & van Lange, P. A. M. (2001). Why prosocials exhibit greater cooperation than proselfs: The roles of social responsibility and reciprocity. *European Journal of Personality, 15,* 5–18.

Deese, J. (1959). Influence of inter-item associative strength upon immediate free recall. *Psychological Reports, 5,* 305–312.

Deffenbacher, K. A., Bernstein, B. H., & Penrod, S. D. (2006). Mugshot exposure effects: Retroactive interference, mugshot commitment, source confusion, and unconscious transference. *Law and Human Behavior, 30,* 287–307.

Degen, L., Matzinger, D., Drewe, J., & Beglinger, C. (2001). The effect of cholecystokinin in controlling appetite and food intake in humans. *Peptides, 22,* 1265–1269.

deGeus, E. J. C. (2000). Aerobics in stress reduction. In G. Fink (Ed.), *Encyclopedia of stress.* San Diego, CA: Academic Press.

Dehaene, S., Izard, V., Pica, P., & Spelke, E. (2006). Core knowledge of geometry in an Amazonian indigene group. *Science, 311,* (5759), 381–384.

Delahunt, P. B., Ball, K. K., Roenker, D. L., Hardy, J. L., Mahncke, H. W., & Merzenich, M. M. (2009). Computer-based cognitive training to facilitate neural plasticity. *Gerontechnology, 8,* 52–53.

Delgado, A. R., & Prieto, G. (2009). Stereotype threat as validity threat: The anxiety–sex–threat interaction. *Intelligence, 37,* 635–640.

Dell, P. F., & O'Neil, J. A. (Eds.). (2009). *Dissociation and the dissociative disorders: DSM-V and beyond.* New York: Routledge/Taylor & Francis Group.

Della Sala, S. (Ed.). (2007). *Tall tales about the mind and brain.* Oxford, England: Oxford University Press.

DeLongis, A. (2000). Coping skills. In G. Fink (Ed.), *Encyclopedia of stress.* San Diego, CA: Academic Press.

Demarest, J., & Allen, R. (2000). Body image: Gender, ethnic, and age differences. *Journal of Social Psychology, 140,* 465–472.

Dement, W. C. (2005). History of sleep medicine. *Neurologic Clinics, 23,* 945–965.

Démonet, J. F., Thierry, G., & Cardebat, D. (2005). Renewal of the neurophysiology of language:

Functional neuroimaging. *Physiological Reviews, 85*, 49–95.

DeMoranville, B. M., Jackson, I., Ader, R., Madden, K. S., Felten, D. L., & Bellinger, D. L. (2000). Endocrine and immune systems. In B. S. Fogel, R. B. Schiffer, & S. M. Rao (Eds.), *Synopsis of neuropsychiatry*. Philadelphia: Lippincott-Raven.

Denollet, J., Nyklicek, I., & Vingerhoets, A. (Eds.). (2007). *Emotional regulation: Conceptual and clinical issues*. New York: Springer.

Depue, R. A., & Collins, P. F. (1999). Neurobiology of the structure of personality: Dopamine, facilitation of incentive motivation, and extraversion. *Behavioral and Brain Sciences, 22*, 491–569.

Depue, R. A., & Lenzenweger, M. F. (2005). A neurobehavioral dimensional model of personality disorders. In M. F. Lenzenweger & J. F. Clarkin (Eds.), *Major theories of personality disorder*. New York: Guilford Press.

Der, G., Batty, G. D., & Deary, I. J. (2009). The association between IQ in adolescence and a range of health outcomes at 40 in the 1979 US National Longitudinal Study of Youth. *Intelligence, 37*, 573–580.

DeRegnier, R. A., Wewerka, S., Georgieff, M. K., Mattia, F., & Nelson, C. A. (2002). Influences of postconceptional age and postnatal experience on the development of auditory recognition memory in the newborn infant. *Developmental Psychobiology, 41*, 216–225.

Deregowski, J. B. (1989). Real space and represented space: Cross-cultural perspectives. *Behavior and Brain Sciences, 12*, 51–119.

De Silva, P., & Rachman, J. (1998). *Obsessive-compulsive disorders*. New York: Oxford University Press.

DeStefano, D., & LeFevre, J. (2004). The role of working memory in mental arithmetic. *European Journal of Cognitive Psychology, 16*, 353–386.

DeSteno, D., Dasgupta, N., Bartlett, M. Y., & Cajdric, A. (2004). Prejudice from thin air: The effect of emotion on automatic intergroup attitudes. *Psychological Science, 15*, 319–324.

DeVries, H., Mudde, A. N., Dijkstra, A., & Willemsen, M. C. (1998). Differential beliefs, perceived social influences, and self-efficacy expectations among smokers in various motivational phases. *Preventive Medicine, 27*, 681–689.

de Win, M. M. L., Jager, G., Booij, J., Reneman, L., Schilt, T., Lavini, C., et al. (2008). Neurotoxic effects of Ecstasy on the thalamus. *British Journal of Psychiatry, 193*, 289–296.

DeYoung, C. G., & Gray, J. R. (2009). Personality neuroscience: Explaining individual differences in affect, behavior, and cognition. In P. J. Corr & G. Matthews (Eds.), *The Cambridge handbook of personality psychology*. Cambridge, England: Cambridge University Press.

De Zeeuw, C. I., & Cicirata, F. (Eds.). (2005). *Creating coordination in the cerebellum*. St. Louis: Elsevier Sciences/Mosby.

Dhabhar, F. S., & McEwen, B. S. (2001). Bidirectional effects of stress and glucocorticoid hormones on immune function: Possible explanations for paradoxical observations. In R. Ader, D. L. Feiten, & N. Cohen (Eds.), *Psychoneuroimmunology* (Vol. 1). San Diego, CA: Academic Press.

Diacon, S., & Hasseldine, J. (2007). Framing effects and risk perception: The effect of prior performance presentation format on investment fund choice. *Journal of Economic Psychology, 28*, 31–52.

Dickinson, C. A., & Intraub, H. (2009). Spatial asymmetries in viewing and remembering scenes: Consequences of an attentional bias? *Attention, Perception, & Psychophysics, 71*, 1251–1262.

DiClemente, C. C. (2003). *Addiction and change: How addictions develop and addicted people recover*. New York: Guilford Press.

Diener, E. (2000). Subjective well-being: The science of happiness and a proposal for a national index. *American Psychologist, 55*, 34–43.

Diener, E. (2009). *The science of well-being*. New York: Springer.

Diener, E., & Biswas-Diener, R. (2008). *Happiness: Unlocking the mysteries of psychological wealth*. Malden, MA: Blackwell.

Diener, E., & Diener, C. (1996). Most people are happy. *Psychological Science, 7*, 181–185.

Diener, E., & Seligman, M. E. P. (2002). Very happy people. *Psychological Science, 13*, 81–84.

Diener, E., Suh, E., Lucas, R. E., & Smith, H. L. (1999). Subjective well-being: Three decades of progress. *Psychological Bulletin, 125*, 276–302.

Diener, E., Tamir, M., & Scollon, C. N. (2006). Happiness, life satisfaction, and fulfillment: The social psychology of subjective well-being. In P. A. M. van Lange (Ed.), *Bridging social psychology: Benefits of transdisciplinary approaches*. Mahwah, NJ: Erlbaum.

Dienes, Z., Brown, E., Hutton, S., Kirsch, I., Mazzoni, G., & Wright, D. B. (2009). Hypnotic suggestibility, cognitive inhibition, and dissociation. *Consciousness and Cognition: An International Journal, 18*, 837–884.

Dillard, J. P., & Anderson, J. W. (2004). The role of fear in persuasion. *Psychology & Marketing, 21*, 909–926.

Dimidjian, S., Hollon, S. D., Dobson, K. S., Schmaling, K. B., Kohlenberg, R. J., & Addis, M. E., et al. (2006). Randomized trial of behavioral activation, cognitive therapy, and antidepressant medication in the acute treatment of adults with major depression. *Journal of Consulting and Clinical Psychology, 74*, 658–670.

Dindia, K. (2002). Self-disclosure research: Knowledge through meta-analysis. In M. Allen, R. W. Preiss, B. M. Gayle, & N. A. Burrell (Eds.), *Interpersonal communication research: Advances through meta-analysis*. Mahwah, NJ: Erlbaum.

Dishman, R. K. (1982). Compliance/adherence in health-related exercise. *Health Psychology, 1*, 237–267.

Dishman, R. K. (1994). *Advances in exercise adherence*. Champaign, IL: Human Kinetics.

Dixon, N. F. (1981). *Preconscious processing*. New York: Wiley.

Dobson, K. S. (Ed.). (2010). *Handbook of cognitive-behavior therapies*. Washington, DC: American Psychological Association.

Docherty, N. M., St-Hillaire, A., Aakre, J. M., et al. (2009). Life events and high trait reactivity predict psychotic symptom increase in schizophrenia. *Schizophrenia Bulletin, 35*, 638–645.

Dodge, K. A. (1986). A social information processing model of social competence in children. *Cognitive perspectives on children's social behavioral development. The Minnesota symposium on child psychology, 18*, 77–125.

Doka, K. J. (1995). Coping with life-threatening illness: A task model. *Omega: Journal of Death and Dying, 32*, 111–122.

Dolezal, H. (1982). *Living in a world transformed: Perceptual and performatory adaptation to a visual distortion*. New York: Academic Press.

Dolins, F. L., & Mitchell, R. W. (2010). *Spatial perception, spatial cognition*. New York: Cambridge University Press.

Domhoff, G. W. (2001). A new neurocognitive theory of dreams. *Dreaming: Journal of the Association for the Study of Dreams, 11*, 13–33.

Domhoff, G. W. (2005). Refocusing the neurocognitive approach to dreams: A critique of the Hobson versus Solms debate. *Dreaming, 15*, 3–20.

Domhoff, G. W., & Schneider, A. (2008). Similarities and differences in dream content at the cross-cultural, gender, and individual levels. *Consciousness and Cognition: An International Journal, 17*, 1257–1265.

Domino, G. (2000). *Psychological testing*. Upper Saddle River, NJ: Prentice Hall.

Domjan, M. (2000a). *The essentials of conditioning and learning* (2nd ed.). Belmont, CA: Wadsworth/ Thomson.

Domjan, M. (2000b). General process learning theory: Challenges from response and stimulus factors. *International Journal of Comparative Psychology, 13*, 101–118.

Donnerstein, E., & Malamuth, N. (1997). Pornography: Its consequences on the observer. In L. B. Schlesinger & E. Revitch (Eds.), *Sexual dynamics of anti-social behavior* (2nd ed.). Springfield, IL: Charles C Thomas.

Doppelt, J. E., & Wallace, W. L. (1955). Standardization of the Wechsler Adult Intelligence Scale for older persons. *Journal of Abnormal and Social Psychology, 51*, 312–330.

Dossenbach, M., & Dossenbach, H. D. (1998). *All about animal vision*. Chicago: Blackbirch Press.

Dovidio, J. F. (1984). Helping behavior and altruism: An empirical and conceptual overview. In L. Berkowitz (Ed.), *Advances in experimental social psychology* (Vol. 17). New York: Academic Press.

Dovidio, J. F., Piliavin, J. A., Schroeder, D. A., & Penner, L. (2006). *The social psychology of prosocial behavior*. Mahwah, NJ: Erlbaum.

Downey, G., & Feldman, S. L. (1996). Implications of rejection sensitivity for intimate relationships. *Journal of Personality and Social Psychology, 70*, 1327–1343.

Draguns, J. G. (2009). Personality in cross-cultural perspective. In P. J. Corr & G. Matthews (Eds.), *The Cambridge handbook of personality psychology*. Cambridge, England: Cambridge University Press.

Drake, M. E., Pakalnis, A., & Denio, L. C. (1988). Differential diagnosis of epilepsy and multiple personality: Clinical and EEG findings in 15 cases. *Neuropsychiatry, Neuropsychology, and Behavioral Neurology, 1*, 131–140.

Driscoll, T. R., Grunstein, R. R., & Rogers, N. L. (2007). A systematic review of the neurobehavioural and physiological effects of shiftwork systems. *Sleep Medicine Review, 11*, 179–194.

Drukin, K. (1998). Implicit content and implicit processes in mass media use. In K. Kirsner et al. (Eds.), *Implicit and explicit mental processes*. Mahwah, NJ: Erlbaum.

Dryden, W. (Ed.). (2002). *Handbook of individual therapy*. Thousand Oaks, CA: Sage.

Ducci, F., & Goldman, D. (2008). Genetic approaches to addiction: Genes and alcohol. *Addiction, 103,* 1414–1428.

Duda, J. L., & Treasure, D. C. (2010). Motivational processes and the facilitation of quality engagement in sport. In J. M. Williams (Ed.), *Applied sport psychology: Athletic excellence to personal growth.* New York: McGraw-Hill.

Duman, S., & Margolin, G. (2007). Parents' aggressive influences and children's aggressive problem solutions with peers. *Journal of Clinical Child and Adolescent Psychology, 36,* 42–55.

Dunlosky, J., & Lipko, A. R. (2007). Metacomprehension: A brief history and how to improve its accuracy. *Current Directions in Psychological Science, 16,* 228–232.

Dunn, J., & Plomin, R. (1990). *Separate lives: Why siblings are so different.* New York: Basic Books.

Dunne, M. P., Bailey, J. M., Kirk, K. M., & Martin, N. G. (2000). The subtlety of sex-atypicality. *Archives of Sexual Behavior, 29,* 549–565.

Durkin, K. (1998). Implicit content and implicit processes in mass media use. In K. Kirsner & M. Mayberry (Eds.), *Implicit content and implicit processes in mass media use.* Mahway, NJ: Erlbaum.

Durrant, J. E. (2000). Trends in youth crime and well-being since the abolition of corporal punishment in Sweden. *Youth and Society, 31,* 437–455.

Durrant, J. E., Trocmé, N., Fallon, B., Black, T., & Milne, C. (2009). Child and adolescent maltreatment: Protection of children from physical maltreatment in Canada: An evaluation of the Supreme Court's definition of reasonable force. *Journal of Aggression, Maltreatment & Trauma, 18,* 64–87.

Dutton, D. G. (2006). *The abusive personality: Violence and control in intimate relationships.* New York: Guilford Press.

Duvander, A. Z. E. (1999). The transition from cohabitation to marriage: A longitudinal study of the propensity to marry in Sweden in the early 1990s. *Journal of Family Issues, 20,* 698–717.

Dweck, C. (1999). *Self theories: Their role in motivation, personality, and development.* Philadelphia: Psychology Press/Taylor and Francis.

Dwyer, D. (Ed.) (2007). *The pharmacology of neurogenesis and neuroenhancement.* New York: Academic Press.

Dying to be thin. (2000). *Nova* [Television series]. Boston: WGBH.

Eacott, M. J., & Crawley, R. A. (1998). The offset of childhood amnesia: Memory for events that occurred before age 3. *Journal of Experimental Psychology: General, 127,* 22–33.

Eagly, A. H., & Crowley, M. (1986). Gender and helping behavior: A meta-analytic review of the social psychological literature. *Psychological Bulletin, 100,* 283–308.

Eagly, A. H., & Wood, W. (1999). The origins of sex differences in human behavior: Evolved dispositions versus social roles. *American Psychologist, 54,* 408–423.

Eagly, A. H., & Wood, W. (2006). Three ways that data can misinform: Inappropriate partialling, small samples, and, anyway, they're not playing our song. *Psychological Inquiry, 17,* 131–137.

Eastman, C. I., Gazda, C. J., Burgess, H. J., Crowley, S. J., & Fogg, L. F. (2005). Advancing circadian rhythms before eastward flight: A strategy to prevent or reduce jet lag. *Sleep, 28,* 33–44.

Eastwick, P. W., & Gardner, W. L. (2009). Is it a game? Evidence for social influence in the virtual world. *Social Influence, 4,* 18–32.

Eaton, J. (2001). Management communication: The threat of groupthink. *Corporate Communications, 6,* 183–192.

Ebbinghaus, H. (1964). *Über das Gedächtnis: Untersuchungen Zur Experimentellen Psychologie [Memory: A contribution to experimental psychology]* (H. A. Ruger & C. E. Bussenius, Trans.). New York: Dover. (Original work published 1885)

Eccles, J. (1991). Gender-role socialization. In R. M. Baron, W. G. Graziano, & C. Stangor (Eds.), *Social psychology.* Ft. Worth, TX: Holt, Rinehart & Winston.

Eckensberger, L. H., & Zimba, R. F. (1997). The development of moral judgment. In J. W. Berry, P. R. Dasen, & T. S. Saraswathi (Eds.), *Handbook of cross-cultural psychology* (2nd ed., Vol. 2). Boston: Allyn & Bacon.

Edser, S. J. (2002). Hypnotically facilitated counter conditioning of anticipatory nausea and vomiting associated with chemotherapy: A case study. *Australian Journal of Clinical Hypnotherapy and Hypnosis, 23,* 18–30.

Edvardsen, J., Torgersen, S., Røysamb, E., Lygren, S., Skre, I., Onstad, S., & Øien, P. A. (2009). Unipolar depressive disorders have a common genotype. *Journal of Affective Disorders, 117,* 30–41.

Edwards, R. R., Smith, M. T., Stonerock, G., & Haythornewaite, J. A. (2006). Pain-related catastrophizing in healthy women is associated with greater temporal summation of and reduced habituation to pain. *Clinical Journal of Pain, Oct. 22 (8),* 730–737.

Eelen, P., & Vervliet, B. (2006). Fear conditioning and clinical implications: What can we learn from the past? In M. G. Craske, D. Hermans, & D. Vansteenwegen (Eds.), *Fear and learning: From basic processes to clinical implications.* Washington, DC: American Psychological Association.

Ehlers, C. L., Gizer, I. R., Vieten, C., Gilder, D. A., Stouffer, G. M., Lau, P., & Morrow, A. L. (2010). Cannabis dependence in the San Francisco family study: Age of onset of use, DSM-IV symptoms, withdrawal, and heritability. *Addictive Behaviors, 35,* 102–110.

Ehrman, J. (2003). *Clinical exercise psychology.* Champaign, IL: Human Kinetics.

Eid, M., & Larsen, R. J. (Eds.). (2008). *The science of subjective well-being.* New York: Guilford Press.

Eisenberg, N. (2000). Emotion, regulation, and moral development. *Annual Review of Psychology, 51,* 665–697.

Eisenberg, N. (2002). Emotion related regulation and its relation to quality of social functioning. In W. Hartup & R. A. Weinberg (Eds.), *Child psychology in retrospect and prospect: In celebration of the 75th anniversary of the Institute of Child Development. The Minnesota symposia on child psychology* (Vol. 32). Mahwah, NJ: Erlbaum.

Eisenberg, N. (2004). Prosocial and moral development in the family. In T. A. Thorkildsen & H. J. Walberg (Eds.), *Nurturing morality: Issues in children's and families' lives.* New York: Kluwer Academic/Plenum Press.

Eisenberger, N. I., Lieberman, M. D., & Williams, K. D. (2003). Does rejection hurt? An fMRI study of social exclusion. *Science, 302,* 290–292.

Ekman, P. (1973). Cross-cultural studies of facial expression. In P. Ekman (Ed.), *Darwin and facial expression.* San Diego, CA: Academic Press.

Ekman, P., & Friesen, W. V. (1987). *Facial Action Coding System.* Palo Alto, CA: Consulting Psychologists Press.

Ekman, P., Friesen, W. V., & Ellsworth, P. (1972). *Emotion in the human face: Guidelines for research and an integration of findings.* Oxford, England: Pergamon Press.

Elbeheri, G., Everatt, J., Reid, G., & al Mannai, H. (2006). Dyslexia assessment in Arabic. *Journal of Research in Special Educational Needs, 6,* 143–152.

Elbert, T., Pantev, C., Wienbruch, C., Rockstroh, B., & Taub, E. (1995). Increased cortical representation of the fingers of the left hand in string players. *Science, 270,* 305–307.

Eldevik, S., Jahr, E., Eikeseth, S., Hastings, R. P., & Huges, C. J. (2010). Cognitive and adaptive behavior outcomes of behavioral intervention for young children with intellectual disability. *Behavior Modification, 34,* 16–34.

Elfenbein, H. A., & Ambady, N. (2003). Universals and cultural differences in recognizing emotions. *Current Directions in Psychological Science, 12,* 159–164.

Eliassen, J. C., Souza, T., & Sanes, J. N. (2003). Experience-dependent activation patterns in human brain during visual-motor associative learning. *Journal of Neuroscience, 23,* 10540–10547.

Elkind, D. (1967). Egocentrism in adolescence. *Child Development, 38,* 1025–1034.

Elliot, A. J., & McGregor, H. A. (2001). A 2×2 achievement goal framework. *Journal of Personality and Social Psychology, 80,* 501–519.

Elliot, A. J., & Thrash, T. M. (2002). Approach-avoidance motivation in personality: Approach and avoidance temperaments and goals. *Journal of Personality and Social Psychology, 82,* 804–818.

Ellwood, S., Pallier, G., Snyder, A., & Gallate, J. (2009). The incubation effect: Hatching a solution? *Creativity Research Journal, 21,* 6–14.

Elovainio, M., & Kivimaki, M. (2009). Models of personality and health. In P. J. Corr & G. Matthews (Eds.), *The Cambridge handbook of personality psychology.* Cambridge, England: Cambridge University Press.

Elsey, B., & Fujiwara, A. (2000). Kaizen and technology transfer instructors as work-based learning facilitators in overseas transplants: A case study. *Journal of Workplace Learning, 12,* 333–342.

Emens, J. S., Yuhas, K., Rough, J., Kochar, N., Peters, D., & Lewy, A. J. (2009). Phase angle of entrainment in morning- and evening-types under naturalistic conditions. *Chronobiology International, 26,* 474–493.

Emerson, R. M. (1966). Mount Everest: A case study of communication feedback and sustained group goalstriving. *Sociometry, 29,* 213–227.

Emlen, S. T. (1975, August). The stellar-orientation system of a migratory bird. *Scientific American,* 102–111.

Epley, N., Savitsky, K., & Kachelski, R. (1999). What every skeptic should know about subliminal persuasion. *The Skeptical Inquirer, 23,* 40–46.

Epstein, M. A., & Bottoms, B. L. (2002). Explaining the forgetting and recovery of abuse and trauma memories: Possible mechanisms. *Child*

Maltreatment: Journal of the American Professional Society on the Abuse of Children, 7, 210–225.

Epstein, R., Kirshnit, C. E., Lanza, R. P., & Rubin, L. C. (1984). "Insight" in the pigeon: Antecedents and determinants of an intelligent performance. *Nature, 308,* 61–62.

Epstein, S. (1983). Aggregation and beyond: Some basic issues on the production of behavior. *Journal of Personality, 51,* 360–392.

Erdberg, P. (2000). Rorschach assessment. In G. Goldstein & M. Hersen (Eds.), *Handbook of psychological assessment* (3rd ed.). New York: Elsevier.

Erdelyi, M. H. (2001). Defense processes can be conscious or unconscious. *American Psychologist, 56,* 761–762.

Erford, B. T. (2010). *Group work: Processes and applications.* New York: Prentice-Hall.

Ericsson, K. A., Chase, W. G., & Faloon, S. (1980). Acquisition of a memory skill. *Science, 208,* 1181–1182.

Ericsson, K. A., Delaney, P. F., Weaver, G., & Mahadevan, R. (2004). Uncovering the structure of a memorist's superior "basic" memory capacity. *Cognitive Psychology, 49,* 191–237.

Ericsson, K. A., Krampe, R. T., & Tesch R. C. (1993). The role of deliberate practice in the acquisition of expert performance. *Psychological Review, 100,* 363–406.

Ericsson, K. A., & Polson, P. G. (1988). An experimental analysis of the mechanisms of a memory skill. *Journal of Experimental Psychology: Learning, Memory, and Cognition, 14,* 305–316.

Erikson, E. H. (1968). *Identity, youth and crisis.* New York: Norton.

Erikson, E. H. (1980). *Identity and the life cycle.* New York: Norton. (Original work published 1959.)

Eron, L. D. (1987). The development of aggressive behavior from the perspective of a developing behaviorism. *American Psychologist, 42,* 435–442.

Eron, L. D. (2000). A psychological perspective. In V. B. Van Hasselt & M. Hersen (Eds.), *Aggression and violence: An introductory text.* Boston: Allyn & Bacon.

Esparza, J., Fox, C., Harper, I. T., Bennett, P. H., Schulz, L. O., Valencia, M. E., & Ravussin, E. (2000). Daily energy expenditure in Mexican and USA Pima Indians: Low physical activity as a possible cause of obesity. *International Journal of Obesity and Related Metabolic Disorders, 24,* 55–59.

Essau, C., & Petermann, F. (1999). *Depressive disorders in children and adolescents: Epidemiology, risk factors, and treatment.* Northvale, NJ: Aronson.

Essau, C., & Trommsdorff, G. (1996). Coping with university-related problems: A cross-cultural comparison. *Journal of Cross-Cultural Psychology, 27,* 315–328.

Esser, J. K., & Lindoerfer, J. S. (1989). Groupthink and the space shuttle *Challenger* accident: Toward a quantitative case analysis. *Journal of Behavioral Decision Making, 2,* 167–177.

Estes, T. H., & Vaughn, J. L. (1985). *Reading and learning in the content classroom: Diagrams and instructional strategies* (3rd ed.). Boston: Allyn & Bacon.

Ettinger, C. (2009). *Psychopharmacology.* New York: Prentice-Hall.

Evans-Martin, F. F. (2007). *Emotion and stress.* New York: Facts on File.

Evers, K. E., Harlow, H. L., Redding, C. A., & LaForge, R. G. (1998). Longitudinal changes in stages of change for condom use in women. *American Journal of Health Promotion, 13,* 19–25.

Exner, J. E. (1991). *The Rorschach—A comprehensive system: Assessment of personality and psychopathology* (Vol. 2). New York: Wiley.

Eysenck, H. J. (1964). *Crime and personality.* Boston: Houghton Mifflin.

Eysenck, H. J. (1967). *The biological basis of personality.* Springfield, IL: Charles C. Thomas.

Eysenck, H. J. (1990). Biological dimensions of personality. In L. A. Pervin (Ed.), *Handbook of personality: Theory and research.* New York: Guilford Press.

Fabbro, F. (2001). The bilingual brain: Bilingual aphasia. *Brain & Language, 79,* 201–210.

Facon, B., Sahiri, S., & Rivière, V. (2008). A controlled single-case treatment of severe long-term selective mutism in a child with mental retardation. *Behavior Therapy, 39,* 313–321.

Fagan, J. F., & Holland, C. R. (2009). Culture-fair prediction of academic achievement. *Intelligence, 37,* 62–67.

Fagley, N. S. (1987). Positional response bias in multiple-choice tests of learning: Its relation to testwiseness and guessing strategy. *Journal of Educational Psychology, 79,* 95–97.

Faith, M. S., Matz, P. E., & Jorge, M.A. (2002). Obesity depression associations in the population. *Journal of Psychosomatic Research, 53,* 935–942.

Fallon, A. E., & Rozin, P. (1985). Sex differences in perceptions of desirable body shape. *Journal of Abnormal Psychology, 94,* 102–105.

Falsetti, S. A., Monnier, J., & Resnick, H. S. (2005). Intrusive thoughts in posttraumatic stress disorder. In D. A. Clark (Ed.), *Intrusive thoughts in clinical disorders: Theory, research, and treatment.* New York: Guilford Press.

Fanselow, M. S., & Poulos, A. M. (2005). The neuroscience of mammalian associative learning. *Annual Review of Psychology, 56,* 207–234.

Fantz, R. L. (1961, May). The origin of form perception. *Scientific American, 204,* 66–72.

Farmer, E. M. Z., Compton, S. N., Burns, B. J., & Robertson, E. (2002). Review of the evidence base for treatment of childhood psychopathology: Externalizing disorders. *Journal of Consulting and Clinical Psychology, 71,* 1267–1302.

Faust, J. (1991). Same-day surgery preparation: Reduction of pediatric patient arousal and distress through participant modeling. *Journal of Consulting and Clinical Psychology, 59,* 473–478.

Fayad, J. N., Otto, S. R., Shannon, R. V., & Brackmann, D. E. (2008). Cochlear and brainstem auditory prostheses for hearing restoration: Cochlear and brain stem implants. *Proceedings of the IEEE, 96,* 1085–1095.

Fazio, R. H., Jackson, J. R., Dunton, B. C., & Williams, C. J. (1995). Variability in automatic activation as an unobtrusive measure of racial attitudes: A bona fide pipeline? *Journal of Personality and Social Psychology, 69,* 1013–1027.

Fazio, R. H., & Roskos-Ewoldsen, D. R. (2005). Acting as we feel: When and how attitudes guide behavior. In T. C. Brock & M. C. Green (Eds.), *Persuasion: Psychological insights and perspectives* (2nd ed., pp. 41–62). Thousand Oaks, CA: Sage.

Federal Interagency Forum on Aging-Related Statistics. (2006). *Older Americans update 2006: Key indicators of well-being.* Retrieved February 20, 2007, from http://www.agingstats.gov/update2006/Health_Status.pdf

Feigelman, S., Dubowitz, H., Lane, W., Prescott, L., Meyer, W., Tracy, J. K., et al. (2009). Screening for harsh punishment in a pediatric primary care clinic. *Child Abuse & Neglect, 33,* 269–277.

Fein, S., & Spencer, S. J. (1997). Prejudice as self-image maintenance: Affirming the self through derogating others. *Journal of Personality and Social Psychology, 73,* 31–44.

Feingold, A., & Mazzella, R. (1998). Gender differences in body image are increasing. *Psychological Science, 9,* 190–195.

Feldman, R., Masalha, S., & Derdikman-Eiron, R. (2010). Conflict resolution in the parent–child, marital, and peer contexts and children's aggression in the peer group: A process-oriented cultural perspective. *Developmental Psychology, 46,* 310–325.

Feldman-Barrett, L., Niedenthal, P. M., & Winkielman, P. (Eds.) (2007). *Emotion and consciousness.* New York: Guilford Press.

Felmlee, D. H. (1998). "Be careful what you wish for . . . ": A quantitative and qualitative investigation of "fatal attractions." *Personal Relationships, 5,* 235–253.

Fenichel, G. (2006). *Neonatal neurology.* St. Louis: Mosby.

Fenton, W. S., & McGlashan, T. H. (1991a). Natural history of schizophrenia subtypes: I. Longitudinal study of paranoid, hebephonic, and undifferentiated schizophrenia. *Archives of General Psychiatry, 48,* 969–977.

Fenton, W. S., & McGlashan, T. H. (1991b). Natural history of schizophrenia subtypes: II. Positive and negative symptoms and long-term course. *Archives of General Psychiatry, 48,* 978–986.

Ferguson, C. J. (2008). The school shooting/violent video game link: Causal relationship or moral panic? *Journal of Investigative Psychology and Offender Profiling, 5,* 25–37.

Ferguson, C. J. (2009). Media violence effects: Confirmed truth or just another X-file? *Journal of Forensic Psychology Practice, 9,* 103–126.

Ferguson, C. J., & Kilburn, J. (2009). The public health risks of media violence: A meta-analytic review. *Journal of Pediatrics, 154,* 759–763.

Ferguson, C. J., & Kilburn, J. (2010). Much ado about nothing: The misestimation and overinterpretation of violent video game effects in Eastern and Western nations: Comment on Anderson et al. (2010). *Psychological Bulletin, 136,* 174–178.

Ferguson, C. J., Rueda, S. M., Cruz, A. M., Ferguson, D. E., Fritz, S., & Smith, S. M. (2008). Violent video games and aggression: Causal relationship or byproduct of family violence and intrinsic violence motivation? *Criminal Justice and Behavior, 35,* 311–332.

Ferguson, E. D. (2000). *Motivation: A biosocial and cognitive integration of motivation and emotion.* New York: Oxford University Press.

Fernald, A., Taeschner, T., Dunn, J., Papousek, M., De Boysson-Bardies, B., & Fukui, I. (1989). A cross-cultural study of prosodic modification in mothers' and fathers' speech to preverbal infants. *Journal of Child Language, 16,* 477–501.

Ferster, C. B., & Skinner, B. F. (1957). *Schedules of reinforcement.* Englewood Cliffs, NJ: Prentice Hall.

Festinger, L. (1954). A theory of social comparison processes. *Human Relations, 2,* 117–140.

Festinger, L. (1957). *A theory of cognitive dissonance.* Stanford, CA: Stanford University Press.

Festinger, L., & Carlsmith, J. M. (1959). Cognitive consequences of forced compliance. *Journal of Abnormal and Social Psychology, 58,* 203–210.

Festinger, L., Pepitone, A., & Newcomb, T. (1952). Some consequences of deindividuation in a group. *Journal of Abnormal Psychology, 47,* 382–389.

Fiedler, K., Nickel, S., Muehlfriedel, T., & Unkelbach, C. (2001). Is mood congruency an effect of genuine memory or response bias? *Journal of Experimental Social Psychology, 37,* 201–214.

Field, T. (2000). Infant massage therapy. In C. H. Zeanah, Jr. (Ed.), *Handbook of infant mental health* (2nd ed.). New York: Guilford Press.

Field, T. (2001). Massage therapy facilitates weight gain in preterm infants. *Current Directions in Psychological Science, 10,* 51–54.

Field, T., Diego, M. A., Hernandez-Reif, M., Deeds, O., & Figuereido, B. (2006). Moderate versus light pressure massage therapy leads to greater weight gain in preterm infants. *Infant Behavior & Development, 29,* 574–578.

Field, T. M., Schanberg, S. M., Scafidi, F., Bauer, C. R., Vega-Lahr, N., Garcia, R., Nystrom, J., & Kuhn, C. M. (1986). Tactile/kinesthetic stimulation effects on preterm neonates. *Pediatrics, 77,* 654–658.

Fields, H. L. (2005). *Pain: Mechanisms and management.* New York: McGraw-Hill.

Fink, G. (Ed.). (2010). *Stress science: Neuroendocrinology.* New York: Academic Press.

Fish, J. M. (2002). The myth of race. In J. M. Fish (Ed.), *Race and intelligence: Separating science from myth.* Mahwah, NJ: Erlbaum.

Fishbein, M., & Ajzen, I. (1974). Attitudes toward objects as predictors of single and multiple behavioral criteria. *Psychological Review, 81,* 59–74.

Fisher, S., & Greenberg, R. P. (1996). *Freud scientifically reappraised: Testing the theories and therapy.* New York: Wiley.

Fiske, K. E., & Pillemer, D. B. (2006). Adult recollections of earliest childhood dreams: A cross-cultural study. *Memory, 14,* 57–67.

Flavell, J. H. (1970). Developmental studies of mediated behavior. In H. W. Reese and L. P. Lipsett (Eds.), *Advances in child development and behavior* (Vol. 5). New York: Academic Press.

Flavell, J. H. (2004). Theory-of-mind development: Retrospect and prospect. *Merrill-Palmer Quarterly, 50,* 274–290.

Fleeson, W. (2004). Moving personality beyond the person-situation debate. *Current Directions in Psychological Science, 13,* 83–87.

Flegal, K. M., Carroll, M. D., Ogden, C. L., & Johnson, C. L. (2002). Prevalence and trends in obesity among U.S. adults, 1999–2000. *Journal of the American Medical Association, 288,* 1723–1727.

Fliessbach, K., Weis, S., Klaver, P., Elger, C. E., & Weber, B. (2006). The effect of word concreteness on recognition memory. *NeuroImage, 32,* 1413–1421.

Flinn, M. V. (1997). Culture and the evolution of social learning. *Evolution and Human Behavior, 18,* 23–67.

Flores, J. A., Galan-Rodriguez, B., Ramiro-Fuentes, S., & Fernandez-Espejo, E. (2006). Role for dopamine neurons of the rostral linear nucleus and periaqueductal gray in the rewarding and sensitizing properties of heroin. *Neuropsychopharmacology, 31,* 1475–1488.

Floyd, R. L., O'Connor, M. J., Sokol, R. J., Bertrand, J. , & Cordero, J. F. (2005). Recognition and prevention of fetal alcohol syndrome. *Obstetrics & Gynecology, 106,* 1059–1064.

Flynn, J. R. (1987). Massive IQ gains in 14 nations: What IQ tests really measure. *Psychological Bulletin, 101,* 171–191.

Flynn, J. R. (1998). IQ gains over time: Toward finding the causes. In U. Neisser et al. (Eds.), *The rising curve: Long-term gains in IQ and related measures.* Washington, DC: American Psychological Association.

Foa, E. B., Riggs, D. S., & Gershuny, B. S. (1995). Arousal, numbing, and intrusion: Symptom structure of posttraumatic stress disorder following assault. *American Journal of Psychology, 152,* 116–120.

Foa, E. B., Zoellner, L. A., Feeny, N. C., Hembree, E. A., & Alvarez-Conrad, J. (2002). Does imaginal exposure exacerbate PTSD symptoms? *Journal of Consulting and Clinical Psychology, 70,* 1022–1028.

Folkard, S. (2008). Shift work, safety, and aging. *Chronobiology International, 25,* 183–198.

Follette, W. C., & Davis, D. (2009). Clinical practice and the issue of repressed memories: Avoiding an ice patch on the slippery slope. In W. O'Donohue & S. R. Graybar (Eds.), *Handbook of contemporary psychotherapy: Toward an improved understanding of effective psychotherapy.* Thousand Oaks, CA: Sage.

Fordyce, W. E. (1988). Pain and suffering: A reappraisal. *American Psychologist, 43,* 276–283.

Fosse, R., Stickgold, R., & Hobson, J. A. (2001). Brain-mind states: Reciprocal variation in thoughts and hallucinations. *Psychological Science, 2001, 12,* 30–36.

Foster, D. J., Weigand, D. A., & Baines, D. (2006). The effect of removing superstitious behavior and introducing a pre-performance routine on basketball free-throw performance. *Journal of Applied Sport Psychology, 18,* 167–171.

Foulkes, D. (1982). REM-dream perspectives on the development of affect and cognition. *Psychiatric Journal of the University of Ottawa, 7,* 48–55.

Foulks, F. F., Bland, I. J., & Shervington, D. (1995). Psychotherapy across cultures. *Review of Psychiatry, 14,* 511.

Fournier, J. C., DeRubeis, R. J., Hollon, S. D., et al. (2010). Antidepressant drug effects and depression severity: A patient-level meta-analysis. *Journal of the American Medical Association, 303,* 47–53.

Fouts, R. S., Fouts, D. H., & Van Cantfort, T. E. (1989). The infant Loulis learns signs from other cross-fostered chimpanzees. In R. A. Gardner, B. T. Gardner, & T. E. Van Cantfort (Eds.), *Teaching sign language to chimpanzees.* Albany: State University of New York Press.

Fox, D. K., Hopkins, B. L., & Anger, W. K. (1987). The long-term effects of a token economy on safety performance in open-pit mining. *Journal of Applied Behavior Analysis, 20,* 215–224.

Fox, N. A., Henderson, H. A., Marshall, P. J., Nichols, K. E., & Ghera, M. M. (2005).

Behavioral inhibition: Linking biology and behavior within a developmental framework. *Annual Review of Psychology, 56,* 235–262.

Fox News.com (2010, January 4). *Study: Spanked children may grow up to be happier, more successful.* Retrieved January 16, 2010, from http://www.foxnews.com/story/0,2933,581882,00.html

Fraley, R. C., & Shaver, P. R. (2008). Attachment theory and its place in contemporary personality theory. In O. P. John, R. W. Robins, & L. A. Pervin (Eds.), *Handbook of personality theory and research* (3rd ed.). New York: Guilford Press.

Frances, A., & Widiger, T. A. (1986). Methodological issues in personality disorder diagnosis. In T. Millon & G. L. Klerman (Eds.), *Contemporary directions in psychopathology: Toward the DSM-IV.* New York: Guilford Press.

Frank, J. (1961). *Persuasion & healing: A comparative study of psychotherapy.* Baltimore: Johns Hopkins University Press.

Frank, N. C., Spirito, A., Stark, L., & Owens-Stively, J. (1997). The use of scheduled awakenings to eliminate childhood sleepwalking. *Journal of Pediatric Psychology, 22,* 345–353.

Franklin, B. *Remarks Concerning the Savage of North America.* (1784).

Franklin, T. R., Acton, P. D., Maldjian, J. A., Gray, J. D., Croft, J. R., Dackis, C. A., O'Brien, C. P., & Childress, A. R. (2002). Decreased gray matter concentration in the insular, orbitofrontal, cingulate, and temporal cortices of cocaine patients. *Biological Psychiatry, 51,* 134–142.

Frayser, S. G. (1985). *Varieties of sexual experience: An anthropological perspective on human sexuality.* New Haven, CT: HRAF.

Frazier, P., Tennen, H., Gavian, M., et al. (2009). Does self-reported posttraumatic growth reflect genuine positive change? *Psychological Science, 20,* 912–919.

Fredrickson, B. L. (1998). What good are positive emotions? *Review of General Psychology, 2,* 300–319.

Freeman, C., & Power, M. (2007). *Handbook of evidence-based psychotherapy.* Hoboken, NJ: Wiley.

French, S. J., & Cecil, J. E. (2001). Oral, gastric and intestinal influences on human feeding. *Physiology and Behavior, 74,* 729–734.

Freud, S. (1923). *The ego and the id.* New York: Norton.

Freud, S. (1935). *A general introduction to psychoanalysis.* New York: Washington Square Press.

Freud, S. (1953). The interpretation of dreams. In J. Strachey (Ed.), *The standard edition of the complete psychological works of Sigmund Freud* (Vols. 4 and 5). London: Hogarth. (Original work published 1900.)

Freud, S. (1957). Mourning and melancholia. In J. Strachey (Ed.), *The standard edition of the complete psychological works of Sigmund Freud* (Vol. 14). London: Hogarth. (Original work published 1917.)

Freud, S. (1965). *The interpretation of dreams.* New York: Avon. (Original work published 1900.)

Frijda, N. (2006). *The laws of emotion.* Mahwah, NJ: Erlbaum.

Frijda, N. H., Manstead, A. S. R., & Bem, S. (Eds.). (2005). *Emotions and beliefs: How feelings influence thoughts.* New York: Cambridge University Press.

Frisby, J. P. (1980). *Seeing: Illusion, brain and mind.* Oxford, England: Oxford University Press.

Frisco, M. L., & Williams, K. (2003). Perceived housework equity, marital happiness, and divorce in dual earner households. *Journal of Family Issues, 24,* 51–73.

Fritsch, J. (1999, May 25). 95% regain lost weight. Or do they? *New York Times,* p. F7.

Fritzsche, B. A., Finkelstein, M. A., & Penner, L. A. (2000). To help or not to help: Capturing individuals' decision policies. *Social Behavior and Personality, 28,* 561–578.

Froger, C., Taconnat, L., Landré, L., Beigneux, K., & Isingrini, M. (2008). Effects of level of processing at encoding and types of retrieval task in mild cognitive impairment and normal aging. *Journal of Clinical and Experimental Neuropsychology, 31,* 312–321.

Fuligni, A. J. (1998). Authority, autonomy, and parent-adolescent conflict and cohesion: A study of adolescents from Mexican, Chinese, Filipino, and European backgrounds. *Developmental Psychology, 34,* 782–792.

Funder, D. C. (2008). Persons, situations, and person-situation interactions. In O. P. John, R. W. Robins, & L. A. Pervin (Eds.), *Handbook of personality theory and research* (3rd ed.). New York: Guilford Press.

Furmark, T., Tillfors, M., Marteinsdottir, I., Fischer, H., Pissiota, A., Langstroem, B., & Fredrikson, M. (2002). Common changes in cerebral blood flow in patients with social phobia treated with citalopram or cognitive-behavioral therapy. *Archives of General Psychiatry, 59,* 425–433.

Furnes, B., & Samuelsson, S. (2009). Preschool cognitive and language skills predicting kindergarten and grade 1 reading and spelling: A cross-linguistic comparison. *Journal of Research in Reading, 32,* 275–292.

Furukawa, T. A., Watanabe, N., & Churchill, R. (2006). Psychotherapy plus antidepressant for panic disorder with or without agoraphobia: Systematic review. *British Journal of Psychiatry, 188,* 305–312.

Gabbard, C., & Anmar, D. (2008). The effect of response-delay on estimating reachability. *International Journal of Neuroscience, 118,* 1502–1514.

Gabbard, G. O. (1990). *Psychodynamic psychiatry in clinical practice.* Washington, DC: American Psychiatric Press.

Gabbard, G. O. (2004). *Long-term psychodynamic psychotherapy.* Washington, DC: American Psychiatric Publishing.

Gabbard, G. O., Beck, J., & Holmes, J. (2005). *Oxford textbook of psychotherapy.* New York: Oxford University Press.

Gabrieli, J. D. E. (1998). Cognitive neuroscience of human memory. *Annual Review of Psychology, 49,* 87–115.

Gabrieli, J. D. E., Desmond, J. E., Demb, J. B., & Wagner, A. D. (1996). Functional magnetic resonance imaging of semantic memory processes in the frontal lobes. *Psychological Science, 7,* 278–283.

Gainotti, G. (1972). Emotional behavior and hemispheric side of lesion. *Cortex, 8,* 41–55.

Galanter, E. (1962). Contemporary psychophysics. In R. Brown (Ed.), *New directions in psychology.* New York: Holt, Rinehart & Winston.

Galati, D., & Lavelli, M. (1997). Neonate and infant emotion expression perceived by adults. *Journal of Nonverbal Behavior, 21,* 57–83.

Galea, S., Ahern, J., Resnick, H., Kilpatrick, D., Bucuvalas, M., Gold, J., & Vlahov, D. (2002). Psychological sequelae of the September 11 terrorist attacks in New York City. *New England Journal of Medicine, 346,* 982–987.

Galietta, M., Fineran, V., Fava, J., & Rosenfeld, B. (2010). Antisocial and psychopathic individuals. In D. McKay, J. S Abramowitz, & S. Taylor (Eds.), *Cognitive-behavioral therapy for refractory cases: Turning failure into success.* Washington, DC: American Psychological Association.

Gallivan, J. P., Cavina-Pratesi, C., & Culham, J. C. (2009). Is that within reach? fMRI reveals that the human superior parieto-occipital cortex encodes objects reachable by the hand. *The Journal of Neuroscience, 29,* 4381–4391.

Gallup, G. G. (1970). Chimpanzees: Self-recognition. *Science, 167*(3914), 86–87.

Gamon, D., & Bragdon, A. D. (2003). *Building mental muscle.* New York: Walker.

Gangestad, S. W., Haselton, M. G., & Buss, D. M. (2006). Evolutionary foundations of cultural variation: Evoked culture and mate preferences. *Psychological Inquiry, 17,* 75–95.

Gangstad, B., Norman, P., & Barton, J. (2009). Cognitive processing and posttraumatic growth after stroke. *Rehabilitation Psychology, 54,* 69–75.

Ganguli, R. (2000, March 18). Mental illness and misconceptions. *Pittsburgh Post Gazette.* Retrieved December 12, 2009, from http://www.post-gazette.com/forum/20000318gang1.asp

Ganis, G., Thompson, W. L., & Kosslyn, S. M. (2004). Brain areas underlying visual mental imagery and visual perception: An fMRI study. *Cognitive Brain Research, 20,* 226–241.

Garber, J., & Dodge, K. A. (Eds.) (2007). *The development of emotional regulation and dysregulation.* New York: Cambridge University Press.

Garbutt, J. C. (2009). The state of pharmacotherapy for the treatment of alcohol dependence. *Journal of Substance Abuse Treatment, 36,* S15–S23.

Garcia, J., & Koelling, R. A. (1966). The relation of cue to consequence in avoidance learning. *Psychonomic Science, 4,* 123–124.

Garcia, J., Lasiter, P. S., Bermudez, R. F., & Deems, D. A. (1985). A general theory of aversion learning. *Annals of the New York Academy of Sciences, 443,* 8–21.

Gardner, H. (2000). *Multiple intelligences: The theory in practice.* New York: Basic Books.

Gardner, H. (2003). Three distinct meanings of intelligence. In R. J. Sternberg, J. Lautrey, & T. I. Lubart (Eds.), *Models of intelligence: International perspectives.* Washington, DC: American Psychological Association.

Gardner, R. A., & Gardner, B. T. (1969). Teaching language to a chimpanzee. *Science, 165,* 664–672.

Garland, D. J., & Barry, J. R. (1991). Cognitive advantage in sport: The nature of perceptual structures. *American Journal of Psychology, 104,* 211–228.

Garlick, D. (2002). Understanding the nature of the general factor of intelligence: The role of individual differences in neural plasticity as an explanatory mechanism. *Psychological Review, 109,* 116–136.

Garmezy, N. (1983). *Stress, coping and development in children.* New York: McGraw-Hill.

Garnefski, N., & Arends, E. (1998). Sexual abuse and adolescent maladjustment: Differences between male and female victims. *Journal of Adolescence, 21,* 99–107.

Gatchel, R. J. (2005). *Clinical essentials of pain management.* Washington, DC: American Psychological Association.

Gathercole, S. E. (1998). The development of memory. *Journal of Child Psychology and Psychiatry and Allied Disciplines, 39,* 3–27.

Gathercole, S. E., Pickering, S. J., Knight, C., & Stegmann, Z. (2004). Working memory skills and educational attainment: Evidence from national curriculum assessments at 7 and 14 years of age. *Applied Cognitive Psychology, 18,* 1–16.

Gazit, I., & Terkel, J. (2003). Explosives detection by sniffer dogs following strenuous physical activity. *Applied Animal Behaviour Science, 81,* 149–161.

Gazzaniga, M. S., & Smylie, C. S. (1983). Facial recognition and brain asymmetries: Clues to underlying mechanisms. *Annals of Neurology, 13,* 536–540.

Geary, D. C. (2005). *The origin of mind: Evolution of brain, cognition, and general intelligence.* Washington, DC: American Psychological Association.

Geher, G., Bauman, K. P., Hubbard, S. E. K., & Legare, J. R. (2002). Self and other obedience estimates: Biases and moderators. *Journal of Social Psychology, 142,* 677–689.

Gelade, G. A. (2008). IQ, cultural values, and the technological achievement of nations. *Intelligence, 36,* 711–718.

Gelernter, J., & Stein, M. B. (2009). Heritability and genetics of anxiety disorders. In M. M. Antony & M. B. Stein (Eds.), *Oxford handbook of anxiety and related disorders.* New York: Oxford University Press.

Gelman, S. A., Taylor, M. G., & Nguyen, S. P. (2004). Mother-child conversations about gender. *Monographs of the Society for Research in Child Development, 69,* vii–127.

Gentile, D. A., Lynch, P. J., Linder, J. R., & Walsh, D. A. (2004). The effects of violent video game habits on adolescent hostility, aggressive behaviors, and school performance. *Journal of Adolescence, 27,* 5–22.

George, W. H., Stoner, S. A., Norris, J., Lopez, P. A., & Lehman, G. L. (2000). Alcohol expectancies and sexuality: A self-fulfilling prophecy analysis of dyadic perceptions and behavior. *Journal of Studies on Alcohol, 61,* 168–176.

George-Joseph, G., & Smith, E. W. L. (2008). The dream world in Dominica. *Dreaming, 18,* 167–174.

Geracioti, T. D., Loosen, P. T., Ebert, M. H., & Schmidt, D. (1995). Fasting and postprandial cerebrospinal fluid glucose concentrations in healthy women and in an obese binge eater. *International Journal of Eating Disorders, 18,* 365–369.

Geraerts, E., Schooler, J. W., Merckelbach, C., Jelicic, M., Beatrijs, H. B., & Ambadar, Z. (2007). The reality of recovered memories: Corroborating continuous and discontinuous memories of childhood sexual abuse. *Psychological Science, 18,* 564–568.

Gergen, K. (2000). *An invitation to social constructivism.* Thousand Oaks, CA: Sage.

Gershoff, E. T. (2002). Corporal punishment by parents and associated child behaviors and experiences: A meta-analytic and theoretical review. *Psychological Bulletin, 128,* 539–579.

Gershoff, E. T., (2008a). *Principles and practices of effective discipline: Advice for parents.* Columbus, OH: Center for Effective Discipline.

Gershoff, E. T. (2008b). *Report on physical punishment in the United States: What research tells us about its effects on children.* Columbus, OH: Center for Effective Discipline.

Gershon, E. S., Berrettini, W. H., & Golden, L. E. (1989). Mood disorders: Genetic aspects. In H. I. Kaplan & B. J. Sadock (Eds.), *Comprehensive textbook of psychiatry/V.* Baltimore: Williams & Wilkins.

Ghaemi, S. N. (2008). Why antidepressants are not antidepressants: STEP-BD, STAR*D, and the return of neurotic depression. *Bipolar Disorders, 10,* 957–968.

Ghetti, S., Qin, J., & Goodman, G. S. (2002). False memories in children and adults: Age, distinctiveness, and subjective experience. *Developmental Psychology, 38,* 705–718.

Ghodse, H. (2007). "Uppers" keep going up. *British Journal of Psychiatry, 191,* 279–281.

Gibson, E., & Walk, R. D. (1960). The visual cliff. *Scientific American, 202,* 80–92.

Gibson, J. J. (1979). *The ecological approach to visual perception.* Boston: Houghton Mifflin.

Gier, V. S., Kreiner, D. S., & Natz-Gonzalez, A. (2009). Harmful effects of preexisting inappropriate highlighting on reading comprehension and metacognitive accuracy. *Journal of General Psychology, 136,* 287–300.

Gilligan, C. (1982). *In a different voice: Psychological theory and women's development.* Cambridge, MA: Harvard University Press.

Giorgio, A., Watkins, K. E., Chadwick, M., James, S., Winmill, L., Douaud, G., et al. (2010). Longitudinal changes in grey and white matter during adolescence. *NeuroImage, 49,* 94–103.

Givón, T., & Savage-Rumbaugh, S. (2009). Can apes learn grammar? A short detour into language evolution. In J. Guo, E. Lieven, N. Budwig, S. Ervin-Tripp, K. Nakamura, & S. Özçalişkan (Eds.), *Crosslinguistic approaches to the psychology of language: Research in the tradition of Dan Issac Slobin.* New York: Psychology.

Glanzer, M., & Cunitz, A. R. (1966). Two storage mechanisms in free recall. *Journal of Verbal Learning and Verbal Behavior, 5,* 351–360.

Glanzman, D. L. (2009). Habituation in Aplysia: The Cheshire cat of neurobiology. *Neurobiology of Learning and Memory, 92,* 147–154.

Glock, S., & Kneer, J. (2009). Game over? The impact of knowledge about violent digital games on the activation of aggression-related concepts. *Journal of Media Psychology: Theories, Methods, and Applications, 21,* 151–160.

Glucksman, M. L. (2001). The dream: A psychodynamically informative instrument. *Journal of Psychotherapy Practice and Research, 10,* 223–230.

Gobet, F., & Simon, H. A. (2000). Five seconds or sixty? Presentation time in expert memory. *Cognitive Science, 24,* 651–682.

Goddard, A. W., Mason, G. F., Almai, A., et al. (2001). Reductions in occipital cortex GABA levels in panic disorder detected with sup-1H-magnetic resonance spectroscopy. *Archives of General Psychiatry, 58,* 556–561.

Goddard, H. H. (1917). Mental tests and immigrants. *Journal of Delinquency, 2,* 243–277.

Godden, D. R., & Baddeley, A. D. (1975). Context-dependent memory in two natural environments: On land and under water. *British Journal of Psychology, 66,* 325–332.

Goebel, M. U., Meykadeh, N., Kou, W., Schedlowski, M., & Hengge, U. R. (2008). Behavioral conditioning of antihistamine effects in patients with allergic rhinitis. *Psychotherapy and Psychosomatics, 77,* 227–234.

Goffman, E. (1961). *Asylums: Essays on the social situation of mental patients and other inmates.* New York: Doubleday.

Golden, C., Golden, C. J., & Schneider, B. (2003). Cell phone use and visual attention. *Perceptual and Motor Skills, 97,* 385–389.

Goldfried, M. R., & Eubanks-Carter, C. (2004). On the need for a new psychotherapy research paradigm: Comment on Westen, Novotny, & Thompson-Brenner. *Psychological Bulletin, 139,* 669–673.

Goldsmith, S. K. (2003). *Reducing suicide: A national imperative.* Washington, DC: National Academy Press.

Goldstein, B. (2002). *Sensation and perception* (6th ed.). Belmont, CA: Wadsworth.

Goldstein, G. (2000). Comprehensive neuropsychological assessment batteries. In G. Goldstein & M. Hersen (Eds.), *Handbook of psychological assessment* (3rd ed.). New York: Elsevier.

Goldston, D. B., Reboussin, B., & Daniel, S. S. (2006). Predictors of suicide attempts: State and trait components. *Journal of Abnormal Psychology, 115,* 842–849.

Gonzales, P. M., Blanton, H., & Williams, K. J. (2002). The effects of stereotype threat and double minority status on the test performance of Latino women. *Personality and Social Psychology Bulletin, 28,* 659–670.

Gonzalez, E., et al. (2005). The influence of CCL3L1 gene-containing segmental duplications on HIV-1/AIDS susceptibility. *Science, 307,* 1434–1440.

Goodale, M. A. (1995). The cortical organization of visual perception and visuomotor control. In S. Kosslyn & D. N. Osheron (Eds.), *Visual cognition: An invitation to cognitive science* (2nd ed.). Cambridge, MA: MIT Press.

Goodale, M. A. (2000). Perception and action in the human visual system. In M. S. Gazzaniga (Ed.), *The new cognitive neurosciences* (2nd ed.). Cambridge, MA: MIT Press.

Goode, W. J. (1959). The theoretical importance of love. *American Sociological Review, 24,* 38–47.

Goodman, G. S., Quas, J. A., & Ogle, C. M. (2010). Child maltreatment and memory. *Annual Review of Psychology, 61,* 325–351.

Goodman, W. (1982, August 9). Of mice, monkeys and men. *Newsweek,* 61.

Goodwill, A. M., Alison, L. J., & Beech, A. R. (2009). What works in offender profiling? A comparison of typological, thematic, and multivariate models. *Behavioral Sciences and the Law, 27,* 507–529.

Gorman, J. M. (2002). Treatment of generalized anxiety disorder. *Journal of Clinical Psychiatry, 63*(Suppl. 8), 17–23.

Gosling, S. D., Vazire, S., Srivastava, S., & John, O. P. (2004). Should we trust web-based studies? A comparative analysis of six preconceptions about Internet questionnaires. *American Psychologist, 59,* 93–104.

Goswami, U. (2008). The development of reading across languages. *Annals of the New York Academy of Sciences, 1145,* 1–12.

Gotlib, I. H., Kasch, K. L, Traill, S., Joormann, J., Arnow, B. A., & Johnson, S. L. (2004a). Coherence and specificity of information-processing biases in depression and social phobia. *Journal of Abnormal Psychology, 113,* 386–398.

Gotlib, I. H., Krasnoperova, E., Yue, D. N., & Joormann, J. (2004b). Attentional biases for negative interpersonal stimuli in clinical depression. *Journal of Abnormal Psychology, 113,* 127–135.

Gottesman, I. I. (1991). *Schizophrenia genesis: The origins of madness.* New York: Freeman.

Gottfried, A. E., Fleming, J. S., & Gottfried, A. W. (1998). Role of cognitively stimulating home environment in children's academic intrinsic motivation: A longitudinal study. *Child Development, 69,* 1448–1460.

Gottman, J. M., Gottman, J. S., & de Claire, J. (2006). *Ten lessons to transform your marriage: America's love lab experts share their strategies for strengthening your relationship.* New York: Three Rivers.

Gottman, J. M., & Levenson, R. (1992). Marital processes predictive of later dissolution: Behavior, psychology and health. *Journal of Personality and Social Psychology, 63,* 221–233.

Graber, J. A., Seeley, J. R., Brooks-Gunn, J., & Lewinsohn, P. M. (2004). Is pubertal timing associated with psychopathology in young adulthood? *Journal of the American Academy of Child & Adolescent Psychiatry, 43,* 718–726.

Gracely, E. J. (1998). Why extraordinary claims demand extraordinary proof. *Phactum.* Philadelphia Association for Critical Thinking. Retrieved October 11, 2009, from http://www.quackwatch.com/01QuackeryRelatedTopics/extraproof.html

Gracely, R. H., Farrell, M. J., & Grant, M. A. B. (2002). Temperature and pain perception. In H. Pashler & S.Yantis (Eds.), *Steven's handbook of experimental psychology: Vol. 1. Sensation and perception* (3rd ed.). New York: Wiley.

Graham, J. R. (2006). *MMPI-2: Assessing personality and psychopathology.* New York: Oxford University Press.

Graham, S., Hudley, C., & Williams, E. (1992). Attributional and emotional determinants of aggression among African-American and Latino young adolescents. *Developmental Psychology, 28,* 731–740.

Grainger, J. (2008). Cracking the orthographic code: An introduction. *Language and Cognitive Processes, 23,* 1–35.

Grant, H. M., Bredahl, L. C., Clay, J., Ferrie, J., Groves, J. E., McDorman, T. A., & Dark, V. J. (1998). Context-dependent memory for meaningful material: Information for students. *Applied Cognitive Psychology, 12,* 617–623.

Grasshoff, C., Netzhammer, N., Schweizer, J., Antkowiak, B., & Hentschke, H. (2008). Depression of spinal network activity by thiopental: Shift from phasic to tonic GABA$_A$ receptor-mediated inhibition. *Neuropharmacology, 55,* 793–802.

Graw, P., Werth, E., Kraeuchi, K., Gutzwiller, F., Cajochen, C., & Wirz-Justice, A. (2001). Early morning melatonin administration impairs psychomotor vigilance. *Behavioural Brain Research, 121*, 167–172.

Gray, J. A. (1991). Neural systems, emotions, and personality. In J. Madden IV (Ed.), *Neurobiology of learning, emotion, and affect*. New York: Raven Press.

Gray, J. R., & Burgess, G. C. (2004). Personality differences in cognitive control? BAS, processing efficiency, and the prefrontal cortex. *Journal of Research in Personality, 38*, 35–36.

Green, J. P., Page, R. A., Rasekhy, R., Johnson, L. K., & Bernhardt, S. E. (2006). Cultural views and attitudes about hypnosis: A survey of college students across four countries. *International Journal of Clinical and Experimental Hypnosis, 54*, 263–280.

Green, J. T., & Woodruff-Pak, D. S. (2000). Eyeblink classical conditioning: Hippocampal formation is for neutral stimulus associations as cerebellum is for association-response. *Psychological Bulletin, 126*, 138–158.

Green, M. (1999). Diagnosis of attention-deficit/hyperactivity disorder. *Technical Review Number 3, Publication No. 99–0050*. Rockville, MD: Agency for Health Care Policy and Research.

Green, M. F. (1997). *Schizophrenia from a neurocognitive perspective: Probing the impenetrable darkness*. Boston: Allyn & Bacon.

Greenberg, J., Solomon, S., & Pyszynski, T. (1997). Terror management theory of self-esteem and cultural worldviews: Empirical assessments and conceptual refinements. In M. P. Zanna (Ed.), *Advances in experimental social psychology* (Vol. 29). San Diego, CA: Academic Press.

Greenberg, L. S., & Malcolm, W. (2002). Resolving unfinished business: Relating process to outcome. *Journal of Consulting and Clinical Psychology, 70*, 406–416.

Greenberg, L. S., & Rice, L. N. (1997). Humanistic approaches to psychotherapy. In P. L. Wachtel & S. B. Messer (Eds.), *Theories of psychotherapy: Origins and evolution*. Washington, DC: American Psychological Association.

Greene, K., Krcmar, M., Walters, L. H., Rubin, D. L., & Hale, J. L. (2000). Targeting adolescent risk-taking behaviors: The contribution of egocentrism and sensation seeking. *Journal of Adolescence, 23*, 439–461.

Greene, R. L. (1992). *Human memory: Paradigms and paradoxes*. Hillsdale, NJ: Erlbaum.

Greene, R. W., & Ollendick, T. H. (2000). Behavioral assessment of children. In G. Goldstein & M. Hersen (Eds.), *Handbook of psychological assessment* (3rd ed.). New York: Elsevier.

Greenfield, P. M. (1998). The cultural evolution of IQ. In U. Neisser (Ed.), *The rising curve: Long-term gains in IQ and related measures*. Washington, DC: American Psychological Association.

Greenfield, P. M., Lyn, H., & Savage-Rumbaugh, E. S. (2008). Protolanguage in ontogeny and phylogeny: Combining deixis and representation. *Interaction Studies: Social Behaviour and Communication in Biological and Artificial Systems, 9*, 34–50.

Greenwald, A. G. (1992). New look 3: Unconscious cognition reclaimed. *American Psychologist, 47*, 766–779.

Greenwald, A. G., & Banaji, M. R. (1995). Implicit social cognition: Attitudes, self-esteem, and stereotypes. *Psychological Review, 102*, 4–27.

Greenwald, A. G., McGhee, D. E., & Schwartz, J. (1998). Measuring individual differences in implicit cognition: The implicit association test. *Journal of Personality and Social Psychology, 74*, 1464–1480.

Greenwald, A. G., Nosek, B. A., & Sriram, N. (2006). Consequential validity of the Implicit Association Test: Comment on Blanton and Jaccard. *American Psychologist, 61*, 56–61.

Greenwald, A. G., Spangenberg, E. R., Pratkanis, A. R., & Eskenazi, J. (1991). Double-blind tests of subliminal self-help tapes. *Psychological Science, 2*, 119–122.

Gregory, R. J. (1998). *Foundations of intellectual assessment: The WAIS-III and other tests in clinical practice*. Boston: Allyn & Bacon.

Gregory, R. L. (1966). *Eye and brain*. New York: McGraw-Hill.

Gregory, R. L. (2005). *Illusion: The phenomenal brain*. New York: Oxford University Press.

Gregory, R. L., & Gombrich, E. H. (1973). *Illusion in nature and art*. London: Duckworth.

Grice, H. P. (1975). Logic and conversation. In P. Cole & J. L. Morgan (Eds.), *Syntax and semantics: Vol. 3. Speech acts*. New York: Seminar.

Grigorenko, E. L. (2003). Selected links between nutrition and the mind. In R. J. Sternberg, J. Lautrey, & T. I. Lubart (Eds.), *Models of intelligence: International perspectives*. Washington, DC: American Psychological Association.

Grimes, K., & Walker, E. F. (1994). Childhood emotional expressions, educational attainment, and age at onset of illness in schizophrenia. *Journal of Abnormal Psychology, 103*, 784–790.

Grossberg, S., Finkel, L., & Field, D. (Eds.). (2005). *Vision and brain: How the brain sees: New approaches to computer vision*. St. Louis: Elsevier.

Grossman, H., Bergmann, C., & Parker, S. (2006). Dementia: A brief review. *The Mount Sinai Journal of Medicine, 73*, 985–992.

Grossman, P., Niemann, L., Schmidt, S., & Walach, H. (2004). Mindfulness-based stress reduction and health benefits: A meta-analysis. *Journal of Psychosomatic Research, 57*, 35–43.

Groth-Marnat, G. (1999). *Handbook of psychological assessment*. New York: Wiley.

Grove, W. M., & Meehl, P. E. (1996). Comparative efficiency of informal (subjective, impressionistic) and formal (mechanical, algorithmic) prediction procedures: The clinical-statistical controversy. *Psychology, Public Policy, and Law, 2*, 293–323.

Gruest, N., Richer, P., & Hars, B. (2004). Emergence of long-term memory for conditioned aversion in the rat fetus. *Developmental Psychobiology, 44*, 189–198.

Grunwald, M. (2009, April 2). How Obama is using the science of change. *Time*. Retrieved November 20, 2009, from http://www.time.com/time/magazine/article/0,9171,1889153-1,00.html

Guéguen, N. (2002). Foot in the door technique and computer mediated communication. *Computers in Human Behavior, 18*, 11–15.

Guilford, J. P. (1959). Three faces of intellect. *American Psychologist, 14*, 469–479.

Guilford, J. P. (1967). *The nature of human intelligence*. New York: McGraw-Hill.

Guinness book of records. (2000). Stamford, CT: Guinness Media.

Gulevich, G., Dement, W., & Johnson, L. (1966). Psychiatric and EEG observations on a case of prolonged (264 hours) wakefulness. *Archives of General Psychiatry, 15*, 29–35.

Gump, L. S., Baker, R. C., & Roll, S. (2000). Cultural and gender differences in moral judgment: A study of Mexican Americans and Anglo-Americans. *Hispanic Journal of Behavioral Sciences, 22*, 78–93.

Gundelfinger, E. D., Seidenbecher, C., & Schraven, B. (2006). *Cell communication in nervous and immune system*. New York: Springer.

Gur, R. E., Cowell, P., Turetsky, B. I., Gallacher, F., Cannon, T., Bilker, W., & Gur, R. B. (1998). A follow-up magnetic resonance imaging study of schizophrenia: Relationship of neuroanatomical changes to clinical and neurobehavioral measures. *Archives of General Psychiatry, 55*, 145–152.

Gurvitz, I. G., Koenigsberg, H. W., & Siever, L. J. (2000). Neurotransmitter dysfunction in patients with borderline personality disorder. *Psychiatric Clinics of North America, 23*, 27–40.

Gustavson, C. R., Garcia, J., Hankins, W. G., & Rusiniak, K. W. (1974). Coyote predation control by aversive conditioning. *Science, 184*, 581–583.

Gustavson, C. R., & Gustavson, J. C. (1985, June). Predation control using conditioned food aversion methodology: Theory, practice, and implications. *Annals of the New York Academy of Sciences, 443*, 348–356.

Haaga, D. A. F., Dyck, M. J., & Ernst, D. (1991). Empirical status of cognitive theory of depression. *Psychological Bulletin, 110*, 215–236.

Haber, L. R., Haber, R. N., & Furlin, K. R. (1983). Word length and word shape as sources of information in reading. *Reading Research Quarterly, 18*, 165–189.

Hafen, B. Q., & Hoeger, W. W. K. (1998). *Wellness: Guidelines for a healthy lifestyle*. Englewood, CO: Morton.

Haier, R. J., Colom, R., Schroeder, D. H., Condon, C. A., et al. (2009). Gray matter and intelligence factors: Is there a neuro-*g*? *Intelligence, 37*, 136–144.

Haier, R. J., Siegel, B. V., Crinella, F. M., & Buchsbaum, M. S. (1993). Biological and psychometric intelligence: Testing an animal model in humans with positron emission tomography. In D. K. Detterman (Ed.), *Individual differences and cognition: Current topics in human intelligence* (Vol. 3). Norwood, NJ: Ablex.

Hailman, J. P. (1967). The ontogeny of an instinct. *Behaviour Supplements, 15*, 1–159.

Hailman, J. P. (1969). How an instinct is learned. *Scientific American, 221*, 98–106.

Haines, R. F. (1991). A breakdown in simultaneous information processing. In G. Obrecht & L. W. Stark (Eds.), *Presbyopia research*. New York: Plenum Press.

Halari, R., Hines, M., Kumari, V., Mehrotra, R., Wheeler, M., Ng, V., & Sharma, T. (2005). Sex differences and individual differences in cognitive performance and their relationship to endogenous gonadal hormones and gonadotropins. *Behavioral Neuroscience, 119*, 104–117.

Hall, C. S., & Van de Castle, R. (1966). *The content analysis of dreams.* New York: Appleton-Century-Crofts.

Hall, G. C. N., & Okazaki, S. (2003). *Asian American psychology: The science of lives in context.* Washington, DC: American Psychological Association.

Hall, G. S. (1904). *Adolescence* (Vols. 1 and 2). New York: Appleton-Century-Crofts.

Hall, H., Lawyer, G., Sillen, A., et al. (2007). Potential genetic variants in schizophrenia: A Bayesian analysis. *World Journal of Biological Psychiatry, 8,* 12–22.

Hall, W., & Degenhardt, L. (2009). Adverse health effects of non-medical cannabis use. *The Lancet, 37*(9698), 1383–1391.

Haller, M., & Hadler, M. (2006). How social relations and structures can produce happiness and unhappiness: An international comparative analysis. *Social Indicators Research, 75,* 169–216.

Halligan, P. W., Fink, G. R., Marshall, J. C., & Vallar, G. (2003). Spatial cognition: Evidence from visual neglect. *Trends in Cognitive Sciences, 7,* 125–133.

Halpern, B. (2002). Taste. In H. Pashler & S. Yantis (Eds.), *Steven's handbook of experimental psychology: Vol. 1. Sensation and perception* (3rd ed.). New York: Wiley.

Halpern, D. F. (2004). *Sex differences in cognitive abilities* (3rd ed.). Mahwah, NJ: Erlbaum.

Halpern, D. F., & Tan, U. (2001). Stereotypes and steroids: Using a psychobiosocial model to understand cognitive sex differences. *Brain and Cognition, 45,* 392–414.

Haluk, D. M., & Wickman, K. (2010). Evaluation of study design variables and their impact on food-maintained operant responding in mice. *Behavioural Brain Research, 207,* 394–401.

Hamann S., & Mao, H. (2002). Positive and negative emotional verbal stimuli elicit activity in the left amygdala. *Neuroreport, 13*(1), 15–19.

Hamer, D. H., & Copeland, P. (1998). *Living with our genes: Why they matter more than you think.* New York: Doubleday.

Hamilton, R. J. (1985). A framework for the evaluation of the effectiveness of adjunct questions and objectives. *Review of Educational Research, 55,* 47–85.

Hamilton, W. D. (1964). The genetical theory of social behaviour, I, II. *Journal of Theoretical Biology, 12,* 12–45.

Hamm, A. O. (2009). Specific phobias. *Psychiatric Clinics of North America, 16,* 577–591.

Hammen, C. (1991). *Depression runs in families: The social context of risk and resilience in children of depressed mothers.* New York: Springer-Verlag.

Hampson, S. E., & Friedman, H. S. (2008). Personality and health: A lifespan perspective. In O. P. John, R. W. Robins, & L. A. Pervin (Eds.), *Handbook of personality: Theory and research* (3rd ed.). New York: Guilford Press.

Hampstead, B. M., & Koffler, S. P. (2009). Thalamic contributions to anterograde, retrograde, and implicit memory: A case study. *The Clinical Neuropsychologist, 23,* 1232–1249.

Haney, C., & Zimbardo, P. G. (2009). Persistent dispositionalism in interactionist clothing: Fundamental attribution error in explaining prison abuse. *Personality and Social Psychology Bulletin, 35,* 807–814.

Hankin, B. L., Kassel, J. D., & Abela, R. Z. (2005). Adult attachment dimensions and specificity of emotional distress symptoms: Prospective investigations of cognitive risk and interpersonal stress generation as mediating mechanisms. *Personality and Social Psychology Bulletin, 31,* 136–151.

Hanley, S. J., & Abell, S. C. (2002). Maslow and relatedness: Creating an interpersonal model of self-actualization. *Journal of Humanistic Psychology, 42,* 37–56.

Hanly, S., & Vandenberg, B. (2010). Tip-of-the-tongue and word retrieval in dyslexia. *Journal of Learning Disabilities, 43,* 15–23.

Hansen, C. H., & Hansen, R. D. (1988). Finding the face in the crowd: An anger superiority effect. *Journal of Personality and Social Psychology, 54,* 917–924.

Hansen, J., & Wänke, M. (2009). Liking what's familiar: The importance of unconscious familiarity in the mere-exposure effect. *Social Cognition, 27,* 161–182.

Hansen, N. B., Lambert, M. J., & Forman, E. M. (2002). The psychotherapy dose-response effect and its implications for treatment delivery services. *Clinical Psychology: Science and Practice, 9,* 329–343.

Hanson, R. F., Self-Brown, S., Fricker-Elhai, A., Kilpatrick, D. G., Saunders, B. E., & Resnick, H. (2006). Relations among parental substance use, violence, violence exposure, and mental health. *Addictive Behaviors, 31,* 1988–2001.

Happé, F. G. E., Winner, E., & Brownell, H. (1998). The getting of wisdom: Theory of mind in old age. *Developmental Psychology, 34,* 358–362.

Harackiewicz, J. M., Barron, K. E., Tauer, J. M., & Elliot, A. J. (2002). Predicting success in college: A longitudinal study of achievement goals and ability measures as predictors of interest and performance from freshman year through graduation. *Journal of Educational Psychology, 94,* 562–575.

Hare, R. D. (1991). *The Hare Psychopathy Checklist-Revised.* Toronto, Canada: Multi-Health Systems.

Harkness, K. L., & Stewart, J. O. (2009). Symptom specificity and the prospective generation of life events in adolescence. *Journal of Abnormal Psychology, 118,* 278–287.

Harley, K., & Reese, E. (1999). Origins of autobiographical memory. *Developmental Psychology, 35,* 1338–1348.

Harlow, H. F. (1958). The nature of love. *The American Psychologist, 13,* 673–685.

Harlow, H. F., & Suomi, S. J. (1970). The nature of love—simplified. *American Psychologist, 25,* 161–168.

Harlow, J. M. (1868). Recovery from the passage of an iron bar through the head. *Massachusetts Medical Society, 2,* 327.

Harmon-Jones, E., Brehm, J. W., Greenberg, J., Simon, L., & Nelson, D. E. (1996). Evidence that the production of aversive consequences is not necessary to create cognitive dissonance. *Journal of Personality and Social Psychology, 70,* 5–16.

Harris, C. (2002, August 27). Amazing memory for digits still loses track of car keys. *Naples Daily News.*

Harris, S. L. (1981). A letter from the editor on loss and trust. *Clinical Psychologist, 34*(3), 3.

Harrison, J. E., & Baron-Cohen, S. C. (1997). Synaesthesia: A review of psychological theories. In S. C. Baron et al. (Eds.), *Synaesthesia: Classic and contemporary readings.* Oxford, England: Blackwell.

Hart, J. W., Bridgett, D. J., & Karau, S. J. (2001). Coworker ability and effort as determinants of individual effort on a collective task. *Group Dynamics, 5,* 181–190.

Hart, J. W., Karau, S. J., Stasson, M. F., & Kerr, N. A. (2004). Achievement motivation, expected coworker performance, and collective task motivation: Working hard or hardly working? *Journal of Applied Social Psychology, 34,* 984–1000.

Hart, W., Albarracín, D., Eagly, A. H., Lindberg, M. J., Merrill, L., & Brechan, I. (2009). Feeling validated versus being correct: A meta-analysis of selective exposure to information. *Psychological Bulletin, 135,* 555–588.

Hartshorne, H., & May, A. (1928). *Studies in the nature of character: Vol. 1. Studies in deceit.* New York: Macmillan.

Hartwell, L., Hood, L., Goldberg, M. L., et al. (2010). *Genetics: From genes to genome.* New York: McGraw-Hill.

Harway, M. (2005). *Handbook of couples therapy.* New York: Wiley.

Haskell, W. L., Alderman, E. L., Fair, J. M., et al. (1994). Effects of intensive multiple risk factor reduction on coronary atherosclerosis and clinical cardiac events in men and women with coronary artery disease. *Circulation, 89,* 975–990.

Haslam, S. A., & Reicher, S. (2007). Beyond the banality of evil: Three dynamics of an interactionist social psychology of tyranny. *Personality and Social Psychology Bulletin, 33,* 615–622.

Hass, M., & Graydon, K. (2009). Sources of resilience among successful foster youth. *Children and Youth Services Review, 3,* 457–463.

Hassin, R. R., Uleman, J. S., & Bargh, J. A. (2005). *The new unconscious.* New York: Oxford University Press.

Hatfield, E. (1988). Passionate and companionate love. In R. J. Sternberg & M. L. Barnes (Eds.), *The psychology of love.* New Haven, CT: Yale University Press.

Hauri, P. (1982). *The sleep disorders* (2nd ed.). Kalamazoo, MI: Upjohn.

Hausmann, M., Schoofs, D., Rosenthal, H. S., & Jordan, K, (2009). Interactive effects of sex hormones and gender stereotypes on cognitive sex differences—A psychobiosocial approach. *Psychoneuroendocrinology, 34,* 389–401.

Hawkins, D. L., Pepler, D. J., & Craig, W. M. (2001). Naturalistic observations of peer interventions in bullying. *Social Development, 10,* 512–527.

Hawley, P., & Little, T. D. (2002). Evolutionary and developmental perspectives on the agentic self. In D. Cervone & W. Mischel (Eds.), *Advances in personality science.* New York: Guilford Press.

Hayes, S. C., Luoma, J., Bond, F., Masuda, A., & Lillis, J. (2006). Acceptance and Commitment Therapy: Model, processes, and outcomes. *Behaviour Research and Therapy, 44,* 1–25.

Haynes, S. N. (2000). Behavioral assessment of adults. In G. Goldstein & M. Hersen (Eds.), *Handbook of psychological assessment* (3rd ed.). New York: Elsevier.

Hayslip, B., & Panek, P. E. (1989). *Adult development and aging.* New York: Harper & Row.

Hazan, C., & Diamond, L. M. (2000). The place of attachment in human mating. *Review of General Psychology, 4,* 186–204.

Healy, D. (2004). *Let them eat Prozac: The unhealthy relationship between the pharmaceutical industry and depression.* New York: New York University Press.

Hearold, S. (1986). A synthesis of 1043 effects of television on social behavior. In G. Comstock (Ed.), *Public communications and behavior* (Vol. 1). New York: Academic Press.

Heath, A. C., Kendler, K. S., Eaves, L. J., & Martin, N. G. (1990). Evidence for genetic influences on sleep disturbance and sleep pattern in twins. *Sleep, 13,* 318–335.

Heath, R. G. (1972). Pleasure and brain activity in man. *Journal of Nervous and Mental Disease, 154,* 3–18.

Heather, N. (2006). Controlled drinking, harm reduction and their roles in the response to alcohol-related problems. *Addiction Research and Theory, 14,* 7–18.

Heatherton, T. F., Macrae, C. N., & Kelley, W. M. (2004). What the social brain sciences can tell us about the self. *Current Directions in Psychological Science, 13,* 190–193.

Heaton, T. B. (2002). Factors contributing to increasing marital stability in the U.S. *Journal of Family Issues, 23,* 392–409.

Heerey, E. A., Keltner, D., & Capps, L. M. (2003). Making sense of self-conscious emotion: Linking theory of mind and emotion in children with autism. *Emotion, 3,* 394–400.

Heider, F. (1958). *The psychology of interpersonal relations.* New York: Wiley.

Heimpel, S. A., Wood, J. V., Marshall, M. A., & Brown, J. D. (2002). Do people with low self-esteem really want to feel better? Self-esteem differences in motivation to repair negative moods. *Journal of Personality and Social Psychology, 82,* 128–147.

Heine, S. J., Kitayama, S., Lehman, D. R., Takata, T., Ide, E., et al. (2000). *Divergent consequences of success and failure in Japan and North America: An investigation of self-improving motivations and malleable selves.* Vancouver: University of British Columbia.

Heinrichs, R. W. (2001). *In search of madness: Schizophrenia and neuroscience.* New York: Oxford University Press.

Heller, M. A., & Schiff, W. (Eds.). (1991). *The psychology of touch.* Hillsdale, NJ: Erlbaum.

Hellerstein, D., Yankowitch, P., Rosenthal, J., et al. (1993). A randomized double-blind study of fluoxetine versus placebo in the treatment of dysthymia. *American Journal of Psychiatry, 150,* 1169–1175.

Helliwell, J. F., & Putnam, R. D. (2004). The social context of well-being. *Philosophical Transactions of the Royal Society, 359,* 1435–1446.

Helson, R., Jones, C., & Kwan, V. S. Y. (2002). Personality change over 40 years of adulthood: Hierarchical linear modeling analyses of two longitudinal samples. *Journal of Personality and Social Psychology, 83,* 752–766.

Hennessey, T. M., Rucker, W. B., & McDiarmid, C. G. (1979). Classical conditioning in paramecia. *Animal Learning & Behavior, 7,* 417–423.

Henningsen, D. D., Henningsen, M. L. M., Eden, J., & Cruz, M. G. (2006). Examining the symptoms of groupthink and retrospective sensemaking. *Small Group Research, 37,* 36–64.

Herd, S .A., Banich, M. T., & O'Reilly, R. C. (2006). Neural mechanisms of cognitive control: An integrative model of stroop task performance and fMRI data. *Journal of Cognitive Neuroscience, 18,* 22–32.

Herek, G. M. (2000). The psychology of sexual prejudice. *Current Directions in Psychological Science, 9,* 19–22.

Herek, G. M. (2002). Gender gaps in public opinion about lesbians and gay men. *Public Opinion Quarterly, 66,* 40–66.

Herman, D. B., Susser, E. S., Jandorf, L., Lavelle, J., & Bromet, E. J. (1998). Homelessness among individuals with psychotic disorders hospitalized for the first time: Findings from the Suffolk County Mental Health Project. *American Journal of Psychiatry, 155,* 109–113.

Hernandez, L. M., & Blazer, D. G. (2007). *Genes, behavior, and the social environment: Moving beyond the nature/nurture debate.* Washington, DC: National Academies Press.

Hernnstein, R. J., & Murray, C. (1994). *The bell curve: Intelligence and class structure in American life.* New York: Free Press.

Herrington, R., & Lader, M. H. (1996). *Biological treatments in psychiatry* (2nd ed.). New York: Oxford University Press.

Herrmann, D., Raybeck, D., & Gruneberg, M. (2002). *Improving memory and study skills: Advances in theory and practice.* Ashland, OH: Hogrefe & Huber.

Hersen, M. (2002). *Clinical behavior therapy: Adults and children.* New York: Wiley.

Hersen, M. (2003). *Effective brief therapies.* New York: Academic Press.

Hersen, M. (2006). *Clinician's handbook of adult behavioral assessment.* New York: Academic Press.

Herz, M., & Marder, S. (2002). *Schizophrenia: A comprehensive text.* New York: Williams & Wilkins.

Herzog, H. A. (2005). Dealing with the animal research controversy. In C. K. Akins, S. Panicker, & C. L. Cunningham (Eds.), *Laboratory animals in research and teaching: Ethics, care, and methods.* Washington, DC: American Psychological Association.

Hess, E. H. (1959). Imprinting. *Science, 130,* 133–141.

Hess, W. R. (1965). Sleep as phenomenon of the integral organism. In K. Akert, C. Bally, & J. P. Schade (Eds.), *Sleep mechanisms.* New York: Elsevier.

Hetherington, E. M. (1998). Relevant issues in developmental science: Introduction to the special issue. *American Psychologist, 53,* 93–94.

Hetherington, E. M., Bridges, M., & Insabella, G. M. (1998). What matters? What does not? Five perspectives on the association between marital transitions and children's adjustment. *American Psychologist, 53,* 167–184.

Hetherington, E. M., & Stanley-Hagan, M. (2002). Parenting in divorced and remarried families. In M. H. Bornstein (Ed.), *Handbook of parenting: Being and becoming a parent* (2nd ed., Vol. 3). Mahwah, NJ: Erlbaum.

Hewstone, M., Rubin, M., & Willis, H. (2002). Intergroup bias. *Annual Review of Psychology, 53,* 575–604.

Heylighen, F. (1992). A cognitive-systemic reconstruction of Maslow's theory of self-actualization. *Behavioral Science, 37,* 39–58.

Higbee, K. L. (2001). *Your memory: How it works and how to improve it.* New York: Marlowe.

Higgins, E. T. (1996). The "self digest": Self-knowledge serving self-regulatory functions. *Journal of Personality and Social Psychology, 71,* 1062–1083.

Hilgard, E. R. (1977). *Divided consciousness: Multiple controls in human thought and action.* New York: Wiley.

Hilgard, E. R. (1994). Neodissociation. In S. J. Lynn & J. W. Rhue (Eds.), *Dissociation: Clinical and theoretical perspectives.* New York: Guilford Press.

Hill, C. A. (1987). Affiliation motivation: People who need people but in different ways. *Journal of Personality and Social Psychology, 52,* 1008–1018.

Hill, J. L., Brooks-Gunn, J., & Waldfogel, J. (2003). Sustained effects of high participation in an early intervention for low-birth-weight premature infants. *Developmental Psychology, 2003,* 730–744.

Hill, M. M., Dodson, B. B., Hill, E. W., & Fox, J. (1995). An infant sonicguide intervention program for a child with a visual disability. *Journal of Visual Impairment and Blindness, 89,* 329–336.

Hillman, D. C., Siffre, M., Milano, G., & Halberg, F. (1994). Free-running psycho-physiologic circadians and three-month pattern in a woman isolated in a cave. *New Trends in Experimental and Clinical Psychiatry, 10,* 127–133.

Hillman, J. L., Neubrander, J., & Snyder, S. J. (2007). *Childhood autism.* New York: Routledge.

Hines, M. (2005). *Brain gender.* New York: Oxford University Press.

Hirtz, D., Thurman, D. J., Gwinn-Hardy, K., Mohamed, M., Chaudhuri, A. R., & Zalutsky, R. (2007). How common are the "common" neurologic disorders? *Neurology, 68,* 326–337.

Ho, C. S. H., Chan, D. W. O., Leung, P. W. L., Lee, S. H., & Tsang, S. M. (2005). Reading-related cognitive deficits in developmental dyslexia, attention-deficit/hyperactivity disorder, and developmental coordination disorder among Chinese children. *Reading Research Quarterly, 40,* 318–337.

Hobert, O. (Ed.). (2009). *Development of neural circuitry.* New York: Academic Press.

Hobfoll, S. E., Palmieri, P. A., Johnson, P. A., et al. (2009). Trajectories of resilience, resistance, and distress during ongoing terrorism: The case of Jews and Arabs in Israel. *Journal of Consulting and Clinical Psychology, 77,* 138–148.

Hobson, J. A. (1996). *Chemistry of conscious states: How the brain changes its mind.* Boston: Little, Brown.

Hobson, J. A. (2007). Current understanding of cellular models of REM expression. In D. Barrett & P. McNamara (Eds.), *The new science of dreaming: Vol.1. Biological aspects.* Westport, CT: Praeger/Greenwood.

Hodges, J., & Tizard, B. (1989). Social and family relationships of ex-institutional adolescents. *Journal of Child Psychology and Psychiatry, 30,* 77–97.

Hoffart, A., & Martinson, E. W. (1991). Mental health locus of control in agoraphobia and depression: A longitudinal study of inpatients. *Psychological Reports, 68,* 1011–1018.

Hoffer, A., & Youngren, V. R. (2004). Is free association still at the core of psychoanalysis? *International Journal of Psychoanalysis, 85,* 1489–1492.

Hoffman, H. G., Patterson, D. R., Canougher, G. J., & Sharar, S. R. (2001). Effectiveness of virtual reality-based pain control with multiple treatments. *Clinical Journal of Pain, 17,* 229–235.

Hofmann, S. G., Moscovitch, D. A., & Heinrichs, N. (2004). Evolutionary mechanisms of fear and anxiety. In P. Gilbert (Ed.), *Evolutionary theory and cognitive therapy* (pp. 119–136). New York: Springer.

Hogan, R. (1983). A socioanalytic theory of personality. In M. Page & R. Dienstbier (Eds.), *Nebraska Symposium on Motivation, 1982.* Lincoln: University of Nebraska Press.

Holahan, C. J., & Moos, R. H. (1990). Life stressors, resistance factors, and improved psychological functioning: An extension of the stress resistance paradigm. *Journal of Personality and Social Psychology, 58,* 909–917.

Holden, G. W. (2002). Perspectives on the effects of corporal punishment: Comment on Gershoff (2002). *Psychological Bulletin, 128,* 590–595.

Holden, G. W. (2010). *Parenting: A dynamic perspective.* Thousand Oaks, CA: Sage.

Hollon, S. D. (1996). The efficacy and effectiveness of psychotherapy relative to medications. *American Psychologist, 51,* 1025–1030.

Hollon, S. D., & Beck, A. T. (1994). Cognitive and cognitive-behavioral therapies. In A. E. Bergin & S. L. Garfield (Eds.), *Handbook of psychotherapy and behavior change.* New York: Wiley.

Hooper, J., & Teresi, M. (1986). *The three-pound universe.* New York: Macmillan.

Hopf, W. H., Günter, L., & Weiss, R. H. (2008). Media violence and youth violence: A 2-year longitudinal study. *Journal of Media Psychology: Theories, Methods, and Applications, 20,* 79–96.

Hopko, D. R., & Mullane, C. M. (2008). Exploring the relation of depression and overt behavior with daily diaries. *Behaviour Research and Therapy, 46,* 1085–1089.

Horn, J. (1985). Remodeling old models of intelligence. In B. B. Wolman (Ed.), *Handbook of intelligence: Theory, measurement, and application.* New York: Wiley.

Horn, J. L., & Blankston, N. (2005). Foundation for better understanding of cognitive abilities. In D. P. Flanagan & P. L. Harrison (Eds.), *Contemporary intellectual assessment: Theories, tests, and issues* (2nd ed.). New York: Guilford Press.

Horn, J. L., & Cattell, R. C. (1966). Refinement and test of the theory of fluid and crystallized general intelligences. *Journal of Educational Psychology, 57,* 253–270.

Horn, J. L., & Masunaga, H. (2000). On the emergence of wisdom: Expertise development. *Understanding wisdom: Sources, science, & society.* Philadelphia: Templeton Foundation Press.

Horn, J. L., & Noll, J. (1997). Human cognitive capabilities: Gf-Gc theory. In D. P. Flanagan, J. L. Genshaft, & P. L. Harrison (Eds.), *Contemporary intellectual assessment: Theories, tests, and issues.* New York: Guilford Press.

House, J. S., Landis, K. R., & Umberson, D. (1988). Social relationships and health. *Science, 241,* 540–545.

Houser-Marko, L., & Sheldon, K. M. (2008). Eyes on the prize or nose to the grindstone? The effects of level of goal evaluation on mood and motivation. *Personality and Social Psychology Bulletin, 34,* 1556–1569.

Howard, I. P. (2002). Depth perception. In H. Pashler & S.Yantis (Eds.), *Steven's handbook of experimental psychology: Vol. 1. Sensation and perception* (3rd ed.). New York: Wiley.

Howard, K. I., Kopta, S. M., Krause, M. S., & Orlinsky, D. E. (1986). The dose-effect relationship in psychotherapy. *American Psychologist, 41,* 159–164.

Howard, K. I., Lueger, R. J., Maling, M. S., & Martinovich, Z. (1993). A phase model of psychotherapy outcome: Causal mediation of change. *Journal of Consulting and Clinical Psychology, 61,* 678–685.

Hu, Y., Ericsson, K. A., Yang, D., & Lu, C. (2009). Superior self-paced memorization of digits in spite of a normal digit span: The structure of a memorist's skill. *Memory and Cognition, 35,* 1426–1442.

Hubbard, E. M., & Ramachandran, V. S. (2005). Neurocognitive mechanisms of synesthesia. *Neuron, 48,* 509–520.

Hubbell, V. (2009, para. 8). Dislecksia: The movie. *Director's Statement.* Retrieved Nov. 29, 2009, from http://www.capturedtimeproductions .com/films/dislecksia_old.html

Hubel, D. H., & Wiesel, T. N. (1979). Brain mechanisms of vision. *Scientific American, 241,* 150–162.

Hubel, D. H., & Wiesel, T. N. (2005). *Brain and visual perception: The story of a 25-year collaboration.* New York: Oxford University Press.

Hubert, V., Beaunieux, H., Chételat, G., Platel, H., Landeau, B., Viader, F., et al. (2009). Age-related changes in the cerebral substrates of cognitive procedural learning. *Human Brain Mapping, 30,* 1374–1386.

Hublin, C., Kaprio, J., Partinen, M., Heikkila, K., & Koskenvuo, M. (1997). Prevalence and genetics of sleepwalking: A population-based twin study. *Neurology, 48,* 177–181.

Huddy, L., & Virtanen, S. (1995). Subgroup differentiation and subgroup bias among Latinos as a function of familiarity and positive distinctiveness. *Journal of Personality and Social Psychology, 68,* 97–108.

Hudson, W. (1960). Pictorial depth perception in sub-cultural groups in Africa. *Journal of Social Psychology, 52,* 183–208.

Huesmann, L. R. (2010). Nailing the coffin shut on doubts that violent video games stimulate aggression: Comment on Anderson et al. (2010). *Psychological Bulletin, 136,* 179–181.

Huesmann, L. R., Moise-Titus, J., Podolski, C. L., & Eron, L. D. (2003). Longitudinal relations between children's exposure to TV violence and their aggressive and violent behavior in young adulthood: 1977–1992. *Developmental Psychology, 39,* 201–221.

Huesmann, L. R., & Taylor, L. D. (2006). The role of media violence in violent behavior. *Annual Review of Public Health, 27,* 393–415.

Huettel, S. A., Song, A. W., & McCarthy, G. (2005). *Functional magnetic resonance imaging.* New York: Sinauer.

Hugdahl, K., & Davidson, R. A. (Eds.). (2005). *The asymmetrical brain.* Boston: MIT Press.

Hugenberg, K., & Bodenhausen, G. V. (2003). Facing prejudice: Implicit prejudice and the perception of facial threat. *Psychological Science, 14,* 640–643.

Hull, C. L. (1943). *Principles of behavior: An introduction to behavior theory.* New York: Appleton-Century.

Human Genome Project. (2007). Retrieved May 16, 2007, from http://www.genome.gov/

Hunecke, M., Haustein, S., Böhler, S., & Grischkat, S. (2010). Attitude-based target groups to reduce the ecological impact of daily mobility behavior. *Environment and Behavior, 42,* 3–43.

Hunt, E. (1995). The role of intelligence in modern society. *American Scientist, 83,* 356–368.

Hunt, E. (1997). The status of the concept of intelligence. *Japanese Psychological Research, 39,* 1–11.

Hunt, E. (2007). P-FIT: A major contribution to theories of intelligence. *Behavioral and Brain Sciences, 30,* 158–159.

Hunter, C. L., Goodie, J. L., Oordt, M. S., & Dobmeyer, A. C. (2009). Pain disorders. In C. L. Hunter, J. L.Goodie, M. S. Oordt, & A. C. Dobmeyer (Eds.), *Integrated behavioral health in primary care: Step-by-step guidance for assessment and intervention.* Washington, DC: American Psychological Association.

Hunter, J. E., & Hunter, R. F. (1984). Validity and utility of alternative predictors of job performance. *Psychological Bulletin, 96,* 72–98.

Huon, G. F., Mingyi, Q., Oliver, K., & Xiao, G. (2002). A large-scale survey of eating disorder symptomatology among female adolescents in the People's Republic of China. *International Journal of Eating Disorders, 32,* 192–205.

Hussaini, S. A., Komischke, B., Menzel, R., & Lachnit, H. (2007). Forward and backward second-order Pavlovian conditioning in honeybees. *Learning & Memory, 14,* 678–683.

Huttenlocher, P. R. (2002). *Neural plasticity.* Cambridge, MA: Harvard University Press.

Hutton, S. (2009). Multiple choice and true/false test-taking tips. *Education.com.* Retrieved October 24, 2009, from http://www.education.com/magazine/article/Test_Tips_TrueFalse_Multiple/

Huurre, T., Junkkari, H., & Aro, H. (2006). Long-term psychosocial effects of parental divorce: A follow-up study from adolescence to adulthood. *European Archives of Psychiatry and Clinical Neuroscience, 256,* 256–263.

Hyde, J. S., & DeLamater, J. (2003). *Understanding human sexuality* (8th ed.). Boston: McGraw-Hill.

Hyde, M., Ferrie, J., Higgs, P., Mein, G., & Nazroo, J. (2004). The effects of pre-retirement factors and retirement route on circumstances in retirement: Findings from the Whitehall II study. *Ageing & Society, 24,* 279–296.

Iacono, W. G. (2008). Effective policing: Understanding how polygraph tests work and are used. *Criminal Justice and Behavior, 35,* 1295–1308.

Iacono, W. G.) & Patrick, C. J. (2006). Polygraph ("lie detector") testing: Current status and emerging trends. In I. B. Weiner & A. K. Hess (Eds.), *The handbook of forensic psychology* (3rd ed.). Hoboken, NJ: Wiley.

Ickes, W., Holloway, R., Stinson, L. L., & Hoodenpyle, T. G. (2006). Self-monitoring in social interaction: The centrality of self-affect. *Journal of Personality, 74,* 659–684.

Ikemi, Y., & Nakagawa, A. (1962). A psychosomatic study of contagious dermatitis. *Kyushu Journal of Medical Science, 13,* 335–350.

Indlekofer, F., Piechatzek, M., Daamen, M., Glasmacher, C., Lieb, R., Pfister, H., et al. (2009). Reduced memory and attention performance in a population-based sample of young adults with a moderate lifetime use of cannabis, ecstasy and alcohol. *Journal of Psychopharmacology, 23,* 495–509.

Ingelhart, R., & Rabier, J. R. (1986). Aspirations adapt to situations—but why are the Belgians so much happier than the French? A cross-cultural study of the quality of life. In F. M. Andrews (Ed.), *Research on the quality of life*. Ann Arbor, MI: Institute for Social Research, University of Michigan.

Ingold, C. H. (1989). Locus of control and use of public information. *Psychological Reports, 64*, 603–607.

Inhelder, B., & Piaget, J. (1958). *The growth of logical thinking from childhood to adolescence*. New York: Basic Books.

Institute of Education Sciences. (2010). *About us*. Retrieved February 5, 2010, from http://ies.ed.gov/aboutus/

International Dyslexia Association. (2008). *Dyslexia basics*. Retrieved December 14, 2009, from http://www.interdys.org/ewebeditpro5/upload/Basics_Fact_Sheet_5-08-08.pdf

International Union of Psychological Sciences. (2009). *National members*. Retrieved February 5, 2010, from http://www.iupsys.net/index.php/members/national-members

Intraub, H., Gottesman, C. V., Willey, E. V., & Zuk, I. J. (1996). Boundary extension for briefly glimpsed photographs: Do common perceptual processes result in unexpected memory distortions? *Journal of Memory and Language, 35*, 118–134.

Iranzo, A., & Aparicio, J. (2009). A lesson from anatomy: Focal brain lesions causing REM sleep behavior disorder. *Sleep Medicine, 10*, 9–12.

Irie, M., Maeda, M., & Nagata, S. (2001). Can conditioned histamine release occur under urethane anesthesia in guinea pigs? *Physiology and Behavior, 72*, 567–573.

Irwin, A. R., & Gross, A. M. (1995). Cognitive tempo, violent video games, and aggressive behavior in young boys. *Journal of Family Violence, 10*, 337–350.

Irwin, J. R., & McCarthy, D. (1998). Psychophysics: Methods and analyses of signal detection. In K. A. Lattal & M. Perone (Eds.), *Handbook of research methods in human operant behavior: Applied clinical psychology*. New York: Plenum Press.

Irwin, M., Daniels, M., & Weiner, H. (1987). Immune and neuroendocrine changes during bereavement. *Psychiatric Clinics of North America, 10*, 449–465.

Isaacs, K. S. (1998). *Uses of emotion: Nature's vital gift*. New York: Praeger.

Isaacson, R. L. (2002). Unsolved mysteries: The hippocampus. *Behavioral and Cognitive Neuroscience Reviews, 1*, 87–107.

Ishikawa, S. L., Raine, A., Lencz, T., Bihrle, S., & Lacasse, L. (2001). Autonomic stress reactivity and executive functions in successful and unsuccessful criminal psychopaths from the community. *Journal of Abnormal Psychology, 110*, 423–432.

Itard, J. M. G. (1962). *The wild boy of Aveyron* (G. Humphrey & M. Humphrey, Trans.). New York: Appleton-Century-Crofts. (Original work published 1894)

Ito, T. A., & Cacioppo, J. T. (2000). Electrophysiological evidence of implicit and explicit categorization processes. *Journal of Experimental Social Psychology, 36*, 660–676.

Itti, L., & Rees, G. (2005). *Neurobiology of attention*. St. Louis: Elsevier.

Ivey, A. E., D'Andrea, M. D., Ivey, M. B., & Simek-Morgan, L. (2006). *Theories of counseling and psychotherapy: A multicultural perspective*. Boston: Allyn & Bacon.

Iwasa, N. (2001). Moral reasoning among adults: Japan-U.S. comparison. In H. Shimizu & R. A. LeVine (Eds.), *Japanese frames of mind: Cultural perspectives on human development*. New York: Cambridge University Press.

Iwawaki, S., & Sarmany-Schuller, I. (2001). Cross-cultural (Japan-Slovakia) comparison of some aspects of sleeping patterns and anxiety. *Studia Psychologica, 43*, 215–224.

Izac, S. M., & Eeg, T. R. (2006). Basic anatomy and physiology of sleep. *American Journal of Electroneurodiagnostic Technology, 46*, 18–38.

Izard, C. (Ed.). (1982). *Measuring emotions in infants and children*. Cambridge, England: Cambridge University Press.

Izard, C. E. (1989). The structure and functions of emotions: Implications for cognition, motivation, and personality. In I. S. Cohen (Ed.), *The G. Stanley Hall Lecture Series* (Vol. 9). Washington, DC: American Psychological Association.

Jablensky, A., Sartorius, N., Enberg, C., Anker, M., Korten, A., et al. (1992). Schizophrenia: Manifestation, incidence, and course in different cultures: A World Health Organization ten-country study. *Psychological Medicine Monograph Supplement 20*. Cambridge, England: Cambridge University Press.

Jackson, A., Morrow, J., Hill, D., & Dishman, R. (1999). *Physical activity for health and fitness*. Champaign, IL: Human Kinetics.

Jackson, N., & Butterfield, E. (1986). A conception of giftedness designed to promote research. In R. J. Sternberg & J. E. Davidson (Eds.), *Conceptions of giftedness*. New York: Cambridge University Press.

Jackson, P. B., & Williams, D. R. (2006). Culture, race/ethnicity, and depression. In C. L. Keyes & S. H. Goodman (Eds.), *Women and depression: A handbook for the social, behavioral, and biomedical sciences*. New York: Cambridge University Press.

Jacobs, B. L. (2004). Depression: The brain finally gets into the act. *Current Directions in Psychological Science, 13*, 103–106.

Jacobson, N. S., & Christensen, A. (1996). *Integrative couple therapy: Promoting acceptance and change*. New York: Norton.

Jacobson, N. S., Martell, C. R., & Dimidjian, S. (2001). Behavioral activation therapy for depression: Returning to contextual roots. *Clinical Psychology: Science and Practice, 8*, 255–270.

Jaffee, S. R., Moffitt, T. E., Caspi, A., & Taylor, A. (2003). Life with (or without) father: The benefits of living with two biological parents depend on the father's antisocial behavior. *Child Development, 74*, 109–126.

James, W. (1879). Are we automata? *Mind, 4*, 1–22.

James, W. (1950). *Principles of psychology* (Vol. 2). New York: Dover. (Original work published 1890)

Jamison, K. (1995, February). Manic-depressive illness and creativity. *Scientific American*, 63–67.

Jang, C.-G., Lee, S.-Y., Yoo, J.-H., Yan, J.-J., Song, D.-K., Loh, H. H., & Ho, I. K. (2003). Impaired water maze learning performance in mu-opioid receptor knockout mice. *Molecular Brain Research, 117*, 68–72.

Jang, K. (2005). *The behavioral genetics of psychopathology: A clinical guide*. Hillsdale, NJ: Erlbaum.

Janis, I. L. (1982). *Groupthink: Psychological studies of policy decisions and fiascos* (2nd ed.). Boston: Houghton Mifflin.

Janus, S. S., & Janus, C. L. (1993). *The Janus report on sexual behavior*. New York: Wiley.

Jay, T., King, K., & Duncan, T. (2006). Memories of punishment for cursing. *Sex Roles, 55*, 123–133.

Jayaratne, T. E., Gelman, S. A., Feldbaum, M., Sheldon, J. P., Petty, E. M., & Kardia, S. L. (2009). The perennial debate: Nature, nurture, or choice? Black and White Americans' explanations for individual differences. *Review of General Psychology, 13*, 24–33.

Jeffery, K. J. (2008). The place cells—Cognitive map or memory system? In S. J. Y. Mizumori (Ed.), *Hippocampal place fields: Relevance to learning and memory*. New York: Oxford University Press.

Jencks, C., & Phillips, M. (Eds). (1998). *The Black-White test score gap*. Washington, DC: Brookings Institution.

Jenike, M. A. (1998). *Obsessive-compulsive disorders*. St. Louis, MO: Mosby.

Jenkin, M., & Harris, L. (2005). *Seeing spatial form*. New York: Oxford University Press.

Jenkins, J., Simpson, A., Dunn, J., Rasbash, J., & O'Connor, T. G. (2005). Mutual influence of marital conflict and children's behavior problems: Shared and nonshared family risks. *Child Development, 76*, 24–39.

Jennings, B. M. (1990). Stress, locus of control, social support, and psychological symptoms among head nurses. *Research in Nursing & Health, 13*, 393–401.

Jensen, A. (1969). How much can we boost IQ and scholastic achievement? *Harvard Educational Review, 39*, 2.

Jensen, A. (1980). *Bias in mental testing*. New York: Free Press.

Jensen, A. R. (1998). The *g* factor and the design of education. In R. J. Sternberg & W. M. Williams (Eds.), *Intelligence, instruction, and assessment: Theory into practice*. Mahwah, NJ: Erlbaum.

Jensen, L. A., Arnett, J. J., Feldman, S. S., & Cauffman, E. (2004). The right to do wrong: Lying to parents among adolescents and emerging adults. *Journal of Youth and Adolescence, 33*, 101–112.

Jensen, M. P., Turner, J. A., & Romano, J. M. (2001). Changes in beliefs, catastrophizing, and coping are associated with improvement in multidisciplinary pain treatment. *Journal of Consulting and Clinical Psychology, 69*, 655–662.

Jensen, R. (2006). Behaviorism, latent learning, and cognitive maps: Needed revisions in introductory psychology textbooks. *The Behavior Analyst, 29*, 187–209.

Jéquier, E. (2002). Pathways to obesity. *International Journal of Obesity and Related Metabolic Disorders, 26*, 12–17.

Joanisse, M. F. (2009). Model-based approaches to child language disorders. In R. G. Schwartz (Ed.), *Handbook of child language disorders*. New York: Psychology.

John, O. P., & Srivastava, S. (1999). The Big Five trait taxonomy: History, measurement, and theoretical perspectives. In L. A. Pervin & O. P. John (Eds.), *Handbook of personality: Theory and research*. New York: Guilford Press.

Johns, M., Schmader, T., & Martens, A. (2005). Knowing is half the battle: Teaching stereotype threat as a means of improving women's math performance. *Psychological Science, 16*, 175–179.

Johnson, A. M., Wadsworth, J., Wellings, K., & Bradshaw, S. (1992). Sexual lifestyles and HIV risk. *Nature, 360,* 410–412.

Johnson, J. L., & Newport, E. L. (1989). Critical period effects in second language learning: The influence of maturational state on the acquisition of English as a second language. *Cognitive Psychology, 21,* 60–99.

Johnson, M. W., Richards, W. A., & Griffiths, R. R. (2008). Human hallucinogen research: Guidelines for safety. *Journal of Psychopharmacology, 22,* 603–620.

Johnston, L. D., O'Malley, P. M., Bachman, J. G., & Schulenberg, J. E. (2009). *Monitoring the future national survey results on drug use, 1975–2008: Volume II. College students and adults ages 19–50* (NIH Publication No. 09-7403, p. 305). Bethesda, MD: National Institute on Drug Abuse.

Johnston, V. S., Hagel, R., Franklin, M., Fink, B., & Grammer, K. (2001). Male facial attractiveness: Evidence for hormone-mediated adaptive design. *Evolution and Human Behavior, 22,* 251–267.

Joiner, T. E., & Coyne, J. C. (Eds.). (1999). *The interactional nature of depression: Advances in interpersonal approaches.* Washington, DC: American Psychological Association.

Joiner, T. E., Jr., Van Orden, K. A., Witte, T. K., Selby, E. A., et al. (2009). Main predictions of the interpersonal-psychological theory of suicidal behavior: Empirical tests in two samples of young adults. *Journal of Abnormal Psychology, 118,* 634–646.

Jones, B. C., Little, A. C., Feinberg, D. R., Penton-Voak, I. S., Tiddeman, B. P., & Perrett, D. I. (2004). The relationship between shape symmetry and perceived skin condition in male facial attractiveness. *Evolution and Human Behavior, 25,* 24–30.

Jones, E., Cumming, J. D., & Horowitz, M. J. (1988). Another look at the nonspecific hypothesis of therapeutic effectiveness. *Journal of Consulting and Clinical Psychology, 56,* 48–55.

Jones, E. E., & Harris, V. A. (1967). The attribution of attitudes. *Journal of Experimental Social Psychology, 3,* 2–24.

Jones, E. G. (2006). *The thalamus.* New York: Cambridge University Press.

Jones, J. T., Pelham, B. W., Carvallo, M., & Mirenberg, M. C. (2004). How do I love thee? Let me count the Js: Implicit egotism and interpersonal attraction. *Journal of Personality and Social Psychology, 87,* 665–683.

Jones, M. C. (1924). A laboratory study of fear: The case of Peter. *Pedagogical Seminary, 31,* 308–315.

Jones, P. (2010). *The genetic code.* New York: Facts on File, Inc.

Joseph, R. (2000). The evolution of sex differences in language, sexuality, and visual-spatial skills. *Archives of Sexual Behavior, 29,* 35–66.

Josephs, R. A., Bosson, J. K., & Jacobs, C. G. (2003). Self-esteem maintenance processes: Why self-esteem may be resistant to change. *Personality and Social Psychology Bulletin, 29,* 920–933.

Joslyn, S. L., Nadav-Greenberg, L., Taing, M. U., & Nichols, R. M. (2009). The effects of wording on the understanding and use of uncertainty information in a threshold forecasting decision. *Applied Cognitive Psychology, 23,* 55–72.

Julien, R. (2008). *A primer of drug action* (11th ed.). New York: Worth.

Julien, R. M. (2005). *A primer of drug action: A comprehensive guide to the actions, uses, and side effects of psychoactive drugs* (10th ed.). New York: Worth.

Jung, D-I., Ha, J., Kang, B.T., et al. (2009). A comparison of autologous and allogenic marrow-derived myeschemal stem cell transplantation in canine spinal cord injury. *Journal of the Neurological Sciences, 285,* 67–77.

Jung, J. (1995). Ethnic group and gender differences in the relationship between personality and coping. *Anxiety, Stress & Coping: An International Journal, 8,* 113–126.

Jung, R. E., & Haier, R. J. (2007). The Parieto-Frontal Integration Theory (P-FIT) of intelligence: Converging neuroimaging evidence. *Behavioral and Brain Sciences, 30,* 135–154.

Jureidini, J. N., Doecke, C. J., Mansfield, P. R., Haby, M. M., Menkes, D. B., & Tonkin, A. L. (2004). Efficacy and safety of antidepressants for children and adolescents. *British Medical Journal, 328(7444),* 879–883.

Jurist, E. L., Slade, A., & Bergner, S. (2008). *Reflecting on the future of psychoanalysis: Mentalization, internalization, and representation.* New York: Other Press.

Kaas, A., Weigelt, S., Roebroeck, A., Kohler, A., & Muckli, L. (2010). Imagery of a moving object: The role of occipital cortex and human MT/V5+. *NeuroImage, 49,* 794–804.

Kabat-Zinn, J., Massion, A., Kristeller, J., et al. (1992). Effectiveness of a meditation-based stress reduction intervention in the treatment of anxiety disorders. *American Journal of Psychiatry, 149,* 936–943.

Kagan, J. (1989). Temperamental contributions to social behavior. *American Psychologist, 44,* 668–674.

Kagan, J. (1999). The concept of behavioral inhibition. In L. A. Schmidt & J. Schulkin (Eds.), *Extreme fear, shyness, and social phobia: Origins, biological mechanisms, and clinical outcomes.* New York: Oxford University Press.

Kagan, J., & Fox, N. A. (2006). Biology, culture, and individual differences. In N. Eisenberg, W. Damon, & R. M. Lerner (Eds.), *Handbook of child psychology: Vol. 3, Social, emotional, and personality development* (6th ed). Hoboken, NJ: Wiley.

Kagan, J., Kearsley, R. B., & Zelazo, P. (1978). *Infancy: Its place in human development.* Cambridge, MA: Harvard University Press.

Kagan, J., Reznick, S., & Snidman, N. (1988). Biological bases of childhood shyness. *Science, 240,* 167–171.

Kagitçibasi, C. (1997). Individualism and collectivism. In J. W. Berry, M. H. Segall, & C. Kagitçibasi (Eds.), *Handbook of cross-cultural psychology* (Vol. 3). Boston: Allyn & Bacon.

Kahneman, D., & Frederick, S. (2005). A model of heuristic judgement. In K. Holyoak & R. G. Morrison (Eds.), *The Cambridge handbook of thinking and reasoning.* New York: Cambridge University Press.

Kahneman, D., & Klein, G. (2009). Conditions for intuitive expertise: A failure to disagree. *American Psychologist, 64(6),* 515–526.

Kahneman, D., & Tversky, A. (1979). Prospect theory: An analysis of decisions under risk. *Econometrica, 47,* 263–291.

Kaia, L., Pullmann, H., & Allik, J. (2007). Personality and intelligence as predictors of academic achievement: A cross-sectional study from elementary to secondary school. *Personality and Individual Differences, 42,* 444–451.

Kail, R. (1991). Developmental change in speed of processing during childhood and adolescence. *Psychological Bulletin, 109,* 490–501.

Kail, R. V. (2007). Longitudinal evidence that increases in processing speed and working memory enhance children's reasoning. *Psychological Science, 18,* 312–313.

Kaiser, A., Haller, S., Schmitz, S., & Nitsch, C. (2009). On sex/gender related similarities and differences in fMRI language research. *Brain Research Reviews, 61,* 49–59.

Kaku, M. (2004). *Einstein's cosmos: How Albert Einstein's vision transformed our understanding of space and time.* New York: Norton.

Kalb, C. (2008, February 28). Spare the rod? *Newsweek.* Retrieved December 2, 2009, from http://www.newsweek.com/id/116788

Kaltiala-Heino, R., Marttunen, M., Rantanen, P., & Rimpela, M. (2003). Early puberty is associated with mental health problems in middle adolescence. *Social Science & Medicine, 57,* 1055–1064.

Kamakura, T., Ando, J., & Ono, Y. (2007). Genetic and environmental effects of stability in self-esteem during adolescence. *Personality and Individual Differences, 42,* 181–190.

Kampmann, K. M., Volpicelli, J. R., Mulvaney, F., Rukstalis, M., Alterman, A. I., Pettinati, H., et al. (2002). Cocaine withdrawal severity and urine toxicology results from treatment entry predict outcome in medication trials for cocaine dependence. *Addictive Behaviors, 27,* 251–260.

Kandel, E. R. (2001). The molecular biology of memory storage: A dialogue between genes and synapses. *Science, 294,* 1030–1038.

Kane, H. D., & Brand, C. R. (2006). The variable importance of general intelligence (g) in the cognitive abilities of children and adolescents. *Educational Psychology, 26,* 751–767.

Kanfer, F. H., & Goldstein, A. P. (Eds.). (1991). *Helping people change: A textbook of methods* (4th ed.). New York: Pergamon Press.

Kanner, L. (1943) Autistic disturbance of affective contact. *Nervous Child, 12,* 17–50.

Kanter, J., Busch, A., & Rusch, L. (2009). *Behavioral activation: Distinctive features.* New York: Routledge.

Kaplan, H., & Dove, H. (1987). Infant development among the Ache of eastern Paraguay. *Developmental Psychology, 23,* 190–198.

Kapoula, Z., Ganem, R., Poncet, S., Gintautas, D., Eggert, T., Brémond-Gignac, D., et al. (2009). Free exploration of painting uncovers particularly loose yoking of saccades in dyslexics. *Dyslexia: An International Journal of Research and Practice, 15,* 243–259.

Kaprio, J., Koskenvu, M., & Rita, H. (1987). Mortality after bereavement: A prospective study of 95,647 widowed persons. *American Journal of Public Health, 77,* 283–287.

Karama, S. Ad-Dab'bagh, Y., Haier, R. J., Deary, I. J., et al. (2009). Positive association between cognitive ability and cortical thickness in a representative US sample of healthy 6 to 18 year-olds. *Intelligence, 37,* 145–155.

Karau, S. J., & Williams, K. D. (1993). Social loafing: A meta-analytic review and theoretical integration.

Journal of Personality and Social Psychology, 65, 681–706.

Karau, S. J., & Williams, K. D. (2001). Understanding individual motivation in groups: The collective effort model. In M. E. Turner (Ed.), *Groups at work: Theory and research: Applied social research.* Mahwah, NJ: Erlbaum.

Karon, B. P. (2002). Psychoanalysis: Legitimate and illegitimate concerns. *Psychoanalytic Psychology, 19,* 564–571.

Karpicke, J. D. (2009). Metacognitive control and strategy selection: Deciding to practice retrieval during learning. *Journal of Experimental Psychology, 138,* 469–486.

Karremans, J., Stroebe, W., & Claus, J. (2006). Beyond Vicary's fantasies: The impact of subliminal priming and brand choice. *Journal of Experimental Social Psychology, 42,* 792–798.

Kashima, Y., Yamaguchi, S., Kim, U., Choi, S., Gelfand, M., & Yuki, M. (1995). Culture, gender, and self: A perspective from individualism-collectivism research. *Journal of Personality and Social Psychology, 69,* 925–937.

Kassel, J. D., Wardle, M. C., Heinz, A. J., & Greenstein, J. E. (2010). Cognitive theories of drug effects on emotion. In J. D. Kassel (Ed.), *Substance abuse and emotion.* Washington, DC: American Psychological Association.

Kastenbaum, R. (2000). *The psychology of death* (3rd ed.). New York: Springer.

Katapodi, M. C., Facione, N. C., Humphreys, J. C., & Dodd, M. J. (2005). Perceived breast cancer risk: Heuristic reasoning and search for a dominance structure. *Social Science & Medicine, 60,* 421–432.

Katz, J., & Melzack, R. (1990). Pain "memories" in phantom limbs: Review and clinical observations. *Pain, 43,* 319–336.

Kaye, W. H., Strober, M., & Klump, K. L. (2002). Serotonin neuronal function in anorexia nervosa and bulimia nervosa. In F. Lewis Hall et al. (Eds.), *Psychiatric illness in women: Emerging treatments and research.* Washington, DC: American Psychiatric Publishing.

Kazdin, A. E. (1975). The impact of applied behavior analysis on diverse areas of research. *Journal of Applied Behavior Analysis, 8,* 213–229.

Kazdin, A. E. (Ed.). (2003). *Methodological issues and strategies in clinical research* (3rd ed.). Washington, DC: American Psychological Association.

Kazdin, A. E. (2008). Evidence-based treatment and practice: New opportunities to bridge clinical research and practice, enhance the knowledge base, and improve patient care. *American Psychologist, 63,* 146–159.

Keith, S. J., Regier, D. A., & Rae, D. S. (1991). Schizophrenic disorders. In L. N. Robins & D. A. Regier (Eds.), *Psychiatric disorders in America: The Epidemiological Catchment Area Study.* New York: Free Press.

Kelley, H. H. (1973). The process of causal attribution. *American Psychologist, 28,* 107–128.

Kelly, G. (1955). *The psychology of personal constructs.* New York: Norton.

Kelly, G. F. (2001). *Sexuality today: The human perspective* (6th ed.). Boston: McGraw-Hill.

Kelly, J. A., St. Lawrence, J. S., Hood, H. V., & Brasfield, T. L. (1989). Behavioral intervention to reduce AIDS risk activities. *Journal of Consulting and Clinical Psychology, 57,* 60–67.

Kelly, T. A., & Strupp, H. H. (1992). Patient and therapist values in psychotherapy: Perceived changes, assimilation, similarity, and outcome. *Journal of Consulting and Clinical Psychology, 60,* 34–40.

Keltner, D., & Ekman, P. (2000). Facial expression of emotion. In M. Lewis & J. M. Haviland-Jones (Eds.), *Handbook of emotions* (2nd ed.). New York: Guilford Press.

Kemeny, M. E., (2004). The psychobiology of stress. *Current Directions in Psychological Science, 12,* 124–129.

Kempermann, G. (2005). *Adult neurogenesis: Stem cells and neuronal development in the adult brain.* New York: Oxford University Press.

Kenardy, J., Brown, W. J., & Vogt, E. (2001). Dieting and health in young Australian women. *European Eating Disorders Review, 9,* 242–254.

Kendall, D. (1998). *Social problems in a diverse society.* Boston: Allyn & Bacon.

Kenrick, D. T., & Funder, D. C. (1988). Profiting from controversy: Lessons from the person-situation debate. *American Psychologist, 43,* 23–34.

Kensinger, E. A., Ullman, M. T., & Corkin, S. (2001). Bilateral medial temporal lobe damage does not affect lexical or grammatical processing: Evidence from amnesic patient H. M. *Hippocampus, 11,* 347–360.

Kentridge, R. W., Heywood, C. A., & Weiskrantz, L. (2004). Spatial attention speeds discrimination without awareness in blindsight. *Neuropsychologia, 42,* 831–835.

Kernberg, O. F. (1984). *Severe personality disorders: Psychotherapeutic strategies.* New Haven, CT: Yale University Press.

Kernberg, O. F. (2000). *Personality disorders in children and adolescents.* Poulsbo, WA: H-R Press.

Kernberg, O. F., & Caligor, E. (2005). A psychoanalytic theory of personality disorders. In M. F. Lenzenweger & J. F. Clarkin (Eds.), *Major theories of personality disorder.* New York: Guilford Press.

Kerr, M., Lambert, W. W., & Bem, D. J. (1996). Life course sequelae of childhood shyness in Sweden: Comparison with the United States. *Developmental Psychology, 32,* 1100–1105.

Kerstholt, J. H., & Eikelboom, A. R. (2007). Effects of prior interpretation on situation assessment in crime analysis. Decision making and the law (Special issue) *Journal of Behavioral Decision Making, 20,* 455–465.

Kessler, R. C., Berglund, P. A., Demler, O., Jin, R., & Walters, E. E. (2005a). Lifetime prevalence and age-of-onset distributions of DSM-IV disorders in the National Comorbidity Survey Replication (NCS-R). *Archives of General Psychiatry 62,* 593–602.

Kessler, R. C., Chiu, W. T., Demler, O., & Walters, E. E. (2005b). Prevalence, severity, and comorbidity of twelve-month DSM-IV disorders in the National Comorbidity Survey Replication (NCS-R). *Archives of General Psychiatry, 62*(6), 617–627.

Kessler, R. C., McGonagle, K. A., Zhao, S., Nelson, C., et al. (1994). Lifetime and 12-month prevalence of DSM-III-R psychiatric disorder in the United States. *Archives of General Psychiatry, 51,* 8–19.

Kessler, R. C., & Wittchen, H. U. (2002). Patterns and correlates of generalized anxiety disorder in community samples. *Journal of Clinical Psychiatry, 63*(Suppl. 8), 4–10.

Ketellar, T. (1995). *Emotion as mental representations of fitness affordances: I. Evidence supporting the claim that the negative and positive emotions map onto fitness costs and benefits.* Paper presented at the annual meeting of the Human Behavior and Evolution Society, Santa Barbara, CA.

Kety, S. S. (1988). Schizophrenic illness in the families of schizophrenic adoptees: Findings from the Danish national sample. *Schizophrenia Bulletin, 14,* 217–222.

Keyes, C. L. M., & Waterman, M. B. (2003). Dimensions of well-being and mental health in adulthood. In M. H. Bornstein, L. Davidson, C. L. M. Keyes & K. A. Moore (Eds.), *Well-being: Positive development across the life course: Crosscurrents in contemporary psychology.* Mahwah, NJ: Erlbaum.

Keyes, L. M., & Goodman, S. H. (2006). *Women and depression: A handbook for social, behavioral, and biomedical sciences.* New York: Cambridge University Press.

Kharkhurin, A. V. (2008). The effects of linguistic proficiency, age of second language acquisition, and length of exposure to a new cultural environment on bilinguals' divergent thinking. *Bilingualism: Language and Cognition, 11,* 225–243.

Kiecolt-Glaser, J., McGuire, L., Robles, T. F., & Glaser, R. (2002). Emotions, morbidity, and mortality: New perspectives from psychoneuroimmunology. *Annual Review of Psychology, 53,* 83–107.

Kiecolt-Glaser, J. K., Graham, J. E., Malarkey, W. B., Porter, K., Lemeshow, S., & Glaser, R. (2008). Olfactory influences on mood and autonomic, endocrine, and immune function. *Psychoneuroendocrinology, 33,* 328–339.

Kihlstrom, J. (2008). The psychological unconscious. In O. P. John, R. W. Robins, & L. A. Pervin (Eds.), *Handbook of personality theory and research* (3rd ed.). New York: Guilford Press.

Kihlstrom, J. F. (1999). The psychological unconscious. In L. A. Pervin & O. P. John (Eds.), *Handbook of personality: Theory and research.* New York: Guilford Press.

Kihlstrom, J. F. (2007). Consciousness in hypnosis. In P. D. Zelazo, M. Moscovitch, & E. Thompson (Eds.), *The Cambridge handbook of consciousness.* New York: Cambridge University Press.

Kim, E. (2004). Neurobehavioral aspects of aggression. In J. P. Morgan (Ed.), *Focus on aggression research.* Hauppauge, NY: Nova Science.

Kimerling, R., Ouimette, P., & Wolfe, J. (2003). *Gender and PTSD.* New York: Guilford Press.

Kimura, D. (1992). Sex differences in the brain. *Scientific American, 267*(3), 119–195.

Kimura, K., Tachibana, N., Aso, T., Kimura, J., & Shibasaki, H. (1997). Subclinical REM sleep behavior disorder in a patient with corticobasal degeneration. *Sleep, 20,* 891–894.

King, N. J., Dudley, A., Melvin, G., Pallant, J., & Morawetz, D. (2001). Empirically supported treatments for insomnia. *Scandinavian Journal of Behaviour Therapy, 30,* 23–32.

Kinsey, A. C., Pomeroy, W. B., & Martin, C. E. (1948). *Sexual behavior in the human male.* Philadelphia: Saunders.

Kinsey, A. C., Pomeroy, W. B., Martin, C. E., & Gebhard, P. H. (1953). *Sexual behavior in the human female.* Philadelphia: Saunders.

Kirchengast, S., & Hartmann, B. (2003). Nicotine consumption before and during pregnancy affects not only newborn size but also birth modus. *Journal of Biosocial Science, 35,* 175–188.

Kirk, K. M., Bailey, J. M., & Martin, N. G. (2000). Etiology of male sexual orientation in an Australian twin sample. *Psychology, Evolution, and Gender, 2,* 301–311.

Kirkby, J. A., Webster, L. A. D., Blythe, H. I., & Liversedge, S. P. (2008). Binocular coordination during reading and non-reading tasks. *Psychological Bulletin, 134,* 742–763.

Kirmayer, L. J., & Looper, K. (2007). Somatoform disorders. In M. Hersen, S. M. Turner, & D. C. Beidel (Eds.), *Adult psychopathology and diagnosis.* Hoboken, NJ: Wiley.

Kirsch, I. (2001). The response set theory of hypnosis: Expectancy and physiology. *American Journal of Clinical Hypnosis, 44,* 69–73.

Kirsch, I., Moore, T. J., Scoboria, A., & Nicholls, S. S. (2002). The emperor's new drugs: An analysis of antidepressant medication data submitted to the U.S. Food and Drug Administration. *Prevention & Treatment, 5,* 262–279.

Kitayama, S., & Markus, H. (1999). The yin and yang of the Japanese self. In D. Cervone & Y. Shoda (Eds.), *The coherence of personality.* New York: Guilford Press.

Kitayama, S., Markus, H. R., & Kurokawa, M. (2000). Culture, emotion, and well-being: Good feelings in Japan and the United States. *Cognition and Emotion, 14,* 93–124.

Kleim, J. A., Barbay, S., Cooper, N. R., Hogg, T. M., Reidel, C. N., Remple, M. S., & Nudo, R. J. (2002). Motor learning-dependent synaptogenesis is localized to functionally reorganized motor cortex. *Neurobiology of Learning & Memory, 77,* 63–77.

Klein, M. (1975). *The writings of Melanie Klein.* London: Hogarth Press.

Kleiner, M. (Ed). (2002). *Handbook of polygraph testing.* San Diego, CA: Academic Press.

Kleinknecht, R. A., Dinnel, D. L., Kleinknecht, E. E., Hiruma, N., et al. (Eds.). (1997). Cultural factors in social anxiety: A comparison of social phobia symptoms and Taijin Kyofusho. *Journal of Anxiety Disorders, 2,* 157–177.

Kleinman, A. (2004). Culture and depression. *New England Journal of Medicine, 351,* 951–953.

Kleinmuntz, B. (1980). *Essentials of abnormal psychology* (2nd ed.). New York: Harper & Row.

Kleinmuntz, B., & Szucko, J. J. (1984). Lie detection in ancient and modern times: A call for contemporary scientific study. *American Psychologist, 39,* 766–776.

Kleitman, N. (1963). *Sleep and wakefulness* (2nd ed.). Chicago: University of Chicago Press.

Kling, K. C., Hyde, J. S., Showers, C. J., & Buswell, B. N. (1999). Sex differences in self-esteem: A meta-analysis. *Psychological Bulletin, 125,* 475–500.

Kluckhohn, C., & Murray, H. A. (1953). Personality formation: The determinants. In C. Kluckhohn, H. A. Murray, & D. M. Schneider (Eds.), *Personality in nature, society, and culture.* New York: Knopf.

Knafo, D. (2009). Freud's memory erased. *Psychoanalytic Psychology, 26,* 171–190.

Knoblauch, K. (2002). Color vision. In H. Pashler & S. Yantis (Eds.), *Steven's handbook of experimental psychology: Vol. 1. Sensation and perception* (3rd ed.). New York: Wiley.

Kneebone, I. I., & Al-Daftary, S. (2006). Flooding treatment of phobia to having her feet touched by physiotherapists, in a young woman with Down's syndrome and a traumatic brain injury. *Neuropsychological Rehabilitation, 16,* 230–236.

Koch, C. (2004). *The quest for consciousness: A neurobiological approach.* Denver, CO: Roberts.

Kochanska, G., Aksan, N., Knaack, A., & Rhines, H. M. (2004). Maternal parenting and children's conscience: Early security as moderator. *Child Development, 75,* 1229–1242.

Kochanska, G., Casey, R. J., & Fukumoto, A. (1995). Toddlers' sensitivity to standard violations. *Child Development, 66,* 643–656.

Kochanska, G., Forman, D. R., Aksan, N., & Dunbar, S. B. (2005). Pathways to conscience: Early mother-child mutually responsive orientation and children's moral emotion, conduct, and cognition. *Journal of Child Psychology and Psychiatry, 46,* 19–34.

Kocsis, R. N., & Hayes, A. F. (2004). Believing is seeing? Investigating the perceived accuracy of criminal psychological profiles. *International Journal of Offender Therapy and Comparative Criminology, 48,* 149–160.

Koenig, H. G., Pargament, K. L., & Nielsen, J. (1998). Religious coping and health status in medically ill hospitalized older adults. *Journal of Nervous and Mental Disease, 186,* 513–521.

Koestner, R., & McClelland, D. C. (1990). Perspectives on competence motivation. In L. A. Pervin (Ed.), *Handbook of personality theory and research.* New York: Guilford Press.

Kohlberg, L. (1963). The development of children's orientations toward a moral order: I. Sequence in the development of moral thought. *Human Development, 6,* 11–33.

Kohlberg, L. (1984). *The psychology of moral development: Essays on moral development* (Vol. 2). New York: Harper & Row.

Köhler, W. (1925). *The mentality of apes* (Trans. from the 2nd rev. ed. by Ella Winter). New York: Harcourt.

Kohut, H. (1971). *Analysis of the self.* New York: International Universities Press.

Kohut, H. (1977). *The restoration of self.* New York: International Universities Press.

Kolata, G. (2009, November 16). Panel urges mammograms at 50, not 40. *New York Times.* Retrieved February 2, 2010, from http://www.nytimes.com/2009/11/17/health/17cancer.html

Kolb, B., & Whishaw, I. Q. (2003). *Fundamentals of human neuropsychology* (5th ed.). New York: Worth.

Kolb, B., & Whishaw, I. Q. (2005). *An introduction to brain and behavior* (2nd ed.). New York: Worth.

Kollar, E. J., & Fisher, C. (1980). Tooth induction in chick epithelium: Expression of quiescent genes for enamel synthesis. *Science, 207,* 993–995.

Koltko-Rivera, M. (2006). Rediscovering the later version of Maslow's hierarchy of needs: Self-transcendence and opportunities for theory, research, and unification. *Review of General Psychology, 10,* 302–317.

Koluchova, J. (1972). Severe deprivation in twins: A case study. *Journal of Child Psychology and Psychiatry, 13,* 107–114.

Koluchova, J. (1991). Severely deprived twins after 22 years of observation. *Studia Psychologica, 33,* 23–28.

Koons, C. R. (2007). The use of mindfulness interventions in cognitive behavior therapies. In T. Ronen & A. Freeman (Eds.), *Cognitive behavior therapy in clinical social work practice.* New York: Springer.

Koontz, J., & Baskys, A. (2009). The cognitive reserve hypothesis: Truth or fiction? *Directions in Psychiatry, 29,* 15–21.

Koriat, A., & Bjork, R. A. (2005). Illusions of competence in monitoring one's knowledge during study. *Journal of Experimental Psychology: Learning, Memory, and Cognition, 31,* 187–194.

Kortegaard, L., Hoerder, K., Joergensen, J., Gillberg, C., & Kyvik, K. O. (2001). A preliminary population-based twin study of self-reported eating disorder. *Psychological Medicine, 31,* 361–365.

Kosambi, D. D. (1967). Living prehistory in India. *Scientific American, 216,* 105.

Kosslyn, S. M., Ball, T. M., & Reiser, B. J. (1978). Visual images preserve metric spatial information: Evidence from studies of image scanning. *Journal of Experimental Psychology: Human Perception and Performance, 4,* 47–60.

Kosslyn, S. M., Thompson, W. L., Costantini-Ferrando, M. F., Alpert, N. M., & Spiegel, D. (2000). Hypnotic visual illusion alters color processing in the brain. *American Journal of Psychiatry, 157,* 1279–1284.

Kosslyn, S. M., Thompson, W. L., & Ganis, G. (2006). *The case for mental imagery.* New York: Oxford University Press.

Kostanski, M., Fisher, A., & Gullone, E. (2004). Current conceptualisation of body image dissatisfaction: Have we got it wrong? *Journal of Child Psychology and Psychiatry, 45,* 1317–1325.

Kottak, C. P. (2000). *Cultural anthropology* (8th ed.). Boston: McGraw-Hill.

Kovács, A. M. (2009). Early bilingualism enhances mechanisms of false-belief reasoning. *Developmental Science, 12,* 48–54.

Kraft, C. L. (1978). A psychophysical contribution to air safety: Simulator studies of illusions in night visual approaches. In H. L. Pick, Jr., H. W. Leibowitz, J. E. Singer, A. Steinschneider, & H. W. Stevenson (Eds.), *Psychology: From research to practice.* New York: Plenum Press.

Krahé, B., & Altwasser, C. (2006). Changing negative attitudes towards persons with physical disabilities: An experimental intervention. *Journal of Community & Applied Social Psychology, 16,* 59–69.

Krain, A. L., Gotimer, K., Hefton, S., Ernst, M., Castellanos, F. X., Pine, D. S., et al. (2008). A functional magnetic resonance imaging investigation of uncertainty in adolescents with anxiety disorders. *Biological Psychiatry, 63,* 563–568.

Krasnegor, N. A., Lyon, G. R., & Goldman, R. P. S. (1997). *Development of the prefrontal cortex: Evolution, neurobiology, and behavior.* Baltimore, MD: Paul H. Brookes.

Krebs, D. L., & Denton, K. (1997). Social illusions and self-deception: The evolution of biases in person perception. In J. A. Simpson & D. T. Kenrick (Eds.), *Evolutionary social psychology.* Mahwah, NJ: Erlbaum.

Krevans, J., & Gibbs, J. C. (1996). Parents' use of inductive discipline: Relations to children's empathy and prosocial behavior. *Child Development, 67,* 3263–3277.

Kribbs, N. B. (1993). Siesta. In M. A. Carskadon (Ed.), *Encyclopedia of sleep and dreaming.* New York: Macmillan.

Krishna, A. (2009). *Sensory marketing: Research on the sensuality of products*. Chicago: Taylor & Francis.

Krizan, Z., & Baron, R. S. (2007). Group polarization and choice-dilemmas: How important is self-categorization? *European Journal of Social Psychology, 37*, 191–201.

Kroeber, A. L. (1948). *Anthropology*. New York: Harcourt Brace Jovanovich.

Krueger, R. F., & Johnson, W. (2008). Behavioral genetics and personality: A new look at the integration of nature and nurture. In O. P. John, R. W. Robins, & L. A. Pervin (Eds.), *Handbook of personality theory and research* (3rd ed.). New York: Guilford Press.

Kruger, J., Wirtz, D., & Miller, D. T. (2005). Counterfactual thinking and the first instinct fallacy. *Journal of Personality and Social Psychology, 88*, 725–735.

Kruglanski, A. W. (2004). *The psychology of closed mindedness*. New York: Psychology Press.

Ksir, C. J., Hart, C. I., & Ray, O. S. (2008). *Drugs, society, and human behavior*. New York: McGraw-Hill.

Kübler-Ross, E. (1969). *On death and dying*. New York: Macmillan.

Kulik, J. A., & Mahler, H. I. M. (2000). Social comparison, affiliation, and emotional contagion under threat. In J. Suls & L. Wheeler (Eds.), *Handbook of social comparison: Theory and research*. Dordrecht, Netherlands: Kluwer.

Kulik, J. A., Mahler, H. I. M., & Moore, P. J. (1996). Social comparison and affiliation under threat: Effects of recovery from major surgery. *Journal of Personality and Social Psychology, 66*, 301–309.

Kumar, S., Porcu, P., Werner, D. F., Matthews, D. B., Diaz-Granados, J. L., Helfand, R. S., & Morrow, A. L. (2009). The role of GABA$_A$ receptors in the acute and chronic effects of ethanol: A decade of progress. *Psychopharmacology, 205*, 529–564.

Kuncel, N. P., Hezlett, S. A., & Ones, D. S. (2004). Academic performance, career potential, and job performance: Can one construct predict them all? *Journal of Personality and Social Psychology, 86*, 148–161.

Kunkel, D. (2007, June 26). *The effects of television violence on children*. Hearing before the U.S. Senate Committee on Commerce, Science, and Transportation. Retrieved March 3, 2010, from http://www.apa.org/about/gr/pi/advocacy/2008/kunkel-tv.aspx

Kunzendorf, R. G., Watson, G., Monroe, L., Tassone, S., Papoutsakis, E., McArdle, E., et al. (2007). The archaic belief in dream visitations as it relates to "seeing ghosts," "meeting the lord," as well as "encountering extraterrestrials." *Imagination, Cognition and Personality, 27*, 71–85.

Kunzman, U., & Baltes, P. B. (2003). Beyond the traditional scope of intelligence: Wisdom in action. In R. J. Sternberg, J. Lautrey, & T. I. Lubart (Eds.), *Models of intelligence: International perspectives*. Washington, DC: American Psychological Association.

Kuo, J. R., & Linehan, M. M. (2009). Disentangling emotion processes in borderline personality disorder: Physiological and self-reported assessment of biological vulnerability, baseline intensity, and reactivity to emotionally evocative stimuli. *Journal of Abnormal Psychology, 118*, 531–544.

Kuo, P., Kalsi, G., Prescott, C. A., Goldman, D., van den Oord, E. J., Sullivan, P. F., et al. (2009). Associations of glutamate decarboxylase genes with initial sensitivity and age-at-onset of alcohol dependence in the Irish Affected Sib Pair Study of Alcohol Dependence. *Drug and Alcohol Dependence, 101*, 80–87.

Kurzweil, E. (1989). *The Freudians: A comparative perspective*. New Haven, CT: Yale University Press.

LaBar, K. S., & LeDoux, J. E. (2006). Fear and anxiety pathways. In S. O. Moldin & J. L. Rubenstein (Eds.), *Understanding autism: From basic neuroscience to treatment*. Boca Raton, FL: CRC.

LaBar, K. S., & Phelps, E. A. (1998). Arousal-mediated memory consolidation: Role of the medial temporal lobe in humans. *Psychological Science, 9*, 490–493.

Lachman, M. E. (2004). Development in midlife. *Annual Review of Psychology, 55*, 305–331.

Lahey, B. B. (2009). Public health significance of neuroticism. *American Psychologist, 64*, 241–256.

Laible, D., & Thompson, R. A. (2000). Mother-child discourse, attachment security, shared positive affect, and early conscience development. *Child Development, 71*, 1424–1440.

Lambert, M. J., Shapiro, D. A., & Bergin, A. E. (1986). The effectiveness of psychotherapy. In L. Garfield & A. E. Bergin (Eds.), *Handbook of psychotherapy and behavior change* (3rd ed.). New York: Wiley.

Lamborn, S. D., Mounts, N. S., Steinberg, L., & Dornbusch, S. M. (1991). Patterns of competence and adjustment among adolescents from authoritative, authoritarian, indulgent, and neglectful families. *Child Development, 62*, 1049–1065.

Landers, D. M., & Arent, S. (2001). Arousal-performance relations. In J. M. Williams (Ed.), *Applied sport psychology: Personal growth to peak performance* (4th ed.). Boston: McGraw-Hill.

Landesman, S., & Ramey, C. T. (1989). Developmental psychology and mental retardation: Integrating scientific principles with treatment practices. *American Psychologist, 44*, 409–415.

Lane, R. D., Reiman, E. M., Ahern, G. L., & Schwartz, G. E. (1997). Neuroanatomical correlates of happiness, sadness, and disgust. *American Journal of Psychiatry, 154*, 926–933.

Laney, C., & Loftus, E. F. (2010). Truth in emotional memories. In B. H. Bornstein & R. L. Wiener (Eds.), *Emotion and the law: Psychological perspectives*. New York: Springer.

Langan-Fox, J., & Grant, S. (2006). The Thematic Apperception Test: Toward a standard measure of the Big Three motives. *Journal of Personality Assessment, 87*, 277–291.

Langer, E. (1989). *Mindlessness*. Reading, MA: Addison-Wesley.

Langlois, J. H., Kalakanis, L., Rubenstein, A. J., Larson, A., Hallam, M., & Smoot, M. (2000). Maxims or myths of beauty? A meta-analytic and theoretical review. *Psychological Bulletin, 126*, 390–423.

Langlois, J. H., & Roggman, L. A. (1990). Attractive faces are only average. *Psychological Science, 1*, 115–121.

LaPiere, R. T. (1934). Attitudes and actions. *Social Forces, 13*, 230–237.

LaPointe, L. L. (2005). *Aphasia and related neurogenic language disorders* (3rd ed.). New York: Thieme New York.

Larivée, S., Normandeau, S., & Parent, S. (2000). The French connection: Some contributions of French language research in the post Piagetian era. *Child Development, 71*, 823–839.

Larsen, R., & Buss, D. M. (2007). *Personality psychology: Domains of knowledge about human nature* (3rd ed.). Boston: McGraw-Hill.

Larsen, R., & Diener, E. (1985). A multitrait-multimethod examination of affect structure: Hedonic level and emotional intensity. *Personality and Individual Differences, 6*, 631–636.

Larsen, R. J., & Buss, D. M. (2010). *Personality psychology: Domains of knowledge about human nature* (4th ed.). New York: McGraw-Hill.

Larson, K. (2004). *The science of word recognition or how I learned to stop worrying and love the bouma*. Advanced Reading Technology, Microsoft Corporation. Retrieved December 12, 2009, from http://www.microsoft.com/typography/ctfonts/WordRecognition.aspx

Larson, R. W., Hansen, D. M., & Moneta, G. (2006). Differing profiles of developmental experiences across types of organized youth activities. *Developmental Psychology, 42*, 849–863.

Larson, R. W., Moneta, G., Richards, M. H., & Wilson, W. (2002). Continuity, stability, and change in daily emotional experience across adolescence. *Child Development, 73*, 1151–1165.

Larzelere, R. E. (2008). Disciplinary spanking: The scientific evidence. *Journal of Developmental and Behavioral Pediatrics, 29*, 334–335.

Larzelere, R. E., & Baumrind, D. (2010). Are spanking injunctions scientifically supported? *Law & Contemporary Problems, 73*. Invited, in press.

Larzelere, R. E., & Kuhn, B. R. (2005). Comparing child outcomes of physical punishment and alternative disciplinary tactics: A meta-analysis. *Clinical Child and Family Psychology Review, 8*, 1–37.

Lasco, M. S., Jordan, T. J., Edgar, M. A., Petito, C. K., & Byne, W. (2002). A lack of dimorphism of sex or sexual orientation in the human anterior commissure. *Brain Research, 936*, 95–98.

Lashley, K. S. (1950). In search of the engram. *Symposia of the Society for Experimental Biology, 4*, 454–482.

Lassiter, G. D., Diamond, S. S., Schmidt, H. C., & Elek, J. K. (2007). Evaluating videotaped confessions: Expertise provides no defense against the camera-perspective effect. *Psychological Science, 18*, 224–226.

Latané, B., & Bourgeois, M. J. (2001). Successfully simulating dynamic social impact: Three levels of prediction. In J. P. Forgas & K. D. Williams (Eds.), *Social influence: Direct and indirect processes. The Sydney symposium of social psychology*. Philadelphia: Psychology Press.

Latané, B., & Darley, J. M. (1970). *The unresponsive bystander: Why doesn't he help?* New York: Appleton-Century-Crofts.

Latham, G. P., & Locke, E. A. (2006). Enhancing the benefits and overcoming the pirfalls of goal setting. *Organizational Dynamics, 35*, 332–340.

Laumann, E. O., Gagnon, J. H., Michael, R. T., & Michaels, S. (1994). *The social organization of sexuality: Sexual practices in the United States*. Chicago: University of Chicago Press.

Lavergne, G. M. (1997). *A sniper in the tower: The Charles Whitman murders*. Denton: University of North Texas Press.

Lavie, P. (2000). Sleep-wake as a biological rhythm. *Annual Review of Psychology, 52*, 277–303.

Lavigne, J. V., Gibbons, R. D., Christoffel, K. K., & Arend, R. (1996). Prevalence rates and correlates of psychiatric disorders among preschool children. *Journal of the American Academy of Child & Adolescent Psychiatry, 35,* 204–214.

Lawrence, E., Rothman, A. D., Cobb, R. J., & Bradbury, T. N. (2010). Marital satisfaction across the transition to parenthood: Three eras of research. In M. S. Schulz, M. K. Pruett, P. K. Kerig, & R. D. Parke (Eds.), *Strengthening couple relationships for optimal child development: Lessons from research and intervention.* Washington, DC: American Psychological Association.

Lazarus, R. S. (1991). Progress on a cognitive-motivational-relational theory of emotion. *American Psychologist, 46,* 819–834.

Lazarus, R. S. (1998). *Fifty years of the research and theory of R. S. Lazarus: An analysis of historical and perennial issues.* Mahwah, NJ: Erlbaum.

Lazarus, R. S. (2001). Relational meaning and discrete emotions. In B. K. Scherer et al. (Eds.), *Appraisal processes in emotion: Theory, methods, research.* New York: Oxford University Press.

Leary, M. R. (2004). The self we know and the self we show: Self-esteem, self-presentation, and the maintenance of interpersonal relationships. In M. B. Brewer & M. Hewstone (Eds.), *Emotion and motivation: Perspectives on social psychology.* Malden, MA: Blackwell.

Leary, M. R., Kowalski, R. M., Smith, L., & Phillips, S. (2003). Teasing, rejection, and violence: Case studies of the school shootings. *Aggressive Behavior, 29,* 202–214.

Lebrun, M. (2007). *Student depression.* Lanham, MD: Rowman & Littlefield Education.

Lecat, B., Hilton, D. J., & Crano, W. D. (2009). Group status and reciprocity norms: Can the door-in-the-face effect be obtained in an out-group context? *Group Dynamics: Theory, Research, and Practice, 13,* 178–189.

Lechner, S. C., Tennen, H., & Affleck, G. (2009). Benefit-finding and growth. In S. Lopez & C. R. Snyder (Eds.), *Oxford handbook of positive psychology.* New York: Oxford University Press.

LeDoux, J. E. (1998). *The emotional brain.* New York: Simon & Schuster.

LeDoux, J. E. (2000). Emotion circuits in the brain. *Annual Review of Neuroscience, 23,* 155–184.

LeDoux, J. E., & Phelps, E. A. (2000). Emotional networks in the brain. In M. Lewis & J. M. Haviland-Jones (Eds.), *Handbook of emotions* (2nd ed.). New York: Guilford Press.

LeDoux, J. E., Wilson, D. H., & Gazzaniga, M. S. (1977). A divided mind: Observations on the conscious properties of the separated hemispheres. *Annals of Neurology, 2,* 417–421.

Lee, C. H. (2009). Testing the role of phonology in reading: Focus on sentence processing. *Journal of Psycholinguistic Research, 38,* 333–344.

Lee, U., Mashour, G. A., Kim, S., Noh, G. J., & Choi, B. M. (2009). Propofol induction reduces the capacity for neural information integration: Implications for the mechanism of consciousness and general anesthesia. *Consciousness and Cognition: An International Journal, 18,* 56–64.

Lehmann, D., Pascual-Marqui, R. D., Strik, W. K., & Koenig, T. (2010). Core networks for visual-concrete and abstract thought content: A brain electric microstate analysis. *NeuroImage, 49,* 1073–1079.

Lehmann-Haupt, C. (1988, August 4). Books of the times: How an actor found success, and himself. *New York Times,* p. 2.

Leichtman, M. D., & Ceci, S. J. (1995). The effects of stereotypes and suggestions on preschoolers' reports. *Developmental Psychology, 31,* 568–578.

Leising, D., Rogers, K., & Ostner, J. (2009). The undisordered personality: Assumptions underlying personality disorder diagnoses. *Review of General Psychology, 13,* 230–241.

LeMoal, H., (1999). *Dopamine and the brain: From neurons to networks.* New York: Academic Press.

Lenzenweger, M. F., & Clarkin, J. F. (Eds.). (2005). *Major theories of personality disorder.* New York: Guilford Press.

Leon, D. A., Lawlor, D. A., Clark, G. D., & Macintyre, S. (2009). The association of childhood intelligence with mortality risk from adolescence to middle age: Findings from the Aberdeen Children of the 1950s cohort study. *Intelligence, 37,* 517–634.

Leon, G. R., & Roth, L. (1977). Obesity: Psychological causes, correlations, and speculations. *Psychological Bulletin, 84,* 117–139.

Leor, J., Poole, W. K., & Kloner, R. A. (1996). Sudden cardiac death triggered by an earthquake. *New England Journal of Medicine, 334*(7), 413–419.

Lerdboon, P., Pham, V., Green, M., Riel, R., Tho, L. H., Nguyen, T. V., & Kaljee, L. M. (2008). Strategies for developing gender-specific HIV prevention for adolescents in Vietnam. *AIDS Education and Prevention, 20,* 384–398.

Levant, R. F. (2004). The empirically validated treatments movement: A practitioner/educator perspective. *Clinical Psychology; Science and Practice, 11,* 219–224.

Levenson, H. (2010). *Brief dynamic therapy.* Washington, DC: American Psychological Association.

Levine, R., Sato, S., Hashimoto, T., & Verma, J. (1995). Love and marriage in eleven cultures. *Journal of Cross-Cultural Psychology, 26,* 554–571.

Levinson, D. J. (1986). A conception of adult development. *American Psychologist, 41,* 3–13.

Levinson, D. J. (1990). A theory of life structure development in adulthood. In C. N. Alexander & E. J. Langer (Eds.), *Higher stages of human development: Perspectives on adult growth.* New York: Oxford University Press.

Levinson, D. J., Darow, C. N., Klein, E. B., Levinson, M. H., & McKee, B. (1978). *The seasons of a man's life.* New York: Knopf.

Levinthal, C. F. (2007). *Drugs, behavior, and modern society.* New York: McGraw-Hill.

Levitsky, D. A. (2002). Putting behavior back into feeding behavior: A tribute to George Collier. *Appetite, 38,* 143–148.

Levy, B. R., Slade, M. D., Kunkel, S. R., & Kasl, S. V. (2002). Longevity increased by positive self-perceptions of aging. *Journal of Personality and Social Psychology, 83,* 261–270.

Levy, D. A. (2010). *Tools of critical thinking: Meta-thoughts for psychology* (2nd ed.). Prospect Heights, IL: Waveland.

Levy, S., Marrow, L., Bagley, C., & Lippman, M. (1988). Survival hazards analysis in first recurrent breast cancer patients: Seven-year follow-up. *Psychosomatic Medicine, 50,* 520–528.

Lewin, R. (1998). *The origin of modern humans.* New York: American Scientific Library.

Lewin, T. (2009, October 23). No Einstein in your crib? Get a refund. *New York Times.* Retrieved February 5, 2010, from http://www.nytimes.com/2009/10/24/education/24baby.html

Lewinsohn, P. M. (1974). A behavioral approach to depression. In R. J. Friedman & M. Katz (Eds.), *The psychology of depression: Contemporary theory and research.* Oxford, England: Wiley.

Lewinsohn, P. M, Gotlib, I. H., Lewinsohn, M., Seeley, J. R., & Allen, N. B. (1998). Gender differences in anxiety disorders and anxiety symptoms in adolescents. *Journal of Abnormal Psychology, 107,* 109–117.

Lewinsohn, P. M., Hoberman, H., Teri, L., & Hantzinger, M. (1985). An integrative theory of depression. In S. Reiss & R. Bootzin (Eds.), *Theoretical issues in behavior therapy.* New York: Academic Press.

Lewis, M. (1999). On the development of personality. In L. A. Pervin & O. P. John (Eds.), *Handbook of personality: Theory and research.* New York: Guilford Press.

Lewis, M. (2000). The emergence of human emotions. In M. Lewis & J. M. Haviland-Jones (Eds.), *Handbook of emotions* (2nd ed.). New York: Guilford Press.

Lewis, M. W., Misra, S., Johnson, H. L., & Rosen, T. S. (2004). Neurological and developmental outcomes of prenatally cocaine-exposed offspring from 12 to 36 months. *American Journal of Drug and Alcohol Abuse, 30,* 299–320.

Lewy, A., Emens, J., Jackman, A., & Yuhas, K. (2006). Circadian uses of melatonin in humans. *Chronobiology International, 23,* 403–412.

Li, S., Jin, X., Yan, C., Wu, S., Jiang, F., & Shen, X. (2009). Factors associated with bed and room sharing in Chinese school-aged children. *Child: Care, Health, and Development, 35,* 171–177.

Lidz, C. S. (1997). Dynamic assessment approaches. In D. P. Flanagan, J. L. Genshaft, & P. L. Harrison (Eds.), *Contemporary intellectual assessment: Theories, tests, and issues.* New York: Guilford Press.

Lieb, R., Isensee, B., Hoefier, M., Pfister, H., & Wittchen, H. U. (2002). Parental major depression and the risk of depression and other mental disorders in offspring: A prospective-longitudinal community study. *Archives of General Psychiatry, 59,* 365–374.

Lieberman, J. A. (1998). *Psychiatric drugs.* Philadelphia: Saunders.

Lieberman, M. D., & Eisenberger, N. I. (2009). Pains and pleasures of social life. *Science, 323*(5916), 890–891.

Liedtke, W. B. (2006). *TRP ion channel function in sensory transduction and cellular signaling cascades.* San Francisco: Taylor & Francis.

Lilienfeld, S. O., Lynn, S. J., Ruscio, J., & Beyerstein, B. L. (2010). *50 great myths of popular psychology: Shattering widespread misconceptions about human behavior.* Malden, MA: Wiley-Blackwell.

Lilienfeld, S. O., Wood, J. M., & Garb, H. N. (2000). The scientific status of projective techniques. *Psychological Science in the Public Interest, 1,* 25–62.

Lin, J. Y., Murray, S. O., & Boynton, G. M. (2009). Capture of attention to threatening stimuli without perceptual awareness. *Current Biology, 19,* 1118–1122.

Lindell, A. K., & Lamb, J. A. G. (2008). Priming vs. rhyming: Orthographic and phonological representations in the left and right hemispheres. *Brain and Cognition, 68,* 193–203.

Linehan, M. M. (1993). *Cognitive-behavioral treatment of borderline personality disorder.* New York: Guilford Press.

Linehan, M. M., Comtois, K. A., Murray, A. M., et al. (2006). Two-year randomized controlled trial and follow-up of dialectical behavior therapy vs. therapy by experts for suicidal behaviors and borderline personality disorder. *Archives of General Psychiatry, 63,* 757–766.

Linehan, M. M., & Dexter-Mazza, E. T. (2008). Dialectical behavior therapy for borderline personality disorder. In D. H. Barlow (Ed.), *Clinical handbook of psychological disorders: A step-by-step treatment manual* (4th ed.). New York: Guilford Press.

Link, B. G., & Steuve, A. (1998). New evidence on the violence risk posed by people with mental illness. *Archives of General Psychiatry, 55,* 403–404.

Linver, M. R., Brooks-Gunn, J., & Kohen, D. E. (2002). Family processes as pathways from income to young children's development. *Developmental Psychology, 38,* 719–734.

Lippa, R. A. (2005). *Gender, nature, and nurture.* Hillsdale, NJ: Erlbaum.

Lipsitt, L. P. (1990). Learning processes in the human newborn: Sensitization, habituation, and classical conditioning. *Annals of the New York Academy of Sciences, 608,* 113–127.

Litz, B. T. (2004). *Early intervention for trauma and traumatic loss.* New York: Guilford Press.

Liu, W. T., Humayun, M. S., & Liker, M. A. (2008). Implantable biomimetic microelectronics systems. *Proceedings of the IEEE, 96,* 1073–1074.

Livesley, W. J. (2003). *Practical management of personality disorder.* New York: Guilford Press.

Livingstone, M., & Hubel, D. (1994). Segregation of form, color, movement, and depth: Anatomy, physiology, and perception. In H. Gutfreund & G. Toulouse (Eds.), *Biology and computation: A physicist's choice. Advanced series in neuroscience.* Singapore: World Scientific Publishing.

Lloyd, E. A., & Feldman, M. W. (2002). Evolutionary psychology: A view from evolutionary biology. *Psychological Inquiry, 13,* 150–156.

Locke, D. C. (1992). *Increasing multicultural understanding: A comprehensive model.* Thousand Oaks, CA: Sage.

Locke, E. A., & Latham, G. P. (2002). Building a practically useful theory of goal setting and task motivation: A 35-year odyssey. *American Psychologist, 57,* 705–717.

Löckenhoff, C. E., De Fruyt, F., Terracciano, A., McCrae, R. R., De Bolle, M., Costa P. T., Jr., et al. (2009). Perceptions of aging across 26 cultures and their culture-level associates. *Psychology and Aging, 24,* 941–954.

Locsis, R. N., & Hayes, A. F. (2004). Believing is seeing? Investigating the perceived accuracy of criminal psychological profiles. *International Journal of Offender Therapy and Comparative Criminology, 27,* 149–160.

Loehlin, J. C. (1992). *Genes and environment in personality development.* Newbury Park, CA: Sage.

Loehlin, J. C., Willerman, L., & Horn, J. M. (1988). Genetics and human behavior. *Annual Review of Psychology, 39,* 101–134.

Loewenstein, R. J. (1991). Psychogenic amnesia and psychogenic fugue: A comprehensive review. In A. Tasman & S. M. Goldfinger (Eds.), *American Psychiatric Press review of psychiatry* (Vol. 10). Washington, DC: American Psychiatric Association.

Loftus, E. F., & Palmer, J. C. (1974). Reconstruction of automobile destruction: An example of the interaction between language and memory. *Journal of Verbal Learning and Verbal Behavior, 13,* 585–589.

Logie, R. H., & Maylor, E. A. (2009). An internet study of prospective memory across adulthood. *Psychology and Aging, 24,* 767–774.

Logue, A. W. (1991). *The psychology of eating and drinking* (2nd ed.). New York: Freeman.

Lomber, S. J., & Eggermont, J. J. (2006). *Reprogramming the cerebral cortex: Plasticity following central and peripheral lesions.* New York: Oxford University Press.

London, K., Bruck, M., Wright, D. B., & Ceci, S. J. (2008). Review of the contemporary literature on how children report sexual abuse to others: Findings, methodological issues, and implications for forensic interviewers. *Memory, 16,* 29–47.

Long, M. (2005). Problems with supposed counter-evidence to the critical period hypothesis. *International Review of Applied Linguistics, 43,* 287–317.

Lonnqvist, J-E., Verkasalo, M., Haukka, J., et al. (2009). Premorbid personality factors in schizophrenia and bipolar disorder: Results from a large cohort study of male conscripts. *Journal of Abnormal Psychology, 118,* 418–423.

Lonsdorf, E. V. (2006). What is the role of mothers in the acquisition of termite-fishing behaviors in wild chimpanzees (*Pan troglodytes schweinfurthii*)? *Animal Cognition, 9,* 36–46.

Lopez, R. (2009, November 6). 911 tape released in Bay Area gang rape. *Los Angeles Times.* Retrieved November 24, 2009, from http://articles.latimes.com/2009/nov/06/local/me-gang-rape6

Lopez, S. R., & Guarnaccia, P. J. (2000). Cultural psychopathology: Uncovering the social world of mental illness. *Annual Review of Psychology, 51,* 571–598.

Lorenz, K. (1937). The companion in the bird's world. *Auk, 54,* 245–273.

Lorenzen, L. A., Grieve, F. G., & Thomas, A. (2004). Exposure to muscular male models decreases men's body satisfaction. *Sex Roles, 51,* 743–748.

Lovaas, O. I. (1977). *The autistic child.* New York: Irvington.

Lovallo, W. (Ed.). (2005). *Stress and health: Biological and psychological interactions.* Newbury Park, CA: Sage.

Lovallo, W. R., & Gerin, W. (2003). Psychophysiological reactivity: Mechanisms and pathways to cardiovascular disease. *Psychosomatic Medicine, 65,* 36–45.

Lovibond, P. (2006). Fear and avoidance: An integrated expectancy model. In M. G. Craske, D. Hermans, & D. Vansteenwegen (Eds.), *Fear and learning: From basic processes to clinical implications.* Washington, DC: American Psychological Association.

Low, L-F., & Anstey, K. J. (2009). Dementia literacy: Recognition and beliefs on dementia of the Australian public. *Alzheimer's & Dementia, 5,* 43–49.

Lubinski, D. (2004). Introduction to the special section on cognitive abilities: 100 years after Spearman's (1904) "'General intelligence,' objectively determined and measured." *Journal of Personality and Social Psychology, 86,* 96–111.

Luborsky, L., Rosenthal, R., Diguer, L., Andrusyna, T. P., Berman, J. S., Jeffrey, S., Levitt, J. T., Seligman, D. A., & Krause, E. D. (2002). The dodo bird verdict is alive and well—mostly. *Clinical Psychology: Science and Practice, 9,* 2–12.

Lucas, R. E., Clark, A. E., Georgellis, Y., & Diener, E. (2004). Unemployment alters the set point for life satisfaction. *Psychological Science, 15,* 8–13.

Luchins, A. J. (1942). Mechanization in problem solving: The effect of Einstellung. *Psychological Monographs, 54*(6, Whole No. 248).

Luciana, M. (2010). Adolescent brain development: Current themes and future directions: Introduction to the special issue. *Brain and Cognition, 72,* 1–5.

Luciano, M., Wright, M. J., Smith, G. A., Geffen, G. M., Geffen, L. B., & Martin, N. G. (2001). Genetic covariance among measures of information processing speed, working memory, and IQ. *Behavior Genetics, 31,* 581–592.

Luck, S. J., & Vecera, S. P. (2002). Attention. In H. Pashler & S. Yantis (Eds.), *Steven's handbook of experimental psychology: Vol. 1. Sensation and perception* (3rd ed.). New York: Wiley.

Luders, E., Narr, K. L., Thompson, P. M., & Toga, A. W. (2009). Neuroanatomical correlates of intelligence. *Intelligence, 37,* 156–163.

Luna, B., Garver, K. E., Urban, T. A., Lazar, N. A., & Sweeney, J. A. (2004). Maturation of cognitive processes from late childhood to adulthood. *Child Development, 75,* 1357–1372.

Luo, S., & Zhang, G. (2009). What leads to romantic attraction: Similarity, reciprocity, security, or beauty? Evidence from a speed-dating study. *Journal of Personality, 77,* 933–964.

Luria, A. R. (1968). *The mind of a mnemonist: A little book about a vast memory.* New York: Basic Books.

Lurigio, A. J. (2009). The rotten barrel spoils the apples: How situational factors contribute to detention officer abuse toward inmates: A review of *The Lucifer Effect,* by Philip Zimbardo. The special issue on the history of prisons and punishment. *The Prison Journal, 89*(Suppl. 1), 70S–80S.

Lutz, W., Leon, S., Martinovich, Z., Lyons, J. S., & Stiles, W. B. (2007). Therapist effects in outpatient psychotherapy: A three-level growth curve approach. *Journal of Counseling Psychology, 54,* 32–39.

Lykken, D. T. (1981). *A tremor in the blood: Uses and abuses of the lie detector.* New York: Plenum.

Lykken, D. T. (1984). Polygraph interrogation. *Nature, 307,* 681–684.

Lykken, D. T. (2006). The mechanism of emergenesis. *Genes, Brain, & Behavior, 5,* 306–310.

Lykken, D. T., & Tellegen, A. (1996). Happiness is a stochastic phenomenon. *Psychological Science, 7,* 186–189.

Lynn, R. (2009). What has caused the Flynn effect? Secular increases in the Development Quotients of infants. *Intelligence, 37,* 16–24.

Lynn, S. J., Boycheva, E., Deming, A., Lilienfeld, S. O., & Hallquist, M. N. (2009). Forensic hypnosis: The state of the science. In K. S. Douglas, J. L. Skeem, & S. O. Lilienfeld (Eds.), *Psychological science in the courtroom: Consensus and controversy.* New York: Guilford Press.

Lyon, G. R., Shaywitz, S. E., & Shaywitz, B. A. (2003). A definition of dyslexia. *Annals of Dyslexia, 53,* 1–14.

Lyons, L. (2005, November 1). Paranormal beliefs come (super)naturally to some. *Gallup USA.* Retrieved January 12, 2009, from http://www.gallup.com/poll/19558/Paranormal-Beliefs-Come-SuperNaturally-Some.aspx

Lyons, M. J., Schultz, M., Neale, M., Brady, K., Eisen, S., Toomey, R., Rhein, A., Faraone, S., & Tsuang, M. (2006). Specificity of familial vulnerability for alcoholism versus major depression in men. *The Journal of Nervous and Mental Disease, 194,* 809–817.

Lytton, H., & Romney, D. M. (1991). Parents' differential socialization of boys and girls: A meta-analysis. *Psychological Bulletin, 109,* 267–296.

MacAndrew, C., & Edgerton, R. B. (1969). *Drunken comportment: A social explanation.* Chicago: Aldine.

Maccoby, E. E., & Maccoby, N. (1954). The interview: A tool of social science. In G. Lindzey (Ed.), *Handbook of social psychology.* Cambridge, MA: Addison-Wesley.

Maccoby, E. E., & Martin, J. A. (1983). Socialization in the context of the family: Parent-child interaction. In E. M. Hetherington (Ed.), *Handbook of child psychology: Socialization, personality, and social development.* New York: Wiley.

MacCoun, R. J. (1998). Toward a psychology of harm reduction. *American Psychologist, 53,* 1199–1208.

MacDonald, S., Uesiliana, K., & Hayne, H. (2000). Cross-cultural and gender differences in childhood amnesia. *Memory, 8,* 365–376.

MacDonald, T. K., Fong, G. T., Zanna, M. P., & Martineau, A. M. (2003). Alcohol myopia and condom use: Can alcohol intoxication be associated with more prudent behavior? In P. Salovey & A. J. Rothman (Eds.), *Social psychology of health. Key readings in social psychology.* New York: Psychology Press.

MacDonald, T. K., Zanna, M. P., & Fong, G. T. (1995). Decision making in altered states: Effects of alcohol on attitudes toward drinking and driving. *Journal of Personality and Social Psychology, 68,* 973–985.

MacGregor, J. N., Ormerod, T. C., & Chronicle, E. P. (2001). Information processing and insight: A process model of performance on the nine-dot and related problems. *Journal of Experimental Psychology: Learning, Memory, and Cognition, 27,* 176–201.

Mack, A. (2003). Inattentional blindness: Looking without seeing. *Current Directions in Psychological Science, 12,* 180–184.

Maddux, J. E. (1999). Personal efficacy. In V. J. Derlega, B. A. Winstead, & W. H. Jones (Eds.), *Personality: Contemporary theory and research.* Chicago: Nelson Hall.

Madon, S., Willard, J., Guyll, M., Trudeau, L., & Spoth, R. (2006). Self-fulfilling prophecy effects of mothers' beliefs on children's alcohol use: Accumulation, dissipation, and stability over time. *Journal of Personality and Social Psychology, 90,* 911–926.

Maes, H. H. M., Neale, M. C., & Eaves, L. J. (1997). Genetic and environmental factors in relative body weight and human adiposity. *Behavior Genetics, 27,* 325–351.

Magnuson, S. (1986, March 10). "A serious deficiency": The Rogers Commission faults NASA's

"flawed" decision-making process. *Time* (Intl. ed.), 40–42.

Magora, F., Cohen, S., Shochina, M., & Davan, E. (2006). Visual reality immersion method of distraction to control experimental ischemic pain. *Israel Medical Association Journal, 8,* 261–265.

Maher, L., & Ho, H. T. (2009). Overdose beliefs and management practices among ethnic Vietnamese heroin users in Sydney, Australia. *Harm Reduction Journal.* Advanced online publication. doi: 10.1186/1477-7517-6-6.

Mahler, M. (1968). *On human symbiosis and the vicissitudes of individuation: Infantile psychosis.* New York: Basic Books.

Maier, S. F., & Watkins, L. R. (1999). Bidirectional communication between the brain and the immune system: Implications for behaviour. *Animal Behaviour, 57*(4), 741–751.

Mäkelä, K. (1997). Drinking, the majority fallacy, cognitive dissonance and social pressure. *Addiction, 92,* 729–736.

Malamuth, N. M., Addison, T., & Koss, M. (2000). Pornography and sexual aggression: Are there reliable effects and can we understand them? *Annual Review of Sex Research, 11,* 26–91.

Maldonado, R., & Rodriguez de Fonseca, F. (2002). Cannabinoid addiction: Behavioral models and neural correlates. *Journal of Neuroscience, 22,* 3326–3331.

Malina, R. M., Pena-Reyes, M. E., Tan, S. K., & Little, B. B. (2004). Secular change in age at menarche in rural Oaxaca, southern Mexico: 1968–2000. *Annals of Human Biology, 31,* 634–646.

Malouf, J. M., Rooke, S. E., & Schutte, N. S. (2008). The heritability of human behavior: Results of aggregating meta-analyses. *Current Psychology, 27,* 153–161.

Maner, J. K., DeWall, C. N., Baumeister, R. F., & Schaller, M. (2007). Does social exclusion motivate interpersonal reconnection? Resolving the "porcupine problem." *Journal of Personality and Social Psychology, 92,* 42–55.

Mann, L. (1981). The baiting crowd in episodes of threatened suicide. *Journal of Personality and Social Psychology, 41,* 703–709.

Manson, J. E., Colditz, G. A., Stampfer, M. J., et al. (1990). A prospective study of obesity and risk of coronary heart disease in women. *New England Journal of Medicine, 322,* 882–888.

Manson, S. M. (1994). Culture and depression: Discovering variations in the experience of illness. In W. J. Lonner & R. S. Malpass (Eds.), *Psychology and culture.* Boston: Allyn & Bacon.

Mäntylä, T. (1986). Optimizing cue effectiveness: Recall of 500 and 600 incidentally learned words. *Journal of Experimental Psychology: Learning, Memory, and Cognition, 12,* 66–71.

Marangell, L. B. (2002). Concise guide to psychopharmacology. Washington, DC: American Psychiatric Publishing.

Marata, T., Colligan, R., Malinchok, & Offord, K. (2000). Optimists vs. pessimists: Survival rate among medical patients over a 30-year period. *Mayo Clinic Proceedings, 75,* 140–143.

Marcia, J. E. (1966). Development and validation of ego identity status. *Journal of Personality and Social Psychology, 3,* 551–558.

Marcia, J. E. (2002). Adolescence, identity, and the Bernardone family. *Identity, 2,* 199–209.

Markey, P. M. (2000). Bystander intervention in computer mediated communication. *Computers in Human Behavior, 16,* 183–188.

Markovits, H., & Nantel, G. (1989). The belief-bias effect in the production and evaluation of logical conclusions. *Memory and Cognition, 17,* 11–17.

Marks, D. M., Pae, C. U., & Patkar, A. A. (2008). Triple reuptake inhibitors: The next generation of antidepressants. *Current Neuropharmacology, 6,* 338–343.

Marks, I. M. (1977). Phobias and obsessions: Clinical phenomena in search of laboratory models. In J. Maser & M. E. P. Seligman (Eds.), *Psychopathology: Experimental models.* San Francisco: Freeman.

Marks, I. M. (1991). Self-administered behavioural treatment. *Behavioural Psychotherapy, 19,* 42–46.

Marks, I. M. (2002). The maturing of therapy: Some brief psychotherapies help anxiety/depressive disorders but mechanisms of action are unclear. *British Journal of Psychiatry, 180,* 200–204.

Markus, H. R., & Kitayama, S. (1991). Culture and the self: Implications for cognition, emotion, and motivation. *Psychological Review, 98,* 224–253.

Marlatt, G. A. (1996). Taxonomy of high-risk situations for alcohol relapse: Evolution and development of a cognitive-behavioral model. *Addiction, 91*(Suppl.), S37–S49.

Marlatt, G. A. (Ed.). (1998). *Harm reduction: Pragmatic strategies for managing high-risk behaviors.* New York: Guilford Press.

Marlatt, G. A., Blume, A. W., & Parks, G. A. (2001). Integrating harm reduction therapy and traditional substance abuse treatment. *Journal of Psychoactive Drugs, 33,* 13–21.

Marlatt, G. A., & Gordon, J. R. (1985). *Relapse prevention: Maintenance strategies in the treatment of addiction.* New York: Guilford Press.

Marr, M. J. (2007). The emergence of emergents: One behaviorist's perspective. In D. A. Washburn (Ed.), *Primate perspectives on behavior and cognition.* Washington, DC: American Psychological Association.

Marschark, M., & Mayer, T. S. (1998). Interactions of language and memory in deaf children and adults. *Scandinavian Journal of Psychology, 39,* 145–148.

Marsh, H. W. (1990). A multidimensional, hierarchical model of self-concept: Theoretical and empirical justification. *Educational Psychology Review, 2,* 77–172.

Marshall, L. H., & Magoun, H. W. (1997). *Discoveries in the human brain: Neuroscience prehistory, brain structure, and function.* New York: Humana Press.

Marshall, N. L. (2004). The quality of early child care and children's development. *Current Directions in Psychological Science, 13,* 165–168.

Marshall, P. J., & Fox, N. A. (2000). Emotion regulation, depression, and hemispheric asymmetry. In S. L. Johnson & A. M. Hayes (Eds.), *Stress, coping, and depression.* Mahwah, NJ: Erlbaum.

Marsiglio, W., Amato, P., Day, R. D., & Lamb, M. E. (2000). Scholarship on fatherhood in the 1990s and beyond. *Journal of Marriage and the Family, 62,* 1173–1191.

Marsland, A. L., Cohen, S., Rabin, B. S., & Manuck, S. B. (2001). Associations between stress, trait negative affect, acute immune reactivity, and antibody response to Hepatitis B injection in healthy young adults. *Health Psychology, 20,* 4–11.

Martell, C., Addis, M., & Dimidjian, S. (2004). Finding the action in behavioral activation: The search for empirically supported interventions and mechanisms of change. In S. C. Hayes, V. M. Follette, & M. M. Linehan (Eds.), *Mindfulness and acceptance: Expanding the cognitive-behavioral tradition*. New York: Guilford Press.

Martell, C. R., Dimidjian, S., & Herman-Dunn, R. (2010). *Behavioral activation for depression: A clinician's guide*. New York: Guilford Press.

Martin, C. L., & Ruble, D. (2004). Children's search for gender cues: Cognitive perspectives on gender development. *Current Directions in Psychological Science, 13*, 67–70.

Martin, G. L., & Pear, J. (2010). *Behavior modification*. Piscataway, NJ: Prentice Hall.

Martin, J. E., & Dubbert, P. M. (1985). Adherence in exercise. In R. I. Terjung (Ed.), *Exercise and sport sciences review* (Vol. 13). New York: Macmillan.

Martinez, M., & Raul, E. (2000). Conducta sexual procesos psicologicos moduladores, en mujeres y hombres [Sexual behavior and modulating psychological processes in women and men]. *Archivos Hispanoamericanos de Sexologia, 6*, 133–152.

Maruta, T., Colligan, R., Malinchoc, M., & Offord, K. (2000). Optimists vs. pessimists: Survival rate among medical patients over a 30-year period. *Mayo Clinic Proceedings, 75*, 140–143.

Mascaro, N., & Rosen, H. (2006). The role of existential meaning as a buffer against stress. *Journal of Humanistic Psychology, 46*, 168–190.

Mascolo, M. E., & Li, J. (Eds.). (2004). *Culture and developing selves: Beyond dichotomization*. San Francisco, CA: Jossey-Bass.

Mash, E. J., & Barkley, R. A. (2003). *Child psychopathology* (2nd ed.). New York: Guilford Press.

Maslow, A. H. (1954). *Motivation and personality*. New York: Harper.

Mason, M. F., Tatkow, E. P., & Macrae, C. N. (2005). The look of love: Gaze shifts and person perception. *Psychological Science, 16*, 236–239.

Massad, P. M., & Hulsey, T. L. (2006). Exposure therapy renewed. *Journal of Psychotherapy Integration, 16*, 417–428.

Massen, C., Vaterrodt-Plünnecke, B., Krings, L., & Hilbig, B. E. (2009). Effects of instruction on learners' ability to generate an effective pathway in the method of loci. *Memory, 17*, 724–731.

Masten, A. S. (2001). Ordinary magic: Resilience processes in development. *American Psychologist, 56*, 227–238.

Masten, A. S., & Coatsworth, J. D. (1998). The development of competence in favorable and unfavorable environments: Lessons from research on successful children. *American Psychologist, 53*, 205–220.

Masterpasqua, F. (2009). Psychology and epigenetics. *Review of General Psychology, 13*, 194–201.

Masters, W., & Johnson, V. (1966). *Human sexual response*. London: Churchill.

Masters, W. H., Johnson, V. E., & Kolodny, R. C. (1988). *Human sexuality* (3rd ed.). Boston: Little, Brown.

Mata, J., Silva, M. N., Vieira, P. N., et al. (2009). Motivational "spill-over" during weight control: Increased self-determination and exercise intrinsic motivation predict eating self-regulation. *Health Psychology, 28*, 709–716.

Mather, G. (2006). *Foundations of perception*. Hove, England: Psychology Press/Erlbaum (UK).

Mathews, C. O. (1929). Erroneous first impressions on objective tests. *Journal of Educational Psychology, 20*, 280–286.

Matson, J. L. (Ed.). (2009). *Practitioner's guide to applied behavior analysis for children with autism spectrum disorders*. New York: Springer.

Matsumoto, D., & Hull, P. (1994). Cognitive development and intelligence. In D. Matsumoto (Ed.), *People: Psychology from a cultural perspective*. Pacific Grove, CA: Brooks/Cole.

Matt, G. E., & Navarro, A. M. (1997). What meta-analyses have and have not taught us about psychotherapy effects: A review and future directions. *Clinical Psychology Review, 17*, 1–32.

Matthen, M. (2007). *Seeing, doing, and knowing: A philosophical theory of sense perception*. New York: Oxford University Press.

Matthews, G., Roberts, R. D., & Zeidner, M. (2004). Seven myths about emotional intelligence. *Psychological Inquiry, 15*, 179–196.

Mattys, S. L. (2000). The perception of primary and secondary stress in English. *Perception & Psychophysics, 62*, 253–265.

May, M. (2007). *Sensation and perception*. New York: Chelsea House.

May, R. (1961). The emergence of existential psychology. In R. May (Ed.), *Existential psychology*. New York: Random House.

Mayall, K., Humphreys, G. W., & Olson, A. (1997). Disruption to word or letter processing? The origins of case-mixing effects. *Journal of Experimental Psychology: Learning, Memory, and Cognition, 23*, 1275–1286.

Mayer, J. D. (2008). Personal intelligence expressed: A theoretical analysis. *Review of General Psychology, 13*, 46–58.

Mayer, J. D., Roberts, R. D., & Barsade, S. G. (2008). Human abilities: Emotional intelligence. *Annual Review of Psychology, 59*, 507–536.

Mayer, R. E. (2000). Intelligence and education. In R. J. Sternberg (Ed.), *Handbook of intelligence*. New York: Cambridge University Press.

Mayr, U. (2009). Sticky plans: Inhibition and binding during serial-task control. *Cognitive Psychology, 59*, 123–153.

McAdams, D. P., & de St. Aubin, E. (Eds.). (1998). *Generativity and adult development: How and why we care for the next generation*. Washington, DC: American Psychological Association.

McAdams, D. P., & Olson, B. D. (2010). Personality development: Continuity and change over the life course. *Annual Review of Psychology, 61*, 517–542.

McAdams, S., & Drake, C. (2002). Auditory perception and cognition. In H. Pashler & S. Yantis (Eds.), *Steven's handbook of experimental psychology: Vol. 1. Sensation and perception* (3rd ed.). New York: Wiley.

McArdle, S., & Duda, J. K. (2002). Implications of the motivational climate in youth sports. In F. L. Smoll & R. E. Smith (Eds.), *Children and youth in sport: A biopsychosocial perspective*. Dubuque, IA: Kendall/Hunt.

McAuley, E. (1992). The role of efficacy cognitions in the prediction of exercise behavior in middle-aged adults. *Journal of Behavioral Medicine, 15*, 65–88.

McCann, U. D., Szabo, Z., Scheffel, U., Dannals, R. F., & Ricaurte, G. A. (1998). Positron emission tomographic evidence of toxic effect of MDMA ("Ecstasy") on brain serotonin neurons in human beings. *Lancet, 352*(9138), 1433–1437.

McCarley, R. W. (1998). Dreams: Disguise of forbidden wishes or transparent reflections of a distinct brastate? In R. M. Bilder & F. F. LeFever (Eds.), *Neuroscience of the mind on the centennial of Freud's Project for a Scientific Psychology: Annals of the New York Academy of Sciences* (Vol. 843). New York: New York Academy of Sciences.

McCaul, K. D., & Malott, J. J. (1984). Distraction and coping with pain. *Psychological Bulletin, 95*, 516–533.

McClelland, D. C. (1989). *Human motivation*. New York: Cambridge University Press.

McClelland, D. C., Atkinson, J. W., Clark, R. A., & Lowell, E. L. (1953). *The achievement motive*. New York: Appleton-Century-Crofts.

McClintock, M. K. (1971). Menstrual synchrony and suppression. *Nature, 291*, 244–245.

McConnell, J. V. (1962). Memory transfer through cannibalism in planarians. *Journal of Neuropsychiatry, 3*(Suppl. 1), 542–548.

McCown, D., & Reibel, D. (2010). Mindfulness and mindfulness-based stress reduction. In D. A. Monti & B. D. Beitman (Eds.), *Integrative psychiatry*. New York: Oxford University Press.

McCracken, L. M. (1998). Learning to live with pain: Acceptance of pain predicts adjustment in persons with chronic pain. *Pain, 74*, 21–27.

McCrae, R. R., & Costa, P. T. (2003). *Personality in adulthood: A Five-Factor Theory perspective*. New York: Guilford Press.

McCrae, R. R., & Costa, P. T. (2008). The five-factor theory of personality. In O. P. John, R. W. Robins, & L. A. Pervin (Eds.), *Handbook of personality theory and research* (3rd ed.). New York: Guilford Press.

McCullough, M. E., Worthington, E. L., Jr., & Rachal, K. C. (1997). Interpersonal forgiving in close relationships. *Journal of Personality and Social Psychology, 73*, 321–336.

McDaniel, M. A. (2005). Big-brained people are smarter: A meta-analysis of the relationship between in vivo brain volume and intelligence. *Intelligence, 33*, 337–346.

McDaniel, M. A., Einstein, G. O., Stout, A. C., & Morgan, Z. (2003). Aging and maintaining intentions over delays: Do it or lose it. *Psychology and Aging, 18*, 823–835.

McElroy, S. L., Kotwal, R., & Keck, P. E. (2006). Comorbidity of eating disorders with bipolar disorder and treatment implications. *Bipolar Disorders, 8*, 686–695.

McEvoy, S. P., Stevenson, M. R., McCartt, A.T., Woodward, M., Haworth, C., Palamara, P., & Cercarelli, R. (2005). Role of mobile phones in motor vehicle crashes resulting in hospital attendance: A case-crossover study. *British Medical Journal, 331*, 428. Retrieved December 2, 2006, from http://www.bmj.com/cgi/content/full/bmj;331/7514/428.

McFarland, S., & Carnahan, T. (2009). A situation's first powers are attracting volunteers and selecting participants: A reply to Haney and Zimbardo (2009). *Personality and Social Psychology Bulletin, 35*, 815–818.

McFarlane, J. (1975). Olfaction in the development of social preferences in the human neonate.

In M. Hofer (Ed.), *Parent-infant interaction.* Amsterdam: Elsevier.

McGinnis, M. (1994). The role of behavioral research in national health policy. In S. J. Blumenthal, K. Matthews, & S. M. Weiss (Eds.), *New research frontiers in behavioral medicine: Proceedings of the national conference.* Washington, DC: NIH Publications.

McGlashan, T. H., & Fenton, W. S. (1992). The positive-negative distinction in schizophrenia: Review of natural history validators. *Archives of General Psychiatry, 49,* 63–72.

McGlone, J. (1977). Sex differences in the cerebral organization of verbal functions in patients with unilateral brain lesions. *Brain, 100,* 775–793.

McGregor, H. A., & Elliot, A. J. (2002). Achievement goals as predictors of achievement-relevant processes prior to task engagement. *Journal of Educational Psychology, 94,* 381–395.

McGrew, K. S. (2009). CHC theory and the Human Cognitive Abilities Project: Standing on the shoulders of the giants of psychometric intelligence research. *Intelligence, 37,* 1–10.

McGuffin, P., Owen, M. J., & Gottesman, I. I. (Eds.). (2005). *Psychiatric genetics and genomics.* New York: Oxford University Press.

McIntosh, D. N., Silver, R. C., & Wortman, C. B. (1993). Religion's role in adjustment to a negative life event: Coping with the loss of a child. *Journal of Personality and Social Psychology, 65,* 812–821.

McIntyre, R. B., Paulson, R. M., & Lord, C. G. (2003). Alleviating women's mathematics stereotype threat through salience of group achievements. *Journal of Experimental Social Psychology, 39,* 83–90.

McKenna, M. C., Zevon, M. A., Corn, B., & Rounds, J. (1999). Psychological factors and the development of breast cancer: A meta-analysis. *Health Psychology, 18,* 520–531.

McKenna, P. (2007). *Schizophrenia.* Philadelphia: Taylor & Francis.

McKenna, P., & Oh, T. (2003). *Formal thought disorder in schizophrenia.* New York: Cambridge University Press.

McKenzie, C. R. M., Liersch, M. J., & Yaniv, I. (2008). Overconfidence in interval estimates: What does expertise buy you? *Organizational Behavior and Human Decision Processes, 107,* 179–191.

McKey, R., Conndelli, L., Gansin, H., Barrett, B., McConkey, C., & Plantz, M. (1985). *The impact of Head Start on children, families and communities (Final report of the Head Start Evaluation, Synthesis and Utilization Project).* Washington, DC: CSR, Inc.

McKimmie, B. M., Terry, D. J., & Hogg, M. A. (2009). Dissonance reduction in the context of group membership: The role of metaconsistency. *Group Dynamics: Theory, Research, and Practice, 13,* 103–119.

McKnight, P. E., & Kashdan, T. B. (2009). Purpose in life as a system that creates and sustains health and well-being: An integrative, testable theory. *Review of General Psychology, 13,* 242–251.

McKown, C. (2005). Applying ecological theory to advance the science and practice of school-based prejudice reduction interventions. *Educational Psychologist, 40,* 177–189.

McMurran, M., Conor, D., Christopher, G., & Huband, N. (2007). The relationship between personality disorders and social problem solving in adults. *Personality and Individual Differences, 42,* 145–155.

McNally, R. J., & Geraerts, E. (2009). A new solution to the recovered memory debate. *Perspectives on Psychological Science, 4,* 126–134.

McNeil, E. B. (1967). *The quiet furies: Man and disorder.* Englewood Cliffs, NJ: Prentice Hall.

McNulty, J. K., & Karney, B. R. (2004). Positive expectations in the early years of marriage: Should couples expect the best or brace for the worst? *Journal of Personality and Social Psychology, 86,* 729–743.

McWilliams, N. (2004). *Psychoanalytic psychotherapy: A practitioner's guide.* New York: Guilford Press.

Meaney, M. J., Mitchell, J. B., Aitken, D. H., & Bhatnagar, S. (Eds.). (1991). The effects of neonatal handling on the development of the adrenocortical response to stress: Implications for neuropathology and cognitive deficits in later life. *Psychoneuroendocrinology, 16,* 85–103.

Mebane-Sims, I. (2009). 2009 Alzheimer's disease facts and figures. *Alzheimer's & Dementia, 5,* 234–270.

Mechan, A. O., Moran, P. M., Elliot, J. M., Young, A. M. J., Joseph, M. H., & Green, A. R. (2002). A study of the effect of a single neurotoxic dose of 3,4-methylenedioxymethamphetamine (MDMA; "ecstasy") on the subsequent long-term behaviour of rats in the plus maze and open field. *Psychopharmacology, 159,* 167–175.

Meddis, R., Pearson, A. J., & Langford, G. (1973). An extreme case of healthy insomnia. *Electroencephalography and Clinical Neurophysiology, 35,* 213–214.

Medeiros, J. A. (2006). *Cone shape and color vision: Unification of structure and perception.* Blountsville, AL: Fifth Estate.

Meehl, P. E. (1995). "Is psychoanalysis one science, two sciences, or no science at all? A discourse among friendly antagonists": Comment. *Journal of the American Psychoanalytic Association, 43,* 1015–1023.

Meehl, P. E. (1997). Credentialed persons, credentialed knowledge. *Clinical Psychology: Science and Practice, 4,* 91–98.

Meeus, W. H. J., & Raaijmakers, Q. A. W. (1986). Administrative obedience: Carrying out orders to use psychological-administrative violence. *European Journal of Social Psychology, 16,* 311–324.

Megargee, E. I. (1966). Undercontrolled and overcontrolled personality types in extreme antisocial aggression. *Psychological Monographs, 80*(Whole No. 611).

Mehnert, T., Krauss, H. H., Nadler, R., & Boyd, M. (1990). Correlates of life satisfaction in those with disabling conditions. *Rehabilitation Psychology, 35,* 3–17.

Meleski, M. E., & Damato, E. G. (2003). HIV exposure: Neonatal considerations. *Journal of Obstetric, Gynecologic, and Neonatal Nursing, 32,* 109–116.

Meltzoff, A. N. (2002). Elements of a developmental theory of imitation. In A. N. Meltzoff, N. Andrew, & W. Prinz (Eds.), *The imitative mind: Development, evolution, and brain bases. Cambridge studies in cognitive perceptual development.* New York: Cambridge University Press.

Melzack, R. (1998). Pain and stress. Clues toward understanding chronic pain. In M. Sabourin et al. (Eds.), *Advances in psychological science.* Hove, England: Psychology Press/Erlbaum.

Melzack, R., & Wall, P. D. (1982). *The challenge of pain.* New York: Basic Books.

Menzies, R. G., & Clarke, J. C. (1995). The etiology of acrophobia and its relationship to severity and individual response patterns. *Behaviour Research and Therapy, 33,* 795–803.

Merrill, E. C., & Lookadoo, R. (2004). Selective search for conjunctively defined targets by children and young adults. *Journal of Experimental Child Psychology, 89,* 72–90.

Mersch, P. P. A., Middendorp, H. M., Bouhuys, A. L., Beersma, D. G. M., & van den Hoofdakker, R. H. (1999). Seasonal affective disorder and latitude: A review of the literature. *Journal of Affective Disorders, 53,* 35–48.

Mersky, J. P., & Topitzes, J. (2009). Comparing early adult outcomes of maltreated and non-maltreated children: A prospective longitudinal investigation. *Children and Youth Services Review.* Advance online publication. doi:10.1016/j.childyouth.2009.10.018

Merz, C. J., Tabbert, K., Schweckendiek, J., Klucken, T., Vaitl, D., Stark, R., & Wolf, O. T. (2010). Investigating the impact of sex and cortisol on implicit fear conditioning with fMRI. *Psychoneuroendocrinology, 35,* 33–46.

Mesquita, B., Frijda, N. H., & Scherer, K. R. (1997). Culture and emotion. In J. W. Berry et al. (Eds.), *Handbook of cross-cultural psychology: Vol. 2. Basic processes and human development* (2nd ed.). Boston: Allyn & Bacon.

Mesquita, B., & Markus, H. R. (2005). Culture and emotion: Models of agency as sources of cultural variation in emotion. In A. S. R. Manstead, N. H. Frijda, A. H. Fischer, & K. Oatley (Eds.), *Feelings and emotions: The Amsterdam Symposium.* New York: Cambridge University Press.

Messner, M., Reinhard, M., & Sporer, S. L. (2008). Compliance through direct persuasive appeals: The moderating role of communicator's attractiveness in interpersonal persuasion. *Social Influence, 3,* 67–83.

Methot, L. L., & Huitema, B. E. (1998). Effects of signal probability on individual differences in vigilance. *Human Factors, 40,* 78–90.

Metrik, J., Rohsenow, D. J., Monti, P. M., McGeary, J. C., Travis, A. R., de Wit, H., et al. (2009). Effectiveness of a marijuana expectancy manipulation: Piloting the balanced-placebo design for marijuana. *Experimental and Clinical Psychopharmacology, 17,* 217–225.

Meyer, C. B., & Taylor, S. E. (1986). Adjustment to rape. *Journal of Personality and Social Psychology, 50,* 1226–1234.

Meyer, G. J., Finn, S. E., Eyde, L. D., Kaye, G. G., Moreland, K. L., Dies, R., et al. (2001). Psychological testing and psychological assessment: A review of evidence and issues. *American Psychologist, 56,* 128–165.

Meyer, R. G., & Osborne, Y. H. (1987). *Case studies in abnormal behavior* (2nd ed.). Boston: Allyn & Bacon.

Meyer, T. A., Svirsky, M. A., Kirk, K. I., & Miyamoto, R. T. (1998). Improvements in speech perception by children with profound prelingual hearing loss: Effects of device, communication mode, and chronological age. *Journal of Speech, Language, and Hearing Research, 41,* 846–858.

Meyersburg, C. A., Bogdan, R., Gallo, D. A., & McNally, R. J. (2009). False memory propensity in people reporting recovered memories of past lives. *Journal of Abnormal Psychology, 118,* 399–404.

Mezulis, A. H., Abramson, L. Y., Hyde, J. S., & Hankin, B. L. (2004). Is there a universal positivity bias in attributions? A meta-analytic review of individual, developmental, and cultural differences in the self-serving attributional bias. *Psychological Bulletin, 130,* 711–747.

Mezulis, A. H., Hyde, J. S., & Abramson, L. Y. (2006). The developmental origins of cognitive vulnerability to depression: Temperament, parenting, and negative life events in childhood as contributors to negative cognitive style. *Developmental Psychology, 42,* 1012–1025.

Michael, R. T., Gagnon, J. H., Laumman, E. O., & Kolata, G. (1994). *Sex in America: A definitive survey.* Boston: Little, Brown.

Mignot, E. (1998). Genetic and familial aspects of narcolepsy. *Neurology, 50,* S16–S22.

Miklowitz, D. J. (2007). Mood disorders: Bipolar disorders. In M. Hersen, S. M. Turner, & D. C. Beidel (Eds.), *Adult psychopathology and diagnosis.* Hoboken, NJ: Wiley.

Mikulincer, M., & Shaver, P. R. (2009). Attachment theory: II, Developmental, psychodynamic, and optimal-functioning aspects. In P. J. Corr & G. Matthews (Eds.), *The Cambridge handbook of personality psychology.* Cambridge, England: Cambridge University Press.

Mikulincer, M., Shaver, P. R., & Pereg, D. (2003). Attachment theory and affect regulation: The dynamics, development, and cognitive consequences of attachment-related strategies. *Motivation & Emotion, 27,* 77–102.

Miles, C., & Hardman, E. (1998). State-dependent memory produced by aerobic exercise. *Ergonomics, 41,* 20–28.

Milgram, S. (1974). *Obedience to authority: An experimental view.* New York: Harper & Row.

Miller, A. G. (2004). What can the Milgram obedience experiments tell us about the Holocaust? Generalizing from the social psychology laboratory. In A. G. Miller (Ed.), *The social psychology of good and evil.* New York: Guilford Press.

Miller, B. C., Fan, X., Christensen, M., Grotevant, H. D., & van Dulmen, M. (2000). Comparisons of adopted and nonadopted adolescents in a large, nationally representative sample. *Child Development, 71,* 1458–1473.

Miller, G. A. (1956). The magical number seven, plus or minus two: Some limits on our capacity for processing information. *Psychological Review, 63,* 81–97.

Miller, G. E., Chen, E., & Zhou, E. E. (2007). If it goes up, must it come down? Chronic stress and the hypothalamic-pituitary-adrenocortical axis in humans. *Psychological Bulletin, 133,* 25–45.

Miller, J. G. (1984). Culture and the development of everyday social explanation. *Journal of Personality and Social Psychology, 46,* 961–978.

Miller, J. G., Bersoff, D. M., & Harwood, R. L. (1990). Perceptions of social responsibility in India and in the United States: Moral imperatives or personal decisions? *Journal of Personality and Social Psychology, 58,* 33–47.

Miller, N. E. (1944). Experimental studies of confiict. In J. McV. Hunt (Ed.), *Personality and the behavior disorders* (Vol. 1). New York: Ronald Press.

Miller, S. D., Blackburn, T., Scholes, G., White, G. L., & Mamales, N. (1991). Optical differences in multiple personality disorder: A second look. *Journal of Nervous and Mental Disease, 179,* 132–135.

Miller, W. R., & Brown, S. A. (1997). Why psychologists should treat alcohol and drug problems. *American Psychologist, 52,* 1269–1279.

Miller, W. R., & Rollnick, S. (2002). *Motivational interviewing* (2nd ed.). New York: Guilford Press.

Miller, W. R., & Rose, G. S. (2009). Toward a theory of motivational interviewing. *American Psychologist, 64,* 527–537.

Milling, L. S. (2008). Recent developments in the study of hypnotic pain reduction: A new golden era of research? *Contemporary Hypnosis, 25,* 165–177.

Millon, T., & Davis, R. (2000). *Personality disorders in modern life.* New York: Wiley.

Millon, T., Millon, C. M., Meagher, D., Meagher, S., Grossman, S., & Ramnath, R. (2004). *Personality disorders in modern life* (2nd ed.). New York: Wiley.

Milner, A. D., & Dijkerman, H. C. (2001). Direct and indirect visual routes to action. In B. De Gelder, E. H. F. De Haan, & C. A. Heywood (Eds.), *Out of mind: Varieties of unconscious processes.* London: Oxford University Press.

Milner, B. (1965). Memory disturbances after bilateral hippocampal lesions. In P. Milner & S. Glickman (Eds.), *Cognitive processes and the brain.* Princeton, NJ: Van Nostrand.

Milton, J., & Wiseman, R. (1999). Does psi exist? Lack of replication of an anomalous process of information transfer. *Psychological Bulletin, 125,* 387–391.

Milton, J., & Wiseman, R. (2001). Does psi exist? Reply to Storm and Ertel (2001). *Psychological Bulletin, 127,* 434–438.

Milyavskaya, M. G., Gingras, I., Mageau, G. A., Koestner, R., et al. (2009). Balance across contexts: Importance of balanced need satisfaction across various life domains. *Personality and Social Psychology Bulletin, 35,* 1031–1045.

Mineka, S., Watson, D., & Clark, L. A. (1998). Co-morbidity of anxiety and unipolar mood disorder. *Annual Review of Psychology, 49,* 377–412.

Mintz, J., Drake, R. E., & Crits-Christoph, P. (1996). Efficacy and effectiveness of psychotherapy: Two paradigms, one science. *American Psychologist, 51,* 1084–1085.

Mischel, W. (1999). Personality coherence and dispositions in a cognitive-affective personality system (CAPS) approach. In D. Cervone & Y. Shoda (Eds.), *The coherence of personality.* New York: Guilford Press.

Mischel, W., & Shoda, Y. (1999). Integrating dispositions and personality dynamics within a unified theory of personality: The cognitive-affective personality system (CAPS). In L. Pervin & O. John (Eds.), *Handbook of personality: Theory and research* (2nd ed.). New York: Guilford Press.

Mischel, W., Shoda, Y., & Mendoza-Denton, R. (2002). Situation-behavior profiles as a locus of consistency in personality. *Current Directions in Psychological Science, 11,* 50–54.

Mischel, W., Shoda, Y., & Smith, R. E. (2004). *Introduction to personality: Toward an integration* (7th ed.). New York: Wiley.

Mistlberger, R. E., Antle, M. C., Glass, J. D., & Miller, J. D. (2000). Behavioral and serotonergic regulation of circadian rhythms. *Biological Rhythm Research, 31,* 240–283.

Mitchell, K. J., & Zaragoza, M. S. (2001). Contextual overlap and eyewitness suggestibility. *Memory and Cognition, 29,* 616–626.

Mitka, M. (2009). College binge drinking still on the rise. *JAMA: Journal of the American Medical Association, 302,* 836–837.

Moen, P., Kim, J. E., & Hofmeister, H. (2001). Couples' work/retirement transitions, gender, and marital quality. *Social Psychology Quarterly, 64,* 55–71.

Moffitt, T., Caspi, A., & Rutter, M. (2006). Measured gene-environment interactions in psychopathology: Concepts, research strategies, and implications for research, intervention, and public understanding of genetics. *Perspectives on Psychological Science. 1,* 5–27.

Mokdad, A. H., Marks, J. S., Stroup, D. F., & Gerberding, J. L. (2004). Actual causes of death in the United States, 2000. *Journal of American Medical Association, 291,* 1238–1245.

Molfese, D. L., & Molfese, V. J. (2002). *Developmental variations in learning: Applications to social, executive function, language, and reading skills.* Mahwah, NJ: Erlbaum.

Möller, I., & Krahé, B. (2009). Exposure to violent video games and aggression in German adolescents: A longitudinal analysis. *Aggressive Behavior, 35,* 75–89.

Monk, C. A., Trafton, J. G., & Boehm-Davis, D. A. (2008). The effect of interruption duration and demand on resuming suspended goals. *Journal of Experimental Psychology: Applied, 14,* 299–313.

Monk, T. H., Buysse, D. J., Welsh, D. K., Kennedy, K. S., & Rose, L. R. (2001). A sleep diary and questionnaire study of naturally short sleepers. *Journal of Sleep Research, 10,* 173–179.

Monk, T. H., Folkard, S., & Wedderburn, A. I. (1996). Maintaining safety and high performance on shiftwork. *Applied Ergonomics, 27,* 17–23.

Monroe, S. M., & Peterman, A. M. (1988). Life stress and psychopathology. In L. H. Cohen (Ed.), *Life events and psychological functioning: Theoretical and methodological issues.* Newbury Park, CA: Sage.

Montgomery, H., Lipshitz, R., & Brehmer, B. (Eds.). (2005). *How professionals make decisions.* Mahwah, NJ: Erlbaum.

Moody, M. S. (1997). Changes in scores on the Mental Rotations Test during the menstrual cycle. *Perceptual and Motor Skills, 84,* 955–961.

Moon, C., & Fifer, W. P. (1990). Syllables as signals for 2-day-old infants. *Infant Behavior and Development, 13,* 377–390.

Moore, D. W. (2005, June 16). Three in four Americans believe in paranormal. *Gallup USA.* Retrieved January 12, 2009, from http://www.gallup.com/poll/16915/Three-Four-Americans-Believe-Paranormal.spx

Moore, K. A., Guzman, L., Hair, E., Lippman, L., & Garrett, S. (2004). Parent-teen relationships and interactions: Far more positive than not. *Child Trends Research Brief,* publication no. 2004–25. Retrieved February 20, 2007, from http://www.childtrends.org/Files/Parent_TeenRB.pdf

Moore, T. M., Scarpa, A., & Raine, A. (2002). A meta-analysis of serotonin metabolite 5 HIAA and antisocial behavior. *Aggressive Behavior, 28,* 299–316.

Morales, E. S. (2009). Contextual community prevention theory: Building interventions with community agency collaboration. *American Psychologist, 64*, 805–816.

Moreland, J. L., Dansereau, D. F., & Chmielewski, T. L. (1997). Recall of descriptive information: The roles of presentation format, annotation strategy, and individual differences. *Contemporary Educational Psychology, 22*, 521–533.

Morewedge, C. K., & Norton, M. I. (2009). When dreaming is believing: The (motivated) interpretation of dreams. *Journal of Personality and Social Psychology, 96*, 249–264.

Morford, J. P. (2003). Grammatical development in adolescent first-language learners. *Linguistics, 41*, 681–721.

Morgan, J. D., Laungani, P., & Palmer, S. (Eds.). (2009). *Death and bereavement around the world: Vol. 5. Reflective essays.* Amityville, NY: Baywood.

Morgan, O., Vicente, J., Griffiths, P., & Hickman, M. (2008). Trends in overdose deaths from drug misuse in Europe: What do the data tell us? *Addiction, 103*, 699–700.

Morgan, W. (1997). *Physical activity and mental health.* Philadelphia: Taylor & Francis.

Morgan, W. P., Horstman, D. H., Cymerman, A., & Stokes, J. (1983). Facilitation of physical performance by means of a cognitive strategy. *Cognitive Therapy and Research, 7*, 251–264.

Moro, V., Berlucchi, G., Lerch, J., Tomaiuolo, F., & Aglioti, S. M. (2008). Selective deficit of mental visual imagery with intact primary visual cortex and visual perception. *Cortex, 44*, 109–118.

Morrell, M. J., Dixen, J. M., Carter, C. S., & Davidson, J. M. (1984). The influence of age and cycling status on sexual arousability in women. *American Journal of Obstetrics and Gynecology, 148*, 66–71.

Morris, D., Collett, P., Marsh, P., & O'Shaughnessy, M. (1979). *Gestures.* New York: Stein & Day.

Morris, J., & Dolan, R. (2001). The amygdala and unconscious fear processing. In B. De Gelder, E. H. F. De Haan, & C. A. Heywood (Eds.), *Out of mind: Varieties of unconscious processes.* London: Oxford University Press.

Morris, R., & Becker, J. (2005). *Cognitive neuropsychology of Alzheimer's disease.* New York: Oxford University Press.

Morrison, A. (2005). Psychosis and the phenomena of unwanted intrusive thoughts. In D. A. Clark (Ed.), *Intrusive thoughts in clinical disorders: Theory, research, and treatment.* New York: Guilford Press.

Morrison, D. C. (1988). Marine mammals join the navy. *Science, 242*, 1503–1504.

Morrison, S. (2006). *Hypothalamus: Brainstem interactions in homeostasis.* New York: Springer.

Moscovici, S. (1985). Social influence and conformity. In G. Lindzey & E. Aronson (Eds.), *Handbook of social psychology* (3rd ed.). New York: Random House.

Moss, C. S. (1972). *Recovery with aphasia.* Urbana, IL: University of Illinois Press.

Mousikou, P., Coltheart, M., Saunders, S., & Yen, L. (2010). Is the orthographic/phonological onset a single unit in reading aloud? *Journal of Experimental Psychology: Human Perception and Performance, 36*, 175–194.

Mowrer, O. H. (1947). On the dual nature of learning: A reinterpretation of "conditioning" and "problem solving." *Harvard Educational Review, 17*, 102–150.

Muenchow, S., & Marsland, K. W. (2007). Beyond baby steps: Promoting the growth and development of U.S. child-care policy. In J. L. Aber, S. J. Bishop-Josef, S. M. Jones, K. T. McLearn, & D. A. Phillips (Eds.), *Child development and social policy: Knowledge for action.* Washington, DC: American Psychological Association.

Mulligan, N. W., & Dew, I. T. Z. (2009). Generation and perceptual implicit memory: Different generation tasks produce different effects on perceptual priming. *Memory and Cognition, 35*, 1522–1538.

Mulvey, E. P., Odgers, C., Skeem, J., Gardner, W., Schubert, C., & Lidz, C. (2006). Substance use and community violence: A test of the relation at a daily level. *Journal of Consulting and Clinical Psychology, 74*, 743–754.

Munafo, M. R. (2009). Behavioral genetics: from variance to DNA. Shaver, P. R., & Mikulincer, M. (2009). Attachment theory: I, Motivational, individual differences and structural aspects. In P. J. Corr & G. Matthews (Eds.), *The Cambridge handbook of personality psychology.* Cambridge, UK: Cambridge University Press.

Murdin, L., & Scott, A. (Eds.) (2007). *Transference in counseling and psychotherapy: The power of patterns.* New York: Palgrave Macmillan.

Murphy, S. L. (2000). Deaths: Final data for 1998. *National Vital Statistics Reports* (NCHS), pp. 26, 73.

Murray, C. (1998). *Income, inequality, and IQ.* Washington, DC: American Enterprise Institute.

Murray, J. P. (2008). Media violence: The effects are both real and strong. *American Behavioral Scientist, 51*, 1212–1230.

Murray, R., Jones, P., Van Oss, J., et al. (2003). *The epidemiology of schizophrenia.* New York: Cambridge University Press.

Murray, S. L., Griffin, D. W., Rose, P., & Bellavia, G. (2006). For better or worse? Self-esteem and the contingencies of acceptance in marriage. *Personality and Social Psychology Bulletin, 7*, 866–880.

Murthy, P., Kudlur, S., George, S., & Mathew, G. (2009). A clinical overview of fetal alcohol syndrome. *Addictive Disorders & Their Treatment, 8*, 1–12.

Musicek, F. E., & Baran, J. (2006). *The auditory system: Anatomy, physiology, and clinical correlates.* Boston: Allyn & Bacon.

Myers, B., Latter, R., & Abdollahi-Arena, M. K. (2006). The court of public opinion: Lay perceptions of polygraph testing. *Law and Human Behavior, 10*, 509–523.

Myin-Germeys, I., van Os, J., Schwartz, J. E., Stone, A. A., & Delespaul, P. A. (2001). Emotional reactivity to daily life stress in psychosis. *Archives of General Psychiatry, 58*, 1137–1144.

Mynttinen, S., Sundström, A., Vissers, J., Koivukoski, M., Hakuli, K., & Keskinen, E. (2009). Self-assessed driver competence among novice drivers—A comparison of driving test candidate assessments and examiner assessments in a Dutch and Finnish sample. *Journal of Safety Research, 40*, 301–309.

Mythbusters. (2007, April 11). Voice flame extinguisher. Discovery Channel. Season 5, Episode 76.

Nadler, A., & Ben-Slushan, D. (1989). Forty years later: Long-term consequences of massive traumatization as manifested by holocaust survivors from the city and the Kibbutz. *Journal of Consulting and Clinical Psychology, 57*, 287–293.

Naff, C. F. (2010). *Deafness and hearing impairment.* London, England: Greenhaven Press.

Nakayama, K., & Tyler, C. W. (1981). Psychophysical isolation of movement sensitivity by removal of familiar position cues. *Vision Research, 21*, 427–433.

Narrow, W. E., Rae, D. S., Robins, L. N., & Regier, D. A. (2002). Revised prevalence based estimates of mental disorders in the United States: Using a clinical signficance criterion to reconcile 2 surveys' estimates. *Archives of General Psychiatry, 59*, 115–123.

Nathan, P. E., & Lagenbucher, J. W. (1999). Psychopathology: Description and classification. *Annual Review of Psychology, 50*, 79–107.

National Center for Education Statistics. (2008). *Bachelor's degrees conferred by degree-granting institutions, by field of study: Selected years, 1970–71 through 2006–07. Table 27.1.* United States Department of Education. Retrieved May 19, 2009, from http://nces.ed.gov/programs/digest/d08/tables/dt08_271.asp

National Center for Health Statistics. (2004). *Health and longevity in the United States.* Retrieved October 27, 2004, from http://www.cdc.gov

National Center for Health Statistics. (2006). *Health in America, 2006.* Hyattsville, MD: Author.

National Center for Health Statistics. (2008). *Health, United States 2008.* Hyattsville, MD: Author.

National Center for Health Statistics. (2009). *Health in America, 2008.* Hyattsville, MD: Author.

National Center on Addiction and Drug Abuse. (2005). *National survey of American attitudes on substance abuse X: Teens and parents.* Retrieved March 4, 2007, from http://www.casacolumbia.org/Absolutenm/articlefiles/ Teen_Survey_Report_2005.pdf

National Highway Traffic Safety Administration. (2006). *Traffic safety facts 2005 data. (DOT HS 810 616).* Retrieved January 13, 2007, from http://www-nrd.nhtsa.dot.gov/pdf/nrd-30/NCSA/TSF2005/AlcoholTSF05.pdf

National Institute of Mental Health. (2008). The numbers count: Mental disorders in America. Retrieved November 19, 2009, from http://www.nimh.nih.gov/health/publications/the-numbers-count-mental-disorders-in-america/index.shtml

National Institute of Mental Health. (2009). Suicide in the U.S.: Statistics and prevention. Retrieved February 22, 2010, at http://www.nimh.nih.gov/health/publications/suicide-in-the-us-statistics-and-prevention/index/shtml

National Institutes of Health. (2002). *Alzheimer's disease: Unraveling the mystery.* NIH Publication 02-3782. Bethesda, MD. Available online: http://www.alzheimers.org/unraveling/unraveling.pdf

National Institutes of Health. (2010). Human Genome Project Information. Retrieved January 9, 2010, from http://www.nlm.nih.gov/medlineplus/genetictesting.html

National Safety Council. (1992). *Blood alcohol level and risk of having an automobile accident.* Washington, DC: Author.

National Sleep Foundation. (2004). *Final report: 2004 sleep in America poll.* Retrieved January 8, 2010, from http://www.sleepfoundation.org/sites/default/files/2004SleepPollFinalReport.pdf

National Sleep Foundation. (2009). *2009 sleep in America poll: Summary of findings.*

Retrieved January 8, 2010, from http://www.sleepfoundation.org/sites/default/files/2009%20Sleep%20in%20America%20SOF%20EMBARGOED.pdf

Natsoulas, T. (1999). An ecological and phenomenological perspective on consciousness and perception: Contact with the world at the very heart of the being of consciousness. *Review of General Psychology, 3*, 224–245.

Needham, A., Barrett, T., & Peterman, K. (2002). A pick me up for infants' exploratory skills: Early simulated experiences reaching for objects using "sticky" mittens enhances young infants' object exploration skills. *Infant Behavior and Development, 25*, 279–295.

Neisser, U., Bouchard, T. J., Jr., Boykin, A. W., Brody, N., Ceci, S. J., Halpern, D. F., Loehlin, J. C., Perloff, R., Sternberg, R. J., & Urbina, S. (1998). Intelligence: Knowns and unknowns. In M. E. Hertzig et al. (Eds.), *Annual progress in child psychiatry and child development: 1997.* Bristol, PA: Brunner/Mazel.

Neisser, U., & Harsch, N. (1993). Phantom flashbulbs: False recollections of hearing the news about *Challenger.* In E. Winograd & U. Neisser (Eds.), *Affect and accuracy in recall: Studies of "flashbulb" memories.* New York: Cambridge University Press.

Nelson, L. J. (2009). An examination of emerging adulthood in Romanian college students. *International Journal of Behavioral Development, 33*, 402–411.

Nelson, L. J., Badger, S., & Wu, B. (2004). The influence of culture in emerging adulthood: Perspectives of Chinese college students. *International Journal of Behavioral Development, 28*, 26–36.

Nettle, D. (2006). The evolution of personality in humans and other animals. *American Psychologist, 61*, 622–631.

Neumäker, K. J. (2000). Mortality rates and causes of death. *European Eating Disorders Review, 8*, 181–187.

Neumeister, A. (2004). Neurotransmitter depletion and seasonal affective disorder: Relevance for the biologic effects of light therapy. *Primary Psychiatry, 11*, 44–48.

Neuschatz, J. S., Lampinen, J., Preston, E. L., Hawkins, E. R., & Toglia, M. P. (2002). The effect of memory schemata on memory and the phenomenological experience of naturalistic situations. *Applied Cognitive Psychology, 16*, 687–708.

Neuschatz, J. S., Lawson, D. S., Swanner, J. K., Meissner, C. A., & Neuschatz, J. S. (2008). The effects of accomplice witnesses and jailhouse informants on jury decision making. *Law and Human Behavior, 32*, 137–149.

Newcombe, N. S., & Uttal, D. H. (2006). Whorf versus Socrates, round 10. *Trends in Cognitive Sciences, 10*, 394–396.

Newell, A., & Simon, H. A. (1972). *Human problem solving.* Englewood Cliffs, NJ: Prentice Hall.

Newlin, D. B., & Thomson, J. B. (1997). Alcohol challenge with sons of alcoholics: A critical review and analysis. In G. A. Marlatt & G. R. VandenBos (Eds.), *Addictive behaviors: Readings on etiology, prevention and treatment.* Washington, DC: American Psychological Association.

Newman, D. L., Caspi, A., Moffitt, T. E., & Silva, P. A. (1997). Antecedents of adult interpersonal functioning: Effects of individual differences in age 3 temperament. *Developmental Psychology, 33*, 206–217.

Newman, D. L., Moffit, T. E., Caspi, A., Silva, P. A., & Stanton, W. R. (1996). Psychiatric disorder in a birth cohort of young adults: Prevalence, comorbidity, clinical significance, and new case incidence from ages 11–21. *Journal of Consulting and Clinical Psychology, 64*, 552–562.

Newson, R. S., & Kemps, E. B. (2006). The influence of physical and cognitive activities on simple and complex cognitive tasks in older adults. *Experimental Aging Research, 32*, 341–362.

Newsweek. (2002, March 11), p. 19.

New York Times. (1986, March 18), p. C12.

Nezami, E., & Butcher, J. N. (2000). Objective personality assessment. In G. Goldstein & M. Hersen (Eds.), *Handbook of psychological assessment* (3rd ed.). New York: Elsevier.

Nezlek, J. B., Hampton, C. P., & Shean, G. (2000). Clinical depression and day-to-day social interaction in a community sample. *Journal of Abnormal Psychology, 109*, 11–19.

Nezu, A. M., Nezu, C. M., & D'Zurilla, T. (2000). Problem-solving skills training. In G. Fink (Ed.), *Encyclopedia of stress.* San Diego, CA: Academic Press.

NICHD Early Child Care Research Network. (2001). Child care and family predictors of preschool attachment and stability from infancy. *Developmental Psychology, 37*, 847–862.

NICHD Early Child Care Research Network. (2002). Early child care and children's development prior to school entry: Results from the NICHD Study of Early Child Care. *American Educational Research Journal, 39*, 133–164.

NICHD Early Child Care Research Network. (2006). Child-care effect sizes for the NICHD Study of Early Child Care and Youth Development. *American Psychologist, 61*, 99–116.

Nicholls, J. (1989). *The competitive ethos and democratic education.* Cambridge, MA: Harvard University Press.

Nichols, M. P., & Schwartz, R. C. (2010). *The essentials of family therapy.* Washington, DC: American Psychological Association.

Nichols, P. L. (1984). Familial mental retardation. *Behavior Genetics, 14*, 161–170.

Nickerson, R. S., & Adams, M. J. (1979). Long-term memory for a common object. *Cognitive Psychology, 11*, 287–307.

Niemiec, C. P., Ryan, R. M., & Deci, E. L (2009). The path taken: Consequences of attaining intrinsic and extrinsic aspirations in post-college life. *Journal of Research in Personality, 43*, 291–306.

Nigg, J. T., Lohr, N. E., Westen, D., & Gold, L. J. (1992). Malevolent object representation in borderline personality disorder and major depression. *Journal of Abnormal Psychology, 101*, 61–67.

Nintendo. (2007, para. 3). *Brain Age².* Retrieved February 9, 2010, from http://www.brainage.com/launch/index.jsp

Nisbett, R. (2009). *Intelligence and how to get it: While schools and culture count.* New York: Norton.

Nisbett, R. E. (1998). Race, genetics, and IQ. In C. Jencks et al. (Eds.), *The Black-White test score gap.* Washington, DC: Brookings Institution.

Nisbett, R. E. (2003). *The geography of thought: How Asians and Westerners think differently . . . and why.* New York: Free Press.

Nisbett, R. E., Peng, K., & Choi, I. (2008). Culture and systems of thought: Holistic versus analytic cognition. In J. E. Adler & L. J. Lance (Eds.), *Reasoning: Studies of human inference and its foundations.* New York: Cambridge University Press.

Nixon, K., & Crews, F. T. (2004). Temporally specific burst in cell proliferation increases hippocampal neurogenesis in protracted abstinence from alcohol. *Journal of Neuroscience, 24*, 9714–9722.

Noback, C. R., Strominger, N. L., & Ruggiero, D. A. (Eds.). (2005). *The human nervous system: Structure and function.* New York: Humana Press.

Noice, T., & Noice, H. (2002a). The expertise of professional actors: A review of recent research. *High Ability Studies, 13*, 7–20.

Noice, T., & Noice, H. (2002b). Very long-term recall and recognition of well-learned material. *Applied Cognitive Psychology, 16*, 259–272.

Nolen-Hoeksema, S. (1990). *Sex differences in depression.* Stanford, CA: Stanford University Press.

Noll, R. (2007). *The encyclopedia of manic-depression and other depressive disorders.* New York: Facts on File.

Normann, R. A., Maynard, E. M., Guillory, K. S., & Warren, D. J. (1996). Cortical implants for the blind. *IEEE Spectrum, 33*, 54–59.

Normann, R. A., Maynard, E. M., Rousche, P. J., & Warren, D. J. (1999). A neural interface for a cortical vision prosthesis. *Vision Research, 39*, 2577–2587.

Norton, G. R., Harrison, B., Haunch, J., & Rhodes, L. (1985). Characteristics of people with infrequent panic attacks. *Abnormal Psychiatry, 94*, 216–221.

Nossal, C. J. V., & Hall, E. (1995). Choices following antigen entry: Antibody formation or immunologic tolerance? *Annual Review of Immunology, 13*, 171–204.

Nourkova, V., Bernstein, D. M., & Loftus, E. F. (2004). Altering traumatic memory. *Cognition & Emotion, 18*, 575–585.

Nunn, J. A., Gregory, L. J., Brammer, M., et al. (2002). Functional magnetic resonance imaging of synesthesia: Activation of V4/V8 by spoken words. *Nature Neuroscience, 5*, 371–375.

Nussbaum, A. D., & Steele, C. M. (2007). Situational disengagement and persistence in the face of adversity. *Journal of Experimental Social Psychology, 43*, 127–134.

Nyberg, J. M., Vekovischeva, O., & Sandnabba, N. K. (2003). Anxiety profiles of mice selectively bred for intermale aggression. *Behavior Genetics, 33*, 503–511.

Ockene, J. K. (2001). Strategies to increase adherence to treatment. In L. E. Burke & I. S. Okene (Eds.), *Compliance in healthcare and research.* Armonk, NY: Futura.

O'Connor, D. B., Archer, J., Hair, W. M., & Wu, F. C. W. (2002). Exogenous testosterone, aggression, and mood in eugonadal and hypogonadal men. *Physiology and Behavior, 75*, 557–566.

O'Connor, S. C., & Rosenblood, L. K. (1996). Affiliation motivation in everyday experience: A theoretical comparison. *Journal of Personality and Social Psychology, 70*, 513–522.

Oehman, A., Flykt, A., & Esteves, F. (2001). Emotion drives attention: Detecting the snake in the grass. *Journal of Experimental Psychology, 130*, 466–478.

Ohayon, M. M. (2008). From wakefulness to excessive sleepiness: What we know and still need to know. *Sleep Medicine Reviews, 12*, 129–141.

Ohayon, M. M., Guilleminault, C., & Priest, R. G. (1999). Night terrors, sleepwalking, and confusional arousals in the general population: Their frequency and relationship to other sleep and mental disorders. *Journal of Clinical Psychiatry, 60,* 268–276.

Öhman, A. (2008). Fear and anxiety: Overlaps and dissociations. In M. Lewis, J. Haviland-Jones, & L. F. Barrett (Eds.), *Handbook of emotions* (3rd ed.). New York: Guilford Press.

Öhman, A., & Mineka, S. (2001). Fears, phobias, and preparedness: Toward an evolved module of fear and fear learning. *Psychological Review, 108,* 483–522.

Öhman, A., & Soares, J. J. F. (1998). Emotional conditioning to masked stimuli: Expectancies for aversive outcomes following nonrecognized fear-relevant stimuli. *Journal of Experimental Psychology: General, 127,* 69–82.

Öhman, A., & Wiens, S. (2005). The concept of an evolved fear. In A. S. R. Manstead, N. H. Frijda, A. H. Fischer, & K. Oatley (Eds.), *Feelings and emotions: The Amsterdam Symposium.* New York: Cambridge University Press.

Okado, Y., & Stark, C. E. (2005). Neural activity during encoding predicts false memories created by misinformation. *Learning & Memory, 12,* 3–11.

Olds, J. (1958). Self-stimulation of the brain. *Science, 127,* 315–324.

O'Leary, E., & Murphy, M. (Eds.). (2006). *New approaches to integration in psychotherapy.* New York: Routledge/Taylor & Francis Group.

Oleson, T. (2002). Auriculotherapy stimulation for neuro-rehabilitation. *NeuroRehabilitation, 17,* 49–62.

Ollendick, T. H., Öst, L., Reuterskiöld, L., et al. (2009). One-session treatment of social phobia in youth. *Journal of Consulting and Clinical Psychology, 77,* 504–516.

Olness, K., & Ader, R. (1992). Conditioning as an adjunct in the pharmacotherapy of lupus erythematosus. *Journal of Developmental and Behavioral Pediatrics, 13,* 124–125.

Olshan, J., & Livingston, I. (2009, January 17). Quiet air hero is Captain America: Superpilot lauded from apple to DC. *New York Post.* Retrieved November 28, 2009, from http://www.nypost.com/p/news/regional/item_Goem4fAiUd2hsctASfAjGJ

Olson, M. A., & Fazio, R. H. (2003). Relations between implicit measures of prejudice: What are we measuring? *Psychological Science, 14,* 636–639.

Olsson, A., & Phelps, E. A. (2004). Learned fear of "unseen" faces after Pavlovian, observational, and instructed fear. *Psychological Science, 15,* 822–828.

Olweus, D. (2004). Bullying at school. Prevalence estimation, a useful evaluation design, and a new national initiative in Norway. *Association for Child Psychology and Psychiatry Occasional Papers, 23,* 5–17.

Orbuch, T. L., House, J. S., Mero, R. P., & Webster, P. S. (1996). Marital quality over the life course. *Social Psychology Quarterly, 59,* 162–171.

Orne, M. T. (1959). The nature of hypnosis: Artifact and essence. *Journal of Abnormal and Social Psychology, 58,* 277–299.

Orne, M. T., & Evans, F. J. (1965). Social control in the psychological experiment: Antisocial behavior and hypnosis. *Journal of Personality and Social Psychology, 1,* 189–200.

Ornstein, R. (1997). *Right mind.* Ft. Worth, TX: Harcourt Brace.

Orth, U., Robins, R. W., Trzesniewski, K. H., Maes, J., & Scmitt, M. (2009). Low self-esteem is a risk factor for depressive symptoms from young adulthood to old age. *Journal of Abnormal Psychology, 118,* 472–478.

Orth, U., & Wieland, E. (2006). Anger, hostility and posttraumatic stress disorder in trauma-exposed adults: A meta-analysis. *Journal of Consulting and Clinical Psychology, 74,* 698–706.

Ortiz, J., & Raine, A. (2004). Heart rate level and antisocial behavior in children and adolescents: A meta-analysis. *Journal of the American Academy of Child & Adolescent Psychiatry, 43,* 154–162.

Ost, J., Granhag, P. A., Udell, J., & Roos af Hjelmsäter, E. (2008). Familiarity breeds distortion: The effects of media exposure on false reports concerning media coverage of the terrorist attacks in London on 7 July 2005. *Memory, 16,* 76–85.

Ost, J., Vrij, A., Costall, A., & Bull, R. (2002). Crashing memories and reality monitoring: Distinguishing between perceptions, imaginations and false memories. *Applied Cognitive Psychology, 16,* 125–134.

Öst, L. G. (2008). "Efficacy of the third wave of behavioral therapies: A systematic review and meta-analysis." *Behaviour research and therapy, 46,* 296–321.

Ostacher, M. J., & Eidelman, P. (2006). Suicide in bipolar depression. In R. S. El-Mallakh & S. N. Ghaemi (Eds.), *Bipolar depression: A comprehensive guide.* Arlington, VA: American Psychiatric Publishing.

Ostrovsky, Y., Andalman, A., & Sinha, P. (2007). Vision following extended congenital blindness. *Psychological Science, 17,* 1009–1014.

Ouyang, M., Hellman, K., Abel, T., & Thomas, S. A. (2004). Adrenergic signaling plays a critical role in the maintenance of waking and in the regulation of REM sleep. *Journal of Neurophysiology, 92,* 2071–2082.

Owen, P. R., & Laurel-Seller, E. (2000). Weight and shape ideals: Thin is dangerously in. *Journal of Applied Social Psychology, 30,* 979–990.

Paffenbarger, R. S., Jr., Hyde, R. T., Wing, A. L., & Hsieh, C. C. (1986). Physical activity, all-cause mortality, and longevity of college alumni. *New England Journal of Medicine, 314,* 605–613.

Paivio, A. (1969). Mental imagery is associative learning and memory. *Psychological Review, 76,* 241–263.

Paivio, A. (2006). *Mind and its evolution: A dual coding theoretical approach.* Mahwah, NJ: Erlbaum.

Pajer, K. (2000). Hysteria. In G. Fink (Ed.), *Encyclopedia of stress.* San Diego, CA: Academic Press.

Palfai, T., & Jankiewicz, H. (1991). *Drugs and human behavior.* Dubuque, IA: Wm. C. Brown.

Palmer, J. A., & Palmer, L. K. (Eds.). (2002). *Evolutionary psychology: The ultimate origins of human behavior* (Vol. 15). Needham Heights, MA: Allyn & Bacon.

Palmer, S. E. (2002). Perceptual organization in vision. In H. Pashler & S. Yantis (Eds.), *Steven's handbook of experimental psychology: Vol. 1. Sensation and perception* (3rd ed.). New York: Wiley.

Palmiero, M., Belardinelli, M. O., Nardo, D., Sestieri, C., DiMatteo, R., D'Ausilio, A., et al. (2009). Mental imagery generation in different modalities activates sensory-motor areas. *Cognitive Processing, 10* (Suppl. 2), S268–S271.

Pammer, K. (2009). What can MEG neuroimaging tell us about reading? *Journal of Neurolinguistics, 22,* 266–280.

Panksepp, J. (2005). Basic affects and the instinctual emotion system of the brain: The primordial sources of sadness, joy and seeking. In A. S. R. Manstead, N. H. Frijda, A. H. Fischer, & K. Oatley (Eds.), *Feelings and emotions: The Amsterdam Symposium.* New York: Cambridge University Press.

Pantev, C., Dinnesen, A., Ross, B., Wollbrink, A., & Knief, A. (2006). Dynamics of auditory plasticity after cochlear implantation: A longitudinal study. *Cerebral Cortex, 16,* 31–36.

Papadatou-Pastou, M., Martin, M., Munafo, M. R., & Gregory, V. (2008). Sex differences in left-handedness: A meta-analysis of 144 studies. *Psychological Bulletin, 134,* 677–699.

Papanicolaou, A. C. (1989). *Emotion: A reconsideration of the somatic theory.* New York: Gordon & Breach.

Papini, M. R. (2002). Pattern and process in the evolution of learning. *Psychological Review, 109,* 186–201.

Parapsychology Association. (2008). *Frequently asked questions.* Retrieved October 3, 2009, from http://www.parapsych.org/faq_file2.html#11

Paris, J. (1993). *Borderline personality disorder.* Washington, DC: American Psychiatric Press.

Park, C. L., Armeli, S., & Tennen, H. (2004). Appraisal-coping goodness of fit: A daily internet study. *Personality and Social Psychology Bulletin, 30,* 558–569.

Park, D. C., & Gutchess, A. H. (2005). Long-term memory and aging: A cognitive neuroscience perspective. In R. Cabeza, L. Nyberg, & D. Park (Eds.), *Cognitive neuroscience of aging: Linking cognitive and cerebral aging.* London: Oxford University Press.

Park, N., Peterson, C., & Brunwasser, S. M. (2010). Positive psychology and therapy. In N. Kazantzis, M.A. Reinecke, & A. Freeman (Eds.), *Cognitive and behavioral theories in clinical practice.* New York: Guilford Press.

Parker, C. R., Bolling, M. Y., & Kohlenberg, R. J. (1998). Operant theory of personality. In D. F. Barone, M. Hersen, & V. B. Van Hasselt (Eds.), *Advanced personality.* New York: Plenum Press.

Parker, L. A., Kwiatkowska, M., & Mechoulam, R. (2006). Delta-9-tetrahydrocannabinol and cannabidiol, but not ondansetron, interfere with conditioned retching reactions elicited by a lithium-paired context in *Suncus murinus:* An animal model of anticipatory nausea and vomiting. *Physiology & Behavior, 87,* 66–71.

Parkinson, A. J., Parkinson, W. S., Tyler, R. S., Lowder, M. W., & Gantz, B. J. (1998). Speech perception performance in experienced cochlear-implant patients receiving the SPEAK processing strategy in the Nucleus Spectra-22 cochlear implant. *Journal of Speech, Language, and Hearing Research, 41,* 1073–1087.

Passie, T., Halpern, J. H., Strichenoth, D. O., Emrich, H. M., & Hintzen, A. (2008). The pharmacology of lysergic acid diethylamide: A review. *CNS Neuroscience & Therapeutics, 14,* 295–314.

Patil, P. G., & Turner, D. A. (2008). The development of brain-machine interface neuroprosthetic devices. *Neurotherapeutics 5,* 137–146.

Patry, M. W., Stinson, V., & Smith, S. M. (2009). Supreme Court of Canada addresses admissibility of posthypnosis witness evidence: *R. v. Trochym* (2007). *Canadian Psychology/PsychologieCanadienne, 50,* 98–105.

Patterson, D. R. (2004). Treating pain with hypnosis. *Current Directions in Psychological Science, 13,* 252–255.

Patterson, G. R., Littman, R. A., & Bricker, W. (1967). Assertive behavior in children: A step toward a theory of aggression. *Monographs of the Society for Research in Child Development, 32*(Whole No. 5).

Paul, G. L., & Lentz, R. J. (1977). *Psychosocial treatment of chronic mental patients: Milieu versus social learning programs.* Cambridge, MA: Harvard University Press.

Paulson, T. (2004, December 14). Thought powers computer. *Seattle Post-Intelligencer,* p. A1.

Paunonen, S. V. (2003). Big Five factors of personality and replicated predictions of behavior. *Journal of Personality and Social Psychology, 84,* 411–424.

Pavlov, I. P. (1928). *Lectures on conditioned reflexes: Twenty-five years of objective study of the higher nervous activity (behaviour) of animals* (W. H. Gantt, Trans.). New York: International Publishers. (Original work published 1923)

Peacock, K. W. (2010). *Biotechnology and genetic engineering.* New York: Facts on File, Inc.

Pearlin, L. I., & Schooler, C. (1978). The structure of coping. *Journal of Health and Social Behavior, 19,* 2–21.

Pearsall, M. J., Christian, M. S., & Ellis, A. P. J. (2010). Motivating interdependent teams: Individual rewards, shared rewards, or something in between. *Journal of Applied Psychology, 95,* 183–191.

Pedersen, W. C., Miller, L. C., PutchaBhagavatula, A. D., & Yang, Y. (2002). Evolved sex differences in the number of partners desired? The long and short of it. *Psychological Science, 13,* 157–161.

Pedrotti, F. L., & Pedrotti, L. S. (1997). *Optics and vision.* Englewood Cliffs, NJ: Prentice Hall.

Pelham, W. E., Jr., Massetti, G. M., Wilson, T., Kipp, H., Myers, D., Standley, B. B., Billheimer, S., & Waschbusch, D. A. (2005). Implementation of a comprehensive schoolwide behavioral intervention: The ABC Program. *Journal of Attention Disorders, 9,* 248–260.

Pelletier, D. L., & Frongillo, E. A. (2003). Changes in child survival are strongly associated with changes in malnutrition in developing countries. *Journal of Nutrition, 133,* 107–119.

Pelli, D. G., Farell, B., Moore, D. C. (2003). The remarkable inefficiency of word recognition. *Nature, 423,* 752–756.

Pellino, T. A., & Ward, S. E. (1998). Perceived control mediates the relationship between pain severity and patient satisfaction. *Journal of Pain and Symptom Management, 15,* 110–116.

Pendlebury, S. T. (2007). *Neurological case histories.* New York: Oxford University Press.

Peplau, L. A., Garnets, L. D., Spalding, L. R., Conley, T. D., & Veniegas, R. C. (1998). A critique of Bem's "Exotic Becomes Erotic" theory of sexual orientation. *Psychological Review, 105,* 387–394.

Pepperberg, I. M. (2007). Grey parrots do not always "parrot": The roles of imitation and phonological awareness in the creation of new labels from existing vocalizations. *Language Sciences, 29,* 1–13.

Perdue, C. W., Dovidio, J. F., Gurtman, M. B., & Tyler, R. B. (1990). Us and them: Social categorization and the process of intergroup bias. *Journal of Personality and Social Psychology, 59,* 475–486.

Perrett, D. I., Lee, K. J., Penton-Voak, I., Rowland, D., Yoshikawa, S., Burt, D. M., Henzi, S. P., Castles, D. L., & Akamatsu, S. (1998). Effects of sexual dimorphism on facial attractiveness. *Nature, 394,* 884–887.

Pervin, L. A., Cervone, D., & John, O. (2005). *Personality: Theory and research.* New York: Wiley.

Peterson, C., & Seligman, M. E. P. (2004). *Character strengths and virtues: A handbook and classification.* Washington, DC: American Psychological Association.

Peterson, C., & Whalen, N. (2001). Five years later: Children's memory for medical emergencies. *Applied Cognitive Psychology 15,* 7–24.

Peterson, L. R., & Peterson, M. J. (1959). Short-term retention of individual verbal items. *Journal of Experimental Psychology, 58,* 193–198.

Petrill, S. (2003). The development of intelligence: Behavior genetics approaches. In R. J. Sternberg, J. Lautrey, & T. I. Lubart (Eds.), *Models of intelligence: International perspectives.* Washington, DC: American Psychological Association.

Petrosini, L., De Bartolo, P., Foti, F., Gelfo, F., Cutuli, D., Leggio, M. G., et al. (2009). On whether the environmental enrichment may provide cognitive and brain reserves. *Brain Research Reviews, 61,* 221–239.

Petrovic, P., & Ingvar, M. (2002). Imaging cognitive modulation of pain processing. *Pain, 95,* 1–5.

Petrovic, P., Kalso, E., Petersson, M. K., & Ingvar, M. (2002, February). Placebo and opioid analgesia: Imaging a shared neuronal network. *Science Express Reports,* 17–22.

Pettigrew, T. F., & Meertens, R. W. (1995). Subtle and blatant prejudice in western Europe. *European Journal of Social Psychology, 25,* 57–76.

Petty, R. E., & Cacioppo, J. T. (1986). *Communication and persuasion: Central and peripheral routes to attitude change.* New York: Springer-Verlag.

Petty, R. E., Cacioppo, J. T., Strathman, A. J., & Priester, J. R. (2005). To think or not to think: Exploring two routes to persuasion. In T. C. Brock & M. C. Green (Eds.), *Persuasion: Psychological insights and perspectives* (2nd ed., pp. 81–116). Thousand Oaks, CA: Sage.

Petty, R. E., Fleming, M. A., Priester, J. R., & Feinstein, A. H. (2001). Individual versus group interest violation: Surprise as a determinant of argument scrutiny and persuasion. *Social Cognition, 19,* 418–442.

Pfeifer, M., Goldsmith, H. H., & Davidson, R. R. M. (2002). Continuity and change in inhibited and uninhibited children. *Child Development, 73,* 1474–1485.

Pfiffner, L. J., McBurnett, K., & Rathouz, P. (2001). Father absence and familial antisocial characteristics. *Journal of Abnormal Child Psychology, 29,* 357–367.

Phelps, E. A. (2005). The power of the subliminal: On subliminal persuasion and other potential applications. In R. R. Hassin, J. S. Uleman, & J. A. Bargh (Eds.), *The new unconscious.* New York: Oxford University Press.

Phillips, M., Brooks, G. J., Duncan, G. J., Klebanov, P., & Crane, J. (1998). Family background, parenting practices, and the Black-White test score gap. In C. Jencks & M. Phillips (Eds.), *The Black-White test score gap.* Washington, DC: Brookings Institution.

Phillipson, S. N., & McCann, M. (2007). *Conceptions of giftedness: Socio-cultural perspectives.* Mahwah, NJ: Erlbaum.

Piaget, J. (1926). *The language and thought of the child.* New York: Meridian Books.

Piaget, J. (1970). Piaget's theory. In P. H. Mussen (Ed.), *Carmichael's manual of child psychology* (Vol. 1). New York: Wiley.

Piaget, J. (1977). *The development of thought: Equilibration of cognitive structure.* New York: Viking.

Pickering, A. D., & Gray, J. A. (1999). The neuroscience of personality. In L. A. Pervin & O. P. John (Eds.), *Handbook of personality: Theory and research.* New York: Guilford Press.

Pigliucci, M., & Mueller, G. B. (2010). *Evolution: The extended synthesis.* Cambridge, MA: MIT Press.

Pilbeam, D. (1984). The descent of hominoids and hominids. *Scientific American, 250,* 84–97.

Pilcher, J. J., & Huffcutt, A. J. (1996). Effects of sleep deprivation on performance: A meta-analysis. *Sleep, 19,* 318–326.

Pilcher, J. J., & Walters, A. S. (1997). How sleep deprivation affects psychological variables related to college students' cognitive performance. *Journal of American College Health, 46,* 121–126.

Pinker, S. (2000). Language as an adaptation to the cognitive niche. In M. Christiansen & S. Kirby (Eds.), *Language evolution: Reports from the research frontier.* New York: Oxford University Press.

Pinquart, M., & Sörensen, S. (2003). Differences between caregivers and noncaregivers in psychological health and physical health: A meta-analysis. *Psychology & Aging, 18,* 250–267.

Piper, A., & Merskey, H. (2004). The persistence of folly: A critical examination of dissociative identity disorder. Part I. The excesses of an improbable concept. *Canadian Journal of Psychiatry, 49,* 592–600.

Pitman, R. K., Shalev, A. Y., & Orr, S. P. (2000). Posttraumatic stress disorder: Emotion, conditioning, and memory. In M. S. Gazzaniga (Ed.), *The new cognitive neurosciences* (2nd ed.). Cambridge, MA: MIT Press.

Piven, J., Saliba, K., Bailey, J., & Arndt, S. (1997). An MRI study of autism: The cerebellum revisited. *Neurology, 13,* 546–551.

Plant, E. A., & Peruche, B. M. (2005). The consequences of race for police officers' responses to criminal suspects. *Psychological Science, 16,* 180–183.

Plant, E. A., Peruche, B. M., & Butz, D. A. (2005). Eliminating automatic racial bias: Making race non-diagnostic for responses to criminal suspects. *Journal of Experimental Social Psychology, 41,* 141–156.

Plomin, R. (1997). *Behavioral genetics.* New York: St. Martin's Press.

Plomin, R., & Caspi, A. (1999). Behavior genetics and personality. In L. A. Pervin & O. P. John (Eds.), *Handbook of personality: Theory and research.* New York: Guilford Press.

Plomin, R., & Crabbe, J. (2000). DNA. *Psychological Bulletin, 126,* 806–828.

Plomin, R., & Craig, I. (2002). "Genetic research on cognitive ability": Author's reply. *British Journal of Psychiatry, 180,* 185–186.

Plomin, R., DeFries, J. C., & Fulker D. W. (2007). *Nature and nurture during infancy and early childhood*. New York: Cambridge University Press.

Plomin, R., & Haworth, C. M. A. (2009). Genetics of high cognitive abilities. *Behavior Genetics, 39*, 347–349.

Plomin, R., & Spinath, F. M. (2004). Intelligence: Genetics, genes, and genomics. *Journal of Personality and Social Psychology, 86*, 112–129.

Ploner, M., Gross, J., Timmerman, L., & Schnitzler, A. (2006). Pain processing is faster than tactile processing in the human brain. *Journal of Neuroscience, 26*(42), 10879–10882.

Plotkin, S. A. (2006). The history of rubella and rubella vaccination leading to elimination. *Clinical Infectious Diseases, 43*, S164–S168.

Plous, S. (1996a). Attitudes toward the use of animals in psychological research and education: Results from a national survey of psychologists. *American Psychologist, 51*, 1167–1180.

Plous, S. (1996b). Attitudes toward the use of animals in psychological research and education: Results from a national survey of psychology majors. *Psychological Science, 7*, 352–358.

Plutchik, R. (1994). *Psychology of emotion*. Reading, MA: Addison-Wesley.

Pollack, I., & Pickett, J. M. (1964). Intelligibility of excerpts from fluent speech: Auditory vs. structural context. *Journal of Verbal Learning and Verbal Behavior, 3*, 79–84.

Pompili, M., Serafini, G., Del Casale, A., et al. (2009). Improving adherence in mood disorders: The struggle against relapse, recurrence and suicide risk. *Expert Reviews in Neurotherapy, 9*, 985–1004.

Pool, R. (1994). *The dynamic brain*. Washington, DC: National Academy Press.

Poremba, M., & Poremba, A. (2007). *Attention-deficit/hyperactivity disorder (ADHD)*. New York: Chelsea House.

Pornari, C. D., & Wood, J. (2010). Peer and cyber aggression in secondary school: The role of moral disengagement, hostile attribution bias, and outcome expectancies. *Aggressive Behavior, 36*, 81–94.

Porter, N. P., & Geis, F. L. (1981). Women and nonverbal leadership cues: When seeing is not believing. In C. Mayo & N. M. Henley (Eds.), *Gender and nonverbal behavior*. New York: Springer-Verlag.

Porter, S., Bellhouse, S., McDougall, A., ten Brinke, L., & Wilson, K. (2010). A prospective investigation of the vulnerability of memory for positive and negative emotional scenes to the misinformation effect. *Canadian Journal of Behavioural Science/Revue Canadienne des Sciences du Comportement, 42*, 55–61.

Porterfield S. P., & White, B. A. (2007). *Endocrine physiology*. St. Louis: Mosby.

Portocarrero, J. S., Burright, R. G., & Donovick, P. J. (2007). Vocabulary and verbal fluency of bilingual and monolingual college students. *Archives of Clinical Neuropsychology, 22*, 415–422.

Posada, G., Jacobs, A., Richmond, M. K., Carbonell, O. A., Alzate, G., Bustamante, M. R., & Quiceno, J. (2002). Maternal caregiving and infant security in two cultures. *Developmental Psychology, 38*, 67–78.

Posit Science. (2010). *Brain training software*. Retrieved February 9, 2010, from http://www.positscience.com/

Posner, M. I., & Rothbart, M. K. (2007a). Learning to look. In M. I. Posner & M. K. Rothbart (Eds.), *Educating the human brain*. Washington, DC: American Psychological Association.

Posner, M. I., & Rothbart, M. K. (2007b). *Educating the human brain*. Washington, DC: American Psychological Association.

Posthuma, D., & de Geus, E. J. C. (2006). Progress in the molecular-genetic study of intelligence. *Current Directions in Psychological Science, 15*, 151–155.

Postman, L., & Phillips, L. W. (1965). Short-term temporal changes in free recall. *Quarterly Journal of Experimental Psychology, 17*, 132–138.

Postman, L., & Underwood, B. J. (1973). Critical issues in interference theory. *Memory and Cognition, 1*, 19–40.

Postmes, T., & Spears, R. (1998). Deindividuation and antinormative behavior: A meta-analysis. *Psychological Bulletin, 123*, 238–259.

Poteat, V. P., & Rivers, I. (2010). The use of homophobic language across bullying roles during adolescence. *Journal of Applied Developmental Psychology, 31*, 166–172.

Potter, W. Z. (2009). Benefits exceed risks of newer antidepressant medications in youth—Maybe not. *Clinical Pharmacology and Therapy, 86*, 357–359.

Powell, R. W., & Curley, M. (1976). Instinctive drift in nondomesticated rodents. *Bulletin of the Psychonomic Society, 8*, 175–178.

Powley, T. L., & Keesey, R. E. (1970). Relationship of body weight to the lateral hypothalamic feeding syndrome. *Journal of Comparative and Physiological Psychology, 70*, 25–36.

Prati, G., & Pietrantoni, K. (2009). Optimism, social support and coping strategies as factors contributing to posttraumatic growth: A meta-analysis. *Journal of Loss and Trauma, 14*, 364–388.

Pressman, J. D. (1998). *Last resort: Psychosurgery and the limits of medicine*. New York: Cambridge University Press.

Pressman, M. R. (2007). Factors that predispose, prime and precipitate NREM parasomnias in adults: Clinical and forensic implications. *Sleep Medicine Reviews*. Retrieved January 15, 2007, from http://www.sciencedirect.com/science/article/B6WX7-4MRND2K-1/2/b6953b1caca433bb779eed834d7c6d2f

Preti, G., Cutler, W. B., Garcia, G. R., Huggins, G. R., & Lawley, J. J. (1986). Human axillary secretions influences women's menstrual cycles: The role of donor extract from females. *Hormones and Behavior, 20*, 473–480.

Prigerson, H., Maciejewski, P. K, & Rosenheck, R. A. (2002). Population attributable fractions of psychiatric disorders and behavioral outcomes associated with combat exposure among U.S. men. *American Journal of Public Health, 92*(1), 59–63.

Priluck, R., & Till, B. D. (2004). The role of contingency awareness, involvement, and need for cognition in attitude formation. *Journal of the Academy of Marketing Science, 32*, 329–344.

Pritchard, R. M. (1961, June). Stabilized images on the retina. *Scientific American*, 72–78.

Probst, L. R., Ostrom, R., Watkins, P., Dean, T., & Mashburn, D. (1992). Comparative efficacy of religious and non-religious cognitive-behavioral therapy for the treatment of clinical depression in religious individuals. *Journal of Consulting and Clinical Psychology, 60*, 94–103.

Prochaska, J., & DiClemente, C. (1984). *The transtheoretical approach: Crossing traditional boundaries of therapy*. Illinois: Dow Jones-Irwin.

Prochaska, J. O., Norcross, J. C., & DiClemente, C. C. (1994). *Changing for good*. New York: Avon Books.

Project MATCH Research Group. (1997). Matching alcoholism treatments to client heterogeneity: Project MATCH posttreatment drinking outcomes. *Journal of Studies on Alcohol, 58*, 7–29.

Pruden, S. M., Hirsh-Pasek, K., & Golinkoff, R. M. (2006). The social dimension in language development: A rich history and a new frontier. In P. J. Marshall & N. A. Fox (Eds.), *The development of social engagement: Neurobiological perspectives*. New York: Oxford University Press.

Ptacek, J. T., Smith, R. E., & Zanas, J. (1992). Gender, appraisal, and coping: A longitudinal analysis. *Journal of Personality, 60*, 747–769.

Pugh, G. E. (1977). *The biological origin of human values*. New York: Basic Books.

Pull, C. B. (2007). Combined pharmacotherapy and cognitive-behavioural therapy for anxiety disorders. *Current Opinion in Psychiatry, 20*, 30–35.

Putman, P., van Honk, J., Kessels, R. P. C., Mulder, M., & Koppeschaar, H. P. F. (2004). Salivary cortisol and short- and long-term memory for emotional faces in healthy young women. *Psychoneuroendocrinology, 29*, 953–960.

Putnam, F. W. (1989). *Diagnosis and treatment of multiple personality disorder*. New York: Guilford Press.

Putnam, F. W. (2000). Dissociative disorders. In A. J. Sameroff & M. Lewis (Eds.), *Handbook of developmental psychopathology* (2nd ed.). New York: Cambridge University Press.

Qu, T., Brannen, C. L., Kim, H. M., & Sugaya, K. (2001). Human neural stem cells improve cognitive function of aged brain. *Neuroreport: for Rapid Communication of Neuroscience Research, 12*(6), 1127–1132.

Quilty, L. C., Oakman, J. M., & Farvolden, P. (2007). Behavioural inhibition, behavioural activation, and the preference for familiarity. *Personality and Individual Differences, 42*, 291–303.

Quintero, N. (1980, February). Coming of age the Apache way. *National Geographic, 157*(2), 262–271.

Rachman, S. (1998). *Anxiety*. Mahwah, NJ: Erlbaum.

Rachman, S. J., & Hodgson, R. J. (1980). *Obsessions and compulsions*. Englewood Cliffs, NJ: Prentice Hall.

Radcliffe, R. A., Erwin, V. G., Bludeau, P., Deng, X., Fay, T., Floyd, K. L., & Deitrich, R. A. (2009). A major QTL for acute ethanol sensitivity in the alcohol tolerant and non-tolerant selected rat lines. *Genes, Brain & Behavior, 8*, 611–625.

Radin, D. I. (2006). *Entangled minds: Extrasensory experiences in a quantum reality*. New York: Simon & Schuster.

Radoeva, P. D., Prasad, P., Brainard, D. H., & Aguirre, G. K. (2008). Neural activity within area VI reflects unconscious visual performance in a case of blindsight. *Journal of Cognitive Neuroscience, 20*, 1927–1939.

Rahman, Q. (2005). Fluctuating asymmetry, second to fourth finger length ratios and human sexual orientation. *Psychoneuroendocrinology, 30*, 382–391.

Raine, A. (2002). Annotation: The role of prefrontal deficits, low autonomic arousal and early health factors in the development of antisocial and aggressive behavior in children. *Journal of Child Psychology and Psychiatry and Allied Disciplines, 43*, 417–434.

Raine, A. (2008). From genes to brain to antisocial behavior. *Current Directions in Psychological Science, 17*, 323–328.

Raine, A., Lencz, T., Bihrle, S., LaCasse, L., & Colletti, P. (2000). Reduced prefrontal gray matter volume and reduced autonomic activity in antisocial personality disorder. *Archives of General Psychiatry, 57*, 119–127.

Raine, A., Mellingen, K., Liu, J. Venables, P., & Mednick, S. A. (2003). Effects of environmental enrichment at ages 3–5 years on schizotypal personality and antisocial behavior at ages 17 and 23 years. *American Journal of Psychiatry, 160*, 1627–1635.

Raine, A., Venables, P. H., & Williams, M. (1996). Better autonomic conditioning and faster electrodermal half-recovery time at age 15 years as possible protective factors against crime at age 29 years. *Developmental Psychology, 32*, 624–630.

Ramey, C., & Ramey, S. (1998). Early intervention. *American Psychologist, 53*, 210–225.

Ramey, C. T., Ramey, S. L., & Lanzi, R. G. (1998). Differentiating developmental risk levels for families in poverty: Creating a family typology. In M. Lewis & C. Feiring (Eds.), *Families, risks, and competence*. Mahwah, NJ: Erlbaum.

Ramsey, J. L., Langlois, J. H., Hoss, R. A., Rubenstein, A. J., & Griffin, A. M. (2004). Origins of a stereotype: Categorization of facial attractiveness by 6-month-old infants. *Developmental Science, 7*, 201–211.

Rao, R. (2001). Cannabis: Some psychiatric aspects. *Primary Care Psychiatry, 7*, 101–105.

Ratcliff, R., Thapar, A., & McKoon, G. (2006). Aging and individual differences in rapid two-choice decisions. *Psychonomic Bulletin & Review, 13*, 626–635.

Raudenbush, B., & Meyer, B. (2003). Muscular dissatisfaction and supplement use among male intercollegiate athletes. *Journal of Sport & Exercise Psychology, 25*, 161–170.

Raval, V. V., & Martini, T. S. (2009). Maternal socialization of children's anger, sadness, and physical pain in two communities in Gujarat, India. *International Journal of Behavioral Development, 33*, 215–229.

Raven, J. (1962). *Colored progressive matrices*. New York: Psychological Corp.

Ravussin, E., & Gautier, J. F. (1999). Metabolic predictors of weight gain. *International Journal of Obesity and Related Metabolic Disorders, 23*(Suppl. 1), 37–41.

Rawlinson, G. (1999, May 29). Reibadailty. *New Scientist*. Retrieved February 5, 2010, from http://www.newscientist.com/issue/2188

Ray, O. S., & Ksir, C. J. (2004). *Drugs, society and human behavior* (9th ed.). Boston: McGraw-Hill.

Rayner, K., White, S. J., Johnson, R. L., & Liversedge, S. P. (2006). Raeding wrods with jumbled lettres: There is a cost. *Psychological Science, 17*, 192–193.

Regal, B. (2005). *Human evolution: A guide to the debates*. Santa Barbara, CA: ABC-CLIO, Inc.

Reich, T. W. (2006). *Personality disorders research*. London: Brunner-Routledge.

Reilly, T. (2009). The body clock and athletic performance. *Biological Rhythm Research, 40*, 37–44.

Rendell, P. G., & Thomson, D. M. (1999). Aging and prospective memory: Differences between naturalistic and laboratory tasks. *Journals of Gerontology: Series B: Psychological Sciences and Social Sciences, 54B*(4), 256–269.

Rensink, R. A. (2002). Change detection. *Annual Review of Psychology, 53*, 247–277.

Renzulli, J. S. (2002). Emerging conceptions of giftedness: Building a bridge to the new century, *Exceptionality, 10*, 67–75.

Repovs, G., & Baddeley, A. (2006). The multi-component model of working memory: Explorations in experimental cognitive psychology. *Neuroscience, 28*, 5–21.

Reppucci, N. D., Wollard, J. L., & Fried, C. S. (1999). Social, community, and preventive interventions. *Annual Review of Psychology, 1*, 387–415.

Rescorla, R. A. (1968). Probability of shock in the presence and absence of CS in fear. *Journal of Comparative and Physiological Psychology, 66*, 1–5.

Rescorla, R. A., & Solomon, R. L. (1967). Two-process learning theory: Relationships between Pavlovian conditioning and instrumental learning. *Psychological Review, 74*, 151–182.

Rescorla, R. A., & Wagner, A. R. (1972). A theory of Pavlovian conditioning: Variations in the effectiveness of reinforcement and nonreinforcement. In A. H. Black & W. F. Prokasky (Eds.), *Classical conditioning: II. Current research and theory*. New York: Appleton-Century-Crofts.

Resick, P. (2005). *Stress and trauma*. San Francisco: Taylor & Francis.

Resnick, S. M., Pham, D. L., Kraut, M. A., Zonderman, A. B., & Davatzikos, C. (2003). Longitudinal magnetic resonance imaging studies of older adults: A shrinking brain. *Journal of Neuroscience, 23*, 3295–3301.

Revell, V. L., & Eastman, C. I. (2005). How to trick Mother Nature into letting you fly around or stay up all night. *Journal of Biological Rhythms, 20*, 353–365.

Rey, J. M., & Walter, G. (1997). Half a century of ECT use in young people. *American Journal of Psychiatry, 154*, 595–602.

Rezayof, A., Alijanpour, S., Zarrindast, M. R., & Rassouli, Y. (2008). Ethanol state-dependent memory: Involvement of dorsal hippocampal muscarinic and nicotinic receptors. *Neurobiology of Learning and Memory, 89*, 441–447.

Rhea, P. (2009). Parents ask: Am I risking autism if I vaccinate my children? *Journal of Autism and Developmental Disorders, 39*, 962–963.

Rhodes, G., Yoshikawa, S., Clark, A., Lee, K., McKay, R., & Akamatsu, S. (2001). Attractiveness of facial averageness and symmetry in non-Western cultures: In search of biologically based standards of beauty. *Perception, 30*, 611–625.

Rholes, W. S., Simpson, J. A., & Friedman, M. (2006). Avoidant attachment and the experience of parenting. *Personality and Social Psychology Bulletin, 32*, 275–285.

Richard, S., Davies, D. C., & Faure, J. M. (2000). The role of fear in one-trial passive avoidance learning in Japanese quail chicks genetically selected for long or short duration of the tonic immobility reaction. *Behavioural Processes, 48*, 165–170.

Richardson, D. R. (1991). Interpersonal attraction and love. In R. M. Baron, W. G. Graziano, & C. Stangor (Eds.), *Social psychology*. Ft. Worth, TX: Holt, Rinehart & Winston.

Riesen, A. H. (1965). Effects of early deprivation of photic stimulation. In S. F. Osler & R. E. Cooke (Eds.), *The biosocial basis of mental retardation*. Baltimore, MD: Johns Hopkins University Press.

Rilling, M. (1996). The mystery of the vanished citations: James McConnell's forgotten 1960s quest for planarian learning, a biochemical engram, and celebrity. *American Psychologist, 51*, 589–598.

Rimm, D. C., & Masters, J. C. (1979). *Behavior therapy: Techniques and empirical findings* (2nd ed.). New York: Academic Press.

Rinck, M., & Denis, M. (2004). The metrics of spatial distance traversed during mental imagery. *Journal of Experimental Psychology: Learning, Memory, and Cognition, 30*, 1211–1218.

Rips, L. J. (1997). Goals for a theory of deduction: Reply to Johnson-Laird. *Minds and Machines, 7*, 409–424.

Ritblatt, S. N. (2000). Children's level of participation in a false-belief task, age, and theory of mind. *Journal of Genetic Psychology, 161*, 53–64.

Ritchie, C. W., Ames, D., Clayton, T., & Lai, R. (2004). Metaanalysis of randomized trials of the efficacy and safety of donepezil, galantamine, and rivastigmine for the treatment of Alzheimer disease. *American Journal of Geriatric Psychiatry, 12*, 358–369.

Roberts, B., Helson, R., & Klohnen, E. C. (2002). Personality development and growth in women across 30 years: Three perspectives. *Journal of Personality, 70*, 79–102.

Roberts, B. W., Kuncel, N. R., Shiner, R., Caspi, A., & Goldberg, L. R. (2007). The power of personality: The comparative validity of personality traits, socioeconomic status, and cognitive ability for predicting important life outcomes. *Perspectives on Psychological Science, 2*, 313–345.

Roberts, B. W., Wood, D., & Caspi, A. (2008). The development of personality traits in adulthood. In O. P. John, R. W. Robins, & L. A. Pervin (Eds.), *Handbook of personality theory and research* (3rd ed.). New York: Guilford Press.

Robins, R. W., Fraley, R. C., & Krueger, R. F. (2007). *Handbook of research methods in personality psychology*. New York: Guilford Press.

Robins, R. W., Gosling, S. D., & Craik, K. H. (1999). An empirical analysis of trends in psychology. *American Psychologist, 54*, 117–128.

Robinson, D. (1997). *Neurobiology*. New York: Springer-Verlag.

Robinson, D. S. (2006). Antidepressant discontinuation syndrome. *Primary Psychiatry, 13*, 23–24.

Robinson, M. D., & Sedikedes, C. (2009). Traits and the self: Toward an integration. In P. J. Corr & G. Matthews (Eds.), *The Cambridge handbook of personality psychology*. Cambridge, England: Cambridge University Press.

Robinson, M. D., Vargas, P. T., Tamir, M., & Solberg, E. C. (2004). Using and being used by categories. *Psychological Science, 15*, 521–526.

Robles, T. F., Shaffer, V. A., Malarkey, W. B., & Kiecolt-Glaser, J. K. (2006). Positive behaviors during marital conflict: Influences on stress hormones. *Journal of Social and Personal Relationships, 23,* 305–325.

Rodin, J., Bartoshuk, L., Peterson, C., & Schank, D. (1990). Bulimia and taste: Possible interactions. *Journal of Abnormal Psychology, 99,* 32–39.

Rodin, J., & Salovey, P. (1989). Health psychology. *Annual Review of Psychology, 40,* 533–579.

Roebers, C. M. (2002). Confidence judgments in children's and adults' recall and suggestibility. *Developmental Psychology, 38,* 1052–1067.

Roediger, H. L., III, & McDermott, K. B. (1995). Creating false memories: Remembering words not presented in lists. *Journal of Experimental Psychology: Learning, Memory, and Cognition, 21,* 803–814.

Roediger, H. L., III, & McDermott, K. B. (2000). Tricks of memory. *Current Directions in Psychological Science, 9,* 123–127.

Roelofs, K., Hoogduin, K. A. L., Keijsers, G. P. J., Naering, G. W. B., Moene, F. C., & Sandijck, P. (2002). Hypnotic susceptibility in patients with conversion disorder. *Journal of Abnormal Psychology, 111,* 390–395.

Rogers, C. R. (1951). *Client-centered therapy.* Boston: Houghton Mifflin.

Rogers, C. R. (1959). A theory of therapy, personality and interpersonal relationships, as developed in the client-centered framework. In S. Koch (Ed.), *Psychology: A study of a science* (Vol. 3). New York: McGraw-Hill.

Rogers, C. R. (1980). *A way of being.* Boston: Houghton Mifflin.

Rohrer, D., & Taylor, K. (2006). The effects of overlearning and distributed practise on the retention of mathematics knowledge. *Applied Cognitive Psychology, 20,* 1209–1224.

Rohrer, D., Taylor, K., Pashler, H., Wixted, J. T., & Cepeda, N. J. (2005). The effect of overlearning on long-term retention. *Applied Cognitive Psychology, 19,* 361–374.

Rollman, G. (1998). Culture and pain. In S. S. Kazarian et al. (Eds.), *Cultural clinical psychology: Theory, research, and practice.* New York: Oxford University Press.

Rolls, B. J., Rolls, E. T., Rowe, E. A., & Sweeney, K. (1981). Sensory specific satiety in man. *Physiology and Behavior, 27,* 137–142.

Rolls, E. T. (2000). Memory systems in the brain. *Annual Review of Psychology, 5,* 599–630.

Rolls, E. T. (2010). The affective and cognitive processing of touch, oral texture, and temperature in the brain. *Neuroscience and Biobehavioral Reviews, 34,* 237–245.

Rolls, E. T., & Deco, G. (2002). *Computational neuroscience of vision.* London: Oxford University Press.

Rosch, E. (1973). On the internal structure of perceptual and semantic categories. In T. E. Moore (Ed.), *Cognitive development and the acquisition of language.* New York: Academic Press.

Rosch, E. (1977). Human categorization. In N. Warren (Ed.), *Advances in cross-cultural psychology* (Vol. 1). London: Academic Press.

Rosen, C. S. (2000). Integrating stage and continuum models to explain processing of exercise messages and exercise initiation among sedentary college students. *Health Psychology, 19,* 172–180.

Rosenbaum, J., Arana, G. W., Fava, M., et al. (2009). *Psychiatric drugs.* Chicago: Lippincott.

Rosenhan, D. L. (1973). On being sane in insane places. *Science, 179,* 250–258.

Rosenhan, D. L., & Seligman, M. E. P. (1989). *Abnormal psychology* (2nd ed.). New York: Norton.

Rosenman, R. H., Brand, R. J., Jenkins, C. D., Friedman, M., Straus, R., & Wurm, M. (1975). Coronary disease in the Western Collaborative Group Study. Final follow-up experience of 8½ years. *Journal of the American Medical Association, 233,* 872–877.

Rosenthal, J. Z., & Rosenthal, N. E. (2006). Seasonal affective disorder. In D. J. Stein, D. J. Kupfer, & A. F. Schatzberg (Eds.), *The American Psychiatric Publishing textbook of mood disorders.* Washington, DC: American Psychiatric Publishing, Inc.

Rosenthal, R. (1985). From unconscious experimenter bias to teacher expectancy effects. In J. B. Dusek, V. C. Hall, & W. J. Meyer (Eds.), *Teacher expectancies.* Hillsdale, NJ: Erlbaum.

Rosenthal, R., Archer, D., DiMatteo, M. R., Koivumaki, J. H., & Rogers, P. L. (1974). Body talk and tone of voice: The language without words. *Psychology Today, 8,* 64–71.

Rosenzweig, M. R. (1984). Experience, memory, and the brain. *American Psychologist, 39,* 365–376.

Rosenzweig, M. R., & Bennett, E. L. (1996). Psychobiology of plasticity: Effects of training and experience on brain and behavior. *Behavioural Brain Research, 78,* 57–65.

Rosenzweig, S. (1992). Freud and experimental psychology: The emergence of idiodynamics. In S. Koch & D. E. Leary (Eds.), *A century of psychology as science.* Washington, DC: American Psychological Association.

Rosqvist, J., & Hersen, M. (2006). *Exposure treatments for anxiety disorders.* New York: Brunner-Routledge.

Ross, C. A. (2009). Errors of logic and scholarship concerning dissociative identity disorder. *Journal of Child Sexual Abuse, 18,* 221–231.

Ross, L. (2001). Getting down to fundamentals: Lay dispositionism and the attributions of psychologists. *Psychological Inquiry, 12,* 37–40.

Ross, L., & Nisbett, R. E. (1991). *The person and the situation: Perspectives of social psychology.* New York: McGraw-Hill.

Ross, M., & Wilson, A. E. (2003). Autobiographical memory and conceptions of self: Getting better all the time. *Current Directions in Psychological Science, 12,* 66–69.

Rossell, S. L., Bullmore, E. T., Williams, S. C. R., et al. (2002). Sex differences in functional brain activation during a lexical visual field task. *Brain and Language, 80,* 97–105.

Roth, A., & Fonagy, P. (2005). *What works for whom? A critical review of psychotherapy research* (2nd ed). New York: Guilford Press.

Roth, G., Assor, A., Niemiec, C. P., Ryan, R. M., & Deci, E. L. (2009). The emotional and academic consequences of parental conditional regard: Comparing conditional positive regard, conditional negative regard, and autonomy support as parenting practices. *Developmental Psychology, 45,* 1119–1142.

Rothbart, M. K., Sheese, B. E., & Conradt, E. D. (2009). Childhood temperament. In P. J. Corr & G. Matthews (Eds.), *The Cambridge handbook of personality psychology.* Cambridge, England: Cambridge University Press.

Rotheram-Borus, M. J., Desmond, K., Comulada, W. S., Arnold, E. M., & Johnson, M. (2008). Reducing risky sexual behavior and substance abuse among currently and formerly homeless adults living with HIV. *American Journal of Public Health, 98,* 409–417.

Rothman, J. (2008). Why all counter-evidence to the critical period hypothesis in second language acquisition is not equal or problematic. *Language and Linguistics Compass, 2,* 1063–1088.

Rottenberg, J., & Johnson, S. L. (2007). *Emotion and psychopathology: Bridging affective and clinical science.* Washington, DC: American Psychological Association.

Rotter, J. B. (1954). *Social learning and clinical psychology.* Englewood Cliffs, NJ: Prentice Hall.

Rotter, J. B. (1966). Generalized expectancies for internal versus external control of reinforcement. *Psychological Monographs, 80* (Whole No. 609).

Rouw, R., & Scholte, H. S. (2007). Increased structural connectivity in grapheme-color synesthesia. *Nature Neuroscience, 10,* 792–797.

Rovere, H., Rossini, S., & Reimão, R. (2008). Quality of life in patients with narcolepsy: A WHOQOL-bref study. *Arquivos de Neuro-Psiquiatria, 66,* 163–167.

Rowley, J. T., Stickgold, R., & Hobson, J. A. (1998). Eyelid movements and mental activity at sleep onset. *Consciousness and Cognition: An International Journal, 7,* 67–84.

Rubin, D. C., & Kozin, M. (1984). Vivid memories. *Cognition, 16,* 81–95.

Rubin, K. H., Cheah, C., & Menzer, M. M. (2010). Peers. In M. H. Bornstein (Ed.), *Handbook of cultural developmental science.* New York: Psychology Press.

Rubin, M., & Badea, C. (2010). The central tendency of a social group can affect ratings of its intragroup variability in the absence of social identity concerns. *Journal of Experimental Social Psychology.* Advanced online publication. doi:10.1016/j.jesp.2010.01.001

Rubin, R. T. (2000). Depression and manic-depressive illness. In G. Fink (Ed.), *Encyclopedia of stress.* San Diego, CA: Academic Press.

Rubonis, A. V., & Bickman, L. (1991). Psychological impairment in the wake of disaster: The disaster-psychopathology relationship. *Psychological Bulletin, 109,* 384–399.

Rudatsikira, E., Muula, A. S., & Siziya, S. (2008). Variables associated with physical fighting among US high-school students. *Clinical Practice and Epidemiology in Mental Health, 4*(May). Online publication. doi:10.1186/1745-0179-4-16.

Ruffman, R., Perner, J., Naito, M., Parkin, L., & Clements, W. A. (1998). Older (but not younger) siblings facilitate false belief understanding. *Developmental Psychology, 34,* 161–174.

Rumelhart, D. E., McClelland, J. L., & the PDP Research Group. (Eds.). (1986). *Parallel distributed processing* (Vol. 1). Cambridge, MA: MIT Press.

Rumstein, M. O., & Hunsley, J. (2001). Interpersonal and family functioning of female survivors of childhood sexual abuse. *Clinical Psychology Review, 21,* 471–490.

Ruscio, J. (2005). Exploring controversies in the art and science of polygraph testing. *Skeptical Inquirer, 29,* 34–39.

Ruscio, J., Zimmerman, M., McGlinchey, J. B., Chelminski, I., & Young, D. (2007). Diagnosing major depressive disorder XI: A taxometric investigation of the structure underlying DSM-IV symptoms. *Journal of Nervous and Mental Disease, 195*, 10–19.

Rush, A. J., Warden, D., Wisniewski, S. R., et al. (2009). STAR*D: Revising conventional wisdom. *CNS Drugs, 23*, 627–647.

Rushton, J. P. (1989). Genetic similarity, human altruism, and group selection. *Behavioral and Brain Sciences, 12*, 503–559.

Rushton, J. P. (2009). Brain size as an explanation of national differences in IQ, longevity, and other life-history variables. *Personality and Individual Differences*, September 1.

Rushton, J. P., & Davison, A. C. (2009). Whole brain size and general mental ability: A review. *International Journal of Neuroscience, 119*, 691–731.

Russell, G. (2006). Review of understanding eating disorders: Conceptual and ethical issues in the treatment of anorexia and bulimia nervosa. *British Journal of Psychiatry, 189*, 288–289.

Russell, J. A. (1994). Is there universal recognition of emotion from facial expressions? A review of the cross-cultural studies. *Psychological Bulletin, 115*, 102–141.

Rutter, M. (2000). Genetic studies of autism: From the 1970s into the millennium. *Journal of Abnormal Child Psychology, 28*, 3–14.

Rutter, M. L. (1997). Nature-nurture integration: The example of antisocial behavior. *American Psychologist, 52*, 390–398.

Ryan, R. M., & Lynch, J. (1989). Emotional autonomy versus detachment: Revisiting the vicissitudes of adolescence and young adulthood. *Child Development, 60*, 340–356.

Ryle, A. (2010). Cognitive analytic therapy. In N. Kazantzis, M. A. Reinecke, & A. Freeman (Eds.), *Cognitive and behavioral theories in clinical practice*. New York: Guilford Press.

Sachse, R., & Elliott, R. (2002). Process-outcome research on humanistic therapy variables. In D. J. Cain (Ed.), *Humanistic psychotherapies: Handbook of research and practice*. Washington, DC: American Psychological Association.

Sack, R. L., Hughes, R. J., Edgar, D. M., & Lewy, A. J. (1997). Sleep-promoting effects of melatonin: At what dose, in whom, under what conditions, and by what mechanisms? *Sleep, 20*, 908–915.

Sacks, O. (1985). *The man who mistook his wife for a hat and other clinical tales*. New York: Summit Books and Simon & Schuster.

Sacks, O. (1999). *Awakenings*. Westminster, MD: Knopf.

Saczynski, J. S., Willis, S. L., & Schaie, K. W. (2002). Strategy use in reasoning training with older adults. *Aging, Neuropsychology and Cognition, 9*, 48–60.

Saklofske, D. H., Austin, E. J., Galloway, J., & Davidson, K. (2007). Individual difference correlates of health-related behaviours: Preliminary evidence for links between emotional intelligence and coping. *Personality and Individual Differences, 42*, 491–502.

Saling, L. L., & Phillips, J. G. (2007). Automatic behaviour: Efficient not mindless. *Brain Research Bulletin, 73*, 1–20.

Salovey, P., & Pizzaro, D. A. (2003). The value of emotional intelligence. In R. J. Sternberg, J. Lautrey, & T. I. Lubart (Eds.), *Models of intelligence: International perspectives*. Washington, DC: American Psychological Association.

Salthouse, T. (2006). Mental exercise and mental aging. *Perspectives on Psychological Science, 1*, 68–87.

Salthouse, T. A. (2004). What and when of cognitive aging. *Current Directions in Psychological Science, 13*, 140–144.

Sanchez-Armass, O., & Barabasz, A. F. (2005). Mexican norms for the Stanford Hypnotic Susceptibility Scale, Form C. *International Journal of Clinical and Experimental Hypnosis, 53*, 321–331.

Sandler, J. (1986). Aversion methods. In F. H. Kanfer & A. P. Goldstein (Eds.), *Helping people change: A textbook of methods* (3rd ed.). New York: Pergamon Press.

Santonastaso, P., Scicluna, D., Colombo, G., Zanetti, T., & Favaro, A. (2006). Eating disorders in Maltese and Italian female students. *Psychopathology, 39*, 153–157.

Sarason, I. G., Sarason, B. R., Pierce, G. R., Shearin, E. N., & Sayers, M. H. (1991). A social learning approach to increasing blood donations. *Journal of Applied Social Psychology, 21*, 896–918.

Saremi, M., Grenèche, J., Bonneford, A., Rohmer, O., Eschenlauer, A., & Tassi, P. (2008). Effects of nocturnal railway noise on sleep fragmentation in young and middle-aged subjects as a function of type of train and sound level. *International Journal of Psychophysiology, 70*, 184–191.

Sarkar, U., Ali, S., & Whooley, M. (2009). Self-efficacy as a marker of cardiac function and predictor of heart failure hospitalization and mortality in patients with stable coronary heart disease: Findings from the Heart and Soul Study. *Health Psychology, 28*, 166–173.

Sasseville, A., Benhaberou-Brun, D., Fontaine, C., Charon, M. C., & Hébert, M. (2009). Wearing blue-blockers in the morning could improve sleep of workers on a permanent night schedule: A pilot study. *Chronobiology International, 26*, 913–925.

Sataloff, J., & Thayer, R. (2006). *Hearing loss*. New York: Marcel Dekker.

Satcher, D. (1999). *Mental health: A report of the Surgeon General*. Washington, DC: U.S. Department of Health and Human Services.

Satir, V. (1967). *Conjoint family therapy*. Palo Alto, CA: Science and Behavior Books.

Savage, J., & Yancey, C. (2008). The effects of media violence exposure on criminal aggression: A meta-analysis. *Criminal Justice and Behavior, 35*, 772–791.

Savage-Rumbaugh, E. S., McDonald, K., Sevcik, R. A., Hopkins, W. D., & Rupert, E. (1986). Spontaneous symbol acquisition and communicative use by pygmy chimpanzees (*Pan paniscus*). *Journal of Experimental Psychology: General, 115*, 211–235.

Savage-Rumbaugh, E. S., Murphy, J., Sevcik, R. A., Brakke, K. E., et al. (1993). Language comprehension in ape and child. *Monographs of the Society for Research in Child Development, 58*(233), 1–254.

Saxvig, I. W., Lundervold, A. J., Grønli, J., Ursin, R., Bjorvatn, B., & Portas, C. M. (2008). The effect of a REM sleep deprivation procedure on different aspects of memory function in humans. *Psychophysiology, 45*, 309–317.

Scarr, S. (1992). Developmental theories for the 1990s: Development and individual differences. *Child Development, 63*, 1–19.

Scarr, S., & McCartney, K. (1983). How do people make their own environments? A theory of genotype environment effects. *Child Development, 54*, 424–435.

Scarr, S., & Weinberg, R. A. (1977). Intellectual similarities within families of both adopted and biological children. *Intelligence, 32*, 170–190.

Schabus, M. (2009). Still missing some significant ingredients: Commentary on Genzel et al. Slow wave sleep and REM sleep awakenings do not affect sleep dependent memory consolidation. *Sleep, 32*, 302–310.

Schachter, S. (1959). *The psychology of affiliation: Experimental studies of the sources of gregariousness*. Stanford, CA: Stanford University Press.

Schachter, S. (1966). The interaction of cognitive and physiological determinants of emotional state. In C. D. Spielberger (Ed.), *Anxiety and behavior*. New York: Academic Press.

Schachter, S. (1982). Recidivism and self-cure of smoking and obesity. *American Psychologist, 37*, 436–444.

Schacter, D. L. (1992). Understanding implicit memory: A cognitive neuroscience approach. *American Psychologist, 47*, 559–569.

Schaefer, A., & Philippot, P. (2005). Selective effects of emotion on the phenomenal characteristics of autobiographical memories. *Memory, 13*, 148–160.

Schaeffer, E. L., Novaes, B. A., da Silva, E. R., et al. (2009). Strategies to promote differentiation of newborn neurons into mature functional cells in Alzheimer brain. *Progress in Neuro-Pharmacology & Biological Psychiatry, 33*, 1087–1102.

Schaie, K. W. (1994). The course of adult intellectual development. *American Psychologist, 49*, 304–313.

Schaie, K. W. (1998). The Seattle longitudinal studies of adult intelligence. In M. Lawton & T. Salthouse (Eds.), *Essential papers on the psychology of aging*. New York: New York University Press.

Schaie, K. W. (2005). *Developmental influences on adult intelligence: The Seattle longitudinal study*. London: Oxford University Press.

Schaller, M. (2006). Parasites, behavioral defenses, and the social psychological mechanisms through which cultures are evoked. *Psychological Inquiry, 17*, 96–100.

Schaller, M., & Crandall, C. S. (Eds.). (2004). *The psychological foundations of culture*. Mahwah, NJ: Erlbaum.

Schaller, M., Norenzayan, A., Heine, S. J., Yamagishi, T., & Kameda, T. (Eds.). (2010). *Evolution, culture, and the human mind*. New York: Psychology Press.

Schanberg, S. M., Ingledue, V. F., Lee, J. Y., Hannun, Y. A., & Bartolome, J. V. (2003). PKC alpha mediates maternal touch regulation of growth-related gene expression in infant rats. *Neuropsychopharmacology, 28*, 1026–1030.

Schatschneider, C., & Torgesen, J. K. (2004). Using our current understanding of dyslexia to support early identification and intervention. Learning disabilities, attention-deficit hyperactivity disorder, and psychiatric comorbid conditions. *Journal of Child Neurology, 19*, 759–765.

Schatzberg, A. F., Cole, J. O., & DeBattista, C. (2010). *Manual of clinical psychopharmacology*. Washington, DC: American Psychiatric Publishing.

Scheff, T. J. (1966). *Being mentally ill: A sociological theory.* Chicago: Aldine.

Scheier, M. F., & Carver, C. S. (1985). Optimism, coping, and health: Assessment and implications of generalized outcome expectancies. *Health Psychology, 4,* 219–247.

Scheier, M. F., Carver, C. S., & Bridges, M. W. (1994). Distinguishing optimism from neuroticism (and trait anxiety, self-mastery, and self-esteem): A re-evaluation of the Life Orientation Test. *Journal of Personality and Social Psychology, 67,* 1063–1078.

Schellenberg, G. D., Dawson, G., Sung, Y. J., Estes, A., Munson, J., Rosenthal, E., et al. (2006). Evidence for genetic linkage of autism to chromosomes 7 and 4. *Molecular Psychiatry, 11,* 979–989.

Schenck, C. H., Hurwitz, T. D., Bundlie, S. R., & Mahowald, M. W. (1991). Sleep-related eating disorders: Polysomnographic correlates of a heterogeneous syndrome distinct from daytime eating disorders. *Sleep: Journal of Sleep Research and Sleep Medicine, 14,* 419–431.

Schenck, C. H., Milner, D. M., Hurwitz, T. D., & Bundlie, S. R. (1989). A polysomnographic and clinical report on sleep-related injury in 100 adult patients. *American Journal of Psychiatry, 146,* 1166–1173.

Schendan, H. E., & Lucia, L. C. (2009). Visual object cognition precedes but also temporally overlaps mental rotation. *Brain Research, 1294,* 91–105.

Schiff, M., & Lewontin, R. (1986). *Education and class: The irrelevance of IQ genetic studies.* Oxford, England: Clarendon Press.

Schiff, W., & Foulke, E. (Eds.). (2010). *Tactual perception: A sourcebook.* New York: Cambridge University Press.

Schimanski, L. A., & Nguyen, P. V. (2005). Impaired fear memories are correlated with subregion-specific deficits in hippocampal and amygdalar LTP. *Behavioral Neuroscience, 119,* 38–54.

Schimmack, U., Oishi, S., Furr, M., & Funder, D. C. (2004). Personality and life satisfaction: A facet-level analysis. *Personality and Social Psychology Bulletin, 30,* 1062–1075.

Schlegel, A., & Barry, H. (1991). *Adolescence: An anthropological inquiry.* New York: Free Press.

Schlesinger, L. B. (Ed.). (2007). *Explorations in criminal psychopathology: Clinical syndromes with forensic implications.* Springfield, IL: Charles C Thomas.

Schmidt, F. L., & Hunter, J. (2004). General mental ability in the world of work: Occupational attainment and job performance. *Journal of Personality and Social Psychology, 86,* 162–173.

Schmitt, B. (2007, May 15). 91-year-old battered by carjacking, but getting better. Knight Ridder Tribune News Service, p. l. Retrieved May 20, 2007, from http://proquest.uml.com

Schmitt, D. P., Shackelford, T. K., & Buss, D. M. (2001). Are men really more "oriented" toward short-term mating than women? A critical review of theory and research. *Psychology, Evolution and Gender, 3,* 211–239.

Schnall, E., Wassertheil-Smoller, S., Swencionis, C., et al. (2008). The relationship between religion and cardiovascular outcomes and all-cause morality in the Women's Health Initiative Observational Study. *Psychology and Health, 8,* 1–15.

Schneer, J. A., & Reitman, F. (1997). The interrupted managerial career path: A longitudinal study of MBAs. *Journal of Vocational Behavior, 51,* 411–434.

Schneider, W., Kron, V., Hunnerkopf, M., & Krajewski, K. (2004). The development of young children's memory strategies: First findings from the Wurzburg Longitudinal Memory Study. *Journal of Experimental Child Psychology, 88,* 193–209.

Schredl, M., & Reinhard, I. (2008). Gender differences in dream recall: A meta-analysis. *Journal of Sleep Research, 17,* 125–131.

Schul, Y., Mayo, R., & Burnstein, E. (2004). Encoding under trust and distrust: The spontaneous activation of incongruent cognitions. *Journal of Personality and Social Psychology, 86,* 668–679.

Schunk, D. H., Pintrich, P. R., & Meese, J. (2007). *Motivation in education: Theory, research, and application.* Englewood Cliffs, NJ: Prentice Hall.

Schwartz, B. L. (1998). Illusory tip-of-the-tongue states. *Memory, 6,* 623–642.

Schwartz, C. E., Wright, C. I., Shin, L. M., Kagan, J., & Rauch, S. L. (2003). Inhibited and uninhibited children "grown up": Amygdalar responses to novelty. *Science, 300,* 1952–1953.

Schwartz, R. (1984). Body weight regulation. *University of Washington Medicine, 10,* 16–20.

Schwartz, S., & Maquet, P. (2002). Sleep imaging and the neuro-psychological assessment of dreams. *Trends in Cognitive Sciences, 6,* 23–30.

Schwarz, J. (2009, June 11). If the shoe fits, duck: A real-life example of humans' dual vision system. University of Washington News and Information. Retrieved November 17, 2009, from www.uwnews.org

Schwarzer, R. (1998). Stress and coping from a social-cognitive perspective. *Annals of the New York Academy of Sciences, 851,* 531–537.

Schweinhart, L. J., & Weikart, D. P. (1998). High/Scope Perry Preschool Program effects at age twenty-seven. In J. Crane (Ed.), *Social programs that work.* New York: Russell Sage.

Schweitzer, I., McGuire, K., & Ng, C. (2009). Sexual side-effects of contemporary antidepressants: A review. *Australian/New Zealand Journal of Psychiatry, 43,* 795–808.

ScienceDaily. (2009, November 11). Human-machine interface is essential link in groundbreaking prosthetic hand. Retrieved December 7, 2009, from http://www.sciencedaily.com/releases/2009/11/091104132708.htm

Scoboria, A., Mazzoni, G., Kirsch, I., & Milling, L. S. (2002). Immediate and persisting effects of misleading questions and hypnosis on memory reports. *Journal of Experimental Psychology: Applied, 8,* 26–32.

Scott, T. R. (1992). Taste, feeding, and pleasure. In A. N. Epstein et al. (Eds.), *Progress in psychobiology and physiological psychology.* San Diego, CA: Academic Press.

Scott, T. R., & Giza, B. K. (1993). Gustatory control of ingestion. In D. A. Booth et al. (Eds.), *Neurophysiology of ingestion. Pergamon studies in neuroscience.* Oxford, England: Pergamon Press.

Scott, W. D., & Cervone, D. (2002). The impact of negative affect on performance standards: Evidence for an affect as information mechanism. *Cognitive Therapy and Research, 26,* 9–37.

Sears, R. R. (1977). Sources of life satisfaction of the Terman gifted men. *American Psychologist, 32,* 119–128.

Seattle Times. (1997, December 11). Paralyzed woman is good Samaritan, p. B3.

Sedikides, C., Gaertner, L., & Toguchi, Y. (2003). Pancultural self-enhancement. *Journal of Personality and Social Psychology, 84,* 60–79.

Segal, D. L., & Coolidge, F. A. (2007). Structured interviewing and DSM classification. In M. Hersen, S. M. Turner, & D. C. Beidel (Eds.), *Adult psychopathology and diagnosis.* Hoboken, NJ: Wiley.

Segall, M. H., Campbell, D. T., & Herskowitz, M. J. (1966). *The influence of culture on visual perception.* New York: Pergamon Press.

Segerdahl, P., Fields, W., & Savage-Rumbaugh, E. S. (2006). *Kanzi's primal language: The cultural initiation of primates into language.* New York: Palgrave Macmillan.

Segerstrom, S. C., & Miller, G. E. (2004). Psychological stress and the human immune system. A meta-analytic study of 30 years of inquiry. *Psychological Bulletin, 130,* 601–630.

Sekuler, R., Watamaniuk, S., & Blake, R. (2002). In H. Pashler & S. Yantis (Eds.), *Steven's handbook of experimental psychology: Vol. 1. Sensation and perception* (3rd ed.). New York: Wiley.

Selby, E. A., Anestis, M. D., Bender, T. W., & Joiner, T. E. (2009). An exploration of the emotional cascade model in borderline personality disorder. *Journal of Abnormal Psychology, 118,* 375–387.

Selby, E. A., & Joiner, T. E. (2009). Cascades of emotion: The emergence of borderline personality disorder from emotional and behavioral dysregulation. *Review of General Psychology, 13,* 219–229.

Self, D. W., & Staley, J. K. (Eds.). (2009). *Behavioral neuroscience of drug addiction.* New York: Springer.

Seligman, M. E. P. (1971). Phobias and preparedness. *Behavior Therapy, 2,* 307–320.

Seligman, M. E. P. (1991). *Learned optimisim.* New York: Knopf.

Seligman, M. E. P. (1995). The effectiveness of psychotherapy: The *Consumer Reports* study. *American Psychologist, 50,* 965–974.

Seligman, M. E. P. (2002). *Authentic happiness: Using the new positive psychology to realize your potential for lasting fulfillment.* New York: Free Press.

Seligman, M. E. P., & Isaacowitz, D. M. (2000). Learned helplessness. In G. Fink (Ed.), *Encyclopedia of stress.* San Diego, CA: Academic Press.

Seligman, M. E. P., & Peterson, C. R. (Eds.). (2004). *Human strengths: A classification manual.* New York: Oxford University Press.

Selye, H. (1976). *The stress of life* (Rev. ed.). New York: McGraw-Hill.

Sergios, P. A., & Cody, J. (1985–1986). Importance of physical attractiveness and social assertiveness skills in male homosexual dating behavior and partner selection. *Journal of Homosexuality, 12,* 71–84.

Serpell, R. (2000). Intelligence and culture. In R. J. Sternberg (Ed.), *Handbook of intelligence.* New York: Cambridge University Press.

Sexton, M. M. (1979). Behavioral epidemiology. In O. F. Pomerleau & J. P. Brady (Eds.), *Behavioral Medicine: Theory and Practice.* Baltimore, MD: Williams & Wilkins.

Shaffer, D. R. (1989). *Developmental psychology: Childhood and adolescence* (2nd ed.). Pacific Grove, CA: Brooks/Cole.

Shallice, T., & Burgess, P. (1991). Higher-order cognitive impairments and frontal-lobe lesions in man. In H. S. Levin, H. M. Eisenberg, & A. L. Benton (Eds.), *Frontal lobe function and dysfunction*. New York: Oxford University Press.

Shanab, M. E., & Yahya, L. A. (1977). A behavioral study of obedience in children. *Journal of Personality and Social Psychology, 35*, 530–536.

Shanahan, M., & Baars, B. (2005). Applying global workspace theory to the frame problem. *Cognition, 98*, 157–176.

Shanks, D. R. (2010). Learning: From association to cognition. *Annual Review of Psychology, 61*, 273–301.

Shapiro, A. K., & Shapiro, E. (1997). *The powerful placebo: From ancient priest to modern physician*. Baltimore: Johns Hopkins University Press.

Shapiro, C. M., Bortz, R., Mitchell, D., Bartel, P., & Jooste, P. (1981). Slow-wave sleep: A recovery period after exercise. *Science, 214*, 1253–1254.

Shapiro, J. R., King, E. B., & Quiñones, M. A. (2007). Expectations of obese trainees: How stigmatized trainee characteristics influence training effectiveness. *Journal of Applied Psychology, 92*, 239–249.

Shaver, P., Hazan, C., & Bradshaw, D. (1988). Love as attachment: The integration of three behavioral systems. In R. J. Sternberg & M. L. Barnes (Eds.), *The psychology of love*. New Haven, CT: Yale University Press.

Shaver, P. R., & Clark, C. L. (1996). Forms of adult romantic attachment and their cognitive and emotional underpinnings. In G. G. Noam et al. (Eds.), *Development and vulnerability in close relationships. The Jean Piaget symposium series*. Mahwah, NJ: Erlbaum.

Shaver, P. R., & Mikulincer, M. (2009). Attachment theory: I, Motivational, individual differences and structural aspects. In P. J. Corr & G. Matthews (Eds.), *The Cambridge handbook of personality psychology*. Cambridge, England: Cambridge University Press.

Shaywitz, B. A., Shaywitz, S. E., Pugh, K. R., et al. (1995). Sex difference in the organization of the brain for language. *Nature, 373*, 607–609.

Shaywitz, S. E., Morris, R., & Shaywitz, B. A. (2008). The education of dyslexic children from childhood to young adulthood. *Annual Review of Psychology, 59*, 451–475.

Sheehan, P. W., Green, V., & Truesdale, P. (1992). Influence of rapport on hypnotically induced pseudomemory. *Journal of Abnormal Psychology, 101*, 690–700.

Sheldon, K. M., Joiner, T. E., Pettit, J. W., & Williams, G. (2003). Reconciling humanistic ideals and scientific clinical practice. *Clinical Psychology: Science and Practice, 10*, 302–315.

Sheldon, K. M., & Kasser, T. (2001). Getting older, getting better? Personal strivings and psychological maturity across the life span. *Developmental Psychology, 37*, 491–501.

Shepard, R. N., & Metzler, J. (1971). Mental rotation of three-dimensional objects. *Science, 171*, 701–703.

Shepherd, C., McCann, H., & Halliday, G. M. (2009). Variations in the neuropathology of familial Alzheimer's disease. *Neuropathologica, 118*, 37–52.

Shepherd, G. (1997). *The synaptic organizer of the brain*. New York: Oxford University Press.

Shepperd, J. A., Grace, J., Cole, L. J., & Kline, C. (2005). Anxiety and outcome predictions. *Personality and Social Psychology Bulletin, 31*, 267–275.

Sherif, M. (1935). A study of some social factors in perception. *Archives of Psychology* (No. 187).

Shibuya, A., Sakamoto, A., Ihori, N., & Yukawa, S. (2008). The effects of the presence and contexts of video game violence on children: A longitudinal study in Japan. *Simulation & Gaming, 39*, 528–539.

Shiner, L. (2009, February 18). Sully's tale. *Air & Space Magazine*. Retrieved November 28, 2009, from http://www.airspacemag.com/flight-today/Sullys-Tale.html

Shneidman, E. S. (1976). A psychological theory of suicide. *Psychiatric Annals, 6*, 51–66.

Shneidman, E. S. (1998). *The suicidal mind*. New York: Oxford University Press.

Shoda, Y., & Mischel, W. (2000). Reconciling contextualism with the core assumptions of personality psychology. *European Journal of Personality, 14*, 407–428.

Shoda, Y., Mischel, W., & Wright, J. C. (1994). Intra-individual stability and patterning of behavior: Incorporating psychological situations into the idiographic analysis of personality. *Journal of Personality and Social Psychology, 67*, 674–687.

Shorey, H. S., & Snyder, C. R. (2006). The role of adult attachment styles in psychopathology and psychotherapy outcomes. *Review of General Psychology, 10*, 1–20.

Shorter, E. (1998). *A history of psychiatry: From the era of the asylum to the age of Prozac*. New York: Wiley.

Shultz, K. S., Morton, K. R., & Weckerle, J. R. (1998). The influence of push and pull factors on voluntary and involuntary early retirees' retirement decision and adjustment. *Journal of Vocational Behavior, 53*, 45–57.

Sia, C. L., Tan, B. C. Y., & Wei, K. K. (2002). Group polarization and computer mediated communication: Effects of communication cues, social presence, and anonymity. *Information Systems Research, 13*, 70–90.

Siegel, A. (2005). *Neurobiology of aggression and rage*. San Francisco: Taylor & Francis.

Siegel, S. (1984). Pavlovian conditioning and heroin overdose: Reports from overdose victims. *Bulletin of the Psychonomic Society, 22*, 428–430.

Siegel, S., Baptista, M. A. S., Kim, J. A., McDonald, R. V., & Weise-Kelly, L. (2000). Pavlovian psychopharmacology: The associative basis of tolerance. *Experimental and Clinical Psychopharmacology, 8*, 276–293.

Siegler, R. S. (1986). *Children's thinking*. Englewood Cliffs, NJ: Prentice Hall.

Siegler, R. S. (1996). *Emerging minds: The process of change in children's thinking*. New York: Oxford University Press.

Sieverding, M., Matterne, U., & Ciccarello, L. (2010). What role do social norms play in the context of men's cancer screening intention and behavior? Application of an extended theory of planned behavior. *Health Psychology, 29*, 72–81.

Sigala, N., & Logothetis, N. K. (2002). Visual categorization shapes feature selectivity in the primate temporal cortex. *Nature, 415*, 318–320.

Silva, M. M., Groeger J. A., & Bradshaw, M. F. (2006). Attention-memory interactions in scene perception. *Spatial Vision, 19*, 9–19.

Silvia, P. J., Martin, C., & Nusbaum, E. C. (2009). A snapshot of creativity: Evaluating a quick and simple method for assessing divergent thinking. *Thinking Skills and Creativity, 4*, 79–85.

Simkin, L. R., & Gross, A. M. (1994). Assessment of coping with high risk situations for exercise relapse among healthy women. *Health Psychology, 13*, 274–277.

Simon, C. (2007). *Neurology*. New York: Oxford University Press.

Simon, H. A. (1990). Invariants of human behavior. *Annual Review of Psychology, 41*, 1–20.

Simons, D. J., & Chabris, C. F. (1999). Gorillas in our midst: Sustained inattentional blindness for dynamic events. *Perception, 28*, 1059–1074.

Simonton, D. K. (1999). Creativity and genius. In L. A. Pervin & O. P. John (Eds.), *Handbook of personality: Theory and research* (2nd ed). New York: Guilford Press.

Simonton, D. K. (2001). Talent development as a multidimensional, multiplicative, and dynamic process. *Current Directions in Psychological Science, 10*, 39–43.

Simpaio, E., Maris, S., & Bach-y-Rita, P. (2001). Brain plasticity: "Visual" acuity of blind persons via the tongue. *Brain Research, 908*, 204–207.

Simpson, J. A., & Beckes, L. (2010). Evolutionary perspectives on prosocial behavior. In M. Mikulincer & P. R. Shaver (Eds.), *Prosocial motives, emotions, and behavior: The better angels of our nature*. Washington, DC: American Psychological Association.

Singer, T., Seymour, B., O'Doherty, J., Kaube, H., Dolan, R. J., & Frith, C. D. (2004). Empathy for pain involves the affective but not sensory components of pain. *Science, 303*, 1157–1162.

Singer, T., Verhaeghen, P., Ghisletta, P., Lindenberger, U., & Baltes, P. B. (2003). The fate of cognition in very old age: Six-year longitudinal findings in the Berlin Aging Study (BASE). *Psychology and Aging, 18*, 318–331.

Sistler, A. B., & Moore, G. M. (1996). Cultural diversity in coping with marital stress. *Journal of Clinical Geropsychology, 2*, 77–82.

Siu, O. (2003). Job stress and job performance among employees in Hong Kong: The role of Chinese work values and organizational commitment. *International Journal of Psychology, 38*, 337–347.

Skinner, B. F. (1938). *The behavior of organisms: An experimental analysis*. New York: Appleton-Century-Crofts.

Skinner, B. F. (1948). *Walden two*. New York: Macmillan.

Skinner, B. F. (1953). *Science and human behavior*. New York: Macmillan.

Skinner, B. F. (1957). *Verbal behavior*. New York: Prentice Hall.

Skinner, B. F. (1968). *The technology of teaching*. New York: Appleton-Century-Crofts.

Skinner, B. F. (1971). *Beyond freedom and dignity*. New York: Knopf.

Skinner, B. F. (1989a). The origins of cognitive thought. *American Psychologist, 44*, 13–18.

Skinner, B. F. (1989b). Teaching machines. *Science, 243*, 1535.

Skinner, B. F. (1990). Can psychology be a science of mind? *American Psychologist, 45*, 1206–1210.

Sklar, L. S., & Anisman, H. (1981). Stress and cancer. *Psychological Bulletin, 89*, 369–406.

Skodol, A. E., & Bender, D. S. (2009). The future of personality disorders in DSM-V. *American Journal of Psychiatry, 166*, 388–391.

Skoyles, J. R. (1997). Evolution's "missing link": A hypothesis upon neural plasticity, prefrontal working memory and the origins of modern cognition. *Medical Hypotheses, 48*, 499–501.

Slater, C. L. (2003). Generativity versus stagnation: An elaboration of Erikson's adult stage of human development. *Journal of Adult Development, 10,* 53–65.

Sloan, D., & Marx, D. (2004). A closer examination of the structured written disclosure procedure. *Journal of Consulting and Clinical Psychology, 72,* 165–175.

Sloana, D. M., Feinstein, B. A., & Marx, B. A. (2009). The durability of beneficial health effects associated with expressive writing. *Anxiety, Stress & Coping, 22,* 509–523.

Slovic, P., Fischhoff, B., & Lichtenstein, S. (1988). Response mode, framing, and information-processing effects in risk assessment. In D. E. Bell & H. Raiffa (Eds.), *Decision making: Descriptive, normative, and prescriptive interactions.* New York: Cambridge University Press.

Slovic, P., & Peters, E. (2006). Risk perception and affect. *Current Directions in Psychological Science, 15,* 322–325.

Smalley, S. L., McGough, J. J., Del'Homme, M., et al. (2000). Familial clustering of symptoms and disruptive behaviors in multiplex families with attention-deficit/hyperactivity disorder. *Journal of the American Academy of Child & Adolescent Psychiatry, 39,* 1135–1143.

Smith, B. D. (1998). *Psychology: Science and understanding.* New York: McGraw-Hill.

Smith, C. A., & Kirby, L. D. (2004). Appraisal as a pervasive determinant of anger. *Emotion, 4,* 133–138.

Smith, C. L., Johnson, J. L., & Hathaway, W. (2009). Personality contributions to belief in paranormal phenomena. *Individual Differences Research, 7,* 85–96.

Smith, C. S., Folkard, S., Schmieder, R. A., Parra, L. F., Spelten, E., Almiral, H., et al. (2002). Investigation of morning-evening orientation in six countries using the preferences scale. *Personality and Individual Differences, 32,* 949–968.

Smith, D. (2002). The theory heard 'round the world. *Monitor on Psychology, 33,* No. 9., October. Retrieved December 18, 2004, from http://www. apa.org/monitor/oct02/theory.html

Smith, E. R., & Zarate, M. A. (1992). Exemplar-based model of social judgment. *Psychological Review, 99,* 3–21.

Smith, G. E., Housen, P., Yaffe, K., Ruff, R., Kennison, R. F., Mahncke, H. W., et al. (2009). A cognitive training program based on principles of brain plasticity: Results from the Improvement in Memory with Plasticity-based Adaptive Cognitive Training (IMPACT) study. *Journal of the American Geriatric Society, 57,* 594–603.

Smith, M. C., & Phillips, M. R., Jr. (2001). Age differences in memory for radio advertisements: The role of mnemonic. *Journal of Business Research, 53,* 103–109.

Smith, M. J., Thirthalli, J., Abdallah, A. B., Murray, R. M., & Cottler, L. B. (2009). Prevalence of psychotic symptoms in substance users: A comparison across substances. *Comprehensive Psychiatry, 50,* 245–250.

Smith, M. L., & Glass, G. V. (1977). Meta-analyses of psychotherapy outcome studies. *American Psychologist, 32,* 752–760.

Smith, R. E. (1989). Effects of coping skills training on generalized self-efficacy and locus of control.

Journal of Personality and Social Psychology, 56, 228–233.

Smith, R. E. (1996). Performance anxiety, cognitive interference, and concentration enhancement strategies in sports. In I. G. Sarason, G. R. Pierce, & B. R. Sarason (Eds.), *Cognitive interference: Theories, methods, and findings.* Mahwah, NJ: Erlbaum.

Smith, R. E., & Shoda, Y. (2009). Personality as a cognitive-affective processing system. In P. J. Corr & G. Matthews (Eds.), *The Cambridge handbook of personality psychology.* Cambridge, England: Cambridge University Press.

Smith, R. E., Smoll, F. L., & Cumming, S. P. (2007). Effects of a motivational climate intervention for coaches on young athletes' sport performance anxiety. *Journal of Sport & Exercise Psychology, 29,* 38–58.

Smith, R. E., Smoll, F. L., & Schultz, R. W. (1990). Measurement and correlates of sport-specific cognitive and somatic trait anxiety: The Sports Anxiety Scale. *Anxiety Research* [now *Anxiety, Stress, & Coping*], *2,* 263–280.

Smith, S. M., McIntosh, W. D., & Bazzini, D. G. (1999). Are the beautiful good in Hollywood? An investigation of the beauty-and-goodness stereotype on film. *Basic and Applied Social Psychology, 21,* 69–80.

Smith, S. M., & Vela, E. (2001). Environmental context dependent memory: A review and meta-analysis. *Psychonomic Bulletin and Review, 8,* 203–220.

Smithson, J., Lewis, S., Cooper, C., & Dyer, J. (2004). Flexible working and the gender pay gap in the accountancy profession. *Work, Employment and Society, 18,* 115–135.

Smoll, F. L., Smith, R. E., Barnett, N. P., & Everett, J. J. (1993). Enhancement of children's self-esteem through social support training for youth sport coaches. *Journal of Applied Psychology, 78,* 602–610.

Smoll, F. L., Smith, R. E., & Cumming, S. P. (2007). Effects of a motivational climate intervention for coaches on young athletes' achievement goal orientations. *Journal of Clinical Sport Psychology, 1,* 23–46.

Snook, B., Cullen, R. M., Bennell, C., Taylor, P. J., & Gendreau, P. (2008). The criminal profiling illusion: What's behind the smoke and mirrors? *Criminal Justice and Behavior, 35,* 1257–1276.

Snook, B., Eastwood, J., Gendreau, P., Goggin, C., & Cullen, R. M. (2007). Taking stock of criminal profiling: A narrative review and meta-analysis. *Criminal Justice and Behavior, 34,* 437–453.

Snow, M. E., Jacklin, C. N., & Maccoby, E. E. (1983). Sex-of-child-differences in father-child interaction at one year of age. *Child Development, 54,* 227–232.

Snyder, C. R., & Lopez, S. J. (2007). *Positive psychology: The scientific and practical explorations of human strengths.* Thousand Oaks, CA: Sage Publications, Inc.

Snyder, M. (1987). *Public appearances/private realities: The psychology of self-monitoring.* New York: Freeman.

Snyder, M., Clary, E. G., & Stukas, A. A. (2000). The functional approach to volunteerism. In G. R. Maio & J. M. Olson, *Why we evaluate: Functions of attitudes.* Mahwah, NJ: Erlbaum.

Snyder, S. H. (1977). Opiate receptors and internal opiates. *Scientific American, 236,* 44–56.

Snyderman, N. (2009, September 18). Hitting other people's kids. *MSNBC.com.* Retrieved October 11, 2009, from http://www.msnbc.msn.com/id/3032619/ns/nightly_news#32915557

Social Psychology Network. (2010). *Tips on taking multiple-choice tests.* Retrieved February 5, 2010, from http://www.socialpsychology.org/testtips.htm

Society for Personality Assessment. (2005). The status of the Rorschach in clinical and forensic practice: An official statement by the Board of Trustees of the Society for Personality Assessment. *Journal of Personality Assessment, 85,* 219–237.

Solms, M. (2002). Dreaming: Cholinergic and dopaminergic hypotheses. In E. Perry, H. Ashton, & A. Young (Eds.), *Neurochemistry of consciousness: Neurotransmitters in mind. Advances in consciousness research.* Amsterdam: Benjamins.

Solms, M. (2007). The interpretation of dreams and the neurosciences. In L. Mayes, P. Fonagy, & M. Target (Eds.), *Developmental science and psychoanalysis: Integration and innovation.* London: Karnac.

Soussignan, R. (2002). Duchenne smile, emotional experience, and autonomic reactivity: A test of the facial feedback hypothesis. *Emotion, 2,* 52–74.

Sowell, E. R., Thompson, P. M., Tessner, K. D., & Toga, A. W. (2001). Mapping continued brain growth and gray matter density reduction in dorsal frontal cortex: Inverse relationships during postadolescent brain maturation. *Journal of Neuroscience, 21,* 8819–8829.

Spanos, N. P. (1991). A sociocognitive approach to hypnosis. In S. J. Lynn & J. W. Rhue (Eds.), *Theories of hypnosis: Current models and perspectives.* New York: Guilford Press.

Spanos, N. P. (1994). Multiple identity enactments and multiple personality disorder: A sociocognitive perspective. *Psychological Bulletin, 116,* 143–165.

Spanos, N. P. (1996). *Multiple identities and false memories: A sociocognitive perspective.* Washington, DC: American Psychological Association.

Spanos, N. P., & Chaves, J. F. (Eds.). (1988). *Hypnosis: The cognitive-behavioral perspective.* Buffalo, NY: Prometheus Books.

Sparks, G. G., & Miller, W. (2001). Investigating the relationship between exposure to television programs that depict paranormal phenomena and beliefs in the paranormal. *Communication Monographs 68,* 98–113.

Spear, L. P. (2000). The adolescent brain and age-related behavioral manifestations. *Neuroscience & Biobehavioral Reviews, 24,* 417–463.

Spearman, C. (1923). *The nature of "intelligence" and the principles of cognition.* London: Macmillan.

Spelke, E. S. (1994). Initial knowledge: Six suggestions. *Cognition, 46,* 29–56.

Sperling, G. (1960). The information available in brief visual presentations. *Psychological Monographs, 74* (Whole No. 11).

Sperling, G. (1984). A unified theory of attention and signal detection. In R. Parasuraman & D. R. Davies (Eds.), *Varieties of attention.* New York: Academic Press.

Sperry, R. W. (1982). Some effects of disconnecting the cerebral hemispheres. *Science, 217,* 1223–1226, 1250.

Spiegler, M. D., & Guevremont, D. C. (2003). *Contemporary behavior therapy.* Belmont, CA: Wadsworth.

Spitzer, R. L., Skodol, A. E., Gibbon, M., & Williams, J. B. W. (1983). *Psychopathology: A casebook.* New York: McGraw-Hill.

Sprafkin, J. N., Liebert, R. M., & Poulos, R. W. (1975). Effects of a prosocial televised example on children's helping. *Journal of Experimental Child Psychology, 20,* 119–126.

Sprecher, S. (2001). A comparison of emotional consequences of and change in equity over time using global and domain specific measures of equity. *Journal of Social and Personal Relationships, 18,* 477–501.

Sprecher, S., & Regan, P. C. (1998). Passionate and companionate love in courting and young married couples. *Sociological Inquiry, 68,* 163–185.

Springer, S. (1997). *Left brain, right brain.* San Francisco: Freeman.

Squier, L. H., & Domhoff, G. W. (1998). The presentation of dreaming and dreams in introductory psychology textbooks: A critical examination with suggestions for textbook authors and course instructors. *Dreaming: Journal of the Association for the Study of Dreams, 8,* 149–168.

Squire, L. R. (1987). *Memory and brain.* Oxford, England: Oxford University Press.

Squire, L. R., Stark, C. E. L., & Clark, R. E. (2004). The medial temporal lobe. *Annual Review of Neuroscience, 27,* 279–306.

Sroufe, L. (2002). From infant attachment to promotion of adolescent autonomy: Prospective, longitudinal data on the role of parents in development. In J. G. Borkowski, S. L. Ramey, & M. Bristol-Power (Eds.), *Parenting and the child's world: Influences on academic, intellectual, and social-emotional development. Monographs in parenting.* Mahwah, NJ: Erlbaum.

Stanley, B. G., Kyrkouli, S. E., Lampert, S., & Leibowitz, S. F. (1986). Neuropeptide Y chronically injected into the hypothalamus: A powerful neurochemical inducer of hyperphagia and obesity. *Peptides, 7,* 1189–1192.

Stanley, S. M., Whitton, S. W., & Markman, H. J. (2004). Maybe I do: Interpersonal commitment and premarital or nonmarital cohabitation. *Journal of Family Issues, 25,* 496–519.

Stark, E. (1989, May). Teen sex: Not for love. *Psychology Today,* 10–11.

Statistics Canada. (2002). English-French Bilingualism. 2001 Census (release date December 10, 2002). Retrieved April 6, 2005, from http://www12.statcan.ca/english/census01/products/analytic/companion/lang/bilingual.cfm

Steadman, H. J., Mulvey, E. P., Monahan, J., Robbins, P. C., Appelbaum, P. S., Grisso, T., Roth, L., & Silver, E. (1998). Violence by people discharged from acute inpatient facilities and by others in the same neighborhoods. *Archives of General Psychiatry, 55,* 393–401.

Stearns, S., & Hoekstra, R. (2005). *Evolution.* New York: Oxford University Press.

Steckler, T., Kalin, N. H., & Reul, J. (2005). *Handbook of stress and the brain: Part 2. Stress: integrative and clinical aspects.* Amsterdam: Elsevier Science and Technology.

Steele, C. M. (1997). A threat in the air: How stereotypes shape intellectual identity and performance. *American Psychologist, 52,* 613–629.

Steele, C. M., & Aronson, J. (1995). Stereotype threat and the intellectual test performance of African Americans. *Journal of Personality and Social Psychology, 69,* 797–811.

Steele, C. M., & Josephs, R. A. (1990). Alcohol myopia: Its prized and dangerous effects. *American Psychologist, 45,* 921–933.

Steele, J., James, J. B., & Barnett, R. C. (2002). Learning in a man's world: Examining the perceptions of undergraduate women in male-dominated academic areas. *Psychology of Women Quarterly, 26,* 46–50.

Stein, D. J., & Hollander, E. (2002). *Textbook of anxiety disorders.* Washington, DC: American Psychiatric Press.

Steinberg, L., Lamborn, S. D., Darling, N., & Mount, N. S. (1994). Over-time changes in adjustment and competence among adolescents from authoritative, authoritarian, indulgent, and neglectful families. *Child Development, 65,* 754–770.

Steinvorth, S., Levine, B., & Corkin, S. (2005). Medial temporal lobe structures are needed to re-experience remote autobiographical memories: Evidence from H. M. and W. R. *Neuropsychologia, 43,* 479–496.

Stephan, W. G. (1990). School desegregation: Short-term and long-term effects. In H. Knopke (Ed.), *Opening doors: An appraisal of race relations in America.* Tuscaloosa: University of Alabama Press.

Stern, M. (2006). *Cognitive reserve: Theory and applications.* San Francisco: Taylor & Francis.

Sternberg, R. J. (1988). Triangulating love. In R. J. Sternberg & M. L. Barnes (Eds.), *The psychology of love.* New Haven, CT: Yale University Press.

Sternberg, R. J. (2004). Culture and intelligence. *American Psychologist, 59,* 325–338.

Sternberg, R. J. (2006a). A duplex theory of love. In R. J. Sternberg & K. Weis (Eds.), *The new psychology of love.* New Haven, CT: Yale University Press.

Sternberg, R. J. (2006b). The nature of creativity. *Creativity Research Journal, 18,* 87–98.

Sternberg, R. J., & Davidson, J. E. (Eds.). (2005). *Conceptions of giftedness.* New York: Cambridge University Press.

Sternberg, R. J., Lautrey, J., & Lubart, T. I. (2003). *Models of intelligence: International perspectives.* Washington, DC: American Psychological Association.

Sternberg, R. J., Nokes, C., Geissler, P., Prince, R., Okatcha, F., Bundy, D. A., & Grigorenko, E. L. (2001). The relationship between academic and practical intelligence: A case study in Kenya. *Intelligence, 29,* 401–418.

Sternberg, R. J., Torff, B., & Grigorenko, E. L. (1998). Teaching triarchically improves school achievement. *Journal of Educational Psychology, 90,* 374–384.

Stetson, B. A., Rahn, J. M., Dubbert, P. M., Wilner, B. I., & Mercury, M. G. (1997). Prospective evaluation of the effects of stress on exercise adherence in community-residing women. *Health Psychology, 16,* 515–520.

Steuber, D., Lueck, M., & Roth, G. (2006). The violent brain. *Scientific American Mind, 17,* 20–27.

Stewart, T. L., Latu, I. M., Kawakami, K., & Myers, A. C. (2010). Consider the situation: Reducing automatic stereotyping through situational attribution training. *Journal of Experimental Social Psychology, 46,* 221–225.

Stiles, W., Barkham, M., Connell, J., & Mellor-Clark, J. (2008). Responsive regulation of treatment duration in routine practice in United Kingdom primary care settings: Replication in a larger sample. *Journal of Consulting and Clinical Psychology, 76,* 298–305.

Stine-Morrow, E. A. L., Parisi, J. M., Morrow, D. G., & Park, D. C. (2008). The effects of an engaged lifestyle on cognitive vitality: A field experiment. *Psychology and Aging, 23,* 778–786.

Stoddard, J., Raine, A., Bihrle, S., & Buchsbaum, M. (1997). Prefrontal dysfunction in murderers lacking psychosocial deficits. In A. Raine, P. A. Brennan, D. P. Farrington, & S. A. Mednick (Eds.), *Biosocial bases of violence* (pp. 301–305). New York: Plenum Press.

Stokes, M., Thompson, R., Cusack, R., & Duncan, J. (2009). Top-down activation of shape-specific population codes in visual cortex during mental imagery. *The Journal of Neuroscience, 29,* 1565–1572.

Stone, A. A., Shiffman, S. S., & DeVries, M. (2000). Rethinking our self-report assessment methodologies: An argument for collecting ecologically valid, momentary measurements. In D. Kahneman, E. Diener, & N. Schwarz (Eds.), *Understanding quality of life: Scientific perspectives on enjoyment and suffering.* New York: Russell Sage.

Stone, J., & Cooper, J. (2003). The effect of self-attribute relevance on how self-esteem moderates attitude change in dissonance processes. *Journal of Experimental Social Psychology, 39,* 508–515.

Stone, K., & Church, S. L. (1968). *Personality theories.* San Francisco: Jossey-Bass.

Stone, M., Laughren, T., Jones, M. L., Levenson, M., et al. (2009). Risk of suicidality in clinical trials of antidepressants in adults: Analysis of proprietary data submitted to US Food and Drug Administration. *British Medical Journal, 339,* b3066.

Storm, L., & Ertel, S. (2001). Does psi exist? Comments on Milton and Wiseman's (1999) meta-analysis of Ganzfield research. *Psychological Bulletin, 127,* 424–433.

Stormshak, E. A., Bierman, K. L., McMahon, R. J., Lengua, L. J., & Conduct Problems Prevention Research Group. (2000). Parenting practices and child disruptive behavior problems in early elementary school. *Journal of Clinical Child Psychology, 29,* 17–29.

Stouffer, S. A., Lumsdaine, A. A., Lumsdaine, M. H., & Williams, R. M., Jr. (1949a). *The American soldier: Combat and its aftermath.* Princeton, NJ: Princeton University Press.

Stouffer, S. A., Suchman, E. A., De Vinney, L. C., Star, S. A., & Williams, R. M., Jr. (1949b). *The American soldier: Adjustments during army life.* Princeton, NJ: Princeton University Press.

Stout, P. A., Villegas, J., & Jennings, N. A. (2004). Images of mental illness in the media: Identifying gaps in the research. *Schizophrenia Bulletin, 30,* 543–551.

Strack, F., Martin, L. L., & Stepper, S. (1988). Inhibiting and facilitating conditions of facial expressions: A non-obtrusive test of the facial feedback hypothesis. *Journal of Personality and Social Psychology, 54,* 768–777.

Straus, M. A. (2008). Commentary: The Special Issue on prevention of violence ignores the primordial violence. *Journal of Interpersonal Violence, 23,* 1314–1320.

Straus, M. A., & Stewart, J. H. (1999). Corporal punishment by American parents: National data on prevalence, chronicity, severity, and duration, in relation to child and family characteristics. *Clinical Child and Family Psychology Review, 2*(2), 55–70.

Strauss, E., Sherman, E. M. S., & Spreen, O. (2006). *A compendium of neuropsychological tests: Administration, norms, and commentary.* New York: Oxford University Press.

Strawbridge, W. J., Shema, S. J., Cohen, R. D., Roberts, R. E., & Kaplan, G. A. (1998). Religion buffers effects of some stressors on depression but exacerbates others. *Journal of Gerontology, 53,* 118–126.

Strayer, D. L., & Drews, F. A. (2004). Profiles in driver distraction: Effects of cell phone conversations on younger and older drivers. *Human Factors, 46,* 640–649.

Strayer, D. L., Drews, F. A., & Johnston, W. A. (2003). Cell-phone induced failures of visual attention during simulated driving. *Journal of Experimental Psychology: Applied, 9,* 23–32.

Streissguth, A. P. (1977). Maternal drinking and the outcome of pregnancy: Implications for child mental health. *American Journal of Orthopsychiatry, 47,* 422–431.

Streissguth, A. P. (2001). Recent advances in fetal alcohol syndrome and alcohol use in pregnancy. In D. P. Agarwal & H. K. Seitz (Eds.), *Alcohol in health and disease.* New York: Marcel Dekker.

Streissguth, A. P., Clarren, S. K., & Jones, K. L. (1985). Natural history of the fetal alcohol syndrome: A 10-year follow-up of eleven patients. *The Lancet, 2*(8446), 85–91.

Striedter, G. F. (2005). *Principles of brain evolution.* Springfield, IL: Sinauer.

Stroebe, M., Stroebe, W., & Schut, H. (2001). Gender differences in adjustment to bereavement: An empirical and theoretical review. *Review of General Psychology, 5,* 62–82.

Strong, R. E., Marchant, B. K., Reimherr, F. W., Williams, E., Soni, P., & Mestas, R. (2009). Narrow-band blue-light treatment of seasonal affective disorder in adults and the influence of additional nonseasonal symptoms. *Depression and Anxiety, 26,* 273–278.

Strunk, D. R., & Adler, A. D. (2009). Cognitive biases in three prediction tasks: A test of the cognitive model of depression. *Behaviour Research and Therapy, 47,* 34–40.

Stryer, L. (1987). The molecules of visual excitation. *Scientific American, 257*(1), 42–50.

Stuhlmacher, A. F., Briggs, A. L., & Cellar, D. F. (2009). Workplace safety and personality. In P. J. Corr & G. Matthews (Eds.), *The Cambridge handbook of personality psychology.* Cambridge, England: Cambridge University Press.

Sturges, J. W., Sims, J. M., Omar, K., et al. (2009). It doesn't feel good: The biggest obstacle to condom use among college students. *The Behavior Therapist, 32,* 36–40.

Suarez, L. M., Bennett, S. M., Goldstein, C. R., & Barlow, D. H. (2009). Understanding anxiety disorders from a "triple vulnerability" framework. In M. M. Antony & M. B. Stein (Eds.), *Oxford handbook of anxiety and related disorders.* New York: Oxford University Press.

Subramanian, K. N. S., Yoon, H., & Toral, J. C. (2002, October 31). *Extremely low birth weight infant.* Available online: http://www.emedicine.com/ped/topic2784.htm

Sue, D. W., & Sue, D. (1990). *Counseling the culturally different: Theory and practice.* New York: Wiley.

Sue, S. (1998). In search of cultural competence in psychotherapy and counseling. *American Psychologist, 53,* 440–448.

Sue, S., & Chu, J. (2003). The mental health of ethnic minority groups: Challenges posed by the U.S. Surgeon General. *Culture, Medicine and Psychiatry, 27,* 447–465.

Sue, S., Fujino, D., Hu, L., Takeuchi, D., & Zane, N. (1991). Community mental health services for ethnic minority groups: A test of the cultural responsiveness hypothesis. *Journal of Consulting and Clinical Psychology, 59,* 533–540.

Sue, S., & Zane, N. (1987). The role of culture and cultural techniques in psychotherapy. *American Psychologist, 42,* 37–45.

Sugita, Y. (2004). Experience in early infancy is indispensable for color perception. *Current Biology, 14,* 1267–1271.

Suh, E., Diener, E., Oishi, S., & Triandis, H. (1998). The shifting basis of life satisfaction judgments across cultures: Emotions versus norms. *Journal of Personality and Social Psychology, 74,* 482–493.

Suinn, R. M., Osborne, D., & Winfree, P. (1962). The self-concept and accuracy of recall of inconsistent self-related information. *Journal of Clinical Psychology, 18,* 473–474.

Suls, J. M., & Wallston, K. A. (2003). *Social psychological foundations of health and illness.* New York: Blackwell.

Sun, M.-K. (Ed.). (2005). *Cognition and mood interactions.* Hauppauge, NY: Nova Science.

Sun, W. L., & Rebec, G. V. (2005). The role of prefrontal cortex D1-like and D2-like receptors in cocaine-seeking behavior in rats. *Psychopharmacology, 177,* 315–323.

Sunnafrank, M., Ramirez, A., Jr., & Metts, S. (Ed.). (2004). At first sight: Persistent relational effects of get-acquainted conversations. *Journal of Social and Personal Relationships, 21,* 361–379.

Super, D. E. (1957). *The psychology of careers.* New York: Harper & Row.

Surette, R. (2002). Self-reported copycat crime among a population of serious and violent juvenile offenders. *Crime & Delinquency, 48,* 46–69.

Sutton, S. K. (2002). Incentive and threat reactivity: Relations with anterior cortical activity. In D. Cervone & W. Mischel (Eds.), *Advances in personality science.* New York: Guilford Press.

Swann, W. B., & Bosson, J. K. (2008). Identity negotiation: A theory of self and social interaction. In O. P. John, R. W. Robins, & L. A. Pervin (Eds.), *Handbook of personality theory and research* (3rd ed.). New York: Guilford Press.

Swann, W. B., Jr., Stein-Seroussi, A., & Giesler, R. B. (1992). Why people self-verify. *Journal of Personality and Social Psychology, 62,* 392–401.

Swartz, C. (1995). Setting the ECT stimulus. *Psychiatric Times, 12*(6). (Reprint addition)

Sweeny, T. D., Grabowecky, M., Suzuki, S., & Paller, K. A. (2009). Long-lasting effects of subliminal affective priming from facial expressions. *Consciousness and Cognition: An International Journal of Neuroscience, 118,* 929–938.

Syka, J., & Merzenich, M. M. (2005). *Plasticity and signal representation in the auditory system.* New York: Springer.

Szameitat, A. J., Shen, S., & Sterr, A. (2007). Effector-dependent activity in the left dorsal premotor cortex in motor imagery. *European Journal of Neuroscience, 26,* 3303–3308.

Szelenberger, W., Niemcewicz, S., & Dabrowska, A. J. (2005). Sleepwalking and night terrors: Psychopathological and psychophysiological correlates. *International Review of Psychiatry, 17,* 263–270.

Szkrybalo, J., & Ruble, D. N. (1999). "God made me a girl": Sex-category constancy judgments and explanations revisited. *Developmental Psychology, 35,* 392–402.

Tajfel, H., & Turner, J. C. (1986). The social identity theory of intergroup behavior. In S. Worchel & W. G. Austin (Eds.), *The psychology of intergroup relations* (2nd ed.). Chicago: Nelson Hall.

Takahashi, Y. (1990). Is multiple personality disorder really rare in Japan? *Dissociation: Progress in the Dissociative Disorders, 3,* 57–59.

Takeuchi, S. A. (2006). On the matching phenomenon in courtship: A probability matching theory of mate selection. *Marriage & Family Review, 40,* 25–51.

Talarico, J. M. (2009). Freshman flashbulbs: Memories of unique and first-time events in starting college. *Memory, 17,* 256–265.

Talarico, J. M., & Rubin, D. C. (2003). Confidence, not consistency, characterizes flashbulb memories. *Psychological Science, 14,* 455–461.

Tal-Or, N., & Papirman, Y. (2007).The fundamental attribution error in attributing fictional figures' characteristics to the actors. *Media Psychology, 9,* 331–345.

Tanaka-Matsumi, J. (1979). Taijin Kyofushu: Diagnostic and cultural issues in Japanese psychiatry. *Culture, Medicine, and Psychiatry, 3,* 231–245.

Tanaka-Matsumi, J., & Draguns, J. G. (1997). Culture and psychopathology. In J. W. Berry, M. H. Segall, & C. Kagitçibasi (Eds.), *Handbook of cross-cultural psychology* (Vol. 3). Boston: Allyn & Bacon.

Tarbox, R. S. F., Ghezzi, P. M., & Wilson, G. (2006). The effects of token reinforcement on attending in a young child with autism. *Behavioral Interventions, 21,* 155–164.

Tatlisumak, T., & Fisher, M. (Eds.) (2006). *Handbook of experimental neurology: Methods and techniques in animal research.* New York: Cambridge University Press.

Taylor, A. K., & Kowalski, P. (2004). Naïve psychological science: The prevalence, strength, and sources of misconceptions. *Psychological Record, 54,* 15–25.

Taylor, R. D., & Wang, M. C. (Eds.). (2000). *Resilience across contexts: Family, work, culture, and community.* Mahwah, NJ: Erlbaum.

Taylor, S. (2010). Posttraumatic stress disorder. In D. McKay, J. S. Abramowitz, & S. Taylor, (Eds.), *Cognitive-behavioral therapy for refractory cases: Turning failure into success.* Washington, DC: American Psychological Association.

Taylor, S. E. (2006). Tend and befriend: Biobehavioral bases of affiliation under stress. *Current Directions in Psychological Science, 15,* 273–277.

Taylor, S. E. (2009). *Health psychology* (7th ed.). New York: McGraw-Hill.

Taylor, S. E., & Brown, J. D. (1988). Illusion and well-being: A social psychological perspective on mental health. *Psychological Bulletin, 103,* 193–210.

Taylor, S. E., Klein, L. C., Lewis, B., Gruenewald, T. L., Gurung, R. A. R., & Updegraff, J. A. (2000). Biobehavioral responses to stress in females: Tend-and-befriend, not fight-or-flight. *Psychological Review, 107*, 411–429.

Taylor, S. E., Lerner, J. S., Sherman, D. K., Sage, R. M., & McDowell, N. K. (2003). Portrait of the self-enhancer: Well adjusted and well liked or maladjusted and friendless? *Journal of Personality and Social Psychology, 84*, 165–176.

Teachman, B. A., Gapinski, K. D., Brownell, K. D., Rawlins, M., & Jeyaram, S. (2003). Demonstrations of implicit anti-fat bias: The impact of providing causal information and evoking empathy. *Health Psychology, 22*, 68–78.

Tedeschi, R. G., & Calhoun, L. G. (1995). *Trauma and transformation: Growing in the aftermath of suffering.* Thousand Oaks, CA: Sage.

Teghtsoonian, R. (1971). On the exponents in Stevens' law and the constant in Ekman's law. *Psychological Review, 78*, 71–80.

Tellegen, A., Lykken, D. T., Bouchard, T. J., Wilcox, K. J., Segal, N. L., & Rich, S. (1988). Personality similarity in twins reared apart and together. *Journal of Personality and Social Psychology, 54*, 1031–1039.

Ten-Berge, M. A., Maaike, A., & De-Raad, B. (2002). The structure of situations from a personality perspective. *European Journal of Personality, 16*, 81–102.

Tenenbaum, H. R., & Leaper, C. (2003). Parent-child conversations about science: The socialization of gender inequities? *Developmental Psychology, 39*, 34–47.

Teplin, L. A., McClelland, G. M., Abram, K. M., & Weiner, D. A. (2005). Crime victimization in adults with severe mental illness: Comparison with the National Crime Victimization Survey. *Archives of General Psychiatry, 62*, 911–921.

Terman, L. M., & Merrill, M. A. (1972). *Stanford-Binet intelligence scale, third edition, form L–M.* Boston: Houghton Mifflin.

Terracciano, A., Costa, P. T., & McCrae, R. R. (2006). Personality plasticity after age 30. *Personality and Social Psychology Bulletin, 32*, 999–1009.

Terrace, H. S. (1979). *Nim.* New York: Knopf.

Tesser, A. (2004). Self-esteem. In M. B. Brewer & M. Hewstone (Eds.), *Emotion and motivation: Perspectives on social psychology.* Malden, MA: Blackwell.

Tesser, A., & Shaffer, D. (1990). Attitudes and attitude change. *Annual Review of Psychology, 41*, 479–523.

Thase, M. E. (2009). Newer medications for complicated depression. *Journal of Clinical Psychiatry, 70*, e33.

The Early Show. (2009, September 25). Healthwatch: Spanking may affect IQ. New York: WCBS. Retrieved December 2, 2009, from http://www.cbsnews.com/video/watch/?id=5339033n&tag=related;photovideo

The Today Show. (2009, September 25). Study: Spanked kids have lower IQs. New York: WNBC. Retrieved December 2, 2009, from http://www.msnbc.msn.com/id/33013187/ns/health-kids_and_parenting/#hybrid_video

Thibaut, J. W., & Kelley, H. H. (1959). *The social psychology of groups.* New York: Wiley.

Thiede, K. W., & Anderson, M. C. M. (2003). Summarizing can improve metacomprehension accuracy. *Contemporary Education Psychology, 28*, 129–160.

Thomas, A., & Chess, S. (1977). *Temperament and development.* New York: Brunner/Mazel.

Thomas, L. (1974). *The lives of a cell.* New York: Viking Press.

Thomas, S. A., & Palmiter, R. D. (1997). Disruption of the dopamine Beta-hydroxylase gene in mice suggests roles for norepinephrine in motor function, learning, and memory. *Behavioral Neuroscience, 111*, 579–589.

Thompson, C. P., Cowan, T. M., & Frieman, J. (1993). *Memory search by a memorist.* Hillsdale, NJ: Erlbaum.

Thompson, R. F. (1985). *The brain: An introduction to neuroscience.* New York: Freeman.

Thompson-Brenner, H., Glass, S., & Westen, D. (2003). A multidimensional meta-analysis of psychotherapy for bulimia nervosa. *Clinical Psychology: Science and Practice, 10*, 269–287.

Thorndike, E. L. (1898). *Animal intelligence: An experimental study of the associative processes in animals.* New York: Macmillan.

Thorndike, E. L. (1911). *Animal intelligence: Experimental studies.* New York: Macmillan.

Thurstone, L. L. (1938). *Primary mental abilities.* Chicago: University of Chicago Press.

Tilker, H. A. (1970). Socially responsible behavior as a function of observer responsibility and victim feedback. *Journal of Personality and Social Psychology, 14*, 95–100.

Tinbergen, N. (1951). *The study of instinct.* Oxford, England: Clarendon Press.

Tinsley-Li, S., & Jenkins, S. (2007). Impact of race and ethnicity on the expression, assessment, and diagnosis of psychopathology. In M. Hersen, S. M. Turner, & D. C. Beidel (Eds.), *Adult psychopathology and diagnosis.* Hoboken, NJ: Wiley.

Tizard, B., & Hodges, J. (1978). The effect of early institutional rearing on the development of eight-year-old children. *Journal of Child Psychology and Psychiatry, 19*, 99–118.

Tobin, J. J., & Friedman, J. (1983). Spirits, shamans, and nightmare death: Survivor stress in a Hmong refugee. *American Journal of Orthopsychiatry, 53*, 439–448.

Tobin, S. J., & Raymundo, M. M. (2009). Persuasion by causal arguments: The motivating role of perceived causal expertise. *Social Cognition, 27*, 105–127.

Todd, A. R., Seok, D., Kerr, N. L., & Messe, L. A. (2006). Social compensation: Fact or social-comparison artifact? *Group Processes & Intergroup Relations, 9*, 431–442.

Todorov, A., & Bargh, J. A. (2002). Automatic sources of aggression. *Aggression and Violent Behavior, 7*, 53–68.

Tollefson, G. D. (1993). Major depression. In D. L. Dunner (Ed.), *Current psychiatric therapy.* Philadelphia: Saunders.

Tollison, C. D., Satterswaithe, J. R., & Tollison, J. W. (2002). *Practical pain management.* New York: Williams & Wilkins.

Tolman, E. C. (1948). Cognitive maps in rats and men. *Psychological Review, 55*, 189–208.

Tolman, E. C., & Honzik, C. H. (1930). Introduction and removal of reward and maze performance in rats. *University of California Publications in Psychology, 4*, 257–275.

Toma, C., & Butera, F. (2009). Hidden profiles and concealed information: Strategic information sharing and use in group decision making. *Personality and Social Psychology Bulletin, 35*, 793–806.

Tomarken, A. J., & Keener, A. D. (1998). Frontal brain asymmetry and depression: A self-regulatory perspective. Special Issue: Neuropsychological perspectives on affective and anxiety disorders. *Cognition & Emotion, 12*(3), 387–420.

Tomkins, S. S. (1991). *Affect, imagery, and consciousness.* New York: Springer-Verlag.

Tooby, J., & Cosmides, L. (1992). The psychological foundations of culture. In J. H. Barkow, L. Cosmides, & J. Tooby (Eds.), *The adapted mind.* New York: Oxford University Press.

Tooby, J., & Cosmides, L. (2005). Conceptual foundations of evolutionary psychology. In D. M. Buss (Ed.), *The handbook of evolutionary psychology.* Hoboken, NJ: Wiley.

Torgerson, S. (2000). Genetics of patients with borderline personality disorder. *Psychiatric Clinics of North America, 23*, 1–9.

Torgerson, S., Kringlen, E., & Cramer, V. (2001). The prevalence of personality disorders in a community sample. *Archives of General Psychiatry, 58*, 590–596.

Törnros, J., & Bolling, A. (2006). Mobile phone use—effects of conversation on mental workload and driving speed in rural and urban environments. *Transportation Research Part F: Traffic Psychology and Behaviour, 9*, 298–306.

Torres, A. N., Boccaccini, M. T., & Miller, H. A. (2006). Perceptions of the validity and utility of criminal profiling among forensic psychologists and psychiatrists. *Professional Psychology: Research and Practice, 37*, 51–58.

Torrey, E. F. (1997). *Out of the shadows: Confronting America's mental illness crisis.* New York: Wiley.

Torrey, E. F., & Zdanowicz, M. (2001). Outpatient commitment: What, why, and for whom. *Psychiatric Services, 52*, 337–341.

Toy, E. C. (2007). *Case files: Neurology.* New York: McGraw-Hill.

Trae, H. C., & Deighton, R. M. (2000). Emotional inhibition. In G. Fink (Ed.), *Encyclopedia of stress.* San Diego, CA: Academic Press.

Travers, K. R., & Lyvers, M. (2005). Mood and impulsivity of recreational Ecstasy users in the week following a "rave." *Addiction Research & Theory, 13*, 43–52.

Treasure, J. (2005). *Essential handbook of eating disorders.* New York: Wiley.

Tremblay, L. K., Naranjo, C. A., Cardenas, L., Hermann, N., & Busto, U. E. (2002). Probing brain reward system function in major depressive disorder: Altered response to dextroamphetamine. *Archives of General Psychiatry, 59*, 409–417.

Tremblay, M. A., Blaanchard, C. M., Taylor, S., & Pelletier, L. G. (2009). Work Extrinsic and Intrinsic Motivation Scale: Its value for organizational psychology research. *Canadian Journal of Behavioural Science, 41*, 213–226.

Triandis, H. C. (2001). Individualism-collectivism and personality. *Journal of Personality, 69*, 907–924.

Triandis, H. C., & Suh, E. M. (2002). Cultural influences on personality. *Annual Review of Psychology, 53*, 133–160.

Trimble, M. (2003). *Somatoform disorders.* New York: Cambridge University Press.

Triplett, N. (1898). The dynamogenic factors in pacemaking and competition. *American Journal of Psychology, 9,* 507–533.

Trivers, R. (1971). The evolution of reciprocal altruism. *Quarterly Review of Biology, 46,* 35–57.

Trivers, R. L. (1972). Parental investment and sexual selection. In B. Campbell (Ed.), *Sexual selection and the descent of man.* Chicago: Aldine-Atherton.

Troyer, L., & Youngreen, R. (2009). Conflict and creativity in groups. *Journal of Social Issues, 65,* 409–427.

Trull, T. J., & Geary, D. C. (1997). Comparison of the Big-Five Factor structure across samples of Chinese and American adults. *Journal of Personality Assessment, 69,* 324–341.

Truscott, S. D., & Frank, A. J. (2001). Does the Flynn effect affect IQ scores of students classified as LD? *Journal of School Psychology, 39,* 319–334.

Trzesniewski, K. H., Donnellan, M. B., & Robins, R. W. (2003). Stability of self-esteem across the life span. *Journal of Personality and Social Psychology, 84,* 205–220.

Tseng, W. S., Asai, M., Liu, J., Pismai, W., et al. (1990). Multi-cultural study of minor psychiatric disorders in Asia: Symptom manifestations. *International Journal of Social Psychiatry, 36,* 252–264.

Tucker, V. A. (2000). The deep fovea, sideways vision and spiral flight paths in raptors. *Journal of Experimental Biology, 203,* 3745–3754.

Tudor, K., & Worrall, M. (2006). *Person-centered therapy: A clinical philosophy.* New York: Routledge.

Tuiten, A., Van Honk, J., Koppeschaar, H., Bernaards, C., Thijssen, J., & Verbaten, R. (2000). Time course of effects of testosterone administration on sexual arousal in women. *Archives of General Psychiatry, 57,* 149–153.

Tulsky, D. S., Saklofske, D. H., Chelune, G. J., Heaton, R. K., Ivnik, R. J., Bornstein, R., Prifitera, A., & Ledbetter, M. F. (Eds.). (2003). *Clinical interpretation of the WAIS-III and WMS-III.* San Diego, CA: Academic Press.

Tulving, E., & Thomson, D. M. (1973). Encoding specificity and retrieval processes in episodic memory. *Psychological Review, 80,* 359–380.

Tung, M. C., Huang, J. Y., Keh, H. C., & Wai, S. S. (2009). Distance learning in advanced military education: Analysis of joint operations course in the Taiwan military. *Computers & Education, 53,* 653–666.

Tupala, E., & Tiihonen, J. (2004). Dopamine and alcoholism: Neurobiological basis of ethanol abuse. *Progress in Neuro-Psychopharmacology & Biological Psychiatry, 28,* 1221–1247.

Turk, D. C. (2001). Physiological and psychological bases of pain. In A. Baum & T. A. Revenson (Eds.), *Handbook of health psychology.* Mahwah, NJ: Erlbaum.

Turk, D. C., & Melzack, R. (2001). *Handbook of pain assessment* (2nd ed.). New York: Guilford Press.

Turk, D. C., & Winter, F. (2006). *The pain survival guide: How to reclaim your life.* Washington, DC: American Psychological Association.

Turkheimer, E., Haley, A., Waldron, N., D'Onofrio, B., & Gottesman, I. I. (2003). Socioeconomic status modifies heritability of IQ in young children. *Psychological Science, 14,* 623–628.

Turnbull, C. M. (1961). Some observations concerning the experiences and behavior of the BaMbuti Pygmies. *American Journal of Psychology, 74,* 304–308.

Turner, J. A., Deyo, R. A., Loeser, J. D., et al. (1994). The importance of placebo effects in pain treatment and research. *Journal of the American Medical Association, 271,* 1609–1614.

Turner, M. E., Pratkanis, A. R., & Struckman, C. K. (2007). Groupthink as social identity maintenance. In A. R. Pratkanis (Ed.), *The science of social influence: Advances and future progress.* New York: Psychology.

Tusing, K. J., & Dillard, J. P. (2000). The psychological reality of the door-in-the-face: It's helping, not bargaining. *Journal of Language and Social Psychology, 19,* 5–25.

Tversky, A., & Kahneman, D. (1982). Judgments of and by representativeness. In D. Kahneman, P. Slovic, & A. Tversky (Eds.), *Heuristics and biases.* Cambridge University Press.

Tversky, B., & Tuchin, M. (1989). A reconciliation of the evidence on eyewitness testimony: Comments on McCloskey and Zaragoza. *Journal of Experimental Psychology: General, 118,* 86–91.

Tyrka, A. R., Waldron, I., Graber, J. A., & Brooks-Gunn, J. (2002). Prospective predictors of the onset of anorexic and bulimic syndromes. *International Journal of Eating Disorders, 32,* 282–290.

Tyson, J. E., Parikh, N. A., Langer, J., Green, C., & Higgins, R. D. (2008). Intensive care for extreme prematurity—Moving beyond gestational age. *New England Journal of Medicine, 358,* 1672–1681.

Tzeng, O. J., Hung, W., Cohen, F. J., & Wang, P. (1979). Visual lateralization effect in reading Chinese characters. *Nature, 282,* 499–501.

Tzeng, S. F. (1997). Neural progenitors isolated from newborn rat spinal cords differentiate into neurons and astroglia. *Journal of Biomedical Science, 9*(1), 10–16.

Ulmer, S. (2009). *fMRI: Basics and clinical applications.* New York: Springer.

U.S. Census Bureau. (2002). *Demographic Trends in the 20th Century: Census 2000 Special Reports, CENSR-4, November.* Available online: http://www.census.gov/population/www/cen2000/briefs.html

U.S. Census Bureau. (2003). *Married-couple and unmarried-partner households: 2000. Census 2000 Special Reports, CENSR-5.* Available online: http://www.census.gov/population/www/cen2000/briefs.html

U.S. Census Bureau. (2005a). *Children's characteristics. 2005 American Community Survey.* Retrieved on December 12, 2007, from: http://factfinder.census.gov/servlet/STTable?_bm=y&-geo_id=01000US&-qr_name=ACS_2005_EST_G00_S0901&-ds_name=ACS_2005_EST_G00_&-redoLog=false

U.S. Census Bureau. (2005b). *U.S. population projections for selected age groups by state: 2005–2030.* Retrieved February 25, 2007, from http://www.aoa.gov/prof/Statistics/future_growth/State-5-yr-age-projections-2005-2030.pdf

U.S. Census Bureau. (2005c). *American Community Survey*: Table C16001. Language spoken at home by ability to speak English for the population 5 years and over. Retrieved February 18, 2007, from http://factfinder.census.gov/servlet/DTTable?_bm=y&-geo_id=0100...lang=en&-mt_name=ACS_2005_EST_G2000_C16001&-format=&-CONTEXT=dt

U.S. Department of Health and Human Services. (2002). *National Comorbidity Survey, 1990–92.* Available online: http://www.icpsr.umich.edu/SAMHDA/STUDIES/ncs.html (Substance Abuse and Mental Health Data Archive [SAMHDA])

U.S. Office of Behavior Technology. (1990). *Provision of professional services to the physically handicapped.* Washington, DC: Author.

U.S. Public Health Service. (1979). *Healthy people: The Surgeon General's report on health promotion and disease prevention.* Washington, DC: U.S. Government Printing Office.

Ungerleider, L. G., & Mishkin, M. (1982). Two cortical visual systems. In D. J. Ingle, M. A. Goodale, & R. J. W. Mansfield (Eds.), *Analysis of visual behavior.* Cambridge, MA: MIT Press.

United Nations. (2002). *Report on the global reach of AIDS.* New York: Author.

Unsworth, G., Devilly, G. J., & Ward, T. (2007). The effect of playing violent video games on adolescents: Should parents be quaking in their boots? *Psychology, Crime & Law, 13,* 383–394.

Unverzagt, F. W., Gao, S., Baiyewu, O., Ogunniyi, A. O., Gureje, O., Perkins, A., et al. (2001). Prevalence of cognitive impairment: Data from the Indianapolis Study of Health and Aging. *Neurology, 57,* 1655–1662.

Vaccarino, F. M., & Smith, K. M. (2009). Increased brain size in autism—What it will take to solve a mystery. *Biological Psychiatry, 66,* 313–315.

Valberg, A. (2006). *Light vision color.* New York: Wiley.

Valent, P. (1998). Effects of the Holocaust on Jewish child survivors: Traumas and latent disturbances 50 years later. *Psyche: Zeitschrift fuer Psychoanalyse und ihre Anwendungen, 52,* 751–771.

Valent, P. (2000). Stress effects of the Holocaust. In G. Fink (Ed.), *Encyclopedia of stress.* San Diego, CA: Academic Press.

Valin, R. D. V., Jr. (2009). Some remarks on universal grammar. In J. Guo, E. Lieven, N. Budwig, S. Ervin-Tripp, K. Nakamura, & S. Özçalişkan (Eds.), *Crosslinguistic approaches to the psychology of language: Research in the tradition of Dan Issac Slobin.* New York: Psychology.

Valles, R., Rocha, A., & Nation, J. R. (2006). The effects of acquisition training schedule on extinction and reinstatement of cocaine self-administration in male rats. *Experimental and Clinical Psychopharmacology, 14,* 245–253.

Vallone, R. P., Griffin, D., Lin, S., & Ross, L. (1990). Overconfident prediction of future actions and outcomes by self and others. *Journal of Personality and Social Psychology, 58,* 582–592.

Valsiner, J., & Lawrence, J. A. (1997). Human development in culture across the life span. In J. W. Berry, P. R. Dasen, & T. S. Saraswathi (Eds.), *Handbook of cross-cultural psychology* (Vol. 2). Boston: Allyn & Bacon.

Valverde, C. (2010). *Genetic screening of newborns: An ethical inquiry.* New York: Nova Science Publishers.

van Beest, I., & Williams, K. D. (2006). When inclusion costs and ostracism pays, ostracism still hurts. *Journal of Personality and Social Psychology, 91,* 918–928.

Vandell, D. L., Burchinal, M. R., Belsky, J., Owen, M. T., Friedman, S. L., Clarke-Stewart, A., McCartney, K., & Weinraub, M. (2005). *Early child care and children's development in the primary grades: Follow-up results from the NICHD Study of Early Child Care.* Paper presented at the biennial meeting of the Society for Research in Child Development, Atlanta, Georgia.

Van der Borght, K., Meerlo, P., Luiten, P., Eggen, B., & Van der Zee, E. A. (2005). Effects of active shock avoidance learning on hippocampal neurogenesis and plasma levels of corticosterone. *Behavioural Brain Research, 157,* 23–30.

van der Hart, O., & Nijenhuis, E. (2009). Dissociative disorders. In P. H. Blaney & T. Millon (Eds.), *Oxford textbook of psychopathology* (2nd ed). New York: Oxford University Press.

van de Rijt, A., & Macy, M. W. (2006). Power and dependence in intimate exchange. *Social Forces, 84,* 1455–1470.

Van Goozen, S., Fairchild, G., Snoek, H., & Harold, G. (2007). The evidence for a neurobiological model of childhood antisocial behavior. *Psychological Bulletin, 133,* 149–182.

van Ijzendoorn, M. (1995). Adult attachment representations, parental responsiveness, and infant attachment: A meta-analysis of the Adult Attachment Interview. *Psychological Bulletin, 117,* 387–403.

van Jaarsveld, C. H. M., Fidler, J. A., Simon, A. E., & Wardle, J. Persistent impact of pubertal timing on trends in smoking, food choice, activity, and stress in adolescence. *Psychosomatic Medicine, 69,* 798–806.

van Laar, C., & Levin, S. (2006). The experience of stigma: Individual, interpersonal, and situational influences. In S. Levin & C. van Laar (Eds.), *Stigma and group inequality: Social psychological perspectives.* Mahwah, NJ: Erlbaum.

Vanman, E. J., Saltz, J. L., Nathan, L. R., & Warren, J. A. (2004). Racial discrimination by low-prejudiced Whites: Facial movements as implicit measures of attitudes related to behavior. *Psychological Science, 15,* 711–714.

van Praag, H. M. (2004). *Stress, vulnerability and depression.* New York: Cambridge University Press.

Van Yperen, N. W. (2006). A novel approach to assessing achievement goals in the context of the 2 x 2 framework: Identifying distinct profiles of individuals with different dominant achievement goals. *Personality and Social Psychology Bulletin, 32,* 1432–1445.

Van Zomeren, A. H., & Brouwer, W. H. (1994). *Clinical neuropsychology of attention.* New York: Oxford University Press.

Vargha-Khadem, F., Gadian, D. G., Watkins, K. E., Connelly, A., Van Paesschen, W., & Mishkin, M. (1997). Differential effects of early hippocampal pathology on episodic and semantic memory. *Science, 277,* 376–380.

Vasilaki, E. I., Hosier, S. G., & Cox, W. M. (2006). The efficacy of motivational interviewing as a brief intervention for excessive drinking: A meta-analytic review. *Alcohol and Alcoholism, 41,* 328–335.

Vaughan, P. W., Rogers, E. M., Singhal, A., & Swalehe, R. M. (2000). Entertainment-education and HIV/AIDS prevention: A field experiment in Tanzania. *Journal of Health Communication, 5,* 81–100.

Velotis, C. M. (2006). *New developments in anxiety disorders research.* Hauppauge, NY: Nova Biomedical Books.

Verleger, R., Schuknecht, S. V., Jaskowski, P., & Wagner, U. (2008). Changes in processing of masked stimuli across early-and-late-night sleep: A study on behavior and brain potentials. *Brain and Cognition, 68,* 180–192.

Vernon, D. (2009). *Human potential: Exploring techniques used to enhance human performance.* New York: Routledge.

Verona, E., & Carbonell, J. L. (2000). Female violence and personality: Evidence for a pattern of overcontrolled hostility among one-time violent female offenders. *Criminal Justice and Behavior, 27,* 176–195.

Verplanken, B., & Holland, R. W. (2002). Motivated decision making: Effects of activation and self centrality of values on choices and behavior. *Journal of Personality and Social Psychology, 82,* 434–447.

Vertes, R. P., & Eastman, K. E. (2003). The case against memory consolidation in REM sleep. In E. F. Pace-Schott, M. Solms, M. Blagrove, & S. Harnad (Eds.), *Sleep and dreaming: Scientific advances and reconsiderations.* New York: Cambridge University Press.

Vetter, H. J. (1969). *Language behavior and psychopathology.* Chicago: Rand McNally.

Villar, I., Izuel, M., Carrizo, S., Vicente, E., & Marin, J. M. (2009). Medication adherence and persistence in severe obstructive sleep apnea. *Journal of Sleep and Sleep Disorders Research, 32,* 623–628.

Villarreal, D. M., Do, V., Haddad, E., & Derrick, B. E. (2002). NMDA receptor antagonists sustain LTP and spatial memory: Active processes mediate LTP decay. *Nature Neuroscience, 5,* 48–52.

Vincent, N., Cox, B., & Clara, I. (2009). Are personality dimensions associated with sleep length in a large nationally representative sample? *Comprehensive Psychiatry, 50,* 158–163.

Vinden, P. G. (2002). Understanding minds and evidence for belief: A study of Mofu children in Cameroon. *International Journal of Behavioral Development, 26,* 445–452.

Virnig, B., Huang, Z., Lurie, N., Musgrave, D., McBean, M., & Dowd, B. (2004). Does Medicare managed care provide equal treatment for mental illness across races? *Archives of General Psychiatry, 61,* 201–205.

Vitaliano, P. P., Young, H. M., & Zhang, J. (2004). Is caregiving a risk factor for illness? *Current Directions in Psychological Science, 13,* 13–16.

Vittengl, J. R., Clark, L. A., & Jarrett, R. B. (2009). Continuation-phase cognitive therapy's effects on remission and recovery from depression. *Journal of Consulting and Clinical Psychology, 77,* 367–371.

Vogels, W. W. A., Dekker, M. R., Brouwer, W. H., & deJong, R. (2002). Age-related changes in event-related prospective memory performance: A comparison of four prospective memory tasks. *Brain and Cognition, 49,* 341–362.

Vouloumanos, A., & Werker, J. F. (2007). Listening to language at birth: Evidence for a bias for speech in neonates. *Developmental Science, 10,* 159–164.

Vral, A., Thierens, H., Baeyens, A., & De Ridder, L. (2002). The micronucleus and g(2)-phase assays for human blood lymphocytes as biomarkers of individual sensitivity to ionizing radiation: Limitations imposed by intraindividual variability. *Radiation Research, 157,* 472–477.

Vrij, A. (2008). *Detecting lies and deceit: Pitfalls and opportunities.* New York: Wiley.

Vurpillot, E. (1968). The development of scanning strategies and their relation to visual differentiations. *Journal of Experimental Child Psychology, 6,* 632–650.

Vygotsky, L. S. (1978). *Mind in society: The development of higher psychological processes.* Cambridge, MA: Harvard University Press. (Original work published 1935)

Wadden, T. A., Brownell, K. D., & Foster, G. D. (2002). Obesity: Responding to the global epidemic. *Journal of Consulting and Clinical Psychology, 70,* 510–525.

Wadden, T. A., Vogt, R. A., Andersen, R. E., et al. (1997). Exercise in the treatment of obesity: Effects of four interventions on body composition, resting energy expenditure, appetite, and mood. *Journal of Consulting and Clinical Psychology, 654,* 269–277.

Wade, K. A., Sharman, S. J., Garry, M., Memon, A., Mazzoni, G., et al. (2007). False claims about false memory research. *Consciousness and Cognition: An International Journal, 16,* 18–28.

Wade, P., & Bernstein, B. (1991). Culture sensitivity training and counselor's race: Effects on Black female clients' perceptions and attrition. *Journal of Counseling Psychology, 38,* 9–15.

Wadlington, E., Elliot, C., & Kirylo, J. (2008). The dyslexia simulation: Impact and implications. *Literacy Research and Instruction, 47,* 264–272.

Wadlington, E., & Wadlington, P. (2005). What do educators believe about dyslexia? *Reading Improvement, 42,* 16–33.

Wagner, K. D., Ambrosini, P., Rynn, M., Wohlberg, C., Yang, R. Y., Greenbaum, M. S., et al. (2003). Efficacy of sertraline in the treatment of children and adolescents with major depressive disorder: Two randomized controlled trials. *Journal of the American Medical Association, 290*(8), 1033–1041.

Wagstaff, G. F. (2008). Hypnosis and the law: Examining the stereotypes. *Criminal Justice and Behavior, 35,* 1277–1294.

Wagstaff, G. F. (2009). Is there a future for investigative hypnosis? *Journal of Investigative Psychology and Offender Profiling, 6,* 43–57.

Wagstaff, G. F., Cole, J., Wheatcroft, J., Anderton, A., & Madden, H. (2008). Reducing and reversing pseudomemories with hypnosis. *Contemporary Hypnosis, 25,* 178–191.

Wahlstrom, D., Collins, P., White, T., & Luciana, M. (2010). Developmental changes in dopamine neurotransmission in adolescence: Behavioral implications and issues in assessment. *Brain and Cognition, 72,* 146–159.

Wakefield, J. C. (2006). Personality disorder as harmful dysfunction: DSM's cultural deviance criterion reconsidered. *Journal of Personality Disorders, 20,* 157–169.

Wakefield, M., Reid, Y., Roberts, L., Mullins, R., & Gillies, R. (1998). Smoking and smoking cessation among men whose partners are pregnant: A qualitative study. *Social Science Medicine, 47,* 657–664.

Walen, S. R., & Roth, D. (1987). A cognitive approach. In J. H. Geer & W. T. O'Donohue (Eds.), *Theories of human sexuality.* New York: Plenum Press.

Walker, M. P. (2008). Cognitive consequences of sleep and sleep loss. *Sleep Medicine, 9*(Suppl. 1), S29–S34.

Walker, P. L. (2001). A bioarchaeological perspective on the history of violence. *Annual Review of Anthropology, 30,* 573–596.

Walker, W. R., Skowronski, J., Gibbons, J., Vogl, R., & Thompson, C. (2003). On the emotions that accompany autobiographical memories: Dysphoria disrupts the fading affect bias. *Cognition & Emotion, 17,* 703–723.

Walker, W. R., Skowronski, J. J., & Thompson, C. P. (2003). Life is pleasant—and memory helps to keep it that way! *Review of General Psychology, 7,* 203–210.

Walker, W. R., Vogl, R. J., & Thompson, C. P. (1997). Autobiographical memory: Unpleasantness fades faster than pleasantness over time. *Applied Cognitive Psychology, 11,* 399–413.

Wallbott, H., & Scherer, K. (1988). How universal and specific is emotional experience? Evidence from 27 countries and five continents. In K. Scherer (Ed.), *Facets of emotion: Recent research.* Hillsdale, NJ: Erlbaum.

Wallenius, M., & Punamäki, R. L. (2008). Digital game violence and direct aggression in adolescence: A longitudinal study of the roles of sex, age, and parent-child communication. *Journal of Applied Developmental Psychology, 29,* 286–294.

Wallentin, M. (2009). Putative sex differences in verbal abilities and language cortex: A critical review. *Brain and Language, 108,* 175–183.

Walsh, B. T., & Devlin, M. J. (1998). Eating disorders: Progress and problems. *Science, 280,* 1387–1390.

Walster, E., Aronson, V., Abrahams, D., & Rottman, L. (1966). The importance of physical attractiveness in dating behavior. *Journal of Personality and Social Psychology, 4,* 508–516.

Wang, C. A., Inhoff, A. W., & Radach, R. (2009). Is attention confined to one word at a time? The spatial distribution of parafoveal preview benefits during reading. *Attention, Perception, & Psychophysics, 71,* 1487–1494.

Wang, P. S., Demler, O., & Kessler, R. C. (2002). Adequacy of treatment for serious mental illness in the United States. *American Journal of Public Health, 92,* 92–98.

Wang, Q. (2001). Culture effects on adults' earliest childhood recollection and self-description: Implications for the relation between memory and the self. *Journal of Personality and Social Psychology, 81,* 220–233.

Wang, Q. (2006). Earliest recollections of self and others in European American and Taiwanese young adults. *Psychological Science, 17,* 708–714.

Wang, S., Baillargeon, R., & Paterson, S. (2005). Detecting continuity violations in infancy: A new account and new evidence from covering and tube events. *Cognition, 95,* 129–173.

Wang, S. H., & Morris, R. G. M. (2010). Hippocampal-neocortical interactions in memory formation, consolidation, and reconsolidation. *Annual Review of Psychology, 61,* 49–79.

Wang, T., Brownstein, R., & Katzev, R. (1989). Promoting charitable behaviour with compliance techniques. *Applied Psychology: An International Review, 38,* 165–183.

Ward, J. (2008). *The frog who croaked blue: Synesthesia and the mixing of the senses.* London: Routledge.

Ward, S. L., & Overton, W. F. (1990). Semantic familiarity, relevance, and the development of deductive reasoning. *Developmental Psychology, 26,* 488–493.

Warga, C. (1987). Pain's gatekeeper. *Psychology Today, 21,* 50–59.

Wasserman, D., & Wachbroit, R. (2001). *Genetics and criminal behavior.* New York: Cambridge University Press.

Watanabe, H., Sato, C., Kuramochi, T., Nishino, H., & Mizunami, M. (2008). Salivary conditioning with antennal gustatory unconditioned stimulus in an insect. *Neurobiology of Learning and Memory, 90,* 245–254.

Waterhouse, J., & Reilly, T. (2009). Managing jet lag. *Sleep Medicine Reviews, 13,* 247–248.

Waters, A., Hill, A., & Waller, G. (2001). Bulimics' responses to food cravings: Is binge-eating a product of hunger or emotional state? *Behaviour Research and Therapy, 39,* 877–886.

Waters, A. M., Henry, J., & Neumann, D. L. (2009). Aversive Pavlovian conditioning in childhood anxiety disorders: Impaired response inhibition and resistance to extinction. *Journal of Abnormal Psychology, 118,* 311–321.

Watkins, K., Al-Samarrai, S., Bella, N., Benavot, A., Liebnitz., P. M. B, Buonomo, M., et al. (2008). *EFA Global Monitoring Report 2009.* Paris: UNESCO.

Watkins, L. R., & Maier, S. F. (2003). When good pain turns bad. *Current Directions in Psychological Science, 12,* 232–236.

Watson, D. L., & Tharp, R. G. (1997). *Self-directed behavior: Self-modification for personal adjustment* (7th ed.). Belmont, CA: Brooks/Cole.

Watson, J. B. (1925). *Behaviorism.* New York: People's Institute.

Watson, J. B., & Rayner, R. (1920). Conditioned emotional reactions. *Journal of Experimental Psychology, 3,* 1–14.

Watson, J. C., & Greenberg, L. S. (1998). The therapeutic alliance in short-term humanistic and experiential therapies. In J. D. Safran & C. J. Muran (Eds.), *The therapeutic alliance in brief psychotherapy.* Washington, DC: American Psychological Association.

Watt, C. A., & Irwin, H. J. (2010). Processes underlying the phenomena of mysterious minds: Laboratory evidence for ESP. In S. Krippner & H. L. Friedman (Eds.), *Mysterious minds: The neurobiology of psychics, mediums, and other extraordinary people.* Santa Barbara, CA: Praeger/ABC-CLIO.

Wauterickx, N., Gouwy, A., & Bracke, P. (2006). Parental divorce and depression: Long-term effects on adult children. *Journal of Divorce & Remarriage, 45,* 43–68.

Webb, T. M., Beech, J. R., Mayall, K. M., & Andrews, A. S. (2006). It's what's on the outside that matters: An advantage for external features in children's word recognition. *Journal of Experimental Child Psychology, 94,* 163–181.

Webb, W. B. (1974). Sleep as an adaptive response. *Perceptual and Motor Skills, 38,* 1023–1027.

Webb, W. B. (1994). Prediction of sleep onset. In R. D. Ogilvie & J. R. Harsh (Eds.), *Sleep onset: Normal and abnormal processes.* Washington, DC: American Psychological Association.

Webster, D. M., Richter, L., & Kruglanski, A. W. (1996). On leaping to conclusions when feeling tired: Mental fatigue effects on impressional primacy. *Journal of Experimental Social Psychology, 32,* 181–195.

Wechsler, H., Davenport, A., Dowdall, G., Hoeykins, B., & Castillo, S. (1994). Health and behavioral consequences of binge drinking in college: A national survey of students at 140 campuses. *Journal of the American Medical Association, 272,* 1672–1677.

Wechsler, H., Lee, J. E., Kuo, M., & Lee, H. (2000). College binge drinking in the 1990s: A continuing problem. *Journal of American College Health, 48,* 199–210.

Wechsler, H., Lee, J. E., Kuo, M., Seibring, M., Nelson, T. F., & Lee, H. (2002). Trends in college binge drinking during a period of increased prevention efforts: Findings from 4 Harvard School of Public Health College Alcohol Study surveys. *Journal of American College Health, 50,* 203–217.

Weiland, J. D., & Humayun, M. S. (2008). Visual prosthesis. *Proceedings of the IEEE, 96,* 1076–1084.

Weinberger, D. R., & McClure, R. K. (2002). Neurotoxicity, neuroplasticity, and magnetic resonance imaging morphometry: What is happening in the schizophrenic brain? *Archives of General Psychiatry, 59,* 553–559.

Weiner, B. (1992). *Human motivation: Metaphors, theories, and research.* Newbury Park, CA: Sage.

Weinert, F. E., & Hany, E. A. (2003). The stability of individual differences in intellectual development. In R. J. Sternberg, J. Lautrey, & T. I. Lubart (Eds.), *Models of intelligence: International perspectives.* Washington, DC: American Psychological Association.

Weingardt, K. R., & Marlatt, G. A. (1998). Harm reduction and public policy. In G. A. Marlatt (Ed.), *Harm reduction: Pragmatic strategies for managing high-risk behaviors.* New York: Guilford Press.

Weingarten, H. P. (1983). Conditioned cues elicit feeding in sated rats: A role for learning in meal initiation. *Science, 220,* 431–433.

Weissman, M. M., Geshon, E. S., Kidd, K. K., Prusoff, B. A., Leckman, J. F., Dibble, E., Hamovit, J., Thompson, W. D., Pauls, D. L., & Guroff, J. J. (1984). Psychiatric disorders in the relatives of probands with affective disorders. *Archives of General Psychiatry, 41,* 13–21.

Weissman, M. M., & Markowitz, J. C. (1994). Interpersonal psychotherapy: Current status. *Archives of General Psychiatry, 51,* 599–606.

Weissman, M. M., Markowitz, J. C., & Klerman, G. L. (2007). *Clinician's quick guide to interpersonal psychotherapy.* New York: Oxford University Press.

Weitlauf, J., Smith, R. E., & Cervone, D. (2000). Generalization effects of coping skills training: Influences of self-defense training on women's efficacy beliefs, assertiveness, and aggression. *Journal of Applied Psychology, 85,* 625–633.

Weitzenhoffer, A. M., & Hilgard, E. R. (1962). *Stanford Hypnotic Susceptibility Scale: Form C.* Palo Alto, CA: Consulting Psychologists.

Weller, A., & Weller, L. (1997). Menstrual synchrony under optimal conditions: Bedouin families. *Journal of Comparative Psychology, 111,* 143–151.

Weller, L., Weller, A., Koresh, H. K., & Shoshan, B. R. (1999). Menstrual synchrony in a sample of working women. *Psychoneuroendocrinology, 24,* 449–459.

Wender, P. H., Kety, S. S., Rosenthal, D., Schulsinger, F., Ortmann, J., & Lunde, I. (1986). Psychiatric disorders in the biological and adoptive families of adopted individuals with affective disorders. *Archives of General Psychiatry, 43,* 923–929.

Wenzlaff, R. M., Wegner, D. M., & Roper, D. W. (1988). Depression and mental control: The resurgence of unwanted negative thoughts. *Journal of Personality and Social Psychology, 55,* 882–892.

Werner, E. E., & Smith, R. S. (1982). *Vulnerable and invincible: A longitudinal study of resilient children.* New York: McGraw-Hill.

Wernig, M., & Brustle, O. (2002). Fifty ways to make a neuron: Shifts in stem cell hierarchy and their implications for neuropathology and CNS repair. *Journal of Neuropathology and Experimental Neurology, 61*(2), 101–110.

Werth, J. L., Jr., Blevins, D., Toussaint, K. L., & Durham, M. R. (2002). The influence of cultural diversity on end of life care and decisions. *American Behavioral Scientist, 46,* 204–219.

Wertheimer, M. (1912). Experimentelle studien über das Gesehen von Bewegung. *Zeitschrift fuer Psychologie, 61,* 161–265.

West, S. A., Pen, I., & Griffin, A. S. (2002). Cooperation and competition between relatives. *Science, 296,* 72–75.

Westen, D. (1998). The scientific legacy of Sigmund Freud: Toward a psychodynamically informed psychological science. *Psychological Bulletin, 24,* 333–371.

Westen, D., Gabbard, G. O., & Ortigo, K. M. (2008). Psychoanalytic approaches to personality. In O. P. John, R. W. Robins, & L. A. Pervin (Eds.), *Handbook of personality theory and research* (3rd ed.). New York: Guilford Press.

Westen, D., & Morrison, K. (2001). A multidimensional meta-analysis of treatments for depression, panic, and generalized anxiety disorder: An empirical examination of the status of empirically supported therapies. *Journal of Consulting and Clinical Psychology, 69,* 875–899.

Westen, D., Novotny, C. M., & Thompson-Brenner, H. (2004). The empirical status of empirically supported psychotherapies: Assumptions, findings, and reporting in controlled clinical trials. *Psychological Bulletin, 130,* 631–663.

Wethington, E. (2000). Expecting stress: Americans and the "midlife crisis." *Motivation and Emotion, 24,* 85–103.

Whalen, P. J. (2003). Remembering people: Neuroimaging takes on the real world. *Learning & Memory, 10,* 240–241.

Whalley, L. J., & Deary, I. J. (2001). Longitudinal cohort study of childhood IQ and survival up to age 76. *British Medical Journal, 322,* 819–822.

Wheeler, L., & Miyake, K. (1992). Social comparison in everyday life. *Journal of Personality and Social Psychology, 62,* 760–773.

Wheeler, M. E., & Fiske, S. T. (2005). Controlling racial prejudice: Social-cognitive goals affect amygdala and stereotype activation. *Psychological Science, 16,* 56–63.

Whitam, F. L., & Mathy, R. M. (1991). Childhood cross-gender behavior of homosexual females in Brazil, Peru, the Philippines, and the United States. *Archives of Sexual Behavior, 20,* 151–170.

White, K. M., Hogg, M. A., & Terry, D. J. (2002). Improving attitude behavior correspondence through exposure to normative support from a salient ingroup. *Basic and Applied Social Psychology, 24,* 91–103.

White, P. A. (2009). Property transmission: An explanatory account of the role of similarity information in causal inference. *Psychological Bulletin, 135,* 774–793.

Whitehouse, W. G., Orne, E. C., & Dinges, D. F. (2008). Eyewitness memory: Can suggestion be minimized in the investigative interview? *The Forensic Examiner, 17,* 66–75.

Whorf, B. L. (1956). Science and linguistics. In J. B. Carroll (Ed.), *Language, thought and reality: Selected writings of Benjamin Lee Whorf.* Cambridge, MA: MIT Press.

Whyte, J., & Kavey, N. B. (1990). Somnambulistic eating: A report of three cases. *International Journal of Eating Disorders, 9,* 577–581.

Widiger, T. A., Livesley, T. A., & Clark, L. A. (2009). An integrative dimensional classification of personality disorder. *Psychological Assessment, 21,* 243–255.

Widiger, T. A., & Smith, G. T. (2008). Personality and psychopathology. In O. P. John, R. W. Robins, & L. A. Pervin (Eds.), *Handbook of personality: Theory and research* (3rd ed.). New York: Guilford Press.

Wiederhold, B. K., & Wiederhold, M. D. (2005). *Virtual reality therapy for anxiety disorders.* Washington, DC: American Psychological Association.

Wiens, A. N., & Menustik, C. E. (1983). Treatment outcome and patient characteristics in an aversion therapy program for alcoholism. *American Psychologist, 38,* 1089–1096.

Wierzbicka, A. (1986). Human emotions: Universal or culture-specific? *American Anthropologist, 52,* 759–781.

Wilbrecht, L., & Nottebohm, F. (2003). Vocal learning in birds and humans. *Mental Retardation and Developmental Disabilities Research Reviews, 9,* 135–148.

Wilcox, S., & Storandt, M. (1996). Relations among age, exercise, and psychological variables in a community sample of women. *Health Psychology, 15,* 110–113.

Wilder, D. A., Austin, J., & Casella, S. (2009). Applying behavior analysis in organizations: Organizational behavior management. *Psychological Services, 6,* 202–211.

Willenberg, H. S., Bornstein, S. R., & Crousos, G. P. (2000). Stress-induced disease: Overview. In G. Fink (Ed.), *Encyclopedia of stress.* San Diego, CA: Academic Press.

Williams, D., & Skoric, M. (2005). Internet fantasy violence: A test of aggression in an online game. *Communication Monographs, 72,* 217–233.

Williams, K. D., Cheung, C. K. T., & Choi, W. (2000). Cyberostracism: Effects of being ignored over the Internet. *Journal of Personality and Social Psychology, 79,* 748–762.

Williams, T. J., Pepitone, M. E., Christensen, S. E., Cooke, B. M., Huberman, A. D., & Breedlove, N. J. (2000). Finger length patterns and human sexual orientation. *Nature, 404,* 455–456.

Williams, W. L., & Burkholder, E. (2008). Response chaining. In W. T. O'Donohue & J. E. Fisher, (Eds.), *Cognitive behavior therapy: Applying empirically supported techniques in your practice* (2nd ed.). Hoboken, NJ: Wiley.

Williamson, P. (2006). *Mind, brain, and schizophrenia.* New York: Oxford University Press.

Willingham, W. W., Rock, D. A., & Pollack, J. (1990). Predictability of college grades: Three tests and three national samples. In W. W. Willingham & C. Lewis (Eds.), *Predicting college grades: An analysis of institutional trends over two decades.* Princeton, NJ: Educational Testing Service.

Willis, S. L., & Schaie, K. W. (1986). Training the elderly on the ability factors of spatial orientation and inductive reasoning. *Psychology and Aging, 1,* 239–247.

Wills, A. J. (2005). Association and cognition. In A. J. Wills (Ed.), *New directions in human associative learning.* Mahwah, NJ: Erlbaum.

Wilson, B. J., & Gottman, J. M. (2002). Marital conflict, repair, and parenting. In M. H. Bornstein (Ed.), *Handbook of parenting: Vol. 4. Social conditions and applied parenting* (2nd ed.). Mahwah, NJ: Erlbaum.

Wilson, D. A., Best, A. R., & Sullivan, R. M. (2004). Plasticity in the olfactory system: Lessons for the neurobiology of memory. *Neuroscientist, 10,* 513–524.

Wilson, J. P., & Keane, T. M. (2004). *Assessing psychological trauma and PTSD.* New York: Guilford Press.

Wilson, R. S., & Bennett, D. A. (2003). Cognitive activity and risk of Alzheimer's disease. *Current Directions in Psychological Science, 12,* 87–91.

Wilson, S. J., Lipsey, M. W., & Derzon, J. H. (2003). The effects of school-based intervention programs on aggressive behavior: A meta-analysis. *Journal of Consulting and Clinical Psychology, 71,* 136–149.

Wilson, S. L. (2003). Post-institutionalization: The effects of early deprivation on development of Romanian adoptees. *Child and Adolescent Social Work Journal, 20,* 473–483.

Windholz, G. (1997). Ivan P. Pavlov: An overview of his life and psychological work. *American Psychologist, 52,* 941–946.

Winkler, I., Korzyukov, O., Gumenyuk, V., Cowan, N., Linkenkaer, H. K., Ilmoniemi, R. J., Alho, K., & Naeaetaenen, R. (2002). Temporary and longer-term retention of acoustic information. *Psychophysiology, 39,* 530–534.

Winne, P. H., & Hadwin, A. F. (1998). Studying as self-regulated learning. In D. J. Hacker, J. Dunlosky, & A. C. Graesser (Eds.), *Metacognition in educational theory and practice.* Mahwah, NJ: Erlbaum.

Winnepenninckx, B., Rooms, L., & Kooy, R. F. (2003). Mental retardation: A review of the genetic causes. *British Journal of Developmental Disabilities, 49,* 29–44.

Winner, E. (2000). The origins and ends of giftedness. *American Psychologist, 55,* 159–169.

Winningham, R. G. (2010). *Train your brain.* Amityville, NY: Baywood.

Winson, J. (1990). The meaning of dreams. *Scientific American, 260*(11), 86–96.

Winston, J. S., Strange, B. A., O'Doherty, J., & Dolan, R. J. (2002). Automatic and intentional brain responses during evaluation of trustworthiness of faces. *Nature Neuroscience, 5,* 277–283.

Witelson, S. F., Kigar, D. L., & Harvey, T. (1999). The exceptional brain of Albert Einstein. *Lancet, 353,* 2149–2153.

Witkiewicz, K., & Marlatt, G. A. (2004). Relapse prevention for alcohol and drug problems. *American Psychologist, 59,* 224–235.

Wixted, J. T. (2005). A theory about why we forget what we once knew. *Current Directions in Psychological Science, 14,* 6–9.

Wolberg, L. R. (1967). *The technique of psychotherapy* (2nd ed.). New York: Grune & Stratton.

Wolff, P. H., & Melngailis, I. (1996). Reversing letters and reading transformed text in dyslexia: A reassessment. *Reading and Writing, 8,* 341–355.

Wolken, J. J. (1995). *Light detectors, photoreceptors, and imaging systems in nature.* New York: Oxford University Press.

Wolpe, J. (1958). *Psychotherapy by reciprocal inhibition.* Stanford, CA: Stanford University Press.

Wong, I. C. K., Besag, F. M. C., Santosh, P. J., & Murray, M. L. (2004). Use of selective serotonin reuptake inhibitors in children and adolescents. *Drug Safety, 27*(13).

Wong, M. M., & Csikszentmihalyi, M. (1991). Affiliation motivation and daily experience: Some issues on gender differences. *Journal of Personality and Social Psychology, 60,* 154–164.

Wood, S. L., & Swait, J. (2002). Psychological indicators of innovation adoption: Cross-classification based need for cognition and need for change. *Journal of Consumer Psychology, 12,* 1–13.

Wood, W., Lundgren, S., Ouellete, J. A., Busceme, S., & Blackstone, T. (1994). Minority influence: A meta-analytic review of social influence processes. *Psychological Bulletin, 115,* 323–345.

Wood, W., Rhodes, N., & Whelan, M. (1989). Sex differences in positive well-being: A consideration of emotional style and marital status. *Psychological Bulletin, 106,* 249–264.

Woodruff-Pak, D. S. (1993). Eyeblink classical conditioning in H. M.: Delay and trace paradigms. *Behavioral Neuroscience, 107,* 911–925.

Woods, S. C., & Seeley, R. J. (2002). Hunger and energy homeostasis. In H. Pashler & R. Gallistel (Eds.), *Steven's handbook of experimental psychology: Vol. 3. Learning, motivation, and emotion* (3rd ed.), New York: Wiley.

Word, C. O., Zanna, M. P., & Cooper, J. (1974). The nonverbal mediation of self-fulfilling prophecies in interracial interaction. *Journal of Experimental Social Psychology, 10,* 109–120.

Worell, J., & Remer, P. P. (2003). *Feminist perspectives in therapy: Empowering diverse women.* New York: Wiley.

World Health Organization. (2004). *Global summary of the AIDS epidemic, December, 2004.* Geneva, Switzerland: Author.

Wouters-Adriaens, M., & Westerterp, K. (2006). Basal metabolic rate as a proxy for overnight energy expenditure: The effect of age. *British Journal of Nutrition, 95,* 1166–1170.

Wyman, A. J., & Vyse, S. (2008). Science versus the stars: A double-blind test of the validity of the NEO five-factor inventory and computer-generated astrological natal charts. *Journal of General Psychology, 135,* 287–300.

Wynn, K. (1992). Addition and subtraction by human infants. *Nature, 358,* 749–750.

Wynn, K. (1998). An evolved capacity for number. In D. D. Cummins & C. Allen (Eds.), *The evolution of mind* (pp. 107–126). New York: Oxford University Press.

Wynne, C. D. L. (2007). What the ape said. *Ethology, 113,* 411–413.

Yang, L., Krampe, R. T., & Baltes, P. B. (2006). Basic forms of cognitive plasticity extended into the oldest-old: Retest learning, age, and cognitive functioning. *Psychology and Aging, 21,* 372–378.

Yang, Y., Raine, A., Lencz, T., Bihrle, S., LaCasse, L., & Colletti, P. (2005). Volume reduction in prefrontal gray matter in unsuccessful criminal psychopaths. *Biological Psychiatry, 57,* 1103–1108.

Yen, S., Shea, T., Pagano, M., Sanislow, C. A., Grilo, C. M., McGlashan, T., et al. (2003). Axis I and Axis II disorders as predictors of prospective suicide attempts: Findings from the Collaborative Longitudinal Personality Disorders Study. *Journal of Abnormal Psychology, 112,* 375–381.

Yerkes, R. M., & Dodson, J. D. (1908). The relation of strength of stimulus to rapidity of habit-formation. *Journal of Comparative and Physiological Psychology, 18,* 459–482.

Yi, J. P., Smith, R. E., & Vitaliano, P. P. (2005). Stress-resilience, illness, and coping: A person-centered investigation of young women athletes. *Journal of Behavioral Medicine, 28,* 257–265.

Yin, T. C. T., & Kuwada, S. (1984). Neuronal mechanisms of binaural interaction. In G. M. Edelman, W. M. Cowan, & W. E. Gall (Eds.), *Dynamic aspects of neocortical function.* New York: Wiley.

Young, A. W. (2003). Face recognition with and without awareness. In A. Cleeremans (Ed.), *The unity of consciousness: Binding, integration, and dissociation.* New York: Oxford University Press.

Young, L. R., & Joffe, R. T. (1997). *Bipolar disorder: Biological models and their clinical application.* New York: Marcel Dekker.

Youngstedt, S. D., O'Connor, P. J., & Dishman, R. K. (1997). The effects of acute exercise on sleep: A quantitative synthesis. *Sleep, 20,* 203–214.

Yrizarry, N., Matsumoto, D., Imai, C., Kooken, K., & Takeuchi, S. (2001). Culture and emotion. In L. L. Adler & U. P. Gielen (Eds.), *Cross-cultural topics in psychology* (2nd ed.). Westport, CT: Praeger.

Yuan, Y., Zhang, Z., Bai, F., You, J., Yu, H., Shi, Y., et al. (2009). Genetic variation in apolipoprotein E alters regional gray matter volumes in remitted late-onset depression. *Journal of Affective Disorders, 121,* 273–277.

Yuste, R. (2010). *Dendritic spines.* New York: Springer.

Zadra, A., Pilon, M., & Montplaisir, J. (2008). Polysomnographic diagnosis of sleepwalking: Effects of sleep deprivation. *Annals of Neurology, 63,* 513–519.

Zahava, S., Shklar, R., Singer, Y., & Mikulincer, M. (2006). Reactions to combat stress in Israeli war veterans twenty years after the 1982 Lebanon war. *Journal of Mental and Nervous Disease, 194,* 935–939.

Zajonc, R. B., Murphy, S. T., & Inglehart, M. (1989). Feeling and facial efference: Implications of a vascular theory of emotion. *Psychological Review, 96,* 395–416.

Zakzanis, K. K. (1998). Neuropsychological correlates of positive vs. negative schizophrenic symptomatology. *Schizophrenia Research, 29,* 227–233.

Zald, D., & Rauch, S. (Eds.) (2006). *The orbitofrontal cortex.* New York: Oxford University Press.

Zanker, J. (2010). *Sensation, perception, and action: A functional perspective.* New York: Macmillan.

Zatzick, D. F., & Dimsdale, J. E. (1990). Cultural variations in response to painful stimuli. *Psychosomatic Medicine, 52,* 544–557.

Zautra, A. J. (2003). *Emotions, stress, and health.* New York: Oxford University Press.

Zayas, V., & Shoda, Y. (2007). Predicting preferences for dating partners from past experiences of psychological abuse: Identifying the psychological ingredients of situations. *Personality and Social Psychology Bulletin, 33,* 123–138.

Zebrowitz, L. A., Voinescu, L., & Collins, M. A. (1996). "Wide-eyed" and "crooked-faced": Determinants of perceived and real honesty across the life span. *Personality and Social Psychology Bulletin, 22,* 1258–1269.

Zechner, U., Wilda, M., Kehrer-Sawatzki, H., Vogel, W., Fundele, R., & Hameister, H. (2001). A high density of X-linked genes for general cognitive ability: A runaway process shaping human evolution? *Trends in Genetics, 17,* 697–701.

Zee, P. C., & Lu, B. S. (2008). Insomnia and circadian rhythm in sleep disorders. *Psychiatric Annals, 38,* 583–589.

Zhang, Y., Proenca, R., Maffei, M., Barone, M., Leopold, L., & Friedman, J. M. (1994). Positional cloning of the mouse obese gene and its human homologue. *Nature, 372,* 425–432.

Zhu, Y., Zhang, L., Fan, J., & Han, S. (2007). Neural basis of cultural influence on self-representation. *NeuroImage, 34,* 1310–1317.

Zimbardo, P. G. (2004). A situationist perspective on the psychology of evil: Understanding how good people are transformed into perpetrators. In A. G. Miller (Ed.), *The social psychology of good and evil.* New York: Guilford Press.

Zimbardo, P. G., Haney, C., Banks, W. C., & Jaffe, D. (1973, April 8). The mind is a formidable jailer: A Pirandellian prison. *New York Times Magazine,* pp. 38–60.

Zimmer, C. (2008). The search for intelligence. *Scientific American, 299*(4), 68–75.

Zimmerman, F. J., Christakis, D. A., & Meltzoff, A. N. (2007). Associations between media viewing and language development in children under age 2 years. *The Journal of Pediatrics, 151,* 364–368.

Zinbarg, R. E., Barlow, D. H., Brown, T. A., & Hertz, R. M. (1992). Cognitive-behavioral approaches to the nature and treatment of anxiety disorders. *Annual Review of Psychology, 43,* 235–268.

Zinovieva, I. L. (2001). Why do people work if they are not paid? An example from Eastern Europe. In D. R. Denison (Ed.), *Managing organizational change in transition economies.* Mahwah, NJ: Erlbaum.

Zoellner, L. A., Feeny, N. C., & Bittinger, J. N. (2009). What you believe is what you want: Modeling PTSD-related treatment preferences for sertraline or prolonged exposure. *Journal of Behaviour Therapy and Experimental Psychiatry, 40,* 455–467.

Zolotor, A. J., Theodore, A. D., Chang, J. J., Berkoff, M. C., & Runyan, D. K. (2008). Speak softly—and forget the stick: Corporal punishment and child physical abuse. *American Journal of Preventive Medicine, 35,* 364–369.

Zubieta, J.-K., Smith, Y. R., Bueller, J. A., et al. (2001). Regional *mu* opioid receptor regulation of sensory and affective dimensions of pain. *Science, 293,* 311–315.

Zucker, T. P., Flesche, C. W., Germing, U., Schroeter, S., Willers, R., Wolf, H. H., & Heyll, A. (1998). Patient-controlled versus staff-controlled analgesia with pethidine after allogeneic bone marrow transplantation. *Pain, 75,* 305–312.

Zuckerman, M. (2005). *Psychobiology of personality* (2nd ed.). New York: Cambridge University Press.

Zuckerman, M., Hall, J. A., DeFrank, R. S., & Rosenthal, R. (1976). Encoding and decoding of spontaneous and posed facial expressions. *Journal of Personality and Social Psychology, 34,* 966–977.

Zuroff, D. C., & Blatt, S. J. (2006). The therapeutic relationship in the brief treatment of depression: Contributions to clinical improvement and enhanced adaptive capacities. *Journal of Consulting and Clinical Psychology, 74,* 130–140.

Credits

TEXT AND LINE ART CREDITS

Chapter 1

Table 1.2 From R. Levine, S. Sato, T. Hashimoto & J. Verma, 1995, "Love and Marriage in Eleven Cultures," *Journal of Cross-Cultural Psychology*, 26 (5), 554–571, Table 2. Copyright © 1995 Sage Publications. Reprinted by permission of Sage Publications, Inc. **Figure 1.24** Copyright © 2009 by the American Psychological Association. Adapted with permission from Table 4, "Employment Characteristics of APA Members by Membership Status, 2009" from *2009 APA Directory*. Compiled by Center for Workforce Studies. American Psychological Association. 2009 (http://www.apa.org/workforce/publications/09-member/table-04.pdf). No further reproduction or distribution is permitted without written permission from the American Psychological Association.

Chapter 2

Figure 2.3 From Latané/Darley, *Unresponsive Bystander: Why Doesn't He Help?*, Figure "Helping in an Emergency," © 1971 Appleton-Century-Crofts. Reproduced by permission of Pearson Education, Inc.

Chapter 3

Figure 3.6 Drawing from J.P. Hailman, 1969, "How an Instinct Is Learned," *Scientific American*, 221, 98–106. Reprinted by permission of Eric Mose, Jr.

Chapter 5

Figure 5.6 Drawing from R.M. Pritchard, 1961, "Stabilized Images on the Retina," *Scientific American*, 72–78. Reprinted by permission of Eric Mose, Jr. **Figure 5.15** from K. Koch, *The Quest for Consciousness: A Neurobiological Approach*, Fig 2.2, p. 30, 2004. Greenwood Village, CO: Roberts & Company Publishers. Reprinted by permission. **Figure 5.20** from B.D. Smith, *Psychology: Science and Understanding*, Fig 4.33. Copyright © 1998 The McGraw-Hill Companies. Reprinted by permission of The McGraw-Hill Companies, Inc. **Figure 5.40a** from B.D. Smith, *Psychology: Science and Understanding*, Fig 4.21. Copyright © 1998 The McGraw-Hill Companies. Reprinted by permission of The McGraw-Hill Companies, Inc. **Figure 5.48b** from W. Hudson, 1960, "Pictorial Depth Perception in Sub-Cultural Groups in Africa," *Journal of Social Psychology*, 52, 183–208. Copyright © 1960 Heldref Publications. Reprinted with permission of the publisher (Heldref Publications, www.heldref.org). **Figure 5.49** Adapted by permission from Macmillan Publishers Ltd.: *Nature*, 228, 477–478. C. Blakemore & G.F. Cooper, "Development of the Brain Depends on Visual Environment." Copyright © 1970, Nature Publishing Group.

Chapter 6

Figure 6.6 Reprinted from *Applied Ergonomics*, 27(1), T.H. Monk, S. Folkard & A.I. Wedderburn, "Maintaining Safety and High Performance on Shift Work," 17–23, Fig 1. Copyright © 1996 with permission from Elsevier. **Table 6.1** Reprinted from *Personality and Individual Differences*, 32 (6), C.S. Smith, S. Folkard, R.A. Schmeider, L.F. Parra, E. Spelten & H. Almiral, 2002. "Investigation of Morning-Evening Orientation in Six Countries Using the Preference Scale," 949–968, Table 3. Copyright © 2002 with permission from Elsevier. **Figure 6.7** Reproduced from *The New York Times*, December 29, 1993, p. B7. Copyright © 1993 by *The New York Times*. Reprinted by permission; (data to right of map): Reprinted from *Journal of Affective Disorders*, 53 (1), P. Mersch, H.M. Middendorp, A. Bouhuys, D. Beersma, R. van den Hoofdakker,

1999, "Seasonal Affective Disorder and Latitude: A Review of the Literature," pp. 35–48. Copyright © 1999 with permission from Elsevier. **Figure 6.14** Adapted from H.P. Roffwarg, J.N. Muzio & W.C. Dement, "Ontogenic Development of Human Dream-Sleep Cycle," *Science*, 152, 604, Fig 1. Copyright © 1966, AAAS. Reprinted with permission from AAAS. **Figure 6.17** from R. Fosse, R. Stickgold & J. A. Hobson, 2001, "Brain-Mind States: Reciprocal Variation in Thoughts and Hallucinations," *Psychological Science*, 12 (1), 33, Fig 3. Copyright © 2001 Association for Psychological Science. Reprinted by permission of Sage Publications. **Figure 6.19** From Morewedge, C.K., & Norton, M.I., "When dreaming is believing: The (motivated) interpretation of dreams." *Journal of Personality and Social Psychology*, Vol 96 (2), Feb. 2009. Pp. 249–264, Figure 1, p. 253. Copyright © 2009 American Psychological Association. Reprinted by permission of the American Psychological Association. **Figure 6.31** From S.M. Kosslyn, W.L. Thompson, M.F. Constantini-Ferrando, N.M. Alpert & D. Spieel, 2000, "Hypnotic Visual Illusion Alters Color Processing in the Brain," *American Journal of Psychiatry*, 157, 1279–1284, Fig 1. Copyright 2000 by American Psychiatric Association (Journals). Reproduced with permission of the author and American Psychiatric Association (Journals) in the format Textbook via Copyright Clearance Center.

Chapter 7

Figure 7.15 Reprinted from *Behavior Therapy*, 39, Facon, B., Sahiri, S., & Riviere, V. "A controlled single-case treatment of severe long-term selective mutism in a child with mental retardation." Pp. 313–321. Figure 1, p. 317. Copyright © 2008 Elsevier. Reprinted by permission.

Chapter 8

Figure 8.1 From B. Milner, 1965, "Memory Disturbances After Bilateral Hippocampal Lesions," in *Cognitive Processes and the Brain*, Peter Milner & S.G. Glickman, eds., p. 108, Fig 6. Reprinted with permission. **Figure 8.2** Reprinted from *The Psychology of Learning and Motivation: Advances in Theory and Research*, Vol. 2, K.W. Spence & J.T. Spence, eds. R.C. Atkinson & R. M. Shiffrin, "Human Memory: A Proposed System and Its Control Processes." Copyright © 1968 by Elsevier. Reprinted by permission. **Figure 8.5** Reprinted from *Neuroscience*, 139(1), G. Repovs & A. Baddeley, 2006, "The Multi-component Model of Working Memory: Explorations in Experimental Cognitive Psychology," pp. 5–21, Fig 1. Copyright © 2006 by Elsevier. Reprinted by permission. **Figure 8.6** Reprinted from *Journal of Verbal Learning and Verbal Behavior* (now *Journal of Memory and Language*), 5, M. Glanzer & A. Cunitz, "Two Storage Mechanisms in Free Recall," pp. 351–360, Fig. 2. Copyright © 1966, Elsevier. Reprinted by permission. **Figure 8.11** from A.M. Collins & E.F. Loftus, 1975, "A Spreading Activation Theory of Semantic Processing," *Psychological Review*, 82, 412, Figure 1. Copyright © 1975 by the American Psychological Association. Reprinted by permission of the author and the publisher. **Figure 8.14** from D.R. Godden & A.D. Baddeley, 1975, "Context-Dependent Memory in Two Natural Environments: On Land and Under Water," *British Journal of Psychology*, 66, 325–331. Reprinted by permission of the author. **Figure 8.17** Reprinted from *Cognitive Psychology*, 11 (3), R.S. Nickerson & M.J. Adams, 1979, "Long-Term Memory for a Common Object," pp. 287–307. Copyright © 1979 Elsevier. Reprinted by permission. **Figure 8.20** from H.P. Bahrick, L.K. Hall & S.A. Berger, 1996, "Accuracy and Distortion in Memory for High School Grades," *Psychological Science*, 7(5), 265–271, Table 2. Copyright © 1996 Association for Psychological Science. Reprinted by permission of Sage Publications. **Figure 8.21b** from H. Intraub, C.V. Gottesman,

E.V. Willey, & I. J. Zuk, 1996, "Boundary Extension for Briefly Glimpsed Pictures: Do Common Perceptual Processes Result in Unexpected Memory Distortions?" *Journal of Memory and Language*, 35, 118–134. Reprinted by permission of the author.

Chapter 9

Figure 9.8 From E. Bialystok & M. Martin, 2004, "Attention Inhibition in Bilingual Children: Evidence from the Dimensional Change Card Sort Tasks," *Developmental Science*, 7 (3), 325–339, Fig. 1b. Copyright © 2004 Wiley/Blackwell. Reprinted by permission of Blackwell Publishers. **Figure 9.12b** From E.S. Savage-Rumbaugh, K. McDonald, R.A. Sevick, W.D. Hopkins & E. Rupert, 1986, "Spontaneous Symbol Acquisition and Communicative Use by Pygmy Chimpanzees (*Pan Paniscus*), Journal of Experimental Psychology: General, 115, 220, Fig 1. Copyright © 1986 by the American Psychological Association. Reprinted by permission. **Figure 9.26b** From Baltes, P.B., & Smith, J. (2008). The fascination of wisdom: Its nature, ontogeny, and function. *Perspectives on Psychological Science*, Vol. 3, Issue 1, p. 58, Fig 56. Copyright © 2008 Sage Publications. Reprinted by permission. **Figure 9.27** Reprinted from *Contemporary Educational Psychology*, 28 (2), K.W. Thiede & M. Anderson, 2003, "Summarizing can improve metacomprehension accuracy," pp. 129–160, Fig. 3. Copyright © 2003 Elsevier. Reprinted by permission. **Figure 9.28** Adapted from R.N. Shepard & J. Metzler, 1971, "Mental Rotation of Three-Dimensional Objects," *Science*, 171, Figures 1 & 2. Reprinted with permission from the American Association for the Advancement of Science. **Figure 9.29** From S. M. Kosslyn, T.M. Ball & B.J. Reiser, 1978, "Human Perception and Performance." *Journal of Experimental Psychology*, 4, 51, Fig 2. Copyright © 1978 by the American Psychological Association. Reprinted by permission of the author and the publisher.

Chapter 10

Table 10.1 Copyright © 1973 by The Riverside Publishing Company, "Sample Problems from the Stanford-Binet Intelligence Test That Should Be Answered Correctly at Particular Ages," from the *Stanford-Binet Intelligence Scales*, Form L-M, reproduced with permission of the publisher. All rights reserved. **Table 10.3** L.L. Thurstone, 1938, *Primary Mental Abilities*. Copyright © 1938 by The University of Chicago Press. Reprinted with permission. **Figure 10.5** "A Modern Model of Intellect," from *Human Cognitive Abilities: A Survey of Factor-Analytic Studies*, by J.B. Carroll (Appendix B: Hierarchical Factor Matrix Files). Copyright © Cambridge University Press, 1993. Reprinted with permission. **Figure 10.13** Adapted from P.A. Carpenter, M.A. Just & P. Shell, 1990, "What One Intelligence Test Measures," *Psychological Review*, 97, 404–431, Fig 2. Copyright © 1990 by the American Psychological Association. Reprinted by permission. **Figure 10.16** Schweinhart, Lawrence J., and David P. Weikart. Figure 5.1, "Major Findings at Age Twenty-Seven." In *Social Programs That Work*. © 1998 Russell Sage Foundation, 112 East 64th Street, New York, NY 10021. Reprinted with permission. **Figure 10.19** From D. Kimura, 1992, "Sex Differences in the Brain," *Scientific American*, 267(3), 121–122, Fig 1. Reprinted by permission of Jared Schneidman Design. **Figure 10.20** From C.M. Steele, 1997, "A Threat in the Air: How Stereotypes Shape Intellectual Identity and Performance." *American Psychologist*, 52, 620–621, Figures 1 & 2. Copyright © 1997 by the American Psychological Association. Reprinted by permission of the author and the publisher. **Table 10.5** From *Diagnostic and Statistical Manual of Mental Disorders IV-TR*, 2000. Reprinted with permission from the *Diagnostic and Statistical Manual of Mental Disorders*. Copyright © 2000. American Psychiatric Association. Reprinted by permission.

Chapter 11

Figure 11.14 From *Sex in America* by Robert T. Michael, John Gagnon, Edward O. Laumann and Gina Kolata. Copyright © 1994 by Robert T. Michael, John H. Gagnon, Edward O. Laumann and Gina Kolata. Reprinted by permission of Little, Brown & Company (U.S. and U.K.), and Brockman, Inc. **Figure 11.17** From *Sex in America* by Robert T. Michael, John Gagnon, Edward O. Laumann and Gina Kolata. Copyright © 1994 by Robert T. Michael, John H. Gagnon, Edward O. Laumann and Gina Kolata. Reprinted by permission of Little, Brown & Company (U.S. and U.K.), and Brockman, Inc. **Figure 11.18** from R. Blanchard & A.F. Bogaert, 1996, "Homosexuality in Men and Number of Older Brothers," *American Journal of Psychiatry*, 153, 27–31. Reprinted with permission from the American Journal of Psychiatry. Copyright © 1996 American Psychiatric Association. **Figure 11.34** From J. Speisman, R. S. Lazarus, A. Mordkoff & L. Davidson, 1964, "Experimental Reduction of Stress Based on Ego-Defense Theory," *Journal of Abnormal and Social Psychology*, 68, 373, Fig. 1. Copyright © 1964 by the American Psychological Association. Reprinted by permission of the author and the publisher.

Chapter 12

Figure 12.15 Reprinted from *Journal of Experimental Child Psychology*, 6(4), E. Vurpillot, "The Development of Scanning Strategies and Their Relation to Visual Differences," pp. 632–650, Fig 1. Copyright © 1968, Elsevier. Reprinted with permission. **Figure 12.16** Reprinted from *Journal of Experimental Child Psychology*, 45(3), R. Kail, "Development Functions for Speeds of Cognitive Processes," pp. 339–364, Fig 7. Copyright © 1991 Elsevier. Reprinted with permission. **Figure 12.17** Adapted by permission from Macmillan Publishers Ltd: K. Wynn, 1992, "Addition and Subtraction by Human Infants," *Nature*, August 27, 1992, 358 (6389) 749. Copyright © 1992. **Figure 12.23** From E.E. Maccoby & J.A. Martin, 1983, "Socialization in the Context of the Family: Parent-Child Interaction," in *Handbook of Child Psychology*, 4th ed., E.M. Hetherington, Ed. Reprinted with permission of John Wiley & Sons, Inc. **Figure 12.24** From K. Crowley, M.A. Callahan, H.R. Tenenbaum, & E. Allen, 2001, "Parents Explain More Often to Boys than to Girls During Shared Scientific Thinking," *Psychological Science*, 12(3), 258–261, Fig. 1. Copyright © 2001 Association for Psychological Science. Reprinted by permission of Sage Publications. **Table 12.3** From L. Kohlberg, *The Psychology of Moral Development: Essays on Moral Development*, Vol. 2, 176–177, Table 2. Copyright © 1984, Harper & Row. Reprinted by permission of HarperCollins, Inc. **Figure 12.30b** From J. Piaget, *The Growth of Logical thinking from Childhood to Adolescence*. Copyright © 1958 Jean Piaget. Reprinted by permission of Basic Books, a member of the Perseus Books Group. **Figure 12.31** Based on K.W. Schaie, *Developmental Influences on Adult Intelligence: The Seattle Longitudinal Study*, 2005, Oxford University Press, pp. 123–124. Reprinted by permission of Oxford University Press, Inc. **Figure 12.33** With kind permission from Springer Science & Business Media: *Journal of Youth and Adolescence*, "The Right to Do Wrong: Lying to Parents Among Adolescents and Emerging Adults," 33 (2), 2004, p. 106, Jensen et al., Fig 1. **Figure 12.34** With kind permission from Springer Science & Business Media: *Journal of Adult Development*, "Conceptions of the Transition to Adulthood," 8(2), 2001, p. 140, J. Arnett, Fig 2. **Figure 12.36** From V.L. Bengtson, 2001, "Beyond the Nuclear Family: The Increasing Importance of Multigenerational Bonds," *Journal of Marriage and the Family*, 63(1), 1–16, Fig 2. www.interscience.wiley.com. Reprinted by permission of the publisher.

Chapter 13

P. 459 Excerpt from *A Sniper in the Tower: The Charles Whitman Murders*, by G. M. Lavergne, 1997, University of North Texas Press. Copyright © 1997 Gary M. Lavergne. Reprinted with permission. **Figure 13.4** Adapted from B.D. Smith, *Psychology: Science and Understanding*, Fig 14.2, 1998. New York: McGraw-Hill. Reprinted by permission of The McGraw-Hill Companies, Inc. **Table 13.5** From *Personality in Adulthood: A Five-Factor Theory Perspective*, by R.R. McCrae & P.T. Costa, 2003, New York: Guilford Press. Reprinted by permission of Guilford Publications, Inc. **Table 13.6** From M.F. Scheier, C.S. Carver & M.W. Bridges, 1994, "Distinguishing Optimism from Neuroticism (and Trait Anxiety, Self-Mastery, and Self-Esteem): A Reevaluation of the Life Orientation Test," *Journal of Personality and Social Psychology*, 67, 1073, Table 6. Copyright © 1994 by the American Psychological Association. Reprinted by permission of the author and the publisher. **Table 13.8** From A. Tellegen, D.T. Lykken, T.J. Bouchard, K.L. Wilcox, N.L. Segal & S. Rich, 1988, "Personality Similarity in Twins Reared Apart and Together," *Journal of Personality and Social Psychology*, 54, 1036, Table 5. Copyright © 1988 by the American Psychological Association. Reprinted by permission of the author and the publisher. **Figure 13.13b** From *The Biological Basis of Personality*, by H. J. Eysenck, 1967, Charles C. Thomas Publishers. Reprinted with permission. **Table 13.9** Copyright © 1966 by the American Psychological Association. Adapted with permission of the author and the publisher from Rotter, Julian B. (1966), "Generalized expectancies for internal versus external control of reinforcement," *Psychological Monographs: General & Applied*, Vol 80 (1), Whole No. 609, 1–28. Table 1, pp. 11–12. No further reproduction or distribution is permitted without written permission from the American Psychological Association. **Table 13.10** From Mischel, 1999, Personality coherence and dispositions in a cognitive-affective personality system (CAPS) approach. In D. Cervone & Y. Shoda, eds., *The Coherence of Personality*, Guilford Press. Reprinted with permission. **Figure 13.23** From Cousins, S.D. (1989). "Culture and Self-Perception in the United States and Japan," *Journal of Personality and Social Psychology*, 56, 124–131, Table 2 (adapted). Doi: 10.1037/0022-3514.56.1.124. Copyright © 1989 by the American Psychological Association. Reprinted by permission of the author and the publisher.

Chapter 14

Figure 14.11 From *Relapse Prevention: Maintenance Strategies in the Treatment of Addiction*, by G.A. Marlatt & J.R. Gordon, 1985, p. 38, Figure 1–4. New York: Guilford Press. Reprinted by permission of Guilford Publications, Inc. **Figure 14.14** Figure, "Hans Selye's General Adaptation Syndrome," from *The Stress of Life*, 2nd ed., by Hans Selye, p. 476, 1976. New York: McGraw-Hill. Reprinted by permission of The McGraw-Hill Companies, Inc. **Figure 14.18** From B.R. Levy, M.D. Slade, S. R. Kinkel, & S.V. Kasl, 2002, "Longevity Increased by Positive Self-Perceptions of Aging," *Journal of Personality and Social Psychology*, 83, 264, Fig 1. Copyright © 2002, American Psychological Association. Reprinted by permission of the author and the publisher. **Figure 14.22** With kind permission from Springer Science + Business Media: *Journal of Behavioral Medicine*, "Stress-Resilience, Illness, and Coping: A Person-Focused Investigation of Young Women Athletes," vol. 28 (3), 2005, p. 261, by Yi et al., Fig 1. **Table 14.5** From Frazier, P., Tennen, H., Gavian, M., Park, C., Tomich, P., Tashiro, T. "Does Self-Reported Posttraumatic Growth Reflect Genuine Positive Change?" *Psychological Science*, Vol 20, No. 7, Table 1, p. 915. Copyright © 2009 Association for Psychological Science. Reprinted by permission of Sage Publications. **Figure 14.23** From drawings based on photographs by D.D. Kosambi, 1967, "Living Prehistory in India," *Scientific American*, 216, 110–111.

Chapter 15

Figure 15.31 Reprinted from *Biological Psychiatry*, Vol 57, Yaling Yang, Adrian Raine, Todd Lencz, Susan Bihrie, Lori LaCasse, Patrick Colletti, "Volume Reduction in Prefrontal Gray Matter in Unsuccessful Criminal Psychopaths." p. 1106, Figure 1. Copyright © 2005, Elsevier. Reprinted by permission.

Chapter 16

Pp. 591–592 Excerpt "Can We Talk? The Schizophrenic Patient in Psychotherapy," *American Journal of Psychiatry*, 143, 68–70. Reprinted with permission from the American Journal of Psychiatry. Copyright © 1986 American Psychiatric Association. **Figure 16.4** From Baldwin, S.A., Berkeljan, A., Atkins, D.C., & Nielsen, J.A., (2009). *Journal of Consulting and Clinical Psychology*, 2009, Vol 77 (2) Figure 1, p. 207. Copyright © 2009 American Psychological Association. Reprinted by permission. **Pp. 597–598** Excerpt from Carl R. Rogers, *Client-Centered Therapy*, p. 49. Copyright © 1951 by Cengage Learning, Inc. Reproduced by permission. www.cengage.com/permissions. **Pp. 600–601** Excerpt from A.T. Beck, A.J. Rush, B.F. Shaw & G. Emery, *Cognitive Therapy of Depression*, pp. 145–146, 1979. New York: Guilford. Reprinted by permission of Guilford Publications, Inc. **Figure 16.26** From Foa, E.B., Hearst-Ikeda, D. & Perry, K. J. (1995), "Evaluation of a Brief Cognitive-Behavioral Program for the Prevention of PTSD in Recent Assault Victims," *Journal of Consulting and Clinical Psychology*, 63(6), p. 952, Fig 1. Doi: 10.1037/0022-006X.63.6.948. Copyright © 1995 by the American Psychological Association. Reprinted by permission of the author and the publisher.

Chapter 17

Figure 17.4 From J.G. Miller, 1984, "Culture and the Development of Everyday Social Explanation," *Journal of Personality and Social Psychology*, 46, 961–978, Table 2. Copyright © 1984 by the American Psychological Association. Reprinted by permission of the author and the publisher. **Figure 17.15** From Janis, *Groupthink*, 2nd Ed. © 1982 Wadsworth, a part of Cengage Learning, Inc. Reproduced by permission. www.cengage.com/permissions. **Figure 17.23a** From *The Psychology of Rumor*, by G.W. Allport & L. Postman, 1947, Henry Holt & Co. Reprinted by permission of Robert Allport. **Figure 17.24** From M. Johns et al., 2005, "Knowing Is Half the Battle," *Psychological Science*, 16(3), 175–179, Fig 1. Copyright © 2005 Association for Psychological Science. Reprinted by permission of Sage Publications. **Figure 17.30** From E. Verona & J.L. Carbonell, 2000, "Female Violence and Personality: Evidence for a Pattern of Overcontrolled Hostility Among One-Time Violent Female Offenders," *Criminal Justice and Behavior*, 27 (2), 187, Fig 1. Reprinted by permission of Sage Publications, Inc.

PHOTO CREDITS

Chapter 1

Page 1: © Medioimages/Getty; **p. 3 (top):** © StockTrek/Getty; **p. 3 (middle):** © Gabe Palmer/Corbis; **p. 3 (bottom):** © Brand X Pictures; **p. 10 (left):** Courtesy of Neal E. Miller; **p. 10 (middle):** © Phanie/Photo Researchers, Inc.; **p. 10 (right):** © Michael Freeman/Corbis; **p. 12 (top):** © Archives of the History of American Psychology—The University of Akron; **p. 12 (middle):** © Science Photo Library/Photo Researchers; **p. 12 (bottom):** © Archives of the History of American Psychology; **p. 13:** Library of Congress Image number 3b19621; **p. 14 (left):** © Culver Pictures; **p. 14 (right):** © Sam Falk/Photo Researchers; **p. 15 (top):** © Linda A. Cicero/Stanford News Service; **p. 15 (bottom):** © Diego Azubel/epa/Corbis; **p. 16:** © Eric Lessing/Art Resource; **p. 17:** © Siner Jeff; **p. 18 (top left):** AP Photo/Elizabeth Dalziel; **p. 18 (top right):** © Eldad Rafaeli/Corbis; **p. 18 (bottom):** Library of Congress Image #LC-USZ62-112521; **p. 20 (top left):** © Archives of the History of American Psychology; **p. 20 (top right):** © Michael Phelps; **p. 20 (bottom):** Library of Congress Prints and Photographs Division #LC-USZ62-52389; **p. 21:** © Michael Willmer Forbes Tweedie/Photo Researchers, Inc.; **p. 24:** Courtesy of Dr. Shelly Taylor; **p. 25:** AP Photo/Susan Walsh.

Chapter 2

Page 31: © Masterfile; **p. 32:** © Allan Tannenbaum/Gamma; **p. 37 (left):** © Comstock Images/Getty; **p. 37 (middle):** © Richard T. Nowitz/Photo Researchers; **p. 37 (right):** © Spencer Grant/PhotoEdit; **p. 41 (left):** © Annabella Bluesky/Photo Researchers, Inc.; **p. 41 (right):** © Volker Steger/Photo Researchers, Inc.; **p. 42:** © Chaiwat Subprasom/Reuters/Corbis; **p. 43:** © Bill Aron/PhotoEdit; **p. 49:** Courtesy of Human Factors and Ergonomics Society; **p. 54:** © C Squared Studios/Getty; **p. 60:** Used by permission of the Skeptical Inquirer magazine (www.csicop.org).

Chapter 3

Page 65: © H. Singh/Getty; **p. 66 (both):** © Michael Nichols/Magnum; **p. 67:** © Bettmann/Corbis; **p. 70 (left):** © Barbara Penoyar/Getty; **p. 70 (right):** © Imagestate Media/John Foxx/Imagestate; **p. 72 (top):** © L. Clarke/Corbis; **p. 72 (bottom):** © Jim Whitmer; **p. 75 (left):** © Oan Connell/The Image Works; **p. 75 (right):** © George Holton/Photo Researchers, Inc.; **p. 76 (top):** © 3D4Medical.com/Getty Images; **p. 76 (middle):** © Lisette Le Bon/SuperStock; **p. 76 (bottom):** © Siri Stafford/Getty Images; **p. 83:** © Thomas Nebbia/Woodfin Camp & Associates; **p. 84:** Illustration by J. H. Matternes, 2009; **p. 86 (left):** © Ryan McVay/Getty; **p. 86 (middle):** © Royalty-Free/Corbis; **p. 86 (right):** © 2009 Jupiterimages Corporation; **p. 88:** AP Photo/Jennifer Graylock.

Name Index